T0189664

Lecture Notes in Computer Science 11365

Commenced Publication in 1973
Founding and Former Series Editors:
Gerhard Goos, Juris Hartmanis, and Jan van Leeuwen

More information about this series at http://www.springer.com/series/7412

C. V. Jawahar · Hongdong Li ·
Greg Mori · Konrad Schindler (Eds.)

Computer Vision – ACCV 2018

14th Asian Conference on Computer Vision
Perth, Australia, December 2–6, 2018
Revised Selected Papers, Part V

Springer

Editors
C. V. Jawahar
IIIT Hyderabad
Hyderabad, India

Greg Mori
Simon Fraser University
Burnaby, BC, Canada

Hongdong Li
ANU
Canberra, ACT, Australia

Konrad Schindler ⓘ
ETH Zurich
Zurich, Zürich, Switzerland

ISSN 0302-9743   ISSN 1611-3349 (electronic)
Lecture Notes in Computer Science
ISBN 978-3-030-20872-1   ISBN 978-3-030-20873-8 (eBook)
https://doi.org/10.1007/978-3-030-20873-8

LNCS Sublibrary: SL6 – Image Processing, Computer Vision, Pattern Recognition, and Graphics

This Springer imprint is published by the registered company Springer Nature Switzerland AG
The registered company address is: Gewerbestrasse 11, 6330 Cham, Switzerland

Preface

The Asian Conference on Computer Vision (ACCV) 2018 took place in Perth, Australia, during December 2–6, 2018. The conference featured novel research contributions from almost all sub-areas of computer vision.

This year we received a record number of conference submissions. After removing the desk rejects, 979 valid, complete manuscripts were submitted for review. A pool of 34 area chairs and 1,063 reviewers was recruited to conduct paper reviews. Like previous editions of ACCV, we adopted a double-blind review process to determine which of these papers to accept. Identities of authors were not visible to reviewers and area chairs; nor were the identities of the assigned reviewers and area chairs visible to authors. The program chairs did not submit papers to the conference.

Each paper was reviewed by at least three reviewers. Authors were permitted to respond to the initial reviews during a rebuttal period. After this, the area chairs led discussions among reviewers. Finally, a physical area chairs was held in Singapore, during which panels of three area chairs deliberated to decide on acceptance decisions for each paper. At the end of this process, 274 papers were accepted for publication in the ACCV 2018 conference proceedings, of which five were later withdrawn by their authors.

In addition to the main conference, ACCV 2018 featured 11 workshops and six tutorials.

We would like to thank all the organizers, sponsors, area chairs, reviewers, and authors. Special thanks go to Prof. Guosheng Lin from Nanyang Technological University, Singapore, for hosting the area chair meeting. We acknowledge the support of Microsoft's Conference Management Toolkit (CMT) team for providing the software used to manage the review process.

We greatly appreciate the efforts of all those who contributed to making the conference a success.

December 2018

C. V. Jawahar
Hongdong Li
Greg Mori
Konrad Schindler

Organization

General Chairs

Kyoung-mu Lee	Seoul National University, South Korea
Ajmal Mian	University of Western Australia, Australia
Ian Reid	University of Adelaide, Australia
Yoichi Sato	University of Tokyo, Japan

Program Chairs

C. V. Jawahar	IIIT Hyderabad, India
Hongdong Li	Australian National University, Australia
Greg Mori	Simon Fraser University and Borealis AI, Canada
Konrad Schindler	ETH Zurich, Switzerland

Advisor

Richard Hartley	Australian National University, Australia

Publication Chair

Hamid Rezatofighi	University of Adelaide, Australia

Local Arrangements Chairs

Guosheng Lin	Nanyang Technological University, Singapore
Ajmal Mian	University of Western Australia, Australia

Area Chairs

Lourdes Agapito	University College London, UK
Xiang Bai	Huazhong University of Science and Technology, China
Vineeth N. Balasubramanian	IIT Hyderabad, India
Gustavo Carneiro	University of Adelaide, Australia
Tat-Jun Chin	University of Adelaide, Australia
Minsu Cho	POSTECH, South Korea
Bohyung Han	Seoul National University, South Korea
Junwei Han	Northwestern Polytechnical University, China
Mehrtash Harandi	Monash University, Australia
Gang Hua	Microsoft Research, Asia

Rei Kawakami	University of Tokyo, Japan
Tae-Kyun Kim	Imperial College London, UK
Junseok Kwon	Chung-Ang University, South Korea
Florent Lafarge	Inria, France
Laura Leal-Taixé	TU Munich, Germany
Zhouchen Lin	Peking University, China
Yanxi Liu	Penn State University, USA
Oisin Mac Aodha	Caltech, USA
Anurag Mittal	IIT Madras, India
Vinay Namboodiri	IIT Kanpur, India
P. J. Narayanan	IIIT Hyderabad, India
Carl Olsson	Lund University, Sweden
Imari Sato	National Institute of Informatics
Shiguang Shan	Chinese Academy of Sciences, China
Chunhua Shen	University of Adelaide, Australia
Boxin Shi	Peking University, China
Terence Sim	National University of Singapore, Singapore
Yusuke Sugano	Osaka University, Japan
Min Sun	National Tsing Hua University, Taiwan
Robby Tan	Yale-NUS College, USA
Siyu Tang	MPI for Intelligent Systems
Radu Timofte	ETH Zurich, Switzerland
Jingyi Yu	University of Delaware, USA
Junsong Yuan	State University of New York at Buffalo, USA

Additional Reviewers

Ehsan Abbasnejad	Ognjen Arandjelovic	Nick Barnes
Akash Abdu Jyothi	Anil Armagan	Peter Barnum
Abrar Abdulnabi	Chetan Arora	Joe Bartels
Nagesh Adluru	Mathieu Aubry	Paul Beardsley
Antonio Agudo	Hossein Azizpour	Sima Behpour
Unaiza Ahsan	Seung-Hwan Baek	Vasileios Belagiannis
Hai-zhou Ai	Aijun Bai	Boulbaba Ben Amor
Alexandre Alahi	Peter Bajcsy	Archith Bency
Xavier Alameda-Pineda	Amr Bakry	Ryad Benosman
Andrea Albarelli	Vassileios Balntas	Gedas Bertasius
Mohsen Ali	Yutong Ban	Ross Beveridge
Saad Ali	Arunava Banerjee	Binod Bhattarai
Mitsuru Ambai	Monami Banerjee	Arnav Bhavsar
Cosmin Ancuti	Atsuhiko Banno	Simone Bianco
Vijay Rengarajan Angarai	Aayush Bansal	Oliver Bimber
Pichaikuppan	Dániel Baráth	Tolga Birdal
Michel Antunes	Lorenzo Baraldi	Horst Bischof
Djamila Aouada	Adrian Barbu	Arijit Biswas

Soma Biswas
Henryk Blasinski
Vishnu Boddeti
Federica Bogo
Tolga Bolukbasi
Terrance Boult
Thierry Bouwmans
Abdesselam Bouzerdoum
Ernesto Brau
Mathieu Bredif
Stefan Breuers
Marcus Brubaker
Anders Buch
Shyamal Buch
Pradeep Buddharaju
Adrian Bulat
Darius Burschka
Andrei Bursuc
Zoya Bylinskii
Weidong Cai
Necati Cihan Camgoz
Shaun Canavan
Joao Carreira
Dan Casas
M. Emre Celebi
Hakan Cevikalp
François Chadebecq
Menglei Chai
Rudrasis Chakraborty
Tat-Jen Cham
Kwok-Ping Chan
Sharat Chandran
Chehan Chang
Hyun Sung Chang
Yi Chang
Wei-Lun Chao
Visesh Chari
Gaurav Chaurasia
Rama Chellappa
Chen Chen
Chu-Song Chen
Dongdong Chen
Guangyong Chen
Hsin-I Chen
Huaijin Chen
Hwann-Tzong Chen

Jiacheng Chen
Jianhui Chen
Jiansheng Chen
Jiaxin Chen
Jie Chen
Kan Chen
Longbin Chen
Ting Chen
Tseng-Hung Chen
Wei Chen
Xi'ai Chen
Xiaozhi Chen
Xilin Chen
Xinlei Chen
Yunjin Chen
Erkang Cheng
Hong Cheng
Hui Cheng
Jingchun Cheng
Ming-Ming Cheng
Wen-Huang Cheng
Yuan Cheng
Zhi-Qi Cheng
Loong Fah Cheong
Anoop Cherian
Liang-Tien Chia
Chao-Kai Chiang
Shao-Yi Chien
Han-Pang Chiu
Wei-Chen Chiu
Donghyeon Cho
Nam Ik Cho
Sunghyun Cho
Yeong-Jun Cho
Gyeongmin Choe
Chiho Choi
Jonghyun Choi
Jongmoo Choi
Jongwon Choi
Hisham Cholakkal
Biswarup Choudhury
Xiao Chu
Yung-Yu Chuang
Andrea Cohen
Toby Collins
Marco Cristani

James Crowley
Jinshi Cui
Zhaopeng Cui
Bo Dai
Hang Dai
Xiyang Dai
Yuchao Dai
Carlo Dal Mutto
Zachary Daniels
Mohamed Daoudi
Abir Das
Raoul De Charette
Teofilo Decampos
Koichiro Deguchi
Stefanie Demirci
Girum Demisse
Patrick Dendorfer
Zhiwei Deng
Joachim Denzler
Aditya Deshpande
Frédéric Devernay
Abhinav Dhall
Anthony Dick
Zhengming Ding
Cosimo Distante
Ajay Divakaran
Mandar Dixit
Thanh-Toan Do
Jose Dolz
Bo Dong
Chao Dong
Jingming Dong
Ming Dong
Weisheng Dong
Simon Donne
Gianfranco Doretto
Bruce Draper
Bertram Drost
Liang Du
Shichuan Du
Jean-Luc Dugelay
Enrique Dunn
Thibaut Durand
Zoran Duric
Ionut Cosmin Duta
Samyak Dutta

Pinar Duygulu
Ady Ecker
Hazim Ekenel
Sabu Emmanuel
Ian Endres
Ertunc Erdil
Hugo Jair Escalante
Sergio Escalera
Francisco Escolano Ruiz
Bin Fan
Shaojing Fan
Yi Fang
Aly Farag
Giovanni Farinella
Rafael Felix
Michele Fenzi
Bob Fisher
David Fofi
Gian Luca Foresti
Victor Fragoso
Bernd Freisleben
Jason Fritts
Cheng-Yang Fu
Chi-Wing Fu
Huazhu Fu
Jianlong Fu
Xueyang Fu
Ying Fu
Yun Fu
Olac Fuentes
Jan Funke
Ryo Furukawa
Yasutaka Furukawa
Manuel Günther
Raghudeep Gadde
Matheus Gadelha
Jürgen Gall
Silvano Galliani
Chuang Gan
Zhe Gan
Vineet Gandhi
Arvind Ganesh
Bin-Bin Gao
Jin Gao
Jiyang Gao
Junbin Gao

Ravi Garg
Jochen Gast
Utkarsh Gaur
Xin Geng
David Geronimno
Michael Gharbi
Amir Ghodrati
Behnam Gholami
Andrew Gilbert
Rohit Girdhar
Ioannis Gkioulekas
Guy Godin
Nuno Goncalves
Yu Gong
Stephen Gould
Venu Govindu
Oleg Grinchuk
Jiuxiang Gu
Shuhang Gu
Paul Guerrero
Anupam Guha
Guodong Guo
Yanwen Guo
Ankit Gupta
Mithun Gupta
Saurabh Gupta
Hossein Hajimirsadeghi
Maciej Halber
Xiaoguang Han
Yahong Han
Zhi Han
Kenji Hara
Tatsuya Harada
Ali Harakeh
Adam Harley
Ben Harwood
Mahmudul Hasan
Kenji Hata
Michal Havlena
Munawar Hayat
Zeeshan Hayder
Jiawei He
Kun He
Lei He
Lifang He
Pan He

Yang He
Zhenliang He
Zhihai He
Felix Heide
Samitha Herath
Luis Herranz
Anders Heyden
Je Hyeong Hong
Seunghoon Hong
Wei Hong
Le Hou
Chiou-Ting Hsu
Kuang-Jui Hsu
Di Hu
Hexiang Hu
Ping Hu
Xu Hu
Yinlin Hu
Zhiting Hu
De-An Huang
Gao Huang
Gary Huang
Haibin Huang
Haifei Huang
Haozhi Huang
Jia-Bin Huang
Shaoli Huang
Sheng Huang
Xinyu Huang
Xun Huang
Yan Huang
Yawen Huang
Yinghao Huang
Yizhen Huang
Wei-Chih Hung
Junhwa Hur
Mohamed Hussein
Jyh-Jing Hwang
Ichiro Ide
Satoshi Ikehata
Radu Tudor Ionescu
Go Irie
Ahmet Iscen
Vamsi Ithapu
Daisuke Iwai
Won-Dong Jang

Dinesh Jayaraman
Sadeep Jayasumana
Suren Jayasuriya
Hueihan Jhuang
Dinghuang Ji
Mengqi Ji
Hongjun Jia
Jiayan Jiang
Qing-Yuan Jiang
Tingting Jiang
Xiaoyi Jiang
Zhuolin Jiang
Zequn Jie
Xiaojie Jin
Younghyun Jo
Ole Johannsen
Hanbyul Joo
Jungseock Joo
Kyungdon Joo
Shantanu Joshi
Amin Jourabloo
Deunsol Jung
Anis Kacem
Ioannis Kakadiaris
Zdenek Kalal
Nima Kalantari
Mahdi Kalayeh
Sinan Kalkan
Vicky Kalogeiton
Joni-Kristian Kamarainen
Martin Kampel
Meina Kan
Kenichi Kanatani
Atsushi Kanehira
Takuhiro Kaneko
Zhuoliang Kang
Mohan Kankanhalli
Vadim Kantorov
Nikolaos Karianakis
Leonid Karlinsky
Zoltan Kato
Hiroshi Kawasaki
Wei Ke
Wadim Kehl
Sameh Khamis
Naeemullah Khan

Salman Khan
Rawal Khirodkar
Mehran Khodabandeh
Anna Khoreva
Parmeshwar Khurd
Hadi Kiapour
Joe Kileel
Edward Kim
Gunhee Kim
Hansung Kim
Hyunwoo Kim
Junsik Kim
Seon Joo Kim
Vladimir Kim
Akisato Kimura
Ravi Kiran
Roman Klokov
Takumi Kobayashi
Amir Kolaman
Naejin Kong
Piotr Koniusz
Hyung Il Koo
Dimitrios Kosmopoulos
Gregory Kramida
Praveen Krishnan
Ravi Krishnan
Hiroyuki Kubo
Hilde Kuehne
Jason Kuen
Arjan Kuijper
Kuldeep Kulkarni
Shiro Kumano
Avinash Kumar
Soumava Roy Kumar
Kaustav Kundu
Sebastian Kurtek
Yevhen Kuznietsov
Heeseung Kwon
Alexander Ladikos
Kevin Lai
Wei-Sheng Lai
Shang-Hong Lai
Michael Lam
Zhenzhong Lan
Dong Lao
Katrin Lasinger

Yasir Latif
Huu Le
Herve Le Borgne
Chun-Yi Lee
Gim Hee Lee
Seungyong Lee
Teng-Yok Lee
Seungkyu Lee
Andreas Lehrmann
Na Lei
Spyridon Leonardos
Marius Leordeanu
Matt Leotta
Gil Levi
Evgeny Levinkov
Jose Lezama
Ang Li
Chen Li
Chunyuan Li
Dangwei Li
Dingzeyu Li
Dong Li
Hai Li
Jianguo Li
Stan Li
Wanqing Li
Wei Li
Xi Li
Xirong Li
Xiu Li
Xuelong Li
Yanghao Li
Yin Li
Yingwei Li
Yongjie Li
Yu Li
Yuncheng Li
Zechao Li
Zhengqi Li
Zhengqin Li
Zhuwen Li
Zhouhui Lian
Jie Liang
Zicheng Liao
Jongwoo Lim
Ser-Nam Lim

Kaimo Lin
Shih-Yao Lin
Tsung-Yi Lin
Weiyao Lin
Yuewei Lin
Venice Liong
Giuseppe Lisanti
Roee Litman
Jim Little
Anan Liu
Chao Liu
Chen Liu
Eryun Liu
Fayao Liu
Huaping Liu
Jingen Liu
Lingqiao Liu
Miaomiao Liu
Qingshan Liu
Risheng Liu
Sifei Liu
Tyng-Luh Liu
Weiyang Liu
Xialei Liu
Xianglong Liu
Xiao Liu
Yebin Liu
Yi Liu
Yu Liu
Yun Liu
Ziwei Liu
Stephan Liwicki
Liliana Lo Presti
Fotios Logothetis
Javier Lorenzo
Manolis Lourakis
Brian Lovell
Chen Change Loy
Chaochao Lu
Feng Lu
Huchuan Lu
Jiajun Lu
Kaiyue Lu
Xin Lu
Yijuan Lu
Yongxi Lu

Fujun Luan
Jian-Hao Luo
Jiebo Luo
Weixin Luo
Khoa Luu
Chao Ma
Huimin Ma
Kede Ma
Lin Ma
Shugao Ma
Wei-Chiu Ma
Will Maddern
Ludovic Magerand
Luca Magri
Behrooz Mahasseni
Tahmida Mahmud
Robert Maier
Subhransu Maji
Yasushi Makihara
Clement Mallet
Abed Malti
Devraj Mandal
Fabian Manhardt
Gian Luca Marcialis
Julio Marco
Diego Marcos
Ricardo Martin
Tanya Marwah
Marc Masana
Jonathan Masci
Takeshi Masuda
Yusuke Matsui
Tetsu Matsukawa
Gellert Mattyus
Thomas Mauthner
Bruce Maxwell
Steve Maybank
Amir Mazaheri
Scott Mccloskey
Mason Mcgill
Nazanin Mehrasa
Ishit Mehta
Xue Mei
Heydi Mendez-Vazquez
Gaofeng Meng
Bjoern Menze

Domingo Mery
Pascal Mettes
Jan Hendrik Metzen
Gregor Miller
Cai Minjie
Ikuhisa Mitsugami
Daisuke Miyazaki
Davide Modolo
Pritish Mohapatra
Pascal Monasse
Sandino Morales
Pietro Morerio
Saeid Motiian
Arsalan Mousavian
Mikhail Mozerov
Yasuhiro Mukaigawa
Yusuke Mukuta
Mario Munich
Srikanth Muralidharan
Ana Murillo
Vittorio Murino
Armin Mustafa
Hajime Nagahara
Shruti Nagpal
Mahyar Najibi
Katsuyuki Nakamura
Seonghyeon Nam
Loris Nanni
Manjunath Narayana
Lakshmanan Nataraj
Neda Nategh
Lukáš Neumann
Shawn Newsam
Joe Yue-Hei Ng
Thuyen Ngo
David Nilsson
Ji-feng Ning
Mark Nixon
Shohei Nobuhara
Hyeonwoo Noh
Mehdi Noroozi
Erfan Noury
Eyal Ofek
Seong Joon Oh
Seoung Wug Oh
Katsunori Ohnishi

Iason Oikonomidis
Takeshi Oishi
Takahiro Okabe
Takayuki Okatani
Gustavo Olague
Kyle Olszewski
Mohamed Omran
Roy Or-El
Ivan Oseledets
Martin R. Oswald
Tomas Pajdla
Dipan Pal
Kalman Palagyi
Manohar Paluri
Gang Pan
Jinshan Pan
Yannis Panagakis
Rameswar Panda
Hsing-Kuo Pao
Dim Papadopoulos
Konstantinos Papoutsakis
Shaifali Parashar
Hyun Soo Park
Jinsun Park
Taesung Park
Wonpyo Park
Alvaro Parra Bustos
Geoffrey Pascoe
Ioannis Patras
Genevieve Patterson
Georgios Pavlakos
Ioannis Pavlidis
Nick Pears
Pieter Peers
Selen Pehlivan
Xi Peng
Xingchao Peng
Janez Perš
Talita Perciano
Adrian Peter
Lars Petersson
Stavros Petridis
Patrick Peursum
Trung Pham
Sang Phan
Marco Piccirilli

Sudeep Pillai
Wong Ya Ping
Lerrel Pinto
Fiora Pirri
Matteo Poggi
Georg Poier
Marius Popescu
Ronald Poppe
Dilip Prasad
Andrea Prati
Maria Priisalu
Véronique Prinet
Victor Prisacariu
Hugo Proenca
Jan Prokaj
Daniel Prusa
Yunchen Pu
Guo-Jun Qi
Xiaojuan Qi
Zhen Qian
Yu Qiao
Jie Qin
Lei Qin
Chao Qu
Faisal Qureshi
Petia Radeva
Venkatesh Babu
  Radhakrishnan
Ilija Radosavovic
Bogdan Raducanu
Hossein Rahmani
Swaminathan Rahul
Ajit Rajwade
Kandan Ramakrishnan
Visvanathan Ramesh
Yongming Rao
Sathya Ravi
Michael Reale
Adria Recasens
Konstantinos Rematas
Haibing Ren
Jimmy Ren
Wenqi Ren
Zhile Ren
Edel Garcia Reyes
Hamid Rezatofighi

Hamed Rezazadegan
  Tavakoli
Rafael Rezende
Helge Rhodin
Alexander Richard
Stephan Richter
Gernot Riegler
Christian Riess
Ergys Ristani
Tobias Ritschel
Mariano Rivera
Antonio Robles-Kelly
Emanuele Rodola
Andres Rodriguez
Mikel Rodriguez
Matteo Ruggero Ronchi
Xuejian Rong
Bodo Rosenhahn
Arun Ross
Peter Roth
Michel Roux
Ryusuke Sagawa
Hideo Saito
Shunsuke Saito
Parikshit Sakurikar
Albert Ali Salah
Jorge Sanchez
Conrad Sanderson
Aswin Sankaranarayanan
Swami Sankaranarayanan
Archana Sapkota
Michele Sasdelli
Jun Sato
Shin'ichi Satoh
Torsten Sattler
Manolis Savva
Tanner Schmidt
Dirk Schnieders
Samuel Schulter
Rajvi Shah
Shishir Shah
Sohil Shah
Moein Shakeri
Nataliya Shapovalova
Aidean Sharghi
Gaurav Sharma

Pramod Sharma
Li Shen
Shuhan Shen
Wei Shen
Xiaoyong Shen
Zhiqiang Shen
Lu Sheng
Baoguang Shi
Guangming Shi
Miaojing Shi
Zhiyuan Shi
Takashi Shibata
Huang-Chia Shih
Meng-Li Shih
Sheng-Wen Shih
Atsushi Shimada
Nobutaka Shimada
Daeyun Shin
Young Min Shin
Koichi Shinoda
Tianmin Shu
Zhixin Shu
Bing Shuai
Karan Sikka
Jack Sim
Marcel Simon
Tomas Simon
Vishwanath Sindagi
Gurkirt Singh
Maneet Singh
Praveer Singh
Ayan Sinha
Sudipta Sinha
Vladimir Smutny
Francesco Solera
Amir Arsalan Soltani
Eric Sommerlade
Andy Song
Shiyu Song
Yibing Song
Humberto Sossa
Concetto Spampinato
Filip Šroubek
Ioannis Stamos
Jan Stuehmer
Jingyong Su

Jong-Chyi Su
Shuochen Su
Yu-Chuan Su
Zhixun Su
Ramanathan Subramanian
Akihiro Sugimoto
Waqas Sultani
Jiande Sun
Jin Sun
Ju Sun
Lin Sun
Min Sun
Yao Sun
Zhaohui Sun
David Suter
Tanveer Syeda-Mahmood
Yuichi Taguchi
Jun Takamatsu
Takafumi Taketomi
Hugues Talbot
Youssef Tamaazousti
Toru Tamak
Robert Tamburo
Chaowei Tan
David Joseph Tan
Ping Tan
Xiaoyang Tan
Kenichiro Tanaka
Masayuki Tanaka
Jinhui Tang
Meng Tang
Peng Tang
Wei Tang
Yuxing Tang
Junli Tao
Xin Tao
Makarand Tapaswi
Jean-Philippe Tarel
Keisuke Tateno
Joao Tavares
Bugra Tekin
Mariano Tepper
Ali Thabet
Spiros Thermos
Shangxuan Tian
Yingli Tian

Kinh Tieu
Massimo Tistarelli
Henning Tjaden
Matthew Toews
Chetan Tonde
Akihiko Torii
Andrea Torsello
Toan Tran
Leonardo Trujillo
Tomasz Trzcinski
Sam Tsai
Yi-Hsuan Tsai
Ivor Tsang
Vagia Tsiminaki
Aggeliki Tsoli
Wei-Chih Tu
Shubham Tulsiani
Sergey Tulyakov
Tony Tung
Matt Turek
Seiichi Uchida
Oytun Ulutan
Martin Urschler
Mikhail Usvyatsov
Alexander Vakhitov
Julien Valentin
Ernest Valveny
Ian Van Der Linde
Kiran Varanasi
Gul Varol
Francisco Vasconcelos
Pascal Vasseur
Javier Vazquez-Corral
Ashok Veeraraghavan
Andreas Velten
Raviteja Vemulapalli
Jonathan Ventura
Subhashini Venugopalan
Yashaswi Verma
Matthias Vestner
Minh Vo
Jayakorn Vongkulbhisal
Toshikazu Wada
Chengde Wan
Jun Wan
Renjie Wan

Baoyuan Wang
Chaohui Wang
Chaoyang Wang
Chunyu Wang
De Wang
Dong Wang
Fang Wang
Faqiang Wang
Hongsong Wang
Hongxing Wang
Hua Wang
Jialei Wang
Jianyu Wang
Jinglu Wang
Jinqiao Wang
Keze Wang
Le Wang
Lei Wang
Lezi Wang
Lijun Wang
Limin Wang
Linwei Wang
Pichao Wang
Qi Wang
Qian Wang
Qilong Wang
Qing Wang
Ruiping Wang
Shangfei Wang
Shuhui Wang
Song Wang
Tao Wang
Tsun-Hsuang Wang
Weiyue Wang
Wenguan Wang
Xiaoyu Wang
Xinchao Wang
Xinggang Wang
Yang Wang
Yin Wang
Yu-Chiang Frank Wang
Yufei Wang
Yunhong Wang
Zhangyang Wang
Zilei Wang
Jan Dirk Wegner

Ping Wei
Shih-En Wei
Wei Wei
Xiu-Shen Wei
Zijun Wei
Bihan Wen
Longyin Wen
Xinshuo Weng
Tom Whelan
Patrick Wieschollek
Maggie Wigness
Jerome Williams
Kwan-Yee Wong
Chao-Yuan Wu
Chunpeng Wu
Dijia Wu
Jiajun Wu
Jianxin Wu
Xiao Wu
Xiaohe Wu
Xiaomeng Wu
Xinxiao Wu
Yi Wu
Ying Nian Wu
Yue Wu
Zheng Wu
Zhirong Wu
Jonas Wulff
Yin Xia
Yongqin Xian
Yu Xiang
Fanyi Xiao
Yang Xiao
Dan Xie
Jianwen Xie
Jin Xie
Fuyong Xing
Jun Xing
Junliang Xing
Xuehan Xiong
Yuanjun Xiong
Changsheng Xu
Chenliang Xu
Haotian Xu
Huazhe Xu
Huijuan Xu

Jun Xu
Ning Xu
Tao Xu
Weipeng Xu
Xiangmin Xu
Xiangyu Xu
Yong Xu
Yuanlu Xu
Jia Xue
Xiangyang Xue
Toshihiko Yamasaki
Junchi Yan
Luxin Yan
Wang Yan
Keiji Yanai
Bin Yang
Chih-Yuan Yang
Dong Yang
Herb Yang
Jianwei Yang
Jie Yang
Jin-feng Yang
Jufeng Yang
Meng Yang
Ming Yang
Ming-Hsuan Yang
Tien-Ju Yang
Wei Yang
Wenhan Yang
Yanchao Yang
Yingzhen Yang
Yongxin Yang
Zhenheng Yang
Angela Yao
Bangpeng Yao
Cong Yao
Jian Yao
Jiawen Yao
Yasushi Yagi
Mang Ye
Mao Ye
Qixiang Ye
Mei-Chen Yeh
Sai-Kit Yeung
Kwang Moo Yi
Alper Yilmaz

Xi Yin
Zhaozheng Yin
Xianghua Ying
Ryo Yonetani
Donghyun Yoo
Jae Shin Yoon
Ryota Yoshihashi
Gang Yu
Hongkai Yu
Ruichi Yu
Shiqi Yu
Xiang Yu
Yang Yu
Youngjae Yu
Chunfeng Yuan
Jing Yuan
Junsong Yuan
Shanxin Yuan
Zejian Yuan
Xenophon Zabulis
Mihai Zanfir
Pablo Zegers
Jiabei Zeng
Kuo-Hao Zeng
Baochang Zhang
Cha Zhang
Chao Zhang
Dingwen Zhang
Dong Zhang
Guofeng Zhang
Hanwang Zhang
He Zhang
Hong Zhang
Honggang Zhang
Hua Zhang
Jian Zhang

Jiawei Zhang
Jing Zhang
Kaipeng Zhang
Ke Zhang
Liang Zhang
Linguang Zhang
Liqing Zhang
Peng Zhang
Pingping Zhang
Quanshi Zhang
Runze Zhang
Shanghang Zhang
Shu Zhang
Tianzhu Zhang
Tong Zhang
Wen Zhang
Xiaofan Zhang
Xiaoqin Zhang
Xikang Zhang
Xu Zhang
Ya Zhang
Yinda Zhang
Yongqiang Zhang
Zhang Zhang
Zhen Zhang
Zhoutong Zhang
Ziyu Zhang
Bin Zhao
Bo Zhao
Chen Zhao
Hengshuang Zhao
Qijun Zhao
Rui Zhao
Heliang Zheng
Shuai Zheng
Stephan Zheng

Yinqiang Zheng
Yuanjie Zheng
Zhonglong Zheng
Guangyu Zhong
Huiyu Zhou
Jiahuan Zhou
Jun Zhou
Luping Zhou
Mo Zhou
Pan Zhou
Yang Zhou
Zihan Zhou
Fan Zhu
Guangming Zhu
Hao Zhu
Hongyuan Zhu
Lei Zhu
Menglong Zhu
Pengfei Zhu
Shizhan Zhu
Siyu Zhu
Xiangxin Zhu
Yi Zhu
Yizhe Zhu
Yuke Zhu
Zhigang Zhu
Bohan Zhuang
Liansheng Zhuang
Karel Zimmermann
Maria Zontak
Danping Zou
Qi Zou
Wangmeng Zuo
Xinxin Zuo

Contents – Part V

Oral Session O5: 3D Vision and Pose

Creatures Great and SMAL: Recovering the Shape and Motion of Animals from Video

Benjamin Biggs[1](✉), Thomas Roddick[1](✉), Andrew Fitzgibbon[2](✉), and Roberto Cipolla[1](✉)

[1] Department of Engineering, University of Cambridge, Trumpington Street, Cambridge CB2 1PZ, UK
{bjb56,tr346,rc10001}@cam.ac.uk
[2] Microsoft Research, 21 Station Road, Cambridge CB1 2FB, UK
awf@microsoft.com

Abstract. We present a system to recover the 3D shape and motion of a wide variety of quadrupeds from video. The system comprises a machine learning front-end which predicts candidate 2D joint positions, a discrete optimization which finds kinematically plausible joint correspondences, and an energy minimization stage which fits a detailed 3D model to the image. In order to overcome the limited availability of motion capture training data from animals, and the difficulty of generating realistic synthetic training images, the system is designed to work on silhouette data. The joint candidate predictor is trained on synthetically generated silhouette images, and at test time, deep learning methods or standard video segmentation tools are used to extract silhouettes from real data. The system is tested on animal videos from several species, and shows accurate reconstructions of 3D shape and pose.

1 Introduction

Animal welfare is an important concern for business and society, with an estimated 70 billion animals currently living under human care [1]. Monitoring and assessment of animal health can be assisted by obtaining accurate measurements of an individual's shape, volume and movement. These measurements should be taken without interfering with the animal's normal activity, and are needed around the clock, under a variety of lighting and weather conditions, perhaps at long range (e.g. in farm fields or wildlife parks). Therefore a very wide range of cameras and imaging modalities must be handled. For small animals in captivity, a depth camera might be possible, but techniques which can operate solely from intensity data will have a much wider range of applicability.

Electronic supplementary material The online version of this chapter (https://doi.org/10.1007/978-3-030-20873-8_1) contains supplementary material, which is available to authorized users.

© Springer Nature Switzerland AG 2019
C. V. Jawahar et al. (Eds.): ACCV 2018, LNCS 11365, pp. 3–10, 2019.
https://doi.org/10.1007/978-3-030-20873-8_1

Fig. 1. System overview: input video (a) is automatically processed using DeepLabv3+ [2] to produce silhouettes (b), from which 2D joint predictions are regressed in the form of heatmaps (c). Optimal joint assignment (OJA) finds kinematically coherent 2D-to-3D correspondences (d), which initialize a 3D shape model, optimized to match the silhouette (e). Alternative view shown in (f).

We address this problem using techniques from the recent human body and hand tracking literature, combining machine learning and 3D model fitting. A discriminative front-end uses a deep hourglass network to identify candidate 2D joint positions. These joint positions are then linked into coherent skeletons by solving an optimal joint assignment problem, and the resulting skeletons create an initial estimate for a generative model-fitting back-end to yield detailed shape and pose for each frame of the video.

Although superficially similar to human tracking, animal tracking (AT) has some interesting differences that make it worthy of study:

Variability. In one sense, AT is simpler than human tracking as animals generally do not wear clothing. However, variations in surface texture are still considerable between individuals, and the variety of shape across and within species is considerably greater. If tracking is specialized to a particular species, then shape variation is smaller, but training data is even harder to obtain.

Training Data. For human tracking, hand labelled sequences of 2D segmentations and joint positions have been collected from a wide variety of sources [3–5]. Of these two classes of labelling, animal *segmentation* data is available in datasets such as MSCOCO [4], PASCAL VOC [6] and DAVIS [7]. However this data is considerably sparser than human data, and must be "shared" across species, meaning the number of examples for a given animal shape class is considerably fewer than is available for an equivalent variation in human shape. While segmentation data can be supplied by non-specialist human labellers, it is more difficult to obtain *joint position* data. Some joints are easy to label, such as "tip of snout", but others such as the analogue of "right elbow" require training of the operator to correctly identify across species.

Of more concern however, is 3D skeleton data. For humans, motion capture (mocap) can be used to obtain long sequences of skeleton parameters (joint positions and angles) from a wide variety of motions and activities. For animal tracking, this is considerably harder: animals behave differently on treadmills than in their quotidian environments, and although some animals such as horses and dogs have been coaxed into motion capture studios [8], it remains impractical to consider mocap for a family of tigers at play.

These concerns are of course alleviated if we have access to synthetic training data. Here, humans and animals share an advantage in the availability of parameterized 3D models of shape and pose. The recent publication of the Skinned Multi-Animal Linear (SMAL) model [9] can generate a wide range of quadruped species, although without surface texture maps. However, as with humans, it remains difficult to generate RGB images which are sufficiently realistic to train modern machine learning models. In the case of humans, this has been overcome by generating depth maps, but this then requires a depth camera at test time [10]. The alternative, used in this work, is to generate 2D silhouette images so that machine learning will predict joint heatmaps from silhouettes only.

Taking into account the above constraints, this work applies a novel strategy to animal tracking, which assumes a machine-learning approach to extraction of animal silhouettes from video, and then fits a parameterized 3D model to silhouette sequences. We make the following contributions:

- A machine-learned mapping from silhouette data of a large class of quadrupeds to generic 2D joint positions.
- A novel optimal joint assignment (OJA) algorithm extending the bipartite matching of Cao *et al.* [11] in two ways, one which can be cast as a quadratic program (QP), and an extension optimized using a genetic algorithm (GA).
- A procedure for optimization of a 3D deformable model to fit 2D silhouette data and 2D joint positions, while encouraging temporally coherent outputs.
- We introduce a new benchmark animal dataset of joint annotations (BADJA) which contains sparse keypoint labels and silhouette segmentations for eleven animal video sequences. Previous work in 3D animal reconstruction has relied on bespoke hand-clicked keypoints [9,12] and little quantitative evaluation of performance could be given. The sequences exhibit a range of animals, are selected to capture a variety of animal movement and include some challenging visual scenarios such as occlusion and motion blur.

The system is outlined in Fig. 1. The remainder of the paper describes related literature before a detailed description of system components. Joint accuracy results at multiple stages of the pipeline are reported on the new BADJA dataset, which contains ground truths for real animal subjects. We also conduct experiments on synthetic animal videos to produce joint accuracy statistics and full 3D mesh comparisons. A qualitative comparison is given to recent work [9] on the related single-frame 3D shape and pose recovery problem. The paper concludes with an assessment of strengths and limitations of the work.

2   Related Work

3D animal tracking is relatively new to the computer vision literature, but animal breed identification is a well studied problem [13]. Video tracking benchmarks often use animal sequences [14,15], although the tracking output is typically limited to 2D affine transformations rather than the detailed 3D mesh that we propose. Although we believe our work is the first to demonstrate dense 3D tracking of animals in video without the need for user-provided keypoints, we do build on related work across computer vision:

Morphable Shape Models. Cashman and Fitzgibbon [16] obtained one of the first 3D morphable animal models, but their work was limited to small classes of objects (e.g. dolphins, pigeons), and did not incorporate a skeleton. Their work also showed the use of the 2D silhouette for fitting, which is key to our method. Reinert et al. [17] meanwhile construct 3D meshes by fitting generalized cylinders to hand-drawn skeletons. Combined skeletal and morphable models were used by Khamis et al. [18] for modelling the human hand, and Loper et al. [19] in the SMPL model which has been extensively used for human tracking.

The SMPL model was extended to animals by Zuffi et al. [9], where the lack of motion capture data for animal subjects is cleverly overcome by building the model from 41 3D scans of toy figurines from five quadruped families in arbitrary poses. Their paper demonstrates single-frame fits of their model to real-world animal data, showing that despite the model being built from "artists' impressions" it remains an accurate model of real animals. This is borne out further by our work. Their paper did however depend on per-frame human annotated keypoint labels, which would be costly and challenging to obtain for large video sequences. This work was recently extended [12] with a refinement step that optimizes over model vertex positions. This can be considered independent to the initial SMAL model fit and would be trivial to add to our method.

Shape from Silhouette. Silhouette images have been shown to contain sufficient shape information to enable their use in many 3D recovery pipelines. Chen et al. [20] demonstrate single-view shape reconstruction from such input for general object classes, by building a shape space model from 3D samples. More related to our work, Favreau et al. [21] apply PCA to silhouette images to extract animal gaits from video sequences. The task of predicting silhouette images from 2D input has been effectively used as a proxy for regressing 3D model parameters for humans [22,23] and other 3D objects [24].

Joint Position Prediction. There is an extensive body of prior work related to joint position prediction for human subjects. Earlier work used graphical approaches such as pictorial structure models [5,25,26], which have since been replaced with deep learning-based methods [11,27]. Few works predict animal joint positions directly owing to the lack of annotated data, although Mathis *et al.* [28] demonstrate the effectiveness of human pose estimation architectures for restricted animal domains. Our method instead trains on silhouette input, allowing the use of synthetic training imagery. The related task of animal part segmentation [29,30] has seen some progress due to general object part datasets [31,32].

2.1 Preliminaries

We are given a deformable 3D model such as SMAL [9] which parametrizes a 3D mesh as a function of *pose* parameters $\theta \in \mathbb{R}^P$ (e.g. joint angles) and *shape* parameters $\beta \in \mathbb{R}^B$. In detail, a 3D mesh is an array of vertices $\nu \in \mathbb{R}^{3 \times V}$ (the vertices are columns of a $3 \times V$ matrix) and a set of triangles represented as integer triples (i, j, k), which are indices into the vertex array. A deformable model such as SMPL or SMAL may be viewed as supplying a set of triangles, and a function

$$\nu(\theta, \beta) : \mathbb{R}^P \times \mathbb{R}^B \mapsto \mathbb{R}^{3 \times V} \tag{1}$$

which generates the 3D model for a given pose and shape. The mesh topology (i.e. the triangle vertex indices) is provided by the deformable model, and is the same for all shapes and poses we consider, so in the sequel we shall consider a mesh to be defined only by the 3D positions of its vertices.

In any given image, the model's 3D *position* (i.e. translation and orientation) is also unknown, and will be represented by a parametrization ϕ which may be for example translation as a 3-vector and rotation as a unit quaternion. Application of such a transformation to a $3 \times V$ matrix will be denoted by $*$, so that

$$\phi * \nu(\theta, \beta) \tag{2}$$

represents a 3D model of given pose and shape transformed to its 3D position.

We will also have occasion to talk about model *joints*. These appear naturally in models with an explicit skeleton, but more generally they can be defined as some function mapping from the model parameters to an array of 3D points analogous to the vertex transformation above. We consider the joints to be defined by post-multiplying by a $V \times J$ matrix K. The jth column of K defines the 3D position of joint j as a linear combination of the vertices (this is quite general, as ν may include vertices not mentioned in the triangulation). A general camera model is described by a function $\pi : \mathbb{R}^3 \mapsto \mathbb{R}^2$. This function incorporates details of the camera intrinsics such as focal length, which are assumed known. Thus

$$\kappa(\phi, \theta, \beta) := \pi(\phi * \nu(\theta, \beta)\text{K}) \tag{3}$$

is the $2 \times J$ matrix whose columns are 2D joint locations corresponding to a 3D model specified by (position, pose, shape) parameters (ϕ, θ, β).

The model is also assumed to be supplied with a rendering function R which takes a vertex array in camera coordinates, and generates a 2D binary image of the model silhouette. That is,

$$R\big(\phi * \nu(\theta, \beta)\big) \in \mathbb{B}^{W \times H} \tag{4}$$

for an image resolution of $W \times H$. We use the differentiable renderer of Loper et al. [33] to allow derivatives to be propagated through R.

3   Method

The test-time problem to be solved is to take a sequence of input images $\mathcal{I} = [I_t]_{t=1}^T$ which are segmented to the silhouette of a single animal (i.e. a video with multiple animals is segmented multiple times), producing a sequence of binary silhouette images $\mathcal{S} = [S_t]_{t=1}^T$.

The computational task is to output for each image the shape, pose, and position parameters describing the animal's motion.

As outlined above, the method has three parts. (1). The discriminative front-end extracts silhouettes from video, and then uses the silhouettes to predict 2D joint positions, with multiple candidates per joint. (2). Optimal joint assignment (OJA) corrects confused or missing skeletal predictions by finding an optimal assignment of joints from a set of network-predicted proposals. Finally, (3). a generative deformable 3D model is fitted to the silhouettes and joint candidates as an energy minimization process.

3.1   Prediction of 2D Joint Locations Using Multimodal Heatmaps

The goal of the first stage is to take, for each video frame, a $W \times H$ binary image representing the segmented animal, and to output a $W \times H \times J$ tensor of heatmaps. The network architecture is standard: a stacked hourglass network [34] (details in supplementary material), using synthetically generated training data, but the training procedure is augmented using "multi-modal" heatmaps.

For standard unimodal heatmaps, training data comprises (S, κ) pairs, that is pairs of binary silhouette images, and the corresponding 2D joint locations as a $2 \times J$ matrix. To generate each image, a random shape vector β, pose parameters θ and camera position ϕ are drawn (see supplementary material), and used to render a silhouette $R\big(\phi * \nu(\theta, \beta)\big)$ and 2D joint locations $\kappa(\phi, \theta, \beta)$, which are encoded into a $W \times H \times J$ tensor of heatmaps, blurring with a Gaussian kernel of radius σ.

This training process generalizes well from synthetic to real images due to the use of the silhouette, but the lack of interior contours in silhouette input data often results in confusion between joint "aliases": left and right or front and back legs. When these predictions are wrong and of high confidence, little probability mass is assigned to the area around the correct leg, meaning no available proposal is present after non-maximal suppression.

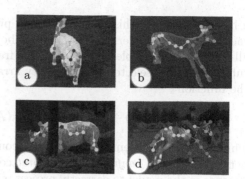

Fig. 2. Example predictions from a network trained on unimodal (top) and multi-modal (bottom) ground-truth for front-left leg joints.

Fig. 3. Example outputs from the joint prediction network, with maximum likelihood predictions linked into skeleton.

We overcome this by explicitly training the network to assign some probability mass to the "aliased" joints. For each joint, we define a list of potential aliases as weights $\lambda_{j,j'}$ and linearly blend the unimodal heatmaps G to give the final training heatmap H:

$$H_j(p) = \sum_{j'} \lambda_{j,j'} G(p; \kappa_{j'}, \sigma) \tag{5}$$

For non-aliased joints j (all but the legs), we simply set $\lambda_{j,j} = 1$ and $\lambda_{j,j'} = 0$, yielding the unimodal maps, and for legs, we use 0.75 for the joint, and 0.25 for the alias. We found this ratio sufficient to ensure opposite legs have enough probability mass to pass through a modest non-maximal suppression threshold without overly biasing the skeleton with maximal predicted confidence. An example of a heatmap predicted by a network trained on multimodal training samples is illustrated in Fig. 2.

3.2 Optimal Joint Assigment (OJA)

Since heatmaps generated by the joint predictor are multi-modal, the non-maximum suppression procedure yields multiple possible locations for each joint. We represent the set of joint proposals $X = \{x_{jp}\}$, where x_{jp} indicates the 2D position of proposal $p \in \{1, ..., N_j\}$ associated with joint $j \in J$. Before applying the optimizer, we must select a subset of proposals $X^* \subseteq X$ which form a complete skeleton, i.e. precisely one proposal is selected for every joint. In this section we consider how to choose the optimal subset by formulating the problem as an extended optimal assignment problem.

In order to select a complete skeleton proposal from the set of joint proposals $\{x_{jp}\}$, we introduce a binary indicator vector $\bar{a}_j = \{a_{jp}\} \in \{0,1\}^{N_j+1}$, where $a_{jp} = 1$ indicates that the pth proposal for joint j is a correct assignment, and the $p = N_j + 1$ position corresponds to a *null proposal*, indicating that joint

j has no match in this image. The null proposals are handled as described in each of the energy terms below. Let A be the jagged array $[\bar{a}_j]_{j=1}^J$ containing all assignment variables (for the current frame), and let $X^* = X(A)$ denote the subset of points selected by the binary array A. Optimal assignment minimizes the function

$$L(A) = L_{\mathrm{prior}}(A) + L_{\mathrm{conf}}(A) + L_{\mathrm{temp}}(A) + L_{\mathrm{cov\text{-}sil}}(A) + L_{\mathrm{cov\text{-}bone}}(A) \qquad (6)$$

which balances agreement of the joint configuration with a learned *prior*, the network-supplied *confidences*, *temporal* coherence, and *coverage* terms which encourage the model to correctly project over the silhouette. Without the coverage terms, this can be optimized as a quadratic program, but we obtain better results by using the coverage terms, and using a genetic algorithm. In addition, the parameters A must satisfy the J constraints $\sum_{p=1}^{N_j+1} a_{jp} = 1$, that exactly one joint proposal (or the null proposal) must be selected for each joint.

L_{prior}: We begin by defining the prior probability of a particular skeletal configuration as a multivariate Gaussian distribution over selected joint positions. The mean $\mu \in \mathbb{R}^{2J}$ and covariance $\Sigma \in \mathbb{R}^{2J \times 2J}$ terms are obtained from the training examples generated as above. The objective of OJA is to select a configuration X^* which maximizes the prior, which is equivalent to minimizing the Mahalanobis distance $(x^* - \mu)^T \Sigma^{-1}(x^* - \mu)$, which is given by the summation

$$L_{\mathrm{prior}}(A) = \sum_j^J \sum_p^{N_j} \sum_k^J \sum_q^{N_k} a_{jp} a_{kq} (x_{jp} - \mu_j) \Sigma_{jk}^{-1}(x_{kq} - \mu_k) \qquad (7)$$

This is a quadratic function of A, so $L_{\mathrm{prior}}(A) = \mathrm{vec}(A)^\top Q \mathrm{vec}(A)$ for a fixed matrix Q, and can be formulated as a quadratic program (QP). Null proposals are simply excluded from the sum, equivalent to marginalizing over their position.

L_{conf}: The next energy term comes from the output of the joint prediction network, which provides a confidence score y_{jp} associated with each joint proposal x_{jp}. Then $L_{\mathrm{conf}}(A) = \sum_j \sum_p -\lambda \log(y_{jp}) a_{jp}$ is a linear function of A, and λ_{conf} is a tunable parameter to control the relative contribution of the network confidences compared with that of the skeleton prior. Null proposals pay a fixed cost λ_{null}, effectively acting as a threshold whereby the null proposal will be selected if no other proposal is of sufficient likelihood.

L_{temp}: A common failure case of the joint prediction network is in situations where a joint position is highly ambiguous, for example between the left and right legs. In such cases, the algorithm will commonly alternate between two equally likely predictions. This leads to large displacements in joint positions between consecutive frames which are difficult for the later model fitting stage to recover from. This can be addressed by introducing a temporal term into the OJA. We impose a prior on the distance moved by each joint between frame t_0 and t_1, which is given by a normal distribution with zero mean and variance $\sigma^2 = e^{\tau|t_1 - t_0 - 1|}$. The parameter τ controls the strength of the interaction between distant frames. This results in an additional quadratic term in our objective function, which has the form $L_{temp} = a^\top T^{(t_0,t_1)} a$ for matrix $T^{(t_0,t_1)}$ given by

$$\left[T^{(t_0,t_1)}\right]_{jp,kq} = \begin{cases} e^{-\alpha|t_1-t_0-1|}||x_{jp}^{(t_0)} - x_{kq}^{(t_1)}||^2 & \text{if } j = k \\ 0 & \text{otherwise} \end{cases} \tag{8}$$

QP Solution. Thus far, all terms in $L(A)$ are quadratic or linear. To optimize over an entire sequence of frames, we construct the block diagonal matrix $\hat{Q}$ whose diagonal elements are the prior matrices $Q^{(t)}$ and the block symmetric matrix $\hat{T}$ whose off-diagonal elements are the temporal matrices $T^{(t_0,t_1)}$. The solution vector for the sequence $\hat{A}$ is constructed by stacking the corresponding vectors for each frame. The quadratic program is specified using the open source CVXPY library [35] and solved using the *"Suggest-and-Improve"* framework proposed by Park and Boyd [36]. It is initialized by choosing the proposal with the highest confidence for each joint. Appropriate values for the free parameters $\lambda_{\text{conf,temp}}$ and α were chosen empirically via grid search.

$L_{\text{cov-\{sil,bone\}}}$: The above quadratic formulation is sufficient to correct many errors in the raw output (which we later demonstrate in the experimental section), but suffers from an 'overcounting' problem, in which leg joint predictions both cover the same silhouette leg region, leaving another leg empty. We therefore extend the definition of $L(A)$ to include two additional terms.

$L_{\text{cov-sil}}$: penalizes large silhouette areas with no nearby selected joint. This term requires a precomputed set of silhouette sample points $Z \subseteq \mathbb{R}^2$, which we aim to "cover" as best as possible with the set of selected joints. Intuitively, the silhouette is considered well-covered if all sample points are close to *some* selected joint proposal. The set Z is generated from the medial axis transform (MAT) [37] of the silhouette, $Z^t = \text{MAT}(S^t)$ with a 3-norm loss encoding a (gently) soft max:

$$L_{\text{cov-sil}}(A^t; X^t, Z^t) = \sum_i \min_j ||Z_i^t - \hat{X}_j^t||_3 \tag{9}$$

$L_{\text{cov-bone}}$: is used to prevent bones crossing the background. The joint hierarchy is stored in a kinematic tree structure $K = \{\{j,k\}$ if joints j, k are connected by a bone$\}$.

$$L_{\text{cov-bone}}(A^t; X^t, S^t, K) = \sum_{\{j,k\}\in K} \left(1 - \min_{\lambda\in[0:0.1:1]} S^t(\hat{X}_j^t + \lambda(\hat{X}_j^t - \hat{X}_k^t))\right) \tag{10}$$

GA Solution. We minimize this more complex objective using a genetic algorithm (GA) [38], which requires defining a fitness function, "genes", an initial population, crossover procedure, and mutation procedure. The *fitness function* is precisely the energy $L(A)$ given above, and the *genes* are vectors of J integers, rather than one-hot encodings. We begin with a population size of 128 genes, in which the first 32 are set equal to the max confidence solutions given by the

Fig. 4. Silhouette coverage loss. The error (shown in red) is the distance between the median axis transform (right) and the nearest point on an approximate rendering (left). (Color figure online)

Fig. 5. Bone coverage loss. One of the back-right leg joints is incorrectly assigned (left), leading to a large penalty since the lower leg bone crosses outside the dilated silhouette (right).

network in order to speed up convergence. The remaining 96 are generated by selecting a random proposal for each joint. *Crossover* is conducted as standard by slicing genes in two parts, and pairing first and second parts from different parents to yield the next generation. In each generation, each gene has some probability of undergoing a *mutation*, in which between 1 and 4 joints have new proposals randomly assigned. Weights were set empirically and we run for 1000 generations. Examples of errors corrected by these two energy terms are shown in Figs. 4 and 5.

3.3 Generative Model Optimization

The generative model optimization stage refines model parameters to better match the silhouette sequence $\mathcal{S}$, by minimizing an energy which sums 4 terms:

Silhouette Energy. The silhouette energy E_{sil} compares the rendered model to a given silhouette image, given simply by the L2 difference between the OpenDR rendered image and the given silhouette:

$$E_{\text{sil}}(\phi, \theta, \beta; S) = \|S - R(\phi * \nu(\theta, \beta))\| \qquad (11)$$

Prior Energy. The prior term E_{prior} encourages the optimization to remain near realistic shapes and poses. It can constrain pose only weakly because of the lack of training data from real poses. We adopt three prior energy terms from the SMAL model. The Mahalanobis distance is used to encourage the model to remain close to: (1) a distribution over shape coefficients given by the mean and covariance of SMAL training samples of the relevant animal family, (2) a distribution of pose parameters built over a walking sequence. The final term ensures the pose parameters remain within set limits.

$$E_{\text{lim}}(\theta) = \max\{\theta - \theta_{\text{max}}, 0\} + \max\{\theta_{\text{min}} - \theta, 0\}. \qquad (12)$$

Joints Energy. The joints energy E_{joints} compares the rendered model joints to the OJA predictions, and therefore must account for missing and incorrect joints. It is used primarily to stabilize the nonlinear optimization in the initial iterations, and its importance is scaled down as the silhouette term begins to enter its convergence basin.

$$E_{\text{joints}}(\phi, \theta, \beta; X^*) = \|X^* - \phi * \nu(\theta, \beta)K(:, j)\| \tag{13}$$

Temporal Energy. The optimizer for each frame is initialized to the result of that previous. In addition, a simple temporal smoothness term is introduced to penalize large inter-frame variation:

$$E_{\text{temp}}(\phi, \theta, \beta; X^*) = (\phi_t - \phi_{t+1})^2 + (\beta_t - \beta_{t+1})^2 \tag{14}$$

The optimization is via a second order dogleg method [39].

4   Experiments

Datasets. In order to quantify our experiments, we introduce a new benchmark animal dataset of joint annotations (BADJA) comprising several video sequences with 2D joint labels and segmentation masks. These sequences were derived from the DAVIS video segmentation dataset [7], as well as additional online stock footage for which segmentations were obtained using Adobe's UltraKey tool [40]. A set of twenty joints on the 3D SMAL mesh were labeled, illustrated in Fig. 6. These joints were chosen on the basis of being informative to the skeleton and being simple for a human annotator to localize. To make manual annotation feasible and to ensure a diverse set of data, annotations are provided for every fifth frame.

The video sequences were selected to comprise a range of different quadrupeds undergoing various movement typical of their species. Although the dataset is perhaps insufficient in size to train deep neural networks, the variety in animal shape and pose renders it suitable for evaluating quadruped joint prediction methods.

4.1   Joint Prediction

Joint accuracy is evaluated with the Probability of Correct Keypoint (PCK) metric defined by Yang and Ramanan [41]. The PCK is the percentage of predicted keypoints which are within a threshold distance d from the ground truth keypoint location. The threshold distance is given by $d = \alpha\sqrt{|S|}$ where $|S|$ is the area of the silhouette and α is a constant factor which we set to $\alpha = 0.2$ for these experiments.

Figure 3 shows a selection of maximum likelihood joint predictions on real world images. Note that despite being trained only on synthetic data, the network generalizes extremely well to animals in the wild. The performance extends

Fig. 6. Example joint annotations from the BADJA dataset. A total of 11 video sequences are in the dataset, annotated every 5 frames with 20 joint positions and visibility indicators.

even to species which were not present in the SMAL model, such as the impala and rhino. The network is also robust to challenging poses (3b), occlusions (3c) and distraction objects such as the human rider in (3d). It is however susceptible to situations where the silhouette image is ambiguous, for example if the animal is facing directly towards or away from the camera. The supplementary material contains examples of failure modes.

4.2   Optimal Joint Assignment

Following non-maximum suppression of the joint heatmaps obtained in Sect. 4.1, we apply OJA to select an optimal set of joints with which to initialize the final optimization stage. It can be seen that the OJA step is able to address many of the failure cases introduced by the joint prediction network, for example by eliminating physically implausible joint configurations (Fig. 7, row 1) or by resolving the ambiguity between the left and right legs (Fig. 7, row 2). Table 1 summarizes the performance of both the raw network predictions and results of the two OJA methods. Over most of the sequences in the BADJA dataset it can be seen that the use of coverage terms (employed by the OJA-GA model) improves skeleton accuracy. In particular, the bear, camel and rs_dog sequences show substantial improvements. The method does however struggle on the horsejump_high sequence, in which part of the silhouette is occluded by the human rider which adversely affects the silhouette coverage term. Across all sequences the selected OJA-GA method improves joint prediction accuracy by 7% compared to the raw network output.

4.3   Model Fitting

The predicted joint positions and silhouette are input to the optimization phase, which proceeds in four stages. The first stage solves for the model's global rotation and translation parameters, which positions the camera. We follow SMPLify [42] by solving this camera stage for torso points only, which remain largely fixed through shape and pose variation. We then solve for all shape, pose and translation parameters and gradually decrease the emphasis of the priors. The silhouette term is introduced in the penultimate stage, as otherwise we find this can lead to the optimizer finding unsatisfactory local minima.

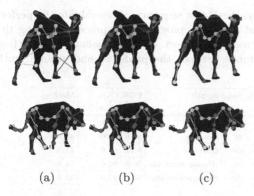

(a)   (b)   (c)

Fig. 7. Example skeletons from raw predictions (a), processed with OJA-QP (b), and OJA-GA (c).

Table 1. Accuracy of OJA on BADJA test sequences.

	Raw	QP	GA
Bear	83.1	83.7	**88.9**
Camel	73.3	74.1	**87.1**
Cat	58.5	**60.1**	58.4
Cows	89.2	88.4	**94.7**
Dog	**66.9**	66.6	**66.9**
Horsejump-high	26.5	**27.7**	24.4
Horsejump-low	26.9	27.0	**31.9**
Tiger	76.5	88.8	**92.3**
rs_dog	64.2	63.4	**81.2**
Average	62.8	64.4	**69.5**

The final outputs of our optimization pipeline are shown in Fig. 9. In each of the cases illustrated the optimizer is able to successfully find a set of pose and shape parameters which, when rendered, closely resembles the input image. The final row of Fig. 9 demonstrates the generalizability of the proposed method: the algorithm is able to find a reasonable pose despite no camel figurines being included in the original SMAL model.

Comparison to Other Work. We compare our approach visually to that given by Zuffi *et al.* [9]. Recall that their results require hand-clicked keypoints whereas ours fits to points predicted automatically by the hourglass network, which was trained on synthetic animal images. Further, their work is optimized for single frame fitting and is tested on animals in simple poses, whereas we instead focus on the more challenging task of tracking animals in video. Figure 8 shows the application of our model to a number of single frame examples from the SMAL result data [9].

Quantitative Experiments. There is no existing ground truth dataset for comparing reconstructed 3D animal meshes, but an estimate of quantitative error is obtained by testing on synthetic sequences for a range of quadruped species. These are generated by randomly deforming the model and varying the camera position to animate animal motion (see supplementary material). Table 2 shows results on these sequences.

4.4   Automatic Silhouette Prediction

While not the main focus of our work, we are able to perform the full 3D reconstruction process from an input image with no user intervention. We achieve this by using the DeepLabv3+ network [2] as a front-end segmentation engine to automatically generate animal silhouettes. This network was trained on the PASCAL VOC 2012 dataset, which includes a variety of animal quadruped classes. An example result generated using the fully automatic pipeline is shown in Fig. 1.

Table 2. Quantitative evaluation on synthetic test sequences. We evaluate the performance of the raw network outputs and quadratic program post-processing using the probability of correct keypoint (PCK) metric (see Sect. 4.1). We evaluate mesh fitting accuracy by computing the mean distance between the predicted and ground truth vertices.

Seq.	Family	PCK (%)		Mesh	Seq.	Family	PCK (%)		Mesh
		Raw	OJA-GA				Raw	OJA-GA	
01	Felidae	91.8	91.9	38.2	06	Equidae	84.4	84.8	19.2
02	Felidae	94.7	95.0	42.4	07	Bovidae	94.6	95.0	40.6
03	Canidae	87.7	88.0	27.3	08	Bovidae	85.2	85.8	41.5
04	Canidae	87.1	87.4	22.9	09	Hippopotamidae	90.5	90.6	11.8
05	Equidae	88.9	89.8	51.6	10	Hippopotamidae	93.7	93.9	23.8

RGB   SMAL [9]   **Ours**

Fig. 8. Our results are comparable in quality to SMAL [9], but note that we do not require hand-clicked keypoints.

Fig. 9. Example results on various animals. From left to right: RGB input, extracted silhouette, network-predicted heatmaps, OJA-processed joints, overlay 3D fit and alternative view.

5   Conclusions

In this work we have introduced a technique for 3D animal reconstruction from video using a quadruped model parameterized in shape and pose. By incorporating automatic segmentation tools, we demonstrated that this can be achieved with no human intervention or prior knowledge of the species of animal being considered. Our method performs well on examples encountered in the real world, generalizes to unseen animal species and is robust to challenging input conditions.

Acknowledgment. The authors would like to thank GlaxoSmithKline for sponsoring this work.

References

1. Food and Agriculture Organization of the United Nations: FAOSTAT statistics database (2016). Accessed FAOSTAT 21 Nov 2017
2. Chen, L., Zhu, Y., Papandreou, G., Schroff, F., Adam, H.: Encoder-decoder with atrous separable convolution for semantic image segmentation (2018)
3. Andriluka, M., Pishchulin, L., Gehler, P., Schiele, B.: 2D human pose estimation: new benchmark and state of the art analysis. In: Proceedings of CVPR (2014)
4. Lin, T.-Y., et al.: Microsoft COCO: common objects in context. In: Fleet, D., Pajdla, T., Schiele, B., Tuytelaars, T. (eds.) ECCV 2014. LNCS, vol. 8693, pp. 740–755. Springer, Cham (2014). https://doi.org/10.1007/978-3-319-10602-1_48
5. Johnson, S., Everingham, M.: Clustered pose and nonlinear appearance models for human poseestimation. In: Proceedings of BMVC, pp. 12.1–12.11 (2010)
6. Everingham, M., Van Gool, L., Williams, C.K.I., Winn, J., Zisserman, A.: The PASCAL Visual Object Classes Challenge 2012 (VOC2012) Results (2012)
7. Perazzi, F., Pont-Tuset, J., McWilliams, B., Van Gool, L., Gross, M., Sorkine-Hornung, A.: A benchmark dataset and evaluation methodology for video object segmentation. In: Proceedings of CVPR (2016)
8. Wilhelm, N., Vögele, A., Zsoldos, R., Licka, T., Krüger, B., Bernard, J.: Furyexplorer: visual-interactive exploration of horse motion capture data. In: Visualization and Data Analysis 2015, vol. 9397, p. 93970F (2015)
9. Zuffi, S., Kanazawa, A., Jacobs, D., Black, M.J.: 3D menagerie: modeling the 3D shape and pose of animals. In: Proceedings of CVPR, pp. 5524–5532. IEEE (2017)
10. Shotton, J., et al.: Real-time human pose recognition in parts from a single depth image. In: Proceedings of CVPR. IEEE (2011)
11. Cao, Z., Simon, T., Wei, S.E., Sheikh, Y.: Realtime multi-person 2D pose estimation using part affinity fields. In: Proceedings of CVPR, vol. 1, p. 7 (2017)
12. Zuffi, S., Kanazawa, A., Black, M.J.: Lions and tigers and bears: capturing nonrigid, 3D, articulated shape from images. In: Proceedings of CVPR (2018)
13. Deng, J., Dong, W., Socher, R., Li, L.J., Li, K., Fei-Fei, L.: ImageNet: a large-scale hierarchical image database. In: Proceedings of CVPR (2009)
14. Li, X., et al.: Video object segmentation with re-identification. In: The 2017 DAVIS Challenge on Video Object Segmentation - CVPR Workshops (2017)
15. Khoreva, A., Benenson, R., Ilg, E., Brox, T., Schiele, B.: Lucid data dreaming for object tracking. In: The 2017 DAVIS Challenge on Video Object Segmentation - CVPR Workshops (2017)

16. Cashman, T.J., Fitzgibbon, A.W.: What shape are dolphins? Building 3D morphable models from 2Dimages. IEEE TPAMI **35**, 232–244 (2013)
17. Reinert, B., Ritschel, T., Seidel, H.P.: Animated 3D creatures from single-view video by skeletal sketching. In: Graphics Interface, pp. 133–141 (2016)
18. Khamis, S., Taylor, J., Shotton, J., Keskin, C., Izadi, S., Fitzgibbon, A.: Learning an efficient model of hand shape variation from depth images. In: Proceedings of CVPR. IEEE (2015)
19. Loper, M., Mahmood, N., Romero, J., Pons-Moll, G., Black, M.J.: SMPL: a skinned multi-person linear model. ACM Trans. Graph. **34**, 248:1–248:16 (2015). (Proceedings of SIGGRAPH Asia)
20. Chen, Y., Kim, T.-K., Cipolla, R.: Inferring 3D shapes and deformations from single views. In: Daniilidis, K., Maragos, P., Paragios, N. (eds.) ECCV 2010. LNCS, vol. 6313, pp. 300–313. Springer, Heidelberg (2010). https://doi.org/10.1007/978-3-642-15558-1_22
21. Favreau, L., Reveret, L., Depraz, C., Cani, M.P.: Animal gaits from video. In: Proceedings of the 2004 ACM SIGGRAPH/Eurographics Symposium on Computer Animation, pp. 277–286 (2004)
22. Tan, V., Budvytis, I., Cipolla, R.: Indirect deep structured learning for 3D human body shape and pose prediction. In: Proceedings of BMVC (2017)
23. Kanazawa, A., Black, M.J., Jacobs, D.W., Malik, J.: End-to-end recovery of human shape and pose. In: Computer Vision and Pattern Recognition (CVPR) (2018)
24. Wiles, O., Zisserman, A.: SilNet: single-and multi-view reconstruction by learning from silhouettes. In: Proceedings of BMVC (2017)
25. Andriluka, M., Roth, S., Schiele, B.: Monocular 3D pose estimation and tracking by detection. In: Proceedings of CVPR, pp. 623–630. IEEE (2010)
26. Pishchulin, L., Andriluka, M., Gehler, P., Schiele, B.: Poselet conditioned pictorial structures. In: Proceedings of CVPR, pp. 588–595. IEEE (2013)
27. Bulat, A., Tzimiropoulos, G.: Human pose estimation via convolutional part heatmap regression. In: Leibe, B., Matas, J., Sebe, N., Welling, M. (eds.) ECCV 2016. LNCS, vol. 9911, pp. 717–732. Springer, Cham (2016). https://doi.org/10.1007/978-3-319-46478-7_44
28. Mathis, A., et al.: DeepLabCut: markerless pose estimation of user-defined body parts with deep learning. Technical report, Nature Publishing Group (2018)
29. Wang, P., Shen, X., Lin, Z., Cohen, S., Price, B., Yuille, A.L.: Joint object and part segmentation using deep learned potentials. In: Proceedings of ICCV, pp. 1573–1581 (2015)
30. Wang, J., Yuille, A.L.: Semantic part segmentation using compositional model combining shape and appearance. In: Proceedings of CVPR, pp. 1788–1797 (2015)
31. Chen, X., Mottaghi, R., Liu, X., Fidler, S., Urtasun, R., Yuille, A.: Detect what you can: detecting and representing objects using holistic models and body parts. In: Proceedings of CVPR (2014)
32. Zhou, B., Zhao, H., Puig, X., Fidler, S., Barriuso, A., Torralba, A.: Scene parsing through ADE20K dataset. In: Proceedings of CVPR (2017)
33. Loper, M.M., Black, M.J.: OpenDR: an approximate differentiable renderer. In: Fleet, D., Pajdla, T., Schiele, B., Tuytelaars, T. (eds.) ECCV 2014. LNCS, vol. 8695, pp. 154–169. Springer, Cham (2014). https://doi.org/10.1007/978-3-319-10584-0_11
34. Newell, A., Yang, K., Deng, J.: Stacked hourglass networks for human pose estimation. In: Leibe, B., Matas, J., Sebe, N., Welling, M. (eds.) ECCV 2016. LNCS, vol. 9912, pp. 483–499. Springer, Cham (2016). https://doi.org/10.1007/978-3-319-46484-8_29

35. Diamond, S., Boyd, S.: CVXPY: a Python-embedded modeling language for convex optimization. J. Mach. Learn. Res. **17**, 1–5 (2016)
36. Park, J., Boyd, S.: General heuristics for nonconvex quadratically constrained quadratic programming (2017)
37. Blum, H.: A transformation for extracting new descriptors of shape. Models Percept. Speech Vis. Forms **1967**, 362–380 (1967)
38. Holland, J.H.: Adaptation in Natural and Artificial Systems: An Introductory Analysis with Applications to Biology, Control, and Artificial Intelligence. MIT Press, Cambridge (1992)
39. Lourakis, M., Argyros, A.A.: Is Levenberg-Marquardt the most efficient optimization algorithm for implementing bundle adjustment? In: Proceedings of ICCV, pp. 1526–1531 (2005)
40. Adobe Systems Inc.: Creating a green screen key using ultra key. https://helpx. adobe.com/premiere-pro/atv/cs5-cs55-video-tutorials/creating-a-green-screen-key-using-ultra-key.html. Accessed 14 Mar 2018
41. Yang, Y., Ramanan, D.: Articulated human detection with flexible mixtures of parts. TPAMI **35**, 2878–2890 (2013)
42. Bogo, F., Kanazawa, A., Lassner, C., Gehler, P., Romero, J., Black, M.J.: Keep it SMPL: automatic estimation of 3D human pose and shape from a single image. In: Leibe, B., Matas, J., Sebe, N., Welling, M. (eds.) ECCV 2016. LNCS, vol. 9909, pp. 561–578. Springer, Cham (2016). https://doi.org/10.1007/978-3-319-46454-1_34

EdgeStereo: A Context Integrated Residual Pyramid Network for Stereo Matching

Xiao Song, Xu Zhao$^{(\boxtimes)}$, Hanwen Hu, and Liangji Fang

Department of Automation, Shanghai Jiao Tong University, Shanghai, China
{song_xiao,zhaoxu,huhanwen,fangliangji}@sjtu.edu.cn

Abstract. Recent convolutional neural networks, especially end-to-end disparity estimation models, achieve remarkable performance on stereo matching task. However, existed methods, even with the complicated cascade structure, may fail in the regions of non-textures, boundaries and tiny details. Focus on these problems, we propose a multi-task network EdgeStereo that is composed of a backbone disparity network and an edge sub-network. Given a binocular image pair, our model enables end-to-end prediction of both disparity map and edge map. Basically, we design a context pyramid to encode multi-scale context information in disparity branch, followed by a compact residual pyramid for cascaded refinement. To further preserve subtle details, our EdgeStereo model integrates edge cues by feature embedding and edge-aware smoothness loss regularization. Comparative results demonstrates that stereo matching and edge detection can help each other in the unified model. Furthermore, our method achieves state-of-art performance on both KITTI Stereo and Scene Flow benchmarks, which proves the effectiveness of our design.

Keywords: Stereo matching · Edge detection · Multi-task learning

1 Introduction

Stereo matching is a fundamental problem in computer vision. It has a wide range of applications, such as robotics and autonomous driving [1,29]. Given a rectified image pair, the main goal is to find corresponding pixels from stereo images. Most traditional stereo algorithms [14,39] follow the classical four-step pipeline [28], including matching cost computation, cost aggregation, disparity calculation and disparity refinement. However the hand-crafted features and multi-step regularized functions limit their improvements.

Since [38], CNN based stereo methods extract deep features to represent image patches and compute matching cost. Although the performance on several benchmarks is significantly promoted, there remains some difficulties, including the limited receptive fields and complicated regularized functions.

This research is supported by the funding from NSFC programs (61673269, 61273285, U1764264).

ⓒ Springer Nature Switzerland AG 2019
C. V. Jawahar et al. (Eds.): ACCV 2018, LNCS 11365, pp. 20–35, 2019.
https://doi.org/10.1007/978-3-030-20873-8_2

Fig. 1. Examples on KITTI (top) and Scene Flow (bottom) datasets. Left: left stereo images. Middle up and right up: colorized error maps (wrong estimates in orange) predicted without context pyramid and by *EdgeStereo*. Middle down and right down: colorized disparity map predicted without edge branch and by *EdgeStereo*. As shown in the red boxes in top row, predicted disparities are more accurate in ill-posed regions such as shadowed road, under the guidance of context cues. In bottom row, *EdgeStereo* produces accurate estimates in details under the guidance of edge cues. (Color figure online)

Recently end-to-end disparity estimation networks [16,24,27] achieve state-of-the-art performance, however drawbacks still exist. Firstly, it is difficult to handle local ambiguities in ill-posed regions. Secondly, the cascade structures or 3D convolution based structures are computationally expensive. Lastly, disparity predictions of thin structures or near boundaries are not accurate.

Humans, on the other hand, can find stereo correspondences easily by utilizing edge cues. Accurate edge contours can help discriminating between different objects or regions. In addition, humans perform binocular alignment well in texture-less or occluded regions based on global perception at different scales.

Based on these observations, we design a multi-task network *EdgeStereo* that cooperates edge cues and edge regularization into disparity prediction pipeline. Firstly, we design a disparity network for *EdgeStereo*, called context pyramid based residual pyramid network (*CP-RPN*). Two modules are designed for *CP-RPN*: a context pyramid to encode multi-scale context information for ill-posed regions, and an one-stage residual pyramid to simplify the cascaded refinement structure. Secondly an edge detection sub-network is designed and employed in our unified model, to preserve subtle details with edge cues. Interactions between two tasks are threefold: (i) Edge features are embedded into disparity branch providing local and low-level representations. (ii) The edge map, acting as an implicit regularization term, is fed to residual pyramid. (iii) The edge map is also utilized in *edge-aware smoothness loss*, which further guides disparity learning.

In disparity branch of *EdgeStereo*, we use a siamese network with a correlation operation [9] to extract image features and compute matching cost volumes, followed by a context pyramid. Based on different representations (unary features, edge features and matching cost volumes), context pyramid can encode contextual cues from different sub-regions on multiple scales. Then they are aggregated as a hierarchical scene prior. After that, we employ an hour-glass structure to regress the full-size disparity map. Different with the decoder in DispNetC or the cascade encoder-decoder in CRL, decoder in *EdgeStereo* is replaced by the proposed residual pyramid. We predict the disparity map on the smallest scale and learn disparity residuals on other scales. Hence learning and refining are conducted in a single decoder, making *CP-RPN* as an one-stage disparity estimation model. Based on experimental results in Table 1, our residual pyramid is better and faster than other cascade structures. In edge branch of *EdgeStereo*, the shallow part of backbone network is shared with *CP-RPN*. Edge feature and edge map are embedded into the disparity branch, under the guidance of *edge-aware smoothness loss*.

Both edge and disparity branches are fully-convolutional so that end-to-end training can be conducted for *EdgeStereo*. As there is no dataset providing both ground-truth disparities and edge labels, we propose a multi-phase training strategy. We adopt the supervised disparity regression loss and our adapted edge-aware smoothness loss to train the entire *EdgeStereo*, achieving a high accuracy on Scene Flow dataset [24]. We further finetune our model on KITTI 2012 and 2015 datasets, achieving state-of-the-art performance on KITTI stereo benchmarks. After multi-task learning, both disparity estimation and edge detection tasks are improved in both quantitatively and qualitatively.

In summary, our main contribution is threefold.

(1) We propose *EdgeStereo* to support the joint learning of scene matching and edge detection, where edge cues and edge-aware smoothness loss serve as important guidance for disparity learning. The multi-task labels are not required during training due to our proposed multi-phase training strategy.
(2) The effective context pyramid is designed to handle ill-posed regions, and the efficient residual pyramid is designd to replace cascade refinement structures.
(3) Our unified model *EdgeStereo* achieves state-of-the-art performance on Scene Flow dataset, KITTI stereo 2012 and 2015 benchmarks.

2   Related Work

Stereo Matching. Among non-end-to-end deep stereo algorithms, each step in traditional stereo pipeline could be replaced by a network. For example, Luo *et al.* [23] train a simple multi-label classification network for matching cost computation. Shaked and Wolf [32] introduce an initial disparity prediction network pooling global information from cost volume. Gidaris *et al.* [11] substitute hand-crafted disparity refinement functions with a three-stage refinement network.

For end-to-end deep stereo algorithms, all steps in traditional stereo pipeline are combined for joint optimization. To train end-to-end stereo networks, Mayer *et al.* [24] propose a baseline model called DispNet with an encoder-decoder structure. Based on DispNet, Pang *et al.* [27] cascade a residual learning network for further refinement. Kendall *et al.* [16] propose GC-Net that incorporates contextual information by means of 3D convolutions over a feature volume. Based on GC-Net, Yu *et al.* [37] add an explicit cost aggregation structure. An unsupervised method is proposed in [41]. Liang *et al.* [18] formulate the disparity refinement task as Bayesian inference process for joint learning. Chang *et al.* [5] utilizes spatial pyramid pooling and 3D CNN to regularize cost volumes. Yang

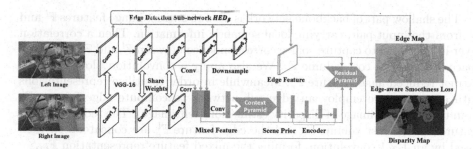

Fig. 2. The overview of *EdgeStereo* architecture, consisting of a disparity network and an edge sub-network. In disparity branch, context pyramid extract multi-scale context cues from the mixed feature representation. The hierarchical scene prior is encoded then decoded by our one-stage residual pyramid, producing a full-size disparity map. To preserve subtle details, the edge branch cooperates edge cues into disparity estimation pipeline by embedding edge features and the *edge-aware smoothness loss*.

et al. [36] integrate semantic segmentation with stereo matching, which reaches state-of-the-art level on KITTI benchmarks.

Combining Stereo Matching with Other Tasks. Bleyer *et al.* [4] first solve stereo and object segmentation problems together. Guney and Geiger [13] propose Displets which utilizes foreground object recognition to help stereo matching. More tasks are fused through a slanted plane in [35]. However, these hand-crafted multi-task methods are not robust.

Edge Detection. To preserve details in disparity maps, we resort to edge detection task to supplement features and regularization. Inspired by FCN [22], Xie *et al.* [34] first design an end-to-end edge detection network named holistically-nested edge detector (HED) based on VGG-16 network. Recently, Liu *et al.* [21] modify the structure of HED, combining richer convolutional features from VGG backbone. These fully-convolutional edge networks can be easily incorporated.

Deep Learning Based Multi-task Structure. Cheng *et al.* [7] propose an end-to-end network called SegFlow, which enables the joint learning of video object segmentation and optical flow. The segmentation branch and flow branch are iteratively trained offline. Our *EdgeStereo* is a different multi-task structure where multi-phase training is conducted rather than iterative training. Hence disparity branch can exploit more stable boundary information from pretrained edge branch. In addition, *EdgeStereo* does not require multi-task labels from a single dataset, hence it is easier to find proper datasets for training.

3   Approach

3.1   Basic Architecture

The overall architecture of our *EdgeStereo* is shown in Fig. 2. To combine two tasks efficiently, edge branch shares the shallow computation with disparity branch at the backbone network.

The shallow part of backbone network is used to extract image features $\mathbb{F}^l$ and $\mathbb{F}^r$ from the input pair, carrying local semantic information. Then a correlation layer in [8] is used to capture coarse correspondence between $\mathbb{F}^l$ and $\mathbb{F}^r$ in feature space, obtaining a cost volume $\mathbb{F}_c$. We also apply a convolution block on $\mathbb{F}^l$ to extract reduced image feature $\mathbb{F}_r^l$. Meanwhile in order to utilize representations with edge cues, we employ an edge sub-network to compute edge feature $\mathbb{F}_e^l$ from the reference image of disparity estimation (left image). The reduced image feature $\mathbb{F}_r^l$, the cost volume $\mathbb{F}_c$ and the edge feature $\mathbb{F}_e^l$ are concatenated then fused by an 1×1 convolution, forming the mixed feature representation $\mathbb{F}_m$.

Taking $\mathbb{F}_m$ as input, context pyramid collects contextual information at four scales and aggregate them into a hierarchical scene prior for disparity estimation. Each scale in context pyramid captures context cues from different sub-regions with different receptive fields. Next we feed the scene prior to an hour-glass structure to predict full-size disparity map, where the encoder is a stack of convolution layers to sub-sample feature maps and the decoder is formulated by our residual pyramid. Multi-scale processing is conducted in residual pyramid, where the disparity map is directly regressed on the smallest scale and residual maps are predicted for refinement on other scales. Edge features and edge map are fed to each scale in residual pyramid, helping preserving details in disparity map. The edge map also guides disparity or residual learning under *edge-aware smoothness loss regularization*. These are the key components of our framework. More settings are detailed in Sect. 4.1.

3.2   Context Pyramid

Context information is widely used in many tasks [19,26]. For stereo matching, it can be regarded as the relationship between an object and its surroundings or its sub-regions, which can help inferring correspondences especially for ill-posed regions. Many stereo methods learn these relationships by stacking lots of convolution blocks. Differently we encode context cues explicitly through context pyramid, hence learning stereo geometry of the scene is easier. Moreover, single-scale context information is insufficient because objects with arbitrary sizes are existed. Over-focusing on global information may neglect small-size objects, while disparities of big stuff might be inconsistent or discontinuous if the receptive field is small. Hence the proposed context pyramid aims at capturing multi-scale context cues in an efficient way.

We use four parallel branches with similar structures in the context pyramid. As mentioned in [40], the size of receptive field roughly indicates how much we use context. Hence four branches own different receptive fields to capture context information at different scales. The largest context scale corresponds to the biggest receptive field. To our knowledge, convolution, pooling and dilation [6] operations can enlarge the receptive field. Hence we design *convolution context pyramid, pooling context pyramid and dilation context pyramid* respectively. They are detailed in Sect. 4.1. The best one is embedded in *EdgeStereo*.

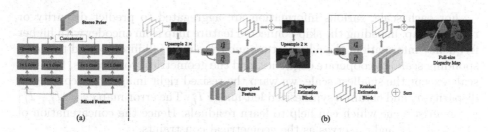

Fig. 3. (a) An example of context pyramid (pooling context pyramid). (b) One-stage residual pyramid. Disparity map is first predicted on the smallest scale then residual signals are predicted on other scales. Aggregated feature is the concatenation of edge cues, feature maps from encoder and geometrical constraints. Each estimation block is used to predict disparity or residual map, detailed in Sect. 4.1.

As shown in Fig. 3, outputs of four branches as well as the input $\mathbb{F}_m$ are concatenated as the hierarchical scene prior, carrying both low-level semantic information and global context cues for disparity estimation.

3.3 Residual Pyramid

Many stereo methods [11,27] use a cascade structure for disparity estimation, where the first network generates initial disparity predictions and the second network produces residual signals to rectify initial disparities. However these residual signals are hard to learn (residuals are always close to zero), because initial disparity predictions are pretty good. Moreover these multi-stage structures are computationally expensive. In order to optimize the cascade structure, we design a residual pyramid so that initial disparity learning and disparity refining can be conducted in a single network.

To make multi-scale disparity estimation easier, we refer to the idea "From Easy to Tough" from curriculum learning [3]. In other words, it is easier to regress disparity map on the smallest scale because searching range is narrow and few details is needed. To get larger disparity maps, we estimate residual signals relative to the disparity map at the smallest scale. The formulation of residual pyramid makes *EdgeStereo* an effective one-stage structure. Besides, the residual pyramid can be beneficial for overall training because it alleviates the problem of over-fitting.

Scale number S in residual pyramid is consistent with the encoder structure. As shown in Fig. 3, the smallest scale in residual pyramid produces a disparity map d_S ($\frac{1}{2^{S-1}}$ of the full resolution), then it is continuously upsampled and refined with the residual map r_s on a larger scale, until the full-size disparity map d_0 is obtained. The formulation is shown in Eq. (1), where $u(\cdot)$ denotes upsampling by a factor of 2 and s denotes the pyramid scale (e.g. 0 represents the full-resolution).

$$d_s = u(d_{s+1}) + r_s, \ 0 \le s < S. \tag{1}$$

For each scale, various information are aggregated to predict disparity or residual map, including the skip-connected feature map from encoder with higher frequency information, the edge feature and edge map (all interpolated to corresponding scale) to cooperate edge cues, and the geometrical constraints. For each scale except the smallest scale, we warp the resized right image I_R^s according to disparity d_s and obtain a synthesized left image $\overline{I_L^s}$. The error map $e_s = |I_L^s - \overline{I_L^s}|$ is a heuristic cue which can help to learn residuals. Hence the concatenation of I_L^s, I_R^s, d_s, $\overline{I_L^s}$ and e_s serves as the geometrical constraints.

3.4   Cooperation of Edge Cues

Basic disparity estimation network *CP-RPN* works well on ordinary and texture-less regions, where matching cues are clear or context cues can be easily captured through the context pyramid. However as shown in the second row of Fig. 1, details in disparity map are lost, due to too many convolution and down-sampling operations. Hence we utilize edge cues to help refining disparity maps.

Firstly we cooperate edge cues by embedding edge features. On the one hand, in front of context pyramid, we combine the interpolated edge feature $\mathbb{F}_e^l$ with the image feature $\mathbb{F}_r^l$ and the cost volume $\mathbb{F}_c$. By concatenation, we expect context pyramid can consider both local semantic information, matching cost distribution and edge representations when extracting context cues. On the other hand, edge features are interpolated and concatenated to each scale in residual pyramid. This feature embedding alleviates the issue that residual pyramid lacks low-level representations to produce accurate disparities and residual signals.

Secondly we resize and feed the edge map to each scale in residual pyramid. The edge map acts as an implicit regularization term which can help smoothing disparities in non-edge regions and preserving edges in disparity map. Hence the edge sub-network does not behave like a black-box.

Finally we regularize the edge map into an edge-aware smoothness loss, which is an effective guidance for disparity estimation. For disparity smoothness loss $\mathcal{L}_{ds}$, we encourage disparities to be locally smooth and the loss term penalizes depth changes in non-edge regions. To allow for depth discontinuities at object contours, previous methods [12,41] weight this regularization term according to image gradients. Differently, we weight this term based on gradients of edge map, which is more semantically meaningful than intensity variation. As shown in Eq. (2), N denotes the number of pixels, ∂d denotes disparity gradients and $\partial \mathcal{E}$ denotes gradients of edge probability map.

$$\mathcal{L}_{ds} = \frac{1}{N} \sum_{i,j} |\partial_x d_{i,j}| e^{-|\partial_x \mathcal{E}_{i,j}|} + |\partial_y d_{i,j}| e^{-|\partial_y \mathcal{E}_{i,j}|}. \tag{2}$$

3.5   Multi-phase Training Strategy and Objective Function

In order to conduct multi-task learning for *EdgeStereo*, we propose a multi-phase training strategy where the training phase is split into three phases. Weights of the backbone network are fixed in all three phases.

In the first phase, edge sub-network is trained on a dataset for edge detection task, guided by a class-balanced cross-entropy loss proposed in [21].

In the second phase, we supervise the regressed disparities across S scales on a stereo dataset. Deep supervision is adopted, forming the total loss as the sum $C = \sum_{s=0}^{S-1} C_s$ where C_s denotes the loss at scale s. Besides the disparity smoothness loss, we adopt the disparity regression loss $\mathcal{L}_r$ for supervised learning, as shown in Eq. (3).

$$\mathcal{L}_r = \frac{1}{N} \| d - \hat{d} \|_1, \tag{3}$$

where $\hat{d}$ denotes the ground truth disparity map. Hence the overall loss at scale s becomes $C_s = \mathcal{L}_r + \lambda_{ds}\mathcal{L}_{ds}$, where λ_{ds} is a loss weight for smoothness loss. In addition, weights of the edge sub-network are fixed.

In the third phase, all layers in *EdgeStereo* except for the backbone are optimized on the same stereo dataset used in the second phase. Similarly we also adopt the deep supervision across S scales. However the edge-aware smoothness loss is not used in this phase, because edge contours in the second phase are more stable than those in the third phase. Hence the loss at scale s is $C_s = \mathcal{L}_r$.

4 Experiments

Experiment settings and results are presented in this section. Firstly we evaluate key components of *EdgeStereo* on Scene Flow [24] dataset. We also compare our approach with other state-of-the-art stereo matching methods on KITTI benchmarks. In addition, we demonstrate that better edge maps can be obtained after multi-task learning.

4.1 Model Specifications

The backbone network is VGG-16 [33]. The shallow part of backbone shared by two tasks is conv1_1 to conv3_3. Hence the extracted unary features $\mathbb{F}^l$ and $\mathbb{F}^r$ have a 1/4 spatial size to raw images. For cost volume computation, the max displacement in 1D-correlation layer is set to 40.

The encoder contains convolution layers with occasional strides of 2, resulting in a total down-sampling factor of 64. Correspondingly there are 7 output scales in residual pyramid. For each scale, the estimation block consists of four 3×3 convolution layers and the last convolution layer regresses disparity or residual map. Each convolution layer except the output is followed by a ReLU layer.

We modify the structure of HED [34] and propose an edge sub-network called HED_β, where low-level edge features are easier to obtain and the produced edge map is more semantic-meaningful. HED_β uses the VGG-16 backbone from conv1_1 to conv5_3. In addition, we design five side branches from conv1_2, conv2_2, conv3_3, conv4_3 and conv5_3 respectively. Each side branch consists of two 3×3 convolution layers, an upsampling layer and an 1×1 convolution layer producing the edge probability map. In the end, feature maps from each upsampling layer in each side branch are concatenated as the final edge feature, meanwhile edge probability maps in each side branch are fused as the final edge map. The final edge feature and edge map are of full size.

Finally we describe the structure of each context pyramid.

Convolution Context Pyramid. Each branch consists of two convolution layers with a same kernel size. Kernel size for the largest context scale is biggest. For example, 7×7, 5×5, 3×3 and 1×1 for each branch, denoted as $C\text{-}7\_5\_3\_1$.

Pooling Context Pyramid. Each branch consists of an average pooling layer with different pooling kernels, followed by an 1×1 convolution layer, then an upsampling layer to get the representation with a same spatial size as $\mathbb{F}_m$. For the largest context scale, output size of pooling layer is smallest. For example, 1×1, 2×2, 4×4 and 8×8 for each branch respectively, denoted as $P\text{-}1\_2\_4\_8$.

Dilation Context Pyramid. Inspired by [6], each branch consists of a 3×3 dilated convolution layer, followed by an 1×1 convolution layer to reduce dimensions. Dilation rate for the largest context scale is biggest. For example, 6, 3, 2 and 1 for each branch respectively, denoted as $D\text{-}6\_3\_2\_1$.

4.2   Datasets and Evaluation Metrics

Scene Flow dataset [24] is a synthesised dataset containing 35454 training and 4370 test image pairs. Dense ground-truth disparities are provided and we perform the same screening operation as CRL [27]. The real-world KITTI dataset includes two subsets with sparse ground-truth disparities. KITTI 2012 [10] contains 194 training and 195 test image pairs while KITTI 2015 [25] consists of 200 training and 200 test image pairs.

To pretrain the edge sub-network, we adopt the BSDS500 [2] dataset containing 300 training and 200 test images. Consistent with [20,21], we combine the training data in BSDS500 with PASCAL VOC Context dataset [26].

To evaluate the stereo matching results, we apply the end-point-error (EPE) which measures the average Euclidean distance between estimated and ground-truth disparity. We also use the percentage of bad pixels whose disparity errors are greater than a threshold ($> t\,px$), denoted as t-pixel error.

4.3   Implementation Details

Our model is implemented based on Caffe [15]. The model is optimized using the Adam method [17] with $\beta_1 = 0.9$, $\beta_2 = 0.999$. In the first training phase, HED_β is trained on BSDS500 dataset for $30k$ iterations. The batch size is 12 and the initial learning rate is 10^{-6} which is divided by 10 at the $15k$-th and $25k$-th iterations. The second and third training phases are all conducted on Scene Flow dataset with a batch size of 2. In the second phase, we train for $400k$ iterations with a fixed learning rate of 10^{-4}. The loss weight λ_{ds} for edge-aware smoothness loss is set to 0.1. Afterwards in the third phase, we train for $600k$ iterations with a learning rate of 10^{-4} which is halved at the $300k$-th and $500k$-th iterations. When finetuning on KITTI datasets, the initial learning rate

Table 1. Ablation studies on Scene Flow dataset. $\mathbb{F}_h$ denotes the hybrid feature, which is the aggregation of unary feature and cost volume then fused by an 1×1 convolution. $\mathbb{F}_h$ is equivalent to the mixed feature $\mathbb{F}_m$ without edge feature embedding. $\mathbb{F}_h$ is only used in pure disparity networks.

Model	$> 3\,px(\%)$	EPE	Time(s)
Basic ablation studies			
DispFulNet [27] (unary feature + encoder-decoder)	8.61	1.75	0.07
Our unary feature + encoder-decoder in DispFulNet	6.83	1.38	0.14
$\mathbb{F}_h$ + encoder-decoder in DispFulNet	6.70	1.37	0.14
$\mathbb{F}_h$ + our encoder-decoder (residual pyramid)	5.96	1.28	0.19
$\mathbb{F}_h$ + P-2_4_8_16 + our encoder-decoder (*CP-RPN*)	**5.33**	**1.15**	0.19
$\mathbb{F}_h$ + P-2_4_8_16 + encoder-decoder in DispFulNet	5.95	1.28	0.13
Context pyramid comparisons			
CP-RPN with convolution pyramid C-7_5_3_1	5.85	1.26	0.24
CP-RPN with convolution pyramid C-9_7_5_3	5.70	1.21	0.26
CP-RPN with convolution pyramid C-11_9_7_5	5.79	1.23	0.28
CP-RPN with pooling pyramid P-1_2_4_8	5.61	1.19	0.22
CP-RPN with pooling pyramid P-2_4_8_16	**5.33**	**1.15**	**0.19**
CP-RPN with dilation pyramid D-6_3_2_1	5.81	1.24	0.23
CP-RPN with dilation pyramid D-12_9_6_3	5.52	1.17	0.24
CP-RPN with dilation pyramid D-24_18_12_6	5.88	1.26	0.24
One-stage *vs* Multi-stage refinement			
$\mathbb{F}_h$ + P-2_4_8_16 + encoder-decoder in DispFulNet + DRR [11]	5.48	1.17	0.47
$\mathbb{F}_h$ + P-2_4_8_16 + encoder-decoder and refinement in CRL [27]	5.34	1.16	0.31
$\mathbb{F}_h$ + P-2_4_8_16 + our one-stage encoder-decoder	**5.33**	**1.15**	**0.19**
Benefits from edge cues			
CP-RPN with C-7_5_3_1	5.85	1.26	0.24
CP-RPN with C-7_5_3_1 + edge cues	5.40	1.14	0.32
$\mathbb{F}_h$ + D-6_3_2_1 + encoder-decoder in DispFulNet	6.31	1.33	0.17
$\mathbb{F}_m$ + D-6_3_2_1 + encoder-decoder in DispFulNet + edge cues	5.98	1.27	0.25
$\mathbb{F}_h$ + P-2_4_8_16 + our encoder-decoder	5.33	1.15	0.19
$\mathbb{F}_m$ + P-2_4_8_16 + our encoder-decoder + edge cues (*EdgeStereo*)	**4.97**	**1.11**	0.29

is set to 2×10^{-5} which is halved at the $20k$-th and $80k$-th iterations. Since ground-truth disparities provided by the KITTI datasets are sparse, invalid pixels are neglected in $\mathcal{L}_r$.

4.4 Ablation Studies

In this section, we conduct several ablation studies on Scene Flow dataset to evaluate key components in the *EdgeStereo* model. The one-stage DispFulNet [27] (a simple variant of DispNetC [24]) serves as the baseline model in our experiments. All results are shown in Table 1.

Hybrid Feature Extraction. Firstly we replace the unary feature extraction part in DispFulNet with the shallow part of VGG-16 bcakbone, 3-pixel error is reduced from 8.61% to 6.83%. Next we apply an 1×1 convolution with 128 channels on the concatenation of unary feature and cost volume, forming the hybrid feature $\mathbb{F}_h$. The 3-pixel error is further reduced to 6.70% because it can help fusing various information such as local semantic features and matching cost distributions. For clarification, hybrid feature $\mathbb{F}_h$ is equivalent to the mixed feature $\mathbb{F}_m$ in Sect. 3.1 without edge feature embedding.

Context Pyramid. Firstly we choose a context pyramid (P-2_4_8_16), then train a model consisting of the hybrid feature extraction part, the selected context pyramid and the encoder-decoder of DispFulNet. Compared with the model without context pyramid, 3-pixel error is reduced from 6.70% to 5.95%. Furthermore, as shown in the "Context Pyramid Comparisons" part in Table 1, adopting other context pyramids can also lower the 3-pixel error. Hence we argue that multi-scale context cues are beneficial for dense disparity estimation task.

Encoder-Decoder (Residual Pyramid). We use the same encoder as DispFulNet and we adopt residual pyramid as the decoder. To prove its effectiveness, we train a model consisting of the hybrid feature extraction part and our encoder-decoder. Compared with the model containing the encoder-decoder in DispFulNet, 3-pixel error is reduced from 6.70% to 5.96%. Hence our multi-scale residual learning mechanism is superior to direct disparity regression.

Finally we train *CP-RPN* consisting of the hybrid feature extraction part, context pyramid P-2_4_8_16 and our encoder-decoder. The 3-pixel error is 5.33% and the EPE is 1.15, outperforming the baseline model by 3.28%/0.60.

Context Pyramid Comparisons. We train different *CP-RPN* models with different context pyramids. As shown in Table 1, convolution context pyramids don't work well, reducing the 3-pixel error by only 0.11%, 0.26% and 0.17% respectively. In addition, the large dilation rate is harmful for extracting context cues. The 3-pixel error of D-12_9_6_3 is 5.52% while 5.88% for D-24_18_12_6. P-2_4_8_16 has the best performance, achieving a 3-pixel error of 5.33%. Hence pooling context pyramid P-2_4_8_16 is embedded in the final model.

Comparisons with Multi-stage Refinement. Firstly we compare with the three-stage refinement structure DRR [11]. We replace our encoder-decoder with encoder-decoder in DispFulNet, then three additional networks are cascaded for refinement. *CP-RPN* outperforms this model by 0.15% meanwhile being 2.3 times faster. Next we compare with the two-stage cascade structure CRL [27]. We replace our encoder-decoder with disparity prediction and disparity refinement networks in [27]. As can be seen, performance is almost equal but our model is faster with less parameters, which proves the effectiveness of residual pyramid.

Benefits from Edge Cues. We conduct several experiments where different disparity networks are cooperated with our edge sub-network. As can be seen, all stereo matching models are improved. We also present visual demonstrations as shown in Fig. 4. When edge cues are cooperated into the disparity estimation pipeline, subtle details are preserved hence the error rate is reduced.

Table 2. Comparisons of stereo matching methods on Scene Flow dataset.

Metric	SGM	SPS-st	MC-CNN	DRR	DispNet	DispFulNet	CRL	GC-Net	CA-Net	EdgeStereo
> 3 px	12.54	12.84	13.70	7.21	9.67	8.61	6.20	7.20	5.62	**4.97**
EPE	4.50	3.98	3.79	-	1.84	1.75	1.32	-	-	**1.11**

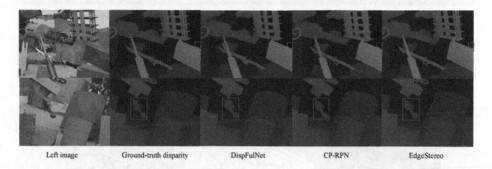

Left image   Ground-truth disparity   DispFulNet   CP-RPN   EdgeStereo

Fig. 4. Comparisons of different stereo models on Scene Flow dataset.

4.5 Comparisons with Other Stereo Methods

In this section, we compare *EdgeStereo* with state-of-the-art stereo matching methods on Scene Flow dataset as well as KITTI 2012 and 2015 benchmarks.

Scene Flow Results. Firstly we compare with several non-end-to-end methods, including SGM [14], SPS-St [35], MC-CNN-fst [38] and DRR [11]. We also compare with the most advanced end-to-end stereo networks, including DispNetC [24], DispFulNet [27], CRL [27], GC-Net [16] and CA-Net [37]. The comparisons are presented in Table 2, *EdgeStereo* achieves the best performance in terms of two evaluation metrics. As shown in Fig. 4, disparities predicted by *EdgeStereo* are very accurate, especially in thin structures and near boundaries.

KITTI Results. For KITTI 2012, *EdgeStereo* is finetuned on all 194 training image pairs, then test results are submitted to KITTI stereo 2012 benchmark. For evaluation, we use the percentage of erroneous pixels in non-occluded (Noc) and all (All) regions. We also conduct comparisons in challenging reflective (Refl) regions such as car windows. The results are shown in Table 3. By leveraging context and edge cues, our *EdgeStereo* model is able to handle challenging scenarios with large occlusion, texture-less regions and thin structures.

For KITTI 2015, we also finetune *EdgeStereo* on the whole training set. The test results are also submitted. For evaluation, we use the 3-pixel error of background (D1-bg), foreground (D1-fg) and all pixels (D1-all) in non-occluded and all regions. The results are shown in Table 4. *EdgeStereo* achieves state-of-the-art performance on KITTI 2015 benchmark and our one-stage structure is faster than most stereo models. Figure 7 gives qualitative results on KITTI test sets. As can be seen, *EdgeStereo* produces high-quality disparity maps in terms of global scene and object details. We also provide visual demonstrations for "stereo benefits from edge" on KITTI datasets, as shown in Fig. 5.

Fig. 5. Benefits from edge detection on KITTI dataset. As can be seen, after incorporating edge cues, the predicted disparities are more accurate in thin structures, near boundaries and the upper part of the images.

Fig. 6. Visual demonstrations for better edge maps after multi-task learning. As can be seen, details are highlighted in the produced edge maps.

Table 3. Results on the KITTI stereo 2012 benchmark. The online leaderboard ranks all methods according to the 3-pixel error in "Noc" regions.

	> 3px			> 4px			> 5px		
	Noc	All	Refl	Noc	All	Refl	Noc	All	Refl
PSMNet [5]	**1.49**	**1.89**	8.36	**1.12**	**1.42**	5.89	**0.90**	**1.15**	4.58
iResNet [18]	1.71	2.16	7.40	1.30	1.63	5.07	1.06	1.32	3.82
GC-Net [16]	1.77	2.30	10.80	1.36	1.77	8.13	1.12	1.46	6.59
L-ResMatch [32]	2.27	3.40	15.94	1.76	2.67	12.92	1.50	2.26	11.14
SGM-Net [31]	2.29	3.50	15.31	1.83	2.80	12.18	1.60	2.36	10.39
SsSMNet [41]	2.30	3.00	14.02	1.82	2.39	10.87	1.53	2.01	8.96
PBCP [30]	2.36	3.45	16.78	1.88	2.28	13.40	1.62	2.32	11.38
Displets v2 [13]	2.37	3.09	8.99	1.97	2.52	6.92	1.72	2.17	5.71
MC-CNN-acrt [38]	2.43	3.63	17.09	1.90	2.85	13.76	1.64	2.39	11.72
EdgeStereo (ours)	1.73	2.18	**7.01**	1.30	1.64	**4.83**	1.04	1.32	**3.73**

Table 4. Results on the KITTI stereo 2015 benchmark. The online leaderboard ranks all methods according to the D1-all error of "All Pixels".

| | All pixels | | | Non-occluded pixels | | | Runtime |
	D1-bg	D1-fg	D1-all	D1-bg	D1-fg	D1-all	(s)
PSMNet [5]	**1.86**	4.62	**2.32**	**1.71**	4.31	**2.14**	0.41
iResNet [18]	2.25	**3.40**	2.44	2.07	**2.76**	2.19	0.12
CRL [27]	2.48	3.59	2.67	2.32	3.12	2.45	0.47
GC-Net [16]	2.21	6.16	2.87	2.02	5.58	2.61	0.9
DRR [11]	2.58	6.04	3.16	2.34	4.87	2.76	0.4
SsSMNet [41]	2.70	6.92	3.40	2.46	6.13	3.06	0.8
L-ResMatch [32]	2.72	6.95	3.42	2.35	5.74	2.91	48
Displets v2 [13]	3.00	5.56	3.43	2.73	4.95	3.09	265
SGM-Net [31]	2.66	8.64	3.66	2.23	7.44	3.09	67
MC-CNN-acrt [38]	2.89	8.88	3.88	2.48	7.64	3.33	67
DispNetC [24]	4.32	4.41	4.34	4.11	3.72	4.05	0.06
EdgeStereo (ours)	2.27	4.18	2.59	2.12	3.85	2.40	0.27

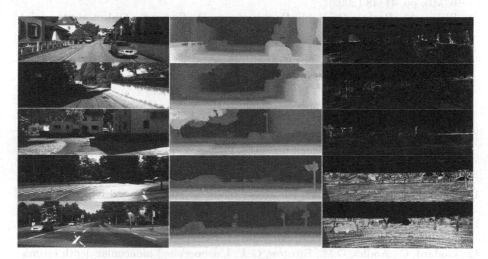

Fig. 7. Qualitative results on the KITTI datasets. The top three rows are from KITTI 2012 test set and the following rows are from KITTI 2015 test set. From left: left stereo input image, disparity prediction, error map.

4.6   Better Edge Map

We can't evaluate on a stereo dataset whether the edge detection task is improved or not after multi-task learning, because the ground-truth edge map is not provided. Hence we first give visual demonstrations on Scene Flow dataset, as shown in Fig. 6. *EdgeStereo* produces edge maps with finer details, compared with HED_β without multi-task learning. We argue that the learned geometrical knowledge from disparity branch can help highlighting image boundaries.

5   Conclusion

In this paper, we present a multi-task architecture *EdgeStereo* where edge cues are incorporated into the disparity estimation pipeline. Also the proposed context pyramid and residual pyramid enable our unified model to handle challenging scenarios with an effective one-stage structure. Our method achieves state-of-the-art performance on Scene Flow dataset and KITTI stereo benchmarks, demonstrating the effectiveness of our design.

References

1. Achtelik, M., Bachrach, A., He, R., Prentice, S., Roy, N.: Stereo vision and laser odometry for autonomous helicopters in GPS-denied indoor environments. In: Unmanned Systems Technology XI, vol. 7332, p. 733219 (2009)
2. Arbelaez, P., Maire, M., Fowlkes, C., Malik, J.: Contour detection and hierarchical image segmentation. TPAMI **33**(5), 898–916 (2011)
3. Bengio, Y., Louradour, J., Collobert, R., Weston, J.: Curriculum learning. In: ICML, pp. 41–48 (2009)
4. Bleyer, M., Rother, C., Kohli, P., Scharstein, D., Sinha, S.: Object stereo—joint stereo matching and object segmentation. In: CVPR, pp. 3081–3088 (2011)
5. Chang, J.R., Chen, Y.S.: Pyramid stereo matching network. In: CVPR (2018)
6. Chen, L.C., Papandreou, G., Kokkinos, I., Murphy, K., Yuille, A.L.: Deeplab: Semantic image segmentation with deep convolutional nets, atrous convolution, and fully connected CRFs. TPAMI **40**(4), 834–848 (2018)
7. Cheng, J., Tsai, Y.H., Wang, S., Yang, M.H.: SegFlow: joint learning for video object segmentation and optical flow. In: ICCV, pp. 686–695 (2017)
8. Dosovitskiy, A., Fischer, P., Ilg, E., Hausser, P., Hazirbas, C.: Flownet: learning optical flow with convolutional networks. In: ICCV, pp. 2758–2766 (2015)
9. Dosovitskiy, A., Fischery, P., Ilg, E., HUsser, P.: Flownet: learning optical flow with convolutional networks. In: ICCV, pp. 2758–2766 (2015)
10. Geiger, A., Lenz, P., Urtasun, R.: Are we ready for autonomous driving? The Kitti vision benchmark suite. In: CVPR, pp. 3354–3361 (2012)
11. Gidaris, S., Komodakis, N.: Detect, replace, refine: deep structured prediction for pixel wise labeling. In: CVPR, pp. 5248–5257 (2017)
12. Godard, C., Aodha, O.M., Brostow, G.J.: Unsupervised monocular depth estimation with left-right consistency. In: CVPR, pp. 6602–6611 (2017)
13. Guney, F., Geiger, A.: Displets: resolving stereo ambiguities using object knowledge. In: CVPR, pp. 4165–4175 (2015)
14. Hirschmuller, H.: Accurate and efficient stereo processing by semi-global matching and mutual information. In: CVPR, pp. 807–814 (2005)
15. Jia, Y., et al.: Caffe: convolutional architecture for fast feature embedding. In: ACMMM, pp. 675–678 (2014)
16. Kendall, A., Martirosyan, H., Dasgupta, S., Henry, P., Kennedy, R.: End-to-end learning of geometry and context for deep stereo regression. In: ICCV (2017)
17. Kingma, D.P., Ba, J.: Adam: a method for stochastic optimization. arXiv preprint arXiv:1412.6980 (2014)
18. Liang, Z., Feng, Y., Guo, Y., Liu, H.: Learning deep correspondence through prior and posterior feature constancy. arXiv preprint arXiv:1712.01039 (2017)

19. Liu, W., Rabinovich, A., Berg, A.C.: ParseNet: looking wider to see better. In: ICLR (2016)
20. Liu, Y., Lew, M.S.: Learning relaxed deep supervision for better edge detection. In: CVPR, pp. 231–240 (2016)
21. Liu, Y., Cheng, M.M., Hu, X., Wang, K., Bai, X.: Richer convolutional features for edge detection. In: CVPR, pp. 5872–5881 (2017)
22. Long, J., Shelhamer, E., Darrell, T.: Fully convolutional networks for semantic segmentation. In: CVPR, pp. 3431–3440 (2015)
23. Luo, W., Schwing, A.G., Urtasun, R.: Efficient deep learning for stereo matching. In: CVPR, pp. 5695–5703 (2016)
24. Mayer, N., et al.: A large dataset to train convolutional networks for disparity, optical flow, and scene flow estimation. In: CVPR, pp. 4040–4048 (2016)
25. Menze, M., Geiger, A.: Object scene flow for autonomous vehicles. In: CVPR, pp. 3061–3070 (2015)
26. Mottaghi, R., Chen, X., Liu, X., Cho, N.G., Lee, S.W.: The role of context for object detection and semantic segmentation in the wild. In: CVPR, pp. 891–898 (2014)
27. Pang, J., Sun, W., Ren, J., Yang, C., Yan, Q.: Cascade residual learning: a two-stage convolutional neural network for stereo matching. In: ICCV Workshop, vol. 3, pp. 1057–7149 (2017)
28. Scharstein, D., Szeliski, R.: A taxonomy and evaluation of dense two-frame stereo correspondence algorithms. IJCV **47**(1–3), 7–42 (2002)
29. Schmid, K., Tomic, T., Ruess, F., Hirschmüller, H., Suppa, M.: Stereo vision based indoor/outdoor navigation for flying robots. In: IROS, pp. 3955–3962 (2013)
30. Seki, A., Pollefeys, M.: Patch based confidence prediction for dense disparity map. In: BMVC, vol. 2, p. 4 (2016)
31. Seki, A., Pollefeys, M.: SGM-nets: semi-global matching with neural networks. In: CVPR, pp. 21–26 (2017)
32. Shaked, A., Wolf, L.: Improved stereo matching with constant highway networks and reflective confidence learning. In: CVPR, pp. 4641–4650 (2017)
33. Simonyan, K., Zisserman, A.: Very deep convolutional networks for large-scale image recognition. In: ICLR (2015)
34. Xie, S., Tu, Z.: Holistically-nested edge detection. In: ICCV, pp. 1395–1403 (2015)
35. Yamaguchi, K., McAllester, D., Urtasun, R.: Efficient joint segmentation, occlusion labeling, stereo and flow estimation. In: Fleet, D., Pajdla, T., Schiele, B., Tuytelaars, T. (eds.) ECCV 2014. LNCS, vol. 8693, pp. 756–771. Springer, Cham (2014). https://doi.org/10.1007/978-3-319-10602-1_49
36. Yang, G., Zhao, H., Shi, J., Deng, Z., Jia, J.: SegStereo: exploiting semantic information for disparity estimation. In: Ferrari, V., Hebert, M., Sminchisescu, C., Weiss, Y. (eds.) ECCV 2018. LNCS, vol. 11211, pp. 660–676. Springer, Cham (2018). https://doi.org/10.1007/978-3-030-01234-2_39
37. Yu, L., Wang, Y., Wu, Y., Jia, Y.: Deep stereo matching with explicit cost aggregation sub-architecture. In: AAAI (2018)
38. Zbontar, J., LeCun, Y.: Stereo matching by training a convolutional neural network to compare image patches. JMLR **17**(1–32), 2 (2016)
39. Zhang, L., Seitz, S.M.: Estimating optimal parameters for mrf stereo from a single image pair. TPAMI **29**(2), 331–342 (2007)
40. Zhao, H., Shi, J., Qi, X., Wang, X., Jia, J.: Pyramid scene parsing network. In: CVPR, pp. 2881–2890 (2017)
41. Zhong, Y., Dai, Y., Li, H.: Self-supervised learning for stereo matching with self-improving ability. In: CVPR (2017)

Rectification from Radially-Distorted Scales

James Pritts[1,2]([✉]), Zuzana Kukelova[2], Viktor Larsson[3], and Ondřej Chum[2]

[1] Czech Institute of Informatics, Robotics and Cybernetics (CIIRC),
Czech Technical University in Prague, Prague, Czechia
prittjam@cvut.cz
[2] Visual Recognition Group (VRG), FEE, Czech Technical University in Prague,
Prague, Czechia
[3] Department of Computer Science, ETH Zürich, Zürich, Switzerland

Abstract. This paper introduces the first minimal solvers that jointly estimate lens distortion and affine rectification from repetitions of rigidly-transformed coplanar local features. The proposed solvers incorporate lens distortion into the camera model and extend accurate rectification to wide-angle images that contain nearly any type of coplanar repeated content. We demonstrate a principled approach to generating stable minimal solvers by the Gröbner basis method, which is accomplished by sampling feasible monomial bases to maximize numerical stability. Synthetic and real-image experiments confirm that the solvers give accurate rectifications from noisy measurements if used in a RANSAC-based estimator. The proposed solvers demonstrate superior robustness to noise compared to the state of the art. The solvers work on scenes without straight lines and, in general, relax strong assumptions about scene content made by the state of the art. Accurate rectifications on imagery taken with narrow focal length to fisheye lenses demonstrate the wide applicability of the proposed method. The method is automatic, and the code is published at https://github.com/prittjam/repeats.

Keywords: Rectification · Radial lens distortion · Repeated patterns

1 Introduction

This paper proposes minimal solvers that jointly estimate affine rectification and lens distortion from local features extracted from arbitrarily repeating coplanar texture. Wide-angle lenses with significant radial lens distortion are common in consumer cameras like the GoPro series of cameras. In the case of Internet

V. Larsson—This work was done while Viktor Larsson was at Lund University.

Electronic supplementary material The online version of this chapter (https://doi.org/10.1007/978-3-030-20873-8_3) contains supplementary material, which is available to authorized users.

© Springer Nature Switzerland AG 2019
C. V. Jawahar et al. (Eds.): ACCV 2018, LNCS 11365, pp. 36–52, 2019.
https://doi.org/10.1007/978-3-030-20873-8_3

Fig. 1. *Solver Variants.* (top-left image) The input to the method is a single image. (bottom-left triptych, contrast enhanced) The three configurations—222, 32, 4—of affine frames that are inputs to the proposed solvers variants. Corresponded frames have the same color. (top row, right) Undistorted outputs of the proposed solver variants. (bottom row, right) Cutouts of the dartboard rectified by the proposed solver variants. The affine frame configurations—222, 32, 4—are transformed to the undistorted and rectified images. (Color figure online)

imagery, the camera and its metadata are often unavailable for use with off-line calibration techniques. The state of the art has several approaches for rectifying (or partially calibrating) a distorted image, but these methods make restrictive assumptions about scene content by assuming, *e.g.*, the presence of sets of parallel lines [1,2]. The proposed solvers relax the need for special scene structure to unknown repeated structures (see Table 1). The solvers are fast and robust to noisy feature detections, so they work well in robust estimation frameworks like RANSAC [3]. The proposed work is applicable for several important computer vision tasks including symmetry detection [4], inpainting [5], and single-view 3D reconstruction [6].

The proposed solvers enforce the affine invariant that rectified repeated regions have the same scale. We introduce three variants (see Fig. 1) that use different configurations of coplanar repeated features as input, which allows for flexible sampling during robust estimation. Lens distortion is parameterized by the division model, which Fitzgibbon [7] first used to model lens distortion and showed that it accurately models significant distortions. The use of the division model is crucial because other typical distortion models result in unsolvable constraint equations (see Sect. 2.1). A fourth solver variant is proposed that assumes the pinhole camera model. The pinhole variant is also novel because it does not linearize the rectifying transformation, which is the approach of the state of the art [8–10] (Table 2 and Fig. 8).

The polynomial system of equations encoding the rectifying constraints is solved using an algebraic method based on Gröbner bases. Automated solver generators using the Gröbner basis method [11,12] have been used

Table 1. *Scene Assumptions.* Solvers [1,2] require distinct sets of parallel scene lines as input and multi-model estimation for rectification. Pritts et al. [15] is restricted to scenes with translational symmetries. The proposed solvers directly rectify from as few as 4 rigidly transformed repeats.

	Wildenauer et al. [1]	Antunes et al. [2]	Pritts et al. [15]	Proposed
Feature Type	fitted circles	fitted circles	affine-covariant	affine-covariant
Assumption	3 & 3 parallel lines	3 & 4 parallel lines	2 trans. repeats	4 repeats
Rectification	multi-model	multi-model	direct	direct

to generate solvers for several camera geometry estimation problems [11–15]. However, straightforward application of automated solver generators to the proposed constraints resulted in unstable solvers (see Sect. 5). Recently, Larsson et al. [16] sampled feasible monomial bases, which can be used in the action-matrix method. In [16] basis sampling was used to minimize the size of the solver. We modified the objective of [16] to maximize for solver stability. Stability sampling generated significantly more numerically stable solvers (see Fig. 3).

Several state-of-the-art methods can rectify from imaged coplanar repeated texture, but these methods assume the pinhole camera model [5,8–10,17–19]. A subset of these methods use algebraic constraints induced by the equal-scale invariant of affine-rectified space [8–10]. These methods linearize the rectifying transformation and use the Jacobian determinant to induce local constraints on the imaged scene plane's vanishing line. The Jacobian determinant measures the local change-of-scale of the rectifying transformation. In contrast, the proposed solvers are the first to directly encode the unknown scale of a rectified region as the joint function of the measured region, vanishing line, and undistortion parameter. The direct approach eliminates the need for iterative refinement due to the linearization of the rectifying homography.

Pritts et al. [20] recover rectification with distortion using a two-step approach: a rectification estimated from a minimal sample using the pinhole assumption is refined by a nonlinear program that incorporates lens distortion. However, even with relaxed thresholds, a robust estimator like RANSAC [3] discards measurements around the boundary of the image since this region is the most affected by radial distortion and cannot be accurately modeled with a pinhole camera. Neglecting lens distortion during the segmentation of good and bad measurements, as done during the verification step of RANSAC, can give fits that are biased to barrel distortion [14], which degrades rectification accuracy. Pritts et al. [15] were the first to propose minimal solvers that jointly estimate affine rectification and lens distortion, but this method is restricted to scene content with translational symmetries (see Table 1). Furthermore, we show that the conjugate translation solvers of [15] are more noise sensitive than the proposed scale-based solvers (see Figs. 3 and 4).

There are two recent methods that affine-rectify lens distorted images by enforcing the constraint that scene lines are imaged as circles with the division model [1, 2]. The input into these solvers are circles fitted to contours extracted from the image. Sets of circles whose preimages are coplanar parallel lines are used to induce constraints on the division model parameter and vanishing points. These methods require two distinct sets of imaged parallel lines (6 total lines for [1] and 7 for [2]) to estimate rectification, which is a strong scene-content assumption. In addition, these methods must perform a multi-model estimation to label distinct vanishing points as pairwise consistent with vanishing lines. In contrast, the proposed solvers can undistorty and rectify from as few as 4 coplanar repeated local features (see Table 1).

2 Problem Formulation

An affine-rectifying homography H transforms the image of the scene plane's vanishing line $l = (l_1, l_2, l_3)^\top$ to the line at infinity $l_\infty = (0, 0, 1)^\top$ [21]. Thus any homography H satisfying the constraint

$$l = H^\top l_\infty = [h_1\ h_2\ h_3] \begin{pmatrix} 0 \\ 0 \\ 1 \end{pmatrix}, \tag{1}$$

where l is an imaged scene plane's vanishing line, is an affine-rectifying homography. Constraint (1) implies that $h_3 = l$, and that the line at infinity is invariant to rows $h_1^\top$ and $h_2^\top$ of H. Thus the affine-rectification of image point x to the affine-rectified point x' is defined as

$$\alpha x' = Hx \quad \text{such that } H = \begin{bmatrix} 1 & 0 & 0 \\ 0 & 1 & 0 \\ & l^\top & \end{bmatrix} \text{ and } \alpha \neq 0. \tag{2}$$

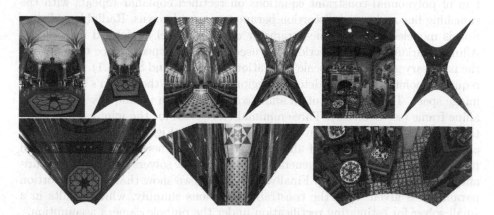

Fig. 2. *Wide-Angle Results.* Input (top left) is an image of a scene plane. Outputs include the undistorted image (top right) and rectified scene planes (bottom row). The method is automatic.

2.1 Radial Lens Distortion

Rectification as given in (2) is valid only if $\mathbf{x}$ is imaged by a pinhole camera. Cameras always have some lens distortion, and the distortion can be significant for wide-angle lenses. For a lens distorted point, denoted $\tilde{\mathbf{x}}$, an undistortion function f is needed to transform $\tilde{\mathbf{x}}$ to the pinhole point $\mathbf{x}$. A common parameterization for radial lens distortion is the one-parameter division model of Fitzgibbon et al. [7], which has the form

$$\mathbf{x} = f(\tilde{\mathbf{x}}, \lambda) = \left(\tilde{x}, \tilde{y}, 1 + \lambda(\tilde{x}^2 + \tilde{y}^2)\right)^\top, \tag{3}$$

where $\tilde{\mathbf{x}} = \left(\tilde{x}, \tilde{y}, 1\right)^\top$ is a feature point with the distortion center subtracted. Substituting (3) into (2) gives

$$\alpha \mathbf{x}' = \left(\alpha x', \alpha y', \alpha\right)^\top = \mathtt{H}\mathbf{x} = \mathtt{H}f(\tilde{\mathbf{x}}, \lambda) =$$
$$\left(\tilde{x}, \tilde{y}, l_1\tilde{x} + l_2\tilde{y} + l_3(1 + \lambda(\tilde{x}^2 + \tilde{y}^2))\right)^\top. \tag{4}$$

The unknown division model parameter λ and vanishing line $\mathbf{l}$ appear only in the homogeneous coordinate α. This property simplifies the solvers derived in Sect. 3. We also generated a solver using the standard second-order Brown-Conrady model [21–23]; however, these constraints generated a very larger solver with 85 solutions because the radial distortion coefficients appear in the inhomogeneous coordinates.

3 Solvers

The proposed solvers use the invariant that rectified coplanar repeats have equal scales. In Sects. 3.1 and 3.2 the equal-scale invariant is used to formulate a system of polynomial constraint equations on rectified coplanar repeats with the vanishing line and radial distortion parameters as unknowns. Radial lens distortion is modeled with the one-parameter division model as defined in Sect. 2.1. Affine-covariant region detections are used to model repeats since they encode the necessary geometry for scale estimation (see Fig. 1 and Sect. 4.1). The solvers require 3 points from each detected region to measure the region's scale in the image space. The geometry of an affine-covariant region is uniquely given by an affine frame (see Sect. 3.1). Three minimal cases exist for the joint estimation of the vanishing line and division-model parameter (see Fig. 1 and Sect. 3.2). These cases differ by the number of affine-covariant regions needed for each detected repetition. The method for generating the minimal solvers for the three variants is described in Sect. 3.3. Finally, in Sect. 3.4, we show that if the distortion parameter is given, then the constraint equations simplify, which results in a small solver for estimating rectification under the pinhole camera assumption.

3.1 Equal Scales Constraint from Rectified Affine-Covariant Regions

The geometry of an oriented affine-covariant region $\mathcal{R}$ is given by an affine frame with its origin at the midpoint of the affine-covariant region detection [24, 25]. The affine frame is typically given as the orientation-preserving homogeneous transformation A that maps from the right-handed orthonormal frame (normalized descriptor space) to the image space as

$$\begin{bmatrix} \mathbf{y} & \mathbf{o} & \mathbf{x} \end{bmatrix} = A \begin{bmatrix} 0 & 0 & 1 \\ 1 & 0 & 0 \\ 1 & 1 & 1 \end{bmatrix},$$

where $\mathbf{o}$ is the origin of the linear basis defined by $\mathbf{x}$ and $\mathbf{y}$ in the image coordinate system [24, 25]. Thus the matrix $\begin{bmatrix} \mathbf{y} & \mathbf{o} & \mathbf{x} \end{bmatrix}$ is a parameterization of affine-covariant region $\mathcal{R}$, which we call its *point-parameterization*.

Let $\begin{bmatrix} \tilde{\mathbf{x}}_{i,1} & \tilde{\mathbf{x}}_{i,2} & \tilde{\mathbf{x}}_{i,3} \end{bmatrix}$ be the point parameterization of an affine-covariant region $\tilde{\mathcal{R}}_i$ detected in a radially-distorted image. Then by (4) the affine-rectified point parameterization of $\tilde{\mathcal{R}}$ is $\begin{bmatrix} Hf(\tilde{\mathbf{x}}_{i,1}, \lambda) & Hf(\tilde{\mathbf{x}}_{i,2}, \lambda) & Hf(\tilde{\mathbf{x}}_{i,3}, \lambda) \end{bmatrix} = \begin{bmatrix} \alpha_{i,1}\mathbf{x}'_{i,1} & \alpha_{i,2}\mathbf{x}'_{i,2} & \alpha_{i,3}\mathbf{x}'_{i,3} \end{bmatrix}$, where $\alpha_{i,j} = \mathbf{l}^\top f(\tilde{\mathbf{x}}_{i,j}, \lambda)$. Thus the affine-rectified scale s_i of $\tilde{\mathcal{R}}$ is

$$s_i = \frac{\det\left(\begin{bmatrix} \alpha_{i,1}\mathbf{x}'_{i,1} & \alpha_{i,2}\mathbf{x}'_{i,2} & \alpha_{i,3}\mathbf{x}'_{i,3} \end{bmatrix}\right)}{\alpha_{i,1}\alpha_{i,2}\alpha_{i,3}} = \frac{1}{\alpha_{i,1}\alpha_{i,2}\alpha_{i,3}} \cdot \begin{vmatrix} \tilde{x}_{i,1} & \tilde{x}_{i,2} & \tilde{x}_{i,3} \\ \tilde{y}_{i,1} & \tilde{y}_{i,2} & \tilde{y}_{i,3} \\ \alpha_{i,1} & \alpha_{i,2} & \alpha_{i,3} \end{vmatrix} =$$

$$\frac{\alpha_{i,1} \cdot \begin{vmatrix} \tilde{x}_{i,2} & \tilde{x}_{i,3} \\ \tilde{y}_{i,2} & \tilde{y}_{i,3} \end{vmatrix} - \alpha_{i,2} \cdot \begin{vmatrix} \tilde{x}_{i,1} & \tilde{x}_{i,3} \\ \tilde{y}_{i,1} & \tilde{y}_{i,3} \end{vmatrix} + \alpha_{i,3} \cdot \begin{vmatrix} \tilde{x}_{i,1} & \tilde{x}_{i,2} \\ \tilde{y}_{i,1} & \tilde{y}_{i,2} \end{vmatrix}}{\alpha_{i,1}\alpha_{i,2}\alpha_{i,3}}. \tag{5}$$

The numerator in (5) depends only on the distortion parameter λ and l_3 due to cancellations in the determinant. The sign of s_i depends on the handedness of the detected affine-covariant region. See Sect. 3.6 for a method to use reflected affine-covariant regions with the proposed solvers.

3.2 Eliminating the Rectified Scales

The affine-rectified scale in s_i (5) is a function of the unknown undistortion parameter λ and vanishing line $\mathbf{l} = \begin{pmatrix} l_1, l_2, l_3 \end{pmatrix}^\top$. A unique solution to (5) can be defined by restricting the vanishing line to the affine subspace $l_3 = 1$ or by fixing a rectified scale, e.g., $s_1 = 1$. The inhomogenous representation for the vanishing line is used since it results in degree 4 constraints in the unknowns λ, l_1, l_2 and s_i as opposed to fixing a rectified scale, which results in complicated equations of degree 7.

Let $\tilde{\mathcal{R}}_i$ and $\tilde{\mathcal{R}}_j$ be repeated affine-covariant region detections. Then the affine-rectified scales of $\tilde{\mathcal{R}}_i$ and $\tilde{\mathcal{R}}_j$ are equal, namely $s_i = s_j$. Thus the unknown rectified scales of a corresponded set of n affine-covariant repeated regions

$s_1, s_2, \ldots, s_n$ can be eliminated in pairs, which gives $n - 1$ algebraically independent constraints and $\binom{n}{2}$ linearly independent equations. After eliminating the rectified scales, 3 unknowns remain, $\mathbf{l} = (l_1, l_2, 1)^\top$ and λ, so 3 constraints are needed. There are 3 minimal configurations for which we derive 3 solver variants: (i) 3 affine-covariant region correspondences, which we denote as the 222-configuration; (ii) 1 corresponded set of 3 affine-covariant regions and 1 affine-covariant region correspondence, denoted the 32-configuration; (iii) and 1 corresponded set of 4 affine-covariant regions, denoted the 4-configuration. The notational convention introduced for the input configurations—(222, 32, 4)—is extended to the bench of state-of-the-art solvers evaluated in the experiments (see Sect. 5) to make comparisons between the inputs of the solvers easy. See Fig. 1 for examples of all input configurations and results from their corresponding solver variant, and see Table 2 for a summary of all tested solvers.

The system of equations is of degree 4 regardless of the input configuration and has the form

$$\alpha_{j,1}\alpha_{j,2}\alpha_{j,3} \sum_{k=1}^{3}(-1)^k M_{3,k}\alpha_{i,k} = \alpha_{i,1}\alpha_{i,2}\alpha_{i,3} \sum_{k=1}^{3}(-1)^k M_{3,k}\alpha_{j,k}, \tag{6}$$

where $M_{i,j}$ is the (i, j)-minor of matrix $[\alpha_{i,1}\mathbf{x}'_{i,1} \ \alpha_{i,2}\mathbf{x}'_{i,2} \ \alpha_{i,3}\mathbf{x}'_{i,3}]$. Note that the minors $M_{3,.}$ of (6) are constant coefficients. The 222-configuration results in a system of 3 polynomial equations of degree 4 in three unknowns l_1, l_2 and λ; the 32-configuration results in 4 equations of degree 4, and the 4-configuration gives 6 equations of degree 4. Only 3 equations are needed, but we found that for the 32- and 4-configurations that all $\binom{n}{2}$ equations must be used to avoid spurious solutions that arise from vanishing $\alpha_{i,j}$ when the rectified scales are eliminated. For example, if only equations $s_1 = s_2$, $s_1 = s_3$, $s_1 = s_4$ are used for the 4-configuration

$$\alpha_{i,1}\alpha_{i,2}\alpha_{i,3} \sum_{k=1}^{3}(-1)^k M_{3,k}\alpha_{1,k} = \alpha_{1,1}\alpha_{1,2}\alpha_{1,3} \sum_{k=1}^{3}(-1)^k M_{3,k}\alpha_{i,k} \quad i = 2, 3, 4,$$

then λ can be chosen such that $\sum_{k=1}^{3}(-1)^k M_{3,k}\alpha_{1,k} = 0$, and the remaining unknowns l_1 or l_2 chosen such that $\alpha_{1,1}\alpha_{1,2}\alpha_{1,3} = 0$, which gives a 1-dimensional family of solutions. Thus, adding two additional equations removes all spurious solutions. Furthermore, including all equations simplified the elimination template construction. In principle a solver for the 222-configuration can be used to solve the 32- and 4-configurations. However, this decouples the scales within each group of regions, and there will exist additional solutions that do not satisfy the original constraints.

3.3 Creating the Solvers

We used the automatic generator from Larsson et al. [12] to make the polynomial solvers for the three input configurations (222, 32, 4). The solver corresponding to each input configuration is denoted $H_{222}1\lambda$, $H_{32}1\lambda$, and $H_41\lambda$, respectively. The resulting elimination templates were of sizes 101×155 (54 solutions), 107×152 (45 solutions), and 115×151 (36 solutions). The equations have coefficients of very different magnitude (e.g. both image coordinates $x_i, y_i \approx 10^3$ and their squares in $x_i^2 + y_i^2 \approx 10^6$). To improve numerical conditioning, we re-scaled both the image coordinates and the squared distances by their average magnitudes. Note that this corresponds to a simple re-scaling of the variables in (λ, l_1, l_2), which is reversed once the solutions are obtained.

Experiments on synthetic data (see Sect. 5.1) revealed that using the standard GRevLex bases in the generator of [12] gave solvers with poor numerical stability. To generate stable solvers we used the recently proposed basis sampling technique from Larsson et al. [16]. In [16] the authors propose a method for randomly sampling feasible monomial bases, which can be used to construct polynomial solvers. We generated (with [12]) 1,000 solvers with different monomial bases for each of the three variants using the heuristic from [16]. Following the method from Kuang et al. [26], the sampled solvers were evaluated on a test set of 1,000 synthetic instances, and the solvers with the smallest median equation residual were kept. The resulting solvers have slightly larger elimination templates (133×187, 154×199, and 115×151); however, they are significantly more stable. See Sect. 5.1 for a comparison between the solvers using the sampled bases and the standard GRevLex bases (default in [12]).

3.4 The Fixed Lens Distortion Variant

Finally, we consider the case of known division-model parameter λ. Fixing λ in (6) yields degree 3 constraints in only 2 unknowns l_1 and l_2. Thus only 2 correspondences of 2 repeated affine-covariant regions are needed. The generator of [12] found a stable solver (denoted $H_{22}1$) with an elimination template of size 12×21, which has 9 solutions. Basis sampling was unneeded in this case. There is second minimal problem for 3 repeated affine-covariant regions; however, unlike the case of unknown distortion, this minimal problem is equivalent to the H_{22} variant. It also has 9 solutions and can be solved with the H_{22} solver by duplicating a region in the input. The $H_{22}1$ solver contrasts to the solvers proposed in [8–10] in that it is generated from constraints directly induced by the rectifying homography rather than its linearization.

3.5 Degeneracies

The solvers have two degeneracies. If the vanishing line passes through the image origin $l = (l_1, l_2, 0)^\top$, then the radial term in the homogeneous coordinate of (4) vanishes. If the scene plane is fronto-parallel to the camera and corresponding points from the affine-covariant regions fall on circles centered at the image origin, then the radial distortion is unobservable. The proposed solvers do not have the degeneracy of the $H_{22}ls_i$ solver of [10], which occurs if the centroids of the sampled affine-covariant regions are colinear.

3.6 Reflections

In the derivation of (6), the rectified scales s_i were eliminated with the assumption that they had equal signs (see Sect. 3.3). Reflections will have oppositely signed rectified scales; however, reversing the orientation of left-handed affine frames in a simple pre-processing step that admits the use of reflections. Suppose that $\det\left(\left[\tilde{\mathbf{x}}_{i,1}\,\tilde{\mathbf{x}}_{i,2}\,\tilde{\mathbf{x}}_{i,3}\right]\right) < 0$, where $(\tilde{\mathbf{x}}_{i,1}, \tilde{\mathbf{x}}_{i,2}, \tilde{\mathbf{x}}_{i,3})$ is a distorted left-handed point parameterization of an affine-covariant region. Then reordering the point parameterization as $(\tilde{\mathbf{x}}_{i,3}, \tilde{\mathbf{x}}_{i,2}, \tilde{\mathbf{x}}_{i,1})$ results in a right-handed point-parameterization such that $\det\left(\left[\tilde{\mathbf{x}}_{i,3}\,\tilde{\mathbf{x}}_{i,2}\,\tilde{\mathbf{x}}_{i,1}\right]\right) > 0$, and the scales of corresponded rectified reflections will be equal.

4 Robust Estimation

The solvers are used in a LO-RANSAC based robust-estimation framework [27]. Minimal samples are drawn according to the solver variant's requirements (see Table 2 and Fig. 1). Affine rectifications and undistortions are jointly hypothesized by the solver. A metric upgrade is directly attempted using the minimal sample (see [20]), and the consensus set is estimated in the metric-rectified space by verifying the congruence of the basis vectors of the corresponded affine frames. Models with the maximal consensus set are locally optimized in a method similar to [20]. The metric-rectified images are presented in the results.

4.1 Local Features and Descriptors

Affine-covariant region detectors are highly repeatable on the same imaged scene texture with respect to significant changes of viewpoint and illumination [28, 29]. Their proven robustness in the multi-view matching task makes them good candidates for representing the local geometry of repeated textures. In particular, we use the Maximally-Stable Extremal Region and Hesssian-Affine detectors [24, 30]. The affine-covariant regions are given by an affine transform (see Sect. 3), equivalently 3 distinct points, which defines an affine frame in the image space [31]. The image patch local to the affine frame is embedded into a descriptor vector by the RootSIFT transform [32, 33].

4.2 Appearance Clustering and Robust Estimation

Affine frames are tentatively labeled as repeated texture by their appearance. The appearance of an affine frame is given by the RootSIFT embedding of the image patch local to the affine frame. The RootSIFT descriptors are agglomeratively clustered, which establishes pair-wise tentative correspondences among connected components. Each appearance cluster has some proportion of its indices corresponding to affine frames that represent the same repeated scene content, which are the *inliers* of that appearance cluster. The remaining affine frames are the *outliers*.

Table 2. State-of-the-art vs. proposed (shaded in grey) solvers. The proposed solvers return more solutions, but typically only 1 solution is feasible (see Fig. 5).

	$H_2lus\lambda$	$H_{22}luvs\lambda$	$H_{22}ls_i$	$H_{22}\lambda$	$H_{22}l$	$H_{222}l\lambda$	$H_{32}l\lambda$	$H_4l\lambda$
Reference	[15]	[15]	[10]	[7]				
Rectifies	✓	✓	✓		✓	✓	✓	✓
Undistorts	✓	✓		✓		✓	✓	✓
Motion	trans.	trans.	rigid	rigid[a]	rigid	rigid	rigid	rigid
# regions	2	4	4	4	4	6	5	4
# sols.	2	4	1	18	9	54	45	36
Size	24x26	76x80	4x4	18x18	12x21	133x187	154x199	115x151

[a]Correspondences must induce the same rigid transform in the scene plane.

Samples for the minimal solvers are either 2 correspondences of 2 covariant regions (the $H_{22}\cdot$ solvers), a corresponded set of 3 covariant regions (the $H_{32}l\lambda$ solver) and a correspondence of 2 covariant regions, and a corresponded set of 4 covariant regions (the $H_4l\lambda$ solver). An appearance cluster is selected with the probability given by its relative size to the other appearance clusters. The consensus is measured by the number of pairs of affine frames that are mutually consistent with a rigid transform within the appearance group, normalized by the size of each respective group. A non-linear optimizer following [20] is used as the local optimization step.

5   Experiments

The stabilities and noise sensitivities of the proposed solvers are evaluated on synthetic data. We compare the proposed solvers to a bench of 4 state-of-the-art solvers (see Table 2). We apply the denotations for the solvers introduced in Sect. 3 to all the solvers in the benchmark, *e.g.*, a solver requiring 2 correspondences of 2 affine-covariant regions will be prefixed by H_{22}, while the proposed solver requiring 1 corresponded set of 4 affine-covariant regions is prefixed H_4.

Included are two state-of-the-art single-view solvers for radially-distorted conjugate translations, denoted $H_2lus\lambda$ and $H_{22}luvs\lambda$ [15]; a full-homography and radial distortion solver, denoted $H_{22}\lambda$ [7]; and the change-of-scale solver for affine rectification of [10], denoted $H_{22}ls_i$. The sensitivity benchmarks measure the performance of rectification accuracy by the warp error (see Sect. 5.1) and the relative error of the division parameter estimate. Stability is measured with respect to the estimated division-model parameter. The $H_{22}\lambda$ solver is omitted from the warp error since the vanishing line is not estimated, and the $H_{22}ls_i$ and $H_{22}l$ solvers are omitted from benchmarks involving lens distortion since the solvers assume a pinhole camera.

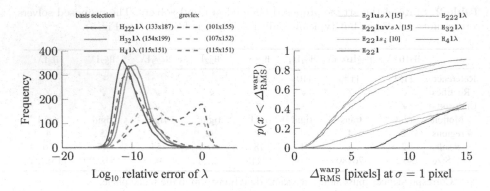

Fig. 3. (left) *Stability study.* Shows that the basis selection method of [16] is essential for stable solver generation. (right) *Proposal Study.* Reports the cumulative distributions of raw warp errors (see Sect. 5.1) for the bench of solvers on 1000 synthetic scenes 1-σ pixel of imaging white noise. The proposed solvers (with distortion) give significantly better proposals than the state of the art.

5.1   Synthetic Data

The performance of the proposed solvers on 1000 synthetic images of 3D scenes with known ground-truth parameters is evaluated. A camera with a random but realistic focal length is randomly placed with respect to a scene plane such that it is mostly in the camera's field-of-view. The image resolution is set to 1000×1000 pixels. Conjugately translated affine frames are generated on the scene plane such that their scale with respect to the scene plane is realistic. The motion is restricted to conjugate translations so that [15] can be included in the benchmark. Figure A.1 of the supplemental includes experiments for rigidly transformed affine frames. The modeling choice reflects the use of affine-covariant region detectors on real images (see Sect. 3). The image is distorted according to the division model. For the sensitivity experiments, isotropic white noise is added to the distorted affine frames at increasing levels. Performance is characterized by the relative error of the estimated distortion parameter and by the warp error, which measures the accuracy of the affine-rectification.

Warp Error. Since the accuracy of scene-plane rectification is a primary concern, the warp error for rectifying homographies proposed by Pritts et al. [34] is reported, which we extend to incorporate the division model for radial lens distortion [7]. A scene plane is tessellated by a 10×10 square grid of points $\{\mathbf{X}_i\}_{i=1}^{100}$ and imaged as $\{\tilde{\mathbf{x}}_i\}_{i=1}^{100}$ by the lens-distorted ground-truth camera. The tessellation ensures that error is uniformly measured over the scene plane. A round trip between the image space and rectified space is made by affine-rectifying $\{\tilde{\mathbf{x}}_i\}_{i=1}^{100}$ using the estimated division model parameter $\hat{\lambda}$ and rectifying homography $\hat{\mathbf{H}}$ and then imaging the rectified plane by the ground-truth camera. Ideally, the ground-truth camera images the rectified points onto $\{\tilde{\mathbf{x}}_i\}_{i=1}^{100}$. There is an affine

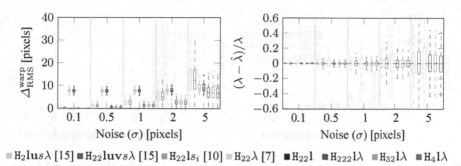

Fig. 4. *Sensitivity Benchmark.* Comparison of two error measures after 25 iterations of a simple RANSAC for different solvers with increasing levels of white noise added to the affine frame correspondences. (left) Reports the warp error as $\Delta_{\mathrm{RMS}}^{\mathrm{warp}}$ and (right) Reports the relative error of the estimated division model parameter. The proposed solvers are significantly more robust.

ambiguity, denoted $\mathtt{A}$, between $\hat{\mathtt{H}}$ and the ground-truth camera matrix $\mathtt{P}$. The ambiguity is estimated during computation of the warp error,

$$\Delta^{\mathrm{warp}} = \min_{\mathtt{A}} \sum_i d^2(\tilde{\mathbf{x}}, f^d(\mathtt{PA}\hat{\mathtt{H}}f(\tilde{\mathbf{x}}, \hat{\lambda})), \hat{\lambda}), \tag{7}$$

where $d(\cdot, \cdot)$ is the Euclidean distance, f^d is the inverse of the division model (the inverse of (3)), and $\{\tilde{\mathbf{x}}_i\}_{i=1}^{100}$ are the imaged grid points of the scene-plane tessellation. The root mean square warp error for $\{\tilde{\mathbf{x}}_i\}_{i=1}^{100}$ is reported and denoted as $\Delta_{\mathrm{RMS}}^{\mathrm{warp}}$. Note that the vanishing line is not directly estimated by the solver $\mathtt{H}_{22}\lambda$ of [7], so it is not reported.

Numerical Stability. The stability study compares the solver variants generated using the standard GRevLex bases versus solvers generated with bases chosen by basis sampling using [16] (see Sect. 3.3). The generator of Larsson et al. [12] et al. was used to generate both sets of solvers. Stability is measured by the relative error of the estimated division model parameter for noiseless affine-frame correspondences across realistic synthetic scenes, which are generated as described in the introduction of Sect. 5.1. The ground-truth parameter of the division model λ is drawn uniformly from the interval $[-8, 0.5]$. As a reference, the normalized division parameter $\lambda = -4$ is typical for wide field-of-view cameras like the GoPro, where the image is normalized by $1/(\text{width} + \text{height})$. Figure 3 (left) reports the histogram of $\log_{10}$ relative error of the estimates of the division model parameter, and Fig. 3 shows that the basis selection method of [16] significantly improves the stability of the generated solvers. The basis-sampled solvers are used for the remainder of the experiments.

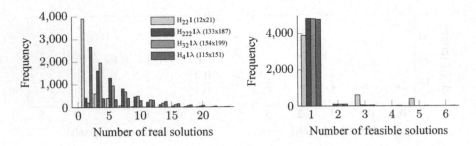

Fig. 5. (left) *Real Solutions*. The histogram of real solutions for the proposed solvers. (right) *Feasible Solutions*. There is typically only 1 feasible real solution.

Noise Sensitivity. The proposed and state-of-the-art solvers are tested with increasing levels of white noise added to the point parameterizations (see Sect. 3.1) of the affine-covariant region correspondences, which are conjugately translated (see [15,35]). The amount of white noise is given by the standard-deviation of a zero-mean isotropic Gaussian distribution, and the solvers are tested at noise levels of $\sigma \in \{0.1, 0.5, 1, 2, 5\}$. The ground-truth normalized division model parameter is set to $\lambda = -4$, which is typical for GoPro-type imagery in normalized image coordinates.

The proposal study in the right panel of Fig. 3 shows that for 1-pixel white noise, the proposed solvers—$H_{222}1\lambda, H_{32}1\lambda$ and $H_41\lambda$—give significantly more accurate estimates than the state-of-the-art conjugate translation solvers of [15]. If 5 pixel RMS warp error is fixed as a threshold for a good model proposal, then 50% of the models given by the proposed solvers are good versus less than 20% by [15]. The proposed $H_{22}1$ solver and $H_{22}1s_i$ [10] both give biased proposals since they don't estimate lens distortion.

For the sensitivity study in Fig. 4, the solvers are wrapped by a basic RANSAC estimator, which minimizes the RMS warp error Δ_{RMS}^{warp} over 25 minimal samples of affine frames. The RANSAC estimates are summarized in boxplots for 1000 synthetic scenes. The interquartile range is contained within the extents of a box, and the median is the horizontal line dividing the box. As shown in Fig. 4, the proposed solvers—$H_{222}1\lambda, H_{32}1\lambda$ and $H_41\lambda$—give the most accurate lens distortion and rectification estimates. The proposed solvers are superior to the state of the art at all noise levels. The proposed distortion-estimating solvers give solutions with less than 5-pixel RMS warp error Δ_{RMS}^{warp} 75% of the time and estimate the correct division model parameter more than half the time at the 2-pixel noise level. The fixed-lens distortion solvers $H_{22}1$ and $H_{22}1s_i$ of [10] give biased solutions since they assume the pinhole camera model.

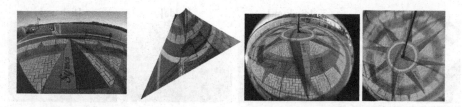

Fig. 6. (left pair) The pre-image of the waterfront is a circle, which violates the plumb-line assumption. (right pair) A reasonable rectification is estimated by the proposed method even with a fish-eye lens.

Feasible Solutions and Runtime. Figure 5 (left) shows the number of real solutions given by the proposed solvers for 5000 synthetic scenes, and Fig. 5 (right) shows the subset of feasible solutions as defined by the estimated normalized division-model parameter solution falling in the interval $[-8, 0.5]$. All solutions are considered feasible for the $H_{22}l$ solver. Figure 5 (right) shows that in 97% of the scenes only 1 solution is feasible, which means that nearly all incorrect solutions can be quickly discarded. The runtimes of the MATLAB implementation of the solvers on a standard desktop are 2 ms for $H_{222}l\lambda$, 2.2 ms for $H_{32}l\lambda$, 1.7 ms for $H_4l\lambda$, and 0.2 ms for $H_{22}l$.

5.2 Real Images

The field-of-view experiment of Fig. 7 evaluates the proposed $H_{222}l\lambda$ solver on real images taken with narrow, medium, and wide-angle lenses as well as a fisheye lens. Images with diverse scene content were chosen. Figure 7 shows that the $H_{222}l\lambda$ gives accurate rectifications for all lens types. Additional results for wide-angle lenses are included in Section A of the supplemental. Figure 8 compares the proposed $H_{222}l\lambda$ and $H_{22}l$ solvers to the state-of-the-art solvers on images with increasing levels of radial lens distortion (top to bottom) that contain either translated or rigidly-transformed coplanar repeated patterns. Only the proposed $H_{222}l\lambda$ accurately rectifies on both pattern types and at all levels of distortion. The results are after a local optimization and demonstrate that the method of Pritts et al. [20] is unable to accurately rectify without a good initial guess at the lens distortion. The proposed fixed-distortion solver $H_{22}l$ gave a better rectification than the change-of-scale solver of Chum et al. [10]. Figure 6 shows the rectifications of a deceiving picture of a landmark taken by wide-angle and fisheye lenses. From the wide-angle image it is not obvious which lines are really straight in the scene making undistortion with the plumb-line constraint difficult.

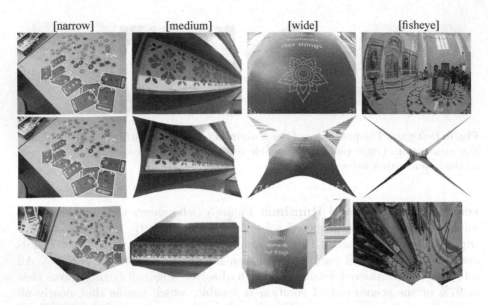

Fig. 7. *Field-of-View Study.* The proposed solver $\mathtt{H_{222}1\lambda}$ gives accurate rectifications across all fields-of-view: (left-to-right) Android phone, GoPro Hero 4 at the medium- and wide-FOV settings, and a Panasonic DMC-GM5 with a Samyang 7.5 mm fisheye lens. The outputs are the undistorted (middle row) and rectified images (bottom row).

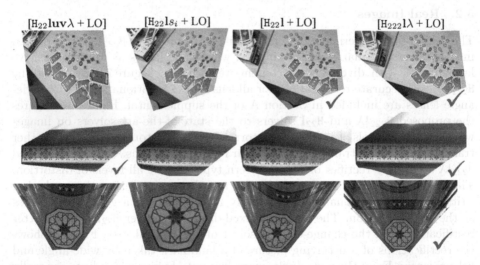

Fig. 8. *Solver Comparison.* The state-of-the art solvers $\mathtt{H_{22}luv\lambda}$ and $\mathtt{H_{22}1s_i}$ [10,15] are compared with the proposed solvers $\mathtt{H_{222}1\lambda}$ and $\mathtt{H_{22}1}$ on images containing either translated or rigidly-transformed coplanar repeated patterns with increasing amounts of lens distortion. (top) small distortion, rigidly-transformed; (middle) medium distortion, translated; (bottom) large distortion, rigidly-transformed. Accurate rectifications for all images is only given by the proposed $\mathtt{H_{222}1\lambda}$.

6   Conclusion

This paper proposes solvers that extend affine-rectification to radially-distorted images that contain essentially arbitrarily repeating coplanar patterns. Synthetic experiments show that the proposed solvers are more robust to noise with respect to the state of the art while being applicable to a broader set of image content. The paper demonstrates that robust solvers can be generated with by the basis selection method of [16] by maximizing for numerical stability. Experiments on difficult images with large radial distortions confirm that the solvers give high-accuracy rectifications if used inside a robust estimator. By jointly estimating rectification and radial distortion, the proposed minimal solvers eliminate the need for sampling lens distortion parameters in RANSAC.

Acknowledgements. James Pritts acknowledges the European Regional Development Fund under the project Robotics for Industry 4.0 (reg. no. CZ.02.1.01/0.0/0.0/15_003/0000470) and the grants MSMT LL1303 ERC-CZ and SGS17/185/OHK3/3T/13; Zuzana Kukelova the ESI Fund, OP RDE programme under the project International Mobility of Researchers MSCA-IF at CTU No. CZ.02.2.69/0.0/0.0/17_050/0008025; and Ondrej Chum the grant MSMT LL1303 ERC-CZ.

References

1. Wildenauer, H., Micusík, B.: Closed form solution for radial distortion estimation from a single vanishing point. In: BMVC (2013)
2. Antunes, M., Barreto, J.P., Aouada, D., Ottersten, B.: Unsupervised vanishing point detection and camera calibration from a single manhattan image with radial distortion. In: CVPR (2017)
3. Fischler, M.A., Bolles, R.C.: Random sample consensus: a paradigm for model fitting with applications to image analysis and automated cartography. CACM **24**, 381–395 (1981)
4. Funk, C., et al.: 2017 ICCV challenge: detecting symmetry in the wild. In: ICCV Workshop (2017)
5. Lukáč, M., et al.: Nautilus: recovering regional symmetry transformations for image editing. ACM Trans. Graph. **36**, 108:1–108:11 (2017)
6. Wu, C., Frahm, J.M., Pollefeys, M.: Repetition-based dense single-view reconstruction. In: CVPR (2011)
7. Fitzgibbon, A.W.: Simultaneous linear estimation of multiple view geometry and lens distortion. In: CVPR (2001)
8. Ohta, T., Maenobu, K., Sakai, T.: Obtaining surface orientation from texels under perspective projection. In: IJCAI (1981)
9. Criminisi, A., Zisserman, A.: Shape from texture: homogeneity revisited. In: BMVC (2000)
10. Chum, O., Matas, J.: Planar affine rectification from change of scale. In: ACCV (2010)
11. Kukelova, Z., Bujnak, M., Pajdla, T.: Automatic generator of minimal problem solvers. In: Forsyth, D., Torr, P., Zisserman, A. (eds.) ECCV 2008. LNCS, vol. 5304, pp. 302–315. Springer, Heidelberg (2008). https://doi.org/10.1007/978-3-540-88690-7_23

12. Larsson, V., Åström, K., Oskarsson, M.: Efficient solvers for minimal problems by syzygy-based reduction. In: CVPR (2017)
13. Larsson, V., Åström, K., Oskarsson, M.: Polynomial solvers for saturated ideals. In: ICCV (2017)
14. Kukelova, Z., Heller, J., Bujnak, M., Pajdla, T.: Radial distortion homography. In: CVPR (2015)
15. Pritts, J., Kukelova, Z., Larsson, V., Chum, O.: Radially-distorted conjugate translations. In: CVPR (2018)
16. Larsson, V., Oskarsson, M., Astrom, K., Wallis, A., Kukelova, Z., Pajdla, T.: Beyond grobner bases: basis selection for minimal solvers. In: CVPR (2018)
17. Ahmad, S., Cheong, L.F.: Robust detection and affine rectification of planar homogeneous texture for scene understanding. Int. J. Comput. Vis. **126**, 822–854 (2018)
18. Aiger, D., Cohen-Or, D., Mitra, N.J.: Repetition maximization based texture rectification. Comput. Graph. Forum **31**, 439–448 (2012)
19. Zhang, Z., Ganesh, A., Liang, X., Ma, Y.: TILT: transform invariant low-rank textures. Int. J. Comput. Vis. **99**, 1–24 (2012)
20. Pritts, J., Chum, O., Matas, J.: Detection, rectification and segmentation of coplanar repeated patterns. In: CVPR (2014)
21. Hartley, R.I., Zisserman, A.W.: Multiple View Geometry in Computer Vision, 2nd edn. Cambridge University Press, Cambridge (2004). ISBN 0521540518
22. Brown, D.C.: Decentering distortion of lenses. Photom. Eng. **32**, 444–462 (1966)
23. Conrady, A.: Decentering lens systems. Mon. Not. R. Astron. Soc. **79**, 384–390 (1919)
24. Mikolajczyk, K., Schmid, C.: Scale & affine invariant interest point detectors. Int. J. Comput. Vis. **60**, 63–86 (2004)
25. Vedaldi, A., Fulkerson, B.: VLFeat: an open and portable library of computer vision algorithms (2008). http://www.vlfeat.org/
26. Kuang, Y., Åström, K.: Numerically stable optimization of polynomial solvers for minimal problems. In: Fitzgibbon, A., Lazebnik, S., Perona, P., Sato, Y., Schmid, C. (eds.) ECCV 2012. LNCS, vol. 7574, pp. 100–113. Springer, Heidelberg (2012). https://doi.org/10.1007/978-3-642-33712-3_8
27. Chum, O., Matas, J., Obdržálek, S.: Enhancing RANSAC by generalized model optimization. In: ACCV (2004)
28. Mikolajczyk, K., Schmid, C.: A performance evaluation of local descriptors. IEEE Trans. Pattern Anal. Mach. Intell. **27**, 1615–1630 (2005)
29. Mishkin, D., Radenović, F., Matas, J.: Repeatability is not enough: learning affine regions via discriminability. In: Ferrari, V., Hebert, M., Sminchisescu, C., Weiss, Y. (eds.) ECCV 2018. LNCS, vol. 11213, pp. 287–304. Springer, Cham (2018). https://doi.org/10.1007/978-3-030-01240-3_18
30. Matas, J., Chum, O., Urban, M., Pajdla, T.: Robust wide baseline stereo from maximally stable extremal regions. In: BMVC (2002)
31. Obdržálek, Š., Matas, J.: Object recognition using local affine frames on distinguished regions. In: BMVC (2002)
32. Arandjelović, R., Zisserman, A.: Three things everyone should know to improve object retrieval. In: CVPR (2012)
33. Lowe, D.G.: Distinctive image features from scale-invariant keypoints. Int. J. Comput. Vis. **60**, 91–110 (2004)
34. Pritts, J., Rozumnyi, D., Kumar, M.P., Chum, O.: Coplanar repeats by energy minimization. In: BMVC (2016)
35. Schaffalitzky, F., Zisserman, A.: Geometric grouping of repeated elements within images. In: BMVC (1998)

Self-supervised Learning of Depth and Camera Motion from 360° Videos

Fu-En Wang[1(✉)], Hou-Ning Hu[1(✉)], Hsien-Tzu Cheng[1(✉)],
Juan-Ting Lin[1(✉)], Shang-Ta Yang[2(✉)], Meng-Li Shih[1(✉)],
Hung-Kuo Chu[2(✉)], and Min Sun[1(✉)]

[1] Department of Electrical Engineering, National Tsing Hua University,
Hsinchu, Taiwan
{fulton84717,eborboihuc,hsientzucheng,brade31919,
shihsml}@gapp.nthu.edu.tw, sunmin@ee.nthu.edu.tw
[2] Department of Computer Science, National Tsing Hua University,
Hsinchu, Taiwan
{sundadenny,hkchu}@gapp.nthu.edu.tw

Abstract. As 360° cameras become prevalent in many autonomous systems (e.g., self-driving cars and drones), efficient 360° perception becomes more and more important. We propose a novel self-supervised learning approach for predicting the omnidirectional depth and camera motion from a 360° video. In particular, starting from the SfMLearner, which is designed for cameras with normal field-of-view, we introduce three key features to process 360° images efficiently. Firstly, we convert each image from equirectangular projection to cubic projection in order to avoid image distortion. In each network layer, we use Cube Padding (CP), which pads intermediate features from adjacent faces, to avoid image boundaries. Secondly, we propose a novel "spherical" photometric consistency constraint on the whole viewing sphere. In this way, no pixel will be projected outside the image boundary which typically happens in images with normal field-of-view. Finally, rather than naively estimating six independent camera motions (i.e., naively applying SfM-Learner to each face on a cube), we propose a novel camera pose consistency loss to ensure the estimated camera motions reaching consensus. To train and evaluate our approach, we collect a new PanoSUNCG dataset containing a large amount of 360° videos with groundtruth depth and camera motion. Our approach achieves state-of-the-art depth prediction and camera motion estimation on PanoSUNCG with faster inference speed comparing to equirectangular. In real-world indoor videos, our approach can also achieve qualitatively reasonable depth prediction by acquiring model pre-trained on PanoSUNCG.

1 Introduction

Thanks to the emergence of Virtual Reality (VR) applications, 360° cameras have become very popular. Nowadays, one can easily find a few 360° cameras

---

F.-E. Wang, H.-N. Hu and H.-T. Cheng—Contribute equally to this paper.

© Springer Nature Switzerland AG 2019
C. V. Jawahar et al. (Eds.): ACCV 2018, LNCS 11365, pp. 53–68, 2019.
https://doi.org/10.1007/978-3-030-20873-8_4

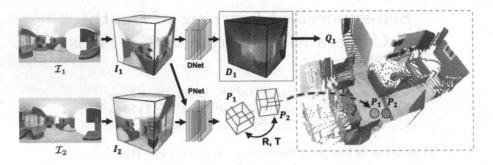

Fig. 1. Overview of 360° depth and camera motion estimation. In training phase, we use two 360° images ($\mathcal{I}_1$ and $\mathcal{I}_2$) as our input. We first project them into cubemaps (I_1 and I_2) which consist of 6 faces with 90° FoV. The DispNet (DNet) estimates depth of I_1 and PoseNet (PNet) predicts explainability map and camera motion (i.e., rotation R and translation T) between I_1 and I_2. With depth map D_1, we reproject our image I_1 to 3D point cloud Q_1. To update our network, depth and camera motion are used to calculate spherical photometric loss (Sect. 3.4) as our self-supervised objective.

supporting real-time streaming with 4K resolution and 30 frames-per-second (fps) at a consumer price. As a result, watching 360° photos and videos is becoming a common experience on sites like YouTube and Facebook. For humans, they enjoy the immersive experience in 360° videos as they can freely move their viewing angle. However, we argue that the ability to capture all surrounding at once in high-resolution and high frame-rate is immersively more critical for autonomous systems than for entertaining humans (Fig. 1).

All autonomous systems need to perceive the surrounding in order to act in the world safely. This includes self-driving cars, indoor/outdoor robots, drones, and even underwater robots. Using a single traditional camera, the autonomous system will need to turn its viewing direction many times in order to explore the environment. To avoid such inefficiency, high-end autonomous systems are typically equipped with multiple cameras. However, this introduces extra cost and technical challenge to maintain a stable and well calibrated multiple camera system. In this case, modern 360° cameras are a great alternative since they are well-calibrated, low-cost, and supporting real-time streaming with high-resolution. Hence, we believe in the future, 360° cameras will be widely adopted in all kinds of autonomous systems.

A few recent methods have proposed to tackle different perception tasks on 360° videos. Caruso et al. [2] propose a robust SLAM algorithm leveraging the wide FoV in 360° videos. Su and Grauman [25] propose to learn spherical convolution for fast and robust object detection in 360° images. Huang et al. [32] propose to recognize place robustly given 360° images. To the best of our knowledge, predicting depth from a monocular 360° camera has not been well studied. We argue that perceiving depth is one of the most important perception ability for autonomous systems since stereo cameras or lidars is the must-have equipment on self-driving cars.

In this paper, we propose a novel deep-learning based model to efficiently predict the depth of each panoramic frame and camera motion between two consecutive frames in a 360° video. We propose to train our method under different levels of self-supervision: (1) just raw 360° video, (2) noisy ground truth camera motion and 360° video, and (3) ground truth camera motion and 360° video. Intuitively, higher depth prediction accuracy can be achieved with a higher level of supervision. In practice, noisy ground truth camera motion can be measured by IMU. Our idea of self-supervision is inspired by SfMLearner [33]. However, since it is designed for traditional cameras with normal field-of-view (NFoV), we introduce several key features to incorporate the unique properties in 360° video.

In this paper, our contributions are:

Spherical Photo-Consistency Loss. We propose to compute photo-consistency loss on the whole viewing sphere (Fig. 3). In this way, no pixel will be projected outside the image boundary which typically happens in images with normal field-of-view.

Robust Motion Estimate. Rather than naively estimating six independent camera motions (i.e., naively applying SfMLearner to each face on the cube), we propose a novel pose consistency loss to ensure the estimated camera motions reaching consensus (Fig. 3).

PanoSUNCG Dataset. To train and evaluate our approach, we collect a new PanoSUNCG dataset containing a large amount of 360° videos with ground truth depth and camera motion.

We compare our method with variants of our method not including all three key features. Our full method achieves state-of-the-art depth prediction and camera motion estimation on PanoSUNCG with faster inference speed comparing to equirectangular. Once pre-trained on PanoSUNCG, our method can easily be fine-tuned on real-world 360° videos and obtain reasonably good qualitative results.

2   Related Work

Single View Depth Estimation. In navigation and self-driving application, an accurate depth map is usually required to help agent to make a decision. In general, depth can come from LiDAR or stereo images. As we know, LiDAR provides us accurate depth. However, the high cost of such sensor makes these application challenging to productize. To reduce the cost, using a stereo camera is also common to get depth. By this way, the quality of depth will be sensitive to the calibration, which means a small error in calibration will reduce the depth accuracy. As deep neural network prospers in recent years, some researches are working on estimating depth map only from a single RGB image. Laina et al. [16] uses fully convolutional architecture with feature map upsampling to improve the regression of prediction and ground truth. With the method in [16,28] uses it as depth initialization and combines it with LSD-SLAM [5] to much improve the quality of reconstruction. With the photometric warping loss, the deep neural network can unsupervisedly learn single depth prediction by using image pairs from unstructured videos. [29] unsupervisedly split the scene into several rigid body motion and masks, which is proposed in [1], and use motion to transform point cloud coming from depth prediction. Zhou et al. [33] uses a multiscale method to predict single view depth and relative pose from unstructured image pairs. For each scale, they apply warping and smoothing loss to each of them. They also propose explainability masks to weight sum photometric error to prevent occlusion and moving object problems. There are also some recent works improve the unsupervised method by adding differentiable 3D losses [18], replacing pose prediction by Direct Visual Odometry (DVO) [30]. However, all the works above cannot be directly applied to 360° images due to the different geometry of spherical projection.

360° Perception. Omni-directional cameras has an emerging potential in a variety of applications. Häne et al. [10] proposed an autonomous driving system with 360° FoV input. A series of works address semantic saliency [15], focus preference [17] and NFoV viewing assistant [11,26,27] in 360° panoramic videos. Current methods deal with an equirectangular image or further process them into NFoV crops, while our system process a cubemap which can reach more than 200% FPS (Fig. 7) in high resolution. Surrounding scene recorded into a single image frame gives a great advantage to autonomous systems since 360° view ensures full coverage of every detail all around.

With the entire field of view, 360° camera is more robust to rotation and translation movements compared to normal perspective camera [22]. There are some recent methods aim to tackle 360° perception tasks. Su and Grauman [25] propose spherical convolution for fast object detection in 360° images. Huang et al. [32] propose a new system in 360° images that able to recognize place robustly. Cheng et al. [4] found using cubemap representation can help network to predict 360° saliency map very well. Although a significant amount of information carried by a 360° view, it can hardly be used in a perspective camera system without being explicitly designed. Therefore, several works have been proposed in solving 3D reconstruction problems [12,23], such as SLAM [2], Structure from Motion [3,9,20], camera motion estimation [13], etc.

However, none of the works above adapts learning-based method to directly mitigate the re-projection problem raised by the nature of 360° FoV. We thus focus on solving the problem regarding speed and robustness by considering a whole panoramic view in one forward.

3 Our Approach

In this section, the method that jointly estimates depth and motion from 360° videos is introduced. Note that spherical photometric constraints are proposed so as to adapt the model input from NFoV videos to 360° videos. We describe the important components in our method including spherical projection (Sect. 3.2), 360° depth and camera motion estimation (Sect. 3.3), self-consistency constraints for self-supervision learning (Sect. 3.4), and 2D image-based constraints (Sect. 3.5). Before that, we first introduce the notations used in our formulation in Sect. 3.1.

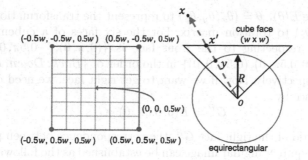

Fig. 2. Spherical projection

3.1 Preliminaries and Notations

Given a cubemap, the set of 6 faces—Back, Down, Front, Left, Right, and Up—are denoted as $\mathcal{F} = \{B, D, F, L, R, U\}$, respectively. In general, we define 2D equirectangular map as $\mathcal{M}$, and the cubemaps $M = \{M^f | f \in \mathcal{F}\}$, where M^f corresponds to the f face. We define a function Φ to transform equirectangular map to cubemap by $M = \Phi(\mathcal{M})$. Note that $\mathcal{M}$ represents an image, a feature map, or a depth map when we consider the input, the intermediate feature maps, or output of the network, respectively.

Given a 360° video sequence with T frames, we define the equirectangular frames $\mathcal{I} = \{\mathcal{I}_i | 1 \leq i \leq T\}$, the corresponding cubemap frames $I = \{I_i = \Phi(\mathcal{I}_i) | 1 \leq i \leq T\}$, the depth map $D = \{D_i | 1 \leq i \leq T\}$ and the relative camera pose $P = \{P_{ij} | 1 \leq i, j \leq T\}$ where P_{ij} denotes the relative camera pose from I_i to I_j. Besides, each relative pose P_{ij} consists of rotation R_{ij} and translation T_{ij} so we can also represent P_{ij} as (R_{ij}, T_{ij}).

After the depth D_i is attained, it can be projected into a 3D point cloud $Q_i = \Psi(D_i)$. To further use photometric consistency as our training loss, we define a warping function $\hat{I}_i = \xi(Q_i, I_j)$ to sample on I_j by the point cloud of I_i. The details of Ψ and ξ will be explained in Sect. 3.2.

3.2 Spherical Projection

For a perfect 360° camera, we can treat its imaging plane as a sphere as shown in Fig. 2 (Right). So any point x in world coordinate can be projected onto this sphere as the new point y and this is what we call spherical projection. If we want to reproject points on the sphere onto a cube face, we can assume a new pinhole camera with 90° FoV and its dimension is $w \times w$. Because we know its FoV is 90°, we can obtain that its focal length is $\frac{w}{2}$. For a pinhole camera, we can assume the 3D coordinate of each pixel in imaging plane is divided equally. So we can get a 3D grid G of this imaging plane as in Fig. 2 (Left). Notice that all the z value will be $0.5w$.

Now we use $E(\theta)$, $\theta = (\theta_x, \theta_y, \theta_z)$ to represent the transformation from euler angle $(\theta_x, \theta_y, \theta_z)$ to rotation matrix. For the six faces of a cubemap, the relative rotation respecting to the front face is $\{(0, \pi, 0), (-0.5\pi, 0, 0), (0, 0, 0),$ $(0, -0.5\pi, 0), (0, 0.5\pi, 0), (0.5\pi, 0, 0)\}$ in the order of $\{Back, Down, Front, Left,$ $Right, Up\}$ respectively. Now if we want to get right face, we need calculate the grid of right face by

$$G^R = E(0, 0.5\pi, 0) \cdot G.$$

With the grid of the right face G^R, the correspondence between pixels on the cubemap and equirectangular image can be established as the following equation:

$$X = \frac{arctan2(\frac{x}{z})}{\pi}, \tag{1}$$

$$Y = \frac{arcsin(\frac{y}{0.5w})}{0.5\pi}. \tag{2}$$

where X and Y are normalized pixel location on the equirectangular image and (x, y, z) is 3D point in the grid G^R. With the correspondence between pixel in cube face and equirectangular image, we can simply use inverse warping interpolation to transform 360° image to any cube faces. In this paper, we refer Φ as the function to project an equirectangular image to a cubemap with 6 faces.

In Sect. 3.1, we use the function Ψ to convert depth map of 6 cube faces to point cloud. The transformation is to scale up the unit grid G^i, where $i \in \mathcal{F}$, according to the depth. Take the right face for example, if we want to convert a pixel which location is (X, Y) and depth is d, we just need to normalize the corresponding grid location (x, y, z) in G^R and scale up to the same length as the depth. For the warping function, we use $\hat{I}_i = \xi(P_{ij} \cdot Q_i, I_j)$ to indicate the warping between I_i and I_j, the term $P_{ij} \cdot Q_i$ simply means the new point cloud transformed by the relative camera pose. And ξ means projecting point cloud to pixel coordinate of another sphere by Eqs. 1 and 2 and then applying interpolation.

3.3   Model for Depth and Camera Motion Estimation

Similar to [33], we adopt two networks for depth and camera motion estimation individually and join them to train together with spherical photometric and pose constraints. For DispNet, we utilize architecture refer to [19] that takes a single RGB image to predict the corresponding depth map. For PoseNet, refer to [33], our network takes the concatenation of target view with all the source views as input, then output relative poses between target and source. Another output is explainability mask (elaborated in Sect. 3.5) which can improve depth network accuracy by masking out ambiguity areas like occlusion and non-static patches. In our entire networks, every layer with 2D operations, such as convolution, pooling, etc., are incorporated with Cube Padding module as proposed by [4] to connect the intermediate features at adjacent faces and make the six faces spatially continuous.

3.4 Self Consistency Constraints

To get supervision from the 3D environment and spherical camera geometry, here we introduce two self-consistency constraints: photometric consistency and camera pose consistency constraints for self-learning.

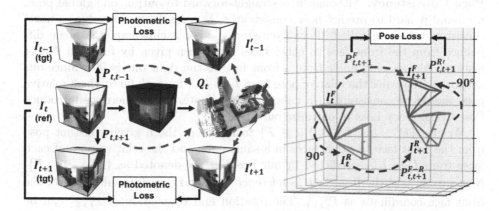

Fig. 3. Spherical photometric constraints. Left panel: photometric consistency loss. Right panel: pose consistency loss. In the left panel, I_{t-1} and I_{t+1} are target (tgt) frames of the reference (ref) I_t with relative pose $P_{t,t-1}, P_{t,t+1}$. Firstly, Q_t is projected by I_t through D_t. I'_{t-1} and I'_{t+1} are generated by transforming Q_t via $P_{t,t-1}, P_{t,t+1}$ and sampling from I_{t-1}, I_{t+1}, respectively. Then, we compute the photometric loss of reprojected I'_{t-1} and I'_{t+1} with I_t . On the right side, the original relative pose between I_t^F and I_{t+1}^F is denoted as $P_{t,t+1}^F$. Regarding the 90° rotation between cube faces, we can get $P_{t,t+1}^{R'}$ from the right face $P_{t,t+1}^R$ through $P_{t,t+1}^{F-R}$. Eventually we can compute pose consistency loss between $P_{t,t+1}^{R'}$ and $P_{t,t+1}^F$.

Photometric Consistency. By synthesizing a target view, given the relative pose, depth, and visibility in nearby views, the difference between the warped image and target image can be treated as a supervision cue [6–8,33] which is referred to as the photometric consistency constraint. Figure 3 shows the overview of 3D projections between the reference and target views while computing photometric consistency loss. Differ from the previous synthesis methods, we should consider the spherical nature of 360° to project between our cubemap and 3D point cloud.

Given a pair of cubemap which have total N pixels (reference I_i, target I_j) with reference depth D_i, reference explainability mask X_i (described in Sect. 3.5) and relative pose P_{ij}, the photometric consistency loss is defined as:

$$\mathcal{L}_{rec} = \frac{1}{N} \sum_i \sum_p^N X_i(p) \cdot |I_i(p) - \hat{I}_i(p)|, \tag{3}$$

which can be derived by the difference between I_i and projected $\hat{I}_i$ from I_j

$$\hat{I}_i = \xi(P_{ij} \cdot Q_i, I_j), \tag{4}$$
$$Q_i = \Psi(D_i). \tag{5}$$

Pose Consistency. Although it is straight-forward to output one global pose, we found it hard to predict pose consistently. As a result, we introduce a novel consistency loss we called "Pose Consistency". For a cubemap, the angle difference from the front face to other faces have been given by function Φ. For instance, the viewing angle from a front face to the right one is $90°$. Since our network will predict the relative pose from I_t to I_{t+1} for each faces, the 6 relative pose should be consistent in a cubemap coordinate. Hence, here we introduce Pose Consistency Loss to optimize our PoseNet.

We use $\{P_c^{F-i} = (R_c^{F-i}, 0)|i \in \mathcal{F}\}$ to represent the 6 given constant pose from the front face to other faces in a same cube and the relative pose of each faces from I_t to I_{t+1} predicted by our PoseNet are denoted as $\{P_{t,t+1}^i|i \in \mathcal{F}\}$. Now we can take the front face as reference view and transform all $P_{t,t+1}^i$ to the front face coordinate as $P_{t,t+1}^{i'}$. The rotation and translation of $P_{t,t+1}^{i'}$ can be derived as Eq. 6.

$$P_{t,t+1}^{i'} = (R_c^{i-F} \cdot R_{t,t+1}^i \cdot R_c^{F-i}, \ R_c^{i-F} \cdot T_{t,t+1}^i), \tag{6}$$

where $R_{t,t+1}^i, T_{t,t+1}^i$ is the rotation and translation of $P_{t,t+1}^i$. Optimally, all $P_{t,t+1}^{i'}$ should be close to each other because camera poses of each faces are innately coherent. A simple case is when $i = R$ as shown in Fig. 3. We first rotate the zero pose P_c^{F-F} by $90°$ and multiply $P_{t,t+1}^R$ to it to get an intermediate pose $P_{t,t+1}^{F-R}$. And then rotate this pose by $-90°$ to get the final transformed pose $P_{t,t+1}^{R'}$. To use this relation as a constraint to improve our PoseNet, we can try to minimize the discrepancy of all $P_{t,t+1}^{i'}$. For this purpose, we use standard derivation as our Pose Consistency Loss as in Eq. 7.

$$\mathcal{L}_{pose} = \sqrt{\frac{\sum\limits_{i \in f} (P_{t,t+1}^{i'} - P_{t,t+1}^*)^2}{6}}, \tag{7}$$

where $P_{t,t+1}^* = \frac{1}{6} \sum\limits_{i \in f} P_{t,t+1}^{i'}$, the mean of 6 poses.

3.5   2D Image-Based Constraints

In addition to the 3D constraints, we further adopt several 2D constraints in our training objectives.

Explainability Mask. To tackle the non-static objects and occlusion between views, our PoseNet outputs explainability masks in levels corresponding to depth prediction. [33] proposed a useful explainability mask learning objective

Frame	Inverse Depth	Frame	Inverse Depth

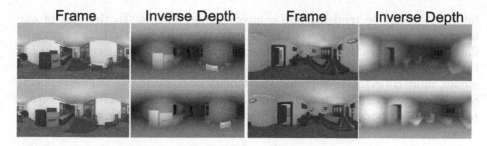

Fig. 4. Dataset examples. We randomly pick 2 scenes, 2 consecutive timesteps for each, and show equirectangular RGB frames and inverse depth maps. Our dataset consists of abundant indoor scenes with high-quality depth groundtruth.

$$\mathcal{L}_{exp} = -\frac{1}{N} \sum_i \sum_p^N \log X_i(p), \tag{8}$$

where p denotes the pixel position and N is the total amount of pixels. Equation 8 can be seen as a cross-entropy loss with constant "one" label. We found that the masks learn to interpret occlusion and high-frequency areas where photometric consistency mis-matched.

Smoothness Regularization. A smoothness loss is commonly employed for regularizing the depth prediction. One type as [7,8,33] is to derive the gradients directly from spatial regions of depth.

$$\mathcal{L}_{sm} = \sum_i |\nabla^2 D_i| \tag{9}$$

3.6 Final Model

Considering all mentioned loss terms, we train our model with the overall objective to optimize both photometric and pose constraints together with spatial smoothing and regularization:

$$\mathcal{L}_{all} = \mathcal{L}_{rec} + \lambda_{pose}\mathcal{L}_{pose} + \lambda_{sm}\mathcal{L}_{sm} + \lambda_{exp}\mathcal{L}_{exp} \tag{10}$$

4 Dataset

To evaluate the accuracy of our method, we collect a new dataset called—
PanoSUNCG. This dataset consists of 103 scenes with about $25k$ 360° images. To collect the dataset, we build up an environment with Unity using SUNCG [24]. We asked the annotators to draw 5 trajectories in each of 103 scenes, which should be reasonable path avoiding obstacles. Some sample snapshots are shown in Fig. 4. Following a trajectory in the 3D synthetic scene, all view and depth

information can be rendered into equirectangular images. To the best of our knowledge, the proposed PanoSUNCG dataset is the first 360° indoor video dataset with panorama depth and camera pose groundtruth sequence. By using the synthetic environment, this dataset can be easily scaled up to have more scenes, more trajectories, or even better quality of rendering. In our experiment, 80 of scenes are used for training and 23 are used for testing. To foster future research in 360° videos, we provide PanoSUNCG dataset at our website[1].

5   Experiments

We conduct several experiments to evaluate our method. In Sect. 5.1 we describe our training details and the incremental training method, then we describe different settings and variants in Sect. 5.2. Lastly in Sect. 5.3 we show the result of depth and camera pose estimation.

5.1   Implementation Detail

Training Details. We implemented our network using PyTorch [21] framework. The network is modified based on SfMLearner [33] backbone. During optimization, we used Adam optimizer with $\beta_1 = 0.9$, $\beta_2 = 0.999$, initial learning rate of 0.0006 and mini-batch size of 4. For the hyperparameters of our training loss, we found that $\lambda_{pose} = 0.1$, $\lambda_{sm} = 0.04$ and $\lambda_{exp} = 0.3$ balance each term in loss dropping. We train all our model 30k−50k iterations.

Incremental Training. Theoretically, PoseNet and DispNet can improve each other simultaneously. However, we found that, at the beginning of training, the two networks are unstable and will suppress each other. When this occurs, both depth and camera motion estimation have problematic convergence behaviors. To increase training stability, we first fit both networks with a relatively small dataset (4 batch size) to initialize the parameters to a stable state. During our training, we gradually increase the amount of our training dataset. When average loss is lower than an update threshold γ, we double our data and update γ with a factor of 1.2. In our experiments, we found 0.16 as a good initial γ.

5.2   Experimental Setups

In the real case when 360° depth is acquired, there might be an additional input: camera motion signal from the camera device. To verify the capacity of our method in different types of supervision signals, we set up different conditions to train our model. Also, we compare our approach with the method which directly using an equirectangular image as input to prove cubemap representation can improve 360° depth prediction.

---

[1] https://aliensunmin.github.io/project/360-depth/.

No PoseGT (fully unsupervised)—Our network can provide a reasonable camera motion estimation without any given labels. By applying spherical photo consistency, the self-supervised network can learn by watching 360° videos without access to camera motions. With cube padding [4] that enhances the bounding of 6 faces, our network can learn inter cube face relationship at no cost.

Noisy PoseGT—In the real world, estimated signals carry bias more or less. And small inertial sensor error can accumulate to a drastically erroneous influence along with time. According to [14], a normal cell phone has about 8.1 mrad/s biases in gyroscope and $15\,mg_0$ for X- and Y-axes, $25\,mg_0$ for Z-axes biases in accelerometer measurements. We apply this constant bias error with scale on PoseGT to examine the robustness of our model.

PoseGT—With our dataset, we can leverage the available camera motion information as a self-supervision signal. By exploring in a simulated environment, error-free motions can be seen as the output of optimal PoseNet, and positively improve the depth network reconstruction accuracy. As a result, we can view this setting as the ideal situation in a real-world application.

Equirectangular (EQUI)—The equirectangular images instead of its cubemaps are adopted as the inputs of the network.

Single pose—To prove applying pose consistency in Sect. 3.4 can improve the performance of pose prediction, in the PoseNet, we concatenate all bottleneck features from the six faces and apply a 2D convolution and global average pooling along the width and height dimensions, which is similar to [33], to make PoseNet output only one pose.

5.3   Evaluation of Depth and Camera Motion Estimation

We conduct experiments to benchmarking our performance with variants in Sect. 5.2. In the following, we will visualize our depth estimation result and show quantitative results of both depth and camera motion on PanoSUNCG. In addition, to prove the potential of practical applications using our method, we conducted experiments on real-world videos.

Results on PanoSUNCG. To test the reliability of our method, we evaluate the accuracy on PanoSUNCG. As shown in Table 1, Figs. 5 and 6, by considering spherical photometric consistency and pose consistency, our method can predict better depth than other baselines described in Sect. 5.2. For camera motion estimation, we use Relative Pose Error (RPE) as our evaluation metric and Table 2 is our pose accuracy. The single pose baseline is using the global pose from PoseNet as described in Sect. 5.2, which is worse than our method. We also tried to train our model (both EQUI and cubemap) by the method proposed in [33], but it ended up with bad depth and camera motion quality. It is obvious that pinhole model projection in [33] is not suitable for our 360° geometry.

Results on Real-World Videos. To demonstrate the usability of our method on real-world cases, we record our own 360° videos by RICOH THETA V. We

Table 1. Depth prediction result on PanoSUNCG. Following metrics used in [7,8, 33], we compare our method with ablation settings, baselines, and different level of supervision. Note that the numbers in the first 4 columns are the lower the better, and the last 3 columns higher the better.

Method	Abs Rel	Sq Rel	RMSE	$RMSE_{log}$	$\delta < 1.25$	$\delta < 1.25^2$	$\delta < 1.25^3$
Ours (full model)	**0.337**	**4.986**	**8.589**	0.611	**0.647**	**0.829**	**0.899**
Ours w/o $\mathcal{L}_{pose}$	0.418	7.113	9.916	0.698	0.580	0.790	0.876
EQUI	0.395	7.279	9.405	**0.493**	0.623	0.803	0.880
Ours w/PoseGT	0.254	3.554	7.126	0.513	0.752	0.880	0.927
Ours w/Noisy PoseGT	0.283	4.200	7.636	0.498	0.722	0.867	0.919

Table 2. RPE of camera motion estimation. RPE-R and RPE-T is rotation (in degree) and translation error, respectively. Our full method predicts better camera motion than other baselines.

Method	RPE-R	RPE-T
Ours (full model)	**6.98**	**0.025**
Ours w/o $\mathcal{L}_{pose}$	7.37	0.039
Single pose	7.49	0.026
EQUI	7.06	0.025

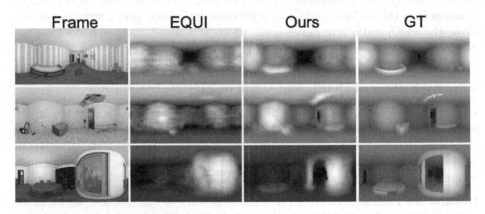

Fig. 5. Our depth prediction in PanoSUNCG comparing to equirectangular (EQUI) baseline.

extract the videos at 5 fps and finetune the PanoSUNCG-pretrained model on a train split. Figure 8 shows the qualitative result of image and predicted depth pairs by our proposed self-supervised method.

For clearer visualization, we also plot the point cloud from the predicted depth. The results show that our proposed method produces promising results in real-world scenarios.

5.4 Time Evaluation

For equirectangular images, there exists a considerable distortion in the field near two polars, consisting of a lot of unnecessary pixels. Fortunately, for a cubemap, there are no redundant pixels because it consists of 6 perspective images. As a result, the most significant benefit of using cubemap is the huge reduction in computing time. In Fig. 7, we plot frame rate and their speed up ratio as a function of image resolution. We denote the height of the equirectangular image as resolution. Our method, therefore, takes cubemap with width equals to $resolution/2$. The time computation of our method includes both converting equirectangular image to cubemap and converting cubemap depth back to equirectangular depth, which is a fair comparison. As we could see, the efficiency gap is getting larger as we have larger image resolution. Therefore, using cubemap can significantly reduce the computation cost, which means our method is much more suitable to be productized in an autonomous system or robotics application. Similar comparisons to other baseline methods are shown in the technical report [31].

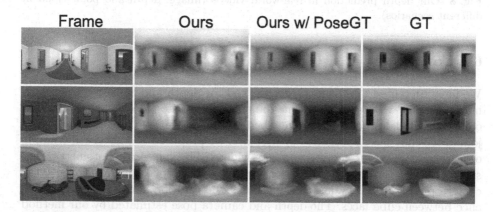

Fig. 6. Our depth prediction in PanoSUNCG using different level of supervision.

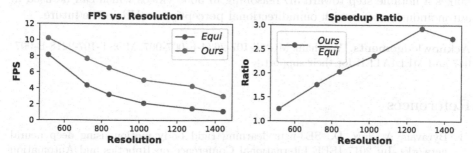

Fig. 7. Frame per second measurement of EQUI and Our method. Our method can perform faster inference speed than EQUI baseline. The speedup ratio increase more than 200% given higher input resolution.

Fig. 8. Our depth prediction in real-world videos (image, depth and point cloud in different scenarios).

6 Conclusion

We have presented a self-supervised method for depth and camera motion estimation in 360° videos. To overcome the projection distortion of equirectangular, our entire model processes data in cubemap, incorporating Cube Padding [4] to join every cube faces spatially. Furthermore, we proposed two novel self-training objectives tailored for geometry in 360° videos. The spherical photometric consistency loss is to minimize the difference between warped spherical images; the camera pose consistency loss is to optimize the rotation and translation difference between cube faces. The depth and camera pose estimated by our method outperform baseline methods in both quality and inference speed. Our work makes a notable step toward 3D reasoning in 360° videos which can be used in autonomous systems with omnidirectional perception or VR in the future.

Acknowledgements. We thank MOST-107-2634-F-007-007, MOST-107-2218-E-007-047 and MEDIATEK for their support.

References

1. Byravan, A., Fox, D.: SE3-nets: learning rigid body motion using deep neural networks. In: 2017 IEEE International Conference on Robotics and Automation (ICRA), pp. 173–180. IEEE (2017)
2. Caruso, D., Engel, J., Cremers, D.: Large-scale direct slam for omnidirectional cameras. In: 2015 IEEE/RSJ International Conference on Intelligent Robots and Systems (IROS), pp. 141–148. IEEE (2015)

3. Chang, P., Hebert, M.: Omni-directional structure from motion. In: Proceedings of the 2000 IEEE Workshop on Omnidirectional Vision, pp. 127–133 (2000)
4. Cheng, H.T., Chao, C.H., Dong, J.D., Wen, H.K., Liu, T.L., Sun, M.: Cube padding for weakly-supervised saliency prediction in 360° videos. In: The IEEE Conference on Computer Vision and Pattern Recognition (CVPR), June 2018
5. Engel, J., Schöps, T., Cremers, D.: LSD-SLAM: large-scale direct monocular SLAM. In: Fleet, D., Pajdla, T., Schiele, B., Tuytelaars, T. (eds.) ECCV 2014. LNCS, vol. 8690, pp. 834–849. Springer, Cham (2014). https://doi.org/10.1007/978-3-319-10605-2_54
6. Flynn, J., Neulander, I., Philbin, J., Snavely, N.: Deepstereo: learning to predict new views from the world's imagery. In: Proceedings of the IEEE Conference on Computer Vision and Pattern Recognition, pp. 5515–5524 (2016)
7. Garg, R., B.G., V.K., Carneiro, G., Reid, I.: Unsupervised CNN for single view depth estimation: geometry to the rescue. In: Leibe, B., Matas, J., Sebe, N., Welling, M. (eds.) ECCV 2016. LNCS, vol. 9912, pp. 740–756. Springer, Cham (2016). https://doi.org/10.1007/978-3-319-46484-8_45
8. Godard, C., Mac Aodha, O., Brostow, G.J.: Unsupervised monocular depth estimation with left-right consistency. In: CVPR, vol. 2, p. 7 (2017)
9. Guan, H., Smith, W.A.P.: Structure-from-motion in spherical video using the von mises-fisher distribution. IEEE Trans. Image Process. **26**(2), 711–723 (2017)
10. Häne, C., et al.: 3D visual perception for self-driving cars using a multi-camera system: calibration, mapping, localization, and obstacle detection. Image Vis. Comput. (IMAVIS) **68**, 14–27 (2017). Special Issue "Automotive Vision"
11. Hu, H.N., Lin, Y.C., Liu, M.Y., Cheng, H.T., Chang, Y.J., Sun, M.: Deep 360 pilot: learning a deep agent for piloting through 360° sports videos. In: CVPR (2017)
12. Im, S., Ha, H., Rameau, F., Jeon, H.-G., Choe, G., Kweon, I.S.: All-around depth from small motion with a spherical panoramic camera. In: Leibe, B., Matas, J., Sebe, N., Welling, M. (eds.) ECCV 2016. LNCS, vol. 9907, pp. 156–172. Springer, Cham (2016). https://doi.org/10.1007/978-3-319-46487-9_10
13. Kangni, F., Laganiere, R.: Orientation and pose recovery from spherical panoramas. In: 2007 IEEE 11th International Conference on Computer Vision, pp. 1–8, October 2007
14. Kos, A., Tomazic, S., Umek, A.: Evaluation of smartphone inertial sensor performance for cross-platform mobile applications. Sensors **16**, 477 (2016)
15. Lai, W.S., Huang, Y., Joshi, N., Buehler, C., Yang, M.H., Kang, S.B.: Semantic-driven generation of hyperlapse from 360° video. TVCG **24**(9), 2610–2621 (2017)
16. Laina, I., Rupprecht, C., Belagiannis, V., Tombari, F., Navab, N.: Deeper depth prediction with fully convolutional residual networks. In: 2016 Fourth International Conference on 3D Vision (3DV), pp. 239–248. IEEE (2016)
17. Lin, Y.C., Chang, Y.J., Hu, H.N., Cheng, H.T., Huang, C.W., Sun, M.: Tell me where to look: investigating ways for assisting focus in 360° video. In: CHI (2017)
18. Mahjourian, R., Wicke, M., Angelova, A.: Unsupervised learning of depth and ego-motion from monocular video using 3D geometric constraints. In: The IEEE Conference on Computer Vision and Pattern Recognition (CVPR), June 2018
19. Mayer, N., et al.: A large dataset to train convolutional networks for disparity, optical flow, and scene flow estimation. In: Proceedings of the IEEE Conference on Computer Vision and Pattern Recognition, pp. 4040–4048 (2016)
20. Pagani, A., Stricker, D.: Structure from motion using full spherical panoramic cameras. In: 2011 IEEE International Conference on Computer Vision Workshops (ICCV Workshops), pp. 375–382, November 2011

21. Paszke, A., Chintala, S.: Pytorch. https://github.com/apaszke/pytorch-dist
22. Pathak, S., Moro, A., Fujii, H., Yamashita, A., Asama, H.: 3D reconstruction of structures using spherical cameras with small motion. In: 2016 16th International Conference on Control, Automation and Systems (ICCAS), pp. 117–122, October 2016
23. Schönbein, M., Geiger, A.: Omnidirectional 3D reconstruction in augmented manhattan worlds. In: 2014 IEEE/RSJ International Conference on Intelligent Robots and Systems, pp. 716–723, September 2014
24. Song, S., Yu, F., Zeng, A., Chang, A.X., Savva, M., Funkhouser, T.: Semantic scene completion from a single depth image. In: IEEE Conference on Computer Vision and Pattern Recognition (2017)
25. Su, Y.C., Grauman, K.: Learning spherical convolution for fast features from 360° imagery. In: NIPS (2017)
26. Su, Y.C., Grauman, K.: Making 360° video watchable in 2D: learning videography for click free viewing. In: CVPR (2017)
27. Su, Y.C., Jayaraman, D., Grauman, K.: Pano2Vid: automatic cinematography for watching 360° videos. In: ACCV (2016)
28. Tateno, K., Tombari, F., Laina, I., Navab, N.: CNN-SLAM: real-time dense monocular slam with learned depth prediction. In: IEEE Conference on Computer Vision and Pattern Recognition (CVPR) (2017)
29. Vijayanarasimhan, S., Ricco, S., Schmid, C., Sukthankar, R., Fragkiadaki, K.: SfMnet: learning of structure and motion from video. CoRR abs/1704.07804 (2017)
30. Wang, C., Miguel Buenaposada, J., Zhu, R., Lucey, S.: Learning depth from monocular videos using direct methods. In: The IEEE Conference on Computer Vision and Pattern Recognition (CVPR), June 2018
31. Wang, F.E., et al.: Technical report of self-supervised 360 depth (2018). https://aliensunmin.github.io/project/360-depth/
32. Wang, T.H., Huang, H.J., Lin, J.T., Hu, C.W., Zeng, K.H., Sun, M.: Omnidirectional CNN for Visual Place Recognition and Navigation. CoRR abs/1803.04228v1 (2018)
33. Zhou, T., Brown, M., Snavely, N., Lowe, D.G.: Unsupervised learning of depth and ego-motion from video. In: CVPR, vol. 2, p. 7 (2017)

Domain Transfer for 3D Pose Estimation from Color Images Without Manual Annotations

Mahdi Rad[2]([envelope])[iD], Markus Oberweger[2]([envelope])[iD], and Vincent Lepetit[1,2]([envelope])[iD]

[1] Laboratoire Bordelais de Recherche en Informatique, Université de Bordeaux, Bordeaux, France
[2] Institute for Computer Graphics and Vision, Graz University of Technology, Graz, Austria
{rad,oberweger,lepetit}@icg.tugraz.at

Abstract. We introduce a novel learning method for 3D pose estimation from color images. While acquiring annotations for color images is a difficult task, our approach circumvents this problem by learning a mapping from paired color and depth images captured with an RGB-D camera. We jointly learn the pose from synthetic depth images that are easy to generate, and learn to align these synthetic depth images with the real depth images. We show our approach for the task of 3D hand pose estimation and 3D object pose estimation, both from color images only. Our method achieves performances comparable to state-of-the-art methods on popular benchmark datasets, without requiring any annotations for the color images.

Keywords: Domain transfer · 3D object pose estimation · 3D hand pose estimation · Synthetic data

1 Introduction

3D pose estimation is an important problem with many potential applications. Recently, Deep Learning methods have demonstrated great performance, when a large amount of training data is available [1–5]. To create training data, the labeling is usually done with the help of markers [6,7] or a robotic system [8], which in both cases is very cumbersome, expensive, or sometimes even impossible, especially from color images. For example, markers cannot be used for 3D hand labeling of color images, as they change the appearance of the hand.

Another direction is to use synthetic images for training. However, synthetic images do not exactly look like real images. Generative Adversarial Networks (GANs) [9–12] or transfer learning techniques [13–16] can be used to bridge the domain gap between real and synthetic images. However, these approaches still require some annotated real images to learn the domain transfer. [2] relies on registered real images to compute a direct mapping between the image features of real and synthetic images, but it also requires some labeled real images.

© Springer Nature Switzerland AG 2019
C. V. Jawahar et al. (Eds.): ACCV 2018, LNCS 11365, pp. 69–84, 2019.
https://doi.org/10.1007/978-3-030-20873-8_5

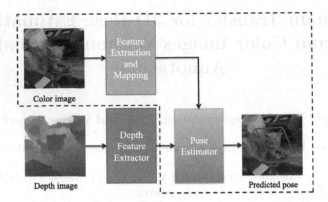

Fig. 1. Method overview. We train a depth feature extractor (red box) together with a pose estimator (blue box). We also train a second network (green box), which extracts image color features and maps them to the depth space, given color images and their corresponding depth images. At run-time, given a color image, we map color features to depth space in order to use the pose estimator to predict the 3D pose of the object (dashed lines). This removes the need for labeled color images. (Color figure online)

In this paper, we propose a method that learns to predict a 3D pose from color images, without requiring labeled color images. Instead, it exploits labeled depth images. These depth images can be real depth images, which are easier to label than color images, and are already readily available for some problems. More interestingly, they can also be synthetic depth images: Compared to color images, synthetic depth images are easier to render, as there is no texture or illumination present in these images.

An overview of our approach is shown in Fig. 1. Our main idea is to bridge the domain gap between color images and these synthetic depth images in two steps, each one solving an easier problem than the original one. We use an RGB-D camera to capture a set of pairs made of color and depth images that correspond to the same view. Capturing such a set can be done by simply moving the camera around. We apply [2] to this set and learn to map the features from the color images to corresponding depth images. However, this mapping alone is not sufficient: A domain gap between the depth images captured by the RGB-D camera and the available labeled depth images remains, since the labeled depth images could be captured with another RGB-D camera or rendered synthetically. Fortunately, this remaining gap is easier to bridge than the domain gap between real and synthetic color images, since illumination and texture effects are not present in depth images. To handle it, we use Maximum Mean Discrepancy (MMD) [17] to measure and minimize the distance between the means of the features of the real and synthetic depth images mapped into a Reproducing Kernel Hilbert Space (RKHS). MMD is a popular in domain transfer method [16] since it does not require correspondences to align the features of different domains and can be efficiently implemented.

Fig. 2. Our method allows very accurate 3D pose estimation from color images without annotated color images. In case of 3D rigid object pose estimation we draw the bounding boxes, where green is the ground truth bounding box and blue the bounding box of our predicted pose. For 3D hand pose estimation, we show the 3D joint locations projected to the color image, blue denoting the ground truth and green our estimation. (Color figure online)

Our approach is general, and not limited to rigid objects. It can be applied to many other applications, such as 3D hand pose estimation, human pose estimation, etc. Furthermore, in contrast to color rendering, no prior information about object's texture has to be known. Figure 2 shows applications to two different problems: 3D rigid object pose estimation and 3D hand pose estimation from color images, on the LINEMOD [6] and STB [18] datasets, respectively. Our method achieves performance comparable to state-of-the-art methods on these datasets without requiring any annotations for the color images.

In the remainder of this paper, we discuss related work, then present our approach and its evaluation.

2   Related Work

We first review relevant works for 3D pose estimation from color images, and then review related methods on domain transfer learning.

2.1   3D Pose Estimation from Color Images

Inferring the 3D pose from depth images has achieved excellent results [1,5,19,20], however, inferring the 3D pose from color images still remains challenging. [4] presented an approach for 3D object pose estimation from color images by predicting the 2D locations of the object corners and using PnP to infer the 3D pose, similar to [3,21]. Also, [22] first predicts the 2D joint locations for hand pose estimation, and then lifts these prediction to 3D estimates. [23] predicts 2D and 3D joint locations jointly, and then applies inverse kinematics to align these predictions. Similarly, [24] uses inverse kinematics to lift predicted 2D joint locations to 3D. All these approaches are fully supervised and require annotated color images, which are cumbersome to acquire in practice. Recently, [25] uses synthetically generated color images from 3D object models with pretrained features, however, they require extensive refinement of the initial network predictions, and we will show that we can reach better performances without annotations for real color images when using no refinement. To generalize synthetically generated color images to real images, [26] proposed to use a domain randomization method, however, the generalization is still limited, and outperformed by our approach as we show in the Evaluation section.

2.2 Domain Transfer Learning

As we mentioned in the introduction, it is difficult to acquire annotations for real training data, and training on synthetic data leads to poor results [4,25]. This is an indication for a domain gap between synthetic and real training data. Moreover, using synthetic data still requires accurately textured models [4,8, 25,27] that require large amount of engineering to model. On the other hand, synthetic depth data is much simpler to produce, but still it requires a method for domain transfer.

A popular method is to align the distributions for the extracted features from the different domains. Generative Adversarial Networks (GANs) [10] and Variational Autoencoders (VAEs) [28] can be used to learn a common embedding for the different domains. This usually involves learning a transformation of the data such that the distributions match in a common subspace [13–15]. [29] learns a shared embedding of images and 3D poses, but it requires annotations for the images to learn this mapping. Although GANs are able to generate visually similar images between different domains [12], the synthesized images lack precision required to train 3D pose estimation methods [2,9]. Therefore, [23] developed a sophisticated GAN approach to adapt the visual appearance of synthetically rendered images to real images, but this still requires renderings of high-quality synthetic color images.

To bridge this domain gap, [2] predicts synthetic features from real features and use these predicted features for inference, but this works only for a single modality, i.e.depth or color images, and requires annotations from both modalities. Similarly, [30] transfers supervision between images from different modalities by learning representations from a large labeled modality as a supervisory signal for training representations for a new unlabeled paired modality. In our case, however, we have an additional domain gap between real and synthetic depth data, which is not considered in their work. Also, [31] aims at transforming the source features into the space of target features by optimizing an adversarial loss. However, they have only demonstrated this for classification, and this approach works poorly for regression [2]. [16] proposed a Siamese Network for domain adaptation, but instead of sharing the weights between the two streams, their method allows the weights to differ and only regularizes them to keep them related. However, it has been shown in [2] that the adapted features are not accurate enough for 3D pose estimation.

Differently, [32] transfers real depth images to clean synthetic-looking depth images. However, this requires extensive hand-crafted depth image augmentation to create artificial real-looking depth images during training, and modeling the noise of real depth cameras is difficult in practice. [33] proposed to randomize the appearance of objects and rendering parameters during training, in order to improve generalization of the trained model to real-world scenarios. However, this requires significant engineering effort and there is no guarantee that these randomized renderings cover all the visual appearances of a real-world scene.

Several works [34,35] propose a fusion of features from different domains. [34] fuses color and depth features by using labeled depth images for a few categories and adapts a color object detector for a new category such that it can use depth images in addition to color images at test time. [35] propose a combination method that selects discriminative combinations of layers from the different source models and target modalities and sums the features before feeding them to a classifier. However, both works require annotated images in all domains. [36] uses a shared network that utilizes one modality in both source and target domain as a bridge between the two modalities, and an additional network that preserves the cross-modal semantic correlation in the target domain. However, they require annotations in both domains, whereas we only require annotations in one, i.e.the synthetic, domain that are much easier to acquire.

When comparing our work to these related works on domain transfer learning, these methods either require annotated examples in the target domain [2,23, 31,34–36], are restricted to two domains [2,30,31,34,35], or require significant engineering [32,33]. By contrast, our method does not require any annotations in the target domain, i.e.color images, and can be only trained on synthetically rendered depth images that are easy to generate, and the domain transfer is trained from real data that can be easily acquired using a commodity RGB-D camera.

3   Method

Given a 3D model of a target object, it is easy to generate a training set made of many depth images of the object under different 3D poses. Alternatively, we can use an existing dataset of labeled depth images. We use this training set to train a first network to extract features from such depth images, and a second network, the *pose estimator*, to predict the 3D pose of an object, given the features extracted from a depth image. Because it is trained on many images, the pose estimator performs well, but only on depth images.

To apply the pose estimator network to color images, we train a network to map features extracted from color images to features extracted from depth images, as was done in [2] between real and synthetic images. To learn this mapping, we capture a set of pairs of color and depth images that correspond to the same view, using an RGB-D camera. In order to handle the domain gap between the real and synthetic depth images of two training sets, we apply the Maximum Mean Discrepancy (MMD) [17], which aims to map features of each training set to a Reproducing Kernel Hilbert Space (RKHS) and then minimizes the distance between the means of the mapped features of the two training sets. An overview of the proposed method is shown in Fig. 3.

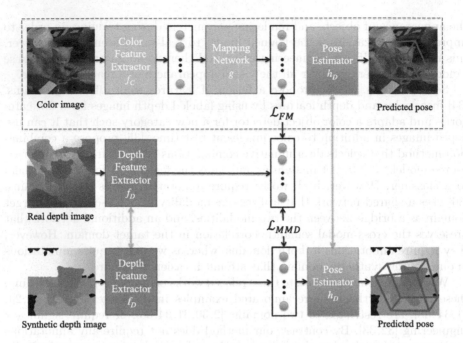

Fig. 3. Detailed overview of our approach. It consists of three data streams, one for each domain. The lower two streams take depth images as input, *i.e.*synthetic and real depth images, respectively, and extract features using the network $f_\mathcal{D}$. The upper stream takes color images as input and uses the mapping network g to map the color features to the depth features used for pose prediction with network $h_\mathcal{D}$. The parameters of the depth feature extractor $f_\mathcal{D}$ and pose predictor $h_\mathcal{D}$ are shared between the synthetic and real depth image (green arrows). Between the synthetic and the real depth feature we have the MMD loss $\mathcal{L}_{MMD}$ and between the real color and real depth features we use the feature mapping loss $\mathcal{L}_{FM}$. For inference at test time, we use only the upper stream within the dashed lines that takes a real color image as input, extracts features using the network $f_\mathcal{C}$, maps these features to the depth space using g, and uses the pose estimator $h_\mathcal{D}$ to predict the 3D pose. (Color figure online)

3.1   Learning the Mapping

More formally, let $\mathcal{T}^S = \{(\mathbf{x}_i^S, \mathbf{y}_i)\}_i$ be a training set of synthetically rendered depth images $\mathbf{x}_i^S$ using a 3D renderer engine under 3D poses $\mathbf{y}_i$. A second training set $\mathcal{T}^{\text{RGB-D}} = \{(\mathbf{x}_i^\mathcal{R}, \mathbf{x}_i^\mathcal{D})\}_i$ consists of pairs of color images $\mathbf{x}_i^\mathcal{R}$, and their corresponding depth images $\mathbf{x}_i^\mathcal{D}$. We jointly train four networks: the feature extractor for depth images $f_\mathcal{D}$, the feature extractor for color images $f_\mathcal{C}$, the pose estimator $h_\mathcal{D}$, and the feature mapping network g, on the training sets $\mathcal{T}^\mathcal{D}$ and $\mathcal{T}^{\text{RGB-D}}$.

We optimize the following loss function over the parameters of networks $f_\mathcal{D}$, $h_\mathcal{D}$, $f_\mathcal{C}$, and g as:

$$
\begin{aligned}
&\mathcal{L}(\theta_D, \theta_h, \theta_C, \theta_g; \mathcal{T}^S, \mathcal{T}^{\text{RGB-D}}) = \\
&\mathcal{L}_P(\theta_D, \theta_h; \mathcal{T}^S) + \beta \mathcal{L}_{FM}(\theta_D, \theta_C, \theta_g; \mathcal{T}^{\text{RGB-D}}) + \gamma \mathcal{L}_{MMD}(\theta_D; \mathcal{T}^S, \mathcal{T}^{\text{RGB-D}}),
\end{aligned}
\tag{1}
$$

where θ_D, θ_h, θ_C, and θ_g are the parameters of networks f_D, h_D, f_C, and g, respectively. The losses $\mathcal{L}_P$ for the pose, $\mathcal{L}_{FM}$ for the feature mapping between color and depth features, and $\mathcal{L}_{MMD}$ for the MMD between synthetic and real depth images are weighted by meta parameters β and γ.

$\mathcal{L}_P$ is the sum of the errors for poses predicted from depth images:

$$\mathcal{L}_P(\theta_D, \theta_h; \mathcal{T}^{\mathcal{S}}) = \sum_{(\mathbf{x}_i^{\mathcal{S}}, \mathbf{y}_i) \in \mathcal{T}^{\mathcal{S}}} \|h_D(f_D(\mathbf{x}_i^{\mathcal{S}}; \theta_D); \theta_h) - \mathbf{y}_i\|^2 . \tag{2}$$

$\mathcal{L}_{FM}$ is the loss used to learn to map features extracted from depth images to features extracted from their corresponding color images:

$$\mathcal{L}_{FM}(\theta_D, \theta_C, \theta_g; \mathcal{T}^{\text{RGB-D}}) = \sum_{(\mathbf{x}_i^{\mathcal{R}}, \mathbf{x}_i^{\mathcal{D}}) \in \mathcal{T}^{\text{RGB-D}}} \|g(f_C(\mathbf{x}_i^{\mathcal{R}}; \theta_C); \theta_g) - f_D(\mathbf{x}_i^{\mathcal{D}}; \theta_D)\|^2 . \tag{3}$$

Finally, $\mathcal{L}_{MMD}$ is the Maximum Mean Discrepancy [17] loss to minimize the domain shift between the distribution of features extracted from real and synthetic depth images of these training sets:

$$\mathcal{L}_{MMD}(\theta_D; \mathcal{T}^{\mathcal{S}}, \mathcal{T}^{\text{RGB-D}}) = \left\| \frac{1}{|\mathcal{T}^{\text{RGB-D}}|} \sum_{\mathbf{x}_i^{\mathcal{D}} \in \mathcal{T}^{\text{RGB-D}}} \phi(f_D(\mathbf{x}_i^{\mathcal{D}}; \theta_D)) - \frac{1}{|\mathcal{T}^{\mathcal{S}}|} \sum_{\mathbf{x}_i^{\mathcal{S}} \in \mathcal{T}^{\mathcal{S}}} \phi(f_D(\mathbf{x}_i^{\mathcal{S}}; \theta_D)) \right\|^2 , \tag{4}$$

where $\phi(\cdot)$ denotes the mapping to kernel space, but the exact mapping is typically unknown in practice. By applying the kernel trick, this rewrites to:

$$\mathcal{L}_{MMD}(\theta_D; \mathcal{T}^{\mathcal{S}}, \mathcal{T}^{\text{RGB-D}}) = \frac{1}{|\mathcal{T}^{\text{RGB-D}}|^2} \sum_{i,i'} k(f_D(\mathbf{x}_i^{\mathcal{D}}; \theta_D), f_D(\mathbf{x}_{i'}^{\mathcal{D}}; \theta_D))$$
$$- \frac{2}{|\mathcal{T}^{\text{RGB-D}}||\mathcal{T}^{\mathcal{S}}|} \sum_{i,j} k(f_D(\mathbf{x}_i^{\mathcal{D}}; \theta_D), f_D(\mathbf{x}_j^{\mathcal{S}}; \theta_D)) \tag{5}$$
$$+ \frac{1}{|\mathcal{T}^{\mathcal{S}}|^2} \sum_{j,j'} k(f_D(\mathbf{x}_j^{\mathcal{S}}; \theta_D), f_D(\mathbf{x}_{j'}^{\mathcal{S}}; \theta_D)) ,$$

where $k(\cdot, \cdot)$ denotes a kernel function. In this work, we implement $k(\cdot, \cdot)$ as an RBF kernel, such that

$$k(\mathbf{x}, \mathbf{y}) = e^{-\frac{\|\mathbf{x}-\mathbf{y}\|^2}{2\sigma^2}} , \tag{6}$$

where we select the bandwidth $\sigma = 1$. Note that our method is not sensitive to the exact value of σ.

At run-time, given a real color image $\mathbf{x}^{\mathcal{R}}$, we extract its features in color space and map them to the depth feature space by the networks f_C and g, respectively, and then use the pose estimator h_D to predict the 3D pose $\hat{\mathbf{y}}$ of the object:

$$\hat{\mathbf{y}} = h_D(g(f_C(\mathbf{x}^{\mathcal{R}}))) . \tag{7}$$

3.2 Network Details and Optimization

3D Object Pose Estimation. For the depth feature extraction network f_D, we use a network architecture similar to the 50-layer Residual Network [37], and remove the Global Average Pooling [37] as done in [2,5,19]. The convolutional layers are followed by two fully-connected layers of 1024 neurons each. The pose estimator h_D consists of one single fully-connected layer with 16 outputs, which correspond to the 2D projections of the 8 corners of objects' 3D bounding box [4]. The 3D pose can then be computed from these 2D-3D correspondences with a PnP algorithm.

In order to do a fair comparison to [2,4] we use the same feature extractor, which consists of the first 10 pretrained convolutional layers of the VGG-16 network [38] and two fully-connected layers with 1024 neurons for the color feature extractor f_C.

3D Hand Pose Estimation. The architectures of f_D and h_D are the same as the ones used for 3D object pose estimation, except h_D outputs 3 values for each of the 21 joints, 63 in total. Additionally, we add a 3D pose prior [5] as a bottleneck layer to the pose estimator network h_D, which was shown to efficiently constrain the 3D hand poses and also gives better performance in our case.

For the color feature extractor f_C, we use the same architecture as the depth feature extractor, which makes the feature extractor comparable to the one used in [23,29].

Mapping Network and Optimization. Following [2], we use a two Residual blocks [39] network g for mapping the features of size 1024 from color space to depth space. Each fully-connected layer within the Residual block has 1024 neurons.

In practice, we use $\beta = 0.02$ and $\gamma = 0.01$ for the meta parameters of the objective function in Eq. 1 for all our experiments. We first pretrain f_D and h_D on the synthetic depth dataset $\mathcal{T}^S$. We also pretrain f_C by predicting depth from color images [40]. Pretraining is important in our experiments for improving convergence. We then jointly train all the networks together using the ADAM optimizer [41] with a batch size of 128 and an initial learning rate of 10^{-4}.

4   Evaluation

In this section, we evaluate our method on two different 3D pose estimation problems. We apply our method first on 3D rigid object pose estimation, and then on 3D hand pose estimation, both from color images only.

4.1   3D Object Pose Estimation from Color Images

We use the LINEMOD dataset [6] for benchmarking 3D object pose estimation. It consists of 13 texture-less objects, each registered with about 1200 real color images and corresponding depth images under different viewpoints, and provided with the corresponding ground truth poses. For evaluating 3D object pose estimation methods using only color images, [1,2,4,42] use 15% of the images of the LINEMOD dataset for training and the rest for testing. This amounts to about 180 images per object for training, which had to be registered in 3D with the help of markers. In contrast to these methods, our approach does *not* require any labeled color image. Instead, it uses pairs of real images and depth images to learn mapping the features from color space to depth space.

Table 1. Evaluation on the LINEMOD dataset [6]. The left part evaluates the impact of our proposed approach, where all methods predict the 3D object pose using the 2D projections of the objects' 3D bounding box [4], given the ground truth 2D object center without using pose refinement. Both BB8 [4] and Feature Mapping [2] use annotated color images, while our method achieves better performance than BB8 and similar performance to Feature Mapping without using any annotated color images at all. The middle and right parts show comparison of different pose estimation methods without using pose refinement, where no annotated color image is used for training. Our approach performs best.

Detection	Ground truth detection			Real detection					
Metric method	2D Projection [42]			2D Projection [42]			ADD [6]		
	BB8 [4]	Feature mapping [2]	Ours	SSD-6D [25]	[26]	Ours	SSD-6D [25]	[26]	Ours
Ape	94.0	**96.6**	**97.3**	3.5	36.4	**96.9**	2.6	4.0	**19.8**
Bench vise	90.0	**96.3**	92.7	0.9	30.5	**88.6**	15.1	20.9	**69.0**
Camera	81.7	**94.8**	83.4	1.0	56.0	**77.4**	6.1	30.5	**37.6**
Can	94.2	**96.6**	93.2	3.0	49.1	**91.3**	27.3	35.9	**42.3**
Cat	94.7	98.0	**98.7**	9.1	59.3	**98.0**	9.3	17.9	**35.4**
Driller	64.7	**83.3**	75.7	1.4	16.7	**72.2**	12.0	24.0	**54.7**
Duck	94.4	**96.3**	95.5	1.2	51.0	**91.8**	1.3	4.9	**29.4**
Egg box	93.5	96.1	**97.1**	1.5	73.5	**92.0**	2.8	81.0	**85.2**
Glue	94.8	96.9	**97.3**	11.0	78.3	**92.4**	3.4	45.5	**77.8**
Hole puncher	87.2	95.7	**97.2**	2.8	48.2	**96.8**	3.1	17.6	**36.0**
Iron	81.0	**92.3**	88.8	1.9	32.1	**85.9**	14.6	32.0	**63.1**
Lamp	76.2	83.5	**84.8**	0.5	30.8	**81.8**	11.4	60.5	**75.1**
Phone	70.6	88.2	**90.0**	5.3	53.3	**85.2**	9.7	33.8	**44.8**
Average	85.9	**93.4**	91.7	3.3	47.3	**88.5**	9.1	28.7	**51.6**

In order to do a fair comparison and not learn any context of the scene, we extract the objects from both color images and depth images for generating the training set $\mathcal{T}^{\text{RGB-D}}$. We follow the protocol of [4] to augment the training data by rescaling the target object, adding a small pixel shift from the center of the image window and superimpose it on a random background. We pick random backgrounds from the RGB-D dataset [43] as they provide color images together with corresponding depth images.

For generating the training set $\mathcal{T}^{\mathcal{S}}$, given the CAD model of the target object, we randomly sample poses from the upper hemisphere of the object, within a range of $[-45°, +45°]$ for the in-plane rotation and a camera distance within a range of $[65\,\text{cm}, 115\,\text{cm}]$. We also superimpose the rendered objects on a random depth background picked from the RGB-D dataset [43]. We apply a 5×5 median filter to mitigate the noise along the object boundaries. For both training sets $\mathcal{T}^{\text{RGB-D}}$ and $\mathcal{T}^{\mathcal{S}}$, we use image windows of size 128×128, and normalize them to the range of $[-1, +1]$.

To evaluate the impact of our approach, we first compare it to [4] and [2], which, similar to us, predict the 2D projection of the 3D object bounding box, followed by a PnP algorithm to estimate the 3D pose. The left part of Table 1 shows a comparison with these methods on the LINEMOD dataset by using 15% of real images for training and the ground truth 2D object center. We use the widely used 2D Projection metric [42] for comparison. We significantly outperform [4] and achieve similar performance to [2], which is the current state-of-the-art on the LINEMOD dataset. Most notably, we do not require any annotations for the color images. By using all the available pairs of real images and depth images, our approach performs with an accuracy of 95.7%. This shows that our approach almost eliminates the needs of the expensive task of annotating, simply by capturing data using an RGB-D camera.

We further compare to the approach of [25][1] without the extensive refinement step, which uses only synthetic color images for training. They obtain an accuracy of 3.3% on the 2D Projection metric. [4] trained only on synthetic color images also performs poorly with an accuracy of 12% on the same metric. This shows that while synthetic color images do not resemble real color images for training 3D pose estimation methods, our approach can effectively transfer features between color images and synthetic depth images. Although the domain randomization of [26] helps to increase the accuracy using synthetically generated images and generalize to different cameras, it is still not enough to bridge the domain gap. The comparisons are shown in Table 1.

Finally, we evaluate the domain adaption technique of [13] that aims to learn invariant features with respect to the shift between the color and depth domains. However, this performs with an accuracy of 2% using the 2D Projection metric, which shows that although this technique helps for general applications such as classification, the features are not well suited for 3D pose estimation.

4.2   3D Hand Pose Estimation from Color Images

We use the Stereo Hand Pose Benchmark (STB) [18] and the Rendered Hand Dataset (RHD) [22] for training and testing our approach for 3D hand pose estimation. The STB dataset contains 6 sequences each containing 1500 images of a stereo camera, and an RGB-D camera. It shows an user performing diverse hand gestures in front of different backgrounds. Each image is annotated with the corresponding 3D hand pose with 21 joints. The RHD dataset contains over 40k synthetically rendered images of humans performing various hand articulations. It consists of pairs of depth and color images, each with hand segmentation and 3D pose annotations of the same 21 joints.

We follow the protocol of [22,23,29], which use the first two sequences from the STB dataset for testing. The remaining ten sequences from the STB dataset

---

[1] We used their public code to obtain accuracies on 2D Projection and ADD metrics.

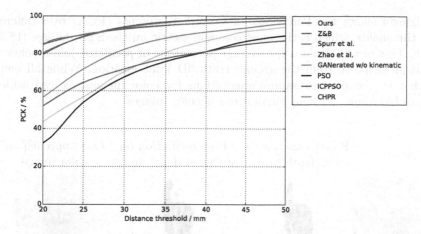

Fig. 4. 3D PCK curves for comparison to state-of-the-art 3D hand pose estimation methods on the STB dataset [18]. Note that all other approaches use annotated color images for training, whereas we do not use any annotations for the color images.

together with the RHD dataset are used for the training set $T^{\mathrm{RGB\text{-}D}}$, since they both contain aligned depth and color images. Creating synthetic depth maps for hands is a relatively simple problem. For generating the training set T^{S} we use the publicly available 3D hand model of [44] to render synthetic depth images of a hand. We use 5M synthetic images of the hand that are rendered online during training from poses of the NYU 3D hand pose dataset [44] perturbed with randomly added articulations. Furthermore, [22,23] align their 3D prediction to the ground truth wrist which we also do for comparison.

We use the pipeline provided by [5] to preprocess the depth images: It crops a 128×128 patch around the hand location, and normalizes its depth values to the range of $[-1, +1]$. For the color image we also crop a 128×128 patch around the corresponding hand location and subtract the mean RGB values. When a hand segmentation mask is available, such as for the RHD dataset [22], we superimpose the segmented hand on random color backgrounds from the RGB-D dataset [43]. During training, we randomly augment the hand scale, in-plane rotation, and 3D translation, as done in [5].

We compare to the following methods: GANerated [23][2], which uses a GAN to adapt synthetic color images for training a CNN; Z&B [22], which uses a learned prior to lift 2D keypoints to 3D locations and the similar approach of Zhao *et al.* [45]; Zhang *et al.* [18], which use stereo images to estimate depth and apply a depth-based pose estimator with variants denoted PSO, ICPPSO, and CHPR; Spurr *et al.* [29], which project color images to a common embedding that is shared between images and 3D poses.

---

[2] The results reported in the paper [23] are tracking-based and include an additional inverse kinematics step. In order to make their results more comparable to ours, we denote results predicted for each frame separately without inverse kinematics kindly provided by the authors.

Figure 4 shows the Percentage of Correct Keypoints (PCK) over different error thresholds, which is the most common metric on the STB dataset [18, 22, 23, 29]. This metric denotes the average percentage of predicted joints below an Euclidean distance from the ground truth 3D joint location. While all methods that we compare to require annotations for color images, we can achieve comparable results without annotations of color images.

Color image	Pose prediction on real depth image	Pose prediction on predicted depth image	Our approach on color image

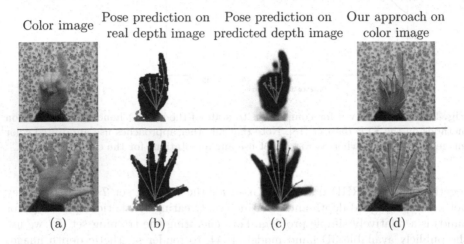

| (a) | (b) | (c) | (d) |

Fig. 5. We use the paired color and depth images shown in (a) and (b) to predict depth from color images [40] shown in (c). We further apply a 3D pose estimator [5] on these images. These predictions from the predicted and real depth images are shown in (b) and (c), respectively. Although the predicted depth images look visually close, the accuracy of the estimated 3D pose is significantly worse compared to using the real depth images. The results from our method are shown in (d) and provide a significantly higher accuracy. Our predictions are shown in blue and the ground truth in green. (Color figure online)

3D hand pose estimation methods work very well on depth images [5, 19]. Since we have paired color and depth images, we can train a CNN to predict the depth image from the corresponding color image [40]. Since the pose estimator works on cropped image patches, we only use these cropped image patches for depth prediction, which makes the task easier. We then use the predicted depth image for a depth-based 3D hand pose estimator with the pretrained model provided by the authors [5]. Although this approach also does not require any annotations of color images, our experiments show that this performs significantly worse on the STB dataset compared to ours. The 3D pose estimator gives an average Euclidean joint error of 17.6 mm on the real depth images and 39.8 mm on the predicted depth images. We show a qualitative comparison in Fig. 5.

4.3 Qualitative Results

We show some qualitative results of our method for 3D object pose estimation and 3D hand pose estimation in Fig. 6. These examples show our approach predicts very close pose to the ground truth.

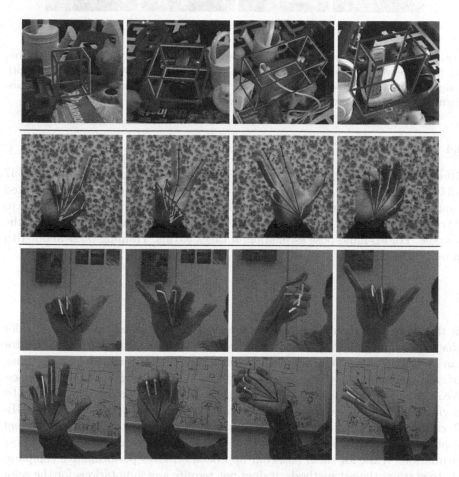

Fig. 6. Qualitative results of our method for 3D rigid object pose estimation on the LINEMOD dataset [6] (top row), and 3D hand pose estimation on the STB dataset [18] (middle row). Green denotes ground truth and blue corresponds to the predicted pose. We applied our trained network on real world RGB images of different users to estimate the 3D hand joint locations (bottom rows). (Color figure online)

Figure 7 illustrates some failure cases that occur due to the challenges of the test sets, such as partial occlusion that can easily be handled by training the networks with partially occluded examples, or missing poses in the paired dataset $\mathcal{T}^{\text{RGB-D}}$ that can be simply resolved by capturing additional data with an RGB-D camera.

(a)   (b)   (c)   (d)

Fig. 7. Some failure cases for 3D object pose estimation due to (a) partial occlusion, (b) not generalizing to every poses because of lack of corresponding color and depth images in the training set. Failure cases for 3D hand pose estimation due to (c) misalignment/confusion of the fingers, (d) severe self occlusion.

4.4 Computation Times

All experiments are implemented using Tensorflow and run on an Intel Core i7 3.3 GHz desktop with a Geforce TITAN X. Given an image window extracted around the object, our approach takes 3.2 ms for 3D object pose estimation to extract color features, map them to the depth feature space, and estimate the 3D pose. For 3D hand pose estimation, it takes 8.6 ms. Training takes about 10 h in our experiments.

5 Conclusion

In this work we presented a novel approach for 3D pose estimation from color images, without requiring labeled color images. We showed that a pose estimator can be trained on a large number of synthetic depth images, and at run-time, given a color image, we can map its features from color space to depth space. We showed that this mapping between the two domains can easily be learned by having corresponding color and depth images captured by a commodity RGB-D camera. Our approach is simple, general, and can be applied to different application domains, such as 3D rigid object pose estimation and 3D hand pose estimation. While for these tasks our approach achieves performances comparable to state-of-the-art methods, it does not require any annotations for the color images.

Acknowledgement. This work was supported by the Christian Doppler Laboratory for Semantic 3D Computer Vision, funded in part by Qualcomm Inc. We would like to thank Franziska Müller and Martin Sundermeyer for kindly providing additional evaluation results. Prof. V. Lepetit is a senior member of the *Institut Universitaire de France* (IUF).

References

1. Xiang, Y., Schmidt, T., Narayanan, V., Fox, D.: PoseCNN: A Convolutional Neural Network for 6D Object Pose Estimation in Cluttered Scenes. RSS (2018)
2. Rad, M., Oberweger, M., Lepetit, V.: Feature mapping for learning fast and accurate 3D pose inference from synthetic images. In: CVPR (2018)
3. Tekin, B., Sinha, S.N., Fua, P.: Real-time seamless single shot 6D object pose prediction. In: CVPR (2018)
4. Rad, M., Lepetit, V.: BB8: a scalable, accurate, robust to partial occlusion method for predicting the 3D poses of challenging objects without using depth. In: ICCV (2017)
5. Oberweger, M., Lepetit, V.: DeepPrior++: improving fast and accurate 3D hand pose estimation. In: ICCV Workshops (2017)
6. Hinterstoisser, S., et al.: Model based training, detection and pose estimation of texture-less 3D objects in heavily cluttered scenes. In: Lee, K.M., Matsushita, Y., Rehg, J.M., Hu, Z. (eds.) ACCV 2012. LNCS, vol. 7724, pp. 548–562. Springer, Heidelberg (2013). https://doi.org/10.1007/978-3-642-37331-2_42
7. Hodan, T., Haluza, P., Obdrzalek, S., Matas, J., Lourakis, M., Zabulis, X.: T-LESS: an RGB-D dataset for 6D pose estimation of texture-less objects. In: WACV (2017)
8. Calli, B., et al.: Yale-CMU-Berkeley dataset for robotic manipulation research. IJRR **36**, 261–268 (2017)
9. Bousmalis, K., Trigeorgis, G., Silberman, N., Krishnan, D., Erhan, D.: Domain separation networks. In: NIPS (2016)
10. Goodfellow, I.J., et al.: Generative adversarial networks. In: NIPS (2014)
11. Shrivastava, A., Pfister, T., Tuzel, O., Susskind, J., Wang, W., Webb, R.: Learning from simulated and unsupervised images through adversarial training. In: CVPR (2016)
12. Zhu, J.Y., Park, T., Isola, P., Efros, A.A.: Unpaired image-to-image translation using cycle-consistent adversarial networks. In: ICCV (2017)
13. Ganin, Y., Lempitsky, V.: Unsupervised domain adaption by backpropagation. In: ICML (2015)
14. Muandet, K., Balduzzi, D., Schölkopf, B.: Domain generalization via invariant feature representation. In: ICML (2013)
15. Pan, S., Tsang, I., Kwok, J., Yang, Q.: Domain adaptation via transfer component analysis. In: IJCAI (2009)
16. Rozantsev, A., Salzmann, M., Fua, P.: Beyond sharing weights for deep domain adaptation. In: CVPR (2017)
17. Gretton, A., Borgwardt, K., Rasch, M.J., Schölkopf, B., Smola, A.J.: A kernel method for the two-sample problem. In: NIPS (2006)
18. Zhang, J., Jiao, J., Chen, M., Qu, L., Xu, X., Yang, Q.: 3D hand pose tracking and estimation using stereo matching. ArXiv (2016)
19. Müller, F., Mehta, D., Sotnychenko, O., Sridhar, S., Casas, D., Theobalt, C.: Real-time hand tracking under occlusion from an egocentric RGB-D sensor. In: ICCV (2017)
20. Krull, A., Brachmann, E., Michel, F., Yang, M.Y., Gumhold, S., Rother, C.: Learning analysis-by-synthesis for 6D pose estimation in RGB-D images. In: ICCV (2015)
21. Oberweger, M., Rad, M., Lepetit, V.: Making deep heatmaps robust to partial occlusions for 3D object pose estimation. In: Ferrari, V., Hebert, M., Sminchisescu, C., Weiss, Y. (eds.) ECCV 2018. LNCS, vol. 11219, pp. 125–141. Springer, Cham (2018). https://doi.org/10.1007/978-3-030-01267-0_8

22. Zimmermann, C., Brox, T.: Learning to estimate 3D hand pose from single RGB images. In: ICCV (2017)
23. Müller, F., et al.: GANerated hands for real-time 3D hand tracking from monocular RGB. In: CVPR (2018)
24. Panteleris, P., Oikonomidis, I., Argyros, A.: Using a single RGB frame for real time 3D hand pose estimation in the wild. In: WACV (2018)
25. Kehl, W., Manhardt, F., Tombari, F., Ilic, S., Navab, N.: SSD-6D: making RGB-based 3D detection and 6D pose estimation great again. In: ICCV (2017)
26. Sundermeyer, M., Marton, Z.-C., Durner, M., Brucker, M., Triebel, R.: Implicit 3D orientation learning for 6D object detection from RGB images. In: Ferrari, V., Hebert, M., Sminchisescu, C., Weiss, Y. (eds.) ECCV 2018. LNCS, vol. 11210, pp. 712–729. Springer, Cham (2018). https://doi.org/10.1007/978-3-030-01231-1_43
27. Hinterstoisser, S., Lepetit, V., Wohlhart, P., Konolige, K.: On Pre-Trained Image Features and Synthetic Images for Deep Learning. ArXiv (2017)
28. Kingma, D.P., Welling, M.: Auto-encoding variational bayes. In: ICLR (2014)
29. Spurr, A., Song, J., Park, S., Hilliges, O.: Cross-modal deep variational hand pose estimation. In: CVPR (2018)
30. Gupta, S., Hoffman, J., Malik, J.: Cross modal distillation for supervision transfer. In: CVPR (2016)
31. Cai, G., Wang, Y., Zhou, M., He, L.: Unsupervised Domain Adaptation with Adversarial Residual Transform Networks. ArXiv (2018)
32. Zakharov, S., Planche, B., Wu, Z., Hutter, A., Kosch, H., Ilic, S.: Keep it Unreal: Bridging the Realism Gap for 2.5D Recognition with Geometry Priors Only. ArXiv (2018)
33. Tobin, J., Fong, R., Ray, A., Schneider, J., Zaremba, W., Abbeel, P.: Domain randomization for transferring deep neural networks from simulation to the real world. In: IROS (2017)
34. Hoffman, J., Gupta, S., Leong, J., Guadarrama, S., Darrell, T.: Cross-modal adaptation for RGB-D detection. In: ICRA (2016)
35. Song, X., Jiang, S., Herranz, L.: Combining models from multiple sources for RGB-D scene recognition. In: IJCAI (2017)
36. Huang, X., Peng, Y., Yuan, M.: Cross-modal common representation learning by hybrid transfer network. In: IJCAI (2017)
37. He, K., Zhang, X., Ren, S., Sun, J.: Deep residual learning for image recognition. In: CVPR (2016)
38. Simonyan, K., Vedaldi, A., Zisserman, A.: Learning local feature descriptors using convex optimisation. PAMI 36(8), 1573–1585 (2014)
39. He, K., Zhang, X., Ren, R., Sun, J.: Delving deep into rectifiers: surpassing human-level performance on imagenet classification. In: ICCV (2015)
40. Eigen, D., Puhrsch, C., Fergus, R.: Depth map prediction from a single image using a multi-scale deep network. In: NIPS (2014)
41. Kingma, D.P., Ba, J.: Adam: a method for stochastic optimization. In: ICML (2015)
42. Brachmann, E., Michel, F., Krull, A., Yang, M.M., Gumhold, S., Rother, C.: Uncertainty-driven 6D pose estimation of objects and scenes from a single RGB image. In: CVPR (2016)
43. Lai, K., Bo, L., Ren, X., Fox, D.: A large-scale hierarchical multi-view RGB-D object dataset. In: ICRA (2011)
44. Tompson, J., Stein, M., LeCun, Y., Perlin, K.: Real-time continuous pose recovery of human hands using convolutional networks. TOG 33, 169 (2014)
45. Zhao, R., Wang, Y., Martinez, A.: A Simple, Fast and Highly-Accurate Algorithm to Recover 3D Shape from 2D Landmarks on a Single Image. ArXiv (2016)

Partially Occluded Hands:
A Challenging New Dataset for Single-Image Hand Pose Estimation

Battushig Myanganbayar, Cristina Mata, Gil Dekel, Boris Katz,
Guy Ben-Yosef, and Andrei Barbu(✉)

CSAIL, MIT, Cambridge, MA 02139, USA
{btushig,cfmata,dekelg,boris,gby,abarbu}@mit.edu

Abstract. Recognizing the pose of hands matters most when hands are
interacting with other objects. To understand how well both machines
and humans perform on single-image 2D hand-pose reconstruction from
RGB images, we collected a challenging dataset of hands interacting
with 148 objects. We used a novel methodology that provides the same
hand in the same pose both with the object being present and occluding the hand and without the object occluding the hand. Additionally,
we collected a wide range of grasps for each object designing the data
collection methodology to ensure this diversity. Using this dataset we
measured the performance of two state-of-the-art hand-pose recognition
methods showing that both are extremely brittle when faced with even
light occlusion from an object. This is not evident in previous datasets
because they often avoid hand-object occlusions and because they are
collected from videos where hands are often between objects and mostly
unoccluded. We annotated a subset of the dataset and used that to show
that humans are robust with respect to occlusion, and also to characterize human hand perception, the space of grasps that seem to be considered, and the accuracy of reconstructing occluded portions of hands. We
expect that such data will be of interest to both the vision community for
developing more robust hand-pose algorithms and to the robotic grasp
planning community for learning such grasps. The dataset is available at
occludedhands.com.

Keywords: Partial occlusion · Dataset ·
RGB hand-pose reconstruction

1 Introduction

Understanding what humans are doing nearly always requires reconstructing the
poses of their bodies and in particular their hands. While body pose recognition

This work was supported, in part, by the Center for Brains, Minds and Machines
(CBMM) NSF STC award 1231216, the Toyota Research Institute, and the MIT-IBM
Brain-Inspired Multimedia Comprehension project.

© Springer Nature Switzerland AG 2019
C. V. Jawahar et al. (Eds.): ACCV 2018, LNCS 11365, pp. 85–98, 2019.
https://doi.org/10.1007/978-3-030-20873-8_6

from single RGB images has advanced significantly [1–5], hand-pose recognition from this type of data has received far less attention. Despite this, recent publications have shown results that reconstruct hand models to within a few pixels of human annotations [6,7]. Here we investigate the performance of such models, introducing a challenging new dataset consisting of common grasps of common objects where those grasps are shown both with the objects occluding the hand and without the object present. We also provide the first measurements of human hand-pose reconstruction accuracy as a function of the proportion of the hand that is occluded against ground-truth annotations. In brief, we discover that existing machine vision systems are brittle with respect to occlusion while humans are robust and vastly outperform machines; we also introduce a new benchmark and target for hand-pose estimation algorithms.

Our dataset is large, consisting of 11,840 images of grasps of 148 object instances. Unlike in most other prior datasets, here each image is collected individually and not from a longer video. We eschew shooting videos and collecting frames from them despite the convenience of doing so because the resulting frames are highly correlated and, due to the mechanical constraints of humans the images, tend to display unoccluded hands moving from place to place. The correlation between the grasps and object types was minimized by asking subjects to perform multiple grasps with the same object. We annotated 400 images with 21 keypoints 4 times over in order to compute human inter-coder agreement. The dataset contains images of hands grasping objects followed by that same grasp but without the presence of the object. This allows us to compute the accuracy of human perception for partially occluded hands against the ground truth hand poses. We then provide a human benchmark on this dataset, finding that humans have 5.31 pixel agreement, which allows us to quantify the state of the art in hand-pose construction and the difference between human and machine perception. While on most other datasets hand-pose reconstruction works well, e.g., average Euclidean distance of 4 to 5 pixels on the Dexter datasets [8–10], the dataset we provide has an average error of 20 pixels making it far more challenging.

The contributions of this work are:

1. a new hand-pose dataset that focuses on recovering hand pose when it matters most: during hand-object interactions,
2. demonstrating that current hand-pose recognizers are brittle and fail when faced with occlusion despite scoring extremely well on previous datasets,
3. a novel methodology for gathering hand-pose datasets that allows us to produce, for the first time, a large set of pairs of hand grasps both with the object present and without the object occluding the hand,
4. an approach to gather many varied stable grasps per object,
5. the first baseline for human hand pose recognition accuracy showing that existing approaches vastly underperform humans.

2 Related Work

Several hand-pose datasets already exist. Historically, most have focused on depth images rather than RGB images and few have had any hand-object interactions. Notably, the NYU Hand Pose Dataset [11] contains several long video sequences but is only geared toward use as a depth dataset as the RGB images are rectified rendering them unusable for single-image hand-pose reconstruction. We do not discuss depth-only datasets further and point the reader to a recent survey of such [12]. The MPII Human Pose dataset [13] contains 11,701 test RGB images of humans engaging in common actions. While these are natural videos from YouTube and the frames are selected to be fairly far apart (at least five seconds, to ensure that they are decorrelated), in most frames hands do not grasp any object. We focus in particular on grasps because they naturally result in high occlusion and because they are so critical to understanding how others are manipulating objects. Few images in the MPII Human Pose dataset are annotated with hand poses. The Yale Human hand grasping dataset [14], while very large at 27.7 h of video, contains 9100 RGB images of hands grasping 11 object classes shot from an egocentric point of view. As these are derived from a small number of video sequences where subjects performed repetitive tasks with a small number of objects, the same grasps reoccur many times.

Dexter+Object   EgoDexter   **Ours**

Fig. 1. A comparison of grasps from Dexter+Object, EgoDexter, and our dataset. Note that previous datasets are designed to remove occlusions and have subjects engage in careful grasps to do so. In our dataset, most subjects were naive having no background in computer vision and only a generic knowledge of how the dataset would be used. This leads to much more natural grasps that significantly occlude the hands.

The closest datasets to the one presented here are Dexter [8], Ego-Dexter [9], and Dexter+Object [10]. They are all collected using the same general procedures. Video sequences are shot of humans changing their hand pose, in the latter two cases while interacting with objects. Since these datasets are collected by shooting videos rather than images, both the grasps in adjacent frames and the pixel values of the frames themselves are highly correlated. This effectively reduces their dataset size significantly. More fundamentally, even though they contain hand-object interactions, hands must travel to arrive at objects and manipulate them. This means that many of the frames do not actually contain hand-object interactions. The three Dexter datasets were collected by subjects who were motivated to make their grasps and interactions as plain, simple, and obvious as possible. See Fig. 1 for an example of what we mean here; the grasps in Dexter avoid hand occlusion and are designed to be easy. Most of our subjects were naive, they were paid for their data collection services, essentially all of the data was collected by subjects not connected to this publication, and they were generally only vaguely aware of the purpose of the dataset. This resulted in grasps that are far more natural and, when combined with our methodology to increase the variety of grasps, resulted in a much larger range of hand poses. It is simply a consequence of natural human object grasps that they result in images where the hands are highly occluded. The biases of subjects and those inherent in data collection protocols have been shown to lead to a significant overstating of machine accuracy in other domains such as natural language processing [15] (Table 1).

Table 1. A comparison of statistics of RGB hand-pose datasets. Within a sequence, poses are highly correlated meaning that the datasets are effectively far smaller than it may first appear. This is in part because most previous datasets are collections of video snippets. In our case, dataset size is effectively reduced by a factor of two because the dataset contains the same hand pose both occluded and unoccluded by an object. The dataset presented here is much larger than previous datasets, with many more decorrelated hand poses and with more controls to provide a variety of hand poses

Dataset	# of sequences	# of frames	# of objects
Dexter	7 videos	1,750	N/A
Dexter+Object	6 videos	3,151	1
Ego-Dexter	4 videos	3,194	17
Ours	**5,920**	**11,840**	**148**

Previous investigations have attempted to characterize human hand perception although no concrete results exist showing the agreement and accuracy of human hand-pose recognition. Santello *et al.* provide a recent overview of the neural and biological basis for hand control [16]. Existing datasets have at most one annotation and rarely have any ground truth data. This means measuring the accuracy of human perception on this task, and, by extension, determining how far away machine results are from human-level performance, is not possible.

In robotics, grasp planning has been investigated [17]. This has included large datasets of grasps but they consist generally of images or videos of attempted robotic grasps [18]. In some cases, such datasets have been synthesized automatically, a potentially useful approach for human hand-pose recognition [19]. The stability of a grasp is of key importance to robotics and its prediction plays a role in some datasets [20]. While we do not consider physical stability in this publication, we do intend to, in the future, investigate if perception is affected by notions of stability using this data.

3   A Dataset of Partially Occluded Hands

We collected a dataset of 11,840 images of hands holding objects. We chose 148 object instances, initially 150 objects but two were damaged during imaging thereby changing their appearance and prompting their removal. Human subjects were asked to hold those objects. Each time a subject held an object, it was then taken from them while they remained in the same pose and another image was shot. This provides the same grasp, up to some minor error, both as it would appear naturally occluded by the object being grasped and unoccluded by the object. Since many objects have a default use, humans tend to grasp them in a consistent manner. To avoid this, and to prevent merely learning and evaluating the default grasp thereby giving the appearance of hand-pose recognition without there being any, we asked subjects to then hold the object in a different way, as determined by the subjects. Each trial then consists of a quad of a hand holding an object in two ways, each both with the object and then without. In what follows we describe the rationale, methodology, and contents of the dataset.

The 148 object instances, almost all from different object classes, were chosen to reflect common objects present in homes that might be of interest to both activity recognition in households and to robot grasping. The chosen objects were opaque to ensure that they could properly occlude the hand and large enough to do so; this ruled out some common but far too small objects like most cutlery. Both deforamble and non-deformable objects were included; with 20 out of the 148 objects being deformable. An overview of the objects selected is shown in Fig. 2. The dataset is balanced with respect to the object instances with 80 images for each object. The objects have a diverse set of possible grasps since they serve different purposes; they were chosen to have different topologies, and have different weights putting constraints on the possible stable grasps.

We designed the data collection procedure to increase the set of grasps that were employed by the subjects. First, an image was collected of a subject grasping an object. Next, that object was removed from the grasp of the subject and another image was collected. In this second image the grasp is evident as it is no longer occluded by the object. It proved to be critical that another individual remove the object from the grasp of the subject so that they could maintain their hand in the same pose. Then the subject was asked to grasp that same object but in a different manner. We did not control for this but subjects were given several instructions to help them identify other reasonable grasps such as imagining the object being much heavier, imagining that part of the object is hot, or that it is being given to someone else at some distance and orientation from the subject. Two more images were collected just as in the initial conditions with the subjects holding the object and then having the same grasp but without the object. This produces a quad where the first pair of the quad is likely a more intuitive grasp while the second is likely a more special-purpose grasp.

The dataset consists of 10 quads for each object collected in 10 different locations by approximately two dozen subjects, although the dataset is not balanced with respect to the identity of the subject. However, it is balanced with respect

Fig. 2. The 148 objects imaged as part of this dataset. These are common objects found in households and offices with a wide range of purposes.

to the locations, an equal number of images having been shot in each. Within a location, we intentionally did not specify a position or viewpoint for the camera leading to more varied backgrounds but multiple images were shot from the same viewpoint in a location. Locations are areas such as hallways, rooms, or outdoor patios. Examples from the dataset are shown in Fig. 3.

Images were collected using portable tripods and subjects' cellphone cameras. Subjects were allowed to use both hands when grasping and were not instructed about the space of allowable grasps. Our intention is to collect images of as a varied set of grasps as possible. Additionally, subjects were chosen such that a variety of skin tones is represented, although we did not balance with respect to skin tone. Most existing hand datasets feature almost exclusively light skin tones which both biases learning and the evaluation of hand pose recognizers. We de-identified subjects by using a face detector and coarsely pixelating their faces. Faces almost never overlapped with grasps.

Since our dataset features the hand poses unobstructed by the object and due to the fairly good performance of existing hand-pose recognizers in such favorable conditions, approximate ground truth exists for every image; we merely copy over the annotation from the unoccluded hand to the occluded hand. This allows us to validate the accuracy of the hand-pose recognizers on all images in the dataset even without any human annotation. Yet this would not allow us to understand how well humans perform on this task of reconstructing interacting and partially-occluded hands. To do so subjects annotated 400 images, 200 pairs of unoccluded and occluded images, with anatomical 21-keypoints—4 for each finger and one at the wrist. Multiple annotators provided judgments for each image, with four annotations per image. We use this to compute human agreement on partially-occluded hand annotations. With our unique design that results in pairs of images of the same hand occluded and unoccluded images, we can test the robustness of human perception of partially-occluded hands. These two experiments help characterize human performance on hand-pose recognition and have not been performed before. Finally, we can also use human annotations to verify the performance of machines where we show that on unoccluded hands, performance is quite good and then quickly decreases with any occlusion.

The methodology described above results in a novel dataset with both the occluded and unoccluded hands in the same poses, which is balanced with respect to the object instances, while encouraging a varied set of grasps.

4 Experiments

After discussing the statistics of the dataset, in Sect. 4.1, we evaluate the performance of state-of-the-art computer vision systems on our dataset, in Sect. 4.2, provide the first account for human hand-pose recognition performance, in Sect. 4.3, and then compare machines against humans putting the state of computer vision into context, in Sect. 4.4. Two recently-published single-image hand-pose recognition systems are evaluated: that of Zimmermann and Brox [6], which we refer to as ZB, and OpenPose [7]. We extensively surveyed the past three years of major computer vision conferences and these were the only two such systems with publicly available runnable source code and pretrained models. Note that we do not fine-tune on this dataset, much as many other systems do not fine

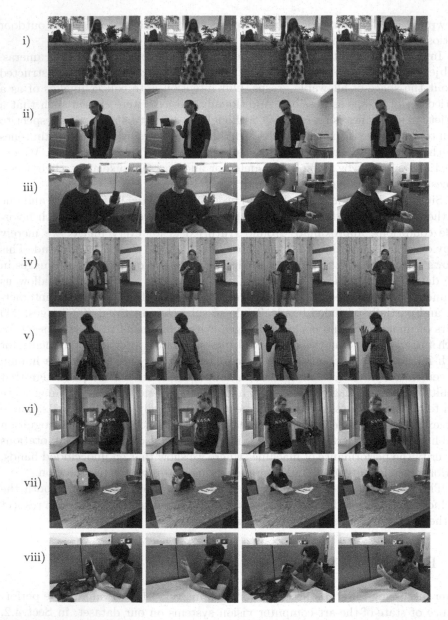

Fig. 3. Eight examples from the dataset. Each row is a quad, a series of four images taken in quick succession. In the first two images, the leftmost two, the subject uses their default grasp of the object. In the next two, the rightmost two, subjects are asked to choose another unspecified grasp. Each pair of images has one image in which the hand is holding the object followed by another in which the hand is in the same pose but without the object.

tune on the Dexter datasets, and to discourage fine-tuning on this data we do not provide a training and test split.

4.1   Dataset Statistics

The dataset consists of 11,840 images of the 148 object instances shown in Fig. 2 with 80 images per instance half of which are of grasps holding an object and the other half are of those same grasps without holding the object. The dataset is balanced with respect to the object identity. Deformable objects account for 15% of the data. Hands were annotated with 21 keypoints over 400 images which were annotated 4 times over to measure human inter-coder agreement. The likelihood of any one keypoint being under self-occlusion, i.e., being occluded in the nominally unoccluded view, is 21.9% and is fairly uniform, shown in Fig. 4(a), as is the likelihood of a keypoint being occluded by the object which is 42.3%, shown in Fig. 4(b). We did not control for the distribution over occlusions per keypoint, as there is no practical way to do so; we merely report the statistics of the grasps that humans employ. While high-resolution images will be provided, on average 4065×2972, for consistency all numbers reported here use the same image dimensions as the Dexter datasets [8–10], namely 640×480. Note that both systems were run at their full native resolution with the full image; we merely report distances rescaled to this standard resolution. The average area of a hand in the dataset was approximately 2400 pixels, roughly 48×48, as computed by a bounding box encompassing the extremities of the hand, while the average size of an object is approximately 2200 pixels, roughly 47×47, about the same size as the hand.

4.2   Machine Performance

First we evaluate how well machines perform against their own judgments. Given that we have both an occluded and unoccluded image, we can directly ask, assuming that the reconstructed pose in the unoccluded images are correct: how much does occlusion degrade machine performance? We find that occlusion is a major contributor to poor machine performance, i.e., it changes how machines interpret hands, leading to a 20 and 75 average pixel Euclidean distance for OpenPose and ZB respectively. The PCK, the probability that a keypoint is within a given threshold distance in the occluded image relative to the unoccluded one, is shown in Fig. 5(a).

The overall distribution of distances for each keypoint is shown in Fig. 5(b). Error on visible keypoints is around 15 pixels while many of the occluded keypoints are never identified, representing the peak at 48 pixels. Since the average hand is about 48×48 pixels we fix the maximum penalty for not finding a hand to this dimension—not scoring these would lead to perfect performance while penalizing them the entire length of the image is arbitrary. It is telling that in any one image roughly half of the keypoints are occluded. At first it may seem like ZB has lower error from Fig. 5(b), but note that the tail is extremely long. ZB makes make confident but wrong predictions for hands which are spurious.

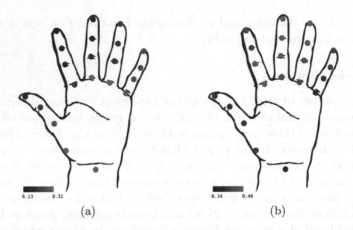

Fig. 4. The 21 annotated keypoints. (a) The likelihood that a keypoint is under self-occlusion by the hand. (b) The likelihood that a keypoint is occluded by an object. The likelihood that any one keypoint is occluded is fairly uniform regardless of the source of the occlusion. For any one grasp, 21.9% of the keypoints are occluded by the hand and 42.3% are occluded by the object. Note that the latter usually also includes the points from the former meaning the two sources of occlusion are not mutually-exclusive.

We did not cap the maximum error of either OpenPose or ZB, but had we capped both, ZB would have a mean error closer to 40.

To investigate the source of errors further, in Fig. 5(c) we show pixel-wise error as a function of the occlusion of each keypoint in each image. We restricted the plot to within 50 pixels of the correct value after which the data is fairly uniform. Again the line at 48 represents the pixels which could not be detected. There are far more of these failed detections at higher occlusion levels but the plot hides this information. OpenPose seems significantly more resilient to occlusion although the trend where additional occlusion worsens results is clear. Whether a keypoint was occluded was determined by humans, but otherwise we do not use any human annotations in this experiment. Overall the robustness of machines to occlusion is quite poor; we will return to this in Sect. 4.4 when machines are compared to humans.

4.3 Human Performance

We provide the first quantitative measurements of humans on hand-pose reconstruction. On 400 images, 200 pairs of occluded and unoccluded images, we collected 4 annotations. One was collected in-house while three were collected on Mechanical Turk. Overall humans agree strongly with each other having a mean distance of 5.3 pixels and standard deviation of 1.7. In Fig. 6, we show the inter-annotator agreement by keypoint separating (a) unoccluded form (b) occluded keypoints. Agreement is far higher on unoccluded keypoints with a mean error of just 2.7 pixels (variance 1.0) while it is significantly lower on

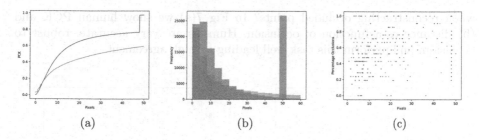

(a)   (b)   (c)

Fig. 5. Performance for OpenPose, shown in blue, and ZB, shown in red. (a) The distance between keypoints in the occluded hand and those in the same hand pose unoccluded by any object. (b) The distribution of the errors by distance for each keypoint. (c) The error as a function of the occlusion of the entire hand up to 50 pixels. (Color figure online)

occluded keypoints with a mean of 7.8 (variance 2.5). Performance depends on the keypoint in part because some keypoints are more likely to be occluded than others and in part because some keypoints, particularly the wrist, are less well defined anatomically. This indicates that humans might be much more robust to occlusion since they agree with each other, although at the same time all humans might share the same systematic biases.

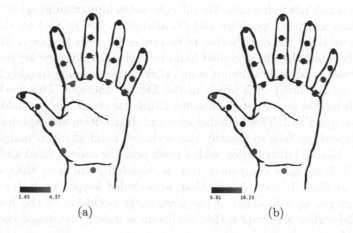

(a)   (b)

Fig. 6. The inter-annotator agreement by hand keypoint showing that some keypoints have higher agreement than others. Overall agreement is far higher than in the machine case. (a) shows only the unoccluded keypoints while (b) shows only the occluded keypoints. The color encodes the mean pixel error for that keypoint across four annotators. (Color figure online)

To investigate human performance, rather than just agreement, we use the occluded and unoccluded images of the same hand pose and compare human performance between the two. In essence this asks: how accurate are humans when reconstructing occluded points? In Fig. 7(a) we show human PCK and (b) distance as a function of occlusion. Humans are very accurate, robust to occlusion, and perform this task well leading to high agreement.

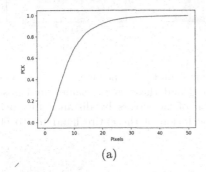
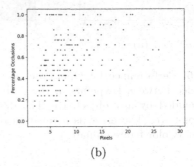

(a)   (b)

Fig. 7. The performance of humans when reconstructing partially-occluded hands showing (a) PCK and the (b) error as a function of occlusion.

4.4   Machine vs. Human Performance

Finally, having established how well humans perform at hand-pose recognition, we compare machines to humans. We take the mean human annotation to be the gold standard and test OpenPose and ZB against it. In Fig. 8(a) we show PCK and in (b) we show the distribution of distances for each keypoint. We report these numbers only for the occluded hand in each pair. Average keypoint error on this dataset is far higher than it is on other datasets, being roughly 20 pixels while it is on the order of 5 pixels in the Dexter datasets. This performance difference is further accentuated since our hands are smaller in the field of view, as can be seen in Fig. 1. This high distance and distribution are explained by the fact that OpenPose fails to identify the occluded hand at all in many images, leading to a bimodal distribution with a peak near the correct hand and another extremely high variance component that is essentially uniform. Since occluded keypoints are likely harder to infer than unoccluded keypoints, in (c) we show the performance as a function of the percentage occlusion of the hand. This confirms the earlier observation that occlusion is indeed the major contributor to poor performance.

5   Discussion

We describe a challenging new dataset for single-image hand pose estimation, made difficult by the fact that the natural grasps that humans use tend to occlude the hand, and make that data available. On other datasets per-keypoint error is around 4 to 5 pixels while on this dataset it is roughly 20 pixels with

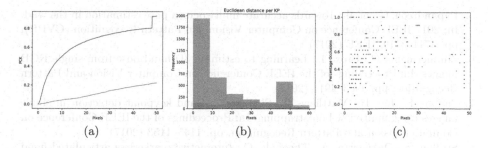

Fig. 8. Performance of OpenPose, shown in blue, and ZB, shown in red against human annotations. (a) PCK for the partially-occluded hands. (b) The distribution of the errors by distance. (c) The pixel error plotted against the percentage occlusion of the hand. (Color figure online)

the mean hand dimensions being 48 × 48 pixels when the images are rescaled to 640 × 480. The per-keypoint error is roughly half the size of a hand. Hand-pose recognizers do not seem to be robust to partial occlusions while in the real world human hands tend to be occluded when hand-object interactions occur. Resilience to partial occlusions is generally not exercised by current datasets, in hand pose recognition or other areas of computer vision. More datasets for object recognition and other tasks where occlusion plays a large role may drive research toward new approaches.

Humans were found to be highly robust to partial occlusions with performance only being weakly related with respect to the percentage of the keypoints which are occluded. We are following up with experiments to understand how much viewing time is required for this robustness to manifest in humans—a long processing time may indicate the necessity for more than feed-forward networks. We hope this dataset will lead to new approaches to robust hand-pose recognition given the importance of this task for action recognition and human-robot interactions.

References

1. Presti, L.L., La Cascia, M.: 3D skeleton-based human action classification: a survey. Pattern Recogn. **53**, 130–147 (2016)
2. Perez-Sala, X., Escalera, S., Angulo, C., Gonzalez, J.: A survey on model based approaches for 2D and 3D visual human pose recovery. Sensors **14**, 4189–4210 (2014)
3. Wei, S.E., Ramakrishna, V., Kanade, T., Sheikh, Y.: Convolutional pose machines. In: Proceedings of the IEEE Conference on Computer Vision and Pattern Recognition, pp. 4724–4732 (2016)
4. Cao, Z., Simon, T., Wei, S.E., Sheikh, Y.: Realtime multi-person 2D pose estimation using part affinity fields. In: Proceedings of the IEEE Conference on Computer Vision and Pattern Recognition, pp. 7291–7299 (2017)

5. Papandreou, G., et al.: Towards accurate multi-person pose estimation in the wild. In: 2017 IEEE Conference on Computer Vision and Pattern Recognition (CVPR), pp. 3711–3719. IEEE (2017)
6. Zimmermann, C., Brox, T.: Learning to estimate 3D hand pose from single RGB images. In: Proceedings of the IEEE Conference on Computer Vision and Pattern Recognition, pp. 4903–4911 (2017)
7. Simon, T., Joo, H., Matthews, I., Sheikh, Y.: Hand keypoint detection in single images using multiview bootstrapping. In: Proceedings of the IEEE Conference on Computer Vision and Pattern Recognition, pp. 1145–1153 (2017)
8. Sridhar, S., Oulasvirta, A., Theobalt, C.: Interactive markerless articulated hand motion tracking using RGB and depth data. In: Proceedings of the IEEE International Conference on Computer Vision, pp. 2456–2463 (2013)
9. Mueller, F., Mehta, D., Sotnychenko, O., Sridhar, S., Casas, D., Theobalt, C.: Real-time hand tracking under occlusion from an egocentric RGB-D sensor. In: Proceedings of International Conference on Computer Vision (ICCV) (2017)
10. Sridhar, S., Mueller, F., Zollhöfer, M., Casas, D., Oulasvirta, A., Theobalt, C.: Real-time joint tracking of a hand manipulating an object from RGB-D input. In: Leibe, B., Matas, J., Sebe, N., Welling, M. (eds.) ECCV 2016. LNCS, vol. 9906, pp. 294–310. Springer, Cham (2016). https://doi.org/10.1007/978-3-319-46475-6_19
11. Tompson, J., Stein, M., Lecun, Y., Perlin, K.: Real-time continuous pose recovery of human hands using convolutional networks. ACM Trans. Graph. **33**, 169 (2014)
12. Huang, Y., Bianchi, M., Liarokapis, M., Sun, Y.: Recent data sets on object manipulation: a survey. Big Data **4**, 197–216 (2016)
13. Andriluka, M., Pishchulin, L., Gehler, P., Schiele, B.: 2D human pose estimation: new benchmark and state of the art analysis. In: Proceedings of the IEEE Conference on computer Vision and Pattern Recognition, pp. 3686–3693 (2014)
14. Bullock, I.M., Feix, T., Dollar, A.M.: The yale human grasping dataset: grasp, object, and task data in household and machine shop environments. Int. J. Robot. Res. **34**, 251–255 (2015)
15. Berzak, Y., Huang, Y., Barbu, A., Korhonen, A., Katz, B.: Anchoring and agreement in syntactic annotations. In: Proceedings of the 2016 Conference on Empirical Methods in Natural Language Processing, pp. 2215–2224 (2016)
16. Santello, M., et al.: Hand synergies: integration of robotics and neuroscience for understanding the control of biological and artificial hands. Phys. Life Rev. **17**, 1–23 (2016)
17. Bohg, J., Morales, A., Asfour, T., Kragic, D.: Data-driven grasp synthesis–a survey. IEEE Trans. Robot. **30**, 289–309 (2014)
18. Levine, S., Pastor, P., Krizhevsky, A., Ibarz, J., Quillen, D.: Learning hand-eye coordination for robotic grasping with deep learning and large-scale data collection. Int. J. Robot. Res. **37**, 421–436 (2018)
19. Goldfeder, C., Ciocarlie, M., Dang, H., Allen, P.K.: The Columbia grasp database. In: 2009 IEEE International Conference on Robotics and Automation, ICRA 2009, pp. 1710–1716. IEEE (2009)
20. Chebotar, Y., et al.: BIGS: biotac grasp stability dataset. In: ICRA 2016 Workshop on Grasping and Manipulation Datasets (2016)

Cross Pixel Optical-Flow Similarity
for Self-supervised Learning

Aravindh Mahendran$^{(\boxtimes)}$ (iD), James Thewlis (iD), and Andrea Vedaldi

Visual Geometry Group, University of Oxford, Oxford, UK
{aravindh,jdt,vedaldi}@robots.ox.ac.uk

Abstract. We propose a novel method for learning convolutional neural image representations without manual supervision. We use motion cues in the form of optical-flow, to supervise representations of static images. The obvious approach of training a network to predict flow from a single image can be needlessly difficult due to intrinsic ambiguities in this prediction task. We instead propose a much simpler learning goal: embed pixels such that the similarity between their embeddings matches that between their optical-flow vectors. At test time, the learned deep network can be used without access to video or flow information and transferred to tasks such as image classification, detection, and segmentation. Our method, which significantly simplifies previous attempts at using motion for self-supervision, achieves state-of-the-art results in self-supervision using motion cues, and is overall state of the art in self-supervised pre-training for semantic image segmentation, as demonstrated on standard benchmarks.

Keywords: Self-supervised learning · Motion · Convolutional neural network

1 Introduction

Self-supervised learning has emerged as a promising approach to address one of the major shortcomings of deep learning, namely the need for large supervised training datasets. All self-supervised learning methods are based on the same basic premise, which is to identify problems that can be used to train deep networks without the expense of collecting data annotations. In this spirit, an amazing diversity of supervisory signals have been proposed, from image generation to colorization, in-painting, jigsaw puzzle solving, orientation estimation, counting, artifact spotting, and many more (see Sect. 2). Furthermore, the recent work of [9] shows that combining several such cues further helps performance.

In this paper, we consider the case of *self-supervision using motion cues* to learn a convolutional neural network (CNN) for static images. Here, a deep network is trained to predict, from a single video frame, how the image *could change*

Electronic supplementary material The online version of this chapter (https://doi.org/10.1007/978-3-030-20873-8_7) contains supplementary material, which is available to authorized users.

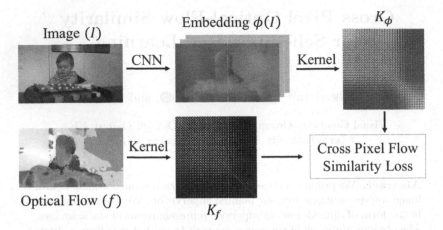

Fig. 1. We propose a novel method to exploit motion information represented as optical-flow, to supervise the learning of deep CNNs. We learn a network that predicts per-pixel embeddings $\phi(I)$ such that the kernel computed over these embeddings (K_ϕ) is similar to that over corresponding optical-flow vectors (K_f). This allows the network to learn from motion cues while avoiding the inherent ambiguity of motion prediction from a single frame. (Color figure online)

over time. Since predicted changes can be verified automatically by looking at the actual video stream, this approach can be used for self-supervision. Furthermore, predicting motion may induce a deep network to learn about objects in images. The reason is that objects are a major cause of motion regularity and hence predictability: pixels that belong to the same object are much more likely to "move together" than pixels that do not.

Besides giving cues about objects, motion has another appealing characteristic compared to other signals for self-supervision. Many other methods are, in fact, based on destroying information in images (e.g. by removing color, scrambling parts) and then tasking a network with undoing such changes. This has the disadvantage of learning the representation on distorted images (e.g. gray scale). On the other hand, extracting a single frame from a video can be thought of as removing information only along the temporal dimension and allows one to learn the network on undistorted images.

There is however a key challenge in using motion for self-supervision: ambiguity. Even if the deep network can correctly identify all objects in an image, this is still not enough to predict the specific direction and intensity of the objects' motion in the video, given just a single frame. This ambiguity makes the direct prediction of the appearance of future frames particularly challenging [54,59], and overall an overkill if the goal is to learn a general-purpose image representation for image analysis. Instead, the previous most effective method for self-supervision using motion cues [42] is based on first extracting motion tubes from videos (using off-the-shelf optical-flow and motion tube segmentation algorithms) and then training the deep network to predict the resulting per-frame segments rather than motion directly. Thus they map a complex self-supervision task into one of classic foreground-background segmentation.

While the approach of [42] sidesteps the difficult problem of motion prediction ambiguity, it comes at the cost of pre-processing videos using a complex handcrafted motion segmentation pipeline, which includes many heuristics and tunable parameters. In this paper, we instead propose a new method that can ingest cues from optical-flow *directly*, without the need for any complex data pre-processing.

Our method, presented in Sect. 3 and illustrated in Fig. 1, is based on a new cross pixel flow similarity loss layer. As noted above, the key challenge is that specific details about the motion, such as its direction and intensity, are usually difficult if not impossible to predict from a single frame. We address this difficulty in two ways. First, we learn to embed pixels into vectors that cluster together when the model believes that the corresponding pixels *are likely to move together*. This is obtained by encouraging the inner product of the learned pixel embeddings to correlate with the similarity between their corresponding optical-flow vectors. This does not require the model to explicitly estimate specific motion directions or velocities. However, this is still not sufficient to address the ambiguity completely; in fact, while different objects may be *able* to move independently, they *may not do so* all the time. For example, often objects stand still, so their velocities are all zero grouping them together in optical-flow. We attempt to address this second challenge by using a contrastive loss.

In Sect. 4 we extensively validate our model against other self-supervised learning approaches. First, we show that our approach works as well or better than [42], establishing a new state-of-the-art method for self-supervision using motion cues. Second, to put this into context, we also compare the results to all recent approaches for self-supervision that use cues other than motion. In this case, we show that our approach has state-of-the-art performance for semantic image segmentation, at the time of submission.

The overall conclusion (Sect. 5) is that our method significantly simplifies leveraging motion cues for self-supervision and does better than existing alternatives for this modality; it is also competitive with self-supervision methods that use other cues, making motion a sensible choice for self-supervision by itself or in combination with other cues [9].

2   Related Work

Self-supervised learning, of which our method is an instance, has become very popular in the community. We discuss here the methods for training generic features for image understanding as opposed to methods with specific goals such as learning object keypoints. We group them according to the supervision cues they use.

Video/Motion Based: LSTM RNNs can be trained to predict future frames in a video [51]. This requires the network to understand image dynamics and extrapolate it into the future. However, since several frames are observed simultaneously, these methods may learn something akin to a tracker, with limited abstraction. On the other hand, we learn to predict properties of optical-flow from a **single input image**, thus learning a static image representation rather than a dynamic one. Closely related to our work is the use of *video segmentation* by [42]. They use an off-the-shelf video segmentation method [15] to construct a foreground-background segmentation dataset in an unsupervised manner. A CNN trained on this proxy task transfers well when fine-tuned for object recognition and detection. We differ from them in that we do not require a sophisticated pre-existing pipeline to extract video segments, but use optical-flow directly. Also closely related to us is the work of [2]. They train a Siamese style convolutional neural network to predict the transformation between two images. The individual base networks in their Siamese architecture share weights and can be used as feature extractors for single images at test time. This late fusion strategy forces the learning of abstractions, but our **no-fusion approach** pushes the model even further to learn better features. The polar opposite of these is to do early fusion by concatenating two frames as in FlowNet [11]. This was used as a pretraining strategy by [16] to learn representations for **pairs of frames**. This is different from our objective as we aim to learn a **static image representation**. This difference becomes clearer when looking at the evaluation. While we evaluate on image classification, detection, and segmentation; [16] evaluate on dynamic scene and action recognition.

Temporal context is a powerful signal. [32,35,57] learn to predict the correct ordering of frames. [24] exploit both temporal and spatial co-occurrence statistics to learn visual groups. [25] extend slow feature analysis using higher order temporal coherence. [55] track patches in a video to supervise their embedding via a triplet loss while [17] do the same but for spatio-temporally matched region proposals. Temporal context is applied in the imitation learning setting by Time Contrastive Networks [49].

Videos contain more than just temporal information. Some methods exploit audio channels by predicting audio from video frames [40,48]. [3] train a two stream architecture to classify whether an image and sound clip go together or not. Temporal information is coupled with ego-motion in [26]. [56] use videos along with spatial context pretraining [8] to construct an image graph. Transitivity in the graph is exploited to learn representations with suitable invariances.

Colorization: [31,60] predict colour information given greyscale input and show competitive pre-training performance. [61] generalize to arbitrary pairs of modalities.

Spatial Context: [41] solve the in-painting problem, where a network is tasked with filling-in partially deleted parts of an image. [8] predict the relative position of two patches extracted from an image. In a similar spirit, [37,38] solve a jigsaw puzzle problem. [38] also cluster features from a pre-trained network to generate pseudo labels, which allows for knowledge distillation from larger networks into smaller ones. The latest iteration on context prediction [36] obtains state-of-the-art on some benchmarks.

Adversarial/Generative: BiGAN based pretrained models [10] show competitive performance on various recognition benchmarks. [27] adversarially learn to generate and spot defects. [45] obtain self-supervision from synthetic data and adapt their model to the domain of real images by training against a discriminator. [5] predict noise-as-targets via an assignment matrix which is optimized on-line. Their approach is domain agnostic. More in general, generative unsupervised layer-wise pretraining was extensively used in deep learning before AlexNet [30]. An extensive review of these and more recent unsupervised generative models is beyond the scope of this paper.

Transformations: [12] create surrogate classes by applying a set of transformations to each image and learn to become invariant to them. [19] do the opposite and try to estimate the transformation (just one of four rotations in their case) given the transformed image. The crop-concatenate transformation is implicit in the learning by counting method of [39].

Others: A combination of self-supervision approaches was explored by [9]. They report results only with ResNet models making it hard to compare with concurrent work, but closely matching ImageNet-pretrained networks in performance on the PASCAL VOC detection task. A widely-applicable trick that helps in transfer learning is the re-balancing method of [29]. Lastly, our optical-flow classification baseline is based on the work of [4]. They learn a sparse hypercolumn model to predict surface normals from a single image and use this as a pretraining strategy. Our baseline flow classification model is the same but with AlexNet for discretized optical-flow.

3   Method

In this section, we describe our novel method, illustrated in Fig. 1, for self-training deep neural networks via direct ingestion of optical-flow. Once learned, the resulting image representation could be used for classification, detection, segmentation and other tasks with minimal supervision.

Our goal is to learn the parameters of a neural network that maps a single image or frame to a field of pixel embeddings, one for each pixel. Notation - Let $\Omega \subset \mathbb{R}^2$ be the set of pixels; $I : \Omega \to \mathbb{R}^3$ is an image; Our CNN is the per-pixel mapping $\phi(I, p | \Theta) \in \mathbb{R}^D$ producing D dimensional embeddings. In order to learn this CNN, we require the **similarity** between **pairs** of embedding vectors to align with the similarity between the corresponding flow vectors. This is sufficient to capture the idea that things that move together should be grouped together, popularly known as the **Gestalt principle of common fate** [53].

Formally, given D-dimensional CNN embedding vectors $\phi(I, p | \Theta), \phi(I, q | \Theta) \in \mathbb{R}^D$ for pixels $p, q \in \Omega$ and their corresponding flow vectors $f_p, f_q \in \mathbb{R}^2$, we match the kernel matrices

$$\forall p, q \in \Omega : \quad K_\phi \Big(\phi(I, p | \Theta), \phi(I, q | \Theta) \Big) \approx K_f(f_p, f_q) \tag{1}$$

where $K_\phi : \mathbb{R}^D \times \mathbb{R}^D \to \mathbb{R}$, $K_f : \mathbb{R}^2 \times \mathbb{R}^2 \to \mathbb{R}$ are kernels that measure the similarity of the CNN embeddings and flow vectors, respectively.

In this formulation, in addition to the choice of CNN architecture ϕ, the key design decisions are the choice of kernels K_ϕ, K_f and how to translate constraint Eq. 1 into a loss function. The rest of the section discusses these choices.

3.1   Kernels

In order to compare CNN embedding vectors and flow vectors, we choose the (scaled) cosine similarity kernel and the Gaussian/RBF kernel respectively. Using the shorthand notation $\phi_p = \phi(I, p|\Theta)$ for readability, these are:

$$K_\phi(\phi_p, \phi_q) := \frac{1}{4} \frac{\phi_p^T \phi_q}{\|\phi_p\|_2 \|\phi_q\|_2}, \qquad K_f(f_p, f_q) := \exp\left(-\frac{\|f_p - f_q\|_2^2}{2\sigma^2}\right). \quad (2)$$

Note that these kernels, when restricted to the set of pixels Ω, are matrices of size $|\Omega| \times |\Omega|$. Each row or column of this matrix can be thought of as a heatmap capturing the similarity of a given pixel with respect to all other pixels and thus can be visualized as an image. We present such visualizations for both of our kernels in Fig. 2.

We use the Gaussian kernel for the flow vectors as this is consistent with the Euclidean interpretation of optical-flow as a displacement. Reducing kernel bandwidth (σ) would result in a localized kernel that pushes our embeddings to distinguish between different movable objects. In some experiments, the value of σ is learned along with the weights of the CNN in the optimization. This localized kernel, with learned $\sigma^2 = 0.0036$, is shown in the second row of Fig. 2.

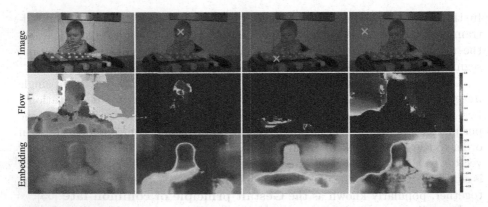

Fig. 2. Visualization of flow and embedding kernels, in the second and third rows respectively. For three pixels p, we plot the row $K_*(p, \cdot)$ reshaped into an image, showing which pixels go together from the kernel's perspective. Note the localized nature of the flow kernel which is obtain by setting a low bandwidth for the RBF kernel. $\sigma^2 = 0.0036$ in this example. In the first column, optical-flow and embeddings (after a random $16D \to 3D$ projection) are visualized as color images. (Color figure online)

We use the cosine kernel for the learned embedding as the CNN effectively computes a *kernel feature map*, so that in principle it can approximate any kernel via the inner product. However, note that the expression normalizes vectors in L^2 norm, so that this inner product is the cosine of the angle between embedding vectors.

3.2   Cross Pixel Optical-Flow Similarity Loss Function

The constraint in Eq. (1) requires kernels K_ϕ and K_f to be similar. We experiment with three loss functions for this task - kernel target alignment, cross-entropy, and cross-entropy reversed.

Kernel Target Alignment (KTA): KTA [7] is a conventional metric to measure the similarity between kernels. KTA for two kernel matrices K, K', is given by

$$\mathcal{L}_{KTA}(K, K') = \sum_{pq} K_{pq} K'_{pq} \Big/ \sqrt{\sum_{pq} K^2_{pq} \sum_{pq} K'_{pq}{}^2} \qquad (3)$$

Cross-Entropy (CE): Our second loss function treats pixels as classes and kernel values as logits of a distribution over pixels. The cross entropy of these two distributions measures the distance between them. We compute this loss in two steps. First, we re-normalize each column $K_*(\cdot, q)$ of each kernel matrix into a probability distribution $S_*(\cdot, q)$. $S_f(\cdot, q)$ describes which image pixels p are likely to belong to the same segment as pixel q, according to optical-flow. $S_\phi(\cdot, q)$ describes the same but from the CNN embedding's perspective. These distributions, arising from CNN and optical-flow kernels, are compared by using cross entropy, summed over columns:

$$\mathcal{L}_{CE}(\Theta) = -\sum_q \sum_p S_f(p, q) \log S_\phi(p, q). \qquad (4)$$

Normalization uses the softmax operator. We reduce the contribution of diagonal terms in the kernel matrix before this normalization because each pixel is trivially similar to itself and would skew the softmax. Formally:

$$S_*(p, q) = \begin{cases} 1 / \left(\sum_{q' \neq p} \exp(K_*(p, q')) + 1 \right), & \text{if } p = q, \\ \exp(K_*(p, q)) / \left(\sum_{q' \neq p} \exp(K_*(p, q')) + 1 \right), & \text{if } p \neq q. \end{cases} \qquad (5)$$

Cross-Entropy Reversed (CE-rev): Note that the particular ordering of distributions inside the cross entropy loss of Eq. 4 treats the distribution induced by the optical-flow kernel (S_f) as ground truth. The embedding is tasked with inducing a kernel such that its corresponding distribution S_ϕ matches S_f. As an ablation study we also experiment with the order of distributions reversed. In other words we use,

$$\mathcal{L}_{CE-rev}(\Theta) = -\sum_q \sum_p S_\phi(p, q) \log S_f(p, q). \qquad (6)$$

The intuition here is as follows: For a given pixel p, the distribution $S_\phi(\cdot, q)$ must be a delta distribution around $q' = \text{argmax}\, S_f(\cdot, q)$. This is the natural effect of a flipped cross entropy loss. This delta distribution can be best approximated by aligning the two embeddings $\phi_p \cong \phi_{q'}$ and making all others anti-correlated $\phi_p \cong -\phi_q\, \forall\, q \neq q'$. Note however that this degenerate solution forces all $\phi_q, \phi_{q''}$ such that $q, q'' \neq q'$ to align as well. This coincidental alignment would, in general, significantly increase the loss function. Thus the embedding is forced to induce a non degenerate distribution S_ϕ. We consider it interesting to experiment with this loss.

Thus we have three cross pixel flow similarity losses - Kernel Target Alignment (CPFS-KTA), Cross Entropy (CPFS-CE) and Cross Entropy reversed (CPFS-CE-rev).

3.3   CNN Embedding Function

Lastly, we discuss the architecture of the CNN function ϕ itself. It maps the image into a per-pixel embedding. Recall that $\forall\, p \in \Omega$, $\phi(I, p|\Theta) \in \mathbb{R}^D$. We design the embedding CNN as a hypercolumn head [22] over a conventional CNN backbone such as AlexNet. The hypercolumn concatenates features from multiple depths so that our embedding can exploit high resolution details normally lost due to max-pooling layers. For training, we use the sparsification trick of [31] and restrict prediction and loss computation to a few randomly sampled pixels in every iteration. This reduces memory consumption and improves training convergence as pixels in the same image are highly correlated and redundant; via sampling we can reduce this correlation and train more efficiently [4].

In more detail, the backbone is a CNN with activations at several layers: $\{\phi_{c_1}(I|\Theta), \cdots, \phi_{c_n}(I|\Theta)\} \in \mathbb{R}^{H_1 \times W_1 \times D_1} \times \cdots \times \mathbb{R}^{H_n \times W_n \times D_n}$. We follow [31] and interpolate values for a given pixel location and concatenate them to form a hypercolumn $\phi_H(I, p|\Theta) \in \mathbb{R}^{D_1 + \cdots + D_n}$. The hypercolumn is then projected non-linearly to the desired embedding $\phi(I, p|\Theta) \in \mathbb{R}^D$ using a multi-layer perceptron (MLP). Details of the model architecture are discussed in Sect. 4.1.

4   Experiments

We extensively assess our approach by demonstrating its effectiveness in learning features that we show as useful for several tasks. In order to make our results comparable to most of the related papers in the literature, we consider an AlexNet [30] backbone and four tasks: classification in ImageNet [47] and classification, detection, and segmentation in PASCAL VOC [13,14].

4.1   Backbone Details

We adapt the AlexNet version used by Pathak et al. [42]. The modifications are minor (mostly related to padding), to make it suitable to attach a hypercolumn head. Sparse hypercolumns are built from the conv1, pool1, conv3, pool5 and fc7 AlexNet activations. Embeddings are generated using a multi-layer percep-tron (MLP) with a single hidden layer and are L2-normalized. The embeddings are $D = 16$ dimensional (this number could be improved via cross validation, although this is expensive). The exact model specification, in the caffe text pro-tocol buffer format (.prototxt), is included in the supplementary material.

4.2   Dataset

We train the above AlexNet model, using various CPFS losses, on a dataset of RGB-optical-flow image pairs. Inspired by the work of Pathak *et al.* [42], we built a dataset from $\sim$204k videos in the YFCC100m dataset [52]. The latter consists of Flickr videos made publicly-available under the creative commons license. We extract 8 random frames from each video and compute optical-flow between those at times t and $t+5$ using the same (handcrafted) optical-flow method of [33,42]. Overall, we obtain 1.6M image-flow pairs.[1] Example training sample crops along with optical-flow fields are shown in Fig. 3. The noisy nature of both the images and optical-flow in such large-scale non-curated video collections makes it all the more challenging for self-supervision.

Optical-flow vectors (f_x, f_y) are normalized logarithmically to lie between $[-1, 1]$ during training, so that occasional large flows do not dominate learning. More precisely, the normalization is given by:

$$f' = \begin{bmatrix} \text{sign}(f_x) \min\left(1, \frac{\log(|f_x|+1)}{\log(M+1)}\right) \\ \text{sign}(f_y) \min\left(1, \frac{\log(|f_y|+1)}{\log(M+1)}\right) \end{bmatrix} \tag{7}$$

where M is a loose upper bound on the flow-magnitude set to 56.0 in our exper-iments.

Fig. 3. Image and optical-flow training pairs post scale-crop-flip data augmentation. The noisy nature of both images and optical-flows illustrate the challenges in using motion as a self-supervision signal. Optical-flow is visualized as a colour image using the toolbox of [6]. (Color figure online)

---

[1] Optical-flow is stored in fixed point 16bit PNG files similar to KITTI [18] for com-pression.

Despite the large size of this data and aggressive data augmentation during training, AlexNet overfits on our self-supervision task. We use early stopping to reduce over-fitting by monitoring the loss on a validation set. The validation set consists of 5000 image-flow pairs computed from the YouTube objects dataset [43]. Epic-Flow [46], with initial matches from Deep-Matching [58], was used to compute optical-flow for these frames.

4.3   Learning Details

We use the Adam optimizer [28] with $\beta_1 = 0.9, \beta_2 = 0.999, \epsilon = 10^{-8}$ and initial learning rate 10^{-4}. No weight decay is used because it resulted in our model reaching a worse local minima before over-fitting started. Pixels are sampled uniformly at random for the sparse hypercolumns. Sampling more pixels gives more information per image but also consumes more memory and is computationally expensive. We use 512 pixels per image to balance this trade-off. This allows for a large batch size of 96 frames. Scale, horizontal flip and crop augmentation with crop size 224×224 are applied during training. Color augmentation: shifting the hue by up to 0.1, random contrast between 0.2–1.8, random brightness by up to 0.12 (based on 0–1 normalised colours); is also applied. Parameter-free batch-normalization [23] is used throughout the network; the moving average mean and variance are absorbed into convolution kernels after self-supervised training, so that, for evaluation, AlexNet does not contain batch normalization layers. The implementation using TensorFlow [1] will be publicly available on GitHub.

Fig. 4. Per-pixel embeddings are visualized by randomly projecting them to RGB colors. From top to bottom: Validation images, RGB-mapped embeddings, optical-flow. (Color figure online)

Fig. 5. Neuron maximization results for conv5 features [34]. Left: Neurons in a randomly initialized AlexNet. Right: Neurons in AlexNet trained using our approach: significantly more structure emerges.

4.4 Qualitative Results

In this section we visualize the AlexNet model pre-trained using the CPFS-CE loss function (Eq. (4)).

Embedding Visualizations: While our learned pixel embeddings are not meant to be used directly (instead their purpose is to pre-train a neural network parametrization that can be transferred to other tasks), nevertheless it is informative to visualize them. Since embeddings are 16D, we first project them to 3D vectors via random projections and then map the resulting coordinates to RGB space. We show results on the YouTube objects validation set in Fig. 4. Note that pixels on a salient foreground object tend to cluster together in the embedding (see, for example, the aircraft in column 4, the motor cyclist in column 3 and the cat in column 6).

Neuron Maximization: We use per-neuron activation maximization [34] to visualize individual neurons in the fifth convolutional layer (Fig. 5). This figure presents the estimated optimal stimulus for each of these neurons, made interpretable using a natural image prior. We observe abstract patterns including a human form (row 2, column 4) that are obviously not present in a random network, suggesting that the representation may be learning concepts useful for general-purpose image analysis.

4.5 Quantitative Results

We follow standard practice in the self-supervised learning community and fine-tune the learned representation on various recognition benchmarks. We evaluate our features, pre-trained using various CPFS losses, by transfer learning on PASCAL VOC 2007 detection and classification [13], PASCAL VOC 2012 segmentation [14], and ILSVRC12 linear probing [60] (in the latter case, the representation is frozen). We provide details on the evaluation protocol next and compare against other self-supervised models with results reported for AlexNet-like-architectures in Tables 1 and 2. Different from other approaches, we did not

Table 1. Pascal VOC Comparison for three benchmarks: VOC2007-classification (column 4) %mAP, VOC2007-Detection (Column 5) %mAP and VOC2012-Segmentation (Column 6) %mIoU. The rows are grouped into four blocks (1) The limits of no-supervision and human supervision, (2) motion/video based self-supervision, (3) Our models and the baseline, (4) others. The third column [ref] indicates which publication the reported numbers are borrowed from. Full table in supplementary material.

	Method	Supervision	[Ref]	Cls.	Detection	Seg.
	Krizhevsky *et al.* [30]	Class labels	[60]	79.9	56.8	48.0
	Random	-	[41]	53.3	43.4	19.8
Motion cues	Agrawal *et al.* [2]	Egomotion	[10]	63.1	43.9	-
	Jayaraman *et al.* [26]	Egomotion	[26]	-	41.7	-
	Lee *et al.* [32]	Time-order	[32]	63.8	46.9	-
	Misra *et al.* [35]	Time-order	[35]	-	42.4	-
	Pathak *et al.* [42]	Video-seg	[42], Self	61.0	50.2	-
	Wang *et al.* [55]	Track + Rank	[29,55]	63.1	47.5	-
	CPFS-CE	Optical-flow	Self	64.2	**50.8**	41.4
	CPFS-CE-rev	Optical-flow	Self	63.6	49.9	39.5
	CPFS-KTA	Optical-flow	Self	**65.3**	50.5	**41.5**
	Ours direct cls.	Optical-flow	Self	63.2	46.1	38.8
	Other Cues	Varied	[19,36,38]	73.3	55.5	40.6
	State of the art		[19]	[38]	[36]	

benefit from the re-balancing trick of [29] and hence we report results without it. This is possibly due to the use of batch normalization layers.

Baseline: Our main hypothesis is that the cross pixel flow similarity matching method, rather than the direct prediction of optical-flow, is more appropriate for exploiting optical-flow as a self-supervisory signal. We validate this hypothesis by comparing against a direct optical-flow prediction baseline, using the same CNN architecture as our method but a different loss function: while we use flow-similarity matching losses, this baseline does a standard per-pixel softmax cross entropy across 16 discrete optical-flow classes, once for each spatial dimension— x and y. To this end, since the flow is normalized in $[-1, 1]$ (Eq. 7), this interval is discretized uniformly. Note that direct L^2 regression of flow vectors is also possible, but did not work as well in preliminary experiments. This may be because continuous regression is usually harder for deep networks compared to classification, especially for ambiguous tasks. It was beneficial to use a faster initial learning rate of 0.01 for this baseline model.

VOC2007-detection: We finetune our AlexNet backbone end-to-end using the Fast-RCNN model [20] using code from [44] to obtain results for PASCAL VOC 2007 detection [13]. Finetuning follows the protocol of [29] to use multi-scale training and single-scale testing. We report mean average precision (mAP) in Table 1 (col. 5) along with results of other self-supervised learning methods. We achieve the state-of-the-art among methods that use temporal information

Table 2. ImageNet LSVRC-12 linear probing evaluation. A linear classifier is trained on the (downsampled) activations of each layer in the pretrained model. Top-1 accuracy is reported on ILSVRC-12 validation set. The column [ref] indicates which publication the reported numbers are borrowed from. We finetune Pathak *et al.*'s [42] model along with ours as they do not report these benchmark in their paper.

	Method	Supervision	[ref]	Conv1	Conv2	Conv3	Conv4	Conv5
	Krizhevsky *et al.* [30]	Class labels	[61]	19.3	36.3	44.2	48.3	50.5
	Random	-	[61]	11.6	17.1	16.9	16.3	14.1
	Random-rescaled [29]	-	[29]	17.5	23.0	24.5	23.2	20.6
Motion	Pathak *et al.* [42]	Video-seg	Self	**15.8**	23.2	29.0	29.5	25.4
	CPFS-CE	Optical-Flow	Self	14.9	**25.0**	**29.5**	**30.1**	**29.1**
	CPFS-CE-rev	Optical-Flow	Self	15.3	24.8	27.7	27.8	26.3
	CPFS-KTA	Optical-Flow	Self	14.8	24.6	29.2	29.5	28.1
	Ours direct cls.	Optical-Flow	Self	14.0	23.0	26.4	26.7	24.8
Other cues	Doersch *et al.* [8]	Context	[61]	16.2	23.3	30.2	31.7	29.6
	Gidaris *et al.* [19]	Rotation	[19]	18.8	31.7	**38.7**	38.2	**36.5**
	Jenni *et al.* [27]	-	[27]	19.5	**33.3**	37.9	**38.9**	34.9
	Mundhenk *et al.* [36]	Context	[36]	**19.6**	31.4	37.0	37.8	33.3
	Noroozi *et al.* [37]	Jigsaw	[39]	18.2	28.8	34.0	33.9	27.1
	Noroozi *et al.* [39]	Counting	[39]	18.0	30.6	34.3	32.5	25.7
	Noroozi *et al.* [38]	Jigsaw++	[38]	18.2	28.7	34.1	33.2	28.0
	Noroozi *et al.* [38]	CC+Jigsaw++	[38]	18.9	30.5	35.7	35.4	32.2
	Pathak *et al.* [41]	In-Painting	[61]	14.1	20.7	21.0	19.8	15.5
	Zhang *et al.* [60]	Colorization	[61]	13.1	24.8	31.0	32.6	31.8
	Zhang *et al.* [61]	Split-Brain	[61]	17.7	29.3	35.4	35.2	32.8

in videos for self-supervision. This table summarizes the state of the art among methods that use cues other than motion. Please see the supplementary material for a complete table of all relevant methods.

VOC2007 Classification: We finetune our pretrained AlexNets to minimize the softmax cross-entropy loss over the PASCAL VOC 2007 *trainval* set for image classification across 20 Pascal classes. The initial learning rate is 10^{-3} and drops by a factor of 2 every 10k iterations for a total of 80k iterations and predictions are averaged over 10 random crops at test time in keeping with [29]. We use the code provided by [31] and report mean average precision (mAP) on VOC2007-test in the fourth column of Table 1. We achieve state-of-the-art among methods that derive self-supervision from motion cues; in particular, we outperform [42] by a large margin.

ILSVRC12 Linear Probing: We follow the protocol and code of [61] to train a linear classifier on activations of our pre-trained network. The activation tensors produced by various convolutional layers (after ReLU) are down-sampled using bilinear interpolation to have roughly 9,000–10,000 elements before being fed into a linear classifier. The CNN parameters are frozen and only the linear classifier weights are trained on the ILSVRC-12 training set. Top-1 classification accuracy is reported on the ILSVRC-12 validation set (Table 2). We achieve the state-of-the-art among motion-based self-supervision methods, except for "conv1" features.

VOC2012 Segmentation: We use the two staged fine-tuning approach of [31] who finetune their AlexNet for semantic segmentation using a sparse hypercolumn head instead of the conventional FCN-32s head. We do so because it is a better fit for our sparse hypercolumn pre-training, although the hypercolumn itself is built using different layers (conv1 to conv5 and fc6 to fc7). Thus the MLP predicting the embedding ϕ from hypercolumn features is replaced with a new one before fine-tuning for segmentation. Also, our model has a fully convolutional structure but is pre-trained on a non-convolutional proxy task. We obtain a mere 31.3 %mIoU using FCN-32s. The training data consists of the PASCAL VOC 2012 [14] training set augmented with additional annotations from [21]. Thus the training-validation split has 10582 training images and 1449 validation images. Test results are reported as mean intersection-over-union (mIoU) scores on the PASCAL VOC 2012 validation set (Column 6 of Table 1). We achieve the state of the art on this benchmark among all self-supervised learning methods, even ones that use other supervisory signals than motion (at the time of submission).

Other Architectures: We experimented with a VGG-16 [50] backbone[2] and followed the protocol of [31] to evaluated on VOC2007-classification and VOC12-segmentation. Our CPFS-CE model achieved 76.4% mAP for VOC2007 classification comparable to Larsson *et al.*'s 77.2% [31]; and 51.7% mIoU for VOC2012-segmentation which fell short of [31]'s 56.0%. VGG-16 has many more parameters than AlexNet. We argue that it may benefit from the extra 2.1M images used by [31] which might explain this performance gap.

4.6 Discussion

We can take home several messages from these experiments. First, in all cases our approach outperforms the baseline of predicting optical-flow directly. This is true for all three cross pixel flow similarity loss functions. This supports our hypothesis that direct single-frame optical-flow prediction is either too difficult due to its intrinsic ambiguity or a distraction from the goal of learning a powerful representation. It also supports our claim that predicting pairwise flow similarities partially addresses this ambiguity and allows us to learn useful CNN representations from optical-flow.

Second, the cross entropy loss is comparable in performance to kernel target alignment (KTA). We know that KTA aligns kernels uniformly and doing so is still highly ambiguous. Thus there is more room for improvement in the loss

---

[2] Full model: 'pool 1–5', and 'fc7' (projected to 256 channels using a 1×1 convolution for faster training) constitute the hypercolumn head for pre-training on the dataset (Sect. 4.2).

function design. Also, surprisingly, reversed cross entropy performs well although not as well as the other two.

Third, our method is the state of the art for self-supervision using motion cues. This is notable as our approach is significantly simpler than the previous state of the art [42]. By ingesting optical-flow information directly, it does not require data pre-processing via a video segmentation algorithm.

Finally, we also observe that all video/motion based methods for self-supervised learning are generally not as effective as methods that use other cues; particularly in image classification benchmarks. However, our approach still sets the overall state of the art for semantic image segmentation suggesting that the learned representation may be more suitable for per-pixel applications. Therefore further progress in this area of motion based self-supervision may be possible and is worth seeking. At the same time, authors of [9] find that combinations of different cues may result in the best performance.

5   Conclusion

We have presented a novel method for self-supervision using motion cues based on cross-pixel optical-flow similarity loss functions. We trained an AlexNet model using this scheme on a large unannotated video data-set. Visualizations of individual neurons in a deep layer and of the output embedding show that the representation captures structure in the image. We established the effectiveness of the resulting representation by transfer learning for several recognition benchmarks. Compared to the previous state of the art motion based method [42], our method works just as well and in some cases noticeably better despite a significant algorithmic simplification. We also outperform all other self-supervision strategies in semantic image segmentation (VOC12). This is reasonable as we train on a per-pixel proxy task on undistorted RGB images and use a hypercolumn model for fine-tuning. Finally, we see our contribution as an instance of self-supervision using multiple modalities, RGB and optical-flow, which poses our work as a special case of this broader area of research.

Acknowledgements. The authors gratefully acknowledge ERC IDIU, AIMS CDT (EPSRC EP/L015897/1) and AWS Cloud Credits for Research program. The authors thank Ankush Gupta and David Novotný for helpful discussions, and Christian Rupprecht, Fatma Guney and Ruth Fong for proof reading the paper. We thank Deepak Pathak for help with reproducing some of the results from [42].

References

1. Abadi, M., et al.: TensorFlow: large-scale machine learning on heterogeneous distributed systems. arXiv preprint arXiv:1603.04467 (2016)
2. Agrawal, P., Carreira, J., Malik, J.: Learning to see by moving. In: ICCV (2015)
3. Arandjelović, R., Zisserman, A.: Look, listen and learn. In: ICCV (2017)
4. Bansal, A., Chen, X., Russell, B., Gupta, A., Ramanan, D.: PixelNet: representation of the pixels, by the pixels, and for the pixels. arXiv:1702.06506 (2017)

5. Bojanowski, P., Joulin, A.: Unsupervised learning by predicting noise. In: ICML (2017)
6. Butler, D.J., Wulff, J., Stanley, G.B., Black, M.J.: A naturalistic open source movie for optical flow evaluation. In: Fitzgibbon, A., Lazebnik, S., Perona, P., Sato, Y., Schmid, C. (eds.) ECCV 2012. LNCS, vol. 7577, pp. 611–625. Springer, Heidelberg (2012). https://doi.org/10.1007/978-3-642-33783-3_44
7. Cristianini, N., et al.: An Introduction to Support Vector Machines. CUP, Cambridge (2000)
8. Doersch, C., Gupta, A., Efros, A.A.: Unsupervised visual representation learning by context prediction. In: ICCV (2015)
9. Doersch, C., et al.: Multi-task self-supervised visual learning. In: ICCV (2017)
10. Donahue, J., et al.: Adversarial feature learning. In: ICLR (2017)
11. Dosovitskiy, A., et al.: FlowNet: learning optical flow with convolutional networks. In: ICCV (2015)
12. Dosovitskiy, A., et al.: Discriminative unsupervised feature learning with exemplar convolutional neural networks. IEEE PAMI **38**(9), 1734–1747 (2016)
13. Everingham, M., et al.: The PASCAL visual object classes challenge 2007 results (2007)
14. Everingham, M., et al.: The PASCAL visual object classes challenge 2012 results (2012)
15. Faktor, A., Irani, M.: Video segmentation by non-local consensus voting. In: BMVC (2014)
16. Gan, C., Gong, B., Liu, K., Su, H., Guibas, L.J.: Geometry guided convolutional neural networks for self-supervised video representation learning. In: CVPR (2018)
17. Gao, R., Jayaraman, D., Grauman, K.: Object-centric representation learning from unlabeled videos. In: Lai, S.-H., Lepetit, V., Nishino, K., Sato, Y. (eds.) ACCV 2016. LNCS, vol. 10115, pp. 248–263. Springer, Cham (2017). https://doi.org/10.1007/978-3-319-54193-8_16
18. Geiger, A., Lenz, P., Urtasun, R.: Are we ready for autonomous driving? The KITTI vision benchmark suite. In: CVPR (2012)
19. Gidaris, S., Singh, P., Komodakis, N.: Unsupervised representation learning by predicting image rotations. In: Proceedings of ICLR (2018)
20. Girshick, R.B.: Fast R-CNN. In: ICCV (2015)
21. Hariharan, B., et al.: Semantic contours from inverse detectors. In: ICCV (2011)
22. Hariharan, B., Arbeláez, P., Girshick, R., Malik, J.: Hypercolumns for object segmentation and fine-grained localization. In: CVPR, pp. 447–456 (2015)
23. Ioffe, S., Szegedy, C.: Batch normalization: accelerating deep network training by reducing internal covariate shift. In: ICML (2015)
24. Isola, P., Zoran, D., Krishnan, D., Adelson, E.H.: Learning visual groups from co-occurrences in space and time. In: ICLR Workshop (2015)
25. Jayaraman, D., Grauman, K.: Slow and steady feature analysis: higher order temporal coherence in video. In: CVPR, pp. 3852–3861 (2016)
26. Jayaraman, D., et al.: Learning image representations tied to ego-motion. In: ICCV (2015)
27. Jenni, S., Favaro, P.: Self-supervised feature learning by learning to spot artifacts. In: CVPR (2018)
28. Kingma, D., Ba, J.: Adam: a method for stochastic optimization. arXiv:1412.6980 (2014)
29. Krähenbühl, P., et al.: Data-dependent initializations of convolutional neural networks. In: ICLR (2016)

30. Krizhevsky, A., Sutskever, I., Hinton, G.E.: ImageNet classification with deep convolutional neural networks. In: NIPS, pp. 1106–1114 (2012)
31. Larsson, G., Maire, M., Shakhnarovich, G.: Colorization as a proxy task for visual understanding. In: CVPR (2017)
32. Lee, H.Y., Huang, J.B., Singh, M.K., Yang, M.H.: Unsupervised representation learning by sorting sequence. In: ICCV (2017)
33. Liu, C.: Beyond pixels: exploring new representations and applications for motion analysis. Ph.D. thesis, Massachusetts Institute of Technology, USA (2009)
34. Mahendran, A., Vedaldi, A.: Visualizing deep convolutional neural networks using natural pre-images. IJCV **120**, 1–23 (2016)
35. Misra, I., Zitnick, C.L., Hebert, M.: Shuffle and learn: unsupervised learning using temporal order verification. In: Leibe, B., Matas, J., Sebe, N., Welling, M. (eds.) ECCV 2016. LNCS, vol. 9905, pp. 527–544. Springer, Cham (2016). https://doi.org/10.1007/978-3-319-46448-0_32
36. Mundhenk, T., Ho, D., Chen, B.Y.: Improvements to context based self-supervised learning. In: CVPR (2017)
37. Noroozi, M., Favaro, P.: Unsupervised learning of visual representations by solving Jigsaw puzzles. In: Leibe, B., Matas, J., Sebe, N., Welling, M. (eds.) ECCV 2016. LNCS, vol. 9910, pp. 69–84. Springer, Cham (2016). https://doi.org/10.1007/978-3-319-46466-4_5
38. Noroozi, M., Vinjimoor, A., Favaro, P., Pirsiavash, H.: Boosting self-supervised learning via knowledge transfer. In: CVPR (2018)
39. Noroozi, M., et al.: Representation learning by learning to count. In: ICCV (2017)
40. Owens, A., Wu, J., McDermott, J.H., Freeman, W.T., Torralba, A.: Ambient sound provides supervision for visual learning. In: Leibe, B., Matas, J., Sebe, N., Welling, M. (eds.) ECCV 2016. LNCS, vol. 9905, pp. 801–816. Springer, Cham (2016). https://doi.org/10.1007/978-3-319-46448-0_48
41. Pathak, D., et al.: Context encoders: feature learning by inpainting. In: CVPR (2016)
42. Pathak, D., et al.: Learning features by watching objects move. In: CVPR (2017)
43. Prest, A., et al.: Learning object class detectors from weakly annotated video. In: CVPR (2012)
44. Ren, S., He, K., Girshick, R., Sun, J.: Faster R-CNN: towards real-time object detection with region proposal networks. In: NIPS (2015)
45. Ren, Z., Lee, Y.J.: Cross-domain self-supervised multi-task feature learning using synthetic imagery. In: CVPR (2018)
46. Revaud, J., Weinzaepfel, P., Harchaoui, Z., Schmid, C.: EpicFlow: edge-preserving interpolation of correspondences for optical flow. In: CVPR (2015)
47. Russakovsky, O., et al.: ImageNet large scale visual recognition challenge. IJCV **115**, 211–252 (2015)
48. de Sa, V.R.: Learning classification with unlabeled data. In: NIPS, pp. 112–119 (1994)
49. Sermanet, P., et al.: Time-contrastive networks: self-supervised learning from video. In: Proceedings of International Conference on Robotics and Automation (2018)
50. Simonyan, K., Zisserman, A.: Very deep convolutional networks for large-scale image recognition. arXiv:1409.1556 (2014)
51. Srivastava, N., Mansimov, E., Salakhudinov, R.: Unsupervised learning of video representations using LSTMs. In: ICML (2015)
52. Thomee, B., et al.: YFCC100M: the new data in multimedia research. ACM (2016)
53. Todorovic, D.: Gestalt principles. Scholarpedia **3**(12), 5345 (2008). revision #91314

54. Walker, J.: Data-driven visual forecasting. Ph.D. thesis, Carnegie Mellon University (2018)
55. Wang, X., Gupta, A.: Unsupervised learning of visual representations using videos. In: ICCV, pp. 2794–2802 (2015)
56. Wang, X., He, K., Gupta, A.: Transitive invariance for self-supervised visual representation learning. In: ICCV, pp. 2794–2802 (2017)
57. Wei, D., et al.: Learning and using the arrow of time. In: CVPR, pp. 8052–8060 (2018)
58. Weinzaepfel, P., Revaud, J., Harchaoui, Z., Schmid, C.: DeepFlow: large displacement optical flow with deep matching. In: ICCV, pp. 1385–1392 (2013)
59. Xue, T., Wu, J., Bouman, K.L., Freeman, W.T.: Visual dynamics: stochastic future generation via layered cross convolutional networks. IEEE PAMI (2018). https://ieeexplore.ieee.org/document/8409321. https://doi.org/10.1109/TPAMI.2018.2854726
60. Zhang, R., Isola, P., Efros, A.A.: Colorful image colorization. In: Leibe, B., Matas, J., Sebe, N., Welling, M. (eds.) ECCV 2016. LNCS, vol. 9907, pp. 649–666. Springer, Cham (2016). https://doi.org/10.1007/978-3-319-46487-9_40
61. Zhang, R., Isola, P., Efros, A.A.: Split-brain autoencoders: unsupervised learning by cross-channel prediction. In: CVPR (2017)

Poster Session P2

DSNet: Deep and Shallow Feature Learning for Efficient Visual Tracking

Qiangqiang Wu, Yan Yan, Yanjie Liang, Yi Liu, and Hanzi Wang[✉]

Fujian Key Laboratory of Sensing and Computing for Smart City,
School of Information Science and Engineering, Xiamen University, Xiamen, China
{qiangwu,liuyitan}@stu.xmu.edu.cn, {yanyan,hanzi.wang}@xmu.edu.cn,
yanjieliang@yeah.net

Abstract. In recent years, Discriminative Correlation Filter (DCF) based tracking methods have achieved great success in visual tracking. However, the multi-resolution convolutional feature maps trained from other tasks like image classification, cannot be naturally used in the conventional DCF formulation. Furthermore, these high-dimensional feature maps significantly increase the tracking complexity and thus limit the tracking speed. In this paper, we present a deep and shallow feature learning network, namely DSNet, to learn the multi-level same-resolution compressed (MSC) features for efficient online tracking, in an end-to-end offline manner. Specifically, the proposed DSNet compresses multi-level convolutional features to uniform spatial resolution features. The learned MSC features effectively encode both appearance and semantic information of objects in the same-resolution feature maps, thus enabling an elegant combination of the MSC features with any DCF-based methods. Additionally, a channel reliability measurement (CRM) method is presented to further refine the learned MSC features. We demonstrate the effectiveness of the MSC features learned from the proposed DSNet on two DCF tracking frameworks: the basic DCF framework and the continuous convolution operator framework. Extensive experiments show that the learned MSC features have the appealing advantage of allowing the equipped DCF-based tracking methods to perform favorably against the state-of-the-art methods while running at high frame rates.

Keywords: Visual tracking · Correlation filter · Deep neural network

1 Introduction

Given the initial state of a target at the first frame, generic visual object tracking is to accurately and efficiently estimate the trajectory of the target at subsequent frames. In recent years, Discriminative Correlation Filter (DCF) based tracking methods have shown excellent performance on canonical object tracking benchmarks [31,32]. The key reasons to their success are the mechanism of enlarging training data by including all shifted samples of a given sample, and the efficiency of DCF by solving the ridge regression problem in the frequency domain.

© Springer Nature Switzerland AG 2019
C. V. Jawahar et al. (Eds.): ACCV 2018, LNCS 11365, pp. 119–134, 2019.
https://doi.org/10.1007/978-3-030-20873-8_8

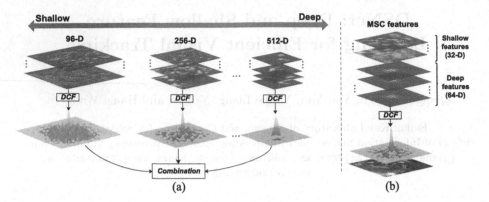

Fig. 1. Comparison between (a) the DCF-based tracking methods [9,20] with deep convolutional features trained from the image classification task and (b) the DCF-based tracking method with our MSC features.

Features play an important role in designing a high-performance tracking method. In recent years, significant progress has been made in exploiting discriminative features for DCFs. For example, hand-crafted features like HOG [5], Color Names [30] or the combinations of these features, are commonly employed by DCFs for online object tracking. Despite the fast tracking speed achieved by these methods, they usually cannot obtain high tracking accuracy due to the less discriminative features they use. Recently, the outstanding success of deep convolutional neural networks (CNNs) has been made in a variety of computer vision tasks [15,19,23]. Inspired by the success of CNNs, the visual tracking community has exploited the advantages of CNNs, and shown that deep convolutional features trained from other tasks like image classification, are also applicable for the visual tracking task [24]. On one hand, the deep features extracted from the shallow convolutional layers, which provide high spatial resolution, are more helpful for the accurate localization of the object. On the other hand, the deep features extracted from the deeper layers encode the semantic information and are more robust to target appearance variations (e.g., deformation, rotation and motion blur). The combination of these two types of features shows excellent tracking performance in both locating the target accurately and modeling the target appearance variations online. However, the conventional DCF formulation is limited to single-resolution feature maps. Deep and shallow features (i.e., multi-resolution feature maps) cannot be naturally used in the conventional DCF framework. Thus, how to effectively fuse the deep and shallow features in the DCF framework is still an open and challenging problem.

Recently, several works have been developed to fuse multi-resolution feature maps in the DCF framework [6,9]. A straightforward strategy is to explicitly resample both deep and shallow features from different spatial resolutions to the same resolution. However, such a strategy introduces artifacts, which severely limit the tracking performance. To overcome the above issue, an online learning formulation is presented in C-COT [9] to integrate multi-resolution feature maps. Despite the promising performance achieved by C-COT, it still has several limitations: (1) The online learning formulation is time-consuming due to the high-dimensional deep features. (2) In order to fuse multi-resolution feature maps, multiple DCFs need to be trained. (3) The method employs the deep features trained from other tasks like image classification. These features are not specifically designed for visual tracking and may limit the tracking performance.

In this paper, instead of designing an online learning formulation to integrate deep and shallow features (i.e., multi-resolution feature maps) in the DCF framework, we propose to learn multi-layer same-resolution compressed (MSC) features in an end-to-end offline manner for efficient online tracking. To achieve this, a deep and shallow feature learning network architecture (called as DSNet) is developed in this paper. The proposed DSNet aggregates multi-level convolutional features and integrates them into the same-resolution feature maps. In the training stage, a correlation filter layer is added in DSNet, enabling to learn the discriminative MSC features for visual tracking. In the test stage, DSNet acts as a feature extractor without relying on the time-consuming online fine-tuning step. In general, our MSC features learned by the proposed DSNet have the following characteristics:

(1) MSC features effectively incorporate both the deep and shallow features of objects but with the same spatial resolution. This enables MSC features to be naturally fused in any DCF-based tracking methods without using any online combination strategies.
(2) Due to the low-dimension and uniform spatial resolution of MSC features, the tracking model complexity can be significantly decreased (see Fig. 1). Generally, our MSC features can be naturally incorporated by a single DCF instead of multiple DCFs, thus leading to highly efficient online object tracking.

To demonstrate the effectiveness of MSC features learned by the proposed DSNet, we incorporate the MSC features into two state-of-the-art tracking frameworks: the basic DCF framework [15] and the continuous convolution operator framework [9], namely MSC-DCF and MSC-CCO, respectively. Experiments demonstrate that our MSC features have the important advantage of allowing the equipped MSC-DCF and MSC-CCO methods to perform favorably against the state-of-the-art methods at high frame rates.

In summary, this paper has the following contributions:

(1) We propose a deep and shallow feature learning network architecture, namely DSNet, enabling to learn multi-level same-resolution compressed (MSC) features for efficient online object tracking in an end-to-end offline manner.
(2) Based on the observation that several feature channels have low channel reliability scores, an online channel reliability measurement (CRM) method is presented to further refine the learned MSC features.
(3) We show that our MSC features are applicable for any CF-based tracking methods. Based on the MSC features, two MSC-trackers (MSC-DCF

and MSC-CCO) are presented. Experiments demonstrate that the presented trackers can achieve favorable performance while running at high frame rates.

2   Related Work

In this section, we give a brief review to the methods closely related to our work.

Correlation Filter Tracking. Correlation filter (CF) based tracking methods [8,9,15] have attracted considerable attention due to their computational efficiency and favorable tracking performance. For example, MOOSE [3] is the initially proposed CF-based tracking method, which uses grayscale images to train the regression model. KCF [15] further extends MOOSE by using multi-channel features and mapping the input features to a kernel space. Staple [1] combines both HOG and Color Name features in a CF framework. Despite the fast tracking speed of their methods, the employed hand-crafted features are still not discriminative enough to handle different challenges. To overcome this problem, several deep feature based tracking methods have been proposed. For example, CF2 [20] and DeepSRDCF [7] employ the convolutional features extracted from VGGNet [4]. HDT [24] merges multiple CFs trained on the different layers of VGGNet. In [9], an online learning formulation of convolutional features is developed on the spatial domain. ECO [6] further alleviates the over-fitting problem in [9], and decreases the computational complexity. Despite significant improvements made by these methods, they still suffer from the problems of low tracking speed and less discriminative deep features. To alleviate these problems, in this work, we propose to learn the multi-layer same-resolution compressed (MSC) features in an end-to-end offline manner. The learned MSC features are specifically designed for visual tracking, and they can be easily incorporated into any CF-based tracking methods without using the time-consuming online fine-tuning steps.

Feature Representation Learning. Feature representation is the core of many computer vision tasks, including semantic segmentation [23], object detection [25] and object tracking [1]. For the object detection task, many works on feature learning have been proposed. For example, in R-CNN [10], a region proposal based CNN is proposed to learn better feature representations in an end-to-end manner. Due to the learned discriminative features, R-CNN significantly outperforms other detection methods. In addition, SSD [19] and HyperNer [17] combine multi-layer convolution features to further improve the detection performance. For the visual tracking task, CFNet [28] firstly proposes to add a correlation filter layer in a CNN architecture, thus enabling to learn more discriminative features for CF-based methods. The similar feature learning method is also introduced in DCFNet [29]. Despite the success of these methods, these methods only focus on learning single-layer convolutional features, which may limit their performance. To encode both the low-level and high-level information of objects, we propose to learn multi-layer convolutional features in an end-to-end manner for visual tracking.

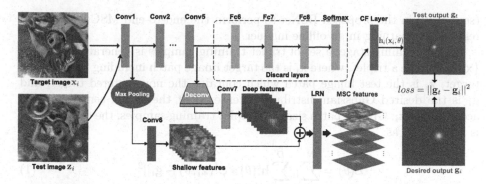

Fig. 2. Overall architecture of the proposed deep and shallow feature learning network (DSNet). (Color figure online)

3 Proposed DSNet for Feature Learning

In this section, we firstly introduce the proposed DSNet framework. Secondly, the feature learning of MSC features is presented. Thirdly, we detail the feature extraction step of MSC features. Finally, we introduce the channel reliability measurement (CRM) method to further refine the learned MSC features.

3.1 DSNet Framework

The proposed DSNet framework is illustrated in Fig. 2. As can be seen, DSNet mainly consists of three parts: a backbone network (the blue part), a shallow feature extraction branch (the red part) and a deep feature extraction branch (the orange part). The backbone network is a pre-trained image classification network, which can be any classification CNNs, such as AlexNet [18] and ResNet [13]. In this work, we select the imagenet-vgg-2048 network [4] as our backbone network. In the shallow and deep feature extraction branches, in order to combine multi-layer multi-resolution feature maps at the same spatial resolution, a max pooling layer (a 7×7 kernel with a stride of 2) and a deconvolution layer [23] (a 4×4 kernel with a stride of 4) are added to perform downsampling and upsampling, respectively. Then, the Conv6 and Conv7 layers (i.e., the 1×1 convolutional layers) are employed to compress the shallow and deep features, respectively. Moreover, a local response normalization (LRN) layer [18] is employed to normalize these features. Finally, we concatenate the normalized features to a single output cube, and obtain our multi-layer same-resolution compressed (MSC) features. In order to effectively train the MSC features, a correlation filter is interpreted as a differentiable layer, which is added at the last layer of DSNet in the training stage.

3.2 End-to-End Feature Learning

In order to effectively train the proposed DSNet and make the learned MSC features suitable for correlation filter tracking, we add a correlation filter layer (see Fig. 2) in the proposed DSNet to perform the end-to-end MSC feature representation learning in an offline manner.

In the training stage, a set of triplet training samples is generated. Let $T = \{\mathbf{x}_i, \mathbf{z}_i, \mathbf{g}_i\}$ be a triplet, where $\mathbf{x}_i$ is the target image patch including the centered target, $\mathbf{z}_i$ is the test image patch which contains the non-centered target, and $\mathbf{g}_i$ is the desired Gaussian distribution centered at the target center position according to $\mathbf{z}_i$. Given a batch size of N triplet training samples, the cost function is formulated as:

$$\mathcal{L}(\theta) = \sum_{i=1}^{N} || \sum_{l=1}^{D} \mathbf{h}_i^l(\theta) * \varphi^l(\mathbf{z}_i, \theta) - \mathbf{g}_i ||^2, \tag{1}$$

where

$$\mathbf{h}_i^l(\theta) = \mathcal{F}^{-1}\left(\frac{\hat{\varphi}^l(\mathbf{x}_i, \theta) \odot \hat{\mathbf{g}}_i^*}{\sum_{k=1}^{D} \hat{\varphi}^k(\mathbf{x}_i, \theta) \odot (\hat{\varphi}^k(\mathbf{x}_i, \theta))^* + \lambda} \right) \tag{2}$$

and $\mathbf{h}_i^l(\theta)$ is the desired correlation filter for the l-th channel feature map, θ refers to the parameters of our DSNet, $\varphi^l(\mathbf{x}_i, \theta)$ is the extracted features of l-th channel with the parameters θ corresponding to the input $\mathbf{x}_i$, and λ is a regularization parameter. Furthermore, $\mathcal{F}^{-1}$ denotes the inverse Fourier transform, $*$ is the circular correlation operation, D represents the channel numbers, $\odot$, $\hat{\ }$ and $*$ denote the Hadamard product, discrete Fourier transform and complex conjugation, respectively. By applying the multivariable chain rule, the derivation of the loss function in Eq. (1) can be rewritten as:

$$\frac{\partial \mathcal{L}}{\partial \theta} = \sum_l \frac{\partial \mathcal{L}}{\partial \varphi^l(\mathbf{x}_i, \theta)} \frac{\partial \varphi^l(\mathbf{x}_i, \theta)}{\partial \theta} + \sum_l \frac{\partial \mathcal{L}}{\partial \varphi^l(\mathbf{z}_i, \theta)} \frac{\partial \varphi^l(\mathbf{z}_i, \theta)}{\partial \theta}. \tag{3}$$

Specifically, $\frac{\partial \varphi^l(\mathbf{x}_i, \theta)}{\partial \theta}$ and $\frac{\partial \varphi^l(\mathbf{z}_i, \theta)}{\partial \theta}$ in the above can be efficiently calculated by recent deep learning toolkits. According to [28, 29], the prior two terms ($\frac{\partial \mathcal{L}}{\partial \varphi^l(\mathbf{x}_i, \theta)}$ and $\frac{\partial \mathcal{L}}{\partial \varphi^l(\mathbf{z}_i, \theta)}$) in (3) can be formulated as:

$$\frac{\partial \mathcal{L}}{\partial \varphi^l(\mathbf{x}_i, \theta)} = \mathcal{F}^{-1}\left(\frac{\partial \mathcal{L}}{\partial (\hat{\varphi}^l(\mathbf{x}_i, \theta))^*} + \left(\frac{\partial \mathcal{L}}{\partial \hat{\varphi}^l(\mathbf{x}_i, \theta)} \right)^* \right), \tag{4}$$

$$\frac{\partial \mathcal{L}}{\partial \varphi^l(\mathbf{z}_i, \theta)} = \mathcal{F}^{-1}\left(\frac{\partial \mathcal{L}}{\partial (\hat{\varphi}^l(\mathbf{z}_i, \theta))^*} \right). \tag{5}$$

3.3 Feature Extraction

In the online tracking stage, DSNet acts as a feature extractor, which first extracts multi-layer convolutional feature maps as shown in Fig. 2. Next, the shallow and deep feature extraction branches in our DSNet aggregate multi-level convolutional feature maps and compress them to the uniform spatial resolution features. Finally, the MSC features are obtained by normalizing the compressed convolutional features. Specifically, the obtained MSC features (with the size

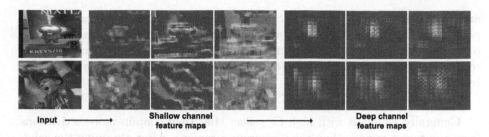

Input ⟶   Shallow channel
feature maps   ⟶   Deep channel
feature maps

Fig. 3. Visualization of the shallow and deep channel feature maps in the learned MSC features.

of $52 \times 52 \times 96$) consist of two parts of features: shallow convolutional features with the size of $52 \times 52 \times 32$ and deep convolutional features with the size of $52 \times 52 \times 64$. To better understand the learned MSC features, several channel feature maps of MSC features are visualized in Fig. 3. As can be seen, the shallow channel feature maps usually capture the detailed information of objects, while the deep channel feature maps generally encode the semantic information. These two types of features can complement each other, and the combination of them is beneficial for online tracking.

3.4 Channel Reliability Measurement

Several channel feature maps of MSC features may have small target activations, which indicates that these feature channels are more sensitive to the background regions rather than the target regions. To measure the reliability of these channels, the channel-wise ratio of the l-th channel is formulated as:

$$R^l = \frac{||S_t^l||_1}{||S_e^l||_1 + \zeta}. \tag{6}$$

Here, S_e^l refers to the entire l-th channel feature map, S_t^l is the target region of S_e^l, ζ is a penalty parameter and $||\cdot||_1$ is the l_1 norm.

The channel-wise ratio shows the ratio of the target responses to the overall responses, however, it cannot fully reflect the channel reliability in some cases. For example, when the background responses are equal to zero, even $||S_t^l||_1$ is a small value, a quite large channel-wise ratio R^l will be obtained. To overcome the above problem, A^l is defined to measure the target activations of the l-th channel feature map:

$$A^l = \begin{cases} 1 & Z(S_t^l) > W_t H_t / \eta \\ 0 & \text{otherwise,} \end{cases} \tag{7}$$

where

$$Z(S_t^l) = \sum_{w=1}^{W_t} \sum_{h=1}^{H_t} sign(|S_t^l(w, h)|), \tag{8}$$

and $sign()$ is the sign function, $S_t^l(w, h)$ returns the activation value at the position (w, h) of S_t^l, W_t and H_t are the width and height of S_t^l, respectively. η is a penalty parameter that controls the measurement of the target region responses. Finally, the reliability score of the l-th feature channel is calculated by:

$$C^l = R^l \times A^l. \tag{9}$$

Generally, channels with high C^l reflect that they contain more activations from the target regions than the background regions. After obtaining the reliability scores of feature channels, we sort these channels in the descending order. The top ranked K feature channels are selected to perform online tracking.

4   MSC-Trackers

In this section, we show how the learned MSC features can be incorporated into different DCF-based tracking frameworks. We select two state-of-the-art tracking frameworks, i.e., the basic DCF framework [15] and the continuous convolutional operator framework [9].

4.1   MSC Features for the Basic DCF Framework

A typical DCF learns a correlation filter $\mathbf{h}^l$ by solving a Ridge Regression problem:

$$\min_{\mathbf{h}^l} || \sum_{l=1}^{D} \mathbf{h}^l * \varphi^l(\mathbf{x}, \theta) - \mathbf{g} ||^2 + \lambda_D \sum_{l=1}^{D} ||\mathbf{h}^l||^2, \tag{10}$$

where $\varphi^l(\mathbf{x}, \theta)$ is the extracted MSC features of l-th channel with the DSNet parameters θ corresponding to the training image patch $\mathbf{x}$, $\mathbf{g}$ is the desired Gaussian distribution, λ_D is a regularization parameter that alleviates the overfitting problem. The learned correlation filter $\mathbf{h}^l$ can be obtained as [15]:

$$\hat{\mathbf{h}}^l = \frac{\hat{\varphi}^l(\mathbf{x}, \theta) \odot \hat{\mathbf{g}}^*}{\sum_{k=1}^{D} \hat{\varphi}^k(\mathbf{x}, \theta) \odot (\hat{\varphi}^k(\mathbf{x}, \theta))^* + \lambda_D}. \tag{11}$$

Given the test image patch $\mathbf{z}$ and the extracted features $\varphi(\mathbf{z}, \theta)$, the online detection process is formulated as:

$$\mathbf{f} = \mathcal{F}^{-1}(\sum_{l=1}^{D} \hat{\mathbf{h}}^{l^*} \odot \hat{\varphi}^l(\mathbf{z}, \theta)), \tag{12}$$

where $\mathbf{f}$ is the response map. The target center position can be estimated by searching the maximum value in $\mathbf{f}$. During the tracking process, at the $(t + 1)$-th frame, the numerator $A_{(t+1)}^l$ and denominator $B_{(t+1)}^l$ in Eq. (11) are respectively updated by using a moving average strategy with a learning rate μ. Then the correlation filter model at the $(t + 1)$-th frame is updated by $\hat{\mathbf{h}}_{(t+1)}^l = A_{(t+1)}^l/(B_{(t+1)}^l + \lambda_D)$. We use the scale estimation similar to [29].

Note that the conventional DCF framework is restricted to single-resolution feature maps. In comparison, the proposed MSC features can be naturally fused into the DCF framework (see Fig. 1). For briefly, this MSC features based DCF tracker is named as MSC-DCF.

4.2   MSC Features for the Continuous Convolution Operator Framework

The continuous convolution operator is proposed in C-COT [9]. Let y_j denote a training sample, which contains D feature channels $y_j^1, y_j^2, ..., y_j^D$. N_D is the number of spatial samples in y_j^d. Here, the feature channel y_j^d can be viewed as a function $y_j^d[n]$, where n is the discrete spatial variable $n \in \{0, ..., N_d - 1\}$. Assume that the spatial support of the feature map is the continuous interval $[0, P) \subset \mathbb{R}$. The interpolation operator J_d is formulated as:

$$J_d\{y^d\}(p) = \sum_{n=1}^{N_d} y^d[n] b_d(p - \frac{P}{N_d}n), \tag{13}$$

where b_d is the interpolation function, p denotes the location in the image, $p \in [0, P)$. In the continuous formulation, the convolution operator is estimated by a set of convolution filters $f = (f^1, f^2, ..., f^D) \in L^2(P)$. The convolution operator is defined as:

$$Q_f\{y\} = \sum_{d=1}^{D} f^d \circledast J_d\{y^d\}. \tag{14}$$

Here, f^d is the continuous filter for the d-th channel (see [9] for more details), $\circledast$ is the circular convolution operation: $L^2(T) \times L^2(T) \to L^2(T)$. As can be seen, for each interpolated sample $J_d\{y^d\}(p)$, it is convolved with the corresponding filter f^d. At last, the final confidence map is obtained by summing up the convolution responses from all the filters.

In Eqs. (13) and (14), the interpolation operator J_d and convolution filter f^d are learned for each feature channel. Thus, the high-dimensional convolutional features (e.g., the 608-dimensional features used in CCOT), significantly limit the online tracking speed. In comparison, the learned MSC features have much less channels (i.e., 96), and they can be regarded as one layer convolutional features to be fused in the continuous convolution operator framework without any modifications. We call this MSC features based tracker as MSC-CCO.

5   Experiments

Implementation Details: To avoid overfitting, we select the large scale video detection dataset (ILSVRC-2015) [26] to train the proposed DSNet. This dataset contains 4417 videos of 30 different objects. We use 3862 videos in this dataset for training and the remaining videos for validation. The triplet training samples

T are generated as described in [12]. The proposed DSNet is trained for 200 epochs with a batch size of 16 and an initial learning rate of 1×10^{-5} by using the SGD solver. The momentum and weight decay are respectively set to 9×10^{-1} and 5×10^{-4}. In the tracking stage, for MSC-DCF, the learning rate μ and the padding area are respectively set to 0.012 and 1.65. The searching scale number is set to 3. For MSC-CCO, we set the learning rate and the padding area to 9.4×10^{-3} and 3.62, respectively. Similar to [6], except for MSC features, MSC-CCO also employs HOG features, and the MSC features are further compressed to 38-D by using PCA. The other parameters in MSC-DCF and MSC-CCO are respectively set to be the same as in [29] and [6]. For the CRM method, we apply it to refine the deep feature channels in MSC features, where K in MSC-DCF and MSC-CCO are respectively set to 50 and 58. The penalty parameters η and ζ are set to 3 and 1×10^{-5}, respectively. In addition, we implement our method on a computer equipped with an Intel 6700K 4.0 GHz CPU and an NVIDIA GTX 1080 GPU.

Evaluation Methodology: Both the distance precision (DP) and overlap success (OS) plots are adopted to evaluate trackers on OTB-2013 [31], OTB-2015 [32] and OTB-50. We report both the DP rates at the conventional threshold of 20 pixels (DPR) and the OS rates at the threshold of 0.5 (OSR). The Area Under the Curve (AUC) is also used to evaluate the trackers.

Comparison Scenarios: We evaluate the proposed MSC-trackers (MSC-DCF and MSC-CCO) in four experiments. The first experiment is conducted to demonstrate the effectiveness of the learned MSC features by comparing our MSC features with both hand-crafted features and deep features. At the second experiment, we compare the proposed highly efficient MSC-trackers with the state-of-the-art real-time trackers, which shows the superiority of our MSC-trackers. The third experiment compares our MSC-trackers with the top-performing CF-based trackers with deep features. The last experiment makes an ablation study on MSC-trackers to show the effectiveness of the proposed CRM method.

5.1 Feature Comparison

To demonstrate the effectiveness of the learned MSC features, we compare the MSC features with different commonly used features. For fair comparison, all the compared features are incorporated into the same tracking framework, i.e., the DCF framework described in Sect. 4.1 for this experiment. We compare MSC features with raw RGB pixels (RGB), HOG [5], the first (Conv1) and fifth (Conv5) layer convolutional features in imagenet-vgg-2048, the combination of HOG and RGB (HOG+RGB) features and the combination of Conv1 and Conv5 (Conv1+Conv5) features. In order to combine the Conv1 and Conv5 features, the bilinear interpolation method is employed to upsample the Conv5 features to the same size as the Conv1 features.

Table 1 shows a comparison of our MSC features with different types of features on OTB-2013. As can be seen, our MSC features achieve the best DPR

Table 1. Comparison of our MSC features with both the hand-crafted features and deep convolutional features within the DCF framework on OTB-2013. Note that * indicates the GPU speed, otherwise the CPU speed. The first, second and third best features are shown in color.

	MSC	Conv1	Conv5	HOG	RGB	HOG+RGB	Conv1+Conv5
DPR (%)	83.7	76.2	69.4	74.4	47.4	77.7	78.5
OSR (%)	78.3	72.6	53.7	73.5	38.7	75.2	75.7
Feat. size.	52×52	109×109	13×13	52×52	52×52	52×52	109×109
Feat. dimen.	96	96	512	32	3	35	608
Avg. FPS	68.5*	51.0*	58.1*	56.0	328.1	49.6	2.6*

(83.7%) and OSR (78.3%) on OTB-2013, significantly outperforming both the hand-crafted features and deep convolutional features with large margins. In particular, the Conv1 and Conv5 features are extracted from the imagenet-vgg-2048 network, which is also the backbone network in DSNet. Despite the similar network architecture, our MSC features improve 7.5% and 14.4% of the DPRs obtained by the Conv1 and Conv5 features on OTB-2013, respectively. Compared with the Conv1 and Conv5 features, the combination Conv1+Conv5 features have more feature channels (608) and achieve better performance, with a DPR of 78.5%. Although much more feature channels are included in the Conv1+Conv5 features, our MSC features still provide improved performance, with a DPR of 83.7%, while achieving the fast tracking speed of 68.5 FPS, which is about 26 times faster than the Conv1+Conv5 features. This empirically shows that the MSC features are compact and can lead to highly efficient online tracking.

5.2   Comparison with Real-Time Trackers

We compare the proposed highly efficient MSC-trackers (MSC-DCF and MSC-CCO) with 12 state-of-the-art trackers that can achieve real-time tracking speed (FPS>20) for fair comparison, including SiamFC [2], CFNet [28], Staple [1], DCFNet [29], DCF$_{CA}$ [22], LCT [21], DSST [8], KCF [15], GOTURN [14], Re3 [11], DCF [15], and TLD [16].

Figure 4 compares the proposed MSC-trackers with the state-of-the-art real-time trackers, showing that our MSC-trackers achieve the best performance on OTB-2015. More specifically, MSC-CCO achieves the best DPR (89.2%) followed by MSC-DCF (79.8%) and CFNet (77.7%). Note that CFNet is the winner of the VOT-17 real-time challenge. Similar to MSC-DCF, CFNet also employs the traditional DCF framework. However, different from CFNet, our MSC-DCF learns complementary multi-layer features instead of single-layer features, thus achieving better performance than CFNet in terms of both DPR and AUC.

As can be seen from Table 2, the proposed MSC-trackers achieve the best accuracy over all the three datasets. Specifically, MSC-CCO achieves the best

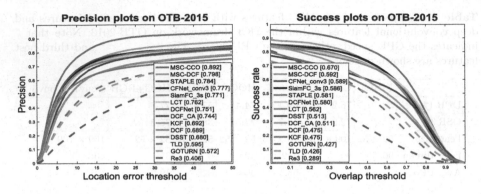

Fig. 4. Precision (left) and success (right) plots obtained by our MSC-DCF and MSC-CCO compared with the other 12 state-of-the-art real-time trackers on OTB-2015. DPRs and AUCs are reported in left and right brackets, respectively.

Table 2. DPRs (%) and speed (* indicates the GPU speed, otherwise the CPU speed) obtained by our MSC-DCF and MSC-CCO trackers as well as the state-of-the-art real-time trackers on OTB datasets. The results of top 8 performing trackers are given. The first, second and third best trackers are shown in color.

	MSC-CCO	MSC-DCF	CFNet	SiamFC	DCFNet	Staple	DCF$_{CA}$	LCT
OTB-2013	90.5	83.7	82.2	80.3	79.5	79.3	78.4	84.8
OTB-2015	89.2	79.8	77.7	77.1	75.1	78.4	74.4	76.2
OTB-50	86.6	75.2	72.3	69.4	68.3	68.1	71.2	69.1
Avg. DPR	88.8	79.6	77.4	75.6	74.3	75.3	74.7	76.7
Avg. FPS	20.6*	66.8*	67.0*	86.0*	65.0*	48.3	179.2	21.0

accuracy (86.6%) on OTB-50 followed by MSC-DCF (75.2%). For the average DPR, the best two results belong to our MSC-trackers, followed by CFNet (77.4%) and SiamFC (75.6%). This comparison highlights the high accuracy achieved by our tracker among the state-of-the-art real-time trackers. The average tracking speed of different trackers are also reported in Table 2. Compared with other trackers, MSC-DCF achieves the fast tracking speed of 66.8 FPS while demonstrating its competitive tracking performance. In addition, higher accuracy of MSC-CCO is obtained at the cost of lower speed compared to MSC-DCF, but MSC-CCO still maintains quasi-real-time tracking speed of 20.6 FPS.

5.3   Comparison with Deep Feature-Based Trackers

We compare the proposed MSC-trackers with 6 state-of-the-art deep feature-based CF trackers: CCOT [9], MCPF [33], CREST [27], DeepSRDCF [7], CF2 [20] and HDT [24].

Figure 5 and Table 3 show the comparison of our MSC-trackers with several deep CF trackers with deep features on OTB datasets. More particularly, the

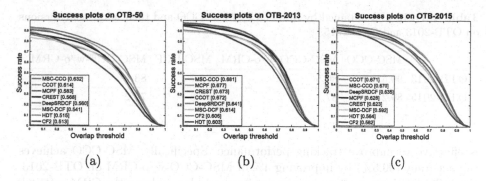

(a)   (b)   (c)

Fig. 5. Success plots obtained by the proposed MSC-trackers (MSC-CCO and MSC-DCF) and the top-performing deep feature-based CF trackers on (a) OTB-50, (b) OTB-2013 and (c) OTB-2015. AUCs are illustrated in brackets.

Table 3. OSRs (%) and speed (* indicates the GPU speed, otherwise the CPU speed) obtained by MSC-CCO and MSC-DCF as well as the state-of-the-art deep feature-based CF trackers on OTB-2013, OTB-2015 and OTB-50. The first, second and third best trackers are highlighted in color.

	MSC-CCO	MSC-DCF	CCOT	MCPF	DeepSRDCF	HDT	CF2	CREST
OTB-2013	83.7	78.3	83.2	85.8	79.4	73.7	74.0	86.0
OTB-2015	82.1	73.3	82.0	78.0	77.2	65.7	65.5	77.6
OTB-50	77.6	67.1	74.9	71.0	67.6	58.4	58.2	70.5
Avg. OSR	81.1	72.9	80.0	78.3	74.7	65.9	65.9	78.0
Avg. FPS	20.6*	66.8*	0.22*	0.56*	<1.0*	11.1*	10.5*	1.0*

AUC and OSR obtained by MSC-DCF are higher than those obtained by CF2 and HDT. MSC-CCO achieves the best OSR (77.6%) on OTB-50, significantly outperforming the second best tracker CCOT with a large margin of 2.7%. Furthermore, the average OSR obtained by MSC-CCO is 81.1%, which is ranked at the first and followed by CCOT (80.0%) and MCPF (78.3%). In terms of the tracking speed reported in Table 5, compared with the other deep feature based trackers, MSC-DCF can run at 66.8 FPS, which is significantly faster than the compared trackers. In addition, MSC-CCO achieves the quasi-real-time tracking speed of 20.6 FPS, which is almost 94 times faster than CCOT and 37 times faster than MCPF. In the meanwhile, MSC-CCO achieves the best overall performance over all the three datasets.

5.4   Ablation Study

To demonstrate the effectiveness of the proposed CRM method, we evaluate MSC-DCF and MSC-CCO with additional versions, i.e., MSC-DCF and MSC-CCO without using the CRM method, namely MSC-DCF-w/o-CRM and MSC-CCO-w/o-CRM, respectively. As can be seen from Table 4, the CRM method

Table 4. DPRs (%) obtained by MSC-DCF, MSC-CCO and their additional versions on OTB-2013 and OTB-2015.

	MSC-CCO	MSC-CCO-w/o-CRM	MSC-DCF	MSC-DCF-w/o-CRM
OTB-2013	90.5	86.5	83.7	83.1
OTB-2015	89.2	87.1	79.8	79.2

is effective to improve tracking performance. Specifically, MSC-CCO achieves the accuracy (90.5%) by improving 4% of MSC-CCO-w/o-CRM on OTB-2013. For MSC-DCF, the performance is also improved by applying the CRM method. These results demonstrate the effectiveness of the CRM method, which is mainly due to the fact that the CRM method filters the feature channels that are more sensitive to the background regions while retaining the high-quality channels that are more beneficial for robust visual tracking.

6   Conclusions

In this work, we propose a deep and shallow feature learning network (called as DSNet) to learn the multi-level same-resolution compressed (MSC) features, which effectively incorporate both deep and shallow features with the same spatial resolution for efficient online tracking. The proposed DSNet compresses multi-layer convolutional features and can be effectively trained in an end-to-end offline manner. The MSC features are generic and can be easily applied to any CF-based trackers. In addition, we propose an effective channel reliability measurement method to further refine the learned MSC features. To demonstrate the effectiveness of our MSC features, two MSC features based trackers are presented, namely MSC-DCF and MSC-CCO, respectively. Experiments on several large scale benchmarks show that the proposed methods perform favorably against state-of-the-art tracking methods.

Acknowledgments. This work is supported by the National Natural Science of China (Grant No. U1605252, 61872307, 61472334 and 61571379) and the National Key Research and Development Program of China under Grant No. 2017YFB1302400.

References

1. Bertinetto, L., Valmadre, J., Golodetz, S., Miksik, O., Torr, P.H.S.: Staple: complementary learners for real-time tracking. In: Computer Vision and Pattern Recognition (CVPR), pp. 1401–1409 (2016)
2. Bertinetto, L., Valmadre, J., Henriques, J.F., Vedaldi, A., Torr, P.H.S.: Fully-convolutional siamese networks for object tracking. In: Hua, G., Jégou, H. (eds.) ECCV 2016. LNCS, vol. 9914, pp. 850–865. Springer, Cham (2016). https://doi.org/10.1007/978-3-319-48881-3_56

3. Bolme, D.S., Beveridge, J.R., Draper, B.A., Lui, Y.M.: Visual object tracking using adaptive correlation filters. In: Computer Vision and Pattern Recognition (CVPR), pp. 2544–2550 (2010)
4. Chatfield, K., Simonyan, K., Vedaldi, A., Zisserman, A.: Return of the devil in the details: delving deep into convolutional nets (2014). arXiv preprint arxiv:1405.3531
5. Dalal, N., Triggs, B.: Histograms of oriented gradients for human detection. In: Computer Vision and Pattern Recognition (CVPR), pp. 886–893 (2005)
6. Danelljan, M., Bhat, G., Khan, F.S., Felsberg, M.: ECO: efficient convolution operators for tracking. In: Computer Vision and Pattern Recognition (CVPR), pp. 21–26 (2017)
7. Danelljan, M., Hager, G., Khan, F.S., Felsberg, M.: Convolutional features for correlation filter based visual tracking. In: International Conference on Computer Vision Workshops, pp. 58–66 (2015)
8. Danelljan, M., Häger, G., Khan, F.S., Felsberg, M.: Discriminative scale space tracking. IEEE Trans. Pattern Anal. Mach. Intell. **39**(8), 1561–1575 (2017)
9. Danelljan, M., Robinson, A., Shahbaz Khan, F., Felsberg, M.: Beyond correlation filters: learning continuous convolution operators for visual tracking. In: Leibe, B., Matas, J., Sebe, N., Welling, M. (eds.) ECCV 2016. LNCS, vol. 9909, pp. 472–488. Springer, Cham (2016). https://doi.org/10.1007/978-3-319-46454-1_29
10. Girshick, R., Donahue, J., Darrell, T., Malik, J.: Rich feature hierarchies for accurate object detection and semantic segmentation. In: Computer Vision and Pattern Recognition (CVPR), pp. 580–587 (2014)
11. Gorden, D., Farhadi, A., Fox, D.: Re3: real-time recurrent regression networks for object tracking (2017). arXiv preprint arxiv:1705.06368
12. Gundogdu, E., Alatan, A.A.: Good features to correlate for visual tracking (2017). arXiv preprint arxiv:1704.06326
13. He, K., Zhang, X., Ren, S., Sun, J.: Deep residual learning for image recognition. In: Computer Vision and Pattern Recognition (CVPR), pp. 770–778 (2016)
14. Held, D., Thrun, S., Savarese, S.: Learning to track at 100 fps with deep regression networks. In: Leibe, B., Matas, J., Sebe, N., Welling, M. (eds.) ECCV 2016. LNCS, vol. 9905, pp. 749–765. Springer, Cham (2016). https://doi.org/10.1007/978-3-319-46448-0_45
15. Henriques, J.F., Caseiro, R., Martins, P., Batista, J.: High-speed tracking with kernelized correlation filters. IEEE Trans. Pattern Anal. Mach. Intell. **37**(3), 583–596 (2015)
16. Kalal, Z., Mikolajczyk, K., Matas, J.: Tracking-learning-detection. IEEE Trans. Pattern Anal. Mach. Intell. **34**(7), 1409–1422 (2012)
17. Kong, T., Yao, A., Chen, Y., Sun, F.: HyperNet: towards accurate region proposal generation and joint object detection. In: Computer Vision and Pattern Recognition (CVPR), pp. 845–853 (2016)
18. Krizhevsky, A., Sutskever, I., Hinton, G.E.: ImageNet classification with deep convolutional neural networks. In: Advances in Neural Information Processing Systems (NIPS), pp. 1097–1105 (2012)
19. Liu, W., et al.: SSD: single shot multibox detector. In: Leibe, B., Matas, J., Sebe, N., Welling, M. (eds.) ECCV 2016. LNCS, vol. 9905, pp. 21–37. Springer, Cham (2016). https://doi.org/10.1007/978-3-319-46448-0_2
20. Ma, C., Huang, J.B., Yang, X., Yang, M.H.: Hierarchical convolutional features for visual tracking. In: International Conference on Computer Vision (ICCV), pp. 3074–3082 (2015)
21. Ma, C., Yang, X., Zhang, C., Yang, M.H.: Long-term correlation tracking. In: Computer Vision and Pattern Recognition (CVPR), pp. 5388–5396 (2015)

22. Mueller, M., Smith, N., Ghanem, B.: Context-aware correlation filter tracking. In: Computer Vision and Pattern Recognition (CVPR), pp. 1387–1395 (2017)
23. Noh, H., Hong, S., Han, B.: Learning deconvolution network for semantic segmentation. In: International Conference on Computer Vision (ICCV), pp. 1520–1528 (2015)
24. Qi, Y., et al.: Hedged deep tracking. In: Computer Vision and Pattern Recognition (CVPR), pp. 4303–4311 (2016)
25. Redmon, J., Divvala, S., Girshick, R., Farhadi, A.: You only look once: unified, real-time object detection. In: Computer Vision and Pattern Recognition (CVPR), pp. 779–788 (2016)
26. Russakovsky, O., Deng, J.: ImageNet large scale visual recognition challenge. Int. J. Comput. Vis. **115**(3), 211–252 (2015)
27. Song, Y., Ma, C., Gong, L., Zhang, J., Lau, R.W., Yang, M.H.: CREST: convolutional residual learning for visual tracking. In: International Conference on Computer Vision (ICCV), pp. 2574–2583 (2017)
28. Valmadre, J., Bertinetto, L., Henriques, J., Vedaldi, A., Torr, P.H.S.: End-to-end representation learning for correlation filter based tracking. In: Computer Vision and Pattern Recognition (CVPR), pp. 5000–5008 (2017)
29. Wang, Q., Gao, J., Xing, J., Zhang, M., Hu, W.: DCFNet: discriminant correlation filters network for visual tracking (2017). arXiv preprint arxiv:1704.04057
30. Weijer, J.V.D., Schmid, C., Verbeek, J., Larlus, D.: Learning color names for real-world applications. IEEE Trans. Image Process. **18**(7), 1512–1523 (2009)
31. Wu, Y., Lim, J., Yang, M.H.: Online object tracking: a benchmark. In: Computer Vision and Pattern Recognition (CVPR), pp. 2411–2418 (2013)
32. Wu, Y., Lim, J., Yang, M.H.: Object tracking benchmark. IEEE Trans. Pattern Anal. Mach. Intell. **37**(9), 1834–1848 (2015)
33. Zhang, T., Xu, C., Yang, M.H.: Multi-task correlation particle filter for robust object tracking. In: Computer Vision and Pattern Recognition (CVPR), pp. 4819–4827 (2017)

Back-Projection Lightweight Network for Accurate Image Super Resolution

Chia-Yang Chang[✉] and Shao-Yi Chien

Media IC and System Lab, Graduate Institute of Electronics Engineering,
National Taiwan University, Taipei, Taiwan
cychang@media.ee.ntu.edu.tw, sychien@ntu.edu.tw

Abstract. Recently, deep neural networks have led to tremendous advances in image super-resolution and achieved remarkable results. However, most deep learning methods attain appreciable performance by increasing model parameters and complexity. Consequently, they are difficult to utilize in common devices despite significant results. With respect to application in resource-limited devices, the goal of the present study involves designing a compact network that exhibits good scalability. We proposed a back projection network (BPnet) as we were inspired by a traditional image super-resolution technique, namely iterative back projection (IBP). Our proposed network is composed of different modules. Each module performs the enlarging function based on the result of the previous module, which is similar to an iteration in IBP. The input of each module network corresponds to the previous down-sampled output minus the low-resolution input image. Additionally, the output of the network is the residual between the ground truth high-resolution image and previous output. The non-linear property of a neural network is maximized through the sparsity of residual input/output. Thus, we can achieve a lightweight network without sacrificing the quality of the results. The experiments indicate that the number of parameters of the proposed BPnet can be less than quarter of those proposed in the state-of-the-art papers and still have comparable results.

1 Introduction

The aim of single image super-resolution (SISR) involves boosting resolution of a low-resolution image. The technology is widely used in surveillance, satellite, and medical cameras. Additionally, it is an important tool to enhance old pictures. In order to tackle the problem, numerous SISR methods were proposed over the last few decades. They include interpolation-based, self-similarity-based [5,12], and dictionary-based methods [25,30,34].

Recently, deep learning achieved significant success in different computer vision areas. Several deep learning based SISR methods were examined. First, Dong *et al.* proposed SRCNN [3] that exhibits a simple three-layer structure. Although the performance improvement is limited, SRCNN inspired several convolutional neural network(CNN) methods. Subsequently, Kim *et al.* reinvestigated neural network properties and proposed the VDSR [17] net that

© Springer Nature Switzerland AG 2019
C. V. Jawahar et al. (Eds.): ACCV 2018, LNCS 11365, pp. 135–151, 2019.
https://doi.org/10.1007/978-3-030-20873-8_9

contains global skip connection and trains with adjustable gradient clipping. The aforementioned technologies exhibit significant improvements in performance and are widely explored in follow-up research. In order to further increase network capacity and ease training difficulty, a few advanced neural network techniques appear in the super-resolution network. Zhang et al. [35] used the Batch-Norm [14] layer in VDSR, and Jiao et al. proposed a similar idea in a general residual form [16]. As opposed to pooling and unpooling layers, Mao et al. used convolutional and deconvolutional layers to design an encoder–decoder network [24]. The well-known ResNet [10] is also adapted for image regression [21,23] and achieves state-of-the-art results. Recently, two different architectures [33,37] are proposed based on DenseNet [11]. Furthermore, a few networks are also constructed based on traditional image processing methods. Lai et al. developed LapSRN [20] from the laplacian pyramid, and LapSRN exhibits good ability with respect to a large scaling factor. Haris et al. proposed DPBN [8] which up-scales and down-scales hidden features iteratively.

Based on the recent studies on challenges with respect to super-resolution [29, 32], improvements in the performance of deep networks have led to increases in their depth. The high number of parameters constitutes a practical problem. Kim et al. first proposed the recursive method for image super-resolution. They folded VDSR into a single convolutional layer with the exception of feature extraction and reconstruction layers. Although the recurrent network was adapted, the parameters exceed those of the VDSR. Subsequently, Tai et al. proposed DRRN [27]. The DRRN contains multi-path local skip connections and recursive units. Based on the DRRN, Tai et al. proposed MemNet [28]. Dense connections exist between recursive units in MemNet. Additionally, the latest hidden features of each recursive unit are concatenated to reconstruct a better final image. Despite the fact that the number of parameters in the network are significantly reduced by DRRN and MemNet, the demand of multiply-accumulates (MACs) increases. This is because the number of convolutions in the inference phase increases.

Conversely, a low-cost network is proposed to tackle the aforementioned problem. Specifically, FSRCNN [4] proposed by Dong et al. is a compact model of SRCNN. They attempt to reduce feature channels in the hidden layers and avoid pre-upscaling the input image. Shi et al. also constructed a compact model termed as ESPCN [26] that only exhibits two convolutional layers and a sub-pixel layer. Both FSRCNN and ESPCN exhibit a reasonable count of parameters and MACs. However, the quality of their super-resolved images is also not comparable to that of deeper models.

In order to achieve a lightweight model with adequate quality, we re-inspect network model capacity. The reason as to why VDSR achieves significant results corresponds to the global skip connection. Thus, it is necessary for the network to only predict the residual between ground-truth and approximate up-sampled image. The sparse residual reduces the complexity of mapping the input to output. Bae et al. [1] used persistent homology to prove the aforementioned property and realized that it improves furthermore if the input is also sparse. Therefore, they used wavelet transform to decompose the input into four parts. However, the

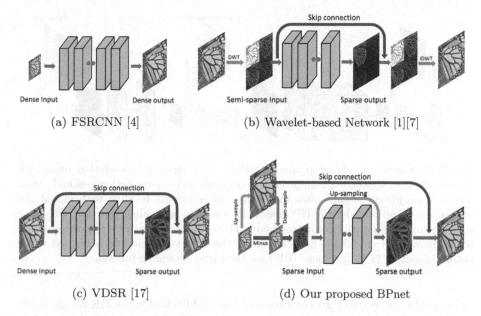

(a) FSRCNN [4]   (b) Wavelet-based Network [1][7]

(c) VDSR [17]   (d) Our proposed BPnet

Fig. 1. This figure concludes different type of input/output. (a) illustrates the direct end-to-end learning methods. Either pre-upsampling [3] or not, the input and output are also dense images. In (c), the global skip connection simplifies the output to the residual frame. It is the popular style in major literature [29,32]. The (b) shows the wavelet-based methods. Based on global skip connection, this type further reduce the complexity of input. Considering there still low-frequency information in any signal transformation, we use the self-constraint to obtain a fully sparse input. The flow chart of our proposed schemes is shown in (d).

low-frequency part still corresponds to a dense image, and the quality improvement is also limited. Inspired by traditional iterative back-projection(IBP) [15], we determined that the image input can correspond to its own residual. By performing down-sample after up-sample, the result exhibits a minor difference to input low-resolution image. Specifically, in the flat region, the difference is almost zero. The IBP up-samples the difference and adds back to the previous result for further enhancement. The most used up-sampling function in IBP corresponds to the bicubic function [31]. Thus, we adapt CNN to learn a better mapping function to replace bicubic interpolation. Given the sparsity, the network maps the input to output well without massive parameters and MACs. The experiments indicate that the proposed method uses a shallow network to achieve the performance of a deep network in which the input corresponds to a dense image. Figure 1 shows the differences in the input/output between the proposed model and other models.

Furthermore, based on the iterative step of IBP, we construct the full model in a module-based manner. Figure 2 shows an overview of the complete model. The output of each network module adds to the previous super-resolved result to

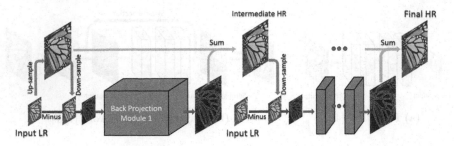

Fig. 2. The overview of our proposed BPnet. The input low-resolution image will first produce an approximate high-resolution image and low-resolution residual. Then, the back projection module aims to enlarge low-resolution residual with global skip connection. If we consider the BP module as a mature up-scaling function, the whole step is similar to iterative back projection. Then, the iterations of IBP corresponding to the number of modules. The difference is that our every module is trained as the optimal function to its iteration; IBP uses the same up-scaling function.

improve the successive high-resolution image. Additionally, the HR image down-samples to low-resolution and computes the residual for the adjacent module. Each module is considered as one iteration of IBP. Furthermore, the outputs of each module are supervised by the ground-truth high-resolution image. The strategy is also analogous to deep-supervision and is proven to aid the large scaling factor [20].

In summary, the main contributions of the study are as follows:

1. **Scalability.** Given the module-based design, our whole network exhibits good scalability. The function of each module involves enhancing the previous high-resolution output. It can be bypassed if the quality of the previous output image is desirable or the computing resources are limited.
2. **Residual to residual learning.** To the best of our knowledge, it is the first network that uses residual to residual learning. As shown in Fig. 1, in a manner different from the pre-defined decomposition such as wavelet or discrete cosine transform, the residual corresponds to difference up-sampling followed by down-sampling. It can be entirely sparse. When combined with module-based design, our complete model can be considered as deep-learning IBP.
3. **Lightweight network.** Benefit from residual to residual learning, the power of the proposed network concentrates on where the residual is not zero. The non-zero regions almost correspond to the high-frequency part of an image. The optimization of network capacity to handle a difficult region is conducive to minimizing the counts of the parameter and MACs. The whole model achieves state-of-the-art results with a lightweight network.

2   Related Work

Section 1 includes a brief introduction on neural network based super-resolution methods. In this section, we discuss related works in detail including lightweight/low-cost network, special domain based network, and iterative back projection.

2.1   Lightweight/Low-Cost Network

As previously mentioned, the recursive method exhibits the ability to reduce the count of parameters. However, the demand for MACs still exists. A few resource-limited devices, such as mobile phone, surveillance cameras, or digital TVs, do not handle massive computing. Specifically, FSCRNN [4] attempts to address the problem via compressing hidden feature channels. After the first feature extraction convolutional layer, the hidden features feed into a 1×1 convolutional layer. The feature channels are reduced from 56 to 12, and the total number of parameters approximately correspond to a quarter that of SRCNN [3]. Additionally, the run-time of FSRCNN is 40 times faster than that of SRCNN. Conversely, the aim of ESPCN [26] involves using shallow network architecture for parameters and computational reduction. There are only two convolutional layers and one sub-pixel layer in ESPCN. The count of parameters and MACs almost corresponds to the same order as FSRCNN. The sub-pixel layer is considered as a compact version of a deconvolutional layer. Based on that, Shi *et al.* extends ESPCN to a video super-resolution version [2]. Both ESPCN and FSRCNN share an identical key factor in which the input image does not pre-upscale to a high resolution via a certain pre-defined up-sampling function. Hence, the dimension of hidden features remains in a low-resolution scale. However, given the limited parameters, it is not possible to compare the results to those of deeper models such as VDSR and DRRN.

Similarly, Liang *et al.* proposed a lightweight network [22] "R-basic" based on ResBlock [10] and monotonically increased shape. However, the result of R-basic is worse than that of VDSR, and the parameters remain in the order of a million.

2.2   Special Domain Based Network

Kim *et al.* commenced from an end-to-end learning network termed as SRCNN and determined that the mapping of a dense image is complicated for a neural network. Therefore, they added the global skip connection to deal with the problem. Thus, the network focused on the residual as opposed to a whole image. The same issue was discussed in traditional dictionary-based [34] and regressor-based methods [25,30]. The residual is considered as a collapsed manifold when compared with the original image. Thus, mapping to residual exhibits less complexity than end-to-end training. The global skip connection is widely used in a super-resolution network [27,29,32] to increase quality.

Beyond empirical research, Bae *et al.* measured topological complexity [1] to theoretically prove why the global residual connection works well. Moreover, prior to feeding into a neural network, they first applied discrete wavelet transformation (DWT) to the input image. The network is trained to predict the wavelet residual from the input wavelet image. Zero dimensional barcodes indicated that transformed input exhibited less topological complexity when compared with that of the original image. Similarly, Gue *et al.* also used the wavelet transformation to simplify the network input. The results indicated that the wavelet network [7,29] extends beyond VDSR with half depth.

In addition to the wavelet transform, Guo *et al.* recently proposed the ORDSR [6]. Specifically, the ORDSR exploits discrete cosine transform (DCT) as an input transformation and rearranges the DCT coefficient with a zig-zag order. However, the sparsity of DCT is weaker than that of the DWT. This was proven in the compression standard (JPEG vs. JPEG2000). The ORDSR requires three-quarter the depth of VDSR to achieve the same performance. This indicates the importance of input sparsity.

2.3   Iterative Back Projection

Iterative back projection [15] was proposed by Irani *et al.* to enhance multi-frame super-resolution. It also acts as a useful refinement for single image super-resolution to minimize reconstruction error. Specifically, IBP employs iterative down-sampling of the super-resolution result and adds back the up-sampling residual to constrain the final reconstruction in a manner consistent with the input low-resolution image. Although it is necessary to know the exact down-sampling kernel in the original function, a few studies [12] demonstrate that the direct use of bicubic or bilinear up-/down-sampling still exhibits a good performance. Additionally, Timofte *et al.* indicated that IBP further improved the super-resolution result as a post-processing method for learning approaches including SRCNN.

Zhang *et al.* presented a convex function with reconstruction error and regularization error in [36]. After inferring the convex function and solving it via gradient descent, each iteration to reduce the reconstruction error corresponds to the same operator of IBP. This numerically proves that back projection reduces the reconstruction error of super-resolved results. Therefore, we formulate the IBP refinement into our BPnet to enhance our results in a step by step manner.

3   Proposed Method

In this section, we first describe the design methodology of the proposed back projection model. Subsequently, we introduce the details of the module, the connection between modules, and the loss function with deep supervision. We then present a few training and implementation details.

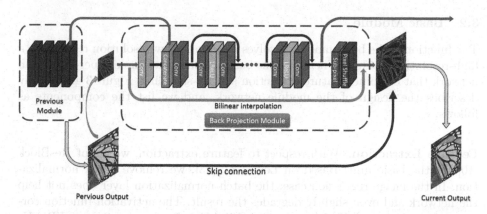

Fig. 3. Overview of our proposed BP module. The structure of our BP module is simple but effective. First, we use one convolutional layer to extract features and concatenate them with the hidden features from the previous module. It is an effective strategy. Subsequently, we compress the feature channels with 1×1 convolution to avoid the network parameters growth. After passing through some ResBlocks, the sub-pixel layer up-scale to high-resolution dimension.

3.1   Back Projection Net

As previously mentioned, we construct our complete model to emulate iterative back projection. Each stage of our model can be considered as a step in IBP. As shown in Fig. 2, an input low-resolution image is first enlarged to a high-resolution approximation via a simple up-scale function. Additionally, the approximation HR image down-samples back to low-resolution dimension. Hence, the low resolution residual is the difference between the input LR image and approximation LR image. As discussed in Sect. 2.3, the up-/down-sample methods that are used need not be identical to exact ones. Subsequently, the low-resolution residual corresponds to the input of the module network. The output of the module network corresponds to the high-resolution residual. The final high-resolution image of a module is the sum of high-resolution approximation image, up-sampled input low-resolution residual, and high-resolution residual. We add global skip connections in a module network to further simplify the network output.

Following the first module, the first high-resolution result replaces the high-resolution approximation. The down-sampled approximation in the following modules is attributed to the previous result. Additionally, the previous result is a part of the next high-resolution image. The proposed BPnet can contain a couple of basic modules. The exact number of modules depends on the task or computing resources; and there is a discussion in Sect. 4.1.

3.2   Basic Module

The function of the basic module involves mapping a low-resolution residual to a high-resolution residual. Therefore, the basic module is a simple super-resolution network that combines feature extraction and up-sampling. Figure 3 graphically describes the design of the module network, and we list the components as follows:

Feature Extraction. With respect to feature extraction, we adapt ResBlock [10] for the basic unit. Based on Lee *et al.* [23], we remove batch normalization. In the image regression case, the batch normalization layer does not help the network and even slightly degrades the result. The activation function corresponds to leaky rectified linear units (LReLUs). In the experiment, LReLUs with a negative slope of 0.2 out-performs other activation functions in the proposed model. This is due to the fact that the input and output of the module network are both sparse, and thus it is not necessary to cascade a large number of ResBlocks. Conversely, we prefer to increase the module units. The count of the module units aids in enhancing the final super-resolution image.

Upsampling Layer. As in a few previous studies [4,20,26], the input of our module network is low-resolution although the output is high-resolution. There are several options to tackle the problem including the convolutional transposed layer, sub-pixel layer, and un-pooling layer followed by convolution. Un-pooling layer followed by convolution is not suitable for our purpose since it processes in a high-resolution dimension. Finally, we select the sub-pixel layer although the convolutional transposed layer can substitute for the same.

Feature Concatenate. With respect to fully leveraging each module, the hidden features before the sub-pixel layer act as a good hint for successive module. Borrowing the idea from DRCN [18] and MemNet [28], we concatenate the last hidden features of the previous module to the present one. Subsequently, a 1×1 convolutional layer reduces the feature channels. It avoids the growth of the parameters. The concatenation position can correspond to hidden features after the first convolution or before the sub-pixel layer. Additionally, we can either concatenate the hidden features only from the previous one or from all of the preceding modules. Based on our experiments, if we concatenate the hidden features only from the previous module to the first layer, then there are improvements in the final image. In Sect. 4.1, we analyze different concatenation methods in detail.

Loss Function. In a manner different from other super-resolution networks, each module of our entire back projection model produces a high-resolution image. In most cases, only the latest one is our goal, and the loss function focuses on the goal. However, we refer to deep-supervision and we penalize all the intermediate outputs in the loss function. As opposed to minimizing the mean square error (MSE) loss, we select the ℓ_1-loss as our final objective function since ℓ_1-loss is better than MSE-loss in our experiments.

3.3   Implementation Detail

In the proposed back projection net, either the convolutional layer or sub-pixel layer exhibits the same spatial support 3×3. The filter number of the sub-pixel layer depends on the scaling factor [23]. Subsequently, the filter number and layer number of the convolutional layer correspond to the design factor. We performed a few ablation studies and discussed in Sect. 4.1. With respect to the down-sample layer, we use average pooling with the same spatial support as scaling factor. The average pooling exhibits the same functionality as bilinear downsampling, and thus we use bilinear interpolation as our up-sampling method. Both the down-sample and up-sample layer are derivatives, and therefore the entire back projection model can be fully trained.

Recently, Timofte *et al.* proposed the DIV2K dataset that consists of 800 high-quality training images, 100 validation images, and 100 testing images. In a manner similar to several extant studies [8,23,37] and super-resolution image challenge [29,32], we also select it as our training data. Additionally, we use traditional training dataset (BSDS200, Train91) to fine-tune our BPnet. We found that the strong textures and edges in Train91 aided in improving the accuracy of the network. We generate low-resolution image with a MATLAB built-in bicubic down-sample function. In each batch, we randomly sample 64 sub-images with a size of 32×32 from low-resolution images. The size of the corresponding high-resolution sub-images depends on the scaling factor. There are approximately 8,000 iterations in one epoch. With respect to a few ablation studies, we only use half of the training data to accelerate the training process. The optimizer we used is Adam [19] by setting $\beta_1 = 0.9$, $\beta_2 = 0.999$, and $\epsilon = 10^{-8}$. The learning rate begins at 10^{-5} and is halved every 5 epochs. The weights of all the filters are initialized by [9], and biases are set to zeros.

4   Experimental Result

We first analyze the properties of the proposed BPnet. It includes the number of filters, layers, and modules, loss function design, and concatenation strategies. Subsequently, we compare our back projection network with the state-of-the-art algorithms on standard benchmark datasets and discuss model complexities.

4.1   Network Properties

Network Parameters. In most cases, increases in the network parameters are effective in enhancing network accuracy. With respect to our back projection network, there are three methods to increase parameters as follows: cascading

Table 1. This table summarizes the performance gain of parameter settings. In the first experiment, we fix two of the settings and change the last setting. The other experiment is the comparison between the number of modules and ResBlocks. We use different settings to obtain the same depth model.

	Set5, scaling factor = 3							Set5, sf = 4		
Modules	1	2	3	3	3	3	3	2	3	4
ResBlocks	2	2	2	3	4	2	2	6	4	3
Filters	64	64	64	64	64	32	128	64	64	64
PSNR (dB)	33.72	33.97	34.07	34.15	34.19	33.82	34.20	31.84	31.96	32.05

more modules, stacking more ResBlock in each module, and increasing the filter number for each layer. We analyze the aforementioned three methods and summarize the same in Table 1.

The first experiment is the quantitative test of the different factors. It is observed that increasing the modules, ResBlock, or filters strengthens the performance. An interesting observation corresponds to "the deeper, the better." In the proposed BPnet, either cascading more modules or increasing the ResBlocks in each module attains a deeper model. The main difference is that cascading modules collapse hidden features back to the image in adjacent modules. However, with the aid of feature concatenation and deep supervision, the performance of the cascading module extends beyond increasing the ResBlocks in each module. This is more noticeable in the hard case (e.g. 4× super-resolution).

Loss Function Design. As discussed in Sect. 3.2, the high-resolution images from each module can be supervised via ground truth image. We indicated the effectiveness of deep supervision in Table 1. In the quantitative experiment, the final results with deep supervision are 0.07 dB higher than those without it. Another advantage of deep supervision is that the whole model is modular. The high-resolution of each module corresponds to the final output if the computing resource of a device is limited. Figure 4 shows the input/output of each module in a four-modules-net.

Concatenation Strategies. The hidden features of the previous module are advantageous. Specifically, when the number of ResBlocks in a module is low, the feature extraction of modules is not sufficient. It is necessary to concatenate hidden features to optimize the successive module. We evaluate different concatenation strategies in Set5 with a scale factor of 3. First, the average PSNR is approximately 33.58 dB if we do not concatenate hidden features. The concatenation of all the previous hidden features in the last layer of the present module increases the PSNR to 33.82 dB. Subsequently, if we concatenate the previous hidden feature or all the preceding hidden features in the first layer, then the PSNR corresponds to 34.11 dB and 34.09 dB, respectively. We consider that concatenating hidden features in the first layer as equivalent to increasing

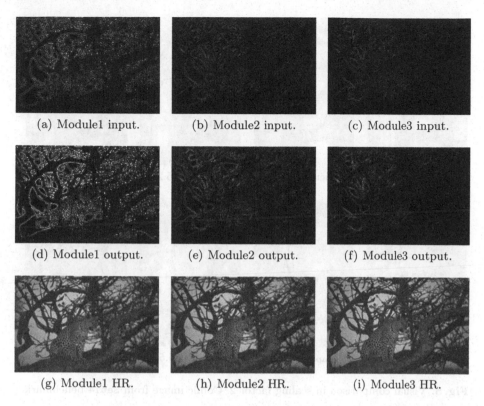

(a) Module1 input.   (b) Module2 input.   (c) Module3 input.

(d) Module1 output.   (e) Module2 output.   (f) Module3 output.

(g) Module1 HR.   (h) Module2 HR.   (i) Module3 HR.

Fig. 4. We visualize each module input and output in this figure. After the first module, the input and output become quite spares. This property helps the module network focus on the important part of the image.

the receptive field. The performance increase is significant when compared to the concatenation of the last layer.

4.2 Performance Evaluation

In this section, we compare our proposed BP model to existing neural network super-resolution methods including SRCNN [3], FSRCNN [4], VDSR [17], DRCN [18], LapSRN [20], DRRN [27], MemNet [28], and IDN [13]. We construct three different types of models. The first model corresponds to the normal model, and it contains three modules and two ResBlocks in each module. The model is denoted as BP-normal. Another model corresponds to the light model, and it includes two modules. Furthermore, each module also exhibits two ResBlocks. We let BP-light denote the light model. The BP-light model is actually a part of the BP-normal. We remove the last module to demonstrate the scalability of our proposed model. The filter size of both BP-normal and BP-light corresponds to 64. The final model corresponds to an ultralight model, which is termed as BP-ultralight. The BP-ultralight includes only one module

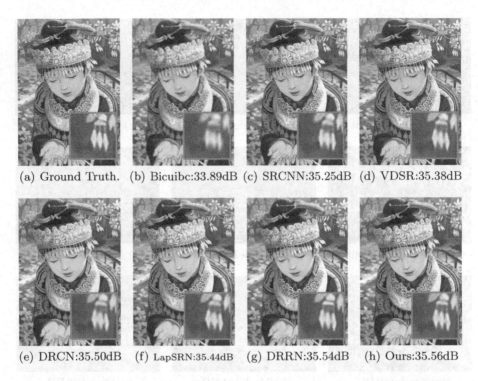

(a) Ground Truth. (b) Bicuibc:33.89dB (c) SRCNN:35.25dB (d) VDSR:35.38dB

(e) DRCN:35.50dB (f) LapSRN:35.44dB (g) DRRN:35.54dB (h) Ours:35.56dB

Fig. 5. Visual comparison in scaling factor 2. Comic image from Set14 benchmark.

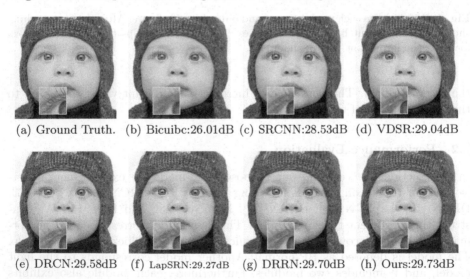

(a) Ground Truth. (b) Bicuibc:26.01dB (c) SRCNN:28.53dB (d) VDSR:29.04dB

(e) DRCN:29.58dB (f) LapSRN:29.27dB (g) DRRN:29.70dB (h) Ours:29.73dB

Fig. 6. Visual comparison in scaling factor 3. Baby image from Set5 benchmark.

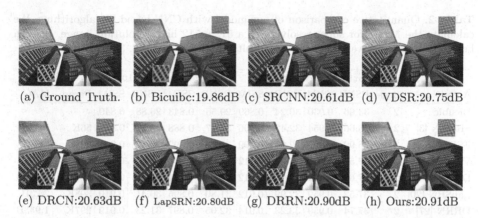

(a) Ground Truth. (b) Bicuibc:19.86dB (c) SRCNN:20.61dB (d) VDSR:20.75dB

(e) DRCN:20.63dB (f) LapSRN:20.80dB (g) DRRN:20.90dB (h) Ours:20.91dB

Fig. 7. Visual comparison in scaling factor 4. 62 image from Urban100 benchmark. (Color figure online)

and three ResBlocks. Furthermore, the filter size in BP-ultralight is only 32. This indicates that BP-ultralight corresponds to the alternative SRResNet [21] with sparse input. We compared 2, 3, and 4 scaling factors in Set5, Set14, B100, and Urban100 datasets.

Table 2 summarizes the objective measurement. Additionally, we compare the parameters and multiply-accumulate (MAC) of our proposed BP-net with those of existing algorithms. We assume that the dimension of the output super-resolution image is 512×512. All the existing algorithms with the exception of FSRCNN require billion-level MACs. A few methods need trillion-level MACs. Our proposed BPnet only requires MACs that are less by a factor of ten when compared with that in the aforementioned algorithms. We note that the proposed method does not perform well in the Urban100 benchmark. Specifically, there is a more significant decrease in the quality of BP-light and BP-ultralight when compared with that of the BP-normal. This is potentially caused by the repeated structure in the urban scene, which produces aliasing artifacts while down-sampling the repeated scene. The aliasing area sometimes exceeds our receptive field since it does not exhibit a very deep structure. The DRRN and MemNet exhibit relatively deeper structures (52 layers and 80 layers), and thus they handle the urban scene well. We show the visual comparison in Figs. 5, 6, and 7. In the 2× and 3× visual comparison, the proposed BPnet exhibits a more sharp edge when compared with other algorithms. This is potentially due to the iterative back projection strategy. A case of failure of our BP-net was also observed in Fig. 7. This corresponds to a difficult case from the urban scene. In the yellow window, the proposed BPnet also generates a sharper edge. However, in the blue window, the proposed BPnet produces a more serious aliasing artifact when compared with the deeper models.

Table 2. Quantitative comparison of our model with CNN-based SR algorithms. We calculate the MACs for super-resolving to a 512×512 high resolution image. In each benchmark dataset, we evaluation the results of scaling factor 2, 3, and 4.

Algorithm	Scale	Set5		Set14		B100		Urban100		Param.	MAC
		PSNR	SSIM	PSNR	SSIM	PSNR	SSIM	PSNR	SSIM		
Bicubic	2	33.66	0.930	30.24	0.869	29.56	0.843	26.88	0.840	-	-
SRCNN [3]	2	36.66	0.954	32.42	0.906	31.37	0.888	29.53	0.895	56K	14.8B
FSRCNN [4]	2	36.99	0.955	32.63	0.909	31.52	0.892	29.87	0.901	12K	817M
VDSR [17]	2	37.53	0.959	33.03	0.912	31.90	0.896	30.76	0.914	665K	174B
DRCN [18]	2	37.63	0.959	33.04	0.912	31.85	0.894	30.75	0.913	1774K	2,939B
LapSRN [20]	2	37.52	0.959	32.99	0.912	31.80	0.895	30.41	0.910	398K	26.3B
DRRN [27]	2	37.74	0.959	33.23	0.914	32.05	0.897	31.23	0.919	297K	1,933B
MemNet [28]	2	37.78	0.960	33.28	0.914	32.08	0.898	31.31	0.920	667K	451B
IDN [13]	2	37.83	0.960	33.30	0.915	32.08	0.899	31.27	0.920	655K	42.9B
BP-normal	2	37.91	0.961	33.36	0.915	32.11	0.899	31.30	0.920	599K	30.5B
BP-light	2	37.74	0.959	33.15	0.914	32.02	0.897	31.11	0.918	375K	20.2B
BP-ultralight	2	37.51	0.958	33.02	0.912	31.89	0.896	30.74	0.911	57K	3.70B
Bicubic	3	30.39	0.868	27.55	0.774	27.21	0.739	24.46	0.735	-	-
SRCNN [3]	3	32.75	0.909	29.32	0.825	28.41	0.787	26.25	0.801	56K	14,8B
FSRCNN [4]	3	33.16	0.914	29.37	0.825	28.54	0.791	26.43	0.808	12K	364M
VDSR [17]	3	33.66	0.921	29.77	0.831	28.82	0.798	27.14	0.828	655K	174B
DRCN [18]	3	33.82	0.923	29.76	0.831	28.80	0.796	27.15	0.828	1774K	2,939B
LapSRN [20]	3	33.81	0.922	29.79	0.833	28.82	0.798	27.07	0.828	796K	198B
DRRN [27]	3	34.03	0.924	29.96	0.835	28.95	0.800	27.53	0.838	297K	1,933B
MemNet [28]	3	34.09	0.925	30.00	0.835	28.96	0.801	27.56	0.838	667K	451B
IDN [13]	3	34.11	0.925	29.99	0.835	28.95	0.801	27.42	0.836	655K	19.2B
BP-normal	3	34.16	0.927	30.03	0.836	28.97	0.801	27.45	0.836	608K	13.9B
BP-light	3	33.91	0.924	29.91	0.834	28.90	0.800	27.18	0.829	382K	9.17B
BP-ultralight	3	33.63	0.920	29.75	0.829	28.80	0.797	27.08	0.825	58K	1.69B
Bicubic	4	28.42	0.810	26.00	0.703	25.96	0.668	23.14	0.658	-	-
SRCNN [3]	4	30.48	0.862	27.49	0.750	26.91	0.712	24.53	0.724	56K	14.8B
FSRCNN [4]	4	30.71	0.866	27.59	0.754	26.97	0.714	24.61	0.727	12K	204M
VDSR [17]	4	31.35	0.884	28.01	0.767	27.29	0.725	25.18	0.752	655K	174B
DRCN [18]	4	31.53	0.885	28.02	0.767	27.23	0.723	25.14	0.751	1774K	2,939B
LapSRN [20]	4	31.54	0.885	28.09	0.770	27.32	0.728	25.21	0.756	796K	110B
DRRN [27]	4	31.68	0.889	28.21	0.772	27.38	0.728	25.44	0.764	297K	1,933B
MemNet [28]	4	31.74	0.889	28.26	0.772	27.40	0.728	25.50	0.763	667K	451B
IDN [13]	4	31.82	0.890	28.25	0.773	27.41	0.739	25.41	0.763	655K	10.7B
BP-normal	4	31.89	0.891	28.28	0.773	27.43	0.732	25.40	0.762	620K	7.97B
BP-light	4	31.65	0.888	28.13	0.771	27.38	0.727	25.15	0.750	389K	5.27B
BP-ultralight	4	31.33	0.881	27.98	0.765	27.26	0.724	25.03	0.741	60K	980M

5   Conclusions

In the study, we presented a lightweight network based on traditional iterative back-projection. The proposed BPnet indicated that the shallow model also exhibited comparable high-resolution results with sparse input and output. Additionally, with respect to the modular design, our BPnet exhibits good scalability. A whole trained model jettisoned the last modules to reduce the computational complexity although it still exhibited excellent quality. The property can be useful for edge computing. In the future, we will attempt to use a recursive manner to further reduce the number of parameters. Furthermore, to overcome the limitation of an insufficient receptive field, dilation convolution or other spatial-transform convolution methods can be adapted in the model.

References

1. Bae, W., Yoo, J., Ye, J.C.: Beyond deep residual learning for image restoration: persistent homology-guided manifold simplification. In: IEEE Conference on Computer Vision and Pattern Recognition Workshops, pp. 145–153 (2017)
2. Caballero, J., et al.: Real-time video super-resolution with spatio-temporal networks and motion compensation. In: IEEE Conference on Computer Vision and Pattern Recognition, pp. 2848–2857 (2017)
3. Dong, C., Loy, C.C., He, K., Tang, X.: Image super-resolution using deep convolutional networks. IEEE Trans. Pattern Anal. Mach. Intell. 38(2), 295–307 (2016)
4. Dong, C., Loy, C.C., Tang, X.: Accelerating the super-resolution convolutional neural network. In: Leibe, B., Matas, J., Sebe, N., Welling, M. (eds.) ECCV 2016. LNCS, vol. 9906, pp. 391–407. Springer, Cham (2016). https://doi.org/10.1007/978-3-319-46475-6_25
5. Glasner, D., Bagon, S., Irani, M.: Super-resolution from a single image. In: IEEE International Conference on Computer Vision, pp. 349–356 (2009)
6. Guo, T., Mousavi, H.S., Monga, V.: Orthogonally regularized deep networks for image super-resolution. In: IEEE International Conference on Acoustics, Speech, and Signal Processing (2018)
7. Guo, T., Mousavi, H.S., Vu, T.H., Monga, V.: Deep wavelet prediction for image super-resolution. In: IEEE Conference on Computer Vision and Pattern Recognition Workshops (2017)
8. Haris, M., Shakhnarovich, G., Ukita, N.: Deep back-projection networks for super-resolution. In: IEEE Conference on Computer Vision and Pattern Recognition (2018)
9. He, K., Zhang, X., Ren, S., Sun, J.: Delving deep into rectifiers: surpassing human-level performance on ImageNet classification. In: IEEE International Conference on Computer Vision, pp. 1026–1034 (2015)
10. He, K., Zhang, X., Ren, S., Sun, J.: Deep residual learning for image recognition. In: IEEE Conference on Computer Vision and Pattern Recognition, pp. 770–778 (2016)
11. Huang, G., Liu, Z., Weinberger, K.Q., van der Maaten, L.: Densely connected convolutional networks. In: IEEE Conference on Computer Vision and Pattern Recognition, vol. 1, p. 3 (2017)

12. Huang, J.B., Singh, A., Ahuja, N.: Single image super-resolution from transformed self-exemplars. In: IEEE Conference on Computer Vision and Pattern Recognition, pp. 5197–5206 (2015)
13. Hui, Z., Wang, X., Gao, X.: Fast and accurate single image super-resolution via information distillation network. In: IEEE Conference on Computer Vision and Pattern Recognition, pp. 723–731 (2018)
14. Ioffe, S., Szegedy, C.: Batch normalization: accelerating deep network training by reducing internal covariate shift. In: IEEE International Conference on Machine Learning, pp. 448–456 (2015)
15. Irani, M., Peleg, S.: Improving resolution by image registration. CVGIP: Graph. Model. Image Process. **53**(3), 231–239 (1991)
16. Jiao, J., Tu, W.C., He, S., Lau, R.W.: FormresNet: formatted residual learning for image restoration. In: IEEE Conference on Computer Vision and Pattern Recognition Workshops, pp. 1034–1042 (2017)
17. Kim, J., Kwon Lee, J., Mu Lee, K.: Accurate image super-resolution using very deep convolutional networks. In: IEEE Conference on Computer Vision and Pattern Recognition, pp. 1646–1654 (2016)
18. Kim, J., Kwon Lee, J., Mu Lee, K.: Deeply-recursive convolutional network for image super-resolution. In: IEEE Conference on Computer Vision and Pattern Recognition, pp. 1637–1645 (2016)
19. Kingma, D.P., Ba, J.: Adam: a method for stochastic optimization. arXiv preprint arXiv:1412.6980 (2014)
20. Lai, W.S., Huang, J.B., Ahuja, N., Yang, M.H.: Deep Laplacian pyramid networks for fast and accurate super-resolution. In: IEEE Conference on Computer Vision and Pattern Recognition, pp. 624–632 (2017)
21. Ledig, C., et al.: Photo-realistic single image super-resolution using a generative adversarial network. In: IEEE Conference on Computer Vision and Pattern Recognition (2017)
22. Liang, Y., Yang, Z., Zhang, K., He, Y., Wang, J., Zheng, N.: Single image super-resolution via a lightweight residual convolutional neural network. arXiv preprint arXiv:1703.08173 (2017)
23. Lim, B., Son, S., Kim, H., Nah, S., Lee, K.M.: Enhanced deep residual networks for single image super-resolution. In: IEEE Conference on Computer Vision and Pattern Recognition Workshops, vol. 1, p. 3 (2017)
24. Mao, X., Shen, C., Yang, Y.B.: Image restoration using very deep convolutional encoder-decoder networks with symmetric skip connections. In: Advances in Neural Information Processing Systems, pp. 2802–2810 (2016)
25. Schulter, S., Leistner, C., Bischof, H.: Fast and accurate image upscaling with super-resolution forests. In: IEEE Conference on Computer Vision and Pattern Recognition, pp. 3791–3799 (2015)
26. Shi, W., et al.: Real-time single image and video super-resolution using an efficient sub-pixel convolutional neural network. In: IEEE Conference on Computer Vision and Pattern Recognition, pp. 1874–1883 (2016)
27. Tai, Y., Yang, J., Liu, X.: Image super-resolution via deep recursive residual network. In: IEEE Conference on Computer Vision and Pattern Recognition, vol. 1 (2017)
28. Tai, Y., Yang, J., Liu, X., Xu, C.: MemNet: a persistent memory network for image restoration. In: IEEE International Conference on Computer Vision, pp. 4539–4547 (2017)

29. Timofte, R., Agustsson, E., Van Gool, L., Ming-Hsuan, Y., et al.: NTIRE 2017 challenge on single image super-resolution: methods and results. In: IEEE Conference on Computer Vision and Pattern Recognition Workshops (2017)
30. Timofte, R., De Smet, V., Van Gool, L.: A+: adjusted anchored neighborhood regression for fast super-resolution. In: Asian Conference on Computer Vision, pp. 111–126 (2014)
31. Timofte, R., Rothe, R., Van Gool, L.: Seven ways to improve example-based single image super resolution. In: IEEE Conference on Computer Vision and Pattern Recognition, pp. 111–126 (2016)
32. Timofte, R., Shuhang, G., Jiqing, W., Van Gool, L., et al.: NTIRE 2018 challenge on single image super-resolution: methods and results. In: IEEE Conference on Computer Vision and Pattern Recognition Workshops (2018)
33. Tong, T., Li, G., Liu, X., Gao, Q.: Image super-resolution using dense skip connections. In: IEEE International Conference on Computer Vision, pp. 4809–4817 (2017)
34. Yang, J., Wright, J., Huang, T.S., Ma, Y.: Image super-resolution via sparse representation. IEEE Trans. Image Process. 19(11), 2861–2873 (2010)
35. Zhang, K., Zuo, W., Chen, Y., Meng, D., Zhang, L.: Beyond a Gaussian denoiser: residual learning of deep cnn for image denoising. IEEE Trans. Image Process. 26(7), 3142–3155 (2017)
36. Zhang, K., Tao, D., Gao, X., Li, X., Xiong, Z.: Learning multiple linear mappings for efficient single image super-resolution. IEEE Trans. Image Process. 24(3), 846–861 (2015)
37. Zhang, Y., Tian, Y., Kong, Y., Zhong, B., Fu, Y.: Residual dense network for image super-resolution. In: IEEE Conference on Computer Vision and Pattern Recognition (2018)

Loss Guided Activation for Action Recognition in Still Images

Lu Liu[1]([✉]), Robby T. Tan[1,2], and Shaodi You[3,4]

[1] ECE Department, National University of Singapore, Singapore, Singapore
lliu@u.nus.edu
[2] Yale-NUS College, Singapore, Singapore
robby.tan@yale-nus.edu.sg
[3] DATA61-CSIRO, Canberra, Australia
shaodi.you@data61.csiro.au
[4] Australian National University, Canberra, Australia

Abstract. One significant problem of deep-learning based human action recognition is that it can be easily misled by the presence of irrelevant objects or backgrounds. Existing methods commonly address this problem by employing bounding boxes on the target humans as part of the input, in both training and testing stages. This requirement of bounding boxes as part of the input is needed to enable the methods to ignore irrelevant contexts and extract only human features. However, we consider this solution is inefficient, since the bounding boxes might not be available. Hence, instead of using a person bounding box as an input, we introduce a human-mask loss to automatically guide the activations of the feature maps to the target human who is performing the action, and hence suppress the activations of misleading contexts. We propose a multi-task deep learning method that jointly predicts the human action class and human location heatmap. Extensive experiments demonstrate our approach is more robust compared to the baseline methods under the presence of irrelevant misleading contexts. Our method achieves 94.06% and 40.65% (in terms of mAP) on Stanford40 and MPII dataset respectively, which are 3.14% and 12.6% relative improvements over the best results reported in the literature, and thus set new state-of-the-art results. Additionally, unlike some existing methods, we eliminate the requirement of using a person bounding box as an input during testing.

Keywords: Image action recognition · Loss guided activation · Human-mask loss

1 Introduction

Action recognition from a single image is generally still challenging. An input image can contain multiple objects and humans, with occlusions, cluttered

Electronic supplementary material The online version of this chapter (https://doi.org/10.1007/978-3-030-20873-8_10) contains supplementary material, which is available to authorized users.

© Springer Nature Switzerland AG 2019
C. V. Jawahar et al. (Eds.): ACCV 2018, LNCS 11365, pp. 152–167, 2019.
https://doi.org/10.1007/978-3-030-20873-8_10

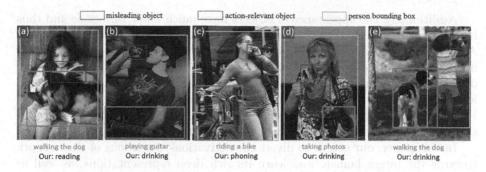

Fig. 1. Examples of irrelevant objects that mislead human action predictions. The wrong predictions using previous holistic method [13] are marked in red. Our proposed method implicitly suppresses the activations of misleading contexts and therefore can correctly identify the actions (marked in black). (Color figure online)

backgrounds, viewpoint variations, and articulated human poses, making the task of action recognition much more challenging than standard image classification task. Existing methods have exploited cues such as human body pose [3, 4, 22], interactive objects [8, 14], body part appearances [7, 12, 25], and multiple instance learning [13] to handle the aforementioned problems.

Particularly for deep-learning based methods, human action recognition can be misled by irrelevant objects or backgrounds in the input image. Mining contextual object cues can be helpful to recognize human actions that involve objects, but can also be unreliable under the presence of misleading contexts. An input image may contain multiple objects, some of which are relevant and discriminative to recognize the action, but some are irrelevant and misleading to recognize the action. Some examples of misleading objects and action-relevant objects are shown in Fig. 1. These irrelevant cues can be salient (e.g. the dog in Fig. 1(a)(e)) and interactive with human (e.g. the dog, guitar, bike, camera in Fig. 1(a-d)), making them even harder to be ignored by recognition algorithms. Intuitively, human action prediction should focus on the target humans with priority. However, most of the existing methods are significantly driven by training data, which can be biased for non-human objects and backgrounds. Consequently, instead of focusing on humans, the attention of the algorithms can be shifted to irrelevant contextual cues, leading to a wrong prediction.

To address the misleading contexts problem, existing approaches usually use person bounding boxes as input [8, 9, 11–14, 17, 21, 25] in both training and testing stages. This is needed to extract features of the target human and then to combine them with contextual features from the whole image. However, we consider that using a person bounding box as an additional input is not effective to exclude irrelevant cues in the image. This form of hard attention does not tackle the underlying problem, because the extracted features of the misleading contexts can have higher response than action-related contexts, due to some probable bias in the dataset for object manipulation type of actions, leading to a wrong prediction.

Additionally, the appearance of objects have much fewer variations and thus higher consistency than the appearance of human body in the training data. As a result, deep neural networks learn richer representations of objects and other contexts than the human body. The unbalanced feature activations among objects and humans make the existing methods sensitive to the irrelevant misleading contexts, and hence these methods perform poorly under their presence. For example, in Fig. 1(a), the presence of a dog makes the action to be misclassified as "walking the dog" by previous holistic methods [4,13].

In this paper, our goal is to divert the activations/attentions of the network towards the target human, and learn its rich deep representations, as well as simultaneously learn compact representations of action-relevant objects and contexts. We propose a multi-task deep learning framework that jointly predicts the human action class and human location heatmap (Fig. 3). Instead of adding the person bounding boxes in the input [13,25] or modifying the extracted feature maps by multiplying them with an saliency map [4], we use a novel human-mask loss to automatically guide the activations of the feature maps to the human who is performing the action, and hence suppress the influences of the misleading objects or backgrounds. To our knowledge, it is the first time that we explicitly show the class activation map can be influenced by a human-mask loss. The practical benefit of this is that we do not need bounding boxes during testing. Evaluations on two popular and challenging datasets: Stanford40 Action dataset [23] and MPII Human Pose dataset [1] show the effectiveness of our method. To sum up, our main contributions are three-fold:

- We propose a new human-mask loss to automatically guide the activation of the network into the human regions to learn rich deep representations of humans. This eliminates the requirement of bounding boxes as part of the input in testing stage.
- We propose a multi-task deep learning method that jointly predicts the action class and human location heatmap.
- Our method achieves 94.06% and 40.65% (in terms of mean Average Precision, mAP) on Stanford40 and MPII dataset respectively, which are 3.14% and 12.6% relative improvements over the best results reported in the literature, and thus set new state-of-the-art results.

The rest of the paper is organized as follows. Section 2 reviews the related work of action recognition from still images. Section 3 describes our approach, which is a multi-task learning framework. Section 4 shows experimental results and our evaluations quantitatively and qualitatively. Finally, Sect. 5 provides a brief summary of our method and some practical future works.

2   Related Work

Compared to action recognition from videos, which highly relies on motion, action recognition from a single image depends on static cues, such as human pose, body parts, and interactive objects. Existing methods can be grouped into three categories: holistic methods, part-based methods, context-based methods.

Holistic Methods: Holistic methods extract features from the human in the given bounding box and combine them with contextual features from the whole image to predict human actions [3,13,22]. Early works [3,22] use a graphical model on the human body pose to infer actions. Recently, Mallya and Lazebnik [13] propose a simple fusion network that concatenates features extracted from a bounding box with features from the whole image for action prediction. Overall, holistic methods follow the most straightforward strategy and do not involve many pre-processing steps. However, holistic methods can be easily misled by the presence of irrelevant objects or backgrounds. To resolve this problem, our approach introduces a human-mask loss to guide the activations of the network into human regions, and hence suppresses the response of irrelevant contexts.

Part-Based Methods: Part-based approaches detect multiple bounding boxes on various body parts and combine their features with global features to predict actions [7,12,25]. Gkioxari et al. [7] train body part detectors on 'pool5' features in a sliding window manner and combine them with the ground-truth box to train a CNN for action classification. Recently, Zhao et al. [25] incorporate mid-level body part actions (e.g. head: laughing) to infer body actions. However, this method requires an external human pose estimation technique to localize body keypoints and crop out part patches in both training and testing stages. Moreover, the "hard-coded attention" limits the regions to be around the human. Instead of using body parts' patches as input, our approach learns rich representations of humans by using our human-mask loss.

Context-Based Methods: Contextual algorithms exploit contextual cues, such as interactive objects. CAI [27] utilizes language information of the context (i.e. subject and object) labels, and encodes them into semantic space to learn context-dependent classifier for visual relationship detection. R*CNN [8] applies selective search [20] to generate object proposals to discover proper interactive objects. However, these proposals are required for both training and testing stages, and the sampling over potential proposals might also be computationally expensive. Moreover, R*CNN uses two hyper-parameters to define the overlap between the person bounding box and the proposal box. Our approach achieves this overlapping by introducing a human-mask loss, which can automatically divert the attention into the most discriminative image regions around the human, in a soft and learnable way.

Weakly-Supervised Localization: All the aforementioned methods require the prior knowledge of the ground-truth bounding boxes in both training and testing stages, making them difficult to scale to real-world applications. There have been a number of recent works exploring weakly-supervised object localization or soft attention [4,14,24]. Oquab et al. [14] transfer mid-level image representations obtained from image classification to action recognition. Zhang et al. [24] generate a foreground action mask using a five-step iterative optimization method, then extract features from the action mask for recognition purpose. However, this method suffers from high optimization complexity. Recently, Girdhar and Ramanan [4] propose a pooling method that scales the score map with a saliency map. This method potentially assumes that the salient objects are the most useful cues for identifying actions. However, there could be salient but irrelevant objects (see Fig. 1) that can lead to wrong predictions. Our approach implicitly models attention via a number of feature activation maps. We show that it is unnecessary to explicitly model the attention map, but by training the network to predict the human location heatmap. Doing this, we implicitly divert the attention from the misleading contexts to the human regions.

Multi-task Learning: Some prior works have shown that jointly learning multiple tasks that relate to each other boosts the individual performances of all the tasks. To name a few, HyperFace [16] jointly learns face detection, landmarks localization, pose estimation and gender recognition tasks, and improves individual performances. Simonyan and Zisserman [18] use multi-task learning to decrease over-fitting by jointly training two video datasets. We observe a similar performance boost, where a multi-task learning approach detecting human, as a by-product, improves action classification performance. By jointly predicting the location of the human, the network learns rich representations of the human who is performing the action, and thus achieves better action prediction results.

3   Our Approach

The presence of misleading objects or backgrounds can pose a major problem for human action recognition. To address this, existing methods attempt to turn the focus more on the target human. Their strategies to turn the focus on the target human can be categorized into: Input modification and feature modification. An example of input modification is Zhao et al.'s method [25], which crops the region of the given person bounding box to extract the features of the human. Another example is an approach by [8,13], which uses box coordinates and a Regions Of Interest (ROI) pooling layer [5] on top of the last convolutional feature maps to extract features on the human. One example of feature modification is to reweight the extracted image feature maps by scaling them with either a human pose heatmap or with a saliency map [4].

However, neither input modification nor feature modification can resolve the problem. Since, for input modification, a person bounding box may still include irrelevant contexts due to the viewpoint, and the close spatial relationship between the human and these contexts. For feature modification, a saliency map produced by a data-driven deep learning model can magnify the effect of misleading contexts rather than suppress them, and hence, can lead to incorrect action predictions.

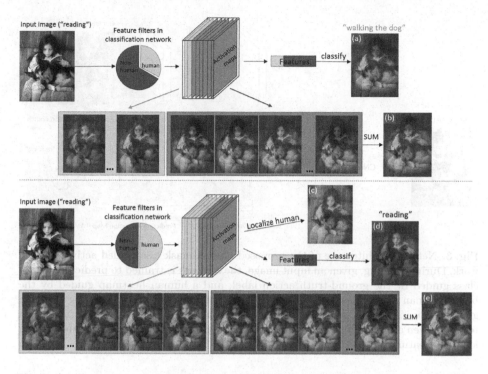

Fig. 2. An illustration of a classification network trained without and with our human-mask loss. The multi-task learning framework achieves balanced activations between humans and non-human contexts, which is more robust under the presence of irrelevant misleading contexts.

3.1 Key Idea: Human-Mask Loss

Our key idea is to use a novel human-mask loss to automatically divert the activation of the network into the human regions to learn rich representations of humans, as illustrated in Fig. 2. Under the guidance of human-mask loss, the network is forced to learn more features of humans in order to produce the final human location heatmap, and hence enhance the influence of humans in the final decision. After all, human action recognition must be firstly about human, not the surrounding objects or backgrounds.

As illustrated in Fig. 2, by visualizing the Sum of Activation Maps (SAM) of the network trained with only an action classification loss (Fig. 2(b)), we observe that the final feature maps have much higher activations on salient objects (see the dog), but much lower activations on the human body. This unbalanced activation could probably be the reason why the existing deep learning methods [4,8,13,14] are fragile to misleading contexts.

We input only the whole image into the network, by training the network to predict the human location heatmap, we encourage the network to learn rich representations about humans (see the highlighted face of the reading girl in Fig. 2(e) compared to (b)). Thus, with the balanced activations on humans and

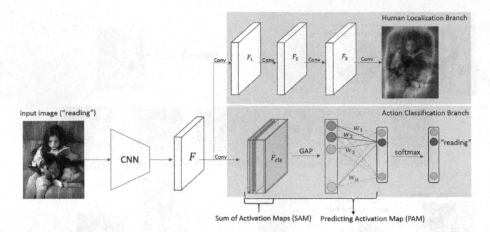

Fig. 3. Network architecture of the proposed human-mask loss guided activation network. During training, given an input image, the network is trained to predict an action class guided by the ground-truth action label, and a human heatmap guided by the binary human mask. The groundtruth human mask images for the training data are generated using the person bounding box information given in the dataset. During testing, given an input image, the network jointly predicts the action class and human location heatmap.

contexts, the network gives the correct action prediction, and the final Predicting Activation Map (PAM) (i.e. the Class Activation Map (CAM [26]) of the predicted class) shifts attention from the irrelevant objects or backgrounds (e.g. the dog in Fig. 2(a)) to the human's body parts (e.g. the holding hand in Fig. 2(d)), as well as the action-related interactive objects (e.g. the book in Fig. 2(d)) around that human.

3.2 Network Architecture

The architecture of our proposed network is shown in Fig. 3. There are two branches in the network: Action classification branch that predicts the action class, and human localization branch that produces the human location heatmap. Given an input image, we first use a CNN (Inception-ResNet-v2 [19]) to extract feature maps [1] from the last convolutional layer. By jointly predicting the human location heatmap, the network is forced to learn rich representations of humans, and hence suppresses the influences of irrelevant misleading contexts.

Action Classification Branch: On top of the backbone features F, we use a convolutional layer to further reduce the number of channels to extract compact features F_{cls} for classification. Since this convoluational layer is only trained using classification loss, it provides the classification task with more flexibility and capacity. Then, we perform global average pooling (GAP) on the feature

---

[1] This backbone feature is shared by both two branches.

maps F_{cls} to obtain a feature vector V, and use it to train a softmax classifier to predict the action class. We use only one fully-connected (FC) layer for predicting action labels, so that the weights of the FC layer can be projected back on to the convolutional feature maps F_{cls}, indicating image regions that have been used by the network to recognize that action class.

Human Localization Branch: Our goal is to divert the activations of the feature maps into the human regions to learn rich representations of the target human and the surrounding interactive objects. To accomplish this, we add the human localization branch to create a human heatmap guided by the binary human mask M^{gt} (we use gt to denote ground-truth). In the mask, $M^{gt}(i) = 1$ means the pixel i is inside the person bounding box[2], otherwise it belongs to the background regions. Note that, we only generate this groundtruth human mask for training data. Based on the backbone feature maps F, we further apply four convolutional layers to generate a 2D human location heatmap M^*. To obtain a mask with a proper spatial resolution, these convolutional layers preserve the spatial dimension and only reduce the number of channels gradually. Finally, we compute the L2-norm distance between the output map M^* and the ground-truth mask M^{gt} and back-propagate the error.

Loss Function: We use cross-entropy loss for action classification task, and the L2-norm distance between the predicted human-mask M^* and the ground-truth human mask M^{gt} as the loss function for human localization task (Eq. 1). We combine the two losses with equal weights $L = L_{cls} + L_{mask}$, where:

$$L_{cls} = - \log\left(\frac{\exp(S_{c^{gt}})}{\sum_c \exp(S_c)}\right); \quad L_{mask} = ||M^{gt} - M^*||_2^2, \tag{1}$$

where S_c is the score before softmax of class c, and c^{gt} is the ground-truth class.

3.3 Loss-Guided Activation

We summarize all channels of the final activation map F_{cls} to obtain a 2D map, denoted as SAM (Sum of Activation Maps). By visualizing SAM, we are able to evaluate the distribution of the feature kernels learnt by the network trained with and without our human-mask loss. To investigate based on which image regions that the CNN is making its decision, we further compute the weighted sum of the activation maps at the predicted class c^* (i.e. CAM at the predicted class), denoted as PAM (Predicting Activation Map). Here are the definitions of SAM and PAM, respectively:

$$\text{SAM}(i, j) = \sum_k F_{cls}^k(i, j); \quad \text{PAM}(i, j) = \sum_k w_{c^*}^k F_{cls}^k(i, j), \tag{2}$$

where F_{cls}^k is the kth channel of the final activation map F_{cls}, (i, j) is the spatial location, c^* is the predicted action class, and $w_{c^*}^k$ is the learnt weight of the kth feature for predicted class c^*.

---

[2] The person bounding box coordinates are given by the dataset.

4   Experiments

We use two challenging action datasets: (1) Stanford40 Action Dataset [23] consisting of 9532 images of people performing 40 actions. The dataset is split into training and test sets with 4000 and 5532 images each. (2) MPII Human Pose Dataset [1] containing 20,916 images classified into one of the 393 action classes. It is split into training, validation (from authors of [8]) and test sets, with 8219, 6988 and 5709 images each. The final test mAP results are obtained by emailing our results to authors of [1]. The annotations do not include a ground-truth bounding box explicitly, but provide the location of 16 human body keypoints. This information is used to generate human-mask images for the training data. Among all coordinates of body joints, the min and max coordinates are picked to composite a tight box covering the human body joints. Then we expand the box by 50% to cover the whole body, and generate human-mask images for training.

To obtain the final activation maps of resolution 14×14, the test images are resized to 448×448 and inputted to the network. We train two backbone CNNs: ResNet [10] and Inception-ResNet-v2 [19] initialized with ImageNet [2] weights. On top of the backbone feature maps, (i) In action classification branch, we use one convolutional layer with 1024 kernels (3×3 kernel size, stride 1) and ReLu nonlinearity to obtain the final feature maps F_{cls} ($1024 \times 14 \times 14$). This F_{cls} is then global average pooled to a feature vector for training the softmax classifier; (ii) In human localization branch, we apply four Conv-ReLu layers (all 3×3 kernel size, stride 1) to gradually reduce the channel numbers ($512 \rightarrow 64 \rightarrow 32 \rightarrow 1$) to generate the final human location heatmap. The learning rate is set to be 10^{-5}, and batch size is 12. Three kinds of data augmentations are employed: horizontal flipping, random rotation (range of 0–$10°$), and random zoom (0.9–1.1).

4.1   Comparisons with Existing Methods

Stanford40 Action Dataset. Table 1 shows the results on Stanford40 dataset [23]. Using Inception-ResNet-v2 as backbone CNN, our method achieves a mAP of 94.06% on Stanford40 test set, which is the state-of-the-art. Performance varies from 76.7% for "waving hands" to 100% for "playing violin". For all the 40 categories, the improvement of using our human-mask loss comes from two sources: (1) Test samples that contain irrelevant misleading objects and backgrounds; (2) Confusing action pairs such as "waving hands" and "applauding". Figure 4 shows the AP performance per action on the test set. In comparison with previous best approach PAN [25] (mAP of 91.2%), which uses bounding boxes in the input image, our method's performance is comparable (mAP of 91.1%). In fact, PAN uses body part bounding boxes (in addition to the person bounding boxes) and additional body part action annotations, thus ours uses less information. The benefit of our method compared to PAN is that we do not need the bounding boxes in the testing, which in terms of practicality is a significant improvement.

Table 1. mean Average Precision (mAP) on Stanford40 dataset

Methods	mAP(%)
Action Mask [24]	82.64
ResNet50[a] [10]	87.23
Inception-ResNet-v2[a] [19]	90.38
VGG-16, R*CNN [8]	90.90
ResNet50, Part Action Network [25]	91.20
Ours - ResNet50, w/o human-mask loss	88.80
Ours - ResNet50, w human-mask loss	91.10
Ours - Inception-ResNet-v2, w/o human-mask loss	91.42
Ours - Inception-ResNet-v2, w human-mask loss	**94.06**

[a]A standard classification network, trained with the same experimental configurations as ours, but without adding one convolutional layer on top of the backbone CNN.

Effectiveness of Our Human-Mask Loss. We train action classification network with/without our human-mask loss to compare the effectiveness of our introduced human-mask loss. Our human-mask loss improves the mAP by 2.3% and 2.64% for both ResNet50 and Inception-ResNet-v2 based network respectively. Jointly predicting human location heatmap significantly boosts action classification performance. Figure 4 shows the AP comparison between a network trained with and without our human-mask loss. Our method significantly improves mAP on the top confusing pair "waving hands" and "applauding" by 7.33% and 5.06% respectively. It also obtains large gains on object manipulation type of actions, such as "texting message" (+11.09%), "brushing teeth" (+7.31%), "pouring liquid" (+5.98%), "phoning" (+5.59%). There is an accuracy drop for "cutting vegetables". The misclassification happens because the knife is lying on the table and the hand is holding the vegetables.

MPII Dataset. Table 2 shows the comparison on MPII test and validation sets. We use the validation set shared by the authors of [8] to compare with [4,8]. Performance on the test set is obtained by submitting our prediction scores to authors of [1]. The previous best approach is Attn.Pool [4], which achieves a mAP of 36.1% on test set. Using Inception-ResNet-v2 as backbone CNN with our human-mask loss, our method achieves a mAP of 40.65% on MPII test set, surpassing previous benchmark by 12.6% (relative improvement).

Effectiveness of Our Human-Mask Loss. Our human-mask loss improves the mAP by 1.21% and 1.90% for both ResNet101 and Inception-ResNet-v2 based network respectively on validation set. For all 393 categories, we observe that the top improved actions are those whose critical cues are about humans rather than contexts, which may contain irrelevant objects and cluttered backgrounds. For example, our human-mask loss significantly improves "sitting, in

Table 2. mean Average Precision (mAP) on MPII dataset

Methods	Val mAP(%)	Test mAP(%)
Dense Trajectories+Pose [15]	-	5.5
VGG-16, Scene-RCNN [8]	16.5	-
VGG-16, R*CNN[a] [8]	21.7	26.7
VGG-16, Fusion [13]	-	32.3
Inception-v2, Attn.Pool [4]	24.3	-
ResNet101, Attn.Pool [4]	30.3	36.0
ResNet101, Attn.Pool+Pose [4]	30.6	36.1
Ours - ResNet101, w/o human-mask loss	30.77	-
Ours - ResNet101, w human-mask loss	31.98	-
Ours - Inception-ResNet-v2, w/o human-mask loss	32.38	-
Ours - Inception-ResNet-v2, w human-mask loss	**34.28**	**40.65**

[a]R*CNN reports the test AP of 1.1% for both "cooking or food preparation" and "video exercise workout" actions, while our method achieves 25.64%, and 11.11% on the two action classes respectively.

class, general, including note-taking or class discussion" by 40.1%, "woodwind, sitting" by 36.4%, "laughing, sitting" by 25.58% on validation set.

4.2 Visualization of Activation Maps

We visualize the activation maps of the network (Inception-ResNet-v2 based) trained with/without our human-mask loss. Figure 5 shows the shifted attention on SAM and PAM using our human-mask loss. Note for a fair comparison between a classification network trained with and without a human-mask loss, we use min-max normalization to normalize each channel of F_{cls} to [0,1] before summation. Given an input image as shown in Fig. 5(a), the network jointly predicts the action class and human location heatmap as shown in Fig. 5(f). By comparing SAM trained with and without a human-mask loss in Fig. 5(b)(c), we

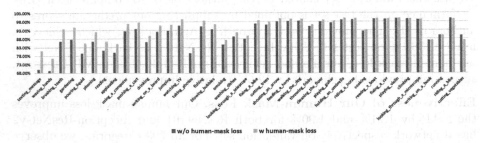

Fig. 4. AP (%) comparison between a network (Inception-ResNet-v2 based) trained with and without our human-mask loss on Stanford40 dataset. The results of all actions are shown in descending order of their absolute AP improvements. The mean AP improvement across all actions is 2.64%.

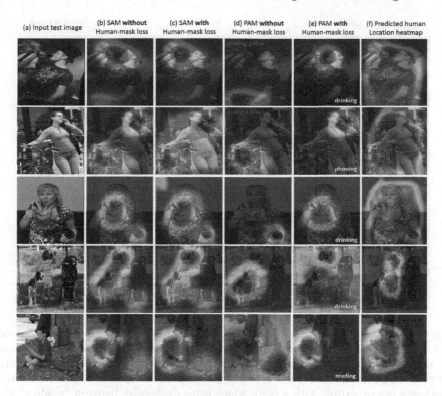

Fig. 5. Examples of the SAM and PAM obtained from the network trained with/without human-mask loss. Wrong predictions are marked in red, and correct ones (ours) are marked in white. Using our human-mask loss, the final predicting attention shifts from the misleading objects (e.g. guitar, bike, camera, dog) or backgrounds (e.g. garden) to the human regions. (Color figure online)

observe that our human-mask loss successfully drives more activations into the human regions, such as the boy besides the dog, and the human carrying the guitar. Therefore, the final PAM (Fig. 5(d)(e)) shifts the attention from the misleading objects (e.g. guitar, bike, camera, dog) or backgrounds (e.g. garden) into the human regions. Our proposed human-mask loss guides the network to focus more into the discriminative image regions where humans and the non-human contexts have balanced contributions for predicting actions.

Additionally, we observe some corrections using human-mask loss benefit from learning better representations of humans. Figure 6 shows examples of two confusing pairs of "applauding" vs. "waving hands", and "reading" vs. "writing on a book". For instance, Surprisingly, by attending on humans, the network captures more discriminative body pose features, which helps distinguish between "applauding" and "waving hands". The key to distinguish between "applauding" and "waving hands" is the pose of the upper body. Usually, "waving hands" requires one hand, while "applauding" requires two hands. Under the guidance

164 L. Liu et al.

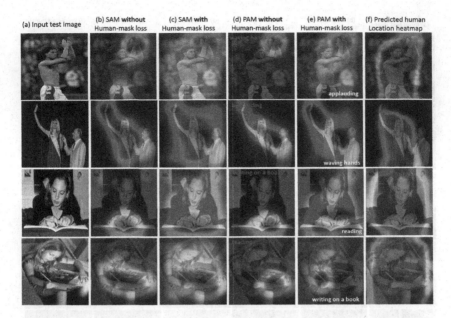

Fig. 6. Examples of two confusing action pairs. Wrong predictions are marked in red, and correct ones (ours) are marked in white. Surprisingly, by attending on humans, the network captures more discriminative body pose features, which helps distinguish between "applauding" and "waving hands", as well as the specific way of interaction (holding a pen or writing with a pen), which helps distinguish between "reading" and "writing on a book". (Color figure online)

of our human-mask loss, the network is able to capture the overall pose of the human's upper body rather than purely focusing on the local hand regions.

4.3 Comparison and Discussion

We show some predictions obtained by our method and existing methods in Fig. 7. R*CNN [8] can misclassify an action when the misleading objects are selected as its secondary box with highest response score (Fig. 7(a)). PAN [25] focuses on local body parts and can misclassify when body parts are occluded (Fig. 7(b-e)). Fusion [13] can make a wrong prediction when the misleading objects are inside the person bounding box (Fig. 7(f)(g)). Attn.Pool [4] can magnify the response of misleading contexts, leading to a wrong prediction (Fig. 7(h-j)). Compared to the aforementioned methods, our method applies human-mask loss and successfully diverts the activations of the network to human, and hence gives correct action predictions, as shown in (Fig. 7(a-j)).

In the last row of Fig. 7(k-o), we show some misclassified samples by our method. There are mainly three reasons: (1) Misleading objects are too dominant (i.e. occupy a larger portion of the image than the human does) to be ignored (see the big car in front of the applauding man in Fig. 7(k)). (2) Action-

Fig. 7. Predictions obtained by our method and existing methods on Stanford40 test set. The correct predictions are marked in black, and wrong ones are in red. Results show that our method is more robust than existing methods under the presence of irrelevant misleading contexts (see first two rows). Our approach also has certain limitations when misleading objects are too dominant, or action-relevant objects are largely occluded, or have no direct interaction with the human in the presence of multiple objects in the image (see third row). (Color figure online)

relevant objects are largely occluded (the brush and TV in Fig. 7(l)(m)). (3) Indirect interaction between human and action-relevant objects in the presence of multiple objects (Fig. 7(n)(o)). Our human-mask loss implicitly increases the activations of the objects that are close to the target human. We believe that by explicitly detecting the interactive objects using human-object interaction models such as [6], our method can perform even better. We leave this for our future work.

5   Conclusion

In this paper, we propose a multi-task learning method to solve the problem of irrelevant misleading contexts for action recognition in still images. Our goal is to divert the activations of the network to focus on humans, and hence the activations of the misleading objects or backgrounds can be suppressed. We introduce a novel human-mask loss to automatically guide the activations of the feature maps to the target human. We propose a multi-task deep learning method that jointly predicts the human action class and human location heatmap. Our method achieves state-of-the-art results: 94.06% on Stanford40 and 40.65% on MPII dataset, surpassing the previous benchmarks. Additionally, we eliminate the requirement of using a person bounding box as an input in the testing stage. Future work involves combining human-object interaction technique to better exploit action-relevant contexts in the given images.

Acknowledgement. This research is supported by the National Research Foundation, Prime Ministers Office, Singapore under its Strategic Capability Research Centres Funding Initiative. R.T. Tan's work is supported in part by Yale-NUS College Start-Up Grant. Lu Liu is supported by Yale-NUS College PhD Scholarship.

References

1. Andriluka, M., Pishchulin, L., Gehler, P., Schiele, B.: 2D human pose estimation: new benchmark and state of the art analysis. In: Proceedings of the IEEE Conference on computer Vision and Pattern Recognition, pp. 3686–3693 (2014)
2. Deng, J., Dong, W., Socher, R., Li, L.J., Li, K., Fei-Fei, L.: ImageNet: a large-scale hierarchical image database. In: 2009 IEEE Conference on Computer Vision and Pattern Recognition, CVPR 2009, pp. 248–255. IEEE (2009)
3. Desai, C., Ramanan, D.: Detecting actions, poses, and objects with relational phraselets. In: Fitzgibbon, A., Lazebnik, S., Perona, P., Sato, Y., Schmid, C. (eds.) ECCV 2012. LNCS, vol. 7575, pp. 158–172. Springer, Heidelberg (2012). https://doi.org/10.1007/978-3-642-33765-9_12
4. Girdhar, R., Ramanan, D.: Attentional pooling for action recognition. In: NIPS (2017)
5. Girshick, R.: Fast R-CNN. In: 2015 IEEE International Conference on Computer Vision (ICCV), pp. 1440–1448. IEEE (2015)
6. Gkioxari, G., Girshick, R., Dollár, P., He, K.: Detecting and recognizing human-object interactions. arXiv preprint arXiv:1704.07333 (2017)
7. Gkioxari, G., Girshick, R., Malik, J.: Actions and attributes from wholes and parts. In: Proceedings of the IEEE International Conference on Computer Vision, pp. 2470–2478 (2015)
8. Gkioxari, G., Girshick, R., Malik, J.: Contextual action recognition with R*CNN. In: Proceedings of the IEEE International Conference on Computer Vision, pp. 1080–1088 (2015)
9. Gupta, S., Malik, J.: Visual semantic role labeling. arXiv preprint arXiv:1505.04474 (2015)
10. He, K., Zhang, X., Ren, S., Sun, J.: Deep residual learning for image recognition. In: Proceedings of the IEEE Conference on Computer Vision and Pattern Recognition, pp. 770–778 (2016)
11. Hoai, M.: Regularized max pooling for image categorization. In: Proceedings of the British Machine Vision Conference. BMVA Press (2014)
12. Maji, S., Bourdev, L., Malik, J.: Action recognition from a distributed representation of pose and appearance. In: 2011 IEEE Conference on Computer Vision and Pattern Recognition (CVPR), pp. 3177–3184. IEEE (2011)
13. Mallya, A., Lazebnik, S.: Learning models for actions and person-object interactions with transfer to question answering. In: Leibe, B., Matas, J., Sebe, N., Welling, M. (eds.) ECCV 2016. LNCS, vol. 9905, pp. 414–428. Springer, Cham (2016). https://doi.org/10.1007/978-3-319-46448-0_25
14. Oquab, M., Bottou, L., Laptev, I., Sivic, J.: Learning and transferring mid-level image representations using convolutional neural networks. In: 2014 IEEE Conference on Computer Vision and Pattern Recognition (CVPR), pp. 1717–1724. IEEE (2014)

15. Pishchulin, L., Andriluka, M., Schiele, B.: Fine-grained activity recognition with holistic and pose based features. In: Jiang, X., Hornegger, J., Koch, R. (eds.) GCPR 2014. LNCS, vol. 8753, pp. 678–689. Springer, Cham (2014). https://doi.org/10.1007/978-3-319-11752-2_56

16. Ranjan, R., Patel, V.M., Chellappa, R.: HyperFace: a deep multi-task learning framework for face detection, landmark localization, pose estimation, and gender recognition. IEEE Trans. Pattern Anal. Mach. Intell. **41**, 121–135 (2017)

17. Sharma, G., Jurie, F., Schmid, C.: Expanded parts model for semantic description of humans in still images. IEEE Trans. Pattern Anal. Mach. Intell. **39**(1), 87–101 (2017)

18. Simonyan, K., Zisserman, A.: Two-stream convolutional networks for action recognition in videos. In: Advances in Neural Information Processing Systems, pp. 568–576 (2014)

19. Szegedy, C., Ioffe, S., Vanhoucke, V., Alemi, A.A.: Inception-v4, inception-ResNet and the impact of residual connections on learning. In: AAAI, vol. 4, p. 12 (2017)

20. Uijlings, J.R., Van De Sande, K.E., Gevers, T., Smeulders, A.W.: Selective search for object recognition. Int. J. Comput. Vis. **104**(2), 154–171 (2013)

21. Yang, H., Tianyi Zhou, J., Zhang, Y., Gao, B.B., Wu, J., Cai, J.: Exploit bounding box annotations for multi-label object recognition. In: Proceedings of the IEEE Conference on Computer Vision and Pattern Recognition, pp. 280–288 (2016)

22. Yao, B., Fei-Fei, L.: Action recognition with exemplar based 2.5D graph matching. In: Fitzgibbon, A., Lazebnik, S., Perona, P., Sato, Y., Schmid, C. (eds.) ECCV 2012. LNCS, vol. 7575, pp. 173–186. Springer, Heidelberg (2012). https://doi.org/10.1007/978-3-642-33765-9_13

23. Yao, B., Jiang, X., Khosla, A., Lin, A.L., Guibas, L., Fei-Fei, L.: Human action recognition by learning bases of action attributes and parts. In: 2011 IEEE International Conference on Computer Vision (ICCV), pp. 1331–1338. IEEE (2011)

24. Zhang, Y., Cheng, L., Wu, J., Cai, J., Do, M.N., Lu, J.: Action recognition in still images with minimum annotation efforts. IEEE Trans. Image Process. **25**(11), 5479–5490 (2016)

25. Zhao, Z., Ma, H., You, S.: Single image action recognition using semantic body part actions. In: 2017 IEEE International Conference on Computer Vision (ICCV), Venice, pp. 3411–3419 (2017)

26. Zhou, B., Khosla, A., Lapedriza, A., Oliva, A., Torralba, A.: Learning deep features for discriminative localization. In: 2016 IEEE Conference on Computer Vision and Pattern Recognition (CVPR), pp. 2921–2929. IEEE (2016)

27. Zhuang, B., Liu, L., Shen, C., Reid, I.: Towards context-aware interaction recognition for visual relationship detection. In: 2017 IEEE International Conference on Computer Vision (ICCV), pp. 589–598. IEEE (2017)

Visual Odometry for Indoor Mobile Robot by Recognizing Local Manhattan Structures

Zhixing Hou, Yaqing Ding, Ying Wang, Hang Yang, and Hui Kong[✉]

School of Computer Science and Engineering,
Nanjing University of Science and Technology,
Nanjing 210094, People's Republic of China
{zxhou,konghui}@njust.edu.cn

Abstract. In this paper, we propose a novel 3-DOF visual odometry method to estimate the location and pose (yaw) of a mobile robot when the robot is navigating indoors. Particularly, we mainly aim at dealing with the corridor-like scenarios where the RGB-D camera mounted on the robot can capture apparent planar structures such as floor or walls. The novelties of our method lie in two-folds. First, to fully exploit the planar structures for odometry estimation, we propose a fast plane segmentation scheme based on efficiently extracted inverse-depth induced histograms. This training-free scheme can extract dominant planar structures by only exploiting the depth image of the RGB-D camera. Second, we regard the global indoor scene as a composition of some local Manhattan-like structures. At any specific location, we recognize at least one local Manhattan coordinate frame based on the detected planar structures. Pose estimation is realized based on the alignment of the camera coordinate frame to one dominant local Manhattan coordinate frame. Knowing pose information, the location estimation is carried out by a combination of a one-point RANSAC method and the ICP algorithm depending on the number of point matches available. We evaluate our work extensively on real-world data, the experimental result shows the promising performance in term of accuracy and robustness.

Keywords: Visual odometry · Manhattan structure · RGB-D camera · Plane segmentation

1 Introduction

In recent years, visual odometry (VO) has been an active field in computer vision as well as robotics. It mainly involves a real-time estimation of the relative pose between two consecutive camera or robot (if the camera is installed rigidly on the robot) locations. Over the past decades, many VO methods have been proposed based on utilizing different sensors, such as monocular or stereo cameras, Lidars and RGB-D cameras, for a variety of application scenarios.

© Springer Nature Switzerland AG 2019
C. V. Jawahar et al. (Eds.): ACCV 2018, LNCS 11365, pp. 168–182, 2019.
https://doi.org/10.1007/978-3-030-20873-8_11

In this paper, we focus on estimating the poses and the locations of a wheeled robot when the robot is roaming in an indoor corridor-like structured environment. The RGB-D camera is installed rigidly on the top of a robot, and the pitch and roll angles of the camera can be estimated initially based on the detected floor. In general, the indoor floor is flat. We assume that the pitch and roll angles remain constant throughout the whole process. Given the estimation of the pitch and roll angles, we rectify the RGB-D camera by rotating the generated point cloud so that the pitch and roll angles are approximately equal to zeros. It means that we only need to care about a three degree-of-freedom (DOF) visual odometry problem (given the location and yaw unknown) for such an application scenario (Fig. 1).

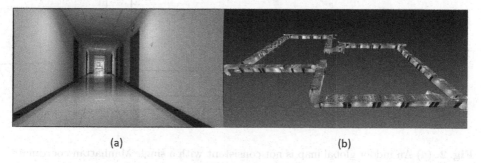

(a)   (b)

Fig. 1. (a) An RGB image in the office building. (b) A 3D structure built from our method.

The indoor corridor-like structures mainly consist of floor, walls and doors. In general, the global indoor structure may not completely match a single Manhattan-world coordinate system. However, we can assume that it usually consists of a few (if not one) local Manhattan-like structures. Figure 2(a) illustrates that this approximation totally makes sense, where each subgraph represented by a specific color can be well approximated by a Manhattan-like structure, although the global map is not a single one.

With the above assumptions, we propose a novel 3-DOF visual odometry method to estimate the location and pose (yaw) of a mobile robot when the robot is navigating indoors. Particularly, we mainly aim at dealing with the corridor-like scenarios where the RGB-D camera mounted on the robot can capture apparent planar structures such as floor or walls. The novelties of our method lie in two-folds. First, to fully exploit the planar structures for odometry estimation, we propose a fast plane segmentation scheme based on efficiently extracted inverse-depth induced histograms. This training-free scheme can extract dominant planar structures by only exploiting the depth image of the RGB-D camera. Second, we regard the whole indoor scene as a composition of several (if not one) local Manhattan structures. At any specific location, we recognize at least one local Manhattan coordinate frame based on the detected planar structures. Then pose estimation is realized based on the alignment of the camera coordinate frame to one optimally selected (the dominant) local Manhattan coordinate frame. Given pose information, the location estimation is carried out by a combination of a one-point RANSAC method and the ICP algorithm depending on the number of point matches available.

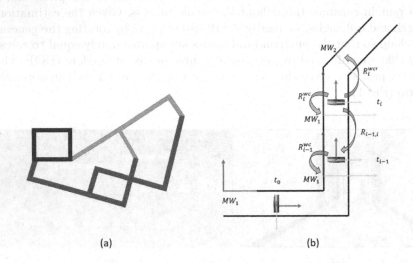

(a)   (b)

Fig. 2. (a) An indoor global map is not consistent with a single Manhattan coordinate system, although it is composed of several local Manhattan-like structures (e.g., each color representing a single Manhattan-like structure). (b) Rotation between two successive cameras. The local Manhattan structures denoted by MW_1 and MW_2. At time t_i, multiple local Manhattan coordinates are recognized, and we can calculate multiple rotations of the camera with respect to the local Manhattan coordinate respectively.

2   Related Work

In either the VO or SLAM area, the widely used methods are the feature-based ones, which generally track keypoints and minimize geometric projection error to estimate the camera poses. They can be classified into two categories: the filter-based [3,17] and pose-graph based methods [10,18]. Both rely on sufficient and reliable keypoints detection and matching. In the low-textured scenes where there are no enough tracked feature points, however, these point-based approaches tend to produce a large drift error and even fail to work.

To address this problem, some line- and plane-based methods have emerged prominently. Among these methods, Paul et al. use two end-points to represent the line segment in [22], and the other similar works are in [13,23]. Besides, by employing an RGB-D camera, Yan et al. detect and match line segments in 2D grayscale image and then apply back-projection to obtain the correspondences of 3D line segments [16]. Furthermore, some algorithms not only employ one type of feature, but also use the combination of points and line segments to improve robustness, such as [20,25] for a monocular camera, [6,28] for a stereo camera and [15] for an RGB-D camera. Li et al. propose a method [14] that use lines to guide keypoint selection rather than acting as features, since they believe that points on a line are treated as stronger keypoints than those in the other parts of the image. Zhou et al. find structure lines [27] and to get them aligned with the dominant directions of the building to improve the accuracy of the SLAM system.

Besides points and lines, planes are often used as important features in some low-textured indoor scenes. Usually planes are extracted from the RGB and depth images of the RGB-D camera, and the ego-motion is estimated by a plane-to-plane registration [21] or minimizing the geometric and photometric error simultaneously [8]. In [26], the authors propose a pop-up 3D plane model to measure the plane for both state estimation and dense mapping. Concha et al. propose a direct-SLAM framework where the planes are segmented based on the assumption that homogeneous-color regions belong to approximately planar areas [2]. Thabet et al. propose a method to correct and complete the unreliable depth data, which can be adopted to improve the result of the plane segmentation [24].

In addition, the Manhattan-world constraints have also been exploited in a variety of scene-parsing and SLAM algorithms for indoor applications. For example, the line-based methods can also be integrated with the Manhattan assumption to provide an ego-motion of the camera [27]. Kim et al. jointly use lines and planes to estimate a rotational motion and then track keypoints to estimate a translational motion utilizing environmental regularity [9]. Ghanem et al. propose a framework [5] for estimating the Manhattan frame from a single RGB-D image, simultaneously estimating the surfaces that are aligned with the dominant directions as well as the outlier surfaces. In [4], the authors demonstrate a real-time SLAM method being capable of modeling floor, ceiling and walls leveraging the Manhattan assumption and the vanishing point. Le et al. [12] exploit the dynamic programming technique to parse the structure of the indoor environment using both the RGB and depth image sequences. Then they propose an accurate rotation estimation scheme combining plane registration and point matching. Thanks to the Manhattan assumption, most of the approaches mentioned above yield an ego-motion with small accumulated rotational error.

Similar to the work of [9,12], we decouple the rotation and translation estimation so that the orientational drift is eliminated to the least extent. However, the difference between our work and the others is that we do not need to segment the corridor-like scene into very accurate plane regions. Instead, a rough plane-segmentation result is enough for the subsequent normal estimation of the planes. To meet the need of real-world applications, we design a fast plane segmentation method by using only the depth image, where we use the inverse-depth induced horizontal and vertical histograms to detect planes instead of segmenting the huge point cloud directly. In addition, only depth image is used for rotational motion estimation as well.

Another difference between ours and the previous methods is that we are able to recognize at least one dominant local Manhattan-like frame at any moment from the plane segmentation results, and the rotational motion estimation is realized by the alignment of the dominant local Manhattan-like frame to the world coordinate frame.

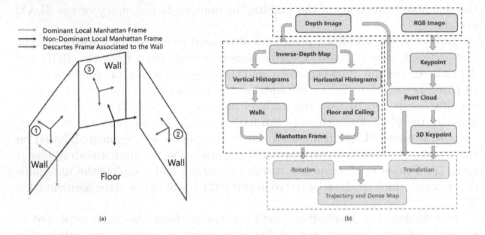

(a)   (b)

Fig. 3. (a) Three walls are denoted by three different Descartes frames (Green). Descartes frame 1 and 2 are aligned with the first Manhattan frame (Red) and Descartes frame 3 is aligned with the second Manhattan frame (purple). (b) Flow chart of the whole method. (Color figure online)

3   Approach

The pipeline of our method is given in Fig. 3(b). In our algorithm, the depth image plays a dual role on both extracting planes and constructing Manhattan coordinate frame which can serve rotation and translation estimation. We decouple rotational and translational motion estimation so that a drift-free rotation estimation can be obtained according to the local Manhattan frame alignment. Based on the accurate rotational motion, we can get a very robust estimation of translational motion employing a combination of a one-point RANSAC method and the ICP algorithm [1]. As a consequence, we build a 2D trajectory and a dense 3D detailed map of the corridor-like environment.

3.1   Plane Segmentation

In plane segmentation, we propose a fast method based on the inverse-depth induced histograms. The definition of the inverse-depth induced histograms is inspired by the u-v disparity of stereo vision [11].

As the inverse depth map is equivalent to the disparity map in stereo vision up to a scale, we convert the depth map in Fig. 4(a) to the equivalent disparity one based on the following equation:

$$d(u, v) = s \cdot \frac{1}{z} \tag{1}$$

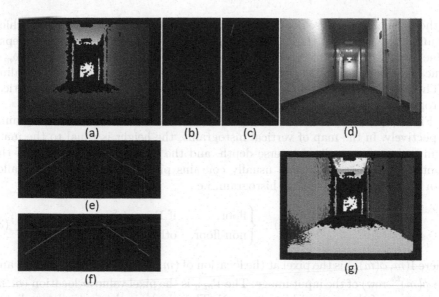

Fig. 4. Plane segmentation from the depth image. (a) the depth image. (b) the horizontal histogram map. (c) the line structures in the horizontal histogram map. (d) the RGB image. (e) the vertical histogram map. (f) the line structures in the vertical histogram map. (g) the plane segmentation.

where $d(u, v)$ is the equivalent disparity of point $p = (u, v)^T$ in the image, s being a scale factor used to normalize the inverse depth so that it is equivalent to the disparity in stereo vision, and z is the corresponding depth value at $p = (u, v)^T$ of the depth map.

Actually, this scale factor can be selected based on the real disparity observed by a stereo camera which is placed at the approximate location of the RGB-D camera. Since we only need to extract an approximate plane region based on the histograms of the normalized inverse depth, the scale factor can be a rough value. Specifically, the horizontal and vertical histograms of the normalized inverse depth are defined as follows:

$$\mathcal{H}_n^t = \sum_{m=0}^{cols} \delta_{m,n}$$

$$\mathcal{V}_m^t = \sum_{n=0}^{rows} \delta_{m,n} \tag{2}$$

$$\delta_{m,n} = \begin{cases} 1, & \text{if } d(m, n) = t \\ 0, & \text{otherwise} \end{cases}$$

where $\mathcal{H}_n^t$ represents a horizontal histogram, which accumulates horizontally the number of pixels whose normalized inverse-depth value equals t on the nth row in the normalized inverse depth map. $\mathcal{V}_m^t$ represents a vertical histogram, which accumulates vertically the number of pixels whose normalized inverse-depth value equals t on the mth column in the normalized inverse depth map. $\delta_{m,n}$ indicates whether pixel at $(m,n)^T$ has normalized inverse-depth value equaling t. Therefore, we can get a map of horizontal histograms and a map of vertical histograms of the normalized inverse depth, respectively.

Figure 4(b) and (e) shows the maps of the horizontal and vertical histograms, respectively. In the map of vertical histograms, the height is equal to the maximum value of normalized inverse depth, and the width is equal to that of the input image. The floor region usually contains pixels of small values (smaller than 3) in the map of vertical histogram, i.e.,

$$I(m, \phi(m)_n) \in \begin{cases} \text{floor}, & \text{if } \mathcal{V}_{m,n} < \delta_{\mathcal{V}} \\ \text{non-floor}, & \text{otherwise} \end{cases} \tag{3}$$

where $I(m, \phi(m)_n)$ is the pixel at the location of $(m, \phi(m)_n)$ (the mth column and the $\phi(m)_n^{th}$ row) of the input image. The $\mathcal{V}_{m,n}$ is the pixel value at location (m,n) of the map of the vertical histograms $\mathcal{V}$. The $\phi(m)_n$ is the vertical-coordinate of a pixel in the mth column of the color image whose normalized inverse depth value is n. The $\delta_{\mathcal{V}}$ is a threshold that is used to decide whether $I(m, \phi(m)_n)$ belongs to floor or non-floor region.

In the map of horizontal histograms, the height is equal to that of the input image, and the width is equal to the maximum value of the normalized inverse depth. Based on Eq. 2, the normalized inverse depth values of the pixels in floor and ceiling regions are histogramed into two linear structures in the horizontal histogram map, shown in Fig. 4(b). The two linear structures can represent the floor and ceiling profiles, respectively, and they can be fitted by the RANSAC (Random Sample Consensus) algorithm. Likewise, the normalized inverse depth values of the pixels in the wall areas are histogramed into the linear structure in the vertical histogram map, shown in Fig. 4(e).

In the following, we take the floor profile line as an example to illustrate how to find the floor region quickly based on the fitted line in the map of horizontal histograms. We assume that the line equation is $v_i = k \cdot u_i + b$, where (u_i, v_i) are the set of points on the line, and u_i is the set of normalized inverse depth values. Theoretically, this line can classify the point clouds into floor region, positive and negative obstacles (if any). Given a 3D point $P = (x, y, z)^T$ in the RGB-D camera system, its projection onto the image frame is (m, n). We know its normalized inverse depth value, denoted as $d(m, n)$. Specifically, P can belong to one of the three classes based on (4).

$$P = \begin{cases} \text{floor}, & d(m,n) == (n-b)/k, \\ \text{positive obstacle}, & d(m,n) > (n-b)/k, \\ \text{negative obstacle}, & d(m,n) < (n-b)/k, \end{cases} \tag{4}$$

In reality, because of the noise in measuring depth by the RGB-D camera, the floor is not a perfect plane in 3D space. Therefore, we specify two tolerance margins to contain floor points as completely as possible, written as follows:

$$\begin{cases} n = k \cdot m + \alpha b, & \alpha > 1, \quad \text{upper bound} \\ n = k \cdot m + \beta b, & \beta < 1, \quad \text{lower bound} \end{cases} \tag{5}$$

In this way, we can roughly obtain the classification of floor and obstacles. For a certain scanning row n, the bottom and top margins of its normalized inverse depth can be denoted by $B(n)$ and $T(n)$, respectively. Assuming that $d(m, n)$ is the normalized inverse depth value of a point, if $d(m, n) < B(n)$, this point is lower than the floor plane, belonging to negative obstacle. If $d(m, n) > T(n)$, this point is higher than the floor plane, belonging to positive obstacle. If $B(n) <= d(m, n) <= T(n)$, this point is nearly on the floor plane, belonging to the floor. In practice, we can calculate a floor probability map where the probability value at pixel (m, n) in the nth row is calculated as

$$\text{prob}(m, n) = \frac{|d(m, n) - \frac{n - b}{k}|}{\max(|d(:, n) - \frac{n - b}{k}|)} \tag{6}$$

where b and k correspond to the equation of the fitted straight line in the map of horizontal histograms. The $d(:, n)$ is the set of normalized inverse depth values on the nth row of map of the horizontal histograms.

3.2   Visual Odometry

As shown in Fig. 2(a), we regard a global indoor structure as a composition of multiple local Manhattan frames. Each color indicates a single local Manhattan structure. When the robot roaming in the same color, we can recognize one Manhattan coordinate at most, but there arc at least two Manhattan coordinates when the robot passes by the joint location of two different colors.

Given a detected wall, its normal is perpendicular to that of the floor, and it defines an associated Descartes coordinate frame (Fig. 3(a)) where the z-axis corresponds to the floor normal, the x-axis corresponding to the normal of the wall and the y-axis is the cross product of them. Note that the x-axis may not be perpendicular to the z-axis perfectly because of the error of fitting planes, so we use the cross product of z-axis and y-axis instead of the normal of the wall as the x-axis to ensure orthogonality of three axes.

Generally, we may detect multiple walls at the same time which correspond to a couple of different Descartes coordinate frames (Fig. 3(a)). We first search for the dominant Manhattan frame based on the specified Descartes coordinate frames attached to the walls. To do that, we calculate an evaluation score for each Descartes coordinate frame. Each score is calculated as the area of all the walls in the RGB image whose normal (in the depth image) is approximately parallel or perpendicular to each other. We consider the Descartes coordinate frame with the largest score as the dominant local Manhattan frame, e.g., the first and second walls belonging to the dominant local Manhattan frame. Meanwhile, the other walls belong to the minor Manhattan frames (Fig. 3(a)), and they will be available when the robot passes by the joint of two local Manhattan structures.

Once the dominant Manhattan frame has been determined at each moment, the drift-free rotation between two successive camera locations can be obtained (Fig. 2(b)). Let the camera coordinate frame at time t_i be C_i. We can estimate only one rotation $R_{i-1,i}$ of C_i with respect to C_{i-1} if there is only one local Manhattan structure (frame), denoted by MW_1, at t_{i-1} and t_i.

$$R_{i-1,i} = (R_{i-1}^{wc})^T R_i^{wc} \tag{7}$$

where R_{i-1}^{wc} and R_i^{wc} are the rotations of C_{i-1} and C_i with respect to the local Manhattan coordinate, respectively.

Next, we need to recognize the situation where the dominant local Manhattan coordinate frame at t_i is different from the one at t_{i-1}, which means the robot is at the joint location of two local Manhattan structures (frames). To do that, we judge whether the following two criteria are satisfied:

(1) *whether the relative rotation $R_{i-1,i}$ is larger than a certain angle θ_t.*
    We suppose that the motion is continuous and, in that case, the rotational estimation is small enough if two cameras are in the same dominant local Manhattan frame.
(2) *whether there are more than one local Manhattan frame detected at t_i.*
    If there is only one local Manhattan frame, even if the first criterion is satisfied, the cameras at two moments are regarded in the same local dominant Manhattan frame.

If both of the criteria are satisfied, at least two local Manhattan coordinate frames are recognized at t_i. So we have to use the non-dominant Manhattan coordinate to estimate the relative pose $R'_{i-1,i} = (R_{i-1}^{wc})^T R_i^{'wc}$. If $R'_{i-1,i}$ is a smaller rotation and less than θ_t, we regard it as the relative rotation of two camera locations while the angle between $R_{i-1,i}$ and $R'_{i-1,i}$ will be used to update the relative pose between local Manhattan structure in the global map.

Knowing the accurate pose information, the location estimation is carried out by a single 3D keypoint match or the ICP algorithm. We extract and match corner points from two successive RGB images and then back-project the 3D point match using the depth images. The relative position of two cameras is equal to that of the two corresponding 3D points. Because of the outliers, we implement a RANSAC routine for more accuracy, which selects the best corresponding point to estimate the relative translation. If there is not enough corner points matches in two images, we carry on down-sampling on two successive point clouds from the back-projection of the depth image and estimate relative translation by the ICP algorithm.

4   Experiment

In this section, we evaluate the performance of our method in different scenarios. The first datasets are captured by ourselves with an RGB-D camera mounted on a robot. We pass through only once for each corridor when we collected our dataset. The resolution of these images is 960×540. The other datasets are from [12], called Le's data, at a resolution of 640×480. Both datasets do not have groundtruth.

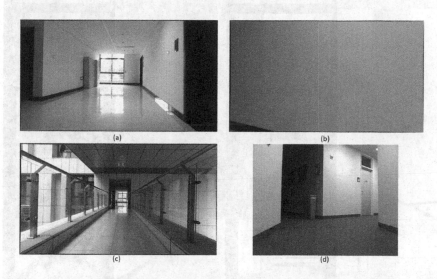

Fig. 5. (a) Light reflection: some features in the reflective area will bring about wrong matching. (b) when the robot turns a corner, there may be only a low-textured wall in front of the camera. (c) Glass walls on both sides of the corridor. (d) Multiple Manhattan structures.

All the experiments are run at 10 FPS on a desktop computer with an Intel Core i5-4460 3.20 GHz CPU and without GPU acceleration. To demonstrate the accuracy of our method, we build a 2D trajectory and a dense 3D point cloud map for every video sequence. We also compare our approach with the ORB-SLAM [19], one of the state-of-the-art keypoint based SLAM methods which include visual odometry, local mapping and loop closing. In addition, we also compare the trajectories built from our method with those built from the Google's cartographer method [7] using a single-line laser mounted on the same robot as the RGB-D camera.

Our method is applicable in corridor-like indoor scenarios, and we capture such kind of image sequences used for our experiment, where there are large areas of mirror reflection, very low textured walls (Fig. 5(a) (b)). When there are glass walls in the scenes (Fig. 5(c)), the single-line Lidar often fails in obtaining the scan points. Furthermore, the datasets we used contains multiple Manhattan structures (Fig. 5(d)).

Some results of the plane segmentation in typical scenes are shown in Fig. 6, where we use different colors to represent the different planes. We set α to 1.01 and β to 0.99 in Eq. 5. Figure 7(a) and (b) show the resulting trajectories of

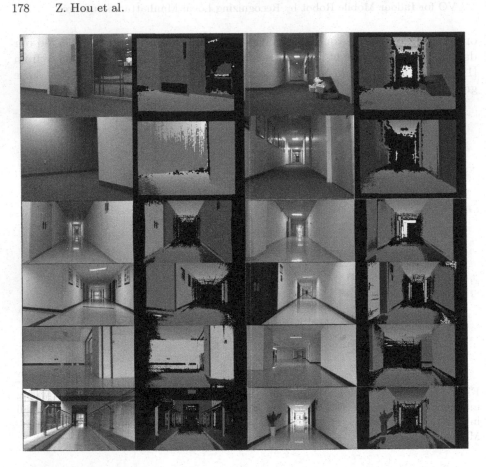

Fig. 6. Results of the plane segmentation.

Le's data obtained by the ORB-SLAM method and ours, respectively. Since the height of the camera is fixed, we only plot the 2D trajectories. Le's dataset (1) is a ring corridor and dataset (2) includes more than one local Manhattan structure. Due to the low-textured floor and walls, the ORB-SLAM often loses the point tracking around the corner, thus failing in generating the complete trajectory. In contrast, our method exhibits good performance. We remove the planes whose width is lower than 15 pixels in the image and set θ_t to 20°. For convenience, we project the walls onto the floor and plot a 2D trajectory for every data sequence. Note that the planes between different frames don't have any association and merging.

For further evaluation, we implement the experiment on our own datasets and our method outperform other compared ones shown in Fig. 8. The same as the Le's data, the ORB-SLAM fails to complete the entire image sequence. What's worse is that the ORB-SLAM finds wrong loop closure in our building with very similar repetitive structures. Because our dataset contains single-

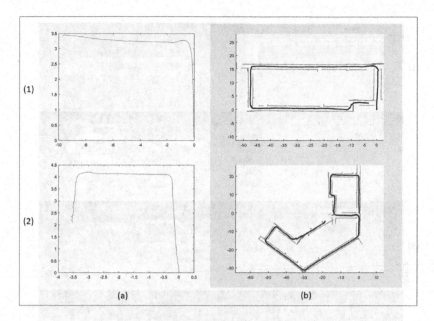

Fig. 7. Results on Le's data. (Not the same scales) (a) Trajectories built from the ORB-SLAM. (b) Trajectories built from our method. (Green: the trajectories. Magenta: the walls projected to the floor.) (Color figure online)

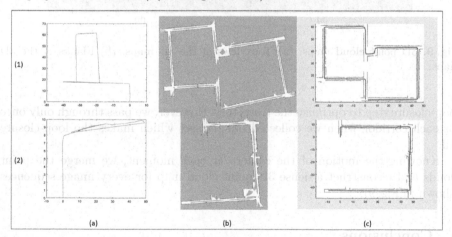

Fig. 8. Results on our data. (Not the same scales) (a) Trajectories built from the ORB-SLAM. (b) 2D maps generated by the Google's Cartographer (without loop closing). (c) Trajectories built from our method. (Green: the trajectories. Magenta: the walls projected to the floor.) (Color figure online)

line Lidar data, we also compare our method with the Google's Cartographer, which can generate a 2D map with a single-line Laser. By comparison, the Google's Cartographer method is worse than ours since it depends heavily on the

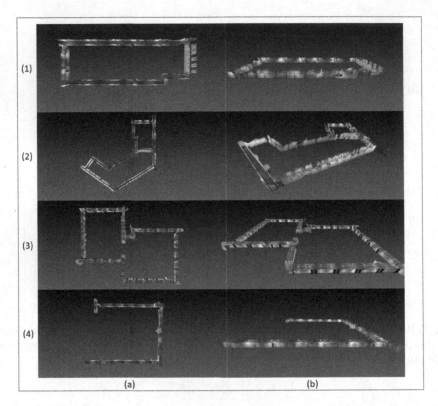

Fig. 9. 3D point cloud maps. (a) Top views of the 3D maps. (b) Flanks of the 3D maps.

loop-closure step to optimize the trajectory. However, we pass through only once for each corridor when we collected our dataset which makes the loop-closure fail.

Knowing the motion of the camera at each moment, we merge the point clouds and reconstruct a dense 3D point cloud map for every image sequences (shown in Fig. 9).

5   Conclusions

We propose a novel 3-DOF visual odometry method to estimate the location and pose (yaw) of a mobile robot, which is suitable for indoors especially in the corridor-like scenarios where the RGB-D camera can capture apparent planar structures in this paper. Unlike previous work, we estimate odometry with the planar structures that are segmented based on efficiently extracted inverse-depth induced histograms. Our visual odometry system recognize at least one local Manhattan coordinate at each time based on detected floor and walls. Pose estimation is drift-free since we align the camera coordinate system to one optimally selected local Manhattan-world coordinate system. Experiments on real-world data shows that our method outperforms other compared ones such as the ORB-SLAM and the Google's Cartographer. We can complete the entire image sequences and exhibit excellent rotation estimation without loop closing even if there is no texture.

Acknowledgement. This work was supported in part by the Jiangsu Province Natural Science Foundation under Grant BK20151491 and in part by the Natural Science Foundation of China under Grant 61672287.

References

1. Besl, P.J., McKay, N.D.: Method for registration of 3-D shapes. In: Sensor Fusion IV: Control Paradigms and Data Structures, vol. 1611, pp. 586–607. International Society for Optics and Photonics (1992)
2. Concha, A., Civera, J.: DPPTAM: dense piecewise planar tracking and mapping from a monocular sequence. In: 2015 IEEE/RSJ International Conference on Intelligent Robots and Systems (IROS), pp. 5686–5693. IEEE (2015)
3. Davison, A.J., Reid, I.D., Molton, N.D., Stasse, O.: MonoSLAM: real-time single camera SLAM. IEEE Trans. Pattern Anal. Mach. Intell. **29**(6), 1052–1067 (2007)
4. Flint, A., Mei, C., Reid, I., Murray, D.: Growing semantically meaningful models for visual SLAM. In: 2010 IEEE Conference on Computer Vision and Pattern Recognition (CVPR), pp. 467–474. IEEE (2010)
5. Ghanem, B., Thabet, A., Carlos Niebles, J., Caba Heilbron, F.: Robust Manhattan frame estimation from a single RGB-D image. In: Proceedings of the IEEE Conference on Computer Vision and Pattern Recognition, pp. 3772–3780 (2015)
6. Gomez-Ojeda, R., Zuñiga-Noël, D., Moreno, F.A., Scaramuzza, D., Gonzalez-Jimenez, J.: PL-SLAM: a stereo SLAM system through the combination of points and line segments. arXiv preprint arXiv:1705.09479 (2017)
7. Hess, W., Kohler, D., Rapp, H., Andor, D.: Real-time loop closure in 2D LIDAR SLAM. In: 2016 IEEE International Conference on Robotics and Automation (ICRA), pp. 1271–1278. IEEE (2016)
8. Hsiao, M., Westman, E., Zhang, G., Kaess, M.: Keyframe-based dense planar SLAM. In: 2017 IEEE International Conference on Robotics and Automation (ICRA), pp. 5110–5117. IEEE (2017)
9. Kim, P., Coltin, B., Kim, H.J.: Low-drift visual odometry in structured environments by decoupling rotational and translational motion. In: 2018 IEEE international conference on Robotics and automation (ICRA)
10. Klein, G., Murray, D.: Parallel tracking and mapping for small AR workspaces. In: 6th IEEE and ACM International Symposium on Mixed and Augmented Reality 2007, ISMAR 2007, pp. 225–234. IEEE (2007)
11. Labayrade, R., Aubert, D., Tarel, J.P.: Real time obstacle detection in stereovision on non-fat road geometry through "v-disparity" representation. In: Proceedings of the IEEE Intelligent Vehicles Symposium 2002, pp. 646–651. IEEE (2002)
12. Le, P.H., Košecka, J.: Dense piecewise planar RGB-D SLAM for indoor environments. In: 2017 IEEE/RSJ International Conference on Intelligent Robots and Systems (IROS), pp. 4944–4949. IEEE (2017)

13. Lemaire, T., Lacroix, S.: Monocular-vision based SLAM using line segments. In: 2007 IEEE International Conference on Robotics and Automation, pp. 2791–2796. IEEE (2007)
14. Li, S.J., Ren, B., Liu, Y., Cheng, M.M., Frost, D., Prisacariu, V.A.: Direct line guidance odometry. In: 2018 IEEE international conference on Robotics and automation (ICRA) (2018)
15. Lu, Y., Song, D.: Robust RGB-D odometry using point and line features. In: Proceedings of the IEEE International Conference on Computer Vision, pp. 3934–3942 (2015)
16. Lu, Y., Song, D.: Robustness to lighting variations: an RGB-D indoor visual odometry using line segments. In: 2015 IEEE/RSJ International Conference on Intelligent Robots and Systems (IROS), pp. 688–694. IEEE (2015)
17. Montemerlo, M., Thrun, S., Koller, D., Wegbreit, B., et al.: FastSLAM: a factored solution to the simultaneous localization and mapping problem. In: pp. 593–598. AAAI/IAAI (2002)
18. Mur-Artal, R., Montiel, J.M.M., Tardos, J.D.: ORB-SLAM: a versatile and accurate monocular SLAM system. IEEE Trans. Robot. **31**(5), 1147–1163 (2015)
19. Mur-Artal, R., Tardós, J.D.: ORB-SLAM2: an open-source SLAM system for monocular, stereo, and RGB-D cameras. IEEE Trans. Robot. **33**(5), 1255–1262 (2017)
20. Pumarola, A., Vakhitov, A., Agudo, A., Sanfeliu, A., Moreno-Noguer, F.: PL-SLAM: real-time monocular visual SLAM with points and lines. In: 2017 IEEE International Conference on Robotics and Automation (ICRA), pp. 4503–4508. IEEE (2017)
21. Raposo, C., Lourenço, M., Antunes, M., Barreto, J.P.: Plane-based Odometry using an RGB-D camera. In: BMVC (2013)
22. Smith, P., Reid, I.D., Davison, A.J.: Real-time monocular SLAM with straight lines (2006)
23. Sola, J., Vidal-Calleja, T., Devy, M.: Undelayed initialization of line segments in monocular SLAM. In: IEEE/RSJ International Conference on Intelligent Robots and Systems 2009, IROS 2009, pp. 1553–1558. IEEE (2009)
24. Thabet, A.K., Lahoud, J., Asmar, D., Ghanem, B.: 3D aware correction and completion of depth maps in piecewise planar scenes. In: Cremers, D., Reid, I., Saito, H., Yang, M.-H. (eds.) ACCV 2014. LNCS, vol. 9004, pp. 226–241. Springer, Cham (2015). https://doi.org/10.1007/978-3-319-16808-1_16
25. Yang, S., Scherer, S.: Direct monocular odometry using points and lines. In: 2017 IEEE International Conference on Robotics and Automation (ICRA), pp. 3871–3877. IEEE (2017)
26. Yang, S., Song, Y., Kaess, M., Scherer, S.: Pop-up SLAM: semantic monocular plane SLAM for low-texture environments. In: 2016 IEEE/RSJ International Conference on Intelligent Robots and Systems (IROS), pp. 1222–1229. IEEE (2016)
27. Zhou, H., Zou, D., Pei, L., Ying, R., Liu, P., Yu, W.: StructSLAM: visual SLAM with building structure lines. IEEE Trans. Veh. Technol. **64**(4), 1364–1375 (2015)
28. Zuo, X., Xie, X., Liu, Y., Huang, G.: Robust visual SLAM with point and line features. arXiv preprint arXiv:1711.08654 (2017)

Capsule Based Image Synthesis
for Interior Design Effect Rendering

Fei Yang[1], Zheng Lu[2], Guoping Qiu[3], Jing Lin[4], and Qian Zhang[2(✉)]

[1] International Doctoral Innovation Centre, University of Nottingham Ningbo China,
Ningbo 315100, China
`fei.yang@nottingham.edu.cn`
[2] School of Computer Science, University of Nottingham Ningbo China,
Ningbo 315100, China
`{zheng.lu,qian.zhang}@nottingham.edu.cn`
[3] College of Information Engineering, Shenzhen University, Shenzhen 518052, China
`qiu@szu.edu.cn`
[4] School of Architecture and Urban Planning, Shandong Jianzhu University,
Jinan 250101, China
`songf@sdjzu.edu.cn`

Abstract. Effect rendering that renders 3D model to 2D images with various coloring and lighting effects, is an important step in home interior design. Traditional way of manual rendering using professional software is very labor intensive and time consuming. In this paper, we present a novel capsule based conditional generative adversarial network that can automatically synthesize an indoor image with realistic and aesthetically pleasing rendering effect from a given plain image rendered without any effects from a interior designed 3D model. By adapting capsule blocks in both generator and discriminator and a novel multi-way loss function inside discriminator, our framework is able to generate more realistic rendering effect at both detail and global levels. In addition, a novel line preservation loss is introduced not only to help preserve the properties that are independent of lighting effect, but also improves the lighting effect along those lines. We apply our technique on a dataset specially prepared for interior design effect rendering and systematically compare our approach with multiple state-of-the-art methods.

Keywords: Capsule · GAN · Image synthesize · Rendering

1 Introduction

Interior design concerns how to enhance the interior of a building for a healthier and more aesthetically pleasing environment. Traditional way for a interior designer to show his/her work to the customer is to design the interior 3D model with desired layout and decoration in professional software such as 3D Max. And then the designer use the software to render the model with desired color tone and lighting effect from various viewing angles to several static indoor images for

© Springer Nature Switzerland AG 2019
C. V. Jawahar et al. (Eds.): ACCV 2018, LNCS 11365, pp. 183–198, 2019.
https://doi.org/10.1007/978-3-030-20873-8_12

Fig. 1. Demonstration of our interior design effect rendering results. Details are shown on the right.

ease of viewing from customer's perspective. The rendering step is very important as a plain 3D model without any color and lighting effect would significantly hinder the customers' appreciation of the functionality and aesthetics of the original design.

While being able to produce the best rendering result, the conventional way of interior effect rendering using professional software requires a significant amount of human labor work and very time consuming. Interior designers need manually adding textures of the indoor objects, such as walls and furniture, and adjusting lighting effects by setting different light types, intensity and direction. This is usually done through a trial-and-error approach with lot of rounds of trials. Our survey shows that on average it takes about two working days for an experienced interior designer to render several images with desired effects using software.

In recent years, image generation, concerning synthesizing new images based on input and training data, has attracted tremendous attention in the research community. Representative works include synthesizing fake but real-like images using deep generative networks with various loss functions [5,6,8]. These approaches aim to translate the input image into the output with certain styles as target general images, instead of focusing on rendering effects of indoor images, hence disregard useful information such as lighting, layouts of walls and furniture, during the learning process. Another line of work focuses specifically on indoor images such as indoor navigation or VR/AR [21,25], depth estimation [19,21], or 3D to 2D rendering [20], etc. Despite focusing on indoor images, these works do not concern the rendering effect at all.

In our work, we devise a novel capsule based conditional Generative Adversarial Network (cGAN) approach to synthesize images for interior design effect rendering, with prior domain knowledge of pairs of plain images and well rendered images. Our method can generate an image in less than one second automatically. The use of cGAN enables our framework to learn a better generator by simultaneously training a discriminator to distinguish the generated synthetic images from rendered images. Noting the advantage of using capsules [18] instead of scalar based neurons in deep learning networks, our approach incorporates capsules blocks inside both generator and discriminator to encourage strong part-to-whole relationship for better coloring effect. In addition, a multi-way loss discriminator including both capsule blocks and conventional fully connected neurons (patchGAN [8]) is designed to simultaneously capture low and high frequencies during the training process. To facilitate generating realistic lighting effect, we introduce the line preservation loss to constraint the layout of the plain image. Together with pixel level loss, our line preservation loss not only helps preserve the properties that are independent of lighting effect, but also improves the lighting effect along those lines which are crucial to the effect of interior design (see Fig. 1).

Contributions. Our main contribution is the idea of applying capsule based deep learning techniques to image synthesis for interior design effect rendering; to our best knowledge, ours is the first image generation work to explicitly target interior design effect rendering. To accomplish this, our technical contributions are: (1) we adapt cGAN for synthesizing rendering effect from a training set of plain and rendered images; (2) we incorporate capsule blocks inside both generator and discriminator (multi-way) for more realistic rendering effects; (3) we introduce a novel line preservation loss to help preserve content layout of indoor images while improve lighting effect; (4) we perform an extensive evaluation and analysis to compare the proposed approach to several baselines on our Home Interior Design Effect Rendering Dataset, HIDER. Our experiment results confirm that our method produces synthetic images with a much better rendering effects. At last, we contribute to the research community by publishing our dataset for further exploration of image synthesis techniques. To our best knowledge, HIDER is the first dataset specifically designed for such task.

2 Related Work

In the initial explorations of indoor image understanding, the majority of works have put effort in traditional segmentation and recognition tasks, contributing to applications like indoor navigation, virtual/augmented reality (VR/AR), robotic vision, and etc. [21,25]. One key part to achieve these subsequent intention is to identify the object types, boundaries and learn the corresponding spatial relationship between them. Therefore, object depth estimation and RGB-D image based research take a great part in this field [19,21]. To facilitate the data-driven based approaches, some of these works [13,19,20,25] attempt to render 2D indoor images from 3D models. Our work differs in that the emphasis is put into the visual effect of synthetic images, targeting efficient interior design effect rendering, instead of modeling the visual variations caused by viewpoint changes [14,20]. To our best knowledge, due to the high-level requirement of professionalism and extreme dependency of labor/computing cost, there is a lack of extensive use of rendering data and no previous research has been dedicated to the area of synthesizing interior design rendering images.

Recent years, Generative Adversarial Networks (GANs) [6] have attracted tremendous amount of attention, which train a generator and a discriminator in an adversarial way for the purpose of generating non-existent samples. Instead of feeding randomly sampled data, conditional GAN (cGAN) is widely adopted to solve image-to-image translation problems, such as cityscapes generation [2],

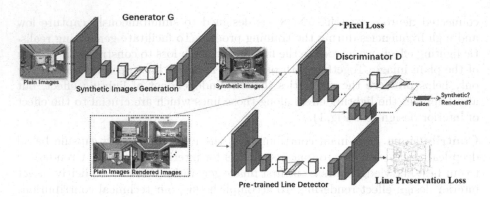

Fig. 2. The proposed image synthesis framework. The generator G, with capsule blocks built in, synthesizes the rendering effect images conditioned on the input plain images. A two-branch discriminator distinguishes the rendered ("real") and synthetic ("fake") images. The line preservation loss helps preserve the properties that are independent of lighting and coloring effect and improve the lighting effect along those lines.

aerial map translation [8], black-white colorization [24], photo generation from edges or sketch [4,23,27], day-night transformation [10], and image style transfer [9]. It attempts to output sharp and realistic local image patches by restricting its attention in the local patch [12], whereas merely considered the part-to-whole structural relationships. As a result, in the problem of rendering effect synthesis, the output images may contain ghosting artifacts that are caused by inconsistent color distribution, unreasonable lighting effect and lack of lighting reflection between objects. Unlike the other cGAN based image translation methods, our work attempts to encrypt the lighting effect as well as a part-to-whole relationships in the structural loss to maximize the rendering effect.

3   Methodology

3.1   Overview

As the name suggested, a typical cGAN trains both a generator G and a discriminator D iteratively with two adversarial objectives: (1) G aims to generate synthetic data very similar to the real data that D has trouble to distinguish; (2) D aims to discriminate the real data from the synthetic ones generated from G. Specifically, the image cGAN takes an image as the input for G and the following min-max function (Eq. (1)) concerning both G and D are optimized.

$$\min_{G} \max_{D} V(D,G) = E_{x,y \sim P_{data}(x,y)}[logD(x,y)]$$
$$+ E_{x \sim P_{data}(x)}[log(1 - D(x,G(x)))] \tag{1}$$

where x represents a plain image and y represent a rendered image from data distribution P_{data}. In our work, generator G learns a mapping $x \rightarrow y$ to produce

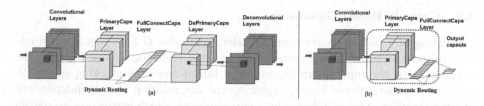

Fig. 3. (a) Capsule blocks in the Generator; (b) Capsule block in the discriminator. The red dotted area shows the original CapsNet structure introduced by [18] (Color figure online)

a synthetic image, whereas discriminator D learns to distinguish the rendered images from the ones generated by G while observing the plain image.

To facilitate realistic rendering effect, we use multiple loss in our objective function to guide the training so that our framework can generate coloring and lighting effect while keeping the content/structure information, such as base colors, shapes, and edges, from the original plain images. In particular, generator G embedded with *capsule blocks* attempts to encourage the condition in a part-to-whole manner. The *two-branch discriminator* with two branches forces G to produce images maintaining a consistent appearance (color, light, texture, and style) distribution throughout the image while keeping each local patch as real as possible. A simple L1 loss in the image space, ensures the low-frequency difference between synthetic images and their targeting rendered images as small as possible. Our *line preservation loss* encourages the preservation of the indoor layout by minimizing the L1 distance in a high-level feature space that embedding line and lighting effect information. The overall structure is shown as Fig. 2.

3.2 Capsule with Dynamic Routing

One shortcoming of Convolutional Neuron Networks (CNNs) is that the scalar representation and the additive nature for each neuron are ineffective to capture precise spatial relationships, such as part-to-whole [7]. To overcome this, Hinton et al. [7] proposed the concept of capsule, using a vector to replace scalar for each neuron in traditional neural networks. These vectorized neurons, called capsules, form a capsule layer with each of them connected to the capsules in the next layer through a *dynamic routing* algorithm [18]. Dynamic routing computes the similarity between a capsule and each of its connected capsules, while assigning corresponding weights. A larger connecting weight indicates a higher similarity. The capsule structure is shown by red dotted rectangle in Fig. 3(b). Compared with common recognition tasks, effect rendering process relies significantly on spatial relationships in the image, such as the relative positions between lights and furniture. Hence, we incorporate capsules and dynamic routing because of better capability of capturing and representing such information.

3.3 Capsule Based Generator

Consisting of a pair of encoder and decoder, generator G only requires a single forward pass to generate an synthetic image with rendering effects. Initially, the encoder maps the input plain image into a latent space by stacking several 2-step stride convolutional layers, capturing the information that is independent of lighting effect. This is followed by a capsule block which learns precise spatial relationship. Then, the decoder synthesizes the images with coloring and lighting effects by several deconvolutional layers according to the learned feature from the capsule block.

Our capsule block is composed of three layers, PrimaryCaps layer, Full-ConnectionCaps layer, and DePrimaryCaps layer, as shown in yellow boxes in Fig. 3(a). The PrimaryCaps layer is a convolutional capsule layer [18] that uses N convolutional filters to output a N-dimension capsule map for each channel. Multiple capsule maps with the same dimension of N are calculated. The Full-ConnectionCaps layer is a set of capsules fully connected with capsules from the PrimaryCaps layer with weights calculated by dynamic routing. The DePrimaryCaps layer is a set of capsule maps, which is the same size of those from PrimaryCaps layer, fully connected to the FullConnectionCaps layer with dynamic routing again. The capsule maps of this layer are calculated by deconvolutional filters after stacking all of them according to the capsule dimension into the form of conventional CNN feature maps.

In our case, it is important that the contribution of every pixel matters and adjacent pixels should contribute the same way. This is achieved by applying convolution kernels with stride of 2 to remap the feature maps, instead of using max-pooling and upsampling layers. We employ batch normalization (BN) and ReLU non-linear activation after each convolutional layer and drop-out to avoid overfitting.

3.4 Capsule Based Discriminator

Discriminator D learns to distinguish whether an image x is from real rendered data or synthesized data from G by calculating the probability of being from real data. Denoting the distribution of plain images and rendered image as $x \sim P_p(x)$ and $y \sim P_r(y)$, ultimately the distribution of synthetic images from G ($G(x) \sim P_g$ conditioned on $P_p(x)$) should be equivalent to $P_r(y)$ when the training reaches the optimum.

After several layers of convolutional filters, the network is separated into two branches, the capsule based one and the patchGAN [8] based one. The capsule based branch is expected to distinguish the "real" and "fake" rendering effects based on information learned from the whole image emphasizing on spatial part-to-whole relationship. The patchGAN branch tries to distinguish the input of the discriminator at local level by observing each patch from the feature map of the last convolutional layer. Our aim is to make the discriminator distinguish the images in both low and high frequencies, the global rendering effects and the local details.

The discriminator structure is shown in Fig. 2 and a closer view of the capsule branch is shown in Fig. 3(b). The capsule branch consists of a PrimaryCaps Layer, a FullConnectionCaps layer and two output capsules, which represent the instances of "rendered" and "synthetic". The cost function is calculated as the margin loss [18] out of the two capsules. The patchGAN branch stacks three more convolutional layers and calculates the average patch-wise binary cross entropy classification loss on the last feature map. Specifically, the loss functions of the capsule branch, $\mathcal{L}_{caps\_D}$ and $\mathcal{L}_{caps\_G}$, for the optimization of D and G respectively are written as in Eqs. (2) and (3)

$$\mathcal{L}_{caps\_D} = E_{x\sim P_p(x), y\sim P_r(y)}[\mathcal{L}_M(D_{caps}(x,y), [0,1]) + \mathcal{L}_M(D_{caps}(x, G(x)), [0,1])]$$
$$(2)$$

$$\mathcal{L}_{caps\_G} = E_{x\sim P_p(x)}\mathcal{L}_M(D_{caps}(x, G(x)), [0,1]) \qquad (3)$$

where $\mathcal{L}_M$ is the margin loss as in [18], and D_{caps} is the output of capsule branch.

The loss functions of patchGAN branch, $\mathcal{L}_{patchG\_D}$ and $\mathcal{L}_{patchG\_G}$, optimizing D and G respectively, are written as in Eqs. (4) and (5)

$$\mathcal{L}_{patchG\_D} = E_{x\sim P_p(x), y\sim P_r(y)}Aver(log(1 - D_{patchG}(x,y)) + log(D_{patchG}(x, G(x))))$$
$$(4)$$

$$\mathcal{L}_{patchG\_G} = E_{x\sim P_p(x)}Aver(log(1 - D_{patchG}(x, G(x)))) \qquad (5)$$

where D_{patchG} is the output of patchGAN branch, and $Aver(\cdot)$ calculates the mean of the data. Thus, the overall discriminator loss functions, $\mathcal{L}_{disc\_D}$ and $\mathcal{L}_{disc\_G}$, optimizing D and G respectively, are written as in Eqs. (6) and (7)

$$\mathcal{L}_{disc\_D} = \mathcal{L}_{caps\_D} + \lambda_1\mathcal{L}_{patchG\_D} \qquad (6)$$

$$\mathcal{L}_{disc\_G} = \mathcal{L}_{caps\_G} + \lambda_1\mathcal{L}_{patchG\_G} \qquad (7)$$

where λ_1 is the weight balancing the two branches.

3.5   Line Preservation

Unlike general images, the line shapes of the objects in indoor images, such as wall, decorations, or furniture, are massive and important in reflecting the overall and local lighting effects. Due to the variety of light directions, some line shapes are omitted and some "light lines" (lighting effect along the lines) appears. Therefore, we introduce a line constraint on G to improve lighting effects by preserving line shapes. In particular, besides generator G described in Sect. 3.3, we add another generator (with the same structure) as our line detector L that takes an plain image as input and output a image with lines that are important to effect rendering. Our dedicated line detector L is specially trained on millions of indoor images [26] with the groundtruth generated using FastLine [11]. Compared to simply applying the state-of-the-art line detection techniques, our line detector can capture lines that appears in and are important to indoor images with rendering effects. We use the same discrimination loss as introduced in Sect. 3.4 and L1 distance loss to model the mapping in L.

In particular, our line detector L is appended to G as the *Line Preservation Loss* formulated as $\mathcal{L}_{line}$ in Eq. (8). Our *Line Preservation Loss* ensures the preservation of the line shapes of the synthetic image under the rendering lighting effects and guides the learning process in this way.

$$\mathcal{L}_{line} = E_{x \sim P_p(s), y \sim P_r(y)}[\|L(y) - L(G(x))\|_1] \tag{8}$$

where $L(\cdot)$ is the output of L and $\mathcal{L}_{line}$ is passed back to G without updating the parameters of L, while performing the adversarial training.

3.6   Objective and Optimization Functions

Previous research show that image cGANs benefit from extra supervision signals during the adversarial learning [8,15]. Therefore, we use pixel loss to penalize the difference between $G(x)$ and the groundtruth of $y \sim P_r$, see Eq. (9). Instead of L2 distance, we use L1 distance as we find that L1 works the best during the optimization in our work, especially when D finds improper distinguishable features.

$$\mathcal{L}_{pixel} = E_{x \sim P_p(x), y \sim P_r(y)}[\|y - G(x)\|_1] \tag{9}$$

By combining Eqs. (6), (7), (8) and (9), our final objective functions, Obj_G and Obj_D, for G and D respectively are formulated as in Eqs. (10) and (11).

$$Obj_G = \arg \min_G [\mathcal{L}_{disc\_G} + \lambda_2 \mathcal{L}_{line} + \lambda_3 \mathcal{L}_{pixel}] \tag{10}$$

$$Obj_D = \arg \min_D \mathcal{L}_{disc\_D} \tag{11}$$

where λ_2 and λ_3 are balancing weights to control the loss contribution from the line preservation and pixel loss.

4   Dataset - HIDER

To our best knowledge, there is no image dataset dedicated to interior design effect rendering, which maps the plain to the rendered images. Therefore, we propose our Home Interior Design Effect Rendering dataset, HIDER, containing image pairs of plain and rendered images. We employed 20 professionals to design 300 home interior design models using the software *3D Max* [1]. The models are designed for various rooms including living room, study room, bedroom, and dinning room, and various styles including modern, post-modern, European, and Chinese. 1−3 pairs of images were rendered from a single model from different view angles. Various light types, illumination, and lit angless are also adjusted for best rendering effects. In total, 584 pairs of 1300×939 plain and rendered images are generated in our dataset. We also prepared a 512×512 version to benefit current state-of-the-art frameworks. Examples are shown in Fig. 4.

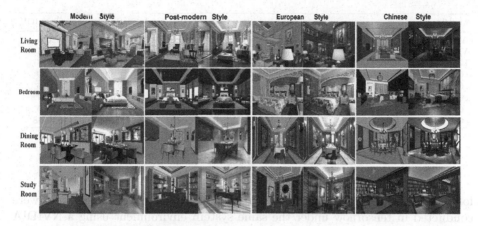

Fig. 4. Examples from our HIDER dataset with four room types and four styles.

4.1 Data Preparation and Implementation Details

Data Preparation. We use the 512-sized version of our HIDER dataset to train the proposed network. The dataset is randomly separated into training and testing sets with a ratio 8:2. Prior to feeding the images into our network, data augmentation is adopted by performing cropping and mirror flipping on both plain and rendered images. In our experiments, to ensure each input image maintains majority visual content, we first resize images into 600×600 pixels and then crop and flip them into ten 512×512 pixels image patches, resulting 4600 training pairs.

Implementation Details. As demonstrated in Fig. 2, the architecture of G starts with eight 2-step stride convolutional layers, followed by the capsule block and the corresponding deconvolutional layers. In the capsule block inside G, 64 channels of 8D convolutional capsule layers are used in both the PrimaryCaps and DePrimaryCaps layers, fully connecting to 64 16D capsules in the FullConnectionCaps layer. Similar to the experimental setting in [18], we set the number of iterations for dynamic routing as three.

Discriminator D is constructed by three 2-step stride convolutional layers, followed by a two-branch stacking layers. The capsule branch consists of a PrimaryCaps layer with 32 channels of 8D convolutional capsule and a FullConnectionCaps layer with 10 8D capsules, outputting two 8D capsules representing the probability of rendered image (real) and synthetic image (fake). The patchGAN branch stacks three convolutional layers and output a 1D feature map with size of 30×30 for patch-wise discrimination.

Both G and D are trained iteratively according to objective Obj_G and Obj_D specified in Sect. 3.6. The line detector L and pixel losses only contribute to the training of G without updating the parameters of L. The loss balancing weights are empirically set as $\lambda_1 = 0.2$, $\lambda_2 = 10$, $\lambda_3 = 10$. We use Adam optimizer with a learning rate of 0.0001. All our experiment setups are trained

Models	nrmse(L2)	L1	psnr	ssim	Per-pixel acc.	Per-class acc.	Class IOU
AE[23]	0.4135	0.1956	13.74	0.5889	0.8728	0.2849	0.2081
VAE[17]	0.4293	0.2092	13.23	0.5907	0.8912	0.2615	0.2231
U-net[18]	0.3327	0.1552	14.17	0.6537	0.9031	0.3276	0.2737
cGAN[9]	0.3160	0.1626	14.71	0.6271	0.9126	0.3901	0.3200
cGAN+Caps(our method)	0.2779	0.1273	15.85	0.7184	**0.9202**	0.3653	0.3056
cGAN+Caps^2(our method)	0.3081	0.1375	15.08	0.6440	0.9157	0.3733	0.3087
cGAN+Caps+line(our method)	**0.2063**	**0.1073**	**16.91**	**0.7356**	0.9166	0.3807	0.3105
cGAN+Caps^2+line(our method)	0.2600	0.1160	15.77	0.6542	0.9123	**0.4308**	**0.3368**

Fig. 5. Quantitative evaluation results using various metrics.

for 200 epochs on the HIDER dataset with batch size 4. All the experiments were conducted in tensorflow under the same system environment using a NVIDIA GPU, GTX1080TI or TITAN X (Pascal).

4.2   Performance Comparison and Analysis

We evaluate our approach by analyzing the performance of each proposed components and comparing with the state-of-the-art methods. We choose our baselines including image Autoencoder (AE) [22], Variational Autoencoder (VAE) [16], U-net [8,17], and cGAN (pix2pix) [8]. For our proposed network architecture, we perform ablation studies to interpret the performance of line preservation term, capsule block term, together with the discriminator using a single branch against our discriminator using two branches, respectively. Our experimental model settings are denoted by $[cGAN + Caps]$, $[cGAN + Caps + line]$, $[cGAN + Caps^2]$ and $[cGAN + Caps^2 + line]$, where $[cGAN]$ is the base image cGAN model, $[* + Caps]$ means the network using capsule blocks, $[* + Caps^2]$ shorts for the two-branch-discriminator implementation, and $[* + line]$ represents the use of line preservation loss. In all these settings, we keep the pixel loss since this is not considered as our contribution.

Quantitative Evaluation. Quantitative evaluation is challenging in the field of image synthesis. In this experiment, we evaluate and compare our proposed generative models from three perspectives: (1) using mean-squared error (mse) and L1 distance to measure the similarity between synthesized and target image at the pixel level; (2) adopting the peak signal to noise ratio (psnr) and structural similarity index (ssim) metric to measure the quality of synthesized image at signal level; (3) applying FCN-score to measure the discriminability of the generated image at semantic level, as suggested by [8]. For the FCN-score, we use the pre-trained FCN-8s [3] classifiers to segment both the rendered and the synthetic images, and compute the per-pixel accuracy, per-class accuracy and class IOU.

Figure 5 shows the evaluation results. Note that baseline AE, VAE and U-net are generative models without discriminator, while the cGAN [8] having a patchGAN discriminator contributing to high frequency visual content. By comparing cGAN [8] against U-net [17], we can observe the trade-off between

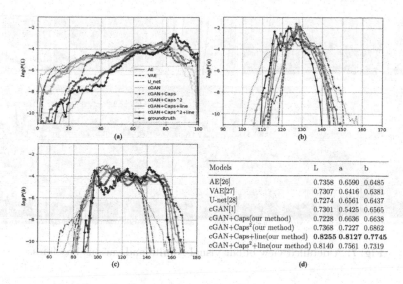

The table shown as part (d) of the figure:

Models	L	a	b
AE[26]	0.7358	0.6590	0.6485
VAE[27]	0.7307	0.6416	0.6381
U-net[28]	0.7274	0.6561	0.6437
cGAN[1]	0.7301	0.5425	0.6565
cGAN+Caps(our method)	0.7228	0.6636	0.6638
cGAN+Caps^2(our method)	0.7368	0.7227	0.6862
cGAN+Caps+line(our method)	**0.8255**	**0.8127**	**0.7745**
cGAN+Caps^2+line(our method)	0.8140	0.7561	0.7319

Fig. 6. Color distribution in Lab space and histogram intersection scores results calculated against ground truth distribution. (Color figure online)

pixel and semantic level metrics results, where cGAN shows much better FCN-score results with a lower ssim and L1 scores.

The quantitative results show that all of our proposed models outperform the three generative models in both tables and our $cGAN + Caps^2 + line$ model boosts the per-class accuracy and class IOU scores greatly compared to previous best cGAN based [8] model, indicating that our approach can simultaneously encourage low and high frequency correctness throughout the image at both pixel and semantic level. In addition, we can see that our adoption of capsule blocks alone can boost the pixel and signal level scores while maintaining good results in FCN-Score. Our line preservation loss can further improve the result at both the pixel and semantic level by comparing the proposed model with/without the line preservation loss. Compared with a single capsule-block-branch discriminator, a decrease in pixel/signal level metrics while a performance boosting in semantic level metric can be observed with if two-branch discriminator is applied. This is because the two-branch discriminator also penalize the synthetic images in a patch-wise fashion, guiding the generator producing images with fine details. The results is consistent with the comparison between U-net and cGAN [8]. Combining all quantitative results, we could see our $cGAN + Caps + line$ model outperform all the other methods in the pixel/signal level, while our $cGAN + Caps^2 + line$ model obtain a better performance in a semantic level.

Color and Lighting Fidelity Evaluation. Color plays an important role in synthesizing images, especially for effects rendering. To further investigate the performance of our models from a visual perspective, we plot the color distribution in the Lab color space and compute the histogram intersection scores between the synthetic and ground truth images. The result is shown in Fig. 6.

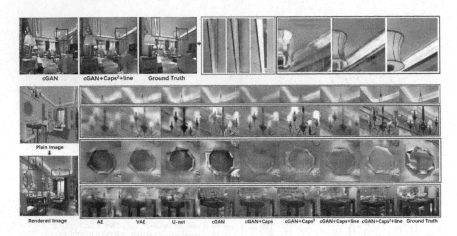

Fig. 7. A detailed view of our visual results and various baselines.

The ground truth distribution are shown as black lines. We can see that both our $cGAN + Caps + line$ and $cGAN + Caps^2 + line$ models obtain very similar distribution compared with the ground truth in all channels, and they outperform all the other models greatly in the histogram score results.

The color distribution shows the use of capsule blocks encourages ground truth alike lighting effect while avoiding grayish pattern caused by the averaging attempt guided by uncertainty in AE, VAE and U-net. Unsurprisingly, the lighting effect encouraged by the line preservation loss can also be observed in Fig. 6(a). In Fig. 6(b) and (c), we can see that the pure generative model based methods (AE, VAE and U-net) tend to produce a narrower color distribution in the green-red space. On the other hand, the cGAN [8] tends to produce much wider distribution, resulting unrealistic visual pattern. In addition, models from AE, VAE, U-net, and cGAN [8] all tend to synthesize images with blue (cool-toned) pattern closer to plain images while producing less red alike (warm-toned) pattern that closer to ground truth images.

Rendering Effect Fidelity Evaluation. We acknowledge that the quantitative results and color distribution is not enough to measure whether the synthetic images contain aesthetically pleasing rendering effect. Therefore, a more comprehensive evaluation is provided with visual analysis to match the visual sense of human perception.

We illustrate the synthesized images from different methods in Fig. 8 and demonstrate visual details in Fig. 7, starting with input plain images and ending with the ground truth images. As shown in the Fig. 8, AE, VAE and U-net tend to generate greyish and blury images because of the absent of discriminator, resulting in relatively low pixel-wise distance but hard to recognize structures at semantic level. The results are unacceptable in the context of interior design effect rendering. Compared to pure generative models, the output of cGAN [8] is able to preserve more local details by using patchGAN discriminator and

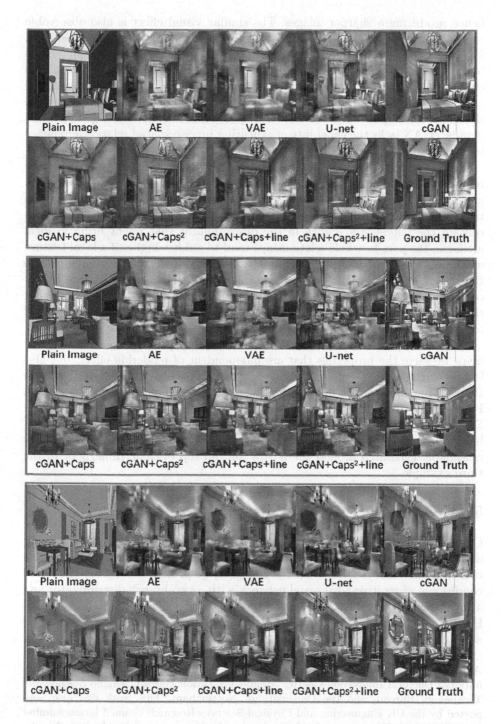

Fig. 8. Visual comparison of our approach and various baselines.

hence producing a sharper images. The similar visual effect is also observable in our models, where two-branch discriminator encourages more detailed local features. However, the overall coloring effect of the results from cGAN [8] tend to be distorted and cool-tone instead of warm-tone. If we take a deeper look at the cGAN [8] output, both the background wall of the TV in the second example and floor from the third example seem locally real but appear abruptly from the whole image point of view. This is because, while being able to generate fine details, cGAN lacks the capability of capturing precise spatial relationship hence tends to produce incoherent rendering effects.

In contrast, our capsule based method ensures capturing the part-to-whole relationships among the whole images. It is very obvious that all of our proposed capsule block based output obtain a closer coloring compared with the ground truth image. Although both $cGAN + Caps^2$ and $cGAN + Caps^2 + line$ models contain the patchGAN branch in the discriminator that might bring in local artifacts, the part-to-whole relationships tend to guide whether if a local texture or the coloring and lighting effect is reasonable globally. For example, unlike the cGAN [8] result in the second example, the artifacts in TV is kept in our results while fake lighting effect on the background wall is restricted. Similarly, the floor texture of the third example is maintained consistent throughout all of our proposed methods' output.

The visual results also demonstrate that our line preservation loss not only helps preserve the properties that are independent of rendering effect, but also improves these effects along the lines. It is clearly observable that light and shade is more distinctive and the lighting effect is well captured in our results. For example, in the images synthesized by $cGAN + Caps + line$ and $cGAN + Caps^2 + line$, the chandelier is sharper and the lighting effect along the light belt is more realistic in all three examples. In addition, the lighting reflection is reasonably generated around the mirror and on top of chair/table/floor in the third example.

5   Conclusion

Our work brings the idea of image translation to automatically synthesize rendering effect for interior design with the need for manual rendering from software in a trial-and-error manner. Towards this goal, we present a novel capsule based conditional generative adversarial network with a two-branch discriminator and a novel line preservation loss. Our extensive experiments and analysis on our HIDER dataset shows that our framework is able to generate more realistic and aesthetically pleasing rendering effect at both detail and semantic levels.

Acknowledgement. The author acknowledges the financial support from the International Doctoral Innovation Centre, Ningbo Education Bureau, Ningbo Science and Technology Bureau, and the University of Nottingham. This work was also supported by the UK Engineering and Physical Sciences Research Council [grant number EP/L015463/1]. We are grateful for access to the University of Nottingham Ningbo China High Performance Computing Facility.

References

1. Autodesk: 3D max. https://www.autodesk.com/products/3ds-max/overview
2. Cordts, M., et al.: The cityscapes dataset for semantic urban scene understanding. In: Proceedings of the IEEE Conference on Computer Vision and Pattern Recognition (CVPR), pp. 3213–3223 (2016)
3. Dai, J., Li, Y., He, K., Sun, J.: R-FCN: object detection via region-based fully convolutional networks. In: Advances in Neural Information Processing Systems (NIPS), pp. 379–387 (2016)
4. Eitz, M., Hays, J., Alexa, M.: How do humans sketch objects? ACM Trans. Graph. **31**(4), 44:1–44:10 (2012)
5. Gatys, L.A., Ecker, A.S., Bethge, M.: Image style transfer using convolutional neural networks. In: 2016 IEEE Conference on Computer Vision and Pattern Recognition (CVPR), pp. 2414–2423. IEEE (2016)
6. Goodfellow, I.J., et al.: Generative adversarial nets. In: International Conference on Neural Information Processing Systems (ICONIP), pp. 2672–2680 (2014)
7. Hinton, G.E., Krizhevsky, A., Wang, S.D.: Transforming auto-encoders. In: Honkela, T., Duch, W., Girolami, M., Kaski, S. (eds.) ICANN 2011. LNCS, vol. 6791, pp. 44–51. Springer, Heidelberg (2011). https://doi.org/10.1007/978-3-642-21735-7_6
8. Isola, P., Zhu, J.Y., Zhou, T., Efros, A.A.: Image-to-image translation with conditional adversarial networks. In: 2017 IEEE Conference on Computer Vision and Pattern Recognition (CVPR), pp. 5967–5976. IEEE (2017)
9. Johnson, J., Alahi, A., Fei-Fei, L.: Perceptual losses for real-time style transfer and super-resolution. In: Leibe, B., Matas, J., Sebe, N., Welling, M. (eds.) ECCV 2016. LNCS, vol. 9906, pp. 694–711. Springer, Cham (2016). https://doi.org/10.1007/978-3-319-46475-6_43
10. Laffont, P.Y., Ren, Z., Tao, X., Qian, C., Hays, J.: Transient attributes for high-level understanding and editing of outdoor scenes. ACM Trans. Graph. (TOG) **33**(4), 149 (2014)
11. Lee, J.H., Lee, S., Zhang, G., Lim, J., Chung, W.K., Suh, I.H.: Outdoor place recognition in urban environments using straight lines. In: 2014 IEEE International Conference on Robotics and Automation (ICRA), pp. 5550–5557. IEEE (2014)
12. Li, C., Wand, M.: Precomputed real-time texture synthesis with Markovian generative adversarial networks. In: Leibe, B., Matas, J., Sebe, N., Welling, M. (eds.) ECCV 2016. LNCS, vol. 9907, pp. 702–716. Springer, Cham (2016). https://doi.org/10.1007/978-3-319-46487-9_43
13. Movshovitz-Attias, Y., Kanade, T., Sheikh, Y.: How useful is photo-realistic rendering for visual learning? In: Hua, G., Jégou, H. (eds.) ECCV 2016. LNCS, vol. 9915, pp. 202–217. Springer, Cham (2016). https://doi.org/10.1007/978-3-319-49409-8_18
14. Movshovitz-Attias, Y., Sheikh, Y., Boddeti, V.N., Wei, Z.: 3D pose-by-detection of vehicles via discriminatively reduced ensembles of correlation filters. In: British Machine Vision Conference (BMVC) (2014)
15. Pathak, D., Krahenbuhl, P., Donahue, J., Darrell, T., Efros, A.A.: Context encoders: feature learning by inpainting. In: Proceedings of the IEEE Conference on Computer Vision and Pattern Recognition (CVPR), pp. 2536–2544 (2016)
16. Pu, Y., et al.: Variational autoencoder for deep learning of images, labels and captions. In: Advances in Neural Information Processing Systems (NIPS), pp. 2352–2360 (2016)

17. Ronneberger, O., Fischer, P., Brox, T.: U-Net: convolutional networks for biomedical image segmentation. In: Navab, N., Hornegger, J., Wells, W.M., Frangi, A.F. (eds.) MICCAI 2015. LNCS, vol. 9351, pp. 234–241. Springer, Cham (2015). https://doi.org/10.1007/978-3-319-24574-4_28
18. Sabour, S., Frosst, N., Hinton, G.E.: Dynamic routing between capsules. In: Advances in Neural Information Processing Systems (NIPS), pp. 3859–3869 (2017)
19. Song, S., Yu, F., Zeng, A., Chang, A.X., Savva, M., Funkhouser, T.: Semantic scene completion from a single depth image. In: 2017 IEEE Conference on Computer Vision and Pattern Recognition (CVPR), pp. 190–198. IEEE (2017)
20. Su, H., Qi, C.R., Li, Y., Guibas, L.J.: Render for CNN: viewpoint estimation in images using CNNs trained with rendered 3D model views. In: Proceedings of the IEEE International Conference on Computer Vision (ICCV), pp. 2686–2694 (2015)
21. Taira, H., et al.: InLoc: indoor visual localization with dense matching and view synthesis. In: Proceedings of the IEEE Conference on Computer Vision and Pattern Recognition (CVPR), pp. 7199–7209 (2018)
22. Xie, G.-S., Zhang, X.-Y., Liu, C.-L.: Efficient feature coding based on auto-encoder network for image classification. In: Cremers, D., Reid, I., Saito, H., Yang, M.-H. (eds.) ACCV 2014. LNCS, vol. 9003, pp. 628–642. Springer, Cham (2015). https://doi.org/10.1007/978-3-319-16865-4_41
23. Yu, A., Grauman, K.: Fine-grained visual comparisons with local learning. In: Proceedings of the IEEE Conference on Computer Vision and Pattern Recognition (CVPR), pp. 192–199 (2014)
24. Zhang, R., Isola, P., Efros, A.A.: Colorful image colorization. In: Leibe, B., Matas, J., Sebe, N., Welling, M. (eds.) ECCV 2016. LNCS, vol. 9907, pp. 649–666. Springer, Cham (2016). https://doi.org/10.1007/978-3-319-46487-9_40
25. Zhang, Y., et al.: Physically-based rendering for indoor scene understanding using convolutional neural networks. In: 2017 IEEE Conference on Computer Vision and Pattern Recognition (CVPR), pp. 5057–5065. IEEE (2017)
26. Zhang, Y., Yu, F., Song, S., Xu, P., Seff, A., Xiao, J.: Large-scale scene understanding challenge: room layout estimation (2015). Accessed 15 Sep 2015
27. Zhu, J.-Y., Krähenbühl, P., Shechtman, E., Efros, A.A.: Generative visual manipulation on the natural image manifold. In: Leibe, B., Matas, J., Sebe, N., Welling, M. (eds.) ECCV 2016. LNCS, vol. 9909, pp. 597–613. Springer, Cham (2016). https://doi.org/10.1007/978-3-319-46454-1_36

Deep Upright Adjustment of 360 Panoramas Using Multiple Roll Estimations

Junho Jeon, Jinwoong Jung, and Seungyong Lee[⊠]

POSTECH, Pohang, South Korea
{zwitterion27,jinwoong.jung,leesy}@postech.ac.kr

Abstract. Misalignment of the orientations between a 360 camera and the scene results in a wavy and distorted spherical panorama image, which may look unstable and have poor perceptual quality. To automatically correct such mis-oriented 360 panoramas, this paper proposes a novel upright adjustment framework based on a convolutional neural network. Instead of directly predicting the 3D rotation of the camera on a given panorama image, our method estimates the rotation by analyzing the projected 2D rotations of multiple images sampled from the panorama. To accurately estimate the rotations of 2D sampled images, we train a 2D roll estimation network using a large-scale labeled image dataset generated by cropping 360 spherical panoramas with various view orientations. Experimental results demonstrate that the proposed method accurately and robustly handles upright adjustment of rotated panoramas while outperforming the previous methods on test datasets that consist of a variety of scenes.

1 Introduction

With the progress of imaging sensors, consumer-level 360 panorama cameras (e.g., Ricoh Theta S, Samsung Gear 360) become cheaper and popular. Typical 360 cameras do not have viewfinder screens while simultaneously capturing the entire view directions (omni-direction) in any poses, so casual users tend not to care about the camera orientations during the capture. However, misalignment of the orientations between the camera and the scene results in wavy and distorted panorama images (Fig. 1a). The wavy horizon and distorted objects look visually unstable, especially when the panorama is used for a VR application with a narrow field-of-view display, such as HMD [14]. Moreover, the objects on the wavy horizon may suffer from severe deformations, which drastically reduce the perceptual quality of panorama images as salient parts of a scene are usually located around the horizon.

Electronic supplementary material The online version of this chapter (https://doi.org/10.1007/978-3-030-20873-8_13) contains supplementary material, which is available to authorized users.

(a) input distorted panorama   (b) upright adjustment result

Fig. 1. Our upright adjustment method works accurately and robustly for a severely rotated 360 spherical panorama even when the vanishing structures are not clearly detectable.

Correction of this mis-orientation of the camera is called *upright adjustment* [19], and it requires the estimation of the 3D camera rotation relative to the scene. Few recent works [3,14] addressed upright adjustment of 360 panoramas by analyzing the structural features of the scene, especially horizontal and vertical lines as well as vanishing points. Unfortunately, these methods work well only if the given scene follows the specific assumption on the orthogonality of scene structures, such as Manhattan or Atlanta world [6,26], which could be violated in many cases, e.g., natural scenes.

In this paper, we propose a novel automatic upright adjustment framework for 360 panorama images based on a deep convolutional neural network. Instead of using hand-crafted features extracted from a given 360 spherical panorama, our method indirectly estimates the camera rotation by analyzing the projected 2D rotations estimated from multiple narrow field-of-view images sampled from the input panorama. Our proposed framework exploits the semantically trained CNN features rather than straight line segments and vanishing points, and can robustly handle a variety of scenes no matter whether they follow the Manhattan or Atlanta world assumption.

Various experiments on a test dataset show that our method achieves the state-of-the-art performance in both accuracy and robustness, compared to previous methods that are based on straight lines and vanishing points detected in the scene. Furthermore, our method works well on datasets of various scene categories which do not follow the Manhattan and Atlanta world assumptions, demonstrating the benefits of our deep neural network based approach that could learn the semantic upright direction of the scene even when the horizontal and vertical lines are not clearly detectable.

In summary, the key contributions of our work are as follows:

- we propose a 3D camera rotation estimation method for 360 spherical panoramas by exploiting the geometric relationship between a 3D rotation and projected 2D rotations.
- we generate a large-scale labeled narrow field-of-view image dataset that can be used for supervised learning of roll (in-plane image rotation) angle estimation, by cropping 360 spherical panoramas using various view orientations.

- our trained convolutional neural network shows mean absolute error (MAE) about 1° in roll angle estimation for a 2D image.
- our 3D camera rotation estimation for 360 panoramas shows the state-of-the-art performance in both accuracy and robustness, and can handle a variety of scenes where the Manhattan or Atlanta world assumption is not satisfied.

2 Related Work

2.1 Upright Adjustment and Camera Orientation Estimation

Automatic correction of a tilted photograph has been researched for a decade, and the existing works are mainly based on vanishing structure analysis [2,8,10, 23]. Recently Lee et al. [18,19] proposed a set of criteria to straighten-up slanted photos while minimizing perceptual distortions.

Camera calibration estimates the relative orientation of a camera in the environment. With the Manhattan and Atlanta world assumptions [6,26], scene structure analysis for camera calibration has been actively studied. Bazin et al. [4] proposed a method to estimate the globally optimal vanishing points in a Manhattan world. Joo et al. [12] presented a precise Atlanta direction estimation algorithm with inlier set maximization. Recently Zhai et al. [29] proposed a horizon and vanishing point detection algorithm without assuming the Manhattan or Atlanta world.

2.2 Upright Adjustment of 360 Spherical Panoramas

Although omnidirectional vision has been actively researched in computer vision and robotics [5,15,17,25], estimation of 3D camera rotation for 360 panoramas, i.e., upright adjustment of a single 360 panorama image, has not been much studied yet. Bazin et al. [3] presented a top-down approach for rotation estimation of an omnidirectional camera based on vanishing point detection with the Manhattan world assumption. Jung et al. [14] proposed vertical/horizontal line clustering and iterative optimization to robustly estimate 360 camera rotation under the Atlanta world assumption.

These methods [3,14] assume the environment as a Manhattan or Atlanta world, and may fail for panoramas which do not follow the assumption. In addition, as the methods depend on detecting and clustering straight line segments and vanishing points, lack of such features would incur inaccurate and unstable upright adjustment results. In this paper, we overcome these limitations by proposing a deep learning based approach that does not assume any specific scene structure.

2.3 CNN-Based Upright Adjustment

With the success of deep learning on image analysis and understanding, there have been a few attempts to apply deep learning for image orientation estimation.

Fischer et al. [9] trained a CNN with an artificially rotated image dataset to predict in-plane image rotation (roll). Olmschenk et al. [24] proposed a network to estimate pitch and roll at the same time for a given image. Recently Joshi and Guerzhoy [13] trained a CNN classifier to distinguish the orientation of an image in four directions $\{0°, 90°, 180°, 270°\}$.

All these existing methods focus on ordinary images with conventional field-of-views, and a deep learning based approach has not been exploited yet for upright adjustment of 360 spherical panoramas.

3   3D Rotation Estimation of 360 Spherical Panoramas

A 360 spherical panorama captured with a rotated camera shows wavy and distorted appearance when it is represented using equirectangular projection. A narrow field-of-view projection of the panorama shows a tilted image, as the 3D rotated world is projected onto the 2D image plane. In this section, we formulate the relationship between a 3D camera rotation and a projected 2D rotation, and propose a novel framework to compute the 3D rotation using multiple samples of 2D rotation estimates.

3.1   Rotation of 360 Spherical Panorama

Upright adjustment of a 360 spherical panorama can be considered as 3D rotation estimation for a 360 camera from the input panorama. Once we have estimated the camera rotation, the given panorama can easily be made upright by applying the inverse rotation. Since a 3D rotation can be represented by various conventions, we first clarify the notation before describing the relationship between 2D and 3D rotations.

A 3D rotation that should be estimated for upright adjustment of 360 panoramas has only two degree-of-freedoms (DOFs) as it can be modeled as a position change of the north pole on the globe [14], as illustrated in Fig. 2a. In the previous work [14], a 3D rotation is represented with two rotation angles, tilt and roll. For better understanding, in this paper, we use a different but equivalent definition of a 3D *intrinsic* rotation of a 360 camera using *yaw* α and *roll* β. Intrinsic rotation means that each element rotation (yaw and roll) occurs with the intrinsic vertical axis attached to the camera itself. As shown in Fig. 2a, an arbitrary camera rotation (α, β) is performed in two steps. The viewing direction of the camera is first rotated by α around the vertical axis, and then the camera with the vertical axis is rotated by β around the rotated viewing direction.

As shown in Fig. 2b, an equirectangular panorama captured by a rotated 360 camera shows a wavy horizon along the horizontal centerline of the image. If we crop the panorama into perspective images with narrow field-of-views, which we call *sampled images*, this wavy horizon would be shown as tilted (slanted horizon) or nodded (higher or lower eye level) in accordance with the viewing directions. Intuitively, the horizon is most slanted when the viewing direction

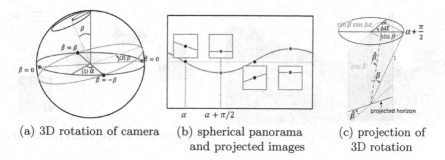

(a) 3D rotation of camera   (b) spherical panorama   (c) projection of
                            and projected images   3D rotation

Fig. 2. Relation between 3D and 2D rotations. (a) 3D rotation (α, β) of the camera and the captured 360 panorama image. (b) Original ground plane (blue) becomes a wavy horizon when projected along the horizontal centerline of the rotated 360 camera (red). Perspective projections of the panorama with a narrow field-of-view produce tilted or nodded images according to the viewing directions (small rectangles). (c) The angle between the original upright direction and a rotated direction (roll of a 2D image) becomes smaller as it is projected onto a rotated image plane. (Color figure online)

agrees with the yaw α of the 3D rotation, while the horizon becomes flat for the viewing direction orthogonal to the yaw.

With this observation, we can develop an algorithm that estimates a 3D rotation (α, β) for a given distorted (rotated) 360 spherical panorama by analyzing the rotations of multiple sampled images. To this end, we formulate the relationship between the 3D rotation of a 360 camera and the 2D rotations of sampled images in the following section.

3.2 3D Rotation Estimation from Multiple 2D Sampled Images

The geometric derivation between 2D and 3D rotations in a spherical panorama can be explained with Fig. 2. The blue vertical line in Fig. 2a represents the vertical axis perpendicular to the ground. As shown in Fig. 2c, when the vertical axis is projected to a rotated image plane (gray), the angle $\hat{\beta}$ between the vertical axis of the camera (solid red line) and the projected vertical axis (dashed blue line) can be derived using a trigonometric relationship.

We call $\hat{\beta}$ as the *projected roll* because the angle is identical to the in-plane rotation angle of the projected horizon. When the view direction is rotated with an angle $\Delta\alpha$ from the yaw α, the projection image plane is also rotated away from $\alpha + \pi/2$ by the amount of $\Delta\alpha$. We can then derive the following function f that relates the rotation angle $\Delta\alpha$ with the projected roll $\hat{\beta}$:

$$\tan\hat{\beta} = \frac{\sin\beta\cos(\Delta\alpha)}{\cos\beta}$$

$$\hat{\beta} = f(\Delta\alpha; \beta) = \tan^{-1}\left(\tan\beta\cos(\Delta\alpha)\right),$$

where the function $f(\Delta\alpha; \beta)$ is a periodic function that has the maximum β and minimum $-\beta$ at $\Delta\alpha = 0$ and $\Delta\alpha = \pi$, respectively.

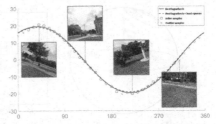

(a) input spherical panorama   (b) estimated samples and fitted curve

Fig. 3. Estimation of 3D rotation function $f(\hat{\alpha}; \alpha, \beta)$. (a) input panorama image. (b) sample estimates (blue dots) and some corresponding images with the best hypothesis (black dashed curve) and the least squares solution (green curve). (Color figure online)

To measure the yaw angle α, we introduce an auxiliary variable $\hat{\alpha}$, where $\hat{\alpha} = 0$ at the leftmost of the panorama image, and define $\Delta\alpha$ as the difference between $\hat{\alpha}$ and the yaw angle α, i.e., $\Delta\alpha = \hat{\alpha} - \alpha$. Then the function f can be represented as follows:

$$\hat{\beta} = f(\hat{\alpha}; \alpha, \beta) = \tan^{-1}\left(\tan\beta\cos\left(\hat{\alpha} - \alpha\right)\right).$$

If we know two distinct points $(\hat{\alpha}_1, \hat{\beta}_1)$, $(\hat{\alpha}_2, \hat{\beta}_2)$ on $f(\hat{\alpha}; \alpha, \beta)$, we can determine a unique solution for α and β, i.e., 3D rotation of the camera. However, for more robust estimation, we determine a 3D rotation (α, β) using the roll estimation results from multiple sampled images. Figure 3 illustrates the pipeline of our framework and the detailed steps are in the following.

1. Sample N narrow field-of-view images $\{I_i\}_{i=1}^{N}$ around the horizontal centerline of a given spherical panorama using uniformly distributed viewing angles $\{\hat{\alpha}_i\}_{i=1}^{N}$.
2. Estimate the projected roll $\{\hat{\beta}_i\}_{i=1}^{N}$ of the sample images using our *roll estimation network*, which will be described in the following section. Now we have multiple yaw/roll pairs $\{(\hat{\alpha}_i, \hat{\beta}_i)\}_{i=1}^{N}$.
3. Use exhaustive search to find the best hypothesis (α', β'), which maximizes the number of inlier samples among the multiple pairs.
4. Determine the function parameters (α, β) using the least-squares fitting of inlier samples.

Through all experiments in this paper, we used 36 uniformly sampled images (i.e., $N = 36$) with 60° for the field-of-view. As the number of samples are only 36, we use an exhaustive search to find the best hypothesis for outlier rejection. If a larger number of samples are used for better accuracy, RANSAC could be an option, instead of the exhaustive search, for avoiding too much increase of the computation time.

Even though we use outlier rejection and least-squares fitting with inlier samples for robust estimation, the performance of our algorithm would highly depend

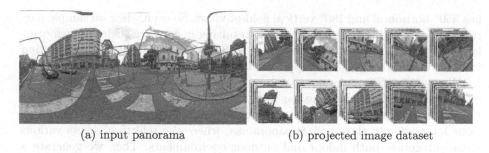

(a) input panorama   (b) projected image dataset

Fig. 4. Large-scale dataset generation with various perspective projections.

on the accuracy and reliability of 2D roll estimation of sampled images. As described in Sect. 2, previous rotation estimation methods for 2D images mainly utilize hand-crafted features, such as lines and vanishing points, with specific assumptions on the scene structure, i.e., the Manhattan or Atlanta world. To overcome the limitations, we present a CNN-based approach that can precisely estimate the rotation of a 2D image (Fig. 4).

4   CNN-Based 2D Roll Estimation

In this section, we first present a massive 2D image dataset, where individual images are labeled with how much they have been rotated. The dataset is generated by cropping 360 spherical panoramas into perspective narrow field-of-view images. Our CNN is trained with the dataset to estimate the projected roll angle $\hat{\beta}$ of a given sampled image.

4.1   Rotated Image Dataset Generation Using 360 Panoramas

Recent tremendous success of image understanding using deep learning is built upon large-scale labeled datasets [7,21]. Similarly we need a large-scale dataset for training our roll estimation network. However, it would be time-consuming to label the rotation angles for many captured images, and applying artificial rotations to upright images [9] may suffer from information losses due to the cropping after image rotation. To annotate the ground truth rotation angles, Olmsschenk et al. [24] used the camera poses of a RGB-D stream estimated by 3D reconstruction, and additionally utilized the onboard accelerometer of a RGB-D sensor to extend the dataset. However, as the RGB-D dataset only consists of images captured from indoor environments, the dataset is not suitable for 2D images sampled from 360 spherical panoramas that may come from a variety of scenes.

In this paper, we generate a novel large-scale dataset for 2D image roll estimation using an existing 360 spherical panorama dataset. A 360 spherical panorama has 360° horizontal and 180° vertical field-of-views. So even when we sample narrow field-of-view images multiple times, resulting images are seldom much overlapped with each other. In addition, as a 360 panorama contains information from all view directions, no cropping is needed for a rotated image.

We use SUN360 panorama dataset [28]. The dataset consists of 30K high-resolution 360 spherical panoramas from a large variety of scene categories. Since the dataset contains non-upright panoramas, we manually correct the 3D rotations for randomly chosen 2000 panoramas, where the selection covers various scene categories, both indoor and outdoor environments. Then we generate a labeled image dataset by projecting the panoramas onto intentionally rotated viewing angles and image frames as follows.

For the purpose of uniform sampling, we first divided the 360° yaw angle into 10 uniform intervals. Then we randomly sampled a yaw value from each interval, and for each yaw value, we sampled 30 images with random rotations, where the angle ranges are $-20° \leq$ pitch $\leq 20°$ and $-40° \leq$ roll $\leq 40°$. We used 45° and 60° for the field-of-views to obtain perspective diversity of feature learning. Consequently, 600 narrow field-of-view images were sampled from each 360 spherical panorama with random 3D rotations. The ground truth label for a sampled image becomes the roll angle used for the sampling. As a result, we generated 1.2M randomly sampled images labeled with rotation angles in total.

We randomly chose 100 out of 2000 panoramas for a validation set and sampled training and validation images from the disjoint sets of panoramas. We used 1140K training images and 60K validation images for training our roll estimation network.

4.2   Network Structure and Training Details

We choose Deep Residual Network (ResNet) [11] as our base network architecture, and modify the last layer to produce a single real value that represents the rotation angle of a given image, instead of the original 1000 class probabilities. To reduce the burden for exploring semantic features from scratch, we use a ResNet34 model pretrained for ImageNet-1K classification task. The network parameters are trained using stochastic gradient descent algorithm [16] for 142K iterations (16 epochs) with mini-batch size of 128. We set the initial learning rate to 5e–4, and decrease the learning rate by 0.1 times when the validation error does not drop for two epochs. The final learning rate was 5e–7 after training. We use L1 loss to minimize the absolute error between the prediction and ground truth angles.

5   Experimental Results

In this section, we present various experimental results that show our method achieves the state-of-the-art performance on upright adjustment of 360 spherical panoramas. We first show some 2D image upright adjustment results to demonstrate the performance of our trained network. We then compare our 360 upright

(a) (b) (c) (d)

Fig. 5. Correction of slanted 2D images (top: input images, bottom: results). Our network precisely predicts the rotation angles of images sampled from spherical panoramas (a, b) and works even for natural images that were captured by ordinary perspective cameras (c, d). We selected the test natural images in (c, d) from DIV2K dataset [1].

adjustment results qualitatively and quantitatively on a test dataset [14]. In addition, with a newly constructed test dataset, we show that our method produces robust results for input panoramas violating the Manhattan and Atlanta world assumptions.

Implementation Details. For outlier rejection, we set the inlier threshold to $2°$, which is the distance between a sample and the hypothesis function. We used the Levenberg–Marquardt algorithm [20,22] for the non-linear least squares fitting of function $f(\hat{\alpha}; \alpha, \beta)$ to obtain the final 3D rotation. We tested our algorithm on an Intel i7-6700K 4.00 GHz CPU, 32 GB RAM and NVIDIA GeForce GTX 1080. For an input image of size 9104×4552, our algorithm takes about 0.6 s on average. Jung et al. [14] consumes less than one second, and Bazin et al. [3] takes about five seconds with a MATLAB implementation.

5.1 Rotation Estimation for 2D Images

After network training, the average absolute error on the validation set is $1.08°$. We also define the in-k accuracy as the percentage of samples whose error is less then $k°$, which is similar to top-k accuracy in classification tasks. Our network shows 67.5%, 94.9%, and 97.9% on the validation set for in-1, 3, and 5 accuracies, respectively.

Although our CNN is trained on images sampled from 360 spherical panoramas, it shows satisfying prediction results on ordinary perspective images. Figure 5 shows 2D roll correction results on different images, where the correction works well even when the image is cluttered and does not have enough straight lines.

Table 1. Numerical comparison with existing 360 panorama upright adjustment methods on Jung et al.'s test dataset [14] and our newly generated test datasets with four categories. We measured the average absolute angular error between the predicted rotation and the ground truth label.

	Jung et al.'s dataset [14]	Our test datasets				
		Street	Indoor	Park	Mountain	Total
Bazin et al. [3]	3.66°	3.76°	4.13°	13.29°	17.67°	9.71°
Jung et al. [14]	1.12°	1.78°	2.21°	3.75°	12.98°	5.18°
Ours (best hypothesis)	1.02°	1.14°	1.09°	1.58°	3.85°	1.92°
Ours (best hypothesis+lsq.)	**0.84°**	0.96°	0.81°	1.50°	3.80°	**1.77°**

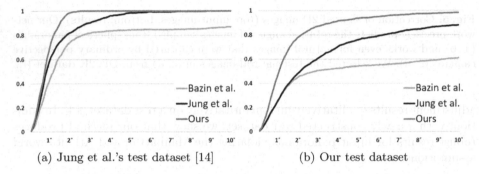

(a) Jung et al.'s test dataset [14]   (b) Our test dataset

Fig. 6. Cumulative histograms of the errors of different methods on Jung et al.'s test dataset [14] and our dataset. Our method outperforms previous methods on both datasets.

5.2   New Test Datasets

To evaluate the performance of our framework, we use two different kinds of test datasets. Jung et al. [14] constructed a test dataset by applying various rotations to 360 panoramas that have been carefully taken with no camera rotations. It consists of 840 test images generated from 14 panoramas. As Jung et al.'s work [14] assumes the Atlanta world for the scene, most of test images in the dataset follow the assumption well. In contrast, our method does not assume any specific scene structures, and the dataset would not be enough to thoroughly evaluate the performance in various situations.

To this end, we built a new test dataset by collecting four scene categories from SUN360 dataset [28]: street, indoor, park, and mountain. Intuitively, street and indoor scenes usually follow the Manhattan or Atlanta world assumption, and contain lots of structural features useful for rotation estimation. However, park scenes consist of mainly natural structures, such as trees, which may yield many false vanishing structures. Lastly, mountain scenes contain images captured at mountain tops, which rarely include straight lines and vanishing structures and hardly follow the Atlanta world assumption. We manually corrected the randomly chosen 50 panoramas from each category in SUN360 dataset, 200

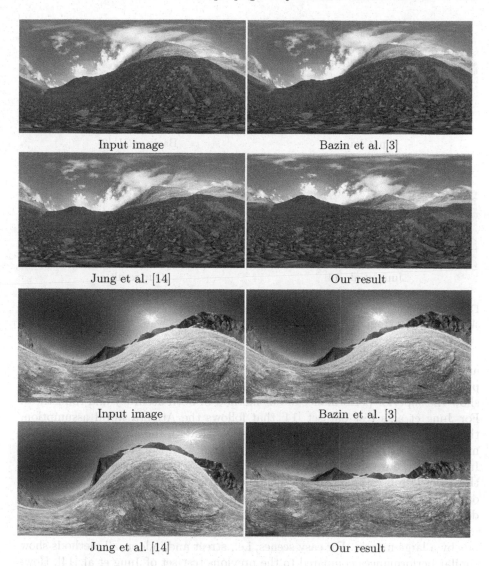

Fig. 7. Visual comparisons of the upright adjustment results on 360 panorama images from mountain scenes that do not contain strong structural features.

panoramas in total. Then we randomly rotated each panorama image with 10 different rotations within a range of ±30°, resulting in 2000 labeled test cases in total.

5.3 Comparisons and Quantitative Evaluation

We quantitatively evaluated our method on two test datasets: Jung et al.'s and ours. We measured the angular error between the predicted vertical direction of the rotated camera and the ground truth label. Table 1 shows average absolute

Input image   Bazin et al. [3]

Jung et al. [14]   Our result

Fig. 8. Comparison on a scene not following the Atlanta world assumption (e.g., the slide in the playground).

angular errors on both datasets. Figure 6 shows the cumulative histograms of prediction errors comparing with existing methods [3,14]. The table and figure show the superior performance of our method in both accuracy and robustness. For Jung et al.'s test dataset [14] that follows the Atlanta world assumption, the average error of our method reaches the state-of-the-art performance and more than 99% of test panoramas are corrected with the errors less than 2.2°. Interestingly, our errors of upright adjustment of 360 panoramas are lower than those of 2D roll estimation network. The reason would be our framework uses outlier rejection and least-squares fitting to robustly find the best 3D rotation despite possible mistakes in roll predictions.

For our newly generated test dataset, our method outperforms previous methods by a large margin. For easy scenes, i.e., street and indoor, all methods show similar performances compared to the previous test set of Jung et al. [14]. However, as can be expected, for the test images from the hard case of mountain scenes, previous methods easily fail as the scenes rarely contain strong structural features such as straight lines. In contrast, our method uses a roll estimation network trained with a large-scale dataset, and robustly estimates semantically correct upright directions regardless of the existences of structural features. Figure 7 shows visual comparisons of the upright adjustment results for some mountain scenes.

In addition, as shown in Fig. 8, our method works well on a scene that does not follow the Atlanta world assumption. Various examples of our algorithm in Fig. 9 and the supplementary material show that our method can robustly and accurately handle spherical panoramas from a variety of scenes.

| Input image | Our upright adjustment result |

Fig. 9. Additional results of our method for a variety of scenes.

6   Conclusions

Upright adjustment of a mis-oriented 360 spherical panorama improves the perceptual quality by correcting the wavy horizon and distorted objects. In this paper, we presented a novel upright adjustment framework for 360 spherical panoramas which indirectly uses a convolutional neural network. By exploiting the relationship between a 3D camera rotation and projected 2D rotations of multiple sampled images, our method accurately estimates the 3D camera rotation relative to the scene from a given single 360 panorama. Differently from existing methods based on straight lines and vanishing points, our method uses a CNN for 2D roll estimation by training it using a massively generated 2D image dataset, enabling the network to learn semantic upright directions (e.g., standing people). Extensive experiments on test datasets demonstrate that our method provides highly accurate and robust results for upright adjustment of 360 panoramas even when existing methods could fail.

There remains a limitation of our method. A uniform sampling along the horizontal centerline of the image could crop only the ground or sky when the camera has been severely rotated, introducing many outliers in roll estimation. Adaptive sampling based on saliency or objectness would improve our method.

Directly applying CNN to a 360 spherical panorama has not been straightforward due to severe distortions around the north and south poles of the panorama and the lack of a large-scale labeled dataset. In this paper, to avoid the difficulties, we took an indirect approach that uses CNN to estimate rotations of 2D sampled images and computes the 3D rotation from the estimated 2D rotations. Recently Su and Grauman [27] proposed a novel approach to extract CNN features directly from a spherical panorama image by adjusting the shapes of pre-trained convolution kernels according to the spherical distortions. Directly predicting the 3D camera rotation using CNN from a given panorama would be interesting future work.

Acknowledgements. This work was supported by the Ministry of Science and ICT, Korea, through IITP grant (IITP-2015-0-00174), NRF grant (NRF-2017M3C4A7066317), and Giga Korea grant (GK18P0300).

References

1. Agustsson, E., Timofte, R.: NTIRE 2017 challenge on single image super-resolution: dataset and study. In: Proceedings of the IEEE Conference on Computer Vision and Pattern Recognition (CVPR) Workshops, vol. 3, p. 2 (2017)
2. Antone, M.E., Teller, S.: Automatic recovery of relative camera rotations for urban scenes. In: Proceedings of the IEEE Conference on Computer Vision and Pattern Recognition (CVPR), vol. 2, pp. 282–289. IEEE (2000)
3. Bazin, J.C., Demonceaux, C., Vasseur, P., Kweon, I.: Rotation estimation and vanishing point extraction by omnidirectional vision in urban environment. Int. J. Rob. Res. **31**(1), 63–81 (2012)
4. Bazin, J.C., et al.: Globally optimal line clustering and vanishing point estimation in Manhattan world. In: Proceedings of the IEEE Conference on Computer Vision and Pattern Recognition (CVPR), pp. 638–645. IEEE (2012)
5. Bosse, M., Rikoski, R.J., Leonard, J.J., Teller, S.J.: Vanishing points and 3D lines from omnidirectional video. In: Proceedings of the IEEE International Conference on Image Processing (2002)

6. Coughlan, J.M., Yuille, A.L.: The Manhattan world assumption: regularities in scene statistics which enable Bayesian inference. In: Advances in Neural Information Processing Systems, pp. 845–851 (2001)
7. Deng, J., Dong, W., Socher, R., Li, L.J., Li, K., Fei-Fei, L.: ImageNet: a large-scale hierarchical image database. In: Proceedings of the IEEE Conference on Computer Vision and Pattern Recognition (CVPR), pp. 248–255 (2009)
8. Denis, P., Elder, J.H., Estrada, F.J.: Efficient edge-based methods for estimating Manhattan frames in urban imagery. In: Forsyth, D., Torr, P., Zisserman, A. (eds.) ECCV 2008. LNCS, vol. 5303, pp. 197–210. Springer, Heidelberg (2008). https://doi.org/10.1007/978-3-540-88688-4_15
9. Fischer, P., Dosovitskiy, A., Brox, T.: Image orientation estimation with convolutional networks. In: Gall, J., Gehler, P., Leibe, B. (eds.) GCPR 2015. LNCS, vol. 9358, pp. 368–378. Springer, Cham (2015). https://doi.org/10.1007/978-3-319-24947-6_30
10. Gallagher, A.C.: Using vanishing points to correct camera rotation in images. In: Proceedings of the Canadian Conference on Computer and Robot Vision, pp. 460–467. IEEE (2005)
11. He, K., Zhang, X., Ren, S., Sun, J.: Deep residual learning for image recognition. In: Proceedings of the IEEE Conference on Computer Vision and Pattern Recognition (CVPR), pp. 770–778 (2016)
12. Joo., K., Oh., T.H., Kwon., I.S., Bazin., J.: Globally optimal inlier set maximization for Atlanta frame estimation. In: Proceedings of the IEEE Conference on Computer Vision and Pattern Recognition (CVPR), pp. 2408–2415. IEEE (2018)
13. Joshi, U., Guerzhoy, M.: Automatic photo orientation detection with convolutional neural networks. In: Conference on Computer and Robot Vision (CRV), pp. 103–108. IEEE (2017)
14. Jung, J., Kim, B., Lee, J.Y., Kim, B., Lee, S.: Robust upright adjustment of 360 spherical panoramas. Vis. Comput. **33**(6–8), 737–747 (2017)
15. Kamali, M., Banno, A., Bazin, J.C., Kweon, I.S., Ikeuchi, K.: Stabilizing omnidirectional videos using 3D structure and spherical image warping. In: Proceedings of the IAPR Conference on Machine Vision Applications, pp. 177–180 (2011)
16. Kiefer, J., Wolfowitz, J., et al.: Stochastic estimation of the maximum of a regression function. Ann. Math. Stat. **23**(3), 462–466 (1952)
17. Kopf, J.: 360° video stabilization. ACM Trans. Graph. **35**(6), 195 (2016)
18. Lee, H., Shechtman, E., Wang, J., Lee, S.: Automatic upright adjustment of photographs. In: Proceedings of the IEEE Conference on Computer Vision and Pattern Recognition (CVPR), pp. 877–884. IEEE (2012)
19. Lee, H., Shechtman, E., Wang, J., Lee, S.: Automatic upright adjustment of photographs with robust camera calibration. IEEE Trans. Pattern Anal. Mach. Intell. **36**(5), 833–844 (2014)
20. Levenberg, K.: A method for the solution of certain non-linear problems in least squares. Q. Appl. Math. **2**(2), 164–168 (1944)
21. Lin, T.Y., et al.: Microsoft COCO: common objects in context. In: Fleet, D., Pajdla, T., Schiele, B., Tuytelaars, T. (eds.) ECCV 2014. LNCS, vol. 8693, pp. 740–755. Springer, Cham (2014). https://doi.org/10.1007/978-3-319-10602-1_48
22. Marquardt, D.W.: An algorithm for least-squares estimation of nonlinear parameters. J. Soc. Ind. Appl. Math. **11**(2), 431–441 (1963)
23. Martins, A.T., Aguiar, P.M.Q., Figueiredo, M.A.T.: Orientation in Manhattan: equiprojective classes and sequential estimation. IEEE Trans. Pattern Anal. Mach. Intell. **27**(5), 822–827 (2005)

24. Olmschenk, G., Tang, H., Zhu, Z.: Pitch and roll camera orientation from a single 2D image using convolutional neural networks. In: Conference on Computer and Robot Vision (CRV), pp. 261–268. IEEE (2017)
25. Scaramuzza, D.: Omnidirectional vision: from calibration to robot motion estimation. Ph.D. thesis, ETH Zurich (2008)
26. Schindler, G., Dellaert, F.: Atlanta world: an expectation maximization framework for simultaneous low-level edge grouping and camera calibration in complex man-made environments. In: Proceedings of the IEEE Conference on Computer Vision and Pattern Recognition (CVPR), pp. 203–209 (2004)
27. Su, Y.C., Grauman, K.: Learning spherical convolution for fast features from 360 imagery. In: Advances in Neural Information Processing Systems, pp. 529–539 (2017)
28. Xiao, J., Ehinger, K.A., Oliva, A., Torralba, A.: Recognizing scene viewpoint using panoramic place representation. In: Proceedings of the IEEE Conference on Computer Vision and Pattern Recognition (CVPR), pp. 2695–2702. IEEE (2012)
29. Zhai, M., Workman, S., Jacobs, N.: Detecting vanishing points using global image context in a non-manhattan world. In: Proceedings of the IEEE Conference on Computer Vision and Pattern Recognition (CVPR), pp. 5657–5665 (2016)

DN-ResNet: Efficient Deep Residual Network for Image Denoising

Haoyu Ren$^{(\boxtimes)}$, Mostafa El-khamy, and Jungwon Lee

SOC R&D, Samsung Semiconductor Inc.,
9868 Scranton Road, San Diego, CA 92121, USA
{haoyu.ren,mostafa.e,jungwon2.lee}@samsung.com

Abstract. A deep learning approach to blind denoising of images without complete knowledge of the noise statistics is considered. We propose DN-ResNet, which is a deep convolutional neural network (CNN) consisting of several residual blocks (ResBlocks). With cascade training, DN-ResNet is more accurate and more computationally efficient than the state of art denoising networks. An edge-aware loss function is further utilized in training DN-ResNet, so that the denoising results have better perceptive quality compared to conventional loss function. Next, we introduce the depthwise separable DN-ResNet (DS-DN-ResNet) utilizing the proposed Depthwise Seperable ResBlock (DS-ResBlock) instead of standard ResBlock, which has much less computational cost. We propose cascade evolution of DS-DN-ResNet from DN-ResNet by incrementally transforming the ResBlocks to DS-ResBlocks, while building on the previous training. As a result, high accuracy and good computational efficiency are achieved concurrently. Whereas previous state of art deep learning methods focused on denoising either Gaussian or Poisson corrupted images, we consider denoising images having the more practical Poisson with additive Gaussian noise as well. The results show that DN-ResNets are more efficient, robust, and perform better denoising than current state of art deep learning methods, as well as the popular variants of the BM3D algorithm, in cases of blind and non-blind denoising of images corrupted with Poisson, Gaussian or Poisson-Gaussian noise. Our network also works well for other image enhancement task such as compressed image restoration.

Keywords: Denoising · Depth-aware · Cascade involving · ResNet · CNN

1 Introduction

Denoising is an active topic in image processing since it is a key step in many practical applications, such as image and video capturing. It aims to generate a clean image X from a given noisy image Y which follows an image degradation model $Y = D(X)$. For the widely used additive Gaussian noise (AWGN) model, the ith observed pixel is

$$y_i = D(x_i) = x_i + n_i \tag{1}$$

© Springer Nature Switzerland AG 2019
C. V. Jawahar et al. (Eds.): ACCV 2018, LNCS 11365, pp. 215–230, 2019.
https://doi.org/10.1007/978-3-030-20873-8_14

where $n_i \sim \mathcal{N}(0, \sigma^2)$ is i.i.d Gaussian noise with zero mean and variance σ^2. AWGN has been used to model the signal-independent thermal noise and other system imperfections. Degradation due to low light shot noise is signal dependent and has often been modeled using Poisson noise

$$y_i = D(x_i) = p_i, \quad p_i \sim \mathcal{P}(x_i) \tag{2}$$

where $\mathcal{P}(x_i)$ is a Poisson random variable with mean x_i. However, this noise approaches a Gaussian distribution for average light conditions as $\mathcal{P}(\lambda) \approx \mathcal{N}(\lambda, \lambda)$, for large enough λ. Hence, the noise due to capturing by an imaging device is better modeled as a Poisson noise with AWGN, referred to as Poisson-Gaussian noise, such that

$$y_i = D(x_i) = \alpha p_i + n_i, \quad \alpha > 0 \tag{3}$$

which has been verified by experimental results [7].

Recently, the state of art denoising accuracy is achieved by deep neural networks [22, 26], which construct a mapping between the noisy image and clean image. Unfortunately, most of existing denoising networks cannot be executed in real-time due to their large network size. In addition, it is relatively difficult to set the hyperparameters when learning a very deep network, such as the weight initialization, the learning rate, and the weight decay rate. With inappropriate parameters, the training might fall into local minimum or not converge at all.

In this paper, we propose a Denoising Residual Network (DN-ResNet) which is more efficient and accurate than prior art. DN-ResNet consists of residual blocks (ResBlock) which are gradually inserted into the network stage by stage during the training. This training strategy not only allows the resulting DN-ResNet to converge faster, but also allows it to be more computationally efficient than prior art denoising networks. Even better perceptual quality have been observed by using the proposed edge-aware loss function instead of the conventional mean square error (MSE). In addition, we introduce the depthwise separable ResBlock (DS-ResBlock) into DN-ResNet to construct the depthwise separable ResNet (DS-DN-ResNet). DS-DN-ResNet is generated by the proposed incremental evolution from DN-ResNet, where the ResBlocks in DN-ResNet are replaced by DS-ResBlocks stage by stage. As a result, we may obtain a 2.5 times complexity reduction for DN-ResNet, with less than 0.1 dB PSNR loss. To our knowledge, DN-ResNet is the first unified deep CNN trained for the problem of blind denoising of images corrupted by multiple type of noises. By cascading only 5 ResBlocks, DN-ResNet and DS-DN-ResNet achieve the state of art performance on all three denoising problems, Gaussian, Poisson, and Poisson-Gaussian, for both cases of non-blind denoising (known noise level for noisy input) and blind denoising (unknown noise level for noisy input). The speed is also much faster than prior art denoising networks. Moreover, we show that DN-ResNet works well for compressed image restoration. This implies that DN-ResNet can be generalized to other applications.

As summary, our contributions are three folds:

1. We show that ResNet is effective for image denoising, and using edge-aware loss function significantly improves the perceptual quality. The resulting DN-ResNet achieves the state of art accuracy, and is 4 times less complicate than existing networks;
2. We introduce the depthwise separable ResBlock (DS-ResBlock) to construct DS-DN-ResNet. The incrementally evolved DS-DN-ResNet is 2.5 times faster than DN-ResNet, without significant accuracy loss;
3. We show that the proposed DN-ResNet works well for all types of noises, even without knowing the noise level. It can be generalized to other image enhancement task such as compressed image restoration;

2 Related Work

2.1 Image Denoising

During the past years, numerous approaches have been exploited for modeling image priors for denoising, such as nonlocal self-similarity (NSS) [8] and sparse coding [5]. The block matching with 3D collaborative filtering (BM3D) [4] and its variants such as iterative BM3D with variance stabilizing transforms (I+VST+BM3D) [1] and generalized Anscombe variance stabilizing transform with BM3D (GAT-BM3D) [13] are widely used. These methods generally involve a complex optimization problem in the testing stage, which makes the denoising process time-consuming. To improve the efficiency, learning-based methods are proposed to get rid of the iterative optimization procedure, such as the trainable nonlinear reaction diffusion (TNRD) [3], and Gaussian conditional random field [20] for non-blind image deblurring. Unfortunately, the accuracy of these methods is still limited due to the use of specific image prior. It is also difficult to set the handcrafted parameters during the stage-wise learning.

Recently, deep neural networks have been deployed for image denoising due to their significant improvement of the accuracy [2]. Zhang et al. [26] constructed a 20-layer feed-forward denoising convolutional neural networks with residual learning for Gaussian denoising. Remez et al. trained 20-layer CNNs for each object category respectively and showed good performance for either Gaussian denoising [15] or Poisson denoising [16]. Zhang et al. [27] proposed FFDNet adopting orthogonal regularization to enhance the generalization ability of Gaussian denoising. Tai et al. designed MemNet [22], where the feature map concatenations and skip connections are utilized to construct a network for image super resolution, Gaussian denoising, and JPEG deblocking. 1×1 convolutions are adopted to integrate the long-term memorization, which shows significant accuracy improvements. Most of the existing networks are designed for single type of noise only. Due to the high computational cost, they can not be executed in real-time. In contrast, our DN-ResNet is far more efficient. The same network architecture can be utilized for Gaussian, Poisson, and Poisson-Gaussian noise, as well as other image enhancement tasks.

2.2 Deep Learing Based Compressed Image Restoration

Compressed image restoration aims to reduce the artifacts of decoded compressed images, so that the images can be stored or transmitted at low bit rates. Most of existing work design an end-to-end network including both the encoding (compression) and decoding procedure. Toderici et al. [24] presented a set of full-resolution lossy image compression methods using recurrent neural network based encoder and decoder with entropy coding. Theis et al. [23] constructed the compression network by deep autoencoders with a sub-pixel structure. In these work, although a low bit rate can be achieved, both of the encoding and decoding procedure are replaced by deep neural networks. As a result, it is difficult to integrate them into real system, where efficient image compression algorithms such as JPEG are implemented. In this paper, we consider the compressed image restoration as a 'denoising' problem, where the noise comes from image compression algorithms. DN-ResNet is trained to refine the quality of decoded compressed image. Since our network can be considered as a post-processing step, it can be applied to any existing image compression algorithms.

3 Denoising Residual Network

3.1 DN-ResNet

We aim to train a deep convolution neural network for image denoising. The network takes a noisy image Y as input and predicts a clean image X as its output. Given a training set $\{X_i, Y_i\}, i = 1, \ldots, N$ with N samples, our goal is to learn a model S that predicts the clean image $\hat{X}_i = S(Y_i)$.

ResNet [9] has demonstrated considerable performance in computer vision applications such as image classification. The basic element of our proposed denoising residual network (DN-ResNet) is a simplified ResBlock, as shown in Fig. 1(b). Different from the standard ResBlock in Fig. 1(a), we remove the batch normalization layers and the ReLU layer after the addition, because removing these layers will not harm the performance of feature-map based ResNet [12].

We construct our DN-ResNet by concatenating the ResBlocks in Fig. 1(b). We observed that as the network goes deeper, the training and the hyperparameter tuning become more difficult. To solve this problem, we follow the cascade training [18], which separates the whole training into stages and proceeds one by one. The training of DN-ResNet starts from a simple 3-layer CNN model. The first layer consists of 64 9 × 9 filters. The second layer consist of 32 5 × 5 filters. There is only one 5 × 5 filter in the last layer. All convolutions have stride one, and all the weights are randomly initialized from a Gaussian distribution with $\sigma = 0.001$. After the 3-layer CNN is trained, we start cascading the ResBlocks stage by stage, as shown in Fig. 2. When the training of current stage is finished, e.g., the training loss of current stage is 3% lower than previous stage, the training will proceed to next stage, and the network is cascaded to a deeper network. In each stage, one new ResBlock is inserted. So the training starts from

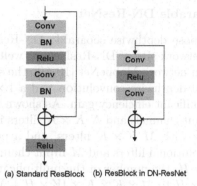

(a) Standard ResBlock   (b) ResBlock in DN-ResNet

Fig. 1. ResBlocks in DN-ResNet. (a) Standard ResBlock (b) ResBlock in DN-ResNet.

3 layers, and proceeds to 5 layers, 7 layers, etc. Each convolutional layer in the ResBlock consists of 32 3×3 filters. It ensures a smaller network when going deeper. The new layers are inserted just before the last 5×5 layer. The weights of pre-existing layers are inherited from the previous stage, and the weights of the new ResBlocks are randomly initialized (Gaussian with $\sigma = 0.001$). Hence, only a few weights of DN-ResNet are randomly initialized at each stage, so the convergence will be relatively easy. We find that using a fixed learning rate 0.0001 for all layers without any decay is feasible.

Since new convolutional layers will reduce the size of the feature map, we zero pad 2 pixels in each new 3×3 layer. As a result, all the stages in cascade training have the same size as the output, so that the training samples could be shared. When cascading 5 ResBlocks, the resulting DN-ResNet will have $5 \times 2 + 3 = 13$ convolutional layers. Our experiments show that such DN-ResNet-13 has already achieved the state of art accuracy on all type of noises.

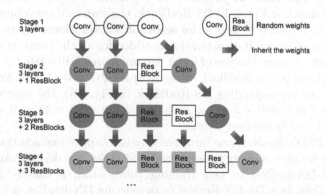

Fig. 2. Cascade training of DN-ResNet. Circle denotes standard convolutional layer, rectangle denotes ResBlock.

3.2   Depthwise Separable DN-ResNet

In this section, we propose depthwise separable DN-ResNet (DS-DN-ResNet) to further reduce the network size of DN-ResNet, as well as the computational cost. In the classification network MobileNet [10,19], the standard convolutional layer is factorized into a depthwise convolution and a 1×1 pointwise convolution, which achieves significant efficiency gain. As shown in Fig. 3, the standard convolution with M input channels and N $K \times K$ filters is replaced by a depthwise convolutional layer with M $K \times K$ filters, and a pointwise convolutional layer with N 1×1 convolutional filters and M input channels. Assume the input feature map size is $W \times H$, the number of the multiplications are reduced from $M \times K \times K \times N \times W \times H$ to $M \times K \times K \times W \times H + M \times N \times W \times H$.

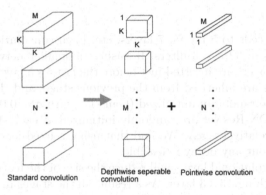

Fig. 3. Depthwise separable convolution. The standard convolution (left) is replaced by depthwise convolution (middle) and pointwise convolution (right).

Inspired by this idea, we propose the depthwise separable ResBlock (DS-ResBlock), as shown in Fig. 4. In DS-ResBlock, the standard convolutional layers in ResBlock are replaced by depthwise separable convolutional layers and pointwise convolutional layers. Relu activation is added for all the convolutional layers in DS-ResBlock. Assume the size of input feature map is 640×480, the number of the multiplications in the ResBlock in Fig. 4(a) is $640 \times 480 \times 3 \times 3 \times 32 \times 32 \times 2 = 5.6 \times 10^9$. In the corresponding DS-ResBlock in Fig. 4(b), the number of multiplications is $640 \times 480 \times 3 \times 3 \times 32 + 640 \times 480 \times 32 \times 32 = 9 \times 10^8$. The computational cost is reduced 6 times.

To train DS-DN-ResNet, one intuitive way is to apply cascade training from scratch. Since we have already trained the DN-ResNet, we describe another way to obtain DS-DN-ResNet to save training time, which is called 'incremental evolution'. To obtain a DS-DN-ResNet from existing DN-ResNet, a feasible way is to replace all ResBlocks by DS-ResBlocks, and fine-tune the whole network. If this procedure is done in a one-shot way, the fine-tuning will not converge well (see Table 3 for details). In the incremental evolution, the ResBlocks are replaced stage by stage. In each stage, only one-ResBlock is replaced by DS-ResBlock,

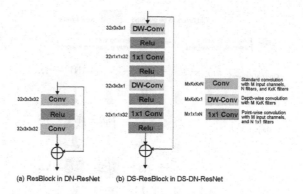

(a) ResBlock in DN-ResNet   (b) DS-ResBlock in DS-DN-ResNet

Fig. 4. Comparison between the ResBlock in DN-ResNet and the DS-ResBlock in DS-DN-ResNet.

and followed by a fine-tuning, as shown in Fig. 5. Similar to cascade training, the weights in the new DS-ResBlock are randomly initialized, and the weights in all other layers are inherited. The replacement starts from the tail side to ensure a smaller influence to the whole network. In the implementation, we first train 13-layer DN-ResNet, and then evolve it to DS-DN-ResNet. The learning rate is the same as cascade training. The fine-tuning will last 10 epochs for each evolution stage.

After incremental evolution, there are still three standard convolutional layers (1st, 2nd, and the last one) in DS-DN-ResNet. The overall complexity of DS-DN-ResNet is about 2.5 times less compared to DN-ResNet, without significant accuracy loss (<0.1 dB PSNR, see Table 3 for details). We do not replace the 1st and 2nd standard convolutional layers by depthwise version because it will decrease the accuracy a lot (>0.3 dB PSNR).

3.3 Edge-Aware Loss Function

Most of existing denoising networks aim to minimize the Mean Square Error (MSE) $\frac{1}{N}\sum_{i=1}^{N}||X_i - \hat{X}_i||^2$ over the training set. In this paper, we propose an edge-aware loss function, where the pixels in the edges are granted higher weights compared to non-edge pixels

$$loss = \frac{1}{N}\sum_{i=1}^{N}||X_i - \hat{X}_i||^2 + w \times \frac{1}{N}\sum_{i=1}^{N}||X_iM_i - \hat{X}_iM_i||^2. \qquad (4)$$

In Eq. (4), X_i is the ground truth of ith clean image, $\hat{X}_i$ is the ith denoised image, M is an edge map, N is the number of images, and w is a constant to control the trade-off between edge and non-edge pixels.

There are two advantages of applying such edge-aware loss function. Firstly, one of the major challenge in image denoising is that the edges are difficult to be retrieved from a noisy image, especially when the noise level is high. Adding

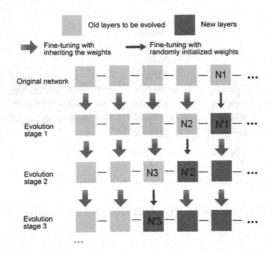

Fig. 5. Incremental evolution from DN-ResNet to DS-DN-ResNet.

a corresponding constraint in the loss function is reasonable. Secondly, the high-frequency information such as edge is very sensitive in human vision. Increasing the denoising accuracy of edge pixels will contribute to the perceptual quality.

We try two ways to construct M, including (a) gradient magnitude from Sobel filter, and (b) binary edge mask by thresholding (a). In the experiments, we show that using such edge-aware loss function can grant us better perceptual quality. The SSIM (structural similarity measure) is significantly improved.

4   Experiments

4.1   Experiment Setting

For image denoising, we use the PASCAL VOC 2010 dataset [6]. We follow the same training and testing split as [15], 1,000 testing images are used to evaluate the performance of the proposed DN-ResNet, while the remaining images are used for training. Random Gaussian/Poisson/Poisson-Gaussian noisy images are generated with different noise levels. We consider AWGN with different noise variances σ^2, where $\sigma \in \{10, 25, 50, 75\}$. We follow the same way as [1,16], before corrupting with Poisson noise, the input image pixel values are scaled to have a max peak value from the set $peak \in \{1, 2, 4, 8\}$. For the Poisson-Gaussian noise, we follow the same setting as [13], where $\sigma \in \{0.1, 0.2, 0.5, 1, 2, 3, 6, 12\}, peak = 10 \times \sigma$. 33×33 noisy patches and the corresponding 17×17 clean patches are cropped for training. For more comparison to other existing methods, we also use the Set14 [25], and BSD [14] datasets in the testing.

For compressed image restoration, we utilize the dataset provided by the challenge on learned image compression (CLIC) [11]. The commonly-used image

Table 1. PSNR (dB) evaluation of DN-ResNets with different layers for different denoising problems on PASCAL VOC 2010 dataset. Noise level is known. Bold fold indicates the best. Conventional MSE loss function is utilized for all models.

DN-ResNet	Sigma/peak	3-layer	5-layer	7-layer	9-layer	11-layer	13-layer	13-layer-os
Parameters	-	57,184	75,616	94,048	112,480	130,912	149,344	149,344
Gaussian	10	34.43	34.56	34.71	34.80	34.93	**34.99**	34.70
	25	29.86	30.03	30.10	30.30	30.44	**30.52**	30.27
	50	26.86	27.05	27.22	27.29	27.38	**27.50**	27.14
	75	25.24	25.43	25.55	25.63	25.81	**25.89**	25.61
Poisson	1	22.51	22.66	22.74	22.88	22.95	**23.06**	22.80
	2	23.66	23.74	23.92	24.05	24.14	**24.23**	23.96
	4	24.67	24.80	24.91	25.14	25.27	**25.39**	25.01
	8	26.01	26.24	26.35	26.55	26.64	**26.77**	26.49
Poisson-Gaussian	0.1/1	22.11	22.27	22.36	22.50	22.65	**22.73**	22.30
	0.2/2	22.99	23.14	23.22	23.40	23.59	**23.75**	23.44
	0.5/5	24.54	24.61	24.77	24.90	25.00	**25.10**	24.78
	1/10	25.61	25.69	25.77	25.91	25.99	**26.14**	25.67
	2/20	26.59	26.71	26.89	26.99	27.14	**27.29**	26.88
	3/30	27.10	27.22	27.37	27.50	27.61	**27.77**	27.41
	6/60	27.87	27.98	28.16	28.32	28.48	**28.59**	28.11
	12/120	28.19	28.30	28.44	28.58	28.72	**28.88**	28.50

Table 2. PSNR (dB)/SSIM evaluation of 13-layer DN-ResNets with different loss functions and blind/non-blind denoising. Bold fold indicates the best SSIM. 'edge' means the network is trained by edge-aware loss function. In 'edge-a', the edge map in the edge-aware loss function is the gradient magnitude from Sobel filter. In 'edge-b', the edge map is a binary mask by thresholding the Sobel map with 150. We have tried different thresholds to obtain the binary edge mask and find that 150 is the best one.

DN-ResNet	Sigma/peak	Non-blind	Blind	Blind+'edge-a'	Blind+'edge-b'
Parameters	-	149,344	149,344	149,344	149,344
Gaussian	10	34.99/0.9224	34.88/0.9217	34.88/**0.9271**	34.85/0.9266
	25	30.52/0.8383	30.47/0.8369	30.45/**0.8441**	30.44/0.8433
	50	27.50/0.7464	27.44/0.7458	27.41/0.7499	27.42/**0.7502**
	75	25.89/0.6881	25.80/0.6880	25.80/0.6947	25.77/**0.6950**
Poisson	1	23.06/0.5958	22.99/0.5949	23.00/**0.6050**	22.95/0.6038
	2	24.23/0.6403	24.17/0.6377	24.15/**0.6501**	24.15/0.6488
	4	25.39/0.6858	25.33/0.6829	25.30/**0.6911**	25.31/0.6899
	8	26.77/0.7332	26.72/0.7329	26.71/**0.7388**	26.71/0.7371
Poisson-Gaussian	0.1/1	22.73/0.5938	22.65/0.5936	22.64/**0.6044**	22.60/0.6019
	0.2/2	23.75/0.6345	23.69/0.6337	23.68/**0.6402**	23.66/0.6400
	0.5/5	25.10/0.6878	24.98/0.6860	24.95/**0.6955**	24.91/0.6933
	1/10	26.14/0.7263	26.07/0.7255	26.05/**0.7334**	26.05/0.7330
	2/20	27.29/0.7613	27.18/0.7600	27.15/**0.7677**	27.15/0.7659
	3/30	27.77/0.7785	27.64/0.7770	27.59/**0.7844**	27.61/0.7840
	6/60	28.59/0.8010	28.51/0.8001	28.50/0.8068	28.50/**0.8077**
	12/120	28.88/0.8147	28.80/0.8122	28.77/**0.8180**	28.78/0.8166

Table 3. PSNR (dB)/SSIM evaluation of 13-layer DN-ResNets with different Res-Blocks for blind denoising. 'DN' is DN-ResNet, 'DS-DN' is DS-DN-ResNet constructed by incremental evolution from DN-ResNet. 'DS-DN-os' is the DS-DN-ResNet constructed by one-shot fine-tuning from DN-ResNet. 'edge-a' denotes that the network is trained by edge-aware loss function. MACs are calculated for 640×480 input.

DN-ResNet	Sigma/peak	DN	DS-DN	DS-DN-os	DN+'edge-a'	DS-DN+'edge-a'
Parameters	-	149,344	63,728	63,728	149,344	63,728
MACs (Billion)	-	45.9	19.6	19.6	45.9	19.6
Gaussian	10	34.88/0.9217	34.79/0.9206	34.41/0.9088	34.88/0.9271	34.79/0.9259
	25	30.47/0.8369	30.36/0.8355	30.00/0.8240	30.45/0.8441	30.36/0.8433
	50	27.44/0.7458	27.34/0.7439	26.99/0.7298	27.41/0.7499	27.32/0.7484
	75	25.80/0.6880	25.74/0.6878	25.32/0.6759	25.80/0.6947	25.72/0.6939
Poisson	1	22.99/0.5949	22.89/0.5933	22.59/0.5870	23.00/0.6050	22.89/0.6040
	2	24.17/0.6377	24.11/0.6364	23.77/0.6302	24.15/0.6501	24.09/0.6499
	4	25.33/0.6829	25.26/0.6811	24.88/0.6733	25.30/0.6911	25.24/0.6899
	8	26.72/0.7329	26.62/0.7314	26.30/0.7265	26.71/0.7388	26.60/0.7377
Poisson-Gaussian	0.1/1	22.65/0.5936	22.57/0.5919	22.17/0.5830	22.64/0.6044	22.56/0.6038
	0.2/2	23.69/0.6337	23.58/0.6322	23.20/0.6269	23.68/0.6402	23.54/0.6389
	0.5/5	24.98/0.6860	24.93/0.6843	24.65/0.6788	24.95/0.6955	24.93/0.6941
	1/10	26.07/0.7255	25.99/0.7239	25.66/0.7188	26.05/0.7334	26.00/0.7330
	2/20	27.18/0.7600	27.12/0.7596	26.80/0.7524	27.15/0.7677	27.11/0.7666
	3/30	27.64/0.7770	27.57/0.7755	27.24/0.7700	27.59/0.7844	27.53/0.7839
	6/60	28.51/0.8001	28.46/0.7991	28.16/0.7929	28.50/0.8068	28.45/0.8061
	12/120	28.80/0.8122	28.74/0.8108	28.44/0.8059	28.77/0.8180	28.68/0.8177

compression algorithms, JPEG, JPEG 2000, and BPG (Better Portable Graphics) are utilized to obtain the decoded images. 33×33 decoded patches and the corresponding 17×17 clean patches are further extracted for training.

Our networks are trained on y/cb/cr channels[1]. For non-blind denoising, multiple networks are trained for each noise level respectively. In contrast, only one DN-ResNet is trained for blind denoising by mixing all training samples corrupted by Gaussian/Poisson/Poisson-Gaussian noises. Peak-Signal-to-Noise-Ratio (PSNR) and SSIM are utilized as evaluation protocol.

4.2 Experiments on Image Denoising

We first test the DN-ResNets up to 13 layers on non-blind Gaussian, Poisson, and Poisson-Gaussian denoising. These DN-ResNets are trained by cascading the ResBlocks in Fig. 1(b). The conventional MSE loss is utilized for all networks. In Table 1, we find that for all the above three denoising problems, the PSNR consistently increases along with using more layers. Although the deepest network we show is 13-layer DN-ResNet, the accuracy could still be further improved by cascading more layers. This is consistent with 'the deeper, the better'. We also compare the cascade training versus one-shot training ('13-layer-os' in Table 1), where an end-to-end 13-layer DN-ResNet is trained from unsupervised weight

---

[1] In the quantitative evaluation, we show the PSNR/SSIM of the networks trained on y-channel only for fair comparison to existing work.

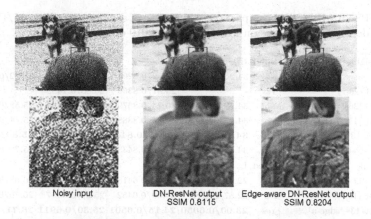

Noisy input   DN-ResNet output   Edge-aware DN-ResNet output
SSIM 0.8115   SSIM 0.8204

Fig. 6. Example outputs of different Poisson-Gaussian blind denoising networks. Left:noisy input. Mid:DN-ResNet output. Right:edge-aware DN-ResNet output.

initialization. We observe that such one-shot training results in 0.3 dB PSNR degradation compared to cascade training. This result makes sense because cascade training can be considered as a 'partial-supervised weight initialization', its convergence will be easier compared to one-shot training based on unsupervised weight initialization.

Next, we test the DN-ResNets trained by edge-aware loss function described in Sect. 3.3, as well as utilizing DN-ResNet for blind denoising. In Table 2, we observe that utilizing DN-ResNet for blind denoising will not decrease the accuracy much compared to non-blind denoising. This trade-off is valuable since blind denoising does not require a time-consuming noise level estimation. In addition, we show that utilizing edge-aware loss function (blind+'edge-a'/'edge-b') improves the SSIM 0.005–0.01, without degrading the PSNR much. Since the conventional MSE has the same equation as PSNR, the slightly degradation in PSNR of the edge-aware DN-ResNet is reasonable. Using the edge map generated by Sobel gradient magnitude (blind+'edge-a', $w = 0.025$ in Eq. (4)) is better than binary edge mask (blind+'edge-b', $w = 4$). The perceptual quality is clearly improved as well, as illustrated in Fig. 6. It can be seen that the output from edge-aware DN-ResNet has sharper edge and higher SSIM compared to the output from ordinary DN-ResNet. This shows the effectiveness of emphasizing edge pixels during the training.

Moreover, we evaluate the DN-ResNets constructed by different ResBlocks for the blind denoising problem. In Table 3, We observe that DS-DN-ResNet (DS-DN) has less than 0.1 dB PSNR degradation and less than 0.002 SSIM degradation compared to DN-ResNet, but the computational cost (MACs, number of multiplications and accumulations) and the network size are significantly reduced. We also notice that if the DS-DN-ResNet is constructed by one-shot fine-tuning DN-ResNet (DS-DN-os), both the PSNR and SSIM will decrease a lot. This indicates that the proposed incrementally evolved DS-DN-ResNet is able to improve the efficiency of DN-ResNet. Using the DS-ResBlock together

Table 4. PSNR (dB)/SSIM comparison to the state of art Gaussian/Poisson/Poisson-Gaussian denoising algorithms on PASCAL VOC 2010 dataset.

Gaussian sigma	Blind	10	25	50	75
BM3D [4]	No	34.26/0.9197	29.62/0.8294	26.61/0.7404	25.12/0.6852
DN-CNN-3 [26]	Yes	-	29.87/0.8350	26.85/0.7439	-
DN-CNN-S [26]	No	34.79/0.9216	30.23/0.8379	27.29/0.7444	25.58/0.6888
DenoiseNet [15]	No	34.87/0.9219	30.36/0.8388	27.32/0.7447	25.74/0.6899
DN-ResNet-13+'edge-a'	Yes	**34.88/0.9271**	**30.45/0.8441**	**27.41/0.7499**	**25.80/0.6947**
DS-DN-ResNet-13+'edge-a'	Yes	34.79/0.9259	30.36/0.8433	27.32/0.7484	25.72/0.6939
Poisson peak	Blind	1	2	4	8
IVST+BM3D [1]	No	22.71/0.5920	23.70/0.6418	24.78/0.6815	26.08/0.7297
DenoiseNet [16]	No	22.87/0.5989	24.09/0.6452	25.26/0.6857	26.70/0.7329
DN-ResNet-13+'edge-a'	Yes	**23.00/0.6050**	**24.15/0.6501**	**25.30/0.6911**	**26.71/0.7388**
DS-DN-ResNet-13+'edge-a'	Yes	22.89/0.6040	24.09/0.6499	25.24/0.6899	26.60/0.7377
Poisson-Gaussian sigma/peak	Blind	0.1/1	0.2/2	0.5/5	1/10
GAT+BM3D [13]	No	21.28/0.5451	22.56/0.5795	24.13/0.6478	25.38/0.7008
DN-ResNet-13+'edge-a'	Yes	**22.64/0.6044**	**23.68/0.6402**	**24.95/0.6905**	**26.05/0.7334**
DS-DN-ResNet-13+'edge-a'	Yes	22.56/0.6038	23.54/0.6389	24.93/0.6941	26.00/0.7330
Poisson-Gaussian sigma/peak	Blind	2/20	3/30	6/60	12/120
GAT+BM3D [13]	No	26.50/0.7249	27.07/0.7587	27.87/0.7849	28.43/0.7962
DN-ResNet-13+'edge-a'	Yes	**27.15/0.7677**	**27.59/0.7844**	**28.50/0.8068**	**28.77/0.8180**
DS-DN-ResNet-13+'edge-a'	Yes	27.11/0.7666	27.53/0.7839	28.45/0.8061	28.68/0.8177

Table 5. PSNR (dB)/SSIM evaluation of different blind Gaussian/Poisson denoising methods on multiple datasets. The speed is tested in single Titan-X GPU and 512 × 512 image.

Gaussian sigma = 50	Set14	BSD200	VOC2010	Network size	Speed (ms)
MemNet [22]	26.99/0.7794	25.89/0.7207	27.02/0.7422	667K	343.28
DN-CNN [26]	27.05/0.7788	25.83/0.7214	26.85/0.7439	650K	55.44
DN-ResNet-13+'edge-a'	**27.15/0.7849**	**25.99/0.7270**	**27.41/0.7499**	149K	17.92
DS-DN-ResNet-13+'edge-a'	27.05/0.7826	25.87/0.7247	27.32/0.7484	**64K**	**8.33**
Poisson peak = 8	Set14	BSD200	VOC2010	Network size	Speed (ms)
MemNet [22]	25.14/0.7198	25.77/0.7031	26.34/0.7321	667K	343.28
DN-ResNet-13+'edge-a'	**25.25/0.7242**	**25.91/0.7075**	**26.71/0.7388**	149K	55.44
DS-DN-ResNet-13+'edge-a'	25.10/0.7220	25.79/0.7061	26.60/0.7374	**64K**	**8.33**

with the edge-aware loss function, we can achieve considerable accuracy, good perceptual quality, and less computational cost at the same time.

4.3   Comparison to the State of Art Denoising Algorithms

In Table 4, we compare the proposed DN-ResNet to the state of art denoising algorithms in PASCAL VOC dataset. For fair comparison, we retrain other networks using the same VOC dataset. We observe that DN-ResNet-13 blind denoising network clearly outperforms other blind and non-blind Gaussian denoising

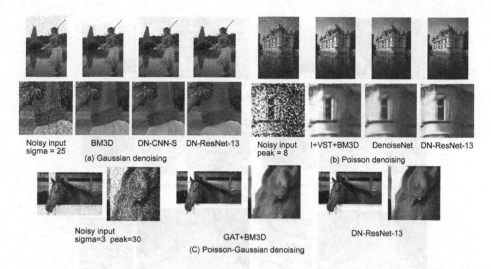

Noisy input   BM3D   DN-CNN-S   DN-ResNet-13   Noisy input   I+VST+BM3D   DenoiseNet   DN-ResNet-13
sigma = 25   peak = 8
          (a) Gaussian denoising   (b) Poisson denoising

Noisy input
sigma=3 peak=30   GAT+BM3D   DN-ResNet-13
                                 (C) Poisson-Gaussian denoising

Fig. 7. Example outputs of different algorithms for Gaussian, Poisson, and Poisson-Gaussian denoising.

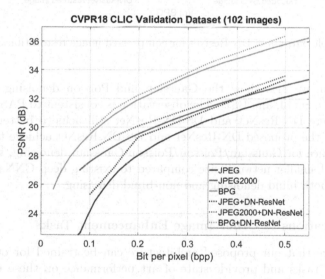

Fig. 8. Bit per pixel vs. PSNR in CLIC validation dataset.

algorithms. Compared to the 20-layer DN-CNN-S [26], DenoiseNet [15], and MemNet [22] which contain more than 600K parameters, DN-ResNet achieves competitive performance, but the network size (150K parameters) is 4 times smaller. DN-ResNet takes 15–20 ms to process a 512×512 image on single Titan X GPU, compared to 50–60 ms for DN-CNN and DenoiseNet. DS-DN-ResNet only takes 8–10 ms to process a 512×512 image, with the cost of less than 0.1 dB accuracy loss. These results show the effectiveness of DN-ResNet for Gaussian denoising. Example outputs are given in Fig. 7.

Fig. 9. Example outputs of DN-ResNet for compressed image restoration at 0.15 bpp.

In Table 5, we also show the Gaussian and Poisson denoising results on other datasets, Set14, and BSD. The observation is consistent to PASCAL VOC datasets, where DN-ResNet and DS-DN-ResNet still achieve better accuracy. As summary, the proposed DN-ResNet and DS-DN-ResNet achieve the state of art performance for Gaussian/Poisson/Poisson-Gaussian denoising, with better efficiency and smaller network size compared to existing deep CNNs. They are effective for both blind denoising and non-blind denoising.

4.4   Applications to Other Image Enhancement Tasks

We emphasize that our proposed architecture can be trained for other image enhancement tasks and provide state of art performance on these tasks, with relatively low complexity.

Image Restoration: We evaluate the proposed DN-ResNet on compressed image restoration. In Fig. 8, the curves of compression ratio (bpp, bit per pixel) versus PSNR of the decoded compressed image and restored image are given. We can find that DN-ResNet is able to improve the quality of the decoded images for all compression methods. 1–2 dB, 0.5–0.7 dB, and 0.3–0.4 dB gain can be observed for JPEG, JPEG 2000, and BPG respectively. Figure 9 shows some restored images at 0.15 bit per pixel, where DN-ResNet clearly improves the perceptual quality of the decoded compressed images.

Image Super Resolution: We cascade our DN-ResNet to 19 layers and apply it for image super resolution [17]. The low-resolution images are considered as noisy input, and the high-resolution images are considered as clean image. Our DN-ResNet achieved state of art SR performance with much less computational complexity. For example, it achieves 0.5, 0.3, 0.2 dB PSNR gain and 0.003, 0.001, 0.001 better SSIM for the SR scales 2, 3, and 4 in Set 14, while having only 1/3rd of the network size compared to existing networks such as MemNet networks such as MemNet [22] or DRRN [21].

5 Conclusion

In this paper, we presented the DN-ResNet for image denoising achieving both high accuracy and efficiency. We show that cascade training is effective in training efficient deep ResNets. The perceptual quality can be enhanced by using edge-aware loss function. We further propose the depthwise separable ResBlock and incrementally evolve the DN-ResNet to DS-DN-ResNet, which reduced the computational cost of DN-ResNet 2.5 times with less than 0.1 dB degradation in PSNR. For both cases of blind and non-blind denoising, our experimental results on benchmark datasets show that the proposed DN-ResNet achieves better accuracy and efficiency compared to the state of art denoising networks on all types of noises, including Gaussian, Poisson, and Poisson-Gaussian. The same network architecture can be utilized for other image enhancement applications as well.

References

1. Azzari, L., Foi, A.: Variance stabilization for Noisy+Estimate combination in iterative Poisson denoising. IEEE Signal Process. Lett. **23**(8), 1086–1090 (2016)
2. Burger, H.C., Schuler, C.J., Harmeling, S.: Image denoising: can plain neural networks compete with BM3D? In: IEEE Conference on Computer Vision and Pattern Recognition (2012)
3. Chen, Y., Pock, T.: Trainable nonlinear reaction diffusion: a flexible framework for fast and effective image restoration. IEEE Trans. Pattern Anal. Mach. Intell. **39**(6), 1256–1272 (2017)
4. Dabov, K., Foi, A., Katkovnik, V., Egiazarian, K.: Image denoising by sparse 3-D transform-domain collaborative filtering. IEEE Trans. Image Process. **16**(8), 2080–2095 (2007)
5. Dong, W., Zhang, L., Shi, G., Li, X.: Nonlocally centralized sparse representation for image restoration. IEEE Trans. Image Process. **22**(4), 1620–1630 (2013)
6. Everingham, M., Van Gool, L., Williams, C.K., Winn, J., Zisserman, A.: The PASCAL visual object classes (VOC) challenge. Int. J. Comput. Vis. **88**(2), 303–338 (2010)
7. Foi, A., Trimeche, M., Katkovnik, V., Egiazarian, K.: Practical Poissonian-Gaussian noise modeling and fitting for single-image raw-data. IEEE Trans. Image Process. **17**(10), 1737–1754 (2008)
8. Gu, S., Zhang, L., Zuo, W., Feng, X.: Weighted nuclear norm minimization with application to image denoising. In: IEEE Conference on Computer Vision and Pattern Recognition (2014)
9. He, K., Zhang, X., Ren, S., Sun, J.: Deep residual learning for image recognition. In: IEEE Conference on Computer Vision and Pattern Recognition (2016)

10. Howard, A.G., et al.: MobileNets: efficient convolutional neural networks for mobile vision applications. arXiv:1704.04861 (2017)
11. Workshop and challenge on learned image compression (CLIC) (2018). http://www.compression.cc/
12. Lim, B., Son, S., Kim, H., Nah, S., Lee, K.M.: Enhanced deep residual networks for single image super-resolution. In: IEEE Conference on Computer Vision and Pattern Recognition Workshops (2017)
13. Makitalo, M., Foi, A.: Optimal inversion of the generalized Anscombe transformation for Poisson-Gaussian noise. IEEE Trans. Image Process. 22(1), 91–103 (2013)
14. Martin, D., Fowlkes, C., Tal, D., Malik, J.: A database of human segmented natural images and its application to evaluating segmentation algorithms and measuring ecological statistics. In: IEEE International Conference on Computer Vision, vol. 2, pp. 416–423 (2001)
15. Remez, T., Litany, O., Giryes, R., Bronstein, A.M.: Deep class-aware image denoising. In: International Conference on Sampling Theory and Applications (2017)
16. Remez, T., Litany, O., Giryes, R., Bronstein, A.M.: Deep convolutional denoising of low-light images. arXiv:1701.01687 (2017)
17. Ren, H., El-Khamy, M., Lee, J.: Image super resolution based on fusing multiple convolution neural networks. In: 2017 IEEE Conference on Computer Vision and Pattern Recognition Workshops (CVPRW), pp. 1050–1057. IEEE (2017)
18. Ren, H., El-Khamy, M., Lee, J.: CT-SRCNN: cascade trained and trimmed deep convolutional neural networks for image super resolution (2018)
19. Sandler, M., Howard, A., Zhu, M., Zhmoginov, A., Chen, L.C.: MobileNetv 2: Inverted residuals and linear bottlenecks. In: IEEE Conference on Computer Vision and Pattern Recognition (2018)
20. Schmidt, U., Jancsary, J., Nowozin, S., Roth, S., Rother, C.: Cascades of regression tree fields for image restoration. IEEE Trans. Pattern Anal. Mach. Intell. 38(4), 677–689 (2016)
21. Tai, Y., Yang, J., Liu, X.: Image super-resolution via deep recursive residual network (2017)
22. Tai, Y., Yang, J., Liu, X., Xu, C.: MemNet: a persistent memory network for image restoration. In: Proceedings of the IEEE Conference on Computer Vision and Pattern Recognition, pp. 4539–4547 (2017)
23. Theis, L., Shi, W., Cunningham, A., Huszár, F.: Lossy image compression with compressive autoencoders. arXiv:1703.00395 (2017)
24. Toderici, G., et al.: Full resolution image compression with recurrent neural networks. In: IEEE Conference on Computer Vision and Pattern Recognition, pp. 5435–5443 (2017)
25. Zeyde, R., Elad, M., Protter, M.: On single image scale-up using sparse-representations. In: Boissonnat, J.D., et al. (eds.) Curves and Surfaces 2010. LNCS, vol. 6920, pp. 711–730. Springer, Heidelberg (2012). https://doi.org/10.1007/978-3-642-27413-8_47
26. Zhang, K., Zuo, W., Chen, Y., Meng, D., Zhang, L.: Beyond a Gaussian denoiser: residual learning of deep cnn for image denoising. IEEE Trans. Image Process. 26(7), 3142–3155 (2017)
27. Zhang, K., Zuo, W., Zhang, L.: FFDnet: toward a fast and flexible solution for CNN based image denoising. arXiv:1710.04026 (2017)

TKDN: Scene Text Detection
via Keypoints Detection

Yuanshun Cui[1,2], Jie Li[1,2], Hu Han[1,3(✉)], Shiguang Shan[1,2,4],
and Xilin Chen[1,2]

[1] Key Laboratory of Intelligent Information Processing of Chinese Academy
of Sciences (CAS), Institute of Computing Technology, CAS, Beijing 100190, China
{yuanshun.cui,jie.li}@vipl.ict.ac.cn, {hanhu,sgshan,xlchen}@ict.ac.cn
[2] University of Chinese Academy of Sciences, Beijing 100049, China
[3] Peng Cheng Laboratory, Shenzhen, China
[4] CAS Center for Excellence in Brain Science and Intelligence Technology,
Shanghai, China

Abstract. In the past few years, great efforts have been devoted to
scene text detection. Nevertheless, efficient text detection in the wild
remains a challenging problem. Methods for general object detection
usually have limitations in handling the arbitrary orientations and large
aspect ratios of scene text. In this paper, we present a novel scene text
detection method which treats text detection as a text keypoint detection task performed in a coarse-to-fine scheme (text keypoint detection
network, TKDN). Specifically, in TKDN we first generate the coarse
text instance regions using feature pyramid network (FPN) as well as
region proposal network (RPN) and ResNet50. Within the coarse text
regions, we then perform text keypoint detection, bounding box classification and regression, and text region segmentation in a multi-task way.
In the inference stage, an effective post-processing algorithm is designed
to combine the outputs from three branches and obtain the final text
keypoint detection results. The proposed TKDN approach outperforms
the state-of-the-art approach and achieves an F-measure of 82.0% on the
public-domain ICDAR2015 database.

1 Introduction

Scene text detection has drawn increasing attentions in recent years because of
its wide applications in practical scenarios (such as autonomous driving, image
retrieval, and blind-navigation). While documental text detection techniques are
becoming mature, scene text detection remains a challenging problem because of
many factors such as blur, noise, illumination, and occlusion. In addition, there
are also some internal factors of the text, such as random orientations, language
categories, large aspect ratios, and different fonts.

In the past few years, studies on the topic of scene text detection are emerging, and some representative approaches have been proposed to resolve the scene
text detection problem, such as the sliding window based methods [3,15,30,35]

© Springer Nature Switzerland AG 2019
C. V. Jawahar et al. (Eds.): ACCV 2018, LNCS 11365, pp. 231–246, 2019.
https://doi.org/10.1007/978-3-030-20873-8_15

and connected component based methods [5,24]. While these approaches give reasonably good results on scene text detection, there remain a few limitations. (i) The sliding window methods intensively search candidate text regions and classify text/non-text regions through traditional machine learning algorithm. Due to the dense search and multi-scale operation, these methods are relatively slow. (ii) The latter approach often contains multiple steps, such as character or text component detection, component filtering, text line construction, and word splitting. (iii) Both approaches are not good at dealing with complicated scenarios in text detection, e.g., arbitrary orientations and large aspect ratios.

Benefiting from recent advances in general object detection using Convolutional Neural Networks (CNNs), the performance of scene text detection based on CNNs has been significantly improved. For example, representative object detection approaches such as Faster R-CNN [26] and SSD [19] have been improved w.r.t. the scene text detection task. The best known performance on ICDAR2015 [14] has been improved from 53.6% to 80.7% in terms of F-measure in recent three years.

However, scene text is a special type of instance, which has unique appearance variations that are different from general objects, and thus it requires special designs from the feature representation to the classifier. Recent efforts include utilizing semantic segmentation based approaches such as Fully Convolutional Networks (FCN) [20] to perform text detection [4,37,38] via pixel-wise prediction of text or non-text such as [37], EAST [38] and PixelLink [4]. These methods show good performance in scene text detection, but they usually require complicated post-processing steps to resolve the region overlapping issue.

Inspired by human pose estimation approaches, e.g., [1,2], and the corner detection based scene detection method [22], we propose a Text Keypoints Detection Network (TKDN) for scene text detection. As shown in Fig. 1, we regard the scene text detection task as a text keypoints detection task. *The terminology of text keypoint used in this work has the same meaning with text corner; however, we choose to use text keypoint because we would like to extend the approach into a more general scenario in which variable number of keypoints can be used to define the text region.* We perform scene text detection in a coarse-to-fine strategy. Specifically, we first use FPN and RPN [26] to generate coarse text region proposals, which are followed by three branches: text keypoint detection branch, bounding box classification and regression branch, and text region segmentation branch, performed within the coarse text region proposal following a multi-task learning scheme [8]. During inference, the outputs of the three branches were integrated to get the final keypoint detection result.

The main contributions of this paper are three folds: (1) we transform the scene text detection task into a coarse-to-fine text keypoints detection task, leading to improved robustness against text appearance variations in scale, orientations, aspect variations, etc; (2) the proposed coarse-to-fine detection strategy effectively eliminates the overlap issue of different text instances; and (3) with text instance segmentation as a multi-task learning branch, the missing keypoints can be easily recovered based on the text segmentation results.

Fig. 1. A text region in natural scene image can be defined with a clockwise connection of four keypoints in clockwise *e.g.*, top-left, top-right, bottom-right and bottom-left, respectively.

2 Related Work

2.1 Keypoints Detection

Traditional keypoint detection approaches include SIFT [21], MSER [36], etc., which are widely used for image representation and matching tasks. Recently, keypoint detection has been found to be useful in human pose estimation task [1, 2, 9, 25, 32].

In [2], the keypoints or body parts of the human are detected from the heatmaps and used together with the affinity fields to model the connection between keypoints or parts. In [32], two FCNs are used to extract pose joint features and semantic part features, and then a fully-connected conditional random field (FCRF) is utilized to estimate multi-person pose. In [9], the location of a keypoint is modeled a one-hot mask and MASK-RCNN is utilized to predict the per keypoint mask. In [25], a Parsing Induced Learner method is proposed to estimate the dynamic parameters of the human pose model, and extract complementary features for human pose estimation.

Similar to human pose detection, the scene text detection task is converted into a corner detection task [22], which treats the corner of the text instance region as a small bounding box and utilizes position sensitive segmentation for text detection. Our method is based on both of human pose detection and corner detection. But unlike [22], we detect the keypoints within a coarse text instance region proposals instead of the whole image.

2.2 Scene Text Detection

The early approaches for text detection, based on connected components, try to find the connected regions with the characteristics of text [5,24]. Some early methods are based on sliding window [3,15]. Recently, with the rapid development of deep learning, deep learning based scene text detection approached were proposed [4,16,22,23,27,31,37,38].

SWT [5] utilizes a feature extractor based on stroke width to detect the text stroke regions and connects the regions together to generate the text regions.

Similarly, the method in [24] uses the Maximally Stable Extremal Regions (MSER) to find the extremal regions, which are considered as the text regions. The method in [15] uses a Support Vector Machine (SVM) to predict the probability that the pixel belongs to text regions. The method in [3] makes some block patterns based on the sliding window to find text regions from the source image.

CTPN [31] casts the text detection into localizing a sequence of fine-scale text proposals and then utilizes a Long Short-Term Memory (LSTM) [13] network to connect the fine-scale text proposals. To handle the large aspect ratios of scene text, TextBoxes [16] uses large ratio proposals and large ratio convolutional filters to detect the text region. RRPN [23] uses proposals with rotations to handle the text orientation problem. SegLink [27] predicts a sequence of text segments and links them into a text instance by the linkage prediction. RRD [17] utilizes regression branch and classification branch modules to extract rotation-sensitive and rotation-invariant features, respectively, and then generates text boxes. The method in [22] treats the corners of the text regions as small bounding boxes and then predicts some position sensitive segmentation maps to generate final text boxes.

Different from the above text detection approaches based on general object detection algorithms, [37] extracts a segmentation map and detects the characters regions on the map and finally connects the regions to some text lines. Similarly, EAST [38] also uses a segmentation method to detect the scene text rectangle regions. PixelLink [4] also extracts the segmentation map of text instances and utilizes the connections between pixels to generate the boxes of text regions.

Different from the existing methods, we treat scene text detection task as text keypoints detection task, as shown in Fig. 1. we only detect the keypoints of text given an image, and then connect them to generate the polygon.

3   Proposed Approach

In our approach, we detect the text region based on four keypoints of the text region, *i.e.*, the top-left, bottom-left, top-right, bottom-right keypoints. Given the four detected keypoints, a clock-wise connection of the keypoints gives the text region. Inspired by human pose estimation methods recent and corner detection based scene text detection method in [22], we propose a novel scene text detection approach based on keypoint detection. Different from the previous segmentation based text detection methods [34,38], which usually need complex post-processing, the post-processing of our method is much simpler and clearer. In addition, while previous approaches [4,38] have to carefully deal with region overlappings, our method does not suffer from this issue. Our method performs text keypoint detection using a two-stage coarse-to-fine network based on Mask-RCNN [9]. In the first stage, FPN and RPN are utilized to generate the coarse text region proposals. In the second stage, three tasks, *i.e.*, text vs. not-text classification and location regression, text keypoint detection, and text segmentation, are performed inside each region proposal in a multi-task learning manner.

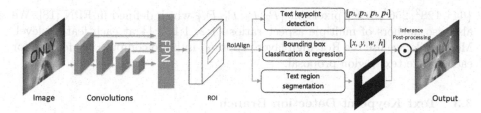

Fig. 2. Overview of the proposed approach for scene text detection, which consists of two stages performed from coarse to fine. In the first stage, ResNet50 and FPN, as well as RPN, are used to extract feature and generate the coarse text regions. In the second stage, three branches (text keypoint detection, bounding box classification and regression, and text region segmentation) are performed inside each region proposal in a multi-task way. The final polygon text region could be computed with an effective post-processing algorithm, denoted by ⊙.

3.1 Network Architecture

As shown in Fig. 2, we use a ResNet50 [10] as the backbone feature extraction module because of its high efficiency and representation ability. The size of scene text varies greatly, so the features are expected to contain more semantic information. FPN [18] which has a top-down architecture with lateral connections to build an in-network feature pyramid can provide rich information for texts with significant different scales. Therefore, we embed FPN to the backbone network to extract features that are shared by the three branches in the second stage.

3.2 Text Region Proposal Generation

As we mentioned before, the large aspect ratios of scene text is a big challenge for text detection. The difficulty lies in the fact that the candidate areas generated by the original RPN [26] cannot cover both the large and small text areas at the same time. The main reason is that the original RPN network is based on a high-level feature map of the backbone. The high-level features contain more abstract information, but the resolution is low. This causes some text areas to be ignored when generating candidate regions, and the recall rate will also decrease. Considering this situation, we embed FPN into the backbone network. FPN connects the high-level abstract features of low-resolution with the low-level detailed features of high-resolution from top to down so that the final feature representation could have rich semantic information. This helps to improve the quality of candidate region generation, and the recall rate for text detection task could increase accordingly.

We made some adjustments to the RPN by replacing the single-scale feature map with FPN. There are two parameters to control the size and shape of anchors, *i.e.*, scale and aspect ratio. The scale parameter determines the size of the anchor, and the aspect ratio controls the ratio of the width to the height for the anchor box. In our approach, we define the anchors to have areas of

$\{64^2, 128^2, 256^2, 512^2\}$ pixels on $\{P_2, P_3, P_4, P_5\}$ which defined in FPN [18]. We also use anchors of multiple aspect ratios $\{1:2, 1:1, 2:1\}$ at each feature level. Meanwhile, we use the RoIAlign layer proposed in [9] to compute the feature for each coarse text region proposal.

3.3   Text Keypoint Detection Branch

The popular text area detection algorithms are based on semantic segmentation, such as [4, 38]. These methods determine the text areas based on the response of score maps and usually rely on complicated post-processing algorithms to get the final text detection result. But for our keypoints detection task, the keypoints are obtained through direct regression, so no additional post-processing operations are required at the keypoint level. For each ground-truth text region, if we define K keypoints, then we can get the coordinates of K points directly. So the superiority of our methods is to decouple the connection between individual point-pairs, making every point of an instance text area to be independent.

In this branch, we adopt a small FCN [20] to predict K masks for K keypoints (e.g. top-left, top-right). We set K to 4 by default. This setting is also catering to the annotation of dataset ICDAR2015. This branch helps demonstrate the progress of using keypoints for text detection.

Considering the differences between general image segmentation and text keypoint detection, we have revised the original FCN so that it can be better adapted to the text keypoint detection task and the point-wise prediction. For each of K keypoints of an instance, the training target is a one-hot $n \times n$ binary mask where only a single pixel is labeled as foreground. During training, given a training set (p, p'), in which p denotes the predicted location and p' denotes the target location, we minimize the cross-entropy loss over a n^2-way softmax output. The loss function is defined as:

$$L_{kpt} = \frac{1}{k} \sum_{i=1}^{k} CrossEntropy(p_i, p_i'). \tag{1}$$

The keypoint detection branch consists of a stack of four 3×3 512-d convolutional layers, followed by a deconvolutional layer and $2\times$ bilinear upscaling, producing an output resolution of 56×56. The overall structure of the text keypoint detection branch is shown in Fig. 3a. In theory, our method can approximate an arbitrary polygon because in our method K can be any integer. Our preliminary results show that the higher resolution of the output mask, the better accuracy of the detected keypoints. However, in this work focus on the text detection ability from a single resolution feature map.

3.4   Bounding Box Classification and Regression Branch

In order to cooperate with the use of FPN for proposal generation, we use two fully connected (fc) layers in bounding box regression branch to do the bounding

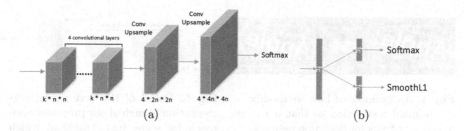

Fig. 3. Details of the text keypoints detection branch and the bounding box classification and regression branch of our proposed approach. (a) Four convolutional layers and two deconvolutional layers with bilinear upsample operations. (b) Two fully connected layers are used for both classification and regression.

box offset regression (see Fig. 3b). Suppose $B = \{b_i\}_{i=1}^n$ is the set of region proposals generated by modified RPN, and t_i is the label for proposal b_i. We use $SmoothL1$ loss defined in Fast R-CNN [26] for backpropagation, which is defined as:

$$L_{loc} = \frac{1}{n} \sum_{i=1}^{n} SmoothL1(b_i, t_i). \tag{2}$$

In contrast to the default setting of Faster R-CNN in which the bounding box should be as tight as possible, we intentionally make the bounding box classification and regression branch to predict a larger box that can wrap around the entire text area. So we made some modifications to the training data so that they can be suited to our network design. We increased the size of the text area in the original annotation data by a certain proportion $w.r.t.$ its original size (see Fig. 4). The reason why we made the above modifications is due to the following considerations: (1) text areas can be covered more comprehensively; (2) since each box is generated from the keypoints, the four keypoints of the text area are respectively located on the four sides of the box. If all the key points are located on side of bounding boxes in training data, the definition of the data will be ambiguous. Our modification to the text bounding annotations resolves the ambiguity issue. In summary, the effect of this modification is to decouple the association between the point and each edge, allowing relatively free distribution per text keypoint.

As for the text classification loss, we directly use the cross-entropy loss L_{cls}, which is defined as:

$$L_{cls} = CrossEntropy(Pr_c, t_c), \tag{3}$$

where Pr_c is the predicted probability of all the boxes belonging to positive or negative, and t_c is the ground-truth label of all boxes, 1 for positive and 0 for negative.

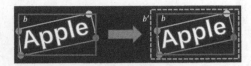

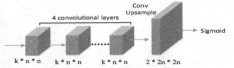

Fig. 4. An example of how we modify the original annotation so that it can fit our text keypoint detection network. Generally speaking, we extend the minimum enclosing rectangle of the text region by a certain percentage.

Fig. 5. Detail of the text region segmentation branch of our proposed approach for scene text detection, which consists of four convolutional layers and one deconvolutional layer with bilinear upsample operation.

3.5   Text Region Segmentation Branch

Since there are significant changes in the scale and shape of the text areas, it is not always easy to directly regress the text keypoints from the feature of each proposal. To obtain more complementary information for these hard cases, we introduce a text region segmentation branch to assist in the text keypoint detection task (see Fig. 5). The text region mask is a finer-grained supervisory signal that facilitates the regression of keypoints during multi-task training.

Similar to the text keypoint detection branch, the text region segmentation branch has a Cn^2-dimensional output for each RoI, which encodes C binary masks of resolution $n \times n$. Each mask defines one class in the segmentation task. Here, for text vs. non-text segmentation, $C = 2$. Per-pixel sigmoid is applied to compute the masks, and an average binary cross-entropy loss is used for backpropagation

$$L_{mask} = \frac{1}{n^2} \sum_{i=1}^{n^2} CrossEntropy(m_i, m_i'),   \tag{4}$$

where m_i denotes a single pixel from the predict mask with the resolution of $n \times n$. The text region segmentation branch consists of a stack of four 3×3 512-d convolutional layers, followed by one deconvolutional layer, producing an output of 28×28. We use a low-resolution mask output here because this auxiliary text region segmentation task does not require very high segmentation accuracy.

3.6   Optimization

We train the three branches (text keypoint detection branch, bounding box classification and regression branch, and text region segmentation branch) in a multi-task way, and the joint loss function L is defined as:

$$L = \frac{1}{N_c}L_{cls} + \frac{\lambda_1}{N_c}L_{loc} + \frac{\lambda_2}{N_k}L_{kpt} + \frac{\lambda_3}{N_s}L_{mask},   \tag{5}$$

where L_{cls}, L_{loc}, L_{kpt} and L_{mask} are defined in (3) (2), (1) and (4), respectively. N_c is the number of positive boxes in a minibatch, N_k is the number of keypoints, N_s is the number of pixels in segmentation maps; they are used to normalize the losses of three branches. We empirically set $\lambda_1 = 10$, $\lambda_2 = 1$, and $\lambda_3 = 1$.

3.7 Post-processing

In most cases, our text keypoint detection works well, and the detection keypoints of each text instance are visible (see Fig. 6a). Under rare cases, some keypoints of a text instance may be missing (see Fig. 6b and c). In this case, we restore the missing points using an efficient post-processing algorithm:

(1) If only one text point is missing, we treat the text polygon as a parallelogram and the missing point can be recovered by the general properties of a parallelogram. For example, $\mathbf{p}_2$ in Fig. 6b can be recovered as

$$\mathbf{p}_2 = \mathbf{p}_3 + (\mathbf{p}_1 - \mathbf{p}_4). \tag{6}$$

(2) If more than one points are missing, we further consider the following two cases. (i) Without text region segmentation branch. In this case, we replace the missing points by corresponding bounding box corner points, such as $\mathbf{p}_2$ and $\mathbf{p}_3$ shown in Fig. 6c; (ii) With text region segmentation branch. In this case, we abandon the detected keypoints of text instance and use the mask of text instance to restore a rectangle instead of a polygon. As shown in Fig. 6d, we use the rectangle with the minimum area which covers the mask of text instance.

The proposed post-processing algorithm is only used in the inference stage of a learned network.

4 Experimental Results

4.1 Database and Settings

We provide evaluations of the proposed approach and comparisons with the state-of-the-art methods on the public-domain ICDAR2015 database [14] and the MSRA-TD500 database [33]. ICDAR2015 is a benchmark of the ICDAR2015 Robust Reading Competition which contains 1, 000 training images and 500 test images. ICDAR2015 is a challenging dataset for scene text detection because it contains arbitrary-oriented text in wild. MSRA-TD500 is collected for detecting arbitrary-oriented long text lines and contains 300 training images and 200 test images.

Since the size of the ICDAR2015 database is relatively small, we have used the SynthText [6] dataset for pre-training, which consists of 800K images with approximately 8 million synthetic word instances. In our experiments, we did not use the entire SynthText dataset, instead, we randomly select 50K images for pre-training.

(a) All keypoints are visible   (b) One keypoint is missing

(c) Two keypoints are missing

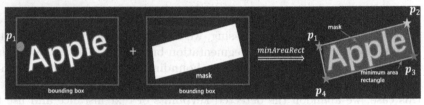

(d) More than two keypoints are missing

Fig. 6. Example of post-processing in the network inference stage when some text keypoints are missing in the keypoint detection by the algorithm in Sect. 3.7. The star points represent the missing and recovered keypoints.

Since our coarse-to-fine approach consists of three tasks (text keypoint detection, bounding box classification and regression, and text region segmentation) in the second stage, we obtain the required supervision signals by converting the original annotations of each database according to the following rules: (1) generate four keypoints of the text area according to the text annotations, which are generally the top-left, bottom-left, top-right, and bottom-right points; (2) generate a bounding box that covers the entire text area based on the coordinates of the keypoints; (3) generate a corresponding mask for text vs. non-text segmentation using the four keypoints. To summarize, the target of the keypoint detection branch is $t_{kpt} = \{p_i | i \in \{1, 2, 3, 4\}\}$, where $p_i = (x_i, y_i)$ is a keypoint coordinate. The target of the bounding box classification and regression branch is already discussed in Sect. 3.4. The target for the text region segmentation branch is a binary map, 1 for the text area and 0 for the background.

We select ResNet50 [10] as the backbone of our model. We first pre-train our model on SynthText50K for one epoch with the learning rate fixed to 2.5×10^{-3}. With the standard SGD optimizer, we set the momentum to 0.9 and set the batch size to 2. Then we finetune our model on other datasets. Note that we don't use any data augmentations. During pre-training stage or finetuning stage, we adopt randomly scale from (512, 640, 672, 704, 736, 768, 800) and set the max size to 1, 333 for input images.

We finetune our model on ICDAR2015 with only 10 epochs based on the pre-trained SynthText50K model. The learning rate is fixed to 2.5×10^{-3} except the last epoch with the learning rate of 2.5×10^{-4}. Note that we don't use any augmentations for the dataset. In testing, we set the scale to 800 and the max size to 1, 333 for input images. The threshold of non-maximum suppression (NMS) is set to 0.5. All the experiments are conducted on a desktop with NVIDIA Titan X GPU and Intel i7-3.60 GHz CPU.

4.2 Evaluation Metric

Following the state-of-the-art text detection methods [22,31,38], we also use precision, recall, and F-measure as the evaluation metric. If an image contains X text instances, and a model gives Y text boxes. Z text boxes shot the ground-truth text instances. Then, Precision = Z/Y, Recall = Z/X, and F-measure = $2 \cdot$ Precision $\cdot$ Recall$/$(Precision + Recall).

Usually, recall reflects the ability of a model on finding out all the ground-truth text regions, and precision reflects the quality (percentage of correct detections) of the detections. F-measure gives a single value measure to the performance of a model.

4.3 Baselines

We compare the proposed approach with a number of the state-of-the-art methods for scene text detection, such as Zhang *et al.* [37], CTPN [31], Yao *et al.* [34], SegLink [27], EAST [38], SSTD [11] and Lyu *et al.* [22]. Yao *et al.* [34] used a FCN model to predict the text regions based on semantic segmentation and post-processing method, and SSTD [11] uses an attention mechanism method based on SSD to detect word-level bounding boxes in a natural image. For all these baseline methods, we directly use the detection accuracies reported in their original papers.

4.4 Text Detection Results

The text detection results by the proposed approach and the state-of-the-art methods on ICDAR2015 are listed in Table 1. We can see that our method outperforms all the state-of-the-art methods in terms of F-measure and Recall rate. In terms of F-measure, the best result by the state-of-the-art methods is reported in [22] (80.7%), while the result by the proposed approach is 82.0%. Similarly, in terms of recall rate, the proposed approach outperforms the state-of-the-art methods by a large margin (*e.g.*, 79.7% vs. 76.8%). This suggests that the proposed approach is able to detect more challenging text instances. Some examples of text detection results by the proposed approach on ICDAR2015 are shown in Fig. 7a. We can see that even when the text areas are tiny *w.r.t.* the entire

Table 1. Comparisons of text detection performance by our method and a number of state-of-the-art text detection methods on the ICDAR2015 dataset.

Method	F-measure	Recall	Precision	FPS
Zhang et al. [37]	53.6	43.0	70.8	0.48
CTPN [31]	60.9	51.6	74.2	7.1
Yao et al. [34]	64.8	58.7	72.3	1.61
SegLink [27]	75.0	76.8	73.1	-
EAST [38]	76.4	72.8	80.5	6.52
SSTD [11]	77.0	73.0	80.0	**7.7**
Lyu et al. [22]	80.7	70.7	**94.1**	3.6
He et al. [12]	81.0	**80.0**	82.0	-
Proposed	**82.0**	79.7	84.5	3.0

image, the proposed approach still works well. We did not use multi-scale strategy [22,38] to do the detection, but we agree it will improve the performance with the cost of additional computations.

We also evaluate our model on MSRA-TD500 [33], which is collected for detecting arbitrary-oriented long text lines. All configurations of our model are the same as those used on ICDAR2015 except that we randomly rotate the input images by 90° or −90° during training and the scale is set to 736 during testing. Moreover, we train our method for 50 epochs in total. The baseline methods, e.g., Zhang et al. [37], Yao et al. [34], EAST [38], SegLink [27], He et al. [12], and Lyu et al. [22], reported 74.0%, 75.9%, 76.1%, 77.0%, 74.0%, and 81.5% F-measure scores, respectively. The proposed approach achieves 81.1% F-measure, which is better than all the baseline methods expect for [22]. The possible reason is that our method is not good at detecting the long multi-line oriented text instances which exist in the MSRA-TD500 database (see Fig. 7b). Because of the coarse-to-fine strategy, our method usually detects a coarse text instance region in the form of bounding box first. In most cases, the coarse text instance region contains little part of other text. But when detecting oriented multi-line long text instances, a coarse text instance region not only contains the currently focused text instance but also the non-negligible parts of other text instances. Then it will confuse the model which part should be focused on. Moreover, from Fig. 7b, we can see that due to the close distance between difficult text instances, some coarse text regions will be filtered out by NMS. So in our future work, we will improve the text region proposal generation algorithm so that it can better handle the oriented multi-line long texts.

4.5   Ablation Experiment

We provide an ablation study of the three branches in the second stage of the proposed approach. Specifically, we gradually remove the branches and train the network using the same configurations as the full network.

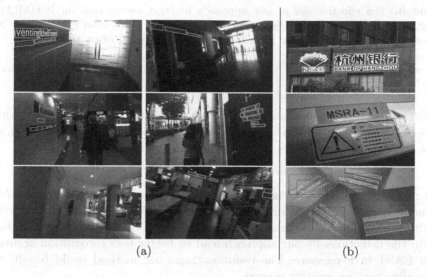

(a)   (b)

Fig. 7. Examples of text detection results by the proposed approach on (a) the ICDAR2015 database, and (b) the MSRA-TD500 database. The last image in (b) shows the limitations of the proposed approach in detecting.

The results by individual ablated models are listed in Table 2. When we only use the bounding box classification and regression branch, the network becomes a Faster R-CNN network, and there is a big performance drop compared with the full method. The main reason should be that it has big limitations in detecting oriented text using a traditional Faster R-CNN framework. The predicted upright bounding box cannot cover the ground-truth with the required IoU threshold. The ablated model without using text segmentation branch leads to degraded performance in both F-measure and recall, although the precision is slightly higher. We find that the main reason lies in the cases in which there are missing keypoints, and the post-processing algorithm is required to recover the missing keypoints. The segmentation masks by the text segmentation branch have been found to be useful in accurately recovering the missing text keypoints (see Fig. 6c and d).

4.6 Effectiveness for Scene Text Recognition

To evaluate our method on its effectiveness for text recognition, we compare our method with a state-of-the-art text detector - EAST [38] using a state-of-the-art

Table 2. Ablation study for the proposed approach on ICDAR2015.

	F-measure	Recall	Precision
BBox Cls. & Reg. alone	73.5	69.7	77.8
BBox Cls. & Reg. + Seg	81.0	79.1	82.9
BBox Cls. & Reg. + Keypoint Det	81.5	77.8	**85.6**
BBox Cls. & Reg. + Keypoint Det. + Seg	**82.0**	**79.7**	84.5

Table 3. The effectiveness of our approach for text recognition on ICDAR2015. "F","R", and "P" represent "F-measure", "Recall", and "Precision". "S", "W", "G" represent the "Strong", "Weak", "Generic" lexicon scenarios, respectively.

Detection method	Accuracy			Recognition method	End-to-End Acc.			Word Spotting Acc.		
	F	R	P		S	W	G	S	W	G
EAST†	80.77	77.23	**84.64**	CRNN*	70.09	65.91	48.04	74.78	70.04	50.97
Proposed	**82.03**	**79.69**	84.53		**71.92**	**67.81**	**49.62**	**76.95**	**72.27**	**52.93**

†We use the pre-trained model in public. *The method is implemented by ourselves.

text recognizer CRNN [28]. As shown in Table 3, our method outperforms EAST in terms of F-measure for text detection on ICDAR2015. When the detection results by EAST and our method are input into CRNN for text recognition; again, the detections by our approach lead to better text recognition accuracy than EAST in F-measure. The result suggests our method could benefit the succeeding text recognition process.

5 Conclusions

In this paper, we propose a novel scene text detection method via coarse-to-fine text keypoint detection (named as Text Keypoints Detection Network (TKDN)). Our TKDN model first generates coarse text region proposals, and then perform text keypoint detection, bounding box classification and regression, and text region segmentation simultaneously within the text region proposals. An efficient post-processing is also proposed to recover missing text keypoints based on the outputs by the three branches. Experimental results on the public-domain ICDAR2015 database show that the proposed approach outperforms the state-of-the-art. Ablation study shows the effectiveness of individual components in the proposed approach. The comparison with EAST on the end-to-end task shows that the proposed approach is more effective for scene text recognition.

Inevitably, our method has its limitations, such as in detecting oriented multi-line long texts. In our future work, we would like to focus on the improvement of our method *w.r.t.* the proposal generations for the oriented multi-line long text scenarios and introducing 3D prior to assist in ambiguity reduction like that widely used in face analysis [7]. In addition, we would like to investigate the possibility of detecting arbitrarily shaped scene text using multiple keypoints, and apply the method for end-to-end text detection and recognition [29].

Acknowledgement. This research was supported in part by the Natural Science Foundation of China (grants 61732004, 61390511, and 61672496), External Cooperation Program of Chinese Academy of Sciences (CAS) (grant GJHZ1843), and Youth Innovation Promotion Association CAS (2018135).

References

1. Alp Güler, R., Neverova, N., Kokkinos, I.: DensePose: dense human pose estimation in the wild. In: IEEE CVPR (2018)
2. Cao, Z., Simon, T., Wei, S., Sheikh, Y.: Realtime multi-person 2D pose estimation using part affinity fields. In: IEEE CVPR (2017)
3. Chen, X., Yuille, A.L.: Detecting and reading text in natural scenes. In: IEEE CVPR (2004)
4. Deng, D., Liu, H., Li, X., Cai, D.: PixelLink: detecting scene text via instance segmentation. In: AAAI (2018)
5. Epshtein, B., Ofek, E., Wexler, Y.: Detecting text in natural scenes with stroke width transform. In: IEEE CVPR (2010)
6. Gupta, A., Vedaldi, A., Zisserman, A.: Synthetic data for text localisation in natural images. In: IEEE CVPR (2016)
7. Han, H., Jain, A.K.: 3D face texture modeling from uncalibrated frontal and profile images. In: IEEE BTAS (2012)
8. Han, H., Jain, A.K., Wang, F., Shan, S., Chen, X.: Heterogeneous face attribute estimation: a deep multi-task learning approach. IEEE Trans. PAMI 40(11), 2597–2609 (2018)
9. He, K., Gkioxari, G., Dollár, P., Girshick, R.B.: Mask R-CNN. In: IEEE ICCV (2017)
10. He, K., Zhang, X., Ren, S., Sun, J.: Deep residual learning for image recognition. In: IEEE CVPR (2016)
11. He, P., Huang, W., He, T., Zhu, Q., Qiao, Y., Li, X.: Single shot text detector with regional attention. In: IEEE ICCV (2017)
12. He, W., Zhang, X.Y., Yin, F., Liu, C.L.: Deep direct regression for multi-oriented scene text detection. In: IEEE ICCV (2017)
13. Hochreiter, S., Schmidhuber, J.: Long short-term memory. Neural Comput. 9(8), 1735–1780 (1997)
14. Karatzas, D., et al.: ICDAR 2015 competition on robust reading. In: ICDAR (2015)
15. Kim, K.I., Jung, K., Kim, J.H.: Texture-based approach for text detection in images using support vector machines and continuously adaptive mean shift algorithm. IEEE Trans. PAMI 25(12), 1631–1639 (2003)
16. Liao, M., Shi, B., Bai, X., Wang, X., Liu, W.: TextBoxes: a fast text detector with a single deep neural network. In: AAAI (2017)
17. Liao, M., Zhu, Z., Shi, B., Xia, G.S., Bai, X.: Rotation-sensitive regression for oriented scene text detection. In: IEEE CVPR (2018)
18. Lin, T., Dollár, P., Girshick, R.B., He, K., Hariharan, B., Belongie, S.J.: Feature pyramid networks for object detection. In: IEEE CVPR (2017)
19. Liu, W., et al.: SSD: single shot multibox detector. In: Leibe, B., Matas, J., Sebe, N., Welling, M. (eds.) ECCV 2016. LNCS, vol. 9905, pp. 21–37. Springer, Cham (2016). https://doi.org/10.1007/978-3-319-46448-0_2
20. Long, J., Shelhamer, E., Darrell, T.: Fully convolutional networks for semantic segmentation. In: IEEE CVPR (2015)
21. Lowe, D.G.: Object recognition from local scale-invariant features. In: IEEE ICCV (1999)
22. Lyu, P., Yao, C., Wu, W., Yan, S., Bai, X.: Multi-oriented scene text detection via corner localization and region segmentation. In: IEEE CVPR (2018)
23. Ma, J., et al.: Arbitrary-oriented scene text detection via rotation proposals. IEEE Trans. Multimedia 20, 3111–3122 (2018)

24. Neumann, L., Matas, J.: A method for text localization and recognition in real-world images. In: Kimmel, R., Klette, R., Sugimoto, A. (eds.) ACCV 2010. LNCS, vol. 6494, pp. 770–783. Springer, Heidelberg (2011). https://doi.org/10.1007/978-3-642-19318-7_60

25. Nie, X., Feng, J., Zuo, Y., Yan, S.: Human pose estimation with parsing induced learner. In: IEEE CVPR (2018)

26. Ren, S., He, K., Girshick, R.B., Sun, J.: Faster R-CNN: towards real-time object detection with region proposal networks. In: NIPS (2015)

27. Shi, B., Bai, X., Belongie, S.J.: Detecting oriented text in natural images by linking segments. In: IEEE CVPR (2017)

28. Shi, B., Bai, X., Yao, C.: An end-to-end trainable neural network for image-based sequence recognition and its application to scene text recognition. IEEE Trans. PAMI 39(11), 2298–2304 (2017)

29. Song, Y., Cui, Y., Han, H., Shan, S., Chen, X.: Scene text detection via deep semantic feature fusion and attention-based refinement. In: ICPR (2018)

30. Sun, L., Huo, Q., Jia, W., Chen, K.: A robust approach for text detection from natural scene images. Pattern Recognit. 48(9), 2906–2920 (2015)

31. Tian, Z., Huang, W., He, T., He, P., Qiao, Y.: Detecting text in natural image with connectionist text proposal network. In: Leibe, B., Matas, J., Sebe, N., Welling, M. (eds.) ECCV 2016. LNCS, vol. 9912, pp. 56–72. Springer, Cham (2016). https://doi.org/10.1007/978-3-319-46484-8_4

32. Xia, F., Wang, P., Chen, X., Yuille, A.L.: Joint multi-person pose estimation and semantic part segmentation. In: IEEE CVPR (2017)

33. Yao, C., Bai, X., Liu, W., Ma, Y., Tu, Z.: Detecting texts of arbitrary orientations in natural images. In: IEEE CVPR (2012)

34. Yao, C., Bai, X., Sang, N., Zhou, X., Zhou, S., Cao, Z.: Scene text detection via holistic, multi-channel prediction. arXiv preprint arXiv:1606.09002 (2016)

35. Yin, X., Yin, X., Huang, K., Hao, H.: Robust text detection in natural scene images. IEEE Trans. PAMI 36(5), 970–983 (2014)

36. Yin, X., Yin, X., Hao, H., Iqbal, K.: Effective text localization in natural scene images with MSER, geometry-based grouping and AdaBoost. In: ICPR (2012)

37. Zhang, Z., Zhang, C., Shen, W., Yao, C., Liu, W., Bai, X.: Multi-oriented text detection with fully convolutional networks. In: IEEE CVPR (2016)

38. Zhou, X., et al.: EAST: an efficient and accurate scene text detector. In: IEEE CVPR (2017)

Scale-Varying Triplet Ranking
with Classification Loss for Facial
Age Estimation

Woobin Im[1], Sungeun Hong[2], Sung-Eui Yoon[1](✉), and Hyun S. Yang[1]

[1] KAIST, Daejeon, Republic of Korea
{iwbn,sungeui}@kaist.ac.kr, hsyang@cs.kaist.ac.kr
[2] SK T-Brain, Seoul, Republic of Korea
csehong@sktbrain.com

Abstract. In recent years, considerable efforts based on convolutional neural networks have been devoted to age estimation from face images. Among them, classification-based approaches have shown promising results, but there has been little investigation of age differences and ordinal age information. In this paper, we propose a ranking objective with two novel schemes jointly performed with an age classification objective to take ordinal age labels into account. We first introduce relative triplet sampling in which a set of triplets is constructed considering the relative differences in ages. This also addresses the problem of having limited triplet candidates, that occurs in conventional triplet sampling. We then propose the scale-varying ranking constraint, which decides the importance of a relative triplet and adjusts a scale of gradients accordingly. Our adaptive ranking loss with relative sampling not only lowers the generalization error but ultimately has a meaningful performance improvement over the state-of-the-art methods on two well-known benchmarks.

Keywords: Age estimation · Triplet ranking · Joint loss · Deep learning

1 Introduction

There has been a growing interest in age estimation from face images due to a variety of potential applications [1–3]. As in other computer vision fields [4–8],

Supported by Institute for Information & Communications Technology Promotion (IITP) grant funded by the Korea government (MSIT) [2016-0-00562 (R0124-16-0002), Emotional Intelligence Technology to Infer Human Emotion and Carry on Dialogue Accordingly], and NRF [NRF-2017M3C4A7066317].

Electronic supplementary material The online version of this chapter (https://doi.org/10.1007/978-3-030-20873-8_16) contains supplementary material, which is available to authorized users.

C. V. Jawahar et al. (Eds.): ACCV 2018, LNCS 11365, pp. 247–259, 2019.
https://doi.org/10.1007/978-3-030-20873-8_16

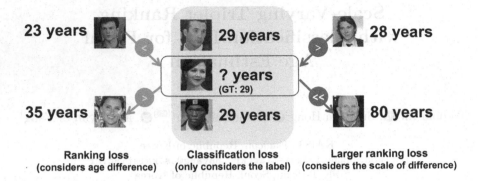

Fig. 1. When we infer the age of the woman in the center, (center) classification loss considers only its label, (left) ranking loss considers the age difference of a triplet, which is an additional clue for inferencing the age, and (right) our adaptive triplet ranking loss considers the scale of differences, so that larger ranking loss is applied to the triplet.

considerable efforts based on Convolutional Neural Networks (CNN) have been devoted to age estimation. Depending on tasks, age estimation can be largely divided into classification of age groups or direct prediction of age values, i.e. the regression task.

In the field of age estimation, CNNs have been widely exploited in a variety of different approaches. To classify age groups, Levi et al. [9] used vanilla CNN with N-class probability outputs, which gives a baseline performance on Adience benchmark dataset [10]. To better estimate ages from face images, studies using transferred CNN [2] and attention models [3] have also been proposed. Meanwhile, studies have been conducted to predict age values beyond the age group classification. Early investigations involved a three-layer CNN regression model with a Gaussian loss [1]. However, recent experiments have shown that training a CNN directly for regression loss is unstable since outliers cause a larger generalization error [11]. This led to different approaches to estimate age values such as distribution-related loss [12–15], ordinal ranking strategy [16,17], bias-analysis [18], and classification loss [3,11]. Among them, methods based on classification [3,11] showed the most simple yet powerful results in large scale datasets in the wild.

Crucially, the classification loss, i.e. cross-entropy loss, however, does not reflect the ordinal characteristics of age labels; it focuses on whether the predicted label is correct, but does not care about the degree of error between a prediction and its target value. As discussed later in the experiment, this leads to a large performance gap between training and validation sets. To address the issue, we take a feature learning approach by an end-to-end learning objective for CNN, which is configured jointly from the proposed ranking constraint as well as the classification loss. The classification loss is used to predict the exact age, while our adaptive ranking constraint, inspired by the triplet ranking loss [19–21] and classification-ranking joint loss [22], acts like a regularizer and consequently

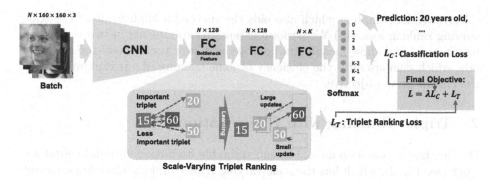

Fig. 2. Overall network framework of our method. In the bottleneck layer, we apply the adaptive triplet ranking strategy (L_T: Eq. 6) by selecting triplets and computing the scale-varying triplet ranking loss. Our final objective jointly includes both the ranking (L_T: Eq. 6) and classification (L_C: Eq. 9) losses simultaneously.

helps improve the performance. Meanwhile, large-margin softmax loss [23,24] is suggested to make the conventional classification loss produce more discriminative feature space which results in better classification performance. However, the approach can be applied when each inter-class relation is the same throughout all pairs of classes; while age pairs have different relations in themselves.

The main difference between conventional triplet loss and our proposed ranking constraint is twofold: relative triplet sampling and scale-varying ranking. Generally, in the conventional triplet loss, triplets consist of two samples with the same label (anchor and positive) and a sample with a different label (negative), and the loss aims to separate the positive pair from the negative pair by a constant margin in the embedding space.

We, however, argue that applying ranking loss by using a constant margin in age estimation cannot fully exploit the ordinal information in age labels. To solve this problem, we first alleviate the existing rigid selection criterion by suggesting relative triplet sampling, where a sample relatively close to the anchor is positive, otherwise negative. The proposed sampling creates more diversity in the triplets than the conventional one, and ultimately makes it possible to apply the following ranking constraint efficiently.

Once the relative triplets are sampled, we then apply the scale-varying ranking loss which automatically decides the importance of a triplet and accordingly adjusts scales of gradients. This enables for a model to learn a ranking without a fixed margin constant and also act like a regularizer, which prevents overfitting of a model. Figure 1 illustrates the concept and purpose of the proposed method.

The main contributions of this study are as follows: (i) We propose an adaptive, scale-varying ranking loss that prevents overfitting of a model by acting as a regularizer, while assisting in the improvement of the estimation performance. To our knowledge, this is the first attempt to utilize a triplet ranking method to efficiently train a model for age estimation. (ii) To address the lack of possible triplets caused by the conventional triplet sampling, we suggest the relative triplet sampling which also aids the successful application of the scale-varying ranking loss. (iii) We perform extensive experiments in two well-known benchmarks and show meaningful improvement over the state-of-the-art methods, which demonstrates the efficiency of joint training of our ranking loss and the classification objective.

2   Triplet Ranking with Classification

Our method is based on an end-to-end trainable deep convolutional neural network (see Fig. 2), which has the scale-varying triplet ranking module and a softmax output. In the network, our final goal is to estimate a correct age by the softmax layer when a face image is given. While not directly related to the age inference, the triplet ranking module accommodates the relative age difference given a triplet, leading to better age estimation. As a result, our final objective function includes both triplet ranking and classification loss. In the next sub-sections, we introduce our suggested loss functions in detail.

2.1   Relative Triplet Sampling

Sampling triplets is an essential part of a triplet ranking loss. Conventional applications utilizing a triplet loss deal with binary labels, i.e., whether or not two samples belong to the same class. In other words, triplet samples, (a, p, n), commonly called an anchor, a positive, and a negative samples, are chosen, when a and p are in the same class, but a and n are not.

While ages of two faces can be treated as the same or not, we found that it is less effective for ordinal classes like age. One aspect is that the pool of possible triplets in this perspective is restricted. Suppose that we have a mini-batch of size N with an equal number of samples from each class and we have K classes of age labels. If we constrain the positive sample to have the same age label as the anchor for the conventional ranking loss, the pool size of the triplets for a mini-batch becomes $O(N^3/K)$. Since K can be large for an age regression task, e.g., MORPH dataset has 60 classes of age, this approach is subject to severely limited combinations of triplets.

When it comes to age, we can better define the positive and the negative samples by a relative measure. Formally, we sample features from a d-dimensional embedding space in $\mathbb{R}^d$, which is built by a CNN, f, embedding an image input x into $f(x) \in \mathbb{R}^d$. Assume that we have a mini-batch X of a size N with its corresponding set of age labels Y, which contains positive real numbers; i.e., $X = \{x_1, x_2, \cdots, x_N\}$ and $Y = \{y_1, y_2, \cdots, y_N\}$. We then sample every possible $(f(x_a), f(x_p), f(x_n))$, simply dented by (f_a, f_p, f_n), such that the relative triplet satisfies $|y_a - y_p| < |y_a - y_n|$. In other words, the set of our chosen triplets is:

$$T = \{(f_a, f_p, f_n) \,|\, a \neq p \neq n \cap |y_a - y_p| < |y_a - y_n|\}. \tag{1}$$

As a result, the chosen relative triplets satisfy that the age difference between the pair of the anchor and the positive must be less than the one between the anchor

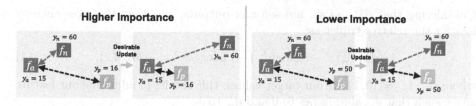

Fig. 3. Schematic visualization of two dimensional embedding space (bottleneck) where similar age samples should be located closer. The left triplet shows a wider discrepancy between age labels and their features in the space, compared to that of the right one. The left triplet should be treated more importantly with its update for learning the feature.

and the negative. This approach creates more diversity in the triplets compared to the traditional methods, since it has a pool of $O(N^3)$ triplets, which is K times diverse than the conventional one. When used with our adaptive ranking loss, this in turn results in better performance (Table 1a) and embedding space (Fig. 5).

2.2   Scale-Varying Triplet Ranking Loss

When a triplet ranking is used for representation learning [19,25,26], its loss formulation directly utilizes a distance function. For instance, [25] used the squared L2 distance between two features:

$$L = \sum_{S} \max(0, d(f_a, f_p) - d(f_a, f_n) + m), \qquad (2)$$

where m is a margin constant, and $d(a, b) = \|a - b\|_2^2$. This loss targets a goal in which the difference between $d(f_a, f_p)$ and $d(f_a, f_n)$ should be larger than m.

Unfortunately, this approach requires the margin constant, and fixing m as a constant for a diverse set of triplets can limit the effectiveness of this strategy. This ineffectiveness is caused, mainly because age triplets may have different importance for learning the feature space – some triplets need a larger m, while others need a smaller m, which is conceptually visualized in Fig. 3.

To design a loss that considers discrepancies in triplets, we propose to use the cross-entropy loss for relative triplets, by normalizing the difference of distances with the softmax function. It enables us to use a loss function, the scale-varying ranking loss, considering our relative triplets, without the margin constant used in the conventional ranking loss.

To compute the loss, we start with a set of relative triplets $\mathcal{T}$. Given $\mathcal{T}$, we calculate a normalized version of positive distance, d_+, and negative distance, d_-. Inspired by [22] we normalize the distances as the following:

$$d_+ = \frac{\exp(d(f_a, f_p))}{\exp(d(f_a, f_p)) + \exp(d(f_a, f_n))}, \; d_- = \frac{\exp(d(f_a, f_n))}{\exp(d(f_a, f_p)) + \exp(d(f_a, f_n))}.$$

$$\qquad (3)$$

Considering that d_+ and d_- are softmax outputs, we apply the cross-entropy loss for the relative triplet as:

$$l_T(d_+, d_-) = -t_- \log(d_-) - t_+ \log(d_+) = -\log(d_-), \tag{4}$$

where $(t_+, t_-) = (0, 1)$ are our target values; this results in adjusting our feature space such that d_+ approaches to 0 and d_- to 1.

Triplets chosen from training datasets (Eq. 1) could have largely varying importance in learning features. For example, the triplet on the left in Fig. 3 is more important case than the one on the right, since a desirable update for the former case should be stronger than the latter due to its larger discrepancy. If we simply use the cross-entropy loss (Eq. 4), gradients of these two triplets with varying importance are computed to be the same, which fails to achieve the desirable updates.

To reflect the varying importance of relative triplets, we introduce a non-uniform weighting function, $\omega(\cdot)$, that measures the importance of a triplet, as the following:

$$\omega(f_a, f_p, f_n) = \frac{1 + \epsilon}{|\bar{y}_a - \bar{y}_p| + \epsilon} - 1, \tag{5}$$

where ϵ is a small constant for preventing zero-division and $\bar{y}_k = (y_k - Y_{\min})/(Y_{\max} - Y_{\min})$ is a normalized label when the range of age labels in a dataset is $[Y_{\min}, Y_{\max}]$. We then multiply it directly to the loss function, and the final ranking loss L_T is given by:

$$L_T = \frac{1}{|T|} \sum_T \omega(f_a, f_p, f_n) \cdot l_T(d_+, d_-). \tag{6}$$

Gradient Analysis. Before moving on to our final training objective considering the classification loss, we would like to point out that the proposed loss has the same gradient as that of the conventional ranking loss, but it is different in that the magnitude of our gradients are adjusted according to the importance of relative triplets. Note that the conventional ranking loss (Eq. 2) has its derivative with regard to f_a, f_p, and f_n:

$$\frac{\partial L}{\partial f_a} = \sum_S 2(f_n - f_p), \quad \frac{\partial L}{\partial f_p} = \sum_S 2(f_p - f_a), \quad \frac{\partial L}{\partial f_n} = \sum_S 2(f_a - f_n), \tag{7}$$

where $S \subset T$ and S includes only triplets whose loss is not zeroed out by $\max(0, \cdot)$, and the derivative equals 0 for $T - S$. Note that the margin constant does not have any effect on these gradients. On the contrary, our loss function (6) has its derivative:

$$\frac{\partial L_T}{\partial f_a} = \sum_T \alpha(f_n - f_p), \quad \frac{\partial L_T}{\partial f_p} = \sum_T \alpha(f_p - f_a), \quad \frac{\partial L_T}{\partial f_n} = \sum_T \alpha(f_a - f_n). \tag{8}$$

where $\alpha = 2d_+\omega(f_i, f_j, f_k)$. We can see that the directions of the derivatives of two different loss functions are exactly the same, but the scale of ours are regulated by two values: d_+ and ω. d_+ is moving toward zero during training, and if d_+ becomes near zero, our loss also comes closer to zero. The benefit of this is that d_+ softly slows down the learning when the training is adequately done, without using any hyper-parameter such as the margin constant m. Note that we have ω as well as d_+, both of which together let the gradient scale depend on the discrepancies of triplets – those with higher importance will have larger updates, and those with less importance will get smaller updates.

2.3 Final Training Objective

Our final goal is to estimate an age value, and we thus set our model to have a classification endpoint alongside the ranking part. To use age values for training the classification network, we discretize the age values into K classes. We then apply softmax to our classifier. Specifically, our classifier model has one hidden layer with ReLU activation and a softmax layer after the embedding layer. To formulate the classification loss, we have a classifier g, resulting in our whole model to be $g \circ f$, where $\circ$ indicates the function composition. Since g gives probabilities of an input x belonging to each age class, g satisfies $g(f(x)) \in \mathbb{R}^K$, $g(f(x))_j > 0$, and $\sum_{j=1}^{K} g(f(x))_j = 1$, where the subscript j is used to represent the probability belonging to the j-th class.

We also apply the softmax cross-entropy for the classification objective, the same as for the relative triplet ranking loss. Our final classification loss is then defined as:

$$L_C = -\frac{1}{N} \sum_{i=0}^{N} \sum_{j=0}^{K} t_{ij} \log(g(f(x_i))_j), \qquad (9)$$

where N is the batch-size, and t_{ij} is an indicator function that has 1 when x_i belongs to the class j, otherwise 0.

Based on our classification and triplet ranking losses, our final training objective function is defined as $L = \lambda L_C + L_T$, where λ is a constant for controlling the balance between L_T and L_C.

3 Experiments

We evaluate our approach with two popular age estimation databases against two different tasks, age regression and age classification: MORPH Album 2 and Adience datasets for each of the tasks respectively.

3.1 Implementation Details

We base our network model on the recent Inception-ResNet-V1 [27] implemented with Tensorflow. We do not start the training from scratch, since our target benchmark databases are relatively small. Instead, we utilize weights pretrained with MS Celeb 1M [28] or ILSVRC2012 datasets.

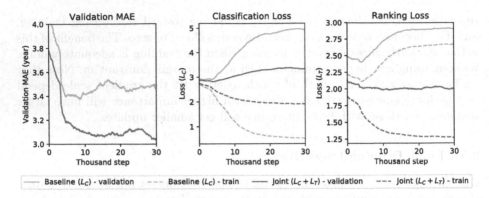

Fig. 4. Training of the baseline and ours on the MORPH Album 2 dataset.

When we train our model, we use Adam optimizer [29] with a small learning rate 5×10^{-4}, with a exponential decay. In all experiments, we set λ to 0.01, and ϵ to 0.1. For stopping policy, we utilize a portion of a training set as a validation set, and stop training when the validation accuracy converges. We augment the training set with random cropping and color jittering including brightness, saturation and hue. In the test phase, we do not use random cropping, rather we obtain 10 samples by cropping and flipping four corners and the center of an image. Then, we average the scores of the last layer from all 10 samples to compute a final decision.

3.2 MORPH Album 2 Dataset

MORPH Album 2 dataset contains 55k facial images of 13k people, and has been widely used by researchers since it provides various labels: identity, gender, age, race, and so on. The MORPH also has been widely used in age estimation field [11,17,30]. As Chang et al. suggested, the protocol for evaluation has been settled – using 80% of image samples for training and the rest for testing.

Interestingly, we found that photos of an identity are taken in a short time frame. Specifically, the max age deviation of a identity is only 1.9 years on average. This implies that by perfectly identifying identities, we can achieve down to 1.9 years for the mean absolute error (MAE). In our settings, we also confirmed that using a baseline network pretrained for face verification with MS-Celeb gives MAE of 2.43 years, which is far better than the state-of-the-art result, 2.96 by [17].

Our Split for Evaluation. To get rid of the effect of identity, we suggest to split the dataset in a way that training and testing sets have no duplicated identities. Thus, we split 13,617 identities into 5 mutually exclusive sets, and perform 5-fold cross-validation for evaluation.

Training-Validation Curves. Figure 4 shows training-validation curves, with regard to MAE and two types of losses. The first graph plotting MAE, our

Table 1. (a) 5-fold cross-validation MAE with the standard error ($\pm e$) on MORPH by our split protocol. We also show the effectiveness of our method over other joint (classification + triplet ranking) losses. (b) Comparison against the state-of-the-art results.

Loss Type	MAE (year)
L_C (Eq. 9)	3.27 ± 0.02
$L_C + L_{c.triplet}$ (Eq, 2)	2.93 ± 0.01
$L_C + L_T$ (without T)	2.91 ± 0.02
$L_C + L_T$ (ours, Eq. 6)	$\mathbf{2.87 \pm 0.02}$

T: relative triplet selection (Eq. 1)

(a)

Method	MAE (year)
MR-CNN [16]	3.27
DEX [11]	3.25
Ranking-CNN [17]	2.96
Ours (random sample)†	**2.38**
Ours (identity sample)‡	**2.87**

†Pretrained on MS-Celeb, ‡Our split

(b)

main target metric, shows a clear gap between the baseline (the solid, light blue curve) and ours (the solid red curve). Especially, we can observe that the baseline overfits in the early stage of training, while our model keeps improving MAE. The second and third plots show that our ranking loss acts as a regularizer that results in lower generalization error to unseen datasets in compensation for a relatively higher training loss than the baseline model.

Comparison Between Loss Types. We report different accuracies obtained by different loss types in Table 1a. The baseline (L_C) does not exploit the ranking loss and has worse MAE than the others. We first compare the baseline to the conventional ranking loss $L_{c.triplet}$ (Eq. 2) adopted from [25] designed for face recognition. Here the results show that the joint loss configuration using classification loss and ranking loss is effective enough in that they improve MAE in a gap of 0.3 years over the baseline; this supports our fundamental condition that a triplet loss aligns the age feature space better than a classification loss alone does, by utilizing relative information in age labels. As we additionally use the components we designed, performance is further improved. Without exploiting the relative triplet selection, our ranking loss L_T shows performance 0.02 years better than $L_{c.triplet}$. Furthermore, ours works even better than the other joint models when combined with the relative sampling method, by showing MAE of 2.87, which is the lowest result among all the tested methods. This improvement is mainly resulted from the relative sampling for diverse set of triplets, and our adaptive scale-varying loss function (Eq. 6) leading to reasonable gradients (Eq. 8) for ordinal classes.

Comparisons Against the State-of-the-Art. In Table 1b, we compare our model to other CNN models. First, we can conclude that if we use a facial domain knowledge, i.e. pretraining on MS-Celeb, we can achieve the highest result based on the previously widely used split protocol, i.e. random split by images [11,17,30]. When we use our harder split, i.e. random split by identity, we achieve MAE of 2.87, which is also better than results from the prior state-of-the-art methods.

(a) Classification: L_C　　(b) Joint: $L_C + L_{c.triplet}$　　(c) Ours: $L_C + L_T$

Fig. 5. Embedding space visualization of a bottleneck feature of the network by T-SNE [31] method. Input from test instances of the MORPH database. Values on the color bar are ages.

Embedding Space Visualization. Figure 5 visualizes the embedding space computed by only classification loss, joint loss with $L_{c.triplet}$ [25], and our joint model. Here, we can clearly observe that ours (Fig. 5c) much coherently aligns the features along the one dimensional curve as a function of age than the others (Fig. 5a–b). That is because the classification loss is only aware of the class difference rather than considering the ordinal characteristics; samples in similar colors (and thus ages) as well as those in totally different colors are thus treated equally, resulting in a rather fuzzy feature space. In the joint loss case (Fig. 5b), the samples are aligned in more neat shape, but not in complete 1D curve, since it has a fixed margin term without considering different importance of triplets. On the other hand, the scale-varying ranking loss deliverately put those in similar colors at close locations while those in different colors are pushed farther, considering how close or far they should be.

3.3　Adience Benchmark

We also evaluate our model to the age classification task using the Adience benchmark database [10]. The database includes 25k cropped face images taken in unconstrained environments. It provides identity, gender, and age group labels for each face image. For performance evaluation, we follow the protocol used by [9]. The dataset consists of 5 splits where 5-fold cross-validation is performed. Its age groups include eight classes: [0, 2], [4, 6], [8, 12], [15, 20], [25, 32], [38, 43], [48, 53], and [60, 100].

Performance Analysis. We report age classification results and compare our results to other methods in Table 2. For a baseline, we first train our baseline model with only classification loss, which produces 60.5% of accuracy. When we train the network with our method, we can clearly see the improvement of ours over the baseline with about 3% of gap in exact and 2% in 1-off results. In regard to the fact that other work [3,9,11] use L_C (Eq. 9) for classification, we can expect that adding our adaptive ranking loss (L_T: Eq. 6) to their classification loss (L_C: Eq. 9) is able to further improve the performance. This concludes that our scale-varying triplet loss acts as a reasonable objective function whether labels are highly dense (i.e. regression), or not (i.e. classification).

Table 2. Comparison to the state-of-the-art deep methods on the Adience benchmark. '1-off' means that 1-off class miss classification is allowed as correct. For 'exact' results, we do not allow any mis-classification. Alongside the accuracy, we report the standard error ($\pm e$) of 5-fold cross-validation results.

Method	Exact (%)	1-off (%)
CNN [9]	50.7 ± 5.1	84.7 ± 2.2
DEX [11]	55.7 ± 6.1	89.7 ± 1.8
Attention CNN [3]	61.8 ± 2.1	95.1 ± 0.03
Squared EMD [13]	62.2	94.3
Baseline (L_C)	60.5 ± 2.2	95.0 ± 0.6
Ours ($L_C + L_T$)	$\mathbf{63.1 \pm 1.0}$	$\mathbf{96.7 \pm 0.4}$

4 Conclusion

We have proposed the adaptive, scale-varying ranking loss jointly used with the classification loss for age estimation. Based on a simple intuition that a triplet ranking loss is helpful for age feature learning, we adapt the conventional one by introducing the relative triplet selection and the weighting scheme to improve the performance of the joint objective for age estimation. By using our proposed joint loss with the relative triplet sampling, we show that our adaptive scale-varying ranking loss reduces the generalization error of a model and better aligns the age features than the baseline. Lastly, our approach achieves meaningful improvements over the state-of-the-art methods in both age regression and classification tasks.

Much interesting future work lies ahead. While the proposed approach was applied mainly to the estimation of facial age in this study, it is not restricted only to this tested application. Since our work uses a relative ranking strategy, it can be applied to other domains where a distance measure between ground-truth labels exists.

References

1. Ranjan, R., et al.: Unconstrained age estimation with deep convolutional neural networks. In: Proceedings of the IEEE International Conference on Computer Vision Workshops, pp. 109–117 (2015)
2. Ozbulak, G., Aytar, Y., Ekenel, H.K.: How transferable are CNN-based features for age and gender classification? In: 2016 International Conference of the Biometrics Special Interest Group (BIOSIG), pp. 1–6. IEEE (2016)
3. Rodríguez, P., Cucurull, G., Gonfaus, J.M., Roca, F.X., Gonzàlez, J.: Age and gender recognition in the wild with deep attention. Pattern Recognit. **72**, 563–571 (2017)
4. Krizhevsky, A., Sutskever, I., Hinton, G.E.: ImageNet classification with deep convolutional neural networks. In: Advances in Neural Information Processing Systems, pp. 1097–1105 (2012)

5. Hong, S., Ryu, J., Im, W., Yang, H.S.: D3: recognizing dynamic scenes with deep dual descriptor based on key frames and key segments. Neurocomputing **273**, 611–621 (2018)
6. Taigman, Y., Yang, M., Ranzato, M., Wolf, L.: DeepFace: closing the gap to human-level performance in face verification. In: Proceedings of the IEEE Conference on Computer Vision and Pattern Recognition, pp. 1701–1708 (2014)
7. Taigman, Y., Yang, M., Ranzato, M., Wolf, L.: Web-scale training for face identification. In: Proceedings of the IEEE Conference on Computer Vision and Pattern Recognition, pp. 2746–2754 (2015)
8. Hong, S., Im, W., Ryu, J., Yang, H.S.: SSPP-DAN: deep domain adaptation network for face recognition with single sample per person. In: International Conference on Image Processing (2017)
9. Levi, G., Hassner, T.: Age and gender classification using convolutional neural networks. In: Proceedings of the IEEE Conference on Computer Vision and Pattern Recognition Workshops, pp. 34–42 (2015)
10. Eidinger, E., Enbar, R., Hassner, T.: Age and gender estimation of unfiltered faces. IEEE Trans. Inf. Forensics Secur. **9**, 2170–2179 (2014)
11. Rothe, R., Timofte, R., Van Gool, L.: Deep expectation of real and apparent age from a single image without facial landmarks. Int. J. Comput. Vis. **126**, 144–157 (2016)
12. Geng, X., Yin, C., Zhou, Z.H.: Facial age estimation by learning from label distributions. IEEE Trans. Pattern Anal. Mach. Intell. **35**, 2401–2412 (2013)
13. Hou, L., Yu, C.P., Samaras, D.: Squared earth mover's distance-based loss for training deep neural networks. arXiv preprint arXiv:1611.05916 (2016)
14. Gao, B.B., Xing, C., Xie, C.W., Wu, J., Geng, X.: Deep label distribution learning with label ambiguity. IEEE Trans. Image Process. **26**, 2825–2838 (2017)
15. Gao, B.B., Zhou, H.Y., Wu, J., Geng, X.: Age estimation using expectation of label distribution learning. In: Proceedings of the Twenty-Seventh International Joint Conference on Artificial Intelligence, IJCAI 2018, pp. 712–718. International Joint Conferences on Artificial Intelligence Organization (2018)
16. Niu, Z., Zhou, M., Wang, L., Gao, X., Hua, G.: Ordinal regression with multiple output CNN for age estimation. In: Proceedings of the IEEE Conference on Computer Vision and Pattern Recognition, pp. 4920–4928 (2016)
17. Chen, S., Zhang, C., Dong, M., Le, J., Rao, M.: Using ranking-CNN for age estimation. In: The IEEE Conference on Computer Vision and Pattern Recognition (CVPR) (2017)
18. Clapés, A., Bilici, O., Temirova, D., Avots, E., Anbarjafari, G., Escalera, S.: From apparent to real age: gender, age, ethnic, makeup, and expression bias analysis in real age estimation. In: Proceedings of the IEEE Conference on Computer Vision and Pattern Recognition Workshops, pp. 2373–2382 (2018)
19. Wang, J., et al.: Learning fine-grained image similarity with deep ranking. In: Proceedings of the IEEE Conference on Computer Vision and Pattern Recognition, pp. 1386–1393 (2014)
20. Parkhi, O.M., Vedaldi, A., Zisserman, A., et al.: Deep face recognition. In: BMVC, vol. 1, p. 6 (2015)
21. Hong, S., Im, W., Yang, H.S.: CBVMR: content-based video-music retrieval using soft intra-modal structure constraint. In: ACM International Conference on Multimedia Retrieval (2018)
22. Simo-Serra, E., Ishikawa, H.: Fashion style in 128 floats: joint ranking and classification using weak data for feature extraction. In: Proceedings of the IEEE Conference on Computer Vision and Pattern Recognition, pp. 298–307 (2016)

23. Liu, W., Wen, Y., Yu, Z., Yang, M.: Large-margin softmax loss for convolutional neural networks. In: ICML, pp. 507–516 (2016)
24. Liu, W., Wen, Y., Yu, Z., Li, M., Raj, B., Song, L.: SphereFace: deep hypersphere embedding for face recognition. In: The IEEE Conference on Computer Vision and Pattern Recognition (CVPR), vol, 1, p. 1 (2017)
25. Schroff, F., Kalenichenko, D., Philbin, J.: FaceNet: a unified embedding for face recognition and clustering. In: Proceedings of the IEEE Conference on Computer Vision and Pattern Recognition, pp. 815–823 (2015)
26. Wang, L., Li, Y., Lazebnik, S.: Learning deep structure-preserving image-text embeddings. In: Proceedings of the IEEE Conference on Computer Vision and Pattern Recognition, pp. 5005–5013 (2016)
27. Szegedy, C., Ioffe, S., Vanhoucke, V., Alemi, A.A.: Inception-v4, inception-ResNet and the impact of residual connections on learning. In: AAAI, pp. 4278–4284 (2017)
28. Guo, Y., Zhang, L., Hu, Y., He, X., Gao, J.: MS-Celeb-1M: a dataset and benchmark for large-scale face recognition. In: Leibe, B., Matas, J., Sebe, N., Welling, M. (eds.) ECCV 2016. LNCS, vol. 9907, pp. 87–102. Springer, Cham (2016). https://doi.org/10.1007/978-3-319-46487-9_6
29. Kingma, D.P., Ba, J.: Adam: a method for stochastic optimization. CoRR abs/1412.6980 (2014)
30. Chang, K.Y., Chen, C.S., Hung, Y.P.: Ordinal hyperplanes ranker with cost sensitivities for age estimation. In: 2011 IEEE Conference on Computer Vision and Pattern Recognition (CVPR), pp. 585–592. IEEE (2011)
31. Van Der Maaten, L., Hinton, G.: Visualizing data using t-SNE. J. Mach. Learn. Res. 9, 2579–2605 (2008)

Large Scale Scene Text Verification
with Guided Attention

Dafang He[1(✉)], Yeqing Li[2], Alexander Gorban[2], Derrall Heath[2], Julian Ibarz[2],
Qian Yu[2], Daniel Kifer[1], and C. Lee Giles[1]

[1] The Pennsylvania State University, University Park, USA
{duh188,giles}@ist.psu.edu, dkifer@cse.psu.edu
[2] Google Inc., Mountain View, USA
{yeqing,gorban,dheath,julianibarz,qyu}@google.com

Abstract. Many tasks are related to determining if a particular text string exists in an image. In this work, we propose a new framework that learns this task in an end-to-end way. The framework takes an image and a text string as input and then outputs the probability of the text string being present in the image. This is the first end-to-end framework that learns such relationships between text and images in scene text area. The framework does not require explicit scene text detection or recognition and thus no bounding box annotations are needed. It is also the first work in scene text area that tackles such a weakly labeled problem. Based on this framework, we developed a model called *Guided Attention*. Our designed model achieves better results than several state-of-the-art scene text reading based solutions for a challenging Street View Business Matching task. The task tries to find correct business names for storefront images and the dataset we collected for it is substantially larger, and more challenging than existing scene text dataset. This new real-world task provides a new perspective for studying scene text related problems.

Keywords: Scene text · Verification · End to end model · Attention · Weakly labeled dataset

1 Introduction

Our streets are full of text such as street names, street numbers, store names, etc. These text are important clues for understanding the real world. With this rapidly growing new source of data, it has become more and more important to learn how to extract useful text information out of images. This task is usually referred to as scene text reading.

Many researchers divide the scene text reading problem into two sub-problems: text detection [2,3,5,12,13,26] and text recognition [6,8,15]. In order to build such an applicable system, the two components are usually combined

---

D. He and Y. Li—Contribute equally.

D. He—The work is done while Dafang is in Internship at Google.

© Springer Nature Switzerland AG 2019
C. V. Jawahar et al. (Eds.): ACCV 2018, LNCS 11365, pp. 260–275, 2019.
https://doi.org/10.1007/978-3-030-20873-8_17

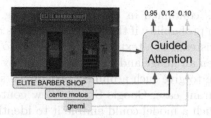

Fig. 1. An example application of scene text verification task. Our model takes a business storefront image and a potential business name, and then directly outputs how likely the storefront image matches the business name. The red text means it is the ground truth for this image and our model gives it a high score. (Color figure online)

sequentially into a complex system even though they are developed separately. In many applications, we don't need to precisely transcribe every single word in an image - we only need to tell if some text prominently exists in an image and we call this problem: **scene text verification**. If we use scene text reading to formulate it, we will be facing several challenges: (1) Building a robust text understanding system is difficult, especially considering the possible differences in the domains of images in real usage and in training. A detector trained on currently available public datasets (e.g. ICDAR 2015 [10]) may have high possibility of failure on the new domain of images the system is deployed on. (2) Scene text is normally highly artistic. Heuristic based text matching is usually applied afterwards for verification, and often error are introduced when connecting these pieces. (3) A large amount of fully annotated data is needed in order to train a detector, which is expensive to obtain. In this work, we argue that we do not need separate text detection and text recognition systems for text verification problem.

We have observed that, in a lot of situations, an explicit text transcriber is unnecessary. Often a context is available, which can be used to narrow down the attention (text candidates). For example, if a person wants to find the reviews of a restaurant, they may want to just take a picture of the restaurant and we should be able to provide the reviews for them. In such cases, the algorithm only needs to pay attention to the name of the restaurant in order to identify it. It does not need to read any other text on the street, such as a 20% off advertising on clothes, or the opening hours on the door. Furthermore, a list of restaurant candidates could be obtained based on the geo-location so as to serve as candidates. Therefore, the actual problem we are trying to solve is instead: how likely is it that a sequence of words is in the image? In answering this question, an undiscriminating transcriber may be harmful since it could provide extra transcriptions that are irrelevant to the question (i.e., noise), and/or provide incorrect transcriptions which confuse the later process.

In order to address the previous concerns, we propose a new, end-to-end framework which takes input the image and the text and predict the possibility that the text string is contained in an image as in Fig. 1. The framework is expected to give a high probability if the input sequence is in the image, and thus it tries to verify the existence of a text string. It could also be regarded as trying to find a match between an image and a text string. Many applications could be built when we are able to give such a unified text-image score. For example, In addition to the restaurant case, Google Street View contains countless images taken on the street. Such a model could enable it to identity the business name from storefront images for back-end data processing.

We design a model called *Guided Attention* based on such framework. It does not need to do any explicit text detection or recognition. Instead it uses an attention mechanism that is guided by the input text string and decides whether the string is in the image or not.

This is the first work that tries to solve this problem in an end-to-end manner, and we study it in the context of business matching—given a storefront image, predict which business it represents. We collect millions of business storefront images through Google Maps API[1] for this task. Each image is associated with a list of candidate business names and the algorithm needs to find correct candidate among them.

We call this the Street View Business Matching (SVBM) dataset, and experiments show the effectiveness of our new framework in solving this challenging real-world problem. Our contributions are:

1. **New Problem.** We study a new problem: scene text verification in an image. It verifies the existence of a certain text string and is closely related to scene text reading. It could be tackled with traditional method based on scene text detection and scene text recognition. It could also been seen as a sub-problem for scene text retrieval.
2. **New Dataset.** We collect a large-scale dataset (SVBM) which contains 1.5M images for experiment. It is substantially larger than any existing public scene text datasets (e.g ICDAR2015 contains only 1500 images). The dataset contains storefront images from google street view, and algorithm needs to verify the existence of the business name in the images. It contains various of different languages and is much more challenging than existing public scene text datasets.
3. **New Framework.** We propose an end-to-end trainable framework to this problem that does not do or require any explicit text detection or recognition. The framework is completely different from traditional method, and only requires image-text pairs for training, as opposed to a fully annotated dataset (e.g., bounding box labels), which are more expensive to create than simple yes/no labels. This greatly reduces the burden of dataset collection. We also propose a model based on this new framework and it achieves better performance in terms of precision/recall curve than existing text reading based solutions on SVBM. This new framework brings new insight into scene text area, and could inspire further research works.

---

[1] https://developers.google.com/maps/.

4. **Extensive Experiments.** We have done extensive experiments to study different properties of the framework. Our major experiments are on SVBM dataset, and we also evaluate the trained model in two public datasets: Uber-Text [25] and FSNS [16]. These experiments confirm that our Guided Attention model is better suited at solving this task than a more traditional scene text reading based solution and by combing the proposed method and traditional method, we can achieve an even better performance in this task. We have also done ablation studies that show how important some design aspects of our model impact performance.

2   Related Work

Scene text detection is usually considered the most challenging part of building an end-to-end system, and many techniques have been developed to solve it. There are usually two approaches. The first approach treats the problem as a semantic segmentation problem, and several further steps are performed to obtain each individual text instance. This category includes methods that use fully convolutional neural networks (FCNs) to do semantic segmentation ón text to extract text blocks [5,26,27]. The second category uses modified region proposal networks (RPNs) to detect text [13,18]. Both approaches achieve state-of-the-art performance on public datasets.

The challenges of scene text recognition are mainly due to the fact that text could be distorted in an image. Most regular (straight) text could be effectively read by first extracting CNN features and then using a RNN to predict the sequence. [6,14] used such techniques and combined them with CTC loss [4] to create powerful models for transcribing straight text. [15,21,22] tried to read curved scene text by using an attention mechanism, and spatial attention [21,22] has achieved the state-of-the-art performance.

Scene text retrieval [9,11], which aims at retrieving images based on text content, is closely related to scene text verification. The verification task could be seen as a subtask for scene text retrieval, as it only cares about the existence of text and no ranking is needed. Retrieval performance will benefits from a better verification model.

An end-to-end scene text reading system would combine the detection and recognition steps sequentially, and a fully annotated dataset is needed to train it. Instead, our proposed framework takes as input a character string and an image, and then verifies the existence of the string in the image in an end-to-end manner. Our framework is unique in that no explicit text detection or recognition is involved, and thus, there is also no need for a fully annotated dataset. The annotation for our framework is thus much easier to obtain since we only need images with corresponding lists of candidate strings and their labels.

Our work also has a loose connection to visual question answering [1] or image text matching [23]. However, our framework also has several unique properties: (1) input text is character sequence instead of words. (2) Simple binary classification is used as evaluation metric. (3) Order of input words shouldn't affect the results. For example, if a sequence of words "Street View Image" is in an image, then "Image Street View" should also be considered as positive.

In experiments, we evaluate our framework and model on the SVBM dataset and two public datasets: UbetText [25], FSNS [16]. SVBM dataset contains image-text pairs without bounding box annotations and it makes training a scene text detector impossible. The model has to learn from both the image and text in order to give a final prediction.

3   Method

3.1   Model Architecture

The architecture is shown in Fig. 2. Our model consists of two major components: (1) a CNN-based image encoder network with coordinate encoding, (2) a guided attention decoder which selectively pools features from the encoded feature map and generates the final result.

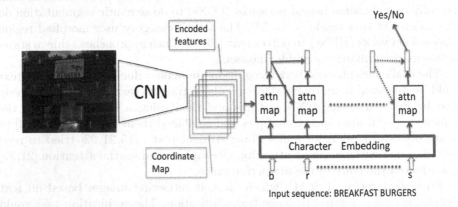

Fig. 2. The architecture of our scene text verification model. The model takes in a sequence of characters and an image, and predict the probability of the input text sequence being present in the input image.

CNN Encoder with Coordinate Map. We trimmed InceptionV3 [17] to construct our image encoder, which builds a deep CNN by stacking some carefully designed sub-network structure with different scales.

Let I be the input image, and CNN encoded visual feature is denoted as $f_v = CNN(I)$. In order to capture the spatial information for each location in the feature map, we follow [21] to create a coordinate map f_{xy} for each image. The equation of such coordinate encoding could be expressed as $f_{xy} = Eocode(i,j)$. i,j denotes the x, and y indices of each spatial location in the feature map. Function $Encode$ computes the one-hot encoding for each positing i,j, and we concatenate the coordinate map f_{xy} with original cnn feature f_v in depth dimension. We use $\tilde{f}$ to denote the features augmented with position information.

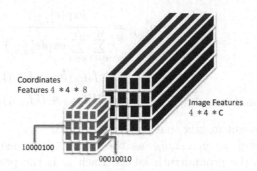

Fig. 3. Illustration of encoding the coordinates as a one-hot feature vector f_{xy} and concatenate it with the original visual features f_v. A feature map with H × W × C will have corresponding coordinate feature map with size H × W × (H+W)

By combining such position information with each feature vector, the following decoding process could refer to them for better attention calculation and achieves better decoding results. Such scheme has been adopted by [21,22] and has been proved to be effective in scene text related tasks. Figure 3 illustrates the coordinate encoding.

Guided Attention Decoder. In the next step, the model tries to decode useful information from the cnn features $\tilde{f}$ guided by the input character string. Let N be the number of characters of the input string and $S = S_1, \ldots, S_N$ be the character level one-hot encoding of it. The embeddings of the characters are represented as $S^e = S_1^e, \ldots, S_N^e$, which is learned end-to-end during training. Our goal is to compute

$$p_{valid} = \mathbb{P}(y = 1 | S_1, \ldots, S_N, I), \tag{1}$$

where $y \in \{0, 1\}$ is the indicator of the existence of the text.

We use LSTM [7] as our recurrent function to encode sequential features. Let us denote h_t as the hidden state of the LSTM in time step t, then the update function of hidden state could be expressed as Eq. 2:

$$h_t = \text{LSTM}(h_{t-1}, S_t^e, \text{CT}(x_t)), \tag{2}$$

where $\text{CT}(x_t)$ represents the context vector generated in time step t. It can be computed based on Eq. 3:

$$\text{CT}(x_t) = \sum_{i=1}^{W} \sum_{j=1}^{H} \alpha_{(i,j)}^t * \tilde{f}_{(i,j)}, \tag{3}$$

where $\alpha_{(i,j)}^t$ represents the attention map. It is computed based on Eq. 4. $e_{(i,j)}^t$ represents how relevant is the feature $\tilde{f}_{(i,j)}$ to the current character embedding S_t^e. In this work, we choose to use attention function as in [19] in Eq. 5:

$$\alpha^t_{(i,j)} = \frac{\exp(e^t_{(i,j)})}{\sum\limits_{u=1}^{W}\sum\limits_{v=1}^{H} \exp(e^t_{(u,v)})},$$

$$e^t_{(i,j)} = f_{attn}(h_{t-1}, \tilde{f}_{(i,j)}), \tag{4}$$

$$f_{attn}(h_{t-1}, \tilde{f}_{(i,j)}) = v^T \tanh(W h_{t-1} + U \tilde{f}_{(i,j)}), \tag{5}$$

where W, V are weight matrix that could be learned.

Let us denotes $y = y_1, \ldots, y_N$ as the output sequence probability and $y' = y'_1, \ldots, y'_N$ as the groundtruth labels. Each y_i is the prediction based on information till character S^e_i. In training, we use cross entropy as our loss function, and we only calculate the loss based on the output of the last time step for each image and candidate pair as in Eq. 6:

$$loss = -\frac{1}{M}\sum_{i=1}^{M}(y'_i \log(y^i_{n_i}) + (1 - y'_i)\log((1 - y^i_{n_i}))), \tag{6}$$

where n_i is the length of the ith candidate and M is the number of training pairs.

3.2 Model Training and Sub-batch Architecture

In our problem setting, each image usually contains several positive (random shuffling of positive words) and a list of negative text.

In order to save the computation, for each image we have M parallel text input for it and the CNN tower will only need to be computed once. The number M is equal to $N_n + N_p$ where N_p, N_n represent the number of positive and negative examples sampled for each image, respectively. The total loss thus becomes a weighted cross entropy based on the ratio between positive examples and negative examples. In our experiment, we usually set N_p to be 1, and N_n to be 4. So there are 5 parallel recurrent sequences for each convolutional tower.

3.3 Hard Negative Mining (HNM)

During model training, the sampling scheme of the N_n number of negative training examples plays an important role for better performance. In our problem, the hardness of a negative candidate could be empirically determined by the edit distance of it with the corresponding positive candidates. Figure 4 illustrates this idea.

We also observe that, in the SVBM dataset, most negative candidates are easy cases as they differ from the positive text by quite a lot. However, the negative samples that really confuse the network are from those hard cases. So we incorporate hard negative example mining as a fine tuning process for our model. We first define the hardness of an example based on Eq. 7.

Ground truth:
centro de estetica body silk
Negative Candidates:
centro de estetica elia ariza
centro medico real sa
gestion juridica boensa
eclypse moda s
audifon euro s l
colorin

Fig. 4. Example showing how we can determine the hardness of a negative example based the corresponding positive candidates. The different color represents the different hardness levels. (Color figure online)

$$\text{Hardness}(n\hat{e}g) = 1 - \min_{\forall p\hat{o}s \in \hat{P}} \frac{\text{edit\_dis}(n\hat{e}g, p\hat{o}s)}{\max(\text{len}(p\hat{o}s), \text{len}(n\hat{e}g))} \tag{7}$$

$\hat{P}$ represents the positive example set for a specific image. $p\hat{o}s$ is one positive sample and $n\hat{e}g$ represents the negative sample that we want to compute. The function edit_dis calculates the edit distance between the positive sample $p\hat{o}s$ and the negative sample $n\hat{e}g$. The hardness of a negative sample is determined by the minimal edit distance between the negative candidate and all the positive samples. The higher the score, the harder the negative sample.

The training process including HNM is thus as follows: (1) Train the network from scratch with evenly sampled positive and negative text for each image. (2) Finetune the network with evenly sampled positive text and evenly sampled negative text whose hardness score is larger than T. In our experiments, we set $T = 0.3$ to keep relatively harder text without removing too much of them. Note that we did this for both training set and testing set, so in the second phase, the testing examples are harder. During the first phase, the classification accuracy reached 95%, but in the beginning of the second phase, the classification accuracy dropped to 88%. This means that the harder examples, based on our definition, are actually more difficult for our model.

4   Experiments

The major experiments are on the SVBM dataset which contains millions of images, and we use it to study different properties of our model as well as the problem of scene text verification. We have also done two experiments on UberText and FSNS datasets with the model trained on SVBM dataset and baseline methods.

4.1   Dataset Description and Experiment Setting

SVBM. The SVBM dataset is based on Street View images, and each image represents one business storefront. The storefront images could be obtained by the method proposed in [24], and all the images have associated geo-locations (for e.g, lat/lng) so that we can retrieve a list of candidate business names by filtering out far-away business. The number of candidates depends on the business density and the search radius. The goal is to find the correct business name among the list of candidates. No text bounding boxes are provided.

The dataset contains 1.39M training images and around 147K testing images. They are collected from various countries such as US, Brazil, England and etc. with various different languages. Each image has a number of candidates ranging from 10 to over 500. One of them is the correct business name, and all others are incorrect. As a preprocessing step, we convert all business names into lower case. So the character set contains a total of 37 alphanumeric characters (including space) plus characters in other languages which have high frequency in training set. We evaluate the dataset based on precision recall curve on a per-candidate basis.

In training, we use rmsprop as our optimization method, and the learning rate is set to 0.001. The batch size is set to 32, and the input image is resized and padded to 400 * 400 with random noise for simplicity. Each image is associated with 5 candidate text during training, and thus the batch size for attention decoder is 160(32 * 5). We use 70 cpu machines for training and it takes over 20 days to converge to an initial checkpoint.

UberText and FSNS. There is currently no public dataset that is suitable for our purpose. We choose two public datasets that are relatively larger with a little bit different evaluation schemes. This study aims at demonstrating that by combining the proposed model with other traditional approaches, a better performance can be achieved for the text verification problem.

UberText [25] is a newly released dataset for scene text related problems. It is currently the largest fully annotated public dataset and contains 10K testing images. We evaluate it using the model trained on SVBM to show that our model can generalize well to other datasets. We choose the words that are of type: "business names" in the dataset and only evaluate the recall of these positive text in the verification problem.

FSNS [16] contains french street signs. The images are much easier than that in SVBM because the text are focused and clear. We randomly sample 49 text as negative text for each image for evaluation purpose.

4.2   Qualitative Results

In this section, we give several visual results illustrating the different properties of our trained guided attention model. More visual examples are in Fig. 9.

Subset of Text. During training and subsequent evaluations, we use the full business name. However, it is interesting and important to study the property of our model when we use subsets of the business name, or a slightly different business name to see how it performs. This is because that during annotation, we

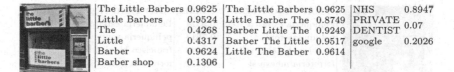

The Little Barbers	0.9625	The Little Barbers	0.9625	NHS	0.8947
Little Barbers	0.9524	Little Barber The	0.8749	PRIVATE	0.07
The	0.4268	Barber Little The	0.9249	DENTIST	
Little	0.4317	Barber The Little	0.9517	google	0.2026
Barber	0.9624	Little The Barber	0.9614		
Barber shop	0.1306				

Fig. 5. A qualitative evaluation on several specific behaviors of our model when we give it the same input image, but different input text. On the left is the input image. The first section in the table on the right shows results when we input a subset of ground truth text. The 2nd section in the table demonstrates when we have randomly shuffled groundtruth text as input. The last section represents results when the input text are not the corresponding business name, but are also in the image.

may not obtain exactly the same text as the actual business name. For example, "The Little Barbers" might be annotated as "Little Barbers", and our model is expected to still give a high score for that. The first section in the table of Fig. 5 shows an example image and several such input text strings with their predicted probabilities.

We can see that, when we use informative subset text (For e.g, "Little Barbers") from the ground truth as input text to the model, the model still gives a pretty high score. This meets our expectation as we care about the existence of the string (words) in the image. However, there are also several interesting findings: (1) If we use non-informative words as input (e.g: "The"), the model gives a relatively low score. (2) If we use text string that contains other words that are not in the image (For e.g, "Barber Shop"), the model gives a low score. These findings are interesting, and we believe that the model is looking for more informative words and makes decisions based on that. "The" is common in business names, so the model gives a lower score if we only use that as input text. "Barber shop" contains other words, which could possibly indicate that it's some other business' name. So our model gives a low score to it even though it contains the word "Barber" that is in the image.

Random Shuffled Text. As we have discussed before, our model should be able to ignore the shuffling of input words. The 2nd section of the table in Fig. 5 shows the results when we try to input shuffled text with the same image into the model. This property is also important, as the order of words in annotation has no relationship with the spacial ordering of those words in image, and thus the trained model should ignore the word order, and only focus on the existence of the collection of words.

We can see that our model is somewhat invariant to the random shuffling of words as all the of them received high scores. This is the property that we expect, and it is important to text verification.

Non-Business Text. The last section of the table in Fig. 5 shows an example where we have text inputs that are not the specific business name in the ground

Before Hard Negative Mining		After Hard Negative Mining	
Peluqueria estetica stela	0.9324	Peluqueria estetica stela	0.8924
peluqueria toni	0.7613	peluqueria toni	0.3293
francisco hidalgo tello	0.2643	francisco hidalgo tello	0.1375
ferreteria mheva sl	0.2232	ferreteria mheva sl	0.1328
puertodental sl	0.1989	puertodental sl	0.1276
Before Hard Negative Mining		After Hard Negative Mining	
ceip santa catalina	0.9324	ceip santa catalina	0.8604
aulario santa catalina	0.9057	aulario santa catalina	0.1294
trastero 16	0.0781	verde limo	0.1186
ropa africana	0.0618	la pizarra	0.0970
verde limon	0.0606	trastero 16	0.0868
peluqueria vanitas	0.0605	apartamento primas	0.0819

Fig. 6. Two visual examples illustrating the performance gain after mining hard negative candidates for training. We observe that after HNM, the gap between the best prediction and the second best prediction has usually been increased.

truth. We can see that the model still gives it a high score since it is in the image, and it also meets our expectation. There is also a failure example when we have "PRIVATE DENTIST" as input. This might happen when text are too small w.r.t the image size, so the attention could not capture it well. In addition to that, since our model is trained on business related text, we believe that this also caused the failure of this non-business text.

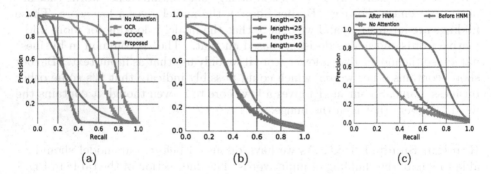

(a)   (b)   (c)

Fig. 7. (a) The Precision-Recall curve of our model compared with other baselines. (b) The Precision-Recall curve of our model w.r.t. different maximum length of text. (c) The Precision-Recall curve comparison before and after HNM.

Hard Negative Mining. Figure 6 shows two examples illustrating the performance of the model trained before and after hard negative mining.

We can see that after hard negative mining, the probability margins between the positive and best negative sample for the two images have increased by 40%. This makes the model trained with HNM much more robust and the quantitative results of such comparison are in the followings.

4.3   SVBM Quantitative Evaluation

Baseline Models. We compare several baseline models with our approach: (1) Google Cloud OCR(GCOCR)[2]. (2) Attention OCR(OCR) [21]. (3) Show and Tell Model [20] with binary classification output.

Model (1) tries to detect and read all the text indiscriminately. Then we do text based matching with the candidates to find the best candidate. This is one typical paradigm for this problem, but the model is trained on other fully annotated dataset. Model (2) is trained on the SVBM dataset directly. We simply force it to transcribe the whole image into the positive business name it represents. Text based matching is performed afterwards. Model (3) is a modification based on [19] (by changing the output as a binary classification). It could also be regarded as removing the attention mechanism in our framework. So we call it "no attention".

Comparison w.r.t Baselines. We first show the comparison of our final model against other baseline methods. Figure 7a shows the Precision/Recall curve. We can see that our end-to-end model (after HNM) outperforms all other baselines by a large margin. This address our two points: (1) text detector and recognizer trained on other fully annotated data couldn't achieve good results in our SVBM dataset because they couldn't accurately find and transcribe the business name. (2) Our task could be learned in an end-to-end way, and it outperforms transcription based method(OCR). In the following two evaluations, we show different settings that can improve the performance.

Evaluation w.r.t Maximum Length. The maximum length of the character sequence could be tuned as an hyperparameter. This is an interesting aspect of our scene text verification problem. It is because when we need to decide which candidate business name the storefront represents, sometimes we only need, for example, the first 20 characters. In the example Fig. 4, we only need the first 15 characters to determine which candidate is the positive one.

Note that this maximum length N only affects those candidates with length longer than it. We simply cut the longer text to keep the first N characters. This is also a difference between our problem w.r.t traditional VQA problem, since usually we will not cut the question in VQA task.

The Precision/Recall curve w.r.t the maximum length is in Fig. 7b. We can see that the peak is when the maximum length set to 40 for our task. However, other lengths also achieve reasonable performance. Besides, the value is dataset dependant. This experiment aims at illustrating an unique property of our problem and is important in deployment since the shorter the sequence, the faster the model could run. So there is a trade-off between the performance and efficiency. We use 40 as our final model choice.

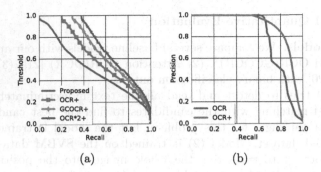

Fig. 8. (a) The recall w.r.t threshold for different models on UberText. We only evaluate positive text here. (b) P-R curve for OCR [21] and the ensembled model on FSNS.

Evaluation w.r.t Hard Negative Mining. Whether to use hard negative mining makes a big difference in terms of the performance of the trained model. In Fig. 7c we show the results of the models trained before and after hard negative mining. Together we also show the results produced by a model with "no attention". We can see that our attention mechanism is important to get good performance for our scene text verification tasks. By further adding hard negative mining process, the performance has been further improved, especially in the high accuracy region of the curve. This is also a difference between our problem with standard VQA problem since we can empirically define the "hardness".

4.4   UberText and FSNS Quantitative Evaluation

In this quantitative study, we study the problem that whether we can combine this model with traditional approaches to better solve text verification problem. The compared ensembled approaches are following: (1) OCR+: Ensemble of Attention OCR [21] and the proposed approach by taking the maximum of the scores output by the two models as the final score. This way of ensemble is used in all of the following compared approaches. (2) GCOCR+: Simple ensemble of GCOCR[1] and the proposed approach. (3) OCR*2+: Simple ensemble of GCOCR[1], OCR [21] and the proposed approach.

Figure 8a, b show the results for UberText and FSNS, respectively. The results show that when combining our model with other traditional approaches, we can achieve a better results than the original model itself. It also demonstrates that the "knowledge" learned from different models are not the same, and our model could also serve as complementary resources of information for traditional approaches.

*Top of the ..	0.696	*H&R Block	0.734	*Advance ..	0.637	*Ralphs	0.921	*Leslie's ...	0.945
Pcrr	0.287	Us Bank	0.280	Access to ..	0.213	KC Produ...	0.338	Hungry n ..	0.567
Ed's Hot ..	0.237	CW Price	0.193	ATM (Webs ...	0.176	Cactusbird ..	0.202	A1 Auto ..	0.437
Christian ..	0.158					Studio Plaza	0.132		
R&B Conco..	0.142					Work Boot ..	0.124		
Candelas ..	0.140					Cardtronics ..	0.081		

*Alagood ..	0.804	*Phillips ..	0.962	*South by ..	0.945	*Lund's Fly ..	0.862	*Xtreme Au..	0.693
Taylor Sar ..	0.276	Dry Down ..	0.246	Teapot Mus..	0.201	The Marti ..	0.443	Rock The ..	0.271
Denton Cou ..	0.155	Coupon	0.240	Old Town ..	0.148	ATM (BP)	0.366	ATM	0.073
		Fresh & Cl..	0.151	Scherer Da ..	0.086	Lazy River	0.338	Just ATMs Inc	0.223
		Plaza Segundo	0.150			First Bapti..	0.230		
		The San Remo	0.146			River Falls	0.167		

*beacon hou ..	0.722	*Nando's ..	0.935	*La Rinno ..	0.963	*Design Con ..	0.957	*Pondok Mes..	0.941
Select	0.155	The Child ..	0.179	Civiche racc...	0.249	Tabac - Pres...	0.295	Beauty Spa 2	0.581
Sinar Kaca	0.575	Scope	0.141	Borse.Pro ..	0.162	Matrix Fe ..	0.270	*T-Mobile	0.119
		CEX - Ent ..	0.135	Intesa Sa ..	0.154	Edf Gdf	0.270	Toko Hous ..	0.333
		Station Way	0.118	DE NIGRIS ..	0.141	Tri Slectif	0.202	Simbah. Net	0.210
		Vodafone	0.109	Il Aria Folli	0.141	Studio Coiff...	0.166	SD Negeri Si...	0.206

Avila	0.684	*Hungry Ho ..	0.419	*A-C Brake ..	0.507	The People ..	0.627	New Kingdom	0.219
Riko's	0.219	Efmark Dep ..	0.193	Christ Wa ..	0.481	Holy Dog	0.580	ATM Express	0.189
Tradicionarius	0.203	Cardtronics ..	0.076			Gene Suttle ..	0.389	*Super Gia..	0.170
*Cornerst ..	0.201					Queen's Hou ..	0.369		
Jordi's	0.177					Jane	0.350		
A Cantina ..	0.177					Nare	0.305		

Fig. 9. Example images from the test set. We only visualize the top predicted candidates. The first three rows show the examples that we give good predictions (high score for positive candidate, low score for negative ones). The last row shows several failure examples. They are either caused by wrong prediction from our model, or by the problem of extremely unclear or non-exists text. It also shows that the dataset is challenging as it contains many practical problems such as extreme distortion. Such problems make it hard to correctly detect and transcribe the text. Our model, without the need to explicitly detect text, can achieve a better performance.

5 Conclusion and Acknowledgement

In this work, we proposed a new problem: verifying the existence of a text string in an image and collected a large-scale dataset (SVBM) for evaluating the performance on this problem. Instead of traditional approaches based on scene text reading, we propose an end-to-end framework which takes both the image and the text as inputs and gives a unified result. We experimentally proved that model designed based on this framework achieved a better performance in SVBM for matching the business with the storefront image. It could also be combined with traditional methods into more powerful models as shown in the experiments in two public datasets. This work does not aim at giving the most sophisticated architecture, but proving that an end-to-end solution could be developed for such task to achieve a better performance without the need to fully annotate images at the text level.

This work was majorly done while Dafang is at internship at Google. We also thank NSF grant CCF 1317560 for support.

References

1. Antol, S., et al.: VQA: visual question answering. In: Proceedings of the IEEE International Conference on Computer Vision, pp. 2425–2433 (2015)
2. Chen, X., Yuille, A.L.: Detecting and reading text in natural scenes. In: Proceedings of the IEEE Computer Society Conference on Computer Vision and Pattern Recognition, CVPR, vol. 2, p. II-366. IEEE (2004)
3. Epshtein, B., Ofek, E., Wexler, Y.: Detecting text in natural scenes with stroke width transform. In: Proceedings of the IEEE Computer Society Conference on Computer Vision and Pattern Recognition, CVPR, pp. 2963–2970. IEEE (2010)
4. Graves, A., Fernández, S., Gomez, F., Schmidhuber, J.: Connectionist temporal classification: labelling unsegmented sequence data with recurrent neural networks. In: Proceedings of the 23rd International Conference on Machine Learning, pp. 369–376. ACM (2006)
5. He, D., et al.: Multi-scale FCN with cascaded instance aware segmentation for arbitrary oriented word spotting in the wild. In: The IEEE Conference on Computer Vision and Pattern Recognition (CVPR), July 2017
6. He, P., Huang, W., Qiao, Y., Loy, C., Tang, X.: Reading scene text in deep convolutional sequences. In: AAAI Conference on Artificial Intelligence (2016)
7. Hochreiter, S., Schmidhuber, J.: Long short-term memory. Neural Comput. 9(8), 1735–1780 (1997)
8. Jaderberg, M., Simonyan, K., Vedaldi, A., Zisserman, A.: Reading text in the wild with convolutional neural networks. Int. J. Comput. Vis. 116(1), 1–20 (2016)
9. Karaoglu, S., Tao, R., Gevers, T., Smeulders, A.W.: Words matter: scene text for image classification and retrieval. IEEE Trans. Multimed. 19(5), 1063–1076 (2017)
10. Karatzas, D., et al.: ICDAR 2015 competition on robust reading. In: 2015 13th International Conference on Document Analysis and Recognition (ICDAR), pp. 1156–1160. IEEE (2015)
11. Mishra, A., Alahari, K., Jawahar, C.: Image retrieval using textual cues. In: Proceedings of the IEEE International Conference on Computer Vision, pp. 3040–3047 (2013)

12. Neumann, L., Matas, J.: Real-time scene text localization and recognition. In: Proceedings of the IEEE Computer Society Conference on Computer Vision and Pattern Recognition, CVPR, pp. 3538–3545. IEEE (2012)

13. Shi, B., Bai, X., Belongie, S.: Detecting oriented text in natural images by linking segments. In: The IEEE Conference on Computer Vision and Pattern Recognition (CVPR), July 2017

14. Shi, B., Bai, X., Yao, C.: An end-to-end trainable neural network for image-based sequence recognition and its application to scene text recognition. IEEE Trans. Pattern Anal. Mach. Intell. **39**, 2298–2304 (2016)

15. Shi, B., Wang, X., Lyu, P., Yao, C., Bai, X.: Robust scene text recognition with automatic rectification. In: Proceedings of the IEEE Conference on Computer Vision and Pattern Recognition, pp. 4168–4176 (2016)

16. Smith, R., et al.: End-to-end interpretation of the French street name signs dataset. In: Hua, G., Jégou, H. (eds.) ECCV 2016. LNCS, vol. 9913, pp. 411–426. Springer, Cham (2016). https://doi.org/10.1007/978-3-319-46604-0_30

17. Szegedy, C., Vanhoucke, V., Ioffe, S., Shlens, J., Wojna, Z.: Rethinking the inception architecture for computer vision. In: Proceedings of the IEEE Conference on Computer Vision and Pattern Recognition, pp. 2818–2826 (2016)

18. Tian, Z., Huang, W., He, T., He, P., Qiao, Y.: Detecting text in natural image with connectionist text proposal network. In: Leibe, B., Matas, J., Sebe, N., Welling, M. (eds.) ECCV 2016. LNCS, vol. 9912, pp. 56–72. Springer, Cham (2016). https://doi.org/10.1007/978-3-319-46484-8_4

19. Vinyals, O., Kaiser, L., Koo, T., Petrov, S., Sutskever, I., Hinton, G.: Grammar as a foreign language. In: Advances in Neural Information Processing Systems, pp. 2773–2781 (2015)

20. Vinyals, O., Toshev, A., Bengio, S., Erhan, D.: Show and tell: a neural image caption generator. In: Proceedings of the IEEE Conference on Computer Vision and Pattern Recognition, pp. 3156–3164 (2015)

21. Wojna, Z., et al.: Attention-based extraction of structured information from street view imagery. arXiv preprint arXiv:1704.03549 (2017)

22. Yang, X., He, D., Zhou, Z., Kifer, D., Giles, C.L.: Learning to read irregular text with attention mechanisms. In: Proceedings of the Twenty-Sixth International Joint Conference on Artificial Intelligence, IJCAI 2017, pp. 3280–3286 (2017). https://doi.org/10.24963/ijcai.2017/458

23. Yan, F., Mikolajczyk, K.: Deep correlation for matching images and text. In: Proceedings of the IEEE Conference on Computer Vision and Pattern Recognition, pp. 3441–3450 (2015)

24. Yu, Q., et al.: Large scale business discovery from street level imagery. arXiv preprint arXiv:1512.05430 (2015)

25. Zhang, Y., Gueguen, L., Zharkov, I., Zhang, P., Seifert, K., Kadlec, B.: Uber-text: a large-scale dataset for optical character recognition from street-level imagery. In: SUNw: Scene Understanding Workshop - CVPR 2017, Hawaii, USA (2017)

26. Zhang, Z., Zhang, C., Shen, W., Yao, C., Liu, W., Bai, X.: Multi-oriented text detection with fully convolutional networks. In: Proceedings of the IEEE Computer Society Conference on Computer Vision and Pattern Recognition, CVPR, June 2016

27. Zhou, X., et al.: East: an efficient and accurate scene text detector. In: The IEEE Conference on Computer Vision and Pattern Recognition (CVPR), July 2017

On Learning Associations
of Faces and Voices

Changil Kim[1]([✉]), Hijung Valentina Shin[2], Tae-Hyun Oh[1], Alexandre Kaspar[1],
Mohamed Elgharib[3], and Wojciech Matusik[1]

[1] MIT CSAIL, Cambridge, MA, USA
changil@csail.mit.edu
[2] Adobe Research, Cambridge, MA, USA
[3] QCRI, Doha, Qatar

Abstract. In this paper, we study the associations between human faces and voices. Audiovisual integration, specifically the integration of facial and vocal information is a well-researched area in neuroscience. It is shown that the overlapping information between the two modalities plays a significant role in perceptual tasks such as speaker identification. Through an online study on a new dataset we created, we confirm previous findings that people can associate unseen faces with corresponding voices and vice versa with greater than chance accuracy. We computationally model the overlapping information between faces and voices and show that the learned cross-modal representation contains enough information to identify matching faces and voices with performance similar to that of humans. Our representation exhibits correlations to certain demographic attributes and features obtained from either visual or aural modality alone. We release our dataset of audiovisual recordings and demographic annotations of people reading out short text used in our studies.

Keywords: Face-voice association ·
Multi-modal representation learning

1 Introduction

"Can machines put a face to the voice?"

We humans often deduce various, albeit perhaps crude, information from the voice of others, such as gender, approximate age and even personality. We even imagine the appearance of the person on the other end of the line when we phone a stranger. Can machines learn such human ability? In this paper we pose questions about whether machines can put faces to voices, or vice versa,

Electronic supplementary material The online version of this chapter (https://doi.org/10.1007/978-3-030-20873-8_18) contains supplementary material, which is available to authorized users.

© Springer Nature Switzerland AG 2019
C. V. Jawahar et al. (Eds.): ACCV 2018, LNCS 11365, pp. 276–292, 2019.
https://doi.org/10.1007/978-3-030-20873-8_18

like humans presumably do, and if they can, how accurately they can do so. To answer these questions, we need to define what "putting a face to a voice" means. We approximate this task by designing a simple discrete test: we judge whether a machine can choose the most plausible facial depiction of the voice it hears, given multiple candidates. This definition has a number of advantages: (1) it is easy to implement in machines, (2) it is possible to conduct the same test on human subjects, and (3) the performance can be quantitatively measured.

Neuroscientists have observed that the multimodal associations of faces and voices play a role in perceptual tasks such as speaker recognition [14,19,44]. Recently, the problem was brought to the computer vision community and it has been shown that such ability can be implemented by machine vision and intelligence [25]. We perform experimental studies both on human subjects and machine models. Compared to prior human-subject studies, we collect a new, larger dataset consisting of audiovisual recordings of human speeches performed by non-celebrity individuals with more diverse demographic distributions, on which human-subject study is conducted to set a more accurate baseline for human performances. Unlike the prior computational model [25], which models the task as an n-way classification, we learn the overlapping information between the two modalities, inspired by the findings of neuroscientists. This allows us to analyze both modalities in the same embedding space by measuring the distance between two modal representations directly, which enables cross-modal retrieval. We analyze what information we have learned, and examine potential connections between our learned representation and modal features of faces and voices alone. We show that our representation has a close connection to certain demographic attributes such as age and gender, some facial features, and prosodic features like voice pitch. We expect our approach to further lead to new opportunities for cross-modal synthesis and editing.

Contributions. Our technical contributions include the following.

- We provide an extensive human-subject study, with both the participant pool and dataset larger and more diverse than those used in prior studies, where we verify that humans are capable of correctly matching unfamiliar face images to corresponding voice recordings and vice versa with greater than chance accuracy. We provide a statistical analysis with diverse controls on demographic attributes and various levels of homogeneity of studied groups.
- We learn the co-embedding of modal representations of human faces and voices, and evaluate the learned representations extensively, revealing unsupervised correlations to demographic, prosodic, and facial features. We compare a number of existing techniques to learn the representation and show that we obtain consistent performances, independent of particular computational models, on the matching task on a par with human performance.
- We present a new dataset of the audiovisual recordings of speeches by 181 individuals with diverse demographic background, totaling over 3 hours of recordings, with the demographic annotations.

Limitations. While we use our own dataset for human-subject studies, we use an existing dataset of celebrities (the VoxCeleb dataset [26]) to train our computational model, due to the two experiments' respective characteristics and practical concern about data collection. Humans have prior knowledge about celebrities, which can affect their performance on VoxCeleb, while the deep neural network we use requires a large amount of data, rendering our dataset short of scale. Further, conducting user studies on such a huge dataset would also require a comparably large number of test participants. Thus, it should be avoided to compare the numbers directly between the two studies; rather, the results should be understood such that both humans and our computational model achieve statistically significant, better than random performances. Collecting a large dataset of non-celebrity audiovisual recordings comparable to VoxCeleb in size is an important and non-trivial task which we leave to future work.

2   Related Work

Studies on face-voice association span multiple disciplines. Among the most relevant to our work are cognitive science and neuroscience, which study human subjects, and machine learning, specifically, cross-modal modeling.

Human Capability for Face-Voice Association. Behavioural and neuroimaging studies of face-voice integration show clear evidence of early perceptual integrative mechanisms between face and voice processing pathways. The study of Campanella and Belin [5] reveals that humans leverage the interface between facial and vocal information for both person recognition and identity processing. This human capability is unconsciously learned by processing a tremendous number of auditory-visual examples throughout their whole life [10], and the ability to learn the associations between faces and voices starts to develop as early as three-months old [4], without intended discipline.[1] This ability has also been observed in other primates [34].

These findings led to the question about to what extent people are able to correctly match which unfamiliar voice and face belong to the same person [16,20,23,36]. Early work [16,20] argued that people could match voices to dynamically articulating faces but not to static photographs. More recent findings of Mavica and Barenholtz [23] and Smith et al. [36] contradicted these results, and presented evidence that humans can actually match *static* facial images to corresponding voice recordings with greater than chance accuracy. In a separate study, Smith et al. also showed that there is a strong agreement between the participants' ratings of a model's femininity, masculinity, age, health and weight made separately from faces and voices [35]. The discrepancy between these sets of studies were attributed to the different experimental procedures. For instance, Kamachi et al. [16] and Lachs and Pisoni [20] presented the stimuli sequentially (participants either heard a voice and then saw two faces or saw

---

[1] In machine learning terminology, this could be seen as natural supervision [28] or self-supervision [9] with unlabeled data.

a face and then heard two voices), while the latter works presented faces and voices simultaneously. In addition, the particular stimuli used could also have led to a difference in performance. For example, Kamachi et al. experimented with Japanese models, whereas Marvica and Barenholtz used Caucasian models. Smith et al. [36] showed that different models vary in the extent to which they look and sound similar, and performance could be highly dependent on the particular stimuli used.

The closest work to our human subject study is Mavica and Barenholtz's experiment. We extend the previous work in several ways. First, we exploit crowdsourcing to collect a larger and more diverse dataset of models. We collected faces and voices of 181 models of different gender, ethnicity, age-group and first-language. This diversity allowed us to investigate a wider spectrum of task difficulties according to varying control factors in demographic parameters. Specifically, whereas previous work only tests on models from a homogenous demographic group (same gender, ethnicity, age group), we vary the homogeneity of the sample group in each experiment and test models from same gender (G), same gender and ethnicity (G/E), same gender, ethnicity, first language and age group (G/E/F/A). By comparing the performances across experiments, we explicitly test the assumption, hereto taken for granted, that people infer demographic information from both face and voice and use this to perform the matching task.

Audiovisual Cross-Modal Learning by Machinery. Inspired by the early findings from cognitive science and neuroscience that humans integrate audiovisual information for perception tasks [15, 24, 32], the machine learning community has also shown increased interest in the visual-auditory cross-modal learning. The key motivation has been to understand whether machine learning models can reveal correlations across different modalities. With the recent advance of deep learning, multi-modal learning leverages neural networks to mine common or complementary information effectively from large-scale paired data. In the real world, the concurrency of visual and auditory information provides a natural supervision [29]. Recent emergence of deep learning has witnessed the understanding of the correlation between audio and visual signals in applications such as: improving sound classification [1] by combining images and their concurrent sound signals in videos; scene and place recognition [2] by transferring knowledge from visual to auditory information; vision-sound cross modal retrieval [28, 29, 37]; and sound source localization in visual scenes [31]. These works focus on the fact that visual events are often positively correlated with their concurrent sound signals. This fact is utilized to learn representations that are modality-invariant. We build on these advances and extend to the face-voice pair.

Nagrani et al. [25] recently presented a computational model for the face-voice matching task. While they see it as a binary decision problem, we focus more on the shared information between the two modalities and extract it as a representation vector residing in the shared latent space, in which the task is modeled as a nearest neighbor search. Other closely related work include Ngiam et al. [27] and Chung et al. [8], which showed that the joint signals from face and audio help disambiguate voiced and unvoiced consonants. Similarly, Hoover et al. [13] and Gebru et al. [11] developed systems to identify active speakers from a video by jointly observing the audio and visual signals. Although the voice-speaker matching task seems similar, these work mainly focus on distinguishing active speakers from non-speakers at a given time, and they do not try to learn cross-modal representations. A different line of work has also shown that recorded or synthesized speech can be used to generate facial animations of animated characters [17,39] or real persons [38].

Our interest is to investigate whether people look and sound similar, i.e., to explore the existence of the learnable relationship between the face and voice. To this end, we leverage the face-voice matching task. We examine whether faces and voices encode redundant identity information and measure to which extent.

3 Study on Human Performance

We conducted a series of experiments to test whether people can match a voice of an unfamiliar person to a static facial image of the same person. Participants were presented with photographs of two different models and a 10-second voice recording of one of the models. They were asked to choose one and only one of the two faces they thought would have a similar voice to the recorded voice ($V \rightarrow F$). We hypothesized that people may rely on information such as gender, ethnicity and age inferred from both face and voice to perform the task. To test this possibility, in each experiment, we added additional constraints on the sample demography and only compared models of the same gender (G - Experiment 1), same gender and ethnicity (G/E - Experiment 2), and finally same gender, ethnicity, first language, and age group (G/E/F/A - Experiment 3), specifically male pairs and female pairs from non-Hispanic white, native speakers in their 20s. For the most constrained condition (G/E/F/A), we also performed a follow-up experiment, where participants were presented with a single facial image and two voice recordings and chose the recording they thought would be similar to the voice of the person in the image ($F \rightarrow V$).

3.1 Dataset

While there exist multiple large-scale audiovisual datasets of human speakers, notably in the context of speech or speaker recognition [8,26], they contain widely known identities, such as celebrities or public figures. Thus, for our human subject study, we used Amazon Mechanical Turk to collect a separate dataset consisting of 239 video clips of 181 unique non-celebrities. Participants recorded themselves through their webcam, while reading out short English scripts. In addition to the video recordings, participants fill out a survey about their demographic information: gender, ethnicity, age, and their first language. The demographic distribution of the acquired dataset is tabulated in Table 2. See our supplementary material for acquisition details and the accompanying dataset to examine samples.

Table 1. The average performance of Amazon Mechanical Turk participants in each of the four experimental conditions.

Demographic constraints	Mean	SD	t (n)	p-value
G	71.4%	13.6%	13.17 (70)	$p < 0.001$
G/E	65.0%	13.0%	9.65 (70)	$p < 0.001$
G/E/F/A	58.4%	13.8%	5.20 (73)	$p < 0.001$
G/E/F/A, F → V	55.2%	12.2%	3.69 (75)	$p < 0.001$

3.2 Protocol

For the face-voice matching experiments, we conducted a separate study also through Amazon Mechanical Turk. Before starting the experiment, participants filled out a questionnaire about their demographic information, identical to the one above presented for data collection. Following the questionnaire, they completed 16 matching tasks, along with 4 control tasks for quality control. Each task consists of comparing two pairs of faces and selecting one of them as matching a voice recording (vice versa for Experiment 4). Two of the four control tasks check for consistency; we repeat a same pair of faces and voice. The other two control for correctness; we add two pairs with one male model and one female model. From preliminary studies we noticed that people are generally very good at identifying gender from face or voice, and indeed less than 3% of the participants incorrectly answered the correctness control questions (11 out of 301 participants). In the analysis, we discarded data from participants who failed in two or more control questions (9/301).

The rest of the 16 tasks comprise of 16 different pairs. Each unique person in the dataset is paired with 8 other persons from the dataset, randomly selected within the experiment's demographic constraint (Experiment 1: same gender, Experiment 2: same gender and ethnicity, Experiments 3 and 4: same gender, ethnicity, age group and first language). Each participant in the experiment was presented with 16 randomly selected pairs (8 male pairs and 8 female pairs). The pairs were presented sequentially. Participants had to listen to the audio recording(s) and choose an answer, before they could move on to the next pair. No feedback was given on whether their choice was correct or not, precluding learning of face-voice pairings. We also discarded data from participants who partook in the data collection (4/301).

3.3 Results

Table 1 shows the average performance across participants for each of the four experimental conditions. Individual t tests found significantly better than chance performance (50%) for each of the four experimental conditions. An ANOVA comparing the four experiments found a significant difference in performance ($F = 21.36$, $p < 0.001$). Tukey's HSD showed that performance in Experiment 1 (G) was significantly better than Experiment 2 (G/E) ($p < 0.05$), and performance in Experiment 2 (G/E) was significantly better than Experiment 3 (G/E/F/A) ($p < 0.05$). However, results from Experiment 3 (V → F) and Experiment 4 (F → V) were not significantly different from one another.

Similarly to Mavica and Barenholtz [23], in order to assess whether some models were more or less difficult to match, for Experiment 3, we also calculated the percentage of trials on which the participants chose the correct response whenever the model's face was presented either as the correct match or as the incorrect comparison. In other words, a high  score for a model means participants are able to correctly match the model's face to its voice as well as reject matching that face to another person's voice. Shown above is the average performance for each of the 42 models (18 male and 24 female) in Experiment 3, sorted by performance. Despite the wide variance in performance, we observe a clear trend toward better-than-chance performance, with 34 of the 42 models (80%) yielding a performance above 50%.

Overall, participants were able to match a voice of an unfamiliar person to a static facial image of the same person at better than chance levels. The performance drop across experimental conditions 1 to 3 supports the view that participants leverage demographic information inferred from the face and voice to perform the matching task. Hence, participants performed worse when comparing pairs of models from demographically more homogeneous groups. This was an assumption taken for granted in previous work, but not experimentally tested. More interestingly, even for the most constrained condition, where participants compared models of the same gender, ethnicity, age group and first language, their performance was better than chance. This result aligns with that of Mavica and Barenholtz [23] that humans can indeed perform the matching task with greater than chance accuracy even with static facial images. The direction of inference (F → V vs. V → F) did not affect the performance.

4   Cross-Modal Metric Learning on Faces and Voices

Our attempt to learn cross-modal representations between faces and voices is inspired by the significance of the overlapping information in certain cognitive tasks like identity recognition, as discussed earlier. We use standard network architectures to learn the latent spaces that represent the visual and auditory modalities for human faces and voices, respectively, and are compatible enough to grasp the associations between them. Analogous to human unconscious learning [10], we train the networks to learn the voice-face pairs from naturally paired face and voice data without other human supervision.

4.1   Network Architecture

The overall architecture is based on the triplet network [12], which is widely used for metric learning. As subnetworks for two modalities, we use VGG16 [33] and

Table 2. The demographic distributions of our dataset for user studies and the Vox-Celeb [26] test set. The fluency denotes whether the English language is the speaker's first language (Y) or not (N). The ethnicity denotes one of the following groups: (1) American Indian; (2) Asian and Pacific Islander; (3) black or African American; (4) Hispanic or Latino; (5) non-Hispanic white; (6) others.

Dataset	Gender		Ethnicity						Fluency		Age group							
	m.	f.	1	2	3	4	5	6	Y	N	≤19	20s	30s	40s	50s	60s	70s	≥80
Ours	95	86	5	30	14	15	97	20	134	47	6	101	53	14	4	3	0	0
VoxCeleb	150	100	1	10	19	13	189	18	223	27	2	27	77	58	43	21	14	8

SoundNet [2], which have shown sufficient model capacities while allowing for stable training in a variety of applications. In particular, SoundNet was devised in the context of transfer learning between visual and auditory signals.

Unlike typical triplet configurations where all three subnetworks share the weights, in our model, two heterogeneous subnetworks are hooked up to the triplet loss. The face subnetwork f_F is based on VGG16, where the conv5_3 layer is average-pooled globally, resulting in 512-d output. It is fed to a 128-d fully connected layer with the ReLU activation, followed by another 128-d fully connected layer but without ReLU, which yields the face representation. The voice subnetwork f_V is based on SoundNet, whose conv6 layer is similarly average-pooled globally, yielding 512-d output. It is then fed to two fully-connected layers with the same dimensions as those in the face subnetwork one after another. In our experiments with the voice as the reference modality, for a single voice subnetwork, there are two face subnetworks with shared weights.

During training, for each random voice sample $\mathbf{v}$, one positive face sample $\mathbf{f}^+$ and one negative sample $\mathbf{f}^-$ are drawn, and the tuple $(\mathbf{v}, \mathbf{f}^+, \mathbf{f}^-)$ is fed forward to the triplet network. Optimizing for the triplet loss

$$\mathcal{L}(\mathbf{v}, \mathbf{f}^+, \mathbf{f}^-) = \left\| \operatorname{softmax}([d^+, d^-]) - [0, 1] \right\|_2^2 \tag{1}$$

minimizes the L_2 distance between the representations of the voice and the positive face, $d^+ = \|f_V(\mathbf{v}) - f_F(\mathbf{f}^+)\|_2$, while maximizing the L_2 distance between those of the voice and the negative face, $d^- = \|f_V(\mathbf{v}) - f_F(\mathbf{f}^-)\|_2$, pushing representations of the same identity closer and pulling those of different identities away.

4.2 Dataset

Our collected dataset of 239 samples was not large enough to train a large deep neural network. Thus, we turned to unconstrained, "in-the-wild" datasets, which provide a large amount of videos mined from video sharing services like YouTube. We use the VoxCeleb dataset [26] to train our network. From the available 21,063 videos, 114,109 video clips of 1,251 celebrities are cut and used. We split these into two sets: randomly chosen 1,001 identities as the training set and the rest 250 identities as the test set. The dataset comes with facial bounding boxes. We first filtered the bounding boxes temporally as there were fluctuations in their sizes and positions, and enlarged them by 1.5 times to ensure that the entire face

Table 3. The performance of our model measured on the VoxCeleb test set. Experiments are controlled with varying demographic grouping: without control (–), within the same gender (G), ethnic group (E), both of the two (G/E), and on the largest and most homogeneous group, i.e., non-Hispanic white, male native speakers in their 30s.

Direction	Demographic grouping of test samples				
	–	G	E	G/E	G/E/F/A
V → F	78.2%	62.9%	76.4%	61.6%	59.0%
F → V	78.6%	61.6%	76.7%	61.2%	56.8%

is always visible. From each clip, the first frame and first 10 s of the audio are used, as the beginning of the clips is usually well aligned with the beginning of utterances. We manually annotated the samples in the test set with demographic attributes, which allowed us to conduct the experiments with the same controls as presented in Sect. 3 and to examine the clustering on such attributes naturally arising in the learned representations (Sect. 4.5). The demographic distributions of the annotated test set are illustrated in Table 2.

4.3   Training

All face images are scaled to 224×224 pixels. Audio clips are resampled at 22,050 Hz and trimmed to 10 s; those shorter than 10 s are tiled back to back before trimming. Training tuples are randomly drawn from the pool of faces and voices: for a random voice, a random but distinct face of the same identity and a random face of a different identity are sampled. We use Adam [18] to optimize our network with $\beta_1 = 0.9$ and $\beta_2 = 0.999$, and the batch size of 8. We use the pretrained models of VGG16 and SoundNet. The fully connected layers are trained from scratch with a learning rate of 10^{-3} and the pretrained part of the network is fine-tuned with a learning rate of 10^{-5} at the same time. The training continues for 240k iterations, while the learning rates are decayed by a factor of 10^{-1} after every 80k iterations. After 120k iterations, the network is trained with *harder* training samples, where 16 tuples are sampled for each batch, from which only the 8 samples with the highest losses are used for back-propagation. See the supplementary material for more details. We train a separate model for each direction: a V → F network with the voice as the reference modality and an F → V network with the face as the reference.

4.4   Results

We conducted the same experiments introduced in Sect. 3 using our trained model. A voice recording is fed to the network along with two candidate face images, resulting in three representation vectors. Then the face candidate closer to the voice in the representation space in L_2 metric is picked as the matching face. The performance of our computational model is tabulated in Table 3.

Similarly to our user study, we measure the test accuracy on a number of different conditions. We replicate the conditions of Experiments 1 (G), 2 (G/E), and

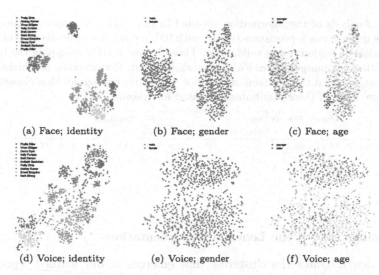

Fig. 1. The t-SNE visualization of face (a–c) and voice (d–f) representations, color-coded with the identity and demographic information. Age (c,f) color-codes continuous values, the legend showing only the two extremes; the rest categorical values. No demographic attribute was used to train representations. (Color figure online)

3 (G/E/F/A) as before but in both directions (thus including Experiment 4), in addition to two more experiments where the accuracy is measured on the same ethnic group (E) and on the entire test set samples (–). For Experiment 3 (G/E/F/A), we show the accuracy on the single, largest homogeneous group of people in the test set (non-Hispanic white, male native speakers in their 30s). Note that we used the age group of 30s instead of 20s, which were the largest group in our user study dataset, as the VoxCeleb test set demography includes more identities in their 30s. These largest groups are marked in boldface in Table 2.

We observe that the gender of the subject provides the strongest cue for our model to decide the matching, as we assume it does for human testers.[2] Unlike the experiments with human participants, conditioning on ethnicity lowers the accuracy only marginally. For the most constrained condition (G/E/F/A) the accuracy shows about 20% drop from the uncontrolled experiment.

These results largely conform to our findings from the user study (Table 1). One noticeable difference is that the performance drop due to the demographic conditioning is less drastic in the machine experiments (~4%) than in the human experiments (~13%), while their accuracies on the most controlled group (G/E/F/A; i.e., the hardest experiment) are similar (59.0% and 58.4%, respectively). Note that the accuracy on the uncontrolled group was not measured on human participants, and the machine's best accuracy should not erroneously be compared to the human best accuracy, which is already measured among same gender candidates.

---

[2] Gender is such a strong cue that we use it for control questions in our user study. See Sect. 3.

Table 4. Analysis of the information encoded in face and voice representations. We report the mean average precisions (mAP) with 99% confidence intervals (CI) obtained from 20 trials of holdout cross validations. Those having a CI overlapping the random chance with a 5% margin (50 ± 5%) are marked in red. Performance not higher than random suggests that the representation is not distinctive enough for that classification task. Again, none of these attributes were used for training.

Modality		Gender	Fluency	Age					Ethnicity					
				<30	30s	40s	50s	≥60	1	2	3	4	5	6
Face repr.	mAP	99.4	65.4	76.8	60.7	59.1	71.9	81.9	84.5	82.5	84.6	74	72	67.3
	CI	±0.2	±7.9	±4.5	±8.9	±7.6	±4.2	±7.0	±11.6	±5.2	±5.3	±5.6	±8.1	±11.1
Voice repr.	mAP	90.4	53.9	60.6	53.3	50.8	53	59.8	84.7	69.6	53.3	58.2	53.8	63.8
	CI	±4.0	±3.8	±7.5	±3.4	±0.6	±4.1	±5.7	±9.3	±7.5	±3.4	±5.1	±4.7	±7.1

4.5   Evaluations of the Learned Representation

Figure 1 demonstrates the clustering that emerges in our learned representation using the t-SNE visualization [22]. The samples in the t-SNE plots are colored so as to denote particular attribute values associated with them (from either their identities or our annotations) and visualize the attribute distribution in the feature space. Bear in mind that both the t-SNE and our network have not seen any such demographic attributes during training, and that at no point has the association between the attributes and our learned representations been introduced to the network. This allows us an unbiased assessment of the attributes' correlation to the feature distribution. We drew 100 random samples for each of 10 unique identities from the VoxCeleb test set for the identity visualization in Fig. 1ad, which shows per-identity clustering. Additionally, we drew 1,000 random samples for demographic attribute visualizations in demographic attribute visualizations Fig. 1bcef. The learned representation forms the clearest clusters regarding gender (Fig. 1be), which explains the performance drop when the experiment is constrained by gender. Also noticeable is the distribution by age (Fig. 1cf). While correlated with gender, it shows a distinct grouping to gender, in particular for face representations. The t-SNE visualization does not reveal similar clustering with respect to the first language or the ethnic group (shown in the supplementary material).

In Table 4, we further evaluate our representation using linear classifiers trained on our representations. We examine whether or not any additionally interpretable information is encoded in the representations, and how much discrepancy there exists between the representations from two modalities. Following the data-driven probing used in Bau et al. [3], we use the demographic attributes as probing data to see how accurately they can be predicted from our representations. Given the set of representations and their corresponding attributes, we train one-vs-all SVM classifiers for each attribute. The results further support that, while the attributes are never used for training, the learned representation encodes a significant amount of attribute information. They also demonstrate that our representation encodes additional information, more prominent in the face modality. Statistical insignificance of the age group classification from voice representations aligns with the t-SNE (Fig. 1f), which shows less obvious patterns than those found in its face counterpart (Fig. 1c). See our supplementary material for more visualizations and further evaluations.

Voice pitch

We show t-SNE with two prosodic features to examine a potential correlation between vocal features and our learned representations. In Fig. 2, our representation forms clusters with respect to voice pitch (fundamental frequency), while it does not with respect to voice loudness. Shown on the right is the t-SNE of G/E/F/A–controlled samples, color-coded with their voice pitch: the voice pitch is found in our learned representations even in the most controlled sample group. This shows that our representation remains informative about voice pitch, which presumably is one of the *residual signals* beyond demographic attributes and affects the performance, among many possible factors. We trained SVM on our representation to predict CelebA attributes [21] and show in Table 5 several attributes suggesting correlation.

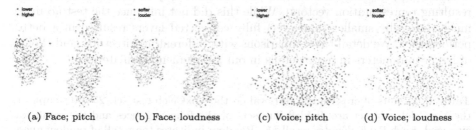

(a) Face; pitch   (b) Face; loudness   (c) Voice; pitch   (d) Voice; loudness

Fig. 2. The t-SNE visualization of face (a,b) and voice (c,d) representations with respect to two prosodic features, voice pitch and loudness.

This demonstrates that our representation encodes certain information related to these attributes without supervision. Each cell shows the mean average precision with 99% confidence intervals.

Table 5. Facial features encoded in our representation. Classification precisions for select CelebA features are shown.

Modality	Big nose	Chubby	Double chin	Baldness
Face repr.	62.9 ± 7.7	69.4 ± 4.7	69.4 ± 5.2	81.0 ± 5.8
Voice repr.	50.4 ± 7.5	57.2 ± 4.3	61.5 ± 9.7	71.0 ± 10.2

The correlation with baldness reveals the attribute's strong gender bias. Like demographic attributes, neither prosodic nor facial features were used for training.

Lastly, we use the learned representations for cross-modal retrieval. Given a face (voice) sample, we retrieve the voice (face) samples closest in the latent space. We report recall@K in Table 6, which measures the portion of queries where the true identity is among the top K retrievals, as in Vendrov et al. [42], for varying K and set sizes. The number of samples per identity was kept the same while samples within the same identity was randomly chosen.

4.6   Discussions

Comparisons and Model Parameter Selection. We experimented the task with a
number of different model components: a Siamese network with the same subnetworks, trained with a contrastive loss [7]; the same triplet network but with
VGG-Vox [26] as voice subnetwork and VGG-Face [30] as face subnetwork; and
finally a binary classification network inspired by the "L^3 network" [1], an audiovisual correlation classifier, and Nagrani et al.'s model [25], which determines,
given a face and a voice, whether or not the two belong to the same identity.
For the classification network, the positive class probability is used as a measurement of the similarity between a face and a voice to determine the matching
candidate. The networks are trained in a similar manner to the network presented in Sect. 4.1 with hyper-parameters manually tuned to ensure the best
possible performances. The results shown in Table 7 present similar performance
on our experiments, which supports the *learnability* of the overlapping information between two modalities regardless of the particular network architecture.
We also measured the test accuracy with varying configurations of the presented
network, e.g., the dimensions of the fully connected layers (and thus those of the
resulting representation vectors). While this did not influence the test accuracy
much, generally smaller (narrower) fully connected layers resulted in a better
performance. We detail the comparisons with different architectures and choices
of hyper-parameters in more details in our supplementary material.

Table 6. Results of cross-modal retrieval on the VoxCeleb test set. 25,000 samples in
the VoxCeleb test set are divided into sets of the following sizes and the recall was
averaged. Each R@K denotes recall@K. Random indicates the recall of random guess.

Direction	Set size	R@1	R@5	R@10	R@50	R@100
V → F	250	3.5%	11.3%	15.1%	51.3%	84.4%
	1,000	1.9%	7.2%	13.7%	41.3%	61.8%
	5,000	2.3%	7.7%	12.7%	34.8%	47.0%
F → V	250	2.7%	8.6%	12.3%	52.6%	82.6%
	1,000	3.3%	10.7%	18.1%	45.2%	65.7%
	5,000	0.7%	7.2%	13.9%	42.6%	61.2%
Random		0.4%	2.0%	4.0%	20.0%	40.0%

Table 7. Performance with alternative model components (for V → F). The results
consistently support the learnability of the associations with comparable performances.

Model configurations	Demographic grouping				
	–	G	E	G/E	G/E/F/A
Siamese net with same subnets	76.5%	59.9%	76.2%	60.7%	57.2%
Triplet net with VGG-Vox & VGG-Face	81.9%	67.3%	81.8%	66.7%	57.5%
Classification network	77.6%	62.2%	77.4%	61.6%	58.4%
Our model	78.2%	62.9%	76.4%	61.6%	59.0%

Table 8. Performance of our model measured on the dataset collected for our user studies (Sect. 3).

Direction	Demographic grouping				
	–	G	E	G/E	G/E/F/A
V → F	71.2%	58.0%	70.7%	55.0%	42.6%
F → V	64.5%	52.4%	65.1%	52.4%	51.4%

(a) Face dist.   (b) Voice dist.

Fig. 3. Distributions of VoxCeleb and our dataset samples.

Representation Asymmetry. We observed that face and voice representations are learned asymmetrically, depending on the modality used as the reference of the triplet. We simply trained two networks, one with the voice as reference for voice-to-face retrieval, and vice versa. A more sophisticated model, such as the quadruplet network [6], could be used to alleviate this issue. In this work, however, we focus more on showing the feasibility of the task using widely-used models, minimizing the complexity and dependency on a particular architecture.

Cross-Domain Generalization. Table 8 indicates that our model trained on the VoxCeleb dataset results in lower performance on our dataset used for user studies—a phenomenon known as "dataset bias" [40]. The t-SNE's of the samples drawn from both datasets in Fig. 3 show that the distributions of VoxCeleb and our dataset do not exactly overlap, which is more prominent for voices: while the faces in our dataset seem to be covered by those of VoxCeleb, the voices tend to be outside of the gamut of the VoxCeleb sample distribution. This is likely attributed to the fact that VoxCeleb is collected from published interviews with professional-quality audio whereas our dataset consists of webcam recordings. It is also suggested that the appearance of celebrities is more diverse and gender-typical than non-celebrities, and its distribution is not dense enough in the regions where most non-celebrity faces are distributed. This could be alleviated by additional fine-tuning on the new dataset or by domain adaptation (e.g., Tzeng et al. [41]), which is left to future work.

Accent and Regional Cues. It is worth noting that cultural or regional cues, such as accent or the subject's appearance, can play a role in the face-voice matching task. In fact, both face and voice contain rich information about a person's identity that cannot be controlled or separated out in a simple way (e.g., it is difficult to imagine a "completely neutral face" devoid of racial, emotional or personality cues). Instead of attempting to factor out all such cues, we use self-reported demographic information to control for the most common and objective identity factors. We manually filtered data with very strong accent or background noise. In the most homogeneous group (controlled by all G/E/F/A), we compare native speakers to minimize the influence of accents. We also cropped images to the facial bounding boxes to minimize subtle hints from background.

5   Conclusion

We studied the associations between human faces and voices through a series of experiments: first, with human subjects, showing the baseline for how well people perform such tasks, and then on machines using deep neural networks, demonstrating that machines perform on a par with humans. We expect that our study on these associations can provide insights into challenging tasks in a broader range of fields, pose fundamental research challenges, and lead to exciting applications.

For example, cross-modal representations such as ours could be used for finding the voice actor that *sounds* like how an animated character *looks*, manipulating synthesized facial animations [17,38,39] to harmonize with corresponding voices, or as an entertaining application to find the celebrity whose voice sounds like a user's face or vice versa. While understanding of the face-voice association at this stage is far from perfect, its advance could potentially lead to additional means towards criminal investigation like lie detection [43], which is still arguable but practically used. However, we emphasize that, similar to lie detectors, such associations should not be used for screening purposes or as hard evidence. Our work suggests the possibility of learning the associations by referring to a part of the human cognitive process, but not their definitive nature, which we believe would be far more complicated than it is modeled as in this work.

Acknowledgments. This work was funded in part by the QCRI–CSAIL computer science research program. Changil Kim was supported by a Swiss National Science Foundation fellowship P2EZP2 168785. We thank Sung-Ho Bae for his help.

References

1. Arandjelovic, R., Zisserman, A.: Look, listen and learn. In: ICCV, pp. 609–617 (2017)
2. Aytar, Y., Vondrick, C., Torralba, A.: SoundNet: learning sound representations from unlabeled video. In: NIPS, pp. 892–900 (2016)
3. Bau, D., Zhou, B., Khosla, A., Oliva, A., Torralba, A.: Network dissection: quantifying interpretability of deep visual representations. In: CVPR, pp. 3319–3327 (2017)
4. Brookes, H., Slater, A., Quinn, P.C., Lewkowicz, D.J., Hayes, R., Brown, E.: Three-month-old infants learn arbitrary auditory-visual pairings between voices and faces. Infant Child Dev. 10(1–2), 75–82 (2001)
5. Campanella, S., Belin, P.: Integrating face and voice in person perception. Trends Cogn. Sci. 11(12), 535–543 (2007)
6. Chen, W., Chen, X., Zhang, J., Huang, K.: Beyond triplet loss: a deep quadruplet network for person re-identification. In: CVPR, pp. 1320–1329 (2017)
7. Chopra, S., Hadsell, R., LeCun, Y.: Learning a similarity metric discriminatively, with application to face verification. In: CVPR, pp. 539–546 (2005)
8. Chung, J.S., Senior, A.W., Vinyals, O., Zisserman, A.: Lip reading sentences in the wild. In: CVPR, pp. 3444–3453 (2017)
9. Doersch, C., Gupta, A., Efros, A.A.: Unsupervised visual representation learning by context prediction. In: ICCV, pp. 1422–1430 (2015)

10. Gaver, W.W.: What in the world do we hear? an ecological approach to auditory event perception. Ecol. Psychol. **5**(1), 1–29 (1993)
11. Gebru, I.D., Ba, S., Evangelidis, G., Horaud, R.: Tracking the active speaker based on a joint audio-visual observation model. In: ICCV Workshop, pp. 15–21 (2015)
12. Hoffer, E., Ailon, N.: Deep metric learning using triplet network. In: Feragen, A., Pelillo, M., Loog, M. (eds.) SIMBAD 2015. LNCS, vol. 9370, pp. 84–92. Springer, Cham (2015). https://doi.org/10.1007/978-3-319-24261-3_7
13. Hoover, K., Chaudhuri, S., Pantofaru, C., Slaney, M., Sturdy, I.: Putting a face to the voice: fusing audio and visual signals across a video to determine speakers. arXiv preprint arXiv:1706.00079 (2017)
14. Joassin, F., Pesenti, M., Maurage, P., Verreckt, E., Bruyer, R., Campanella, S.: Cross-modal interactions between human faces and voices involved in person recognition. Cortex **47**(3), 367–376 (2011)
15. Jones, B., Kabanoff, B.: Eye movements in auditory space perception. Atten. Percept. Psychophys. **17**(3), 241–245 (1975)
16. Kamachi, M., Hill, H., Lander, K., Vatikiotis-Bateson, E.: "Putting the face to the voice": matching identity across modality. Curr. Biol. **13**(19), 1709–1714 (2003)
17. Karras, T., Aila, T., Laine, S., Herva, A., Lehtinen, J.: Audio-driven facial animation by joint end-to-end learning of pose and emotion. ACM Trans. Graph. **36**(4), 94:1–94:12 (2017)
18. Kingma, D.P., Ba, J.: Adam: a method for stochastic optimization. arXiv preprint arXiv:1412.6980 (2014)
19. von Kriegstein, K., Kleinschmidt, A., Sterzer, P., Giraud, A.L.: Interaction of face and voice areas during speaker recognition. J. Cogn. Neurosci. **17**(3), 367–376 (2005)
20. Lachs, L., Pisoni, D.B.: Crossmodal source identification in speech perception. Ecol. Psychol. **16**(3), 159–187 (2004)
21. Liu, Z., Luo, P., Wang, X., Tang, X.: Deep learning face attributes in the wild. In: ICCV, pp. 3730–3738 (2015)
22. van der Maaten, L., Hinton, G.: Visualizing data using t-SNE. JMLR **9**, 2579–2605 (2008)
23. Mavica, L.W., Barenholtz, E.: Matching voice and face identity from static images. J. Exp. Psychol. Hum. Percept. Perform. **39**(2), 307–312 (2013)
24. McGurk, H., MacDonald, J.: Hearing lips and seeing voices. Nature **264**(5588), 746–748 (1976)
25. Nagrani, A., Albanie, S., Zisserman, A.: Seeing voices and hearing faces: cross-modal biometric matching. In: CVPR, pp. 8427–8436 (2018)
26. Nagrani, A., Chung, J.S., Zisserman, A.: VoxCeleb: a large-scale speaker identification dataset. In: INTERSPEECH, pp. 2616–2620 (2017)
27. Ngiam, J., Khosla, A., Kim, M., Nam, J., Lee, H., Ng, A.Y.: Multimodal deep learning. In: ICML, pp. 689–696 (2011)
28. Owens, A., Isola, P., McDermott, J.H., Torralba, A., Adelson, E.H., Freeman, W.T.: Visually indicated sounds. In: CVPR, pp. 2405–2413 (2016)
29. Owens, A., Wu, J., McDermott, J.H., Freeman, W.T., Torralba, A.: Ambient sound provides supervision for visual learning. In: Leibe, B., Matas, J., Sebe, N., Welling, M. (eds.) ECCV 2016. LNCS, vol. 9905, pp. 801–816. Springer, Cham (2016). https://doi.org/10.1007/978-3-319-46448-0_48
30. Parkhi, O.M., Vedaldi, A., Zisserman, A.: Deep face recognition. In: BMVC, pp. 41.1–41.12 (2015)
31. Senocak, A., Oh, T., Kim, J., Yang, M., Kweon, I.S.: Learning to localize sound source in visual scenes. arXiv preprint arXiv:1803.03849 (2018)

32. Shelton, B.R., Searle, C.L.: The influence of vision on the absolute identification of sound-source position. Percept. Psychophys. **28**(6), 589–596 (1980)
33. Simonyan, K., Zisserman, A.: Very deep convolutional networks for large-scale image recognition. arXiv preprint arXiv:1409.1556 (2014)
34. Sliwa, J., Duhamel, J.R., Pascalis, O., Wirth, S.: Spontaneous voice-face identity matching by rhesus monkeys for familiar conspecifics and humans. PNAS **108**(4), 1735–1740 (2011)
35. Smith, H.M., Dunn, A.K., Baguley, T., Stacey, P.C.: Concordant cues in faces and voices: testing the backup signal hypothesis. Evol. Psychol. **14**(1), 1–10 (2016)
36. Smith, H.M., Dunn, A.K., Baguley, T., Stacey, P.C.: Matching novel face and voice identity using static and dynamic facial images. Atten. Percept. Psychophys. **78**(3), 868–879 (2016)
37. Solèr, M., Bazin, J.-C., Wang, O., Krause, A., Sorkine-Hornung, A.: Suggesting sounds for images from video collections. In: Hua, G., Jégou, H. (eds.) ECCV 2016. LNCS, vol. 9914, pp. 900–917. Springer, Cham (2016). https://doi.org/10.1007/978-3-319-48881-3_59
38. Suwajanakorn, S., Seitz, S.M., Kemelmacher-Shlizerman, I.: Synthesizing Obama: learning lip sync from audio. ACM Trans. Graph. **36**(4), 95:1–95:13 (2017)
39. Taylor, S.L., et al.: A deep learning approach for generalized speech animation. ACM Trans. Graph. **36**(4), 93:1–93:11 (2017)
40. Torralba, A., Efros, A.A.: Unbiased look at dataset bias. In: CVPR, pp. 1521–1528 (2011)
41. Tzeng, E., Hoffman, J., Saenko, K., Darrell, T.: Adversarial discriminative domain adaptation. In: CVPR, pp. 2962–2971 (2017)
42. Vendrov, I., Kiros, R., Fidler, S., Urtasun, R.: Order-embeddings of images and language. arXiv preprint arXiv:1511.06361 (2015)
43. Wu, Z., Singh, B., Davis, L.S., Subrahmanian, V.S.: Deception detection in videos. In: AAAI (2018)
44. Zweig, L.J., Suzuki, S., Grabowecky, M.: Learned face-voice pairings facilitate visual search. Psychon. Bull. Rev. **22**(2), 429–436 (2015)

Hand Pose Estimation Based on 3D Residual Network with Data Padding and Skeleton Steadying

Pai-Wen Ting[1], En-Te Chou[1], Ya-Hui Tang[1], and Li-Chen Fu[1,2(✉)]

[1] National Taiwan University, Taipei 10617, Taiwan
ck980046@gmail.com, csjou88@gmail.com, d05922027@csie.ntu.edu.tw,
lichen@ntu.edu.tw
[2] NTU Research Center for AI and Advanced Robotics, Taipei 10617, Taiwan
http://robotlab.csie.ntu.edu.tw/,
http://ai.robo.ntu.edu.tw

Abstract. In this paper, we propose a deep-learning-based approach
for real-time hand pose estimation from a single depth image by using
3D convolutional neural network which takes a 3D voxelized grid generated by a depth image as input. Most of the previous works for hand
pose estimation only take a single 2D depth image as input and estimate
coordinates of the key points of a hand with 2D convolutional neural network. The disadvantage of those methods is that 2D depth image can not
represent the spatial information of 3D data, while the 3D voxelized grid
can represent the point cloud of the surface of the hand in a spatial way.
Hence, we design a 3D convolutional neural network which takes a 3D
voxelized grid with data padding as input and steadying the hand skeleton with an additional loss function for regression. Experiments show
that our approach outperforms previous methods on two public datasets
and can run in real time with a single GPU.

Keywords: Hand pose estimation · Computer vision · Virtual reality

1 Introduction

Accurate hand pose estimation plays an important role in human-computer interaction and its various applications, such as virtual reality and augmented reality,
since this technology can provide a natural way to interact with objects in the
virtual world. This challenged task has been studied for decades because of the
emergence of depth cameras. In recent years, many methods have performed
good results in the area of computer vision including hand pose estimation by

This research was supported in part by the Joint Research Center for AI Technology and
All Vista Healthcare under Ministry of Science and Technology of Taiwan (MOST 107-
2634-F-002-018) and Center for Artificial Intelligence & Advanced Robotics, National
Taiwan University.

C. V. Jawahar et al. (Eds.): ACCV 2018, LNCS 11365, pp. 293–307, 2019.
https://doi.org/10.1007/978-3-030-20873-8_19

successfully applying convolutional neural networks (CNNs) to them. Although these methods outperform the existing approaches using optimization, due to many difficult challenges such as severe self-occlusion, large hand pose variations, and broken depth image, it is still very hard for them to estimate the hand pose accurately. Most of the deep-learning based methods take the 2D depth image as input and output positions of the joints or key points, which are the 3D coordinates. However, we argue that 2D depth images and the features extracted by 2D CNNs can not fit the requirement for 3D hand pose estimation. The pixel value of the depth image is the distance from the depth camera to the hand or object, and it includes the 3D information indeed. Nevertheless, more spatial information can be passed on to convolutional neural network by using 3D voxelized grids than using 2D depth images only. That is, we propose a 3D CNN (HSSNet) which takes 3D voxelized grid transformed by depth image as input and output 3D coordinates of the hand pose. We evaluate our method on two public challenging datasets: NYU dataset [16] and ICVL dataset [15]. The experiment results show that our 3D CNN with data padding and skeleton steadying method outperforms state-of-the-art approaches. In addition, our proposed method can also run in real time with a single GPU. Overall, the advantages of our proposed 3D CNN with data padding and skeleton steadying are listed below:

- We transform a 2D image to a 3D voxelized grid. By doing so, the values of the pixels, which are the distances between the depth camera and the object, are presented as the point cloud in the grid. Compared with 2D depth image, 3D voxelized grid can represent the spatial information much more accurate, and thus 3D CNN can extract more useful features and perform a better result.
- Although the quality of depth image taken by depth camera is pretty good nowadays, there are still some broken places and missing parts, which may cause an inaccurate estimation. Data padding will fill the missing parts. After padding, the 3D data will be more complete and more similar to the hand shape.
- We design an additional loss function to handle the relation between joints of hand by taking the skeleton length ratio into consideration. The overall estimated result can be stable after applying this loss function in the training stage of CNN.

2   Related Work

The approaches for the hand pose estimation from a single depth image can be categorized into three kinds, which are generative approaches, discriminative approaches and hybrid approaches.

2.1   Generative Approaches

Generative approaches predefine a hand model and fit it to a depth image by minimizing a hand-crafted cost function. Optimization algorithms such as Particle

Swarm Optimization (PSO) [13], Iterative Closest Point (ICP) [1] and their combination are commonly used to optimize the result. Accuracies of these methods heavily rely on the hand model and the cost function. In addition, since they usually take temporal information to obtain better result, the error will be accumulated if initialization and previous estimation are inaccurate.

2.2   Discriminative Approaches

Discriminative approaches learn to map the input depth image to regress hand pose joint coordinates from training data. For the methods that use random forest [9,14] which are limited by the hand-crafted features, although they can provide fast and good performance on hand pose estimation, convolutional neural network (CNN) based methods can outperform them easily. Tompson et al. [16] first proposed to apply CNN to predict the 2D heatmaps which represent the probability of the hand joints coordinates from a depth image. Ge et al. [4] extend this method by transforming the depth image to multi-view representation and predicting the heatmaps respectively and finally fusing to better extract the information of depth image. Ge et al. [5] transform the 2D depth image to a 3D representation form by Directional Truncated Signed Distance Function (D - TSDF) and utilize 3D convolution network to estimate the hand joints directly. Guo et al. [7] propose a region ensemble network to extract the features from different regions of a depth image to estimate the hand joint accurately. Chen et al. [2] transform the 3D hand joint coordinate to a spherical part model as a loss function to add the physical constraint into the CNN. Wu et al. [18] propose a skeleton-difference layer which allows CNN to learn the shape of the hand. Oberwegar et al. [12] train a feedback loop CNN to improving the estimated result by iteratively correct the error of the hand pose. Oberwegar et al. [11] enforcing a prior of the 3D hand pose by adding a bottleneck layer in the CNN and [10] improving their work by applying [8] to their network architecture, utilizing data augmentation and a CNN to refine the reference point of the hand.

2.3   Hybrid Approaches

Hybrid approaches combine the generative approach and discriminative approach to estimate the hand pose. Hand tracking technology is more likely to utilize these methods because of the requirement for maintaining the smooth result, which needs temporal information to support. Wan et al. [17] use two generative networks: a variational auto encoder (VAE) and a generative adversarial network (GAN) for modeling and train a discriminator to estimate the posterior of the shared latent space.

3   Methodology

In this paper, we will describe the details of our proposed hand pose estimation method in the following three sections. The next section will briefly introduce the system and overview our method. In the section right after that, we will describe in detail how we preprocess the depth image including 3D projection and data padding. Following then, we will detail the network architecture and training process details.

3.1 System Overview

The goal of our method is to estimate the 3D coordinates of joints of a hand. First, we will convert 2D depth image to 3D voxelized grid by projecting the 2D points with depth information into 3D space. After voxelizing the 2D depth image, we will do an additional preprocessing called data padding. Then, our 3D CNN will take the 3D voxelized grid as input and estimate the 3D coordinates of joints directly. Figure 1 shows the overview of our proposed method. We will then describe each part of the proposed method including input data generating, network architecture and implementation details.

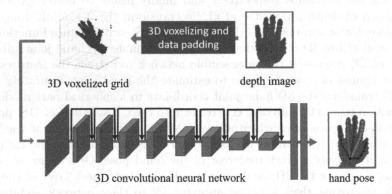

Fig. 1. The system overview of the proposed method. The depth image will first be voxelized into 3D representation and be padded. Then the 3D CNN will take 3D voxelized grid as input and estimate the 3D coordinates of joints directly.

3.2 Input Data Generating

To fit the input size of our proposed method, we should first convert the 2D depth image of hand into 3D voxelized grid representation. First of all, we resize our 2D depth image to the size 96 * 96 pixels and normalize the values at every pixel which are the distance from the depth camera to hand from 0 to 95 so that we can project the hand surface to 3D voxelized grid. After depth normalization, we create a grid with size 96 * 96 * 96 voxels and project the 2D depth image into it. For example, here we denote the 2D depth image as D_2 and 3D voxelized grid as D_3. Then the values of voxels of D_3 will be listed as follows,

$$D_3[x][y][z] = \begin{cases} 1, & if\ D_2[x][y] = z \\ 0, & else \end{cases} \qquad (1)$$

That is, voxel value will be set as 1 if the voxel is occupied by a depth point and be set as 0 if it is not.

After we generate the 3D voxelized grid which contains the information of depth of hand surface, we apply data padding to the 3D voxelized grid. As mentioned above, because of the rise of high quality and commercial depth camera, we can capture the depth image with accurate depth information. However, there are still many missing parts which may occur in the depth image, especially on the margin of the object. For example, where some fingers occlude some part of the hand, the depth values of that part of the hand surrounding those fingers may be missed. We would like to fill in those parts through padding to provide a more complete hand voxels. This problem will cause a very large area of missing parts when we try to convert the 2D depth image into 3D voxelized grid, which leads to the difficulty for CNN to extract the features. Hence, to overcome this problem, we propose a method to pad the voxels which are around the occupied voxels with cubes. We denote the original voxelized grid as D_3 and the padded voxelized grid as D_3^p. If $D_3[x][y][z] = 1$, then $D_3^p[x+i][y+i][z+i] = 1$. Where i is from the range -2 to 2, which is used to pad the shape of cube. By padding the data, we can improve the performance of the results, and the advantages of doing so are listed below:

- When there is a broken part or missing value occurring in the 2D depth image, it is very difficult to recover because of the variation of the hand shape, that is, the method such as interpolation can't recover the missing part perfectly. However, if we convert the 2D depth image into 3D voxelized grid, the depth points are represented in a spatial way. In turn, if we pad the surrounding voxels of the occupied voxels, it does not distort the shape of the hand much while padding the missing part at the same time.
- For the 3D voxelized grid which is projected from the 2D depth image, the maximum number of the occupied voxels is limited by the total number of pixels of the 2D depth image, which is 96 * 96 in our proposed method. The fewer occupied voxels contained in the 3D voxelized grid makes the CNN difficult to learn and influence the final result. But with the padded data, it is much easier for CNN to learn and to perform better.
- As mentioned above, the occupied voxels in the 3D data are very few and only be represented as a surface of hand. By padding the surrounding voxels with a shape of cube, the 3D data may look more like a hand instead of a piece of paper.

3.3 Network Architecture Design and Training Details

In this section, we are going to introduce the design of our proposed network (HSSNet) and implementation details. The section is divided into three parts. For the first part, we will introduce the architecture of our network. For the second part, we will go through the design of our additional loss function. Finally, we will introduce the implement details of our method.

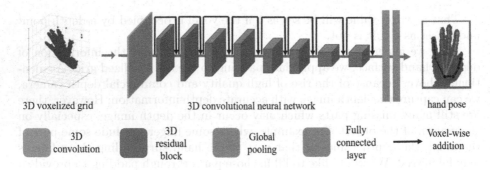

Fig. 2. The proposed architecture of 3D convolutional neural network. This figure shows the design of our proposed network.

Network Architecture. The proposed 3D convolutional neural network takes 3D voxelized grid with size 96 * 96 * 96 as input and output a vector with size 3 * J elements, which are the x, y and z coordinates of J joints of a hand. We design our 3D convolutional neural network architecture inspired by [8]. The 3D voxelized grid will first be input into a convolutional layer, where the kernel size of it is 3 * 3 * 3 with stride 2, which will downsample the input data to half of the size. Then, an activation layer (i.e., ReLU) and a max pooling layer with kernel size 2 are added afterward. After the first convolutional layer, shown as the green block in Fig. 2, the extracted feature map will be input into 4 residual block referred to [8]. The kernel size of residual block is 3 * 3 * 3 with stride 1. Finally, we use a global pooling layer to pool the output high-level feature map, and the last fully connected layer, which has 3 * J neurons, regresses the coordinates of J keypoints. The illustration of our network is shown in Fig. 2.

Loss Function Design. In this part, we will detail the design of our loss function for training 3D convolutional neural network. At the end of the proposed CNN, which is the last layer, the output will be generated as a 3 * J vector which represents the 3D coordinates. Once we have the predicted joint coordinates, we can evaluate the difference between the predicted result and the ground truth. Here, we use the Euclidean distance loss as the basic loss function which is defined as shown below,

$$L_e(H_j) = \sum_{j=1}^{J} \left\| H_j(j_x, j_y, j_z) - H_j^*(j_x, j_y, j_z) \right\|^2 \tag{2}$$

where H_j and H_j^* are the predicted result and the ground truth of the jth joint of the hand, where j_x, j_y and j_z, is the x, y and z coordinate of jth joint. And J is the total number of keypoints of the hand. The Euclidean loss will directly regress the joint position coordinates, and it is also a basic loss function for training a CNN model. So we apply this Euclidean loss as our basic loss function to let CNN learn the spatial information from input 3D voxelized grid to output estimated result. However, for the case of hand pose estimation, Euclidean loss only takes the depth information into consideration and does not consider any physical constraints of a hand. Therefore, in order to add the physical constraints in the training stage, we design an additional novel loss function to control the skeleton of the hand.

Generally, for most of the public datasets, material models or applications which are about hand pose, the reference points are often taken at the joints of the hand. So from now on, when we mention the word "joint", it means the reference point of datasets or material models. The connections between joints can be viewed as bones, and all the joints and the bones will form the structure of a hand. So this structure will be like a tree with the palm as the root, and the edges which do not take palm's joint will be the bones. In our designed loss function, which is called Hand-Skeleton-Steadying loss, we will evaluate the loss, which is exactly the ratio of each finger and the ratio of each bone's length. Hand-Skeleton-Steadying loss function is combined by two different terms, which are finger-length-ratio loss and bone-length-ratio loss, and we will explain them, respectively.

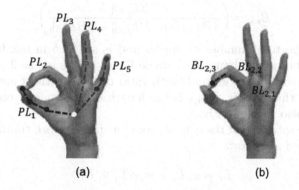

Fig. 3. The illustration of the finger-length-ratio loss and bone-length-ratio loss. (a) shows that the length of each finger is calculated as the length of each line with different color. (b) shows that the length of each bone is calculated as the length of each line with different color. (Color figure online)

For the finger-length-ratio loss, the goal of this function is to steady the ratio of the length between each finger. By applying this loss function, we hope that the length of each finger of predicted result can be in a reasonable range, that is, none of the fingers will be too long or too short compared with other fingers. The loss function is defined as bellow,

$$L_f = \sum_{i=1}^{5} \|P_i - P_i^*\| \tag{3}$$

Where,

$$P_i = \frac{PL_i}{PL_{total}} \tag{4}$$

$$PL_{total} = \sum_{i=1}^{5} PL_i \qquad (5)$$

Here, i is the total number of fingers and is set as 5 in our function. P_i and P_i^* are the predicted ratio and the ground truth ratio of each finger of the total length of five fingers. PL_i means the length of one finger, and it is calculated by the output 3D coordinates, which are the values of x, y and z. The illustration is shown in Fig. 3.

For bone-length-ratio loss, the goal of this function is to steady the length of each bone of a single finger. What we actually want to do is to control the ratio of the three bones of each finger defined by the joints. By doing so, the length of bone of each finger will also be predicted in a reasonable range and let the predicted hand looks more real in the 3D space. The loss function is designed as bellow,

$$L_b = \sum_{i=1}^{5} \sum_{k=1}^{3} \left\| B_{i,k} - B_{i,k}^* \right\| \qquad (6)$$

Where

$$B_{i,k} = \left(\frac{\|BL_{i,k}\|}{\|BL_{i,1}\| + \|BL_{i,2}\| + \|BL_{i,3}\|} \right) \qquad (7)$$

Here, i is the total number of fingers and is set as 5 in our function. And k is total number of the bones of a single finger and is set as 3. $B_{i,k}$ and $B_{i,k}^*$ are the predicted and the ground truth ratio of the length of one bone of the total length of three bones. $BL_{i,k}$ is the length of one bone of one finger. The illustration is also shown in Fig. 3.

Finally, the total loss of the convolutional neural network training procedure will be evaluated as bellow,

$$L_t = w_e L_e + w_{fb}(L_f + L_b) \qquad (8)$$

where L_e, L_f and L_b are Euclidean loss, finger-length-ratio loss and bone-length-ratio loss, respectively. And w_e, w_{fb} are the weights of the two loss functions. Here, we will set w_e as 1 and adjust another weight, which is w_{fb}, to get the best performance.

Implementations Details. The input size of our network is 96 * 96 * 96 and output size is 3 * J which is x, y and z coordinates of J joints of hand where J is set 16 in our method. We train our 3D neural network end-to-end with the dropout rate 0.5 and batch size 5. We apply stochastic gradient descent (SGD), with a learning rate of $1 * 10^{-4}$, to minimize our loss function. Finally, we implement our system with python and Tensorflow and train on a single GPU which is NVIDIA GTX 1080ti.

4 Experiments

In this chapter, we will show the experiments of our proposed method on two public datasets under different conditions. We first introduce the two datasets which we evaluate our method on. Next, we show the experimental results on two datasets and compare with other state-of-the-art works. We will also evaluate the performance of hand pose estimation with and without our proposed improvement method to prove the enhancement of it. We will also give some discussions about the results.

4.1 Datasets

In this section, we will introduce the two public datasets which are used to evaluate our method in our experiments. The two public datasets are ICVL Hand Posture Dataset [15] and NYU Hand Pose Dataset [16]. These two datasets are widely used to evaluate the performance of the hand pose estimation. So we choose these datasets to evaluate our proposed hand pose estimation method and compare with other state-of-the-art works. The introduction is listed below:

- ICVL Hand Posture Dataset: This Dataset is released by Imperial Computer Vision and Learning Lab (ICVL). The total number of the depth images are about 24,000 and are divided into 22.000 depth images for the training set and the rest of 2000 depth images for the testing set. There are total 16 joints annotated on the hand, which are 3 joints for each finger and 1 joint for the palm. Each joint is annotated with the 3D coordinates in the image space.
- NYU Hand Pose Dataset: This is a public dataset released by New York University. They use Microsoft Kinect to capture the depth images of hands from the three different viewpoints of third person's view. The total number of the depth images are about 80,000, which are 72757 training data and 8252 testing data respectively. There are total 36 joints with the 3D coordinates for each joint. Most of the hand pose estimation works use 14 or 16 joints for evaluation, and we use 16 joints here.

4.2 Evaluation Metric

There are two kinds of performance evaluation methods which are commonly used to test the accuracy of hand pose estimation. The evaluation methods are introduced as below:

- Average Euclidean distance error: The evaluation of this method is to compute the Euclidean distance between the position of the estimated joints and the position of the ground truth joints which are defined as the same joint type of the hand in the 3D space. We will finally average the error of each joint from all the frames in the testing data of each dataset to see the overall results.

– The fraction of success under threshold: This evaluation is to compute the fraction of the successfully estimated hand pose frame under different thresholds. A successfully estimated case means that the Euclidean distance error of every joint of a hand pose is under the threshold.

4.3   Results

In this section, we will compare our method with other state-of-the-art methods. In addition, we will also compare our method with the baseline, which is evaluated without the improvement and make some discussions.

Comparison with State-of-the-Art Methods. We compare the performance of proposed method on the two public datasets (ICVL, NYU) with state-of-the-art methods, which include Cascade [14], SDNet [18], Ren-9x6x6 [6], Pose-Ren [3] and DeepPrior++ [10]. We compared with 3DCNN [5] on the curve of NYU dataset since the curve on ICVL dataset is not provided in their paper. As shown in Tables 1, 2 and Figs. 4, 5, 6, 7, our proposed method outperforms other state-of-the-art methods on the two public hand pose datasets. This shows the superiority of our proposed network with data padding and additional loss function. Some qualitative estimated results of two datasets is shown in Fig. 8.

Table 1. Comparison of the proposed method with state-of-the-art methods on ICVL dataset. Mean error distance indicates the average Euclidean distance error.

Methods	Mean error distance (mm)
Cascade	9.9
SDNet	8.45
Ren-9x6x6	7.31
Pose-Ren	6.79
Ours (HSSNet)	**6.67**

Comparison with Baseline. We also compare the proposed method with the baseline which is trained without data padding or Hand-Skeleton-Steadying loss function. For the data padding part, as shown in Table 3, the performance is improved when the padding size increases from $3 \times 3 \times 3$ to $5 \times 5 \times 5$. However, when the padding size comes to $7 \times 7 \times 7$, the performance becomes worse. It is because if the padding size is too large for the data, it will blur the data instead of filling the missing part. The result has shown that $5 \times 5 \times 5$ padding size is the fittest size for our method.

For the Hand-Skeleton-Steadying loss function part, as shown in Table 4, the performance is also improved until the weight increases to 0.5. When the weight

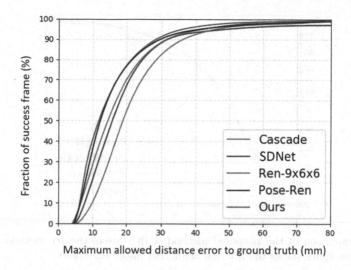

Fig. 4. Comparison of the proposed method with state-of-the-art methods on ICVL dataset. This figure shows the fraction of success under threshold.

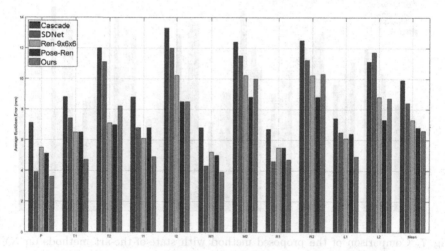

Fig. 5. Comparison of the proposed method with state-of-the-art methods on ICVL dataset. This figure shows the average Euclidean distance error of each joint.

Table 2. Comparison of the proposed method with state-of-the-art methods on NYU dataset. Mean error distance indicates the average Euclidean distance error.

Methods	Mean error distance (mm)
Ren-9x6x6	12.69
DeepPrior++	12.24
Pose-Ren	11.81
Ours (HSSNet)	**11.66**

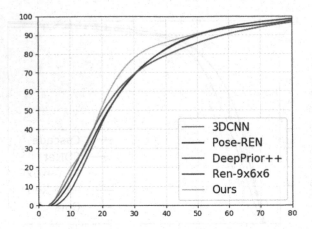

Fig. 6. Comparison of the proposed method with state-of-the-art methods on NYU dataset. This figure shows the fraction of success under threshold.

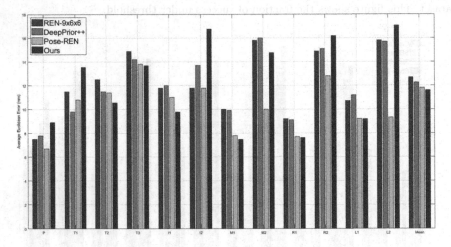

Fig. 7. Comparison of the proposed method with state-of-the-art methods on NYU dataset. This figure shows the average Euclidean distance error of each joint.

is larger than 0.5, the performance becomes worse. This fact indicates that Hand-Skeleton-Steadying loss is an additional knowledge and should not dominate the training process, so it cannot be used individually. Figure 9 shows the visualization results between using Hand-Skeleton-Steadying loss or not. Overall, the testing time of our method is 35 fps in a single GPU environment.

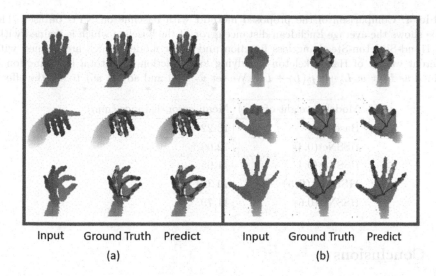

Input   Ground Truth   Predict   Input   Ground Truth   Predict

(a)   (b)

Fig. 8. Example results estimated by the proposed method. (a) Examples of NYU dataset. (b) Examples of icvl dataset.

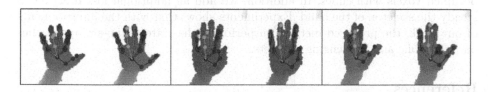

Fig. 9. The left image in a block is the predicting result when not using Hand-Skeleton-Steadying loss. The right is the result when using our loss. Obviously, the performance comes better when using our steadying losses, especially for the fingertip joint.

Table 3. Comparison of the proposed method with baseline on NYU dataset. The table shows the average Euclidean distance error of the baseline which is trained without data padding and other models which are trained with different size of padding.

Models (padding voxels)	Mean error distance (mm)
Baseline	11.87
HSSNet($3 \times 3 \times 3$)	11.79
HSSNet$5 \times 5 \times 5$)	**11.66**
HSSNet($7 \times 7 \times 7$)	11.91

Table 4. Comparison of the proposed method with baseline on NYU dataset. The table shows the average Euclidean distance error of the baseline which is trained without Hand-Skeleton-Steadying loss function and other models which are trained with different weight of Hand-Skeleton-Steadying loss function. The total loss function is defined as $L_t = w_e L_e + w_{fb}(L_f + L_b)$. We set w_e as 1 and adjust w_{fb} to see the effect.

Models (weight of w_{fb})	Mean error distance (mm)
Baseline	13.22
HSSNet(0.3)	12.06
HSSNet(0.4)	11.95
HSSNet(0.5)	**11.66**
HSSNet(0.6)	11.79

5   Conclusions

We propose a real-time, robust 3D CNN for hand pose estimation from single depth image. To overcome the problem of broken image, we transform the data from 2D depth image to 3D voxelized grid and pad the data by replacing the occupied voxels with cubes. In addition, we add an additional loss function to steady the skeleton of the hand. Experiments shows that with the improvements of our work, the proposed method outperforms the state-of-the-art approaches on two public and challenging datasets.

References

1. Andrea, T., Matthias, S., Anastasia, T., Sofien, B., Mario, B., Mark, P.: Robust articulated-ICP for real-time hand tracking. Comput. Graph. Forum **34**(5), 101–114 (2015)
2. Chen, T.Y., Ting, P.W., Wu, M.Y., Fu, L.C.: Learning a deep network with spherical part model for 3D hand pose estimation. In: 2017 IEEE International Conference on Robotics and Automation (ICRA), pp. 2600–2605, May 2017
3. Chen, X., Wang, G., Guo, H., Zhang, C.: Pose guided structured region ensemble network for cascaded hand pose estimation. arXiv preprint arXiv:1708.03416 (2017)
4. Ge, L., Liang, H., Yuan, J., Thalmann, D.: Robust 3D hand pose estimation in single depth images: from single-view CNN to multi-view CNNs. In: Proceedings of IEEE International Conference on Computer Vision and Pattern Recognition (CVPR 2016) (2016)
5. Ge, L., Liang, H., Yuan, J., Thalmann, D.: 3D convolutional neural networks for efficient and robust hand pose estimation from single depth images. In: 2017 IEEE Conference on Computer Vision and Pattern Recognition (CVPR), pp. 5679–5688, July 2017. https://doi.org/10.1109/CVPR.2017.602
6. Guo, H., Wang, G., Chen, X., Zhang, C.: Towards good practices for deep 3D hand pose estimation. arXiv preprint arXiv:1707.07248 (2017)
7. Guo, H., Wang, G., Chen, X., Zhang, C., Qiao, F., Yang, H.: Region ensemble network: improving convolutional network for hand pose estimation. arXiv preprint arXiv:1702.02447 (2017)

8. He, K., Zhang, X., Ren, S., Sun, J.: Deep residual learning for image recognition. In: CVPR, pp. 770–778. IEEE Computer Society (2016)

9. Li, P., Ling, H., Li, X., Liao, C.: 3D hand pose estimation using randomized decision forest with segmentation index points. In: 2015 IEEE International Conference on Computer Vision (ICCV), pp. 819–827, December 2015. https://doi.org/10.1109/ICCV.2015.100

10. Oberweger, M., Lepetit, V.: DeepPrior++: improving fast and accurate 3D hand pose estimation. In: 2017 IEEE International Conference on Computer Vision Workshop (ICCVW), pp. 585–594 (2017)

11. Oberweger, M., Wohlhart, P., Lepetit, V.: Hands deep in deep learning for hand pose estimation. In: Computer Vision Winter Workshop, pp. 1–10 (2015)

12. Oberweger, M., Wohlhart, P., Lepetit, V.: Training a feedback loop for hand pose estimation. In: International Conference on Computer Vision, pp. 1–8 (2015)

13. Oikonomidis, I., Kyriazis, N., Argyros., A.: Efficient model-based 3D tracking of hand articulations using Kinect. In: Proceedings of the British Machine Vision Conferencem pp. 101.1–101.11 (2011)

14. Sun, X., Wei, Y., Liang, S., Tang, X., Sun, J.: Cascaded hand pose regression. In: 2015 IEEE Conference on Computer Vision and Pattern Recognition (CVPR), pp. 824–832, June 2015

15. Tang, D., Chang, H.J., Tejani, A., Kim, T.: Latent regression forest: Structured estimation of 3D articulated hand posture. In: CVPR, pp. 3786–3793. IEEE Computer Society (2014)

16. Tompson, J., Stein, M., Lecun, Y., Perlin, K.: Real-time continuous pose recovery of human hands using convolutional networks. ACM Trans. Graph. **33**, 169:1–169:10 (2014)

17. Wan, C., Probst, T., Gool, L.J.V., Yao, A.: Crossing Nets: combining GANs and VAEs with a shared latent space for hand pose estimation. In: 2017 IEEE Conference on Computer Vision and Pattern Recognition (CVPR), pp. 1196–1205, July 2017

18. Wu, M.Y., Tang, Y.H., Ting, P.W., Fu, L.C.: Hand pose learning: combining deep learning and hierarchical refinement for 3D hand pose estimation. In: British Machine Vision Conference (2017)

Continuous-Time Intensity Estimation
Using Event Cameras

Cedric Scheerlinck[1(✉)], Nick Barnes[1,2], and Robert Mahony[1]

[1] The Australian National University, Canberra, ACT 2600, Australia
cedric.scheerlinck@anu.edu.au
[2] Data61, CSIRO, Canberra, Australia
https://www.data61.csiro.au/

Abstract. Event cameras provide asynchronous, data-driven measurements of local temporal contrast over a large dynamic range with extremely high temporal resolution. Conventional cameras capture low-frequency reference intensity information. These two sensor modalities provide *complementary* information. We propose a computationally efficient, asynchronous filter that continuously fuses image frames and events into a single high-temporal-resolution, high-dynamic-range image state. In absence of conventional image frames, the filter can be run on events only. We present experimental results on high-speed, high-dynamic-range sequences, as well as on new ground truth datasets we generate to demonstrate the proposed algorithm outperforms existing state-of-the-art methods.

Code, Datasets and Video: https://cedric-scheerlinck.github.io/
continuous-time-intensity-estimation.

1 Introduction

Event cameras respond asynchronously to changes in scene-illumination at the pixel level, offering high-temporal-resolution information over a large dynamic range [8, 12, 17, 22, 27]. Conventional cameras typically acquire intensity image frames at fixed time-intervals, generating temporally-sparse, low-dynamic-range image sequences. Fusing image frames with the output of event cameras offers the opportunity to create an image state infused with high-temporal-resolution, high-dynamic-range properties of event cameras. This image state can be queried locally or globally at any user-chosen time-instance(s) for computer vision tasks such motion estimation, object recognition and tracking.

This research was supported by an Australian Government Research Training Program Scholarship, and the Australian Research Council through the "Australian Centre of Excellence for Robotic Vision" CE140100016.

Electronic supplementary material The online version of this chapter (https://doi.org/10.1007/978-3-030-20873-8_20) contains supplementary material, which is available to authorized users.

© Springer Nature Switzerland AG 2019
C. V. Jawahar et al. (Eds.): ACCV 2018, LNCS 11365, pp. 308–324, 2019.
https://doi.org/10.1007/978-3-030-20873-8_20

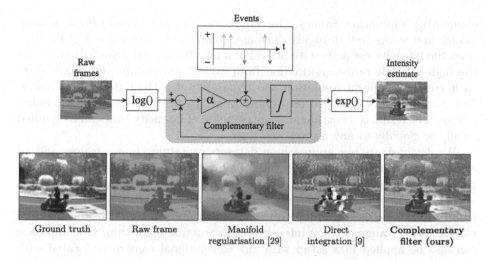

Fig. 1. The complementary filter takes image frames and events, and produces a high-dynamic-range, high-temporal-resolution, continuous-time intensity estimate.

Event cameras produce events; discrete packets of information containing the timestamp, pixel-location and polarity of a brightness change [8,22]. An event is triggered each time the change in log intensity at a pixel exceeds a preset threshold. The result is a continuous, asynchronous stream of events that encodes non-redundant information about local brightness changes. The DAVIS camera [8] also provides low-frequency, full-frame intensity images in parallel. Alternative event cameras output direct brightness measurements with every event [17,27], and may also allow user-triggered, full-frame acquisition.

Due to high availability of contrast event cameras that output polarity (and not absolute brightness) with each event, such as the DAVIS, many researchers have tackled the challenge of estimating image intensity from contrast events [3–5,9,29]. Image reconstruction algorithms that operate directly on the event stream typically perform spatio-temporal filtering [5,29], or take a spatio-temporal window of events and convert them into a discrete image frame [3,4]. Windowing incurs a trade-off between length of time-window and latency. SLAM-like algorithms [11,20,21,28] maintain camera-pose and image gradient (or 3D) maps that can be upgraded to full intensity via Poisson integration [1,2], however, so far these methods only work well for static scenes. Another image reconstruction algorithmic approach is to combine image frames directly with events [9]. Beginning with an image frame, events are integrated to produce inter-frame intensity estimates. The estimate is reset with every new frame to prevent growth of integration error.

In this paper, we present a continuous-time formulation of event-based intensity estimation using complementary filtering to combine image frames with events (Fig. 1). We choose an asynchronous, event-driven update scheme for the complementary filter to efficiently incorporate the latest event information, eliminating windowing latency. Our approach does not depend on a motion-model, and works well in highly dynamic, complex environments. Rather than reset the intensity estimate with arrival of a new frame, our formulation retains the high-dynamic-range information from events, maintaining an image state with greater temporal resolution and dynamic range than the image frames. Our method also works well on a pure event stream without requiring image frames. The result is a continuous-time estimate of intensity that can be queried locally or globally at any user-chosen time.

We demonstrate our approach on datasets containing image frames and an event stream available from the DAVIS camera [8], and show that the complementary filter also works on a pure event stream without image frames. If available, synthetic frames reconstructed from events via an alternative algorithm can also be used as input to the complementary filter. Thus, our method can be used to augment any intensity reconstruction algorithm. Our approach can also be applied in a setup with any conventional camera co-located with an event camera. Additionally, we show how an adaptive gain can be used to improve robustness against under/overexposed image frames.

In summary, the key contributions of the paper are;

- a continuous-time formulation of event-based intensity estimation,
- a computationally simple, asynchronous, event-driven filter algorithm,
- a methodology for pixel-by-pixel adaptive gain tuning.

We also introduce a new ground truth dataset for reconstruction of intensities from combined image frame and event streams, and make it publicly available. Sequences of images taken on a high-speed camera form the ground truth. We retain full frames at 20 Hz, and convert the inter-frame images to an event stream. We compare state-of-the-art approaches on this dataset.

The paper is organised as follows: Sect. 2 describes related works. Section 3 summarises the mathematical representation and notation used, and characterises the full continuous-time solution of the proposed filter. Section 4 describes asynchronous implementation of the complementary filter, and introduces adaptive gains. Section 5 shows experimental results including the new ground truth dataset, and high-speed, high-dynamic-range sequences from the DAVIS. Section 6 concludes the paper.

2   Related Works

Event cameras such as the DVS [22] and DAVIS [8] provide asynchronous, data-driven contrast events, and are widely popular due to their commercial availability. Alternative cameras such as ATIS [27] and CeleX [17,18] are capable of providing absolute brightness with each event, but are not commercially available at the time of writing. Estimating image intensity from contrast events is important because it grants computer vision researchers a readily available high-temporal-resolution, high-dynamic-range imaging platform that can be used for tasks such as face-detection [4], SLAM [11,20,21], or optical flow estimation [3].

Image reconstruction from events is typically done by processing a spatio-temporal window of events [3,4]. Barua et al. [4] learn a patch-based dictionary from simulated event data, then use the learned dictionary to reconstruct gradient images from groups of consecutive event-images. Intensity is obtained using Poisson integration [1,2]. Optical flow [6,7,14,31], together with the brightness constancy equation can be used to estimate intensity. Bardow et al. [3] simultaneously optimise optical flow and intensity estimates within a fixed-length, sliding spatio-temporal window using the primal-dual algorithm [26]. Taking a spatio-temporal window of events imposes a latency cost at minimum equal to the length of the time window, and choosing a time-interval (or event batch size) that works robustly for all types of scenes is not trivial. Reinbacher et al. [29] integrate events over time while periodically regularising the estimate on a manifold defined by the timestamps of the latest events at each pixel; the surface of active events [6]. An alternative approach is to estimate camera pose and map in a SLAM-like framework [11,20,21,28,35]. Intensity can be recovered from the map, for example via Poisson integration of image gradients. These approaches work well for static scenes, but are not designed for dynamic scenes. Belbachir et al. [5] reconstruct intensity panoramas from a pair of 1D stereo event cameras on a single-axis rotational device by filtering events (e.g. temporal high-pass filter).

Combining different sensing modalities (e.g. a conventional camera) with event cameras [8,10,15,19,23,30,32] can overcome limitations of pure events, including lack of information about static or texture-less regions of the scene that do not trigger many events. Brandli et al. [9] combine image frames and event stream from the DAVIS camera to create inter-frame intensity estimates by dynamically estimating the contrast threshold (temporal contrast) of each event. Each new image frame resets the intensity estimate, preventing excessive growth of integration error, but also discarding important accumulated event information. Shedligeri et al. [30] use events to estimate ego-motion, then warp low frame-rate images to intermediate locations. Liu et al. [23] use affine motion models to reconstruct video of high-speed foreground/static background scenes.

We introduce the concept of a continuous-time image state that is asynchronously updated with every event. Our method is motion-model free and can be used with events only, or with image frames to complement events.

3   Approach

3.1   Mathematical Representation and Notation

Let $Y(\boldsymbol{p}, t)$ denote the intensity or irradiance of pixel $\boldsymbol{p}$ at time t of a camera. We will assume that the same irradiance is observed at the same pixel in both a classical and event camera, such as is the case with the DAVIS camera [8]. A classical image frame (for a global shutter camera) is an average of the received intensity over the exposure time

$$Y_j(\boldsymbol{p}) := \frac{1}{\epsilon} \int_{t_j - \epsilon}^{t_j} Y(\boldsymbol{p}, \tau) \mathrm{d}\tau, \quad j \in 1, 2, 3 \dots , \tag{1}$$

where t_j is the time-stamp of the image capture and ϵ is the exposure time. In the sequel we will ignore the exposure time in the analysis and simply consider a classical image as representing image information available at time t_j. Although there will be image blur effects, especially for fast moving scenes in low light conditions (see the experimental results in Sect. 5), a full consideration of these effects is beyond the scope of the present paper.

The approach taken in this paper is to analyse image reconstruction for event cameras in the continuous-time domain. To this end, we define a continuous-time intensity signal $Y^F(\boldsymbol{p}, t)$ as the zero-order hold (ZOH) reconstruction of the irradiance from the classical image frames:

$$Y^F(\boldsymbol{p}, t) := Y_j(\boldsymbol{p}) = Y(\boldsymbol{p}, t_j), \quad t_j \leq t < t_{j+1} \tag{2}$$

Since event cameras operate with log intensity we convert the image intensity into log-intensity:

$$L(\boldsymbol{p}, t) := \log(Y(\boldsymbol{p}, t)) \tag{3}$$
$$L_j(\boldsymbol{p}) := \log(Y_j(\boldsymbol{p})) \tag{4}$$
$$L^F(\boldsymbol{p}, t) := \log(Y^F(\boldsymbol{p}, t)). \tag{5}$$

Note that converting the zero-hold signal into the log domain is not the same as integrating the log intensity of the irradiance over the shutter time. We believe the difference will be insignificant in the scenarios considered and we do not consider this further in the present paper.

Dynamic vision sensors (DVS), or event cameras, are biologically-inspired vision sensors that respond to changes in scene illumination. Each pixel is independently wired to continuously compare the current log intensity level to the last reset-level. When the difference in log intensity exceeds a predetermined threshold (contrast threshold), an event is transmitted and the pixel resets, storing the new illumination level. Each event contains the pixel coordinates, timestamp, and polarity ($\sigma = \pm 1$ for increasing or decreasing intensity). An event can be modelled in the continuous-time[1] signal class as a Dirac-delta function $\delta(t)$. We define an event stream $e_i(\boldsymbol{p}, t)$ at pixel $\boldsymbol{p}$ by

$$e_i(\boldsymbol{p}, t) := \sigma_i^p c\, \delta(t - t_i^p), \ i \in 1, 2, 3 \ldots , \tag{6}$$

where σ_i^p is the polarity and t_i^p is the time-stamp of the ith event at pixel $\boldsymbol{p}$. The magnitude c is the *contrast threshold* (brightness change encoded by one event). Define an *event field* $E(\boldsymbol{p}, t)$ by

$$E(\boldsymbol{p}, t) := \sum_{i=1}^{\infty} e_i(\boldsymbol{p}, t) = \sum_{i=1}^{\infty} \sigma_i^p c\, \delta(t - t_i^p). \tag{7}$$

---

[1] Note that events are continuous-time signals even though they are not continuous functions of time; the time variable t on which they depend varies continuously.

The event field is a function of all pixels $\boldsymbol{p}$ and ranges over all time, capturing the full output of the event camera.

A quantised log intensity signal $L^E(\boldsymbol{p}, t)$ can be reconstructed by integrating the event field

$$L^E(\boldsymbol{p}, t) := \int_0^t E(\boldsymbol{p}, \tau)d\tau = \int_0^t \sum_{i=1}^\infty \sigma_i^p c\, \delta(\tau - t_i^p)d\tau. \tag{8}$$

The result is a series of log intensity steps (corresponding to events) at each pixel. In the absence of noise, the relationship between the log-intensity $L(\boldsymbol{p}, t)$ and the quantised signal $L^E(\boldsymbol{p}, t)$ is

$$L(\boldsymbol{p}, t) = L^E(\boldsymbol{p}, t) + L(\boldsymbol{p}, 0) + \mu(\boldsymbol{p}, t; c), \tag{9}$$

where $L(\boldsymbol{p}, 0)$ is the initial condition and $\mu(\boldsymbol{p}, t; c)$ is the quantisation error. Unlike $L^F(\boldsymbol{p}, t)$, the quantisation error associated with $L^E(\boldsymbol{p}, t)$ is bounded by the contrast threshold; $|\mu(\boldsymbol{p}, t; c)| < c$.

Remark 1. Events can be interpreted as the temporal derivative of $L^E(\boldsymbol{p}, t)$

$$E(\boldsymbol{p}, t) = \frac{\partial}{\partial t}L^E(\boldsymbol{p}, t). \tag{10}$$

3.2 Complementary Filter

We will use a complementary filter structure [13,16,24] to fuse the event field $E(\boldsymbol{p}, t)$ with ZOH log-intensity frames $L^F(\boldsymbol{p}, t)$. Complementary filtering is ideal for fusing signals that have complementary frequency noise characteristics; for example, where one signal is dominated by high-frequency noise and the other by low-frequency disturbance. Events are a temporal derivative measurement (10) and do not contain reference intensity $L(\boldsymbol{p}, 0)$ information. Integrating events to obtain $L^E(\boldsymbol{p}, t)$ amplifies low-frequency disturbance (drift), resulting in poor low-frequency information. However, due to their high-temporal-resolution, events provide reliable *high-frequency* information. Classical image frames $L^F(\boldsymbol{p}, t)$ are derived from discrete, temporally-sparse measurements and have poor high-frequency fidelity. However, frames typically provide reliable *low-frequency* reference intensity information. The proposed complementary filter architecture combines a *high-pass* version of $L^E(\boldsymbol{p}, t)$ with a *low-pass* version of $L^F(\boldsymbol{p}, t)$ to reconstruct an (approximate) all-pass version of $L(\boldsymbol{p}, t)$.

The proposed filter is written as a continuous-time ordinary differential equation (ODE)

$$\frac{\partial}{\partial t}\hat{L}(\boldsymbol{p}, t) = E(\boldsymbol{p}, t) - \alpha\big(\hat{L}(\boldsymbol{p}, t) - L^F(\boldsymbol{p}, t)\big), \tag{11}$$

where $\hat{L}(\boldsymbol{p}, t)$ is the continuous-time log-intensity state estimate and α is the complementary filter gain, or crossover frequency [24] (Fig. 1).

The fact that the input signals in (11) are discontinuous poses some complexities in solving the filter equations, but does not invalidate the formulation. The filter can be understood as integration of the event field with an innovation term $-\alpha(\hat{L}(\boldsymbol{p}, t) - L^F(\boldsymbol{p}, t))$, that acts to reduce the error between $\hat{L}(\boldsymbol{p}, t)$ and $L^F(\boldsymbol{p}, t)$.

The key property of the proposed filter (11) is that although it is posed as a continuous-time ODE, one can express the solution as a set of asynchronous-update equations. Each pixel acts independently, and in the sequel we will consider the action of the complementary filter on a single pixel $\boldsymbol{p}$. Recall the sequence $\{t_i^p\}$ corresponding to the time-stamps of all events at $\boldsymbol{p}$. In addition, there is the sequence of classical image frame time-stamps $\{t_j\}$ that apply to all pixels equally. Consider a combined sequence of monotonically increasing *unique* time-stamps $\hat{t}_k^p$ corresponding to event $\{t_i^p\}$ or frame $\{t_j\}$ time-stamps.

Within a time-interval $t \in [\hat{t}_k^p, \hat{t}_{k+1}^p)$ there are (by definition) no new events or frames, and the ODE (11) is a constant coefficient linear ordinary differential equation

$$\frac{\partial}{\partial t} \hat{L}(\boldsymbol{p}, t) = -\alpha(\hat{L}(\boldsymbol{p}, t) - L^F(\boldsymbol{p}, t)), \quad t \in [\hat{t}_k^p, \hat{t}_{k+1}^p). \tag{12}$$

The solution to this ODE is given by

$$\hat{L}(\boldsymbol{p}, t) = e^{-\alpha(t - \hat{t}_k^p)} \hat{L}(\boldsymbol{p}, \hat{t}_k^p) + (1 - e^{-\alpha(t - \hat{t}_k^p)}) L^F(\boldsymbol{p}, t), \quad t \in [\hat{t}_k^p, \hat{t}_{k+1}^p). \tag{13}$$

It remains to paste together the piece-wise smooth solutions on the half-open intervals $[\hat{t}_k^p, \hat{t}_{k+1}^p)$ by considering the boundary conditions. Let

$$(\hat{t}_{k+1}^p)^- := \lim_{t \to (\hat{t}_{k+1}^p)} t, \quad \text{for } t < \hat{t}_{k+1}^p \tag{14}$$

$$(\hat{t}_{k+1}^p)^+ := \lim_{t \to (\hat{t}_{k+1}^p)} t, \quad \text{for } t > \hat{t}_{k+1}^p, \tag{15}$$

denote the limits from below and above. There are two cases to consider:

New Frame: When the index $\hat{t}_{k+1}^p$ corresponds to a new image frame then the right hand side (RHS) of (11) has bounded variation. It follows that the solution is continuous at $\hat{t}_{k+1}^p$ and

$$\hat{L}(\boldsymbol{p}, \hat{t}_{k+1}^p) = \hat{L}(\boldsymbol{p}, (\hat{t}_{k+1}^p)^-). \tag{16}$$

Event: When the index $\hat{t}_{k+1}^p$ corresponds to an event then the solution of (11) is *not* continuous at $\hat{t}_{k+1}^p$ and the Dirac delta function of the event must be integrated. Integrating the RHS and LHS of (11) over an event

$$\int_{(\hat{t}_{k+1}^p)^-}^{(\hat{t}_{k+1}^p)^+} \frac{d}{d\tau} \hat{L}(\boldsymbol{p}, \tau) d\tau = \int_{(\hat{t}_{k+1}^p)^-}^{(\hat{t}_{k+1}^p)^+} E(\boldsymbol{p}, \tau) - \alpha(\hat{L}(\boldsymbol{p}, \tau) - L^F(\boldsymbol{p}, \tau)) d\tau \tag{17}$$

$$\hat{L}(\boldsymbol{p}, (\hat{t}_{k+1}^p)^+) - \hat{L}(\boldsymbol{p}, (\hat{t}_{k+1}^p)^-) = \sigma_{k+1}^p c, \tag{18}$$

yields a unit step scaled by the contrast threshold and sign of the event. Note the integral of the second term $\int_{(\hat{t}^p_{k+1})_-}^{(\hat{t}^p_{k+1})_+} \alpha(\hat{L}(\boldsymbol{p},\tau) - L^F(\boldsymbol{p},\tau)) d\tau$ is zero since the integrand is bounded. We use the solution

$$\hat{L}(\boldsymbol{p}, \hat{t}^p_{k+1}) = \hat{L}(\boldsymbol{p}, (\hat{t}^p_{k+1})^-) + \sigma^p_{k+1} c, \tag{19}$$

as initial condition for the next time-interval. Eqs. (13), (16) and (19) characterise the full solution to the filter Eq. (11).

Remark 2. The filter can be run on *events only* without image frames by setting $L^F(\boldsymbol{p},t) = 0$ in (11), resulting in a high-pass filter with corner frequency α

$$\boxed{\frac{\partial}{\partial t}\hat{L}(\boldsymbol{p},t) = E(\boldsymbol{p},t) - \alpha\hat{L}(\boldsymbol{p},t).} \tag{20}$$

This method can efficiently generate a good quality image state estimate from pure events. Furthermore, it is possible to use alternative pure event-based methods to reconstruct a temporally-sparse image sequence from events and fuse this with raw events using the proposed complementary filter. Thus, the proposed filter can be considered a method to augment any event-based image reconstruction method to obtain a high temporal-resolution image state.

4   Method

4.1   Adaptive Gain Tuning

The complementary filter gain α is a parameter that controls the relative information contributed by image frames or events. Reducing the magnitude of α decreases the dependence on image frame data while increasing the dependence on events ($\alpha = 0 \rightarrow \hat{L}(\boldsymbol{p},t) = L^E(\boldsymbol{p},t)$). A key observation is that the gain can be time-varying at pixel-level ($\alpha = \alpha(\boldsymbol{p},t)$). One can therefore use $\alpha(\boldsymbol{p},t)$ to dynamically adjust the relative dependence on image frames or events, which can be useful when image frames are compromised, e.g. under- or overexposed.

We propose to reduce the influence of under/overexposed image frame pixels by decreasing $\alpha(\boldsymbol{p},t)$ at those pixel locations. We use the heuristic that pixels reporting an intensity close to the minimum $L_{\min}$ or maximum $L_{\max}$ output of the camera may be compromised, and we decrease $\alpha(\boldsymbol{p},t)$ based on the reported log intensity. We choose two bounds L_1, L_2 close to $L_{\min}$ and $L_{\max}$, then we set $\alpha(\boldsymbol{p},t)$ to a constant (α_1) for all pixels within the range $[L_1, L_2]$, and linearly decrease $\alpha(\boldsymbol{p},t)$ for pixels outside of this range:

$$\alpha(\boldsymbol{p},t) = \begin{cases} \lambda\alpha_1 + (1-\lambda)\alpha_1 \frac{(L^F(\boldsymbol{p},t)-L_{\min})}{(L_1-L_{\min})} & L_{\min} \leq L^F(\boldsymbol{p},t) < L_1 \\ \alpha_1 & L_1 \leq L^F(\boldsymbol{p},t) \leq L_2 \\ \lambda\alpha_1 + (1-\lambda)\alpha_1 \frac{(L^F(\boldsymbol{p},t)-L_{\max})}{(L_2-L_{\max})} & L_2 < L^F(\boldsymbol{p},t) \leq L_{\max} \end{cases} \tag{21}$$

where λ is a parameter determining the strength of our adaptive scheme (we set $\lambda = 0.1$). For α_1, typical suitable values are $\alpha_1 \in [0.1, 10]$ rad/s. For our experiments we choose $\alpha_1 = 2\pi$ rad/s.

Algorithm 1. Per-pixel, Asynchronous Complementary Filter

1: At each pixel:
2: Initialise $\hat{L}_\diamond$, $\hat{t}_\diamond$, $L_\diamond^F$ to zero
3: Initialise $\alpha_\diamond$ to α_1
4: **for** each new event **or** image frame **do**
5:     $\Delta t \leftarrow t - \hat{t}_\diamond$
6:     $\hat{L}_\diamond \leftarrow \exp(-\alpha_\diamond \cdot \Delta t) \cdot \hat{L}_\diamond + (1 - \exp(-\alpha_\diamond \cdot \Delta t)) \cdot L_\diamond^F$ based on (13)
7:     **if** event **then**
8:         $\hat{L}_\diamond \leftarrow \hat{L}_\diamond + \sigma c$ based on (19)
9:     **else if** image frame **then**
10:         Replace $L_\diamond^F$ with new frame
11:         Update $\alpha_\diamond$ based on (21)
12:     $\hat{t}_\diamond \leftarrow t$

4.2   Asynchronous Update Scheme

Given temporally sparse image frames and events, and using the continuous-time solution to the complementary filter ODE (11) outlined in Sect. 3 one may compute the intensity state estimate $\hat{L}(\boldsymbol{p}, t)$ at any time. In practice it is sufficient to compute the image state $\hat{L}(\boldsymbol{p}, t)$ at the asynchronous time instances $\hat{t}_k^p$ (event or frame timestamps). We propose an asynchronous update scheme whereby new events cause state updates (19) *only* at the event pixel-location. New frames cause a global update (16) (note this is not a reset as in [9])[2]. Algorithm 1 describes a per-pixel complementary filter implementation. At a given pixel $\boldsymbol{p}$, let $\hat{L}_\diamond$ denote the latest estimate of $\hat{L}(\boldsymbol{p}, t)$ stored in computer memory, and $\hat{t}_\diamond$ denote the time-stamp of the latest update at $\boldsymbol{p}$. Let $L_\diamond^F$ and $\alpha_\diamond$ denote the latest image frame and gain values at $\boldsymbol{p}$. To run the filter in events only mode (high-pass filter (20)), simply let $L_\diamond^F = 0$.

5   Results

We compare the reconstruction performance of our complementary filter, both with frames (CF$_f$) and without frames in *events only* mode (CF$_e$), against three state-of-the-art methods: manifold regularization (MR) [29], direct integration (DI) [9] and simultaneous optical flow and intensity estimation (SOFIE) [3]. We introduce new datasets: two new ground truth sequences (Truck and Motorbike); and four new sequences taken with the DAVIS240C [8] camera (Night drive, Sun, Bicycle, Night run). We evaluate our method, MR and DI against our ground truth dataset using quantitative image similarity metrics. Unfortunately, as code is not available for SOFIE we are unable to evaluate its performance on our new datasets. Hence, we compare it with our method on the jumping sequence made available by the authors.

---

[2] The filter can also be updated (using (13)) at any user-chosen time instance (or rate). In our experiments we update the entire image state whenever we export the image for visualisation.

Ground truth is obtained using a high-speed, global-shutter, frame-based camera (mvBlueFOX USB 2) running at 168 Hz. We acquire image sequences of dynamic scenes (Truck and Motorbike), and convert them into events following the methodology of Mueggler et al. [25]. To simulate event camera noise, a number of random noise events are generated (5% of total events), and distributed randomly throughout the event stream. To simulate low-dynamic-range, low-temporal-resolution input-frames, the upper and lower 25% of the maximum intensity range is truncated, and image frames are subsampled at 20 Hz. In addition, a delay of 50 ms is applied to the frame time-stamps to simulate the latency associated with capturing images using a frame-based camera.

The complementary filter gain $\alpha(\boldsymbol{p}, t)$ is set according to (21) and updated with every new image frame (Algorithm 1). We set $\alpha_1 = 2\pi$ rad/s for all sequences. The bounds $[L_1, L_2]$ in (21) are set to $[L_{min} + \kappa, L_{max} - \kappa]$, where $\kappa = 0.05(L_{max} - L_{min})$. The contrast threshold (c) is not easy to determine and in practice varies across pixels, and with illumination, event-rate and other factors [9]. Here we assume two constant contrast thresholds (ON and OFF) that are calibrated for each sequence using APS frames. We note that error arising from the variability of contrast thresholds appears as noise in the final estimate, and believe that more sophisticated contrast threshold models may benefit future works. For MR [29], the number of events per output image (events/image) is a parameter that impacts the quality of the reconstructed image. For each sequence we choose events/image to give qualitatively best performance. We set events/image to 1500 unless otherwise stated. All other parameters are set to defaults provided by [29].

Night drive (Fig. 2) investigates performance in high-speed, low light conditions where the conventional camera image frame (Raw frame) is blurry and underexposed, and dark details are lost. Data is recorded through the front wind shield of a car, driving down an unlit highway at dead of night. Our method (CF) is able to recover motion-blurred objects (e.g. roadside poles), trees that are lost in Raw frame, and road lines that are lost in MR. MR relies on spatial smoothing to reduce noise, hence faint features such as distant trees (Fig. 2; zoom) may be lost. DI loses features that require more time for events to accumulate (e.g. trees on the right), because the estimate is reset upon every new image frame. The APS (active pixel sensor in DAVIS) frame-rate was set to 7 Hz.

Sun investigates extreme dynamic range scenes where conventional cameras become overexposed. CF recovers features such as leaves and twigs, even when the camera is pointed directly at the sun. Raw frame is largely over-saturated, and the black dot (Fig. 2; Sun) is a camera artifact caused by extreme brightness, and marks the position of the sun. MR produces a clean looking image, though some features (small leaves/twigs) are smoothed out (Fig. 2; zoom). DI is washed out in regions where the frame is overexposed, due to the latest frame reset. Because the sun generates so many events, MR requires more events/image to recover fine features (with less events the image looks oversmoothed), so we increase events/image to 2500. The APS frame-rate was set to 26 Hz.

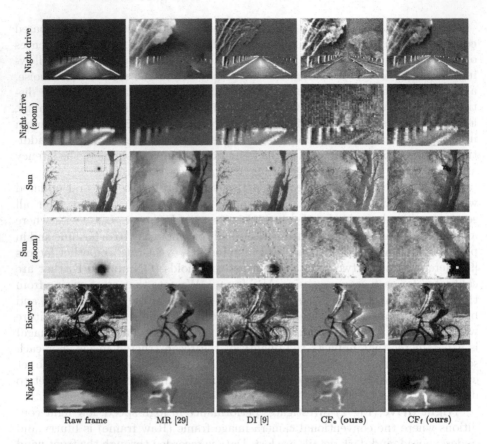

Raw frame   MR [29]   DI [9]   CF$_e$ (ours)   CF$_f$ (ours)

Fig. 2. Night drive: Raw frame is motion-blurred and contains little information in dark areas, but captures road markings. MR is unable to recover some road markings. CF$_f$ recovers sharp road markings, trees and roadside poles. **Sun:** Raw frame is overexposed when pointing directly at the sun (black dot is a camera artifact caused by the sun). In MR, some features are smoothed out (see zoom). DI is washed out due to the latest frame reset. CF captures detailed leaves and twigs. **Bicycle:** Static background cannot be recovered from events alone in MR and CF$_e$. CF$_f$ recovers both background and foreground. **Night run:** Pedestrian is heavily motion-blurred and delayed in Raw frame. DI may be compromised by frame-resets. MR and CF recover sharp detail despite high-speed, low-light conditions.

Bicycle explores the scenario of static background, moving foreground. Raw frame is underexposed in shady areas because of large intra-scene dynamic range. When the event camera is stationary, almost no events are generated by the static background and it cannot be recovered by pure event-based reconstruction methods such as MR and CF$_e$. In contrast, CF$_f$ recovers both stationary and non-stationary features, as well as high-dynamic-range detail. The APS frame-rate was set to 26 Hz.

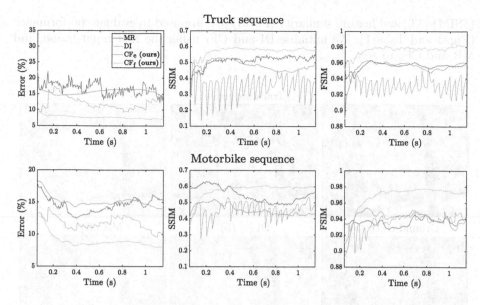

Fig. 3. Full-reference quantitative evaluation of each reconstruction method on our ground truth datasets using photometric error (%), SSIM [33] and FSIM [34].

Table 1. Overall performance of each reconstruction method on our ground truth dataset (Truck and Motorbike). Values are reported as mean ± standard deviation. Our method (CF_f) outperforms state-of-the-art on all metrics.

Method	Truck sequence			Motorbike sequence		
	Photometric error (%)	SSIM	FSIM	Photometric error (%)	SSIM	FSIM
Direct integration [9]	12.25 ± 1.94	0.36 ± 0.07	0.93 ± 0.01	11.78 ± 0.99	0.45 ± 0.05	0.94 ± 0.01
Manifold regularisation [29]	16.81 ± 1.58	0.51 ± 0.03	0.96 ± 0.00	14.53 ± 1.13	0.55 ± 0.05	0.94 ± 0.00
CF_e (ours)	15.67 ± 0.73	0.48 ± 0.03	0.95 ± 0.01	15.14 ± 0.88	0.45 ± 0.03	0.94 ± 0.01
CF_f (ours)	**7.76 ± 0.49**	**0.57 ± 0.03**	**0.98 ± 0.01**	**9.05 ± 1.19**	**0.58 ± 0.04**	**0.97 ± 0.02**

Night run illustrates the benefit in challenging low-light pedestrian scenarios. Here a pedestrian runs across the headlights of a (stationary) car at dead of night. Raw frame is not only heavily motion-blurred, but also significantly delayed, since a large exposure duration is required for image acquisition in low-light conditions. DI is unreliable as an unfortunately timed new image frame could reset the image (Fig. 2). MR and CF manage to recover the pedestrian, and CF_f also recovers the background without compromising clarity of the pedestrian. The APS frame-rate was set to 4.5 Hz.

Ground Truth Evaluation. We evaluate our method with (CF_f) and without (CF_e) 20 Hz input-frames, and compare against DI [9] and MR [29]. To assess similarity between ground truth and reconstructed images, each ground truth frame is matched with the corresponding reconstructed image with the closest time-stamp. Average absolute photometric error (%), structural similarity

(SSIM) [33], and feature similarity (FSIM) [34] are used to evaluate performance (Fig. 3 and Table 1). We initialise DI and CF_f using the first input-frame, and MR and CF_e to zero.

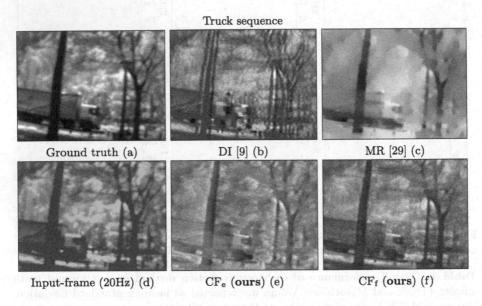

Truck sequence

Ground truth (a)   DI [9] (b)   MR [29] (c)

Input-frame (20Hz) (d) CF_e (ours) (e) CF_f (ours) (f)

Fig. 4. Reconstructed image for each method (DI, MR, CF) on ground truth dataset (Truck) with raw input-frame (d) and ground truth (a) for comparison. DI (b) displays edge artifacts where new events are added directly to the latest input-frame. MR (c) produces smoothed images compared to CF (e), (f).

Figure 3 plots the performance of each reconstruction method over time. Our method shows an initial improvement as useful information starts to accumulate, then maintains good performance over time as new events and frames are incorporated into the estimate. The oscillations apparent in DI arise from image frame resets. Table 1 summarises average performance for each sequence. Our method CF_f achieves the lowest photometric error, and highest SSIM and FSIM scores for all sequences. Figure 4 shows the reconstructed image halfway between two input-frames of Truck ground truth sequence. Pure event-based methods (MR and CF_e) do not recover absolute intensity in some regions (truck body) due to sparsity of events. DI displays artifacts around edges, where many events are generated, because events are directly added to the latest input-frame. In CF_f, event and frame information is continuously combined, reducing edge artifacts (Fig. 4) and producing a more consistent estimate over time (Fig. 3).

SOFIE. The code for SOFIE [3] was not available at the time of writing, however the authors kindly share their pre-recorded dataset (using DVS128 [22]) and results. We use their dataset to compare our method to SOFIE (Fig. 5), and since no camera frames are available, we first demonstrate our method by setting

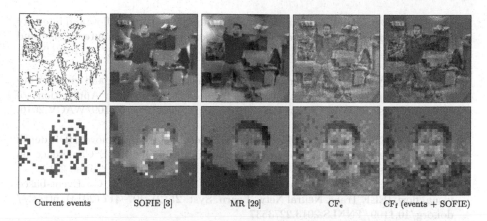

| Current events | SOFIE [3] | MR [29] | CF_e | CF_f (events + SOFIE) |

Fig. 5. SOFIE [3] and MR [29] reconstruct images from a pure event stream. CF can reconstruct images from a pure event stream by either setting input-frames to zero CF_e, or by taking reconstructed images from other methods (e.g. SOFIE) as input-frames CF_f (events + SOFIE).

input-frames to zero (CF_e), then show that reconstructed image frames output from an alternative reconstruction algorithm such as SOFIE can be used as input-frames to the complementary filter (CF_f (events + SOFIE)) to generate intensity estimates.

6 Conclusion

We have presented a continuous-time formulation for intensity estimation using an event-driven complementary filter. We compare complementary filtering with existing reconstruction methods on sequences recorded on a DAVIS camera, and show that the complementary filter outperforms current state-of-the-art on a newly presented ground truth dataset. Finally, we show that the complementary filter can estimate intensity based on a pure event stream, by either setting the input-frame signal to zero, or by fusing events with the output of a computationally intensive reconstruction method.

References

1. Agrawal, A., Chellappa, R., Raskar, R.: An algebraic approach to surface reconstruction from gradient fields. In: International Conference on Computer Vision (ICCV), pp. 174–181 (2005). https://doi.org/10.1109/iccv.2005.31
2. Agrawal, A., Raskar, R., Chellappa, R.: What is the range of surface reconstructions from a gradient field? In: Leonardis, A., Bischof, H., Pinz, A. (eds.) ECCV 2006. LNCS, vol. 3951, pp. 578–591. Springer, Heidelberg (2006). https://doi.org/10.1007/11744023_45

3. Bardow, P., Davison, A.J., Leutenegger, S.: Simultaneous optical flow and intensity estimation from an event camera. In: IEEE Conference on Computer Vision and Pattern Recognition (CVPR), pp. 884–892 (2016). https://doi.org/10.1109/CVPR.2016.102

4. Barua, S., Miyatani, Y., Veeraraghavan, A.: Direct face detection and video reconstruction from event cameras. In: IEEE Winter Conference on Applications of Computer Vision (WACV), pp. 1–9 (2016). https://doi.org/10.1109/WACV.2016.7477561

5. Belbachir, A.N., Schraml, S., Mayerhofer, M., Hofstaetter, M.: A novel HDR depth camera for real-time 3D 360-degree panoramic vision. In: IEEE Conference on Computer Vision and Pattern Recognition Workshops (CVPRW), June 2014

6. Benosman, R., Clercq, C., Lagorce, X., Ieng, S.H., Bartolozzi, C.: Event-based visual flow. IEEE Trans. Neural Netw. Learn. Syst. **25**(2), 407–417 (2014). https://doi.org/10.1109/TNNLS.2013.2273537

7. Benosman, R., Ieng, S.H., Clercq, C., Bartolozzi, C., Srinivasan, M.: Asynchronous frameless event-based optical flow. Neural Netw. **27**, 32–37 (2012). https://doi.org/10.1016/j.neunet.2011.11.001

8. Brandli, C., Berner, R., Yang, M., Liu, S.C., Delbruck, T.: A 240×180 130 dB 3 μs latency global shutter spatiotemporal vision sensor. IEEE J. Solid-State Circuits **49**(10), 2333–2341 (2014). https://doi.org/10.1109/JSSC.2014.2342715

9. Brandli, C., Muller, L., Delbruck, T.: Real-time, high-speed video decompression using a frame- and event-based DAVIS sensor. In: IEEE International Symposium on Circuits and Systems (ISCAS), pp. 686–689, June 2014. https://doi.org/10.1109/ISCAS.2014.6865228

10. Censi, A., Scaramuzza, D.: Low-latency event-based visual odometry. In: IEEE International Conference on Robotics and Automation (ICRA), pp. 703–710 (2014). https://doi.org/10.1109/ICRA.2014.6906931

11. Cook, M., Gugelmann, L., Jug, F., Krautz, C., Steger, A.: Interacting maps for fast visual interpretation. In: International Joint Conference on Neural Networks (IJCNN), pp. 770–776 (2011). https://doi.org/10.1109/IJCNN.2011.6033299

12. Delbruck, T., Linares-Barranco, B., Culurciello, E., Posch, C.: Activity-driven, event-based vision sensors. In: IEEE International Symposium on Circuits and Systems (ISCAS), pp. 2426–2429, May 2010. https://doi.org/10.1109/ISCAS.2010.5537149

13. Franklin, G.F., Powell, J.D., Workman, M.L.: Digital Control of Dynamic Systems, vol. 3. Addison-Wesley, Menlo Park (1998)

14. Gallego, G., Rebecq, H., Scaramuzza, D.: A unifying contrast maximization framework for event cameras, with applications to motion, depth, and optical flow estimation. In: IEEE Conference on Computer Vision and Pattern Recognition (CVPR), pp. 3867–3876 (2018). https://doi.org/10.1109/CVPR.2018.00407

15. Gehrig, D., Rebecq, H., Gallego, G., Scaramuzza, D.: Asynchronous, photometric feature tracking using events and frames. In: Ferrari, V., Hebert, M., Sminchisescu, C., Weiss, Y. (eds.) ECCV 2018. LNCS, vol. 11216, pp. 766–781. Springer, Cham (2018). https://doi.org/10.1007/978-3-030-01258-8_46

16. Higgins, W.T.: A comparison of complementary and kalman filtering. IEEE Trans. Aerosp. Electron. Syst. **3**, 321–325 (1975)

17. Huang, J., Guo, M., Chen, S.: A dynamic vision sensor with direct logarithmic output and full-frame picture-on-demand. In: IEEE International Symposium on Circuits and Systems (ISCAS), pp. 1–4, May 2017. https://doi.org/10.1109/iscas.2017.8050546

18. Huang, J., Guo, M., Wang, S., Chen, S.: A motion sensor with on-chip pixel rendering module for optical flow gradient extraction. In: IEEE International Symposium on Circuits and Systems (ISCAS), pp. 1–5, May 2018. https://doi.org/10.1109/iscas.2018.8351312

19. Huang, J., Wang, S., Guo, M., Chen, S.: Event-guided structured output tracking of fast-moving objects using a CeleX sensor. IEEE Trans. Circuits Syst. Video Technol. **28**(9), 2413–2417 (2018). https://doi.org/10.1109/tcsvt.2018.2841516

20. Kim, H., Handa, A., Benosman, R., Ieng, S.H., Davison, A.J.: Simultaneous mosaicing and tracking with an event camera. In: British Machine Vision Conference (BMVC) (2014). https://doi.org/10.5244/C.28.26

21. Kim, H., Leutenegger, S., Davison, A.J.: Real-time 3D reconstruction and 6-DoF tracking with an event camera. In: Leibe, B., Matas, J., Sebe, N., Welling, M. (eds.) ECCV 2016. LNCS, vol. 9910, pp. 349–364. Springer, Cham (2016). https://doi.org/10.1007/978-3-319-46466-4_21

22. Lichtsteiner, P., Posch, C., Delbruck, T.: A 128×128 120 dB 15 μs latency asynchronous temporal contrast vision sensor. IEEE J. Solid-State Circuits **43**(2), 566–576 (2008). https://doi.org/10.1109/JSSC.2007.914337

23. Liu, H.C., Zhang, F.L., Marshall, D., Shi, L., Hu, S.M.: High-speed video generation with an event camera. Vis. Comput. **33**(6–8), 749–759 (2017). https://doi.org/10.1007/s00371-017-1372-y

24. Mahony, R., Hamel, T., Pflimlin, J.M.: Nonlinear complementary filters on the special orthogonal group. IEEE Trans. Autom. Control. **53**(5), 1203–1218 (2008)

25. Mueggler, E., Rebecq, H., Gallego, G., Delbruck, T., Scaramuzza, D.: The event-camera dataset and simulator: event-based data for pose estimation, visual odometry, and SLAM. Int. J. Robot. Res. **36**, 142–149 (2017). https://doi.org/10.1177/0278364917691115

26. Pock, T., Chambolle, A.: Diagonal preconditioning for first order primal-dual algorithms in convex optimization. In: International Conference on Computer Vision (ICCV), pp. 1762–1769, November 2011. https://doi.org/10.1109/iccv.2011.6126441

27. Posch, C., Matolin, D., Wohlgenannt, R.: A QVGA 143 dB dynamic range frame-free PWM image sensor with lossless pixel-level video compression and time-domain CDS. IEEE J. Solid-State Circuits **46**(1), 259–275 (2011). https://doi.org/10.1109/JSSC.2010.2085952

28. Rebecq, H., Horstschäfer, T., Gallego, G., Scaramuzza, D.: EVO: a geometric approach to event-based 6-DOF parallel tracking and mapping in real-time. IEEE Robot. Autom. Lett. **2**, 593–600 (2017). https://doi.org/10.1109/LRA.2016.2645143

29. Reinbacher, C., Graber, G., Pock, T.: Real-time intensity-image reconstruction for event cameras using manifold regularisation. In: British Machine Vision Conference (BMVC) (2016). https://doi.org/10.5244/C.30.9

30. Shedligeri, P.A., Shah, K., Kumar, D., Mitra, K.: Photorealistic image reconstruction from hybrid intensity and event based sensor. arXiv preprint arXiv:1805.06140 (2018)

31. Stoffregen, T., Kleeman, L.: Simultaneous optical flow and segmentation (SOFAS) using dynamic vision sensor. In: Australasian Conference on Robotics and Automation (ACRA) (2017)

32. Vidal, A.R., Rebecq, H., Horstschaefer, T., Scaramuzza, D.: Ultimate SLAM? Combining events, images, and IMU for robust visual SLAM in HDR and high-speed scenarios. IEEE Robot. Autom. Lett. **3**(2), 994–1001 (2018). https://doi.org/10.1109/lra.2018.2793357

33. Wang, Z., Bovik, A.C., Sheikh, H.R., Simoncelli, E.P.: Image quality assessment: from error visibility to structural similarity. IEEE Trans. Image Process. **13**(4), 600–612 (2004). https://doi.org/10.1109/tip.2003.819861
34. Zhang, L., Zhang, L., Mou, X., Zhang, D.: FSIM: a feature similarity index for image quality assessment. IEEE Trans. Image Process. **20**(8), 2378–2386 (2011). https://doi.org/10.1109/tip.2011.2109730
35. Zhou, Y., Gallego, G., Rebecq, H., Kneip, L., Li, H., Scaramuzza, D.: Semi-dense 3D reconstruction with a stereo event camera. In: Ferrari, V., Hebert, M., Sminchisescu, C., Weiss, Y. (eds.) ECCV 2018. LNCS, vol. 11205, pp. 242–258. Springer, Cham (2018). https://doi.org/10.1007/978-3-030-01246-5_15

Comprehensive Feature Enhancement Module for Single-Shot Object Detector

Qijie Zhao, Yongtao Wang$^{(\boxtimes)}$, Tao Sheng, and Zhi Tang

Institute of Computer Science and Technology, Peking University, Beijing, China
{zhaoqijie,wyt,shengtao,tangzhi}@pku.edu.cn

Abstract. Recent one-stage CNN based detectors attract lots of research interests due to the high detection efficiency. However, their detection accuracy usually is not good enough. The major reason is that with only one regression step, one-stage detectors like SSD build features which are not representative enough for both classification and localization. In this paper, we propose a novel module, Comprehensive Feature Enhancement (CFE) module, for largely enhancing the features of one-stage detectors. The effective yet lightweight module could improve the detection accuracy with only increasing little inference time. Moreover, we propose two new one-stage detectors by assembling CFEs into the original SSD: CFE-SSDv1 and CFE-SSDv2. The CFE-SSDv1 is of simple structure with high efficiency while CFE-SSDv2 is more accurate and improves dramatically on detecting small objects especially. We evaluate the proposed CFE-SSDv1 and CFE-SSDv2 on two benchmarks for general object detection: *PASCAL VOC07* and *MS COCO*. Experimental results show that CFE-SSDv2 outperforms state-of-the-art one-stage methods such as DSSD and RefineDet on these two benchmarks. Moreover, additional ablation study demonstrates the effectiveness of the proposed CFE module. We further test the proposed CFE-SSDv2 on *UA-DETRAC* dataset for vehicle detection and *BDD* dataset for road object detection, and both get accurate detection results compared with other state-of-the-art methods.

1 Introduction

Object detection is one of the most fundamental problems in the field of computer vision, and recent deep neural network (DNN) based methods achieve state-of-the-art results for this problem. The state-of-the-art methods for general object detection can be briefly categorized into one-stage methods (e.g., YOLO [24], SSD [22], Retinanet [19], DSSD [5], RefineDet [36]), and two-stage methods (*e.g.*, Fast/Faster R-CNN [27], FPN [18], Mask R-CNN [9]). Generally speaking, two-stage methods usually have better detection performance while one-stage methods are more efficient.

For many real world applications, *e.g.*, video surveillance and autonomous driving, an adequate object detector should be effective and efficient enough, and has strong ability to detect small objects. For example, regarding the application

© Springer Nature Switzerland AG 2019
C. V. Jawahar et al. (Eds.): ACCV 2018, LNCS 11365, pp. 325–340, 2019.
https://doi.org/10.1007/978-3-030-20873-8_21

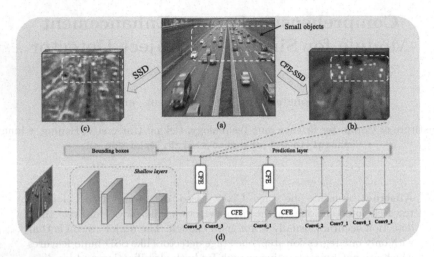

Fig. 1. CFE-SSDv1 effectively enhance the corresponding features for small objects. (a) An image for testing. (b), (c) The feature map for detecting small objects respectively of CFE-SSDv1 and the original SSD. (d) The structure of CFE-SSDv1.

of autonomous driving, the object detector should be very effective to sense the surrounding scenes and also should be very efficient to avoid obstacles in time. Moreover, the ability of detecting small objects is very important in autonomous driving scenes, due to that large portion of small objects appears in these scenes, such as traffic lights, traffic signs and faraway objects. However, state-of-the-art detectors cannot fulfill all the above requirements. Hence, in this work, we make a first attempt to propose a detector can fit all these requirements.

To achieve this goal, we improve the most widely used one-stage detector SSD by enhancing the CNN features for predicting candidate detections, based on our observations: (1) the shallower layer features used to detect small objects doesn't contain rich high-level semantic information thus not discriminative enough for the classification task, and (2) the deeper layer features used to detect large objects are less position-sensitive thus not accurate enough for the bounding box regression task. To be more specific, we propose a novel Comprehensive Feature Enhancement (CFE) module and assemble four CFE modules into the network architecture of SSD for enhancing the CNN features. As illustrated in Fig. 1, CNN features corresponding to small objects are effectively enhanced by the proposed CFE modules. Moreover, experimental results show that CFE module can also promote the detection performance of other one-stage detectors like DSSD [5] and RefineDet [36].

The main contributions of this work are summarized as follows.

- We introduce Comprehensive Feature Enhancement (CFE) module, an effective and flexible module for learning better CNN features to improve the detection accuracy of the single shot object detectors.

- Based on the proposed CFE module, we further propose two one-stage detectors, CFE-SSDv1 and CFE-SSDv2, which are efficient as SSD while have much better detection accuracy than SSD, especially for small objects.
- The proposed CFE-SSDv2 achieves good results on multiple benchmark datasets: outperforms the state-of-the-art one-stage detectors DSSD and RefineDet on VOC07 and MS-COCO datasets for general object detection, gains the best result on UA-DETRAC [33] dataset for vehicle detection, and the second best result on BDD [35] dataset for road object detection.

2   Related Work

Due to DNN based methods become dominate now, we only review them in this section, which can be briefly divided into two groups: two-stage detectors and one-stage detectors.

Two-Stage Detectors. The two-stage detectors consist of a proposal generation stage (*e.g.*, Selective Search [32] for Fast R-CNN [7] and RPN for Faster R-CNN [27]) and a stage for object classification and bounding box regression. The two-stage detectors (*e.g.*, R-CNN [8], Fast R-CNN [7], Faster R-CNN [27], R-FCN [3], HyperNet [15], FPN [18], Mask R-CNN [9], PANet [21]) keep achieving state-of-the-art performance on several challenging datasets such as PASCAL VOC 2007, 2012 [4] and MS COCO [20]). However, their efficiency is not high enough, which is the main drawback of them.

One-Stage Detectors. The one-stage detectors directly perform object classification and bounding box regression over a regular, dense sampling of object locations, scales, and aspect ratios, that is, skip the proposal generation stage. One-stage detectors usually have notably higher efficiency than two-stage detectors. YOLO [24] and SSD [22] are two representative one-stage detectors. YOLO adopts a relatively simple architecture thus very efficient, but cannot deal with dense objects or objects with large scale variants. As for SSD, it could detect objects with different sizes from multi-scale feature maps. Moreover, SSD uses anchor strategy to detect dense objects. Therefore, it achieves a pretty detection performance. In addition, SSD with input size of 512 * 512 can achieve the speed of about 23 FPS on the graphics processing unit (GPU) such as Titan XP. Due to the above advantages, SSD becomes a very practical object detector in industry, which has been widely used for many tasks. However, its detection performance is still not good enough, especially for small objects. For example, on the test-dev set of MSCOCO [20], the average precision (AP) of small objects of SSD is only 10.9%, and the average recall (AR) is only 16.5%. The major reason is that it only uses shallow feature maps to detect small objects, which doesn't contain rich high-level semantic information thus not discriminative enough for classification. Recently proposed one-stage detector RetinaNet [27] show comparable detection performance with the state-of-the-art two-stage detectors. However, its efficiency is not good when the best detection performance is achieved. More recently proposed RefineDet [36] performs best among the existing one-stage

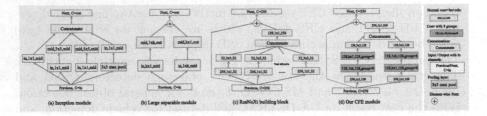

Fig. 2. Example structures for learning representative features: (a) the Inception module [30], (b) the large separable module [16], (c) the ResNeXt module [34] and (d) our CFE module. A Conv represents a combination of Conv+BatchNorm+ReLU layers.

detectors, in both terms of detection accuracy and speed. RefineDet uses an Encode-Decode [5] structure to deepen the network and upsample feature maps so that large-scale feature maps can also learn deeper semantic information. On the other hand, RefineDet uses the idea of cascade regression like Faster-RCNN [27], applying the Encode part to firstly regress coarse positions of the targets, and then use the Decode part to regress out a more accurate position on the basis of the previous step. On MSCOCO test-dev, it gets the average precision of 16.3% and an average recall of 29.3% for small objects. Also, RefineDet with VGG backbone could perform with high efficiency. Although the result achieved by RefineDet is much better, there is still much room for performance improvement.

CNN Structures. In addition, we also review some developments of CNN structure which are also introduced to our CFE module. First, Convolution (Conv) layers have powerful feature learning capabilities, and stacking multiple 3×3 Conv layers can capture advanced semantics [29]. Inspired by NIN [17], Inception module (in Fig. 2a) proposes the split-transform-merge method, decomposing a Conv layer into multiple joint 1×1 and $k \times k$ conv layers combinations. Moreover, Xception [2] and MobileNet [12] take use of connecting depthwise separable convolution and pointwise convolution for weight lighting.

Second, it is necessary to expand the scope of the proximity relationship and learn the high-level semantics from large receptive field. Inside an upgraded version of Inception, like Inception V3 [31], Conv layers with kernel size = 7 are applied for expanding the receptive field. Specifically, after factorization, continuously connecting 1×7 and 7×1 Conv layers can decrease parameter magnitude, while still keeping the area of its receptive field. And shown in Fig. 2b, the large kernel convolution is proposed in [23] to improve semantic segmentation, the large separable module [16] is also implemented after feature extraction in object detection system.

Third, decreasing redundancy is also of great significance. ResNet [11] introduces the Bottleneck structure to achieve this target. Additionally, as shown in Fig. 2c, ResNeXt [34] proposes to group convolution kernels. Specifically, the aggregated transformations of ResNeXt module replace the Conv layers of original ResNet module with blocks of the same topology stacked in parallel. This scheme improves the model without increasing the parameter magnitude.

3   Comprehensive Feature Enhancement (CFE) Module

Our target is to design a module for learning better features, which should have advantages in terms of receptive field and learning capacity, also have less weight redundance and is easy to converge.

As shown in Fig. 2d, the main framework is based on a residual structure, so that module is easy to converge [11]. The output from the right side of the model is multiplied by a value (*i.e.*, α in Eq. (1)) to control its contribution to the final output. Given the input feature $\mathbf{X} \in \mathbb{R}^{B \times C \times W \times H}$, the CFE module $\mathbf{G}_{cfe}$ generate a feature of $\mathbf{Y} \in \mathbb{R}^{B \times \widehat{C} \times \widehat{W} \times \widehat{H}}$, the spatial dimensions of which are downsampled if the striding parameter set to be bigger than 1. The CFE operation can be formulated as:

$$\mathbf{Y} = \mathbf{G}_{cfe}(\mathbf{X}) = \alpha \cdot T\left([F_+(\mathbf{X}), F_-(\mathbf{X})]\right) + g(\mathbf{X}), \tag{1}$$

where $g(\cdot)$ is a short connection of striding function, $T(\cdot)$ is the bottleneck output layer for tuning channels. To be more specific, function $F(\cdot)$ contains four continuous operations: a 1×1 Conv layer for tuning internal channels, two adjacent $1 \times k$ and $k \times 1$ Conv layers and a 3×3 Conv layer. $F_+(\cdot)$ and $F_-(\cdot)$ both contain these convolution layers, the main difference of them is the ordering between $1 \times k$ Conv and $k \times 1$ Conv. As a whole, $\mathbf{G}_{cfe}$ function combines the advantages of residual learning and dual learning, and benefit to convergence in training process.

The motivation of designing function $F(\cdot)$ is to learn more non-linearity relations, we apply the idea of split-transform-merge. In detail, splicing a 1×1 Conv layer before a larger-kernel Conv layer(initially, a $k \times k$ Conv layer), and finally followed by a 1×1 Conv layer to adjust the output dimensions. Note that the inside Conv layer with large kernel is the most significant component for feature learning. To lighten the weight and keep receptive field, we use a combination of $1 \times k$ and $k \times 1$ and its inverse combination to learn more comprehensive features. Obviously, increasing k will expand the receptive field.

After having strengthened the high-level semantics and expanded the receptive field through Conv layers, we also need to consider the problem of weights redundancy [31], which fails to achieve fully training on small-scale dataset, *e.g.*, *Pascal VOC*. Specifically, we should avoid excessive feature redundancy among channels. We use group convolution to increasing sparsity as well as shrinking the redundancy [34], which is proved to be effective by experiment. In order to assure powerful learning ability, we add another 3×3 Conv layer to compensate.

Some other details also should be concerned with. Since a 1×1 Conv layer can be used to adjust channels, the top and bottom 1×1 Conv layers together make our module flexibly inserted into arbitrary positions. Each of these Conv layers in Fig. 2 represents a group of Conv+BN+ReLU layers. In addition, the Conv layer with kernel size k has $(k-1)/2$ padding, so that the shape of input and output features can be unchanged. Alternatively, if we have to apply a striding operation (for a stride size bigger than 1 such as 2), we set striding size of one of the $1 \times k$ kernels to be 2, and then add another Conv layer with stride 2 at

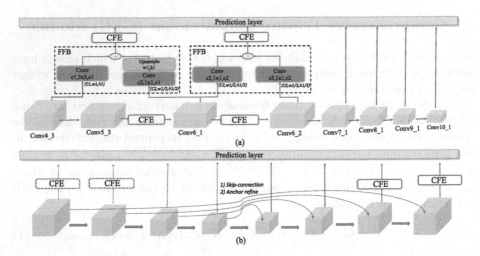

Fig. 3. (a) The way of assembling CFE modules for CFE-SSDv2. (b) The way of assembling CFE modules for DSSD (solid parts) and ReifineDet (dashed parts).

the left side shortcut of the module. All of the Conv layers are initialized using the MSRA [10] method.

4   Detection Networks with CFE

CFE could be assembled into multiple one-stage detectors due to its flexible structure. In this section, we first introduce two architecture based on SSD, CFE-SSDv1 and v2 in section Sect. 4.1. Then we illustrate the strategy to cooperate with other detectors in Sect. 4.2, such as DSSD [5] and RefineDet [36].

4.1   CFE-SSD

CFE-SSDv1. We have analyzed how weak shallow features of SSD influence the detection results of small objects, so our target is to enhance SSD by assembling CFE modules at the most sensitive position. It's noteworthy that adding too many modules excessively is also suboptimal because this operation increase inference time as well as make training process more difficult (*i.e.*, if we broaden the input size, a smaller batch size can't fit very well). As shown in Fig. 1d, we first insert two CFE modules following the output of the backbone. Then we can get the output feature of them respectively, *i.e.*, Conv6_1 and Conv6_2 shown in Fig. 1d. These additional layers effectively increase the depth of the corresponding detection features. In addition, we connect another two separate CFE modules to Conv4_3 and Conv6_1 detection branch respectively. Since the two layers are relatively shallow, and its learned features are not high-level enough. We use CFE modules to deepen the Conv4_3 and Conv6_1 feature layers as well as broaden the receptive fields. Since this scheme only make a simple modification to the SSD architecture, we call it CFE-SSDv1. Moreover, we can find from Fig. 1c and b that Conv4_3 feature indeed generates more distinguishable and position-sensitive features. The CFE modules replace the original 3×3 Conv layers in CFE-SSDv1, so this operation does not increase inference time a lot.

CFE-SSDv2. The network topology is very important for the improvement of detection accuracy. The two feature maps with the largest resolution of CFE-SSDv1 have been enhanced directly, but no other assistance has been obtained to supplement the rich semantic information from the arterial part of the network. To further improve small objects detection, we propose an advanced version, CFE-SSDv2. With the idea of feature fusion, CFE-SSDv2 improves the ability of small objects detection of shallow features compared with the CFE-SSDv1. As shown in Fig. 3a, the two shallowest feature maps are restructured through connecting feature fusion blocks (FFB) between Conv4_3 and Conv6_1, Conv6_1 and Conv6_2. Our goal is to combine a relatively shallower layer with a relatively deeper layer, which respectively represent more accurate spatial information and deeper semantic knowledge. To make models more concise and elegant, we only apply easy operations here, which also improve computing efficiency. FFB has two kinds of variants: FFB_a, shown in Fig. 3a, whose main strategy is element-wise summation; and FFB_b, where the fusion strategy is concatenation. We have compared the two kinds of blocks in experiment Sect. 4. Due to concat operation will double the output channels, so we use the 1×1 Conv layer to slim the channels before feature fusion for fair comparison, and it leads to suboptimal compared with summation operation. Note that the FFB module is intentionally simplistic, to ensure inference efficiency and decrease training complexity. Armed with two FFB modules, CFE-SSDv2 gets more improvement. For both v1 and v2, we use hard-NMS for post-processing after filtering anchor boxes with a confidence score threshold of 0.01.

For one-stage detectors, the bottleneck of accuracy depends on backbone model and input size mostly. However, large input size (*e.g.*, 800×800) and heavy backbone (*e.g.*, SE-ResNeXt101 [13]) make the batch size in training process smaller, which will influence the model's learning ability directly and also make training time longer. According to our experience, it is required that a batch size bigger than 4 per GPU to train well an one-stage detector. So we build CFE-SSD with the consideration that compacting model structure for increasing a larger input size or changing a more powerful backbone. This is why we do not add too many extra layers for CFE-SSD.

4.2   CFE-DSSD and CFE-RefineDet

To evaluate the generalization of CFE modules, we have tested on other base detectors. DSSD [5] and RefineDet [36] are state-of-the-art one-stage detectors. They have such improvements for the original SSD. However, CFE could still benefit them. As shown in Fig. 3b, we add two CFE modules at the positions before prediction layers of the small-objects sensitive layers. In detail, the area of solid lines is for DSSD, and the area of dashed lines is for RefineDet.

We do not consider assembling more CFEs and FFBs on DSSD and RefineDet since their contribution (Encode-Decode structure, cascade regression strategy) somewhat overlaps with the effects of CFE module for helping to detect small objects. CFE modules have better performance on them, but the improvement is much smaller than on original SSD.

5   Training Details

5.1   Data Augmentation

Data augmentation is essential for training. The experiments in SSD illustrate that an appropriate data augmentation strategy helps train a better model. Our strategy is the same as that of SSD [22], including image cropping, expansion, mirroring and distortion. In this work, it improves the results of CFE-SSDv1 and CFE-SSDv2 a lot especially in the term of small-size.

5.2   Design of Anchor

For a fair comparison with SSD and its variants, we identically select 6 feature layers when input size is 300×300, 7 feature layers when input size is 512×512 or 800×800, to regress detection results. As for aspect ratios of anchors, we keep the default settings of SSD except adding (3, 1/3) ratio at the first regression layer when training *Pascal VOC* and *COCO*. For *DETRAC* and *BDD*, we set the parameters of anchors by analyzing the ratio distribution of ground truth. We train anchors adequately with hard negative mining strategy, which helps mitigate the extreme foreground-background class imbalance. Specifically, we select negative anchors that have top loss values to make the ratio between the negatives and positives below 3:1. Note that we judge whether a proposal is positive or not according to its biggest IoU value with ground truth. If it exceeds the threshold (0.5 as default), we treat the proposal as positive.

6   Experiments

Experiments are conducted on four datasets: *PASCAL VOC 2007*, *MS COCO*, *UA-DETRAC* and *BDD*. It's worth nothing that, for a fair comparison, we mainly compare methods based on VGG-16 backbone [29], which is pre-trained on the *ImageNet* dataset. For all experiments based on CFE modules, we start training with warm-up strategy, initialize the learning rate of 2×10^{-3}, and then drop to 2×10^{-4} and 2×10^{-5} when loss stops decreasing. The experiment on CFE-SSDv2 with ResNet-101 backbone is conducted on a machine with 2 V100 GPUs, others are conducted on a machine with 4 Titan X GPUs. Both use CUDA 8.0 and cuDNN v6.

Table 1. Detection results comparison on *PASCAL VOC07* dataset

Method	Data	Backbone	Input size	#Boxes	FPS	mAP
Two-stage:						
Fast R-CNN [7]	07+12 trainval	VGG-16	~1000 × 600	~2000	0.5	70.0
Faster R-CNN [27]	07+12 trainval	VGG-16	~1000 × 600	300	7	73.2
Faster R-CNN [27]	07+12 trainval	ResNet-101	~1000 × 600	300	2.4	76.4
ION [1]	07+12 trainval	VGG-16	~1000 × 600	4000	1.25	76.5
MR-CNN [6]	07+12 trainval	VGG-16	~1000 × 600	250	0.03	78.2
R-FCN [3]	07+12 trainval	ResNet-101	~1000 × 600	300	9	80.5
One-stage:						
YOLO [24]	07+12 trainval	GoogleNet	448 × 448	98	45	63.4
RON384 [14]	07+12 trainval	VGG-16	384 × 384	30600	15	75.4
SSD300* [22]	07+12 trainval	VGG-16	300 × 300	8732	46	77.2
DSOD300 [28]	07+12 trainval	DenseNet-64	300 × 300	8732	17.4	77.7
DSSD321 [5]	07+12 trainval	ResNet-101	321 × 321	17080	9.5	78.6
RefineDet320 [36]	07+12 trainval	VGG-16	320 × 320	6375	40.3	80.0
CFE-SSDv1-300	07+12 trainval	VGG-16	300 × 300	11620	42.2	80.2
CFE-SSDv2-300	07+12 trainval	VGG-16	300 × 300	11620	41.5	**80.5**
YOLOv2 [25]	07+12 trainval	Darknet-19	544 × 544	845	40	78.6
SSD512* [22]	07+12 trainval	VGG-16	512 × 512	24564	19	79.8
DSSD513 [5]	07+12 trainval	ResNet-101	513 × 513	43688	5.5	81.5
RefineDet512 [36]	07+12 trainval	VGG-16	512 × 512	16320	24.1	81.8
CFE-SSDv1-512	07+12 trainval	VGG-16	512 × 512	32756	22.0	81.8
CFE-SSDv2-512	07+12 trainval	VGG-16	512 × 512	32756	21.2	**82.1**

6.1   Results on *PASCAL VOC 2007*

In this experiment, we train our models on the union set of *VOC 2007* and *VOC 2012 trainval* set (approximately 16,500 pictures) with 20 categories and test them on the *VOC 2007 test* set. Stochastic Gradient Descent (SGD) with momentum of 0.9 and weight decay of 0.0005 was used for optimization. Table 1 shows the results.

Compare with Previous State-of-the-Art Methods. In Table 1, SSD300* and SSD512* are the upgraded version of SSD with the new data augmentation methods [22], which are the baselines for one-stage detectors. By integrating our CFE module, the original SSD300 model obtains a mAP of 80.5% at the speed of 42.5 fps. Obviously, CFE-SSDv2 outperforms SSD and also keeps its speed. Compared with state-of-the-art two-stage methods, CFE-SSDv2 300 outperforms most of them and achieves the same accuracy as R-FCN, whose backbone is ResNet-101 and input size is ~ 1000 × 600. By using a larger input size 512 × 512, CFE-SSDv2 512 gets 82.1% mAP, better than most object detection systems for both one-stage and two-stage. In addition, CFE-SSDv2 exceeds another version of modified SSD, DSSD [5], by a large margin. DSSD321 equipped with ResNet101 and broadening the input size to 321 × 321 still gets lower results

Table 2. Comparison of different modules

Module name	CFE-SSD	Result (mAP)
SSD (baseline) [22]	None	77.24
Inception module [31]	v1	78.91
Large separable module (k = 7)[16]	v1	78.10
ResNeXt module [34]	v1	77.44
CFE module (k = 3)	v1	79.96
CFE module (k = 5)	v1	80.05
CFE module (k = 7)	v1	**80.16**
CFE module (k = 7)	v2	**80.49**

Table 3. Results of different groups in CFE (when k = 3)

Groups	Results (mAP)
1	79.31
2	79.58
4	79.64
8	**79.96**
16	79.88
32	79.42
64	78.92

Table 4. Comparison between different CFE-SSD settings

FFB type	FFB	Result (mAP)	Speed (fps)
None (v1)	0	80.16	42.21
Concat	1	80.42	42.01
Concat	2	80.43	41.77
Sum (v2)	2	**80.49**	41.48

Table 5. Results of DSSD and RefineDet with CFE modules

Method	Size	CFEs	VOC07	COCO
DSSD	320	0	77.47	27.4
CFE-DSSD	320	2	**78.86**	**29.5**
RefineDet	320	0	80.01	29.4
CFE-RefineDet	320	2	80.00	**30.5**

by 2% compared with our method. As for input size of 512 (including 513), we still outperform the heavy DSSD and also keep real-time efficiency. RefineDet is another state-of-the-art one-stage method. Both our 300 (including 320) and 512 versions are higher than each of RefineDet. Specifically, CFE-SSDv2 300 not only performs better but is also more accurate. CFE-SSDv2 512 outperforms RefineDet512 as for detection accuracy and achieves state-of-the-art.

Analysis of Different Modules. We conducted experiments to evaluate the components of CFE-SSDv1 and v2, CFE module itself and also test the generalizations of CFE module on DSSD [5] and RefineDet [36]. If not specified, default settings are: the large kernel is k = 7; group convolution of 8; input size is 300 × 300; base architecture is CFE-SSDv1. The results are shown in Tables 2, 3, 4 and 5.

Compare with Different Modules. To prove that CFE does have great effects for improving detection performance, we compare CFE module with other popular modules to assemble in SSD. As shown in Table 2. CFE module with k = 3 already outperforms the existing modules, and increasing k will further improve the accuracy. We have tried a larger k, but the performance begins to drop, it can be concluded that CFE module with k = 7 is enough for keeping a large receptive field. The last line in Table 2 shows the effects of changing the topology structure to CFE-SSDv2.

Groups. We suggest to group convolution kernels to decrease the module weight as well as reducing the FLOPs and find that this operation can also improve detection accuracy. We deduce that group convolution controls the redundancy and even learns better feature on small-scale dataset (*e.g.*, Pascal VOC). As shown in Table 3, grouping convolution kernels to 8 groups is relatively the best.

Table 6. Detection accuracy comparisons in terms of mAP percentage on *MS COCO* test-dev set

Method	Backbone	Input size	Avg. precision, IoU:			Avg. precision, area:		
			0.5:0.95	0.5	0.75	S	M	L
SSD300* [22]	VGG-16	300 × 300	25.1	43.1	25.8	6.6	25.9	41.4
RON384++ [14]	VGG-16	384 × 384	27.4	49.5	27.1	-	-	-
DSSD321 [5]	ResNet-101	321 × 321	28.0	46.1	29.2	7.4	28.1	**47.6**
RefineDet320 [36]	VGG-16	320 × 320	29.4	49.2	31.3	10.0	32.0	44.4
CFE-SSDv1-300	VGG-16	300 × 300	29.3	49.0	31.0	10.6	31.7	44.3
CFE-SSDv2-300	VGG-16	300 × 300	**30.4**	**50.5**	**31.3**	**12.1**	**32.2**	46.4
YOLOv2 [25]	DarkNet-19	544 × 544	21.6	44.0	19.2	5.0	22.4	35.5
YOLOv3 [26]	DarkNet-53	608 × 608	33.0	57.9	34.4	18.3	35.4	41.9
SSD512* [22]	VGG-16	512 × 512	28.8	48.5	30.3	10.9	31.8	43.5
DSSD513 [5]	ResNet-101	513 × 513	33.2	53.3	35.2	13.0	35.4	51.1
RetinaNet500 [19]	ResNet-50	500 × 500	32.5	50.9	34.8	13.9	25.8	46.7
RefineDet512 [36]	VGG-16	512 × 512	33.0	54.5	35.5	16.3	36.3	44.3
RefineDet512 [36]	ResNet-101	512 × 512	36.4	57.5	39.5	16.6	39.9	51.4
CFE-SSDv1-512	VGG-16	512 × 512	33.8	55.1	35.7	16.2	37.2	46.3
CFE-SSDv2-512	VGG-16	512 × 512	35.2	56.4	36.9	17.5	38.3	47.5
CFE-SSDv2-512	ResNet-101	512 × 512	**39.6**	**60.3**	**42.7**	**21.2**	**44.2**	**53.1**
RefineDet320-MS [36]	VGG-16	320 × 320	35.2	56.1	37.7	19.5	37.2	47.0
RefineDet512-MS [36]	VGG-16	512 × 512	37.6	58.7	40.8	22.7	40.3	48.3
RefineDet512-MS [36]	ResNet-101	512 × 512	41.8	62.9	45.7	25.6	45.1	54.1
CFE-SSDv2-300-MS	VGG-16	300 × 300	**36.7**	**58.0**	**39.1**	**21.8**	**39.2**	**47.4**
CFE-SSDv2-512-MS	VGG-16	512 × 512	**39.0**	**60.5**	**41.2**	**25.0**	**42.8**	**48.5**
CFE-SSDv2-512-MS	ResNet-101	512 × 512	**43.1**	**63.2**	**49.2**	**28.9**	**49.1**	**56.1**

FFB. We compare the effectiveness and efficiency of different settings of FFB, CFE-SSDv1 is relatively more efficient while CFE-SSDv2 is more accurate one that achieves a better result. Due to we keep the output channels, concat has only 1/2 input channels as summation operation. Furthermore, we select FFB type of summation (sum shown in Table 4) as the final fusion method for CFE-SSDv2.

CFE on Other Detectors. Moreover, not only SSD, DSSD and RefineDet could also get improvements by the assembling of CFE modules as illustrated in Table 5. The networks are illustrated in Sect. 4. Both of the two detectors insert two CFE modules. The improvement on *Pascal VOC* is relatively less due to the reason that different methods may contribute similarly and somewhat has increased the redundancy instead. We further evaluate it on MS-COCO 2014 minival set and find that the improvement on both detectors is very significant compared with the corresponding original methods.

6.2 Results on *MS COCO*

Besides *Pascal VOC 07*, we also evaluate CFE-SSD on a large detection dataset, *MS COCO*. Although some module congurations may only be suitable for medium/small-scale dataset (*e.g.*, the number of groups may perform differently

Table 7. Comparison between CFE-SSD and state-of-the-art methods on *DETRAC* dataset

Method	Input size	Overall	Easy	Medium	Hard	Cloudy	Night	Rainy	Sunny	FPS
YOLOv2 [25]	544 × 544	57.72	83.28	62.25	42.44	57.97	64.53	47.84	69.75	40
LateralCNN	1000 × 600	67.25	89.56	73.59	51.61	69.11	74.36	55.77	78.66	23.4
SSD [22]	512 × 512	72.56	91.12	77.71	57.83	79.12	73.52	59.03	81.72	22.4
RefineDet [36]	512 × 512	76.38	92.60	83.05	63.03	82.84	78.92	64.19	**87.32**	21.1
CFE-SSDv1	512 × 512	78.72	93.58	84.85	66.15	**84.72**	80.40	69.43	86.97	21.0
CFE-SSDv2	512 × 512	**79.25**	**94.31**	**84.93**	**67.37**	84.35	**80.60**	**70.42**	87.24	20.7
CFE-SSDv2*	512 × 512	**82.68**	**94.60**	**89.71**	**70.65**	**89.81**	**83.02**	**73.35**	**88.11**	-

on larger datasets), we still keep them unchangeable in this experiment for convenience. Except VGG backbone, we also implement experiment with ResNet-101 backbone to compare with state-of-the-art detectors. Table 6 shows the result on *MS COCO* test-dev set. When equipped with VGG, our CFE-SSDv2 300 achieves 30.4% mAP and CFE-SSDv2 512 achieves 35.2% mAP. Specifically, only CFE-SSDv2 exceeds 30% of mAP of the overall detection results when input size is 300 × 300. And the result of small objects exceeds a large margin than other methods, which proves that our method significantly improves to detection small objects. We also compare with the popular efficient network YOLOv3 [26] (19.5 fps), CFE-SSDv2 (16.7 fps) is more accurate with comparable speed. CFE-SSDv2 512 gains 17.5% AP for small objects, 35.2 mAP for overall, which outperforms all of the other one-stage detectors. This emphasizes that the proposed CFE modules largely enhance the detection abilities of shallow layers. When changing to ResNet-101 backbone, the CFE-SSDv2 further get a large improvement. CFE-SSDv2 512 then reaches AP of 39.6 and achieve state-of-the-art results among one-stage detectors, and it also has a speed of 11 fps. In the bottom 6 lines of Table 6, we compare performance with multi-scale inference strategy, both scales of 300 and 512 or VGG and ResNet-101 backbones, CFE-SSDv2 outperforms RefineDet. Notably, The CFE-SSDv2 with multi-scale inference strategy has achieved mAP of 43.1, which is the best accuracy result of one-stage detectors. To demonstrate the targeted improvement of our model, we bolded the best result in Table 6.

6.3 Results on *UA-DETRAC*

UA-DETRAC [33] is a challenging real-world multi-object detection and multi-object tracking benchmark. The dataset contains 10 h of videos captured with a Cannon EOS 550D camera at 24 different locations in China. The videos are recorded at 25 fps, with a resolution of 960 × 540 pixels. Annotation contains 4 categories in total *(car, van, bus, others)*. The difficulty behind this dataset is small and densely distributed cars at varying weather and illuminations (Fig. 4).

As shown in Table 7, *UA-DETRAC* evaluates comprehensive detection results, including Overall, Easy, Medium, Hard, Cloudy, Night, Sunny and Rainy.

Fig. 4. Qualitative result examples. (a) Images from *COCO*, (b) Images from *VOC07*, (c) Images from *UA-DETRAC*, (d) Images from *BDD*.

The result can reflect the complete effectiveness of object detectors. As for comparisons, we select state-of-the-art one-stage detectors, such as SSD and RefineDet. Specifically, CFE-SSD exceeds raw SSD by about 7%, and exceeds

RefineDet nearly by 3%. Our CFE-SSD nearly wins every condition, especially outperforming RefineDet by 4% for hard targets detection. In addition, multi-scale inference strategy make CFE-SSDv2 512 improves to 82.6% finally, ranking first place at the leaderboard. It's noteworthy that the results of RefineDet and SSD are trained and tested by ourselves, while others are from the leaderboard.

6.4   Results on *Berkeley DeepDrive*

BDD [35] is a well-annotated dataset that includes road object detection, instance segmentation, driveable area segmentation and lane markings detection annotations. The road object detection contains 2D bounding boxes annotated on 100,000 images for bus, traffic light, traffic sign, person, bike, truck, motor, car, train, and rider, 10 categories in total. The split ratio of training, validation and testing set is 7:1:2. The evaluated IoU threshold is 0.7 on testing leaderboard.

In experiment, we mainly compare CFE-SSDv2 with original SSD and RefineDet, shown in Table 8. The version with input size of 512 could realize real-time performance while The version with input size of 800 with multi-scale inference strategy achieves the second place of the challenge on the leaderboard. Note that, to evaluate the effects of small object detection, we average the results of *traffic light* and *traffic sign* (denoted by *S-mAP* in Table 8) for comparison.

Table 8. AP and FPS results on BDD

Method	Input size	FPS	mAP (%)	S-mAP (%)
SSD	512 × 512	**23.1**	14.1	9.2
RefineDet [36]	512 × 512	22.3	17.4	13.1
CFE-SSDv2	512 × 512	21.0	**19.1**	**15.4**
CFE-SSDv2	800 × 800	6.2	**22.3**	**18.1**
CFE-SSDv2*	800 × 800	-	**29.7**	**26.0**

7   Conclusions

In this paper, we propose an effective and lightweight feature enhancing module, *i.e.*, CFE module, to improve the detection accuracy of the one-stage detectors. By assembling this module, the performance of the state-of-the-art one-stage detectors can be significantly improved while their efficiency nearly doesn't drop. Specifically, by inserting 4 CFE modules into the network architecture of the most widely used one-stage detector SSD, we get two novel one-stage detectors CFE-SSDv1 and CFE-SSDv2, which have significantly better performance than the original SSD. Experimental results on *PASCAL VOC07* and *MS COCO* datasets show that the CFE-SSDv2 outperforms state-of-the-art methods DSSD and RefineDet, especially for the small objects. Additional ablation study on

PASCAL VOC07 dataset demonstrates the effectiveness of the proposed CFE module. Moreover, CFE-SSDv2 achieves the best result on the *UA-DETRAC* dataset for vehicle detection and ranks second on the *BDD* leaderboard for road object detection, which demonstrate that it is effective for practical applications such as traffic scene video surveillance and autonomous driving.

Acknowledgement. This work is supported by National Natural Science Foundation of China under Grant 61673029. This work is also a research achievement of Key Laboratory of Science, Technology and Standard in Press Industry (Key Laboratory of Intelligent Press Media Technology).

References

1. Bell, S., Zitnick, C.L., Bala, K., Girshick, R.B.: Inside-outside net: detecting objects in context with skip pooling and recurrent neural networks. In: CVPR 2016, pp. 2874–2883 (2016)
2. Chollet, F.: Xception: deep learning with depthwise separable convolutions. In: CVPR 2017, pp. 1800–1807 (2017)
3. Dai, J., Li, Y., He, K., Sun, J.: R-FCN: object detection via region-based fully convolutional networks. In: NIPS (2016)
4. Everingham, M., Gool, L.J.V., Williams, C.K.I., Winn, J.M., Zisserman, A.: The pascal visual object classes (VOC) challenge. Int. J. Comput. Vis. **88**(2), 303–338 (2010)
5. Fu, C., Liu, W., Ranga, A., Tyagi, A., Berg, A.C.: DSSD: deconvolutional single shot detector. CoRR abs/1701.06659 (2017)
6. Gidaris, S., Komodakis, N.: Object detection via a multi-region and semantic segmentation-aware CNN model. In: ICCV 2015, pp. 1134–1142 (2015)
7. Girshick, R.B.: Fast R-CNN. In: ICCV 2015, pp. 1440–1448 (2015)
8. Girshick, R.B., Donahue, J., Darrell, T., Malik, J.: Rich feature hierarchies for accurate object detection and semantic segmentation. In: CVPR 2014, pp. 580–587 (2014)
9. He, K., Gkioxari, G., Dollár, P., Girshick, R.B.: Mask R-CNN. In: ICCV (2017)
10. He, K., Zhang, X., Ren, S., Sun, J.: Delving deep into rectifiers: surpassing human-level performance on imagenet classification. In: ICCV 2015, pp. 1026–1034 (2015)
11. He, K., Zhang, X., Ren, S., Sun, J.: Deep residual learning for image recognition. In: CVPR 2016, pp. 770–778 (2016)
12. Howard, A.G., et al.: MobileNets: efficient convolutional neural networks for mobile vision applications. CoRR abs/1704.04861 (2017)
13. Hu, J., Shen, L., Sun, G.: Squeeze-and-excitation networks. In: CVPR (2018)
14. Kong, T., Sun, F.; Yao, A., Liu, H., Lu, M., Chen, Y.: RON: reverse connection with objectness prior networks for object detection. In: CVPR 2017, pp. 5244–5252 (2017)
15. Kong, T., Yao, A., Chen, Y., Sun, F.: HyperNet: towards accurate region proposal generation and joint object detection. In: CVPR 2016, pp. 845–853 (2016)
16. Li, Z., Peng, C., Yu, G., Zhang, X., Deng, Y., Sun, J.: Light-head R-CNN: in defense of two-stage object detector. CoRR abs/1711.07264 (2017)
17. Lin, M., Chen, Q., Yan, S.: Network in network. In: ICLR (2014)
18. Lin, T., Dollár, P., Girshick, R.B., He, K., Hariharan, B., Belongie, S.J.: Feature pyramid networks for object detection. In: CVPR 2017, pp. 936–944 (2017)

19. Lin, T., Goyal, P., Girshick, R.B., He, K., Dollár, P.: Focal loss for dense object detection. In: ICCV 2017, pp. 2999–3007 (2017)
20. Lin, T.-Y., et al.: Microsoft COCO: common objects in context. In: Fleet, D., Pajdla, T., Schiele, B., Tuytelaars, T. (eds.) ECCV 2014. LNCS, vol. 8693, pp. 740–755. Springer, Cham (2014). https://doi.org/10.1007/978-3-319-10602-1_48
21. Liu, S., Qi, L., Qin, H., Shi, J., Jia, J.: Path aggregation network for instance segmentation. In: CVPR (2018)
22. Liu, W., et al.: SSD: single shot multibox detector. In: Leibe, B., Matas, J., Sebe, N., Welling, M. (eds.) ECCV 2016. LNCS, vol. 9905, pp. 21–37. Springer, Cham (2016). https://doi.org/10.1007/978-3-319-46448-0_2
23. Peng, C., Zhang, X., Yu, G., Luo, G., Sun, J.: Large kernel matters - improve semantic segmentation by global convolutional network. In: 2017 IEEE Conference on Computer Vision and Pattern Recognition, CVPR 2017, Honolulu, HI, USA, 21–26 July 2017, pp. 1743–1751 (2017)
24. Redmon, J., Divvala, S.K., Girshick, R.B., Farhadi, A.: You only look once: unified, real-time object detection. In: CVPR 2016, pp. 779–788 (2016)
25. Redmon, J., Farhadi, A.: YOLO9000: better, faster, stronger. In: CVPR 2017, pp. 6517–6525 (2017)
26. Redmon, J., Farhadi, A.: YOLOv3: an incremental improvement. arXiv (2018)
27. Ren, S., He, K., Girshick, R.B., Sun, J.: Faster R-CNN: towards real-time object detection with region proposal networks. In: Annual Conference on Neural Information Processing Systems 2015, pp. 91–99 (2015)
28. Shen, Z., Liu, Z., Li, J., Jiang, Y., Chen, Y., Xue, X.: DSOD: learning deeply supervised object detectors from scratch. In: ICCV 2017, pp. 1937–1945 (2017)
29. Simonyan, K., Zisserman, A.: Very deep convolutional networks for large-scale image recognition. CoRR abs/1409.1556 (2014)
30. Szegedy, C., et al.: Going deeper with convolutions. In: CVPR 2015, pp. 1–9 (2015)
31. Szegedy, C., Vanhoucke, V., Ioffe, S., Shlens, J., Wojna, Z.: Rethinking the inception architecture for computer vision. In: CVPR 2016, pp. 2818–2826 (2016)
32. Uijlings, J.R.R., van de Sande, K.E.A., Gevers, T., Smeulders, A.W.M.: Selective search for object recognition. Int. J. Comput. Vis **104**(2), 154–171 (2013)
33. Wen, L., et al.: UA-DETRAC: a new benchmark and protocol for multi-object detection and tracking. arXiv CoRR abs/1511.04136 (2015)
34. Xie, S., Girshick, R.B., Dollár, P., Tu, Z., He, K.: Aggregated residual transformations for deep neural networks. In: CVPR 2017, pp. 5987–5995 (2017)
35. Yu, F., et al.: BDD100K: a diverse driving video database with scalable annotation tooling. CoRR abs/1805.04687 (2018)
36. Zhang, S., Wen, L., Bian, X., Lei, Z., Li, S.Z.: Single-shot refinement neural network for object detection. In: CVPR (2018)

SingleGAN: Image-to-Image Translation by a Single-Generator Network Using Multiple Generative Adversarial Learning

Xiaoming Yu, Xing Cai, Zhenqiang Ying, Thomas Li, and Ge Li[✉]

School of Electronic and Computer Engineering, Shenzhen Graduate School,
Peking University, Shenzhen, China
{xiaomingyu,caixing46,zqying}@pku.edu.cn, thomasli@pkusz.edu.cn,
geli@ece.pku.edu.cn

Abstract. Image translation is a burgeoning field in computer vision where the goal is to learn the mapping between an input image and an output image. However, most recent methods require multiple generators for modeling different domain mappings, which are inefficient and ineffective on some multi-domain image translation tasks. In this paper, we propose a novel method, SingleGAN, to perform multi-domain image-to-image translations with a single generator. We introduce the domain code to explicitly control the different generative tasks and integrate multiple optimization goals to ensure the translation. Experimental results on several unpaired datasets show superior performance of our model in translation between two domains. Besides, we explore variants of SingleGAN for different tasks, including one-to-many domain translation, many-to-many domain translation and one-to-one domain translation with multimodality. The extended experiments show the universality and extensibility of our model.

Keywords: GANs · Image-to-image translation

1 Introduction

Recently, more and more attention has been paid to image-to-image translation due to its exciting potential in a variety of image processing applications [9]. Although existing methods show impressive results on one-to-one mapping problems, they need to build multiple generators for modeling multiple mappings, which are inefficient and ineffective in some multi-domain and multi-model image translation tasks. Intuitively, many multi-mapping translation tasks are not independent and share some common features such as scene contents in transformations between different seasons. By sharing a network between related tasks, we can enable our model to generalize better on each separated task. In this paper,

---

X. Yu and X. Cai—Indicates equal contribution.

© Springer Nature Switzerland AG 2019
C. V. Jawahar et al. (Eds.): ACCV 2018, LNCS 11365, pp. 341–356, 2019.
https://doi.org/10.1007/978-3-030-20873-8_22

we propose a single-generator generative adversarial network (GAN), called SingleGAN, to solve multi-mapping translation tasks effectively and efficiently. To indicate a specific mapping, we introduce the domain code as an auxiliary input to the network. Then we integrate multiple optimization goals to learn each specific translation.

As illustrated in Fig. 1, the base SingleGAN model is utilized to learn the bijection between two domains. Since each domain dataset is not required to have the label of other domains, SingleGAN can make full use of the existing different datasets to learn the multi-domain translation.

To explore the potential and generality of SingleGAN, we also extend it to three cross domains translation tasks, which are more complex and practical. The first variant model tries to address the one-to-many domain translation task that processes a source domain input to a different target domains, such as the image style transfer. The Second model explore the many-to-many domain translation task. Unlike the recent method [5] requires detailed annotation of category information to training the auxiliary classifier, we use multiple adversarial objects to help network captures different domain distribution separately. It means that SingleGAN is capable of learning multi-domain mappings by weakly supervised learning since we do not need to label all the training data with detailed annotation. The third variant model attempts to increase the generative diversity by introducing attribute latent code. A similar idea is used in BicycleGAN [33] to address the multimodal translation problem. Our third model can be considered a generalization of BicycleGAN towards unpaired image-to-image translation.

To summarize, our contributions are as follows:

- We propose SingleGAN, a novel GAN that utilizes a single generator and a group of discriminators to accomplish the unpaired image-to-image translation.
- We show the generality and flexibility of SingleGAN by extending it to achieve three different kinds of translation tasks.
- Experimental results demonstrate that our approach is more effective and general-purpose than several state-of-art methods.

2   Related Work

2.1   Generative Adversarial Networks

Influenced by a zero-sum game, a typical GAN model consists of two modules: a generator and a discriminator. While the discriminator learns to distinguish between real and fake samples, the generator learns to generate fake samples that are indistinguishable from real samples. The GANs have shown impressive results in various computer vision tasks such as image generation, image editing [3] and representation learning [21]. Recently, GAN-based conditional image generation has also been actively studied. To be specific, the various of extension GANs have achieved good results in many generation tasks such as image inpainting [20], super-resolution [15], text2image [22], as well as to other domains such as videos [26] and 3D data [27]. In this paper, we propose a scalable GAN framework to achieve image translation based on conditional image generation.

2.2 Image-to-Image Translation

The idea of image-to-image translation goes back to Image Analogies [8], in which Hertzmann *et al.* proposed a network to transfer the texture information from a source modality space onto a target modality space. Image-to-image translation has received more attention since the flourishing growth of GANs. The pioneering work, Pix2pix [9] uses cGAN [19] to perform supervised image translation from paired data. As those methods adopt supervised learning, sufficient paired data are required to train the network. However, preparing paired images can be time-consuming and laborious (*e.g.* artistic stylization) and even impossible for some applications (*e.g.* male to female face transfiguration). To address this issue, For example, CycleGAN [32], DiscoGAN [11] and DualGAN [28] introduce a cycle-consistency constraint, which widely used in visual tracking [25] and language domain [2], to learn convincing mappings across image domains from unpaired images. Based on a shared-latent space assumption, UNIT [16] extends the Coupled GAN [17] to learn a joint distribution of different domains without paired images. FaderNet [14] is also successful in the controlling of attributes by adding the discriminator to the latent space. Even though, these methods have promoted the development of one-to-one mapping image translation, they have limitations in scalability for multi-mapping translation. By introducing an auxiliary classifier in the discriminator, StarGAN [5] achieved translation among different facial attributes with a single generator. However, this method may learn an inefficient domain mapping when the attribute labels are not sufficient for training the auxiliary classifier even if it introduces a mask vector.

3 Base Model

The main architecture is shown in Fig. 1. In order to take advantage of the correlation between two related tasks, SingleGAN adopts a single generator to achieve bi-direction translation.

The goal of the model is to learn a mapping $G : A \leftrightarrow B$. By adding the domain code, G is redefined as

$$
\begin{aligned}
x_B^{fake} &= G(x_A, z_B), \\
x_A^{fake} &= G(x_B, z_A),
\end{aligned}
\tag{1}
$$

where x_*^{fake} is the fake sample generated by the generator, sample x_* belongs to the set of domain χ_* and z_A, z_B are domain code for domain A and domain B respectively.

3.1 Domain Code Injection

For capturing the distribution of different domains with a single generator, it is necessary to indicate the mapping with auxiliary information. Therefore, we introduce the domain code z to label the different mapping in the generator. The domain code is constructed as a one-hot vector and similar to the latent code that is widely used to indicated the attributes of generated image [4,33].

Recent work [29] shows that different injection methods of latent code will effect the performance of generation model. So we adopt the central biasing instance normalization (CBIN) proposed in [29] to inject the domain code in our SingleGAN model. CBIN is defined as

$$\mathrm{CBIN}(x_i) = \frac{x_i - \mathrm{E}[x_i]}{\sqrt{\mathrm{Var}[x_i]}} + \tanh(f_i(z)), \tag{2}$$

where i is the index of feature maps, f_i is affine transformation applied on the domain code z and its parameters are learned for each feature map x_i in one layer. The CBIN aims to adjust the different distributions of input feature maps adaptively with learnable parameters, which makes the domain code able to manage the different tasks. Meanwhile, the distance between the different distributions of input data is also trainable, which means that the coupling degree of different tasks is determined by the model itself. This advantage enables different tasks to share parameters better, so as to promote each other better.

3.2 Loss Functions

GAN Loss. Since our single generator has multi-domain outputs, we set up adversarial objectives for each target domain and employ a group of discriminators. The corresponding discriminator is used to identify the generated images in one domain. The adversarial loss is defined as

$$\begin{aligned}
\mathcal{L}_{adv}(G, D_\mathrm{A}) &= \mathbb{E}_{\chi_\mathrm{A}}[\log(D_\mathrm{A}(x_\mathrm{A}))] + \mathbb{E}_{\chi_\mathrm{B}, z_\mathrm{A}}[\log(1 - D_\mathrm{A}(G(x_\mathrm{B}, z_\mathrm{A})))], \\
\mathcal{L}_{adv}(G, D_\mathrm{B}) &= \mathbb{E}_{\chi_\mathrm{B}}[\log(D_\mathrm{B}(x_\mathrm{B}))] + \mathbb{E}_{\chi_\mathrm{A}, z_\mathrm{B}}[\log(1 - D_\mathrm{B}(G(x_\mathrm{A}, z_\mathrm{B})))].
\end{aligned} \tag{3}$$

By optimizing multiple generative adversarial objectives, the generator recovers different domain distributions that indicated by domain code z.

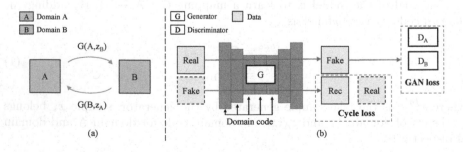

Fig. 1. (a) The base model contains two mapping direction: A → B and B → A. (b) Our base model architecture, which consists of a generator and a group of discriminators.

Cycle Consistency Loss. Although the above GAN loss can complete domain translation, highly under-constrained mapping often leads to a mode collapse. There are many possible mappings that can be inferred without the use of pairing information.

To reduce the space of the possible mappings, we use the cycle-consistency constraint [5,32] in the training stage. The cycle consistency loss is defined as $x_A \approx G(G(x_A, z_B), z_A)$ and $x_B \approx G(G(x_B, z_A), z_B)$ in our model. The formula of the cycle consistency loss is defined as

$$
\begin{aligned}
\mathcal{L}_{cyc}(G) = \mathbb{E}_{\chi_A}\big[\,\|x_A - G(G(x_A, z_B), z_A)\|_1\,\big] + \\
\mathbb{E}_{\chi_B}\big[\,\|x_B - G(G(x_B, z_A), z_B)\|_1\,\big],
\end{aligned}
\tag{4}
$$

where $\|\cdot\|_1$ denotes ℓ_1 norm.

Full Objective. The final objective function is defined as

$$
G^* = arg \min_{G} \max_{D_A, D_B} \sum_{i \in \{A,B\}} \mathcal{L}_{adv}(G, D_i) + \lambda_{cyc} \cdot \mathcal{L}_{cyc}(G)
\tag{5}
$$

where λ_{cyc} controls the relative importance of the two objectives.

4 Extended Models

To explore the potential and generality of SingleGAN, based on the above model, we extend three variants of our model to different tasks: one-to-many domain translation, many-to-many domain translation and one-to-one domain translation with multi-modal mapping.

4.1 One-to-Many Domain Translation

The first trial in Fig. 2(a) applies to unidirectional tasks, for example multi-task detection and image multi-style transfer. As far as image style transfer is concerned, different style transfer from a single input image is a representative

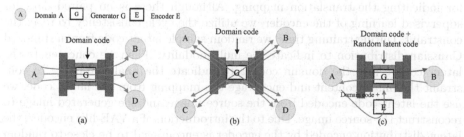

Fig. 2. Extended models: (a) one-to-many domain translation, (b) many-to-many domain translation, (c) one-to-one domain translation with multi-modal mapping.

task of sharing semantics. Our model shares the same texture information of the input image and apply different styles on it. Compared with traditional image style transfer methods, which learn mapping between one content image and one style image, our model learn different mappings between image collections. Such one-to-three translation task are shown in Fig. 2(a), the $\mathcal{L}_{adv}$ is redefined as

$$\mathcal{L}_{adv}(G, D_{\{B,C,D\}}) = \sum_{i \in \{B,C,D\}} (\mathbb{E}_{\chi_i}[\log(D_i(x_i))] + \mathbb{E}_{\chi_A,z_i}[\log(1 - D_i(G(x_A, z_i)))]),$$

(6)

where A is the source domain and B, C, D are target domains. In the meantime, the cycle consistency loss is modified to

$$\mathcal{L}_{cyc}(G) = \sum_{i \in \{B,C,D\}} (\mathbb{E}_{\chi_A}[\|G(G(x_A, z_i), z_A)\|_1] + \mathbb{E}_{\chi_i}[\|G(G(x_i, z_A), z_i)\|_1]).$$

(7)

4.2   Many-to-Many Domain Translation

As illustrated in Fig. 2(b), the second variation shows images in multi-domain translating to each other. In this model, our goal is to train a single generator that can learns mappings among multiple domains and realize the mutual transformation of multiple domains. For a four-domain transfer instance, the $\mathcal{L}_{adv}$ is redefined as

$$\mathcal{L}_{adv}(G, D_{\{A,B,C,D\}}) = \sum_{i,j \in \{A,B,C,D\}} (\mathbb{E}_{\chi_i}[\log(D_i(x_i))] +$$

$$\mathbb{E}_{\chi_j,z_i}[\log(1 - D_i(G(x_j, z_i)))]),$$

(8)

and the $\mathcal{L}_{cyc}$ also needs to be modified like the extended model (a).

4.3   One-to-One Domain Translation with Multi-modal Mapping

To address the multi-modal image-to-image translation problem with unpaired data, we introduce the third variant as show in Fig. 2(c). Inspired by Bicycle-GAN [33], we introduce the VAE-like encoder to extract feature latent code c for indicating the translation mapping. Although there is no paired data for supervised learning of the encoder, we utilize the cycle consistency to relax the constraint. During training time, we random sample latent code from a standard Gaussian distribution to indicate the multimodality. Then we concatenate the latent code c into the domain code z to indicate the final mapping. To constraint the image content and encourage the mapping from the latent code, we use the latent code encoded from the source image and the generated image to reconstruct the source image. Due to the introduction of a VAE-like encoder, the latent distribution encoded by the encoder is encouraged to be close to random Gaussian

$$\mathcal{L}_{KL}(E) = \mathbb{E}_{\chi_B}[D_{KL}(E(x_B)\|\mathcal{N}(0, I))],$$

(9)

where $D_{KL}(p\|q) = -\int p(c)\log\frac{p(c)}{q(c)}dc$. To enforce the generator utilizing the latent code, the reconstruction latent code loss is also used

$$\mathcal{L}_1^{VAE}(G,E) = \mathbb{E}_{\chi_A,c}\|c - E(G(x_A,c))\|_1. \tag{10}$$

Combining these two losses with the loss of base model, our model can solve the problem of the lack of diversity in unpaired image translation. Notice that we only discuss the translation of A-to-B, as the mapping of B-to-A is similar and concurrent during training time.

5 Implementation

5.1 Network Architecture

As in [5,10,29,32], our generator G uses the ResNet [7] structure with an encoder-decoder framework, which contains two stride-2 convolution layers for downsampling, six residual blocks and two stride-2 transposed convolution layers for upsampling. We replace all normalization layers except upsampling layers with CBIN layers. For the discriminators D, we use two discriminators [9] to discriminate the real and fake images in different scales. For the experiment of multi-modal SingleGAN, the encoder model E adopts the ResNet structure [33]. We equip the encoder with CBIN, so it can also extract the latent information from different domain images. Code and model are available at https://github. com/Xiaoming-Yu/SingleGAN.

5.2 Training Details

For all experiments, we train all models with Adam optimizer [12], setting $\beta_1 = 0.5$, $\lambda_{cyc} = 10$, learning rate of 0.001. In the extended multi-modal networks as shown in Fig. 2(c), the weights for $\mathcal{L}_{KL}(E)$ and $\mathcal{L}_1^{VAE}(G,E)$ are 0.1 and 0.5 respectively. To generate higher quality results with stable training, we replace the negative log likelihood objective by a least-squares loss [18].

5.3 Structure of Domain Code

As mentioned in Sect. 3.1, we use the one-hot vector to present the domain code z. To the base model, we use the 2 dimensional domain code for indicating the mapping between domain A $\leftrightarrow$ B. For the one-to-many and many-to-many translation instances illustrated in Fig. 2, the domain code is 4 dimension and represents 4 different domains. In the third variant, the 8 dimensional latent code c is also used for multimodal image translation in the specific domain that indicated by the 2 dimensional domain code.

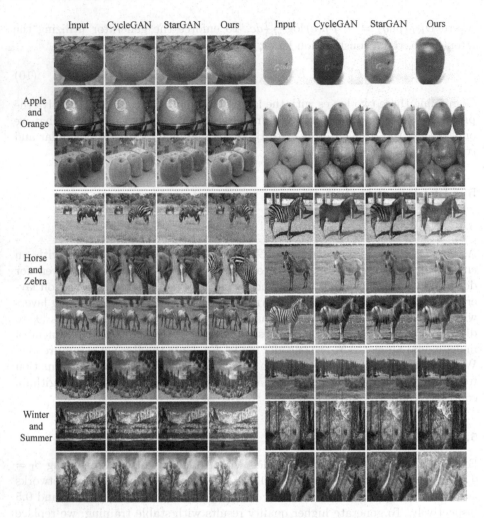

Fig. 3. Visualization and comparison on three unpaired datasets. The first four columns show mapping from domain A to domain B while the next four columns show mapping from domain B to domain A.

6   Experiments

6.1   Datasets

To evaluate the base model, we use three unpaired datasets: Apple↔Orange, Horse↔Zebra, and Summer↔Winter [32]. As for the three extended models, we use Photo↔Art [32] for one-to-many translation, Transient-Attributes [13] for many-to-many translation, and Edges↔Photos [9] for one-to-one multi-model translation. All of the images are scale to 128 × 128 resolution.

Table 1. The classification accuracy for three datasets. Best results are in boldface.

	Horse & Zebra	Apple & Orange	Summer & Winter
Image number	240	480	500
Real image	0.985	0.978	0.827
CycleGAN	0.850	0.935	0.644
StarGAN	0.858	**0.970**	0.689
SingleGAN	**0.859**	0.966	**0.742**

Table 2. The perceptual distance for three datasets. Best results are in boldface. Here A represents horse, apple or summer, and B represents zebra, orange or winter.

	Real image		CycleGAN		StarGAN		SingleGAN	
	A	B	A	B	A	B	A	B
Horse & Zebra	1.198	1.177	**1.141**	**1.133**	1.083	1.081	1.112	1.128
Apple & Orange	1.205	1.499	1.106	1.144	1.128	1.132	**1.152**	**1.164**
Summer & Winter	1.272	1.824	1.223	1.189	1.209	1.173	**1.258**	**1.208**

6.2 Baselines

To compare the performance of our SingleGAN model, we adopt the Cycle-GAN [32] and StarGAN [5] as our baseline models. CycleGAN uses cycle loss to learn the mapping between two different domains. To achieve cycle consistency, CycleGAN requires two generators and discriminators for two different domains. To unify multi-domain translation with single generator, StarGAN introduces an auxiliary classifier trained on image-label pairs in its discriminator to assist the generator to learn the mapping cross multiple domains. We compare our method with CycleGAN and StarGAN on two domains translation tasks.

6.3 Base Model Comparison

In this section, we evaluate the performance of different models. It should be noted that both SingleGAN and StarGAN use a single generator for two domain image translation and CycleGAN uses two generators to achieve the similar mappings.

The qualitative comparison is shown in Fig. 3. We can observe that all these models present pleasant results in the simple case such as the apple to orange transformation. In the translation with complex scene, the performance of these models are degraded especially StarGAN. The possible reason is that the generator of StarGAN introduces the adversarial noise to fool the auxiliary classifier and fails to learn the effective mapping. Meanwhile, we can observer that SingleGAN presents the best results in most cases.

To judge the quality of the generated image quantitatively, we evaluate the classification accuracy of the images generated by these three models at first.

We train three Xception [6] based binary classifiers for each image datasets. The baseline is the classification accuracy in real images. Higher classification accuracy means that the generated images may more easy to distinguish. Second, we compare the domain consistency between real images and generated images by computing average distance in feature space. A similar idea is used for calculating the diversity of multi-modal generation task [29,33]. We use the cosine similarity to evaluate the perceptual distance in the feature space of the VGG-16 network [24] that pre-trained in ImageNet [23]. We sum across the five convolution layers preceding the pool layers. The larger the value, the more similar between two images. In the test stage, we randomly sample the real image and the generated image from same domain to make up the data pair. Then we compute the average distance between 2,000 pairs. The baseline is computed by sampling from 2,000 pairs of real images.

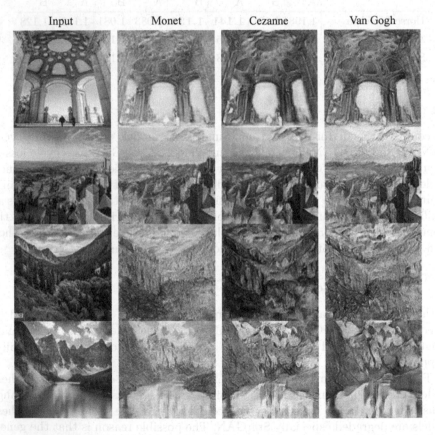

Fig. 4. The one-to-many translation results of multi-style image generation. The first column is the real images and the rest of columns are the translation results that represent different artistic styles.

The quantitative results are shown in Tables 1 and 2. Both SingleGAN and CycleGAN produce the quantitative results that comply with qualitative performance. In contrast, StarGAN gets a higher classification accuracy but the poor performance in domain consistency. It validates our conjecture that the generated image of StarGAN may have the adversarial noise of fooling the classifier in some complex scenes. In StarGAN, the discriminator learns to tell the image is real or fake without considering the classification result of the image while the generator learns to fool the discriminator with an image that can be corrected classified by the auxiliary classifier. So the generator may not get enough encouragement if it generates the adversarial noise to the image. For example, on the task of Summer↔Winter, although the input summer image is expected to translate into winter, the generator of StarGAN tends to just add a tiny adversarial noise to the input image so that the discriminator still tell it is real while the classifier classifies it as the winter. As a result, the generated images will look unchanged to human but win high classification scores. This issue does not exist in SingleGAN and CycleGAN since these models optimizes different mappings with different discriminators. The main difference between SingleGAN and CycleGAN is the number of generators. As shown in Fig. 3 and Tables 1, 2,

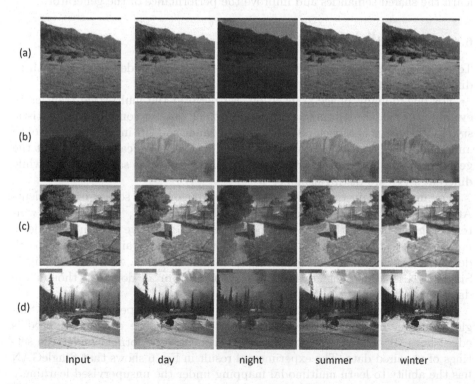

Fig. 5. The many-to-many domain translation results. The first column is the input images from different domains: (a) day, (b) night, (c) summer, (d) winter. The remaining columns are the transfer results.

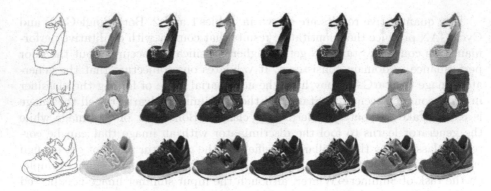

Fig. 6. The multi-modal translation results. The first column shows the input and the other columns show randomly generated samples.

we can observer that SingleGAN has the capacity to learn multiple mapping without performance degradation. By sharing the generator for different domain translation, SingleGAN can see more training data form different domains to learn the shared semantics and improve the performance of the generator.

6.4 Extended Model Evaluation

To explore the potential of SingleGAN, we test the extended models on three different translation tasks.

For one-to-many image translation, we perform the multi-style transfer to evaluate the model performance. Photo↔Art [32] dataset contains three artistic styles (500 images of Monet, 584 images of Cezanne and 401 images of Van Gogh) and 1000 real photos. The results are shown in Fig. 4. We can observe that the generate images have similar artistic styles when we perform same mapping while different styles are distinguishable.

For multi-domain translation, we choose four outdoor scenes in Transient-Attributes dataset [13] to evaluate the model: 'day', 'night', 'summer' and 'winter'. It should be note that the multiple domains do not have to be independent, *e.g.* the subset 'day' contains summer and winter. The training data for each domain do not need to consider other domain information. As shown in Fig. 5, SingleGAN is competent at the transformation from all domains, though the dataset has incomplete labels.

The final experiment is to verify the multi-modal performance of SingleGAN after introducing the attribute latent code. The dataset adopted is edge2shoes [31]. Please Note that this experiment is performed under the settings of unpaired data. The experimental result in Fig. 6 shows that SingleGAN has the ability to learn multimodal mapping under the unsupervised learning.

Fig. 7. Saliency and edge detection results of SingleGAN under paired data setting.

6.5 Translation Under Paired Data Setting

Although the above experiments have the unpaired data assumption, SingleGAN can also perform multi-domain image translation with paired data by replacing the cycle consistency loss $\mathcal{L}_{cyc}$ with ℓ_1 reconstruction loss $\mathcal{L}_{rec}$.

Here we use the salient object dataset DUTS-TR [30] and BSDS500 edge dataset [1] to perform one-to-many image translation. Specify the real image as domain A, salient images as domain B and edge images as domain C. Then the $\mathcal{L}_{rec}$ can define as

$$
\begin{aligned}
\mathcal{L}_{rec}(G) = \mathbb{E}_{\chi_A, \chi_B}\big[\, \|x_B - G(x_A, z_B)\|_1 \,\big] + \\
\mathbb{E}_{\chi_A, \chi_C}\big[\, \|x_C - G(x_A, z_C)\|_1 \,\big].
\end{aligned}
\tag{11}
$$

The results in Fig. 7 demonstrate the effectiveness of SingleGAN.

6.6 Limitations and Discussion

Although SingleGAN can achieve multi-domain image translations, multiple adversarial learning needs to be done simultaneously. This constraint makes SingleGAN only be able to learn limited domain translation at a time since our storage is limited. So it is valuable to explore the transfer learning for the existing models. Besides, the capacity of the network to learning different mappings is also an important problem. We also observe that integrate suitable tasks for one single model may improve the performance of the generator. But what kind of tasks can promote each other remains to be explored in the future work. Nonetheless, we think the method proposed in this paper is valuable for exploring the multi-domain generation works.

7 Conclusion

In this paper we introduce a single generator based model, SingleGAN, for learning multi-mapping image-to-image translation. By introducing multiple adversarial learning for the generator, SingleGAN is able to learn a variety of mappings effectively and efficiently. Contrastive experimental results show quantitatively and qualitatively that our approach is effective in many image translation tasks. Furthermore, to improve the versatility and generality of the model, we present three variants of SingleGAN for different tasks: one-to-many domain transfer, many-to-many domain transfer and one-to-one domain transfer with varying attributes. The experiment results demonstrate these variants improve the corresponding translation effectively.

Acknowledgments. This work was supported in part by the Shenzhen Key Laboratory for Intelligent Multimedia and Virtual Reality (No. ZDSYS20170 3031405467), Project of National Engineering Laboratory for Video Technology - Shenzhen Division, National Natural Science Foundation of China and Guangdong Province Scientific Research on Big Data (No. U1611461), and Shenzhen Municipal Science and Technology Program under Grant JCYJ20170818141146428.

References

1. Arbelaez, P., Maire, M., Fowlkes, C., Malik, J.: Contour detection and hierarchical image segmentation. IEEE Trans. Pattern Anal. Mach. Intell. **33**(5), 898–916 (2011)
2. Brislin, R.W.: Back-translation for cross-cultural research. J. Cross-Cult. Psychol. **1**(3), 185–216 (1970)
3. Brock, A., Lim, T., Ritchie, J.M., Weston, N.: Neural photo editing with introspective adversarial networks. In: ICLR (2017)
4. Chen, X., Duan, Y., Houthooft, R., Schulman, J., Sutskever, I., Abbeel, P.: Infogan: interpretable representation learning by information maximizing generative adversarial nets. In: Advances in Neural Information Processing Systems, pp. 2172–2180 (2016)
5. Choi, Y., Choi, M., Kim, M., Ha, J.W., Kim, S., Choo, J.: Stargan: unified generative adversarial networks for multi-domain image-to-image translation. In: 2018 IEEE Conference on Computer Vision and Pattern Recognition (CVPR) (2018)
6. Chollet, F.: Xception: deep learning with depthwise separable convolutions, pp. 1800–1807 (2016)
7. He, K., Zhang, X., Ren, S., Sun, J.: Deep residual learning for image recognition. In: Proceedings of the IEEE Conference on Computer Vision and Pattern Recognition, pp. 770–778 (2016)
8. Hertzmann, A., Jacobs, C.E., Oliver, N., Curless, B., Salesin, D.H.: Image analogies. In: Proceedings of the 28th Annual Conference on Computer Graphics and Interactive Techniques, pp. 327–340. ACM (2001)

9. Isola, P., Zhu, J.Y., Zhou, T., Efros, A.A.: Image-to-image translation with conditional adversarial networks. In: 2017 IEEE Conference on Computer Vision and Pattern Recognition (CVPR) (2017)

10. Johnson, J., Alahi, A., Fei-Fei, L.: Perceptual losses for real-time style transfer and super-resolution. In: Leibe, B., Matas, J., Sebe, N., Welling, M. (eds.) ECCV 2016. LNCS, vol. 9906, pp. 694–711. Springer, Cham (2016). https://doi.org/10.1007/978-3-319-46475-6_43

11. Kim, T., Cha, M., Kim, H., Lee, J.K., Kim, J.: Learning to discover cross-domain relations with generative adversarial networks. In: International Conference on Machine Learning, pp. 1857–1865 (2017)

12. Kinga, D., Adam, J.B.: A method for stochastic optimization. In: International Conference on Learning Representations (ICLR) (2015)

13. Laffont, P.Y., Ren, Z., Tao, X., Qian, C., Hays, J.: Transient attributes for high-level understanding and editing of outdoor scenes. ACM Trans. Graph. (Proc. SIGGRAPH) 33(4), 149 (2014)

14. Lample, G., Zeghidour, N., Usunier, N., Bordes, A., Denoyer, L., et al.: Fader networks: manipulating images by sliding attributes. In: Advances in Neural Information Processing Systems, pp. 5969–5978 (2017)

15. Ledig, C., et al.: Photo-realistic single image super-resolution using a generative adversarial network. In: 2017 IEEE Conference on Computer Vision and Pattern Recognition (CVPR) (2017)

16. Liu, M.Y., Breuel, T., Kautz, J.: Unsupervised image-to-image translation networks. In: Advances in Neural Information Processing Systems, pp. 700–708 (2017)

17. Liu, M.Y., Tuzel, O.: Coupled generative adversarial networks. In: Advances in Neural Information Processing Systems, pp. 469–477 (2016)

18. Mao, X., Li, Q., Xie, H., Lau, R.Y., Wang, Z., Smolley, S.P.: Least squares generative adversarial networks. In: 2017 IEEE International Conference on Computer Vision (ICCV), pp. 2813–2821. IEEE (2017)

19. Mirza, M., Osindero, S.: Conditional generative adversarial nets. arXiv preprint arXiv:1411.1784 (2014)

20. Pathak, D., Krahenbuhl, P., Donahue, J., Darrell, T., Efros, A.A.: Context encoders: feature learning by inpainting. In: Proceedings of the IEEE Conference on Computer Vision and Pattern Recognition, pp. 2536–2544 (2016)

21. Radford, A., Metz, L., Chintala, S.: Unsupervised representation learning with deep convolutional generative adversarial networks. In: ICLR (2016)

22. Reed, S., Akata, Z., Yan, X., Logeswaran, L., Schiele, B., Lee, H.: Generative adversarial text to image synthesis. In: International Conference on Machine Learning, pp. 1060–1069 (2016)

23. Russakovsky, O., et al.: Imagenet large scale visual recognition challenge. Int. J. Comput. Vis. 115(3), 211–252 (2015)

24. Simonyan, K., Zisserman, A.: Very deep convolutional networks for large-scale image recognition. Computer Science (2014)

25. Sundaram, N., Brox, T., Keutzer, K.: Dense point trajectories by GPU-accelerated large displacement optical flow. In: Daniilidis, K., Maragos, P., Paragios, N. (eds.) ECCV 2010. LNCS, vol. 6311, pp. 438–451. Springer, Heidelberg (2010). https://doi.org/10.1007/978-3-642-15549-9_32

26. Vondrick, C., Pirsiavash, H., Torralba, A.: Generating videos with scene dynamics. In: Advances in Neural Information Processing Systems, pp. 613–621 (2016)

27. Wu, J., Zhang, C., Xue, T., Freeman, B., Tenenbaum, J.: Learning a probabilistic latent space of object shapes via 3D generative-adversarial modeling. In: Advances in Neural Information Processing Systems, pp. 82–90 (2016)

28. Yi, Z., Zhang, H., Tan, P., Gong, M.: Dualgan: unsupervised dual learning for image-to-image translation. In: IEEE International Conference on Computer Vision, pp. 2868–2876 (2017)
29. Yu, X., Ying, Z., Li, T., Liu, S., Li, G.: Multi-mapping image-to-image translation with central biasing normalization. arXiv preprint arXiv:1806.10050 (2018)
30. Zhao, R., Ouyang, W., Li, H., Wang, X.: Saliency detection by multi-context deep learning. In: Proceedings of the IEEE Conference on Computer Vision and Pattern Recognition, pp. 1265–1274 (2015)
31. Zhu, J.-Y., Krähenbühl, P., Shechtman, E., Efros, A.A.: Generative visual manipulation on the natural image manifold. In: Leibe, B., Matas, J., Sebe, N., Welling, M. (eds.) ECCV 2016. LNCS, vol. 9909, pp. 597–613. Springer, Cham (2016). https://doi.org/10.1007/978-3-319-46454-1_36
32. Zhu, J.Y., Park, T., Isola, P., Efros, A.A.: Unpaired image-to-image translation using cycle-consistent adversarial networkss. In: 2017 IEEE International Conference on Computer Vision (ICCV) (2017)
33. Zhu, J.Y., et al.: Toward multimodal image-to-image translation. In: Advances in Neural Information Processing Systems 30 (2017)

Deep Embedding Using Bayesian Risk Minimization with Application to Sketch Recognition

Anand Mishra[1]($\boxtimes$) and Ajeet Kumar Singh[2]

[1] Department of Computational and Data Sciences,
Indian Institute of Science, Bangalore, India
anandmishra@iisc.ac.in
[2] TCS Research, Pune, India
ajeetk.singh1@tcs.com

Abstract. In this paper, we address the problem of hand-drawn sketch recognition. Inspired by the Bayesian decision theory, we present a deep metric learning loss with the objective to minimize the Bayesian risk of misclassification. We estimate this risk for every mini-batch during training, and learn robust deep embeddings by backpropagating it to a deep neural network in an end-to-end trainable paradigm. Our learnt embeddings are discriminative and robust despite of intra-class variations and inter-class similarities naturally present in hand-drawn sketch images. Outperforming the state of the art on sketch recognition, our method achieves 82.2% and 88.7% on *TU-Berlin-250* and *TU-Berlin-160* benchmarks respectively.

Keywords: Bayesian decision theory · Metric learning · Sketch recognition

1 Introduction

Hand-drawn sketches have been effective tools for communication from the ancient times. With the advancements in technology, e.g., touch screen devices, sketching has become much easier and convenient way of communication in the modern era. Moreover, sketch recognition has numerous applications in many real-world areas, examples include education, human-computer interaction, sketch-based search and game design. Considering its importance, research on sketch recognition [6,15,30], sketch-to-image retrieval [14,27,28] and facial sketch recognition [9,23,26] have gained huge interest in past few years.

In this work, we aim to recognize hand-drawn sketch images. It is a challenging task due to following. (i) sketches are abstract description of objects (Fig. 1(a)), (ii) sketches have large intra-class variation and large inter-class similarity (Fig. 1(b)), and (iii) sketches lack visual cues, e.g., absence of color and texture (Fig. 1(c)). Overcoming these challenges to some extent Yu *et al.* [30] and

© Springer Nature Switzerland AG 2019
C. V. Jawahar et al. (Eds.): ACCV 2018, LNCS 11365, pp. 357–370, 2019.
https://doi.org/10.1007/978-3-030-20873-8_23

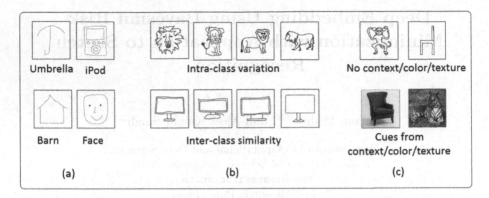

Fig. 1. Challenges in sketch recognition. (a) Hand-drawn sketches are often abstract representation with minimal details, yet they make meaning for us, and we can easily recognize them, e.g., umbrella, barn, etc in this figure. (b) Hand-drawn sketches are the classic examples of inter-class similarity and intra-class variations. Here we show examples of a single category *Lion* in the first row, and examples of two categories *TV* and *Computer Monitor* in the second row. Note: first two images in second row are from *TV* category whereas the next two examples are from *Computer Monitor* category. (c) Object category recognition (natural images) problem often gets benefited from image color, texture and context. On the other hand, these important cues are not present in sketches.

more recently He *et al.* [6] have shown promising performance on sketch recognition. Despite these successful models the problem is far from being solved for real-life applications.

We address the sketch recognition problem by designing robust and category-agnostic representation[1] of sketches using a novel deep metric learning technique. Our proposed method is inspired by the classical Bayesian decision theory [3]. Given a deep neural network $f : X \leftarrow \mathbb{R}^D$ where X is a set of sketches, and x_i is a D-dimensional representation of ith sketch, let $\mathcal{D}_{ij}$ be the distance between two samples. Further, suppose ω^+ and ω^- are classes containing all positive and negative samples respectively, and $P(\omega^+|\mathcal{D}_{ij})$ and $P(\omega^-|\mathcal{D}_{ij})$ are the class conditional probabilities given distance between embeddings of two samples i and j. Now, given these probabilities the Bayesian risk of misclassifying pair of positive samples as negative and the vice-versa, can be easily estimated [3]. We use this risk as a loss and minimize it to learn better representations for sketch images. The learnt representations obtained using this loss function is robust and a naïve linear classifier on these embeddings yields us state-of-the-art performance on sketch recognition.

The contributions of our work are as follows.

1. We propose a novel and principled approach of designing a loss function to learn robust and discriminative embeddings. Design of our loss function is

---

[1] Embedding, feature and representation are interchangeably used in this paper to represent feature vector.

inspired by the classical Bayesian decision theory. Here, we minimize the Bayesian risk of misclassifying a randomly chosen pair of samples from each mini-batch during training in an end-to-end trainable fashion (Sect. 3).

2. We bypass the need of sophisticated sampling strategy like hard negative mining, and careful fine-tuning of parameters like margin, using our loss function, yet we perform better than the related metric learning loss functions. It should be noted that the performance of classical metric loss function such as triplet [19,25] and lifted loss [22] is heavily dependent on sampling strategy and choice of margin parameter (Sect. 3.3).

3. The proposed loss function in combination with a popular pretrained CNN architecture achieves state-of-the-art sketch recognition accuracy on TU-Berlin-250 and TU-Berlin-160 benchmarks (Tables 1 and 2).

This paper is organized as follows. In Sect. 2 we provide a literature survey related to sketch recognition problem and deep metric learning. We then formally describe our loss function in Sect. 3. We then show results on public benchmarks, provide extensive discussions on our results in Sect. 4 and ablation study in Sect. 4.5. We finally conclude our work in Sect. 5.

2   Related Work

Early works on sketch recognition focused on artistic or CAD design drawing with small number of categories [11,32]. The release of public hand-drawn sketch benchmark namely TU-Berlin [4] has triggered the research in hand-drawn sketch recognition. The sketch recognition research in the literature can broadly be categorized into two groups – (i) hand-crafted feature based, and (ii) Deep embedding based methods. Hand-crafted features such as Histogram-of-Oriented-Gradients (HOG) have shown some success on sketch recognition. However, the results are far inferior to human performance [4]. Advancement in deep learning has significantly influenced sketch recognition. The seminal work of "sketch-a-net" by Yu *et al.* [31], for the first time, has shown promising results in sketch recognition by surpassing human performance. Extending this idea further authors tried to improve the sketch recognition performance by introducing and designing smart data augmentation techniques [30]. Leveraging the inherent sequential nature of sketches Sarvadevabhatla *et al.* [15] and more recently He *et al.* [6] addressed the problem of sketch recognition as sequence learning task. These methods can be very successful in online sketch recognition tasks where stroke sequence are available. However, they learn category specific concepts and may not be trivially generalizable to unseen categories. Our method falls in deep embedding based methods where our focus is to address the problem of sketch recognition by learning robust sketch embeddings. To this end, we present a deep metric learning scheme.

Metric Learning. Metric learning is a well-established area in Machine Learning with growing interest in deep methods for this problem in recent years. In this paper we will limit our discussion to deep metric learning methods. However, we encourage the readers to refer [1] for details of classical metric learning techniques. In deep metric learning research the major effort goes into designing a discriminative loss function. The contrastive [5] and triplet loss [19,25] have shown their utility in various Computer Vision tasks and their usage is widespread. However, their drawbacks are (i) they do not use the complete information available in the batch, and (ii) their convergence is often subject to the correct choice of triplets. Other recent line of research include histogram loss [24], lifted-structured embedding [22] and Multi-class N-pair Loss [21]. The histogram loss function is computed based on the histograms of positive and negative pairs. Leveraging this idea, we present a principled approach of loss computation using Bayesian decision theory, and minimize the risk of positive pair getting classified as negative pair and vice-versa.

3   Deep Embedding via Bayesian Risk Minimization

We focus on learning robust representation for hand-drawn sketches using a novel deep metric learning technique. Our proposed method is inspired by the classical Bayesian decision theory [3]. Given a pretrained deep neural network $f : X \leftarrow \mathbb{R}^D$ which maps a set of images to a D-dimensional feature embedding, our goal is to learn f such that the pair of positive examples come closer and pair of negative examples go farther. Suppose x_i and x_j are normalized D-dimensional feature embeddings for two randomly chosen samples i and j respectively. Further, suppose $\mathcal{D}(x_i, x_j)$ denotes the distance between these two embeddings. Now, suppose ω^+ and ω^- are the classes representing all the positive and negative samples respectively, and $P(\omega^+|\mathcal{D}(x_i, x_j))$ and $P(\omega^-|\mathcal{D}(x_i, x_j))$ are class conditional probabilities given distance between embeddings of two samples. Given these notations, the Bayesian risk of misclassification, i.e., classifying positive samples as negative and negative sample as positive is given by.

$$\mathcal{R}(f_\theta) = \int_{-1}^{1} \int_{-1}^{z=\mathcal{D}(x_i,x_j)} P(\omega^+|\mathcal{D}(x_i,x_j))P(\omega^-|\mathcal{D}(x_i,x_j))d^2z. \tag{1}$$

In the above equation, we estimate the class conditional probabilities on each mini-batch during training of deep neural network using the method described in Sect. 3.1 and illustrated in Fig. 2.

3.1   Estimating Class Conditional Probabilities.

Given a mini-batch consisting of feature embedding of n samples and their class, i.e., $x_i, y_{i i=1}^n$ we obtain positive and negative sample sets as follows.

$$S^+ = \{(x_i, x_j) : y_i = y_j\}, \quad S^- = \{(x_i, x_j) : y_i \neq y_j\}. \tag{2}$$

Given these sample sets, we compute distance between each pair of embeddings and denote these distances as $\mathcal{D}(x_i, x_j)$. It should be noted that we define this distance as negative of cosine similarity. Now, to estimate class conditional probabilities, we use histogram fitting approach as follows. Every pair of positive

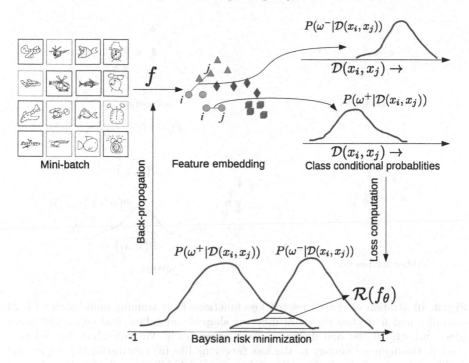

Fig. 2. The Bayesian risk minimization based loss function. The sketch samples of mini-batch are represented using embedding function f. Here f can be defined by any popular deep neural network. Each sample in a mini-batch is represented using this embedding. Here, we show different colors and shape for examples of different categories. The distance between a pair of samples is modeled as two class conditional probabilities. The distance between samples of same class forms positive class conditional distribution, similarly the distance between samples of different classes are used to model negative class conditional distribution. Please refer to Sect. 3 for more details. (Color figure online)

and negative embeddings are mapped as two histograms representing positive and negative class conditional probabilities respectively based on their distance. Since we assume that our embeddings are L2-normalized, and our distance is defined as negative of cosine similarity, the distance $\mathcal{D}$ has a range from $[-1, 1]$. This allows us to fit histograms in a finite range. We use bin size $= R$ for both positive and negative histograms. Further, P_i^+ and P_i^- denote the value at ith bin of positive and negative histogram respectively. In the discrete histogram space, (1) is rewritten as,

$$\mathcal{R}(f_\theta) = \sum_{i=1}^{R}\sum_{j=1}^{r} P_i^+ P_j^-. \tag{3}$$

$$\mathcal{R}(f_\theta) = \sum_{i=1}^{R} P_i^+ \sum_{j=1}^{r} P_j^-. \tag{4}$$

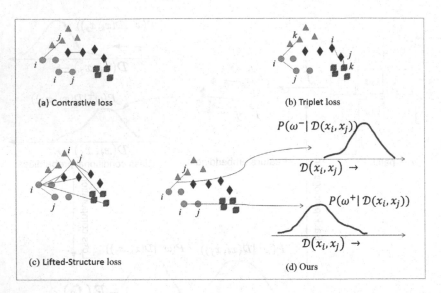

Fig. 3. Illustration of various related loss functions for a training mini-batch with 24 examples and four class shown in different shapes and colors. Red edges and green edges indicate similar and dissimilar pairs respectively. We only show few selected pairs in this figure. Contrary to the loss functions like (a) contrastive (b) triplet and (c) lifted-structured, our loss function is based on probabilistic modeling of similar and dissimilar pairs in the mini-batch. Further, unlike (a), (b) and (c) our loss function does not rely on sample selection strategy.

$$\mathcal{R}(f_\theta) = \sum_{i=1}^{R} P_i^+ \psi(H^-). \tag{5}$$

Here $\psi(H^-)$ is cumulative sum of negative histogram H^-. We use the above risk (shown using shaded area in Fig. 2) as loss function. This loss function is computed as a linear combination of value at ith bin of histogram H^+, and hence is differentiable. We back-propagate this loss to deep neural network, and learn embeddings in an end-to-end trainable framework as discussed in the next section.

3.2 Training and Implementation Details

Our loss function can be used to learn robust embeddings using any of the popular mapping functions. To this end, we use popular pretrained ResNet [7] architecture and fine-tune the convolution layers to improve embeddings with the help of our loss function. Once embeddings are obtained by minimizing our loss function, we use a linear SVM [2] with default parameters to classify sketch images.

The features obtained from the CNN above are normalized using $L2$-normalization. The objective is learned using these normalized features. We scale sketches to $256 \times 256 \times 3$, with each brightness channel tiled equally. We also use data augmentation on these sketches to reduce the risk of over-fitting. Precisely, for each sketch, we perform random affine transformation, random rotation of $10°$, random horizontal flip and pixel jittering.

We implemented our loss function using PyTorch [13]. For training the network using our loss function, we set batch size to 256 and initial learning rate to $1e - 03$. The learning rate is gradually decreased at regular intervals to aid in proper convergence. During training, each sketch is cropped centrally to a 224×224. Then, the data augmentation described above are applied. We used computationally efficient Adam optimizer for updating the network weights. The maximum number of epochs is set to 300, and our stopping criteria is based on the change in validation accuracy.

3.3   Comparison with Related Loss Functions

Max-margin based pair-wise loss functions such as contrastive loss [5], triplet loss [19,25] and more recently lifted structured loss [22] have gained huge interest in deep metric learning research. They have been successful in some selected tasks. However, their major drawbacks are – (i) Their performance heavily depends on sample selection strategy for each mini-batch as noted in [12], (ii) their performance is very sensitive to choice of margin which is often manually tuned, (iii) being non-probabilistic these loss functions do not really leverage the probability distributions of positive and negative pair of samples. Overcoming these drawbacks, our loss function uses the probability distribution of distances of positive and negative samples in principled manner, and does not rely on any hand-tuned parameter (except number of bins whose choice is not that much sensitive to performance as studied in our experimental section), and most importantly does not require any specific sample selection strategy. Comparison between contrastive, triplet, lifted and our loss function is illustrated in Fig. 3. Further, the widely used supervised loss functions, for example, cross-entropy loss is designed to learn category specific feature embeddings with the goal of minimizing classification loss, and does not directly impose the metric learning criteria.

4   Experiments and Results

4.1   Datasets and Evaluation Protocols

In this section, we, first, briefly describe the datasets we use. Then, we evaluate our method qualitatively and quantitatively, and compare it with the state-of-the-art approaches for sketch recognition.

The TU-Berlin [4][2] is a popularly used sketch recognition dataset. It contains $20\,K$ unique sketches of 250 categories. Some of the examples of this dataset

---

[2] http://cybertron.cg.tu-berlin.de/eitz/projects/classifysketch/.

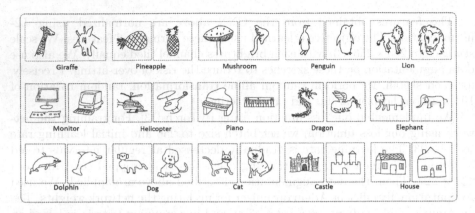

Fig. 4. Some sample images from the TU-Berlin [4] of datasets we use. As it is evident from the images, the dataset has large intra-class variations and inter-class similarities which makes it harder to learn a robust feature representation.

are shown in Fig. 4. Following the protocol in literature [30] we perform 3-fold cross validation with two-fold for training and one-fold for testing and report mean recognition accuracy. We refer to this dataset as *TU-Berlin-250* from here onwards.

The TU-Berlin dataset is extremely challenging. As studied by Elitz *et al.* [4] the human performance on this dataset is 73%. This is primarily due to the fact it is hard to distinguish sketch images of some categories in the TU-Berlin [4] such as *Table* vs *Bench, Monitor* vs *TV, Panda* vs *Teddy Bear* even for human. Considering this Schneider and Tuytelaars [17] have identified 160-category subset of the TU-Berlin dataset which could be unambiguously recognized by humans. This subset was later used by Sarvadevabhatla *et al.* [15] to evaluate sketch recognition performance. In the similar setting, along with full TU-Berlin, i.e. *TU-Berlin-250*, we also use 160 categories subset of TU-Berlin to evaluate our sketch recognition performance. We will refer to this subset as the *TU-Berlin-160* from here onwards.

4.2 Comparable Methods

Since our model uses a deep convolutional neural networks, we compare with popular CNN baselines to evaluate their performance against ours. Specifically, We use (i) AlexNet [8], the seminal deep network with five convolutional and three fully-connected layers, (ii) VGGNet [20] with 16 convolutional layers and (iii) ResNet-18, ResNet-34 and ResNet-50 networks with 18, 34 and 50 convolutional layers.

We also compare our method with classical handcrafted feature based methods and modern state-of-the-art approaches to prove the effectiveness of our proposed method. Here we briefly describe these methods.

1. **Hand-crafted features and classifier pipeline.** Prior to the emergence of successful deep learning models, like in many other Computer Vision tasks. Hand-crafted features were the popular choice for sketch recognition. In these we specifically compare with (i) HOG-SVM [4], which is based on HOG descriptor and the classification is done using SVM classifier, (ii) structured ensemble matching [29], (iii) multi-kernel SVM [10], and (iv) Fisher vector spatial pooling (FV-SP) [18], which is based on SIFT descriptor and Fisher Vector for encoding.
2. **SketchANet** [30,31]. It is a multi-scale and multi-channel framework for sketch recognition. We compare our method with its two versions SN1.0 [31] and SN2.0 [30].
3. **DVSF** [6]. It uses ensemble of networks to learn the visual and temporal properties of the sketches for addressing sketch recognition problem.

We directly use the reported results of these methods whenever available from [6, 15,30].

Table 1. Sketch recognition accuracy on TU-Berlin-250 dataset.

Method	Accuracy (in %)
AlexNet [8]	67.1
VGGNet [20]	74.5
ResNet-18 [7]	74.1
ResNet-34 [7]	74.8
ResNet-50 [7]	75.3
HOG-SVM [4]	56.0
Ensemble [29]	61.5
MKL-SVM [10]	65.8
FV-SP [18]	68.9
SN1.0 [31]	74.9
SN2.0 [30]	77.9
DVSF [6]	79.6
Humans	73.1
Ours	**82.2**

4.3   Our Results on TU-Berlin-250

We first show results on the TU-Berlin-250 of our Bayesian risk minimization based loss function with combination with a simple linear classifier, and compare it with various alternatives as described in 4.2 and human performance. These results are reported in Table 1. Our method clearly outperforms the hand-crafted

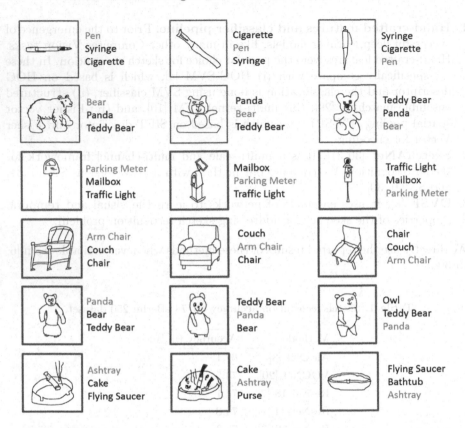

Fig. 5. Few selected example results of our method. We show top-3 predictions (top to down rank wise) for our method. Please note that our method achieves 92% top-3 accuracy. Here words in green color are the ground truth predictions. [Best viewed in color] (Color figure online)

feature based methods and basic deep neural networks. Moreover, beating the human performance by more than 9%, our method also outperforms the seminal work by Yu *et al.* [31] and their improved version [30] by more than 9% and close to 7% respectively. It should also be noted that our method does not use any carefully designed sketch augmentation technique. A more recent work and the state-of-the-art method [6] uses multiple networks to learn the visual and sequential features to achieve an accuracy of 79.6% on TU-Berlin-250 dataset. This is 3.6% inferior to our method which only uses one network to learn the feature embeddings. It should be noted that contrary to our method, most of the comparable baselines use specialized deep architecture suitable for sketch recognition and specialized techniques for sketch data augmentation. The superior performance of our work is primarily attributed to the discriminative feature embedding which we learn using proposed loss function.

Table 2. Sketch recognition accuracy on *TU-Berlin-160* dataset.

Methods	Accuracy (%)
Alexnet-FC GRU	85.1
Alexnet-FC LSTM	82.1
SN1.0 [31]	81.4
Alexnet-FT	83.0
SketchCNN-Sch-FC LSTM [16]	78.8
SketchCNN-Sch-FC GRU [16]	79.
Ours	**88.7**

Examining our results more closely, we found that our method achieves top-3 accuracy of 92% and top-5 accuracy of 95% which is quite encouraging given the challenges in the dataset. We show top-3 predictions of our method in Fig. 5. We observe that similar looking objects are mis-classified more. For example, in Fig. 5, a *pen* is mis-classified as *cigarette* and *syringe*. Similarly, *bear* is mis-classified as *panda* and a *teddy-bear*. However, by observing the top-2 and top-3 predictions, we can safely say that our method is able to distinguish between similar looking sketches. Going further, we also show category-wise accuracy on selected 25 categories in Fig. 6. From the figure we see that the accuracy for *loudspeaker* and *megaphone* classes are less because both these classes looks similar.

4.4 Our Results on the TU-Berlin-160

We next show results on the *TU-Berlin-160* dataset. Here we compare our methods with Alexnet-FC-GRU method proposed by [15], Sketch-a-Net [31] and deep neural networks based baselines provided by authors of [15]. These results are summarized in Table 2. The state-of-the-art results on this subset of *TU-Berlin-160* is method presented by Sarvadevabhatla *et al.* [15] which pose the sketch recognition task as a sequence modeling task using gated recurrent unit (GRU). Our method achieves 88.7% top-1 recognition accuracy and clearly outperforms other methods.

4.5 Ablation Study

Effect of Bin Size. One of the major advantages of our method is that it is not very sensitive to choice of parameter. One of the critical parameter of our loss function is bin size. We choose bin size = 75 for all our experiments. We empirically justify our choice of bin size by conducting following experiment: we vary bin size in range of 70 to 150 and plot bin size vs accuracy in Fig. 7 for a validation set. We observe the best validation accuracy for bin size = 75, and the accuracy does not change more than ±2% for these range of bin size.

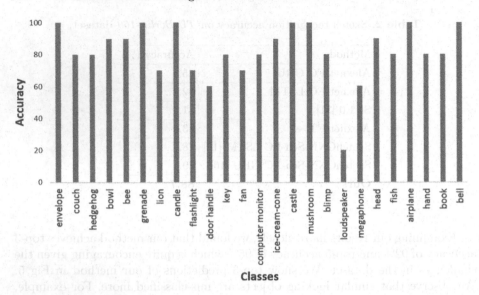

Fig. 6. Category-wise sketch classification results. We show category-wise accuracy for 25 selected categories. The classification accuracy for categories such as *Envelope, Grenade, Candle, Castle, Mushroom, Airplane* are 100%. The worst classification accuracy (20%) is obtained for *Loudspeaker* which often gets misclassified as visually similar category *Megaphone*.

Table 3. Comparison of our methods with various loss functions on sketch recognition task. We also evaluate our method with the combination of cross entropy (CE) loss.

Loss functions	Accuracy
Contrastive [5]	63.5%
Triplet loss [19,25]	70.6%
Lifted loss [22]	75.2%
Ours	82.2%
Ours + CE	82.6%

Comparison with Other Loss Function Used for Metric Learning. We compare our loss function with other related metric learning based loss functions, i.e., contrastive [5], triplet [19,25] and lifted loss [22] for sketch recognition task in Table 3. Here, we show results on *TU-Berlin-250*. We used public implementations of these loss functions. For triplet and lifted loss, we used hard negative sampling strategy as suggested by authors of these loss functions. However, our method does not require any sophisticated sampling strategy. Despite this, we observe that our loss function clearly outperforms others. Further, we evaluate the performance of our loss function when combined with cross entropy (CE) loss. This gave an additional 0.4% boost in sketch recognition accuracy.

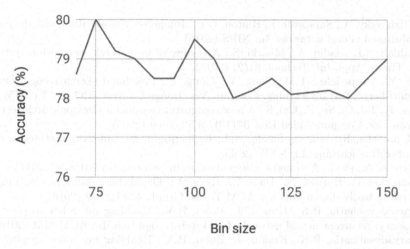

Fig. 7. Bin-size vs validation accuracy. We vary bin size in range of 70 to 150 and observe that best validation accuracy is obtained using bin size = 75, and the accuracy does not change more than ±2% for these range of bin size.

5   Conclusion

We proposed a principled approach for designing metric-learning based loss function, and showed its application to sketch recognition. Our method achieved state-of-the-art performance on sketch recognition on two benchmarks. The learnt sketch embeddings are generic and can be applicable to other sketch related tasks such as sketch-to-photo retrieval and zero-shot or few-shot sketch recognition. We leave these as future works of this paper.

Acknowledgements. Authors would like to thank Dr. Partha Pratim Talukdar from Machine and Language Learning Lab at IISc, Bangalore for providing computational resources used for this work.

References

1. Bellet, A., Habrard, A., Sebban, M.: A survey on metric learning for feature vectors and structured data. CoRR abs/1306.6709 (2013). http://arxiv.org/abs/1306.6709
2. Cortes, C., Vapnik, V.: Support-vector networks. Mach. Learn. **20**(3), 273–297 (1995)
3. Duda, R.O., Hart, P.E., Stork, D.G.: Pattern Classification. Wiley, Hoboken (2001)
4. Eitz, M., Hays, J., Alexa, M.: How do humans sketch objects? ACM Trans. Graph. **31**(4), 44 (2012)
5. Hadsell, R., Chopra, S., LeCun, Y.: Dimensionality reduction by learning an invariant mapping. In: CVPR (2006)
6. He, J., Wu, X., Jiang, Y., Zhao, B., Peng, Q.: Sketch recognition with deep visual-sequential fusion model. In: ACM-MM (2017)
7. He, K., Zhang, X., Ren, S., Sun, J.: Deep residual learning for image recognition. In: CVPR (2016)

8. Krizhevsky, A., Sutskever, I., Hinton, G.E.: ImageNet classification with deep convolutional neural networks. In: NIPS (2012)
9. Lahlali, S.E., Sadiq, A., Mbarki, S.: A review of face sketch recognition systems. J. Theor. Appl. Inf. Technol. 81(2) (2015)
10. Li, Y., Hospedales, T.M., Song, Y., Gong, S.: Free-hand sketch recognition by multi-kernel feature learning. Comput. Vis. Image Underst. **137**, 1–11 (2015)
11. Lu, T., Tai, C., Su, F., Cai, S.: A new recognition model for electronic architectural drawings. Comput. Aided Des. **37**(10), 1053–1069 (2005)
12. Manmatha, R., Wu, C., Smola, A.J., Krähenbühl, P.: Sampling matters in deep embedding learning. In: ICCV (2017)
13. Paszke, A., et al.: Automatic differentiation in pytorch. In: NIPS-W (2017)
14. Sangkloy, P., Burnell, N., Ham, C., Hays, J.: The sketchy database: learning to retrieve badly drawn bunnies. ACM Trans. Graph. **35**(4), 119 (2016)
15. Sarvadevabhatla, R.K., Kundu, J., Babu, R.V.: Enabling my robot to play pictionary: recurrent neural networks for sketch recognition. In: ACM-MM (2016)
16. Sarvadevabhatla, R.K., Kundu, J., Babu, R.V.: Enabling my robot to play pictionary: recurrent neural networks for sketch recognition (2016)
17. Schneider, R., Tuytelaars, T.: Sketch classification and classification-driven analysis using fisher vectors **33**(11), 174:1–174:9 (2014)
18. Schneider, R.G., Tuytelaars, T.: Sketch classification and classification-driven analysis using fisher vectors. In: SIGGRAPH (2014)
19. Schroff, F., Kalenichenko, D., Philbin, J.: Facenet: a unified embedding for face recognition and clustering. In: CVPR (2015)
20. Simonyan, K., Zisserman, A.: Very deep convolutional networks for large-scale image recognition. arXiv preprint arXiv:1409.1556 (2014)
21. Sohn, K.: Improved deep metric learning with multi-class n-pair loss objective. In: NIPS (2016)
22. Song, H.O., Xiang, Y., Jegelka, S., Savarese, S.: Deep metric learning via lifted structured feature embedding. In: CVPR (2016)
23. Tang, X., Wang, X.: Face sketch recognition. IEEE Trans. Circuit Syst. Video Technol. **14**(1), 50–57 (2004)
24. Ustinova, E., Lempitsky, V.S.: Learning deep embeddings with histogram loss. In: NIPS (2016)
25. Wang, J., et al.: Learning fine-grained image similarity with deep ranking. In: CVPR (2014)
26. Wang, N., Li, J., Sun, L., Song, B., Gao, X.: Training-free synthesized face sketch recognition using image quality assessment metrics. arXiv preprint arXiv:1603.07823 (2016)
27. Xu, D., Song, J., Alameda-Pineda, X., Ricci, E., Sebe, N.: Multi-paced dictionary learning for cross-domain retrieval and recognition. In: ICPR (2016)
28. Xu, P., et al.: SketchMate: deep hashing for million-scale human sketch retrieval. In: CVPR (2018)
29. Li, Y., Song, Y.-Z., Gong, S.: Sketch recognition by ensemble matching of structured features. In: Proceedings of the British Machine Vision Conference (2013). (QMUL)
30. Yu, Q., Yang, Y., Liu, F., Song, Y., Xiang, T., Hospedales, T.M.: Sketch-a-Net: a deep neural network that beats humans. Int. J. Comput. Vis. 122(3) 411–425 (2017)
31. Yu, Q., Yang, Y., Song, Y., Xiang, T., Hospedales, T.M.: Sketch-a-Net that beats humans. In: BMVC (2015)
32. Zitnick, C.L., Parikh, D.: Bringing semantics into focus using visual abstraction. In: 2013 IEEE Conference on Computer Vision and Pattern Recognition, Portland, OR, USA, 23–28 June 2013, pp. 3009–3016 (2013)

Geodesic via Asymmetric Heat Diffusion Based on Finsler Metric

Fang Yang[1]([⊠]), Li Chai[1], Da Chen[2], and Laurent Cohen[2]

[1] Engineering Research Center of Metallurgical Automation
and Measurement Technology, Wuhan University of Science and Technology,
Wuhan, China
{yangfang.idif,chaili}@wust.edu.cn
[2] Université Paris Dauphine, PSL Research University, CNRS, UMR 7534,
CEREMADE, 75016 Paris, France
{chenda,Cohen}@ceremade.dauphine.fr

Abstract. Current image segmentation involves strongly non-uniform, anisotropic and asymmetric measures of path length, which challenges available algorithms. In order to meet these challenges, this paper applies the Finsler metric to the geodesic method based on heat diffusion. This metric is non-Riemannian, anisotropic and asymmetric, which helps the heat to flow more on the features of interest. Experiments demonstrate the feasibility of the proposed method. The experimental results show that our algorithm is of strong robustness and effectiveness. The proposed method can be applied to contour detection and tubular structure segmentation in images, such as vessel segmentation in medical images and road extraction in satellite images and so on.

Keywords: Geodesic · Minimal path · Heat diffusion · Finsler metric

1 Introduction

Geodesic refers to the shortest path connecting two points in metric space and plays an important role in image processing and computer vision. It can be applied to tasks such as contour detection, tubular structure segmentation, surface remeshing and so on [19]. In theory, the shortest path problem can be described by a static Hamilton-Jacobi equation or an anisotropic Eikonal partial differential equation (PDE). Numerical methods to compute the discrete geodesic distance on smooth surfaces and images can be classified into two classes: exact methods based on geometry and approximation method based on PDE. Generally, the approximation methods via solving the Eikonal PDE are widely used.

In terms of computation, it is difficult to get the analytical solution of the Eikonal equation directly. Therefore, an iterative relaxation scheme such as Gauss-Seidel is useful to get the numerical solution. In [13], the authors summarize popular numerical solutions to the Eikonal equation on Cartesian grids.

Supported by the National Science Foundation of China (grant 61625305).

The most popular algorithms are the Fast Marching [20] and Fast Sweeping Method [27] *etc.* By comparing the errors, speed, accuracy and robustness of different algorithms, the authors conclude in [13] that the Fast Marching Method outperforms the other methods. However, the Fast Marching Method do not reuse its information, *i.e.*, for the same data, once the initial point is changed, the geodesic distance should be recomputed from scratch.

Recently, the geodesic method based on heat flow has become popular because of its efficiency, robustness and insensitivity to noise. It is originated from the Varadhan's formula [22]:

$$\phi(p_0, p_x) = \lim_{t \to 0} \sqrt{-4t \log u_{p_0}(p_x, t)}, \tag{1}$$

which shows that within a small time t, the geodesic distance $\phi(p_0, p_x)$ between two points p_0 and p_x can be approximated via the heat kernel $u_{p_0}(p_x, t)$.

Inspired by the classical result of Varadhan, Crane *et al.* proposed a different method for computing the geodesic distance on a Riemannian manifold, which is called the heat method [10]. Instead of using the Varadhan's formula directly, the heat method is based on solving a pair of standard linear elliptic problems.

The key observation in [10] is to divide the process of distance computation into two steps: the first step determines the direction along which the distance increases; the second step recovers the distance via solving a Poisson equation by using the normalized gradient of the heat flow. Each step relates to a standard problem in numerical linear algebra. Moreover, the sparse systems from elliptic PDEs can be solved in a very short time that is close to linear time. Therefore, the heat method can be facilitated by using existing algorithms and software, thus improves the efficiency and robustness of distance computation. In addition, for every single data, the Laplacian can be precomputed, *i.e.* recomputation is not necessary even the initial point is changed.

Though fast and efficient, the heat method described in [10] only involves the simplest case – the diffusion coefficient is a constant. To expand the scope of use of the heat method, Yang and Cohen [24] proposed to use the isotropic/anisotropic heat diffusion to obtain geodesic in images and on surfaces. In their method, the diffusion coefficient is no longer a constant, but an isotropic scalar or an anisotropic tensor computed from the image. Based on [24], the authors propose a 2D+Radius heat method for segmenting the centerline and boundary of the tubular structures simultaneously [25]. Besides, the diffusive nature of the heat equation causes instant smoothing, which is the reason why the heat method is robust to noise.

Because of the advantages of the heat method, based on Crane's work, a variety of tasks in computational science and data analysis are developed. For example, Belyaev and Fayolle [4] reinterpret the heat method and achieve more accurate results by either iterating the heat method or by applying more advanced descent strategies. Zou *et al.* [28] use the heat method for efficient tool path planning; Solomon *et al.* [21] use the heat method to facilitate solving optimal transport problems on geometric domains; Lin *et al.* [14] apply this approach to vector-valued data in the context of manifold learning.

The heat method is popular, however, the diffusion coefficient and tensor are constructed on Riemannian manifold, which can not provide asymmetric metric. While current image processing applications involve strongly non-uniform, anisotropic and asymmetric measures of path length, which can not be efficiently solved on Riemannian manifolds. Hence, in this paper, we are motivated to apply asymmetric Finsler metric to the heat method.

Finsler geometry can be described as Riemannian geometry without the quadratic restriction [9]. Riemannian distances are defined by a position dependent inner product, while Finslerian distances are defined by a direction dependent inner product, computed from a position dependent norm. Since the level sets determined by norms can be more complex than those (ellipsoidal) given by an inner product, Finsler metric is more suitable for modeling complex diffusion profiles [3].

In [15], Melonakos et al. proposed a Finsler active contour method by replacing the original potential in [6] into a potential including the normal of the curves. Then Zach et al. [26] proposed a global optimal method for the Finsler active contours. Mirebeau [16] proposes an efficient discretization scheme for the Fast Marching Method on Finsler manifold. Chen et al. [8] introduces a minimal path model with Finsler metric and uses the scheme in [16] to compute the distance. In [7], the authors extend the framework of front propagation from Riemannian manifold to Finsler manifold. The Rander's metric used in their work [7] prevents the fronts leaking problem during the fronts propagation.

The asymmetric metric is successfully applied in the Eikonal PDE, but as mentioned before, the numerical scheme Fast Marching Method is more sensitive to noise than the heat method. In addition, the Fast Marching Method do not reuse information. Therefore, we would like to develop the asymmetric heat method.

The contributions of this paper lie in that:

1. We extend the heat method based on Riemannian metric to Finsler metric;
2. We build two kinds of Rander's metric to detect contours and centerlines;
3. The asymmetric heat diffusion improves the performance comparing with the traditional heat method on image segmentation.

2 Background and Related Work

2.1 Finsler Metric and Minimal Path Model

Similar to the geodesic on Riemannian manifold, the minimal path on Finsler manifold is also obtained by minimizing the length between two fixed points. Let $\Omega \subset \mathbb{R}^N, N \in \{2, 3\}$ denote the image domain, which is equipped with a Finsler metric $\mathcal{F}(x, v) > 0$, where $x \in \Omega$ denotes the position and $v \in \mathbb{R}^N$ denotes the orientation. Generally, the Finsler metric $\mathcal{F}(x, v)$ is asymmetric, i.e., $\mathcal{F}(x, v) \neq \mathcal{F}(x, -v)$. The length of a Lipschitz continuous curve $\gamma(t), 0 \leq t \leq 1$ on a Finsler manifold is defined as:

$$\mathcal{L}_{\mathcal{F}}(\gamma) = \int_0^1 \mathcal{F}(\gamma(t), \gamma'(t)) dt. \tag{2}$$

Note that because of the asymmetry of $\mathcal{F}(x, v)$, the curve on a Finsler manifold and its reverse curve are usually not the same.

The geodesic distance defined in (2) can be generalized to the distance from any point $p \in \Omega$ to a set of points $\mathcal{S} \subset \Omega$, thus defines the geodesic distance map:

$$\phi_{\mathcal{S}}(p) := \inf\{\mathcal{L}_{\mathcal{F}}(\gamma); \gamma(0) = p, \gamma(1) \in \mathcal{S}\}, \tag{3}$$

which is the unique viscosity solution to the following Eikonal PDE:

$$\begin{cases} \mathcal{F}^*(\nabla\phi(p)) = 1, & \forall p \in \Omega \setminus \mathcal{S}, \\ \phi(p) = 0, & \forall p \in \mathcal{S}, \end{cases} \tag{4}$$

where $\mathcal{F}^*$ is the dual metric of $\mathcal{F}$:

$$\mathcal{F}^*(x, u) = \sup_{\|v\| \neq 0} \frac{\langle u, v \rangle}{\mathcal{F}(x, v)}. \tag{5}$$

Once the geodesic distance map ϕ is obtained, the shortest path from p to $\mathcal{S}$ can be tracked by solving an ordinary differential equation (ODE) [17]:

$$\frac{d\gamma(t)}{dt} := \nabla\mathcal{F}^*(\nabla\phi(\gamma(t))). \tag{6}$$

In this paper, we will utilize the Rander's Finsler metric, which is defined by the combination of a symmetric Riemannian metric and an asymmetric linear part:

$$\mathcal{F}(x, v) = \|v\|_{M(x)} + \langle \omega(x), v \rangle. \tag{7}$$

According to [16], the dual to $\mathcal{F}$ is also a Rander's metric $\mathcal{F}^*$ with parameters M_* and ω_*:

$$\mathcal{F}^*(x, v) := \|v\|_{M_*(x)} + \langle \omega_*(x), v \rangle, \tag{8}$$

where M_* and ω_* are some algebraic expressions of M and ω [16]:

$$\eta := 1 - \langle \omega, M^{-1}\omega \rangle, M_* := \frac{(M^{-1}\omega)(M^{-1}\omega)^T + \eta M^{-1}}{\eta^2}, \omega_* := -\frac{M_*^{-1}M^{-1}\omega}{\eta}.$$

Hence, the backtracking ODE on the Rander's metric becomes [17]:

$$\frac{d\gamma(t)}{dt} = \frac{M_*(\gamma(t))\nabla\phi(\gamma(t))}{\|\nabla\phi(\gamma(t))\|_{M_*(\gamma(t))}} + \omega_*(\gamma(t)). \tag{9}$$

Compared with the Riemannian minimal path model [5], the Rander's Finsler minimal path is with an additional linear part, which is able to deal with the asymmetric information of the images.

2.2   Finsler Heat Equation

In this paper, we are dedicated to developping the heat method on the Rander's Finsler manifold. Let us consider the following energy functional:

$$\mathcal{E}(u) := \int_\Omega \|\epsilon\nabla u + g\|_D^2, \tag{10}$$

where D is the conductivity matrix and is positive definite by construction:

$$D = M_* - \omega_* \otimes \omega_*, \tag{11}$$

and we set $g = D^{-1}\omega_*$.

The gradient descent of (10) is interpreted as:

$$\partial_t u = \Delta_\mathcal{F} u, \tag{12}$$

where $\Delta_\mathcal{F}$ is the Finsler Laplace operator [1,18], and (12) is called the Finsler heat equation.

Let us recall the heat method proposed in [24], where the initial condition for the heat equation is $u_{p_0}(p_x, t = 0) = \delta_{p_0}$. Therefore, the initial condition for the Finsler heat method should be the same as in [24]. The Varadhan's formula (1) presents that within a small time $t \to 0$, the heat kernel can be used to approximate geodesic distance. It is proved in [24] that the Varadhan's formula is applicable in Riemannian cases because that the geodesic distance is only related to the coefficients of the second-order derivative of the heat kernel.

In [18], the Finsler Gauss kernel $G_{\mathcal{F}*}$ is presented by the following exponential form:

$$G_{\mathcal{F}*}(x,t) := (4\pi t)^{-\frac{N}{2}} \exp\left(-\frac{\mathcal{F}^*(x)^2}{4t}\right). \tag{13}$$

Let $t \to 0$, put the Finsler heat kernel (13) on the *r.h.s* of the Varadhan's formula (1), according to the L'Hospital's rule, we have:

$$\lim_{t\to 0} \sqrt{-4t\log(G_{\mathcal{F}*})} = \mathcal{F}^*(x). \tag{14}$$

Equation (14) is already well understood in the case of homogeneous heat diffusion on the whole domain $\mathbb{R}^2$, where $\mathcal{F}^*(x) = \|x\|$ and the corresponding distance is Euclidean.

3   Construction of Rander's Metric and Algorithm of the Asymmetric Heat Method

As mentioned in Sect. 2.1, the Rander's metric is composed by a Riemannian symmetric quadratic form plus a linear part. In this section, the construction of the Rander's metric is presented. In addition, we should pay attention that in order to ensure that the metric $\mathcal{F}$ is always positive, the following constraint should be satisfied [7,8]:

$$\langle\omega(x), M^{-1}(x)\omega(x)\rangle < 1, \forall x \in \Omega. \tag{15}$$

Different specific metrics are designed for detecting the boundaries of shapes and centerlines of tubular structures in images.

3.1   Rander's Metric for Boundary Detection

In [23] and [24], the authors use either the magnitude of the gradient as the diffusion coefficient or the structure tensor to enhance the flow-like structures or edge features. Inspired by their work, we adapt these metrics to our method for detecting boundaries.

Denote by $g(x)$ the gradient of the image: $g(x) = \nabla f(x)$, where $f(\cdot)$ is a scalar function computed from the image I. The definite positive symmetric tensor field $M(x)$ can be built by the magnitude of $g(x)$:

$$M_I(x) := (\|g(x)\| + \epsilon)I_d, \tag{16}$$

where $M_I(\cdot)$ represents the tensor field in isotropic case, ϵ is a small constant that prevents the diffusion coefficient from being 0, and I_d is a 2×2 identity matrix.

$M(x)$ can be also built by the tensor product:

$$M_A(x) = \lambda_1(x)e_1(x)e_1^T(x) + \lambda_2(x)e_2(x)e_2^T(x), \tag{17}$$

where $M_A(\cdot)$ denotes the tensor field in anisotropic case, $e_1(x) = g(x)$ and $e_2(x) = g(x)^\perp$ are the eigenvectors of $M_A(x)$, $\lambda_1(x) \geq \lambda_2(x) \geq 0$ are the corresponding eigenvalues. The anisotropy A is defined as:

$$A(x) = \frac{\lambda_1(x) - \lambda_2(x)}{\lambda_1(x) + \lambda_2(x)}. \tag{18}$$

The linear part can be obtained by using the orthogonal of the normalized gradient of the image:

$$\omega(x) = \tau \left(\frac{\nabla I(x)}{\|\nabla I\|_\infty} \right)^\perp, \tag{19}$$

where τ is an adjustable coefficient which is used to satisfy (15).

Note that in [24], M_A behaves better than M_I when the feature of interest is very curved. However, in the proposed method, the difference between M_A and M_I is weakened because of $\omega(x)$.

Figure 1 shows the experimental results on a synthetic image under the same initial condition but different metrics. In (a), only (16) is used as the diffusion coefficient, without adding any additional part, which leads to a shortcut during backtracking from the endpoint to the source point. In (b) and (c), since $\omega(x)$ and $-\omega(x)$ defined in (19) are used as the linear part in the Rander's metric respectively, the heat flows more on the edge of the central black curve. Hence, during the backtracking process, the extracted curves are along the edge of the shape. Note that the closed boundary of the black central curve can be obtained by simply merging the results of (b) and (c).

Figure 1 illustrates clearly that the additional linear part $\omega(x)$ forces the heat to flow more along the direction of $\omega(x)$, i.e., $\omega(x)$ enhance the heat diffusion on the edges.

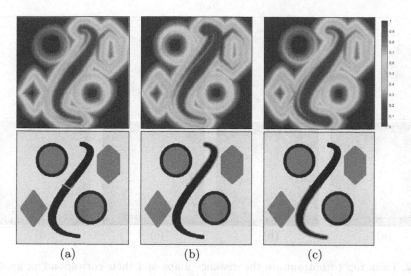

Fig. 1. From top to bottom are the distance maps and their corresponding geodesic respectively, from left to right are the results: (a) by using Riemannian metric M defined in (16), (b) by using Rander's metric whose linear part ω is defined in (19) and (c) by using the Rander's metric, the linear part $-\omega$. In the bottom row, the red and blue points denote the source point and endpoint respectively, the green curves are the geodesic curves. (Color figure online)

Figure 2 presents an example of using different metrics on a 2D Gaussian image. First we show the Euclidean distance with the anisotropy A = 0 and its corresponding geodesic curve, which is in fact a straight line (a). In (b), we use the diffusion tensor defined in (17) as the symmetric part $M_A(x)$ with the anisotropy $A \equiv 0.9$ everywhere. We can see that the heat flows along the direction of $e_2(x)$ and the geodesic line is curved because of the anisotropic diffusion. In (c), we add the linear part $\omega(x)$. Though the geodesic curves in (b) and (c) make no difference visually, it is not hard to distinguish the distance maps from (b) and (c), which are symmetric and asymmetric respectively. In (b) the distance map is symmetric because the diffusion tensor is with quadratic form, while in (c), because of $\omega(x)$, the heat diffusion is becomes asymmetric hence flows more on the direction of $\omega(x)$. In (d), we use $-\omega(x)$ as the linear part, which is opposite to $\omega(x)$, so the heat flows in the inverse direction of (c).

The results in Figs. 1 and 2 not only demonstrate the validity of the metrics designed for boundary detection, but also testify the effectiveness of the Rander's metric. In addition, both examples illustrate that $\mathcal{F}(x, v) \neq \mathcal{F}(x, -v)$.

3.2   Rander's Metric for Centerline Extraction

For the purpose of extracting the centerline, the vessel enhancement method can be considered, e.g. Hessian-based vesselness measures [12] Here we plan to construct the symmetric part of the Rander's metric based on the eigenvalues

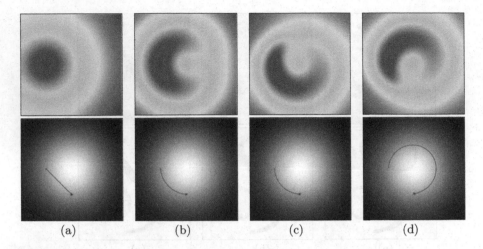

(a)   (b)   (c)   (d)

Fig. 2. From top to bottom are the distance maps and their corresponding geodesic respectively, from left to right are the results: (a) Euclidean, (b) using anisotropic Riemannian metric (17), (c) by using the Rander's metric with the linear part ω defined in (19) and (d) by using the Rander's metric with linear part $-\omega$. In the bottom row, the red and blue points denote the source point and endpoint respectively, the blue curves are the geodesic curves. (Color figure online)

and eigenvectors of the Hessian matrix because of its simplicity. In [12], the authors introduced a multi-scale vessel enhancement method by interpreting geometrically the eigenvalues of the Hessian matrix. The local orientation of the image can be estimated by using the Hessian eigenvectors, which allows us to find out the position of the tubular structures.

First we convolve the image I with a Gaussian kernel $\mathcal{G}(x, \sigma)$:

$$\mathcal{G}(x, \sigma) = \frac{1}{\sqrt{(2\pi)}\sigma} \exp(-\frac{\|x\|^2}{2\sigma^2}) \tag{20}$$

Since σ can be considered as an estimator of the width of the tubular structures, we use different σ in different images. Let $I_{\mathcal{G}}$ be the product after convolution, we obtain the symmetric Hessian matrix $\mathcal{H}$ by computing the second derivative of $I_{\mathcal{G}}$:

$$\mathcal{H} = \begin{bmatrix} \partial_{xx} & \partial_{xy} \\ \partial_{yx} & \partial_{yy} \end{bmatrix} I_{\mathcal{G}} \tag{21}$$

Then we decompose $\mathcal{H}$ to get the corresponding eigenvectors $v_1(x), v_2(x)$ and eigenvalues $\vartheta_1(x), \vartheta_2(x)$ in order to form $M(x)$:

$$M = \vartheta_1(x)v_1(x)v_1^T(x) + \beta\vartheta_2(x)v_2(x)v_2^T(x) \tag{22}$$

where β is a constant controlled by the users to adjust the anisotropy A.

In order to prevent the heat from leaking out the region of tubular structure, we can use the eigenvector $v_1(x)$ as the linear part of the Rander's metric:

$$\omega = \tau v_1 \tag{23}$$

where τ is an adjustable constant which plays the same role as in (19) to ensure that (15) is satisfied.

Figure 3 shows an example on a synthetic U-tube image. In this example, we set σ in (20) to be 4, β in (22) to be 0.1 and $\tau = 1$. In (a), we use the isotropic heat diffusion. The diffusion coefficient is simply obtained by using the graylevel of the image: $\alpha = (1 - (I - I_{x_0}))^n$, $n = 3$ in this case, and $M_I = \alpha I_d$. Clearly, there is a shortcut connecting the source point and the endpoint. In (b), we use the anisotropic heat diffusion where M is the diffusion tensor. The geodesic curve goes along the U tube structure this time. However, our aim is to extract the centerline of the structure. In (c), we use the Rander's metric in heat diffusion by adding ω (23). From the result, we can see that the asymmetric heat diffusion forces the heat to flow more on the main direction v_1, In the bottom row of Fig. 3, although that both curves in (b) and (c) travel along the U tube structure, we can still find that the result by using asymmetric diffusion is closer to the centerline.

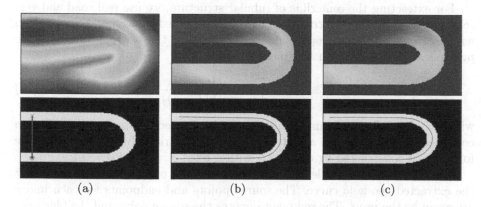

(a)   (b)   (c)

Fig. 3. From top to bottom are the distance maps and their corresponding detected geodesic curves respectively, from left to right are the results by using: (a) isotropic heat diffusion, (b) anisotropic heat diffusion with metric (17), (c) asymmetric heat diffusion with the linear part ω defined in (23).

3.3   Algorithm of the Asymmetric Heat Method

The basic steps of the asymmetric heat method can be described as follows:

In our method, the numerical solution to the Finsler heat equation and the time of diffusion (Step. 2) are determined according to a backward discretization scheme designed for anisotropic heat diffusion, see [11] for details.

Algorithm 1. The Asymmetric Heat Method

---

1. Construct the asymmetric metric $\mathcal{F}(x, u)$, Sect.3.1 and Sect.3.2 ;
2. Integrate the heat flow $\partial_t u = \Delta_{\mathcal{F}} u$ from some source points for some fixed time t;
3. Approximate the distance ϕ using Varadhan's formula;
4. Backtrack the geodesic from a given endpoint to the source point using an ODE (9).

---

4   Experiments and Discussions

4.1   Experiment Data and Settings

We testify the effectiveness of the proposed method on both synthetic and real images. Firstly, we use a 411×411 synthetic image to testify the noise-insensitive performance of the heat method, see Fig. 4. A 12% of pepper and salt noise is added to the original image. The metric is constructed by using (16) and (19), with $\tau = 1$.

For detecting the boundary of shapes in images, we choose some natural images from the BSDS500 dataset [2], see Fig. 5. The gray images are used to construct metrics and initiate the heat flow.

For extracting the centerline of tubular structure, we use real road and vessel images, see Fig. 6. We compare the result obtained by asymmetric diffusion with isotropic and anisotropic diffusion in [24]. For the isotropic diffusion, we preprocess the images with a sigmoid function:

$$f(x) = 1 - \frac{1}{1 + \exp(k(I - \alpha))}, \tag{24}$$

where $k = 10$ and $\alpha = 0.4$ in our tests, and $f(x)$ is used to compute the diffusion coefficient M_I in (16). For anisotropic and asymmetric diffusion, the quadratic form M_A is constructed by using (22) with a fixed $\sigma = 8$ and $\beta = 0.1$.

To display the results clearly, we use either green or blue curves to represent the extracted geodesic curve. The source points and endpoints for each image are given by the users. The red point denotes the source point and the blue ones are the endpoints.

Finally, we evaluate the quality of our algorithm on the images of BSDS500 dataset. Table 1 lists the recall of the detection results by symmetric diffusion method [24] and the proposed method. Note that instead of all the edges, only the geodesic curves between the two chosen points are used to calculate the recall.

4.2   Results and Analysis

(1) Noisy case

In this test, the original synthetic image is corrupted by some pepper and salt noise. As we know that these kind of noise is impulse noise, it affects the image gradient a lot. However, as we can see in Fig. 4(a), most part of the extracted geodesic still goes along the edge of the center curve. Moreover, by adding the additional linear part ω and $-\omega$ (19), both geodesics travel exactly on the boundary of the curve and complete the contour of the center shape. For the result by the fast marching method (d), we use the same metric as in (b), but the result is not as good as in (b) or (c). This test demonstrates that the heat method is robust to noise, since the exponential kernel (13) causes instant smoothing.

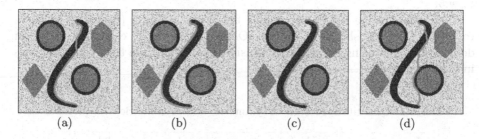

(a)   (b)   (c)   (d)

Fig. 4. Experiment on a synthetic noisy image, from left to right are the results by using: (a) isotropic heat diffusion, (b) asymmetric heat diffusion with linear part ω defined in (19), (c) asymmetric heat diffusion with the linear part $-\omega$, (d) asymmetric fast marching method (the same metric as used in (b)).

(2) Contour Detection

The boundary and contour detection results are displayed in Fig. 5. The comparison experiments are performed by using symmetric heat method in [24] with isotropic metric M_I or anisotropic metric M_A, as shown in Column.1 and Column.3 in Fig. 5. The results of the proposed method are shown in Column.2 and Column.4. By using symmetric diffusion [24], the detected edges do not include some main details, e.g., some elephants and the tree of *elephant*, the long pole, haystack and head of *lakeman*. As mentioned before, because of the diffusive nature of the heat kernel, the heat method can smooth the sharp changes in images, i.e., noise, spurious parts. Hence in such cases, the spurious part of the edges can not be fully detected by using the symmetric heat diffusion. However, after adding the linear part ω, all the missing details are included.

Apparently, the shapes of all images are irregular and asymmetric. Because of the symmetry of the Riemannian metric, the geodesic connecting two points of using Riemmanian metric will surely be the shorter part on the contour of the shape, such as *mushroom*, *redbird* and so on. However, by adding the asymmetric linear part ω, the detected curves can go in the opposite way and thus complete the whole contour of the shape, such as *hawk*, *swan*, *mushroom* and *birds etc*. In addition, for *river*, *waterfall* and *bear*, the background is complex, therefore, the symmetric method fails to extract the edges of these shapes directly and causes some shortcuts. When adding the linear part ω, the curves are forced to go along the edges of the shapes, even the details can be detected.

The reason why asymmetric diffusion using Rander's metric works better is not only because that during the process of diffusion, the heat are more concentrated on the edges, but also on the way of backtracking, the vector field ω^* in (9) is taken into account. However, it is worth mentioning that the proposed method to detect the boundaries are somehow sensitive to the gradient of the image, *e.g.*, the beak of the swan in Row.2, the contour of the bird in Row.5.

The quantitative results of contour detection in Fig. 5 (from left to right, top to bottom) is shown in Table 1. Obviously, in most cases, the recall of detection results using asymmetric diffusion are higher than the symmetric ones in [24].

Table 1. Quantitative results of symmetric and asymmetric heat methods

Image	elephant	river	hawk	swan	lakeman
Symmetric recall	0.365	0.214	0.863	0.628	0.653
Asymmetric recall	0.892	0.878	0.827	0.852	0.936
Image	mushroom	redbird	waterfall	bear	bird
Symmetric recall	0.637	0.774	0.033	0.797	0.913
Asymmetric recall	0.921	0.836	0.866	0.453	0.824

(3) Centerline Detection

The results of detecting centerlines in tubular structures are shown in Fig. 6. For the road image in Row.1, the curves extracted using different metrics are all smooth, despite that there is a lot of noise around the road. This example demonstrates again that the heat method is not sensitive to noise. The Column.1 of Fig. 6 displays the results by using isotropic heat diffusion. As we can see, the extracted lines are not on the centerline, especially for the curved part, there is much deviation from the center. This case can be improved by using the anisotropic diffusion, which helps the heat to concentrate inside the tubular structures. However, the centerlines of the very curved parts and junctions are still not very well detected (Column.2). Finally, we combine the quadratic form with the linear part ω (23) to construct the Rander's metric. The results by using the asymmetric diffusion are shown in Column.3. Thanks to ω the extracted geodesic curves are located much more on the centerlines visually.

Fig. 5. Experiment on several real natural images (from left to right and top to bottom): *elephant, river, hawk, swan, lakeman, mushroom, redbird, waterfall, bear* and *bird*. The red points are the source points and the blue ones are the endpoints, the blue or green curves are the detected geodesic curves.

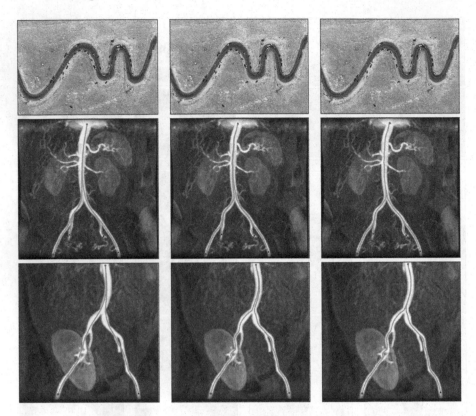

Fig. 6. Experiment on real satellite road image and vessel images, from left to right are the results by using: (a) isotropic heat diffusion, (b) anisotropic heat diffusion, (c) asymmetric heat diffusion.

5   Conclusion

In this paper, we extend the traditional symmetric heat method to asymmetric cases in order to overcome the difficulty on measuring asymmetric path length. Two kinds of Rander's metric are designed for contour detection and centerline extraction. Experimental results show that asymmetric heat diffusion is effective and robust. Thanks to the asymmetric metric, the proposed method performs better than the traditional heat method. However we only consider the Rander's metric in this paper. In future, we will design different Finsler metrics to apply to the heat method according to different image processing tasks.

Acknowledgements. The authors would like to thank Dr. Jean-Marie Mirebeau for his insightful suggestions on the numerical solutions to asymmetric heat diffusion. The authors would also like to thank Dr. Xin Su for his useful comments that allowed us to improve this paper.

References

1. Akagi, G., Ishige, K., Sato, R.: The cauchy problem for the finsler heat equation. arXiv preprint arXiv:1710.00456 (2017)
2. Arbeláez, P., Maire, M., Fowlkes, C., Malik, J.: Contour detection and hierarchical image segmentation. IEEE Trans. Pattern Anal. Mach. Intell. **33**(5), 898–916 (2011)
3. Astola, L., Florack, L.: Finsler geometry on higher order tensor fields and applications to high angular resolution diffusion imaging. Int. J. Comput. Vis. **92**(3), 325–336 (2011)
4. Belyaev, A.G., Fayolle, P.A.: On variational and PDE-based distance function approximations. In: Computer Graphics Forum, vol. 34, pp. 104–118. Wiley (2015)
5. Benmansour, F., Cohen, L.D.: Tubular structure segmentation based on minimal path method and anisotropic enhancement. Int. J. Comput. Vis. **92**(2), 192–210 (2011)
6. Caselles, V., Kimmel, R., Sapiro, G.: Geodesic active contours. Int. J. Comput. Vis. **22**(1), 61–79 (1997)
7. Chen, D., Cohen, L.D.: Fast asymmetric fronts propagation for image segmentation. J. Math. Imaging Vis. **60**, 1–18 (2017)
8. Chen, D., Mirebeau, J.M., Cohen, L.D.: Global minimum for a finsler elastica minimal path approach. Int. J. Comput. Vis. **122**(3), 458–483 (2017)
9. Chern, S.S.: Finsler geometry is just riemannian geometry without the quadratic equation. Not. Am. Math. Soc. **43**(9), 959–963 (1996)
10. Crane, K., Weischedel, C., Wardetzky, M.: Geodesics in heat: a new approach to computing distance based on heat flow. ACM Trans. Graph. (TOG) **32**(5), 152 (2013)
11. Fehrenbach, J., Mirebeau, J.M.: Sparse non-negative stencils for anisotropic diffusion. J. Math. Imaging Vis. **49**(1), 123–147 (2014)
12. Frangi, A.F., Niessen, W.J., Vincken, K.L., Viergever, M.A.: Multiscale vessel enhancement filtering. In: Wells, W.M., Colchester, A., Delp, S. (eds.) MICCAI 1998. LNCS, vol. 1496, pp. 130–137. Springer, Heidelberg (1998). https://doi.org/10.1007/BFb0056195
13. Hysing, S.R., Turek, S.: The Eikonal equation: numerical efficiency vs. algorithmic complexity on quadrilateral grids. In: Proceedings of Algoritmy, vol. 22 (2005)
14. Lin, B., Yang, J., He, X., Ye, J.: Geodesic distance function learning via heat flow on vector fields. In: International Conference on Machine Learning, pp. 145–153 (2014)
15. Melonakos, J., Pichon, E., Angenent, S., Tannenbaum, A.: Finsler active contours. IEEE Trans. Pattern Anal. Mach. Intell. **30**(3), 412–423 (2008)
16. Mirebeau, J.M.: Efficient fast marching with finsler metrics. Numer. Math. **126**(3), 515–557 (2014)
17. Mirebeau, J.M.: Anisotropic fast-marching on cartesian grids using Voronoi's first reduction of quadratic forms (2017)
18. Ohta, S.I., Sturm, K.T.: Heat flow on Finsler manifolds. Commun. Pure Appl. Math. **62**(10), 1386–1433 (2009)
19. Peyré, G., Péchaud, M., Keriven, R., Cohen, L.D., et al.: Geodesic methods in computer vision and graphics. Found. Trends® Comput. Graph. Vis. **5**(3–4), 197–397 (2010)
20. Sethian, J.A.: A fast marching level set method for monotonically advancing fronts. Proc. Nat. Acad. Sci. U.S.A. **93**(4), 1591–1595 (1996)

21. Solomon, J., et al.: Convolutional wasserstein distances: efficient optimal transportation on geometric domains. ACM Trans. Graph. (TOG) **34**(4), 66 (2015)
22. Varadhan, S.R.S.: On the behavior of the fundamental solution of the heat equation with variable coefficients. Commun. Pure Appl. Math. **20**(2), 431–455 (1967)
23. Weickert, J.: Coherence-Enhancing Diffusion Filtering. Kluwer Academic Publishers (1999)
24. Yang, F., Cohen, L.D.: Geodesic distance and curves through isotropic and anisotropic heat equations on images and surfaces. J. Math. Imaging Vis. **55**(2), 210–228 (2016)
25. Yang, F., Cohen, L.D.: Tubular structure segmentation based on heat diffusion. In: Lauze, F., Dong, Y., Dahl, A.B. (eds.) SSVM 2017. LNCS, vol. 10302, pp. 54–65. Springer, Cham (2017). https://doi.org/10.1007/978-3-319-58771-4_5
26. Zach, C., Shan, L., Niethammer, M.: Globally optimal finsler active contours. In: Denzler, J., Notni, G., Süße, H. (eds.) DAGM 2009. LNCS, vol. 5748, pp. 552–561. Springer, Heidelberg (2009). https://doi.org/10.1007/978-3-642-03798-6_56
27. Zhao, H.: A fast sweeping method for Eikonal equations. Math. Comput. **74**(250), 603–627 (2005)
28. Zou, Q., Zhang, J., Deng, B., Zhao, J.: Iso-level tool path planning for free-form surfaces. Comput. Aided Des. **53**, 117–125 (2014)

Putting the Anchors Efficiently: Geometric Constrained Pedestrian Detection

Liangji Fang, Xu Zhao$^{(\boxtimes)}$, Xiao Song, Shiquan Zhang, and Ming Yang

Department of Automation,
Shanghai Jiao Tong University, Shanghai, China
{fangliangji,zhaoxu,song_xiao,sq.zhang,mingyang}@sjtu.edu.cn

Abstract. Anchor box mechanism is of vital importance for deep network based object detection. Current object detectors put anchors uniformly in the entire image, so the false positives along with training and testing costs are increased significantly. In this work, we break through the homogeneity limitation in anchor putting by introducing geometric constraints for pedestrian detection. We first deduce the relationship between the height of the pedestrian and its location in image plane using geometrical priors, for which we only need to know the rough relative height between camera and pedestrian. As a result, we narrow down the distribution space of anchors with a certain pixel height from 2D to 1D. In implementation, we propose a novel Geometric Constrained Loss, by which the new anchor mechanism is embedded into the deep learning architecture. To further remove false positives in inference, Geometric Constrained Suppression is introduced. Complemented with two effective prediction modules, Dilated Double Shots Detector is designed to achieve better performance. Comprehensive experiments conducted on KITTI and Caltech datasets validate the superior performance and generalization ability of our method for both one-stage and two-stage methods, in both training and inference phases.

Keywords: Pedestrian detection · Geometric constrained theorems

1 Introduction

Pedestrian detection aims at recognizing and localizing pedestrians from images. It is a fundamental task in applications like autonomous driving and video surveillance. However, due to complicated background, relatively small size and

This research is supported by the funding from NSFC programs (61673269, 61273285, U1764264).

Electronic supplementary material The online version of this chapter (https://doi.org/10.1007/978-3-030-20873-8_25) contains supplementary material, which is available to authorized users.

Fig. 1. Mis-detections that violate "common sense". The solid and dotted boxes illustrate some abnormal "pedestrians" detected by SSD [24] and MS-CNN [3].

occlusion, pedestrian detection still remains unsolved. Recently, deep learning based object detector becomes mainstream method [6,17,24,29,30,32], where anchor box mechanism has been widely used. In either two-stage detectors like Faster R-CNN [32] and MS-CNN [3] or one-stage detectors like SSD [24] and YOLO [29,30], anchors play an important role in finding object candidates with different scales and aspect ratios at different locations. Essentially, the anchor generating process is equivalent to a discrete sampling process in 2D image space, under the guidance of prior knowledge observed from data.

This mechanism had been validated advantageous as it largely reduces the search space and can be naturally embedded into deep learning architectures. When detecting a pedestrian under current anchor mechanism, however, the entire image need to be searched uniformly with more than thousands of anchors. Due to the homogeneity when putting anchors, the false positives along with training and testing costs are increased significantly with the increase of anchor number. This leads to some new questions: do we really need to put anchors across the whole image for automatic driving and video surveillance? Can prior knowledge be incorporated in anchor generating process? In YOLO v2 [30], k-means clustering is applied to the training set to ascertain reasonable anchor sizes, but anchors at different locations are still treated equally.

A recent psychological research [9] reveals that unlike humans, object detectors like [32] can be fooled by target-shaped distractors that are inconsistent with the expected size of the object, which is also consistent with our experimental results. In Fig. 1, some typical mistakes that current detectors are prone to make on the KITTI dataset [13] are displayed. As can be seen, although these detections own some similar features with pedestrians, e.g. shape and color, predicated as false positives is easy for human vision but hard for machine detectors. For human vision, it is unreasonable that a small pedestrian is hung up in sky or a pedestrian appears as tall as a building. We believe that employing such inherent "common sense" is beneficial for efficient object detection.

Hence our motivation is to find a feasible computational strategy to encode such "common sense" into the current anchor box mechanism, so that the drawbacks introduced with the global homogeneity when putting anchors can be surmounted. In a nutshell, the geometrical constraints extracted from the perspective projection rule can be naturally exploited as corresponding "common sense" to break through the limitations of current anchor mechanism.

In this paper, a novel method is proposed to set up anchors and remove false detection results using geometrical constraints, which is especially useful for autonomous driving. First of all, the relationship between the height of a pedestrian and its location in image plane is derived, under the assumption that pedestrian height (e.g. 1.5 m–2 m) is roughly known and the camera pose does not change greatly. Hence anchors with different sizes are no longer equally distributed in image plane, meanwhile the previous 2D searching process is reduced to 1D for fixed-size anchors.

Different from previous work [1, 2, 19, 28, 36] which applys the geometric constraints in traditional detectors like DPM [10] and HOG [7], we further propose the novel Geometric Constrained Loss and Geometric Constrained Suppression which can be easily embedded into the deep learning framework. Instead of abandoning all anchors not satisfying the geometric constraints, another mitigatory way is adopted in which the losses of those anchors are down weighted during training and their confidence scores are decayed during inference.

To verify the effectiveness of our proposed Geometric Constrained Loss and Suppression, we specially design an one-stage detector called Dilated Double Shots Detector (DDSD) in which new prediction modules are established. To obtain a better classification performance, dilated convolution is utilized to explicitly encode context information with little additional computation cost. To acquire more precise localization results, a double-shots regression module is proposed in which the location of an anchor is regressed twice. Then we embed our geometric constraints into two-stage detector MS-CNN.

To sum up, the main contributions of this paper lie in the following aspects.

(1) The relationship between the size of a pedestrian and its location in image plane is deduced and utilized, hence the homogeneity limitation of anchor mechanism is broken. Accordingly the searching space of a pedestrian is narrowed down from 2D to 1D for fixed-size anchor.

(2) Based on the deduced relationship, we propose a novel Geometric Constrained Loss (GC Loss), by which the new anchor mechanism is embedded into the deep learning architecture. Then Geometric Constrained Suppression (GCS) is designed to remove false positives in inference.

(3) Furthermore, the proposed GC Loss and GCS are embedded into our designed one-stage Dilated Double Shots Detector and existing two-stage MS-CNN. Comprehensive experiments conducted on KITTI and Caltech datasets validate the superiority and generalization ability of our method.

2   Related Work

Pedestrian detection is an important task in object detection. Many works are proposed to improve pedestrian detection [3, 11, 19, 31]. Starting from R-CNN [16], two-stage object detectors are evolved rapidly [15, 32]. Many works focus on the second stage to obtain more precise classification and localization results.

MS-CNN [3] concatenates features extracted from region proposals and contextual regions to encode context information. Loc-Net [14] regards output from the second stage as proposals and refines them iteratively to obtain better results.

Although more precise, two-stage methods tend to be less efficient comparing with one-stage methods. YOLO [29] treats the object detection as an one-stage task which directly regresses the target's category and location within each image grid. Inspired by YOLO, SSD putting anchors with different sizes and aspect ratios on multiple feature maps with different resolutions. In order to encode context information, a recurrent and rolling architecture is proposed in [31] for feature fusion, which obtains good results but increases computation cost. Dilated convolution is utilized in [40,41] to enlarge receptive field meanwhile preserving the resolution for semantic segmentation and classification. However, the speed drops significantly owing to the usage of dilated convolution in backbone network. We reveal that using a simple 3×3 convolution with dilation on the prediction head boosts the encoding for context information while maintaining efficiency. RetinaNet [23] incorporates Focal Loss to solve class imbalance problem in one-stage methods, in which Focal Loss down-weights the classification loss assigned to easy examples.

Both two-stage and one-stage methods deeply rely on a set of predefined anchors. For instance, two-stage detectors can be accelerated by simply reducing the number of proposals [21]. Several papers use geometric priors to improve pedestrian detection accuracy [1,2,19,28,36]. Perspective rule is used in [19] to filter sliding windows in their probabilistic model. A coarse linear relationship between detection's height and its location is used in [28] to penalize the scores of small objects based on a rigid template. In [36], the derived geometric algorithm is embedded into their HOG detector to select valid sliding windows. Depth information is exploited in [1,2] based on stereo images to encode geometric priors. However, the previous work apply the geometric constraints in traditional detectors like DPM [10] and HOG [7]. Different from previous works, we explore how to embed the geometric constraints into deep learning based object detector reasonably. Specifically, we first deduce the relationship between pedestrian's pixel height and location then extend the relationship after using data augmentation. Then we propose our novel Geometric Constrained Loss and Geometric Constrained Suppression which decays the contributions of anchors and remove false detection results that do not meet geometrical constraints.

3   Geometric Constraints

In this section, we deduce the relationship between the height of a pedestrian's bounding box and its location in image based on the perspective projection rule.

3.1   Derivation

Firstly three coordinate systems: the world coordinate system, the camera coordinate system and the image coordinate system are defined. (X, Y, Z),

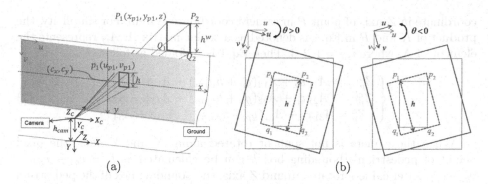

(a)   (b)

Fig. 2. (a) The pinhole camera model. (b) Rotation of the camera along the Z axis. Left shows the circumstance of clockwise rotation while the right shows the anticlockwise rotation. The solid rectangles denote the bounding boxes before rotation while the dash rectangles represent the new boxes after rotation.

(X_c, Y_c, Z_c) and (u, v) are defined as the coordinates corresponding to the three coordinate systems respectively. (c_x, c_y) is the coordinate of the principal point in the image coordinate system. Then we make two assumptions in the scenario like autonomous driving (Fig. 4(a) along with experiment results validate the correctness of our theorem and further prove the reasonability of the assumptions):

(1) The camera with focus length f is equipped on a car and located at $T = (0, -h_{cam}, 0)$ in the world coordinate system, where h_{cam} is denoted as the height of camera above the ground. The three rotation angles between the camera and the world coordinate system are notated as ψ, φ and θ respectively.

(2) The pedestrian can be represented by a rectangle (w^w, h^w, P_1, Q_2) in the world coordinate system, where (w^w, h^w) are the width and the height of the pedestrian, $P_1 = (x_{p1}, y_{p1}, z_{p1})$, $Q_2 = (x_{q2}, y_{q2}, z_{q2})$, P_2 and Q_1 represent four vertexes of the rectangle in the world coordinate system. $p_1 = (u_{p1}, v_{p1})$, $q_2 = (u_{q2}, v_{q2})$, p_2 and q_1 are defined as the coordinates of four vertexes' projection points in the image coordinate system. The perspective projection rule used for derivation and the assumptions are shown in Fig. 2(a).

Our goal is to obtain the relationship between the height of a pedestrian's bounding box and its location in image coordinate system, thereby anchors with a certain size could be put on corresponding locations based on the relationship, and detections violate it can be removed. Point P in world coordinate system is projected into image coordinate system using Eq. 1 [42], notated as p.

$$Z_p^c \widetilde{p} = KR[I \mid -T]\widetilde{P}, \tag{1}$$

where $\widetilde{P} = (x_p, y_p, z, 1)$ and $\widetilde{p} = (u_p, v_p, 1)$ are the homogeneous coordinates of P and p respectively, K denotes the camera intrinsic matrix, R is defined as the rotation matrix from world to camera coordinate system and Z_p^c notates the coordinate in Z-axis of point P in camera coordinate system. For simplicity, the product of K and R in Eq. 1 is denoted as a scalar matrix A. A_{ij} represents the element of A, where $i, j = 1, 2, 3$. Then Eq. 1 is unfolded as follows:

$$\begin{cases} Z_p^c u_p = A_{11} x_p + A_{12}(y_p + h_{cam}) + A_{13}z + A_{14} \\ Z_p^c v_p = A_{21} x_p + A_{22}(y_p + h_{cam}) + A_{23}z + A_{24} \\ Z_p^c = A_{31} x_p + A_{32}(y_p + h_{cam}) + A_{33}z + A_{34} . \end{cases} \quad (2)$$

When the camera is not spun or rotated along X and Y axes, the pixel height of pedestrian's bounding box h can be calculated as $h = v_{q1} - v_{p2} = v_{q2} - v_{p1}$. After camera rotates around Z axis, the bounding box of the pedestrian is changed as illustrated in Fig. 2(b). Under this condition, $v_{q1} - v_{p2} \neq v_{q2} - v_{p1}$. Assuming $|\theta| \ll 90°$, the pixel height of the bounding box h can be calculated by the coordinates of four vertexes in v-axis:

$$h = \begin{cases} v_{q1} - v_{p2} & 0 \le \theta < 90° \\ v_{q2} - v_{p1} & -90° < \theta < 0. \end{cases} \quad (3)$$

As (ψ, φ, θ) are small, we suppose $Z_{p1}^c = Z_{q2}^c$ and $Z_{p2}^c = Z_{q1}^c$. Combining with Eqs. 2, 3 is simplified as follows:

$$h = \begin{cases} \frac{A_{21} w^w + A_{22} h^w}{Z_{p2}^c} & 0 \le \theta < 90° \\ \frac{A_{21} w^w + A_{22} h^w}{Z_{p1}^c} & -90° < \theta < 0. \end{cases} \quad (4)$$

Considering Eqs. 2 and 4, the ultimate relationship is obtained:

$$h = \frac{a u_i + b v_i + c}{d(h_{cam} - h^w)}, i = \{p1, p2\}, \quad (5)$$

where (a, b, c, d) are the constants determined by K, R and P_1 or P_2 (detailed formulation can be found in supplemental material), (u_i, v_i) is the location of the pedestrian's bounding box. i is determined by the sign of θ in Eq. 3. Figure 4 (b) reveals heat maps of the height of pedestrian's bounding box and its location using Eq. 5. Based on the above deduction, Theorem 1 is obtained.

Theorem 1 (general constrain). *A certain pedestrian with pixel height of h is located at (u_p, v_p), satisfying Eq. 5. Apparently, h is in linear relationship with u_p and v_p.*

Suppose the camera is not spun in the following. Then we consider a special case where ψ, φ and θ are equal to 0. Hence $R = I$ and Eq. 1 is simplified:

$$Z_p^c \begin{bmatrix} u_p \\ v_p \\ 1 \end{bmatrix} = \begin{bmatrix} f & 0 & p_x \\ 0 & f & p_y \\ 0 & 0 & 1 \end{bmatrix} \begin{bmatrix} x_p \\ y_p + h_{cam} \\ z \end{bmatrix}, \quad (6)$$

where (p_x, p_y) are the pixel offsets of the principle point. As the rotation of the camera is not considered, hence $h = v_{q1} - v_{p1} = \frac{h^w}{Z^c}$ and $Z^c = Z_{p1}^c = Z_{q2}^c$. Based on Eq. 6, the relationship between the height of the pedestrian's bounding box and its location in the image coordinate system is described in Eq. 7.

$$h = \frac{h^w(v_{p1} - p_y)}{h_{cam} - h^w} = \frac{2h^w(v_c - p_y)}{2h_{cam} - h^w}, \tag{7}$$

where v_c denotes the center point coordinate in v-axis of the pedestrian's bounding box. Finally, Theorem 1 is simplified to Theorem 2. For simplicity, v_c is regarded as the location of the bounding box.

Theorem 2 (special constrain). *When the camera is not spun, pedestrians with a pixel height of h are located at v_c, satisfying Eq. 7. If the top of the pedestrian is located below the camera in the world coordinate system, h is proportional to v_c, otherwise h is inversely proportional to v_c.*

3.2   Translation and Scaling

In this section, we will consider the translation and scaling operations applied to the image to generalize Theorem 2.

Translation. When an image is translated, the coordinate of each pixel is changed. Assuming that the origin of the image is changed to $(\Delta u, \Delta v)$ from $(0, 0)$ after translation, hence the coordinate of certain pedestrian's center point is changed from (u_c, v_c) to $(u_c^t, v_c^t) = (u_c - \Delta u, v_c - \Delta v)$ meanwhile the height of corresponding pedestrian's bounding box will remain constant after translation. Hence the relationship mentioned in Theorem 2 is turned into:

$$h = \frac{2h^w}{2h_{cam} - h^w}(v_c^t + \Delta v - p_y). \tag{8}$$

Scaling. Scaling, namely resizing an image, will simultaneously affect the height of a pedestrian's bounding box and the coordinate of its center point. Let (H_s, W_s), h_s and v_c^s denote the size of image, the pixel height of the pedestrian's bounding box and the coordinate of its center point after scaling respectively. Then we have $h_s = \frac{H_s}{H}h$ and $v_c^s = \frac{H_s}{H}v_c$, where H is the height of the original image. Furthermore Eq. 9 is deduced:

$$h_s = \frac{2h^w}{2h_{cam} - h^w}(v_c^s - \frac{H_s}{H}p_y). \tag{9}$$

4   Geometric Constrained Pedestrian Detector

Based on Theorem 2, the Geometric Constrained Loss is designed to instruct the detector where to look during training while the Geometric Constrained Suppression is proposed to remove the false positives during inference. Taking our designed one-stage Dilated Double Shots Detector (DDSD) as an example, we show how to integrate GC Loss and GCS into deep learning framework.

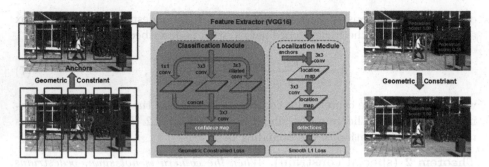

Fig. 3. The whole framework of our proposed GC-DDSD. Firstly Theorem 2 is employed to make distinctions among densely distributed anchors. For better viewing results, we diagram the pattern of directly abandoning illegal anchors. Next, features are extracted from VGG16 network complemented with added layers. Then, the classification and localization modules are designed to refine the anchors. Finally, Theorem 2 is employed again to filtrate false positives.

4.1   Geometric Constrained Loss

Based on Theorem 2, the distribution space of anchors with certain height is narrowed down from 2D to 1D. Hence we only need to put anchors with a height of h on row v_c. In practice, however, we know little about the real and accurate height of the pedestrian h^w. So we hypothesize that h^w is ranged from $h_{min}^w = 1.5$ m to $h_{max}^w = 2.0$ m (Pedestrian). Then a row index interval satisfying Eq. 7 is obtained, which we call security interval (v_c^{min}, v_c^{max}).

Instead of removing all anchors located out of the security interval during training, we preserve those anchor boxes in use and relatively decrease their contributions to the loss. For binary classification, the cross entropy loss can be written as $CEL(p) = -log(p)$, where p is the estimated foreground probability.

We propose our novel Geometric Constrained Loss based on the cross entropy loss, in which the contributions of samples outside the security interval are weakened. Assuming the calculated security interval is determined as (v_c^{min}, v_c^{max}) and the location of an anchor with a height of h is v_c. The normalized distance between an anchor and the security interval is defined in Eq. 10.

$$d = \frac{\max(v_c^{min} - v_c, 0)}{v_c^{min}} + \frac{\max(v_c - v_c^{max}, 0)}{H - v_c^{max}},   \tag{10}$$

where H is the height of the image. Finally, the GC Loss is defined as follows:

$$GCL(p) = -(1 - d)^\gamma log(p).   \tag{11}$$

As the normalized distance increases, the contribution of corresponding anchor to the final loss is decreased.

4.2   Geometric Constrained Suppression

Merely utilizing Theorem 2 in training apparently wastes its powerfulness, it is also capable of benefiting the inference phase. Detection results violating Theorem 2 may less likely be true pedestrians. Hence we propose to lower confidence scores of detections that violate the geometric constrained theorem using Eq. 12. Score of each anchor is multiplied with a polynomial decaying factor derived from its normalized distance d from the security interval defined in Eq. 10.

$$score = score \cdot (1 - d)^\sigma. \qquad (12)$$

However, there is a more efficient way that directly abandoning the anchors and detection results not satisfying the theorem. Experiments show that it works as well as polynomial decaying function.

4.3   Dilated Double Shots Detector

Figure 3 is an overall illustration of the entire framework. The whole network consists of three major components, named as the feature extractor backbone, the classification module and the localization module.

Feature Extractor. As pointed out in [21], the performance of one-stage detectors might slightly rely on the accuracy of its feature extractors (VGG [35], ResNet [18], Inception [22,37,38]). Therefore we adopt the simple but effective VGG-16 backbone, which is pre-trained on ImageNet [33]. Following SSD [24], we convert the fully connected layers fc6 and fc7 to convolutional layers. Lastly, several extra layers are exploited to enhance detection accuracy of large objects.

Dilated Context Embedding. The core task for encoding context information is to obtain a bigger receptive filed. There are three major methods, including (a) aggregated features produced by convolution with bigger kernel sizes, (b) aggregated features produced by deeper layers [12,27] and (c) aggregated features produced by the dilated convolution. For efficiency, we ignore (a). By conducting experiments, we ignore (b) and choose (c). It is worth mentioning that we only incorporate context information into the classification task. Furthermore, as pointed out in [20], using a fixed contextual window of 300 pixels lowering error rate for small objects dramatically. Therefore dilation routines with relatively big rates on lower prediction layers are adopted to enlarge receptive field.

Double Shots Regression. SSD [24] merely utilizes a simple convolution with a kernel size of 3×3 for localization. Motivated by LocNet [14], we design double shots regression module to refine locations of anchors twice, as shown Fig. 3.

4.4   Integration Strategies

Anchors. We put anchors on multiple layers where normalized areas of anchors increase proportional to the depth of layer. Following [30], k-means clustering algorithm is adopted for the bounding boxes in training set in order to get reasonable aspect ratios of anchors. Unlike other methods, anchors with different sizes on different locations are discriminated based on Theorem 2.

Matching Strategy. During training, an anchor is treated as positive sample if the IoU value with a ground truth bounding box is higher than a certain threshold (e.g. 0.6), instead as potential negative sample if IoU values with all ground truth bounding boxes are lower than a certain threshold (e.g. 0.5). Next the online hard example mining (OHEM [34]) strategy is exploited to select hard negative examples based on their confidence losses, meanwhile insuring that the ratio between positive and negative samples are maintained at 1:3.

Data Augmentation. We follow the same data augmentation employed in SSD [24], including random expanding, cropping and flipping operations as well as other photo-metric distortions. After data augmentation, relationship between the height of an anchor and its location in Theorem 2 is changed.

Specifically, expanding operation is first employed in which the input image with size (W, H) is placed randomly on a canvas with a random size of $(\alpha W, \alpha H)(\alpha \geq 1)$ filled with mean pixel values. Next a small patch with size $(\beta \alpha W, \beta \alpha H)(\beta \leq 1)$ in the canvas is cropped. Finally the cropped patch is scaled to (W_r, H_r). Hence two translation and one scaling operations are employed. Based on Eqs. 8 and 9, the relationship in Theorem 2 after data augmentation is obtained (detailed proof can be found in supplemental material):

$$h_r = \frac{2h^w}{2h_{cam} - h^w} [v_c^r + \frac{H_r}{\beta \alpha H}(\Delta v_c - \Delta v_e - p_y)] . \tag{13}$$

Loss. Geometric Constrained Loss proposed in Sect. 4.1 is adopted for classification. If all anchors that violate the geometrical constraint are treated equally (their distances to the security interval are set to 1), it is equivalent to simply neglecting them. Smooth L1 loss defined in [15] is utilized for localization. Finally the multi-task loss is jointly minimized.

5 Experiment

Our proposed Geometric Constrained theorem and one-stage detector GC-DDSD are evaluated on KITTI [13] dataset. Geometric constrained theorem is also applied to the existed two-stage method MS-CNN [3] and evaluated on Caltech dataset [8]. All models are trained and tested on a single Nvidia Titan X GPU.

KITTI Dataset. The KITTI object detection benchmark contains 7481 and 7518 images for training and testing, respectively. We focus on detections with the moderate degree of difficulty because all methods are evaluated based on this metric on KITTI. We divide the trainval set into training and validation sets containing 3712 and 3769 images respectively following [3,5].

Caltech Pedestrian Dataset. The Caltech pedestrian dataset contains approximately 10 hours of video taken from a vehicle. Following MS-CNN, a

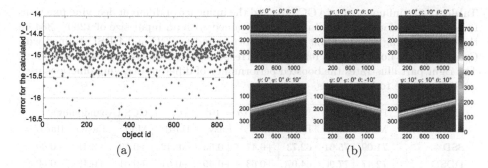

(a)   (b)

Fig. 4. (a) The error distribution between the calculated coordinate using Theorem 2 and the ground truth value. (b) Heatmaps of calculated pixel height h in different locations corresponding to different rotation angles for Theorem 1. Each heatmap corresponds to a 1280×384 image. Box height over twice the image height or negative is set to 0. Better viewed in color. (Color figure online)

7x set of the original training images (32077 images) is employed and the standard test set (4024 images) is used for evaluation.

DDSD Implementation Details. For the following ablation studies, we add extra layers conv8_2, conv9_2, conv10_2 and conv11_2 after VGG-16 [35] body. Feature map's spatial size is halved by the forward propagation of every added layer. All added layers along with conv4_3 and conv7 are used for prediction. Following SSD [24], the L2 normalization operation [25] is utilized on conv4_3. In order to encode context information, we use a 3×3 dilated convolution with a rate of 3 on conv4_3 and conv7 in classification modules and another 3×3 dilated convolution with a rate of 2 on other layers in classification modules. Anchors are put on all layers responsible for prediction and areas of the anchors on each layer vary from $0.1^2 L^2$ to $0.7^2 L^2$, where L denotes the shortest edge of the input image. To obtain denser anchors, 2 additional scales ($2^{1/3}$, $2^{2/3}$ fold than each original scale) on each feature map are complemented. After K-means clustering, aspect ratios are fixed to $\{0.3, 0.4, 0.5, 0.7, 1\}$ for Pedestrian and Cyclist.

5.1   Verification of Geometric Constraints

In order to verify the validity of Theorem 2, we analyse the relationship between the height of a ground truth bounding box and its pixel location among KITTI training set[1]. Based on the given label and info, all variables mentioned in Eq. 7 are known except the principle point offset (set as $p_y = \frac{H}{2}$ manually). Firstly, assuming the center point coordinate of the ground truth object is unknown and it can be easily calculated by Eq. 7. Next the calculated center point coordinate in v-axis notated as v_c is compared with ground truth label. The distribution of error between v_c and corresponding ground truth is revealed in Fig. 4(a). As can

---

[1] Seriously occluded and truncated examples are ignored.

Table 1. The influence of γ to GC Loss and the influence of different decaying functions to GC Suppression (GCS). All models are trained with an input size of 1280×384 on the same training set. The first two rows correspond to SSD and DDSD trained with Cross Entropy Loss and the remaining correspond to DDSD trained with GC Loss. The right part illustrates the boosted performance of different decaying functions used in GCS relative to left models.

Model	γ	Pedestrian			GCS ($\sigma = 10$)			GCS (Abandoning)		
		Mod	Easy	Hard	Mod	Easy	Hard	Mod	Easy	Hard
SSD	-	71.09	75.61	62.73	+0.47	+0.53	+0.42	+0.60	+0.41	+0.60
DDSD	-	72.47	77.90	64.07	+0.63	+0.49	+0.61	+0.61	+0.46	+0.60
GC-DDSD	1	**73.59**	**78.15**	**64.98**	+0.64	+0.52	**+0.66**	+0.61	**+0.70**	**+0.75**
	2	73.39	78.07	64.59	**+0.67**	**+0.77**	+0.55	**+0.62**	+0.54	+0.70
	3	72.54	77.14	63.55	+0.47	+0.63	+0.51	+0.44	+0.41	+0.70
	-	73.08	77.73	64.54	+0.44	+0.49	+0.65	+0.42	+0.42	+0.66

be seen, the calculated error is small and fluctuated within $[-16, -14]$ pixels. Hence the principle point offset is refined as $p_y = \frac{H}{2} - 15$.

5.2 Analysis of Geometric Constraints

Geometric Constrained Loss (GC Loss). The influence of different values of γ to GC Loss in Eq. 11 is shown in the left part of Table 1. The first two rows in Table 1 correspond to SSD [24] and our base model DDSD trained without GC Loss using the same anchor settings respectively. By using powerful prediction modules, DDSD outperforms SSD by almost 1.4%. Specifically, dilated context encoding along boosts the performance by 1% and double shots boosts the performance by 0.5%. According to the experiments, GC Loss is robust to the hyper-parameter γ. When γ is set to 1, the highest mAP is achieved, which is 1.1% higher than that without using GC Loss. Experiment where anchors out of the security interval are directly abandoned, is also conducted. The performance is slightly worse than that using GC Loss, as shown in the last row in Table 1. Hence utilization of all training anchors is akin to a data augmentation method.

Intuitively, most of the anchors violating Theorem 2 are potentially negative samples. By narrowing down the distribution of anchors from 2D to 1D, GC Loss is prone to handling the class imbalance problem mentioned in [23] naturally.

Table 1 also reveals that GC Loss does not perform well on easy objects. Samples violating the geometric constraints have little impact on easy objects because of their distinguished features, however detectors can be easily confused by negative samples violating the geometrical constraints for moderate objects.

Geometric Constrained Suppression (GCS). In inference phase, confidence scores of the detections violating Theorem 2 are decayed before Non-Maxim Suppression. The right part of Table 1 displays the detection performance by employing polynomial decaying function. As can be seen, utilization of Geometric Constrained Suppression boosts the performance by around 0.5% steadily

Table 2. Comparison with other methods on the same KITTI validation and test set. MS-CNN* is trained using the open source code. SSD is trained using the same settings as DDSD. **All models except Monocular 3D are trained and tested with an input size of 1280 × 384 in a single model.**

Model	Validation set (Pedestrian)			Test set (Pedestrian)		
	Mod	Hard	Easy	Mod	Hard	Easy
Monocular 3D [4]	65.10	60.97	72.20	66.66	63.44	77.30
MS-CNN* [3]	71.46	63.80	76.87	69.65	64.34	80.65
HyperLearner [26]	71.25	62.15	78.43	-	-	-
SSD [24]	71.09	62.73	75.61	67.29	62.27	78.83
ours	**74.20**	**65.73**	**78.85**	**71.41**	**65.78**	**82.34**

for different models. However, a relatively plain way that directly abandoning detection candidates that violate the geometric constrained theorem may reduce the computation cost. Table 1 reveals that comparable performance is achieved by abandoning those anchors directly, which indicates that almost all anchors violating the geometrical constraints are harmful to detection performance, verifying the validity of Theorem 2. Although abandoning illegal anchors and detections directly may slightly hurt the recall due to the unknown ground height and other random noises, this scheme can be adopted considering efficiency.

GC Loss and GCS could boost the performance by 1.8% on validation set, which is mainly attributed to the reduction of false positives. The number of false positives and anchors are reduced from 23 to 8 and 108,288 to 22,724 per image using our geometric constraints for DDSD. Meanwhile the speed is accelerated from 19 fps to 22 fps. Detection is the basis for many high-level tasks like Multiple Object Tracking. Using our geometric constraint may reduce the number of false positives (equal to the number of trajectories) by 15.

Finally, Table 2 reveals the performance compared with other methods on the same validation and test sets. Results of MS-CNN, SSD and our GC-DDSD on test set are trained and tested with an input size of 1280 × 384, without tricks like multi-scale testing or ensemble. For MS-CNN [3], we use their default settings to train the model. Our GC-DDSD outperforms SSD by 4.1% and MS-CNN by 1.8%. Figure 5 shows some qualitative results of GC-DDSD.

5.3   Extension to Two-Stage Methods

Our proposed geometric constrained theorem is a general theorem that could be applied to most detectors. Finally, we demonstrate the effectiveness of our proposed geometric constrained theorem on two-stage methods. MS-CNN is adopted as our base model, where Geometric Constrained Loss is utilized on the second stage. In addition, Theorem 1 is employed in inference phase to remove redundant anchors and false proposals.

Fig. 5. Detection results of DDSD (left) and GC-DDSD (right) on KITTI dataset. Green bounding boxes denote the true positives while the red dashed boxes illustrate the false detection results. (Color figure online)

To obtain the necessary parameters in Theorem 1, pose of camera and center-point compensation are estimated on the training set. Next GCS is utilized on the original MS-CNN denoted as MS-CNN-GCS. Figure 6 reveals that only applying GCS to remove false positives in inference phase boosts the performance by 0.5%. Finally, we retrain a MS-CNN model using our proposed geometrical constraint denoted as MS-CNN-GC which is 1.1% higher than MS-CNN, the excellent performance on Caltech Pedestrian dataset is achieved.

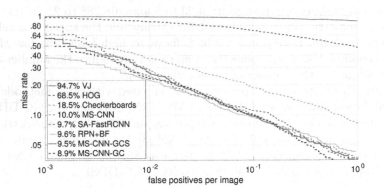

Fig. 6. Results on Caltech test set (reasonable, MR_{-2}). Only methods trained with Caltech images are shown.

6   Conclusion

In this paper, we demonstrate that putting anchors with a certain height covering the whole image is not necessary for autonomous driving. By utilizing geometrical constraints, the spatial distribution of anchors with a certain height is narrowed down from 2D to 1D. Specifically, we propose a novel Geometric Constrained Loss where contributions of samples violating the geometric constrained theorem are decayed. Geometric Constrained Suppression is designed to remove unreasonable anchors and detection candidates in inference. By conducting experiments on the designed one-stage detector DDSD and the extended two-stage method MS-CNN, the superiority of our proposed theorem is proved.

References

1. Benenson, R., Mathias, M., Timofte, R., Van Gool, L.: Pedestrian detection at 100 frames per second. In: CVPR, pp. 2903–2910. IEEE (2012)
2. Benenson, R., Timofte, R., Van Gool, L.: Stixels estimation without depth map computation. In: ICCV Workshops, pp. 2010–2017. IEEE (2011)
3. Cai, Z., Fan, Q., Feris, R.S., Vasconcelos, N.: A unified multi-scale deep convolutional neural network for fast object detection. In: Leibe, B., Matas, J., Sebe, N., Welling, M. (eds.) ECCV 2016. LNCS, vol. 9908, pp. 354–370. Springer, Cham (2016). https://doi.org/10.1007/978-3-319-46493-0_22
4. Chen, X., Kundu, K., Zhang, Z., Ma, H., Fidler, S., Urtasun, R.: Monocular 3D object detection for autonomous driving. In: CVPR, pp. 2147–2156 (2016)
5. Chen, X., et al.: 3D object proposals for accurate object class detection. In: NIPS, pp. 424–432 (2015)
6. Dai, J., Li, Y., He, K., Sun, J.: R-FCN: object detection via region-based fully convolutional networks. In: NIPS, pp. 379–387 (2016)
7. Dalal, N., Triggs, B.: Histograms of oriented gradients for human detection. In: IEEE Computer Society Conference on Computer Vision and Pattern Recognition, 2005. CVPR 2005. vol. 1, pp. 886–893. IEEE (2005)
8. Dollár, P., Wojek, C., Schiele, B., Perona, P.: Pedestrian detection: a benchmark. In: CVPR, pp. 304–311 (2009)
9. Eckstein, M.P., Koehler, K., Welbourne, L.E., Akbas, E.: Humans, but not deep neural networks, often miss giant targets in scenes. Curr. Biol. 27(18), 2827–2832 (2017)
10. Felzenszwalb, P., McAllester, D., Ramanan, D.: A discriminatively trained, multi-scale, deformable part model. In: CVPR, pp. 1–8 (2008)
11. Felzenszwalb, P.F., Girshick, R.B., McAllester, D., Ramanan, D.: Object detection with discriminatively trained part-based models. TPAMI 32(9), 1627–1645 (2010)
12. Fu, C.Y., Liu, W., Ranga, A., Tyagi, A., Berg, A.C.: DSSD: deconvolutional single shot detector. arXiv preprint arXiv:1701.06659 (2017)
13. Geiger, A., Lenz, P., Urtasun, R.: Are we ready for autonomous driving? the KITTI vision benchmark suite. In: CVPR, pp. 3354–3361 (2012)
14. Gidaris, S., Komodakis, N.: LocNet: improving localization accuracy for object detection. In: CVPR, pp. 789–798 (2016)
15. Girshick, R.: Fast R-CNN. In: ICCV, pp. 1440–1448 (2015)
16. Girshick, R., Donahue, J., Darrell, T., Malik, J.: Rich feature hierarchies for accurate object detection and semantic segmentation. In: CVPR, pp. 580–587 (2014)
17. He, K., Gkioxari, G., Dollár, P., Girshick, R.: Mask R-CNN. In: ICCV, pp. 2980–2988 (2017)
18. He, K., Zhang, X., Ren, S., Sun, J.: Deep residual learning for image recognition. In: CVPR, pp. 770–778 (2016)

19. Hoiem, D., Efros, A.A., Hebert, M.: Putting objects in perspective. IJCV **80**(1), 3–15 (2008)
20. Hu, P., Ramanan, D.: Finding tiny faces. In: CVPR, pp. 1522–1530 (2017)
21. Huang, J., et al.: Speed/accuracy trade-offs for modern convolutional object detectors. In: CVPR (2017)
22. Ioffe, S., Szegedy, C.: Batch normalization: accelerating deep network training by reducing internal covariate shift. In: ICML, pp. 448–456 (2015)
23. Lin, T.Y., Goyal, P., Girshick, R., He, K., Dollár, P.: Focal loss for dense object detection. In: ICCV (2017)
24. Liu, W., et al.: SSD: single shot multibox detector. In: Leibe, B., Matas, J., Sebe, N., Welling, M. (eds.) ECCV 2016. LNCS, vol. 9905, pp. 21–37. Springer, Cham (2016). https://doi.org/10.1007/978-3-319-46448-0_2
25. Liu, W., Rabinovich, A., Berg, A.C.: ParseNet: looking wider to see better. arXiv preprint arXiv:1506.04579 (2015)
26. Mao, J., Xiao, T., Jiang, Y., Cao, Z.: What can help pedestrian detection? In: CVPR, p. 3 (2017)
27. Newell, A., Yang, K., Deng, J.: Stacked hourglass networks for human pose estimation. In: Leibe, B., Matas, J., Sebe, N., Welling, M. (eds.) ECCV 2016. LNCS, vol. 9912, pp. 483–499. Springer, Cham (2016). https://doi.org/10.1007/978-3-319-46484-8_29
28. Park, D., Ramanan, D., Fowlkes, C.: Multiresolution models for object detection. In: Daniilidis, K., Maragos, P., Paragios, N. (eds.) ECCV 2010. LNCS, vol. 6314, pp. 241–254. Springer, Heidelberg (2010). https://doi.org/10.1007/978-3-642-15561-1_18
29. Redmon, J., Divvala, S., Girshick, R., Farhadi, A.: You only look once: Unified, real-time object detection. In: CVPR, pp. 779–788 (2016)
30. Redmon, J., Farhadi, A.: YOLO9000: Better, Faster, Stronger. arXiv preprint arXiv:1612.08242 (2016)
31. Ren, J., et al.: Accurate single stage detector using recurrent rolling convolution. In: CVPR, pp. 752–760 (2017)
32. Ren, S., He, K., Girshick, R., Sun, J.: Faster R-CNN: towards real-time object detection with region proposal networks. In: NIPS, pp. 91–99 (2015)
33. Russakovsky, O., et al.: Imagenet large scale visual recognition challenge. IJCV **115**(3), 211–252 (2015)
34. Shrivastava, A., Gupta, A., Girshick, R.: Training region-based object detectors with online hard example mining. In: CVPR, pp. 761–769 (2016)
35. Simonyan, K., Zisserman, A.: Very deep convolutional networks for large-scale image recognition. arXiv preprint arXiv:1409.1556 (2014)
36. Sudowe, P., Leibe, B.: Efficient use of geometric constraints for sliding-window object detection in video. In: Crowley, J.L., Draper, B.A., Thonnat, M. (eds.) ICVS 2011. LNCS, vol. 6962, pp. 11–20. Springer, Heidelberg (2011). https://doi.org/10.1007/978-3-642-23968-7_2
37. Szegedy, C., Ioffe, S., Vanhoucke, V., Alemi, A.A.: Inception-v4, inception-ResNet and the impact of residual connections on learning. In: AAAI, pp. 4278–4284 (2017)
38. Szegedy, C., Vanhoucke, V., Ioffe, S., Shlens, J., Wojna, Z.: Rethinking the inception architecture for computer vision. In: CVPR, pp. 2818–2826 (2016)
39. Uijlings, J.R., Van De Sande, K.E., Gevers, T., Smeulders, A.W.: Selective search for object recognition. IJCV **104**(2), 154–171 (2013)
40. Yu, F., Koltun, V.: Multi-scale context aggregation by dilated convolutions. In: ICLR (2016)

41. Yu, F., Koltun, V., Funkhouser, T.: Dilated residual networks. In: CVPR, p. 2 (2017)
42. Hartley, R., Zisserman, A.: Multiple View Geometry in Computer Vision, 2nd edn., January 2006
43. Zitnick, C.L., Dollár, P.: Edge boxes: locating object proposals from edges. In: Fleet, D., Pajdla, T., Schiele, B., Tuytelaars, T. (eds.) ECCV 2014. LNCS, vol. 8693, pp. 391–405. Springer, Cham (2014). https://doi.org/10.1007/978-3-319-10602-1_26

Multi-label Learning from Noisy Labels with Non-linear Feature Transformation

Mengying Hu[1,2], Hu Han[1,3(✉)], Shiguang Shan[1,2,4], and Xilin Chen[1,2]

[1] Key Laboratory of Intelligent Information Processing of Chinese Academy of Sciences (CAS), Institute of Computing Technology, CAS, Beijing 100190, China
mengying.hu@vipl.ict.ac.cn, {hanhu,sgshan,xlchen}@ict.ac.cn
[2] University of Chinese Academy of Sciences, Beijing 100049, China
[3] Peng Cheng Laboratory, Shenzhen, China
[4] CAS Center for Excellence in Brain Science and Intelligence Technology, Shanghai, China

Abstract. Multi-label classification is an essential problem in image classification, because there are usually multiple related tags associated with each image. However, building a large scale multi-label dataset with clean labels can be very expensive and difficult. Therefore, utilizing a small set of data with verified labels and massive data with noise labels to build a multi-label classification model becomes valuable for practical applications. In this paper, we propose a teacher-student network with non-linear feature transformation, leveraging massive dataset with noisy labels and a small dataset with verified data to learn a multi-label classifier. We use a non-linear feature transformation to map the feature space and the label space. We first pre-train both the teacher and student networks with noisy labels and then train both networks jointly. We build a multi-label dataset based on MS COCO2014 for performance evaluation, in which both noisy label and verified label are given for each image. Experimental results on our dataset and the public-domain multi-label dataset (OpenImage) show that the proposed approach is effective in leveraging massive noisy labels to build multi-label classifiers.

1 Introduction

Multi-label learning has always been an important research topic in image classification, since multiple tags can be jointly associated to a single image. However, high quality annotation of multiple labels per image can be very challenging because different persons often have different understanding or focus on different parts of the same image. Insufficient data has become a common issue in limiting the use of deep learning based multi-label classification in various applications, *e.g.*, attribute learning [8], face recognition and analysis [7,12], etc. While annotating a large multi-label dataset with verified labels can be expensive and slow, it is relatively easy to obtain a huge number of images with unverified (noisy) labels, *e.g.*, either through Internet search or automatic labeling by pre-training

© Springer Nature Switzerland AG 2019
C. V. Jawahar et al. (Eds.): ACCV 2018, LNCS 11365, pp. 404–419, 2019.
https://doi.org/10.1007/978-3-030-20873-8_26

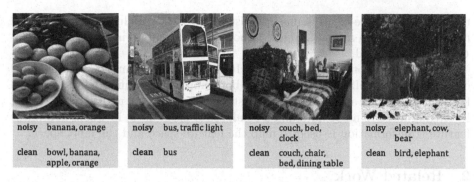

noisy	banana, orange	noisy	bus, traffic light
clean	bowl, banana, apple, orange	clean	bus

Fig. 1. Example images from the *extended MS-COCO*. This dataset contains images from 56 generic objects classes (*e.g.*, *banana, orange, bed, etc*). Most images can correspond to multiple labels because there can be multiple objects in one image. The noisy labels are not always consistent with the clean labels.

models. Therefore, it has drawn increasing attention to build multi-label classifier leveraging massive data with noisy labels and a small set of data with verified labels [11, 28].

In this work, we treat both wrong labels and missing labels as noisy labels. In addition, from the perspective of noisy label ratio per image, noisy labels can be grouped into two groups, single-label noise and multi-label noise. In single-label noise learning, each instance has unique label which is either correct or wrong. Sometimes, the confusing classes have a probability to flip to each other. This provides a precondition of modeling the label flipping process. Compared to single-label noise, multi-label noise is more complex. Since the dataset contains both correct and wrong labels and the relationship between them is hard to model manually.

Instead of modeling the label flipping process manually, Veit et al. [28] learned a linear map (between noisy labels and clean labels) based on image features learned from massive noisy data together with a small set of data with clean labels. This approach avoids using the noise transition probability matrix between labels and can be easily used in different dataset. However, features learned from noisy data can be noisy. In this situation, a linear transformation may not be enough to fit the clean labels. In this work, we introduce a non-linear transformation for noisy feature and evaluate it on MS COCO2014 [16] and OpenImage [13]. The results show that the non-linear transformation is helpful to improve the multi-label model's performance.

MS COCO2014 is widely used for multi-label classification which contains about 120k images of 90 image classes [16]. We extend MS COCO2014 by generating noisy label for each image using an ImageNet [5] pretrained Inception V3 [27] model. We denote this dataset as *extended MS-COCO*. Unlike OpenImages [13] and Fashion550k [11], which have massive noisy labels but very few human verified labels, the *extended MS-COCO* dataset consists of both verified and noisy labels for each image. Therefore, it is possible to investigate the effectiveness of the state-of-art semi-supervised approaches, including the proposed multi-label learning method. Figure 1 shows some examples in the *extended MS-COCO* we compiled.

The contributions of this work include: (1) a compiling of a multi-label dataset based on MS COCO2014 with both noisy and verified labels provided for each image; (2) an efficient teacher-student network for multi-label learning leveraging massive noisy data and a small set of clean data, in which non-linear feature transformation is used to map the feature space and the label space.

2 Related Work

2.1 Direct Learning with Noisy Labels

There are two main approaches for direct learning with noisy labels: removing the noisy data or making algorithm robust to noise. For approaches of the first category, a popular method is to remove the outliers [3,18] under the assumption that outliers are mislabeled. For example, Brodley and Friedl [3] presented a method which used a set of classifiers to filter out outliers before training. [17] used a reweight scheme to force model pay less attention to noisy samples. [24] removed the noise by "bootstrapping" on label prediction. For approaches of the second category, they focuses on improving the model tolerance to noisy labels [2,6,19,21,23,26]. Several algorithms explore new design of the loss function to achieve robustness against noisy labels [6,19]. Patrini [23] used a noise transition matrix T to define the probability of one label being flipped to another, and use it to correct the loss calculation even without human intervention. Some methods tried to model the label changing process in order to achieve better tolerance to noisy labels. Misra et al. [20] proposed a noise model assuming that noise is conditioned on image while some other methods assume that label noise is conditionally independent of input image [21]. Several works also use side information, like knowledge graph [4,15], to reduce the influence of noise. Recently, deep neutral network has been utilized as a simple way to handle noisy labels. Rolnick et al. [25] showed that deep neutral network can be robust to massive label noise without explicit handling of label noise. However, compared to the performance trained on clean labels, there is still a gap between them.

2.2 Semi-supervised Learning

Different from using the noise label solely, semi-supervised learning approaches introduce a small set of clean labels [11,14,28,29]. The difficulty in direct learning with noisy labels is that wrong labels are hard to recognize. However, clean data can relieve the problem to some extent, since it can be a good guide to distinguish noise from clean labels. Xiao et al. [29] divided the label noise into three types and associated them with three semantic meanings, noise-free, pure random and confusing noise. They used this information to model the relationship between images and noisy labels with a probabilistic graphical model and used clean data to pre-train the model. Several works [11,28] used a teacher-student model [10] to reduce label noise. In classification problem of noisy labels, teacher-student model consists of a label cleaning network as teacher and a classification network as student. The label cleaning network utilizes features of images to generates predictions which considered as cleaned labels. And these cleaned labels are used to supervise the student network. Veit et al. [28] proposed to learn a linear map between noisy labels and clean labels based on image features in the label cleaning network and used another linear network to classify. It is treated as a fine-tuning method while a base CNN is just used for extracting features. We follow a similar framework to [28], but we use a non-linear transformation to learn the map between features and labels.

3 Our Approach

We aim at learning a robust multi-label classifier from massive data with noisy labels and a small set of data with clean labels. Our idea is to leverage the small set of data with verified labels to clean (purify) the labels of the massive data. To facilitate the description below, we first give some notations. We use T to denote the data with noisy/unverified labels in the training dataset and use V to denote the small set of data with human verified labels in the training dataset. T consists of tuples of data: image x and its label y, i.e., $T = \{(x_i, y_i)\}_{i=1}^m$ where m denotes the number of data. By contrast, images in V have a noisy label and have a human verified label v_i, and thus can be denoted in triples, i.e., $V = \{(x_j, y_j, v_j)\}_{j=1}^n$ where n denotes the data number. Thus, in practical applications, we can assume $m >> n$. Both the noisy label y_i and verified label v_i are d-D binary labels with 1 denoting the presence of one class of label.

3.1 Teacher-Student Network with Non-linear Transform

As shown in Fig. 2, we use a multi-task learning architecture combining the label cleaning net and the multi-label classification net together. The aim is to train two classifiers with the same network structure utilizing the features extracted by the backbone feature extractor network f. When we learn f using both the noisy data and verified data, it can be not optimal compared with a network learning using a large amount of verified labels.

We regard the label cleaning network g in Fig. 2 as a teacher net that update its parameters using only human verified labels. Different from the method by Veit et al. [28], which use the noisy labels and image features as the input of the label cleaning network, we directly learn a non-linear transformation from image feature space f to the verified label space v. Specifically, we use a sigmoid layer between two linear layers, and use them to perform the transformation from noisy feature space to the label space. Through such transformation, the network can utilize the information in the noisy feature to learn a robust classification model. In our experiments, we find that the performance difference of using different

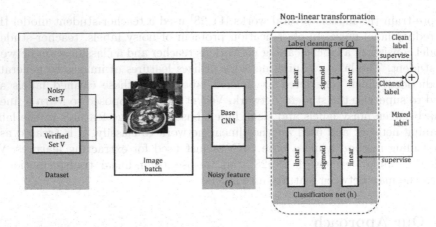

Fig. 2. Overview of our approach. We choose the image batch as a mixture of samples from both the noisy set and the verified set. We extract visual features using a ResNet50 model (denoted as Base CNN) and use these features as shared features by both the label cleaning net and the classification net. We use the same network architecture for both the label cleaning net and the classification net. The only difference between them lies in the supervision signal, *i.e.*, the label cleaning net is supervised by only the clean labels from set V, while the classification net is supervised by the mixed labels of clean labels and hard labels predicted by the label cleaning net.

nonlinear transformations (*e.g.*, sigmoid, tanh, and Relu) is minor. So we use a sigmoid perform.

The reason why we do not use noisy labels of the data as the feature is that when the number of classes or the number of samples is small, the map learned from noisy labels to clean labels can easily gets overfit. In addition, how to combine low dimensional label feature with high dimensional image feature can be a complicated problem itself, which is beyond the discussion in this work. However, we are not arguing that the noisy labels are not useful at all; instead, we find it can be very useful if we use the massive data with noisy labels to perform model pre-training. We will discuss the effect of such pre-training in detail in the experiments.

The output of the classifier g for each sample is a soft label which means it is a float number between 0 and 1, not a binary value like the noisy vector or the verified label vector. To make full use of label, we use a threshold (by default, we use 0.4) to convert a soft label into a hard label (0 or 1). Similarly, we regard the classification network h as a student. It imitates the behavior of network g to produce the similar classification results. The difference between g and h is that h uses mixed labels consisting of both the generated hard labels by g and the verified labels. Similar to the method in [28], the input of h takes input samples from both T and V.

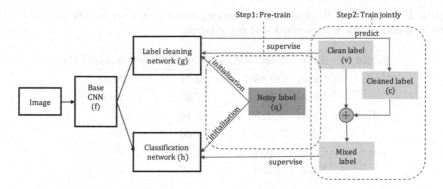

Fig. 3. Two-stage training strategy for the proposed approach. We first use noisy label to initialize the weights of both the label cleaning net and the classification net. In the fine-tune stage, we use clean label and mixed label (clean labels and hard labels predicted by the label cleaning net) to supervise the label cleaning net and the classification net, respectively.

Given the above notations, our goal can be formulated as:

$$\underset{W_1,W_2}{\arg\min} \; L_{classify}(h(f(x), W_2), v, c), \tag{1}$$

where W_1 and c denote the weights and output of the label cleaning network; W_2 and $L_{classify}$ denote the weights and loss of the classification network.

3.2 Network Training

We train a backbone CNN network (*i.e.*, a ResNet50 or Inception V3) on the entire training dataset and the noisy labels, and use it for extracting the shared visual features. And then we train the teacher-student network consisting of the label cleaning net and the multi-label classification net. As shown in Fig. 3, we use a two-stage training strategy to train the proposed approach.

Specifically, we pre-train both the label cleaning network g and the classification network h using all the training data and the noisy labels q_i, q_j with binary cross-entropy loss

$$L_{noise} = - \sum_{k \in V, T} q_k log(o_k), \tag{2}$$

where o denotes the output of g or h.

We then train g and h jointly using two losses, *i.e.*, a label cleaning loss L_{clean} and a classification loss $L_{classify}$. Both are binary cross-entropy loss. The label cleaning network g is supervised by the verified labels c for all samples j in V

$$L_{clean} = - \sum_{j \in V} v_j log(c_j), \tag{3}$$

where c denotes the output of g.

Table 1. Statistics of the training, validation, and the test set for the *extended MS-COCO* dataset with both verified and noisy labels.

Subset	Type	# annotations	Label/Image	Image/Label
Train	Clean	150,854	2.21	2,694
	Noisy	114,527	1.67	2,045
Validation	Clean	36,225	2.16	647
	Noisy	27,910	1.66	498
Test	Clean	37,028	2.20	661
	Noisy	28,039	1.67	501

The classification network h is supervised by mixed labels, which consists of the clean labels from V and the predicted labels generated by g. So, the total loss is a combination of losses from two sets

$$L_{classify} = -\sum_{i \in V} v_i log(p_i) - \sum_{j \in T} c_j^h log(p_j), \qquad (4)$$

where p denotes the output of h and c^h denotes the hard version of c. To prevent a trivial solution, *i.e.*, $c_j^h = p_j = 0$, the cleaned label c_j^h is regarded as a constant.

4 Experiments

4.1 Dataset

MS COCO2014. We extend the MS COCO2014 [16] into a dataset with both clean labels and noisy labels which consists of 101,690 images from 56 generic object classes. Similar to [11,28], we use a pre-trained CNN model (Inception V3 [27]) on ImageNet [5] to generate predicted labels for each image in MS-COCO and treat these predicted labels as noisy or unverified labels. The procedure of generating these labels consists of two main steps.

First, considering that the image classes in ImageNet and MS-COCO are not consistent, we map the classes in ImageNet to the classes in MS-COCO. The map can be complicated since the semantic meaning of classes in two datasets is different. For instance, there are about 100 kinds of birds in ImageNet but there is only one class named *bird* in MS-COCO. Therefore, we map all kinds of bird's classes in ImageNet to the same class *bird* in MS-COCO. And also, we remove the classes which do not appear in ImageNet but exist in MS-COCO (*e.g., giraffe, snowboard*). Eventually, we obtain a subset of 90 original classes which contains 56 overlapped classes.

Second, we choose Inception V3 model pre-trained on ImageNet to annotate all images in MS-COCO automatically, which are used as the noisy/unverified labels. We use the top-8 predictions for each image as possible labels. We map these possible labels to 56 classes to get the final noisy/unverified labels for MS-COCO. If the possible label does not exist in the 56 classes, we just ignore it.

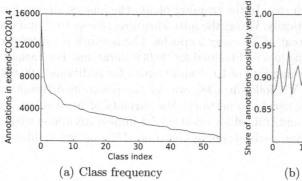 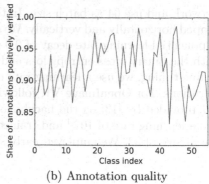

(a) Class frequency   (b) Annotation quality

Fig. 4. Label statistics for the complied *extended MS-COCO* dataset, which contains both clean labels and noisy labels. (a) The class distribution is non-uniform. The most frequent class has over 12,000 annotations while the least frequent class has just less than 1,000 annotations. (b) The annotation quality shows the proportion of verified label in all annotations. It does not show obvious relationship with the class populations. We sort the class indices by the frequency and use the same index order in (a) and (b).

We also remove the images that do not have labels and finally obtain 101,690 images with 170,476 annotations total. Following the split of the original MS-COCO database, we have 68,213 for training, 16,714 for validation and 16,763 for testing. The data distribution statistics of the *extended MS-COCO* dataset is given in Table 1.

As shown in Fig. 4(a), classes in the *extended MS-COCO* are not distributed evenly. For example, the class *dog* has more than 14,000 annotations in the whole dataset while many other classes have less than 1,000 annotations. For the verified/clean labels, we directly use the original annotations provided in MS-COCO. Figure 4(b) shows the annotation quality over all classes. It is not related to per class annotation frequencies. In all noisy labels, about 91.5% are verified. Meanwhile, in all verified labels, about 13.1% are missing. These noisy and missing labels can lead to poor performance of multi-label classification models.

OpenImage V1. OpenImage V1 [13] is widely used for multi-label classification which contains about 9 million images from 6,012 classes. Following the partition in [28], we use all the training data as the training set with noisy labels, a quarter of the validation data (about 40K images) as the verified set and the remaining data in the validation set for testing.

4.2   Experimental Settings and Metrics

Settings. We implement all the models with TensorFlow [1] and optimized with RMSProp. For *extended MS-COCO*, we use ResNet50 [9] as the backbone network and use 64 as batch size. In the training phase, the images are random flipped horizontally and vertically. We set the initial learning rate as 10^{-4} and use exponential learning rate decay of 0.9 every 2 epochs. The network is supervised with the binary cross-entropy loss and trained for 20,000 iterations. For variants of fine-tuning, we use a learning rate of 10^{-4} and trained for additional 100,000 iterations. For OpenImage V1, following [28], we use the pre-trained Inception V3 provided by [13] as the backbone network. For variants of fine-tuning, we use a learning rate of 10^{-4} and trained for additional 4 million iterations with a batch size of 32. We employed early stopping based on AP_{all} on the validation set.

Metrics. We use the mean of class-average precision (mAP) and the class-agnostic average precision (AP_{all}), which are widely used in noisy label classification problem [11,20,28]. mAP computes the mean of average precision (AP) of all binary classification problems. AP uses precision weighting for each positive label. For each class, it is calculated as follow

$$AP_c = \frac{1}{m} \sum_n Presion(i,c) \cdot I(i,c), \tag{5}$$

where m and n denote numbers of positive labels and instances. In our experiments, n is the size of test set. $Presion(i,c)$ is the precision of class c at rank i. $I(i,c)$ is an indicator function which outputs 1 iff the ground truth label at rank i is true. AP_{all} ignores the class of each annotation and treats them as a single class. It consists of $m \times n$ values for both predictions and ground-truth labels. This metric considers each annotation equally which ignores the class difficulties.

4.3 Training Details

When we pre-train the label cleaning network and the classification network on noisy labels, a learning rate of 10^{-4} is used for both *extended MS-COCO* and OpenImage. We then use two pairs of learning rates (3×10^{-4}, 3×10^{-5} for *extended MS-COCO* and 10^{-4}, 10^{-5} for OpenImage) for jointly training the label cleaning network and the classification network, respectively. In each batch, we use batches that contain samples from both V and T (in a ratio of 1:9). Similar to [11,28], we balance the influences of L_{clean} and $L_{classify}$ with the weights of 0.1 and 1.0, respectively.

4.4 Results

Multi-label Classification from Noisy Labels. We evaluated the proposed approach for multi-label classification on the *extended MS-COCO* and Open-Image dataset. One important baseline we used for comparison is Veit et al. [28]. Since the source code of [28] is not publicly available, we implement their method based on the best of our understanding. Our implementation achieves

Table 2. Multi-label classification performance by the proposed approach and several state-of-the-art methods on the *extended MS-COCO* dataset. We choose 5%, 30% and 50% clean labels, and use them as the verified set, respectively.

Model	mAP			AP_{all}		
	5%	30%	50%	5%	30%	50%
ResNet50 (Noisy)	0.4530			0.3914		
ResNet50 (Noisy-FT-W)	0.5471	0.6054	**0.6195**	0.5735	**0.6332**	**0.6442**
ResNet50 (Noisy-FT-L)	0.5554	0.5919	0.5990	0.5781	0.6168	0.6242
ResNet50 (Noisy-FT-M)	0.4803	0.5361	0.5679	0.4343	0.5194	0.5671
Veit et al. [28] (WP)	0.4576	0.4732	0.4748	0.4602	0.4705	0.4722
Veit et al. [28] (TJ)	0.4631	0.4756	0.4784	0.4671	0.4700	0.4760
Proposed	**0.5775**	**0.6078**	0.6118	**0.5975**	0.6287	0.6337
ResNet50 (GT)	0.6516			0.6815		

very similar results to the results reported in [28] on OpenImage database. In this experiment, we use ResNet50 and Inception V3 as backbone network for *extended MS-COCO* and OpenImage, respectively. Besides the state-of-the-art method [28], we also provide the performance of some very related baselines.

Backbone (GT): A backbone network is trained for multi-label classification using all the clean labels in dataset. This can be viewed as the upper bound of the semi-supervised learning methods including the proposed approach.

Backbone (Noisy): A backbone network is trained for multi-label classification by using all the unverified/noisy labels. All the semi-supervised learning methods are expected to achieve higher performance than this baseline.

Backbone (Noisy-FT-L(M)): Fine-tune the last layer of *Backbone (Noisy)* using clean (mixed) labels. We tried to do this fine-tuning with 5%, 30% and 50% clean labels in *extended MS-COCO* and all clean labels in OpenImage, respectively.

Backbone (Noisy-FT-W): Fine-tune the whole nets of *Backbone (Noisy)* using clean labels. We use the fine-tuning setting similar to *Backbone (Noisy-FT-L)*.

The results (in terms of AP_{all} and mAP) for *extended MS-COCO* and Open-Image by the proposed approach and the state-of-the-art methods are reported in Tables 2 and 3 respectively. For *extended MS-COCO*, we can see that the baseline method *ResNet50 (Noisy)* does not work well when directly training a deep model with unverified labels. When this network is fine-tuned with verified labels (e.g., 5%, 30%, 50%), its performance can be improved significantly. This suggests that collecting as many verified labels as possible (without considering the expense of time and money) is an effective way to improved the model performance. However, if the budget is limited, we may seek to use approaches like [28] and the proposed method to improve the system's performance using as few verified labels as possible. We can see that both [28] and our approach is able to improve the multi-label classification performance even when only 5% clean labels are available. However, the method in [28] (including two variants) does not give better results than directly using the clean labels to fine-tune the entire model or just the last layer of the model. The possible reasons are: (i) the number of classes in the *extended MS-COCO* is small, and classes are completely different; it is difficult for [28] to model the relationship between individual classes; (ii) it can be difficult to learn a linear mapping from noisy features to cleaned labels as used in [28]; we will give additional experiments about this in the following sections. By contrast, the proposed approach achieves much better performance than [28], and outperforms the fine-tuning based methods when 5% clean labels are available (0.5975 by our method vs. 0.5735 by *ResNet50* (*Noisy-FT-W*)). When about 30% or more clean labels are used to fine-tune the whole network, the results can be slightly better than our approach. The results are encouraging because in practical applications, manually verifying 5% labels from millions of data is more feasible than manually verifying 30% or more label.

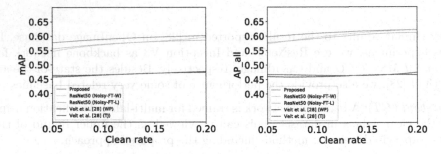

Fig. 5. *mAP*-clean rate and *AP_all*-clean rate curves of the proposed approach and the baseline methods for multi-label classification under a small verified label set.

Table 3. Performance of our approach and the baseline methods on OpenImage.

Model	mAP	AP_{all}
Inception V3 (Noisy)	0.6182	0.8382
Inception V3 (Noisy-FT-W)	0.6153	0.8588
Inception V3 (Noisy-FT-L)	0.6566	0.8957
Inception V3 (Noisy-FT-M)	0.6189	0.8480
Veit et al. [28] (WP)	0.6236	0.8768
Veit et al. [28] (TJ)	0.6238	0.8767
Proposed	**0.6772**	**0.9047**

According to Fig. 5, if the percentage of available clean labels is less than 20% which is the scenario focused by this work, our approach performs much better than the other baseline methods. Moreover, the proposed approach shows the best robustness against noisy labels when the percentage of clean labels is

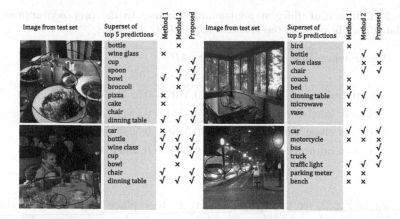

Fig. 6. Multi-label classification results by the proposed approach and the baseline approaches on the test set of the *extended MS-COCO* database. We show the top 5 most confident predictions by *ResNet50 (Noisy)*, *ResNet50 (Noisy-FT-W)*, and the proposed approach, denoted as Method 1, Method 2 and Proposed, respectively. The ground-truth labels are marked with cycle in the images.

Table 4. Comparisons between linear and non-linear feature transformation for the proposed approach on the *extended MS-COCO* database.

Model	mAP		AP_{all}	
	5%	10%	5%	10%
Proposed (Linear Feat. Trans.)	0.5690	0.5773	0.5891	0.5972
Proposed	**0.5775**	**0.5892**	**0.5975**	**0.6095**
ResNet50 (GT)	0.6516		0.6815	
ResNet50 (Noisy)	0.4530		0.3914	

extremely small (*e.g.*, 5%). Figure 6 shows the top 5 predictions by our model, *ResNet50 (Noisy)* and *ResNet50 (Noisy-FT-W)* for some samples from the test set of the *extended MS-COCO*. The proposed approach gives correct estimations for many of the hard cases for which the baseline algorithms do not predict correctly.

For OpenImage, we use about 40k images as clean data which is less than 1% of the noisy data. From Table 3, we can see that our method also gives the best performance among all models in terms of both mAP and AP_{all}. It also outperforms [28] by a large margin (0.6772 by our method vs. 0.6238 by [28]). These results show that our method's effectiveness under extremely small percentage of clean data.

Effect of Non-linear Transformation. We analyze the effect of the proposed non-linear transformation on the *extended MS-COCO*, and compare it with the linear feature transformation (*Linear Feat. Trans.*) under the same framework.

Table 5. Influence of different pre-training schemes to the proposed approach for multi-label classification on the *extended MS-COCO* database.

Pre-training data	mAP		AP_{all}	
	5%	10%	5%	10%
No pre-training	0.5707	0.5834	0.5926	0.6061
Pre-train label cleaning net alone	0.5731	0.5864	0.5955	0.6092
Pre-train classification net alone	0.5758	0.5886	0.5968	0.6090
Pre-train both nets	**0.5775**	**0.5892**	**0.5975**	**0.6095**

As shown in Fig. 2, we use two linear layers to replace the non-linear sigmoid layers. We used 5% and 10% verified labels to do the evaluations. The results using linear feature transformation are given in Table 4. Under the assumption that only a small set of clean labels are available, the proposed non-linear feature transformation works better than linear feature transformation in terms of mAP and AP_{all}. These results suggest that non-linear feature transformation is more helpful to model the mapping from the feature space (learned with noisy labels) to the label space.

Influence of Different Pre-training Schemes. For deep learning models, the pre-training strategy may influence the final performance. We provide the performance of four variants of our model on the *extended MS-COCO*: (i) pre-training the label cleaning net alone, (ii) pre-training the classification net alone, (iii) pre-training both nets, and (iv) no pre-training using 5% and 10% clean labels, respectively. Table 5 gives the influence of these different pre-training schemes to the proposed method. The results show that pre-training is helpful to improve the final classification performance, and pre-training both nets shows the best performance in terms of mAP and AP_{all}. The results also suggest that even the percentage of clean labels is small (5% and 10%), using the data with noisy labels for pre-training is helpful for improving the performance.

Soft vs. Binary Generated Labels. Another aspect worthy of analysis is the choice of soft or hard labels for the output by the label cleaning network. Soft label means an image is labelled with a real value between 0 and 1, and a hard label means the real value is thresholded into either 0 or 1. These labels are then used for supervising the classification network as we described in Sect. 3.1. The results of the *extended MS-COCO* are given in Table 6. We find that using hard labels performs better than using soft labels. The possible reason is that during the training of the label cleaning network, the easy samples should correspond to high confidences at the beginning. However, using a soft label, e.g., 0.8, for an easy sample, its confidence is actually reduced compared with using 1 as its label. The whole training process is similar to the curriculum learning to some extent, *i.e.*, learning with the easy instances first, then the hard instances. Although we

Table 6. A comparison between using soft labels (real values ranging in [0, 1]) and binary labels (0 or 1) for the output of the label cleaning network in our approach on the *extended MS-COCO* database.

Model	mAP		AP_{all}	
	5%	10%	5%	10%
Proposed (soft label)	0.5682	0.5838	0.5884	0.6040
Proposed (hard label)	**0.5775**	**0.5892**	**0.5975**	**0.6095**

do not explicitly utilize the sample difficulties, the training process of the label cleaning network helps to force the student net (classification net) to learn from easy to hard. Such a learning strategy is helpful to improve the classification performance.

5   Conclusions

Utilizing a small number of clean labels and massive unverified labels to learn robust classification models is valuable for many practical applications. In this work, we have proposed a teacher-student network with non-linear feature transformation to learn from massive noisy labels efficiently. We showed that non-linear feature transformation is more helpful than linear feature transformation in mapping from the feature space to the label space. In addition, we have built an *extended MS-COCO* database which consists of both clean labels and noisy labels generated by pre-trained model on ImageNet. Experimental results show that the proposed approach can achieve much better performance than the state-of-the-art method in multi-label classification from noisy labels. It also works better than fine-tuning an entire pre-trained network using clean labels when the available clean label is relative small, *e.g.*, less than 30%.

In our future work, we will consider comprehensive feature transformation to see whether it can better model the mapping between the feature space and the label space. In addition, the label confidences generated by the label cleaning network will be taken into consideration. We also would like to extend the proposed approach into other tasks such as face attribute estimation [8,22].

Acknowledgment. This research was supported in part by the Natural Science Foundation of China (grants 61732004, 61390511, and 61672496), External Cooperation Program of Chinese Academy of Sciences (CAS) (grant GJHZ1843), and Youth Innovation Promotion Association CAS (2018135).

References

1. Abadi, M., et al.: TensorFlow: large-scale machine learning on heterogeneous systems. In: Proceedings of OSDI (2016). http://tensorflow.org/
2. Beigman, E., Klebanov, B.B.: Learning with annotation noise. In: Su, K., Su, J., Wiebe, J. (eds.) Proceedings of ACL, pp. 280–287. The Association for Computer Linguistics (2009)
3. Brodley, C.E., Friedl, M.A.: Identifying mislabeled training data. J. Artif. Intell. Res. **11**(1), 131–167 (2011)
4. Chen, X., Gupta, A.: Webly supervised learning of convolutional networks. In: Proceedings of IEEE ICCV, pp. 1431–1439. IEEE Computer Society (2015)
5. Deng, J., Dong, W., Socher, R., Li, L.J., Li, K., Li, F.F.: Imagenet: a large-scale hierarchical image database. In: Proceedings of IEEE CVPR, pp. 248–255. IEEE Computer Society (2009)
6. Ghosh, A., Kumar, H., Sastry, P.S.: Robust loss functions under label noise for deep neural networks. In: Singh, S.P., Markovitch, S. (eds.) Proceedings of AAAI. AAAI Press (2017)
7. Han, H., Jain., A.K.: 3D face texture modeling from uncalibrated frontal and profile images. In: Proceedings of 5th IEEE International Conference on Biometrics: Theory, Applications and Systems (BTAS), pp. 223–230, September 2012
8. Han, H., Jain, A.K., Wang, F., Shan, S., Chen, X.: Heterogeneous face attribute estimation: a deep multi-task learning approach. IEEE Trans. Pattern Anal. Mach. Intell. (T-PAMI) **40**(11), 2597–2609 (2018)
9. He, K., Zhang, X., Ren, S., Sun, J.: Deep residual learning for image recognition. In: Proceedings of IEEE CVPR, pp. 770–778. IEEE Computer Society (2016)
10. Hinton, G., Vinyals, O., Dean, J.: Distilling the knowledge in a neural network. Comput. Sci. **14**(7), 38–39 (2015)
11. Inoue, N., Simoserra, E., Yamasaki, T., Ishikawa, H.: Multi-label fashion image classification with minimal human supervision. In: Proceedings of IEEE ICCV Workshops, pp. 2261–2267. IEEE Computer Society (2017)
12. Patel, K., Han, H., Jain, A.K.J.: Secure face unlock: spoof detection on smartphones. IEEE Trans. Inf. Forensics Secur. (T-IFS) **11**(10), 2268–2283 (2016)
13. Krasin, I., et al.: Openimages: a public dataset for large-scale multi-label and multi-class image classification. arXiv:1701.01619 (2016)
14. Lee, K.H., He, X., Zhang, L., Yang, L.: CleanNet: transfer learning for scalable image classifier training with label noise. In: Proceedings of IEEE CVPR (2018)
15. Li, Y., Yang, J., Song, Y., Cao, L., Luo, J., Li, L.: Learning from noisy labels with distillation. In: Proceedings of IEEE ICCV, pp. 1928–1936. IEEE Computer Society (2017)
16. Lin, T.-Y., et al.: Microsoft COCO: common objects in context. In: Fleet, D., Pajdla, T., Schiele, B., Tuytelaars, T. (eds.) ECCV 2014. LNCS, vol. 8693, pp. 740–755. Springer, Cham (2014). https://doi.org/10.1007/978-3-319-10602-1_48
17. Liu, T., Tao, D.: Classification with noisy labels by importance reweighting. IEEE Trans. Pattern Anal. Mach. Intell **38**, 447–461 (2016)
18. Liu, W., Hua, G., Smith, J.R.: Unsupervised one-class learning for automatic outlier removal. In: Proceedings of IEEE CVPR, pp. 3826–3833. IEEE Computer Society (2014)
19. Manwani, N., Sastry, P.S.: Noise tolerance under risk minimization. IEEE Trans. Cybern. **43**(3), 1146–1151 (2013)

20. Misra, I., Zitnick, C.L., Mitchell, M., Girshick, R.: Seeing through the human reporting bias: visual classifiers from noisy human-centric labels. In: Proceedings of IEEE CVPR, pp. 2930–2939. IEEE Computer Society (2016)
21. Natarajan, N., Dhillon, I.S., Ravikumar, P., Tewari, A.: Learning with noisy labels. In: Burges, C.J.C., Bottou, L., Ghahramani, Z., Weinberger, K.Q. (eds.) Proceedings of NIPS, pp. 1196–1204 (2013)
22. Pan, H., Han, H., Shan, S., Chen., X.: Mean-variance loss for deep age estimation from a face. In: Proceedings of IEEE CVPR, pp. 5285–5294, June 2018
23. Patrini, G., Rozza, A., Menon, A.K., Nock, R., Qu, L.: Making deep neural networks robust to label noise: a loss correction approach. In: Proceedings of IEEE CVPR, pp. 2233–2241. IEEE Computer Society, July 2017
24. Reed, S., Lee, H., Anguelov, D., Szegedy, C., Erhan, D., Rabinovich, A.: Training deep neural networks on noisy labels with bootstrapping. arXiv:1412.6596 (2014)
25. Rolnick, D., Veit, A., Belongie, S., Shavit, N.: Deep learning is robust to massive label noise. arXiv:1705.10694 (2017)
26. Sukhbaatar, S., Bruna, J., Paluri, M., Bourdev, L., Fergus, R.: Training convolutional networks with noisy labels. In: Proceedings of ICLR Workshops (2015)
27. Szegedy, C., Vanhoucke, V., Ioffe, S., Shlens, J., Wojna, Z.: Rethinking the inception architecture for computer vision. In: Proceedings of IEEE CVPR, pp. 2818–2826. IEEE Computer Society (2016)
28. Veit, A., Alldrin, N., Chechik, G., Krasin, I., Gupta, A., Belongie, S.: Learning from noisy large-scale datasets with minimal supervision. In: Proceedings of IEEE CVPR, pp. 6575–6583. IEEE Computer Society (2017)
29. Xiao, T., Xia, T., Yang, Y., Huang, C., Wang, X.: Learning from massive noisy labeled data for image classification. In: Proceedings of IEEE CVPR, pp. 2691–2699. IEEE Computer Society (2015)

Robust Angular Local Descriptor Learning

Yanwu Xu[1,3]([✉]), Mingming Gong[1], Tongliang Liu[2], Kayhan Batmanghelich[1], and Chaohui Wang[3]

[1] University of Pittsburgh, 4200 Fifth Avenue, Pittsburgh, PA 15260, USA
{yanwuxu,mig73,kayhan}@pitt.edu
[2] The University of Sydney, Camperdown, NSW 2006, Australia
tongliang.liu@sydney.edu.au
[3] Université Paris-Est LIGM (UMR 8049), CNRS, ENPC, ESIEE Paris, UPEM, Marne-la-Vallée, France
chaohui.wang@u-pem.fr

Abstract. In recent years, the learned local descriptors have outperformed handcrafted ones by a large margin, due to the powerful deep convolutional neural network architectures such as L2-Net [1] and triplet based metric learning [2]. However, there are two problems in the current methods, which hinders the overall performance. Firstly, the widely-used margin loss is sensitive to incorrect correspondences, which are prevalent in the existing local descriptor learning datasets. Second, the L2 distance ignores the fact that the feature vectors have been normalized to unit norm. To tackle these two problems and further boost the performance, we propose a robust angular loss which (1) uses cosine similarity instead of L2 distance to compare descriptors and (2) relies on a robust loss function that gives smaller penalty to triplets with negative relative similarity. The resulting descriptor shows robustness on different datasets, reaching the state-of-the-art result on Brown dataset, as well as demonstrating excellent generalization ability on the Hpatches dataset and a Wide Baseline Stereo dataset.

Keywords: Local descriptor · CNNs · Robust loss

1 Introduction

Finding correspondences between local patches across images is an important component in many computer vision tasks, such as image matching [3], image retrieval [4] and object recognition [5]. Since the seminal paper introducing SIFT [6], local patches have been encoded into representative vectors, called descriptors, which are designed to be invariant/robust to various geometric and photometric changes such as scale change, viewpoint change, and illumination change.

Supported by grant Pfizer and organization by SAP SE and CNRS INS2IJCJC-INVISANA.

© Springer Nature Switzerland AG 2019
C. V. Jawahar et al. (Eds.): ACCV 2018, LNCS 11365, pp. 420–435, 2019.
https://doi.org/10.1007/978-3-030-20873-8_27

Given the success of deep learning, hand-crafted descriptors such as SIFT have been outperformed by learned ones [7–9]. Different from the hand-crafted descriptors which extract low-level features such as gradients, the learned descriptors learn a convolutional neural network (CNN) from raw patches with ground-truth correspondences. These descriptor learning networks are trained by metric learning losses and can be divided into two cat-egories by whether there are learnable distance comparison layers in the network. The networks with distance comparison layers output distances directly without explicit descriptors [9–11]. This type of networks showed promising performance in patch verification but cannot be combined with nearest neighbor search. Recently, networks without similarity comparison layers achieved better performances due to more advanced network architectures such as L2Net [1] and training techniques such as triplet loss with hard negative mining [2]. These networks output descriptors which can be compared using simple L2 distance and be matched using fast approximate nearest neighbor search algorithms like Kd-tree [12].

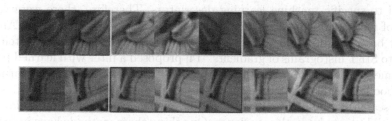

Fig. 1. Examples of false labeled patches, the patches sharing same label of 3D view point are marked by same color box, and different color boxes come from different 3D view point. (Color figure online)

In the descriptor learning networks, the metric learning loss function and the distance/similarity measure between descriptors are two essential components. State-of-the-art methods usually adopt margin-based losses such as the hinge loss [2] to train the descriptor learning networks. Because the number of neg-ative pairs is huge, batch hard negative mining is usually applied to stabilize the training process as well as reduce the computational load [2,13]. However, the current triplet losses are not robust to the incorrect correspondences (out-liers) in the training data, as shown in Fig. 1. The patches at different locations (negative pairs) can exhibit strong similarities and the patches at the same loca-tion (positive pairs) can be very different due to local distortion or corruptions. Additionally, since the local descriptors are normalized to unit norm before com-parison, L2 distance is no longer an appropriate distance measure to compare descriptors.

To target the these two problems, we propose a robust angular loss to train the descriptor learning networks which is called RAL-Net. Instead of using the hinge loss as done in [2], we propose a robust loss function which gives bounded penalty to the triplets with incorrect correspondences. In addition, we propose to utilize cosine similarity to compare two descriptors, which is more appropriate to compare unit-norm vectors. We train our descriptor on the Brown dataset [14] and obtain state-of-the-art results using the same training strategy as [2]. Moreover, our descriptor performs much better than [2] when the sample size and batch size is small, which further verifies the effectiveness of the proposed method. Our codes is released in github[1].

2   Related Works

Recent work on local descriptor designing has gone through a huge change from conventional hand-crafted descriptors to learning-based approaches, which ranges from SIFT [6] and DAISY [15] to latest methods such as DeepCompare, MatchNet, and HardNet [2,7–9]. As for deep learning-based descriptors, there are two study trends including CNN structure designing and negative sampling for embedding learning.

Before CNN models being broadly applied, descriptors learning methods were limited to specific machine learning descriptors. Therefore, there were various kinds of methods inspired by different aspects. Principal Components Analysis (PCA) based SIFT (PCA-SIFT) [16] leads to normalized gradient patch compared to SIFT histograms of gradients. [14] proposed a filter with learned pooling and dimension reduction. Simonyan et al. [11] studied convex sparse learning to learn pooling fields for descriptors. Aside from these descriptors, [17] raised an online search method from a subset of tests which can increase inter-class variance and decrease intra-class variance. One thing these methods have in common is that they all rely on shallow learning architectures.

In the past few years, models based on CNN try to get better performance by designing various convolutional neural network architectures, e.g. [9,10]. [9] choose a two-branched network, a typical Siamese structure for feature extraction and three full connected layers for deep metric learning. [10] explored further on Siamese network with two branches sharing no parameters and proposed a two-channel input structure which is stacked by center cropped patches and plain patches.

Recently methods focused more on loss function design because improving network structure can not give birth to significant improvement of descriptors as before. These works on learning embedding can be summarized as classification loss, contrastive loss, and triplet loss. [18,19] proved the validity classification loss for face recognition ans scene recognition. As the most common pairwise loss, contrastive loss [20,21] aims at increase all of the similarity of positive pairs and push away the negative pairs until bigger than a variant margin. [22] proposed a restricting two sides margin for contrastive learning and this method not only requires distance between positive pairs above the margin but also limits distance between positive pairs under the second margin. Compared to contrastive loss, triplet loss cares about relative similarity between positive pairs and negative pairs rather than absolute value which consists of anchor positive (a, p) and

---

[1] https://github.com/xuyanwu/RAL-Net

anchor negative (a, n) with a shared point anchor a. This method can meet with most of tasks involving large scale embedding learning [23]. However, there is still a great challenge in choosing hinge margin for triplet loss, as well as searching proper negative pairs fed into triplet loss. Distinguished from this embedding learning methods, Histogram loss [24] uses a quadruplet based sampling strategy by estimating distribution of similarity between positive pairs and negative pairs.

From previous studies, the loss functions have their advantages and disadvantages in different learning tasks. A indispensable component of these methods is the negative sampling strategy. In this paper, our main aim is to improve the loss function to further improve the performance of local descriptor learning. Our method can possibly be applied to other related tasks such as face recognition and person re-identification.

3   Proposed Method

In this section, we will discuss the form of our robust triplet loss which similar to [25] and simply introduction to network structure which is based on [1]. In order to explain our loss function, we first review the general forms of triplet loss and contrastive loss then present our difference.

3.1   Loss Function

3.2   The Triplet Loss

Triplet loss has been successfully applied to many tasks, such as image matching, image retrieval, and face identification. The idea is to make positive pairs closer and keep relative negative pairs away from the positive. The very common expression of triplet loss is formulated as follows:

$$L_{triplet} = \frac{1}{N} \sum_{i,j,k} [s(a_i, n_k) - s(a_i, p_j) + m]_+ \tag{1}$$

where a, p and n represent anchor, positive and, negative of triplet tuple and operator $[l]_+$ means $max(l, 0)$ and function $s(x, y)$ represent similarity score between two features. Due to the large amounts of combination among a, p and n, the back propagation of loss is very time-consuming. Thus, an indispensable component is to sample hard negatives for both performance improvement and computation reduction. In the context of descriptor learning, the recent HarNet [2] method searches for the most difficult negative pair with reference to each achor positive pair. However, the hard negative sampling strategy in [2] is unable to fully explore the negative pairs because only negative pairs that share an element with the anchor positive pairs are considered. Due to the margin m, if the similarity between positive pairs and negative pairs is bigger than margin and then the derivation of triplet item will be 0. This will cause information loss, but triplet can help learn a better distribution of descriptors.

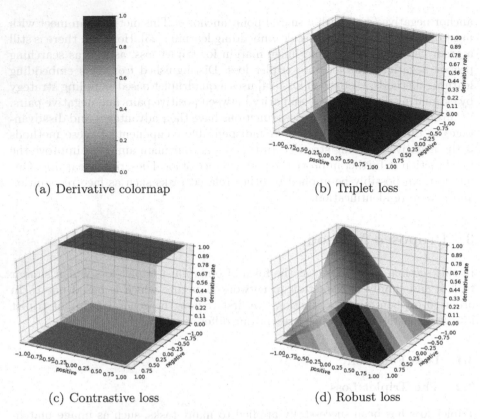

(a) Derivative colormap

(b) Triplet loss

(c) Contrastive loss

(d) Robust loss

Fig. 2. This figure depicts the derivation of three different loss function, (b) triplet loss, (c) contrastive loss, (d) robust loss. The cosine similarity of positive pairs and negative pairs represent x axis and y axis, where z axis denotes the absolute derivative values with respect to the change of x and y. The derivative value becomes larger when approaching red, vice versa when approaching blue. (Color figure online)

3.3   The Contrastive Loss

The difference between the contrastive loss and the triplet loss is that triplet loss aims at comparing relative similarity between positive pairs and negative pairs, while contrastive loss only compares negative pairs with margin and pull positive pairs as close as possible. The general form of contrastive loss is formed as follows:

$$L_{contrastive} = \frac{1}{N} \sum_{i,j,k,l} ([m + s(a_k, n_l)]_+ - s(a_i, p_j)) \tag{2}$$

In contrastive loss, the number of training data pairs grows quadratic with respect to training sample size. Therefore, it is much easier to sample the data pairs than triplet loss, and random sampling is often employed for contrastive loss-based learning. However, as shown in previous works, contrastive loss showed inferior performance to triplet loss in certain tasks. But [26] argues that the inferior performance of contrastive learning is due to the inappropriateness of the random sampling strategy. When combined with the proposed negative sampling strategy, contrastive loss performs as well as triplet loss in the descriptor learning task. The common difficulty for triplet and contrastive loss is that margin cause a great impact in result.

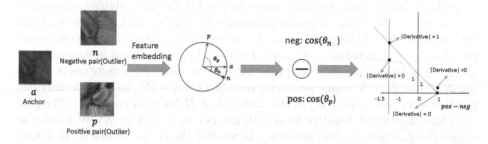

Fig. 3. Proposed descriptor learning model, the negative mining strategy is same as [2]. The features extracted from patches are located in embedding space and cosine similarity between positive pairs is $\cos\theta_p$ and negative pairs are $\cos\theta_{n_1}$ and $\cos\theta_{n_2}$. The curves in the right side represent triplet margin function (solid line), contrastive margin function (dash line) and our robust function (dash-doted line).

As for triplet loss or contrastive loss, these methods all consist of positive pairs, negative pairs and a discriminative margin. The keypoint is the negative search strategy and margin choosing, the later one of which is tricky for metric learning. Thus we propose a robust loss without margin confusion which can keep more relative embedding information as well as applying cosine similarity for our metric learning which is similar to cosine face [27], cause the angle distance is closer to original embedding distribution as a hypersohere. As shown in Fig. 2, assuming margin values for triplet loss and contrastive loss are 1 and 0 separately which are common margin choice. Due to the margin strategy, there is always a part of selected triplet or contrastive items with no derivation, also the selected negative pairs are too sparse, resulting in a large selection bias in the sampling process. Explained in [25], robust regression and classification problem often requires non-convex loss function which can prevent scalable and global training where a natural approach to implement it is cutting out loss vales that exceed threshold, which is similar to triplet and contrastive loss. However, a relaxation of this kind of 'clipping loss' can improve robustness. As for our embedding metric learning problem, we can adopt this intuition.

Thus, we propose a robust version of triplet loss which can offset bias problem to some extent. We consider that selected positive pairs (a_i, p_i) and negative pairs (a_i, n_i) should be more important when their similarity are high and vice versa given less weight rather than set their derivation to be 0. However, we observed that a considerable amount false negative labels exiting which should be positive pairs but marked as negative which is shown in Fig. 3, therefore, we put less weight to triplet items when the cosine distance between negative pairs (a_i, n_i) is much more bigger than positive pairs (a_i, p_i), the derivation of which should be similar to symmetrical arch bridges as shown in Fig. 2(d). Our method performs obviously better when training data by small batch where the effect of bias influences more and reach the best for bigger batch size, which will be discussed later.

We apply the same positive pairs and negative pairs sampling strategy as [2] and the features generated by networks are 128-D and euclidean normalized with length 1. We define a search procedure S_i starting with anchors (a_i) and we search for all of the positive and negative items related to a_i. With regard to a batch which consists of N pairs of matched patches a and p from different given 3D point of view of descriptors, the size of descriptors matrices A and P are $N \times 128$, $N \times N$ cosine similarity matrix $D = A \times P^T$, so there is only one positive item $pos_i = d(a_i, p_i)$ in the diagonal of D for each search S_i. The goal is to find the closest negative item with respect to a_i and p_i. As we know, the bigger the gap between two features, the smaller the cosine similarity is. Please refer to [2] for more sampling details, the formula is organized as follow:

$$D(i, j) = \cos \theta_{i,j} = a_i \cdot p_j,$$
$$pos_i = D(i, i),$$
$$neg_i = D(r_i, c_i),$$
$$(r_i, c_i) = \operatorname{argmax}_{k,l} D(k, l),$$
$$s.t. \quad k, l = 1...n,$$
$$\{k = i \vee l = i\} = True,$$
$$k \neq l. \tag{3}$$

Finally, the triplet items are fed into loss function formed as follow, and our goal is to minimize this loss for each batch. Also, the derivation of L_i with respect to $(pos_i - neg_i)$ is even function as explained above in Fig. 2, and as for better description, Fig. 2 demonstrate the absolute value of derivation.

$$L_{robust} = \frac{1}{N} \sum_{i=1}^{N} (1 - \tanh(pos_i - neg_i)),$$
$$L_i = 1 - \tanh(pos_i - neg_i),$$
$$\frac{\partial L_i}{\partial (pos_i - neg_i)} = \tanh^2((pos_i - neg_i)) - 1. \tag{4}$$

3.4 Network Structure

Following [2], we adopt the L2Net [1] architecture as our main network. The network consists of two parts, the main feature extraction network and the linear decision layer which reduces the feature dimension. For fair comparison, we also make slight modifications by adding 0.3 dropout layer above the bottom layer of network as [2]. For an 32×32 normalized single-channel patch, the output is a

L2 normalized 128-dimensional feature vector. It is worth noting that the whole feature extraction network is built by full convolutional layers, downsampling by two-stride convolutional net. Also, and there is a BN layer and a Relu activation layer in every layer except the last layer, except the bottom layer with no Relu layer. And the whole network is trained with the proposed negative sampling procedure and corresponding loss functions.

4   Experimental Results

We train and test our RAL-Net descriptor on the Brown dataset and test the patch verification performance on Brown dataset. In addition, we use the models trained on the Brown dataset to test its generalization abilities in patch verification, patch matching, and patch retreival on the Hpatches dataset. Finally, we apply our RAL-Net descriptor on the Wide Baseline Stereo dataset to test its invariance properties.

4.1   Brown Dataset

The Brown dataset is the most popular local descriptor learning dataset, which contains three subsets of images taken from different places, including Liberty, Notredame and Yosemite. Keypoints are firstly detected by Difference of Gaussians (DOG) [6] and then vefified with ground truth 3-D view. The patches are extracted around the keypoint locations and are normalized by scale and orientation calculated during keypoint detection. There are about 400k classes of patch pairs with 64×64 size, extracted from different sequences. In practice, the size of 64×64 is unnecessary, and we resized the patches to 32×32 by linear cubic interpolation (Fig. 4).

(a) Liberty

(b) Notredame

(b) Yosemite

Fig. 4. Subsets of brown

Training Setting. On the three Brown subsets, we trained our RAL-Net descriptor in different setting with different training sample size and batch size. In the first setting, we only extracted 200K pairs in total for each subsect respectively. In this setting, we compared the performance of our descriptor with the state-of-the-art HardNet trained with a small batchsize 128. The performance with a small batch size can desmonstrate the effectiveness of the negative sampling strategies. We applied the training strategy different from [2] and [1], which trains data for 50 epochs with learning rate linearly decreasing to 0 in the end. We choose Stochastic Gradient Descent (SGD) as our optimizer and we set the initial learning rate to be 10, and the rest momentum to be 0.9 and weight decay to be 0.0001. In addition, we have tried Adam optimizer and it converge faster than SGD, however SGD can achieve a better result with well chosen training parameters.

In the second setting, which is the standard setting, we extracted 5000K pairs and trained descriptor with batch size 512. As for HardNet, we trained it using batch sizes 512 and 1024, as the performance of HardNet is more sensitive to batch size. In this setting, due to big amount of data, the training is done within 10 epoch which is much less than strategy one but the other training aspects are the same as strategy one. In order to compare our RAL-Net descriptors, we also apply the same training strategy on HardNet and cite several result of recent works. Following previous works, we also applied data augmentation by random filpping and 90° rotation in both training settings.

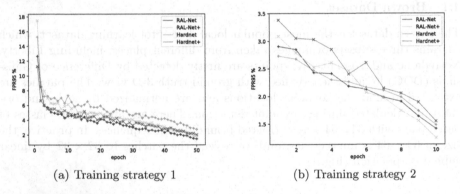

(a) Training strategy 1   (b) Training strategy 2

Fig. 5. The curves describe the result of FPR95 of Hardnet and our RAL-Net tested in Brown dataset. X axis is training epochs and Y is the percent value of FPR95.

Overall Evaluation. The descriptors are trained on one subset and tested on the rest two subsets. As for evaluation, tested subset contains 100k pairs of patches for each subset with 50K matched and 50K unmatched labels. We follow the evaluation protocol [14] and give the results of false positive rate FPR at the recall of 95% true positive rate TPR (FPR95). The training precision alone training epoch is demonstrated in Fig. 5 and the results are shown in Table 1, the best results are shown in bold.

Obviously, our RAL-Net generate the overall best results among all of the representative descriptors as well as the best among the testing subsets. Deep model-based descriptors have surpassed far more than hand-crafted ones, and focus on comparison between our descriptor and the HardNet descriptor.

Table 1. Descriptor performance on Brown dataset for patch verification. False positive rate at 95% true positive rate is displayed. Results of the best are in bold and "+" suffix represent training implemented by data augmentation of random flipping and 90° rotating.

Training	Notredame	Yosemite	Liberty	Yosemite	Liberty	Notredame	Mean
Test	Liberty		Notredame		Yosemite		FPR
SIFT [6]	29.84		22.53		27.29		26.55
MatchNet [9]	7.04	11.47	3.82	5.65	11.6	8.7	8.05
L2Net [1]	3.64	5.29	1.15	1.62	4.43	3.30	3.23
L2Net+ [1]	2.36	4.70	0.72	1.29	2.57	1.71	2.22
CS L2Net [1]	2.55	4.24	0.87	1.39	3.81	2.84	2.61
CS L2Net+ [1]	1.71	3.87	0.56	1.09	2.07	1.3	1.76
HardNetNIPS [2]	3.06	4.27	0.96	1.4	3.04	2.53	2.54
HardNet+NIPS [2]	2.28	3.25	0.57	0.96	2.13	2.22	1.9
Training strategy 1: 200K training pairs for each subset, batch size 128							
HardNet$_{128}$	2.07	3.70	0.77	1.22	3.79	3.33	2.48
HardNet$_{128}$+	2.46	3.55	0.73	1.67	3.54	3.40	2.56
RAL-Net$_{128}$(ours)	**1.46**	**2.63**	**0.51**	**0.91**	**1.95**	**1.40**	**1.48**
RAL-Net$_{128}$+(ours)	1.81	3.80	0.55	1.01	1.96	2.18	1.89
Training strategy 2: 5000k training pairs for each subset, batch size 512							
HardNet$_{512}$	1.54	2.56	0.63	0.92	2.65	2.05	1.73
HardNet$_{512}$+	2.53	2.69	0.54	0.83	2.49	1.70	1.80
HardNet$_{1024}$	1.47	2.67	0.62	0.88	2.14	1.65	1.57
HardNet$_{1024}$+	1.49	2.51	0.53	0.78	1.96	1.84	1.51
RAL-Net$_{512}$(ours)	1.44	2.60	0.48	0.77	1.77	1.43	1.42
RAL-Net$_{512}$+(ours)	**1.30**	**2.39**	**0.37**	**0.67**	**1.52**	**1.31**	**1.26**

In the first training setting, it is interesting that RAL-Net descriptor achieves better results than the HardNet descriptor when both of them are trained with 200K pairs with batch size of 128. Furthermore, our descriptor trained with less data achieves comparable results as Hardnet trained on 5000K data pairs with 512 batch size. We can also notice that data augmentation shows no better effect for small training sample size and even slightly worsen the performance due to the increasing difficulties of negative sampling and less training data with bigger bias. However, the results on the small training dataset and small batchsize verifies the effectiveness of our proposed robust loss training.

In the second setting, we obtain the best results on 5000K data pairs with a batch size of 512. Even in the training without data augmentation, RAL-Net exceeds Hardnet with batch size 512 as well as 1024. It is worth noting that Hardnet descriptor gets improved when enlarging batch size from 512 to 1024, while increasing batchsize from 512 to 1024 leads to almost no enhancement for our descriptor. Thus, we only report the results of our Ral-Net trained with batch size of 512. The experimental results confirm the efficiency and validity of our RAL-Net descriptor. For the rest of experiments, we test HardNet and our descriptor on other datasets by training them on 5000K data pairs with 512 batch size on the Liberty subset.

Ablation Studies. Proving the effectiveness of angular and robust form separately with respect to our RAL loss. We set four variants based on our training strategy 1 without augmentation due to limited time, which are HardNet with angular embedding, HardNet with robust form, original HardNet and our RAL-Net respectively. The result is shown in Table 2. The results indicate that both the angular distance and the robust loss function contribute to the overall performance and the combination of them achieves state-of-the-art performance.

Table 2. Comparision between different combinations.

Training	Notredame	Yosemite	Liberty	Yosemite	Liberty	Notredame	Mean
Test	Liberty			Notredame		Yosemite	FPR
Training strategy 1: 200K training pairs for each subset							
RAL-Net	**1.46**	**2.63**	**0.51**	**0.91**	**1.95**	**1.40**	**1.48**
HardNet/angular embedding	1.63	3.26	0.56	1.24	2.87	2.02	1.93
HardNet/robust form	1.67	3.27	0.57	1.06	2.51	2.15	1.87
HardNet	2.07	3.70	0.77	1.22	3.79	3.33	2.48
L2Net/contrastive	3.52	7.83	1.63	2.75	7.36	6.68	4.96

4.2   Descriptor Generalization Ability on Hpatches Dataset

Recently, Hpatches, a new local descriptor evaluation benchmark, provides a huge dataset and an evaluation criterion for modern descriptors. This dataset consists of 65×65 pixel size of patches extracted from 116 sequences which originate from 6 images. Different from the widely used Brown dataset, Hpatches contains more diversity and noisy changes. The keypoints of this dataset are detected by DOG, Hessian, and Harris detectors from reference images which are then applied to reproject the three different geometric noisy image sequences of easy, hard and tough. A small fraction of the dataset is shown in Fig. 6.

To comprehensively test the generalization abilities of descriptors, Hpatches also propose three different tasks, including patch verification, image matching, and patch retrieval. First, patch verification is used to verify whether two patches match or not by confidence scores. As for a patches pair set $P = \{(x_i, x_i'), y_i), i = 1, ..., N)\}$, consisting of positive pairs and negative pairs (x_i, x_i') with labels $(y_i = 1, -1)$, we calculate the average precision by the ranked confidence scores. The mean average precision (mAP) for all of the rank is finally used as the evaluation criterion. Second, image matching is similar to patch verification, in which we are given patches collection $L_k = (x_{k,i}, i = 1, ..., N)$, where L_r is from the reference image and L_t is from the target image. With respect to $x_{r,i}$ from L_r, we aim to find the maximum matching $x_{t,j}$ from L_t and get the related index

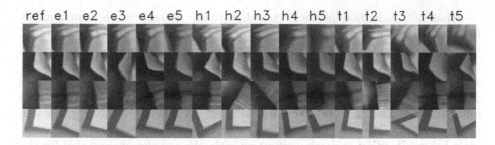

Fig. 6. Hpatches patches image. For each reference patch, there are 5 random geometric changing patches for three different changing range, which can be classified to e(easy), h(hard) and t(tough).

$\{\sigma_i, i = 1, ..., N\}$ of finding $x_{t,j}$. After finding all of the matching, we consider if the found $x_{t,j}$ corresponds to $x_{r,i}$ with a ground truth label, and we get the matching set $M = \{y_i = 2[\sigma_i \overset{?}{=} i] - 1\}$ by whether the found patch is matched with the label. Similar to the first task, we calculate the mAP for AP of set M for all ranks. The final task is patch retrieval, which considers these retrieved patches from the matched images of reference images with a large proportion of distraction, and returns AP of the collection of labels ranked by confidence scores. For more protocol details, please refer to [28]. The result is shown in Fig. 7.

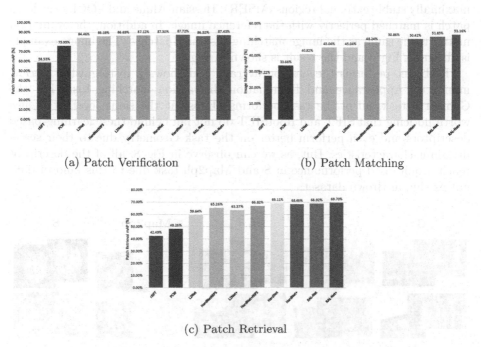

(a) Patch Verification

(b) Patch Matching

(c) Patch Retrieval

Fig. 7. Descriptors performance on three tasks

Hpatches evaluation protocol considers many different aspects of patches from different view points and different illumination as well as patches of intra-class and inter-class, which are implemented from three degree of difficult sequences separately. In order to make a clearer demonstration, we just give the average performance of all different factors. Actually, these descriptors which obtain better average result shown in Fig. 7 also perform better on these different child factors respectively. In terms of the result, RAL-Net generates the best results on the image matching task and the patch retrieval task, and a little behind HardNet in patch verification task. We can also observe that for the hardest image matching task, our descriptor with data augmentation shows an obvious improvement over the competitors. Overall, our descriptor gives almost the same results as L2Net and HardNet. This might be due to the different distributions between the Hpatches data and the Brown data, which needs further consideration and new learning algorithms such as transfer learning.

4.3 WxBS Testing

In order to test the performance of our RAL-Net descriptor in a hard environment with various changing factors, we apply our descriptor on Wide Baseline Stereo [29]. The dataset consists of three different tasks, which are Appearance (A) by environment change, Geometry (G) with different view point, scale variance, etc., Illumination (L) influenced by brightness or image intensity, and Sensor (S) consisting of different type of data. With local feature detected by maximally stable extremal regions (MSER), Hessian-Affine and FOCI, each local patch is matched perfectly with the reference image. In addition, the evaluation metric is the same as the image matching task as Hpatches. The image example is shown as Fig. 8 and the result is shown in Fig. 9.

RAL-Net performs the best on average and shows a distinguished performance on Appearance and Illumination distraction matching task. For the Geometry task, all of the task performs almost at the same level. It is also worth noticing that SIFT and RootSIFT do not fall behind these learning-based descriptors and even perform better on the task Geometry due to their scale-invariant characteristics. But, as we can observe in Fig. 8, all of the descriptor reach a quite bad performance in S and Map2ph task due to this kind of data not exiting in Brown dataset.

G   A   L   Map2ph   S

Fig. 8. Examples of WxBS dataset

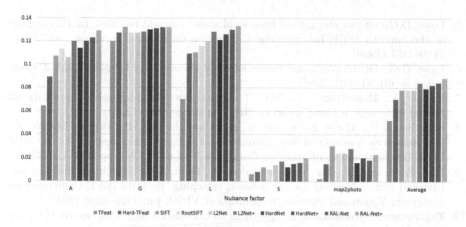

Fig. 9. Descriptors performance on three tasks

5   Conclusions

In this paper, we suggest a robust angular training loss named RAL-Net for deep embedding learning without sensitive parameters to further improve the performance of local descriptor learning, where the similarity between descriptors is defined as cosine distance, it is based on the idea of smooth the margin of triplet by giving different importance to triplet items with regard to the difference between the similarity of positive pairs and the similarity between chosen negative pairs. The loss can learn more information from limited data and performs better if with larger training data and relax the effect that false labels exits in training dataset. We test DigNet on typical Brown dataset, Hpathches dataset and W1BS dataset for diverse tasks verification and our RAL-Net have shown a superiority over existing local descriptors.

References

1. Tian, Y., Fan, B., Wu, F.: L2-net: deep learning of discriminative patch descriptor in euclidean space. In: 2017 IEEE Conference on Computer Vision and Pattern Recognition (CVPR), pp. 6128–6136 (2017)
2. Mishchuk, A., Mishkin, D., Radenovic, F., Matas, J.: Working hard to know your neighbor's margins: local descriptor learning loss. In: Guyon, I., et al. (eds.) Advances in Neural Information Processing Systems 30, pp. 4829–4840. Curran Associates, Inc. (2017)
3. Choy, C.B., Gwak, J., Savarese, S., Chandraker, M.: Universal correspondence network. In: Lee, D.D., Sugiyama, M., Luxburg, U.V., Guyon, I., Garnett, R. (eds.) Advances in Neural Information Processing Systems 29, pp. 2414–2422. Curran Associates, Inc. (2016)
4. Philbin, J., Chum, O., Isard, M., Sivic, J., Zisserman, A.: Object retrieval with large vocabularies and fast spatial matching. In: 2007 IEEE Conference on Computer Vision and Pattern Recognition, pp. 1–8 (2007)

5. Lowe, D.G.: Object recognition from local scale-invariant features. In: Proceedings of the Seventh IEEE International Conference on Computer Vision, vol. 2, pp. 1150–1157 (1999)
6. Lowe, D.G.: Distinctive image features from scale-invariant keypoints. Int. J. Comput. Vis. **60**, 91–110 (2004)
7. Fischer, P., Dosovitskiy, A., Brox, T.: Descriptor Matching with Convolutional Neural Networks: a Comparison to SIFT. ArXiv e-prints (2014)
8. Simo-Serra, E., Trulls, E., Ferraz, L., Kokkinos, I., Fua, P., Moreno-Noguer, F.: Discriminative learning of deep convolutional feature point descriptors. In: 2015 IEEE International Conference on Computer Vision (ICCV), pp. 118–126 (2015)
9. Han, X., Leung, T., Jia, Y., Sukthankar, R., Berg, A.C.: Matchnet: unifying feature and metric learning for patch-based matching. In: 2015 IEEE Conference on Computer Vision and Pattern Recognition (CVPR), pp. 3279–3286 (2015)
10. Zagoruyko, S., Komodakis, N.: Learning to Compare Image Patches via Convolutional Neural Networks. ArXiv e-prints (2015)
11. Simonyan, K., Vedaldi, A., Zisserman, A.: Learning local feature descriptors using convex optimisation. IEEE Trans. Pattern Anal. Mach. Intell. **36**, 1573–1585 (2014)
12. Bentley, J.L.: Multidimensional binary search trees used for associative searching. Commun. ACM **18**, 509–517 (1975)
13. Schroff, F., Kalenichenko, D., Philbin, J.: Facenet: a unified embedding for face recognition and clustering. In: 2015 IEEE Conference on Computer Vision and Pattern Recognition (CVPR), pp. 815–823 (2015)
14. Brown, M., Hua, G., Winder, S.: Discriminative learning of local image descriptors. IEEE Trans. Pattern Anal. Mach. Intell. **33**, 43–57 (2011)
15. Tola, E., Lepetit, V., Fua, P.: A fast local descriptor for dense matching (2008)
16. Ke, Y., Sukthankar, R.: PCA-SIFT: a more distinctive representation for local image descriptors, pp. 506–513 (2004)
17. Balntas, V., Tang, L., Mikolajczyk, K.: Bold - binary online learned descriptor for efficient image matching. In: 2015 IEEE Conference on Computer Vision and Pattern Recognition (CVPR), pp. 2367–2375 (2015)
18. Zhou, B., Lapedriza, A., Xiao, J., Torralba, A., Oliva, A.: Learning deep features for scene recognition using places database. In: Ghahramani, Z., Welling, M., Cortes, C., Lawrence, N.D., Weinberger, K.Q. (eds.) Advances in Neural Information Processing Systems 27, pp. 487–495. Curran Associates, Inc. (2014)
19. Sun, Y., Wang, X., Tang, X.: Deep learning face representation from predicting 10,000 classes. In: 2014 IEEE Conference on Computer Vision and Pattern Recognition, pp. 1891–1898 (2014)
20. Hadsell, R., Chopra, S., LeCun, Y.: Dimensionality reduction by learning an invariant mapping. In: 2006 IEEE Computer Society Conference on Computer Vision and Pattern Recognition (CVPR 2006), vol. 2, pp. 1735–1742 (2006)
21. Varior, R.R., Haloi, M., Wang, G.: Gated siamese convolutional neural network architecture for human re-identification. CoRR abs/1607.08378 (2016)
22. Lin, J., Morère, O., Chandrasekhar, V., Veillard, A., Goh, H.: Deephash: getting regularization, depth and fine-tuning right. CoRR abs/1501.04711 (2015)
23. Chechik, G., Sharma, V., Shalit, U., Bengio, S.: Large scale online learning of image similarity through ranking. J. Mach. Learn. Res. **11**, 1109–1135 (2010)
24. Ustinova, E., Lempitsky, V.: Learning deep embeddings with histogram loss. In: Lee, D.D., Sugiyama, M., Luxburg, U.V., Guyon, I., Garnett, R. (eds.) Advances in Neural Information Processing Systems 29, pp. 4170–4178. Curran Associates, Inc. (2016)

25. Yu, Y., Yang, M., Xu, L., White, M., Schuurmans, D.: Relaxed clipping: a global training method for robust regression and classification. In: NIPS (2010)
26. Wu, C., Manmatha, R., Smola, A.J., Krähenbühl, P.: Sampling matters in deep embedding learning. CoRR abs/1706.07567 (2017)
27. Wang, H., et al.: CosFace: large margin cosine loss for deep face recognition (2018)
28. Balntas, V., Lenc, K., Vedaldi, A., Mikolajczyk, K.: HPatches: a benchmark and evaluation of handcrafted and learned local descriptors. CoRR abs/1704.05939 (2017)
29. Mishkin, D., Matas, J., Perdoch, M., Lenc, K.: WxBS: wide baseline stereo generalizations. CoRR abs/1504.06603 (2015)

Weighted Feature Pooling Network in Template-Based Recognition

Zekun Li$^{(\boxtimes)}$, Yue Wu, Wael Abd-Almageed, and Prem Natarajan

Information Sciences Institute, USC, Los Angeles, CA, USA
zekunl@usc.edu

Abstract. Many computer vision tasks are template-based learning tasks in which multiple instances of a specific concept (e.g. multiple images of a subject's face) are available at once to the learning algorithm. The template structure of the input data provides an opportunity for generating a robust and discriminative unified *template-level* representation that effectively exploits the inherent diversity of feature-level information across instances within a template. In contrast to other feature aggregation methods, we propose a new technique to dynamically predict weights that consider factors such as noise and redundancy in assessing the importance of image-level features and use those weights to appropriately aggregate the features into a single template-level representation. We present extensive experimental results on the MNIST, CIFAR10, UCF101, IJB-A, IJB-B, and Janus CS4 datasets to show that the new technique outperforms statistical feature pooling methods as well as other neural-network-based aggregation mechanisms on a broad set of tasks.

Keywords: Template representation · Feature pooling ·
Attention network

1 Introduction

In many computer vision tasks, the input data comes in the form of grouped instances ("templates") of examples (images, videos) related to the same object or class. For example, in the case of face recognition where the task is to recognize the identity of a subject, many face recognition datasets provide multiple images of each subject, e.g., YouTube Faces (YTF) [1] and IARPA Janus Benchmarks [2,3]. Template-based learning is a natural extension of image-based learning. When the template includes only one image, template-level recognition reduces to image-level recognition. Of course, even in the case of a single-image recognition, there may be scenarios in which it is advantageous to generate a pseudo-template by applying a sequence of augmentations to the base image using other sources of information (e.g., 3D face model) to introduce useful variability.

Template-based learning, like image-based learning, requires an appropriate mechanism to represent instances. Image-level representations or features

C. V. Jawahar et al. (Eds.): ACCV 2018, LNCS 11365, pp. 436–451, 2019.
https://doi.org/10.1007/978-3-030-20873-8_28

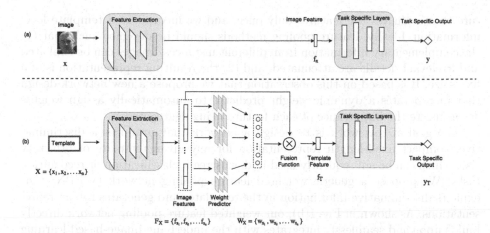

Fig. 1. WFPN can be constructed upon an arbitrary image-based learning network. (a) Image-based learning network (base model). (b) Template-based weighted feature pooling network (WFPN). The red block in feature extractor indicates split node (details in Sect. 3). **Weight predictor** network (green blocks) evaluates features in the same template and generates significance scores. The green blocks share the weights and have the same structure. This weight sharing technique enables WFPN to handle dynamic-sized templates. Fusion function fuses image-level features to template level feature according to the significance scores. (Color figure online)

are easy to obtain from popular deep neural networks such as VGG16 [4] or ResNet [5]. Two fundamental problems need to be overcome or accounted for in using these individual representations in template-based learning: variability across instances and varying numbers of instances from one template to the next. Different images in a given template may reveal different aspects of the underlying object. They may also carry redundant and noisy information [6], and images within the same template may exhibit significant diversity due to variances such as lighting conditions, alternative view angles, or different background scenes. Furthermore, the number of instances varies from one template to another; a natural way to deal with this variability is to generate a single, unified fixed-length representation which we call the "template-level representation".

The most straightforward way to generate a template-level representation is to use the average pooling (or other order statistics) over image-level features, which has been used extensively in recent works [7,8]. Such pooling, however, ignores factors such as noise and redundancy. Importantly, the essence of average pooling is that each feature carries equal weight, which is not true in most cases. For example, certain features from high-resolution images might be more important than those from low-resolution images while other features may be equally important across both conditions. Other neural-network based approaches [9] considered the difference of features by applying convolutional masks on features, but the masking is always constant. The work that aligns most to ours [10] proposed a cascade attention network, while we used a feed-forward structure that evaluates the features only once, and we incorporated template level information. Ideally, feature pooling methods should be designed such that (1) the complementary information from different instances/images can be exploited and irrelevant details are attenuated, and (2) the resulting representation is of a fixed-size. It is based on this observation that we propose a new network design that incorporates a dynamic weight predictor to automatically assign weights according to the importance of each feature being aggregated.

The goal of this work is to design a network that produces a discriminative, compact fixed-length representation for any given template of arbitrary size, which can be subsequently used in downstream classification or recognition tasks. We propose a generic weighted feature pooling network (WFPN) that exploits discriminative information in the templates and generates robust representations. As shown in Fig. 1(b), our weighted feature pooling network directly builds upon and seamlessly integrates with the underlying image-based learning network, i.e., the base model. It is important to note that WFPN takes dynamic-sized templates as input and produces task-specific outputs. Each image inside the template goes through a feature extraction block to generate image-level features. A weight predictor module then assigns weights to the image features according to their importance, where less informative features are assigned lower weights. Image features and weights are then fed into the fusion layer to compute template representations. While we have used linear functions in this work, the fusion layer can use either linear or nonlinear aggregation functions. In our design, the predicted weights should be constrained to sum up to one. WFPN can be trained with the same loss function as in the base model.

The main contribution of this work is the introduction of a new network module (weight predictor) that explicitly and dynamically predicts the importance of image-level features for templates of arbitrary sizes. The proposed WFPN is the integration of weight predictor and the underlying base model. It can deal with various template sizes and generate a discriminative feature that represents the entire template. We quantitatively compared our network with traditional pooling methods as well as neural-network-based approaches, and experiments show superior performance of our WFPN. Furthermore, WFPN is a general end-to-end framework that can be easily extended to solve a broad class of recognition and classification problems. From a computational perspective, compared to its corresponding base models, WFPN provides a significant performance boost while being parsimonious in its addition of parameters.

The remainder of this paper is organized as follows: In Sect. 2 we discuss other feature pooling methods and briefly review related work. Section 3 describes the components of the weighted feature pooling network (WFPN) and show how the weight predictor network is constructed. In Sect. 4 training schemes and evaluation baselines are outlined. In Sect. 5 we evaluate WFPN on multiple datasets. More specifically, with MNIST and CIFAR-10, we show that image-based recognition problems can be easily extended to template-based problems. With IJB-A, IJB-B and Janus CS4, we show that WFPN can deal with dynamic template size on face recognition tasks. With UCF-101, we show WFPN can be applied to action recognition problems. We experimented with various depth and structures of WFPN and observed consistent improvement over statistical pooling and other attention networks.

2   Related Work

The most relevant feature pooling methods can be broadly categorized into two families—transformation-based pooling and neural network-based methods.

Average pooling and max-pooling are the most commonly used statistical pooling methods to generate template representations. Despite their simplicity, these two pooling methods have been remarkably effective in face recognition problems. Hassner et al. [7] used average pooling over images and features that grouped by image quality and head pose to generate template representations. Kawulok et al. [8] applied max pooling over feature descriptors to obtain a single representation from a collection of face images. In the above methods, pooling is performed after feature extraction, and the choice of pooling operations is essentially ad hoc. Some other works [11, 12] formulate the pooling problem as finding orbit of a set of images, where the variations inside the set can be modeled as unitary transforms. This approach is capable of capturing translation, in-plane rotation, out-of-plane rotation, and illumination changes.

Attention networks also have an aggregation process when generating context vector. Given a fixed target output, it loops over all the source hidden states and compares with the current target state to generate scores. Then it uses softmax to normalize all scores and generate attention alignment vector. Then source-side context vector can be computed from the weighted sum of source hidden states according to attention alignment vector. In visual attention networks [13–15], spatial-attention and channel-attention mechanisms are widely used for object recognition and detection, where an attention mask is learned to focus on different regions of image.

In contrast to the approaches mentioned above, our proposed network *explicitly* predicts the importance (or weights) of image features using a weight predictor model. The weight predictor model employed the attention mechanism where the attention mask is determined dynamically based on the input feature and template level information. Different from the attention networks mentioned above, our attention model has a *dynamic*-sized attention window (or attention span) instead of a fixed one. The dynamic-sized window is achieved by the weight-sharing mechanism as illustrated in Fig. 1. Compared with Yang et al. [10], we use one single network instead of a cascaded style to perform weight prediction—thus we only need to look at the features once to determine the weights. Also, their attention-block method employed *local* feature information to learn the mapping, while we also use *template-level information* by introducing a normalization layer after the input layer, which computes template mean and variance to normalize the input data. Moreover, the weight predictor does not have ordering constraint as in [15]. In our WFPN, the significance score depends solely on the current input feature, and the network state is independent of the previous input. Meaningly, even if the ordering of input images has changed, the corresponding weights produced by the weight predictor module remain consistent. In the proposed WFPN model, feature pooling can be adapted to different datasets and employed to solve different problems with the aid of task-specific layers.

3   Template Representation Using Weighted Feature Pooling Network (WFPN)

As mentioned in Sect. 1, template pooling can be utilized for in both image-based and template-based learning tasks. For example, in IJB-A [2] and IJB-B [3] face recognition datasets, a template is defined as a set of images and video frames that contain the face of the same person, whereas in image patch denoising problems [16], a template can be considered as a group of similar 2D image fragments. In single-image-based learning tasks where template does not exist, we can easily create a *pseudo template* from the base image using data augmentation or data adaptation techniques. For instance, in the MNIST dataset [17], we can arbitrarily rotate the images, such that the rotated copies form a pseudo template for base images.

The overall architecture of WFPN is shown in Fig. 1(b). Let $X \in \mathbf{R}^{N \times l}$ be the template that contains an arbitrary number of images, where N is the number of images, and l is the length of the feature. The goal of WFPN is to compute a $X \rightarrow y_T$ mapping where y_T is the task-specific, learned representation. WFPN consists of a quintuple $\{\mathcal{F}, \mathcal{P}, \mathcal{C}, \mathcal{M}\}$, where $\mathcal{F}$ is the underlying feature extraction module (blue block on the left side of Fig. 1b), $\mathcal{P}$ is the weight predictor module (green network in the middle of Fig. 1b), $\mathcal{M}$ is the fusion function that aggregates the image-level representations to produce template-level features using the weights estimated by $\mathcal{P}$, and $\mathcal{C}$ is the underlying, task-specific module (e.g., classifier or regressor). In this section, we describe the above four components of WFPN that perform the $X \rightarrow y_T$ mapping.

One of the main design goals of WFPN is to easily integrate our weight predictor (as a plug and play module) into existing network architectures, without changes to the underlying network. For every visual recognition task, we assume there is an underlying image-based learning network, i.e., base model, that has been developed specifically for the given task, as shown in Fig. 1(a). Since deep learning-based recognition methods generally learn feature extraction along with the recognition task [18], a typical image-based recognition network can be conceptually divided into two parts: feature extraction $\mathcal{F}$ and task-specific layers $\mathcal{C}$ (e.g., classification layers). Therefore, we can define **split node** as the intermediate layer that separates the two parts in the original recognition network. The segment from the input layer to split node will be referred to as the feature extraction block $\mathcal{F}$, and the rest of the network will be thought of as task-specific layers $\mathcal{C}$. The output of the split node can be seen as the feature representation of the input image—as shown in Fig. 1(a). The choice of the split node is not deterministic. Often, the split node is a fully connected layer or global average pooling layer that produces 1D representation. Figure 1(b) shows an example of constructing WFPN from the base model using the above splitting scheme. Built upon the base model, WFPN uses a weight predictor $\mathcal{P}$ to predict the importance of image-level features, and a fusion layer $\mathcal{M}$ takes predicted weights together with image features to compute the final template representation.

Assume object X has a template size N (N can be different among different objects), given the group of images $X = \{x_1, x_2, ...x_N\}$ that belong to the same template, feature extraction layers are applied to get image features, $F_X = \{f_{x_1}, f_{x_2}, ...f_{x_N}\}$, and we want to obtain a template feature f_T that represents all the features in F_X. Those image-level features $F_X = \{f_{x_1}, f_{x_2}, ...f_{x_N}\}$ are fed into the weight predictor module, which is essentially a regression network, to produce corresponding weights $W_X = \{w_{x_1}, w_{x_2}, ..., w_{x_N}\}$. Basically, input features are treated separately by the same network such that each input feature generates a weight value associated with it. In this way, we are able to handle arbitrary template size since all the operations are applied feature-wise instead of template-wise. Finally, the fusion layer computes $f_T = \sum_{i=1}^{N} w_{x_i} f_{x_N}$, which is the template-level feature representation. Note that $\sum_i^N w_{x_i} = 1$.

The weight predictor module is composed of multiple fully connected layers interpolated with drop-out layers (the number of hidden units and dropout rates that may vary depending on the specific task). The last fully connected layer uses 3D softmax activation, since we want the predicted weights to ensure $\sum_i^N w_{x_i} = 1$. All layers are wrapped in a time-distributed layer such that each input feature produces a corresponding weight, as shown in Fig. 1(b). Formally, without loss of generality, suppose the weight predictor has L fully-connected layers, and $x_i \in \mathbb{R}^M$. Then the weight score w_{x_i} can be computed from the following steps.

$$a_{x_i}^{(1)} = W^{(1)} f_{x_i} + b^{(1)} \tag{1}$$

$$g_{x_i}^{(1)} = max\{0, a_{x_i}^{(1)}\} \tag{2}$$

$$... \tag{3}$$

$$a_{x_i}^{(L)} = W^{(L)} g_{x_i}^{(L-1)} + b^{(L)} \tag{4}$$

$$w_{x_i} = \frac{exp(a_{x_i}^{(L)})}{\sum_j exp(a_{x_j}^{(L)})} \tag{5}$$

Notice that $W^{(L)}$ is of shape $(1 \times D)$ where D is the dimension of $g_{x_i}^{(L-1)}$. This constraint ensures that w_{x_i} is scalar. Equation 5 guarantees that the output is a probability distribution.

The above weight predictor network is wrapped in a time-distributed layer which reads in a template tensor $X \in \mathbb{R}^{N \times M}$ and performs the operations (1)–(4) on each slice of X, namely x_i, and their output will be softmax normalized. Each $x_i \in X$ is processed by $\mathcal{P}$, and the parameters of $\mathcal{P}$ are shared by all $x_i, \forall i \in \{1, 2, ...N\}$. The weight predictor looks at each image feature individually and predicts a value that expresses the significance of this feature. As shown above, the weight predictor parameters $\{W^{(1)}, ..., W^{(N)}\}$ are independent of template size. Thus we can use dynamic template size during training and testing, as long as the template size is fixed within each batch.

In some cases, we might want to harness template-level information to assist the weight prediction of each single features. A straightforward way to achieve this is to add a normalization layer before feeding the features into weight predictor, such that features are normalized with the template mean and the template variance. Template-level information is then encoded into image-level features.

4   Training Scheme and Evaluation Methodology

In order to accurately evaluate the contribution of weight predictor versus the underlying feature extraction and classification modules, we first pre-train the base model (see Fig. 1(a)) and then initialize WFPN with pre-trained weights, such that feature extraction and classification blocks in these two models have the learned weights. We further freeze those weights and train the rest of layers in WFPN with randomly initialized weights. The loss is computed using the output of task-specific layers. For example, in classification tasks, we use categorical cross-entropy as our loss function, as shown in Eq. 6.

$$L(p, q) = - \sum_x p(x) log(q(x)) \tag{6}$$

The error is back-propagated end-to-end, although only the weight predictor weights will be updated during the process because we have frozen the feature extraction and classification module.

In terms of evaluation, we compare WFPN performance with three baseline methods: single image classification without pooling, average pooling, and majority voting. For the single-image evaluation, we use the base model as shown in Fig. 1(a) for classification, without template synthesis. For average pooling, we simply average over all features to obtain the template feature $f_T = \frac{1}{T} \sum_{i=1}^{T} f_{x_i}$ and do classification. In majority voting (or hard voting), we do not compute any template feature anymore. Instead, for feature vector $F_X = \{f_{x_1}, f_{x_2}, ... f_{x_T}\}$, we predict a label vector $Y_X = \{y_{x_1}, y_{x_2}, ... y_{x_T}\}$, which each y_{x_i} is the predicted label of f_{x_i} by the classification network. We then carry out voting using Y_X and mark the template label $\tilde{y}_x$ to be the label that received maximum votes. $\tilde{y}_x = argmax_j \sum_i \lambda_{ij} y_{x_i}$, where $j \in C$ is the class label and $\lambda_{ij} = [y_{x_i} = j]$.

5   Experimental Results

5.1   Influence of Template Synthesis Scheme on WFPN

In this section, we study the influence of the template synthesis scheme on WFPN performance and show how to apply the weighted feature pooling network on the MNIST [17] dataset, which is naturally a single-image dataset.

MNIST is a database of handwritten digits. It has 60,000 training images and 10,000 testing images. We randomly split the training set into training and

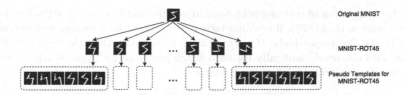

Fig. 2. MNIST pseudo template generation. First augment original MNIST dataset through rotation to generate MNIST-ROTϕ, then generate pseudo templates for MNIST-ROTϕ for different ϕ angles.

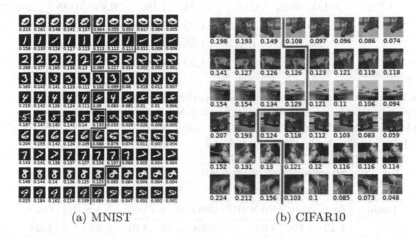

(a) MNIST   (b) CIFAR10

Fig. 3. WFPN-predicted weights on MNIST and CIFAR-10 (base model: Resnet18). Note that weight prediction is performed on features. The red line splits template images into two parts: images on left side have weights above average, images on right side have weights below average. (Color figure online)

validation sets with ratio 5:1. Since all the digits in MNIST were orientation-normalized and centered in a fixed-size image, in order to evaluate the performance of WFPN on different dataset distributions, we need first to create some variations of MNIST that have distinctive distributions. We perturb MNIST by randomly rotating the images by an angle $\Theta = \{\theta_1, \theta_2, ..., \theta_M\}$, where $\theta_i \in U(-\phi, \phi)$. We refer to this perturbed dataset as MNIST-ROTϕ. All the results in this section are reported on MNIST-ROTϕ instead of the original MNIST dataset. By setting $M = 10$, we will have MNIST-ROTϕ containing 500,000 training, 100,000 validation, and 100,000 testing samples.

Since MNIST-ROTϕ does not have the concept of *template*, we need to synthesize the pseudo templates in a meaningful way. Figure 2 illustrates how templates are generated from MNIST-ROTϕ images. An image x in MNIST-ROTϕ is augmented with a sequence of rotations with angle $\Omega = \{\omega_1, \omega_2, ...\omega_T\}$, where $\omega_i \in U(-\phi, \phi)$ and T is the size of the synthesized template. We can use either dynamic or fixed template size for training, and we use template size $\{8,11,20\}$ for testing to better evaluate the performance of WFPN with controlled

Table 1 Comparison of training with fixed/dynamic template size. For testing data of a certain tsize in (8, 11, 20), if training tsize is *fixed*, then the template size of training data is (8, 11, 20) respectively. If training tsize is *dynamic*, then the template size of training data change dynamically for each batch and is range from [8, 20]. (Numbers in the table are errors, the lower the better.)

Err. (%)	tsize	8		11		20	
Rot. range	Img.	Fixed	Dynam.	Fixed	Dynam.	Fixed	Dynam.
5	0.73	0.72	0.71	0.71	0.72	0.71	0.72
15	1.09	0.86	0.88	1.24	1.19	0.83	0.85
45	2.26	1.20	1.14	1.86	1.36	1.17	1.09
75	2.93	2.10	1.88	1.55	1.44	1.43	1.46
90	4.59	2.53	1.88	1.99	1.86	2.19	2.21

Table 2. Comparison of different template synthesizing method. With *rand. rot. angle*, we randomly sample rotation angles for testing. With *fixed rot. sequence*, we use a set of angles with a fixed interval $\Omega = \{\omega_1, \omega_2, ...\omega_T\}$ where $|\omega_{i+1} - \omega_i| = \frac{2\phi}{T}$. (Numbers in the table are errors, the lower the better.)

Err. (%)	Single image: 4.59 ($\phi = 90$)							
	Rand. rot. angles				Fixed rot. sequence			
Tmplt.	Avg.	Vote.	NAN [10]	Ours	Avg.	Vote.	NAN [10]	Ours
8	4.42	8.80	3.62	**2.53**	4.89	3.91	2.42	**1.98**
11	4.12	4.31	2.83	**1.99**	4.90	3.49	2.18	**1.71**
20	9.67	10.24	3.45	**2.19**	5.12	3.33	2.28	**1.77**

variables. Note that the rotation angle range in augmentation should be at least the same as in perturbation because we want all the tilted digits to have a chance to rotate back to their original positions. In this paper, we use the same angle range for perturbation and augmentation (Fig. 3).

We first train an MNIST-CNN network on MNIST-ROTϕ. We use a simple 4-layer convolutional network as the base model.[1] We pre-train MNIST-CNN on MNIST-ROTϕ for 100 epochs with batch size = 128 and get the testing result as our single image classification baseline. For template-based recognition with WFPN, we let the split node be the second-last fully connected layer and use a weight predictor network that has three fully connected layers and three dropout layers. The number of filters is {128, 8, 1} respectively. The dropout layers have dropout rates of 0.25. As mentioned in Sect. 3, all of the above layers are wrapped in time distributed layers. For the choice of ϕ, we experimented with a group of angle ranges: [5, 15, 45, 75, 90]. Thus we have five different perturbed datasets. After training the MNIST-CNN network for each dataset, we obtained the testing error rates shown in Table 1 in column labeled *img*.

---

[1] https://github.com/fchollet/keras/blob/master/examples/mnist_cnn.py.

During training of WFPN we can either use a dynamic template size or fixed template size. When using dynamic template size, the network will learn to handle test sets with arbitrary template size. We compare the results of WFPN against our single image classification baseline. Results are shown in Table 1 (the test sets are generated using randomly sampled rotation angles). We observe that the network trained with dynamic template size has generally better performance than the ones trained with fixed size templates. Also, there are multiple ways of generating templates for testing. We can either randomly sample rotation angles, or we use a set of angles with a fixed interval. The first setting can be used to evaluate the performance of the weight predictor when template generation is random. The second setting guarantees that the existence of an image in our synthesized template is as close to an optimal tilted position as possible. Results are shown in Table 2.

5.2   Influence of Base Model Structure on WFPN

In this section, we study the influence of base model structure on the WFPN performance using CIFAR-10 dataset. CIFAR-10 has 60,000 color images of size 32×32, with 50,000 for training and 10,000 for testing. Those images contain objects from 10 classes. We keep 5,000 for validation and use the rest to train the WFPN network.

We experimented with three base models, Resnet-18 [5], Resnet-20 [5] and adapted-VGG16 on CIFAR-10 [19]. For the first two models, we let the split node be the flatten layer before the last fully connected layer. Then the classification block would be the one fully connected layer (last layer) with softmax activation. The feature extraction block consists of layers in-between the input layer and split node. The output feature dimension is 512 for Resnet-18 and 64 for Resnet-20. For the VGG16 model, the split node is again the flatten layer—thus the classification block has two fully connected layers, and the feature extraction block has 13 convolutional layers. The flatten layer serves as the output of the feature extraction block. With this structure, the feature dimension is 512. During training, we use the loss function defined in Eq. 6. In the corresponding WFPN models, all weight predictors have the same structure: 3 fully connected layers with {128, 8, 1} filters; dropout layers have a dropout rate of 0.25.

WFPN is initialized from the pre-trained base model, such that feature extraction block and classification block weights are loaded. The loaded weights are frozen during the training of WFPN thus only the weight predictor module is trainable. Then the performance change will only be related to feature pooling methods instead of the fine-tuning of feature extractor and classifier.

In this experiment, we synthesize templates by randomly shifting and horizontally flipping the base image. The shifting range is [-6, +6] pixels in all directions, and shift distance is uniformly and randomly selected. The number of augmentations indicates template size. Note that the above augmentation methods can also be used to train our base models described earlier, but the purposes of augmentation are different. During training the base model, augmentation is a common trick used against over-fitting. While training the WFPN

Table 3. Comparison of baselines and WFPN performance. WFPN consistently outperforms baselines and NAN for different network structures with different depth.

Acc. (%)	Img.	Tmplt.	Avg. pool	Voting	NAN [10]	Ours
Resnet20	91.42	3	91.47	90.06	91.64	**92.49**
		5	92.09	91.59	92.09	**93.17**
		8	91.88	90.98	92.71	**93.17**
Resnet18	89.41	3	89.80	88.85	89.69	**90.02**
		5	90.66	89.97	90.36	**90.89**
		8	90.47	89.40	90.63	**90.84**
VGG16	93.59	3	93.69	93.32	93.54	**93.84**
		5	93.88	93.62	**94.11**	93.92
		8	93.66	93.39	93.88	**94.02**

model, augmentation is used to generate templates from one seed image, and the model learns to disregard redundant or noisy information to produce compact and discriminative features.

We compared the performance of WFPN with two baselines and the NAN network in [10]. We observed that WFPN has higher accuracy than mostly all three baselines. Results are shown in Table 3.

5.3 WFPN for Face Recognition

In this section we evaluate WFPN on the face recognition task using the IJB-A [2], IJB-B [3] and Janus CS4 dataset. Our base model is ResFace101 in [20], which is a deep neural network with 101 convolutional layers. Since these datasets have already pre-defined the templates, we do not need to synthesize templates anymore.

In facial recognition problems, we adapt our weight predictor module by adding one extra normalization layer after the input of features. The purpose of this layer is to encode local information within the template, such that even with exactly the same image feature input, the absolute weight value could be different depending on its neighboring features inside the same template. The normalization layer is defined as $g(\mathbf{x_i}) = (\mathbf{x_i} - \bar{\mathbf{x}})/\sigma(X)$, where $X \in \mathbb{R}^{N \times M}$ is a template tensor with template size N and feature length M, $\sigma(X)$ denotes the variance of X, and $\bar{\mathbf{x}} = \frac{1}{N} \sum_{i=1}^{N} \mathbf{x_i}$.

For face recognition problems, we are only interested in the areas that contain faces. However, images in the uncontrolled environment have large illumination, background, and environment variations [18]. Thus necessary preprocessing steps are applied to crop out face regions, detect landmarks, and align the faces [18,24]. The input to face recognition networks should be aligned face images cropped by tight bounding boxes.

For training, we used a combination of three datasets: Microsoft Celeb [25], Oxford VGG face [22] and CASIA WebFace dataset [26]. The combined data

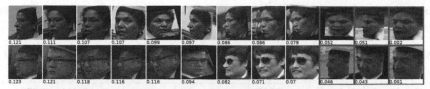

(a) WPFN assigns features from low resolution images less weights

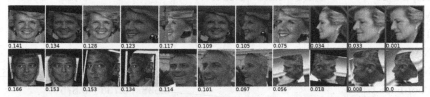

(b) WPFN assigns features from bad augmentations less weights

(c) WPFN is able to distinguish outliers

Fig. 4. Weights visualization of IJB-B.

set has a total of 6,641,205 images from 68,906 subjects, and we split them into three parts—train, val, and test. Training and validation have 6,597,046 images, and the remainder is used for testing. The advantage of using this combined dataset is the huge amount of data. However, this dataset does *not* have the concept of template thus we need to synthesize templates for training weight predictor. In this case, we cannot simply use augmentations as we did for MNIST and CIFAR datasets since synthesized templates from one single image do not provide much information about the subject. Instead, we should select different images for one subject and group them as a template. Since we want our model to be able to handle *dynamic* template size during testing time, we should also train our model with dynamic size templates. In order to decide the appropriate template size, we further studied the IJB-B gallery set and analyzed its template size distribution. We observed that the template size could be fitted using an exponential distribution. Therefore, during training, we determine the template size dynamically according to the exponential probability of mass distribution. The loss function we use is defined in Eq. 6.

The trained network was testing on the IJB-A, IJB-B and CS4 datasets without fine-tuning. There are 1845 subjects in IJB-B dataset with still images,

Table 4. Comparison of WFPN and state-of-the-art networks on IJB-A (*: result reported in [21], †: NAN single attention model, ‡: NAN cascade model)

Method	1:1 Verification TAR@FAR			1:N Identification TPIR@FPIR			
	1e-3	1e-2	1e-1	1e-4	1e-3	1e-2	1e-1
VGG-Face* [22]	-	0.805	-	-	-	0.461	0.670
Triplet [23]	0.813	0.900	0.964	-	-	0.753	0.863
Multi-pose [18]	-	0.787	0.911	-	-	0.876	0.954
Templt-Adapt [21]	0.836	0.939	0.979	-	-	0.774	0.882
NAN†[10]	0.860	0.933	0.979	-	-	0.804	0.909
NAN‡ [10]	0.881	0.941	0.978	-	-	0.817	0.917
Pool-Face [7]	-	-	-	0.538	0.735	0.875	-
WFPN	**0.906**	**0.954**	**0.981**	**0.878**	**0.932**	**0.966**	**0.981**

Table 5. Comparison of average pooling and WFPN on IJB-B and CS4

	IJB-B 1-N identification				CS4 1-N identification			
	Avg.	WFPN	Absolute	Relative	Avg.	WFPN	Absolute	Relative
TAR@FAR = 0.001%	0.484	0.563	0.079	15.31%	0.584	0.651	0.067	16.11%
TAR@FAR = 0.01%	0.748	0.786	0.038	15.08%	0.786	0.814	0.028	13.08%
TAR@FAR = 0.1%	0.891	0.901	0.010	9.17%	0.907	0.915	0.008	8.60%
Rank 1	0.890	0.904	0.014	12.73%	0.895	0.905	0.010	9.52%
Rank 5	0.945	0.950	0.005	9.09%	0.941	0.947	0.006	10.17%
Rank 10	0.960	0.964	0.004	10.00%	0.956	0.960	0.004	9.09%

video frames, and videos collected from the web. CS4 has 3548 subjects with a total of 23,221 templates. Evaluation is performed using the still images and keyframes protocol. Results are shown in Table 5. The last two columns are the absolute improvement and relative improvement respectively. We can better understand the effect of WFPN by visualizing the images and their associated weights. Figure 4 illustrates that WFPN has favorable properties (Table 4).

5.4   WFPN for Action Recognition

In this experiment we apply WFPN on UCF-101 dataset [27], an action recognition dataset that has 101 classes of human actions with 13320 videos. We followed the same pre-processing steps as in [28] and used RGB stream and optical flow streams for our experiments. For optical flow stream, videos are processed using the TV-L1 algorithm [29] with pixel values truncated to $[-20, 20]$ and also resized with short side equals to 256. During training, we randomly crop out a (224×224) region spatially and select 64 consecutive frames temporally. For videos that are not long enough, we replicate the video until it has more than 64 frames, and take the first 64. For testing, we crop out the center region of size (224 × 224) and select 250 time frames. Images are loaded in [0, 255] range and then scaled to [−1, 1] range by multiplying a constant number 255/2 and subtracting 1. Flows are also scaled using the same procedure.

The base model we use to initialize WFPN is the Inflated 3D Convnet (I3D) in [28]. The weights are pretrained on ImageNet and Kinetics and fine-tuned on UCF101 with learning rate 0.1, mini-batch size 6, and weight decay 1e-7. I3D is a two-stream network that operates on both RGB and flow streams, and we treat each stream as the base model. In the base model, a stack of 3D convolutional filters are applied to the input, and then a spatial global average pooling is applied on top of them. The tensor has a temporal receptive field of 99 frames in input RGB stream. In the classifier, each remaining frame predicts a logit distribution of output categories, which are averaged to generate the video logit distribution. The softmax of video logit distribution gives class probability distribution. It is clear that each spatially convolved frame has equal weight in determining the final probability distribution, which might not be optimal. Thus we can insert our weight predictor module into the classifier and perform the soft aggregation. Instead of averaging the logit distributions, the weight predictor takes in all the logit distributions produced by each spatially convolved frame and predicts the importance of each distribution for generating video logit distribution.

Results of WFPN compared with other state-of-the-art networks are shown in Table 6. We can see that WFPN outperforms its corresponding base models [28] and achieves the highest accuracy on this dataset.

Table 6. Comparison of WFPN and other methods on UCF101 dataset. (WFPN initialized from imagenet + kinetics pretrained weights, *: Keras implementation)

	Two-Strm [30]	Conv-TS [9]	TSN [31]	HiddenTSN [32]	I3D [28]	WFPN
RGB	73.0	82.61	84.5	85.7	92.2*	**94.1**
Flow	83.7	86.25	87.2	86.3	94.7*	**96.3**
Joint	88.0	90.62	92.0	92.5	96.0*	**97.8**

6   Conclusion

We present the weighted feature pooling network (WFPN) that is designed for template-based recognition problems. This network is conceptually composed of four parts: feature extractor, weight predictor, fusion function and task-specific layers. Feature extractor produces image-level features for all the images in the same template, and weight predictor predicts the significance of each image and fusion function aggregates image-level features to template-level features according to their significance. This network can extract complementary information, remove noise, and produce a compact and discriminative template feature. WFPN is lightweight and easy to generalize on many tasks such as object classification, face recognition, and video activity recognition.

Acknowledgments. This research is based upon work supported in part by the Office of the Director of National Intelligence (ODNI), Intelligence Advanced Research Projects Activity (IARPA), via IARPA 2014-14071600011. The views and conclusions contained herein are those of the authors and should not be interpreted as necessarily representing the official policies or endorsements, either expressed or implied, of ODNI, IARPA, or the U.S. Government. The U.S. Government is authorized to reproduce and distribute reprints for Governmental purpose notwithstanding any copyright annotation thereon.

References

1. Wolf, L., Hassner, T., Maoz, I.: Face recognition in unconstrained videos with matched background similarity. In: Proceedings of the IEEE Conference on Computer Vision and Pattern Recognition, pp. 529–534 (2011)
2. Klare, B.F., et al.: Pushing the frontiers of unconstrained face detection and recognition: IARPA Janus Benchmark A. In: Proceedings of the IEEE Conference on Computer Vision and Pattern Recognition, pp. 1931–1939 (2015)
3. Whitelam, C., et al.: IARPA Janus Benchmark-B face dataset. In: Proceedings of the IEEE Conference on Computer Vision and Pattern Recognition Workshops (2017)
4. Simonyan, K., Zisserman, A.: Very deep convolutional networks for large-scale image recognition. arXiv preprint arXiv:1409.1556 (2014)
5. He, K., Zhang, X., Ren, S., Sun, J.: Deep residual learning for image recognition. In: Proceedings of the IEEE Conference on Computer Vision and Pattern Recognition, pp. 770–778 (2016)
6. Ma, L., Lu, J., Feng, J., Zhou, J.: Multiple feature fusion via weighted entropy for visual tracking. In: Proceedings of the IEEE International Conference on Computer Vision, pp. 3128–3136 (2015)
7. Hassner, T., et al.: Pooling faces: template based face recognition with pooled face images. In: Proceedings of the IEEE Conference on Computer Vision and Pattern Recognition Workshops, pp. 59–67 (2016)
8. Kawulok, M., Celebi, E., Smolka, B.: Advances in Face Detection and Facial Image Analysis. Springer, Cham (2016). https://doi.org/10.1007/978-3-319-25958-1
9. Feichtenhofer, C., Pinz, A., Zisserman, A.: Convolutional two-stream network fusion for video action recognition. In: Proceedings of the IEEE Conference on Computer Vision and Pattern Recognition, pp. 1933–1941 (2016)
10. Yang, J., Ren, P., Chen, D., Wen, F., Li, H., Hua, G.: Neural aggregation network for video face recognition. arXiv preprint arXiv:1603.05474 (2016)
11. Liao, Q., Leibo, J.Z., Poggio, T.: Learning invariant representations and applications to face verification. In: Advances in Neural Information Processing Systems, pp. 3057–3065 (2013)
12. Pal, D.K., Juefei-Xu, F., Savvides, M.: Discriminative invariant kernel features: a bells-and-whistles-free approach to unsupervised face recognition and pose estimation. In: Proceedings of the IEEE Conference on Computer Vision and Pattern Recognition, pp. 5590–5599 (2016)
13. Luong, M.T., Pham, H., Manning, C.D.: Effective approaches to attention-based neural machine translation. arXiv preprint arXiv:1508.04025 (2015)
14. Wang, P., Cao, Y., Shen, C., Liu, L., Shen, H.T.: Temporal pyramid pooling based convolutional neural networks for action recognition. arXiv preprint arXiv:1503.01224 (2015)

15. Sharma, S., Kiros, R., Salakhutdinov, R.: Action recognition using visual attention. arXiv preprint arXiv:1511.04119 (2015)
16. Alkinani, M.H., El-Sakka, M.R.: Patch-based models and algorithms for image denoising: a comparative review between patch-based images denoising methods for additive noise reduction. EURASIP J. Image Video Process. **2017**, 58 (2017)
17. LeCun, Y., Bottou, L., Bengio, Y., Haffner, P.: Gradient-based learning applied to document recognition. Proc. IEEE **86**, 2278–2324 (1998)
18. AbdAlmageed, W., et al.: Face recognition using deep multi-pose representations. In: Proceedings of the IEEE Winter Conference on Applications of Computer Vision, pp. 1–9 (2016)
19. Liu, S., Deng, W.: Very deep convolutional neural network based image classification using small training sample size. In: Proceedings of the IEEE Asian Conference on Pattern Recognition, pp. 730–734 (2015)
20. Masi, I., Tran, A.T., Hassner, T., Leksut, J.T., Medioni, G.: Do we really need to collect millions of faces for effective face recognition? In: Leibe, B., Matas, J., Sebe, N., Welling, M. (eds.) ECCV 2016. LNCS, vol. 9909, pp. 579–596. Springer, Cham (2016). https://doi.org/10.1007/978-3-319-46454-1_35
21. Crosswhite, N., Byrne, J., Stauffer, C., Parkhi, O., Cao, Q., Zisserman, A.: Template adaptation for face verification and identification. In: Proceedings of the IEEE International Conference on Automatic Face & Gesture Recognition, pp. 1–8. IEEE (2017)
22. Parkhi, O.M., Vedaldi, A., Zisserman, A., et al.: Deep face recognition. In: Proceedings of the British Machine Vision Conference, vol. 1, p. 6 (2015)
23. Sankaranarayanan, S., Alavi, A., Castillo, C.D., Chellappa, R.: Triplet probabilistic embedding for face verification and clustering. In: Proceedings of the IEEE International Conference on Biometrics Theory, Applications and Systems, pp. 1–8 (2016)
24. Masi, I., Hassner, T., Tran, A.T., Medioni, G.: Rapid synthesis of massive face sets for improved face recognition. In: Proceedings of the IEEE Automatic Face & Gesture Recognition, pp. 604–611 (2017)
25. Guo, Y., Zhang, L., Hu, Y., He, X., Gao, J.: MS-Celeb-1M: a dataset and benchmark for large-scale face recognition. In: Leibe, B., Matas, J., Sebe, N., Welling, M. (eds.) ECCV 2016. LNCS, vol. 9907, pp. 87–102. Springer, Cham (2016). https://doi.org/10.1007/978-3-319-46487-9_6
26. Yi, D., Lei, Z., Liao, S., Li, S.Z.: Learning face representation from scratch. arXiv preprint arXiv:1411.7923 (2014)
27. Soomro, K., Zamir, A.R., Shah, M.: Ucf101: a dataset of 101 human actions classes from videos in the wild. arXiv preprint arXiv:1212.0402 (2012)
28. Carreira, J., Zisserman, A.: Quo vadis, action recognition? A new model and the kinetics dataset. In: Proceedings of the IEEE International Conference on Computer Vision and Pattern Recognition, pp. 4724–4733 (2017)
29. Pérez, J.S., Meinhardt-Llopis, E., Facciolo, G.: Tv-l1 optical flow estimation. Image Process. On Line **2013**, 137–150 (2013)
30. Simonyan, K., Zisserman, A.: Two-stream convolutional networks for action recognition in videos. In: Advances in Neural Information Processing Systems, pp. 568–576 (2014)
31. Wang, L., et al.: Temporal segment networks: towards good practices for deep action recognition. In: Leibe, B., Matas, J., Sebe, N., Welling, M. (eds.) ECCV 2016. LNCS, vol. 9912, pp. 20–36. Springer, Cham (2016). https://doi.org/10.1007/978-3-319-46484-8_2
32. Zhu, Y., Lan, Z., Newsam, S., Hauptmann, A.G.: Hidden two-stream convolutional networks for action recognition. arXiv preprint arXiv:1704.00389 (2017)

Efficient Multi-level Correlating
for Visual Tracking

Yipeng Ma[1], Chun Yuan[2(✉)], Peng Gao[1], and Fei Wang[1(✉)]

[1] Shenzhen Graduate School, Harbin Institute of Technology, Shenzhen, China
{mayipeng,pgao}@stu.hit.edu.cn, wangfeiz@hit.edu.cn
[2] Graduate School at Shenzhen, Tsinghua University, Shenzhen, China
yuanc@sz.tsinghua.edu.cn

Abstract. Correlation filter (CF) based tracking algorithms have demonstrated favorable performance recently. Nevertheless, the top performance trackers always employ complicated optimization methods which constrain their real-time applications. How to accelerate the tracking speed while retaining the tracking accuracy is a significant issue. In this paper, we propose a multi-level CF-based tracking approach named MLCFT which further explores the potential capacity of CF with two-stage detection: primal detection and oriented re-detection. The cascaded detection scheme is simple but competent to prevent model drift and accelerate the speed. An effective fusion method based on relative entropy is introduced to combine the complementary features extracted from deep and shallow layers of convolutional neural networks (CNN). Moreover, a novel online model update strategy is utilized in our tracker, which enhances the tracking performance further. Experimental results demonstrate that our proposed approach outperforms the most state-of-the-art trackers while tracking at speed of exceeded 16 frames per second on challenging benchmarks.

Keywords: Visual tracking · Correlation filter ·
Convolutional neural networks · Relative entropy

1 Introduction

Visual object tracking has made considerable progress in the last decades, and it is widely developed in numerous applications, such as intelligent video surveillance, self-driving vehicle and human computer interaction. Despite the great effort that has been made to investigate effective approaches [11,12,14,26,31], visual object tracking is still a tough task owing to complicated factors like severe deformation, abrupt motion, illumination variation, background clutter, occlusion, etc. Due to requirement from many demanding applications, boosting both accuracy and tracking speed has long been pursued.

Recently, CF-based trackers have drawn considerable attention owing to their high tracking speed and good performance. Bolme et al. [2] are the first to exploit

© Springer Nature Switzerland AG 2019
C. V. Jawahar et al. (Eds.): ACCV 2018, LNCS 11365, pp. 452–465, 2019.
https://doi.org/10.1007/978-3-030-20873-8_29

CF for visual tracking. Since then, several extended works are engaged in improving tracking performance. Henriques et al. propose CSK [18] and KCF [19] successively, which introduce circulant structure to interpret CF and generalize to the extension of multi-channel features. Additionally, Danelljan et al. [5] exploit fast scale pyramid estimation to deal with scale variations. Despite the prominent efficiency of these CF-based trackers, intensive computation overhead brought by the complex framework hinders its application in real-time scenarios.

To address the unwanted model drifting issue, Ma et al. [26] propose a complementary re-detection scheme based on an online random fern classifier. Also to address the same issue, Wang et al. [33] conduct a multi-modal target re-detection technique with a support vector machine (SVM) based tracking method. However, because of the directionless re-detection and too much proposals, inaccuracy and redundant computation do exist in these works.

With the great representation capability of deep features, convolutional neural network (CNN) [22] has become popular in a wide range of computer vision tasks like object detection [15,28] and object recognition [20]. Most recently, CNN has been employed for visual tracking and shown its promising performance. Several CNN-based tracking approaches [1,13,27] have shown state-of-the-art results on many object tracking benchmarks. These methods validate the strong capacity of CNN for target representation.

Inspired by previous works, we propose an efficient *multi-level* CF-based framework for visual tracking. Here the so-called *Multi-level* has two meanings: (a) Multiple layers of CNN are used to represent the target. Shallow and deep layers of CNN take the complementary properties into account. (b) A two-level detection scheme is proposed, i.e., primal detection and re-detection. Primal detection is cascaded with an oriented re-detection module. The primal detection delivers the possible candidate locations of the target to the re-detection module. Then, the re-detection module will conduct estimations around those locations and the most possible location is given as the location of the target finally.

The main contributions of our work can be summarized as follows:

- We propose a multi-level CF-based tracking method with features extracted from multiple layers of CNNs. Additionally, an effective fusion method based on relative entropy is applied to improve the tracking performance.
- We employ an oriented re-detection technique to ensure the localization accuracy. Furthermore, an effective adaptive online model update strategy is applied in our tracker.
- We compare our approach with state-of-the-art trackers on several benchmarks: OTB-2013, OTB-2015 and VOT-2017. The results validate that our tracker outperforms the most state-of-the-art trackers in terms of accuracy, robustness and speed.

2   Algorithmic Overview

A brief introduction to the overall framework of our proposed tracker is shown in Fig. 1. We divide our algorithm into four stages: filter learning, primal detection, re-detection and scale estimation followed by adaptive update. In the filter

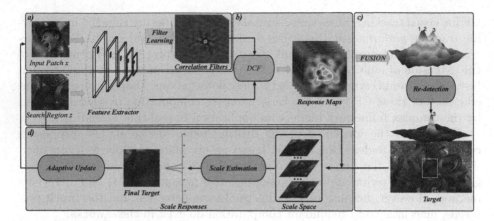

Fig. 1. The overall framework of the proposed method. The tracker can be divided into four parts marked in color: (a) Filter learning; (b) Primal detection; (c) Re-detection module; (d) Scale estimation and adaptive update. (Color figure online)

learning stage, we utilize the pre-trained VGG-Net to extract the feature maps of different convolutional layers from image patch. Then, the corresponding correlation filters are learned with these features and a Gaussian shaped label. In the primal detection stage, each feature map extracted from the search region is correlated by the corresponding correlation filter to generate response maps, respectively. And candidate locations of the target can be obtained in the fusion response map. In case of detection failure, the re-detection module is exploited in our tracker, which effectively avoid target drift during tracking (see Sect. 3.2 for more details). In the last stage, scale estimation and a useful adaptive online model update strategy are applied to adjust to scale variation and adapt model variation of the target.

3 The Proposed Approach

In this section, we first describe the overall framework of our proposed approach in Sect. 3.1. Then, we detail our proposed re-detection module in Sect. 3.2. Finally, we present the adaptive online model update scheme in Sect. 3.3.

3.1 Multi-level Correlation Tracking

Our tracking framework is constructed with the combination of canonical CF-based tracking approach with convolutional deep features. The pre-trained VGG-Net [3] is used to extract the convolutional features to represent the target. We observe the fact that the convolutional features extracted from very deep layer of CNN can capture rich discriminative semantic information, while the features from shallow layers offer more spatial information which is crucial to visual tracking. Therefore, multiple layers of VGG-Net are used to construct several weak trackers and then a fusion method based on Kullback-Leibler (KL) divergence is proposed to unitize response maps produced by weak trackers to obtain an enhanced one.

CF models the appearance of a target using filters w trained over samples x and their corresponding regression target y. Given a feature map extracted from the k-th convolutional layer, denoted $x^k \in \mathbb{R}^{V \times H \times D}$, where V, H and D denote the height, width and the number of feature channels, respectively, and a Gaussian shaped label matrix $y \in \mathbb{R}^{V \times H}$ indicates the regression target. Then, the desired corresponding filter of the k-th convolutional layer can be obtained by minimizing the output ridge loss in the Fourier domain:

$$\arg \min_{\hat{w}^k} \| \sum_{d=1}^{D} \hat{w}_d^k \odot \hat{x}_d^k - \hat{y} \|_2^2 + \lambda \| \hat{w}^k \|_2^2 \tag{1}$$

where the hat $\hat{w} = \mathcal{F}(w)$ denotes the discrete Fourier transform (DFT) of the filter w, $\lambda \geq 0$ is a regularization coefficient to counter model overfitting and $\odot$ indicates Hadamard product. The solution can be quickly computed as [19]:

$$\hat{w}_d^k = \frac{\hat{x}_d^k \odot \hat{y}}{\sum_{d=1}^{D} \hat{x}_d^k \odot (\hat{x}_d^k)^* + \lambda} \tag{2}$$

Here, y^* represents the complex conjugate of a complex number y.

For the detection stage, we aim to acquire the target location in the search frame. Let $z^k \in \mathbb{R}^{V \times H \times D}$ indicate the new feature map of k-th CNN layer in the current frame. We transform it to the Fourier domain $\hat{z}^k = \mathcal{F}(z^k)$, and then the responses can be computed as:

$$R^k = \mathcal{F}^{-1}(\sum_{d=1}^{D} \hat{z}_d^k \odot \hat{w}_d^k) \tag{3}$$

where $\mathcal{F}^{-1}(\cdot)$ denotes the inverse discrete Fourier transform (IDFT) and $R^k \in \mathbb{R}^{V \times H}$ is the k-th response map resized to the same size of the image patch.

Now we obtain K response maps $R = \{R^1, R^2, \ldots, R^k\}$ and our goal is to fuse all response maps into an enhanced one, denoted $Q \in \mathbb{R}^{V \times H}$. Similar to [24], we can treat the fusion as the measurement of correlation between the original response maps R and the fused map Q. Hence, we exploit KL divergence-based method to measure this correlation and ensemble response maps. The desired fused response map Q can be optimized by minimize the distance between the response maps R and the fused response map Q:

$$\arg \min_{Q} \sum_{k=1}^{K} KL(R^k \| Q) \tag{4}$$

$$s.t. \sum q_{i,j} = 1$$

where $KL(R^k \| Q) = \sum_{i,j} r_{i,j}^k \log \frac{r_{i,j}^l}{q_{i,j}}$ denotes the KL divergence, the subscript (i, j) denote the (i, j)-th elements of a matrix. Then, the solution can be deduced by the Lagrange multiplier method:

$$Q = \sum_{k=1}^{K} \frac{R^k}{K} \tag{5}$$

Finally, the target position is regarded as the location of the largest response on the fused response map Q.

3.2   Re-detection Module

The practical tracking environment always undergoes variations, hence the translation estimation module must be robust against challenging conditions like fast motion, illumination variation and occlusion. As Wang et al. described in [33], the detection may be disturbed by similar objects or certain noises in the search region, and this can be reflected as multiple peaks in the response map. This provides an intuitional approach to avoid tracker drift and improve localization precision by re-detecting all possible peaks exhaustively. However, examining all candidate peaks is very time consuming, and re-detecting too many similar objects may lead to inaccuracy.

Similar to [33], we propose a reliable module to ensure the efficiency and robustness of our detector. For the fusion response map $Q(z; w)$ produced by correlation, the multiple peaks are computed by

$$G(z) = Q(z; w) \cdot B \tag{6}$$

where B is a binary matrix with the same size of $Q(z; w)$, whose non-zeros elements identifies the local maxima in $Q(z; w)$. Elements at the location of local maxima in B are set to 1, while the other elements are set to 0.

Without loss of generality, we can always assume that the target has limited translation between consecutive frames, and that the tracker is able to detect it in a constricted search region. It reveals two practical senses that (a) the object has a low probability to locate on the boundary and (b) the object has high chance to appear at the higher peaks. Motivated by these assumptions, we cover a mask M on B to constrain the candidate peaks and reformulate the function:

$$G(z) = Q(z; w) \cdot B \cdot M \tag{7}$$

where M denotes a binary mask matrix with the same size of $Q(z; w)$. The elements of central region in M are set to 1 (the region of ones has a proportion ξ to the size of the response map), while elements in marginal region are set to 0. For each peak, a ratio between its magnitude and that of the highest peak is calculated. Those peaks whose ratio is above a pre-defined threshold θ are called as qualified peaks. Then, all qualified peaks are sorted according to its ratio, and only the top n peaks are selected as candidate re-detection locations. The whole process is illustrated in Fig. 2.

If there existing more than one peak, the corresponding image regions centered at these candidate locations can be re-detected according to Eq. 3. Then, the location of the target can be identified as where the maximum response occurs.

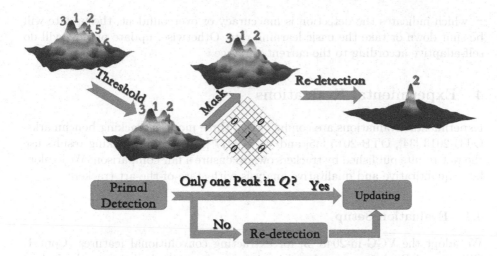

Fig. 2. The process of producing candidate locations for re-detecting. The numbers in each stage indicate the candidate peaks before re-detection. The target will be given by re-detection module finally.

3.3   Adaptive Online Model Update

The online model update is an essential step to adapt appearance variations of the target. The conventional strategy is to update linearly, which may result in tracking failure once the detection is inaccurate. Inspired by previous work, we design an adaptive online model update strategy, which aims to regulate update scheme of the model automatically.

As the maximum score of one response map indicates the degree of correlation between the object and the model learned by CF, we measure the confidence of current frame's detection result through historical scores. Assume the maximum score in current score map is H^t, and the historical maximum scores of previous frames are $\{H^{t-T}|T=1,\ldots,n\}$. So, we can measure the variance between current score and historical scores appropriately by:

$$C^t = S^t - \sum_{T=0}^{n} \frac{H^{t-T}}{n+1} \tag{8}$$

We define a basic learning rate η, which balances the proportion between the old model and the new model. The whole adaptive update strategy can be summarized as:

$$\eta^t = \begin{cases} \eta & C^t > \tau \\ 0 & C^t < -\tau \\ \eta(1+C^t) & \text{otherwise} \end{cases} \tag{9}$$

$$\hat{w}^t_{new} = (1 - \eta^t)\hat{w}^{t-1} + \eta^t \hat{w}^t \tag{10}$$

Learning rate η is replaced by the current adaptive learning rate η^t, Eq. 10 represents that once the absolute value of variance is larger than the threshold

τ, which indicates the detection is inaccuracy or overconfident, the update will be shut down or take the basic learning rate. Otherwise, update process will do self-adaptive according to the current variance.

4 Experimental Evaluations

Experimental evaluations are conducted on three modern tracking benchmarks: OTB-2013 [34], OTB-2015 [35] and VOT-2017 [21]. All the tracking results use the raw results published by trackers own to ensure a fair comparison. We explore both quantitative and qualitative analysis with state-of-the-art trackers.

4.1 Evaluation Setup

We adopt the VGG-m-2048 [3] for extracting convolutional features (Conv-1, Conv-3 and Conv-5 are employed in the experiments). And due to the lack of spatial information and to retain computation efficiency, all layers after layer 15th are removed. We crop search region with twice the size of the target. Then, we resize it to 224×224 pixels to satisfy the VGG-Net input demand. The regularization coefficient is set to $\lambda = 10^{-4}$ in Eq. 1. For the re-detection module, the proportion ξ of the region set to 1 in mask M is 0.4 and the threshold θ is set to 0.7 with the qualified top $n = 3$ peaks selected as candidate re-detection locations (refer to Sect. 3.2 for more details). Similar to [5], we adopt patch pyramid with the scale factors $\{a^n | a = 1.02, n \in ([-\frac{s-1}{2}], \ldots, [\frac{s-1}{2}])\}$ for scale estimation. Finally, for the adaptive online model update strategy, we set the threshold τ to 0.05 and the basic learning rate η is initialed by 0.01 in Eq. 10. Our experiments are conducted in MATLAB R2015b and use the MatConvNet toolbox [32] on a PC with an Intel i7 3770K 3.5 GHz CPU, 8G RAM, and a GeForce GTX 960 GPU in this work.

4.2 Evaluation Metrics

OTB dataset: OTB-2013 [34] contains 50 fully annotated sequences, and OTB-2015 [35] is the extension of OTB-2013 including 100 video sequences. The evaluation is based on two metrics: precision plot and success plot. The precision plot shows the percentage of frames in which the estimated locations are within a given threshold distance of the ground-truth positions. In addition, the value when threshold is 20 pixels is always taken as the representative precision score. The success plot shows the ratio of successful frames when the threshold varies from 0 to 1, where a successful frame means its overlap score is larger than the given threshold. The rank of tracking algorithms is always given by the area under curve (AUC) of each success plot.

VOT dataset: VOT-2017 [21] contains 60 videos, three metrics are used to evaluate the performance: accuracy, robustness and average overlap. The accuracy is defined as average overlap with annotated groundtruth during successful

Table 1. Ablation studies of MLCFT on OTB benchmarks

	OTB-2013			OTB-2015		
	OP (%)	DP (%)	FPS	OP (%)	DP (%)	FPS
MLCFT	67.2	88.4	16.19	66.4	87.6	15.86
MLCFT-nrd	66.2	87.6	18.93	63.5	83.2	19.74
MLCFT-ue	66.8	87.9	17.96	64.4	84.6	18.41

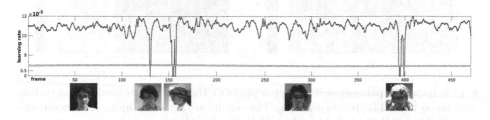

Fig. 3. Adaptive learning rate for the frames in the sequence *David*.

tracking periods. The robustness is defined as how many times the trackers fail to localize the target during tracking. And the expected average overlap (EAO) is an estimator of the average overlap a tracker is expected to attain on a large collection of short-term sequences.

4.3   Ablation Study

To verify our claims and justify our design choice in MLCFT, we conduct several ablation experiments. We first conduct tests with different versions of MLCFT on OTB benchmarks. We denote MLCFT without re-detection module as MLCFT-nrd and with linear update as MLCFT-ue. OP indicates area under curve of each success plot and DP represents precision score at the threshold of 20 pixels.

As shown in Table 1, MLCFT outperforms well above MLCFT-nrd and MLCFT-ue. The results show the importance of the re-detection module, without which AUC may decrease by 1% and 2.9% in OTB-2013 and OTB-2015, respectively.

We visualize the variation of the adaptive learning rate during tracking to demonstrate our proposal. As shown in Fig. 3, the learning rate fluctuates in a small range, i.e., to adaptively adjust itself during the ideal conditions as frame 57 and frame 278 show. However, when the target suffers from significant deformation (frame 130), out-of-plane rotation (frame 158) and illumination variation (frame 307), the learning rate will decrease to 0. The adaptive update module automatically suspends updating process to avoid updating the model with the unconfident target.

Moreover, in re-detection module, we set two priori thresholds as θ and n. In order to demonstrate the choice, the sensitivity analysis is made. As shown in Fig. 4, the best tracking result is always obtained by $\theta = 0.7$ and $n = 3$ both

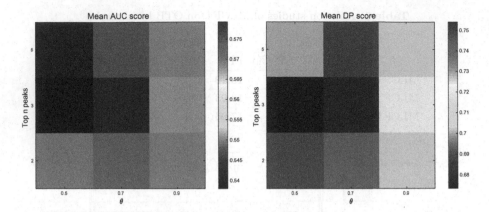

Fig. 4. Impact of parameters θ and top n peaks on tracking results used in re-detection module on the OTB-2013 benchmark. The results are scaled in mean AUC score and mean DP score. Best viewed in color. (Color figure online)

in the mean AUC score and mean DP score. And the tracker performs more sensitive to the threshold θ than the parameter n, i.e., the tracking result varies more dramatically in the horizontal direction than the vertical direction.

4.4 Evaluation on OTB-2013

We evaluate our approach MLCFT with 8 state-of-the-art trackers designed with various improvement, including KCF [19], DSST [5], SAMF [23], SRDCF [7], LMCF [33], LCT [26], HDT [27] and Staple [1]. The one-pass evaluation (OPE) is employed to compare these trackers.

Figure 5 illustrates the precision and success plots of compared trackers. It clearly demonstrates that our proposed tracker MLCFT outperforms those 8 compared trackers significantly in both metrics. Our approach obtains an AUC score of 0.672 in the success plot. Compared with LMCF and LCT which are assembled with re-detection module, MLCFT gains the improvement of 4.4%. And in the precision plot, our approach obtains a score of 0.884, outperforms LMCF and LCT by 4.2% and 3.6%, respectively.

4.5 Evaluation on OTB-2015

In this experiment, we compare our method against most recent trackers, including C-COT [9], ECO [4], CREST [29], BACF [10], MCPF [36], SINT [30], SRD-CFdecon [8], DeepLMCF [33] and DeepSRDCF [6]. The OPE is also employed to compare these trackers.

The precision plots and success plots are illustrated in Fig. 6. MLCFT is close to state-of-the-art in terms of accuracy and is the fastest among all top performers. The CF-based trackers C-COT and its improved version ECO both

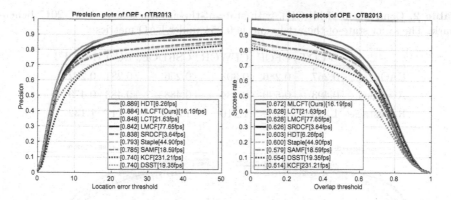

Fig. 5. Precision and success plots on OTB-2013. The forward numbers in the legend indicate the representative precisions at 20 pixels for precision plots, and AUC for success plots. The backward numbers in the legend denotes the speed of trackers. Best viewed in color. (Color figure online)

suffer from low speed, while MLCFT does not sacrifice too much run-time performance due to the simpler framework and the cascade detection scheme based on CF. Quantitatively, compared with the top rank algorithms C-COT [9] and the subsequent ECO [4] tracker, MLCFT sacrifices the accuracy by 1.0% and 3.9% in average under curve (AUC) but provides an 80X and 16X speedup on the OTB-2015 dataset.

The top performance can be attributed to several aspects. Firstly, our method exploits an effectively oriented re-detection module based on CF, which not only avoids the target drift but also retains the computation efficiency. Besides, the ensemble of multiple layers of convolutional layers provides expressive features to represent the target. Finally, the adaptive update strategy also contributes to the improvement of the performance and the acceleration of speed.

4.6   Evaluation on VOT-2017

We compare our MLCFT with state-of-the-art approaches on the VOT-2017 benchmark [21], including C-COT [9], CFCF [16], CFWCR [17], CSRDCF [25] and ECO [4]. Table 2 shows the comparison results over all the sequences on VOT-2017. Among these approaches, CFWCR achieves the best EAO score of 0.303 and ECO gets the best robustness score of 1.117. CFCF achieves the best accuracy score of 0.509. Meanwhile, our MLCFT obtains a second-best robustness score of 1.132 with state-of-the-art EAO score of 0.272 and accuracy score of 0.479. Our MLCFT can be regarded as state-of-the-art tracking approach since the EAO score exceeds the state-of-the-are bound which is defined as 0.251 according to the VOT-2017 report.

Table 2. Comparison of MLCFT with state-of-the-art trackers on VOT-2017 benchmark. The strict state-of-the-art bound is 0.251 under EAO metrics

	C-COT	CFCF	CFWCR	CSRDCF	ECO	MLCFT
EAO	0.267	0.286	0.303	0.256	0.281	0.272
Accuracy	0.493	0.509	0.484	0.488	0.483	0.479
Robustness	1.315	1.169	1.210	1.309	1.117	1.132

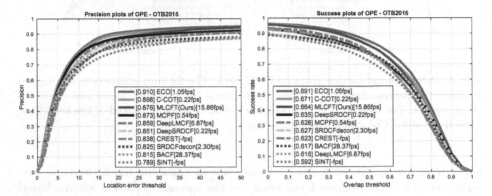

Fig. 6. Precision and success plots on OTB-2015. The forward numbers in the legend indicate the representative precisions at 20 pixels for precision plots, and AUC for success plots. The backward numbers in the legend denotes the speed of trackers. Best viewed in color. (Color figure online)

4.7 Qualitative Evaluation

Qualitative comparisons of our approach with existing state-of-the-art trackers are conducted on OTB benchmarks. Figure 7 illustrates four challenging sequences named *Matrix, Biker, Skating1* and *CarScale* from top to bottom. In the sequence *Matrix* with fast motion and background clutter, both MLCFT and C-COT can handle the translation estimation well, while MLCFT is more capable of dealing with fast scale variations.

In the sequence *Biker*, the compared trackers fail to track under simultaneous fast scale variations and significant deformation. However, MLCFT and DeepLMCF accurately estimate the scale and position, as shown in frame 106. This is attributed to the re-detection module assembled in the tracker, which enhance the robustness of the tracker.

In the sequence *Skating1*, all compared trackers fail or cannot handle scale variations due to the varying lighting conditions. In contrast, our approach provides better robustness and accuracy in these conditions. Additionally, in the sequence *CarScale* with significant scale variations, MLCFT have the best scale estimation among all the compared trackers.

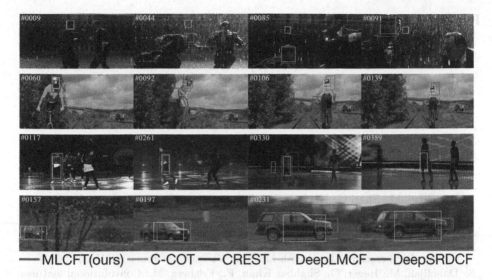

— MLCFT(ours) — C-COT — CREST — DeepLMCF — DeepSRDCF

Fig. 7. Comparisons of our approach with state-of-the-art trackers in challenging scenarios of fast motion, significant deformation, illumination variation and scale variation on the *Matrix*, *Biker*, *Skating1* and *CarScale* sequences. Our tracker is able to avoid target drift more effectively and handle the appearance changes more accurately.

5   Conclusions

In this paper, we propose a multi-level CF-based approach for visual object tracking. With an auxiliary CF-based re-detection module, our tracker shows a satisfactory robustness under challenging scenarios like fast motion, illumination variation and occlusion. Meantime, the characteristic features from multiple CNN layers offer our tracker more capability to discriminate the target. Moreover, our proposed adaptive online model update strategy can automatically handle the adjustment of the model variations, and thus promote the performance of the tracker further. Both quantitative and qualitative evaluations are performed to validate our approach. The results demonstrate that our proposed tracker obtain the state-of-the-art performance according to VOT-2017 report, while retaining higher speed than other state-of-the-art trackers.

Acknowledgements. This work is supported by the NSFC project under Grant No. U1833101, Shenzhen Science and Technologies project under Grant No. JCYJ20160428182137473, the Science and Technology Planning Program of Guangdong Province under Grant No. 2016B090918047, and the Joint Research Center of Tencent & Tsinghua.

The authors would like to thank all the anonymous reviewers for their constructive comments and suggestions.

References

1. Bertinetto, L., Valmadre, J., Henriques, J.F., Vedaldi, A., Torr, P.H.S.: Fully-convolutional siamese networks for object tracking. In: Hua, G., Jégou, H. (eds.) ECCV 2016. LNCS, vol. 9914, pp. 850–865. Springer, Cham (2016). https://doi.org/10.1007/978-3-319-48881-3_56
2. Bolme, D.S., Beveridge, J.R., Draper, B.A., Lui, Y.M.: Visual object tracking using adaptive correlation filters. In: IEEE Conference on Computer Vision and Pattern Recognition (CVPR), pp. 2544–2550 (2010)
3. Chatfield, K., Simonyan, K., Vedaldi, A., Zisserman, A.: Return of the devil in the details: delving deep into convolutional nets. arXiv preprint arXiv:1405.3531 (2014)
4. Danelljan, M., Bhat, G., Khan, F.S., Felsberg, M.: ECO: efficient convolution operators for tracking. In: Conference on Computer Vision and Pattern Recognition (CVPR), pp. 21–26 (2017)
5. Danelljan, M., Häger, G., Khan, F., Felsberg, M.: Accurate scale estimation for robust visual tracking. In: British Machine Vision Conference (BMVC) (2014)
6. Danelljan, M., Hager, G., Shahbaz Khan, F., Felsberg, M.: Convolutional features for correlation filter based visual tracking. In: International Conference on Computer Vision Workshops (ICCVW), pp. 58–66 (2015)
7. Danelljan, M., Hager, G., Shahbaz Khan, F., Felsberg, M.: Learning spatially regularized correlation filters for visual tracking. In: International Conference on Computer Vision, pp. 4310–4318 (2015)
8. Danelljan, M., Hager, G., Shahbaz Khan, F., Felsberg, M.: Adaptive decontamination of the training set: a unified formulation for discriminative visual tracking. In: Computer Vision and Pattern Recognition, pp. 1430–1438 (2016)
9. Danelljan, M., Robinson, A., Shahbaz Khan, F., Felsberg, M.: Beyond correlation filters: learning continuous convolution operators for visual tracking. In: Leibe, B., Matas, J., Sebe, N., Welling, M. (eds.) ECCV 2016. LNCS, vol. 9909, pp. 472–488. Springer, Cham (2016). https://doi.org/10.1007/978-3-319-46454-1_29
10. Galoogahi, H.K., Fagg, A., Lucey, S.: Learning background-aware correlation filters for visual tracking. In: IEEE Conference on Computer Vision and Pattern Recognition (CVPR), pp. 21–26 (2017)
11. Gao, P., et al.: Adaptive object tracking with complementary models. IEICE Trans. Inf. Syst. **E101-D**(11), 2849–2854 (2018)
12. Gao, P., Ma, Y., Song, K., Li, C., Wang, F., Xiao, L.: A complementary tracking model with multiple features. arXiv preprint arXiv:1804.07459 (2018)
13. Gao, P., Ma, Y., Song, K., Li, C., Wang, F., Xiao, L.: Large margin structured convolution operator for thermal infrared object tracking. In: International Conference on Pattern Recognition (ICPR), pp. 2380–2385 (2018)
14. Gao, P., et al.: High performance visual tracking with circular and structural operators. Knowl.-Based Syst. **161**, 240–253 (2018)
15. Girshick, R., Donahue, J., Darrell, T., Malik, J.: Rich feature hierarchies for accurate object detection and semantic segmentation. In: IEEE Conference on Computer Vision and Pattern Recognition (CVPR), pp. 580–587 (2014)
16. Gundogdu, E., Alatan, A.: Good features to correlate for visual tracking. arXiv preprint arXiv:1704.06326 (2017)
17. He, Z., Fan, Y., Zhuang, J., Dong, Y., Bai, H.: Correlation filters with weighted convolution responses. In: IEEE International Conference on Computer Vision (ICCV). IEEE (2017)

18. Henriques, J.F., Caseiro, R., Martins, P., Batista, J.: Exploiting the circulant structure of tracking-by-detection with kernels. In: Fitzgibbon, A., Lazebnik, S., Perona, P., Sato, Y., Schmid, C. (eds.) ECCV 2012. LNCS, vol. 7575, pp. 702–715. Springer, Heidelberg (2012). https://doi.org/10.1007/978-3-642-33765-9_50
19. Henriques, J.F., Caseiro, R., Martins, P., Batista, J.: High-speed tracking with kernelized correlation filters. IEEE Trans. Pattern Anal. Mach. Intell. **37**(3), 583–596 (2015)
20. Karpathy, A., Toderici, G., Shetty, S., Leung, T., Sukthankar, R., Fei-Fei, L.: Large-scale video classification with convolutional neural networks. In: IEEE Conference on Computer Vision and Pattern Recognition (CVPR), pp. 1725–1732 (2014)
21. Kristan, M., et al.: The visual object tracking VOT2017 challenge results. In: International Conference on Computer Vision (ICCV), pp. 1949–1972 (2016)
22. LeCun, Y., Bottou, L., Bengio, Y., Haffner, P.: Gradient-based learning applied to document recognition. Proc. IEEE **86**(11), 2278–2324 (1998)
23. Li, Y., Zhu, J.: A scale adaptive kernel correlation filter tracker with feature integration. In: Agapito, L., Bronstein, M.M., Rother, C. (eds.) ECCV 2014. LNCS, vol. 8926, pp. 254–265. Springer, Cham (2015). https://doi.org/10.1007/978-3-319-16181-5_18
24. Liu, Q., Lu, X., He, Z., Zhang, C., Chen, W.S.: Deep convolutional neural networks for thermal infrared object tracking. Knowl.-Based Syst. **134**, 189–198 (2017)
25. Lukežič, A., Vojíř, T., Čehovin, L., Matas, J., Kristan, M.: Discriminative correlation filter with channel and spatial reliability. In: IEEE Conference on Computer Vision and Pattern Recognition (CVPR), pp. 4847–4856. IEEE (2017)
26. Ma, C., Yang, X., Zhang, C., Yang, M.H.: Long-term correlation tracking. In: Proceedings of the IEEE Conference on Computer Vision and Pattern Recognition, pp. 5388–5396 (2015)
27. Qi, Y., et al.: Hedged deep tracking. In: IEEE Conference on Computer Vision and Pattern Recognition (CVPR), pp. 4303–4311 (2016)
28. Sermanet, P., Eigen, D., Zhang, X., Mathieu, M., Fergus, R., LeCun, Y.: OverFeat: integrated recognition, localization and detection using convolutional networks. arXiv preprint arXiv:1312.6229 (2013)
29. Song, Y., Ma, C., Gong, L., Zhang, J., Lau, R.W., Yang, M.H.: CREST: convolutional residual learning for visual tracking. In: International Conference on Computer Vision (ICCV), pp. 2574–2583 (2017)
30. Tao, R., Gavves, E., Smeulders, A.W.: Siamese instance search for tracking. In: IEEE Conference on Computer Vision and Pattern Recognition (CVPR), pp. 1420–1429 (2016)
31. Valmadre, J., Bertinetto, L., Henriques, J., Vedaldi, A., Torr, P.H.: End-to-end representation learning for correlation filter based tracking. In: IEEE Conference on Computer Vision and Pattern Recognition (CVPR), pp. 5000–5008 (2017)
32. Vedaldi, A., Lenc, K.: MatConvnet: convolutional neural networks for MATLAB. In: ACM International Conference on Multimedia (ACMMM), pp. 689–692 (2015)
33. Wang, M., Liu, Y., Huang, Z.: Large margin object tracking with circulant feature maps. In: IEEE Conference on Computer Vision and Pattern Recognition (CVPR), pp. 21–26 (2017)
34. Wu, Y., Lim, J., Yang, M.H.: Online object tracking: a benchmark. In: Computer Vision and Pattern Recognition (CVPR), pp. 2411–2418 (2013)
35. Wu, Y., Lim, J., Yang, M.H.: Object tracking benchmark. IEEE Trans. Pattern Anal. Mach. Intell. **37**(9), 1834–1848 (2015)
36. Zhang, T., Xu, C., Yang, M.H.: Multi-task correlation particle filter for robust object tracking. In: IEEE Conference on Computer Vision and Pattern Recognition (CVPR) (2017)

Scalable Deep k-Subspace Clustering

Tong Zhang[1,5(✉)], Pan Ji[2,4], Mehrtash Harandi[3,5], Richard Hartley[1,5],
and Ian Reid[2,5]

[1] Australian National University, Canberra, Australia
tong.zhang@anu.edu.au
[2] University of Adelaide, Adelaide, Australia
[3] Monash University, Melbourne, Australia
[4] NEC Labs America, San Jose, USA
[5] Australian Centre for Robotic Vision, Brisbane, Australia

Abstract. Subspace clustering algorithms are notorious for their scalability issues because building and processing large affinity matrices are demanding. In this paper, we introduce a method that simultaneously learns an embedding space along subspaces within it to minimize a notion of reconstruction error, thus addressing the problem of subspace clustering in an end-to-end learning paradigm. To achieve our goal, we propose a scheme to update subspaces within a deep neural network. This in turn frees us from the need of having an affinity matrix to perform clustering. Unlike previous attempts, our method can easily scale up to large datasets, making it unique in the context of unsupervised learning with deep architectures. Our experiments show that our method significantly improves the clustering accuracy while enjoying cheaper memory footprints.

Keywords: Subspace clustering · Deep learning · Scalable

1 Introduction

Subspace Clustering (SC) is the de facto method in various clustering tasks such as motion segmentation [7,10,11,17], face clustering [8,9] and image segmentation [24,36]. As the name implies, the underlying assumption in SC is that samples forming a cluster can be adequately described by a subspace. Such data modeling is natural in many applications. One prime example is face clustering in which it has been shown that the face images of one subject obtained with a fixed pose and varying illumination lie in a low-dimensional subspace [20].

Most recent subspace clustering methods [8,21] assume that data points lie on a union of linear subspaces and construct an affinity matrix for spectral clustering. Although promising results on certain datasets are obtained, the performances degrade significantly when non-linearity arises in the data. Moreover, constructing the affinity matrix and performing clustering demand hefty memory footprints and processing power. To benefit from the concept of SC and its unique features, two issues should be addressed:

© Springer Nature Switzerland AG 2019
C. V. Jawahar et al. (Eds.): ACCV 2018, LNCS 11365, pp. 466–481, 2019.
https://doi.org/10.1007/978-3-030-20873-8_30

Non-linearity: Majority of the SC algorithms target clustering with linear subspaces. This is a very bold assumption and can hardly be met in practice. Some studies [12, 26, 34, 38] employ kernel methods to alleviate this limitation. Nevertheless, kernel methods still suffer from the scalability issues [40]. To make things more complicated, there is no guideline as how to choose the kernel function and its parameters which truly well-suited to subspace clustering.

Scalability: With the current trend in analyzing big data, SC algorithms should be able to deal with large volume of data. However, most of the state-of-the-art methods for SC make use of an affinity matrix along norm regularization (*e.g.*, ℓ_1 [7, 8], ℓ_2 [13] or nuclear [21, 32]). Not only building an affinity matrix demands for solving large scale optimization problems, but also performing spectral clustering on an affinity matrix, whose size is dictated by the number of samples, is overwhelming.

In this paper, instead of constructing the affinity matrix for spectral clustering, we revisit the k-subspace clustering (k-SC) method [2, 5, 30] to design a novel and scalable method. In order to handle non-linear subspaces, we propose to utilize deep neural networks to project data to a latent space where k-SC can be easily applied. Our contributions in this paper are three-folds:

- We bypass the steps of constructing an affinity matrix and performing spectral clustering, which have been used in mainstream subspace clustering algorithms, and accelerate the computation by using a variant of k-subspace clustering. As a result, our method can handle datasets that are orders of magnitudes larger than those considered in traditional methods.
- In order to address non-linearity, we equip deep neural networks with subspace priors. This in return enables us to learn an explicit non-linear mapping of the data that is well-suited for subspace clustering.
- We propose novel strategies to update subspace bases. When the size of the dataset at hand is manageable, we update subspaces in closed-form using Singular Value Decomposition (SVD) with a simple mechanism to rule out outliers. For large datasets, we update subspaces by making use of the stochastic optimization methods on the Grassmann manifolds.

Empirically, evaluations on relatively large datasets such as MNIST and Fashion-MNIST dataset [33] show that our proposed method achieves the state-of-the-art results in terms of clustering accuracies and speed.

2   Related Work

Linear subspace clustering methods can be classified as algebraic algorithms, iterative methods, statistical methods and spectral clustering-based methods [31]. Among them, spectral clustering-based methods [7, 13, 14, 16, 21, 39] have become dominant in the literature. In general, spectral clustering-based methods solve the problem in two steps: encode a notion of similarity between pairs of data points into an affinity matrix; then, apply normalized cuts [29] or spectral clustering [25] on this affinity matrix. To construct the affinity matrix, recent methods tend to rely on the concept of *self-expressiveness*, which seeks to express each point in a cluster as a linear combination of other points sharing some common notions (*e.g.*, coming from the same subspace).

The literature on true end-to-end learning of subspace clustering is surprisingly limited. Furthermore and to the best of our knowledge, none of the deep algorithms can handle medium size datasets, let aside the large ones[1]. In hybrid methods such as [28], hand-crafted features (*e.g.*, SIFT [23] or HOG [6]) are fed into a deep auto-encoder with a sparse subspace clustering (SSC) prior. The final clustering is then obtained by applying k-means or SSC on the learned auto-encoder features. Instead of using hand-crafted features, Deep subspace clustering Networks (DSC-NET) [15] employ the deep convolutional Auto-encoder to nonlinearly map the images to a latent space, and make use of a self-expressive layer between the encoder and the decoder to learn the affinities between all the data points. Through learning affinity matrix within the neural network, state-of-the-art results on several traditional small datasets are reported in [15]. Nevertheless, relying on the whole dataset to create the affinity matrix, DSC-NET cannot scale for large dataset.

The SSC by Orthogonal Matching Pursuit (SSC-OMP) [40] is probably the only subspace clustering which could be considered as "scalable". The main idea is to replace the large scale convex optimization procedure with the OMP algorithm in constructing the affinity matrix. Having said this, SSC-OMP makes use of spectral clustering and hence still fails to really push subspace clustering for large scale datasets.

k-Subspace Clustering [2, 30], an iterative methods, can be considered as a generalization of k-means algorithm. k-SC shows fast convergence behavior and can handle both linear and affine subspaces explicitly. However, k-SC methods are sensitive to outliers and initialization. Attempts to make k-SC methods more robust include the work of Zhang *et al.* [41] and Balzano *et al.* [3]. In the former, best k subspaces from a large number of candidate subspaces are selected using a greedy combinatorial algorithm [41] to make the algorithm robust to data corruptions. Balzano *et al.* propose a variant of k subspaces method named k-GROUSE which can handle the missing data in subspace clustering. However, the resulting methods seem not to producing competitive results compared to methods relying on affinity matrices.

In this paper, we propose k-Subspace Clustering(k-SC) networks which incorporate k-SC into a deep neural network embedding. This lets us not only bypass the affinity construction and spectral clustering procedure, but also handle data points lying in non-linear subspaces.

---

[1] Among all the datasets that have been tested, COIL100 with 7,200 images seems to be the largest one.

3 k-Subspace Clustering(k-SC) Networks

Our k-subspace clustering networks leverage on the properties of deep convolutional auto-encoder and the k-subspaces clustering. In this section we will discuss the k-subspace property and the whole framework in detail.

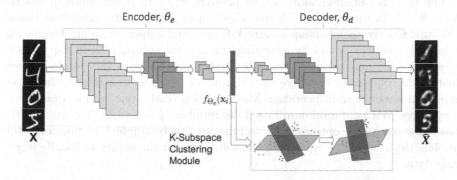

Fig. 1. Scalable deep k-subspace structure. As an example, we show our scalable batch-based subspace clustering with three convolutional encoder layers and three deconvolutional decoder layers. During the training, we first pre-train the deep convolutional auto-encoder by simply reconstructing the corresponding images, and then fine-tune the network using this pre-trained model as initialization. During the fine-tuning, the network minimizes the sum of distances of each sample in the latent space to its closet subspace.

3.1 k-Subspace Clustering

Consider a collection of points $\{\mathbf{x}_1, \mathbf{x}_2, \cdots, \mathbf{x}_n\} \in \mathbb{R}^d$ belonging to a union of k subspaces $\mathbf{S}_1, \mathbf{S}_2, \cdots, \mathbf{S}_k$ of dimensions $p_1, p_2, \cdots, p_k$, respectively[2]. With slight abuse of notation, we will use $\mathbf{S}_i$ to represent the basis of the subspace index by i, that is $\mathbf{S}_i \in \mathbb{R}^{d \times p_i}$ and $\mathbf{S}_i^\top \mathbf{S}_i = \mathbf{I}_{p_i}$ with $\mathbf{I}_p$ denoting $p \times p$ identity matrix. The goal of subspace clustering is to learn the subspaces and assign points to their nearest subspaces. Once every data point is assigned to a subspace, the corresponding subspace basis can be re-calculated by SVD (will be shown shortly). Different from self-expressiveness-based methods which obtain the affinity matrix by solving large-scale optimization problems, k-SC seeks to minimize the sum of residuals of points to their nearest subspaces. The cost function of k-SC can be written as

$$\min_{\{\mathbf{S}_i\}, \{w_{ij}\}} \sum_j^n \sum_i^k w_{ij} \|\mathbf{x}_j - \mathbf{S}_i \mathbf{S}_i^\top \mathbf{x}_j\|_2^2,$$

$$\text{s.t.} \quad w_{ij} \in \{0, 1\} \quad \text{and} \quad \sum_{i=1}^k w_{ij} = 1. \tag{1}$$

---

[2] We assume $p = p_i, \forall i$ in the remainder.

Given the subspace basis $\{\mathbf{S}_1, \cdots, \mathbf{S}_n\}$, the optimal value for w_{ij} can be written as

$$w_{ij} = \begin{cases} 1 & \text{if} \quad i = \arg\min_m \|\mathbf{x}_j - \mathbf{S}_m\mathbf{S}_m^\top\mathbf{x}_j\|_2^2, \\ 0 & \text{otherwise.} \end{cases} \tag{2}$$

For the sake of discussion, let us arrange w_{ij} into a membership matrix $\mathbf{W} \in \mathbb{R}^{k \times n}$. Beginning with an initialization of k candidate subspaces bases, k-SC updates the membership assignments w_{ij} and subspaces in an alternating fashion: (1) cluster points by assigning the nearest subspace as in Eq. (2); (2) re-estimate the new subspace bases by performing SVD on the points of each cluster (the columns of $\mathbf{W}$ where the i-th row is 1). Similar to k-means, the whole algorithm works in an Expectation Maximization (EM) style, and is guaranteed to converge to a local minimum in a finite number of iterations. We will shortly show how stochastic optimization techniques can be applied to minimize the problem depicted in (1), equipping our solution with the ability to handle large-scale data.

3.2 k-SC with Convolutional Auto-Encoder Network

Denoising fully-connected Auto-Encoders (AEs) are widely used with generic clustering algorithms [35,37]. We have found such structures difficult to train (due to the large number of parameters in the fully-connected layers) and propose to use convolutional AEs to learn the embeddings for k-SC.

Specifically, let θ denote the AE parameters, which can be decomposed into encoder parameters θ_e and decoder parameters θ_d. Let $f_{\theta_e}(\cdot)$ be the encoder mapping function and $g_{\theta_d}(\cdot)$ as the decoder mapping function, both of which are composed of a sequence of convolution kernels and nonlinear activation functions. Our overall loss can be written as

$$\ell(\theta, \{\mathbf{S}_i\}, \mathbf{W}) = \ell_{ae}(\theta) + \lambda\ell_{ksc}(\{\mathbf{S}_i\}, \mathbf{W}), \tag{3}$$

where λ is a regularization parameter to balance the reconstruction loss and the k-subspace clustering loss. The auto-encoder reconstruction loss ℓ_{ae} is defined as

$$\ell_{ae}(\theta) = \sum_j \|\mathbf{x}_j - g_{\theta_d}(f_{\theta_e}(\mathbf{x}_j))\|_2^2. \tag{4}$$

The $\ell_{ksc}(\theta)$ is the loss for subspace clustering and is written as

$$\ell_{ksc}(\{\mathbf{S}_i\}, \theta) = \sum_{i,j} w_{ij}\|f_{\theta_e}(\mathbf{x}_j) - \mathbf{S}_i\mathbf{S}_i^\top f_{\theta_e}(\mathbf{x}_j)\|_2^2$$

$$\text{s.t.} \quad \mathbf{S}_i \in \mathcal{G}(d,p), \ w_{ij} \in \{0,1\}, \ \sum_{i=1}^k w_{ij} = 1, \ \forall ij, \tag{5}$$

where $\mathcal{G}(d,p)$ denotes the Grassmann manifold consisting of p-dimensional subspaces with ambient dimension d.

As a pre-processing step, some of traditional algorithms such as [40,41] use PCA to project images onto a low-dimensional space. However, the mapping by PCA projection is linear and fixed. By contrast, our encoder function f_{θ_e} can update its parameters to adapt to a space which is subspace-clustering-friendly.

Algorithm 1. Scalable k-Subspace Clustering (SVD update)

Input: dimensionality of subspaces p, number of class K, epochs number T, batch size b and dataset $\mathbf{x}_j, j = 1, \cdots, N$
Pre-train CAE using $\mathbf{x}_j, j = 1, \cdots, N$
Generate $\{\mathbf{S}_i\}$ based on the pre-trained model and initial cluster labels
for $m = 1 : T$ **do**
    for $n = 1 : b : N$
        Update the CAE parameters θ by Eq. (6)
    end
    Recalculate the latent space for the whole data set,
    $\mathbf{z}_j = f_{\theta_e}(\mathbf{x}_j), j = 1...N$
    Assign the membership for every $\mathbf{z}_i$ as Eq. (2) and
    rule out the farthest 10% points as outliers, for each
    class we have set $\mathbf{Z}_i$
    Update each subspace $\mathbf{S}_i$ through SVD decomposition on the $\mathbf{Z}_i$
end
Output: Subspaces $\{\mathbf{S}_i\}$, and membership assignment w_{ij}

---

4 Optimization

The cost function (3) is highly non-convex and three sets of variables (*i.e.*, $\mathbf{W}, \theta$, and $\{\mathbf{S}_i\}$) should be updated alternatively. It is known that alternating optimization problems are not without difficulties. A strategy such as wake-and-sleep is a common practice to update one set of variables while fixing the others. As mentioned before, we first pre-train a CAE without having any information about $\mathbf{W}$ and $\mathbf{S}_i$. Therefore, it is natural to obtain an initial state for $\mathbf{W}$ and $\{\mathbf{S}_i\}$ directly from the output of the pre-trained CAE. This is exactly how we initialize $\mathbf{W}$ and $\{\mathbf{S}_i\}$.

As shown in Fig. 1, the gradient of the encoder comes from the loss of reconstruction and the loss of k-subspace clustering loss, *i.e.*,

$$\nabla_{\theta_e} \ell = \frac{\partial \ell_{\text{ae}}}{\partial \theta_e} + \lambda \frac{\partial \ell_{\text{ksc}}}{\partial \theta_e}. \tag{6}$$

By fixing $\{\mathbf{S}_i\}$, the assignments $\mathbf{W}$ for a mini-batch can be obtained easily and the required gradient for updating the CAE follows by back-propagating the error. The most difficult part in our problem is to find a way to update the subspaces efficiently and accurately. Here we will explain two approaches to update the subspaces. The first method is based on the SVD decomposition and the second one makes use of the Riemannian geometry of Grassmannian to update the subspaces.

4.1 SVD Update

Although SVD decomposition is computationally more expensive, we empirically observe that the SVD can provide satisfactory results. In our optimization, we update the encoder through back-propagation, batch by batch, and update the subspaces by employing the SVD once per epoch. This is mainly because updating subspaces more frequently hinders the convergence. Intuitively, if the gradient takes the network to a bad direction, updating subspaces accordingly could intensify the negativity and worsen the CAE. Empirically, we observe updating subspaces after every epoch can neutralize the good and the bad directions of the gradient, yielding a stable framework.

The outliers may affect the subspace clustering badly, especially for k-subspace clustering. Therefore, when updating each subspace, we rule out the farthest 10% points as outliers. That is, after back propagation on CAE, we pass all the data through the encoder and assign their membership. We then sort the distance between each sample and the subspace it belongs to, and remove the outliers. Finally, we apply SVD on the remainder of points assigned to a subspace to obtain its new basis. Note that we only need to compute the largest p singular values and corresponding vectors to update a subspace. Specifically, after fixing w_{ij} and θ in Eq. (5), updating the subspace basis $\mathbf{S}_i$ translates to solving the following problem

$$\underset{\mathbf{S}_i \in \mathcal{G}(d,p)}{\arg\min} \|\mathbf{Y}_i - \mathbf{S}_i \mathbf{S}_i^\top \mathbf{Y}_i\|_F^2, \tag{7}$$

where $\mathbf{Y}_i$ consists of $\{f_{\theta_e}(\mathbf{x}_j)\}$ (as columns) that belong to cluster i. The solution to (7) corresponds to the column space $\mathbf{Y}_i$, which can be obtained by applying SVD on $\mathbf{Y}_i$ and taking the top p left singular vectors.

4.2 Gradient Based Update

If more frequent updates are required, the SVD solution can be replaced by a Riemannian gradient descent method based on the geometry of Grassmannian. In particular, let $\nabla \ell_{ksc}(\mathbf{S}_i)$ be the gradient of the loss with respect to $\mathbf{S}_i$ after an iteration (or accumulated gradient after a few iterations). In Riemannian optimization, $\mathbf{S}_i$ is updated according to the following rule;

$$\mathbf{S}_i^{(t+1)} = \Upsilon_{\mathbf{S}_i^{(t)}}\Big(-\eta \Pi_{\mathbf{S}_i^{(t)}}\big(\nabla \ell_{ksc}(\mathbf{S}_i)\big)\Big). \tag{8}$$

We explain Eq. (8) with the aid of Fig. 2. First we note that a global coordinate system on a Riemannian manifold cannot be defined. As such Riemannian techniques make extensive use of the tangent bundle of the manifold to achieve their goal. Note that moving in the direction of $\nabla \ell_{ksc}(\mathbf{S}_i)$ will take us off the manifold. For a Riemannian manifold embedded in a Euclidean space (our case here), an ambient vector such as $\nabla \ell_{ksc}(\mathbf{S}_i)$ can be projected orthogonally on the tangent space at the current solution $\mathbf{S}_i^{(t)}$. We denote this operator by Π in

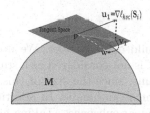

Fig. 2. Illustration of how we update the gradient and keep the subspaces lie on the manifold

Eq. (8). The resulting tangent vector shown by the green arrow in Fig. 2 identifies a geodesic on the manifold. Moving along this geodesic (sufficiently) will guarantee to decrease the loss while preserving the orthogonality of the solution. In Riemannian optimization, this is achieved by a retraction which is local approximation to the exponential map on the manifold. We denote the retraction in Eq. (8) by Υ. The only remaining bit is η which is the learning rate. For the Grassmannian, we have

$$\Pi_{\mathbf{S}}(\boldsymbol{u}) = \left(\mathbf{I}_d - \mathbf{S}\mathbf{S}^\top\right)\boldsymbol{u}, \tag{9}$$

$$\Upsilon_{\mathbf{S}}(\boldsymbol{u}) = \mathrm{qf}\left(\mathbf{S} + \boldsymbol{u}\right), \tag{10}$$

In Eq. (10), qf is the Q part of the QR decomposition which is much faster than SVD. Although the SVD can perform good enough in experiments, we provide the other method which is faster in order to deal with very large datasets.

Algorithm 2. Scalable k-Subspace Clustering(Gradients update)

Input: dimensionality of subspaces p, number of class K, initial $\{\mathbf{S}_i\}$, epochs number T, pre-trained CAE, batch size b and dataset $\mathbf{x}_j$, $j = 1, ..., N$

for $m = 1 : T$ **do**

    for $n = 1 : b : N$

        Assign the membership for every point based on the distance
        to each subspace as Eq. (2)

        Compute the gradients with respect to each subspace as
        Eq. (5) $\ell_{ksc}(\mathbf{S}_i)$ and store them

        Update the CAE parameters Θ by Eq. (6)

    end

    Project the gradients on Grassmannian manifolds
    based on Eq. (9)

    Apply the gradients on the corresponding subspace
    accord to Eq. (10)

end

Output: subspaces $\{\mathbf{S}_i\}$, and membership assignment w_{ij}

---

5   Experiment

We use Tensorflow [1] to build our networks. We used MNIST dataset [19] in our first experiment. MNIST is not considered as a standard dataset for previous subspace clustering algorithms, since the size of this dataset is far beyond the size that traditional algorithms can handle. In addition, the original images do not follow the structure of linear subspaces. Taking advantage of CAE with our k-subspace clustering module, we aim to project all the MNIST data into a space which is more friendly for subspace clustering. In order to enforce our conclusion, we also evaluate our method on Fashion-MNIST dataset [33], a similar dataset to MNIST but with fashion images. Fashion-MNIST has 10 classes, with image being gray scale and of size 28×28. The images of Fashion-MNIST come from the fashion products which are classified based on a certain assortment and manually labeled by in-house fashion experts and reviewed by a separate team. It contains more variations within each class and it is thus more challenging compared to MNIST.

Baseline Methods. For most of the baselines and our method, we evaluate them on the whole datasets of MNIST and Fashion-MNIST with all 70000 images (including both training and testing sets). We compare our solution with the following generic clustering algorithms:

(1) k-Means [22]: k-means finds clusters based on spatial closeness. As an EM method, it heavily relies on good initialization. Hence, for k-means (and other k-means based methods), we run the algorithm 20 times with different centroid seeds and report the best result.

(2) Deep Embedded Clustering (DEC) [35]: A rich structure for the MNIST dataset is proposed in [35] which we follow here. In particular, stacked autoencoder (SAE) [4] along layer-wise pre-training was considered. The structure of the network reads as 784-500-500-2000-10. Image brightness is scaled from 0–1 to 0–5.2 to boost the performance. We observe that this method is highly sensitive to network parameters in the sense that even a small change in the structure will result in a significant performance drop. However, the feature extracted by the pre-trained model is very discriminative, *i.e.*, even simply using k-means on top of it can achieve competitive results. We call the feature extracted by this network the SEA features in the sequel.

(3) Deep Clustering Network (DCN) [37]: Based on the vanilla SAE, Yang *et al.*propose to add k-means clustering loss in addition to the data reconstruction loss of SAE.

(4) Stacked Auto-Encoder followed by k-Means (SAE-KM): Extract features with SAE followed by applying k-means.

(5) PCA followed by k-subspace (PCA-KS): It projects the original data onto a low-dimensional space at first, then use k-subspace to obtain the final results. Since PCA is a linear projection, it helps the readers to understand where the improvements come from compared to our nonlinear projection.

The results are reported based on the 10 trails due to the randomness of initialization when employing k-subspace.

(6) Convolutional Auto-Encoder followed by k-Means (CAE-KM): Extract features with SAE and then apply k-means. This is also the initialization for our method. It also can be considered as an evaluation of the quality of our initialization.

For those subspace clustering algorithms that rely on affinity matrix construction and spectral clustering, since they are not scalable to the whole dataset, we can report their results on the test sets (with 10000 images) only. We list several state-of-the-art subspace clustering algorithms for baselines: Sparse Subspace Clustering (SSC) [8], Low Rank Representation (LRR) [21], Kernel Sparse Subspace Clustering (KSSC) [26], SSC by Orthogonal Matching Pursuit(SSC-OMP) [40] and the latest one Deep Subspace Clustering Networks (DSC-Net) [15].

Evaluation Metric. For all quantitative evaluations, we make use of the unsupervised clustering accuracy rate, defined as

$$\text{ACC } \% = \max_{M} \frac{\sum_{i=1}^{n} \mathbf{1}(l_i = M(s_i))}{n} \times 100\%. \tag{11}$$

where l_i is the ground-truth label, s_i is the subspace assignment produced by the algorithm, and M ranges over all possible one-to-one mappings between subspaces and labels. The mappings can be efficiently computed by the Hungarian algorithm. We also use normalized mutual information (NMI) as the additional quantitative standard. NMI scales from 0 to 1, where a smaller value means less correlation between predict label and ground truth label. Another quantitative metric is the adjusted Rand index (ARI), which is scaled between -1 and 1. The larger the ARI, the better the clustering performance.

Implementation. We build our CAE in a bottle-neck structure, meaning we decrease the number of channels and the size of feature maps layer by layer. We design a six layer convolutional auto-encoder, where the kernel size in the first layer is 5 and in the last two layers of the encoder is 3×3. We set the number of channels in each layer to $20 - 10 - 5$ for the encoder, and the reverse for the decoder since they are symmetric in structure. Between layers, we set the stride to 2 in both horizontal and vertical directions, and use rectified linear unit (ReLU) as the non-linear activations. We use the same structure for both MNIST and Fashion-MNIST datasets.

Instead of greedy layer-wise pre-training [35,37], we pre-trained our network end-to-end from random initialization, until the reconstructed images are similar to the input ones (200 epochs suffice for pre-training). For subspaces initialization, we randomly sampled 2000 images and use DSC network to generate the clusters and corresponding subspaces. We noticed that initialization by the DSC subspaces leads to a model that under-performs in the beginning as compared to the k-Means algorithm. Nevertheless, our algorithm successfully recovers from such an initialization in all the experiments. During the optimization we use

Adam [18] optimizer, an adaptive momentum based gradient descent method, to minimize the loss, where we set the learning rate to 1.0×10^{-3} in both our pre-training and fine-tuning stages. For different datasets, the only two parameters need tuning are the λ in (3) and the subspace ambient dimension n, since the subspace intrinsic dimension p is fixed by the number of feature map of CAE.

5.1   MNIST Dataset

In this section, we will report and discuss results on the MNIST dataset. To the best of our knowledge, existing subspace clustering methods, with raw images as input, have not achieved satisfactory results on this dataset. As far as we know, the best performance reported in [27] is in the range 58%–65%, where the DSIFT features are employed.

On MNIST, we fix our subspace dimension as 7, which means each subspace lies on a Grassmannian manifold $\mathcal{G}(80, 7)$. The λ is set to 0.08, which balances between subspace clustering and CAE data reconstruction. Table 1 reports the results of all the baselines, including both subspace clustering algorithms and generic clustering algorithms. kSCN-S is to update the subspaces by employing the SVD decomposition, and kSCN-G stands for updating the subspaces by the Grassmannian gradients, which empirically is not as stable as the SVD updating scheme, probably due to the stochastic nature of each gradient step. This Grassmannian update, however, runs faster and takes less time to converge. We run our methods 15 times and report the average. The results of DEC are taken from the original paper. We tune the parameters for DCN very carefully and report the best results.

Among all the algorithms, our algorithm achieves the best performance in ACC and ARI. Especially for ACC, ours is 3% higher than the second best, namely DEC. From the results, it is not difficult to conclude that the DEC and DCN perform only marginally better than SAE-KM, which is the initialization for DEC and DCN. Specifically, DEC improvements over the initialization are around 3% and DCN only boosts around 1.5% over SAE-KM. By contrast, our method starts from CAE-KM (with 51% ACC), and improves it by 36.14% to 87.14% ACC. The improvement can be visualized by Fig. 3, which shows the projections of CAE feature space and the latent space of our network in a two-dimensional space. Compared to CAE features, which are all mixed up, our latent space are well separated even though the two-dimensional space is not suitable for visualizing subspace structure as they reside in high-dimensional ambient space.

For traditional subspace clustering algorithms, around 37 Gigabytes of memory is required to store the affinity matrix, which is computationally prohibitive. Therefore, we contrast our algorithm against SSC, LRR, KSSC, SSC-OMP and Deep Subspace Clustering Networks on a smaller experiment, namely only using the 10000 test images of the MNIST dataset (see Table 2 for results). Note that SSC-OMP completely fails in dealing with feature generated by SAE and CAE, achieving around 12% ACC and 2% NMI. Generally speaking, with more samples, better accuracies are expected. We can see that all the subspace clustering

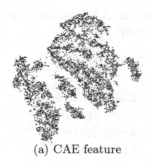
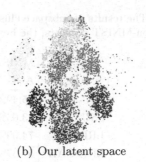

(a) CAE feature   (b) Our latent space

Fig. 3. Visualization using t-SNE on the latent space generated by projecting the testing set images on pre-trained CAE and our network. Points marked with the same color belong to the same class. (Color figure online)

algorithms using the SAE feature perform better compared to using CAE feature. To some extent, it proves that there exists a nonlinear mapping which is more favorable to subspace clustering. At the same time, our algorithm still achieves the best results within all subspace clustering algorithms, even higher that DSC-Net.

Table 1. Results on MNIST (70000 samples).

	SAE-KM	CAE-KM	K-means	PCA-KS	DEC	DCN	kSCN-G	kSCN-S
ACC	81.29%	51%	53%	68.53%	84.3%	83.31%	82.22%	**87.14%**
NMI	73.78%	44.87%	50%	64.17%	80%	**80.86%**	73.93%	78.15%
ARI	67%	33.52%	37%	54.17%	75%	74.87%	71.10%	**75.81%**

5.2   Fashion-MNIST

Unlike MNIST dataset, which only contains simple digits, every class in Fashion-MNIST has different styles and come from different gender groups: men, women, kids and neutral. In Fashion-MNIST, there are 60000 training images and 10000 test images. In our case, we pre-trained and fine-tuned the network using the whole dataset. On Fashion-MNIST, we fix our subspace dimension to 11 and set λ to 0.11.

Consistent with the MNIST dataset, the DCN sightly improves upon its initialization (SAE-KM) in terms of ACC and NMI. Moreover, we find out that the DCN algorithm works better with smaller learning rates, which in turn requires more epochs to converge properly. From Table 3, we can see that our method still improves the accuracy by 24% compared to our initialization, and outperforms other algorithms. The t-SNE maps in Fig. 4 show that there exists a subspace structure in our latent space even in two dimensional space.

Table 2. The results of subspace clustering algorithms on the test sets of the MNIST and Fashion-MNIST datasets, the best two are in bold

	MNIST		Fashion-MNIST	
	ACC	NMI	ACC	NMI
SSC-SAE	75.49%	66.26%	52.33%	51.26%
SSC-CAE	43.03%	56.81%	35.31%	18.10%
LRR-SAE	74.09%	66.97%	**58.09%**	59.19%
LRR-CAE	51.37%	66.59%	34.43%	18.57%
KSSC-SAE	**81.53%**	**84.53%**	57.10%	**60.40%**
KSSC-CAE	56.42%	65.66%	35.41%	18.18%
DSC-Net	53.20%	47.90%	55.81%	54.80%
kSCN-S	**83.30%**	**77.38%**	**60.02%**	**62.30%**

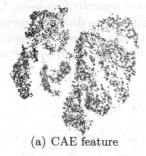

(a) CAE feature   (b) Our latent feature

Fig. 4. Visualization using t-SNE for the latent space generated by pretrained CAE and our network on Fashion-MNIST. Points marked with the same color belong to the same class. (Color figure online)

Table 2 shows that the subspace clustering algorithms also achieve acceptable results on the 10000 test sets, with our algorithm being the best among all. Compared to other subspace clustering algorithms, our algorithm runs much faster, only requiring less than 8 min (including pre-training and fine tuning with subspace clustering) to generate final results, whereas the traditional algorithms need at least 40 min to process these 10000 samples even after the dimensionality reduction.

5.3 Further Discussion

Based on the above experiments, we observe that our algorithm consistently achieves higher accuracies as compared to DCN (even with the initialization using CAE). One may argue that the performance gain over DCN is due to the fact that unlike SAE, CAE can be trained easily[3]. To verify that this is not

---

[3] In our experiments, the number of parameters in SAE is 2600 times more than that of CAE.

Table 3. Results on Fashion-Mnist

	SAE-KM	CAE-KM	K-means	PCA-KS	DCN	kSCN-G	kSCN-S
ACC	54.35%	39.84%	47.58%	53.41%	56.14%	58.67%	**63.78%**
NMI	58.54%	39.80%	51.24%	57.5%	59.4%	52.88%	**62.04%**
ARI	41.86%	25.93%	34.86%	41.17%	43.04%	42%	**48.04%**

the case, we replace the SAE with the CAE in DCN to see whether DCN can generate competitive results. Table 4 demonstrates that even with the CAE, the DCN cannot boost the clustering results as much as ours. On MNIST, DCN-CAE can hardly improve the accuracy and NMI; on Fashion-MNIST, it can increase the accuracy more than 3% (and NMI around 1%). This can be attributed to the loss introduced by k-means in DCN, compared to our k-subspace clustering loss which we believe is more robust. In other words, the subspace structure could be more desirable than cluster centroids in high dimensional space.

Table 4. The performance of the DCN-CAE and its CAE initialization.

	MNIST		Fashion-MNIST	
	ACC	NMI	ACC	NMI
DCN-CAE	51.10%	45.18%	45.64%	47.8%
Initilization	50.98%	44.87%	42.38%	46.75%

6   Conclusions

In this paper, we proposed a scalable deep k-subspace clustering algorithm, which combined the k-subspace clustering and convolutional auto-encoder in a principle way. Our algorithm makes it possible to scale subspace clustering algorithms to large datasets. Furthermore, we proposed two efficient and robust schemes to update the subspaces. These allow our k-SC networks to iteratively fit every sample into its corresponding subspace and update the subspaces accordingly, even from a bad initialization (as observed in our experiments).

Our extensive experiments on MNIST and Fashion-MNIST dataset demonstrated that our deep k-subspace clustering method provides significant improvements over various state-of-the-art subspace clustering solutions in terms of clustering accuracy and efficiency.

Acknowledgement. This research was supported by Australian Research Council (ARC) Discovery Projects funding scheme (project DP150104645), ARC through Laureate Fellowship FL130100102 to IDR and ARC of Excellence for Robotic Vision (project number CE140100016).

References

1. Abadi, M., et al.: TensorFlow: large-scale machine learning on heterogeneous distributed systems. arXiv:1603.04467 (2016)
2. Agarwal, P.K., Mustafa, N.H.: K-means projective clustering. In: Proceedings of the Twenty-Third ACM SIGMOD-SIGACT-SIGART Symposium on Principles of Database Systems, pp. 155–165. ACM (2004)
3. Balzano, L., Szlam, A., Recht, B., Nowak, R.: K-subspaces with missing data. In: 2012 IEEE Statistical Signal Processing Workshop (SSP), pp. 612–615. IEEE (2012)
4. Bengio, Y., Lamblin, P., Popovici, D., Larochelle, H.: Greedy layer-wise training of deep networks. In: NIPS, pp. 153–160 (2007)
5. Bradley, P.S., Mangasarian, O.L.: K-plane clustering. J. Glob. Optim. **16**(1), 23–32 (2000)
6. Dalal, N., Triggs, B.: Histograms of oriented gradients for human detection. In: CVPR 2005, pp. 886–893. IEEE (2005)
7. Elhamifar, E., Vidal, R.: Sparse subspace clustering. In: CVPR, pp. 2790–2797 (2009)
8. Elhamifar, E., Vidal, R.: Sparse subspace clustering: algorithm, theory, and applications. IEEE Trans Pattern Anal. Mach. Intell. **35**(11), 2765–2781 (2013)
9. Ho, J., Yang, M.H., Lim, J., Lee, K.C., Kriegman, D.: Clustering appearances of objects under varying illumination conditions. In: CVPR, vol. 1, pp. 11–18. IEEE (2003)
10. Ji, P., Li, H., Salzmann, M., Dai, Y.: Robust motion segmentation with unknown correspondences. In: Fleet, D., Pajdla, T., Schiele, B., Tuytelaars, T. (eds.) ECCV 2014. LNCS, vol. 8694, pp. 204–219. Springer, Cham (2014). https://doi.org/10.1007/978-3-319-10599-4_14
11. Ji, P., Li, H., Salzmann, M., Zhong, Y.: Robust multi-body feature tracker: a segmentation-free approach. In: CVPR, pp. 3843–3851 (2016)
12. Ji, P., Reid, I., Garg, R., Li, H., Salzmann, M.: Low-rank kernel subspace clustering. arXiv preprint arXiv:1707.04974 (2017)
13. Ji, P., Salzmann, M., Li, H.: Efficient dense subspace clustering. In: IEEE Winter Conference on Applications of Computer Vision (WACV), pp. 461–468. IEEE (2014)
14. Ji, P., Salzmann, M., Li, H.: Shape interaction matrix revisited and robustified: efficient subspace clustering with corrupted and incomplete data. In: ICCV, pp. 4687–4695 (2015)
15. Ji, P., Zhang, T., Li, H., Salzmann, M., Reid, I.: Deep subspace clustering networks. In: Advances in Neural Information Processing Systems, pp. 23–32 (2017)
16. Ji, P., Zhong, Y., Li, H., Salzmann, M.: Null space clustering with applications to motion segmentation and face clustering. In: ICIP, pp. 283–287. IEEE (2014)
17. Kanatani, K.: Motion segmentation by subspace separation and model selection. In: ICCV, vol. 2, pp. 586–591. IEEE (2001)
18. Kingma, D., Ba, J.: Adam: a method for stochastic optimization. arXiv:1412.6980 (2014)
19. LeCun, Y., Bottou, L., Bengio, Y., Haffner, P.: Gradient-based learning applied to document recognition. Proc. IEEE **86**(11), 2278–2324 (1998)
20. Lee, K.C., Ho, J., Kriegman, D.J.: Acquiring linear subspaces for face recognition under variable lighting. TPAMI **27**(5), 684–698 (2005)

21. Liu, G., Lin, Z., Yan, S., Sun, J., Yu, Y., Ma, Y.: Robust recovery of subspace structures by low-rank representation. IEEE Trans Pattern Anal. Mach. Intell. **35**(1), 171–184 (2013)
22. Lloyd, S.: Least squares quantization in PCM. IEEE Trans. Inf. Theory **28**(2), 129–137 (1982)
23. Lowe, D.G.: Distinctive image features from scale-invariant keypoints. IJCV **60**(2), 91–110 (2004)
24. Ma, Y., Derksen, H., Hong, W., Wright, J.: Segmentation of multivariate mixed data via lossy data coding and compression. TPAMI **29**(9), 1546–1562 (2007)
25. Ng, A.Y., Jordan, M.I., Weiss, Y., et al.: On spectral clustering: analysis and an algorithm. In: NIPS, vol. 14, pp. 849–856 (2001)
26. Patel, V.M., Vidal, R.: Kernel sparse subspace clustering. In: ICIP, pp. 2849–2853. IEEE (2014)
27. Peng, X., Feng, J., Xiao, S., Lu, J., Yi, Z., Yan, S.: Deep sparse subspace clustering. arXiv preprint arXiv:1709.08374 (2017)
28. Peng, X., Xiao, S., Feng, J., Yau, W.Y., Yi, Z.: Deep subspace clustering with sparsity prior. In: IJCAI (2016)
29. Shi, J., Malik, J.: Normalized cuts and image segmentation. TPAMI **22**(8), 888–905 (2000)
30. Tseng, P.: Nearest q-Flat to m points. J. Optim. Theory Appl. **105**(1), 249–252 (2000)
31. Vidal, R.: Subspace clustering. IEEE Signal Process. Mag. **28**(2), 52–68 (2011)
32. Vidal, R., Favaro, P.: Low rank subspace clustering (LRSC). Pattern Recognit. Lett. **43**, 47–61 (2014)
33. Xiao, H., Rasul, K., Vollgraf, R.: Fashion-MNIST: a novel image dataset for benchmarking machine learning algorithms (2017)
34. Xiao, S., Tan, M., Xu, D., Dong, Z.Y.: Robust kernel low-rank representation. IEEE Trans. Neural Netw. Learn. Syst. **27**(11), 2268–2281 (2016)
35. Xie, J., Girshick, R., Farhadi, A.: Unsupervised deep embedding for clustering analysis. In: International Conference on Machine Learning, pp. 478–487 (2016)
36. Yang, A.Y., Wright, J., Ma, Y., Sastry, S.S.: Unsupervised segmentation of natural images via lossy data compression. CVIU **110**(2), 212–225 (2008)
37. Yang, B., Fu, X., Sidiropoulos, N.D., Hong, M.: Towards k-means-friendly spaces: simultaneous deep learning and clustering. In: ICML, pp. 3861–3870 (2017)
38. Yin, M., Guo, Y., Gao, J., He, Z., Xie, S.: Kernel sparse subspace clustering on symmetric positive definite manifolds. In: CVPR, pp. 5157–5164 (2016)
39. You, C., Li, C.G., Robinson, D.P., Vidal, R.: Oracle based active set algorithm for scalable elastic net subspace clustering. In: CVPR, pp. 3928–3937 (2016)
40. You, C., Robinson, D., Vidal, R.: Scalable sparse subspace clustering by orthogonal matching pursuit. In: CVPR, pp. 3918–3927 (2016)
41. Zhang, T., Szlam, A., Wang, Y., Lerman, G.: Hybrid linear modeling via local best-fit flats. Int. J. Comput. Vis. **100**(3), 217–240 (2012)

Siamese Generative Adversarial Privatizer for Biometric Data

Witold Oleszkiewicz[1]([✉]), Peter Kairouz[2], Karol Piczak[1], Ram Rajagopal[2], and Tomasz Trzciński[1,3]

[1] Warsaw University of Technology, Warsaw, Poland
witold.oleszkiewicz@pw.edu.pl
[2] Stanford University, Stanford, USA
[3] Tooploox, Wrocław, Poland

Abstract. State-of-the-art machine learning algorithms can be fooled by carefully crafted adversarial examples. As such, adversarial examples present a concrete problem in AI safety. In this work we turn the tables and ask the following question: can we harness the power of adversarial examples to *prevent malicious adversaries from learning identifying information* from data while allowing non-malicious entities to *benefit from the utility* of the same data? For instance, can we use adversarial examples to anonymize biometric dataset of faces while retaining usefulness of this data for other purposes, such as emotion recognition? To address this question, we propose a simple yet effective method, called *Siamese Generative Adversarial Privatizer* (SGAP), that exploits the properties of a Siamese neural network to find discriminative features that convey identifying information. When coupled with a generative model, our approach is able to correctly locate and disguise identifying information, while minimally reducing the utility of the privatized dataset. Extensive evaluation on a biometric dataset of fingerprints and cartoon faces confirms usefulness of our simple yet effective method.

1 Introduction

Large-scale datasets enable researchers to design and apply state-of-the-art machine learning algorithms that can solve progressively challenging problems. Unfortunately, most organizations release datasets rather reluctantly due to the excessive amounts of sensitive information about participating individuals.

Ensuring the privacy of subjects is done by removing all personally identifiable information (e.g. names or birthdates) – this process, however, is not foolproof. Correlation and linkage attacks [15,25] often identify an individual by combining anonymized data with personal information obtained from other sources. Several such cases have been presented in the past, e.g. deanonymization of users' viewing history that was published in the Netflix Prize competition [25], identifying subjects in medical studies based on fMRI imaging data [9], and linking DNA profiles of anonymized participants with data from the Personal Genome Project [32].

C. V. Jawahar et al. (Eds.): ACCV 2018, LNCS 11365, pp. 482–497, 2019.
https://doi.org/10.1007/978-3-030-20873-8_31

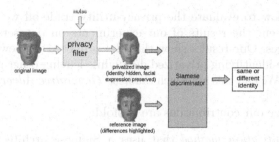

Fig. 1. Basic functionality of the proposed Siamese Generative Adversarial Privatizer: given an original face image, the privacy filter generates a privatized image. The original identity is hidden, at the same time other useful features, e.g. facial expression, are preserved. Siamese discriminator identifies the discriminative features of the images.

Typical approaches to countering the shortcomings of anonymization techniques leverage data randomization. While randomizing datasets with differential privacy [7] provides much stronger privacy guarantees, the utility of machine learning models trained on such randomized data is often significantly impaired [16,18,30]. We therefore believe that there is an ever increasing need for new privatization methods that preserve the value of the data while protecting the privacy of individuals.

The above privacy problem becomes critical when dealing with sensitive biometric and medical images. Several breakthrough applications of computer vision have been proposed in this domain: [12] used machine learning algorithms to parcellate human cerebral cortex, [29] utilized convolutional networks to detect arrhythmia, and [8] used machine learning to realize a precision medicine system. These applications, though critical for the advancement of the domain, rely on the access to highly sensitive data. This calls for novel privatization schemes that allow for the publication of images containing medical and biometric information without sacrificing the utility of the applications discussed above.

1.1   Our Contributions

In this work, we take a new approach towards enabling private data publishing. Instead of adopting worst case, context-free notions of statistical data privacy (such as differential privacy), we present a novel framework that allows the publisher to privatize images in a context-aware manner (Fig. 1). Our framework builds up on the recent work [17] where they propose a Generative Adversarial Privacy (GAP) method that casts the privatization as a constrained minimax game between a privatizer and an adversary that tries to infer private data. The approach we propose here is focused on biometric images and exploits a Siamese neural network architecture to identify image parts that bear the highest discriminative power and perturb them to enforce privatization. Contrary to other works that quantify privacy in a subjective manner using user surveys [28], we define here empirical conditions our privatizer needs to fulfill and propose metrics that allow to evaluate the privacy-utility trade-off we aim to explore. Finally, we present the results of our experiments on datasets of fingerprints and cartoon faces. Our results show that the proposed framework prevents an attacker from re-identifying privatized data while leaving other important image features intact. We call this approach *Siamese Generative Adversarial Privatizer* (SGAP).

To summarize our contributions are twofold:

- a novel *privatization method* that uses a Siamese architecture to identify identity-discriminative image parts and perturbates them to protect privacy, while preserving the utility of the resulting data for other machine learning tasks, and
- an empirical data-driven *privacy metric* (c.f. Sect. 4.2) based on mutual information that allows to quantify the privatization effects on biometric images.

1.2 Paper Outline

The remainder of this paper is organized as follows. In Sect. 2, we provide a brief survey of recent relevant works. In Sect. 3, we present the architectural details of our SGAP model. The main results of our paper are presented in Sect. 4. We conclude our paper in Sect. 5.

2 Related Work

Privatization of data has been an active area of research with multiple works touching on this subject [1,16,18,30]. Our approach extends the concept of context-independent data privatization by incorporating context-dependent information as an input to the privatization algorithm. More precisely, it identifies the discriminative characteristics of the data and distorts them to enforce privacy. Although standard methods of protecting privacy based on erasing personal information have been widely used, correlation and linkage attacks allow to re-identify the users, even when explicitly identifying information is not present in the released datasets [25].

Those kinds of attacks pose an even greater threat to individual privacy when used against publicly available medical databases [14]. [15] show that using publicly available genotype-phenotype correlations, an attacker can statistically relate genotype to phenotype and therefore re-identify individuals. Publicly available profiles in the Personal Genome Project can be linked with names by using demographic data [32]. Also, when considering fRMI imaging data, individual variability across individuals is both robust and reliable, thus can be used to identify single subjects [9].

Although numerous works are focused on finding discriminative patterns within the data [10,34], we use a Siamese neural network architecture [4] since it allows us to learn a discriminant data embedding in an end-to-end fashion. Contrary to the typical goal of a Siamese architecture, i.e. learning similarity, we use it to identify discriminant parts of a pair of images and alter those parts with minimal impact on other useful features. When both examples come from the same individual, this setup allows us to learn a perturbation that carefully disguises the individual's identity, hence protecting their privacy.

One can consider the problem of data anonymization to be conceptually similar to the idea of adversarial examples in neural network architectures [3, 19–21,33]. In the case of adversarial examples, the adversary wants to trick the neural network into misclassifying a slightly perturbed input of a given class. Similarly, our goal is to modify the data points in such a way that the identity of the individual corresponding to the data cannot be correctly classified. The most relevant work is [20], where they use a Generative Adversarial Network (GAN) [13] framework to create adversarial examples and use them in training to increase the robustness of the classifier.

Similar to us, [28] analyses the trade-off between data privacy and utility. In their work, however, privacy and utility metrics are defined based on a user-study, where the users were asked to assess the usefulness of the anonymized images in the context of social media distribution. The privacy, on the other hand, was measured by first enlisting a number of attributes linked to privacy (*e.g.* passport number or registration plates) and then asking the users to validate if a given privacy attribute is visible in the photo or not. We argue that this way of measuring both privacy and utility is limited to a very specific subset of applications. In our work we propose fundamentally different metrics for both privacy and utility that have backing in information theory and machine learning.

Another relevant and recent works [33], [5] address the privatization problem using a generative adversarial approach while providing theoretical privacy-utility trade-offs. The work of [5], which is the most similar to our work, proposes an architecture combining Variational Autoencoder (VAE) and GAN to create an identity-invariant representation of a face image. Their approach differs from ours as they use an additional discriminator, which explicitly controls which useful features of the images are to be preserved, whereas in our approach the model has no information about other features of the images, except that it knows whether a pair of images belongs to the same person or different people. This is a significant contribution because in practice, one cannot expect to know all potential applications of the privatized images. Therefore our approach proves to be more robust towards real-life applications.

[27] presents a similar game-theoretic perspective on image anonymization. However, the difference is that it focuses on adversarial image perturbations (carefully crafted perturbations invisible to human), while our privatizer introduces structural changes to the image. In [31], a head inpainting obfuscation technique is proposed by generating a realistic head inpainting using facial landmarks. On contrary, our goal is to hide the identity of a person without knowing which part of the image is responsible for identity. Thanks to this, our framework is more universal and has a much wider field of application, not only to hide face identity, but also hide identity in cases where there is no prior knowl-

edge of which part of the image should be obfuscated. [23,24] are relevant to our work and deal with a problem similar to ours. However, the formulation of the problem is different from ours. [23,24] transform an input face image in a way such that the transformed image can be successfully used for face recognition (so the identity is preserved) but not for gender classification. Our goal is the opposite, we want to hide identity while maintaining as much other features as possible, without explicitly modeling the non-malicious classification tasks. Another difference is that our model requires only identity labels. The architecture of the models presented in [23] and our work are similar, however we use Siamese discriminator what makes our approach advantageous when applied to large datasets with thousands or even millions of people, since this architecture reduces the output of the discriminator to a binary output rather than create a long list of individual class predictions.

3   Method

The goal of our approach is to develop a privatizer that converts an input image into its privatized version in such a way that: (1) the privacy of the subject is preserved by making sure that the identifying features are hidden, (2) the utility of the original image is maintained by preserving the non-identifying features that are vital for other machine learning tasks, and (3) the privacy-utility trade-off can be adjusted.

3.1   Proposed Approach

To enforce the above conditions, we will use a custom neural network architecture, dubbed *Siamese Generative Adversarial Privatizer*, that consists of two tightly coupled models: a generator $G(\theta_g)$ and a discriminator $D(\theta_d)$. This coupling is inspired by Generative Adversarial Networks (GANs) [13]. Two neural networks compete with each other: the discriminator tries to predict the identity of the person in the image, while the generator tries to generate such an image which fools the discriminator and thus hides the identity of the person.

We use a Siamese architecture [4] for the discriminator. This allows us to extract discriminative and identifying features from images. More importantly, this architecture reduces the output of the discriminator to a single value (from 0 to 1) rather than create a long list of individual class predictions, an approach which would be prohibitive when applied to large datasets with thousands or even millions of people. In this case, we use pairs of images (instead of single images) to train the neural network, and the goal of the Siamese discriminator is to classify whether the two images belong to the same person or to different people.

Furthermore, the above problem is subjected to a distortion constraint, which ensures that the privatized images are not too different from the original images.

We did not use L_2 since it is sensitive to small changes (e.g. shift, rotation, etc.) which do not significantly affect the content of the image. Instead

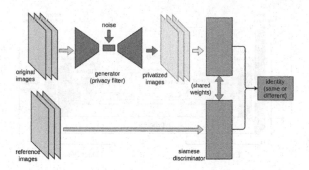

Fig. 2. Overview of our Siamese Generative Adversarial Privatizer model. The generator acts as a privacy filter, which hides the identity of the person in the original images. The Siamese discriminator recognizes whether the person in the privatized image is the same person as in the reference image.

we chose SSIM (structural similarity index) [35] which is sensitive to the structural changes of images, not pixel-by-pixel differences like L_2 [36]. We enforce a constraint on SSIM which allows us to control the level of distortion added to protect identity, and thus ensure that the quality of privatized images is not substantially degraded. The architecture overview can be seen in Fig. 2.

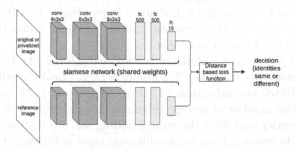

Fig. 3. Discriminator's architecture. We use a Siamese neural network to verify the identities of people in the images. The discriminator classifies whether a pair of images belongs to the same person or to different people. We get the output from the range between 0 and 1 applying distance-based loss function to the output of the last fully connected layer of the Siamese discriminator.

3.2 Architecture

Our discriminator is a Siamese convolutional neural network, which consists of two identical branches with shared weights, as shown in Fig. 3. Each branch consists of 3 blocks of the following form: (1) Convolutional layer (mask 3×3, stride $= 1$, padding $= 0$), (2) Leaky rectified linear unit ($\alpha = 0.1$), (3) Batch normalization, (4) Dropout ($p = 0.2$). The blocks are followed by 2 dense layers

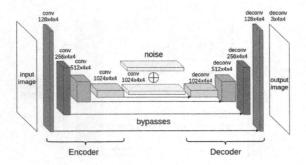

Fig. 4. Generator's architecture. We use Variational Autoencoder-like architecture to generate a privatized image in a context-aware manner based on the original image. At the bottleneck of the generator we get a compressed representation of the image without identity features, and thanks to the bypasses between the layers we preserve other useful features of the original image.

(500 neurons, leaky rectified linear unit, $\alpha = 0.1$) and an output layer (15 neurons). A discriminator network converts two input images to two output representations (embeddings) $D(\boldsymbol{X}_1, \boldsymbol{X}_2) \rightarrow (\boldsymbol{o}_1, \boldsymbol{o}_2)$.

The generator network, as presented in Fig. 4, consists of two parts: the encoding part and the decoding part. The encoder follows the typical architecture of a convolutional neural network. It consists of 5 blocks of the following form: (1) Convolutional layer (mask 4×4, stride $= 2$, padding $= 1$), (2) Leaky rectified linear unit ($\alpha = 0.1$), (3) Batch normalization. At each downsampling step we double the number of feature channels.

The decoder consists of 5 blocks of the following form: (1) Transpose convolutional layer (mask 4×4, stride $= 2$, padding $= 1$), (2) Leaky rectified linear unit ($\alpha = 0.1$), (3) Batch normalization, (4) Dropout ($p = 0.5$). At each upsampling step we halve the number of feature channels. Also we concatenate the feature maps of the decoder part with the corresponding feature map from the encoder part (these are bypasses). Last deconvolutional layer is followed by a hyperbolic tangent activation function.

A noise matrix $\mathbf{Z}$ is added to the bottleneck part of the generator, *i.e.* to the latent space variable representing input image in a low-dimensional space. We use a noise matrix instead of a vector, as we do not use a standard fully-connected layers in our generator and retain convolutional layers instead. The output of generator network is a privatized version of original image: $G(\mathbf{Z}, \boldsymbol{I}) \rightarrow \tilde{\boldsymbol{I}}$.

3.3 Training

When iterating over training dataset we get tuples: $(\boldsymbol{I}_i, \boldsymbol{I}'_i, l_i)$, where $\boldsymbol{I}_i$ and $\boldsymbol{I}'_i$ is a pair of images and l_i is a binary label where $l_i = 0$ if the images have the same identity and $l_i = 1$ for different identities. There are two types of pairs in the training set. Firstly, when the generator is turned off, $\boldsymbol{I}_i, \boldsymbol{I}'_i$ are images from the original training set. Secondly, when the generator is turned on, $\tilde{\boldsymbol{I}}_i = G(\mathbf{Z}_i, \boldsymbol{I}_i)$

is the privatized version of the image I_i from the original training set. I'_i is the reference image, also from the original training set. In both cases mentioned above we use stratified random sampling in order to balance two classes: $l = 0$ and $l = 1$.

The discriminator D takes a pair of images I, I' and outputs a probability that both images come from the same person, i.e. $l = 0$, based on a distance-based metric:

$$D(I, I') \rightarrow \frac{1 + e^{-m}}{1 + e^{d(o,o')^2 - m}} = P(I \overset{\text{sim.}}{\sim} I')$$

where m is a predefined margin and $d(o, o')$ is an Euclidean distance between embeddings o and o' in the last fully connected layer of the discriminator. Given this formulation of the discriminator we use a cross entropy loss for training:

$$\mathcal{L}(l, D(I, I')) = -(1 - l) \log D(I, I') - l \log \left(1 - D(I, I')\right)$$

We train our model similarly to GAN. When the generator training is frozen, our goal is to train the discriminator to recognize whether a pair of images belongs to the same person or to different people. When the generator is trained, there is a minmax game between the generator and the discriminator in which the generator is trying to fool the discriminator and generate an image that hides the identity of the subject. The training equation for our privatization task is:

$$\min_D \max_G \frac{1}{N} \sum_{i=0}^{N-1} \mathcal{L}(l_i, D(I_i, I'_i)) + \frac{1}{N} \sum_{i=0}^{N-1} \mathcal{L}(0, D(I'_i, G(Z_i, I_i)))$$

Furthermore, the above minimax optimization problem is subject to the following critical constraint: $\frac{1}{N} \sum_{i=0}^{N-1} d(I_i, G(Z_i, I_i)) < \delta$, where $d(x, y)$ is a distortion metric and δ is a distortion threshold. The distortion constraint is used to limit all the other image changes except for hiding identity and therefore the utility of the images is preserved. We use Structural Similarity Index as the distortion metric. The above constraint can be incorporated into the main minimax objective function as follows:

$$\min_D \max_G \sum_{i=0}^{N-1} \mathcal{L}(l_i, D(I_i, I'_i)) + \sum_{i=0}^{N-1} \mathcal{L}(0, D(I'_i, G(Z_i, I_i))) + \lambda \sum_{i=0}^{N-1} d(I_i, G(Z_i, I_i))$$
$$(1)$$

Our Siamese Generative Adversarial Privatizer network is trained for 100 epochs using ADAM optimizer with $\beta_1 = 0.9$ and $\beta_2 = 0.999$.

4   Results

In this section, we present the results of evaluation of our method. We first present the datasets and evaluation metrics. Then we show qualitative and quantitative results of our evaluation that confirm usefulness of our approach in the context of data privatization.

4.1   Datasets

Fingerprints. To validate how well our method performs in terms of identity privatization, we evaluate it on a dataset of fingerprints. Although the main purpose of fingerprint datasets is to identify people and therefore their privatization may not be needed in their real-life use cases, we treat this dataset as our toy example and evaluate how well we can hide the privacy of the fingerprint owner. Since there exists a trade-off between the privatization and the utility of the resulting data, we refer to a proxy task of finger type classification to validate how useful our privatization method is. In other words, we try to classify the type of the finger (*e.g.* middle finger, index finger, ring finger) while gradually increasing the privacy of the dataset. Section 4.4 presents the results of this experiment.

We use NIST 8-Bit Gray Scale Images of Fingerprint Image Groups [26]. This database contains 4000 8-bit grayscale fingerprint images paired in couples. Each image is 512-by-512 pixels with 32 rows of white space at the bottom. We use only one image of each pair in our experiments. The dataset contains images for 2000 individuals. For each person there are two different fingerprint shots of the same finger (denoted as: f, s). Our method requires pairs of images as input. In each epoch the dataset is iterated over 4000 pairs of images.

For the first half of the pairs when index of a pair is $i < 2000$ we return a label $l = 0$ and a pair of images (f, s) belonging to the person with $ID = i$.

For the second half of the pairs when index $i >= 2000$ we return a label $l = 1$ and two images. First image is image f of person with $ID = i - 2000$. Second image is an image (f or s) of a different person (selected at random).

This way we have a 50%/50% split over similar/dissimilar pairs and the dataset loader is quasi-deterministic (for a given index i the first image is guaranteed to be constant).

Animated Faces. The second dataset that we use is FERG dataset [2]. FERG is a dataset of cartoon characters with annotated facial expressions. It contains 55769 annotated face images of six characters. The images for each identity are grouped into 7 types of facial expressions, such as: anger, disgust, fear, joy, neutral, sadness and surprise.

In each epoch the dataset is iterated over 10000 pairs of images. For the first half of the pairs we use different randomly selected images of the same person. In this case $l = 0$. For the second half of the pairs we use randomly selected images of different people. In this case $l = 1$. This way we have a 50%/50% split over similar/dissimilar pairs and the dataset loader is quasi-deterministic.

4.2   Evaluation Metrics

To evaluate the performance of our SGAP model and show that it learns privacy schemes that are capable of hiding biometric information even from computationally unbounded adversaries, we propose computing the mutual information between: (a) $X = (X_1, X_2)$ where X_1 is a privatized image and X_2 is an original image, and (b) Y where $Y = 0$ when X_1 and X_2 belong to the same person and $Y = 1$ when they belong to different people. X_1 is privatized using the scheme that is learned in a data-driven fashion using SGAP. By Fano's inequality, if $I(X;Y)$ is low then Y cannot be learned from X reliably (even under computationally infinite adversaries) [6]. In other words, if $I(X;Y)$ is sufficiently small, there's no way we can reliably learn whether or not a privatized image belongs to the same person in another non-privatized image. This ensures that privacy is guaranteed in a strong sense.

In practice, we do not have access to the joint distribution $P(X,Y)$. We instead have access to a dataset of i.i.d observations $\mathcal{D} = \{(X_i, Y_i\}_{i=1}^n\}$. Here, the X_i's are computed after the SGAP training phase is over by applying the learned privacy scheme on a separate test set. We are thus interested in empirically estimating $I(X;Y)$ from $\mathcal{D}$. We will call this estimate "empirical mutual information" and denote it by $\hat{I}(X;Y)$. To compute $\hat{I}(X;Y)$, we can use the following formula:

$$\hat{I}(X;Y) = \hat{H}(X) - \hat{H}(X|Y)$$

where $\hat{H}(X)$ and $\hat{H}(X|Y)$ are the empirical entropies of X and X given Y. To compute these empirical entropies, we use the Kozachenko-Leonenko entropy estimator [11] which we briefly explain next. Letting $R_i = \min_{j, j \neq i} \|X_i - X_j\|$, for $j = 1, \ldots, n$, we get

$$\hat{H}(X) = \frac{1}{n} \sum_{i=1}^n \log\left((n-1)R_i^d\right) + constant$$

$$= \frac{d}{n} \sum_{i=1}^n \log R_i + \frac{1}{n} \sum_{i=1}^n \log(n-1) + constant$$

where d is the dimension of X, i.e. $X_i \in \mathbb{R}^d$. Assuming we have a two-class problem ($Y = 0$ for same identities, $Y = 1$ for different identities), the conditional entropy is given by

$$\hat{H}(X|Y) = \hat{H}(X|Y = 0)\hat{P}(Y = 0) + \hat{H}(X|Y = 1)\hat{P}(Y = 1)$$

Notice that $\hat{P}(Y = 0) = \frac{n_0}{n}$, $\hat{P}(Y = 1) = \frac{n_1}{n}$, where n_0 and n_1 are the counts of samples with label Y equals 0 and 1 respectively. We divide sample X into two partitions. Letting $i_1, i_2, \ldots, i_{n_0}$ be the indices corresponding to $Y_i = 0$, we have a set $\mathcal{X}_0 = \{X_{i_1}, X_{i_2}, \ldots, X_{i_{n_0}}\}$. Automatically we have $i'_1, i'_2, \ldots, i'_{n_0}$, the indices of samples associated with $Y_i = 1$. Thus, we get $\mathcal{X}_1 = \{X_{i'_1}, X_{i'_2}, \ldots, X_{i'_{n_1}}\}$. Therefore we calculate the nearest neighbor distance for each sample within the particular set as follows:

$$R_{i_k} = \min_{l \neq k, l = 1, \ldots, n_0} \|X_{i_k} - X_{i_l}\| \qquad R_{i'_k} = \min_{l \neq k, l = 1, \ldots, n_1} \|X_{i'_k} - X_{i'_l}\|$$

$$\hat{H}(X|Y=0) = \frac{1}{n_0} \sum_{k=1}^{n_0} \log\left((n_0 - 1)R_{i_k}^d\right) + constant$$

$$\hat{H}(X|Y=1) = \frac{1}{n_1} \sum_{k=1}^{n_1} \log\left((n_1 - 1)R_{i'_k}^d\right) + constant$$

Then the empirical mutual information can be expressed as

$$\hat{I}(X,Y) = \hat{H}(X) - \left(\hat{H}(X|Y=0)\hat{P}(Y=0) + \hat{H}(X|Y=1)\hat{P}(Y=1)\right)$$

$$= \frac{1}{n} \sum_{i=1}^{n} \log\left((n-1)R_i^d\right) +$$

$$- \left(\left(\frac{1}{n_0} \sum_{k=1}^{n_0} \log\left((n_0 - 1)R_{i_k}^d\right)\right)\frac{n_0}{n} + \left(\frac{1}{n_1} \sum_{k=1}^{n_1} \log\left((n_1 - 1)R_{i'_k}^d\right)\right)\frac{n_1}{n}\right)$$

To estimate values of R_{i_k} and $R_{i'_k}$ we use L_2 norm between image pixels projected to a 3-dimensional space via t-SNE [22]. We reduce the dimensionality to increase the efficiency of computation, but our metric remains agnostic to image distance calculation and other methods can also be used here.

The second approach to quantify privacy is by measuring an identity mis-classification rate. We measure what percentage of privatized images effectively fool our Siamese discriminator.

To quantify utility of privatized dataset we measure accuracy of the proxy classification task (finger type classification for fingerprint dataset and facial expression classification for faces dataset). More precisely, we evaluate how good in terms of accuracy a separate independent method can be trained for using a privatized dataset. We use fine-tuned ResNet architecture, pre-trained on ImageNet without freezing. In addition we split the dataset into training and validation. The accuracy is measured using k-fold validation ($k = 4$).

4.3   Qualitative Results

In this section, we present the qualitative results of our evaluation, demonstrating the ability of our network to increase the privacy of input data.

Figures 5 and 6 show sample results obtained as an output of our privatization. In Fig. 6 we see that the identities of people have been hidden, while other useful features, in this case facial expressions, have been preserved. Figures 7, 8 and 9 illustrate the trade-off between utility and privacy while tuning λ distortion metric constraint. We see that by tuning the λ parameter we can adjust the level of privacy and utility, finally finding the optimal value for both privacy and utility.

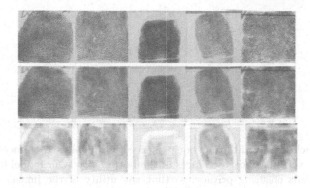

Fig. 5. A toy example of how our privatization method can hide identities of the finger-print owners. Original fingerprints in the upper row. Fingerprints with added artifacts that fool identity discriminator in the middle row. Structural Similarity difference [35] of the original and privatized images is presented in the bottom row. Our Siamese Generative Adversarial Privatizer learns to locate discriminant image features, such as fingerprint minutiae, and substitutes them with anonymizing artifacts. Although in practice fingerprints are used for person identification, we validate if privatized images can be useful (*i.e.* if they can retain utility) for a proxy task of finger type classification. Since our method does not add noise arbitrarily across the image, but only focuses on hiding sensitive personal information, the resulting dataset can be published and used by machine learning for other tasks, e.g. finger type classification or skin disease detection.

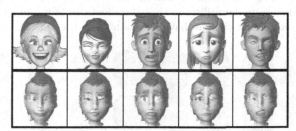

Fig. 6. Original cartoon faces in the upper row. Privatized versions of cartoon faces in the bottom row. Our Siamese Generative Adversarial Privatizer learns to hide the identity of the people, while other important image features, such as facial expression remain intact.

4.4 Quantitative Results

To obtain quantitative results we train our SGAP model with different values of maximal distortion constraint λ (see Eq. 1) in order to adjust the privacy level of the dataset. The goal of our generator is to add such noise to the latent space that privatized image fools the discriminator, which the discriminator in turn has to verify if the pair of images comes from the same person. After SGAP is trained, the generator part can be used to privatize datasets.

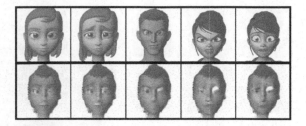

Fig. 7. Too much privacy, utility is not preserved. Original cartoon faces in the upper row. Privatized versions of cartoon faces in the bottom row. Our model has been tuned too much towards ensuring privacy, so that the utility of the images has not been preserved, facial expressions are hard to recognize.

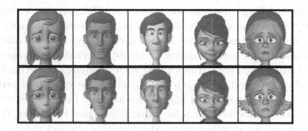

Fig. 8. Not enough privacy, utility is preserved. Original cartoon faces in the upper row. Privatized versions of cartoon faces in the bottom row. Our model has been tuned too much towards preserving utility, so that the identities of the people in the images are not hidden, only minor changes have been added to the images.

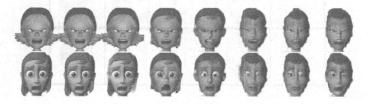

Fig. 9. Images in the first column are the original ones, next there are privatized images generated for different values of distortion constraint $\lambda \in \{10, 8, 6, 4, 2, 1, 0.7\}$. Original images of different identities collapse into an anonymous identity with the expression preserved from the original image.

To measure the utility of the privatized fingerprints dataset, we refer to a proxy task of finger type classification. Although in fingerprints are typically used to identify the identity of an individual, in our case we use the proposed privatization method to hide the identity and anonymize the dataset. The objective of this experiment is to evaluate how increasing data privacy effects the utility of the resulting dataset when used as training data for a machine learning algorithm. Hence, we use a proxy machine learning task, finger type classification. To measure the utility of the privatized cartoon faces dataset, we use

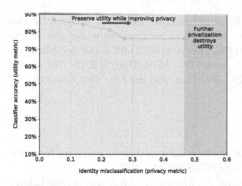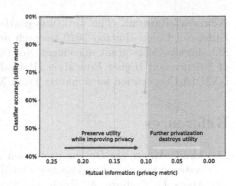

Fig. 10. Left: Graph of identity misclassification rate and the accuracy of a classifier trained with cartoon faces dataset privatized with different maximal constraint distortion thresholds. In green the region where the utility of dataset is preserved while the likelihood of classifying the privatized version of the image as belonging to a given person is reduced. This result proves that by using our privatization method we are able to significantly increase the privacy of the biometric dataset, while not reducing its utility for a task of facial expression classification. Right: Graph of mutual information estimation and the accuracy of a classifier trained with fingerprint dataset privatized with different maximal constraint distortion thresholds. In green the region where the utility of dataset is preserved while the likelihood of classifying the privatized version of the image as belonging to a given person is reduced. This result proves that by using our privatization method we are able to significantly increase the privacy of the biometric dataset, while not reducing its utility for a proxy task of finger type classification. (Color figure online)

facial expression classification as machine learning task. As a classifier, trained on privatized datasets, we use fine-tuned ResNet architecture, pre-trained on ImageNet without freezing. For each dataset generated using different maximal distortion constraint, we calculate classification accuracy and quantify the privacy by estimation of mutual information (fingerprint dataset) or using identity misclassification rate (faces dataset).

Figure 10 shows the results. In both cases we see a significant drop in privacy metric, while for the same range of parameters, the accuracy of the classifier remains stable, indicating that the utility of the dataset is not decreased.

5   Conclusions

We presented the *Siamese Generative Adversarial Privatizer* (SGAP) model for privacy-preserving of biometric data. We proposed a novel architecture combining Siamese neural network, autoencoder, and Generative Adversarial Network to create a context-aware privatizer. Experimental results on two public datasets demonstrate that our approach strikes a balance between privacy preservation and dataset utility.

Acknowledgment. The work was partially supported as RENOIR Project by the European Union Horizon 2020 research and innovation programme under the Marie Skłodowska-Curie grant agreement No. 691152 (project RENOIR) and by Ministry of Science and Higher Education (Poland), grant No. W34/H2020/2016. We thank NVIDIA Corporation for donating Titan Xp GPU that was used for this research.

References

1. Abadi, M., et al.: On the protection of private information in machine learning systems: two recent approaches. CoRR abs/1708.08022 (2017)
2. Aneja, D., Colburn, A., Faigin, G., Shapiro, L., Mones, B.: Modeling stylized character expressions via deep learning. In: Lai, S.-H., Lepetit, V., Nishino, K., Sato, Y. (eds.) ACCV 2016. LNCS, vol. 10112, pp. 136–153. Springer, Cham (2017). https://doi.org/10.1007/978-3-319-54184-6_9
3. Baluja, S., Fischer, I.: Adversarial transformation networks: learning to generate adversarial examples. CoRR abs/1703.09387 (2017)
4. Bromley, J., Guyon, I., LeCun, Y., Säckinger, E., Shah, R.: Signature verification using a "siamese" time delay neural network. In: Advances in Neural Information Processing Systems, vol. 6, pp. 737–744. Morgan-Kaufmann (1994)
5. Chen, J., Konrad, J., Ishwar, P.: VGAN-based image representation learning for privacy-preserving facial expression recognition. CoRR abs/1803.07100 (2018). http://arxiv.org/abs/1803.07100
6. Cover, T.M., Thomas, J.A.: Elements of Information Theory. Wiley Series in Telecommunications and Signal Processing. Wiley, New York (2006)
7. Dwork, C.: Differential privacy: a survey of results. In: International Conference on Theory and Applications of Models of Computation, pp. 1–19 (2008)
8. Famm, K., Litt, B., Tracey, K.J., Boyden, E.S., Slaoui, M.: Drug discovery: a jump-start for electroceuticals. Nature **496**(7444), 159–161 (2013)
9. Finn, E.S., et al.: Functional connectome fingerprinting: identifying individuals using patterns of brain connectivity. Nat. Neurosci. **18**(11), 1664–1671 (2015)
10. Fisher, R.A.: The use of multiple measurements in taxonomic problems. Ann. Eugen. **7**(7), 179–188 (1936)
11. Fournier, N., Delattre, S.: On the Kozachenko-Leonenko entropy estimator. ArXiv e-prints, February 2016
12. Glasser, M.F., et al.: A multi-modal parcellation of human cerebral cortex. Nature **536**(7615), 171–178 (2016)
13. Goodfellow, I., et al.: Generative adversarial nets. In: Advances in Neural Information Processing Systems, vol. 27, pp. 2672–2680 (2014)
14. Gymrek, M., McGuire, A.L., Golan, D., Halperin, E., Erlich, Y.: Identifying personal genomes by surname inference. Science **339**(6117), 321–324 (2013)
15. Harmanci, A., Gerstein, M.: Quantification of private information leakage from phenotype-genotype data: linking attacks. Nat. Methods **13**(3), 251–256 (2016)
16. Hayes, J., Melis, L., Danezis, G., De Cristofaro, E.: LOGAN: evaluating privacy leakage of generative models using generative adversarial networks. ArXiv e-prints (2017)
17. Huang, C., Kairouz, P., Chen, X., Sankar, L., Rajagopal, R.: Context-aware generative adversarial privacy. CoRR abs/1710.09549 (2017)
18. Kairouz, P., Bonawitz, K., Ramage, D.: Discrete distribution estimation under local privacy. CoRR abs/1602.07387 (2016)

19. Kos, J., Fischer, I., Song, D.: Adversarial examples for generative models. CoRR abs/1702.06832 (2017)
20. Lee, H., Han, S., Lee, J.: Generative adversarial trainer: defense to adversarial perturbations with GAN. CoRR abs/1705.03387 (2017)
21. Liang, B., Li, H., Su, M., Li, X., Shi, W., Wang, X.: Detecting adversarial examples in deep networks with adaptive noise reduction. CoRR abs/1705.08378 (2017)
22. van der Maaten, L., Hinton, G.: Visualizing data using t-SNE. J. Mach. Learn. Res. **9**, 2579–2605 (2008). http://www.jmlr.org/papers/v9/vandermaaten08a.html
23. Mirjalili, V., Raschka, S., Namboodiri, A.M., Ross, A.: Semi-adversarial networks: convolutional autoencoders for imparting privacy to face images. CoRR abs/1712.00321 (2017)
24. Mirjalili, V., Ross, A.: Soft biometric privacy: retaining biometric utility of face images while perturbing gender. In: IJCB, pp. 564–573 (2017)
25. Narayanan, A., Shmatikov, V.: Robust de-anonymization of large sparse datasets. In: 2008 IEEE Symposium on Security and Privacy, SP 2008, pp. 111–125. IEEE (2008)
26. NIST: NIST 8-bit gray scale images of fingerprint image groups (FIGS)
27. Oh, S.J., Fritz, M., Schiele, B.: Adversarial image perturbation for privacy protection - a game theory perspective. CoRR abs/1703.09471 (2017)
28. Orekondy, T., Fritz, M., Schiele, B.: Connecting pixels to privacy and utility: automatic redaction of private information in images. In: The IEEE Conference on Computer Vision and Pattern Recognition (CVPR), June 2018
29. Rajpurkar, P., Hannun, A.Y., Haghpanahi, M., Bourn, C., Ng, A.Y.: Cardiologist-level arrhythmia detection with convolutional neural networks. ArXiv e-prints (2017)
30. Raval, N., Machanavajjhala, A., Cox, L.P.: Protecting visual secrets using adversarial nets. In: CVPR Workshop Proceedings (2017)
31. Sun, Q., Ma, L., Oh, S.J., Gool, L.V., Schiele, B., Fritz, M.: Natural and effective obfuscation by head inpainting. CoRR abs/1711.09001 (2017)
32. Sweeney, L., Abu, A., Winn, J.: Identifying participants in the personal genome project by name (a re-identification experiment). CoRR abs/1304.7605 (2013)
33. Tripathy, A., Wang, Y., Ishwar, P.: Privacy-preserving adversarial networks. CoRR abs/1712.07008 (2017)
34. Trzcinski, T., Lepetit, V.: Efficient discriminative projections for compact binary descriptors. In: Fitzgibbon, A., Lazebnik, S., Perona, P., Sato, Y., Schmid, C. (eds.) ECCV 2012. LNCS, vol. 7572, pp. 228–242. Springer, Heidelberg (2012). https://doi.org/10.1007/978-3-642-33718-5_17
35. Wang, Z., Bovik, A.C., Sheikh, H.R., Simoncelli, E.P.: Image quality assessment: from error visibility to structural similarity. IEEE Trans. Image Process. **13**(4), 600–612 (2004)
36. Zhao, H., Gallo, O., Frosio, I., Kautz, J.: Loss functions for neural networks for image processing. CoRR abs/1511.08861 (2015). http://arxiv.org/abs/1511.08861

Exploiting LSTM for Joint Object and Semantic Part Detection

Qi Yao[ID] and Xiaojin Gong[✉][ID]

College of Information Science and Electronic Engineering,
Zhejiang University, Hangzhou, China
yaoqi_isee@zju.edu.cn

Abstract. Object detection and semantic part detection are two tasks that can mutually benefit each other. Thus, in this paper we propose an approach to perform joint detection. Our approach is built upon a proposal-driven detection framework. In order to explore the mutual interaction between two tasks, we integrate an interaction module into the detection framework. The module contains a relationship modeling stage and a feature fusion stage. The former determines the relationship between each object proposal and semantic part proposal by formulating it as a binary classification problem. The second stage adopts Long Short Term Memory networks (LSTMs) to fuse the features of an object and its associated parts, as well as the features of a part and its associated object proposals. Experiments on publicly available datasets show that, with the proposed interaction module, our joint detection approach consistently outperforms the baselines using object or part appearance only. Our approach also shows superior performance when compared to other semantic part detection methods.

Keywords: Object detection · Semantic part detection · Long Short Term Memory network

1 Introduction

Semantic parts, which are object regions interpretable by humans, are of lower intra-class variability and higher robustness to pose variation when compared to whole objects. The detection of semantic parts thus can be beneficial to many vision tasks, including fine-grained classification [16,19], human pose estimation [3,32], attribute prediction [12,27], or even general object detection [20,35,38]. However, most existing works only take parts as support for other vision tasks and rarely focus on part detection itself, let alone the joint detection of both semantic parts and objects.

This work aims to detect both objects and semantic parts simultaneously. In the deep learning framework, these two tasks are complementary and can benefit each other to a great extent because object detection requires larger receptive field while semantic part detection focuses more on local regions. Thus,

© Springer Nature Switzerland AG 2019
C. V. Jawahar et al. (Eds.): ACCV 2018, LNCS 11365, pp. 498–512, 2019.
https://doi.org/10.1007/978-3-030-20873-8_32

on one hand, we can integrate part information into object detection [20,38] to improve the detection robustness to occlusion, pose variation and eliminate the ambiguity across similar object categories; on the other hand, leveraging object-level context for part detection [14] can provide part detection more global and co-occurrence information which will lead to a considerable improvement.

Despite the above-mentioned benefits, the joint detection faces two main challenges when we adopt the successful proposal-based detection frameworks [4, 10,23]. (1) How to determine the relationship between object proposals and part proposals? (2) How to exploit the relationship between objects and parts to boost the performance of both tasks? In this paper, we propose novel solutions to address these problems. We adopt Faster R-CNN [23] as our backbone network and formulate the joint detection problem as a two-stage task. The first stage, called *relationship modeling*, predicts whether to interact or not for a specific pair of object proposal and part proposal by checking their appearance features. The second stage, called *feature fusion*, uses LSTM networks to aggregate the features of associated parts and objects. The fused features are finally leveraged for the classification and regression of both objects and parts.

We evaluate our joint detection approach on the PASCAL-Part dataset [2] and CUB200-2011 dataset [29]. Experimental results demonstrate that our joint detection approach consistently outperforms the baseline using object and part appearance only. We also compare with other semantic part detection methods and show superior performance.

2   Related Work

2.1   Part-Based Object Detection

Due to the low intra-class variability and high robustness to pose variation, local parts have been taken into consideration in various object detection methods. One pioneer work is the pictorial structure model [8], which represented visual objects by a spring-like graph of parts. After that, the deformable part-based model (DPM) [7] and its variants [31,37] had become the leading methods for years. Recently, although deep convolutional neural networks (CNNs), especially the region-based CNNs such as Fast R-CNN [10], Faster R-CNN [23], and R-FCN [4] have significantly improved the detection performance, there are still some works [11,20,38] proposed to integrate part information into the CNN frameworks for object detection. For instance, the DeepPyramid DPM [11] formulated a DPM as a CNN to detect objects. DeepID-Net [20] integrated a deformation constrained pooling layer into a CNN to model the deformation of object parts. CoupleNet [38] coupled local parts and the global structure within R-FCN to improve detection performance. In all above-mentioned methods, the parts they considered are local image patches that are discriminative for objects. In contrast, our work focuses on semantic parts which have actual semantic meanings, like 'person-leg' or 'aeroplane-wing'.

2.2 Semantic Part Detection

Semantic parts play a fundamental role in several visual recognition tasks such as fine-grained classification [16,33] and attribute prediction [12]. Thus, semantic part detection has gained significant attention in recent years. Most existing works detect semantic parts based on their local appearance and treat semantic part detection as a step towards other vision tasks. For instance, fine-grained recognition works [16,33] localized semantic parts first to aggregate more accurate descriptions of objects for classification. [12] performed action recognition and attribute prediction by feeding the given object instance and detected semantic parts inside it into a classification engine. More recently, [14] proposed a deep model that is dedicated to detect semantic parts. It is the work most related to ours. However, although it detects both objects and parts simultaneously at test time, its ultimate goal is to leverage the detected objects as context to boost semantic part detection. In contrast, our work aims to show that object and semantic part detection can benefit mutually, *i.e.* object detection results can be also improved with additional part information.

2.3 LSTM Models

LSTM recurrent neural networks were originally introduced for sequence learning. They have been successfully applied to tasks such as speech recognition, and extended to multi-dimensional learning tasks such as optical character recognition [25,30], image captioning [17,28], and visual question answering [9,22]. LSTM networks can not only automatically learn short and long-range contextual information, but also naturally deal with variable number of inputs or outputs. In our work, since an object may interact with variable number of parts and vice versa, we adopt LSTM to generate a unified representation with variable number of inputs. Further more, we show that LSTM can also capture the dependencies between different spatial regions in a learnable manner and produce powerful feature representations.

3 The Proposed Method

In this section we present our framework for joint detection of objects and semantic parts. The framework is built upon Faster R-CNN [23] and composed of three main modules: (1) a two-stream CNN to extract features for both object proposals and semantic part proposals; (2) an interaction module that consists of relationship modeling and feature fusion components; (3) a region classification and regression module to produce the final detection results. The entire architecture is illustrated in Fig. 1. The details of each module will be introduced in the following subsections.

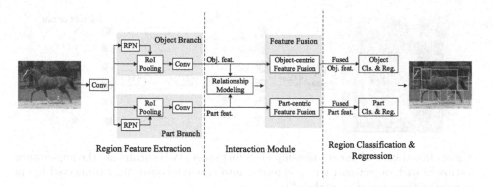

Fig. 1. The overview of our framework for joint object and semantic part detection. It is composed of a two-stream CNN to extract region features for both objects and semantic parts (Sect. 3.1), an interaction module to enhance features of both objects and parts under the guidance of learned relationship (Sect. 3.2) as well as a region classification and regression module to perform multi-way classification and box refinement (Sect. 3.3).

3.1 Feature Extraction Module

We propose a two-stream CNN to generate proposals and extract features for both objects and semantic parts based on the Faster R-CNN framework. Instead of applying two separated backbone networks to extract features for objects and parts respectively, our method shares the convolutional layers in the backbone network for time efficiency.

In each stream, we adopt a region proposal network (RPN) [23] to generate region proposals for either objects or semantic parts. Compared to traditional region proposal methods such as Selective Search [24] or EdgeBoxes [39], RPN is more efficient and effective via using deep features and anchor mechanism. Since semantic parts are usually small and varies in aspect-ratio, we run K-means clustering on training set bounding boxes to get the anchors for semantic parts, which makes it easier for the network to learn to predict well-localized proposals, as validated in [21].

The generated region proposals, together with the feature maps produced by the last convolutional layer, are fed into an RoI pooling layer to generate fixed dimensional feature representations. The pooled features are further transformed into lower dimensions (*i.e.* 4096-d) through two subsequent 1×1 convolutional layers. Their outputs are taken as the final feature representations of object proposals or part proposals, which are further fed into the following interaction module.

3.2 Interaction Module

Object and part features are complementary for detection in two aspect reasons:

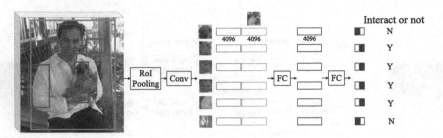

Fig. 2. Illustration of our relationship modeling stage. We concatenate the appearance feature of each object-part pair and feed it into two subsequent fully-connected layers to predict the interaction probability.

- Semantic parts concern more on local structures, leading to a high robustness to variations in viewpoint or pose. This property can benefit object detection especially when objects are suffering from occlusion or non-rigid deformation. Moreover, part information from different positions on objects improves the network's sensibility about the object layout, leading to better localization ability.
- Although high convolutional layers in CNNs can exploit the spatial context information due to their large receptive field, Zhou *et al.* [36] pointed out that the practical receptive field is actually smaller than the theoretical one. Thus it is appealing to explicitly encode the contextual object feature to bring more global information for part detection.

To make the object and part features benefit mutually, we need to address two problems as raised in Sect. 1. To this end, we divide our interaction module into two stages: the relationship modeling stage that aims to predict whether each pair of object proposal and part proposal is interacted or not, and the feature fusion stage that aims to fuse the features of an object proposal and its associated part proposals, as well as the features of a semantic part proposal and its associated objects.

Relationship Modeling. This stage is to predict whether an object proposal and a part proposal are interacted with each other or not. A straightforward condition to select candidate parts for an object is that the parts should lie within the object bounding box. Let $\mathcal{B}_I^p$ represent the set of part proposals in image I. b_k^o and b_j^p denote the k-th object proposal and j-th part proposal respectively. Then, we define the candidate parts that may interact with b_k^o as

$$\mathcal{B}_I^p(b_k^o, \tau_{out}) = \{b_j^p \mid b_j^p \in \mathcal{B}_I^p \ \& \ out(b_k^o, b_j^p) \leq \tau_{out}\}, \tag{1}$$

where $out(b_k^o, b_j^p)$ is a function for measuring how much the part's bounding box exceeds that of the object, and τ_{out} is a tolerance rate($\tau_{out} = 0.2$ in this paper, *i.e.* we allow the part's boundary to exceed the object's for 20% at most).

Given the candidate parts for each object, we formulate the relationship modeling problem as a binary classification task. As shown in Fig. 2, it concatenates the appearance feature of each object-part pair and feeds it into two fully-connected (FC) layers to predict the interaction probability. Cross entropy loss is employed to supervise the learning procedure. Note that we also tried to incorporate spatial information and classification scores of object and part into our module, but they did not bring much performance improvement. Thus, we keep using appearance feature only for simplicity.

During training, a pair of object-part proposal is considered as a positive example if both the object and the part have an Intersection over Union (IoU) overlap higher than 0.5 with their ground-truth boxes and meanwhile they belong to the same object instance. All the rest object-part pairs are treated as negative samples. Since there exists an extremely imbalance between positive and negative samples, optimizing the classification loss of all object-part pairs would bias towards negative samples. For this reason, we randomly sample 256 pairs in each image to compute the classification loss, where the sampled positive and negative examples have a ratio up to 1:3.

Feature Fusion. Once all the interacted object-part pairs are known, we perform feature fusion to enhance the representations of objects or parts. Particularly, the feature of an object proposal will be fused with that of all interacted parts, and the feature of a part will also be fused with all associated object proposals. We build our feature fusion stage on LSTM for three reasons: (1) An object proposal may interact with variable number of parts and vice versa. The LSTM network is naturally capable of handling inputs of variable length. (2) Different semantic parts should contribute differently to the associated object. For example, horse-head is much more discriminative then horse-leg, thus the former part should contribute more to a horse proposal in order to get a more discriminative feature. LSTM can estimate how much the current input contributes to the memory state through the input gate, which is suitable for our demand. (3) LSTM is capable of modeling the dependencies between its inputs, which can be exploited to capture the complex interaction between inertial parts or contextual objects and produce more representative features.

Figure 3 demonstrates the feature fusion stage. For object-centric feature fusion, assume that we want to fuse an object feature with M inertial parts. Let x_t represents the concatenated feature of the object and t-th part, which is the input to the LSTM at t-th time step. Let $W = \{(W_i^x, W_i^h, b_i), (W_f^x, W_f^h, b_f), (W_o^x, W_o^h, b_o), (W_c^x, W_c^h, b_c)\}$ parameterize the four gates of a LSTM unit, namely the input gate, the forget gate, the output gate and the memory cell gate respectively. Let σ and $tanh$ denote the sigmoid and the hyperbolic tangent activation functions respectively. The concatenated feature x_t with output feature from previous step h_{t-1}, is firstly transformed into a memory state space by

$$\tilde{c}_t = tanh(W_c^x x_t + W_c^h h_{t-1} + b_c), \tag{2}$$

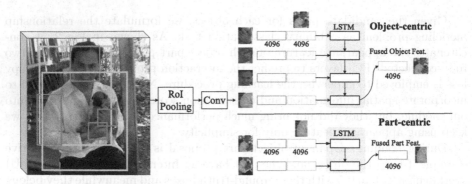

Fig. 3. Illustration of our feature fusion stage. We fuse the features of an object proposal and its associated part proposals (four parts in the above case) to enhance the object feature. Analogously, we fuse the features of a semantic part proposal and its associated objects (two objects in the above case) to enhance the part feature. The LSTM is adopted to handle variable number of input inertial parts or contextual objects.

where $\tilde{c}_t$ is the transformed feature and the memory state stores the information of object and all the previous parts. Then $\tilde{c}_t$ is combined with the old state c_{t-1} to produce the updated state c_t by weighted summation:

$$c_t = f_t \odot c_{t-1} + i_t \odot \tilde{c}_t, \tag{3}$$

where f_t is the output of the forget gate that determines how much information from previous feature should be preserved and i_t is the output of the input gate that determines how much the current input part should contribute to the new feature representation. f_t and i_t are computed by

$$f_t = \sigma(W_f^x x_t + W_f^h h_{t-1} + b_f), \tag{4}$$
$$i_t = \sigma(W_i^x x_t + W_i^h h_{t-1} + b_i). \tag{5}$$

Finally, after gathering the information of all parts, LSTM produces the fused object feature h_M by mapping the final state representation c_M to the output space:

$$h_M = o_M \odot tanh(c_M), \tag{6}$$

where $\odot$ denotes element-wise multiplication, o_M represents the activations of the output gate and is computed by

$$o_M = \sigma(W_o^x x_M + W_o^h h_{M-1} + b_o). \tag{7}$$

The fusion of a semantic part with all of its interacted object proposals is performed in an analogous way. Our LSTM-based feature fusion is superior as it not only learns to fuse the feature of an object-part pair at a single step, but also learns to aggregate the features from different steps to form a final enhanced representation.

3.3 Region Classification and Regression Module

Given the fused features, we perform region classification and regression for both objects and parts in two separate streams. In each stream, two sibling fully-connected layers are attached to the fused feature, one to predict the classification score for each category and the other to predict the per-class bounding box regression offsets. Cross-entropy and smooth L_1 loss are applied to train the classification and regression module respectively. In our paper, we directly employ the corresponding components in Faster R-CNN without any modifications.

4 Experiments

In this section, we first present an ablation study to investigate the effectiveness of our proposed method. Then, our approach is compared to other state-of-the-art methods.

4.1 Ablation Study

Dataset. The ablation study is conducted on PASCAL-Part [2], which has pixel-level part annotations for the images of PASCAL VOC 2010 [6]. We use the box annotations generated by [14], which fits a bounding box to each part segmentation mask and obtains a total of 105 part classes. We train our model on the *train* set and report test results on the *val* set (there is no annotated *test* data in PASCAL-Part).

Experimental Setup. Our model is implemented based on Faster R-CNN [1] in TensorFlow and VGG16 [26] is selected for feature extraction. We present three baseline models for comparison, which are the object baseline, the part baseline and the joint baseline. The object or part baseline model detects object or part by directly applying Faster R-CNN and using all default settings except that we replace the anchor boxes in part baseline by our clustered ones. The joint baseline model is constructed by removing the interaction module from our full model.

Training Details. To train the three baseline models, we follow the same training settings as Faster R-CNN. All the convolutional layers are initialized with weights trained on the ImageNet dataset [5] while the rest of layers, including those in the RPN as well as region classification and regression module, are initialized with [13]. SGD with mini-batch is used for training. The batch size is set to 1, the momentum is 0.9 and the weight decay is 0.0005. Training images are re-scaled so that their shorter side is 600 and no data augmentation except random flipping is applied. We use the default anchor boxes in RPN of object branch and the clustered ones ($K = 9$ in K-means clustering) in part branch.

Table 1. Object and part detection results on PASCAL-Part. * indicates using the default anchor boxes in RPN of part detection baseline.

Method	Object det. mAP(%)	Part det. mAP(%)
Object baseline	67.0	-
Part baseline*	-	42.1
Part baseline	-	46.5
Joint baseline	69.2	48.0
FC fusion	68.8	48.6
Full model	**69.7**	**50.1**

Table 2. PASCAL-Part val object detection average precision (%). 'Obj.' stands for the object baseline and 'Full.' stands for our full model.

Method	mAP	aero	bike	bird	boat	bottle	bus	car	cat	chair	cow	table	dog	horse	mbike	person	plant	sheep	sofa	train	tv
Obj.	67.0	83.4	78.2	74.4	40.3	51.4	81.3	73.6	85.7	37.0	64.3	39.5	84.9	77.8	78.5	75.4	39.7	73.7	49.3	77.4	73.8
Full.	69.7	85.7	78.8	76.7	45.9	52.4	84.8	74.9	88.1	37.2	68.5	43.5	85.2	79.2	81.6	77.1	45.5	79.0	54.1	81.7	73.1

We train the three baseline models for 70k iterations, with learning rate 10^{-3} for the first 50k iterations and 10^{-4} for the rest.

To train our full model, we follow nearly the same settings as the baseline models. The additional layers in the interaction module are initialized with [13]. We choose those object-part pairs with corresponding interaction probability higher than 0.5 to perform feature fusion. We feed the inertial parts and contextual objects into the LSTM in random order for object-centric and part-centric feature fusion respectively. We have also tried different input orders, but found little difference in performance. Our full model is trained for additional 20k iterations compared to the baseline due to more parameters.

Performance Comparison. We measure both object and part detection performance in terms of mean Average Precision (mAP), the same as the PASCAL VOC protocol [6], where a detection is considered to be true positive if its IoU with a ground-truth box is higher than 0.5. The detection performance of all models are presented in Table 1. Our object baseline achieves 67.0% mAP while part detection baseline only reaches 46.5% mAP with the same network architecture, which means part detection is a much more challenging task. Note that replacing the default anchor boxes with the clustered ones improves the part detection performance by 4.4% mAP, indicating that better box priors indeed lead to better predictions. So unless otherwise stated, we use the clustered anchor boxes for part detection in all our experiments. For object detection, the default anchor boxes in RPN are adopted as they are originally designed to fit the object scales in images.

By jointly training for object and part detection without any interaction, the joint baseline improves object detection performance by 2.2% mAP and

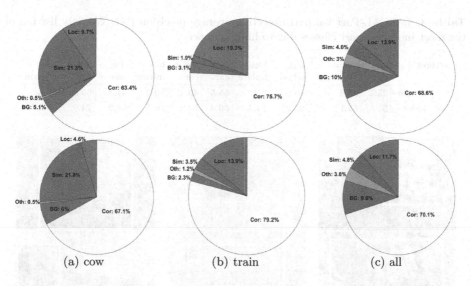

(a) cow   (b) train   (c) all

Fig. 4. False positive analysis: object baseline vs. full model. The first row represents the analysis results of the object baseline and the second shows those of our full model. The text indicates correct or type of error ('Loc' = Localization; 'Sim' = Similar; 'Oth' = Other; 'BG' = Background). Our full model mainly reduces the localization error (5.1% for cow, 5.4% for train and 2.2% on average).

part detection by 1.5% mAP, demonstrating that we can get more expressive representations by sharing the feature extraction step between object and part detection. When incorporating the interaction module, our proposed model consistently improves both object and part detection results (+0.5% mAP for object and +2.1% mAP for part compared to the joint baseline).

To further verify the effectiveness of our proposed feature fusion method, we conduct another experiment that replaces the LSTM feature fusion with a simpler one called *FC fusion*. It concatenates the appearance feature of each object-part pair and feeds them into two subsequent fully connected layers for feature reduction, then performs average pooling along the pair dimension to produce the fused object or part feature. The last two rows in Table 1 demonstrates that our LSTM-based feature fusion method is better than *FC fusion* method.

Detail Analysis. The detailed object detection results of both the object baseline and our full model are presented in Table 2. As we can see from the table, our full model surpasses the object baseline on all the class entries except *tv*. To further investigate how the part information benefits object detection, we use the methodology and tools of [15] to analyze the detailed breakdown of false positives on *val* set. Specifically, For each class, we look at the top N predictions, each of which is either correct (correct class, IoU > 0.5) or belongs to one of the following four types of errors:

Table 3. PASCAL-Part val part detection average precision (%). We only list ten of the most improved part classes due to limited space.

Method	cow leg	train headlight	bus wheel	bus liplate	cow ear	sheep ear	bus mirror	dog paw	horse ear	cow muzzle
Part baseline	25.4	36.9	56.8	3.4	55.5	43.2	10.2	41.4	65.3	69.8
Full model	53.5	55.1	68.2	14.3	66.4	53.9	20.5	51.2	74.9	78.0

Fig. 5. Example object detections of object baseline (blue) and our full model (red). All the predictions above have correct classes, our full model can fit objects more tightly (first row) and avoid duplicate predictions (second row), leading to less localization errors. (Color figure online)

- Localization: correct class, $0.1 < \text{IoU} < 0.5$
- Similar: confused with similar classes, $\text{IoU} > 0.1$
- Other: confused with dissimilar classes, $\text{IoU} > 0.1$
- Background: $\text{IoU} < 0.1$

We choose N to be the number of objects for each class and present the analysis results for two of the most improved classes: *cow* and *train*, together with the results on all 20 classes. As shown in Fig. 4, our full model mainly reduces the localization error. It indicates that our model can make the best of inertial parts to capture the part configuration in objects, leading to better sensing about the object boundary and improving the localization ability.

We also list the average precision for ten of the most improved parts in Table 3. As we can see, most of these parts belong to animals that share similar appearance, like {*cow, sheep, dog*}, and they are usually less discriminative than animal head. When detecting these semantic parts with part appearance feature only, the part classifier may get confused about the actual object class corresponding to the parts. With additional contextual object information, our full model can easily distinguish between *cow_ear* and *sheep_ear*, etc.

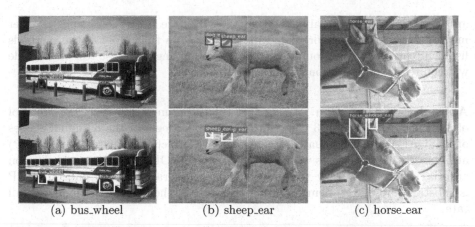

(a) bus_wheel   (b) sheep_ear   (c) horse_ear

Fig. 6. Example part detections of part baseline (first row) and our full model (second row). Our full model can exploit the contextual object information to improve part classification accuracy, it can also detect the part instance missed by part baseline model (see (c)).

Table 4. Comparison to other part detection methods. 'det.' means 'detection'. * indicates that the method uses object ground truth at test time. Note that our method requires no such additional information.

Dataset	PASCAL-Part			CUB200-2011	PASCAL VOC09	
Task	Animal part det.		General part det.	Bird part det.	Human part det.	
Measure	POP	PCP	mAP@0.5	PCP	mAP@0.3	mAP@0.5
Theirs	44.5* [2] 51.3 [14]	70.5* [2] **72.6** [14]	40.1 [14]	74.0* [34] 66.1 [34] 85.0* [19] 91.9 [14] 94.2* [33] 92.7* [14]	65.5 [14]	44.7 [14]
Ours	**59.4**	**72.1**	**46.0**	**95.5**	**75.3**	**63.6**

Example Detections. Figure 5 shows some object detection examples for both the object baseline and our full model. It appears that the baseline model is more likely to be affected by background (see first row, *e.g.* the train) or only focus on the discriminative part of an object (see first row, *e.g.* the sheep). With additional part information, our full model has better sensibility about the object layout and makes less duplicate predictions (see second row).

We also give some part detection examples for both the part baseline and our full model in Fig. 6. For each column, we only present detection results of a specific part class. Our full model can exploit the contextual object information to rectify the part class prediction results (Fig. 6(a), (b)). Moreover, it can also find the part instance missed by part baseline (Fig. 6(c)).

4.2 Comparison to Other Methods

We compare our full model to state-of-the-art methods on part detection task. We use Alexnet [18] as the backbone for animal, bird and human part detection and VGG16 [26] for general part detection, which are the same settings as other methods. All results are presented in Table 4. Note that most of the methods listed in this table use ground-truth object bounding boxes at test time while we require no such additional information.

Animal Part Detection. We conduct this experiment following the protocol of [2] (Sect. 4.3.3 of [2]). 3 parts (head, body and legs) of the 6 animal classes of PASCAL-Part are evaluated. Percentage of Correctly estimated Parts (PCP) and Percentage of Objects with Parts estimated (POP) are taken as evaluation criteria. The results show that our PCP is comparable to [14] and our POP is substantially better, demonstrating that our method has much higher recall rate.

General Part Detection. As we directly use the part annotations from [14], we compare our method with them on the 105 part classes. To make a fair comparison, We use the same VGG16 network for feature extraction and Fast R-CNN for region detection. Our approach outperforms [14] by a large margin(+5.9 mAP), which demonstrates that our LSTM-based method is more effective on part detection. Note that we only use the object feature to guide part detection in our full model while they also adopt object class score as additional information.

Bird Part Detection. We compare our approach to several fine-grained classification works [19,33,34] and the part detection work [14] on CUB200-2011 [29]. Two bird parts (head, torso) are evaluated and PCP is used as performance measurement. As shown in Table 4, our approach outperforms all other methods no matter they use ground-truth object bounding boxes or not at test time.

Human Part Detection. We compare to the part detection work [14] on human part detection following their experiment setting (Sect. 5.2 of [14]). Three human parts (head, torso and legs) are evaluated in terms of mAP. Our method surpasses [14] by a large margin. The performance gap nearly doubles when IoU threshold grows, indicating that our joint detection method has superior localization ability.

5   Conclusion

In this paper, we have presented a joint object and semantic part detection method that makes the two tasks beneficial to each other. Our method integrates an interaction module into a proposal-driven detection framework to perform the joint detection. This module includes two stages: in the *relationship modeling* stage, we decide whether a pair of object and part proposals should interact or not; in the *feature fusion* stage, we enhance object or part representation by fusing the features of inertial parts or contextual objects respectively.

Experiments on PASCAL-Part dataset and CUB200-2011 dataset have showed that our model can improve the object and part detection performance simultaneously.

Acknowledgment. This work was supported in part by the Natural Science Foundation of Zhejiang Province, China under Grant LY17F010007.

References

1. Chen, X., Gupta, A.: An implementation of faster RCNN with study for region sampling. arXiv preprint arXiv:1702.02138 (2017)
2. Chen, X., Mottaghi, R., Liu, X., Fidler, S., Urtasun, R., Yuille, A.L.: Detect what you can: detecting and representing objects using holistic models and body parts. In: CVPR (2014)
3. Chen, X., Yuille, A.L.: Articulated pose estimation by a graphical model with image dependent pairwise relations. In: NIPS (2014)
4. Dai, J., Li, Y., He, K., Sun, J.: R-FCN: object detection via region-based fully convolutional networks. In: NIPS (2016)
5. Deng, J., Dong, W., Socher, R., Li, L.J., Li, K., Fei-Fei, L.: ImageNet: a large-scale hierarchical image database. In: 2009 IEEE Conference on Computer Vision and Pattern Recognition, CVPR 2009, pp. 248–255. IEEE (2009)
6. Everingham, M., Van Gool, L., Williams, C.K., Winn, J., Zisserman, A.: The pascal visual object classes (VOC) challenge. Int. J. Comput. Vis. **88**(2), 303–338 (2010)
7. Felzenszwalb, P.F., Girshick, R.B., McAllester, D., Ramanan, D.: Object detection with discriminatively trained part-based models. IEEE Trans. Pattern Anal. Mach. Intell. **32**(9), 1627–1645 (2010)
8. Fischler, M.A., Elschlager, R.A.: The representation and matching of pictorial structures. IEEE Trans. Comput. **100**(1), 67–92 (1973)
9. Fukui, A., Park, D., Yang, D., Rohrbach, A., Darrell, T., Rohrbach, M.: Multimodal compact bilinear pooling for visual question answering and visual grounding. arXiv preprint arXiv:1606.01847 (2016)
10. Girshick, R.: Fast R-CNN. In: ICCV (2015)
11. Girshick, R., Iandola, F., Darrell, T., Malik, J.: Deformable part models are convolutional neural networks. In: CVPR (2015)
12. Gkioxari, G., Girshick, R., Malik, J.: Actions and attributes from wholes and parts. In: ICCV (2015)
13. Glorot, X., Bengio, Y.: Understanding the difficulty of training deep feedforward neural networks. In: Proceedings of the Thirteenth International Conference on Artificial Intelligence and Statistics, pp. 249–256 (2010)
14. Gonzalez-Garcia, A., Modolo, D., Ferrari, V.: Objects as context for detecting their semantic parts. In: CVPR (2018)
15. Hoiem, D., Chodpathumwan, Y., Dai, Q.: Diagnosing error in object detectors. In: Fitzgibbon, A., Lazebnik, S., Perona, P., Sato, Y., Schmid, C. (eds.) ECCV 2012. LNCS, vol. 7574, pp. 340–353. Springer, Heidelberg (2012). https://doi.org/10.1007/978-3-642-33712-3_25
16. Huang, S., Xu, Z., Tao, D., Zhang, Y.: Part-stacked CNN for fine-grained visual categorization. In: CVPR (2016)
17. Karpathy, A., Fei-Fei, L.: Deep visual-semantic alignments for generating image descriptions. In: CVPR, pp. 3128–3137

18. Krizhevsky, A., Sutskever, I., Hinton, G.E.: ImageNet classification with deep convolutional neural networks. In: NIPS (2012)
19. Lin, D., Shen, X., Lu, C., Jia, J.: Deep LAC: deep localization, alignment and classification for fine-grained recognition. In: CVPR (2015)
20. Ouyang, W., Wang, X., Zeng, X., Qiu, S., Luo, P., Tian, Y.: DeepID-net: deformable deep convolutional neural networks for object detection. In: CVPR (2015)
21. Redmon, J., Farhadi, A.: YOLO9000: better, faster, stronger. In: CVPR (2017)
22. Ren, M., Kiros, R., Zemel, R.: Exploring models and data for image question answering. In: NIPS (2015)
23. Ren, S., He, K., Girshick, R., Sun, J.: Faster R-CNN: towards real-time object detection with region proposal networks. In: NIPS (2015)
24. Van de Sande, K., Uijlings, J., Gevers, T., Smeulders, A.: Segmentation as selective search for object recognition. In: ICCV (2011)
25. Shi, B., Bai, X., Yao, C.: An end-to-end trainable neural network for image-based sequence recognition and its application to scene text recognition. IEEE Trans. Pattern Anal. Mach. Intell. **39**(11), 2298–2304 (2017)
26. Simonyan, K., Zisserman, A.: Very deep convolutional networks for large-scale image recognition. arXiv preprint arXiv:1409.1556 (2014)
27. Vedaldi, A., et al.: Understanding objects in detail with fine-grained attributes. In: CVPR (2014)
28. Vinyals, O., Toshev, A., Bengio, S., Erhan, D.: Show and tell: a neural image caption generator. In: CVPR (2015)
29. Wah, C., Branson, S., Welinder, P., Perona, P., Belongie, S.: The caltech-UCSD birds-200-2011 dataset CNS-TR-2011-001 (2011)
30. Wang, J., Hu, X.: Gated recurrent convolution neural network for OCR. In: NIPS (2017)
31. Wang, X., Bai, X., Yang, X., Liu, W., Latecki, L.J.: Maximal cliques that satisfy hard constraints with application to deformable object model learning. In: NIPS (2011)
32. Yang, Y., Ramanan, D.: Articulated pose estimation with flexible mixtures-of-parts. In: CVPR (2011)
33. Zhang, H., et al.: SPDA-CNN: unifying semantic part detection and abstraction for fine-grained recognition. In: CVPR (2016)
34. Zhang, N., Donahue, J., Girshick, R., Darrell, T.: Part-based R-CNNs for fine-grained category detection. In: Fleet, D., Pajdla, T., Schiele, B., Tuytelaars, T. (eds.) ECCV 2014. LNCS, vol. 8689, pp. 834–849. Springer, Cham (2014). https://doi.org/10.1007/978-3-319-10590-1_54
35. Zhang, Z., Xie, C., Wang, J., Xie, L., Yuille, A.L.: DeepVoting: a robust and explainable deep network for semantic part detection under partial occlusion. In: CVPR (2018)
36. Zhou, B., Khosla, A., Lapedriza, A., Oliva, A., Torralba, A.: Object detectors emerge in deep scene CNNs. arXiv preprint arXiv:1412.6856 (2014)
37. Zhu, L., Chen, Y., Yuille, A.L., Freeman, W.: Latent hierarchical structural learning for object detection. In: CVPR (2010)
38. Zhu, Y., Zhao, C., Wang, J., Zhao, X., Wu, Y., Lu, H.: CoupleNet: coupling global structure with local parts for object detection. In: ICCV (2017)
39. Zitnick, C.L., Dollár, P.: Edge boxes: locating object proposals from edges. In: Fleet, D., Pajdla, T., Schiele, B., Tuytelaars, T. (eds.) ECCV 2014. LNCS, vol. 8693, pp. 391–405. Springer, Cham (2014). https://doi.org/10.1007/978-3-319-10602-1_26

X-GACMN: An X-Shaped Generative Adversarial Cross-Modal Network with Hypersphere Embedding

Weikuo Guo[1] , Jian Liang[2,3] , Xiangwei Kong[4(✉)] , Lingxiao Song[2], and Ran He[2,3]

[1] Dalian University of Technology, Dalian, China
guoweikuo@mail.dlut.edu.cn
[2] University of Chinese Academy of Science (UCAS), Beijing, China
{jian.liang,lingxiao.song,rhe}@nlpr.ia.ac.cn
[3] CRIPAC and NLPR, CASIA, Beijing, China
[4] Zhejiang University, Hangzhou, China
kongxiangwei@zju.edu.cn

Abstract. How to bridge heterogeneous gap between different modalities is one of the main challenges in cross-modal retrieval task. Most existing methods try to tackle this problem by projecting data from different modalities into a common space. In this paper, we introduce a novel X-Shaped Generative Adversarial Cross-Modal Network (X-GACMN) to learn a better common space between different modalities. Specifically, the proposed architecture combines the process of synthetic data generation and distribution adapting into a unified framework to make sure the heterogeneous modality distributions similar to each other in the learned common subspace. To promote the discriminative ability, a new loss function that combines intra-modality angular softmax loss and cross-modality pair-wise consistent loss is further imposed on the common space, hence the learned features can well preserve both inter-modality structure and intra-modality structure on a hypersphere manifold. Extensive experiments on three benchmark datasets show the effectiveness of the proposed approach.

Keywords: Cross-modal retrieval · Generative adversarial network · Hypersphere embedding

1 Introduction

With the help of well-annotated large scale datasets and advancing machine learning techniques, the majority computer vision and pattern recognition tasks have achieved impressive performance, such as machine translation [32], image classification [44], and object detection [13]. However, real-world information often presented in more complex ways at the same time. Tasks that are aiming at solving more complicated problems such as image captioning [18] and visual

C. V. Jawahar et al. (Eds.): ACCV 2018, LNCS 11365, pp. 513–529, 2019.
https://doi.org/10.1007/978-3-030-20873-8_33

question answering [11] always involve more than one modality data form. Over the past few years, multi-modal learning has become a super hot topic with the increase of massive multi-modal data [37]. To make computing equipment understand the world better, representing and matching data from different modalities is crucial and remains challenging.

Data from different modalities are always quite different from each other. Taking image modality and text modality as an example, images are constituted by pixels and show more details while texts are presented in the form of word sequences which contain high-level semantic information. Such differences between different modalities are collectively known as the heterogeneous gap which is one of the most challenging problems to solve in cross-modal retrieval task. Many of existing cross-modal retrieval works try to solve this problem by projecting different modality data into a common space in which similarity between different modality data can be quantitatively measured. Various cross-modal mapping methods [3,12,23,34] with all kinds of common space constraint losses emerge in recent years have achieved noticeable improvement on the cross-modal retrieval task. However, these methods still suffer from the lacking of effective constraint in the common space, which declines the cross-modal retrieval performance.

To make the learned features intra-modality discriminative, the softmax loss is widely used in cross-modal retrieval task. However, softmax loss only learns separable features that are not discriminative enough. Previous works [23,34,39] combine softmax loss with other Euclidean distance based constraints to enhance the discrimination power of features. However, the features learned with original softmax loss have natural angular distribution. Directly combining Euclidean distance based constraint with softmax loss may destroy such angular distribution. To take full advantage of the angular distribution of the original softmax loss, [16,17] make efforts to learn angular distributed features with A-softmax or L-softmax and achieve success in face recognition task.

Inspired by these works above, in this paper, we leverage angular constraint in cross-modal retrieval task to learn angular distributed common space representation. By constraining the hypersphere embedding metric for each modality to be the same and adding cross-modality pair-wise consistent to the original A-softmax, the similarity between different modality representations can be evaluated on a uniformed hypersphere manifold. The proposed cross-modal A-softmax abandon the time-consuming negative instance sampling process in triplet ranking based constraint, which makes it has high computational efficiency and not relying too much on the annotation of data. Besides, to the best of our knowledge, this work is the first work that tries to solve cross-modal retrieval problem with angular constraint, and the experimental result shows the effectiveness of the newly designed cross-modal A-softmax method.

However, the task of cross-modal retrieval expects the learned features to be not only intra-modality discriminative but also inter-modality coherent. Therefore, we should find another constraint to narrow the heterogeneous gap between different modalities. The emergence of Generative Adversarial Networks (GANs)

[7] brings new ideas to many tasks. With the development of GANs, computing equipment can generate different kinds of data adversely. Attempts like generating images with captions [28], and generating captions with images [18] have already proved to be possible. Although these works have different tasks from cross-modal retrieval, they show new possibilities of cross-modal matching. In addition, to generate synthetic data, adversarial training is also widely used in tasks like domain adaption [33] because it can make distributions of the learned features becoming close to each other. The task of cross-modal retrieval also requires that the learned features from different modalities have the same distribution, which makes people intuitively think to use GANs to solve the cross-modal problem. Actually, attempts have already been made in the previous works [23,34] and some of them achieve impressive performance.

Our proposed method tries to combine the process of synthetic data generation and distribution adapting into a unified adversarial training framework to make the learned common space representations to be more modality invariant. A novel X-shaped Generate Adversarial Network (X-GACMN) architecture as shown in Fig. 1 is designed to achieve this. In the proposed X-GACMN model, we first assume that there exists an intermediate state in the middle of the process of cross-modality synthetic data generation. By constraining this intermediate state with adversarial training, we can obtain a common space for different modalities and the heterogeneous gap can be implicitly narrowed.

The contribution of this paper is mainly threefold,

1. An X-shaped generative adversarial cross-modal network (X-GACMN) is designed for cross-modality matching to ensure inter-modality coherent. With two generators to form an information loop and three discriminators to constrain the feature distribution, the correlation between different modalities is maximized and the heterogeneous gap is narrowed.
2. A novel common space angular constraint is applied to learn more intra-modality discriminative features in the common space. With the cross-modal A-softmax constraint, the learned common representations are angularly distributed and can be measured on a hypersphere manifold effectively.
3. Experimental results on three public benchmarks show that the proposed X-GACMN achieves competitive results compared with other state-of-the-art cross-modal retrieval approaches.

2   Related Work

2.1   Cross-Modal Retrieval with GAN

Cross-modal retrieval is the most common and basic task among tasks involve more than one modality. Briefly speaking, cross-modal retrieval aims to bridge the heterogeneous gap between different modalities. Most of the existing cross-modal retrieval method try to solve this by learning common representation and can be divided into two broad categories according to the type of the target representation. Binary representation learning is also called hashing method [3,12],

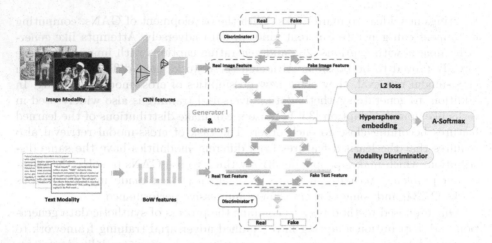

Fig. 1. The architecture of the proposed X-GACMN.

which aims to project original data or features from different modalities into a common hamming space. In the hamming space, the similarity between binary representations can be measured with hamming distance. These hashing methods have high computational efficiency, but sometimes at the cost of retrieval accuracy (effectiveness). The method this paper proposed falls into the other category called real-valued representation learning. Real value representing learning as [37] summarized can be divided into four subclasses: unsupervised [10, 20, 31], pairwise [25, 40, 41, 43], ranking-based [5, 8, 19, 30], and supervised [6, 35, 36, 38, 42] ones. Our approach is a supervised method with generative adversarial networks. Such combination can be seen in some recently published works [9, 23, 34]. In [34], a modality discriminator is directly applied to the learned multi-modal representations to discriminate generated representations from different modalities. The representations from different modalities get close to each other with adversarial learning. [23] involves intra-modality reconstruction constraint through appending discriminators to adversarially make reconstructed features getting close to original ones. Similar to our approach, the method [9] proposed also tries to use data from one modality to generate data from other modality. But their approach tries to use raw images to generate sentences whose performance could be constrained by the scale of the dataset.

Following but not limited to the works mentioned above, our X-GACMN has two generators to perform cross-modal generation. Three discriminators are appended to image feature space, text feature space and the learned common representation space to constrain cross-modal reconstruction and common representation learning process respectively.

2.2   Hypersphere Embedding

The idea of hypersphere embedding is first proposed in [16], and originally designed for face recognition. By modifying softmax loss to A-softmax loss, the original features can be constrained with an angular margin and obtain better recognition performance.

The original softmax loss is designed for classification tasks. Many works try to improve the original softmax loss to make it learn more discriminative features. L-softmax loss [17] also involves the concept of angle but it doesn't normalize the weights, thus the learned features are not constrained to hypersphere manifold and not suitable for open-set problems. Another modified method proposed in [39] combines softmax loss with Euclidean distance constraint by minimizing the distance between intra-class samples and the class center.

In cross-modal retrieval task, softmax loss is also widely used. Previous work like [23,34] combine softmax loss with Euclidean distance based triplet ranking loss to make the learned representations more semantically discriminative. However, it has been proved in [16,17] that the representations learned with original softmax loss have nature angular distribution, immediately combining Euclidean distance based constraint with softmax loss may destroy such angular distribution and cause bad influence.

In the proposed X-GACMN, we follow the above thinking and apply the angular constraint to cross-modal task and designed a cross-modal A-softmax to take full advantage of the angular constraint of softmax loss so as to enhance the retrieval performance.

3   Our Approach

As shown in Fig. 1, the network structure of the proposed X-GACMN is made up of two modules. The feature extracting module extracts original features $\mathcal{V}$ and $\mathcal{T}$ from image modality and text modality respectively. In this paper currently existing feature extracting methods such as CNN modal and BoW are applied. As for the feature projecting module, we will explain it in detail in the following subsections.

3.1   Notation

Without losing generality, we aim to conduct cross-modal representation learning on two modalities e.g., image and text. We assume there exists a multi-modal training dataset which is composed of image-text pairs, denoted as $D = \{(v,t)_i\}_{i=1}^{n}$ where $(v,t)_i$ represents the i-th instance of image-text pair and n is the total number of instances in the dataset. In addition, each instance is assigned a semantic category label $\{c_i\}_{i=1}^{n}$. After feature learning phase, instances can be represented by original features, and the dataset converts to $D = \{\mathcal{V}, \mathcal{T}\}$ where $\mathcal{V} = \{v_{o1}, \ldots, v_{on}\} \in \mathbb{R}^{d_v \times n}$ and $\mathcal{T} = \{t_{o1}, \ldots, t_{on}\} \in \mathbb{R}^{d_t \times n}$ denote the original feature matrixes of image and text respectively and d_v, d_t are the dimensions of the original features.

The original features $v_o \in \mathcal{V}$ and $t_o \in \mathcal{T}$ may follow different complex distributions and have different kinds of statistical properties and dimensions. Thus it is hard to compare them directly. Our primary goal is to find a common subspace $\mathcal{S}$ in which the features after projection is comparable so that the similarity between different modalities can be calculated. The mapping functions for each modality can be formulated as $f_{\mathcal{V}}(v_o; \theta_{\mathcal{V}})$ and $f_{\mathcal{T}}(t_o; \theta_{\mathcal{T}})$. After projection, the original features are transformed into $\mathcal{S}_{\mathcal{V}} \in \mathbb{R}^{d_c \times n}$ and $\mathcal{S}_{\mathcal{T}} \in \mathbb{R}^{d_c \times n}$, where d_c represents the dimension of the common representation. The ultimate goal of the proposed approach X-GACMN is to make $\mathcal{S}_{\mathcal{V}}$ and $\mathcal{S}_{\mathcal{T}}$ modality-invariant and semantically discriminative. To achieve this goal, we apply X-shaped GAN structure to establish an information loop between different modalities and cross-modal A-softmax to maintain the underlying semantic information on a hypersphere manifold.

3.2 X-Shaped Generative Adversarial Cross-Modal Network

X-shaped architectures can be found in some recently published cross-modal researches [2,9]. These X-shaped architectures maximize the correlation between two modality-specific feature spaces by projecting data from one modality into the common representation space and then using the projected common representations to reconstruct data from the other modality. By minimizing the reconstruction loss, the correlation between the two pathways can be maximized. Just like these works, the proposed X-GACMN applies two cross-modal generators G_I and G_T to accomplish the task of cross-modal feature generation. The ultimate goal of these two generators is twofold: (1) to maximize the similarity between the generalized synthetic data and the real data. (2) to make the distribution of the learned common representations in the middle of each generator as close as possible. To accomplish this, three discriminators D_I, D_T and D_C are applied to image feature space, text feature space and common representation space respectively. By training the discriminators and generators iteratively, these two kinds of modal can beat each other with a minimax game, and finally, make the features in the aforementioned three kinds of feature space modality-invariant.

Each generator in the proposed X-GACMN modal is composed by an encoder and a decoder. Original features v_o and t_o are projected to common representations v_c and t_c with encoder $G_{I_{enc}}$ and $G_{T_{enc}}$ respectively. Then the reconstruction representations v_r and t_r can be captured with $G_{I_{dec}}$ and $G_{T_{dec}}$ respectively. The three discriminators are of two kinds. Discriminators D_I and D_T are synthetic data discriminators which are designed to discriminate generated synthetic data from the real ones. The adversarial loss of them can formally be defined as:

$$\mathcal{L}_{D_I} = -\frac{1}{n_{tr}} \sum_{i=1}^{n_{tr}} \left(\log D_I \left(v_{o_i}; \theta_{D_I} \right) + \log \left(1 - D_I \left(v_{r_i}; \theta_{D_I} \right) \right) \right) \tag{1}$$

$$\mathcal{L}_{D_T} = -\frac{1}{n_{tr}} \sum_{i=1}^{n_{tr}} \left(\log D_T \left(t_{o_i}; \theta_{D_T} \right) + \log \left(1 - D_T \left(t_{r_i}; \theta_{D_T} \right) \right) \right) \tag{2}$$

where n_{tr} denotes the total number of instances in training set, θ_{D_I} and θ_{D_T} are the parameters of D_I and D_T respectively.

Discriminators D_C is a modality discriminator which is designed to discriminate projected representations v_c and t_c in the common space. The adversarial loss of D_C can be defined as:

$$\mathcal{L}_{D_C} = -\frac{1}{n_{tr}} \sum_{i=1}^{n_{tr}} \left(\log D_C \left(v_{ci}; \theta_{D_C} \right) + \log \left(1 - D_C \left(t_{ci}; \theta_{D_C} \right) \right) \right) \tag{3}$$

where θ_{D_C} are the parameters of D_C After discriminators D_I, D_T and D_C been optimized, generators G_I and G_T are optimized with θ_{D_I}, θ_{D_T} and θ_{D_C} fixed and the loss of them can be defined as following:

$$\mathcal{L}_{G_i} = \frac{1}{n_{tr}} \sum_{i=1}^{n_{tr}} \left(\log D_T \left(G_I \left(v_o; \theta_{G_I} \right) \right) + \log D_C \left(G_{I_{enc}} \left(v_o; \theta_{G_I} \right) \right) \right) \tag{4}$$

$$\mathcal{L}_{G_t} = \frac{1}{n_{tr}} \sum_{i=1}^{n_{tr}} \left(\log D_I \left(G_T \left(t_o; \theta_{G_T} \right) \right) + \log D_C \left(G_{T_{enc}} \left(t_o; \theta_{G_T} \right) \right) \right) \tag{5}$$

where θ_{G_i} and θ_{G_t} are the parameters of G_i and G_t respectively.

3.3   Common Space Constraint

In this work, we introduce an angular constraint to cross-modal retrieval task and make efforts to adjust it to the multi-modal scenario. The angular constraint ensures the projected representations with different semantic labels be discriminative on a hypersphere manifold. By projecting representations from different modalities onto the same hypersphere manifold, the heterogeneous gap between different modalities can be further narrowed. The proposed angular constraint abandons the time consuming negative sampling and distance calculation process in the Euclidean distance based triplet constraint, which makes it not only preserve the angular feature distribution but also have high computational efficiency without relying too much on the annotation of data. More detailed descriptions are followed in the remainder of this section.

The widely used original softmax loss can be written as

$$\mathcal{L}_{softmax} = \frac{1}{N} \sum_i -\log \left(\frac{e^{f_{y_i}}}{\sum_j e^{f_j}} \right) \tag{6}$$

where N is the number of training instances and f is the posterior probabilities of input feature x_i. The hypothesis function can be represented as $f_j = W_j^T x_i + b_j$ and $f_{y_i} = W_{y_i}^T x_i + b_j$ where W_j^T and $W_{y_i}^T$ denotes the j-th and y_i-th column of the weight metric of the last fully connected layer in the CNN modal. We can rewrite Eq. (6) as follows in angular form:

$$\mathcal{L}_{softmax} = \frac{1}{N} \sum_i -\log \left(\frac{e^{\|W_{y_i}^T\| \|x_i\| \cos(\langle W_{y_i}^T, x_i \rangle) + b_{y_i}}}{\sum_j e^{\|W_j^T\| \|x_i\| \cos(\langle W_j^T, x_i \rangle) + b_j}} \right) \tag{7}$$

where $\langle W_*^T, x_i \rangle$ is the angle between feature x_i and W_*^T.

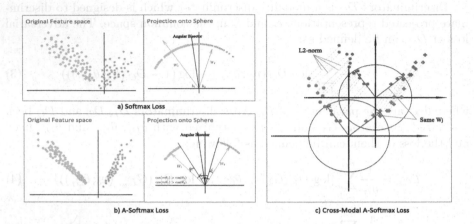

Fig. 2. A Comparison between softmax loss and A-softmax loss.

A-softmax makes ameliorate on the basis of the original softmax by firstly normalize $\|W_j^T\| = 1, \forall j$ and zero the biases, so that the original decision boundary for class i and class j can be presented in an angular margin form $\|x_i\| (\cos(\theta_i) - \cos(\theta_j))$, where θ_* is the angle between W_*^T and x_i. Secondly, A-softmax introduce a lower bound parameter m to quantitatively control the decision boundary and enhance the discrimination power. The decision boundary can be denoted as $\|x_i\| (\cos(m\theta_i) - \cos(\theta_j))$ and $\|x_i\| (\cos(\theta_i) - \cos(m\theta_j))$ for each class respectively. These two steps makes the features learned with A-softmax have angular margin and semantically discriminative. The A-softmax loss can be formulated as:

$$\mathcal{L}_{A-softmax} = \frac{1}{N} \sum_i - \log \left(\frac{e^{\|x_i\|\psi(\langle W_{y_i}^T, x_i \rangle)}}{e^{\|x_i\|\psi(\langle W_{y_i}^T, x_i \rangle)} + \sum_{j \neq y_i} e^{\|x_i\| \cos(\langle W_j^T, x_i \rangle)}} \right) \quad (8)$$

where

$$\psi(\langle W_{y_i}^T, x_i \rangle) = (-1)^k \cos(m \langle W_{y_i}, x_i \rangle) - 2k,$$
$$\langle W_{y_i}, x_i \rangle \in \left[\frac{k\pi}{m}, \frac{(k+1)\pi}{m} \right], k \in [0, m-1] \quad (9)$$

$\psi(\langle W_{y_i}^T, x_i \rangle)$ is a monotonically decreasing angle function which is generalized by expanding the definition range of $\cos(\langle W_{y_i}^T, x_i \rangle)$, $\langle W_{y_i}^T, x_i \rangle \in [0, \frac{\pi}{m}]$. $m \geqslant 1$ is an integer parameter that controls the size of angular margin. With bigger m narrower angular margin can be obtained. The difference between the original softmax loss and A-softmax can be seen in Fig. 2a and b.

The A-softmax has an intuitive hypersphere interpretation. Because A-softmax loss requires $\|W_j\| = 1, b_j = 0$, the original features are projected to a hypersphere manifold, on which the similarity between instances can be quantitatively evaluated by angle or the length of hyperarc. In our cross-modal task, we not only need to make sure instances with different semantic labels be discriminative but also expect items from different modalities can be quantitatively evaluated on the same manifold. Hance for different modalities, we use the same W_j to make sure the original features are projected to the same hypersphere manifold so that the heterogeneous gap between different modalities can be further narrowed. To maximize the correlation between two modalities while at the same time not destroying the inner modality angular distribution, an additional l_2 norm loss is added as a pair-wise consistent constraint to the common space to ensure the representations belong to the same image-text pairs as close as possible. A sketch map of the proposed constraint can be seen in Fig. 2c.

3.4 Loss Function and Optimization

The final objective functions for the generators G_I and G_T can be written as:

$$\mathcal{L}_{G_I} = \lambda_1 \mathcal{L}_{l_2} + \lambda_2 \mathcal{L}_{G_i} + \lambda_3 \mathcal{L}_{A-Softmax_i}, \tag{10}$$

$$\mathcal{L}_{G_T} = \lambda_1 \mathcal{L}_{l_2} + \lambda_2 \mathcal{L}_{G_t} + \lambda_3 \mathcal{L}_{A-Softmax_t}, \tag{11}$$

where λ_1, λ_2 and λ_3 are the weights of l_2 loss, generation loss and A-softmax loss respectively.

The process of optimizing the feature representation is conducted by optimizing the generator loss and the discriminator loss iteratively. The optimization goal of these two stage are opposite, which makes it a minimax game [7] of two sub-processes:

$$\arg\min \left(\mathcal{L}_{G_I} \left(\hat{\theta}_{G_I}, \hat{\theta}_{A-Softmax} \right) - \mathcal{L}_{D_T} - \mathcal{L}_{D_C} \right)$$
$$\arg\min \left(\mathcal{L}_{G_T} \left(\hat{\theta}_{G_T}, \hat{\theta}_{A-Softmax} \right) - \mathcal{L}_{D_I} - \mathcal{L}_{D_C} \right) \tag{12}$$

$$\arg\max \left(\mathcal{L}_{G_I} - \mathcal{L}_{D_T} \left(\hat{\theta_{D_T}} \right) - \mathcal{L}_{D_C} \left(\hat{\theta_{D_C}} \right) \right)$$
$$\arg\max \left(\mathcal{L}_{G_T} - \mathcal{L}_{D_I} \left(\hat{\theta_{D_I}} \right) - \mathcal{L}_{D_C} \left(\hat{\theta_{D_C}} \right) \right) \tag{13}$$

The overall training procedure is presented in Algorithm 1.

4   Experiments

We conduct experiments on three widely-used cross-modal datasets including Wikipedia dataset [24], NUS-WIDE-10k dataset [1] and Pascal Sentence dataset [26]. Comparisons with other state-of-the-art methods on these three datasets verify the effectiveness of our proposed X-GACMN. Additional ablation study and visualization results are presented in the later part in order to dissect our method in detail.

Algorithm 1. Pseudo code of optimizing our X-GACMN.

Require: $\mathcal{V}_{tr}, \mathcal{T}_{tr}$: Training data from both modality; N: Batch size; m, λ_*: hyperparameters;

update until X-GACMN converges:
1: $v_{c_i}, v_{r_i}, t_{c_i}, t_{r_i}$ are generated by G_I and G_T respectively.
2: Calculate loss of D_I, D_T and D_C with equation (1), (2) and (3) respectively.
3: Optimize D_I, D_T and D_C with equation(13))
4: **for** K steps **do**
5:     Calculate loss of G_I, G_T with equation (4) and (5)
6:     Optimize G_I and G_T with equation(12)
7: **end for**
8: **return** Modal parameter $\theta_{G_I}, \theta_{G_T}$ and common space feature $f_{\mathcal{V}}\left(v_o; \theta_{\theta_{G_I}}\right)$ and $f_{\mathcal{T}}\left(t_o; \theta_{G_T}\right)$.

4.1   Datasets and Experimental Setup

Datasets. In this subsection, we briefly introduce the three datasets and the corresponding features in the experiment.

Wikipedia is a widely used dataset for cross-modal retrieval which consists of 2173 training image-text pair and 693 testing image-text pair annotated by 10 semantic labels. In some works, another dataset partition is used by separate the dataset into 1300 training pairs and 1566 testing pairs. In our experiment, we conduct experiments on both partition protocols. 4096-D VGG-19 [29] features and 1000-D BoW features are used for image modality text modality respectively. Besides, for a fair comparison with earlier methods, we also conduct experiments with 128-D SIFT features and 10-D LDA features for each modality.

Pascal Sentence contains 1000 images with 20 semantic labels. Each image is described by 5 sentences. We divide this dataset into 900 training instances and 100 testing instances as [22,34] did, and use the same 4096-D VGG-19 features and 1000-D BoW features for image and text modality respectively.

NUS-WIDE-10k is constructed by sampling 10,000 image text pairs from 10 largest categories of NUS-WIDE without overlaps. Following [22,34], 8000 training pairs and 1000 testing pairs are used in our experiment and 4096-D VGG-19 features and 1000-D BoW features are used for each modality.

Implementation Details. The proposed X-GACMN modal realize feature projection and reconstruction with G_I and G_T which are composed of 6 fully connected layers with tanh as active function. The numbers of hidden units in each network are $V \rightarrow 512 \rightarrow 100 \rightarrow 100 \rightarrow 100 \rightarrow 512 \rightarrow T$ for G_I and $T \rightarrow 512 \rightarrow 100 \rightarrow 100 \rightarrow 100 \rightarrow 512 \rightarrow V$ for G_T. In the middle of each generator, the 100 dimensional output is the common subspace representation to be learned.

Synthetic data discriminator D_I and D_T with structure $V(T) \rightarrow 2000 \rightarrow 2$ are appended to discriminate generated synthetic data from real ones. Modality discriminator D_C with structure $100 \rightarrow 50 \rightarrow 2$ is appended to the common feature space to discriminate learned common space features' modal. An angular softmax layer with the same parameters is appended to both modalities to constrain the learned features to obey angular distribution.

As for hyper-parameters of the modal. The batch size is set to 64 and m is set to 5. λ_1, λ_2 and λ_3 are set to 10, 5 and 100 respectively to make sure the scale of each item balance.

4.2 Experimental Results

Comparison with State-of-the-Art Methods. We first compare our X-GACMN with 13 state-of-the-art methods on three datasets. We choose CCA [10], CCA-3V [6], LCFS [36], JRL [42], JFSSL [35], PACMR [14], SM [27] and SPGCM [15] as traditional cross-modal retrieval methods, Multimodal-DBN [31], Bimodal-AE [20], Corr-AE [4], and CMDN [21], as deep learning based methods and ACMR [34] as GAN based method.

Table 1. Cross-modal retrieval comparison in terms of the mAP on Wikipedia dataset

Protocol	Methods	Shallow feature			Deep feature		
		i2t	t2i	Avg.	i2t	t2i	Avg.
1300/1566 [36]	CCA	0.255	0.185	0.220	0.267	0.222	0.245
	M-DBN	0.149	0.150	0.150	0.204	0.183	0.194
	Bimodal-AE	0.236	0.208	0.222	0.314	0.290	0.302
	SPGCM	0.265	0.207	0.236	0.390	0.362	0.376
	SM	0.260	0.242	0.251	0.475	0.389	0.432
	CCA-3V	0.275	0.224	0.249	0.437	0.383	0.410
	LCFS	0.279	0.214	0.246	0.455	0.398	0.427
	Corr-AE	0.280	0.242	0.261	0.402	0.395	0.398
	JRL	0.344	0.277	0.311	0.453	0.400	0.426
	PACMR	0.318	0.224	0.271	0.468	0.429	0.449
	JFSSL	0.306	0.228	0.267	0.428	0.396	0.412
	CMDN	-	-	-	0.488	0.427	0.458
	ACMR	0.316	0.227	0.272	0.477	0.435	0.456
	X-GACMN	**0.348**	**0.282**	**0.315**	**0.490**	**0.456**	**0.473**
2173/693 [27]	SPGCM	0.254	0.203	0.228	0.351	0.327	0.339
	SM	0.255	0.226	0.205	0.479	0.384	0.431
	LCFS	0.266	0.209	0.238	0.455	0.417	0.436
	PACMR	0.309	0.220	0.264	0.478	0.433	0.456
	ACMR	0.310	0.223	0.267	0.476	0.431	0.454
	X-GACMN	**0.326**	**0.241**	**0.284**	**0.501**	**0.435**	**0.468**

Tables 1 and 2 shows the experimental results in terms of mAP on Wikipedia dataset, Pascal Sentence dataset and the NUS-WIDE-10k dataset. From the

Table 2. Cross-modal retrieval comparison in terms of the mAP on Pascal Sentence dataset and NUS-WIDE-10k dataset

Methods	Pascal sentence			NUS-WIDE-10k		
	i2t	t2i	Avg.	i2t	t2i	Avg.
CCA	0.363	0.219	0.291	0.189	0.188	0.189
M-DBN	0.477	0.424	0.451	0.201	0.259	0.230
Bimodal-AE	0.456	0.470	0.458	0.327	0.369	0.348
LCFS	0.442	0.357	0.400	0.383	0.346	0.365
Corr-AE	0.489	0.444	0.467	0.366	0.417	0.392
JRL	0.504	0.489	0.496	0.426	0.376	0.401
CMDN	0.534	0.534	0.534	0.492	0.515	0.504
ACMR	**0.535**	0.543	0.539	0.447	0.505	0.476
X-GACMN	0.532	**0.547**	**0.540**	**0.501**	**0.526**	**0.514**

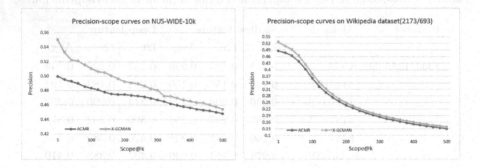

Fig. 3. Precision-scope curves on Wikipedia dataset and NUS-WIDE-10k dataset

results we have the following observations: (1) The proposed X-GACMN outperforms other methods with a big margin on these three datasets. Experimental results on these three datasets which have very distinct properties can testify the effectiveness of the proposed X-GACMN. (2) On Wikipedia dataset, we conduct experiments with shallow features and deep features on two different partition protocols. The performance of the proposed X-GACMN achieves best results with all these four different settings, which can prove the applicability of our method. (3) Compared with our best competitor ACMR which is also a GAN based method, our method obtained better results. This can preliminary shows the superiority of the proposed X-shaped GAN architecture and cross-modal A-softmax. More detailed comparison and analysis of these two methods are in the following subsections. (4) The performance on the Pascal Sentence dataset only be slightly improved, this is mainly because that the training data in Pascal Sentence dataset is limited in number and the X-GACMN model sufferers from

Table 3. Cross-modal retrieval comparison with different loss setting on Wikipedia dataset (1300/1766) in terms of the mAP@50

Methods	t2i	i2t	Avg.
X-GACMN without D_C	0.615	0.477	0.546
X-GACMN without D_I and D_T	0.618	0.482	0.550
X-GACMN without $\mathcal{L}_{A-Softmax}$	0.218	0.188	0.203
X-GACMN without $\mathcal{L}_{l_2}$	0.632	0.472	0.552
X-GACMN with $\mathcal{L}_{Softmax}$	0.598	0.467	0.533
Whole X-GACMN	**0.640**	**0.483**	**0.562**

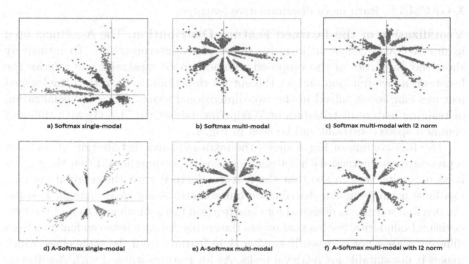

a) Softmax single-modal   b) Softmax multi-modal   c) Softmax multi-modal with l2 norm

d) A-Softmax single-modal   e) A-Softmax multi-modal   f) A-Softmax multi-modal with l2 norm

Fig. 4. The visualization result on Wikipedia dataset (1300/1766).

the overfitting problem, while in the large-scale dataset NUS-WIDE-10k, such problem is mitigated and the performance of our modal is sorted.

To further compare our method with the other GANs based method ACMR [34], we draw precision-scope curves on Wikipedia dataset and NUS-WIDE-10k dataset for additional comparison. The results can be seen in Fig. 3 From the curves we can see that our method outperforms ACMR with all scopes especially when the scopes are small. In real life retrieval scenario, we are more concern about the previous recalls, which means our method is significant in practical applications.

Ablation Study. In this section, we will discuss the effectiveness of each element in the X-GACMN modal. Table 3 summarizes the mAP@50 scores on Wikipedia dataset (2173/693) with different settings. To verify the effectiveness of the three adversarial training processes, we remove two kinds of discriminators respectively. From the first two lines, we can observe that the mAP@50 score drops when the synthetic data discriminators or the modality discriminator is missing, which proves by training the modal adversely with the X-shaped architecture, a better common feature space can be learned.

Line 3, 4, 5 and 6 show the results with different common space constraint loss function. From line 3, we can see that without A-softmax loss the performance drops significantly, which is because the modal is trained unsupervisely without any semantic information. Line 4 shows the experimental results without l_2 norm loss, from the results we can see that the l_2 norm loss as a cross-modal pairwise consistent constraint can improve the performance slightly. To compare the effectiveness of cross-modal A-softmax loss with the original softmax loss, we trained our model with original softmax and the results can be seen in line 5. From the results, we can see that cross-modal A-softmax is beneficial for the X-GACMN to learn more discriminative features.

Visualization of the Learned Feature Distribution. The A-softmax used in our X-GACMN has an intuitive hypersphere interpretation. To intuitively show the properties of the proposed common space constraint, we remove the last tanh active function and set the output dimension to 2, so that the learned features can be visualized in the two-dimensional space. The 2-D visualization of training feature distribution of Wikipedia dataset (2173/693) with different common space constraint can be seen in Fig. 4.

The first column of Fig. 4 shows the intra-modality distribution of common representations learned with softmax loss and A-softmax loss. From the visualization results, we can see that the features learned with the original softmax loss have natural angular distribution but sometimes not clear enough. Besides, the original softmax is designed for classification tasks which aim to find the best decision boundaries. Such a goal makes the cosine distance between features from different classes not necessarily smaller than features from the same class, which makes it not suitable for retrieval tasks. As for features learned with A-softmax, clear angular distributed margins between different classes can be seen. Such property ensures the learned features intra-modality discriminative.

The second and the third column of Fig. 4 shows the inter-modality visualization result. The difference between column 2 and column 3 is whether l_2 loss is applied or not. We can see that features obtained with A-softmax retain the inter-modality angular margin. This is because in our X-GACMN, features from different modalities are projected to a common hypersphere manifold with the same angular constraint. Another observation is by combining l_2 norm with A-softmax, the discrepancy between two different modalities is further diminished, which is because that by constraining distance of features belong to the same image-text pairs, the inter-modality structure can be preserved.

5   Conclusion

In this paper, we proposed a new X-shaped Generative Adversarial Cross-Modal Network (X-GACMN) to learn better common space representations for cross-modal retrieval. Firstly, the proposed X-GACMN designed an X-shaped GAN architecture to combine cross-modal synthetic data generation and distribution adaption together with adversarial training. Secondly, the proposed X-GACMN for the first time exploited the angular constraint in cross-modal retrieval task to increase the discriminative ability of the learned features. With the X-shaped architecture and A-softmax, original features from different modalities are projected to a common hypersphere manifold on which the similarities between instances can be quantitatively evaluated by the magnitude of angle. Extensive experiments on three widely used cross-modal datasets and a detailed analysis of the experimental results demonstrate the effectiveness of our method.

Acknowledgement. We would like to thank anonymous reviewers for their helpful comments on the paper. This research was supported by the National Natural Science Foundation of China (NSFC) under Grant 61772111.

References

1. Chua, T.S., Tang, J., Hong, R., Li, H., Luo, Z., Zheng, Y.: NUS-WIDE: a real-world web image database from national University of Singapore. In: Proceedings of the CIVR, pp. 48:1–48:9 (2009)
2. Eisenschtat, A., Wolf, L.: Linking image and text with 2-way nets. In: Proceedings of the CVPR, pp. 4601–4611 (2017)
3. Erin Liong, V., Lu, J., Tan, Y.P., Zhou, J.: Cross-modal deep variational hashing. In: Proceedings of the ICCV, pp. 4077–4085 (2017)
4. Feng, F., Wang, X., Li, R.: Cross-modal retrieval with correspondence autoencoder. In: Proceedings of the ACM MM, pp. 7–16 (2014)
5. Frome, A., et al.: Devise: a deep visual-semantic embedding model. In: Proceedings of the NIPS, pp. 2121–2129 (2013)
6. Gong, Y., Ke, Q., Isard, M., Lazebnik, S.: A multi-view embedding space for modeling internet images, tags, and their semantics. IJCV **106**(2), 210–233 (2014)
7. Goodfellow, I.J., et al.: Generative adversarial nets. In: Proceedings of the NIPS, pp. 2672–2680 (2014)
8. Grangier, D., Bengio, S.: A discriminative kernel-based approach to rank images from text queries. IEEE TPAMI **30**(8), 1371–1384 (2008)
9. Gu, J., Cai, J., Joty, S.R., Niu, L., Wang, G.: Look, imagine and match: improving textual-visual cross-modal retrieval with generative models. In: Proceedings of the CVPR, pp. 7181–7189 (2018)
10. Hardoon, D.R., Szedmak, S., Shawe-Taylor, J.: Canonical correlation analysis: an overview with application to learning methods. Neural Comput. **16**(12), 2639–2664 (2004)
11. Hu, R., Andreas, J., Rohrbach, M., Darrell, T., Saenko, K.: Learning to reason: end-to-end module networks for visual question answering. In: Proceedings of the ICCV, pp. 804–813 (2017)
12. Jiang, Q.Y., Li, W.J.: Deep cross-modal hashing. In: Proceedings of the CVPR, pp. 3270–3278 (2017)
13. Li, Y., Zhang, J., Huang, K., Zhang, J.: Mixed supervised object detection with robust objectness transfer. IEEE TPAMI **99**, 1–18 (2018)
14. Liang, J., Cao, D., He, R., Sun, Z., Tan, T.: Principal affinity based cross-modal retrieval. In: Proceedings of the ACPR, pp. 126–130 (2015)
15. Liang, J., He, R., Sun, Z., Tan, T.: Group-invariant cross-modal subspace learning. In: Proceedings of the IJCAI, pp. 1739–1745 (2016)

16. Liu, W., Wen, Y., Yu, Z., Li, M., Raj, B., Song, L.: SphereFace: deep hypersphere embedding for face recognition. In: Proceedings of the CVPR, pp. 212–220 (2017)
17. Liu, W., Wen, Y., Yu, Z., Yang, M.: Large-margin softmax loss for convolutional neural networks. In: Proceedings of the ICML, pp. 507–516 (2016)
18. Lu, J., Xiong, C., Parikh, D., Socher, R.: Knowing when to look: adaptive attention via a visual sentinel for image captioning. In: Proceedings of the CVPR, pp. 3242–3250 (2017)
19. Lu, X., Wu, F., Tang, S., Zhang, Z., He, X., Zhuang, Y.: A low rank structural large margin method for cross-modal ranking. In: Proceedings of the SIGIR, pp. 433–442 (2013)
20. Ngiam, J., Khosla, A., Kim, M., Nam, J., Lee, H., Ng, A.Y.: Multimodal deep learning. In: Proceedings of the ICML, pp. 689–696 (2011)
21. Peng, Y., Huang, X., Qi, J.: Cross-media shared representation by hierarchical learning with multiple deep networks. In: Proceedings of the IJCAI, pp. 3846–3853 (2016)
22. Peng, Y., Qi, J., Huang, X., Yuan, Y.: CCL: cross-modal correlation learning with multi-grained fusion by hierarchical network. IEEE TMM **20**(2), 405–420 (2017)
23. Peng, Y., Qi, J., Yuan, Y.: CM-GANs: cross-modal generative adversarial networks for common representation learning. arXiv preprint arxiv:1710.05106 (2017)
24. Pereira, J.C., et al.: On the role of correlation and abstraction in cross-modal multimedia retrieval. IEEE TPAMI **36**(3), 521–535 (2014)
25. Quadrianto, N., Lampert, C.H.: Learning multi-view neighborhood preserving projections. In: Proceedings of the ICML, pp. 425–432 (2011)
26. Rashtchian, C., Young, P., Hodosh, M., Hockenmaier, J.: Collecting image annotations using Amazon's mechanical turk. In: NAACL HLT 2010 Workshop on Creating Speech and Language Data with Amazon's Mechanical Turk, pp. 139–147 (2010)
27. Rasiwasia, N., et al.: A new approach to cross-modal multimedia retrieval. In: Proceedings of the ACM MM, pp. 251–260 (2010)
28. Reed, S., Akata, Z., Yan, X., Logeswaran, L., Schiele, B., Lee, H.: Generative adversarial text to image synthesis. In: Proceedings of the ICML, pp. 1060–1069 (2016)
29. Simonyan, K., Zisserman, A.: Very deep convolutional networks for large-scale image recognition. arXiv preprint arxiv:1409.1556 (2014)
30. Socher, R., Karpathy, A., Le, Q.V., Manning, C.D., Ng, A.Y.: Grounded compositional semantics for finding and describing images with sentences. Trans. Assoc. Comput. Linguist. **2**(1), 207–218 (2014)
31. Srivastava, N., Salakhutdinov, R.R.: Multimodal learning with deep Boltzmann machines. In: Proceedings of the NIPS, pp. 2639–2664 (2012)
32. Su, J., Zeng, J., Xiong, D., Liu, Y., Wang, M., Xie, J.: A hierarchy-to-sequence attentional neural machine translation model. IEEE TASLP **26**(3), 623–632 (2018)
33. Tzeng, E., Hoffman, J., Saenko, K., Darrell, T.: Adversarial discriminative domain adaptation. In: Proceedings of the CVPR, pp. 2962–2971 (2017)
34. Wang, B., Yang, Y., Xu, X., Hanjalic, A., Shen, H.T.: Adversarial cross-modal retrieval. In: Proceedings of the ACM MM, pp. 154–162 (2017)
35. Wang, K., He, R., Wang, L., Wang, W., Tan, T.: Joint feature selection and subspace learning for cross-modal retrieval. IEEE TPAMI **38**(10), 2010–2023 (2016)
36. Wang, K., He, R., Wang, W., Wang, L., Tan, T.: Learning coupled feature spaces for cross-modal matching. In: Proceedings of the ICCV, pp. 2088–2095 (2013)
37. Wang, K., Yin, Q., Wang, W., Wu, S., Wang, L.: A comprehensive survey on cross-modal retrieval. arXiv preprint arxiv:1607.06215 (2016)

38. Wang, W., Yang, X., Ooi, B.C., Zhang, D., Zhuang, Y.: Effective deep learning-based multi-modal retrieval. VLDBJ **25**(1), 79–101 (2016)
39. Wen, Y., Zhang, K., Li, Z., Qiao, Y.: A discriminative feature learning approach for deep face recognition. In: Leibe, B., Matas, J., Sebe, N., Welling, M. (eds.) ECCV 2016. LNCS, vol. 9911, pp. 499–515. Springer, Cham (2016). https://doi.org/10.1007/978-3-319-46478-7_31
40. Yuan, Z., Sang, J., Liu, Y., Xu, C.: Latent feature learning in social media network. In: Proceedings of the ACM MM, pp. 253–263 (2013)
41. Zhai, D., Chang, H., Shan, S., Chen, X., Gao, W.: Multiview metric learning with global consistency and local smoothness. ACM Trans. Intell. Syst. Technol. **3**(3), 53:1–53:22 (2012)
42. Zhai, X., Peng, Y., Xiao, J.: Learning cross-media joint representation with sparse and semisupervised regularization. IEEE TCSVT **24**(6), 965–978 (2014)
43. Zhai, X., Peng, Y., Xiao, J.: Heterogeneous metric learning with joint graph regularization for cross-media retrieval. In: Proceedings of the AAAI, pp. 1198–1204 (2013)
44. Zhu, L., Chen, Y., Ghamisi, P., Benediktsson, J.A.: Generative adversarial networks for hyperspectral image classification. IEEE TGARS **56**(9), 5046–5063 (2018)

Reverse Densely Connected Feature Pyramid Network for Object Detection

Yongjian Xin[1,3], Shuhui Wang[1(✉)], Liang Li[1], Weigang Zhang[2,3], and Qingming Huang[3]

[1] Key Laboratory of Intelligent Information Processing (CAS),
Institute of Computing Technology, CAS, Beijing 100190, China
yongjian.xin@vipl.ict.ac.cn, {wangshuhui,liang.li}@ict.ac.cn
[2] School of Computer Science and Technology, Harbin Institute of Technology,
Weihai 264209, China
wgzhang@hit.edu.cn
[3] University of Chinese Academy of Sciences, Beijing 100049, China
qmhuang@ucas.ac.cn

Abstract. The wide and extreme diversity of object size is an ever-lasting challenging issue in object detection research. To address this problem, we propose Reverse Densely Connected Feature Pyramid Network (Rev-Dense FPN), a novel multi-scale feature transformation and fusion method for object detection. Through reverse dense connection, we directly fuse all the feature maps of higher levels than the current one. This avoids useful contextual information on the higher level to vanish when passed down to lower levels, which is a key disadvantage of widely used feature fusion paradigms such as recursive top-down connection. Therefore, a more powerful hierarchical representation structure can be obtained by effectively aggregating multi-level contexts. We apply Rev-Dense FPN on SSD framework, which reaches 81.1% mAP (mean average precision) on the PASCAL VOC 2007 dataset and 31.2 AP on the MS COCO dataset. The results show that Rev-Dense FPN is more effective in dealing with diversified object sizes.

Keywords: Object detection · Convolutional neural networks · Feature pyramid

1 Introduction

Object detection is one of the key techniques for significant applications in vision research, such as autonomous driving, intelligent video surveillance, and so on. Due to the prevalence of deep convolutional neural networks (CNNs), recent years have witnessed a remarkable progress in object detection literature. Following either the two-stage paradigm stemming from the R-CNN [7] and Faster R-CNN [26] series, or the one-stage framework stemming from YOLO [24] and SSD [21], endeavors have been devoted to improving detection performance.

© Springer Nature Switzerland AG 2019
C. V. Jawahar et al. (Eds.): ACCV 2018, LNCS 11365, pp. 530–545, 2019.
https://doi.org/10.1007/978-3-030-20873-8_34

Among these efforts, a critical class of approaches [15,18,21,28] are proposed to deal with the multi-scale problem caused by a wide and extreme diversity of object sizes, which is an ever-lasting challenging issue in object detection.

Generally, existing works are naturally conducted on the basis of multi-scale detection frameworks, *i.e.*, multi-scale single stage detectors like SSD or multi-scale variants of Faster R-CNN. Then feature fusion techniques are developed to enhance low-level features for small objects, such as FPN [18], TDM [28], FSSD [17], etc. The main idea of these approaches is to recursively fuse deeper-layer features onto shallower layers, making lower-level features more discriminative and boosted by contextual information. However, for a complicated image with multiple objects of different scales, it is hard to determine which upper-layer features above the current layer are helpful. The recursive top-down connection which is widely used in existing model solutions such as FPN or TDM may cause the useful information from higher level to vanish along the layer-by-layer propagation path, which makes it hard for lower-level features to benefit from the contexts delivered by upper-layer features. To address this problem, in this paper, we propose Reverse Densely Connected Feature Pyramid Network (Rev-Dense FPN), a novel multi-scale feature fusion method which obtains feature pyramid by reverse dense connections.

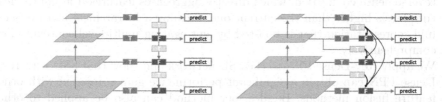

Fig. 1. The recursive top-down connection used in [18,28] (left) vs. the proposed reverse dense connection (right). T denotes a learnable layer and F denotes fusion operation. Different colors of modules indicate different functions. In the left part, blue Ts are lateral layers while yellow ones are top-down layers. The fusion operation F is element-wise addition for FPN and concatenation for TDM. In the right part, blue Ts are layers for adjusting the receptive fields while the yellow ones are layers for channel reduction. F is concatenation. (Color figure online)

As shown in the right part of Fig. 1, for each level of layer, a reverse dense connection directly aggregates features from all the upper-level layers. Through this type of connection, it avoids the aforementioned problem of recursive connection that higher-level contextual information may vanish as it is passed recursively to the lower levels. Since we concatenate several higher-level feature maps with increasing receptive fields, the representation obtained for the current level is highly hierarchical and contains rich multi-level conditional information, thus it tends to be more capable of dealing with the diversified object sizes. Moreover, by applying direct linking, the reverse dense connection also makes information flow forward and backward more smoothly through the network, so that the optimization of deep model parameters can be more sufficient. In our work, we choose a set of feature maps from the backbone network and apply reverse dense connection for each of them. This will generate a new set of feature maps which are taken as our final feature pyramid for the consequent operations. The corresponding feature pyramid transformation is denoted as Rev-Dense FPN since reverse dense connection is the major operation for construction of such pyramidal representation.

We apply Rev-Dense FPN to the SSD detection framework and show that SSD with Rev-Dense FPN can obtain a significant performance gain compared with the original SSD baseline as well as other feature fusion methods. Reaching higher accuracy, our method only suffers a small speed drop. We conduct object detection experiments on the PASCAL VOC 2007 dataset [5] and the MS COCO dataset [20]. Results demonstrate the effectiveness and efficiency of the proposed Rev-Dense FPN. Using only the moderate-sized VGG16 [29] network as backbone, our approach obtains 81.1% mAP on the PASCAL VOC 2007 dataset and 31.2 AP on the MS COCO dataset, outperforming a number of multi-scale feature fusion methods as well as some state-of-the-art detectors.

Our main contributions can be summarized as follows:

- We propose Rev-Dense FPN, a multi-scale feature fusion method based on reverse dense connection, which directly aggregates features from all the feature levels higher than the current one, forming a hierarchical feature pyramid representation that is boosted by aggregating multi-level contexts more comprehensively.
- We apply Rev-Dense FPN to the SSD network and show that SSD with Rev-Dense FPN can obtain a significant performance gain compared with other feature fusion methods. Besides, our method can also be applied to other state-of-the-art object detection frameworks.
- Experimental results demonstrate the effectiveness and efficiency of the proposed Rev-Dense FPN on the PASCAL VOC 2007 dataset and the MS COCO dataset.

2   Related Work

2.1   Two General Frameworks for Object Detectors

One-Stage Detectors. One-stage detector, also called single-stage detector, can be termed as a more powerful class-aware Region Proposal Network (RPN) [26]. Typical works for one-stage detectors include SSD [21], DSSD [6], YOLO v2 [25], RON [14], RetinaNet [19] and so on. Taking a resized image as input, the detector runs in a fully-convolutional manner. Through one forward pass, the detector outputs category probabilities and bounding box offsets for all pre-defined anchors, which are then interpreted and post-processed by removing duplicate boxes. One-stage detectors are usually endowed with relatively faster speed, but with lower potential of accuracy.

Two-Stage Detectors. Another paradigm for CNN-based object detectors is introduced by the R-CNN [7] and Faster R-CNN [26] series, which are called two-stage detectors. Typical works are SPPNet [10], ION [1], R-FCN [3], Mask R-CNN [8], Light-Head R-CNN [16], etc. These detectors first generate a sparse set of candidate boxes (*i.e.*, object proposals or region proposals) via a fully convolutional class-agnostic weak detector, *i.e.*, the Region Proposal Network. Then the generated proposals are processed by a head subnet that classifies these proposals and offsets their locations. Because the feature for each Region-of-Interest (RoI) is better aligned and more fine-grained than the single-stage framework, two-stage approaches usually get high accuracy. The weakness of two-stage methods is their relatively lower detection efficiency.

2.2 Multi-scale Feature Fusion

Detecting objects of a wide range of scales has long been a difficult problem. Before the advent of multi-scale detection frameworks, there have been algorithms that fuse features from different layers to build "hyper-feature map". These methods typically choose one single feature map with the most appropriate spatial scale, pick some features from other layers (often higher-level layers) and then fuse them together to construct the final feature map on which the detection task happens. Such operations have been applied on HyperNet [15], MS-CNN [2] and PVANET [12].

Since a single feature map is hard to cover objects of various scales, there come up multi-scale detectors like SSD and multi-scale Faster R-CNN. Under multi-scale detection frameworks, the feature used for detecting objects is naturally a feature pyramid. Objects with different scales are respectively distributed onto the corresponding levels of the feature pyramid. To enhance pyramidal representation for multi-scale detection, there are several works based on feature pyramid transformation.

Feature Pyramid Network (FPN) [18] is the first work that performs feature pyramid transformation to get better features, especially for the early stage feature maps to which small objects are assigned. The main idea of FPN is to recursively fuse the more discriminative and semantically consistent features from higher levels onto the current one. Through the aggregation, objects assigned to lower levels are better detected. However, FPN uses element-wise addition as its fusion manner, which can make features to be highly miscellaneous. Instead of element-wise addition, TDM [28] uses concatenation to fuse higher level features. But to avoid information loss, TDM keeps a large channel number when applying concatenation, making it computationally inefficient. TDM also keeps recursive linking as used in FPN. This may cause higher-level information to diminish when it is propagated top-down, especially when there are relatively more feature levels. Besides FPN and TDM, FSSD [17] involves another fusion manner which takes some levels in early stages with relatively larger spatial scales and fuses them together, then down-samples the fused feature map to get higher pyramid levels. FSSD is concise and lightweight, but it suffers the drawback of early-stage fusion, which will limit the capacity of the representation.

Additionally, there are also works based on reorganizing features, like STDN [23]. STDN expands a group of smaller feature maps to a larger plane. Since it uses DenseNet [13] as its backbone network which naturally combines features from previous layers, explicit feature aggregation across different layers is not used.

3   Rev-Dense FPN

3.1   Reverse Dense Connection

For convenience of illustration, we first formulate the mechanism of multi-scale detectors (with feature pyramid transformation) as follows:

Given n feature maps of decreasing spatial scales $\mathbf{C} = \{C_i\}_{i=1}^n$ chosen from the backbone network, a group of transformations $\mathbf{\Phi} = \{\phi_i\}_{i=1}^n$ is then conducted on $\mathbf{C}$ to yield a feature pyramid $\mathbf{P} = \{P_i\}_{i=1}^n$. For each ϕ_i, it takes a subset of $\mathbf{C} \cup \{P_k\}_{k=i+1}^n$ as input and outputs P_i. Then a series of detection operations $\{det_i(\cdot)\}_{i=1}^n$ are applied on $\mathbf{P}$ correspondingly to get the detection results $\mathcal{D} = \bigcup_{i=1}^n \mathcal{D}_i$, where $\mathcal{D}_i = det_i(P_i)$. More specific mathematical expression is shown as follows (Algorithm 1):

Algorithm 1. Multi-scale detectors with feature pyramid transformation.

Input: Chosen backbone stages: $\mathbf{C} = \{C_i\}_{i=1}^n$.
Output: Transformed feature pyramid: $\mathbf{P} = \{P_i\}_{i=1}^n$; Detection results: $\mathcal{D} = \bigcup_{i=1}^n \mathcal{D}_i$.
 1: Initialize $\mathbf{P} = \varnothing$, $\mathcal{D} = \varnothing$.
 2: **for** $i = n : -1 : 1$
 3:    select $\mathcal{S}_i \subseteq \mathbf{C} \cup \mathbf{P}$
 4:    $P_i = \phi_i(\mathcal{S}_i)$
 5:    **update** $\mathbf{P} = \mathbf{P} \cup \{P_i\}$
 6: **for** $i = 1 : n$
 7:    $\mathcal{D}_i = det_i(P_i)$
 8:    **update** $\mathcal{D} = \mathcal{D} \cup \mathcal{D}_i$

Through the formulation it is obvious that the transformation procedure $\mathbf{\Phi}$ is critical for the quality of the feature pyramid $\mathbf{P}$ used for detection. For works like FPN [18] and TDM [28], ϕ_i is defined as a recursive aggregating operation, which takes the last-step generated P_{i+1} and the current backbone stage C_i as inputs and outputs the current-level fused feature map P_i. The context information of higher-level layer C_i is first aggregated with C_{i-1} and then passed to lower layers $C_j(i - j \geq 2)$. Such recursive aggregating operation may cause the context information C_i to diminish in $C_j(i - j \geq 2)$, which is swiped away and of no contribution for detection in $C_j(i - j \geq 2)$.

In our work, we introduce reverse dense connection instead of recursive connection and use concatenation as our feature fusion strategy. Specifically, to obtain P_i, we take all $\{C_k\}_{k \geq i}$ as the input of ϕ_i. For each C_k, some operations are applied to either reduce the channel number and match its spatial scale with

C_i or adjust its receptive field. Then the transformed feature maps are concatenated together to form P_i. Since all the feature map levels higher than the current one are taken as the input of ϕ_i and their information is linked to the current level, this type of connection is naturally called reverse dense connection.

There are several advantages of reverse dense connection.

First, our reverse dense connection passes contextual information of various higher levels directly to the current stage, which avoids information to diminish. It is commonly recognized that detecting objects of various scales in a comprehensive image needs contextual information, especially for small objects whose features often appear at shallow layers and are less discriminative. However, due to the high complexity of data, it is hard to distinguish which level of contextual information is helpful for classifying objects on the current one. Therefore, it is better to pass all contextual information of various higher levels directly to the current stage.

Second, concatenating several higher levels that have increasing receptive fields yields hierarchical representation. Boosted by multi-level contexts, such hierarchical representations tend to be more discriminative.

Third, direct linking in reverse dense connection reduces the number of repeating times for stacked learnable modules, leading to more efficient information flow and smoother optimization.

In the next section, we will describe in detail both the formulation of $\{\phi_i\}_{i=1}^n$ and our Rev-Dense FPN based on reverse dense connection.

3.2   Feature Pyramid Transformation for Rev-Dense FPN

In this section we describe in detail Rev-Dense FPN. Suppose we have chosen n backbone stages $\mathbf{C} = \{C_i\}_{i=1}^n$. After the Rev-Dense FPN transformation, it outputs n fused feature pyramid levels $\mathbf{P} = \{P_i\}_{i=1}^n$.

As shown in Fig. 2, for backbone stage C_i, we apply a 3×3 convolution with k_1 output channels. For each backbone stage in $\{C_{i+1}, C_{i+2}, \ldots, C_n\}$, a 1×1 convolution with k_2 output channels is applied, followed by a bilinear up-sample operation to match the spatial scale of C_i. These convolution operations are used for the sake of projecting the representations of $\{C_i, C_{i+1}, \ldots, C_n\}$ into a common space for fusion. Finally, we fuse all the resulted feature maps by concatenation and get P_i.

It should be noted that the 1×1 convolution is performed only once for one certain stage C_i for computation efficiency. And then we apply several bilinear up-sample operations with different spatial outputs to match different scales of $C_1, C_2, \ldots, C_{i-1}$ for later fusion.

k_1, k_2 are tunable parameters. Typically, k_1 is set larger while k_2 is much smaller, similarly to the growth rate in DenseNet [13]. For all the convolution layers used in Rev-Dense FPN, we do not apply non-linearity to their outputs.

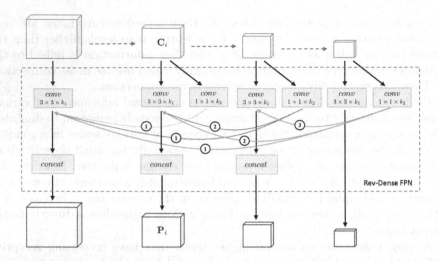

Fig. 2. Structure of Rev-Dense FPN. Taking a set of backbone stages with decreasing spatial scales, it outputs a feature pyramid of the same sizes. The gray dashed arrow lines indicate the propagating direction of the backbone network. Each of the colored arrow lines corresponds to a bi-linear up-sample operation, which is marked by a small circle. The number in the small circle suggests the level number for the targeting spatial size when up-sample is performed. (Color figure online)

According to the description above, the feature pyramid transformation $\Phi = \{\phi_i\}_{i=1}^{n}$ for Rev-Dense FPN can be mathematically formulated as follows:

$$P_i = \phi_i(C_i, C_{i+1}, \ldots, C_n) = \mathcal{F}_{3\times3}^{i}(C_i) \oplus \left(\bigoplus_{k=i+1}^{n} \mathrm{Up}\left(\mathcal{F}_{1\times1}^{k}(C_k), \mathrm{size}(C_i)\right) \right) \quad (1)$$

Where $\mathcal{F}$ denotes convolution, $\oplus$ denotes concatenation and Up is bilinear up-sample operation.

3.3 Network Architecture

We adopt SSD as our baseline algorithm to validate the effectiveness of Rev-Dense FPN. The backbone network is VGGNet which is exactly the same as original SSD.

For input size 300×300, the SSD baseline extracts 6 feature maps to detect objects of different scales. As shown in Fig. 3, the feature maps extracted are $conv4\_3$, $conv7$, $conv8\_2$, $conv9\_2$, $conv10\_2$, and $conv11\_2$. The corresponding spatial scales are 38, 19, 10, 5, 3, 1. To apply Rev-Dense FPN, we first omit the last level $conv11\_2$ for its extreme small spatial size. Then for $conv7$ that has 1024 channels, we add a 1×1 convolution layer followed by relu activation to reduce the channel number to 512. Such channel reduction is for the sake of computation conservation and the reduced feature map is denoted as $conv7'$. Therefore, the chosen backbone stages are $\mathbf{C} = \{conv4\_3, conv7', conv8\_2, conv9\_2, conv10\_2\}$. Then Rev-Dense FPN transformation Φ is applied to $\mathbf{C}$ (with $n = 5$), yielding $\mathbf{P} = \{P_i\}_{i=1}^{5}$. To keep the number of feature levels consistent with baseline, we add $conv11\_2$ in and take $\mathbf{P} \cup \{conv11\_2\}$ as our final feature pyramid. At last we add classification and localization layers on the final feature pyramid to obtain detection outputs.

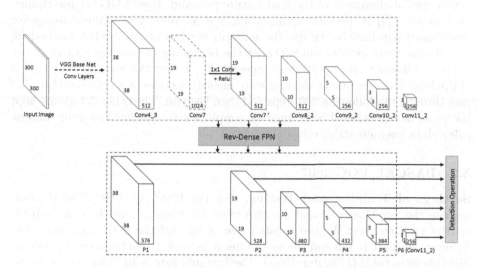

Fig. 3. Network architecture for applying Rev-Dense FPN on SSD300. The blue dashed rectangle encloses the input for Rev-Dense FPN transformation, while the purple dashed rectangle denotes the output. The cube with gray dashed border denotes that it is not contained in the input maps. The channel numbers of the output feature pyramid are in accordance with configuration $k_1 = 384$, $k_2 = 48$. (Color figure online)

For input size 512×512 where there are 7 levels extracted by the baseline SSD, we also adopt similar strategy, *i.e.*, omit the last level when apply Rev-Dense operation, reduce the dimension for 1024-channel map and apply classification and localization layers on the final feature pyramid.

4   Experiments

We conduct experiments on the PASCAL VOC 2007 dataset [5] and the MS COCO dataset [20], which have 20 and 80 categories respectively. In the following sections, we first describe the implementation details of our approach (Sect. 4.1). Then in Sects. 4.2 and 4.3, we will describe training and testing settings on the two datasets and show the experimental results. To demonstrate the flexibility of our method, we also extend Rev-Dense FPN to two-stage method (multi-scale Faster R-CNN with FPN), which is shown in Sect. 4.4.

4.1 Implementation Details

We implement SSD with Rev-Dense FPN using the deep learning framework PyTorch [22]. The training objective is a combination of classification loss and localization loss. And the definitions of both the two components are consistent with the original SSD. Since there are many up-sample operations with large scaling factors in Rev-Dense FPN, we set the weight of localization loss to 1.5 for better spatial alignment of the final feature pyramid. Base VGGNet pre-trained on ImageNet [4] is used for initialization. For all the layers without ImageNet pre-trained parameters, we use the uniform version of the MSRA method [9] to initialize their weights randomly. At the beginning of training procedure, we apply the linear warm-up strategy. Specifically, we set the learning rate to 1/3 of the base learning rate at the first step, linearly increase it to the base learning rate through the following 300 steps and then keep on. The other details are kept the same as the original SSD, such as sampling strategy, hard example mining rules, data augmentation, etc.

4.2 PASCAL VOC 2007

Settings of Training and Testing. For the PASCAL VOC 2007 dataset, we use the *voc07trainval* and *voc12trainval* for training and test the models on the *voc07test* set. We use a batch size of 32 and the SGD optimizer. The momentum is set to 0.9 and the weight decay is 0.0001. We train our models for 250 epochs in total (173k iterations). The learning rate is 10^{-3} for the first 100k iterations (using the warm-up strategy described in Sect. 4.1), 10^{-4} for the next 40k iterations and 10^{-5} for the rest iterations. At the testing stage, NMS (Non-Maximum Suppression) with 0.45 IoU threshold is performed as post-processing operation to remove duplicate boxes. Finally, we evaluate the mean average precision (mAP) on the *voc07test* set.

We train our models with 4 Nvidia GTX 1080Ti GPUs and test on a single GPU. We implement two Rev-Dense FPNs including Rev-Dense FPN (SSD300) and Rev-Dense FPN (SSD512) with input size 300×300 and 512×512 respectively. We set $k_1 = 384$ and $k_2 = 48$ for Rev-Dense FPN (SSD300) and $k_1 = 256$ and $k_2 = 48$ for Rev-Dense FPN (SSD512).

Study on the Effectiveness of Rev-Dense FPN. To demonstrate our argument that reverse dense connection is superior to recursive top-down connection for multi-scale feature fusion or feature pyramid transformation, we conduct the following experiments with SSD300 as baseline:

Transplant FPN to SSD. We transplant FPN to the SSD detector. We implement the connection structure defined by FPN and set output channel number of the lateral layers to 256, which is most commonly used by the community. The backbone stages chosen for the FPN transformation are all the 6 feature maps extracted by the baseline. We do not omit the last feature map. The reason is that in methods based on recursive top-down connection, up-sample operations always happen between two consecutive feature levels. Therefore, there is no extreme scaling factor for up-sampling in FPN. The resulted model reaches 78.3% mAP (see Table 1), which is by 0.9% lower than Rev-Dense FPN.

Transplant TDM to SSD. Similar to transplanting FPN on SSD, we add modules as described in [28] to SSD. The output channel numbers for lateral layers, top-down layers and out layers are set to 128, 128 and 256, respectively. This is slightly different with [28] in which the three numbers are inconsistent at each stage. We choose the largest ones and keep them consistent, since we think this will enhance the representation power of the model. All the 6 feature maps extracted by SSD are taken as the input of TDM. As shown in Table 1, SSD with TDM reaches an mAP of 78.2%, which is by 1.0 point lower than Rev-Dense FPN.

Remove Reverse Dense Connections. To verify that it is the reverse dense connections from higher-level layers that contribute to our method rather than the projection operations which happen on the current levels, we remove reverse dense connections from higher-level layers for ablation study. With the removal of reverse dense connections, the mAP point drops to 77.9% (see Table 1), which is by 1.3 points lower than the model with reverse dense connections from higher levels.

Table 1. Experimental results of recursive top-down connection vs. reverse dense connection for multi-scale feature fusion (feature pyramid transformation). The baseline for this group of experiments is SSD300. All the models are trained on *voc07trainval* and *voc12trainval* and tested on *voc07test*.

Feature pyramid transformation	Connection style	mAP (%)
None (Baseline)	-	77.5
FPN [18]	Recursive top-down	78.3
TDM [28]	Recursive top-down	78.2
Rev-Dense FPN (SSD300) w/o reverse connections	-	77.9
Rev-Dense FPN (SSD300)	Reverse dense	**79.2**

The experiments above validate that reverse dense connection is better than recursive top-down connection. As shown in Table 1, using reverse dense connection, Rev-Dense FPN (SSD300) reaches 79.2% mAP. But for the methods based on recursive top-down connection FPN and TDM, the mAPs are around 1 point lower than our Rev-Dense FPN (SSD300), which supports our point of view. The removal of reverse dense connections as ablation (77.9% mAP vs. 79.2% mAP) also verifies its contribution.

Ablation Study on Which Backbone Stages to Choose. To further study the contributions of different feature levels, we conduct another ablation experiment in which various combinations of input backbone stages are involved. With the basic setting $\{C_1, C_2, C_3, C_4, C_5, C_6\} = \{conv4\_3, conv7', conv8\_2, conv9\_2, conv10\_2, conv11\_2\}$, we consider the following combinations of $\{C_i\}_{i=1}^6$: $(C_2, C_3, C_4, C_5, C_6)$, (C_1, C_3, C_5), (C_1, C_2, C_3, C_4) and $(C_1, C_2, C_3, C_4, C_5)$, using SSD300 as the baseline. The selected stages in a combination are taken as the input of Rev-Dense FPN transformation while the backbone stages excluded are kept the same in the output feature pyramid. Results are shown in Table 2.

Table 2. Ablation study on which backbone stages to choose. The baseline is SSD300. All the models are trained on *voc07trainval* and *voc12trainval* and tested on *voc07test*.

Backbone stages	Number of levels	mAP (%)
None (Baseline)	-	77.5
$(C_2, C_3, C_4, C_5, C_6)$	5	78.4
(C_1, C_3, C_5)	3	78.7
(C_1, C_2, C_3, C_4)	4	78.8
$(C_1, C_2, C_3, C_4, C_5)$	5	**79.2**

As the results suggest, leaving the lowest level out entails the lowest result (78.4% mAP). This indicates that small objects can benefit largely from reverse dense connections. Without being involved in the fusion transformation, low-level features for small objects become less of representation power. Taking the interleaved 3 stages as the input of Rev-Dense FPN yields similar performance as using (C_1, C_2, C_3, C_4) (78.7% mAP vs. 78.8% mAP). But adding C_2 and C_4 back reaches the highest performance (79.2% mAP), which proves their importance. Through the comparison between the last two items, the contribution of level C_5 is also confirmed.

Results on PASCAL VOC 2007. We show the experimental results on PASCAL VOC 2007 for Rev-Dense FPN (SSD300) and Rev-Dense FPN (SSD512). As shown in Table 3, using only the VGGNet as backbone, our Rev-Dense FPN (SSD300) reaches 79.2% mAP, surpassing many other SSD-like detectors, including DSSD321, DSOD300, STDN300 and FSSD300. Reaching high accuracy, Rev-Dense FPN (SSD300) runs at a high speed (70.9 fps), which is only of a small speed drop compared to SSD300 and is faster than FSSD300 as well. For input size 512 × 512, our Rev-Dense FPN (SSD512) reaches 81.1% mAP, which is also higher than STDN513 and FSSD512. Though DSSD513 is slightly higher than our method, it is much slower than out Rev-Dense FPN (SSD512). Note that there is huge gap of model capacity between the two backbone networks (VGGNet [29] for Rev-Dense FPN vs. ResNet-101 [11] for DSSD). ResNet-101 is much more powerful than VGGNet. With such huge gap, our Rev-Dense FPN

(SSD512) is by a small margin lower than DSSD513, which validates the effectiveness of our reverse dense connection.

Table 3. Experimental results on the PASCAL VOC 2007 dataset. The baselines (SSD300 and SSD512) reported here are our own implementation, with SSD300 slightly higher than the original paper (77.2% mAP) and SSD512 the same. For Rev-Dense FPN (SSD300), we set $k_1 = 384$ and $k_2 = 48$. For Rev-Dense FPN (SSD512), we set $k_1 = 256$ and $k_2 = 48$. All the entries listed use *voc07trainval* and *voc12trainval* as training data and use *voc07test* as test data.

Method	Backbone	Input size	GPU	Speed (fps)	mAP (%)
Faster R-CNN [26]	ResNet-101	600 × 1000	K40	2.4	76.4
R-FCN [3]	ResNet-50	600 × 1000	-	-	77.0
SSD300 [21]	VGGNet	300 × 300	1080Ti	**83.3**	77.5
SSD512 [21]	VGGNet	512 × 512	1080Ti	**39.2**	79.8
YOLOv2 [25]	DarkNet-19	544 × 544	Titan X	40	78.6
DSOD300 [27]	DS/64-192-48-1	300 × 300	Titan X	17.4	77.7
DSSD321 [6]	ResNet-101	300 × 300	Titan X	9.5	78.6
DSSD513 [6]	ResNet-101	513 × 513	Titan X	5.5	**81.5**
STDN300 [23]	DenseNet-169	300 × 300	Titan Xp	41.5	78.1
STDN513 [23]	DenseNet-169	513 × 513	Titan Xp	28.6	80.9
FSSD300 [17]	VGGNet	300 × 300	1080Ti	65.8	78.8
FSSD512 [17]	VGGNet	512 × 512	1080Ti	35.7	80.9
Rev-Dense FPN (SSD300)	VGGNet	300 × 300	1080Ti	**70.9**	**79.2**
Rev-Dense FPN (SSD512)	VGGNet	512 × 512	1080Ti	**38.0**	**81.1**

4.3 MS COCO

Settings of Training and Testing. For the MS COCO dataset, we train our model on the *COCO2017 train* set and test on the *COCO test-dev* set. The batch size is 32 and the SGD optimizer is used. We set the momentum and the weight decay to 0.9 and 0.0001. The model is trained for 110 epochs in total (around 403k iterations). The learning rate is 10^{-3} for the first 280k iterations (using the warm-up strategy described in Sect. 4.1), 10^{-4} for the next 90k iterations and 10^{-5} for the rest. At testing stage, NMS with 0.5 IoU threshold is applied.

We implement Rev-Dense FPN (SSD512) on the COCO dataset and set $k_1 = 256$, $k_2 = 48$.

Results on COCO. We evaluate our model on the *COCO test-dev* set, using the official evaluation server. Results are shown in Table 4. On the *COCO test-dev* set, Rev-Dense FPN (SSD512) reaches 31.2 AP, which is by a large margin higher than the SSD512 baseline. It also reaches comparable result as the SSD513 which uses the much powerful ResNet-101 for backbone. Though the AP of Rev-Dense FPN (SSD512) is slightly lower than STDN513 and FSSD512, it is worth noticing

Table 4. Experimental Results on the *COCO test-dev* set. All the entries are trained on the *COCO2017 train* set or the *trainval35k* set which is identical. Column 3~5 show the AP points corresponding to different IoU thresholds (*AP*: AP points averaged over IoU thresholds 0.50:0.05:0.95. AP_{50}, AP_{75}: AP point when IoU threshold is 0.5 or 0.75). The last 3 columns show the AP points corresponding to different object scales. Subscripts S, M, L represent small, medium, large respectively.

Method	Backbone	AP	AP_{50}	AP_{75}	AP_S	AP_M	AP_L
YOLOv2 [25]	DarkNet-19	21.6	44.0	19.2	5.0	22.4	35.5
SSD512 [21]	VGGNet	28.8	48.5	30.3	10.9	31.8	43.5
SSD513 [6]	ResNet-101	31.2	50.4	33.3	10.2	34.5	**49.8**
STDN513 [23]	DenseNet-169	**31.8**	51.0	**33.6**	14.4	**36.1**	43.4
FSSD512 [17]	VGGNet	**31.8**	52.8	33.5	14.2	35.1	45.0
Rev-Dense FPN (SSD512)	VGGNet	31.2	**52.9**	32.4	**15.5**	32.9	43.9

that for the performance on small objects (AP_S), our result is the highest (15.5) among the listed methods. Since small objects are mostly distributed onto lower-level layers which benefit most from reverse dense connections, the result further suggests the effectiveness of reverse dense connection and the representation power of its resulted features boosted by hierarchical multi-level contexts. Some visualized samples are shown in Fig. 4.

4.4   Rev-Dense FPN on Two-Stage Method

To demonstrate the flexibility of Rev-Dense FPN, we apply our approach to a state-of-the-art two-stage detector, Faster R-CNN with Feature Pyramid Network (FPN). In the original configuration of [18], the chosen backbone stages are $\mathbf{C} = \{res2\_2, res3\_3, res4\_5, res5\_2\}$ in ResNet50. Then FPN is applied on these maps, yielding P_1 to P_4. Finally, a 1×1 2-stride max-pooling is performed on P_4 to get P_5. For the experimental settings of ours, we keep the same $\mathbf{C}$ as the input of Rev-Dense FPN. k_1 is set as an increasing sequence of $\{240, 320, 400, 480\}$ and k_2 is set to 80. As FPN does, we use 3×3 convs to post-process the fused maps and output 256 channels. The MS COCO dataset is adopted. We train both models for 180k iterations, using batch size of 8. The learning rate is 0.01 and it is then divided by 10 at 120k and 160k iterations.

Table 5. Results of FPN vs. Rev-Dense FPN for two-stage method. Both models are trained on the *COCO2017 train* (*trainval35k*) set and tested on the *COCO minival* set.

Method	Backbone	Input size	AP	AP_{50}	AP_{75}	AP_S	AP_M	AP_L
FRCN w/FPN [18]	ResNet50	~600 × 1000	35.4	56.8	37.9	18.2	38.5	48.0
FRCN w/Rev-Dense FPN	ResNet50	~600 × 1000	**35.9**	**57.4**	**38.6**	**19.0**	**38.6**	**48.8**

As the results shown in Table 5, with Rev-Dense FPN, the detection performance is better than FPN in all the metrics, suggesting that Rev-Dense FPN is flexible to two-stage method and can make effective improvement as well.

Fig. 4. Some visualized results of Rev-Dense FPN (SSD512) on the *COCO test-dev* set. Score threshold is set to 0.5 for displaying.

5   Conclusions

We develop a new multi-scale feature fusion mechanism for object detection. Our approach, denoted as the Rev-Dense FPN, performs reverse dense connection that directly fuses features from all the higher levels to the current one. Taking a set of feature maps from the base network, for each of them, we first project the current stage, then compress dimension for all the higher levels and concatenate the obtained maps onto the projected current stage after scale matching. By applying Rev-Dense FPN to SSD, we show that Rev-Dense FPN composed by reverse dense connections can achieve higher performance than approaches based on recursive top-down fusion manner. Experimental results demonstrate that reverse dense connection is more effective and Rev-Dense FPN can learn a more powerful representation which benefits from multi-level contexts and contributes to detecting multi-scale objects, especially small objects.

Acknowledgement. This work was supported in part by National Natural Science Foundation of China: 61672497, 61332016, 61771457, 61732007, 61620106009, 61650202 and U1636214, in part by National Basic Research Program of China (973 Program): 2015CB351802, in part by Key Research Program of Frontier Sciences of CAS: QYZDJ-SSW-SYS013, and in part by Shandong Provincial Natural Science Foundation, China: ZR2017MF001.

References

1. Bell, S., Zitnick, C.L., Bala, K., Girshick, R.B.: Inside-outside net: detecting objects in context with skip pooling and recurrent neural networks. In: IEEE CVPR (2016)
2. Cai, Z., Fan, Q., Feris, R.S., Vasconcelos, N.: A unified multi-scale deep convolutional neural network for fast object detection. In: Leibe, B., Matas, J., Sebe, N., Welling, M. (eds.) ECCV 2016. LNCS, vol. 9908, pp. 354–370. Springer, Cham (2016). https://doi.org/10.1007/978-3-319-46493-0_22
3. Dai, J., Li, Y., He, K., Sun, J.: R-FCN: object detection via region-based fully convolutional networks. In: NIPS (2016)
4. Deng, J., Dong, W., Socher, R., Li, L., Li, K., Li, F.: Imagenet: a large-scale hierarchical image database. In: IEEE CVPR (2009)
5. Everingham, M., Gool, L.J.V., Williams, C.K.I., Winn, J.M., Zisserman, A.: The pascal visual object classes (VOC) challenge. IJCV **88**(2), 303–338 (2010)
6. Fu, C., Liu, W., Ranga, A., Tyagi, A., Berg, A.C.: DSSD: deconvolutional single shot detector. CoRR abs/1701.06659 (2017)
7. Girshick, R.B., Donahue, J., Darrell, T., Malik, J.: Rich feature hierarchies for accurate object detection and semantic segmentation. In: IEEE CVPR (2014)
8. He, K., Gkioxari, G., Dollár, P., Girshick, R.B.: Mask R-CNN. In: IEEE ICCV (2017)
9. He, K., Zhang, X., Ren, S., Sun, J.: Delving deep into rectifiers: surpassing human-level performance on imagenet classification. In: IEEE ICCV (2015)
10. He, K., Zhang, X., Ren, S., Sun, J.: Spatial pyramid pooling in deep convolutional networks for visual recognition. IEEE TPAMI **37**(9), 1904–1916 (2015)
11. He, K., Zhang, X., Ren, S., Sun, J.: Deep residual learning for image recognition. In: IEEE CVPR (2016)
12. Hong, S., Roh, B., Kim, K., Cheon, Y., Park, M.: Pvanet: lightweight deep neural networks for real-time object detection. CoRR abs/1611.08588 (2016)
13. Huang, G., Liu, Z., van der Maaten, L., Weinberger, K.Q.: Densely connected convolutional networks. In: IEEE CVPR (2017)
14. Kong, T., Sun, F., Yao, A., Liu, H., Lu, M., Chen, Y.: RON: reverse connection with objectness prior networks for object detection. In: IEEE CVPR (2017)
15. Kong, T., Yao, A., Chen, Y., Sun, F.: Hypernet: towards accurate region proposal generation and joint object detection. In: IEEE CVPR (2016)
16. Li, Z., Peng, C., Yu, G., Zhang, X., Deng, Y., Sun, J.: Light-head R-CNN: in defense of two-stage object detector. CoRR abs/1711.07264 (2017)
17. Li, Z., Zhou, F.: FSSD: feature fusion single shot multibox detector. CoRR abs/1712.00960 (2017)
18. Lin, T., Dollár, P., Girshick, R.B., He, K., Hariharan, B., Belongie, S.J.: Feature pyramid networks for object detection. In: IEEE CVPR (2017)
19. Lin, T., Goyal, P., Girshick, R.B., He, K., Dollár, P.: Focal loss for dense object detection. In: IEEE ICCV (2017)
20. Lin, T.-Y., et al.: Microsoft COCO: common objects in context. In: Fleet, D., Pajdla, T., Schiele, B., Tuytelaars, T. (eds.) ECCV 2014. LNCS, vol. 8693, pp. 740–755. Springer, Cham (2014). https://doi.org/10.1007/978-3-319-10602-1_48
21. Liu, W., et al.: SSD: single shot MultiBox detector. In: Leibe, B., Matas, J., Sebe, N., Welling, M. (eds.) ECCV 2016. LNCS, vol. 9905, pp. 21–37. Springer, Cham (2016). https://doi.org/10.1007/978-3-319-46448-0_2
22. Paszke, A., et al.: Automatic differentiation in pytorch (2017)

23. Peng, Z., Bingbing, N., Cong, G., Jianguo, H., Yi, X.: Scale-transferrable object detection. In: IEEE CVPR (2018)
24. Redmon, J., Divvala, S.K., Girshick, R.B., Farhadi, A.: You only look once: unified, real-time object detection. In: IEEE CVPR (2016)
25. Redmon, J., Farhadi, A.: YOLO9000: better, faster, stronger. In: IEEE CVPR (2017)
26. Ren, S., He, K., Girshick, R.B., Sun, J.: Faster R-CNN: towards real-time object detection with region proposal networks. IEEE TPAMI **39**(6), 1137–1149 (2017)
27. Shen, Z., Liu, Z., Li, J., Jiang, Y., Chen, Y., Xue, X.: DSOD: learning deeply supervised object detectors from scratch. In: IEEE ICCV (2017)
28. Shrivastava, A., Sukthankar, R., Malik, J., Gupta, A.: Beyond skip connections: Top-down modulation for object detection. CoRR abs/1612.06851 (2016)
29. Simonyan, K., Zisserman, A.: Very deep convolutional networks for large-scale image recognition. CoRR abs/1409.1556 (2014)

Image-to-GPS Verification Through a Bottom-Up Pattern Matching Network

Jiaxin Cheng[⊠], Yue Wu, Wael Abd-Almageed, and Prem Natarajan

Information Sciences Institute, University of Southern California,
4746 Admiralty Way, Marina Del Rey, CA 90292, USA
{chengjia,yue_wu,wamageed,pnataraj}@isi.edu

Abstract. The image-to-GPS verification problem asks whether a given image is taken at a claimed GPS location. In this paper, we treat it as an image verification problem – whether a query image is taken at the same place as a reference image retrieved at the claimed GPS location. We make three major contributions: (1) we propose a novel custom bottom-up pattern matching (BUPM) deep neural network solution; (2) we demonstrate that the verification can be directly done by cross-checking a perspective-looking query image and a panorama reference image, and (3) we collect and clean a dataset of 30K pairs query and reference. Our experimental results show that the proposed BUPM solution outperforms the state-of-the-art solutions in terms of both verification and localization.

Keywords: Location verification · Landmark matching ·
Image matching · Panorama

1 Introduction

In recent years we have seen many fake news stories, including but not limited to elections, natural disasters, protests, and riots. With the rapid growth of social networks and easy-to-use publishing applications on mobile devices, fake news can easily be produced and spread to social networks, and consequently to the entire world. Publishing fake news became a "digital gold rush",[1] and detection tools need to be developed.

Many posts on social media are text-only, but it is common to see posts composed of both text and image/video (see samples in Fig. 1), which is preferred by fake news posters, possibly because appealing photos makes fake news more convincing. However, this provides us extra opportunities to identify fake news, because one needs to tell more lies to make up one lie, but we only need to recognize one lie to conclude he/she is a lier.

In this paper, we are interested in identifying fake news by testing location consistency – whether an image is taken at a claimed location. Here, a claimed

---

[1] https://www.wired.com/2017/02/veles-macedonia-fake-news.

© Springer Nature Switzerland AG 2019
C. V. Jawahar et al. (Eds.): ACCV 2018, LNCS 11365, pp. 546–561, 2019.
https://doi.org/10.1007/978-3-030-20873-8_35

Fig. 1. Shall we trust these social network posts? Are these images taken at the claimed places?

position could be inferred or obtained from different sources in a social media post, *e.g.* associated text description, Global Positioning System (GPS) information in image metadata, scene text in an image like street signs/landmark names, etc.

A straight-forward solution to this problem is to use the GPS estimation approach, which estimates a query image's GPS according to visually similar images with known GPS locations in a large, geo-tagged reference database and compares the estimated GPS to the claimed one to make the decision. Depending on the used features, one may further classify existing approaches into two families: (1) 2D-only, which uses image features [5,6,12–15,17] *e.g.*Invariant Feature Transform (SIFT), Speeded-Up Robust Features (SURF) [6,12–14], bag-of-words representation [15], and vocabulary trees [17], to efficiently and effectively retrieve visually similar images first, and estimate the query GPS from nearest neighbors; (2) 2D-to-3D [19,20,25,26], which reconstructs 3D structures of images in a reference database offline, and performs online 2D-to-3D matching for a query.

Unfortunately, this approach does not fit well in the context of image-to-GPS verification for three reasons. First, the premise of a large enough, up-to-date, offline reference database is difficult to achieve for most users because such a database is too expensive to create or maintain. Second, we only have one query image instead of a collection or a sequence of images, and thus violate the working assumptions of methods like [2,28]. Third, similarity-based retrieval works well for city landmarks, but not for visually similar locations, *e.g. Starbucks* stores in different places all over the world.

Alternatively, we approach this problem following the classic image verification paradigm – given a pair of images, one query and one reference, we use a network to decide whether or not they are from the same location, where the reference image can be retrieved at the claimed GPS location from a third-party GPS-based image database *e.g. Google Street View* [3] and *Bing Street Side*. Of course, many existing works on image verification, *e.g.* face verification [1] and object verification [10], can be directly applied to this problem because verification nature does not change, but they are unsuitable since the critical camera information like shooting angle and focal length is unknown and this raises difficulty to retrieve an appropriate reference image to compare against the query. The potential mismatch roots in the fact that a query image is a 2D projection of a 3D scene, while a GPS location is a 2D point.

In this paper, we propose a novel Bottom-Up Pattern Matching (BUPM) based verification network. It directly compares a query image and a panorama reference image collected from a claimed GPS location, and thus completely get rid of the error-prone reference images caused by unknown shooting angle and focal length and largely simplifies the data preparation. It estimates the potential matched patches in both reference and query in a bottom-up manner and makes the decision upon the number of matched patches in a soft way. All modules in the BUPM network are therefore differentiable and learnable. In this way, the BUPM network can be used not only for verification but also for localization, *i.e.* finding the query image in a panorama reference image.

The remainder of this paper is organized as follows: Sect. 2 briefly reviews recent related works; Sect. 3 introduces the image-to-GPS verification problem and proposes the BUPM verification network solution; Sect. 4 discusses the details of training and dataset; Sect. 5 compares performances of different verification solutions; and we conclude this paper in Sect. 6.

2   Related Works

Our problem is closely related to the works in the following two domains: (1) image verification, which answers whether a query image is the *same* as the reference in some sense of interest, *e.g.* scene and landmark, and (2) template matching, which finds a template region in a host image.

Recent advances in location/landmark verification or retrieval, are mainly from deep neural networks [4,9,16,18,21,24,27,28,30]. [16] proposed a generic Siamese network for landmark image matching. [28] quantified 16 millions of images with geo-tags into 26K regions bins, and trained a classification network to predict the region bin of an image belonging to. [4] proposed a generalized VLAD layer to improve classic feature pooling layers for place recognition. [30] introduced a 7 million scene-centric database and the so-called *Places-CNN* for place/scene classification. [18] trains a network but to classify city landmarks, but introduces a new attention layer to provide patches importance and supervision to fuse all patch features into an image feature. [9] showed that extra attention maps, *e.g.*the density map of SIFT keypoints, helped feature aggregation. IM2GPS [27] indexed six million geo-tagged images and estimated a query image's GPS via nearest neighbor search using DNN features.

With regards to template matching, [7] proposed the *best-buddies* similarity score, [23] used the diversity of feature matches as a similarity metric, and [11] introduced an occlusion aware template matching technique. [29] worked on a constrained image splicing localization problem, a general template matching problem, and proposed a learnable deep matching layer to perform matching.

In the context of the image-to-GPS verification problem, a perspective looking query image and a panorama reference image are not directly comparable. A natural solution is to integrate template matching and image verification into a single solution, and this is exactly what the proposed BUPM network is aiming to achieve.

3   The BUPM Network for Image-to-GPS Verification

3.1   Problem Description and Method Overview

The image-to-GPS verification problem can be stated as follows: given a query image Q and a GPS location $(lat., long.)$, how to verify whether or not Q is taken at the claimed location. As mentioned before, we treat it as an image verification problem – whether the visual content of query image Q can be seen in a reference image R retrieved at the claimed location $(lat., long.)$ through a third-party database, *e.g. Google Street View.*

Due to the 2D point nature of a GPS location, we have two choices for the reference image: (1) use many reference images retrieved at the claimed GPS location with different heading angles and focal lengths, verify each one against the query, and aggregate all results for a final decision; and (2) use a panorama reference image, which stitches all scenes spanning over 360° at the claimed GPS location, and verify only this single panorama reference image against the query.

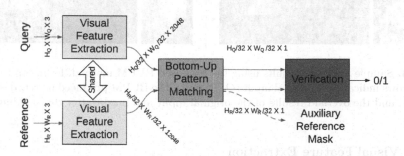

Fig. 2. Overview of the proposed bottom-up pattern matching network. Solid arrows indicate the main network (see Sect. 3); and dashed arrows indicate the auxiliary network to stabilize the main network (see Sect. 4).

In this paper, we choose to use the later one to avoid the annoying and error-prone reference image retrieval for the unknown shooting angle and focal length, and the inefficient use of many reference images. However, as a trade-off, the later choice introduces two additional challenges we have to face:

- visual distortions in a panorama image.
- extra but irrelevant scene content other than the required.

Figure 2 shows the overview of our approach. Specifically, the *Visual Feature Extraction* module represents both query and reference images in terms of two feature tensors, the *Bottom-Up Pattern Matching* module finds matched regions between query and reference, and finally the *Verification* module decides whether or not the visual content of Q is seen in the reference R upon the potential matched patches found in query and reference. It is worth noting that the BUPM network works for image pairs of arbitrary sizes. See Fig. 3 for sample inputs and BUPM matching results. Details of each module as well as our solutions to the above challenges will be discussed in the following sections.

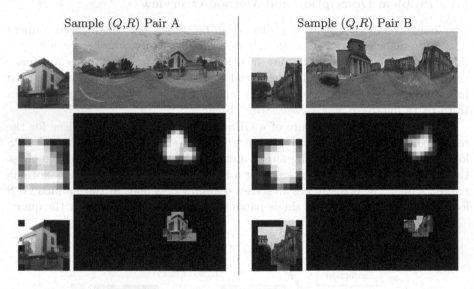

Fig. 3. Sample matching results using the proposed BUPM method. From top to bottom, rows indicate the original input (Q, R) pairs, the BUPM produced matched region masks, and the overlaid results of the original input and mask (after thresholding).

3.2   Visual Feature Extraction

Although a panorama image contains visual distortions, it is clear that such distortions only exist in fairly large patches. For example, a straight line will be distorted to a curve in a panorama image, but this curve can be still considered to be piece-wise linear when we use small patch sizes. This observation indicates that we don't need to worry too much about distortions in a panorama image if we are only interested in local features.

To extract local visual features, we simply use the pretrained *ResNet50* model [8]. More precisely, we crop off all *Dense*(also known as *Fully Connected*) layers and the *Global Pooling* layer in *ResNet50*, while only keeping its *Convolution* layers, because all we need is local visual feature representation while those cropped off layers are for the image classification task. As a result, given a query image of size $H_Q \times W_Q \times 3$, and a reference image of size $H_R \times W_R \times 3$, the *Visual Feature Extraction* module produces query representation F_Q of size $\frac{H_Q}{32} \times \frac{W_Q}{32} \times 2048$, and reference representation F_R of size $\frac{H_R}{32} \times \frac{W_R}{32} \times 2048$, where the denominator 32 is caused by the five times of factor 2 downsampling in *ResNet50*, and the depth dimension 2048 is the number of filters used by the last convolutional layer of *ResNet50*.

3.3 Bottom-Up Pattern Matching

Due to the nature of the panorama image, a reference feature F_R contains much more content than that is required to verify F_Q. Therefore, directly comparing F_R and F_Q makes very little sense – only a small region in F_R is supposed to match with F_Q when R and Q are taken at the same place, while no region should be matched when they are not. Directly comparing these two features means to match signals with the appearance of very heavy noise, and thus its effectiveness and robustness is questionable.

Alternatively, we follow the procedure adopted by a human user, who will first look for regions that are similar to a query, and later decide whether the found regions are matched or not. Specifically, the proposed BUPM module consumes query and reference feature tensors and does three things,

1. computes similarity scores between reference and query from the bottom in the *Patch-wise Similarity* module
2. find best matched patch pairs through *Global MaxPooling*
3. holistic matching based mask detection in the *Mask Detector* module.

This process is illustrated in Fig. 4.

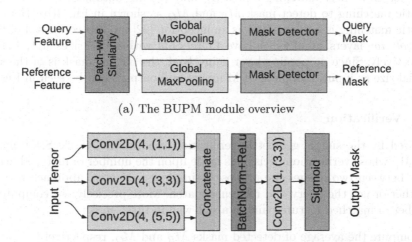

(a) The BUPM module overview

(b) The network architecture of the *Mask Detector* module.

Fig. 4. The proposed bottom-up pattern recognition module.

To match patterns in the bottom-up manner, BUPM views a feature tensor of size $H \times W \times 2048$ as a collection of $H \times W$ patch-wise feature vectors, each of dimension 2048. Consequently, the smallest unit for analysis is of the patch-level. BUPM then computes a pairwise cosine similarity tensor $S = \text{Simi}(F_R, F_Q)$, where each element can be computed as the similarity score between a query patch feature and a reference patch feature as shown in Eq. (1).

$$\text{Simi}(F_R, F_Q)[x, y, i, j] = \frac{F_R[x, y] \cdot F_Q[i, j]}{\|F_R[x, y]\| \cdot \|F_Q[i, j]\|} \tag{1}$$

A larger $\text{Simi}(F_R, F_Q)[x, y, i, j]$ value therefore indicates that reference patch feature $F_R[x, y]$ and query patch feature $F_Q[i, j]$ are more similar. In addition, $S[x, y, :, :]$ stores similarity scores between reference patch feature $F_R[x, y]$ and all query patch features, and $S[:, :, i, j]$ stores similarity scores between query patch feature $F_Q[i, j]$ and all reference features.

To see which reference/query patch is matched, we perform the *Global Max-Pooling* for both query and reference as shown in Eqs. (2) and (3). As one can see, the resulting B_R is of size $\frac{H_R}{32} \times \frac{W_R}{32} \times 1$, and each of its element $B_R[x, y]$ indicates the best matching score we found between the patch feature $F_R[x, y]$ and any feature in F_Q. The resulting B_Q can be interpreted in a similar way.

$$B_R = \max(S, axis = (2, 3)) \tag{2}$$

$$B_Q = \max(S, axis = (0, 1)) \tag{3}$$

Once these best matching scores B_R and B_Q are obtained, BUPM applies holistic matching to detect mask M_R and M_Q as shown in Fig. 4(b). Here, the holistic matching is implemented as an inception [22] module composed of three *Convolution* layers, all of which have 4 filters but with kernel sizes at 1, 3 and 5, respectively. Since no pooling layer is involved, the output mask is of the same spatial size as input. Sample BUPM inputs and outputs can be seen in Fig. 3.

3.4 Verification

Inspired by the simple geometric verification used in the classic SIFT matching [31], whose verification decision is made upon the number of matched feature pairs between two images, we propose a simple yet effective approach to verify whether or not the query and reference match. More precisely, we compute the number of matched feature pairs in a soft way in three steps:

1. compute the average of detected masks M_R and M_Q, respectively
2. concatenate them as a two-dimensional feature V as shown in Eq. (4)
3. learn a multilayer perception (MLP) to make verification decision.

Since the input of the MLP is of dimension two, we simply implement it a shallow DNN composed of three *Dense* layers, which are of 16, 4, and 1 units, and followed by the *Sigmoid* activation.

$$V = [\text{mean}(M_R), \text{mean}(M_Q)]^T \tag{4}$$

It is worthy noting that computing the mean of M_R and M_Q is equivalent to computing the summation of M_R and M_Q, *i.e.* counting the number of matched patched but in a soft and differentiable way.

4   Training the BUPM Network

4.1   Real Training Dataset

To train the BUPM network, we need both positive and negative pairs of perspective-looking query and panorama reference images. Unfortunately, no public available dataset could provide a sufficient number of positive pairs. We therefore collect data for training.

It is noticeable that positive pairs are more important, because negative pairs can be easily *synthesized* by disordering the matched pairs. We start our data collection with downloading quality query images with GPS coordinates. Due to the sensitivity of different GPS sensors/receivers/algorithms, not all query images with GPS locations are considered. Here, we only consider those query images taken by the recent smart phones, *e.g.* Apple iphone 6, which are *typically accurate to within a 4.9 m (16 ft) radius under open sky*[2]. As a result, *Mapillary*[3], a photo sharing website is used as the source of query images, most of whose images are taken by GPS-enabled smart phones and uploaded by users all over the world. Once a query image is obtained, we then download its corresponding panorama image through the *Google Street View* API[4].

In total, we collected 120K raw query images and reference panorama images. The raw data are filtered if violating any of the following condition:

1. no panorama image can be retrieved at a GPS (*e.g.* indoor images)
2. no immovable object like buildings in query (*e.g.* sky images)

The first violation can be easily identified by checking retrieval return values. The second violation can be detected by using any pretrained semantic segmentation model have building classes, *e.g.* the UperNet[5]. Eventually, we successfully harvested 30K positive samples. Rejected and accepted instances can be seen in Fig. 5. We randomly split these $30K$ of paired query and reference positive samples into training and validation dataset of sizes $25K:5K$. We further disorder paired query and reference samples to obtain $5K$ negative samples for validation, respectively. For training, we did not use a fixed negative dataset, but randomly generate negative samples for each batch.

---

[2] https://www.gps.gov/systems/gps/performance/accuracy/.
[3] www.mapillary.com.
[4] https://github.com/Jam3/extract-streetview.
[5] https://github.com/CSAILVision/semantic-segmentation-pytorch.

Accept

Reject

Fig. 5. Rejected and accepted query instances after data filtering.

4.2 Synthetic Training Dataset

Directly training the proposed BUPM network with the real dataset may fail to converge with a great chance. This is because the network may not optimize towards to the desired directions, *i.e.* M_R and M_Q in the proposed BUPM network may not represent the matched regions between query and reference but something different. To enforce this designed feature and stabilize the BUPM training, we prepare a synthetic training dataset with additional M_R targets.

Specifically, for a given panorama image R, we first apply a pretrained building detector to extract a number of region candidates (containing buildings), randomly select one of them, and apply data augmentation to this region to synthesize a query image Q. Because we know where Q is taken in R, we have M_R targets. This process is described in Fig. 6. The used data augmentation includes scaling (range in $[0.5, 2]$), spatial shift (range in $(-20\%, 20\%)$), color adjustment using gamma correction (range in $[0.5, 1.5]$), and random perspective transform.

4.3 Training Details

We implement the BUPM network using the deep learning library *Keras* with the *TensorFlow* backend and 4 *Nvidia Titan-X* GPUs. All weights are randomly initialized except for the *Visual Feature Extraction*, which takes the pretrained *ImageNet* weights from[6]. Our pretrained models and dataset can be found in https://gitlab.vista.isi.edu/chengjia/image-GPS.

The training process is composed of two phases: (1) training with the synthetic dataset, and (2) training with the real dataset. In the first phase, we use synthetic query Q and real reference R images to predict M_R, *i.e.* train the

---

[6] https://keras.io/applications/#resnet50.

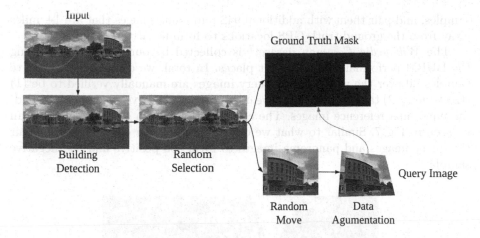

Fig. 6. Synthesizing auxiliary *reference masks* and queries for training.

network until the *BUPM* module (see Fig. 2). We use the *logloss* for the M_R target, optimize the network using the *SGD* optimizer with the initial learning rate *1e-2* without any decay, and use a batch size of 16. Note, the M_Q target is omitted, because its ground truth masks in the context of synthetic data are always 1s, and a constant target somewhat hampers the learning. In the second stage, we use the *binary cross-entropy* for the verification target, optimize the network the *Adam* optimizer with the initial learning rate *1e-3*, and set the batch size to 64 with balanced positive and negative samples. Once the MLP in the BUPM network converges, we unfreeze all weights and optimize the BUPM network end-to-end with the *Adam* optimizer with the initial learning rate *1e-5* until convergence.

It is worthy to mention that we resize query images in a batch to the same square size to speed up training. Depending on data augmentation, the query image size can be one of the sizes in 192, 224, and 256.

5   Experimental Results

5.1   Dataset

We use two dataset in experiment, namely the *Shibuya* dataset and the *Wiki-media Common* dataset. The *Shibuya* dataset [26] is one of very few public dataset with perspective looking query images and panorama reference images. This dataset is originally designed for the location retrieval task, but we reuse all of its 942 query images for our image-to-GPS verification task. It is worthy noting that this is a very challenging dataset in the sense that all reference and query images are densely located in a small geo-region less than 6 square miles but with similar architectures and styles. We pair these 942 query images with 942 panorama images taken at the ground-truth GPS locations to form positive samples, and pair them with additional 942 panorama images that are 1+ miles away from the ground-truth GPS locations to form negative samples.

The *Wikimedia Common* dataset[7] is collected by ourselves for evaluating the BUPM performance on different places. In total, we collected 500 positive samples all over the world, where query images are manually verified to be (1) street-view, (2) taken in recent two years, and (3) visually verified in corresponding panorama reference images. The country distribution of these samples can be seen in Fig. 7. Similar to what we did for the *Shibuya* dataset, we also pair the query images and panorama images to form 500 positive and 500 negative samples.

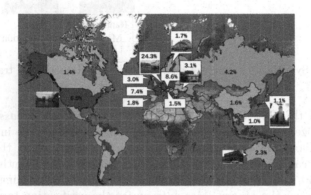

Fig. 7. The country distribution of the Wikimedia Common dataset.

5.2   Baselines

To understand the performance of the proposed BUPM network, we compare its overall performance with the state-of-the-art location-based image retrieval solutions, and its localization performance with the state-of-the-art template matching solutions. For verification baselines, we use

- *NetVLAD* [4] for place recognition.
- *Places-CNN* [30] for place-based scene recognition.
- *DELF* [18] for location based image retrieval.

For template matching baselines, we use

- Best-buddies similarity (*BBS*) [7]
- Deformable diversity similarity (*DDIS*) [23]

All pretrained models/methods are directly taken from their repositories or provided by authors. To make these baselines compatible with the proposed image-to-GPS task, we simply treat them as *feature extractors*, *i.e.* cropping-off the last classification layer of the network if necessary, and use the method defined metric to compute feature-wise similarity score between features of a pair of query and reference images.

---

[7] https://commons.wikimedia.org/wiki/Category:Images.

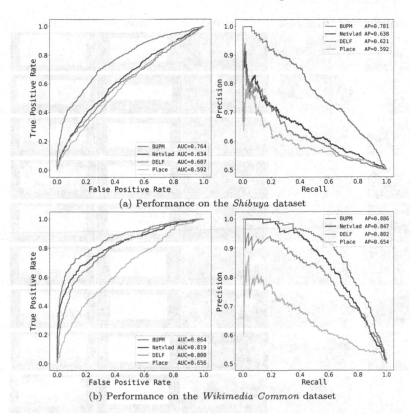

(a) Performance on the *Shibuya* dataset

(b) Performance on the *Wikimedia Common* dataset

Fig. 8. Method performance comparisons using the AUC (left) and precision-recall (right) curves.

5.3   Metrics and Performance

To fairly compare method performance while avoiding additional post-processing, we use (1) *Area Under the Curve* (AUC), and (2) *Precision-Recall* plot. Both are operated on various threshold settings.

Figure 8 show the AUC and precision-recall curves of all baselines and the proposed BUPM method for the *Shibuya* and *Wikimedia Common* dataset, respectively. It is clear that the proposed BUPM solution outperforms the state-of-the art solutions by a large margin, leading the second best approach by 13% (AUC score) and 14% (average precision score) on the *Shibuya* dataset, and by 4% (AUC score) and 4% (average precision score) on the *Wikimedia Common* dataset. The superiority of BUPM is not surprising, because a panorama image contains more contents than required while only the proposed BUPM solution could actively *ignore* these contents.

Due to the lack of ground truth annotation on matched regions, we only assess the localization performance qualitatively. Figure 9 shows the localization results of the proposed BUPM network, BBS, and DDIS, as well as corresponding probability maps where a brighter pixel indicates a higher likelihood of matching. The provided bounding boxes of BUPM are obtained by finding the minimum

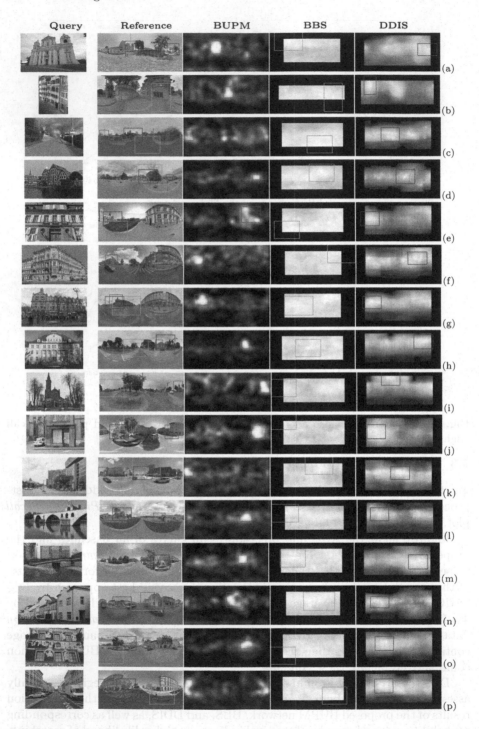

Fig. 9. Localization performance comparisons for BUPM, BBS and DDIS. (Best viewed in digital version. Zoom in for details) Bounding box color: ■ BUPM, ■ BBS, ■ DDIS (Color figure online)

rectangular box of the biggest connected component on the mask (after thresh-olding the predict mask at 0.5), while those of BBS and DDIS are directly taken from the source code outputs.

It is clear that the proposed BUPM network (1) produces fewer bright pixels and thus fewer false alarms than BBS and DDIS; (2) focuses more on immovable objects like buildings as expected, while BBS and DDIS are not (see Fig. 9(c, h)); (3) is more robust against natural variations like day-night change (see Fig. 9(d, h, j, l, n, p)) weather change (see Fig. 9(c)), and season change (see Fig. 9(m)); (4) is capable to handle the extreme case that a panorama image is opened at some place inside of the query scene, which will cause the matched content in a reference locates at both the left- and right-most regions (see Fig. 9(p)).

6 Conclusion

In this paper, we work on the image-to-GPS verification task to fight against fake news. We show that this problem could be formulated as an image verification problem – whether or not a query image and a reference image retrieved at the claimed position are taken from the same position. More precisely, we answer this question by checking visual contents of a query image in one panorama reference image, instead of verifying the query image against many possible reference images. This novel setting not only reduces the number of verification need to perform but also largely simplifies data preparation.

We propose a novel BUPM network to perform the verification task. It is a feed-forward network with multiple stages, each of which is designed to ful-fill one particular goal, e.g. visual feature extraction, similarity matching, etc. Since there is no large enough public dataset for training BUPM, we collect and clean 30K paired positive samples. To ensure the BUPM module to achieve its designed functionality and network convergence, we also introduce a two-stage training scheme. Our experimental results on the real dataset demonstrate that the proposed BUPM network outperforms state-of-the-art image verifica-tion methods in terms of much higher AUC and average precision scores and that it is capable of finding matched patches between query and reference. The bottom-up matching manner further improves matching accuracy and reduces false alarms.

Since the BUPM network solution can be viewed as one way of learnable template matching, it can be applied to related problems, like template matching, constraint splicing detection [29], etc.

Acknowledgement. This work is based on research sponsored by the Defense Advanced Research Projects Agency under agreement number FA8750-16-2-0204. The U.S. Government is authorized to reproduce and distribute reprints for governmental purposes notwithstanding any copyright notation thereon. The views and conclusions contained herein are those of the authors and should not be interpreted as necessarily representing the official policies or endorsements, either expressed or implied, of the Defense Advanced Research Projects Agency or the U.S. Government.

References

1. AbdAlmageed, W., et al.: Face recognition using deep multi-pose representations. In: Proceedings of the IEEE Winter Conference on Applications of Computer Vision, pp. 1–9. IEEE (2016)
2. Agarwal, P., Burgard, W., Spinello, L.: Metric localization using Google street view. In: Proceedings of the IEEE/RSJ International Conference on Intelligent Robots and Systems (IROS), pp. 3111–3118. IEEE (2015)
3. Anguelov, D., et al.: Google street view: capturing the world at street level. Computer **43**(6), 32–38 (2010)
4. Arandjelovic, R., Gronat, P., Torii, A., Pajdla, T., Sivic, J.: NetVLAD: CNN architecture for weakly supervised place recognition. In: Proceedings of the IEEE Conference on Computer Vision and Pattern Recognition, pp. 5297–5307 (2016)
5. Arandjelović, R., Zisserman, A.: DisLocation: scalable descriptor distinctiveness for location recognition. In: Cremers, D., Reid, I., Saito, H., Yang, M.-H. (eds.) ACCV 2014. LNCS, vol. 9006, pp. 188–204. Springer, Cham (2015). https://doi.org/10.1007/978-3-319-16817-3_13
6. Chen, D.M., et al.: City-scale landmark identification on mobile devices. In: Proceedings of the IEEE Conference on Computer Vision and Pattern Recognition, pp. 737–744. IEEE (2011)
7. Dekel, T., Oron, S., Rubinstein, M., Avidan, S., Freeman, W.T.: Best-buddies similarity for robust template matching. In: Proceedings of the IEEE Conference on Computer Vision and Pattern Recognition, pp. 2021–2029 (2015)
8. He, K., Zhang, X., Ren, S., Sun, J.: Deep residual learning for image recognition. In: Proceedings of the IEEE Conference on Computer Vision and Pattern Recognition, pp. 770–778 (2016)
9. Hoang, T., Do, T.T., Le Tan, D.K., Cheung, N.M.: Selective deep convolutional features for image retrieval. In: Proceedings of the ACM on Multimedia Conference, pp. 1600–1608. ACM (2017)
10. Koch, G., Zemel, R., Salakhutdinov, R.: Siamese neural networks for one-shot image recognition. In: Proceedings of International Conference on Machine Learning Deep Learning Workshop, vol. 2 (2015)
11. Korman, S., Milam, M., Soatto, S.: Oatm: occlusion aware template matching by consensus set maximization. In: Proceedings of the IEEE Conference on Computer Vision and Pattern Recognition (2018)
12. Lee, K., Lee, S., Jung, W.J., Kim, K.T.: Fast and accurate visual place recognition using street-view images. Electron. Telecommun. Res. Inst. J. **39**(1), 97–107 (2017)
13. Lefèvre, S., Tuia, D., Wegner, J.D., Produit, T., Nassaar, A.S.: Toward seamless multiview scene analysis from satellite to street level. Proc. IEEE **105**(10), 1884–1899 (2017)
14. Lowe, D.G.: Distinctive image features from scale-invariant keypoints. Int. J. Comput. Vis. **60**(2), 91–110 (2004)
15. Majdik, A.L., Albers-Schoenberg, Y., Scaramuzza, D.: MAV urban localization from Google street view data. In: IEEE/RSJ International Conference on Intelligent Robots and Systems, pp. 3979–3986. IEEE (2013)
16. Melekhov, I., Kannala, J., Rahtu, E.: Siamese network features for image matching. In: Proceedings of the IEEE International Conference on Pattern Recognition, pp. 378–383. IEEE (2016)
17. Nister, D., Stewenius, H.: Scalable recognition with a vocabulary tree. In: Proceedings of the IEEE Conference on Computer Vision and Pattern Recognition, vol. 2, pp. 2161–2168. IEEE (2006)

18. Noh, H., Araujo, A., Sim, J., Weyand, T., Han, B.: Large-scale image retrieval with attentive deep local features. In: Proceedings of the IEEE Conference on Computer Vision and Pattern Recognition, pp. 3456–3465 (2017)
19. Sattler, T., Leibe, B., Kobbelt, L.: Improving image-based localization by active correspondence search. In: Fitzgibbon, A., Lazebnik, S., Perona, P., Sato, Y., Schmid, C. (eds.) ECCV 2012. LNCS, vol. 7572, pp. 752–765. Springer, Heidelberg (2012). https://doi.org/10.1007/978-3-642-33718-5_54
20. Sattler, T., Leibe, B., Kobbelt, L.: Efficient & effective prioritized matching for large-scale image-based localization. IEEE Trans. Pattern Anal. Mach. Intell. **39**(9), 1744–1756 (2017)
21. Schönberger, J.L., Price, T., Sattler, T., Frahm, J.-M., Pollefeys, M.: A vote-and-verify strategy for fast spatial verification in image retrieval. In: Lai, S.-H., Lepetit, V., Nishino, K., Sato, Y. (eds.) ACCV 2016. LNCS, vol. 10111, pp. 321–337. Springer, Cham (2017). https://doi.org/10.1007/978-3-319-54181-5_21
22. Szegedy, C., Vanhoucke, V., Ioffe, S., Shlens, J., Wojna, Z.: Rethinking the inception architecture for computer vision. In: Proceedings of the IEEE Conference on Computer Vision and Pattern Recognition, pp. 2818–2826 (2016)
23. Talmi, I., Mechrez, R., Zelnik-Manor, L.: Template matching with deformable diversity similarity. In: Proceedings of the IEEE Conference on Computer Vision and Pattern Recognition, pp. 1311–1319 (2017)
24. Tolias, G., Sicre, R., Jégou, H.: Particular object retrieval with integral max-pooling of CNN activations (2016)
25. Torii, A., Arandjelović, R., Sivic, J., Okutomi, M., Pajdla, T.: 24/7 place recognition by view synthesis. In: Proceedings of the IEEE Conference on Computer Vision and Pattern Recognition, pp. 1808–1817. IEEE (2015)
26. Torii, A., Sivic, J., Pajdla, T.: Visual localization by linear combination of image descriptors. In: Proceedings of the IEEE International Conference on Computer Vision Workshops, pp. 102–109. IEEE (2011)
27. Vo, N., Jacobs, N., Hays, J.: Revisiting IM2GPS in the deep learning era. In: Proceedings of the IEEE International Conference on Computer Vision, pp. 2640–2649. IEEE (2017)
28. Weyand, T., Kostrikov, I., Philbin, J.: PlaNet - photo geolocation with convolutional neural networks. In: Leibe, B., Matas, J., Sebe, N., Welling, M. (eds.) ECCV 2016. LNCS, vol. 9912, pp. 37–55. Springer, Cham (2016). https://doi.org/10.1007/978-3-319-46484-8_3
29. Wu, Y., Abd-Almageed, W., Natarajan, P.: Deep matching and validation network: an end-to-end solution to constrained image splicing localization and detection. In: Proceedings of the ACM on Multimedia Conference, pp. 1480–1502. ACM (2017)
30. Zhou, B., Lapedriza, A., Xiao, J., Torralba, A., Oliva, A.: Learning deep features for scene recognition using places database. In: Advances in Neural Information Processing Systems, pp. 487–495 (2014)
31. Zhou, Z., Wang, Y., Wu, Q.J., Yang, C.N., Sun, X.: Effective and efficient global context verification for image copy detection. IEEE Trans. Inf. Forensics Secur. **12**(1), 48–63 (2017)

VIPL-HR: A Multi-modal Database for Pulse Estimation from Less-Constrained Face Video

Xuesong Niu[1,2], Hu Han[1,3(✉)], Shiguang Shan[1,2,4], and Xilin Chen[1,2]

[1] Key Laboratory of Intelligent Information Processing of Chinese Academy of Sciences (CAS), Institute of Computing Technology, CAS, Beijing 100190, China
xuesong.niu@vipl.ict.ac.cn, {hanhu,sgshan,xlchen}@ict.ac.cn
[2] University of Chinese Academy of Sciences, Beijing 100049, China
[3] Peng Cheng Laboratory, Shenzhen, China
[4] CAS Center for Excellence in Brain Science and Intelligence Technology, Shanghai, China

Abstract. Heart rate (HR) is an important physiological signal that reflects the physical and emotional activities of humans. Traditional HR measurements are mainly based on contact monitors, which are inconvenient and may cause discomfort for the subjects. Recently, methods have been proposed for remote HR estimation from face videos. However, most of the existing methods focus on well-controlled scenarios, their generalization ability into less-constrained scenarios are not known. At the same time, lacking large-scale databases has limited the use of deep representation learning methods in remote HR estimation. In this paper, we introduce a large-scale multi-modal HR database (named as VIPL-HR), which contains 2,378 visible light videos (VIS) and 752 near-infrared (NIR) videos of 107 subjects. Our VIPL-HR database also contains various variations such as head movements, illumination variations, and acquisition device changes. We also learn a deep HR estimator (named as RhythmNet) with the proposed spatial-temporal representation, which achieves promising results on both the public-domain and our VIPL-HR HR estimation databases. We would like to put the VIPL-HR database into the public domain (http://vipl.ict.ac.cn/database.php).

1 Introduction

Heart rate (HR) is an important physiological signal that reflects the physical and emotional activities, and HR measurement can be useful for many applications, such as training aid, health monitoring, and nursing care. Traditional HR measurement usually relies on contact monitors, such as electrocardiograph (ECG) and contact photoplethysmography (cPPG), which are inconvenient for the users and limit the application scenarios. In recent years, a growing number of studies have been reported on remote HR estimation from face videos [1,3,10,15,16,21,23].

© Springer Nature Switzerland AG 2019
C. V. Jawahar et al. (Eds.): ACCV 2018, LNCS 11365, pp. 562–576, 2019.
https://doi.org/10.1007/978-3-030-20873-8_36

The existing video-based HR estimation methods mainly depend on two kinds of signals: the remote photoplethysmography (rPPG) signals [3,10,15,16,21,23] and the ballistocardiographic (BCG) signals [1]. There is no doubt that the idea of estimating HR from face videos could be a convenient physiological platform for clinical monitoring and health caring in the future. However, most of the existing approaches only provide evaluations on private databases, leading to difficulties in comparing different methods. Although a few public-domain HR databases are available [2,9,18,19,21], the sizes of these databases are very limited (usually smaller than 50 subjects). Moreover, these databases are usually captured in a well-controlled scenario, with minor illumination and motion variations (see Fig. 1(a)). These limitations will lead to two issues for the remote HR estimation: (i) it is hard to analyze the robustness of individual HR estimation algorithms against different variations and acquisition devices; (ii) it is difficult to leverage the deep representation learning approaches in remote HR estimation, which are believed to have the ability to overcome the limitation of hand-crafted methods designed on specific assumptions [13].

To overcome these limitations, we introduce the VIPL-HR database for remote HR estimation, which is a large-scale multi-modal database recorded with various head movement, illumination variations, and acquisition device changes (see Fig. 1(b)).

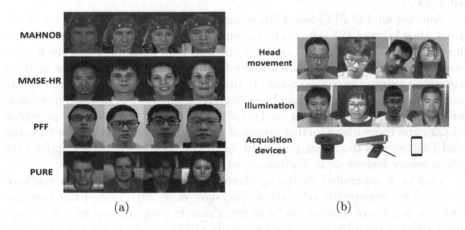

Fig. 1. A comparison between (a) the public domain databases (MAHNOB, MMSE-HR, PFF, PURE) and (b) our VIPL-HR database in terms of the illumination condition, head movement, and acquisition device.

Given the large VIPL-HR database, we further propose a deep HR estimator, named as RhythmNet, for robust heart rate estimation from face. RhythmNet takes an informative spatial-temporal map as input and adopts an effective training strategy to learn the HR estimator. The results of within-database and cross-database experiments have shown the effectiveness of the proposed approach.

The rest of this paper is organized as follow: Sect. 2 discusses the related works of remote HR estimation and existing public-domain HR databases. Section 3 introduces the large-scale VIPL-HR database we have collected. Section 4 provides the details of the proposed RhythmNet. After that, Sect. 5 evaluates the proposed method under both within-database and cross-database protocols. Finally, the conclusions and future work are summarized in Sect. 6.

2   Related Work

2.1   Remote HR Estimation

The possibility of using PPG signals captured by custom color cameras was firstly introduced by Verkruysse et al. [22]. Then many algorithms have been proposed, which can be generally divided into blind signal separation (BSS) methods, model-based methods and data-driven methods.

Poh et al. first applied the blind signal separation (BSS) to remote HR estimation [15,16]. They applied independent component analysis (ICA) to temporal filtered red, green, and blue (RGB) color channel signals to seek the heartbeat-related signal, which they assumed is one of the separated independent components. A patch-level HR signal calculation with ICA was performed later in [8] and achieved the state-of-the-art on the public-available database MAHNOB-HCI [18].

Another kind of PPG-based HR estimation methods focus on leveraging the prior knowledge of the skin model to remote HR estimation. Haan and Jeanne firstly proposed a skin optical model of different color channels under the motion condition and computed a chrominance feature using the combination of RGB signals to reduce the motion noise [3]. In a later work of [24], pixel-wise chrominance features are computed and used for HR estimation. A detailed discussion of different skin optical model used for rPPG-based HR estimation is presented in [23], and the authors further proposed a new projection method for the original RGB signals to extract pulse signals. In [12], Niu et al. further applied the chrominance feature [3] to continuous estimation situations.

Besides hand-crafted methods, there are also some data-driven methods designed for remote HR estimation. Tulyakov et al. [21] divided the face into multiple regions of interest (ROI) to get a matrix temporal representation and used a matrix completion approach to purify rPPG signals. In [2], Hsu et al. generated the time-frequency maps from different color signals and used them to learn an HR estimator. Although the existing data-driven approaches attempted to build learning based HR estimator, they failed to build an end-to-end estimator. Besides, the features they used remain hand-crafted, which may not be optimum for the HR estimation task. In [13], Niu et al. proposed a general-to-specific learning strategy to solve the problem of representing HR signals and lacking data. However, they didn't investigate the choice of color spaces and missing data situation.

Instead of the PPG-based HR measurement methods, the ballistocardiographic (BCG) signals, which is the subtle head motions caused by cardiovascular circulation, can also be used for remote HR estimation. Inspired by the Eulerian magnification method [25], Balakrishnan et al. tracked the key points on face and used PCA to get the pulse signal from the trajectories of feature points. [1]. Since these methods are based on subtle motion, the subjects' voluntary movements will introduce significant influence to the HR signals, leading to limited use in real-life applications.

Although the published methods have made a lot of progress in remote HR measurement, they still have limitations. First, the existing approaches are usually tested on well-controlled small-scale databases, which could not represent the real-life situations. Second, most of the existing approaches are designed in a step-by-step way using hand-crafted features, which are based on some specific assumptions and may fail in some complex conditions. Data-driven methods based on large-scale database are needed. However it is not as simple as visual attribute learning via deep neural network [5], in which the dominant information in the face image is related to the visual attribute learning task. The information in the face image related to the HR estimation task is quite weak.

2.2 Public-Domain Databases for Remote HR Estimation

Many of the published methods reported their performance on private databases, leading to difficulties in performance comparison by other approaches. The first public domain database was introduced by Li et al. [10]. They evaluated their method on the MAHNOB-HCI database [18], which was designed for emotion detection and the subjects performed slight head movement and facial expressions. Later in 2016, Tulyakov et al. introduced a new database MMSE-HR [21], which was part of the MMSE database [26] and the subjects' facial expressions were more various. However, these two databases were originally designed for emotion analysis, and the subjects' motions were mainly limited to facial expression changes, which was far from enough for real-world remote HR estimation.

There are also a few public-available databases specially designed for the task of remote HR estimation. Stricker et al. firstly released the PURE database collected by the camera of a mobile sever robot [19]. Hus et al. released the PFF database containing 10 subjects under 8 different situations [2]. These two databases are limited by the number of subjects and recording situations. In 2018, Xiaobai et al. proposed a database designed for HR and heart rate variability (HRV) measurement [9]. Since this database aims at HRV analysis and all the situations in this database are well-controlled, making it very easy for remote HR estimation.

The existing public-domain databases for remote HR estimation can be found in Table 1. As we can see from Table 1, all these databases are limited in either the number of subjects or the recording situations. A large-scale database recorded under real-life variations is required to push the studies on remote HR estimation.

Table 1. A summary of the public-domain databases and VIPL-HR database.

	Subject	Illumination	Head movement	Recording devices	Video
MAHNOB [18]	27	L	E	C	527
MMSE-HR [21]	40	L	E	C	102
PURE [19]	10	L	S	C	60
PFF [2]	13	L/D	S/SM	C	104
OBF [9]	106	L	S	C/N	2,120
VIPL-HR	**107**	**L/D/B**	**S/LM/T**	**C/N/P**	**3,130**

L = Lab Environment, D = Dark Environment, B = Bright Environment, E = Expression, S = Stable, SM = Slight Motion, LM = Large Motion, T = Talking, C = Color Camera, N = NIR Camera, P = Smart Phone Frontal Camera

3   The VIPL-HR Database

In order to evaluate methods designed for real-world HR estimation, a database containing various face variations, such as head movements and illumination change, and acquisition diversity, is needed. To fill in this gap, we collected the VIPL-HR database, which contains more than one hundred subjects under various illumination conditions and different head movements. All the face videos are recorded by three different cameras and the relative physical measurements, such as HR, SpO2, and blood volume pulse (BVP) signal, are also simultaneously recorded. In this section, we introduce our VIPL-HR database from three aspects: (i) setup and data collection, (ii) video compression, and (iii) database statistics.

3.1   Setup and Data Collection

We design our data collection procedure with two objectives in mind: (i) videos should be recorded under natural conditions (i.e., head movement and illumination change) instead of well-controlled situations; and (ii) videos should be captured using various recording devices to replicate the common case in daily life, i.e., smartphones, RGB-D cameras, and web cameras. The recording setup is arranged based on these two targets, which includes a computer, an RGB web-camera, an RGB-D camera, a smartphone, a finger pulse oximeter, and a filament lamp. The details of the device specifications can be found in Table 2.

Videos recorded from different devices are the core component of VIPL-HR database. In order to test the influence of cameras with different recording quality, we choose the widely used web-camera Logitech C310 and the color camera of RealSense F200 to record the RGB videos. At the same time, while smartphones have become an indispensable part of our daily lives, remote HR estimation from the videos recorded by smart phone cameras has not been studied yet. Thus, we use a HUAWEI P9 smart phone (with its frontal camera) to record the RGB face videos for the potential applications of remote HR estimation on mobile devices. Besides recording the RGB color videos, we also record the NIR

Table 2. Specifications and settings of individual recording devices used in our VIPL-HR database.

Device	Specification	Setting	Output
Computer	Lenovo ThinkCentre	Windows 10 OS	N/A
Color camera	Logitech C310	25 fps 960×720 color camera	Color videos
RGB-D camera	RealSense F200	30 fps, 640×480 NIR camera 1920×1080 color camera	Color videos NIR videos
Smart phone	HUAWEI P9 frontal camera	30 fps, 1920×1080 color camera	Color videos
BVP recoder	CONTEC CMS60C	N/A	HR, SpO2, and BVP signals
Filament lamp	N/A	50 Hz	N/A

face videos using a RealSense F200 to investigate the possibility of remote HR estimation under dim lighting conditions. Related physiological signals, including HR, SpO2, and BVP signals, are synchronously recorded with a CONTEC CMS60C BVP sensor.

The recording environmental setup is illustrated in Fig. 2. The subjects are asked to sit in front of the cameras at two different distances: one meter and 1.5 m. A filament lamp is placed aside the cameras to change the light conditions. Each subject is asked to sit naturally in front of the cameras, and daily activities such as talking and looking around are encouraged during the video recording. HR changes of the subject after exercises are also taken into consideration. The smartphone is first fixed in front of the subject for video recording, and then we asked the subject to hold the smartphone by themselves to record videos like a video chat scenario. Videos under nine different situations are recorded in total for each subject, and the details of these situations are listed in Table 3.

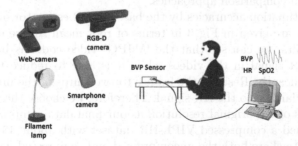

Fig. 2. An illumination of the device setup used in collecting the VIPL-HR database.

Table 3. Details of the nine recording situations in the VIPL-HR database.

Situation	Head movement	Illumination	Distance	Exercise	Phone position
1	S	L	1 m	No	Fixed
2	LM	L	1 m	No	Fixed
3	T	L	1 m	No	Fixed
4	S	B	1 m	No	Fixed
5	S	D	1 m	No	Fixed
6	S	L	1.5 m	No	Fixed
7	S	L	1 m	No	Hand-hold
8	LM	L	1 m	No	Hand-hold
9	S	L	1 m	Yes	Fixed

S = Stable, LM = Large Motion, T = Talking, L = Lab Environment, D = Dark Environment, B = Bright Environment

3.2 Database Compression

As stated in [11], video compression plays an important role in video-based heart rate estimation. The raw data of VIPL-HR we collected is nearly 1.05 TB in total, making it very inconvenient for the public access. In order to balance the convenience of data sharing and completeness of HR signals, we investigate to make a compressed and resized version of our database, which can retain the completeness of the HR signals as much as possible. The compression methods we considered include video compression and frame resizing. The video compression codecs we take into consideration are 'MJPG', 'FMP4', 'DIVX', 'PIM1' and 'X264', which are commonly-used video compression codecs. The resizing scales we consider are 1/2, 2/3, and 3/4 for each dimension of the original frame. We choose one of the widely used remote HR estimation method Haan2013 [3] as a baseline HR estimation method to verify the HR estimation accuracy changes after individual comparison approaches.

The HR estimation accuracies by the baseline HR estimator on various compressed videos are given in Fig. 3 in terms of root mean square error (RMSE). From the results, we can see that the 'MJPG' video codec is better in maintaining the HR signal in the videos while it is able to reduce the size of the database significantly. Resizing the frames to two-thirds of the image resolution leads to little damage to the HR signal. Therefore, we choose the 'MJPG' codec and two-thirds of the original resolution as our final data compression solution, and we obtained a compressed VIPL-HR dataset with about 48 GB. However, we would like to share both the uncompressed and compressed databases to the research community based on the researchers' preference.

3.3 Database Statistics

The VIPL-HR dataset contains a total of 2,378 color videos and 752 NIR videos from 107 participants (79 males and 28 females) aged between 22 and 41. Each

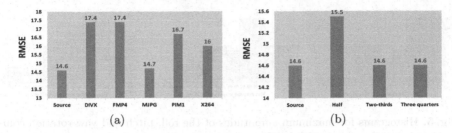

(a)   (b)

Fig. 3. Evaluations of using (a) different video compression codecs and (b) different image resolutions to compress the VIPL-HR database. All the compression methods are tested using Haan2013 [3]. Source represents the test results on uncompressed data.

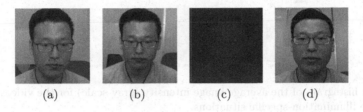

(a)   (b)   (c)   (d)

Fig. 4. Example video frames captured for one subject by different devices: (a) Logitech C310, (b) RealSense F200 color camera, (c) RealSense F200 NIR camera, (4) HUAWEI P9 frontal camera.

video is recorded with a length of about 30 s, and the frame rate is about 30 fps (see Table 1). Some example video frames of one subject captured by different devices are shown in Fig. 4.

To further analyze the characteristics of our VIPL-HR database, we calculated the head pose variations using the OpenFace head pose estimator[1] for the videos with head movement (see Situation 2 in Table 3). Histograms for maximum amplitudes of the three rotation components for all the videos can be found in Fig. 5. From the histograms, we can see that the maximum rotation amplitudes of the subjects vary in a large range, i.e., the maximum rotation amplitudes are 92° in roll, 105° in pitch and 104° in yaw. This is reasonable because every subject is allowed to look around during the video recording.

At the same time, in order to quantitatively demonstrate the illumination changes in VIPL-HR database, we have calculated the mean grey-scale intensity of face area for Situation 1, Situation 4, and Situation 5 in Table 3. The results are shown in Fig. 6. We can see that the mean gray-scale intensity varies from 60 to 212, covering complicated illumination variations.

A histogram of ground-truth HRs is also shown in Fig. 7. We can see that the ground-truth HRs in VIPL-HR vary from 47 bpm to 146 bpm, which covers the typical HR range[2]. The wide HR distribution in VIPL-HR fills the gap between lab-controlled databases and the HR distribution presenting in daily-life scenes.

---

[1] https://github.com/TadasBaltrusaitis/OpenFace.
[2] https://en.wikipedia.org/wiki/Heart_rate.

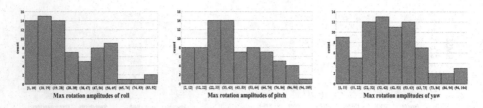

Fig. 5. Histograms for maximum amplitudes of the roll, pitch and yaw rotation components for all the videos with head movement.

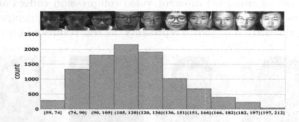

Fig. 6. A histogram of the average image intensity (gray-scale) for the videos recorded under the illumination-specific situations.

The relatively large size of VIPL-HR also makes it possible to use deep learning methods to build data-driven HR estimators.

4   Deeply Learned HR Estimator

With the less-constrained VIPL-HR database, we are able to build a data-driven HR estimator using deep learning methods. Following the idea of [13], we propose a deep HR estimation method, named as RhythmNet. An overview producer of RyhthmNet can be seen in Fig. 8.

4.1   Spatial-Temporal Maps Generation

In order to identify the face area within the video frames, we first use the face detector provided by the open source SeetaFace[3] to get the face location and 81 facial landmarks (see Fig. 9). Since the facial landmarks detection is able to run at a frame rate of more than 30 fps, we perform face detection and landmarks detection on every frame in order to get consistent ROI localization in a face video sequence. A moving average filter is applied to the 81 landmark points to get more stable landmark localizations.

According to [7], the most informative facial parts containing the color changes due to heart rhythms are the cheek area and the forehead area. The ROI containing both the cheek and forehead area is determined using the cheek border and chin locations as shown in Fig. 9. Face alignment is firstly performed

---

[3] https://github.com/seetaface/SeetaFaceEngine.

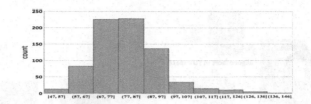

Fig. 7. The histogram showing the ground-truth HR distribution.

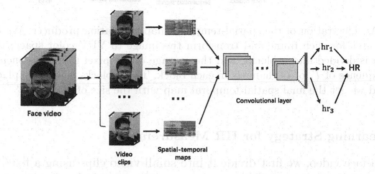

Fig. 8. Overview of RhythmNet. Given an input video sequence, we first divide it into multiple short video clips. Then spatial-temporal maps are generated from the aligned face images within each video clip to represent the HR signals, and a CNN model is trained to predict the HR per video clip. Finally, the average HR estimated for a video sequence is computed as the average of all the HRs.

using the eye center points, and then a bounding box is defined with a width of w (where w is the horizontal distance between the outer cheek border points) and height $1.5 * h$ (where h is the vertical distance between chin location and eye center points). Skin segmentation is then applied to the defined ROI to remove the non-face area such as the eye region and the background area.

According to [13], a good representation of the HR signals is very important for training a deep HR estimator. Niu et al. directly used the average pixel values of RGB channels as the HR signals representation, which may not be the best choice to represent HR signals. As stated in [20], alternative color spaces derived from RGB video are beneficial for getting a better HR signal representation. After testing alternative color spaces, we finally choose the YUV color space for further computing. The color space transform can be formulized as

$$\begin{bmatrix} Y \\ U \\ V \end{bmatrix} = \begin{bmatrix} 0.299 & 0.587 & 0.114 \\ -0.169 & -0.331 & 0.5 \\ 0.5 & -0.419 & -0.081 \end{bmatrix} \begin{bmatrix} R \\ G \\ B \end{bmatrix} + \begin{bmatrix} 0 \\ 128 \\ 128 \end{bmatrix} \quad (1)$$

and the final spatial-temporal map generation producer can be found in Fig. 9.

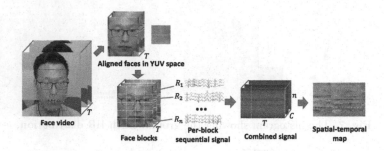

Fig. 9. An illustration of the spatial-temporal map generation producer. We first get the face area for each frame and transform the image to YUV color space, then the face area is divided into n blocks, and the average of the pixel values is concatenated into a sequence of T for C channels in each block. The n blocks is directly placed into rows, and we get the final spatial-temporal map with the size of $n \times T \times C$.

4.2   Learning Strategy for HR Measurement

For each face video, we first divide it into small video clips using a fixed sliding window and then compute the spatial-temporal map, which is used to estimate the HR per video clip. The average HR of the face video is computed as the average of the HRs estimated from each clip. We choose the ResNet18 [6] as our convolutional neural network (CNN) for learning the mapping from spatial-temporal maps to HRs, which is commonly used in various computer vision tasks. The ResNet18 architecture including four blocks made up of convolutional layers and residual link, one convolutional layer and one fully connected layer for the final classification. The output of the network is one single HR value, which is normalized based on the frame rate of the face video. L_1 losses are used for measuring the distance between the predicted HR and ground truth HR.

It is important to leverage the prior knowledge of HR signals during HR estimation. To achieve this purpose, we use the synthetic rhythm data for network pre-training as stated in [13]. Specifically, our training strategy could be divided into three stages. Firstly, we train our model using the large-scale image database ImageNet [17]. Then the synthetic spatial-temporal maps are used to guide the network to learn the prior knowledge of mapping a video sequence into an HR value. With this prior knowledge, we can further fine-tune the neural network for the final HR estimation task using the real-life face videos.

Another situation we need to consider is that the face detector may fail in a short time interval, which commonly happens when the subject's head is moving or rotating. The failing of face detection will cause the missing data of HR signals. In order to handle this issue, we randomly mask (set to zero) the spatial-temporal maps along the time dimension to simulate the missing data situation. The masked spatial-temporal maps are found to be useful to train a robust HR estimator against failing of face detection.

5 Experiments

5.1 Database, Protocol, and Experimental Settings

In this paper, we use the VIPL-HR database for within-database testing and the MMSE-HR database [21] for cross-database evaluation. Details about these two databases can be found in Table 1. We first perform participant-dependent five-fold cross-validation for within-database testing on the VIPL-HR database. Then, we directly train the RhythmNet on the VIPL-HR database and test it on the MMSE-HR database. After that, the RhythmNet pre-trained on the VIPL-HR is fine-tuned and tested on the MMSE-HR.

Different evaluation metrics have been proposed for remote HR estimation, such as the mean and standard deviation (HR_{me} and HR_{sd}) of the HR error, the mean absolute HR error (HR_{mae}), the root mean squared HR error (HR_{rmse}), the mean error rate percentage (HR_{mer}), and Pearsons correlation coefficients r [10,21]. In this paper, we also use these evaluation metrics for all the experiments below.

For each video, a sliding window with 300 frames is used for generating the spatial-temporal maps. We divide the face area into 25 blocks (5×5 grids). The percentage of masked spatial-temporal maps is 50%, and the mask length varies from 10 frames to 30 frames. Since the face sizes in the NIR videos are small for the face detector, only 497 NIR videos with detected faces are involved in the experiments. The RhythmNet is implemented using the PyTorch[4] framework. The Adam solver with an initial learning rate of 0.001 is applied to train the model, and the number of maximum iteration epochs is 50.

5.2 Within-Database Testing

Experiments on Color Face Videos. We first perform the within-database testing on the VIPL-HR database. We use the state-of-the-art methods (Haan2013 [3], Tulyakov2016 [21], Wang2017 [23] and Niu2018 [13]) for comparisons. The results of the individual methods are reported in Table 4.

From the results, we can see that the proposed method could achieve promising results with an HR_{rmse} of 8.94bpm, which is a much lower error than other methods. At the same time, it can also be seen that our method achieves a better consistency on the VIPL-HR database with a much higher Pearsons correlation coefficient r of 0.73.

Experiment on NIR Face Videos. The experiments on NIR face videos are also conducted using the protocol proposed in Sect. 5.1. Since the NIR face videos only have one channel, no color space transformation is used, and we get one-channel spatial-temporal maps for the deep HR estimator. Very few methods have been proposed and evaluated on the NIR data, thus we only report the results based on the RhythmNet in Table 5.

---

[4] https://pytorch.org/.

Table 4. The results of HR estimation on color face videos on VIPL-HR database.

Method	HR_{me} (bpm)	HR_{sd} (bpm)	HR_{mae} (bpm)	HR_{rmse} (bpm)	HR_{mer}	r
Haan2013 [3]	7.63	15.1	11.4	16.9	17.8%	0.28
Tulyakov2016 [21]	10.8	18.0	15.9	21.0	26.7%	0.11
Wang2017 [23]	7.87	15.3	11.5	17.2	18.5%	0.30
RhythmNet	**1.02**	**8.88**	**5.79**	**8.94**	**7.38%**	**0.73**

Table 5. The results of HR estimation on NIR face videos on VIPL-HR database.

Method	HR_{me} (bpm)	HR_{sd} (bpm)	HR_{mae} (bpm)	HR_{rmse}	HR_{mer}	r
RhythmNet	2.87	11.08	8.50	11.44	11.0%	0.53

Table 6. The results of average HR estimation per video using different methods on the MMSE-HR database.

Method	HR_{me} (bpm)	HR_{sd} (bpm)	HR_{rmse} (bpm)	HR_{mer}	r
Li2014 [10]	11.56	20.02	19.95	14.64%	0.38
Haan2013 [3]	9.41	14.08	13.97	12.22%	0.55
Tulyakov2016 [21]	7.61	12.24	11.37	10.84%	0.71
RhythmNet(CrossDB)	−2.26	10.39	10.58	**5.35%**	0.69
RhythmNet(Fine-tuned)	**−1.30**	**8.16**	**8.22**	5.54%	**0.78**

5.3 Cross-Database Testing

The cross-database experiments are then conducted based on the MMSE-HR database. Specifically, we first train our model on the VIPL-HR database and directly test it on the MMSE-HR database. We also fine-tune the model on MMSE-HR to see whether a finetuning could improve the HR estimation accuracy or not. All the results can be found in Table 6. The baseline methods we use for comparisons are Li2014 [10], Haan2013 [3] and Tulyakov2016 [21], and their performances are from [21].

From the results, we can see that the proposed method could achieve a promising performance with an HR_{rmse} of 10.58 bpm, even when we directly test our VIPL-HR pre-trained model on MMSE-HR. The error rate is further reduced to 8.22 bpm when we fine-tune the pre-trained model on MMSE-HR. Both results of the proposed approach are much better than previous methods. These results indicate that the variations of illumination, movement, and acquisition device in the VIPL-HR database are helpful to learn an HR estimator which has good generalization ability to unseen scenarios. In addition, the proposed RhythmNet leverages the diverse information contained in VIPL-HR to learn a robust HR estimator.

6   Conclusion and Further Work

Remote HR estimation from a face video has wide applications; however, accurate HR estimation from the face in the wild is challenging due to the various variations in less-constrained scenarios. In this paper, we introduce a multi-modality VIPL-HR database for remote heart estimation under less-constrained conditions, such as head movement, illumination change, and camera diversity. We also proposed the RhythmNet, a data-driven heart estimator based on CNN, to perform remote HR estimation. Benefited from the proposed spatial-temporal map and the effective training strategy, our approach achieves promising HR accuracies in both within-database and cross-database testing.

In the future, besides investigating new HR signals representations, we are also going to establish models to leverage the relation between adjacent measurements from the sliding windows. Face dense alignment via 3D modeling [4] will also be studied to improve ROI alignment. In addition, detailed analysis of individual methods under various recording situations will be provided using the VIPL-HR database. We would also like to apply the proposed approach into the applications of face presentation attack detection [14], etc.

Acknowledgement. This research was supported in part by the National Key R&D Program of China (grant 2017YFA0700804), Natural Science Foundation of China (grants 61390511, 61672496, 61650202), External Cooperation Program of Chinese Academy of Sciences (grant GJHZ1843).

References

1. Balakrishnan, G., Durand, F., Guttag, J.: Detecting pulse from head motions in video. In: Proceedings of IEEE CVPR, pp. 3430–3437. IEEE (2013)
2. Hsu, G.-S., Ambikapathi, A., Chen, M.S.C.: Deep learning with time-frequency representation for pulse estimation. In: Proceedings of IJCB (2017)
3. de Haan, G., Jeanne, V.: Robust pulse rate from chrominance-based rPPG. IEEE Trans. Biomed. Eng. **60**(10), 2878–2886 (2013)
4. Han, H., Jain, A.K.: 3D face texture modeling from uncalibrated frontal and profile images. In: Proceedings of IEEE BTAS, pp. 223–230. IEEE (2012)
5. Han, H., Jain, A.K., Shan, S., Chen, X.: Heterogeneous face attribute estimation: a deep multi-task learning approach. IEEE Trans. Pattern Anal. Mach. Intell. **40**(11), 2597–2609 (2017)
6. He, K., Zhang, X., Ren, S., Sun, J.: Deep residual learning for image recognition. In: Proceedings of IEEE CVPR, pp. 770–778. IEEE (2016)
7. Kwon, S., Kim, J., Lee, D., Park, K.: ROI analysis for remote photoplethysmography on facial video. In: Proceedings of EMBS, pp. 851–862. IEEE (2015)
8. Lam, A., Kuno, Y.: Robust heart rate measurement from video using select random patches. In: Proceedings of IEEE ICCV, pp. 3640–3648. IEEE (2015)
9. Li, X., et al.: The OBF database: a large face video database for remote physiological signal measurement and atrial fibrillation detection. In: Proceedings of IEEE FG, pp. 242–249. IEEE (2018)

10. Li, X., Chen, J., Zhao, G., Pietikainen, M.: Remote heart rate measurement from face videos under realistic situations. In: Proceedings of IEEE CVPR, pp. 4264–4271. IEEE (2014)
11. McDuff, D.J., Blackford, E.B., Estepp, J.R.: The impact of video compression on remote cardiac pulse measurement using imaging photoplethysmography. In: Proceedings of IEEE FG, pp. 63–70. IEEE (2017)
12. Niu, X., Han, H., Shan, S., Chen, X.: Continuous heart rate measurement from face: a robust rPPG approach with distribution learning. In: Proceedings of IJCB (2017)
13. Niu, X., Han, H., Shan, S., Chen, X.: Synrhythm: learning a deep heart rate estimator from general to specific. In: Proceedings of IEEE ICPR. IEEE (2018)
14. Patel, K., Han, H., Jain, A.K.: Secure face unlock: spoof detection on smartphones. IEEE Trans. Inf. Forensics Secur. 11(10), 2268–2283 (2016)
15. Poh, M.Z., McDuff, D.J., Picard, R.W.: Non-contact, automated cardiac pulse measurements using video imaging and blind source separation. Opt. Exp. 18(10), 10762–10774 (2010)
16. Poh, M.Z., McDuff, D.J., Picard, R.W.: Advancements in noncontact, multiparameter physiological measurements using a webcam. IEEE Trans. Biomed. Eng. 58(1), 7–11 (2011)
17. Russakovsky, O., et al.: Imagenet large scale visual recognition challenge. IJCV 115(3), 211–252 (2015)
18. Soleymani, M., Lichtenauer, J., Pun, T., Pantic, M.: A multimodal database for affect recognition and implicit tagging. IEEE Trans. Affect. Comput. 3(1), 42–55 (2012)
19. Stricker, R., Müller, S., Gross, H.M.: Non-contact video-based pulse rate measurement on a mobile service robot. In: Proceedings of IEEE RO-MAN, pp. 1056–1062. IEEE (2014)
20. Tsouri, G.R., Li, Z.: On the benefits of alternative color spaces for noncontact heart rate measurements using standard red-green-blue cameras. J. Biomed. Opt. 20(4), 048002 (2015)
21. Tulyakov, S., Alameda-Pineda, X., Ricci, E., Yin, L., Cohn, J.F., Sebe, N.: Self-adaptive matrix completion for heart rate estimation from face videos under realistic conditions. In: Proceedings of IEEE CVPR. IEEE (2016)
22. Verkruysse, W., Svaasand, L.O., Nelson, J.S.: Remote plethysmographic imaging using ambient light. Opt. Exp. 16(26), 21434–21445 (2008)
23. Wang, W., den Brinker, A.C., Stuijk, S., de Haan, G.: Algorithmic principles of remote PPG. IEEE Trans. Biomed. Eng. 64(7), 1479–1491 (2017)
24. Wang, W., Stuijk, S., De Haan, G.: Exploiting spatial redundancy of image sensor for motion robust rPPG. IEEE Trans. Biomed. Eng. 62(2), 415–425 (2015)
25. Wu, H.Y., Rubinstein, M., Shih, E., Guttag, J., Durand, F., Freeman, W.: Eulerian video magnification for revealing subtle changes in the world. ACM Trans. Graph. 31(4), 65 (2012)
26. Zhang, Z., et al.: Multimodal spontaneous emotion corpus for human behavior analysis. In: Proceedings of IEEE CVPR, pp. 3438–3446. IEEE (2016)

Multi-level Dense Capsule Networks

Sai Samarth R. Phaye[(✉)], Apoorva Sikka, Abhinav Dhall,
and Deepti R. Bathula

Indian Institute of Technology Ropar, Rupnagar, India
phaye.samarth@gmail.com, {apoorva.sikka,abhinav,bathula}@iitrpr.ac.in

Abstract. Past few years have witnessed an exponential growth of interest in deep learning methodologies with rapidly improving accuracy and reduced computational complexity. In particular, architectures using Convolutional Neural Networks (CNNs) have produced state-of-the-art performances for image classification and object recognition tasks. Recently, Capsule Networks (CapsNets) achieved a significant increase in performance by addressing an inherent limitation of CNNs in encoding pose and deformation. Inspired by such an advancement, we propose Multi-level Dense Capsule Networks (multi-level DCNets). The proposed framework customizes CapsNet by adding multi-level capsules and replacing the standard convolutional layers with densely connected convolutions. A single-level DCNet essentially adds a deeper convolution network, which leads to learning of discriminative feature maps learned by different layers to form the primary capsules. Additionally, multi-level capsule networks uses a hierarchical architecture to learn new capsules from former capsules that represent spatial information in a fine-to-coarser manner, which makes it more efficient for learning complex data. Experiments on image classification task using benchmark datasets demonstrate the efficacy of the proposed architectures. DCNet achieves state-of-the-art performance (99.75%) on the MNIST dataset with approximately twenty-fold decrease in total training iterations, over the conventional CapsNet. Furthermore, multi-level DCNet performs better than CapsNet on SVHN dataset (96.90%), and outperforms the ensemble of seven CapsNet models on CIFAR-10 by +0.31% with seven-fold decrease in the number of parameters. Source codes, models and figures are available at https://github.com/ssrp/Multi-level-DCNet.

Keywords: Deep learning · Computer vision · Image recognition

1 Introduction

In recent years, deep networks have been applied to various challenging tasks in computer vision and machine learning. CNNs have shown unprecedented performance on image classification [5,7,12], object recognition [4,16]. Many variants

---

S. S. R. Phaye and A. Sikka—Equal first authors.

C. V. Jawahar et al. (Eds.): ACCV 2018, LNCS 11365, pp. 577–592, 2019.
https://doi.org/10.1007/978-3-030-20873-8_37

of CNN have been proposed by making them deeper and more complex over the time. However, it has a few drawbacks, which have been highlighted by Sabour et al. [11]. One is that CNNs are not robust to affine transformations i.e. a slight shift in the position of the object make CNNs change their prediction. Although this problem can be reduced to some extent by data augmentation, this does not make network robust to any new poses or variations that might be present in the test data. Another major drawback is that generic CNNs do not consider spatial relationships between objects in an image while making any decision. CNNs only use mere presence of certain local objects in an image to make a decision while actually, the spatial context of objects present is equally important. The primary cause is the pooling operation in the network, which is mainly done to decrease the parameters as the network grows. It gives importance to the presence of features and ignores positional information of features.

To overcome these drawbacks, Sabour et al. [11] proposed a seminal architecture called the capsule networks (CapsNets). In this model, the information is stored in a vector form instead of a scalar (as in the case of the simple neural networks) and these group of neurons acting together is named as a capsule. Sabour et al. have used the concept of routing-by-agreement and layer based squashing to achieve state-of-the-art accuracy on the MNIST dataset and detecting overlapping digits in a better way using reconstruction regularization. CapsNets have proven to be powerful on simpler datasets but their performance on complex datasets such as CIFAR-10 is currently enhanced by using an ensemble of such networks leading to an enormous increase in the network parameters. One reason for low performance of single capsule network could be the network depth as current architecture is using only one layer of convolution followed by single level of capsules. But simply increasing the network depth will make the network parameters huge as no pooling layers are used in CapsNets.

To address these challenges, we propose a new multi-level capsule network architecture which fuses information from multi-level features having varying receptive fields to generate classification. The proposed architecture is a network comprising of multiple levels of capsules capturing various levels of details leading to an improved performance with significant parameter reduction. In addition, we focus on increasing the network depth by adding more convolution layers to improve the performance. But instead of simply stacking CNN layers, we deploy different type of skip connections introduced by Huang et al. known as DenseNets [6] which reduces the number of parameters when compared to a standard CNN. The network adds dense connections between every other layer in a feed-forward manner. An additional benefit is better gradient flow across the network, which allows training deeper networks. We follow the intuition behind DenseNets to design a modified decoder network with concatenated dense layers, which results in improvement in the reconstruction outputs. We demonstrate the potential of proposed methods by experiments on various classification datasets such as the FashionMNIST [19], Street View House Numbers (SVHN) [9], and brain tumor dataset presented in [1,3,21] and discuss the results in Sect. 4. The main objectives behind our work is to: *(a) improve the performance of CapsNet,*

*in terms of faster convergence and better results; (b) achieve better performance
than the CapsNet on complicated datasets such as CIFAR-10; (c) reduce the
model complexity.* The major contributions of this work are as follows:

1. We propose Multi-level capsules build on the prior intuitions and demonstrate
   that it improves the performance of conventional CapsNets in lesser number
   of model parameters (Sect. 3.1).
2. We improve the baseline CapsNets by incorporating DenseNets named as
   DCNets, to create more discriminative features for enhanced training and
   faster convergence. We also redefine the decoder framework resulting in better
   reconstructions (Sect. 3.2).
3. Further, we merge multiple level of capsules in DCNets to obtain a compact
   model, giving improved performance in comparably very less parameters and
   a twenty-fold decrease in training time over the baseline. We also discuss in
   detail the strategy used to improve the training of this model by computing
   separate margin losses for all capsule levels (Sect. 3.3).

2   Background

The literature for CNN is vast. Architectures proposed has increased significantly due to increase in computational power. The CNN tries to learn in a
hierarchical manner from lower to higher layers where lower layers learn basic
features like edges and higher layers learns complex features by a combination
of these lower level features. Adding more depth in various combinations has
lead to significant improvement in performance [7,12,15]. Although deeper networks lead to improvement in performance, they are much more difficult to train
due to a huge increase in the number of parameters. Also, an increase in depth
leads to vanishing gradient problem. This issue has been addressed by Highway
network [14], ResNets [5], FractalNets [8] which trained deeper networks with a
large number of layers. They added bypassing paths to easily train the model to
resolve vanishing gradient problem. Another such network proposed by Huang et
al. [6] created a novel way of adding skip connections by introducing connections
from initial convolution layers to deeper layers, naming it one dense block.

The capsule networks [11] have been recently introduced to overcome the
drawbacks of CNNs discussed in Sect. 1. Capsules are a group of neurons that
depict properties of various entities present in an image. There could be various properties of an image which can be captured like position, size, texture.
Capsules used routing-by-agreement as a routing mechanism where the output
of a lower level (primary) capsule is sent to all higher layered capsules. Each
capsule made a prediction which is sent to all next layered capsules. Now, these
higher level capsules have so many predictions which are then compared with the
actual output of parent capsule. If the outputs matched, the coupling coefficient
between the two capsules is increased. Let u_i be an output of a capsule i, and j
be the parent capsule, the prediction is calculated as:

$$\hat{u}_{i|j} = W_{ij}u_i \tag{1}$$

$$c_{ij} = \frac{exp(b_{ij})}{\sum_k exp(b_{ik})} \qquad (2)$$

In (1) W_{ij} is the weighting matrix that is being learned. Then, coupling coefficients c_{ij} are computed using a simple softmax function as shown. In (2), b_{ij} is log probability of capsule i being coupled with capsule j. This value is zero when routing is started. Finally, input vector to each parent capsule j is computed using prediction vector and coupling coefficient as follows:

$$s_j = \sum_i c_{ij}\hat{u}_{j|i} \qquad (3)$$

$$v_j = \frac{||s_j||^2}{1 + ||s_j||^2} \frac{s_j}{||s_j||} \qquad (4)$$

The output of individual capsule vectors represent the probability that an object represented by capsule is present in given input or not. But the final output of these capsule vectors computed using all lower capsules can exceed one. Thus, a non-linear squashing function is defined which is used to restrict the vector length to 1 as in (4). Here s_j is input to capsule j and v_j is output. The log probabilities are updated by computing the inner product of v_j and $\hat{u}_{j|i}$. If two vectors agreed, the product would be larger leading to longer vector length. In the final layer, a loss value is computed for each capsule. Loss value is high when the capsule has long output instantiation parameters the entity is actually absent. It is defined as:

$$l_k = T_k \, max(0, \, m^+ - ||v^k||)^2 + \lambda(1 - T_k) \, max \, (0, ||v_k|| - m^-)^2 \qquad (5)$$

Here l_k is a margin loss function for a capsule k, T_k is 1 when label is true and 0 otherwise. CapsNet mentioned in [11] applied one convolution layer with 9×9 kernel followed by ReLU to generate 256 feature maps. This first layer act as local feature detector. It is then fed to primary capsule layer where 32, 8D capsules are formed using 9×9 kernel with stride 2 followed by squashing. Finally, a DigitCaps layer is applied which forms final capsules of 16D. Dynamic routing is applied between lower level capsule layer (Primary Capsule Layer) and this higher level capsule layer (DigitCaps). A paper by Afshar et al. [1] showed that capsule networks are powerful enough to work on the images containing complex datasets. We aim to work on empowering capsules by using DenseNets.

3   Proposed Network

We first describe the rationale behind using multi-level capsules and DenseNets that addresses the issues posed by CapsNet. Then we build up on the above intuitions and form the final architecture having faster convergence. We begin by computing the result of a single CapsNet model on CIFAR-10 dataset, keeping the architecture same as used for MNIST dataset. For 150 epochs, we obtained

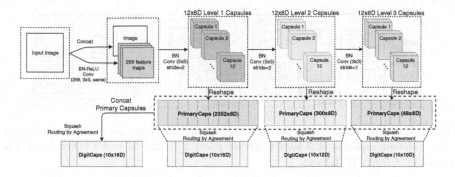

Fig. 1. A simple 3-level CapsNet model (best viewed in color). (Color figure online)

Fig. 2. The pipelines depict the comparison of the part of input images activated by primary capsules of different levels in a Multi-level CapsNet or Multi-level DCNet.

a test accuracy of 68.74%. This low accuracy might be due to the use of simple capsules from a single convolution layer, which is not sufficient to encode the information present in complex images. One way to overcome this problem is to form an ensemble of CapsNet models [11] achieving 89.4% test accuracy, but this leads to exceptionally higher number of model parameters ($7 \times 14.5M$).

3.1 Multi-level Capsules

We investigate CapsNet architecture using guided back-propagation by visualizing the activations of 8D primary capsules of CapsNet and observe that every primary capsule is generated by a small spatial area of the input image. Our belief is that these relations aren't enough to model the information present on these images. We try to overcome this by creating multi-level hierarchical capsules that leverages information from various scales of image. We design these as shown in Fig. 1 by forming twelve 1st level primary capsules using the baseline architecture, which are further used to create another set of twelve 2nd level primary capsules, followed by the 3rd level. The three PrimaryCaps generate three different DigitCaps (output) layers separately and one DigitCaps is generated by concatenation of three PrimaryCaps layers. We add this additional layer to allow the model to learn combined features from various levels of capsules.

A new training strategy instead of simple joint-back propagation as explained in the third subsection is employed. Further, we try to visualize the part of the image activated in a 3-level CapsNet model and it clearly depicts the difference

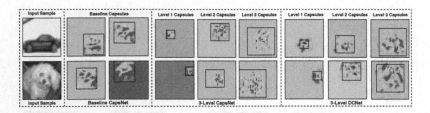

Fig. 3. Activated image region on test image samples by capsules of the baseline CapsNet, different capsules of 3-level CapsNet (Sect. 3.1) and 3-level DCNet (Sect. 3.3), trained on CIFAR-10 dataset.

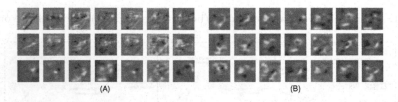

Fig. 4. The motivation for using dense convolutions with CapsNet: Here (A) and (B) are the feature maps at the same depth from DenseNets and CNN, respectively. It is clear that DenseNets learn clearer discriminative features as compared to CNN.

between baseline and 3-level model activations (results shown in Fig. 3, obtained from the pipeline shown in Fig. 2). We achieve 81.26% test accuracy from this model, which is significantly better than the baseline (68.74%) but is substantially lesser than the seven ensemble model (89.40%).

We try to improve the prior 3-level capsule network by adding convolution layers and it resulted in a quick boost in performance (83.75%). We add a convolution layer (256 feature maps, no stride and 3×3 kernel with same padding) in between the consecutive capsule layers and we concatenate the former capsule layer (12×8 feature maps) with this. These $256 + 96$ feature maps lead to generation of subsequent 96 capsules. The results of this simple experiment suggest that the discriminative features from multiple layers are performing better than simpler convolutions. Therefore, we incorporate the idea of adding convolution layers in the Capsule Network as explained the in next section.

3.2 Incorporating DenseNets – DCNets

We try to increase initial convolution layers to two and eight to the baseline CapsNet model, and observe that it did not lead to any improvement as shown in Table 1. We borrow the idea of feature concatenation across layers from DenseNets [6] as it has potential to learn discerning features, which otherwise would require a much deeper network. Thus, we compare a simple architecture having 8 conv-layers with feature concatenation and a simple CNN having same number of layers without concatenation, and both of them having 32 kernels in

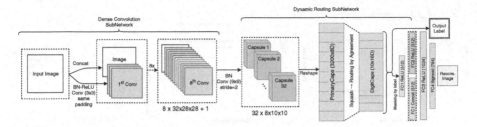

Fig. 5. DCNet – The proposed prediction pipeline for MNIST (best viewed in color). (Color figure online)

each layer. Both quantitative analysis (Table 1) and visualizations (Fig. 4) show that concatenated features were better at capturing diversified features.

This lead to forming DCNets, where we try to modify capsule networks to form a deeper architecture where we create an eight-layered dense convolutional sub-network based on skip connections. Every layer is concatenated to the next layer in a feed-forward manner, adding up to make a final convolution layer.

Figure 5 shows the detailed pipeline of the proposed architecture for MNIST dataset. The input sample goes into 8 levels of convolutions and each of those convolution levels generates 32 new feature maps followed by concatenation with feature maps of all previous layers which results in 257 feature maps (input image is included). These diversified feature maps act as input to the capsule layer which applies a convolution of 9×9 with a stride of 2. The feature maps obtained are the primary capsules of the CapsNet. The work of Sabour et al. [11] focuses on equivariance instead of invariance which we agree with and so, we did not use any of the pooling layers as used in DenseNets, which results in spatial information loss. It is worth noting that while Sabour et al. [11] created the primary capsules from 256 feature maps created by the same complexity level of convolution, DCNet's primary capsules are generated by combining all the features of varied levels of complexity, which further improves the classification.

These feature maps act as thirty-two 8D capsules, which are passed to a squash activation layer, followed by the routing algorithm. 16D final capsules are generated for each of the 10 classes (digits) which further generates one-hot 10D output vector, similar to the conventional capsule network used for MNIST.

Inspired by the dense connections implemented by Huang et al. we modify the reconstruction sub-network of the capsule network. The decoder is a four-layered model with a concatenation of features of the first layer and second layer resulting in better gradient flow, which takes the DigitCaps layer as its input (masked by output label during training). We find that the loss of the modified decoder in the DCNet decrease by a considerable amount (shown in Fig. 7), having same loss multiplier factor as that of CapsNet.

We also assess how different variants of DCNet perform comparing with the baseline CapsNet model, in terms of the number of parameters and achieved accuracy. Results of this experiment is shown in Table 1. Figure 6 shows the test

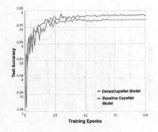 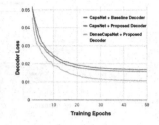 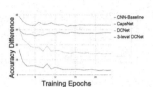

Fig. 6. Performance of DCNet and the Cap-sNet model on MNIST dataset.

Fig. 7. Reconstruction mean squared error loss on MNIST dataset.

Fig. 8. Translated Dataset and affNIST test dataset accuracy difference.

Table 1. Comparison of various model variations after 50 epochs on MNIST dataset.

Model	Description	Parameters	Test Acc.
CapsNet (Baseline)	Conv - Primary capsules - Final capsules	8.2M	99.67%
CapsNet variant	Added one more initial convolution layer having 256 9x9 kernels with same padding, stride = 1	13.5M	99.66%
DCNet variant one	Used 3 convolution layers with 8 feature maps each	6.9M	99.66%
DCNet variant two	No skip connections (simple 8 layered CNN)	4M	99.68%
DCNet variant three	Used 8th convolution layer only (no concatenation)	7.2M	**99.72%**
Final DCNet	DenseConv - Primary capsules - Final capsules	11.8M	**99.75%**

accuracy comparison of CapsNet and DCNet from which we can clearly infer that DCNet has a faster convergence rate. Our experiments show a significant increase in performances over various datasets like MNIST, Fashion-MNIST, SVHN. We notice that DCNet's performance on CIFAR-10 increased over single CapsNet model with same parameters, but it did not outperform the seven ensemble model of CapsNets [11] having 89.40% accuracy. We address this problem by creating multi-level DCNets which learns well on such complex datasets.

3.3 Merging Multi-level CapsNets and DCNets – Multi-level DCNets

The ensemble of seven baseline CapsNet models (by Sabour et al. [11]) resulted in 89.40% accuracy on CIFAR-10 dataset. This might be due to the patches of 24×24 used as input, which increases the effective spatial area used to generate each primary capsule. Although it leads to an increase in accuracy when compared to single CapsNet model, but it also increases the parameters by seven

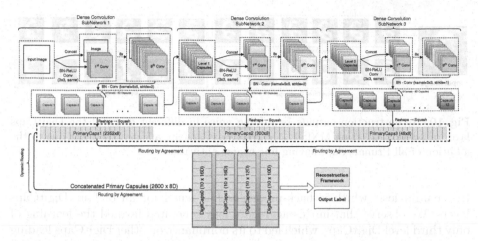

Fig. 9. Pipeline of three-level DCNet for CIFAR-10 (best viewed in color). (Color figure online)

fold which can be reduced for these images. Thus, we focus to model the data while minimizing the parameters by creating multiple levels of capsules learned from densely connected convolutional layers. In the proposed model, we pass the complete image by first down-sampling it to 32×32. A single 3-level DCNet having 13.4M parameters achieves 89.71% test accuracy.

Figure 9 depicts the detailed pipeline of the 3-level DCNet model. It is a hierarchical model where a DCNet is created and its intermediate capsule representation is used as an input to the next DCNet which in turn generates a representation fed to the next DCNet sub-network, creating a three level architecture. There are twelve capsules in each DCNet. Alexey et al. [13] performed experiments on CIFAR-10 dataset and observed that strided-conv if replaced by max-pooling performs on par and outperforms if another conv-layer is added. Thus, a strided convolution (5×5 size and 2 stride) is applied which reduces the size of the image fed to next level which is similar to the concept of Pyramid of Gaussian [2]. This also resembles with the functioning of a brain which separates the information to decide [10]. For example, there are separate pathways for high and low spatial frequency content and color information. Activated image regions generated from the primary capsules of final Multi-level DCNet model are shown in Fig. 3. The activated region is diffused out of the square region because of 'same' padded convolutions in the densely connected convolution layers. We explore two methods of training strategies to train the network with these four different DigitCaps layer outputs:

Joint Prediction. We concatenate the four DigitCaps layers to get a 10×54 dimensional final DigitCaps layer and it creates a single prediction, which is the root mean squared (RMS) value of the concatenated DigitCaps layer. This allows combining low-level and high-level digits to form one prediction. Hence,

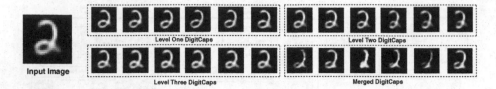

Fig. 10. Reconstruction outputs by adding noise in different digits of the DigitCaps layer of 3-level DCNet on MNIST. Merged DigitCaps are affected the most due to the addition of all PrimaryCaps having fine-coarse activations.

the margin loss, which is back-propagated is equal for all of four DigitCaps layers. We observe that in this aggregate loss generated favored the learning of only third level DigitCaps, which led to its dominance on other DigitCaps leading to a poor learning of the former levels, indicating that routing algorithm didn't help to learn information at first and second level. To overcome this problem, we chose to back-propagate the separate margin losses as explained below.

Four Separate Predictions. Instead of concatenating the DigitCaps layers, we let the model generate four distinct predictions from the corresponding DigitCaps layers. Hence, four margin losses were calculated and back-propagated separately, removing the dominance of any DigitCaps layer on other layers. By creating four different predictions, we let each level of the multi-level DCNet learn their own modeling of the input sample data. Intuitively this means that the first level capsule learned how to perceive objects and classify them by learning finer details (due to small activation area of the input, shown in Fig. 2) and the third (higher) level learned how to classify using the coarser details (due to larger activation area of the input).

Figure 11 shows the output activations of four DigitCaps layers of multi-level DCNet model (16D from concatenating all primary capsules, 16D corresponding to the first level primary capsules, 12D from the second level primary capsules and 10D from the third level primary capsules) obtained both via joint predictions and four separate predictions. It is evident that when the network is jointly trained the lower level capsules did not learn much and only higher level capsules are deciding the class label but on the other hand, in case of separate back-propagation, different levels of capsules have captured varied information leading to better learning. While testing, the four DigitCaps layers are simply concatenated to form a 54D final capsule for each of the ten classes and RMS value is calculated, and the reconstructions were created using one channel of the image using these fifty-four capsules. The reconstructions for CIFAR-10 were not very good, which we believe is due to the dominance of background noise present in the samples and presence of complex information of the image. It is worth noting here that none of the individual DigitCaps performed better than the concatenated vector output. We explore the relative effect of different levels of DigitCaps on the reconstruction outputs and experiment on the MNIST dataset by subtracting 0.2 from each digit one at a time in the 54D DigitCaps. It is observed that the effect on reconstructions decrease from the first level to the last level of capsules (shown in Fig. 10). This could be due to the fact that the first level DigitCaps activates very small area of an image and when perturbations are added to such smaller levels, it leads to an increased overall change in image (and vice versa). Also, it is observed that DigitCaps obtained from the concatenation of PrimaryCaps was most sensitive to this noise.

4   Experiments

We demonstrate the potential of our model on multiple datasets and compare it with the CapsNet architecture. Due to resource constraints, we train all our models for 50 to 100 epochs on one NVIDIA Titan Xp. The initial learning rate is set to 0.001 and decay rate 0.9 with Adam as the optimizer. We change multiplier factor to scale down the reconstruction loss according to the image

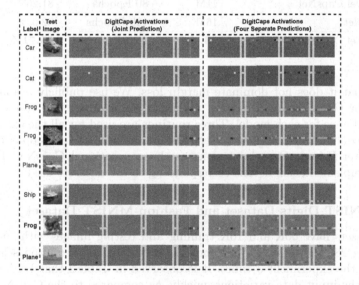

Fig. 11. Comparison of the activations of the DigitCaps layers generated by joint back-propagation (single prediction) and separate back-propagation (four separate predictions). Each row has the true label, the test image (chosen randomly), output DigitCaps activations by joint back-propagation and then by separated back-propagation. Each of the DigitCaps activations is separated by a yellow line, the correct label highlighted by yellow color, followed by another yellow line (*DigitCaps from left to right: 1st - created by concatenating all the PrimaryCaps, 10×16; 2nd - by the first level PrimaryCaps, 10×16; 3rd - by the second level PrimaryCaps, 10×12 and 4th - by the third level PrimaryCaps, 10×10*). The red colored label denote bad examples giving wrong predictions (for example, Plane is getting confused with a Ship in the example shown). It is clear that in case of joint-backpropagation, the first and second level DigitCaps didn't learn via routing algorithm, hence giving de-emphasized activations. (Color figure online)

Table 2. Performance of CapsNets, DCNets and multi-level DCNets over various datasets. NR - No Reconstruction SubNetwork, E - training epochs, BR - baseline Reconstruction SubNetwork.

Model	MNIST	Fashion-MNIST	SVHN	SmallNORB	Tumor Dataset	CIFAR-10
Baseline CapsNet	99.67% (50E) 99.75% (1000E) [11] 99.65% (1000E, NR) [11]	93.65% (100E)	93.23% (100E) 95.70% (> 100E) [11]	89.56% (50E)	78% (10E)[1] 87.50% (50E)	68.74% (150E) 89.40% (7 ensemble) [11]
DCNet	99.75% (50E) 99.71% (50E, NR) 99.72% (50E, BR)	94.64% (100E) 94.59% (100E, NR)	95.58% (50E)	94.43% (50E)	86.8% (10E) 93.04% (50E)	82.63% (single model)
3-level DCNet	99.71% (50E)	94.65% (100E)	96.90% (50E)	95.34% (75E) 95.27% (75E, NR)	71.43% (10E) 95.03% (50E)	89.71% (120E) 89.32% (120E, NR)

Table 3. Analysis of various models on CIFAR-10 Dataset.

Model	Parameters	Training epochs	Test accuracy
Baseline CapsNet	9.6M	160 Epochs	68.74%
Seven ensemble CapsNet [11]	101.5M	>500 Epochs	89.40%
3-level CapsNet	11M	80 Epochs	81.26%
DCNet	16M	100 Epochs	82.63%
3-level DCNet	**13.4M**	**120 Epochs**	**89.71%**

size so that it does not dominate margin loss. We use publicly available code [17,20] for CapsNet and DenseNet to create our models. The test errors are computed once for each model. Three routings are used for all the experiments. For fair comparisons, we mostly keep the parameters of the proposed DCNet model after PrimaryCaps layer same as the conventional CapsNet. Following are the implementation details corresponding to the datasets used:

4.1 MNIST Digits Dataset and Fashion-MNIST Dataset

The datasets have 60K and 10K training and testing images with each image size being 28 × 28 in size. We do not use any data augmentation scheme and repeated the experiment 3 times. It is observed in Table 2 that DCNet is able to learn the input data variations quickly, as compared to the CapsNet, i.e., it is able to achieve 99.75% and 94.64% test accuracy on MNIST and Fashion-MNIST, respectively, with a 20 fold decrease in total iterations. We tried modifying the number of layers and growth parameter in DCNet architecture trained on FashionMNIST. The results of this experiment (Fig. 14) clarify that a deeper DenseNet architecture empowers the CapsNet architecture. Further, we change the stride from two to one in the PrimaryCaps layer of the second level of multi-level DCNet to fit the image. We do not observe any improvement in the performance of multi-level DCNet on MNIST dataset which is as expected because we are capturing fine-to-coarse level features, due to which every tiny variation in the writing of a particular number will be captured from the training set. These 'fine' features might be causing a problem during the testing phase.

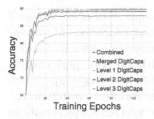
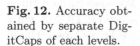

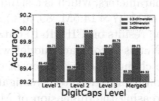

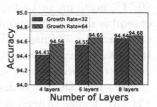

Fig. 12. Accuracy obtained by separate DigitCaps of each levels.

Fig. 13. Effect of Changes in DigitCaps Layer of a 3-level DCNet (CIFAR-10).

Fig. 14. Effect of changes in the dense block of DCNet (FashionMNIST).

Robustness Towards Affine Transformations. We perform a similar experiment as performed by Sabour et al. [11] on a CNN with max-pooling and dropouts, a CapsNet, a DCNet and a 3-level DCNet, trained on translated-digits dataset without reconstruction sub-network. Due to space restrictions, we plot a graph having a difference of test accuracy of Translated MNIST and affNIST datasets against training epochs (shown in Fig. 8). The lesser the value, the better system is performing. The 3-level DCNet model significantly outperforms other models, achieving 93.1% and 96.69% accuracy on affNIST test-set at 99.16% and 99.61% accuracy respectively on translated-dataset, which is an improvement over what Sabour et al. [11] achieved.

MultiMNIST Segmentation Performance. Due to resource constraints, we train CapsNet and DCNet model on three randomly chosen digits classes – 0, 4 and 6. The dataset is created by merging each sample with digit of other class and both the samples are shifted up to four pixels randomly in each direction, resulting in a 36 × 36 image. For each digit, we generate only twelve MultiMNIST examples for training and 30 examples for testing. The final train and test size is 212K, 87.6K. The resultant mean-squared error between segmented digit reconstructions and input samples for CapsNet and DCNet are 0.0271 and 0.0236 respectively. Without segmentation, the mean-squared error values for the merged digit examples and reconstructions are 0.0295 and 0.0245.

4.2 CIFAR-10 Dataset

The CIFAR-10 dataset contains 50K and 10K samples for training and testing. Post normalization (channel mean and std. deviations), we compare our model with the ensemble of four and seven capsule network models [11] for first 50 epochs. We use same DCNet model as used for MNIST and the test accuracy improved over the ensemble of four CapsNet models (implemented by Xi et al. [18]) to 82.68% from 71.55%. The proposed 3-level DCNet model results in

89.71% accuracy in 13.4M parameters, which is a significant improvement over 7 ensemble model by Sabour et al. (7×14.5M, 89.40%) and DCNet (16M parameters for 32×32 image). The results on CIFAR-10 dataset are shown in Table 3. It is clear that 3-level DCNet is a compact model with superior performance and faster convergence. We change the dimension of different DigitCaps layers of the 3-level DCNet trained on CIFAR-10 to investigate its effect (results in the Fig. 13). Unlike others, increasing the dimension of Merge-DigitCaps results in an unexpected trend that could not be readily justified. We also trained three models on CIFAR-10 for 100 epochs – 2-level DCNet, a 3-level DCNet with just the Merge-DigitCaps output and one with just the three DigitCaps without Merge-DigitCaps. All of them achieve lower accuracy compared to the proposed model (88.21%, 87.8% and 89.2% respectively). We also visualize how each DigitCaps of a 3-level DCNet contributes towards the final accuracy of the system (Fig. 12). It can be seen that Level-3 and Merge-DigitCaps layer play a major role in the final performance.

4.3   Other Datasets

SVHN dataset contains 73K and 26K real-life digit images for training and testing. We modify DCNet by using 6D 16 PrimaryCaps with an 8D final capsule from four conv-layers with 18 kernels each. The results of the DCNet model improve over the replicated CapsNet model by +2.36%. We use the same 3-level DCNet model as used for CIFAR-10 dataset, resulting in 96.9% accuracy.

SmallNorb dataset has 24K and 24K images for training and testing. After normalization, we add random noise and contrast to each image. We use the same DCNet and 3-level DCNet model as used for SVHN and results of both improved over the replicated CapsNet model (Table 2).

Brain Tumor dataset contains 3,064 MRI images of 233 patients. Afshar et al. [1] modified CapsNet architecture with initial conv-layer having 64 feature maps. We create an equivalent DCNet model by changing the eight initial conv-layers to four layers with 16 kernels each and 6 PrimaryCaps only. We also change learning rate of our model to $1E - 4$. The 3-level DCNet model is a hierarchical model based on these parameters of DCNet. We train the models on eight-fold cross-validation (Table 2).

5   Conclusion

We introduce two methods that act as the building blocks for the Multi-level DCNet. First is Multi-level CapsNet which aims to learn hierarchical features by creating multiple level of capsules. Another is DCNet, which replaces standard convolution layers in CapsNet with densely connected convolutions. Addition of direct connections between two consecutive layers helps to learn better feature maps, in turn forming better quality primary capsules. The effectiveness of this architecture is demonstrated by state-of-the-art performance (99.75%)

on MNIST data with twenty-fold decrease in total training iterations, over conventional CapsNets. Although the same DCNet model performs better (82.63%) than a single, baseline CapsNet model on CIFAR-10 data, it is below par compared to seven ensemble model of CapsNet with 89.40% accuracy.

Performance of CapsNet on real-life, complex data (CIFAR-10, ImageNet, etc.) is known to be substandard compared to simpler datasets like MNIST. Multi-level DCNets addresses this limitation by importing the multi-level capsules and DenseNets in CapsNets to enhance the representational power of the network. The hierarchical structure helps learn intricate relationships between fine-to-coarse level features. A single 3-level DCNet achieves 89.71% accuracy on CIFAR-10, which is an increase of +0.31% accuracy over seven ensemble CapsNet model with significantly less number of parameters. The proposed networks substantially improve the performance of existing Capsule Networks on other datasets such as SVHN, SmallNORB and Tumor Dataset. Since Capsule Networks have been recently introduced, they have not been researched to be applied to various types of data as Convolutional Neural Networks.

In this work, we try to improve the capsule network and highlight its potential on various datasets. In future, we plan to develop a separate and direct routing for multi-level DCNets and work on reducing the computational complexity of the models even further.

References

1. Afshar, P., Mohammadi, A., Plataniotis, K.N.: Brain tumor type classification via capsule networks. arXiv preprint arXiv:1802.10200 (2018)
2. Burt, P.J., Adelson, E.H.: The laplacian pyramid as a compact image code. In: Readings in computer vision: issues, problems, principles, and paradigms, pp. 671–679. Morgan Kaufmann Publishers Inc., San Francisco (1987). http://dl.acm.org/citation.cfm?id=33517.33571
3. Cheng, J., et al.: Enhanced performance of brain tumor classification via tumor region augmentation and partition. PLoS ONE 10(10), e0140381 (2015)
4. Donahue, J., et al.: Decaf: a deep convolutional activation feature for generic visual recognition. In: International Conference on Machine Learning, pp. 647–655 (2014)
5. He, K., Zhang, X., Ren, S., Sun, J.: Deep residual learning for image recognition. In: Proceedings of the IEEE Conference on Computer Vision and Pattern Recognition, pp. 770–778 (2016)
6. Huang, G., Liu, Z., Weinberger, K.Q., van der Maaten, L.: Densely connected convolutional networks. In: Proceedings of the IEEE Conference on Computer Vision and Pattern Recognition, vol. 1, p. 3 (2017)
7. Krizhevsky, A., Sutskever, I., Hinton, G.E.: Imagenet classification with deep convolutional neural networks. In: Pereira, F., Burges, C.J.C., Bottou, L., Weinberger, K.Q. (eds.) Advances in Neural Information Processing Systems 25, pp. 1097–1105. Curran Associates, Inc. (2012). http://papers.nips.cc/paper/4824-imagenet-classification-with-deep-convolutional-neural-networks.pdf
8. Larsson, G., Maire, M., Shakhnarovich, G.: Fractalnet: Ultra-deep neural networks without residuals. CoRR abs/1605.07648 (2016). http://arxiv.org/abs/1605.07648

9. Netzer, Y., Wang, T., Coates, A., Bissacco, A., Wu, B., Ng, A.Y.: Reading digits in natural images with unsupervised feature learning. In: NIPS Workshop on Deep Learning and Unsupervised Feature Learning, vol. 2011, p. 5 (2011)
10. Rotshtein, P., Vuilleumier, P., Winston, J., Driver, J., Dolan, R.: Distinct and convergent visual processing of high and low spatial frequency information in faces. Cereb. Cortex **17**(11), 2713–2724 (2007)
11. Sabour, S., Frosst, N., Hinton, G.E.: Dynamic routing between capsules. In: Advances in Neural Information Processing Systems, pp. 3859–3869 (2017)
12. Simonyan, K., Zisserman, A.: Very deep convolutional networks for large-scale image recognition. CoRR abs/1409.1556 (2014). http://arxiv.org/abs/1409.1556
13. Springenberg, J.T., Dosovitskiy, A., Brox, T., Riedmiller, M.A.: Striving for simplicity: The all convolutional net. CoRR abs/1412.6806 (2014). http://dblp.uni-trier.de/db/journals/corr/corr1412.html#SpringenbergDBR14
14. Srivastava, R.K., Greff, K., Schmidhuber, J.: Highway networks. CoRR abs/1505.00387 (2015). http://arxiv.org/abs/1505.00387
15. Szegedy, C., et al.: Going deeper with convolutions. CoRR abs/1409.4842 (2014). http://arxiv.org/abs/1409.4842
16. Taigman, Y., Yang, M., Ranzato, M., Wolf, L.: Deepface: closing the gap to human-level performance in face verification. In: Proceedings of the 2014 IEEE Conference on Computer Vision and Pattern Recognition, CVPR 2014, pp. 1701–1708. IEEE Computer Society, Washington, DC (2014). https://doi.org/10.1109/CVPR.2014.220
17. titu1994: Dense net in keras (2017). https://github.com/titu1994/DenseNet
18. Xi, E., Bing, S., Jin, Y.: Capsule network performance on complex data. arXiv preprint arXiv:1712.03480 (2017)
19. Xiao, H., Rasul, K., Vollgraf, R.: Fashion-MNIST: a novel image dataset for benchmarking machine learning algorithms. arXiv preprint arXiv:1708.07747 (2017)
20. XifengGuo: CapsNet-Keras (2017). https://github.com/XifengGuo/CapsNet-Keras
21. Yang, J.Z., Feng, Y., Feng, Q., Chen, W.: Retrieval of brain tumors by adaptive spatial pooling and fisher vector representation. PLoS ONE **11**(6), e0157112 (2016)

DHSGAN: An End to End Dehazing Network for Fog and Smoke

Ramavtar Malav[1]($\boxtimes$), Ayoung Kim[2], Soumya Ranjan Sahoo[1],
and Gaurav Pandey[3]

[1] Indian Institute of Technology Kanpur, Kanpur, India
rmalav15@gmail.com
[2] Korea Advanced Institute of Science and Technology, Daejeon, South Korea
[3] Ford Motor Company, Palo Alto, CA, USA

Abstract. In this paper we propose a novel end-to-end convolution dehazing architecture, called De-Haze and Smoke GAN (DHSGAN). The model is trained under a generative adversarial network framework to effectively learn the underlying distribution of clean images for the generation of realistic haze-free images. We train the model on a dataset that is synthesized to include image degradation scenarios from varied conditions of fog, haze, and smoke in both indoor and outdoor settings. Experimental results on both synthetic and natural degraded images demonstrate that our method shows significant robustness over different haze conditions in comparison to the state-of-the-art methods. A group of studies are conducted to evaluate the effectiveness of each module of the proposed method.

Keywords: Dehazing · Desmoking · GAN · ConvLSTM

1 Introduction

Reduced vision due to haze, smoke, fog, and under-water is a serious problem in many computer vision applications such as object detection, classification, identification, visual navigation, etc. A typical camera works on the principle of pin-hole model and the quality of the image obtained depends upon the amount of light reaching the image sensors through the lens. However, in a turbid medium (due to haze, fog, smoke, etc.) the image contrast and color fidelity reduces due to scattering of light by medium particles. This, in turn, reduces the amount of information content in the resulting hazy image, which cannot be used for any processing until they are dehazed.

The Atmospheric Scattering Model [22], given below, is widely used [3,5,10, 18,27,31,33,36] in computer vision to formulate such degraded/hazy images in dense particle conditions such as fog, smoke, and underwater.

$$I_h(u,v) = \underbrace{I_r(u,v)t(u,v)}_{\text{direct attenuation}} + \underbrace{A(1 - t(u,v))}_{\text{airlight}}, \tag{1}$$

© Springer Nature Switzerland AG 2019
C. V. Jawahar et al. (Eds.): ACCV 2018, LNCS 11365, pp. 593–608, 2019.
https://doi.org/10.1007/978-3-030-20873-8_38

Fig. 1. Image enhancement by DHSGAN on real fog and smoke images. Here, top row shows the real world hazy image and bottom row display the enhancement by DHSGAN.

where $I_h(u, v)$ is hazed pixel intensity at location (u, v) in the query image, $I_r(u, v)$ is the real intensity to be estimated, $t(u, v)$ is the medium transmission and A is global atmospheric light. The transmission value is expressed as $t(u, v) = e^{-\beta d(u,v)}$, where β is attenuation coefficient of the atmosphere and $d(u, v)$ is depth of scene point from the camera. The Eq. (1) indicates that after estimating the transmission $t(u, v)$ and atmospheric light A, the image can be recovered with:

$$\hat{I}_r(u, v) = \frac{I_h(u, v) - \hat{A}(1 - \hat{t}(u, v))}{\hat{t}(u, v)}. \tag{2}$$

Most of the previous works estimate the transmission map and atmospheric light separately to recover the dehazed image. The transmission map estimation is successfully explored using both empirical prior based technique such as dark-channel prior [10], color attenuation prior [36], haze line prior [1,2] and learning based methods [3,18,27,33]. In comparison, atmospheric light is mainly calculated using empirical rules [2,10,31] with the exception of recent methods [18,33] that use deep learning techniques. The most popular method of atmospheric light estimation [10] is based on the observation that the intensity of hazed pixel at very high depth should be equal to atmospheric light A. Therefore, the brightest pixel from the top deep pixels is selected as atmospheric light. It works very well for an image with high depth pixels or high atmospheric light (as maximum intensity pixel is selected), but its performance decreases as atmospheric light decreases, especially, for indoor images with low depth. Recently in [1,2], an atmospheric light estimation algorithm was formulated based on the observation that hazy image can be modelled by haze lines in RGB space which converge at the atmospheric light.

We further notice that although the dehazing is collectively referred to as the problem of image degradation due to fog, smoke, haze, underwater, etc., the recent learning methods [3,18,27,33] include training samples with only high atmospheric light. However, problems of reduced vision due to smoke in situations like fire-rescue emphasize the need of a general algorithm to address the full range of atmospheric light for including both smoke and bad weather conditions such as fog, haze, and mist.

In this paper, we propose an end-to-end deep learning framework for dehazing of images, we call it **DHSGAN**, which models the dehazed image as:

$$\hat{I}_r = \mathcal{G}(\hat{t}, I_h) = \mathcal{G}(\mathcal{T}(I_h), I_h), \qquad (3)$$

where function $\mathcal{G}$ is approximated by a fully end-to-end convolution network, which also implements $\mathcal{T}$ (transmission map) as its inner module. This helps us in addressing the common limitation of most dehazing methods - the scene degradation where atmospheric scattering model (1) becomes invalid. Further, the function $\mathcal{G}$ is learned under a generative adversarial network (GAN) framework. The notion of GAN was first proposed by Goodfellow et al. [7] to learn underlying distribution of training data for generation of realistic images. The overwhelming success of GAN in image generation [7,14] encouraged researchers to employ GAN for solving other low-level vision tasks such as style transfer [35], image enhancement [33,34], and super-resolution [17]. Here we use GAN to generate a clear image from a hazy input and a transmission map which is again estimated by a CNN module within the framework (Fig. 2(a)). The key contributions of the proposed work are:

- A novel end to end dehazing network is proposed which does not use the inverse atmospheric model (2) or any post processing step, rather the clean image is learned and directly generated by the final layer of a fully convolutional network. In addition, the model is trained under the generative adversarial network framework to synthesize realistic clean images. Furthermore, we employ a convolutional recurrent sub-architecture to take advantage of temporal redundancy in case of a video sequence.
- The network is learned on a large number of training samples with high variance to approximate a model that shows robustness on diverse conditions of scene degradation caused by smoke, fog, and haze in both indoor and outdoor settings (See Fig. 1).
- A group of studies are performed to demonstrate the importance of each sub-module of the purposed method. Further, extensive experiments are conducted on both synthetic and real dataset and comparisons are made with recent state of the art methods, showing the robustness of our model.

1.1 Related Work

A variety of approaches have been proposed in the literature to overcome the degradation caused by haze concerning both single image dehazing and video or multiple frames based dehazing [1,2,4,5,10,18–20,31,33,36].

Tan [31] proposed a Markov Random Field based dehazing method, which relies on the observation that clear-day images have more contrast than images affected by bad weather. In [5], Fattal proposed an image dehazing method based on the independent component analysis (ICA). He et al. [10] presented a very simple but promising method based on a key observation that local patches of haze-free images have low-intensity pixels in at least one color channel and in the corresponding hazy image, the intensity of these pixels is mainly contribution of airlight. Zhu et al. [36] identified a new prior based on the statistical observation that brightness and saturation of pixels vary sharply with haze thickness and difference of these two is positively correlated with the scene depth. This statistic was termed as color attenuation prior (CAP). Similarly, Berman et al. [1,2] used a non-local prior (haze-line) to recover the clean image.

Recently, convolution neural networks (CNN) have achieved exemplary results in many application of computer vision such as image classification [12,30], object detection [25] including single image dehazing [3,18,27,33]. In [3], a neural network model is trained to retrieve transmission map from the hazy image. This transmission map is subsequently used with empirical rule [10] based atmospheric light estimation to get the clear image. Most recently, Zhang et al. [33] successfully used a joint architecture for both transmission map and atmospheric light estimation. The [33], uses a math-operation module where the inverse atmospheric model (2) is embedded within the network and a joint discriminator-based generative adversarial network is used to refine the transmission map and dehazed image. This work is closely related to ours as they use a discriminator network to train the sub-networks that estimates the transmission map and atmospheric light. However, estimating the two parameters, transmission and atmospheric light, separately can accumulate errors and potentially amplify each other in the final step of recovery (Eq. (2)). Earlier, Li et al. [18] address this problem by manipulating atmospheric scattering model to linearly embed both transmission map and atmospheric light into one variable and trained a light-weight CNN for its estimation. In the proposed method we do not use the inverse atmospheric model and let the generation network learn this model for a wide range of atmospheric light conditions.

The rest of the paper is organised as follows. In Sect. 2 we describe the proposed framework for dehazing of image sequences. In Sect. 3 we present experimental results of the proposed technique and compare it with various state-of-the-art methods. In Sect. 4 we present some concluding remarks and future works.

2   DHSGAN

In this section, the proposed DHSGAN is explained. Our model can be classified into two sub-modules (see Fig. 2a): T the Transmission Module and the GAN Module, both of which are explained in detail below.

2.1   The Transmission Module

The transmission module T is a fully convolutional recurrent architecture which takes a hazy image as input and estimates its transmission map. The network

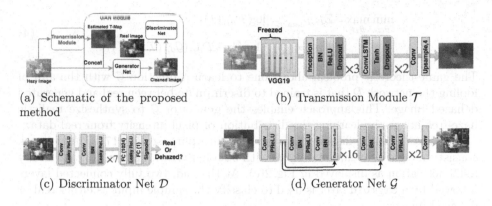

(a) Schematic of the proposed method

(b) Transmission Module $\mathcal{T}$

(c) Discriminator Net $\mathcal{D}$

(d) Generator Net $\mathcal{G}$

Fig. 2. An overview of the proposed DHSGAN. The first module $\mathcal{T}$ estimates the transmission map from hazy image, which in turns concatenated with hazy image and passed to Generator Net $\mathcal{G}$. The generator net $\mathcal{G}$, trained under GAN framework, directly synthesize the realistic clean image without using inverse atmospheric model (2) or any post processing step.

is initialized with VGG19 [29] convolution layers pretrained on ImageNet [16] Dataset. The initial VGG19 [29] convolution layers is proven to be rich feature extractors [26]. The initial 8 convolution layers of VGG19 [29] are excluded from the training. The VGG19 [29] architecture is followed by three Inception [30] modules that simultaneously process the input feature map at multiple scales. We then use two ConvLSTM [24] layers capable of exploiting the temporal correlation of input frames in case of a video stream. The detailed architecture of transmission module is illustrated in Fig. 2(b).

2.2   The GAN Module

The GAN [7] module consists of two CNN architectures: Generative Model $\mathcal{G}$, and Discriminative Model $\mathcal{D}$. We follow the architecture guidelines proposed by Super-Resolution network SRGAN [17]. The transmission map estimated by the transmission module is concatenated with image and passed to $\mathcal{G}$. Our ultimate goal is to learn a generating function $\mathcal{G}$ which recovers the dehazed/clear images given a pair of transmission map and hazed image.

The core module $\mathcal{G}$ as illustrated in Fig. 2(d), contains 16 identical residual blocks [8,12] with 3×3 kernels. Similar to [8,17], we use Batch-Normalization [13] followed by ParametricReLU [11] activation function in each residual block. Each convolution layer in $\mathcal{G}$ is used with zero padding to get the dehazed image with same spatial dimension as input hazy image.

The discriminator model $\mathcal{D}$ is employed to discriminate between real image I_r and dehazed images $\hat{I}_r$. Formally, the models $\mathcal{G}$ and $\mathcal{D}$ with respective learning parameters θ_G and θ_D are alternatively trained to solve the following adversarial min-max function [7]:

$$\min_{\theta_G} \max_{\theta_D} \quad \mathbb{E}_{I \sim P_{\text{data}(I_r)}}[\log \mathcal{D}_{\theta_D}(I)]$$
$$+ \mathbb{E}_{I \sim P_{\text{data}(I_h)}}[\log(1 - \mathcal{D}_{\theta_D}(\mathcal{G}_{\theta_G}(\mathcal{T}(I), I)))]. \quad (4)$$

The game-theoretic problem allows one to learn a function $\mathcal{G}$ with the aim of fooling the network $\mathcal{D}$ that is trained to discriminate between real and generated dehazed image. This approach enables the generator $\mathcal{G}$ to synthesize realistic haze-free images by learning the distribution of pixel intensity from real data.

We use the same discriminator architecture purposed in [17]. The network consists of eight convolutional layers with Batch-Normalization [13] and Leaky ReLU activation as displayed in Fig. 2(c). At the end, two fully connected layers followed by a Sigmoid layer is used to classify the sample input as either real or dehazed image.

2.3   Loss Function

Transmission Module. The Mean Squared Error (MSE) has been commonly used to train transmission estimation model in previous works [3, 27]. We observe that if we assume that the atmospheric light A is known and the transmission map estimated by the network is given by t_e then the dehazed image $\hat{I}_r$ can be obtained from the atmospheric scattering model:

$$\hat{I}_r = \frac{I_h - A}{t_e} + A = I_r \frac{t_r}{t_e} + A \left(1 - \frac{t_r}{t_e}\right). \quad (5)$$

Therefore, the error in the pixel intensity values of the dehazed image is given by

$$error = \left|\hat{I}_r - I_r\right| = \left|(A - I_r)\left(1 - \frac{t_r}{t_e}\right)\right| \quad (6)$$

Based on this observation, we propose a **normalized MSE** loss function for learning the network parameter θ_T of transmission module $\mathcal{T}$, which we define as:

$$\mathcal{L}_{\theta_T}^N = \frac{1}{WH} \sum_{u=1}^{W} \sum_{v=1}^{H} \left(1 - \frac{\mathcal{T}_{\theta_T}(I_h)_{u,v}}{t_r(u,v)}\right)^2 \quad (7)$$

Here, $\mathcal{T}_{\theta_T}(I_h)$ represent the output transmission of $\mathcal{T}$ module, with network parameter θ_T, for a hazy image I_h with $W \times H$ spatial dimension.

It ensures that the penalty for an actual and estimated transmission pair (t_r, t_e) remains the same as for pair $(\alpha t_r, \alpha t_e)$, where α is any constant value. Since the normalized MSE can be unstable when t_r is near zero, we clip the transmission value in training samples to 0.01.

GAN Module. The generative model $\mathcal{G}$ is trained on MSE loss and **VGG-loss** [17, 35] along with the adversarial loss [7] in stage-wise learning. The standard mean squared error (MSE) for hazed image I_h and real image I_r is defined as:

$$\mathcal{L}_{\theta_G}^{MSE} = \frac{1}{WH} \sum_{u=1}^{W} \sum_{v=1}^{H} \left(I_r(u,v) - \mathcal{G}_{\theta_G}(\mathcal{T}(I_h), I_h)_{u,v} \right)^2. \tag{8}$$

The VGG Loss function is formulated as euclidean distance between feature map extracted from intermediate layers of VGG network. VGG loss function allows perceptually more convincing image generation and successfully used in super-resolution [17], style transfer [35], and image enhancement [33, 34]. It is defined as:

$$\mathcal{L}_{\theta_G}^{VGG_{i,j}} = \frac{1}{2WH} \sum_{u=1}^{W} \sum_{v=1}^{H} \left(\mathcal{V}_{i,j}(I_r)_{u,v} - \mathcal{V}_{i,j}(\mathcal{G}_{\theta_G}(\mathcal{T}(I_h), I_h))_{u,v} \right)^2, \tag{9}$$

Where $\mathcal{V}_{i,j}$ represent the feature map extracted after j^{th} convolution activation and before i^{th} max-pooling of VGG network. In our experiments, we used $VGG19_{54}$ for training $\mathcal{G}$. The $\mathcal{L}_{\theta_G}^{VGG_{i,j}}$ loss is multiplied with a rescaling factor of 0.0061 to make it comparable with $\mathcal{L}_{\theta_G}^{MSE}$. In addition to the losses described above, the generator $\mathcal{G}$ is also optimized by the following adversarial loss [7] over training samples:

$$\mathcal{L}_{\theta_G}^{Gadv} = -\log \mathcal{D}(G_{\theta_G}(\mathcal{T}(I_h), I_h)). \tag{10}$$

Here for an input image, $\mathcal{D}(.)$ represent the classification probability, calculated by discriminator $\mathcal{D}$, of the image being from real image distribution. Similarly, the adversarial loss for training Discriminator D is defined as:

$$\mathcal{L}_{\theta_D}^{Dadv} = -\left(\log \mathcal{D}_{\theta_D}(I_r) + \log(1 - \mathcal{D}_{\theta_D}(\mathcal{G}(\mathcal{T}(I_h), I_h))) \right). \tag{11}$$

2.4   Dataset

We use image-depth pairs from publicly available datasets NYU-v2 [28] (indoor), SceneNet [23] (indoor), RESIDE [19] (indoor-outdoor) and KITTI [6] (outdoor) to synthesize training samples {Hazy/Clean/Transmission Map} based on (1). We generated two training sets: **TrainA** and **TrainSeq**. TrainA contains approximately 100,000 training samples synthesized, using (1), from the above four datasets by randomly sampling β from [0.6, 1.8] and A from [0.2, 1.0]. We used a wide range of atmospheric light A for training dataset as compared to previous methods. TrainSeq is synthesized to fine-tune recurrent transmission module $\mathcal{T}$. It is generated from the sequential datasets SceneNet [23] and KITTI [6] and contains 3403 image sequences each containing 4 images. Our training set contains a much larger number of samples and more challenging cases due to higher variance in the atmospheric light component as opposed to previous methods.

For testing, we use RESIDE-SOTS [19] indoor and outdoor test sets. As RESIDE [19] includes images with atmospheric light between [0.7, 1.0] only, we also generate the test set with atmospheric light between [0.25, 0.7] using provided image-depth pairs in the RESIDE-SOTS. RESIDE-SOTS indoor test set contain images generated using last 50 images from NYU-v2. We include additional 49 images from NYU-v2 (which are not used in training) for test data generation with $A \in [0.25, 0.7]$. We denote the overall dataset as **TestAL**, which includes RESIDE-SOTS ($A \in [0.7, 1.0]$) test set along with self generated test set for lower $A \in [0.25, 0.7]$. To further demonstrate the generalization capability of our method we use ICL-NUIM [9] room and office sequences to generate 10 test sequences, denoted as **TestSeq**, having A from 0.25 to 1.0 with an interval of 0.08. Each of the 10 sequences in TestSeq contains 99 images with same A and attenuation coefficient β. For both test sets, the attenuation coefficient β is randomly sampled from [0.6, 1.8].

2.5 Learning

The transmission module is trained separately from the GAN module. Initially, the transmission network $\mathcal{T}$ is optimized using **TrainA** dataset for 20 epochs with 10^{-5} learning rate, followed by fine-tuning using the **TrainSeq** dataset until it converges. We optimize this network $\mathcal{T}$ using the Adam [15] solver with $\beta_1 = 0.9, \beta_2 = 0.999$ as hyper-parameters.

Following the guidelines summarized in [17], we train the GAN module using **TrainA** dataset in three stages. At first step, only the generator $\mathcal{G}$ is trained using only $\mathcal{L}_{\theta_G}^{MSE}$ (8) with a learning rate of 10^{-4}. In the second step, both $\mathcal{G}$ and $\mathcal{D}$ are alternatively trained to jointly minimize overall generator loss $\mathcal{L}_{\theta_G}^{G}$ (12) and discriminator loss $\mathcal{L}_{\theta_D}^{Dadv}$ (11) to solve the adversarial min-max problem (4). The overall generator loss function $\mathcal{L}_{\theta_D}^{Dadv}$ is calculated as:

$$\mathcal{L}_{\theta_G}^{G} = \mathcal{L}_{\theta_G}^{VGG_{5,4}} + 10^{-3} \mathcal{L}_{\theta_G}^{Gadv}. \tag{12}$$

For the first two steps of training, we use the ground truth transmission map along with the corresponding synthesized hazy image and real image samples from the **TrainA** dataset. In the final step, we replace the ground-truth transmission with the output of the trained transmission network $\mathcal{T}$ to further fine-tune $\mathcal{G}$ and $\mathcal{D}$ with a reduced learning rate of 10^{-5}. Similar to the transmission module, the GAN framework is also optimized using Adam [15] with same hyper-parameters.

3 Experimental Results

In this section, we discuss the experiments performed with our model and compare them with the existing state-of-the-art methods to evaluate the robustness of the proposed method.

3.1 Quantitative Evaluation on Synthetic Dataset

In this section, we quantitatively compare the performance of our method with five recent state of the art methods: CAP [36], NLD [1,2], DehazeNet [3], AOD-Net [18], and DCPDN [33]. The availability of ground truth images in synthetic dataset enables us to evaluate our method using Peak Signal-to-Noise Ratio (PSNR) and another well-known metric Structural Similarity Index (SSIM) [32], which is proven to be coherent with human perception.

In Table 1, we compare the mean SSIM and mean PSNR between haze-free images and dehazed images estimated from various methods on the synthesized TestAL dataset. The algorithms CAP [36] and Dehazenet [3], which use the algorithm proposed in DCP [10] for atmospheric light A estimation, perform better for the higher A in comparison to low A, especially, for indoor images. The AOD-Net [18] also follows the same trend as it was trained on samples generated using NYU-v2 [28] images keeping A between $[0.6, 1]$ only. The algorithm NLD [1, 2] which uses haze-line prior to estimate A seems unaffected by different A range but displays low accuracy in both indoor and outdoor dataset. The most recent work DCPDN [33] is trained on 4000 images having $A \in [0.5, 1]$ which was generated using 1000 randomly selected images from NYU-v2 [28]. This makes DCPDN [33] training set overlapping with TestAL indoor test set, which consists of images generated from last 99 images from NYU-v2 [28]. However, in case of outdoor dataset DCPDN [33] shows good generalization capability for all A as it is also trained on a relatively wide range of $A \in [0.5, 1]$. It should be noted that DCPDN [33] recovers the clean image using the inverse atmospheric model (2) embedded within the neural network architecture. DCPDN [33] estimates the transmission map and atmospheric light, separately and then uses (2) to generate the dehazed output. In contrast the proposed DHSGAN generates the output image directly from the generator network, which means it learns the inverse atmospheric model and therefore it is not dependent on separate estimation of atmospheric light. We observe that because our method is purely based on the generation network and is trained on a wide range of atmospheric light it works well in both indoor and outdoor partition of TestAL. As an ablation study,

Table 1. Quantitative comparison using PSNR/SSIM between haze-free images and generated dehazed images on TestAL test set. DCPDN [33] performance on indoor dataset is not computed because the indoor partition of TestAL includes images from NYU-v2 [28] that overlap with the DCPDN [33] training set, this is primarily because DCPDN is trained on randomly selected images from NYU-v2 [28]. Below, we also include performance of two sub-versions of DHSGAN: InvDHSGAN, and DHSGANv0.5. For fair comparison with [33], DHSGANv0.5 is trained on images with atmospheric light between [0.5, 1.0]. To conduct further ablation study, similarly to [33], we add inverse atmospheric model (2) layer after DHSGAN, keeping the existing architecture untouched. This configuration is termed as InvDHSGAN and follows the same training procedure as DHSGAN with same training data.

	NLD [1, 2]	DehazeNet [3]	AOD-Net [18]	DCPDN [33]	InvDHSGAN	DHSGANv0.5	DHSGAN
Indoor $A \in [0.25, 0.5]$	17.4539 / 0.6960	15.7652 / 0.6362	14.2226 / 0.5312	NA	17.9265 / 0.7660	17.8997 / 0.8109	**19.6296 / 0.8356**
Indoor $A \in [0.5, 0.7]$	18.0956 / 0.7211	16.6766 / 0.7101	15.4835 / 0.6587	NA	18.3253 / 0.7785	20.4201 / 0.8523	**20.9710 / 0.8545**
Reside-In [19] $A \in [0.7, 1.0]$	18.9228 / 0.7489	22.9989 / 0.8756	21.1155 / 0.8504	NA	21.3629 / 0.7666	**23.3469** / 0.8388	21.7236 / 0.8120
Outdoor $A \in [0.25, 0.5]$	19.9369 / 0.8140	19.6741 / 0.8029	15.8383 / 0.6275	**23.1771** / 0.8106	21.9664 / 0.8707	22.6735 / **0.8781**	22.7472 / 0.8772
Outdoor $A \in [0.5, 0.7]$	21.0152 / 0.8313	21.1485 / 0.8618	17.4319 / 0.7885	24.2113 / 0.8601	22.5285 / 0.8488	**24.4375** / **0.8821**	23.6601 / 0.8722
Reside-Out [19] $A \in [0.8, 1.0]$	19.9338 / 0.8016	27.2963 / 0.8886	24.3560 / 0.9080	22.6375 / 0.8447	25.9092 / 0.8868	**27.7660** / 0.9009	26.6127 / **0.9105**

Images Count $\Rightarrow$ Indoor: 4 × 99, Outdoor: 2 × 492, RESIDE-In: 500, and RESIDE-Out: 500

Table 2. Quantitative comparison using SSIM on `TestSeq` Indoor Dataset. Here, we also display a subversion of `DHSGAN`, referred as `DHSGANv0`, which forgets the state of `ConvLSTM` [24] after each video frames. It shows the performance improvement by using temporal correlation with `DHSGAN`.

A	CAP [36]	NLD [1,2]	DehazeNet [3]	AOD-Net [18]	DCPDN [33]	DHSGANv0	DHSGAN
Transmission	0.8419	**0.8787**	0.8603	NA	0.8587	0.8473	0.8512
Image	0.7269	0.6467	0.7851	0.7436	0.8304	0.8476	**0.8501**

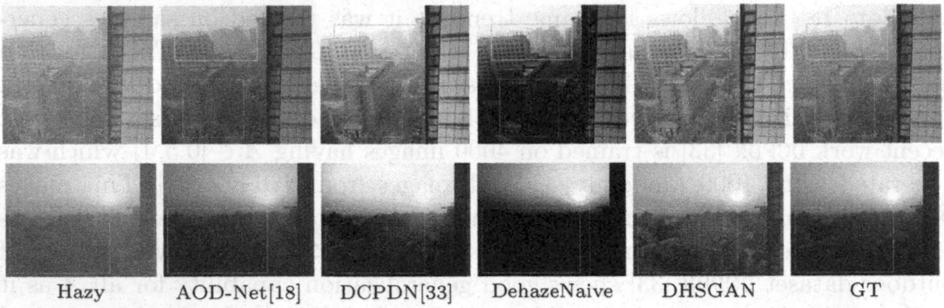

Hazy AOD-Net[18] DCPDN[33] DehazeNaive DHSGAN GT

Fig. 3. Qualitative comparison with recent dehazing methods on synthetic dataset `TestAL`. We notice that our model is generating images which are cleaner than provided ground truth. It shows that quantitative comparison with the ground truth doesn't fully explain the capacity of `DHSGAN`. Further, to demonstrate that generator function $\mathcal{G}$ is not just approximating inverse atmospheric scattering model (2), in column `DehazeNaive` we display the recovered image with (2) by using $\mathcal{T}$ output and known A.

similarly to [33], we add inverse atmospheric model (2) layer after `DHSGAN`, which uses $\mathcal{T}$ module output and generator $\mathcal{G}$ output (now behaving as A estimation module) in (2) to restore the dehazed image. This modification is termed as `InvDHSGAN`. This configuration limits the generator $\mathcal{G}$ capability to just atmospheric light estimation. It is evident from the results shown in Table 1 that removing the inverse atmospheric model (2) layer makes model more accurate and generalized. Further, to show generalization capability of our method, in Table 2 we display the performance of our method on `TestSeq` dataset that is generated using video sequence from `ICL-NUIM` [9] dataset. In this experiment, we deploy a sub-version of our model, termed as `DHSGANv0`, in which we consider image sequence as independent images, i.e. we forget the state of `ConvLSTM` in $\mathcal{T}$ module after each image. We observe that temporal correlations give a some boost to accuracy as observed by difference between `DHSGANv0` and `DHSGAN` SSIM accuracy.

3.2 Qualitative Evaluation on Real and Synthetic Datasets

In this section, we present a visual comparison of our network with other methods by dehazing hazed images. Figure 3 shows the comparison of the proposed method with the state-of-the-art techniques on synthetic set `TestAL`, the output

Fig. 4. Qualitative comparison of DHSGAN with recent state-of-the-art methods on real fog images released by previous authors. From top to bottom: the hazy image, CAP [36], NLD [1,2], DehazeNet [3], AOD-Net [18], DCPDN [33], and DHSGAN.

Fig. 5. Qualitative comparison of DHSGAN with recent methods on real smoke images. From top to bottom: the hazy image, CAP[36], NLD[1,2], DehazeNet[3], AOD-Net[18], DCPDN [33], and DHSGAN. Further to show that DHSGAN is able to preserve the information as opposed to just visual improvement, we employ SSD [21] as person detector. The confidence of object detection model is printed over the detected bounding box.

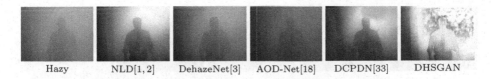

Hazy   NLD[1, 2]   DehazeNet[3]   AOD-Net[18]   DCPDN[33]   DHSGAN

Fig. 6. Qualitative comparison of DHSGAN with recent methods on extreme haze condition.

(a) Hazy   (b) $\beta = 1.0$ (c) $\beta = 2.0$ (d) $\beta = 3.0$ (e) $\mathcal{T}$-$\mathcal{G}$ MSE   (f) DHSGAN

Fig. 7. Effect of different transmission on generator $\mathcal{G}$. In column (b), (c), and (d) we generate scene depth using CAP [36] and use different attenuation coefficient β to generate transmission maps. It can be seen that low transmission (high β) tells generator $\mathcal{G}$ that haze density is high and thus more color shifting occurs. It implies that β can be configured to exploit trade-off between information retrieval and realness. In last two columns, (e) and (f), we show the performance of generator $\mathcal{G}$ with transmission estimated by $\mathcal{T}$ module. In column (e), the generator $\mathcal{G}$ is trained outside GAN framework using only MSE-Loss (8).

of the proposed method looks visually better or at par with the existing methods. In some cases the proposed method recovers the image details so well that it looks better than the ground truth image. This shows that our method is actually learning the clean image colour patterns also as opposed to just learning the inverse Atmospheric model (2). In Fig. 4 we show the results on a standard foggy image dataset, these images contain challenging fog density from outdoor. To further show the robustness of our model on different haze conditions, we also collected indoor smoke images containing high smoke density as displayed in Fig. 5. The smoke in case of fire incidents present challenges to other vision tasks and it's not frequently investigated in recent year as an independent problem.

Figure 4 shows that we are able to clean fog from images without losing any information. As our method is purely network generation based, we are able to provide similar enhancement to the pixels at depth as opposed to other methods. Our method learns what should be the colour compositions of the road, buildings, sky, trees etc., that makes our method resilient to colour shifting and blurring in case of normal fog conditions. In Fig. 5, we present the robustness of our method on a more challenging image degradation due to smoke. It can be seen that we are able to recover richer image content than other dehazing methods, which also

Fig. 8. Performance of DHSGAN on other reduced vision conditions: Underwater [27], Rain [34], and Snow-fall [34].

holds true in extreme situations (Fig. 6). Although, in case of high haze density the information is preserved, some artificial colour appears in the output image (Figs. 5 and 6).

In Fig. 7, we investigate the effect of transmission map on the GAN Module of our model. For this experiment, we estimate the depth of real images using algorithm proposed in [36] and use several attenuation coefficient β value to generate different transmission maps along with the one by $\mathcal{T}$ module. It can be seen that with increasing β the artificial colour becomes dominant but images get cleaner. Further in Fig. 7, we also display the result generated by $\mathcal{G}$ network which is trained on only MSE loss (8) to demonstrate the realness introduced by VGG Loss (9) and GAN [7] framework in our method. Finally, in Fig. 8 we present the performance of our method on other haze conditions such as underwater, raining and snow. It shows that, in future, a single model can be developed to tackle a wide range of image degrading scenarios.

4   Conclusion

In this paper, we have presented a novel end-to-end convolutional network that can directly generate realistic dehazed images in a variety of haze conditions including fog, rain, underwater and smoke. We train our network under GAN framework with a wide range of atmospheric light conditions, which enables the network to learn the distribution of real haze-free images. We do not use the widely used inverse atmospheric model for recovering haze-free images and instead let the generator network learn the dehazing function directly from the training data resulting into a more robust solution. We performed several experiments to demonstrate the superior performance of our method as compared to the state-of-the-art on commonly used real and synthetic datasets. We also showed that the proposed method can be generalized to different types of hazy images including the more challenging smoky images from indoor environments. We show that the proposed method works well even for smoky images with low atmospheric light thereby proving the robustness and the generalization capabilities of the network.

References

1. Berman, D., Treibitz, T., Avidan, S.: Non-local image dehazing. In: 2016 IEEE Conference on Computer Vision and Pattern Recognition, pp. 1674–1682 (2016)
2. Berman, D., Treibitz, T., Avidan, S.: Air-light estimation using haze-lines. In: 2017 IEEE International Conference on Computational Photography, pp. 1–9 (2017)
3. Cai, B., Xu, X., Jia, K., Qing, C., Tao, D.: DehazeNet: an end-to-end system for single image haze removal. IEEE Trans. Image Process. 25(11), 5187–5198 (2016)
4. Chen, C., Do, M.N., Wang, J.: Robust image and video dehazing with visual artifact suppression via gradient residual minimization. In: Leibe, B., Matas, J., Sebe, N., Welling, M. (eds.) ECCV 2016. LNCS, vol. 9906, pp. 576–591. Springer, Cham (2016). https://doi.org/10.1007/978-3-319-46475-6_36
5. Fattal, R.: Single image dehazing. ACM Trans. Graph. (TOG) 27(3), 72 (2008)
6. Geiger, A., Lenz, P., Urtasun, R.: Are we ready for autonomous driving? The KITTI vision benchmark suite. In: 2012 IEEE Conference on Computer Vision and Pattern Recognition, pp. 3354–3361 (2012)
7. Goodfellow, I.J., et al.: Generative adversarial nets. In: Advances in Neural Information Processing Systems 27, pp. 2672–2680 (2014)
8. Gross, S., Wilber, M.: Training and investigating residual nets. Facebook AI Research, CA (2016). http://torch.ch/blog/2016/02/04/resnets.html
9. Handa, A., Whelan, T., McDonald, J., Davison, A.J.: A benchmark for RGB-D visual odometry, 3D reconstruction and SLAM. In: 2014 IEEE International Conference on Robotics and Automation (ICRA), pp. 1524–1531 (2014)
10. He, K., Sun, J., Tang, X.: Single image haze removal using dark channel prior. IEEE Trans. Pattern Anal. Mach. Intell. 33(12), 2341–2353 (2011)
11. He, K., Zhang, X., Ren, S., Sun, J.: Delving deep into rectifiers: surpassing human-level performance on imagenet classification. In: Proceedings of the IEEE International Conference on Computer Vision, pp. 1026–1034 (2015)
12. He, K., Zhang, X., Ren, S., Sun, J.: Deep residual learning for image recognition. In: 2016 IEEE Conference on Computer Vision and Pattern Recognition (CVPR), pp. 770–778 (2016)
13. Ioffe, S., Szegedy, C.: Batch normalization: accelerating deep network training by reducing internal covariate shift. In: International Conference on Machine Learning, pp. 448–456 (2015)
14. Karras, T., Aila, T., Laine, S., Lehtinen, J.: Progressive growing of GANs for improved quality, stability, and variation. In: International Conference on Learning Representations (2018)
15. Kingma, D.P., Ba, J.L.: Adam: a method for stochastic optimization. In: International Conference on Learning Representations (2015)
16. Krizhevsky, A., Sutskever, I., Hinton, G.E.: ImageNet classification with deep convolutional neural networks. In: Advances in Neural Information Processing Systems, pp. 1097–1105 (2012)
17. Ledig, C., et al.: Photo-realistic single image super-resolution using a generative adversarial network. In: 2017 IEEE Conference on Computer Vision and Pattern Recognition (CVPR), pp. 105–114 (2017)
18. Li, B., Peng, X., Wang, Z., Xu, J., Feng, D.: AOD-NET: all-in-one dehazing network. In: 2017 IEEE International Conference on Computer Vision (ICCV), pp. 4780–4788 (2017)
19. Li, B., et al.: Reside: a benchmark for single image dehazing. arXiv preprint arXiv:1712.04143 (2017)

20. Li, Y., You, S., Brown, M.S., Tan, R.T.: Haze visibility enhancement: a survey and quantitative benchmarking. Comput. Vis. Image Underst. **165**, 1–16 (2017)
21. Liu, W., et al.: SSD: single shot multibox detector. In: Leibe, B., Matas, J., Sebe, N., Welling, M. (eds.) ECCV 2016. LNCS, vol. 9905, pp. 21–37. Springer, Cham (2016). https://doi.org/10.1007/978-3-319-46448-0_2
22. McCartney, E.J., Hall, F.F.: Optics of the atmosphere: Scattering by molecules and particles. Phys. Today **30**(5), 76–77 (1977)
23. McCormac, J., Handa, A., Leutenegger, S., Davison, A.J.: Scenenet RGB-D: Can 5M synthetic images beat generic imagenet pre-training on indoor segmentation? In: 2017 IEEE International Conference on Computer Vision, pp. 2697–2706 (2017)
24. Patraucean, V., Handa, A., Cipolla, R.: Spatio-temporal video autoencoder with differentiable memory. arXiv preprint arXiv:1511.06309 (2015)
25. Ren, S., He, K., Girshick, R.B., Sun, J.: Faster R-CNN: towards real-time object detection with region proposal networks. In: NIPS 2015 Proceedings of the 28th International Conference on Neural Information Processing Systems, vol. 1, pp. 91–99 (2015)
26. Sharif Razavian, A., Azizpour, H., Sullivan, J., Carlsson, S.: CNN features off-the-shelf: an astounding baseline for recognition. In: Proceedings of the IEEE Conference on Computer Vision and Pattern Recognition Workshops, pp. 806–813 (2014)
27. Shin, Y.S., Cho, Y., Pandey, G., Kim, A.: Estimation of ambient light and transmission map with common convolutional architecture. In: OCEANS 2016 MTS/IEEE Monterey, pp. 1–7, September 2016. https://doi.org/10.1109/OCEANS.2016.7761342
28. Silberman, N., Hoiem, D., Kohli, P., Fergus, R.: Indoor segmentation and support inference from RGBD images. In: Fitzgibbon, A., Lazebnik, S., Perona, P., Sato, Y., Schmid, C. (eds.) ECCV 2012. LNCS, vol. 7576, pp. 746–760. Springer, Heidelberg (2012). https://doi.org/10.1007/978-3-642-33715-4_54
29. Simonyan, K., Zisserman, A.: Very deep convolutional networks for large-scale image recognition. In: International Conference on Learning Representations (2015)
30. Szegedy, C., et al.: Going deeper with convolutions. In: IEEE Conference on Computer Vision and Pattern Recognition, pp. 1–9 (2015)
31. Tan, R.T.: Visibility in bad weather from a single image. In: 2008 IEEE Conference on Computer Vision and Pattern Recognition, pp. 1–8, June 2008
32. Wang, Z., Bovik, A.C., Sheikh, H.R., Simoncelli, E.P.: Image quality assessment: from error visibility to structural similarity. IEEE Trans. Image Process. **13**(4), 600–612 (2004)
33. Zhang, H., Patel, V.M.: Densely connected pyramid dehazing network. In: Computer Vision and Pattern Recognition, pp. 3194–3203 (2018)
34. Zhang, H., Sindagi, V., Patel, V.M.: Image de-raining using a conditional generative adversarial network. arXiv preprint arXiv:1701.05957 (2017)
35. Zhu, J.Y., Park, T., Isola, P., Efros, A.A.: Unpaired image-to-image translation using cycle-consistent adversarial networks. In: 2017 IEEE International Conference on Computer Vision (ICCV), pp. 2242–2251 (2017)
36. Zhu, Q., Mai, J., Shao, L.: A fast single image haze removal algorithm using color attenuation prior. IEEE Trans. Image Process. **24**(11), 3522–3533 (2015)

Learning Deeply Supervised Good Features to Match for Dense Monocular Reconstruction

Chamara Saroj Weerasekera[1,2]([✉]), Ravi Garg[1,2], Yasir Latif[1,2], and Ian Reid[1,2]

[1] University of Adelaide, Adelaide, Australia
{saroj.weerasekera,ravi.garg,yasir.latif,ian.reid}@adelaide.edu.au
[2] ARC Centre of Excellence for Robotic Vision, Brisbane, Australia

Abstract. Visual SLAM (Simultaneous Localization and Mapping) methods typically rely on handcrafted visual features or raw RGB values for establishing correspondences between images. These features, while suitable for sparse mapping, often lead to ambiguous matches in texture-less regions when performing dense reconstruction due to the aperture problem. In this work, we explore the use of *learned* features for the matching task in dense monocular reconstruction. We propose a novel convolutional neural network (CNN) architecture along with a deeply supervised feature learning scheme for pixel-wise regression of visual descriptors from an image which are best suited for dense monocular SLAM. In particular, our learning scheme minimizes a multi-view matching cost-volume loss with respect to the regressed features at multiple stages within the network, for explicitly learning contextual features that are suitable for dense matching between images captured by a moving monocular camera along the epipolar line. We integrate the learned features from our model for depth estimation inside a real-time dense monocular SLAM framework, where photometric error is replaced by our learned descriptor error. Our extensive evaluation on several challenging indoor datasets demonstrate greatly improved accuracy in dense reconstructions of the well celebrated dense SLAM systems like DTAM, without compromising their real-time performance.

Keywords: Mapping · Visual learning · 3D reconstruction · SLAM

1 Introduction

Visual 3D reconstruction finds its uses in many vision-based autonomous systems, including robotic navigation and interaction. It is a core component of

Supported by the ARC Laureate Fellowship FL130100102 to IR and the Australian Centre of Excellence for Robotic Vision CE140100016.

Electronic supplementary material The online version of this chapter (https://doi.org/10.1007/978-3-030-20873-8_39) contains supplementary material, which is available to authorized users.

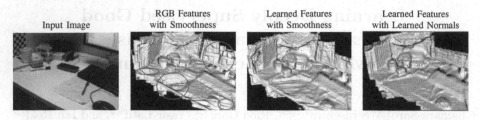

Fig. 1. Replacing color features with learned deep features and hand crafted priors with learned priors improves the reconstruction quality. Notice the dent in table, the very structured error in fusing the depths of the monitor and wrongly reconstructed notebook in the reconstruction which is obtained by using a RGB cost volume with smoothness regularization of DTAM [19]—all of which are fixed using our approach.

structure from motion and visual SLAM systems that work by establishing correspondences between multi-view images, either explicitly or implicitly, and use this information to solve for the locations of both the camera and 3D landmarks. Depending on the method used, and also the application, the reconstructed 3D map varies from being sparse to dense. While sparse mapping is usually sufficient in cases where the desired output is the trajectory of a moving robot, a dense 3D map is useful when a robot is required to reliably interact and move in a given environment. Success of both dense mapping and direct dense tracking given a map crucially depends on the ability to generate accurate dense correspondences between images. Reliance on hand-crafted features or raw RGB pixel values is the major bottleneck of dense SLAM as matching ambiguities arise due lack of unique local texture, repetitive texture in the image, appearance distortion due to change in perspective, change in lightning, motion blur and occlusions. Priors such as smoothness are often used to "fill in" or rectify parts of the map, but they are not always appropriate or sufficient for accurate reconstructions.

Recently, the resurgence of CNNs and their capacity to capture rich scene context directly from data have allowed relatively accurate predictions of surface normals and depths to be made just from a single image [3,7,14]. CNNs have also shown to be capable of accurately solving low-level vision problems like predicting dense image correspondences [12,21] or depth and motion from two-views [27], outperforming traditional vision methods which rely on handcrafted features and loss functions. However they have mainly been used for solving single or two-frame problems. It is not straightforward to extend standard end-to-end learning frameworks to use data from arbitrary number of views without increasing memory and computational requirements while training and testing.

In a typical visual SLAM system where the camera captures images at 30 Hz, it is always beneficial to make use of all the information available. In this work, we take a different approach of learning dense features *good for matching* which are *fast* to compute and can directly be used in existing dense monocular reconstruction systems for reliable correspondence estimation.

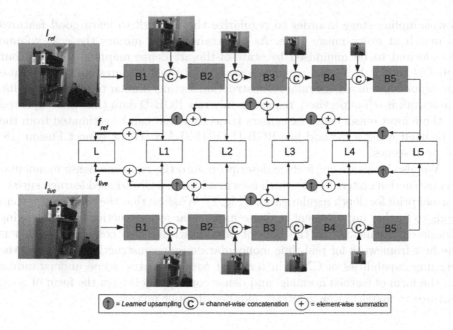

Fig. 2. Overview of the proposed multi-scale network architecture and training setup. At train-time both the reference and live images (I_{ref} and I_{live}) are passed into the network as a batch in two independent streams that share weights. The final 32 dimensional output features ($\mathbf{f_{ref}}$ and $\mathbf{f_{live}}$) for the reference and live image respectively as well as their intermediate output features are used as input to the cost volume loss layers L, L1–L5 for deep feature supervision at every image scale. Note that bold lines do not intersect with thin lines. The forward time for the network for a single image to produce a dense feature map is only ≈ 8 ms on a Nvidia GTX 980 GPU.

More specifically we want to automatically learn features via a CNN to deal with the ambiguities that occur when matching along epipolar lines for per-pixel depth estimation, especially when presented with images captured with a handheld monocular camera. To this end we introduce a novel deeply supervised CNN training scheme for feature descriptor learning, and a fully convolutional multi-scale network design that can help efficiently capture both local and global context around every pixel in the image to regress for the corresponding high dimensional feature vector for these pixels. In contrast to previous feature learning approaches, we propose to construct and minimize a multi-view cost volume loss for feature learning, where the predicted feature for *each* pixel in the reference image is compared with those for a range of pixels along the corresponding epipolar line in the live frame (one of which will be the right match).

The minimization is done with respect to predicted features over the *entire* cost volume during training and thus millions of feature matching instances are incorporated into a single training batch which makes the training very efficient. The efficient computation of our loss is enabled by the large parallel compute capability of GPUs. We apply our cost volume loss after every feature map downsampling stage in order to regularize the network to learn good features to match at every image scale. As our training loss mimics the cost volume loss desired to be minimised by state-of-the-art dense mapping systems, our belief is that it helps the network learn the optimal features suited for dense correspondence in a monocular reconstruction setting. Similar to [23] our training framework is self-supervised, requiring only raw RGB-D data (like that captured by the Kinect sensor) and the camera trajectory that can be estimated from the data itself using a method like RGB-D ORB-SLAM [17] or Kinect Fusion [18] for rigid scenes.

We also integrate our feature descriptors into the real-time dense monocular reconstruction system in [28] which uses in addition a CNN-based learned surface normal prior for depth regularization (Fig. 1). We show that the combined system leads to further improvement in dense monocular reconstructions in challenging indoor environments. To the best of our knowledge this combined system is the first framework for real-time monocular dense reconstruction to harness the learning capabilities of CNNs in terms of *both* geometric scene understanding (in the form of learned normals) and dense correspondence (in the form of good features to match) given arbitrary number of input images.

2   Background

SLAM Methods with Hand Crafted Features: Most popular SLAM methods like PTAM [13] and ORB-SLAM [17] use handcrafted features successfully for sparse matching and solving for a sparse map and camera trajectory. LSD-SLAM [5] uses direct RGB alignment for solving for both pose and map, and is able to generate semi-dense maps aided by depth regularization. DTAM [19] is also based on direct RGB alignment but is able to generate fully dense depth maps by accumulating multiple frames for keyframe reconstruction, and utilizing a smoothness prior to help resolve matching ambiguities. While recent work has begun exploring the use of learned priors for reconstruction [1,6,26,28], these methods still rely on low-level color/feature matching for dense correspondence.

End-to-End CNNs for Two-Frame Reconstruction: Ummenhofer et al. [27] propose to train a network for depth, camera motion, and optical flow prediction from two frames for indoor scenes and Kendel et al. [12] propose to train a deep network end-to-end for disparity prediction outdoors, to give state-of-the-art results for stereo reconstruction in NYU and KITTI datasets respectively. These two-frame reconstruction architectures however are not very easily extensible to use more than two frames – a limitation we address in this work. In particular, our work is inspired by [12], which constructs a cost-volume with learned features for two frames by simply concatenating the features of these images for all possible candidate matches. This stereo cost-volume is further passed to a deep 3D convolutional network which implicitly acts as a regularizer to finally select the correct matches out of these candidates. Instead of learning this regularization network, in our work we propose to make the matching decision on a per-pixel basis directly based on the cost-volume by forcing the correctly matched features to have small distances (and large otherwise). At test time we can then infer the depth of each pixel in the reference image *based on the same/a similar distance metric in the learned feature space summed over multiple live frames*, which end-to-end stereo networks listed above do not allow.

Feature Learning with CNNs for Dense Correspondence: Feature learning methods designed for good matching e.g. MC-CNN [31] or LIFT [30] are often patch-based Siamese like architectures. Unlike these methods, our architecture is fully convolutional allowing for efficient dense feature extraction during training and testing, with flexibility to match each pixel relying potentially on a receptive field as large as the entire image. Also related to our work is [23] that proposed a self-supervised visual descriptor learning method for matching. At test time, their learned features are used for model to frame alignment under extreme scene variations. Another related work is [2] that propose a Universal Correspondence Network for geometric and semantic feature matching. In both [2,23], a correspondence contrastive loss is employed which minimizes the feature distance between positive matches and pushes that of negative matches to be at least margin m away from each other. The cross-entropy loss that we employ enforces a similar effect by forcing the *probability* of the true match to be 1 only at the corresponding location in the other image, and 0 elsewhere, without having to explicitly specify a margin m.

Some other main differences exist between our feature learning method and previous work: (1) we use deep supervision (we minimize the feature matching error at different scales in the network to learn multi-scale features that are good to match), (2) we design and use a significantly faster and efficient neural net architecture specially suited for dense correspondence (which is also independent of spatial transformer layers as used in [2] and [30] to add to efficiency), and (3) previous work on feature learning have relied upon randomly selected negative samples (e.g. nearest neighbor sampling around the true match at *integer* pixel locations in [2])—in our case, by sampling uniformly a fixed number of times along epipolar lines we generate positive and negative training examples at *subpixel* level (through bilinear interpolation in feature space) and this is more reflective of the type of matching during dense reconstruction. Moreover, existing methods have not been extensively analyzed within/integrated into a real-time dense reconstruction framework.

3   Method

In this section we describe our neural network architecture and training and inference time setup, and discuss the motivations behind the design choices.

3.1   Network Architecture

Our network consists of five blocks B1–B5 (Fig. 2), each block consisting of 3 convolutional layers. All convolutional layers have a kernel size of 3×3 and 32 output filters, which we found to be a good middle ground for computational speed and matching accuracy. While we have tried other variations of our network with convolutional kernel sizes 9×9, 7×7, 5×5, the one with convolutional kernel size 3×3 in each block enabled us to achieve the highest matching precision. We believe that this is because explicitly limiting the receptive field, especially at the earlier layers, helps the network learn features that are invariant to appearance distortion.

The first two layers of each block consist of ReLU activation units for adding non-linearity to the network. The first layer of each block has a stride of 2 for 2x downsampling after each subsequent block. Downsampling in Block B1 is optional but adds to the efficiency, at a slight trade-off of precision. The progressive down sampling rapidly increases the receptive field for a pixel without the need for a deeper network and helps the network capture contextual information which is key for successful matching. Not having a very deep network also prevents the network from overfitting to a particular dataset, and helps it learn more generic descriptors that are useful for matching even in completely different types of environments (Fig. 7). In our network, the maximum potential receptive field for a pixel is roughly half the input image resolution which is significantly larger than in work like [31] which limit the receptive field to 9×9 patches.

While coarse features are useful for matching large textureless regions, they are too abstract for fine-grain pixel level matching required for precise depth estimation. Inspired by the U-Net architecture [22] we upsample each coarse prediction and sum it with the preceding fine predictions (Fig. 2) to produce our final feature output. Doing so explicitly embeds local information about a pixel into its contextual representation enabling precise sub-pixel level matching.

The final output of our network is therefore a 32 dimensional feature vector for each pixel in the image, encoding both contextual and low-level image information. Each upsampling operation on the output of each coarse block is done through a single learnable deconvolution layer with a kernel size of 5×5 and stride of 2. Making this layer learnable results in improved results over a simple bilinear upsampling, showing that in this case it is better to allow the network to learn a more appropriate upsampling method. Furthermore, concatenating a bilinearly downsampled version of the input image with the output features from each block before passing them as input into the subsequent coarser blocks also improves the matching result. This shows that there is still information present in the low-level features that can complement the abstract ones in order to benefit the pixelwise matching at lower resolutions. All input RGB images (with values in the range of 0–255) are mean (of training set) subtracted but *not* normalized as this gave the best performance in practice.

Although the multi-scale features from our network can be used independently for course-to-fine matching at test time, we perform matching using just the final *aggregated* high resolution feature output of our network instead as the contextual information contained in it allows for a large basin of convergence and makes the solution less sensitive to initialization (Sect. 4). The fast forward time of our network (≈ 8 ms on a Nvidia GTX 980 GPU) makes it suitable for use as a feature extractor in real-time SLAM. Another advantage of our architecture is that it provides the flexibility for one to discard the courser blocks if needed, as the features that are generated by each block are *explicitly trained* to be suitable for matching through deep supervision (see Sect. 3.2). For example one can choose to remove Blocks B2–B5 and simply use features from Block B1 if further efficiency is desired without compromising too much on accuracy (Fig. 7). One can also reduce the feature vector length from 32 to further improve the matching speed or increase the length to improve the matching accuracy. In our CUDA run-time implementation we make use of $float4$ data structures and 3D texture memory for improving GPU memory access times.

3.2   Training

The output of our network are dense pixelwise features for a given image. Given a pair of images (that are 30 frames apart in our training setup), the goal is to learn suitable features that give a minimum matching cost *only* between a pixel $\mathbf{u}_p$ in the reference image and the corresponding matching pixel in the live image, that lies on the corresponding epipolar line and is defined by the depth of $\mathbf{u}_p$ and the relative camera motion. To do this, first we discretize the (inverse) depth space ρ_p into $K = 256$ bins ($\rho_p = \{\rho_p^1, ..., \rho_p^K\}$, with $\rho_p^1 = 0$ and $\rho_p^K = 4$), and convert the continuous matching problem into a K class classification problem.

More specifically, our goal is to find the optimal features $\mathbf{f}_{ref} = f(\mathbf{w}, I_{ref})$ and $\mathbf{f}_{live} = f(\mathbf{w}, I_{live})$ that are a function f of the shared neural network weights $\mathbf{w}$ and I_{ref} and I_{live} respectively, that maximize the estimated matching probability $P_\phi(\rho_p^l)$ (derived from the cost volume E_ϕ as defined further below) at $\rho_p^l = \rho_p^*$ (the groundtruth inverse depth label), and minimize the probability elsewhere. We achieve this by minimizing the following cross-entropy loss:

$$\sum_p \sum_l P(\rho_p^l)(-lnP_\phi(\rho_p^l, \mathbf{f}_{ref}, \mathbf{f}_{live})) + (1 - P(\rho_p^l))(-ln(1 - P_\phi(\rho_p^l, \mathbf{f}_{ref}, \mathbf{f}_{live}))$$

$$(1)$$

where, $P_\phi(\rho_p^l, \mathbf{f}_{ref}, \mathbf{f}_{live}) = \dfrac{e^{-E_\phi(\rho_p^l, \mathbf{f}_{ref}, \mathbf{f}_{live})}}{\sum_{k=1}^K e^{-E_\phi(\rho_p^k, \mathbf{f}_{ref}, \mathbf{f}_{live})}} = \sigma(-E_\phi(\rho_p^l, \mathbf{f}_{ref}, \mathbf{f}_{live}))$,

$E_\phi(\rho_p, \mathbf{f}_{ref}, \mathbf{f}_{live}) = ||\mathbf{f}_{ref}(\mathbf{u}_p) - \mathbf{f}_{live}(\pi(T_{nr}\pi^{-1}(\mathbf{u}_p, \rho_p)))||_2^2$ and $\sigma(.)$ is the softmax operation. $P(\rho_p^l) = 1$ if $\rho_p^l = \rho_p^*$ and $P(\rho_p^l) = 0$ otherwise.

$T_{nr} \in \mathbb{SE}(3)$ is a matrix describing the transformation of a point from camera coordinates of $\mathbf{I}_r$ to that of $\mathbf{I}_n$. $\pi(.)$ is the projection operation, and $\pi^{-1}(.,.)$ is the back-projection operation, such that $\pi^{-1}(\mathbf{u}_p, \rho_p) = K^{-1}\dot{\mathbf{u}}_p/\rho_p$, where K is the camera intrinsics matrix, and $\dot{\mathbf{u}}_p = (u, v, 1)^T$ is $\mathbf{u}_p$ (a pixel in the reference image) in homogeneous form.

Note that since the length of the epipolar line in the live image (for the specified inverse depth range) can vary depending on the camera baseline and we sample a fixed number of bins, we perform bilinear interpolation in feature space to obtain features corresponding to each inverse depth hypothesis at non-integer pixel locations. Additionally, since the epipolar line for a pixel in the reference image can stretch out of the live image, we set a high cost m (e.g. $m = 10$) for negative matches that fall outside. If, on the other hand, the positive match for a pixel in the reference image falls outside of the live image, we completely mask out the loss for that pixel in the reference image.

Furthermore, in order to mitigate the effects of discretization and enforce a more refined match we minimize the regression loss in the same manner as [12], by performing a dot product between the discrete inverse depth labels and the corresponding set of probabilities $P_\phi(\rho_p^l, \mathbf{f}_{ref}, \mathbf{f}_{live})$, to get a single $\hat{\rho}_p$ for each pixel, and then minimising the squared distance of $\hat{\rho}_p$ to the groundtruth inverse depth ρ_p^*. On top of that we also minimize the squared distance of the inverse of $\hat{\rho}_p$ ($\hat{d}_p$) to the inverse of ρ_p^* (d_p^*). In other words we want to make the expected inverse depth/depth value to be as close as possible to the groundtruth.

Our overall loss function could therefore be written as:

$$\sum_p \sum_l P(\rho_p^l)(-lnP_\phi(\rho_p^l, \mathbf{f}_{ref}, \mathbf{f}_{live})) + (1 - P(\rho_p^l))(-ln(1 - P_\phi(\rho_p^l, \mathbf{f}_{ref}, \mathbf{f}_{live}))$$

$$+ \sum_p \left(\lambda_\rho(\hat{\rho}_p - \rho_p^*)^2 + \lambda_d(\hat{d}_p - d_p^*)^2 \right)$$

$$(2)$$

where, $\hat{\rho}_p = P_\phi(\rho_p^l, \mathbf{f}_{ref}, \mathbf{f}_{live})\rho_p^l$. We experimentally found that using a combination of the aforementioned cross-entropy loss and the two regression losses in both depth and inverse depth space, improved the precision of $\hat{\rho}_p$. We set $\lambda_\rho = 5, \lambda_d = 1$ in order to balance the magnitude of the three types of losses, and to balance the bias in precision between depth and inverse depth label space.

Since our network regresses multi-scale features, similar to [29], we explicitly perform deep supervision by minimizing both cross-entropy and regression losses with respect to the features at each scale independently (L1–L5), as well as the aggregated feature (L in Fig. 2). The camera intrinsics are scaled to suit the output feature resolution at each block, and we obtain groundtruth depth maps at each lower resolution scale through nearest neighbour sampling of the full resolution groundtruth depth map. In comparison, similar works to ours like [2, 23] have relied upon a single contrastive loss function at the end of the network. In addition to providing the flexibility of discarding blocks of the network in trade for computation speed, this deep supervision acts as a good regularizer for the network resulting in fast convergence during training. Our network is trained from scratch with Xavier initialization using the Caffe framework [11].

3.3 Keyframe Reconstruction Using Deep Features

We can use our learned features in the mapping frameworks of [19,28] by simply replacing the RGB cost-volume with the learned deep-features based cost-volume. Our inference loss is:

$$E(\rho) = \sum_{p \in \mathcal{P}} \frac{1}{\lambda} E_\phi(\rho_p) + E_{reg}(\rho_p),$$

$$(3)$$

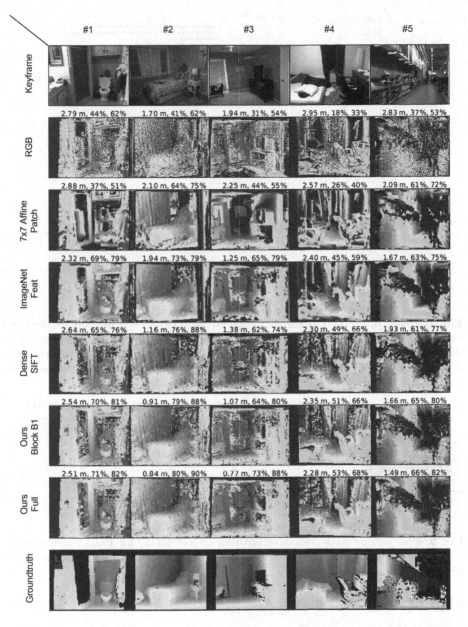

Fig. 3. Comparison of keyframe reconstructions (based purely on matching with 30 frames) using our learned features against those of baselines. The three numbers above each result denote RMSE (m), high precision accuracy ($\delta < 1.1$), and medium precision accuracy ($\delta < 1.25$). (Please refer supplementary material for more examples.)

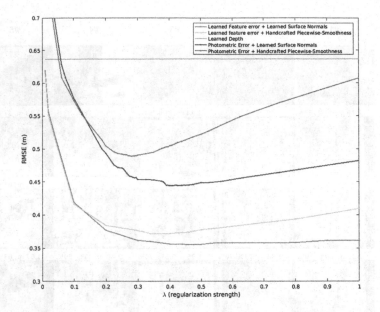

Fig. 4. Plot of RMSE (m) vs regularization strength (λ) for our method (bottom two curves) as well as our baselines. Note that as the cost-volume magnitude depends on the length and range of the used features, for the 2 plots using learned feature error the regularization strength λ is divided by a constant factor of 12.5 for better visualization.

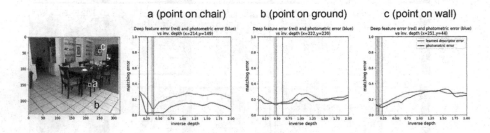

Fig. 5. Cost volume state (matching error vs inverse depth) for RGB features (blue) and learned deep features (red), after accumulating 30 frames, for 3 points in the keyframe. (Color figure online)

where E_ϕ is the data-term defined as:

$$E_\phi(\rho_p) = \frac{1}{N} \sum_{n=1}^{N} ||\mathbf{f}_{ref}(\mathbf{u}_p) - \mathbf{f}_n(\pi(T_{nr}\pi^{-1}(\mathbf{u}_p, \rho_p)))||_1 \tag{4}$$

which computes the descriptor matching error for a pixel in $\mathbf{I}_{ref}$ accumulated over N overlapping frames. Note here that the more robust L1 norm is used rather than square of L2 norm that was used during training. E_{reg} is the regularization energy term. We experiment with the smoothness and normal-based regularizer as two variations. The RGB features replacing $\mathbf{f}$ in (4) forms [19] and [28] as our baselines. λ in each case controls the regularization strength.

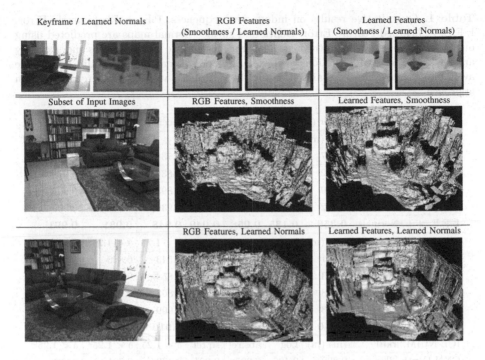

Keyframe / Learned Normals	RGB Features (Smoothness / Learned Normals)	Learned Features (Smoothness / Learned Normals)
Subset of Input Images	RGB Features, Smoothness	Learned Features, Smoothness
	RGB Features, Learned Normals	Learned Features, Learned Normals

Fig. 6. A snapshot of our real-time live reconstruction results on the 'living_room_0075' test sequence from NYUv2 raw dataset, as well as those of our baselines, using live monocular ORB-SLAM tracking.

4   Experiments

We extensively evaluate the matching performance and desirable properties of our learned deep features against several baselines on a large subset of the NYUv2 dataset [24] and follow that up to further explore the generalization capability of the features quantitatively on TUM [25] and ICL-NUIM [9] datasets and qualitatively on KITTI [8] dataset. Note that our features used in all experiments are trained on the raw NYUv2 dataset, excluding all test scenes.

Quantitative and Qualitative Results on NYUv2: We follow the same experimental set-up and the train/test split of NYUv2 dataset as that of [28]. Camera motion (in metric units) for all the NYUv2 train and test sequences were precomputed using [17] to isolate the mapping process. We use our own implementation of [19] and [28] as two very strong mapping baselines for this work. Small sub-sequences of 61 frames (30 past and 30 future frames) were used to reconstruct all the keyframes. We show the improvement in depth estimation by replacing the RGB features by our learned features for cost-volume creation in both the baselines mentioned above and compare the results to quantify the improvements. We evaluate the accuracy of the depth maps on the standard evaluation criteria used on the NYUv2 dataset by [3,28].

Table 1. Quantitative results on indoor test sequences. P.E. = Photometric Error. L.F.E. = Learned Feature Error. Depth and surface normal maps are predicted using our Caffe implementation of the neural network in [3]. The average errors and accuracy are for keyframe reconstructions against Kinect depth maps (where valid depths are available). The results here are those for the optimal λ value of each reconstruction approach.

	Error (lower is better)				Accuracy (higher is better)		
NYU-D V2 Test Set	rms (m)	Log	abs.rel	sq.rel	$\delta < 1.25$	$\delta < 1.25^2$	$\delta < 1.25^3$
CNN Depth [3]	0.637	0.226	0.163	0.135	0.738	0.937	0.982
P.E. + Smoothness	0.522	0.206	0.123	0.111	0.834	0.949	0.979
P.E. + L. Normals	0.449	0.174	0.086	0.076	0.893	0.964	0.985
L.F.E. + Smoothness	0.372	0.143	0.067	0.054	0.936	0.978	0.990
L.F.E. + L. Normals	**0.356**	**0.135**	**0.058**	**0.049**	**0.948**	**0.981**	**0.991**
TUM 'fr2_desk'	rms (m)	Log	abs.rel	sq.rel	$\delta < 1.25$	$\delta < 1.25^2$	$\delta < 1.25^3$
CNN Depth [3]	1.141	0.368	0.227	0.261	0.543	0.820	0.923
P.E. + Smoothness	0.563	0.215	0.106	0.091	0.854	0.924	0.973
P.E. + Normals	0.558	0.215	0.103	0.089	0.863	0.922	0.969
L.F.E. + Smoothness	0.453	0.178	**0.079**	0.061	0.909	0.949	**0.981**
L.F.E. + L. Normals	**0.450**	**0.176**	**0.079**	**0.060**	**0.910**	**0.950**	**0.981**
ICL-NUIM 'lrkt0'	rms (m)	Log	abs.rel	sq.rel	$\delta < 1.25$	$\delta < 1.25^2$	$\delta < 1.25^3$
CNN Depth [3]	0.829	0.426	0.295	0.261	0.472	0.781	0.905
P.E. + Smoothness	0.287	0.118	0.062	0.041	0.943	0.988	0.997
P.E. + Normals	0.214	0.094	0.047	**0.022**	0.963	0.993	**0.998**
L.F.E. + Smoothness	0.285	0.115	0.056	0.043	0.952	0.987	0.996
L.F.E. + L. Normals	**0.213**	**0.090**	**0.043**	**0.022**	**0.972**	**0.994**	**0.998**

To find the optimal hyper-parameter λ for each of the 4 reconstruction approaches, we brute-force search in a sensible range. Figure 4 visualizes the sensitivity of all the reconstruction approaches to the choice of regularization strength λ. After scaling λ for each approach to within a constant normalization factor, it can be seen that all the approaches degrade gracefully when we deviate from the optimal choice of λ while the learned features make this choice less critical.

In Table 1 we report the best reconstruction accuracies obtained on NYUv2 dataset with and without using our learned features. Using our learned features to create the cost-volume gives a significant improvement to the performance (on all the evaluation measures) compared to RGB cost-volume based reconstruction. In particular the percentage of accurately reconstructed points ($\delta < 1.25$) improve from 83.4% to 93.6% with smoothness regularization on the NYU dataset. A similar improvement is observed when learned normals are used as a prior to regularize the depth maps.

Figure 6 shows a visual comparison of the reconstructions obtained using our proposed deep features against those obtained using RGB features, with either learned normals or smoothness prior. The reconstructions were generated in near real-time in parallel with ORB-SLAM monocular visual tracking [16]. We fuse the depth maps of the keyframes obtained using each of the approaches using InfiniTAM [20] as part of our framework for better visualization and the results are shown and analysed in the figures. A significant advantage of the proposed deep features can be easily seen in these results visually.

Generalization Capabilities Across Different Camera Models: Furthermore we quantify the importance of the learned context aware deep features over RGB matching on two more indoor datasets, TUM dataset 'fr2_desk' and ICL-NUIM synthetic dataset 'lr kt0', both of which contain images that possess different properties (e.g. camera intrinsics) from that of NYUv2 raw. As seen in the bottom part of Table 1, the deep features consistently improve the depth estimation accuracy on these datasets without need for fine-tuning. The generalization capability of our network can be clearly observed in the example shown in Fig. 7 where KITTI stereo images are matched using our features learned on the NYU dataset. In this example the camera model, lighting conditions, objects and textures present in the scene, and camera motion significantly vary from the indoor setup. Also notice in the figure how explicitly combining course features with the fine features provides the necessary context to match large textureless regions while maintaining precision.

Comparison with Other Feature Matching Techniques: We compare our learned features against some baselines which are also suited for the dense geometric matching task with their own unique strengths and weaknesses. Apart from raw RGB features as commonly used in dense SLAM systems like DTAM, we chose to use as baselines: 7×7 patches that are affine warped before matching (similar to what is used in DSO [4]), ResNet-50 Conv1 features [10] pre-trained on ImageNet (with a receptive field of 7×7), DenseSIFT (used for dense optic flow in [15]), and features from Block B1 of our network (with a receptive field of 7×7). Results of keyframe reconstructions (based purely on matching with 30 frames) for some examples in and out of NYU dataset are shown in Fig. 3 and the rest in supplementary material. The supplementary material also contains 2-frame matching results.

From the results it can be seen that our learned features (particularly the full network version) consistently produce reconstructions close to groundtruth, and are superior to the baselines in terms of both matching accuracy and precision with minimal piecewise constant depth artifacts that occur in some of the baselines when overlapping images have severe appearance distortion. Although in some examples the number of accurate matches is higher in some of the baselines when matching with two frames, the number of accurate matches when matching based on 30 images is consistently higher using our full learned features. This indicates that the matching performance of the baselines is biased towards particular types of appearance changes present in the overlapping images which is an undesirable property. Please refer supplementary material for the complete set of visual and quantitative comparisons.

Fig. 7. Generalizability of learned features trained on NYU dataset to a completely different type of scene on the KITTI stereo dataset without any finetuning. Note that this is just the pure matching result with no regularization. From Left-Right, Top-Bottom: Reference Image, Live Image, RGB-features based disparity map, Block B1 features-based disparity map, Full network features-based disparity map, Groundtruth.

A Detailed Analysis of Learned Deep Features: A deeper analysis of the cost volumes generated using the proposed learned features (Fig. 5) verses those generated using RGB features highlight three main advantages of using our learned deep features. Particularly, our learned deep features-based cost volume has (1) sharp (non-flat) minima which leads to unambiguous unique matching even in textureless areas without having to rely on priors, (2) small number of local minima leading to a large basin of convergence and favoring gradient based optimization methods which heavily rely on priors and initialization, and most importantly, (3) the global minima corresponds to the correct inverse depth solution in majority of the cases, even with only a few number of overlapping frames (as shown in more detail in the supplementary material).

5 Conclusion

In this work we have presented a novel efficient Convolutional Neural Network architecture and a method for learning context-aware deep features which are "good features to match" in the context of dense mapping. We presented an extensive visual analysis which highlight some of the desirable properties of these deep features (invariance to illumination and viewpoint changes and ability to uniquely match thanks to the large receptive field). With the help of extensive quantitative analysis on three different datasets it was shown that the learned features generalize well across data captured with different cameras to give state-of-the-art reconstructions of indoor scenes in real-time. Initial experiments show promising stereo matching results even in substantially different outdoor scenes of the KITTI dataset where not only the camera but the brightness as well as the scene contents change substantially. We would like to further test the generalization capability of our learned features to different domains (outdoor scenes), and other vision tasks (image classification, retrieval, etc.) and explore if the learned features can be used for accurate camera tracking in a direct image registration framework.

References

1. Bloesch, M., Czarnowski, J., Clark, R., Leutenegger, S., Davison, A.J.: CodeSLAM-learning a compact, optimisable representation for dense visual SLAM. arXiv preprint arXiv:1804.00874 (2018)
2. Choy, C.B., Gwak, J., Savarese, S., Chandraker, M.: Universal correspondence network. In: Advances in Neural Information Processing Systems 30 (2016)
3. Eigen, D., Fergus, R.: Predicting depth, surface normals and semantic labels with a common multi-scale convolutional architecture. In: Proceedings of the IEEE International Conference on Computer Vision, pp. 2650–2658 (2015)
4. Engel, J., Koltun, V., Cremers, D.: Direct sparse odometry. IEEE Trans. Pattern Anal. Mach. Intell. **40**, 611–625 (2017)
5. Engel, J., Schöps, T., Cremers, D.: LSD-SLAM: large-scale direct monocular SLAM. In: Fleet, D., Pajdla, T., Schiele, B., Tuytelaars, T. (eds.) ECCV 2014. LNCS, vol. 8690, pp. 834–849. Springer, Cham (2014). https://doi.org/10.1007/978-3-319-10605-2_54
6. Fácil, J.M., Concha, A., Montesano, L., Civera, J.: Deep single and direct multi-view depth fusion. CoRR abs/1611.07245 (2016). http://arxiv.org/abs/1611.07245
7. Garg, R., B.G., V.K., Carneiro, G., Reid, I.: Unsupervised CNN for single view depth estimation: geometry to the rescue. In: Leibe, B., Matas, J., Sebe, N., Welling, M. (eds.) ECCV 2016. LNCS, vol. 9912, pp. 740–756. Springer, Cham (2016). https://doi.org/10.1007/978-3-319-46484-8_45
8. Geiger, A., Lenz, P., Stiller, C., Urtasun, R.: Vision meets robotics: the KITTI dataset. Int. J. Robot. Res. (IJRR) **32**, 1231–1237 (2013)
9. Handa, A., Whelan, T., McDonald, J., Davison, A.: A benchmark for RGB-D visual odometry, 3D reconstruction and SLAM. In: IEEE International Conference on Robotics and Automation, ICRA, Hong Kong, May 2014
10. He, K., Zhang, X., Ren, S., Sun, J.: Deep residual learning for image recognition. In: Proceedings of the IEEE Conference on Computer Vision and Pattern Recognition, pp. 770–778 (2016)
11. Jia, Y., et al.: Caffe: convolutional architecture for fast feature embedding. arXiv preprint arXiv:1408.5093 (2014)
12. Kendall, A., et al.: End-to-end learning of geometry and context for deep stereo regression. CoRR abs/1703.04309 (2017). http://arxiv.org/abs/1703.04309
13. Klein, G., Murray, D.: Parallel tracking and mapping for small AR workspaces. In: 6th IEEE and ACM International Symposium on Mixed and Augmented Reality 2007, ISMAR 2007, pp. 225–234. IEEE (2007)
14. Laina, I., Rupprecht, C., Belagiannis, V., Tombari, F., Navab, N.: Deeper depth prediction with fully convolutional residual networks. In: 2016 Fourth International Conference on 3D Vision (3DV), pp. 239–248. IEEE (2016)
15. Liu, C., Yuen, J., Torralba, A.: SIFT Flow: dense correspondence across scenes and its applications. In: Hassner, T., Liu, C. (eds.) Dense Image Correspondences for Computer Vision, pp. 15–49. Springer, Cham (2016). https://doi.org/10.1007/978-3-319-23048-1_2

16. Mur-Artal, R., Montiel, J.M.M., Tardós, J.D.: ORB-SLAM: a versatile and accurate monocular SLAM system. IEEE Trans. Robot. **31**(5), 1147–1163 (2015)
17. Mur-Artal, R., Tardós, J.D.: ORB-SLAM2: an open-source SLAM system for monocular, stereo and RGB-D cameras. CoRR abs/1610.06475 (2016). http://arxiv.org/abs/1610.06475
18. Newcombe, R.A., et al.: KinectFusion: real-time dense surface mapping and tracking. In: IEEE ISMAR. IEEE (2011)
19. Newcombe, R.A., Lovegrove, S.J., Davison, A.J.: DTAM: dense tracking and mapping in real-time. In: 2011 IEEE International Conference on Computer Vision (ICCV), pp. 2320–2327. IEEE (2011)
20. Prisacariu, V., et al.: A framework for the volumetric integration of depth images. arXiv e-prints (2014)
21. Ranjan, A., Black, M.J.: Optical flow estimation using a spatial pyramid network. CoRR abs/1611.00850 (2016). http://arxiv.org/abs/1611.00850
22. Ronneberger, O., Fischer, P., Brox, T.: U-Net: convolutional networks for biomedical image segmentation. In: Navab, N., Hornegger, J., Wells, W.M., Frangi, A.F. (eds.) MICCAI 2015. LNCS, vol. 9351, pp. 234–241. Springer, Cham (2015). https://doi.org/10.1007/978-3-319-24574-4_28
23. Schmidt, T., Newcombe, R., Fox, D.: Self-supervised visual descriptor learning for dense correspondence. IEEE Robot. Autom. Lett. **2**(2), 420–427 (2017)
24. Silberman, N., Hoiem, D., Kohli, P., Fergus, R.: Indoor segmentation and support inference from RGBD images. In: Fitzgibbon, A., Lazebnik, S., Perona, P., Sato, Y., Schmid, C. (eds.) ECCV 2012. LNCS, vol. 7576, pp. 746–760. Springer, Heidelberg (2012). https://doi.org/10.1007/978-3-642-33715-4_54
25. Sturm, J., Engelhard, N., Endres, F., Burgard, W., Cremers, D.: A benchmark for the evaluation of RGB-D SLAM systems. In: Proceedings of the International Conference on Intelligent Robot Systems (IROS) (2012)
26. Tateno, K., Tombari, F., Laina, I., Navab, N.: CNN-SLAM: real-time dense monocular slam with learned depth prediction. In: 2017 IEEE Conference on Computer Vision and Pattern Recognition (CVPR), pp. 6565–6574. IEEE (2017)
27. Ummenhofer, B., et al.: DeMoN: depth and motion network for learning monocular stereo. CoRR abs/1612.02401 (2016). http://arxiv.org/abs/1612.02401
28. Weerasekera, C.S., Latif, Y., Garg, R., Reid, I.: Dense monocular reconstruction using surface normals. In: 2017 IEEE International Conference on Robotics and Automation (ICRA), pp. 2524–2531, May 2017. https://doi.org/10.1109/ICRA.2017.7989293
29. Xie, S., Tu, Z.: Holistically-nested edge detection. In: Proceedings of the IEEE International Conference on Computer Vision, pp. 1395–1403 (2015)
30. Yi, K.M., Trulls, E., Lepetit, V., Fua, P.: LIFT: learned invariant feature transform. CoRR abs/1603.09114 (2016). http://arxiv.org/abs/1603.09114
31. Zbontar, J., LeCun, Y.: Stereo matching by training a convolutional neural network to compare image patches. J. Mach. Learn. Res. **17**(1–32), 2 (2016)

DeepAMD: Detect Early Age-Related Macular Degeneration by Applying Deep Learning in a Multiple Instance Learning Framework

Huiying Liu[1], Damon W. K. Wong[1], Huazhu Fu[1], Yanwu Xu[2(✉)],
and Jiang Liu[3]

[1] Institute for Infocomm Research, A*STAR, Singapore, Singapore
{liuhy,wkwong,fuhz}@i2r.a-star.edu.sg
[2] Artificial Intelligence Innovation Business, Baidu Inc., Beijing, China
redkisses121@gmail.com
[3] Cixi Institute of Biomedical Engineering, Ningbo Institute of Industrial Technology,
Chinese Academy of Sciences, Beijing, China
jimmyliu@nimte.ac.cn

Abstract. Automatic screening of Age-related Macular Degeneration (AMD) is important for both patients and ophthalmologists. In this paper, we focus on the task of AMD detection at the very early stage from fundus images. The difficulty of this task is that at the very early stage, the signs, e.g., drusen, are too tiny and subtle to be detected by most of the current methods. To address this issue, we apply deep learning in a multiple instance learning framework to catch these subtle features to detect AMD at the very early stage. The deep networks is able to learn a discriminative representation of the subtle signs of AMD. The multiple instance learning framework helps in two ways. First, It is able to choose the location where AMD happens because it works on image patches instead of the whole image. Second, It works on the image of high resolution instead of down sampling the image which may lead to invisibility of the tiny drusen. The experiments are carried out on a dataset consists of 3596 AMD and 1129 normal fundus images. The final average AUC is 0.79, compared with 0.74 of the same neural network but without multiple instance learning.

1 Introduction

Cataract, glaucoma, and Age-related Macular Degeneration (AMD), are the first three leading causes of blindness worldwide. Among these three ones, AMD is the first leading one in the elderly [1]. Approximately 10% of patients 66 to 74 years of age will have findings of macular degeneration. The prevalence increases to 30% in patients 75 to 85 years of age. According to the statistical data of World Health Organization, till 2010, there were nearly 2 million occurrences of AMD in the United States. The number is projected to be over 5 million in 2050 (http://www.who.int/research/en/).

C. V. Jawahar et al. (Eds.): ACCV 2018, LNCS 11365, pp. 625–640, 2019.
https://doi.org/10.1007/978-3-030-20873-8_40

AMD severely reduces the quality of life due to the vision loss caused by it. AMD happens in and around the macula, which is the central, posterior portion of the retina. Macula contains the densest concentration of photoreceptors within the retina and is responsible for central high-resolution visual acuity, allowing a person to see fine detail, read, and recognize faces. With age, one change that occurs within the eye is the focal deposition of acellular, polymorphous debris in and around macula. These focal deposits are called drusen. AMD results in a loss of vision in the center of the visual field. AMD patients have difficulty in reading, driving, recognizing faces, and some other daily activities [2].

Population bases AMD screening is in necessity for its increasing prevalence and its serious impact on life quality. At the early stage of AMD, the symptoms, e.g., vision blur and distortion, are not obvious to be noticed. When the symptoms are noticed, it is usually too late to save the vision because the vision loss caused by AMD is irreversible and permanent. Therefore, it is of great importance to detect AMD at the early stage, and patients can thus take treatment to prevent it from getting worse. Regular screening is a potential way to detect AMD at early stage. However, there is a conflict between the low and still reducing cost of fundus camera and the high cost of manual detection which is time consuming and labor intensive. More importantly, a certain degree of inaccuracy may be introduced by the subjective grading of human clinicians.

Automatic AMD screening has attracted much research effort in recent years. The major sign of early AMD is the appearance of drusen [3,4]. Drusen appear as yellow-white spot on digital fundus image, which is one of the mainstream and most popular imaging modality for AMD diagnosis. Although in recently years, OCT is occupying higher and higher percentage in the field of ocular imaging, fundus still has its own importance. For example, fundus image can be easily obtained by hand phone now thus automatic fundus image analysis and disease detection will provide great profit for users [5].

AMD is classified into early AMD with only a few small drusen, intermediate AMD with many large drusen, late AMD with geographic atrophy (dry AMD) or exudate (wet AMD). Example fundus images of AMD are shown in Fig. 1. At its early stage, the signs of AMD are very subtle, meaning that there are only a small amount of drusen, of small size. These drusen are very tiny so are very difficult to be detected. They are only visible at high resolution so it is not suitable to down sample the image. They may appear only at a small part of the fundus image but the exact location is unknown. In this paper, we try to address these issues by applying deep learning in the multiple instance learning framework. The reasons we use deep learning include its powerful ability to extract discriminative features automatically and its great success in image classification and recognition. Thanks to the multiple instance learning framework, we keep the high resolution of an image and divide it into multiple sub-images which consist of a "bag". From these bags we train a AMD detector iteratively.

The contribution of this paper is that we propose DeepAMD, a method to detect AMD at the early stage. The major characteristics of this method are two folds. First, it adopts deep learning to extract the discriminative features from

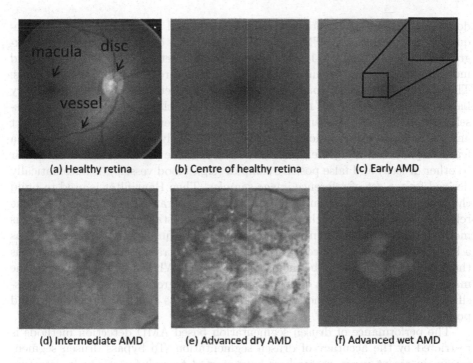

(a) Healthy retina   (b) Centre of healthy retina   (c) Early AMD

(d) Intermediate AMD   (e) Advanced dry AMD   (f) Advanced wet AMD

Fig. 1. Examples of fundus images of AMD. At the early stage, minute amount of small drusen appear (c). At the intermediate stage, there are large drusen clumped together (d). Advanced AMD can be dry with geographic atrophy (e) or wet with exudate (f).

the images. Second, it adopts multiple instance learning to train a classifier from high resolution images with AMD signs at unknown locations.

In the rest of this paper, we will review the state-of-the-art methods in Sect. 2. Then we will detail in Sect. 3 the proposed early AMD detection method. In Sect. 4, we will show the experimental results. Finally, we will conclude this paper with future work in Sect. 5.

2   Related Work

For the importance of automatic AMD screening, in recent years, lots of methods have been proposed for drusen segmentation and AMD detection. The existing drusen segmentation methods can be classified into three major categories. The first category, consisting of the earliest drusen segmentation methods, is based on local maxima, e.g., the geodesic method [6]. These methods first detect local maxima, then further classify the candidates according to contrast, size and shape. The second category consists of the local threshold based methods, e.g., Histogram based Adaptive Local Thresholding (HALT) [7], and Otsu method based adaptive threshold [8]. The third category includes the ones from frequency domain, e.g., wavelet [9], Fourier transform [10], and amplitude-modulation frequency modulation (AM-FM) [11]. There are some other methods, e.g., background modeling method [12] and saliency based method [10]. The background modeling method first segments the healthy structure of eye and blood vessels. The inverse of the healthy parts provide the drusen detection result. The saliency based method first detects the salient regions then classifies them as blood vessel, hard exudates or drusen. In [13], a general framework is proposed to detect and characterize target lesions almost instantaneously. Within the framework, a feature space, including the confounders of both true positive (e.g., drusen near to other drusen) and false positive samples (e.g., blood vessels), is automatically derived from a set of reference image samples. Then Haar filter is used to build the transformation space and PCA is used to generate the optimal filter. One relatively new method is the one using multiple instance learning [14]. In this method, all the local maxima points detected in a fundus image are treated as a bag then multiple instance learning is adopted to train a classifier. Growcut is then applied to obtain the boundary of the drusen. While applying Growcut, the maxima points classified as drusen is treated as foreground points, the ones classified as non-drusen, together with the minima points are treated as background points.

The performance of drusen segmentation based AMD detection methods is restricted by the accuracy of drusen segmentation. To bypass drusen segmentation, in recent years, researchers have started to seek for methods detecting AMD directly from fundus images, without drusen segmentation. These methods describe an image with locally extracted features, where the features are fed into a classifier to decide whether the image contains drusen or not. An early attempt in this direction was a histogram based representation followed by Case-Based Reasoning [15]. Good results were produced, however observations indicated that relying on the retinal image colour distribution alone was not sufficient. Thus, the authors further proposed a method by using a spatial histogram technique to include colour and spatial information [16]. The latest work from the same team comprises a hierarchical image decomposition mechanism, founded on either a circular and angular partitioning or a pyramid partitioning. The resulting decomposition is then stored in a tree structure to which a weighted frequent sub-tree mining algorithm is applied. The identified subgraphs are then incorporated into a feature vector representation (one vector per image) to which classification techniques can be applied [17,18]. The latest methods in this category include Biologically Inspired Feature (BIF) based method [19] and Hierarchical Word Image (HWI) representation and SPIN features based method named Thalia [20]. The BIF based method extracts features in a hierarchical structure simulating the structure of the human visual system the feeds the features into SVM to classify a fundus image into AMD or healthy. In Thalia, dense sampling is first carried out to generate structured pixels which embed local context. These structured pixels are then clustered using hierarchical k-means. The HWI image is subsequently classified using a SVM-based classifier.

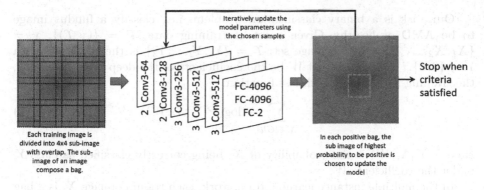

Fig. 2. The flowchart of the proposed method.

In recent years, the success of deep learning has spread into every field of computer vision and pattern recognition. Of cause ocular image analysis is also covered. Some of the works include vessel segmentation of fundus images [21,22], disc and cup segmentation [23], and glaucoma screening [24]. The works applying deep learning to detect AMD include the one feed deep features of fundus images into support vector machine [25] and the one detect AMD from OCT data [26].

All the above methods, both the drusen detection and segmentation based methods and the ones using global feature, can only detect AMD with obvious drusen, meaning large amount and large size. For example, the deep feature based method don't discriminate between healthy fundus and early AMD [25]. The multiple instance learning based method may encounter the problem of failing to converge due to the sparsity of the positive bags which happen in the case of early AMD [14]. In this paper, we focus on detecting the early AMD.

3   DeepAMD

AMD happens at and around macula, which locates at the center of retina. Therefore, we crop the central region around the macula, which is more important for AMD. Given a fundus image, we first detect the fovea, which is center of the macula and appears as the darkest region in a fundus image. The seeded mode tracking method is adopted to detect the fovea [27]. This method is robust to vessels and drusen appear near the fovea. The image region around the fovea will be used for AMD detection.

There are several works about deep multiple instance learning. For example, Xu etc. feed the learned feature using deep learning into a multiple instance learning framework to train a classifier [28]. Wu etc. constructed a model to do image classification and auto-annotation in a dual-multiple instance setting [29]. In [30], the authors used multiple instance learning as the pooling layers of the convolution neural network thus enable training CNNs using full resolution microscopy images with global labels.

Our task is a binary classification problem, i.e., classify a fundus image to be AMD or healthy. Given a set of training data, $\Gamma = \{(\chi, \Upsilon)\}$. $\chi = \{X_1, X_2, \ldots, X_n\}$ is the image set, $\Upsilon = \{Y_1, Y_2, \ldots, Y_3\}$ is the label set, with $Y_i \in \{0, 1\}, i = 1, 2, \ldots, n$. Let W be the coefficients of the deep neural network, the training is to minimize th loss function:

$$L(W) = \sum_{X_i \in |Chi} -\log(P(Y_i|X_i; W)) \tag{1}$$

Here $P(Y_i|X_i; W)$ is the probability of X_i being correctly classified as class Y_i under the coefficients W.

In the multiple instance learning framework, each training image X_i is a bag of sub images, $X_i = \{x_{i1}, x_{i2}, \ldots, x_{im}\}$. Here m is the number of sub images in the bag. It can be different for each bag but in our case it is the same for all the bags. For each training image, if the label is positive, there is at least one sub image is positive. If the label is negative, all the sub images are negative. Then the loss function is re-written as

$$L(W) = \sum_{X_i \in \chi} -\log(\max_{x_{ij} \in X_i} P(Y_i|x_ij; W)) \tag{2}$$

Then we adopt the idea of mi-SVM to train the network. In mi-SVM, each instance label is subjected to constraints determined by the (positive) bag labels. This is to ensure label consistency with the bag label. At the first step, all the samples in a positive bag, in our case, the sub-images of an training image, are treated as positive samples. A classifier is trained under this setting. At the following steps, with the highest probability to be positive is chosen for training. To balance the amount of positive samples and negative samples, from each negative bag, one sample is randomly chosen for training. This iteration continues until the stop criterion is satisfied. The criterion is composed of (1) the accuracy stops increasing, (2) the positive samples stop changing, (3) maximum iteration times. The illustration of this algorithm is shown in Fig. 2.

4   Implementation

To implement the proposed method, we construct a dataset consists of 4725 fundus images with 3596 AMD images and 1129 healthy ones. Each image has a resolution of 3072×2048 and is acquired using a 45 FOV Canon CR-DGi retinal fundus camera with a 10D SLR backing. All the images are macula centered. All the images are clinically diagnosed as early AMD or healthy. In experiment, we randomly choose 500 AMD images and 500 non-AMD images as training data and the rest as test data. The experiments are run for 10 times.

4.1   Choosing Networks

We test different networks and choose one for our task. The networks we considered include VGG16 [31], ResNet50 [32], and InceptionV3 [33]. For a not big

Table 1. The result of fine tuning different networks. The performance is evaluated by the average and standard deviation of accuracy (Acc.), Sensitivity (Sen.), Specificity (Spe.), and the area under ROC (ROC) of 10 random runs.

Acc.	Sen.	Spe.	ROC	Acc.	Sen.	Spe.	ROC	Acc.	Sen.	Spe.	ROC
ResNet50, Layer = 130				ResNet50, Layer = 140				ResNet50, Layer = 152			
0.26	0.14	0.85	0.49	0.25	0.13	0.86	0.52	0.25	0.13	0.87	0.53
0.20	0.30	0.30	0.05	0.13	0.21	0.24	0.08	0.19	0.29	0.30	0.08
InceptionV3, Layer = 183				InceptionV3, Layer = 215				InceptionV3, Layer = 247			
0.41	0.37	0.63	0.49	0.47	0.45	0.54	0.50	0.51	0.52	0.47	0.49
0.25	0.37	0.37	0.05	0.24	0.35	0.34	0.03	0.25	0.37	0.37	0.06
VGG16, Layer = 0				VGG16, Layer = 4				VGG16, Layer = 7			
0.54	0.51	0.68	0.67	0.63	0.65	0.55	0.67	0.66	0.69	0.55	0.68
0.19	0.27	0.20	0.03	0.19	0.28	0.25	0.03	0.10	0.15	0.15	0.03

enough dataset, a reasonable option to train a model is to fine tune the network with weights pre-trained on other datasets. We fine tune the models using the weights trained on ImageNet. During fine tuning, we set the parameters of the first layers to be un-changeable and the ones of other layers to be changeable. The changeable ones will be updated at the training stage.

We fine tune the network and compare the performance, using accuracy (Acc.), sensitivity (Sen.), specificity (Spe.) and the area under ROC (ROC) as metrics. This experiment is performed on the center region of size 224×224 of the images. 224 is about 2 times of the diameter of the macula. For the IncextioinV3 network, the images are resized to 299×299. For each network, 3 settings are tested, meaning that we update the parameters from different layers. For ResNet50, we update the parameters from layers 130, 140, and 152. For InceptionV3, we update the parameter from layers 183, 215, and 247. For VGG16, we update the parameters from layers 0, 4, and 7. The result is shown in Table 1. In the table, each item contains two numbers, one is the average and the other one is the standard deviation. From the result we choose VGG16 as the base model in our work. This model consists of 16 convolution layers, 5 max pooling layers, and 1 soft-max layer. We set the first 6 layers to be un-changeable and the other ones changeable.

4.2   Determining the Size of the Center Region

While determining the size of the image region, we have two consideration. The first one is that at the early stage of AMD, the drusen are so tiny that they are only visible at high resolution. If we down sample the image the drusen may become un-detectable. The other one is that the scope that drusen may appear is larger than suitable for the neural network. The size of the region considered for AMD diagnosis is usually 2 times of the diameter of the disc (please refer

Table 2. The result of different image size. The numbers shown are the average and standard deviation of accuracy (Acc.), Sensitivity (Sen.), Specificity (Spe.), and the area under ROC (ROC) of 10 random runs.

VGG16, Layer = 0				VGG16, Layer = 4				VGG16, Layer = 7			
Acc.	Sen.	Spe.	ROC	Acc.	Sen.	Spe.	ROC	Acc.	Sen.	Spe.	ROC
On the 224 × 224 center region											
0.538	0.51	0.68	0.67	0.63	0.65	0.55	0.67	0.66	0.69	0.55	0.68
0.19	0.27	0.20	0.03	0.19	0.28	0.25	0.03	0.10	0.15	0.15	0.03
On the 801 × 801 center region											
0.64	0.66	0.55	0.66	0.73	0.78	0.47	0.69	0.69	0.71	0.62	0.74
0.10	0.16	0.16	0.01	0.08	0.12	0.14	0.01	0.10	0.15	0.15	0.01

Table 3. Comparison between fine tuning and deep feature. The numbers shown are the average and standard deviation of accuracy (Acc.), Sensitivity (Sen.), Specificity (Spe.), and the area under ROC (ROC) of 10 random runs.

Acc.	Sen.	Spe.	ROC	Acc.	Sen.	Spe.	ROC	Acc.	Sen.	Spe.	ROC
VGG16, Layer = 0				VGG16, Layer = 4				VGG16, Layer = 7			
Fine tune											
0.64	0.66	0.55	0.66	0.73	0.78	0.47	0.69	0.69	0.71	0.62	0.74
0.10	0.16	0.16	0.01	0.08	0.12	0.14	0.01	0.10	0.15	0.15	0.01
Deep feature and SVM											
0.52	0.51	0.56	0.54	0.57	0.57	0.58	0.58	0.59	0.60	0.58	0.59
0.01	0.02	0.02	0.01	0.01	0.01	0.02	0.01	0.01	0.02	0.02	0.01

to Fig. 1 for an illustration of disc). In our case, about 801 × 801. Specifically, the VGG16 network takes 224 × 224 images as input. If we crop the 224 × 224 region around the macula we may miss important information out of this region. If we crop the 801 × 801 region and down sample it to 224 × 224 the drusen may become invisible. We compare these two options. The 801 × 801 image is then resized to 224 × 224. From the result shown in Table 2, we can see that the size 801 × 801 is more suitable for early AMD detection. In our experiment, we then crop the center region of size 801 × 801 and divide it into 4 × 4 sub images of size 224 × 224. The 16 subimages then consists of a bag for the multiple instance learning.

5   Experimental Results

The proposed DeepAMD is implemented in Python, on Keras. The code was run on a server installed with 16 CPUs of 3 GB Hz, an nVidea Tesla K40C graphic card. The memory of the server is 256 GB. While running, each iteration of training needs 35 s. At the prediction stage, each image used 0.08 s.

Table 4. Comparison between DeepAMD and fine tuning VGG16. The numbers shown are the average and standard deviation of accuracy (Acc.), Sensitivity (Sen.), Specificity (Spe.), and the area under ROC (ROC) of 10 random runs.

Acc.	Sen.	Spe.	ROC	Acc.	Sen.	Spe.	ROC
Fine Tune VGG, Layer = 7				DeepAMD, Layer = 7			
0.69	0.74	0.62	0.74	0.70	0.67	0.70	0.79
0.10	0.15	0.15	0.01	0.08	0.11	0.14	0.03

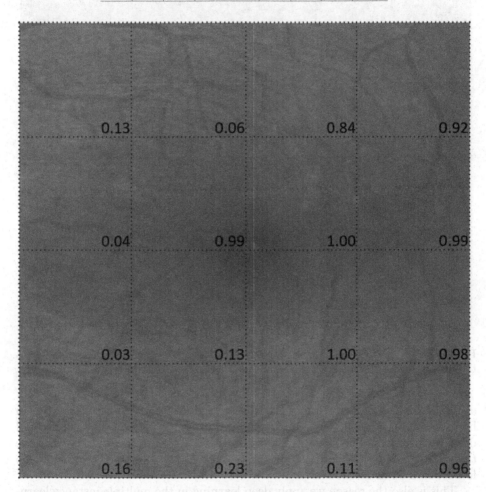

Fig. 3. Result of DeepAMD: an example of true positive. The tiny drusen are correctly detected by the DeepAMD.

5.1 Comparison Between Fine Tune and Deep Feature

As we know, big data sets are needed to train a deep neural network from scratch. For a data set not big enough, extract the output of some layers of the network

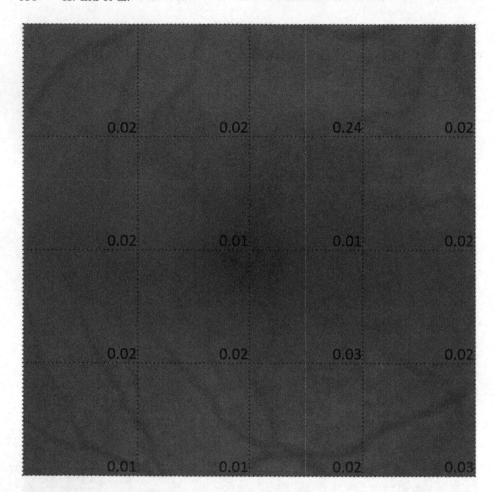

Fig. 4. Result of DeepAMD: an example of false negative. DeepAMD failed to detect the drusen locate at the center of the macula.

as feature, called deep feature, then train a SVM classifier on these features can be a reasonable option. We compare the performance between fine tuning and deep feature here. The result is shown in Table 3. From the result, we can see that fine tune is more suitable for our task of AMD detection, than the deep feature and SVM method.

This is also the reason we apply deep learning in the multiple instance learning framework instead of apply deep feature of each image patch in tradition multiple instance learning, e.g., mi-SVM.

5.2 Result of DeepAMD

Here we show the result of our DeepAMD, compared with the same network without multiple instance learning. The result is shown in Table 4. From the

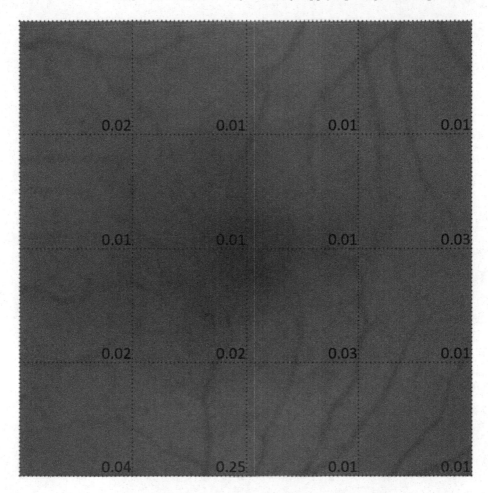

Fig. 5. Result of DeepAMD. The normal fundus image is correctly classified as normal.

result, we can see the improvement of ROC. Four examples are shown in Figs. 3, 4, 5, 6, and 7. In each example, the numbers indicate the probability of the image patch to be classified as AMD.

Figure 3 shows an example of true positive. In this examples, DeepAMD successfully caught the subtle signs of AMD. Figure 4 shows an example of false negative. DeepAMD failed to detect the drusen at the center of the macula. Figure 5 shows an example of true negative. In the example shown in Fig. 6, the drusen like spot is detected as drusen. Figure 7 shown an interesting example. This image is labeled as normal but some large drusen and some small ones appear. The interesting point is that the large drusen are detected as normal because the same sign don't appear in the training set. The small drusen are detected by the system and the image is classified as AMD.

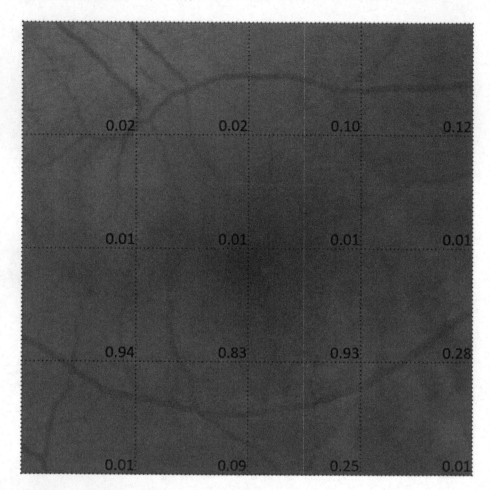

Fig. 6. Result of DeepAMD: an example of false alarm. DeepAMD detects two drusen like image patches from a fundus image labeled as normal.

5.3   Discussion

In experiment, we compared between fine tuning the model with using deep feature which is also a reasonable option. The result verified that fine tuning is more suitable for our task. Then, the results showed that the multiple instance learning improves the performance of the neural network.

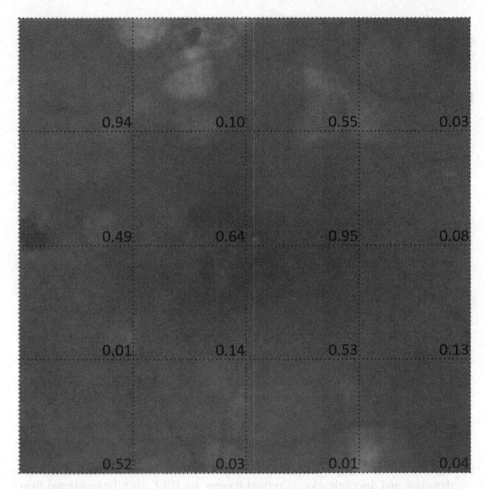

Fig. 7. Result of DeepAMD: another example of false alarm. This image is labeled as normal but detected as AMD.

6   Conclusions

In this paper, we propose DeepAMD, which applies deep learning in a multiple instance learning framework to detect early AMD from fundus images. Extensive experiments verified the performance of the method. In our future work, we will focus our effort on the following topics.

First, further improve the algorithm and also the performance. We will try to tailor a specific network more suitable for our task, instead of the VGG16 which is generic and suitable for the ImageNet dataset.

Second, we will try to collect more data and test the method on a larger and clearer dataset. From the example we shown one can see that there is ambiguity in the dataset.

Finally, we will try to build a system which can classify AMD into different stage, i.e., early AMD, intermediate AMD, and late AMD (dry type and wet type).

References

1. Kawasaki, R., et al.: The prevalence of age-related macular degeneration in Asians: a systematic review and meta-analysis. Ophthalmology **117**, 921–927 (2010)
2. Jager, R.D., Mieler, W.F., Miller, J.W.: Age-related macular degeneration. N. Engl. J. Med. **358**, 2606–2617 (2008)
3. Bressler, N.M., Bressler, S.B., Fine, S.L.: Age-related macular degeneration. Surv. Ophthalmol. **32**, 375–413 (1988)
4. De Jong, P.T.: Age-related macular degeneration. N. Engl. J. Med. **355**, 1474–1485 (2006)
5. Maamari, R.N., Keenan, J.D., Fletcher, D.A., Margolis, T.P.: A mobile phone-based retinal camera for portable wide field imaging. Brit. J. Ophthalmol. **98**, 438–441 (2014)
6. Ben Sbeh, Z., Cohen, L.D., Mimoun, G., Coscas, G.: A new approach of geodesic reconstruction for drusen segmentation in eye fundus images. IEEE Trans. Med. Imaging **20**, 1321–1333 (2001)
7. Rapantzikos, K., Zervakis, M., Balas, K.: Detection and segmentation of drusen deposits on human retina: potential in the diagnosis of age-related macular degeneration. Med. Image Anal. **7**, 95–108 (2003)
8. Smith, R.T., et al.: Automated detection of macular drusen using geometric background leveling and threshold selection. Arch. Ophthalmol. **123**, 200 (2005)
9. Brandon, L., Hoover, A.: Drusen detection in a retinal image using multi-level analysis. In: Ellis, R.E., Peters, T.M. (eds.) MICCAI 2003. LNCS, vol. 2878, pp. 618–625. Springer, Heidelberg (2003). https://doi.org/10.1007/978-3-540-39899-8_76
10. Ujjwal, K., Chakravarty, A., Sivaswamy, J.: Visual saliency based bright lesion detection and discrimination in retinal images. In: IEEE 10th International Symposium on Biomedical Imaging: From Nano to Macro, pp. 1428–1431 (2013)
11. Barriga, E., et al.: Multi-scale AM-FM for lesion phenotyping on age-related macular degeneration. In: IEEE International Symposium on Computer-Based Medical Systems, pp. 1–5 (2009)
12. Köse, C., et al.: A statistical segmentation method for measuring age-related macular degeneration in retinal fundus images. J. Med. Syst. **34**, 1–13 (2010)
13. Quellec, G., Russell, S.R., Abràmoff, M.D.: Optimal filter framework for automated, instantaneous detection of lesions in retinal images. IEEE Trans. Med. Imaging **30**, 523–533 (2011)
14. Liu, H., Xu, Y., Wong, D.W.K., Liu, J.: Effective drusen segmentation from fundus images for age-related macular degeneration screening. In: Cremers, D., Reid, I., Saito, H., Yang, M.-H. (eds.) ACCV 2014. LNCS, vol. 9005, pp. 483–498. Springer, Cham (2015). https://doi.org/10.1007/978-3-319-16811-1_32
15. Hijazi, M.H.A., Coenen, F., Zheng, Y.: Retinal image classification using a histogram based approach. In: IEEE International Joint Conference on Neural Networks, pp. 3501–3507

16. Hijazi, M.H.A., Coenen, F., Zheng, Y.: Retinal image classification for the screening of age-related macular degeneration. In: Bramer, M., Petridis, M., Hopgood, A. (eds.) Research and Development in Intelligent Systems XXVII, pp. 325–338. Springer, London (2011). https://doi.org/10.1007/978-0-85729-130-1_25

17. Hijazi, M.H.A., Jiang, C., Coenen, F., Zheng, Y.: Image classification for age-related macular degeneration screening using hierarchical image decompositions and graph mining. In: Gunopulos, D., Hofmann, T., Malerba, D., Vazirgiannis, M. (eds.) ECML PKDD 2011. LNCS (LNAI), vol. 6912, pp. 65–80. Springer, Heidelberg (2011). https://doi.org/10.1007/978-3-642-23783-6_5

18. Zheng, Y., Hijazi, M.H.A., Coenen, F.: Automated "disease/no disease" grading of age-related macular degeneration by an image mining approach. Invest. Ophthalmol. Vis. Sci. **53**, 8310–8318 (2012)

19. Cheng, J., et al.: Early age-related macular degeneration detection by focal biologically inspired feature. In: IEEE International Conference on Image Processing, pp. 2805–2808 (2012)

20. Wong, D.W.K., et al.: THALIA-an automatic hierarchical analysis system to detect drusen lesion images for AMD assessment. In: IEEE International Symposium on Biomedical Imaging, pp. 884–887 (2013)

21. Li, Q., Feng, B., Xie, L., Liang, P., Zhang, H., Wang, T.: A cross-modality learning approach for vessel segmentation in retinal images. IEEE Trans. Med. Imaging **35**, 109–118 (2016)

22. Fu, H., Xu, Y., Lin, S., Wong, D.W.K., Liu, J.: DeepVessel: retinal vessel segmentation via deep learning and conditional random field. In: Ourselin, S., Joskowicz, L., Sabuncu, M.R., Unal, G., Wells, W. (eds.) MICCAI 2016. LNCS, vol. 9901, pp. 132–139. Springer, Cham (2016). https://doi.org/10.1007/978-3-319-46723-8_16

23. Fu, H., Cheng, J., Xu, Y., Wong, D.W.K., Liu, J., Cao, X.: Joint optic disc and cup segmentation based on multi-label deep network and polar transformation. IEEE TMI **37**, 1597–1605 (2018)

24. Fu, H., et al.: Disc-aware ensemble network for Glaucoma screening from fundus image. IEEE TMI **37**, 2493–2501 (2018)

25. Burlina, P., Freund, D.E., Joshi, N., Wolfson, Y., Bressler, N.M.: Detection of age-related macular degeneration via deep learning. In: 2016 IEEE 13th International Symposium on Biomedical Imaging (ISBI), pp. 184–188. IEEE (2016)

26. Lee, C.S., Baughman, D.M., Lee, A.Y.: Deep learning is effective for classifying normal versus age-related macular degeneration oct images. Ophthalmol. Retina **1**, 322–327 (2017)

27. Wong, D.W.K., et al.: Automatic detection of the macula in retinal fundus images using seeded mode tracking approach. In: 2012 Annual International Conference of the IEEE Engineering in Medicine and Biology Society (EMBC), pp. 4950–4953. IEEE (2012)

28. Xu, Y., et al.: Deep learning of feature representation with multiple instance learning for medical image analysis. In: 2014 IEEE International Conference on Acoustics, Speech and Signal Processing (ICASSP), pp. 1626–1630. IEEE (2014)

29. Wu, J., Yu, Y., Huang, C., Yu, K.: Deep multiple instance learning for image classification and auto-annotation. In: Proceedings of the IEEE Conference on Computer Vision and Pattern Recognition, pp. 3460–3469 (2015)

30. Kraus, O.Z., Ba, J.L., Frey, B.J.: Classifying and segmenting microscopy images with deep multiple instance learning. Bioinformatics **32**, i52–i59 (2016)

31. Simonyan, K., Zisserman, A.: Very deep convolutional networks for large-scale image recognition. arXiv preprint arXiv:1409.1556 (2014)

32. He, K., Zhang, X., Ren, S., Sun, J.: Deep residual learning for image recognition. In: Proceedings of the IEEE Conference on Computer Vision and Pattern Recognition, pp. 770–778 (2016)
33. Szegedy, C., Vanhoucke, V., Ioffe, S., Shlens, J., Wojna, Z.: Rethinking the inception architecture for computer vision. In: Proceedings of the IEEE Conference on Computer Vision and Pattern Recognition, pp. 2818–2826 (2016)

Depth Reconstruction of Translucent Objects from a Single Time-of-Flight Camera Using Deep Residual Networks

Seongjong Song and Hyunjung Shim[✉]

School of Integrated Technology, Yonsei University, Incheon, South Korea
{bell,kateshim}@yonsei.ac.kr

Abstract. We propose a novel approach to recovering translucent objects from a single time-of-flight (ToF) depth camera using deep residual networks. When recording translucent objects using the ToF depth camera, their depth values are severely contaminated due to complex light interactions with surrounding environment. While existing methods suggested new capture systems or developed the depth distortion models, their solutions were less practical because of strict assumptions or heavy computational complexity. In this paper, we adopt deep residual networks for modeling the ToF depth distortion caused by translucency. To fully utilize both the local and semantic information of objects, multiscale patches are used to predict the depth value. Based on the quantitative and qualitative evaluation on our benchmark database, we show the effectiveness and robustness of the proposed algorithm.

1 Introduction

Depth cameras are widely used in various applications including augmented reality, game, human-computer interaction and scene understanding. Owing to their real-time performance, portability, and reasonable price, depth cameras are commercially succeeded, even built in the smartphones. (e.g., iPhone X) Existing depth sensing technologies utilize active light source projected onto the target object, and analyze their light reflection to acquire the depth value of 3-D point.

However, the appearance of translucent object is determined by the complex light interactions associated with the light refraction and transmission. Consequently, when we capture a translucent object using a commercial depth camera, the resultant depth map presents significant errors. Although this issue is well-known and also considered to be critical in research community, it remains unsolved because this error is closely involved with understanding the surroundings of target objects. Lately, several approaches attempt to address this problem by either (1) utilizing controlled environment [3,10,13,30], (2) developing the empirical model of depth error [6,21], or (3) exploiting context information from RGB images [27,33]. Controlling the capture environment formulates the problem of reconstructing the translucent object well-posed. Although they produce high quality geometric models, these solutions are limited to laboratory

© Springer Nature Switzerland AG 2019
C. V. Jawahar et al. (Eds.): ACCV 2018, LNCS 11365, pp. 641–657, 2019.
https://doi.org/10.1007/978-3-030-20873-8_41

experiment, not suitable for practical applications. Later, empirical error models are introduced for releasing the capture conditions. However, their performance is quite limited to the specific types of objects, incapable of handling various shapes and materials in translucent objects. Inspired by the human perceptual ability that recognizes the translucent objects, several studies extract the context information from RGB images and utilize it for understanding the translucent objects. Yet, these approaches do not cover the problem of depth reconstruction.

In this paper, we propose a learning-based approach to compensating depth distortion in translucent objects using a single time-of-flight camera. We utilize both the foreground depth map and background depth map to correct the depth distortion as inputs and recover a correct depth map for the translucent object. Compared to several approaches utilizing RGB images, our algorithm is robust to harsh lighting conditions or dark environment. Also, it is worthwhile noting that the proposed algorithm is a purely data driven approach. That means, we do not require physical constraints [14,28] or controlled environment for developing the model. Consequently, while existing work should be reformulated even with the slight modifications on their assumptions, the proposed framework is extendable to different conditions or scenarios as long as the additional datasets are available.

More specifically, we develop deep convolutional networks for recovering translucent objects from depth maps. Our network architecture is inspired by deep residual network [9], or ResNet, which has been successfully adopted to object classification and image restoration problems [23]. On top of ResNet architecture, our model simultaneously processes multi-scale patches from two input images. In this way, we intend to cope both local characteristics (i.e., small scale patch) and semantic information of target objects (i.e., large scale patch). As a result, the proposed algorithm improves the accuracy of reconstructing translucent objects both quantitatively and qualitatively. Particularly, we show that our algorithm is robust against various levels of sensor noise, which is inevitable in most of time-of-flight depth sensor due to short exposures and the limited amount of emitted light energy. To the best of our knowledge, the proposed algorithm is the first attempt to solving the 3D reconstruction of translucent objects using deep neural networks. We believe our work can serve an important baseline of future work. Our database and code are publicly available at https:// github.com/wtre/deep-translucent-recon.

2   Related Work

Depth Acquisition of Transparent Objects. Recovering 3-D transparent objects is known to be a challenging research problem in computer vision, and numerous techniques have been proposed to address this problem. Previous techniques utilized the laser scan with polarization [3] or with a fluorescent liquid [10] for accurate reconstruction of translucent objects. Tanaka et al. [30] recovered 3D shape of transparent objects utilizing a known refractive index and images captured under controlling the background patterns. Kim et al. [13] analyzed images recorded by projecting several background patterns, and then reconstructed the shape of axially-symmetric transparent objects. Despite of the impressive quality, their capture systems rely on controlled environment, unlikely applicable to practical applications.

Several approaches observe that depth distortions caused by transparent objects provide meaningful clues for understanding their shapes, even in practical situations. Maeno et al. [21] analyzed light field distortion caused by a transparent object (e.g, a glass) and used it for recognizing the object. However, detecting depth distortion features heavily depends on the type of background; for instance, a textureless background or a scene with repeating patterns degrades the detectability. Torres-Gómez and Mayol-Cuevas [32] segmented and roughly reconstructed transparent object from multiple color images by carefully stitching hand-crafted features for translucent objects. Yet, their algorithm is limited to a glass object with a spatially smooth surface.

When acquiring translucent objects using structured light based depth sensors, those target objects often appear invalid, shown as empty holes in the depth map. From this observation, several techniques detect the holes in the depth map and evaluate those holes using its RGB image to classify or localize the translucent objects. That is, Wang et al. [33] sequentially applied traditional image processing algorithms for transparent object localization while Lysenkov et al. [20] adopted the template matching for both localization and pose estimation. Most recently, owing to the rapid progress in machine learning algorithms, the correspondence problem in depth estimation is being addressed by learning based approach [5,8]. Seib et al. [27] extended learning-based approach to an end-to-end framework using Convolutional Neural Network (CNN). They handled depth maps containing transparent objects, yet focusing on classifying and localizing predefined objects exploiting holes of depth image. Yet, it is important to note that our goal is to recover the depth distortion of translucent object, captured by the ToF sensors; depth distortions in ToF sensors produce incorrect depth values instead of holes.

Time-of-Flight Multipath Interference (MPI) Correction. In any case of depth acquisition, the recorded signal might be the result of combining multiple reflected signals from the source, each travels from different paths. This is namely the multi-path interference (MPI), which causes significant depth errors in a concave object or corner of the scene (indirect bounces), in mildly translucent material such as skin or wax (subsurface scattering), or along dense participating media. Alleviating those errors is an active research topic for various imaging systems [4,6,24]. In case of ToF depth sensors, MPI leads to the depth value farther than ground truth because a longer traveling path results in a larger depth. Marco et al. [22] corrected MPI using a single ToF depth image and without any additional information, by learning from simulated data, such as simulated indirect bounces and global illumination. A most recent work by Su et al. [29] proposes ToFNet, a U-Net like architecture to simultaneously solve phase unwrapping of raw ToF sensor data and MPI correction. Naik et al. [24] used high-frequency illumination patterns to resolve ambiguities in multiple possible travel paths, reducing errors caused by sub-surface scattering.

Compared with the MPI problem, recovering transparent or translucent objects should handle a severe case of subsurface scattering. Because translucent objects present light scattering as well as transmission, the amount of depth distortions is considerably larger than the distortions caused by MPI.

Shim and Lee [28] also reported the same analysis, and suggested the depth distortion model based on a ToF depth sensing principle for reconstructing translucent objects. They showed that their model is effective to restore the 3D shape of translucent objects assuming a known background and ignoring the effect of light refraction. Later, Kim and Shim [14] extended the idea of [28] and improved the performance by integrating user interactions. Still, these models assume no refraction, limiting the pose of target object being frontal and the shape being planar. Such assumptions are too strict for practical applications.

Residual Networks. Since AlexNet [16] was announced with outstanding performance in image classification, CNN has been successfully applied in visual recognition tasks. While increasing the number of stacked layers (network depth) of CNN is expected to improve high level feature extraction and boost the performance, the tradeoff is to hinder the training process; it can lead to gradient vanishing during backpropagation. He et al. [9] overcame this drawback by stacking residual blocks, while each block includes an identity mapping to directly link between its input and output. Their invention is called a ResNet architecture, and it is widely applied not only to a visual recognition task or segmentation, but also in more complicated tasks including image restoration [11,23], style/domain transfer [7,19], and depth estimation [2,17,18].

3 Multi-scale Patch Based Residual Networks

To solve the depth reconstruction problem, we introduce three important ideas for developing the network.

First of all, we formulate the depth reconstruction problem by patch-based regression. Several existing techniques [2,18] adopt deep neural networks for estimating depth map from RGB images by interpreting depth estimation as a classification problem via depth binning. Although this leads the depth reconstruction problem being simplified, their results inherently exhibit the quantization errors, and always require post-processing to generate continuous depth maps. To prevent this issue, our network is trained to directly map an input patch to a single depth value. At the last convolutional layer, the patch is reduced to $1 \times 1 \times 1$, and this corresponds to an estimated depth value at the center of patch. Also, our patch-based approach is advantageous for training using the limited database. While the image-based approach learns the overall structures and semantic information better, the corresponding network should be accompanied by much larger amount of model parameters; it requires to establish much larger training database.

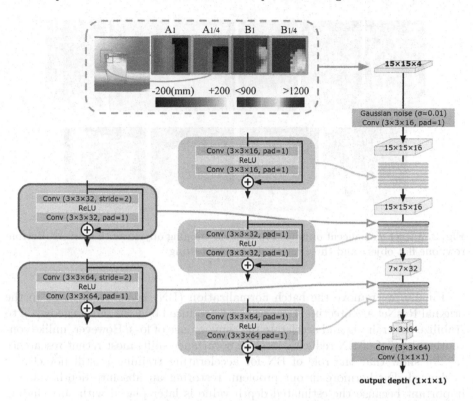

Fig. 1. Illustration of proposed network architecture. Main part of the model consists of 3 groups of 8 stacked residual blocks. Bordered blocks (*on the top of 2nd and 3rd group*) exceptionally have a convolution layer of pad = 0 and stride = 2 to downsample the input size by half

Secondly, we leverage multi-scale patches (i.e., small and large scale patches) for estimating the depth value. For the image generation task, considering both semantic consistency and local details is a difficult yet important problem. One of the means to solve this problem is the multi-scale approach, used by Iizuka et al. [11]. Their model includes two discriminator networks, each processing a different image patch of two different resolutions. Influenced by them, we compose input patches by the concatenation of original image and 1/4 resolution image. By considering the two different scales during training, we effectively increase the receptive field size while maintaining the capability of representing details. Although we add the full-scale image into the input patches, it is different from the image based approach, which transforms the image to a depth map. Because both the full-scale image and the 1/4 scale image are reduced and eventually reach a single depth value after passing those of residual blocks, the number of parameters is still tractable, and is able to be trained on a relatively small size of database.

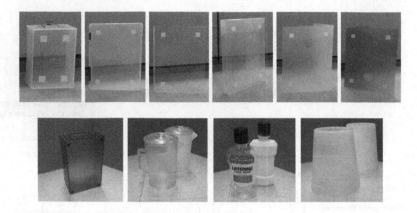

Fig. 2. Target translucent objects. Top row: six training objects with markers. Bottom row: one flat object and three round objects for testing

Finally, we remove the batch normalization (BN) layers as opposed to the original ResNet architecture. BN was first introduced by Ioffe and Szegedy [12] to stabilize the training and accelerate the convergence of loss. However, unlike conventional belief of BN reducing internal covariance shift, most recent researches [15,25] show that the role of BN for accelerating training is still not clearly evidenced. Furthermore in our problem, restoring an absolute depth value is important because the estimated depth value is later placed with surrounding depth values in the final depth map. If the BN layer is adapted into the network, it forces to normalize the data distribution from each batch during the training phase. As a result, during the test phase, the input patch maps to the relative depth value because of the normalization effect. Motivated by [23], we successfully stabilize the training without the BN, by relatively reducing the training batch size and learning rate.

3.1   Acquiring the Database

For supervised learning, it is necessary to obtain ground truth depth data. However, acquiring the ground truth itself can be another research problem in case of translucent objects. Even if the prior for object shape is known by any means, registering the prior shape to the depth map is prone to errors due to severe depth distortions caused by translucency. To bypass the registration issue, we use extra makers to simultaneously register and recover the ground truth shape of training objects, as shown in Fig. 2.

To acquire ground truth depth data regardless of optical characteristics, we utilize the objects with known shapes, particularly planar objects. Four thin and opaque markers are attached to four corners of rectangular objects, 3 cm apart from each boundary. When a raw depth map is captured via ToF camera, we extract depth values at opaque markers on the object and use them as undistorted depth values. We assume the object surface as a projective transformation of a rectangle. Utilizing width and height of the object, and position of four markers on the image, a rectangular mask is able to be fitted into the captured image via projective transform. Note that we can identify the width and height of the target object from the raw depth map because its x and y coordinates are still valid. Four true depth values on the center of each marker are interpolated and extrapolated to fit a plane and fill the depth mask.

To evaluate how much our algorithm is sensitive to shape of the objects, we also collect the ground truth depth maps of three different round objects. For each test object, we prepare two identical objects; serving one for the ground truth depth map and the other for distorted depth map. For acquiring the ground truth depth map, we apply white matt spray to coat its surface. For evaluation, we generate the object mask by thresholding depth difference between background and ground truth depth map. It is important to emphasize that this mask does not input to our network, thus the mask is not required for testing phase. Instead, this mask is utilized only for preparing the training dataset, visualizing the result, and conducting the quantitative evaluation.

We use two types of background, which are differ in both texture and shape. One of them has a corner, which is used to simulate various background distance and orientations for both testing and training. We believe that these variations in background can cover a wide range of refraction effects and distance dependent depth distortion. Nonetheless, adding a variety of background texture could be beneficial for modeling intensity (or color) dependent depth distortion.

We further divide recorded depth maps into patches for constructing the training dataset. Each training sample consists of 4 15×15 images, sampled from the original 248×248 image. Among those four images, two images (A) represent the difference between raw depth and background depth. The other two (B) consist of masked raw depth, whose pixel value is 0 outside the object. Then, each of two images is from either original or 1/4 resolution patch, namely A_1, $A_{1/4}$, B_1 and $B_{1/4}$. To fit those four images into 15×15 resolution, we choose the nearest neighbor interpolation; the 1/4 resolution patch is obtained by sampling pixels with stride of 4. Then, the 2D patches are concatenated to fit into the $15 \times 15 \times 4$ tensor, which is our network input. An example of patch is illustrated in the dashed box of Fig. 1.

3.2   Training Details

We capture depth images of 10 translucent objects with Kinect v2. With data augmentation of horizontal flip, approximately 350k patches from 48 recorded depth maps (corresponding to 10 objects with various background conditions and poses) are used for training. The proposed network is trained on three stages: 10 epochs with learning rate $\eta = 0.0003$, 20 epochs in $\eta = 0.0001$, and 20 epochs in $\eta = 0.000033$. Learning rate greater than 0.0003 triggers sporadic sparks of loss and leads to unstable training. We use RMSProp [31] with momentum of 0.5 and a smooth $L1$ loss as the objective function, and training batch size is 4 through the entire training procedure.

We train our network using six planar objects attached with opaque markers. The remaining planar objects and three additional round objects are used for testing. For evaluation, a 3×3 median filter is applied as post-processing.

4 Experimental Results

4.1 Baseline Models

We evaluate the depth reconstruction accuracy of proposed model compared with that of Shim and Lee [28]. Similar to our model, their approach also compensates depth distortions of translucent object under a known background. Nonetheless, their model is built upon strong assumptions on the orientation and the properties of target object; the object should have a frontal pose and form a thin planar surface. Because their model is formulated by only considering light transmission, these restrictions must be satisfied for their ideal performance.

In addition to the evaluation with the competitor, we investigate the influence of multi-scale patch and exclusion of batch normalization. To analyze the role of multi-scale patch, a network with identical structure as proposed is trained from scratch, using only the patch consists of full resolution. To observe the effect of batch normalization, another network is also trained under identical condition, with the structure modification of added batch normalization layers very next to each convolution layer in all 24 residual blocks.

Table 1. Accuracy comparison with previous work [28] and different network architectures. The best and second best results are boldfaced.

	Planar object			Round objects		
	rms	Rel	$\log_{10}$	rms	Rel	$\log_{10}$
Raw data	203.9	0.21	0.080	165.9	0.16	0.062
Shim and Lee [28]	177.9	0.18	0.069	147.4	0.13	0.053
Batch normalization	82.7	0.08	0.034	154.4	0.14	0.067
Single scale	84.3	0.07	0.033	**87.6**	**0.07**	**0.032**
Proposed	**70.4**	**0.06**	**0.028**	89.1	**0.07**	**0.033**
Proposed(+median filter)	**70.2**	**0.06**	**0.028**	89.0	**0.07**	**0.033**

4.2 Quantitative and Qualitative Evaluation

To quantitatively evaluate our results, following metrics are employed for measuring depth errors.

- Root mean squared error(rms):

$$\sqrt{\frac{1}{|T|} \sum_{d \in T} (\hat{d} - d)^2} \tag{1}$$

(a) Raw depth   (b) GT   (c) Shim & Lee. [28]   (d) Ours   (e) Ours filtered   (f) Ours error

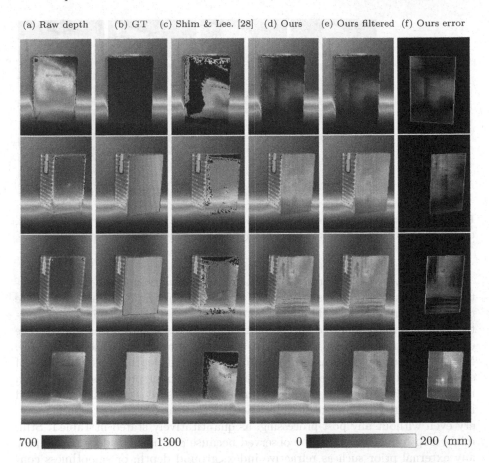

700 ▆▆▆▆▆ 1300   0 ▆▆▆▆▆ 200 (mm)

Fig. 3. Qualitative comparisons on depth map estimation. Depth values outside the target object are identical to the raw depth values. Blue color of the depth map indicates the pixel is close to the camera, as notated at bottom left. Bright yellow of the error map indicates higher error. (Color figure online)

- Mean relative error(Rel):

$$\frac{1}{|T|}\sum_{d\in T}|\hat{d}-d|/d \qquad (2)$$

- Mean $\log_{10}$ error($\log_{10}$):

$$\frac{1}{|T|}\sum_{d\in T}|\log_{10}\hat{d}-\log_{10}d| \qquad (3)$$

$\hat{d}$ and d means the predicted and ground-truth depth value, and T denotes the set of translucent pixels. Pixels that are missing depth in raw data are excluded when computing T.

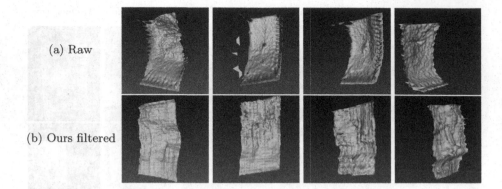

(a) Raw

(b) Ours filtered

Fig. 4. Reconstructing 3D mesh from raw and corrected depth map. From the left, each column corresponds in the same order as the object of each row in Fig. 3

For qualitative evaluation, we demonstrate our results in Fig. 3. Depth distortions by translucent objects are clear as seen by comparing Fig. 3(a) and (b). We compare our results with those of Shim and Lee [28]. This model ignores refraction, thereby is not suitable for handling the slanted surfaces. Consequently, the effect of depth correction is unclear in the second and third case of Fig. 3(c). Meanwhile, our model drastically improves distorted depth maps regardless of surface orientations. Moreover, Shim and Lee's model produces noisy depth maps, thus post-processing throughout multiple exposure is critical as mentioned in their paper. On the contrary, our method performs consistent depth recovery even without any post-processing, as quantitatively stated in Table 1. Still, minor depth fluctuation can be observed because our network does not employ any external prior such as refractive index, ground depth, or smoothness constraint (Fig. 4).

We also show the effectiveness of our ideas for depth reconstruction. The qualitative and quantitative comparison with two degenerated networks are shown in Fig. 5, and left half of Table 1, respectively. The network with a single-scale input (i.e., only a full-scale patch) has smaller receptive field, thereby the region far from edge has no visual clue of relative object structure and produces incorrect depth values, resulting in wiggly reconstructed surfaces. Another network with batch normalization (BN) layers tends to normalize each test batch (i.e., in our implementation, each vertical line forms the batch.). As a result, the recovered depth map exhibits the line-like artifacts as well as significant errors due to depth normalization. The proposed network, on the other hand, suffers from neither artifacts nor normalization error, and outperforms both networks quantitatively and qualitatively as shown in Table 1.

We further evaluate our model using round objects as test objects although the proposed model is trained solely with planar objects. The proposed model reports reasonable performance, even though the objects exhibit completely different characteristics from training dataset, in terms of both 2D outlines and 3D structures. Interestingly, as shown in the right half of Table 2, the network with a

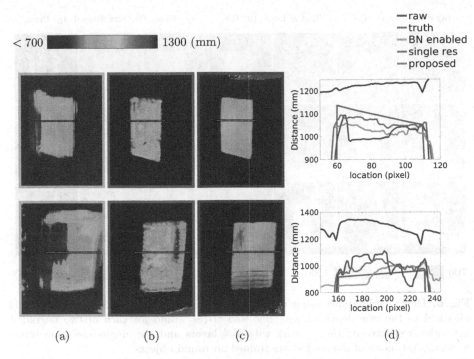

Fig. 5. Comparisons of different network architectures. (a) Network with BN layers, (b) network using the single scale patch, (c) proposed network, (d) center cut for visualizing the shape estimation performance (1-D plots correspond to the depth values along the white line of the images)

single-scale patch input demonstrates marginally better quantitative results than the proposed network for recovering the round objects. In fact, this is expected because the single-scale network focuses on modeling the local surfaces, equivalent to a small receptive field. At the local scale, the curved surface can be reasonably approximated by the piece-wise linear surface. Contrarily, as shown as the qualitative comparisons presented in Fig. 6, the output of the single-scale patch network presents small ripples-like artifacts in the estimated depth maps. These results are analogous to those of planar objects. The proposed model using multi-scale patches generally produces smooth surfaces. Also, our model handles the object with less curved surfaces better. For example, the depth estimation of *Garbage Bin* (Fig. 6, bottom row) is more accurate than others because this object has a larger size and smaller curvatures than others (Fig. 7).

Among round objects, we observe some failure cases. Our reconstruction of a *Plastic pitcher* fails in that we could not restore the overall shape correctly as seen in Fig. 8. This object is particularly challenging because the light transport in a round translucent object is solely governed by light refraction. Such an extreme case has not observed during training. Also, the detailed local structure

(a) Raw   (b) GT   (c) Shim & Lee.   (d) BN   (e) 1-res   (f) Ours filtered   (g) Error

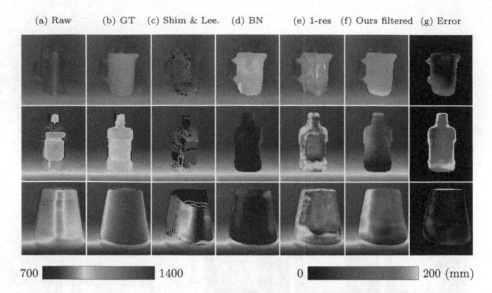

700 ▭ 1400   0 ▭ 200 (mm)

Fig. 6. Depth estimations using round objects. Depth values outside the object is identical to the raw depth values. 'BN' and '1-res' stand for each of two degraded networks, respectively; the network with BN layers and the single-resolution input network. Yet, none of the models are trained on round objects

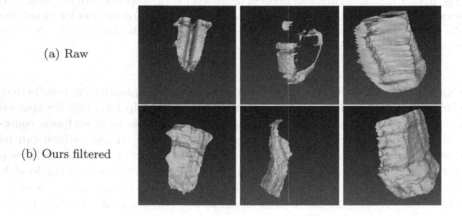

(a) Raw

(b) Ours filtered

Fig. 7. Reconstructing 3D mesh of round objects, from raw and corrected depth map. From the left, each column corresponds in the same order as the object of each row in Fig. 6

such as wavy surfaces on a *Plastic pitcher* is hardly reconstructed by ToF depth sensors even for an opaque object.

(a) Complex object   (b) Raw depth   (c) Ours filtered

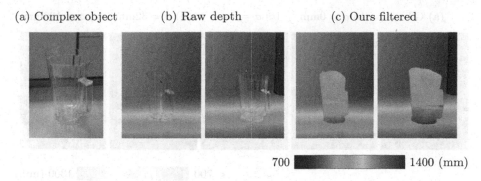

700 ▦ 1400 (mm)

Fig. 8. Failure case. We commonly observe that our model is not successful to model transparent round object with detailed surfaces. This figure shows the example

Table 2. Performance of the proposed model by increasing the standard deviation (σ) of additive white Gaussian noise. Note that no postprocessing is applied

σ (mm)	rms	Rel	$\log_{10}$
0	70.4	0.06	0.028
0.5	70.4	0.06	0.028
1	70.3	0.06	0.028
2	70.5	0.06	0.028
4	70.4	0.06	0.028
8	70.4	0.06	0.028
16	69.4	0.06	0.027
32	72.8	0.07	0.030
64	102.5	0.09	0.044
128	143.8	0.13	0.063

4.3   Noise Robustness

We analyze our performance by increasing the level of input noise. This empirical study is formulated to show how much the proposed model is robust against the input noise. In fact, noise resiliency is a critical property for processing the measurements from depth cameras. It is because (1) active depth sensors always suffer from the lack of emitted light energy, and (2) short exposure is necessary for reducing the motion blurs, thus inevitable for increasing the temporal noise.

To simulate the sensor noise, we refer the empirical noise model by Belhedi et al. [1], thus choose a distance-independent Gaussian distribution as the noise distribution for ToF sensors.

Table 2 and Fig. 9 summarizes quantitative and qualitative results of our model under various levels of input noise. Fortunately, noise with standard deviation of 16 mm or less does not much degrade our performance. In fact, Sarboland et al. [26] report that, except for near-corner pixels, it is unusual for

(a) GT   (b) $\sigma = 0$mm   (c) $\sigma = 8$mm   (d) $\sigma = 32$mm   (e) $\sigma = 128$mm

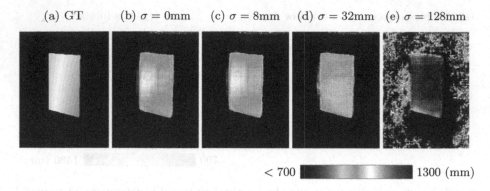

< 700 ▬▬▬▬▬▬▬ 1300 (mm)

Fig. 9. Qualitative performance of depth estimation upon various noise levels

the Tof depth sensor (Kinect v2) to suffer from sensor noise greater than the standard deviation of 20 mm. Therefore, it is reasonable to claim that the proposed model is robust against the shot noise produced by the ToF sensors. In case of the extreme noise variations (after 32 mm), our model starts to malfunction in terms of both overall depth estimation and minor artifacts as seen from Fig. 9(d)–(e).

In addition to sensor noise, another important source of error is light scattering (interreflections) and effects of different illumination conditions. In this paper, we do not explicitly consider them into our model formulation. Because our model is purely data-driven, the light scattering effects are implicitly handled because our training data already includes the scattering effects. Yet, we believe that the rigorous solution for explicitly handle those of scattering and illumination effects is indeed necessary for the future work.

5   Conclusions

We present a deep residual network architecture for recovering depth distortion from translucent object, using a single time-of-flight (ToF) depth camera. We propose multi-scale patch representation and exclusion of batch normalization for developing the network architecture, and show that they are effective to improve the accuracy of reconstructing translucent objects. The quantitative and qualitative evaluations over the competitor clearly demonstrate the superiority of our model; we report higher accuracy and show the robust performance for handling various object poses and optical properties. In addition, the experimental validation of our proposals justifies their positive effects. By showing the robustness of our model across various levels of input noise, we highlight that our model can be a practical solution for real applications. To the best of our knowledge, we propose the first approach to recovering the 3-D translucent object using deep neural networks. We hope that our work can initiate learning based approaches to the problem of recovering translucent objects. In the future, we plan to expand our idea to the large scale dataset, which covers a wide range and shape of translucent objects.

Acknowledgement. This research was supported by the MSIP (Ministry of Science, ICT and Future Planning), Korea, under the University Information Technology Research Center support program (IITP-2016-R2718-16-0014) supervised by the IITP, by the Basic Science Research Program through the National Research Foundation of Korea (NRF) funded by the MSIP (NRF-2016R1A2B4016236), and also by the MIST(Ministry of Science and ICT), Korea, under the "ICT Consilience Creative Program" (IITP-2018-2017-0-01015) supervised by the IITP(Institute for Information & communications Technology Promotion).

References

1. Belhedi, A., Bartoli, A., Bourgeois, S., Gay-Bellile, V., Hamrouni, K., Sayd, P.: Noise modelling in time-of-flight sensors with application to depth noise removal and uncertainty estimation in three-dimensional measurement. IET Comput. Vis. **9**(6), 967–977 (2015)
2. Cao, Y., Wu, Z., Shen, C.: Estimating depth from monocular images asclassification using deep fully convolutional residual networks. IEEE Trans. Circ. Syst. Video Technol. **28**(11), 3174–3182 (2017)
3. Clark, J., Trucco, E., Wolff, L.B.: Using light polarization in laser scanning. Image Vis. Comput. **15**(2), 107–117 (1997)
4. Feigin, M., Bhandari, A., Izadi, S., Rhemann, C., Schmidt, M., Raskar, R.: Resolving multipath interference in kinect: an inverse problem approach. IEEE Sens. J. **16**, 3419–3427 (2015)
5. Francesco, F.S.R., Christoph, R., Murthy, K.A.P., Vladimir, T., David, K., Shahram, I.: Determining depth from structured light using trained classifiers. https://lens.org/103-012-483-114-400
6. Fujimura, Y., Iiyama, M., Hashimoto, A., Minoh, M.: Photometric stereo in participating media considering shape-dependent forward scatter. arXiv preprint arXiv:1804.02836 (2018)
7. Gatys, L.A., Ecker, A.S., Bethge, M.: Image style transfer using convolutional neural networks. In: Proceedings of the IEEE Conference on Computer Vision and Pattern Recognition, pp. 2414–2423 (2016)
8. Hartmann, W., Galliani, S., Havlena, M., Van Gool, L., Schindler, K.: Learned multi-patch similarity. In: International Conference on Computer Vision (ICCV) 2017 (2017)
9. He, K., Zhang, X., Ren, S., Sun, J.: Deep residual learning for image recognition. In: Proceedings of the IEEE Conference on Computer Vision and Pattern Recognition, pp. 770–778 (2016)
10. Hullin, M.B., Fuchs, M., Ihrke, I., Seidel, H.P., Lensch, H.P.: Fluorescent immersion range scanning. ACM Trans. Graph. **27**(3), 87–1 (2008)
11. Iizuka, S., Simo-Serra, E., Ishikawa, H.: Globally and locally consistent image completion. ACM Trans. Graph. (TOG) **36**(4), 107 (2017)
12. Ioffe, S., Szegedy, C.: Batch normalization: accelerating deep network training by reducing internal covariate shift. In: International Conference on Machine Learning, pp. 448–456 (2015)

13. Kim, J., Reshetouski, I., Ghosh, A.: Acquiring axially-symmetric transparent objects using single-view transmission imaging. In: 30th IEEE Conference on Computer Vision and Pattern Recognition (CVPR) (2017)
14. Kim, K., Shim, H.: Robust approach to reconstructing transparent objects using a time-of-flight depth camera. Opt. Exp. **25**(3), 2666–2676 (2017)
15. Kohler, J., Daneshmand, H., Lucchi, A., Zhou, M., Neymeyr, K., Hofmann, T.: Towards a theoretical understanding of batch normalization. arXiv preprint arXiv:1805.10694 (2018)
16. Krizhevsky, A., Sutskever, I., Hinton, G.E.: Imagenet classification with deep convolutional neural networks. In: Advances in Neural Information Processing Systems, pp. 1097–1105 (2012)
17. Lee, J.H., Heo, M., Kim, K.R., Kim, C.S.: Single-image depth estimation based on fourier domain analysis. In: Proceedings of the IEEE Conference on Computer Vision and Pattern Recognition, pp. 330–339 (2018)
18. Li, B., Dai, Y., Chen, H., He, M.: Single image depth estimation by dilated deep residual convolutional neural network and soft-weight-sum inference. arXiv preprint arXiv:1705.00534 (2017)
19. Liao, J., Yao, Y., Yuan, L., Hua, G., Kang, S.B.: Visual attribute transfer through deep image analogy. arXiv preprint arXiv:1705.01088 (2017)
20. Lysenkov, I., Eruhimov, V., Bradski, G.: Recognition and pose estimation of rigid transparent objects with a kinect sensor. Robotics **273**, 273–280 (2013)
21. Maeno, K., Nagahara, H., Shimada, A., Taniguchi, R.I.: Light field distortion feature for transparent object recognition. In: IEEE Conference on Computer Vision and Pattern Recognition (CVPR), pp. 2786–2793. IEEE (2013)
22. Marco, J., et al.: Deeptof: off-the-shelf real-time correction of multipath interference in time-of-flight imaging. ACM Trans. Graph. (TOG) **36**(6), 219 (2017)
23. Nah, S., Kim, T.H., Lee, K.M.: Deep multi-scale convolutional neural network for dynamic scene deblurring, vol. 3. arXiv preprint arXiv:1612.02177 (2016)
24. Naik, N., Kadambi, A., Rhemann, C., Izadi, S., Raskar, R., Bing Kang, S.: A light transport model for mitigating multipath interference in time-of-flight sensors. In: Proceedings of the IEEE Conference on Computer Vision and Pattern Recognition, pp. 73–81 (2015)
25. Santurkar, S., Tsipras, D., Ilyas, A., Madry, A.: How does batch normalization help optimization? (no, it is not about internal covariate shift). arXiv preprint arXiv:1805.11604 (2018)
26. Sarbolandi, H., Lefloch, D., Kolb, A.: Kinect range sensing: structured-light versus time-of-flight kinect. Comput. Vis. Image Underst. **139**, 1–20 (2015)
27. Seib, V., Barthen, A., Marohn, P., Paulus, D.: Friend or foe: exploiting sensor failures for transparent object localization and classification. In: International Conference on Robotics and Machine Vision, vol. 10253, p. 102530I. International Society for Optics and Photonics (2017)
28. Shim, H., Lee, S.: Recovering translucent objects using a single time-of-flight depth camera. IEEE Trans. Circ. Syst. Video Technol. **26**(5), 841–854 (2016)
29. Su, S., Heide, F., Wetzstein, G., Heidrich, W.: Deep end-to-end time-of-flight imaging. In: Proceedings of the IEEE Conference on Computer Vision and Pattern Recognition, pp. 6383–6392 (2018)
30. Tanaka, K., Mukaigawa, Y., Kubo, H., Matsushita, Y., Yagi, Y.: Recovering transparent shape from time-of-flight distortion. In: Proceedings of the IEEE Conference on Computer Vision and Pattern Recognition, pp. 4387–4395 (2016)

31. Tieleman, T., Hinton, G.: Lecture 6.5-RmsProp: divide the gradient by a running average of its recent magnitude. COURSERA: Neural Netw. Mach. Learn. 4(2), 26–31 (2012)
32. Torres-Gómez, A., Mayol-Cuevas, W.: Recognition and reconstruction of transparent objects for augmented reality. In: 2014 IEEE International Symposium on Mixed and Augmented Reality (ISMAR), pp. 129–134. IEEE (2014)
33. Wang, T., He, X., Barnes, N.: Glass object localization by joint inference of boundary and depth. In: 21st International Conference on Pattern Recognition (ICPR), pp. 3783–3786. IEEE (2012)

Predicting Driver Attention in Critical Situations

Ye Xia$^{(\boxtimes)}$, Danqing Zhang, Jinkyu Kim, Ken Nakayama, Karl Zipser, and David Whitney

University of California, Berkeley, CA 94720, USA
yexia@berkeley.edu

Abstract. Robust driver attention prediction for critical situations is a challenging computer vision problem, yet essential for autonomous driving. Because critical driving moments are so rare, collecting enough data for these situations is difficult with the conventional in-car data collection protocol—tracking eye movements during driving. Here, we first propose a new in-lab driver attention collection protocol and introduce a new driver attention dataset, Berkeley DeepDrive Attention (BDD-A) dataset, which is built upon braking event videos selected from a large-scale, crowd-sourced driving video dataset. We further propose Human Weighted Sampling (HWS) method, which uses human gaze behavior to identify crucial frames of a driving dataset and weights them heavily during model training. With our dataset and HWS, we built a driver attention prediction model that outperforms the state-of-the-art and demonstrates sophisticated behaviors, like attending to crossing pedestrians but not giving false alarms to pedestrians safely walking on the sidewalk. Its prediction results are nearly indistinguishable from ground-truth to humans. Although only being trained with our in-lab attention data, the model also predicts in-car driver attention data of routine driving with state-of-the-art accuracy. This result not only demonstrates the performance of our model but also proves the validity and usefulness of our dataset and data collection protocol.

Keywords: Driver attention prediction · BDD-A dataset · Berkeley DeepDrive

1 Introduction

Human visual attention enables drivers to quickly identify and locate potential risks or important visual cues across the visual field, such as a darting-out pedestrian, an incursion of a nearby cyclist or a changing traffic light. Drivers' gaze behavior has been studied as a proxy for their attention. Recently, a large driver

Electronic supplementary material The online version of this chapter (https://doi.org/10.1007/978-3-030-20873-8_42) contains supplementary material, which is available to authorized users.

C. V. Jawahar et al. (Eds.): ACCV 2018, LNCS 11365, pp. 658–674, 2019.
https://doi.org/10.1007/978-3-030-20873-8_42

attention dataset of routine driving [1] has been introduced and neural networks [21,25] have been trained end-to-end to estimate driver attention, mostly in lane-following and car-following situations. Nonetheless, datasets and prediction models for driver attention in rare and critical situations are still needed.

However, it is nearly impossible to collect enough driver attention data for crucial events with the conventional in-car data collection protocol, *i.e.*, collecting eye movements from drivers during driving. This is because the vast majority of routine driving situations consist of simple lane-following and car-following. In addition, collecting driver attention in-car has two other major drawbacks. (i) Single focus: at each moment the eye-tracker can only record one location that the driver is looking at, while the driver may be attending to multiple important objects in the scene with their covert attention, *i.e.*, the ability to fixate one's eyes on one object while attending to another object [6]. (ii) False positive gazes: human drivers also show eye movements to driving-irrelevant regions, such as sky, trees, and buildings [21]. It is challenging to separate these false positives from gazes that are dedicated to driving.

An alternative that could potentially address these concerns is showing selected driving videos to drivers in the lab and collecting their eye movements with repeated measurements while they perform a proper simulated driving task. Although this third-person driver attention collected in the lab is inevitably different from the first-person driver attention in the car, it can still potentially reveal the regions a driver should look at in that particular driving situation from a third-person perspective. These data are greatly valuable for identifying risks and driving-relevant visual cues from driving scenes. To date, a proper data collection protocol of this kind is still missing and needs to be formally introduced and tested.

Another challenge for driver attention prediction, as well as for other driving-related machine learning problems, is that the actual cost of making a particular prediction error is unknown. Attentional lapses while driving on an empty road does not cost the same as attentional lapses when a pedestrian darts out. Since current machine learning algorithms commonly rely on minimizing average prediction error, the critical moments, where the cost of making an error is high, need to be properly identified and weighted.

Here, our paper offers the following novel contributions. First, in order to overcome the drawbacks of the conventional in-car driver attention collection protocol, we introduce a new protocol that uses crowd-sourced driving videos containing interesting events and makes multi-focus driver attention maps by averaging gazes collected from multiple human observers in lab with great accuracy (Fig. 1). We will refer to this protocol as the in-lab driver attention collection protocol. We show that data collected with our protocol reliably reveal where a experienced driver should look and can serve as a substitute for data collected with the in-car protocol. We use our protocol to collect a large driver attention dataset of braking events, which is, to the best of our knowledge, the richest to-date in terms of the number of interactions with other road agents. We call this dataset Berkeley DeepDrive Attention (BDD-A) dataset and will make it

Input raw image

Attention heat maps

Human driver's   Our model prediction

Fig. 1. An example of input raw images (*left*), ground-truth human attention maps collected by us (*middle*), and the attention maps predicted by our model (*right*). The driver had to sharply stop at the green light to avoid hitting two pedestrians running the red light. The collected human attention map accurately shows the multiple regions that simultaneously demand the driver's attention. Our model correctly attends to the crossing pedestrians and does not give false alarms to other irrelevant pedestrians (Color figure online)

publicly available. Second, we introduce Human Weighted Sampling (HWS), which uses human driver eye movements to identify which frames in the dataset are more crucial driving moments and weights the frames according to their importance levels during model training. We show that HWS improve model performance on both the entire testing set and the subset of crucial frames. Third, we propose a new driver attention prediction model trained on our dataset with HWS. The model shows sophisticated behaviors such as picking out pedestrians suddenly crossing the road without being distracted by the pedestrians safely walking in the same direction as the car (Fig. 1). The model prediction is nearly indistinguishable from ground-truth based on human judges, and it also matches the state-of-the-art performance level when tested on an existing in-car driver attention dataset collected during driving.

2   Related Works

Image/Video Saliency Prediction. A large variety of the previous saliency studies explored different bottom-up feature-based models [3,4,9,20,28,32] combining low-level features like contrast, rarity, symmetry, color, intensity and orientation, or topological structure from a scene [12,29,32]. Recent advances in deep learning have achieved a considerable improvement for both image saliency prediction [13,15–17] and video saliency prediction [2,8,18]. These models have achieved start-of-the-art performance on visual saliency benchmarks collected mainly when human subjects were doing a free-viewing task, but models that are specifically trained for predicting the attention of drivers are still needed.

Driver Attention Datasets. DR(eye)VE [1] is the largest and richest existing driver attention dataset. It contains 6 h of driving data, but the data was collected from only 74 rides, which limits the diversity of the dataset. In addition, the dataset was collected in-car and has the drawbacks we introduced earlier, including missing covert attention, false positive gaze, and limited diversity. The driver's eye movements were aggregated over a small temporal window to generate an attention map for a frame, so that multiple important regions of one scene might be annotated. But there was a trade-off between aggregation window length and gaze location accuracy, since the same object may appear in different locations in different frames. Reference [10] is another large driver attention dataset, but only six coarse gaze regions were annotated and the exterior scene was not recorded. References [24] and [27] contain accurate driver attention maps made by averaging eye movements collected from human observers in-lab with simulated driving tasks. But the stimuli were static driving scene images and the sizes of their datasets are small (40 frames and 120 frames, respectively).

Driver Attention Prediction. Self-driving vehicle control has made notable progress in the last several years. One of major approaches is a mediated perception-based approach – a controller depends on recognizing human-designated features, such as lane markings, pedestrians, or vehicles. Human driver's attention provides important visual cues for driving, and thus efforts to mimic human driver's attention have increasingly been introduced. Recently, several deep neural models have been utilized to predict where human drivers should pay attention [21,25]. Most of existing models were trained and tested on the DR(eye)VE dataset [1]. While this dataset is an important contribution, it contains sparse driving activities and limited interactions with other road users. Thus it is restricted in its ability to capture diverse human attention behaviors. Models trained with this dataset tend to become vanishing point detectors, which is undesirable for modeling human attention in urban driving environment, where drivers encounter traffic lights, pedestrians, and a variety of other potential cues and obstacles. In this paper, we provide our human attention dataset as a contribution collected from a publicly available large-scale crowd-sourced driving video dataset [30], which contains diverse driving activities and environments, including lane following, turning, switching lanes, and braking in cluttered scenes.

3   Berkeley DeepDrive Attention (BDD-A) Dataset

Dataset Statistics. The statistics of our dataset are summarized and compared with the largest existing dataset (DR(eye)VE) [1] in Table 1. Our dataset was collected using videos selected from a publicly available, large-scale, crowd-sourced driving video dataset, BDD100k [30,31]. BDD100K contains human-demonstrated dashboard videos and time-stamped sensor measurements collected during urban driving in various weather and lighting conditions. To efficiently collect attention data for critical driving situations, we specifically selected video clips that both included braking events and took place in busy areas (see supplementary materials for technical details). We then trimmed videos to include 6.5 s prior to and 3.5 s after each braking event. It turned out that other driving actions, *e.g.*, turning, lane switching and accelerating, were also included. 1,232 videos (=3.5 h) in total were collected following these procedures. Some example images from our dataset are shown in Fig. 6. Our selected videos contain a large number of different road users. We detected the objects in our videos using YOLO [22]. On average, each video frame contained 4.4 cars and 0.3 pedestrians, multiple times more than the DR(eye)VE dataset (Table 1).

Table 1. Comparison between driver attention datasets

Dataset	# Rides	Durations (hours)	# Drivers	# Gaze providers	# Cars (per frame)	# Pedestrians (per frame)	# Braking events
DR(eye)VE [1]	74	6	8	8	1.0	0.04	464
BDD-A	1,232	3.5	1,232	45	4.4	0.25	1,427

Data Collection Procedure. For our eye-tracking experiment, we recruited 45 participants who each had more than one year of driving experience. The participants watched the selected driving videos in the lab while performing a driving instructor task: participants were asked to imagine that they were driving instructors sitting in the copilot seat and needed to press the space key whenever they felt it necessary to correct or warn the student driver of potential dangers. Their eye movements during the task were recorded at 1000 Hz with an EyeLink 1000 desktop-mounted infrared eye tracker, used in conjunction with the Eyelink Toolbox scripts [7] for MATLAB. Each participant completed the task for 200 driving videos. Each driving video was viewed by at least 4 participants. The gaze patterns made by these independent participants were aggregated and smoothed to make an attention map for each frame of the stimulus video (see Fig. 6 and supplementary materials for technical details).

Psychological studies [11,19] have shown that when humans look through multiple visual cues that simultaneously demand attention, the order in which humans look at those cues is highly subjective. Therefore, by aggregating gazes of independent observers, we could record multiple important visual cues in one frame. In addition, it has been shown that human drivers look at buildings, trees, flowerbeds, and other unimportant objects non-negligibly frequently [1]. Presumably, these eye movements should be regarded as noise for driving-related machine learning purposes. By averaging the eye movements of independent observers, we were able to effectively wash out those sources of noise (see Fig. 2B).

Comparison with In-car Attention Data. We collected in-lab driver attention data using videos from the DR(eye)VE dataset. This allowed us to compare in-lab and in-car attention maps of each video. The DR(eye)VE videos we used were 200 randomly selected 10-second video clips, half of them containing braking events and half without braking events.

We tested how well in-car and in-lab attention maps highlighted driving-relevant objects. We used YOLO [22] to detect the objects in the videos of our

Fig. 2. Comparison between in-car and in-lab driver attention maps. (A) Proportions of attended objects of different categories for in-car and in-lab driver attention maps. In-car attention maps tend to highlight significantly fewer driving-relevant objects than in-lab attention maps. (B) An example of in-car driver attention maps showing irrelevant regions. The in-lab attention map highlights the car in front and a car that suddenly backed up, while the in-car attention map highlights some regions of the building

dataset. We identified three object categories that are important for driving and that had sufficient instances in the videos (car, pedestrian and cyclist). We calculated the proportion of attended objects out of total detected instances for each category for both in-lab and in-car attention maps (see supplementary materials for technical details). The results showed that in-car attention maps highlighted significantly less driving-relevant objects than in-lab attention maps (see Fig. 2A).

The difference in the number of attended objects between the in-car and in-lab attention maps can be due to the fact that eye movements collected from a single driver do not completely indicate all the objects that demand attention in the particular driving situation. One individual's eye movements are only an approximation of their attention [23], and humans can also track objects with covert attention without looking at them [6]. The difference in the number of attended objects may also reflect the difference between first-person driver attention and third-person driver attention. It may be that the human observers in our in-lab eye-tracking experiment also looked at objects that were not relevant for driving. We ran a human evaluation experiment to address this concern.

Human Evaluation. To verify that our in-lab driver attention maps highlight regions that should indeed demand drivers' attention, we conducted an online study to let humans compare in-lab and in-car driver attention maps. In each trial of the online study, participants watched one driving video clip three times: the first time with no edit, and then two more times in random order with overlaid in-lab and in-car attention maps, respectively. The participant was then asked to choose which heatmap-coded video was more similar to where a good driver would look. In total, we collected 736 trials from 32 online participants. We found that our in-lab attention maps were more often preferred by the participants than the in-car attention maps (71% versus 29% of all trials, statistically significant as $p = 1 \times 10^{-29}$, see Table 2). Although this result cannot suggest that in-lab driver attention maps are superior to in-car attention maps in general, it

Table 2. Two human evaluation studies were conducted to compare in-lab human driver attention maps with in-car human driver attention maps and attention maps predicted by our HWS model, respectively. In-car human driver attention maps were preferred in significantly less trials than the in-lab human driver attention maps. The attention maps predicted by our HWS model were not preferred in as many trials as the in-lab human driver attention maps, but they achieved significantly higher preference rate than the in-car human driver attention maps

	# trials	Attention maps	Preference rate
Study 1	736	In-car human driver	29%
		In-lab human driver	71%
Study 2	462	HWS model predicted	41%
		In-lab human driver	59%

does show that the driver attention maps collected with our protocol represent where a good driver should look from a third-person perspective.

In addition, we will show in the Experiments section that in-lab attention data collected using our protocol can be used to train a model to effectively predict actual, in-car driver attention. This result proves that our dataset can also serve as a substitute for in-car driver attention data, especially in crucial situations where in-car data collection is not practical.

To summarize, compared with driver attention data collected in-car, our dataset has three clear advantages: multi-focus, little driving-irrelevant noise, and efficiently tailored to crucial driving situations.

4   Attention Prediction Model

4.1   Network Configuration

Our goal is to predict the driver attention map for a video frame given the current and previous video frames. Our model structure can be divided into a visual feature extraction module, a visual feature processing module, and a temporal processing module (Fig. 3).

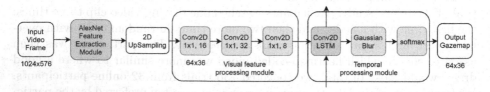

Fig. 3. An overview of our proposed model that predicts human driver's attention from input video frame. We use AlexNet pre-trained on ImageNet as a visual feature extractor. We also use three fully convolutional layers (Conv2D) followed by a convolutional LSTM network (Conv2D LSTM)

The visual feature extraction module is a pre-trained dilated fully convolutional neural network, and its weights are fixed during training. We used ImageNet pre-trained AlexNet [14] as our visual feature extraction module. We chose to use the features from the conv5 layer. In our experiment, the size of the input was set to 1024×576 pixels, and the feature map by AlexNet was upsampled to 64×36 pixels and then fed to the following visual feature processing module.

The visual feature processing module is a fully convolutional neural network. It consists of three convolutional layers with 1×1 kernels and a dropout layer after each convolutional layer. It further processes the visual features from the previous extraction module and reduces the dimensionality of the visual features from 256 to 8. In our experiments, we observed that without the dropout layers, the model easily got stuck in a suboptimal solution which simply predicted a central bias map, i.e. an attention map concentrated in a small area around the center of the frame.

The temporal processor is a convolutional LSTM network with a kernel size of 3×3 followed by a Gaussian smooth layer (σ set to 1.5) and a softmax layer. It receives the visual features of successive video frames in sequence from the visual feature processing module and predicts an attention map for every new time step. Dropout is used for both the linear transformation of the inputs and the linear transformation of the recurrent states. We had also experimented with using an LSTM network for this module and observed that the model tended to incorrectly attend to only the central region of the video frames. The final output of this model is a probability distribution over 64×36 grids predicting how likely each region of the video frame is to be looked at by human drivers. Cross-entropy is chosen as the loss function to match the predicted probability distribution to the ground-truth.

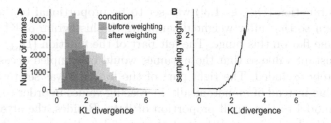

Fig. 4. Human Weighted Sampling: (A) For each video frame, we measure the KL divergence between the collected driver attention maps and the mean attention map for that entire video clip ($\approx 10\,\mathrm{s}$). We use this computed KL divergence as a weight value to sample image frames during training phase, $i.e.$, training a model more often with uncommon attention maps. Histograms show that more uncommon attention maps were selected for training the model, $e.g.$, seeing pedestrians or traffic lights is weighted more than just seeing the vanishing point of roads. (B) Normalized sampling weights as a function of KL divergence values. A normalized sampling weight value of 1 indicates that the video frame is sampled once on average during a single epoch

4.2   Human Weighted Sampling (HWS)

Human driver attention datasets, as well as many other driving related datasets, share a common bias: the vast majority of the datasets consist of simple driving situations such as lane-following or car-following. The remaining small proportion of driving situations, such as pedestrians darting out, traffic lights changing, etc., are usually more crucial, in the sense that making errors in these moments would lead to greater cost. Therefore, ignoring this bias and simply using mean prediction error to train and test models can be misleading. In order to tackle this problem, we developed a new method that uses human gaze data to determine the importance of different frames of a driving dataset and samples the frames with higher importance more frequently during training.

In simple driving situations human drivers only need to look at the center of the road or the car in front, which can be shown by averaging the attention maps of all the frames of one driving video. When the attention map of one frame deviates greatly from the average default attention map, it is usually an important driving situation where the driver has to make eye movements to important visual cues. Therefore, the more an attention map varies from the average attention map of the video, the more important the corresponding training frame is. We used the KL divergence to measure the difference between the attention map of a particular frame and the average attention map of the video. The KL divergence determined the sampling weight of this video frame during training.

The histogram of the KL divergence of all the training video frames of our dataset is shown in Fig. 4. As we expected, the histogram was strongly skewed to the left side. Our goal was to boost up the proportion of the frames of high KL divergence values by weighted sampling. The sampling weight was determined as a function of KL divergence (D_{KL}) illustrated in Fig. 4B. The middle part of this function ($D_{KL} \in [1,3]$) was set to be proportional to the inverse of the histogram so that after weighted sampling the histogram of KL divergence would become flat on this range. The left part of the function ($D_{KL} < 1$) was set to a low constant value so that those frames would be sampled occasionally but not completely excluded. The right part of the function was set to a saturated constant value instead of monotonically increasing values in order to avoid overfitting the model to this small proportion of data. Besides, the attention maps collected in the beginning and the end of each video clip can deviates from the average default attention map merely because the participants were distracted by the breaks between video clips. We therefore restricted the sampling weights of the first second and the last 0.5 s of each video to be less or equal to once per epoch. The histogram of KL divergence after weighted sampling is shown in Fig. 4A. In our experiment, we needed to sample the training frames in continuous sequences of 6 frames. For a particular sequence, its sampling weight was equal to the sum of the sampling weights of its member frames. These sequences were sampled at probabilities proportional to the sequence sampling weights.

5   Results and Discussion

Here, we first provide our training and evaluation details, then we summarize the quantitative and qualitative performance comparison with existing gaze prediction models and variants of our model. To test how natural and reasonable our model prediction look to humans, we conduct a human evaluation study and summarize the results. We further test whether our model trained on in-lab driver attention data can also predict driver attention maps collected in-car.

5.1   Training and Evaluation Details

We made two variants of our model. One was trained with a regular regime, *i.e.*, equal sampling during training, and the other was trained with Human Weighted Sampling (HWS). Except for the sampling method during training, our default model and HWS model shared the same following training settings. We used 926 videos from our BDD-A dataset as the training set and 306 videos as the testing set. We downsampled the videos to 1024×576 pixels and $3\,\mathrm{Hz}$. After this preprocessing, we had about 30k frames in our training set and 10k frames in our testing set. We used cross-entropy between predicted attention maps and human attention maps as the training loss, along with Adam optimizer (learning rate $= 0.001$, $\beta_1 = 0.9$, $\beta_2 = 0.999$, $\epsilon = 1 \times 10^{-8}$). Each training batch contained 10 sequences and each sequence had 6 frames. The training was done for 10,000 iterations. The two models showed stabilized testing errors by iteration 10,000.

To our knowledge, [21] and [25] are the two deep neural models that use dash camera videos alone to predict human driver's gaze. They demonstrated similar results and were shown to surpass other deep learning models or traditional models that predict human gaze in non-driving-specific contexts. We chose to replicate [21] to compare with our work because their prediction code is public. The model designed by [21] was trained on the DR(eye)VE dataset [1]. We will refer to [21]'s model as DR(eye)VE model in the following. The training code of [21] is not available. We implemented code to fine-tune their model on our dataset, but the fine-tuning did not converge to any reasonable solution, potentially due to some training parameter choices that were not reported. We then tested their pre-trained model directly on our testing dataset without any training on our training dataset. Since the goal of the comparison was to test the effectiveness of the combination of model structure, training data and training paradigm as a whole, we think it is reasonable to test how well DR(eye)VE model performs on our dataset without further training. For further comparison, we fine-tuned a publicly available state-of-the-art image gaze prediction model, SALICON [13] on our dataset. We used the open source implementation [26]. We also tested our models against a baseline model that always predicts the averaged human attention map of training videos.

Kullback-Leibler divergence (KL divergence, D_{KL}), Pearson's Correlation Coefficient (CC), Normalized Scanpath Saliency (NSS) and Area under ROC Curve (AUC) are four commonly used metrics for attention map prediction [5,21,25]. We calculated the mean prediction errors in these four metrics on the

Table 3. Performance comparison of human attention prediction. Mean and 95% bootstrapped confidence interval are reported

| | Entire testing set | | | | Testing subset where D_{KL}(GT, Mean) > 2 | | | |
| | KL divergence | | Correlation coefficient | | KL divergence | | Correlation coefficient | |
	Mean	95% CI	Mean	95% CI	Mean	95% CI	Mean	95% CI
Baseline	1.50	(1.45, 1.54)	0.46	(0.44, 0.48)	1.87	(1.80, 1.94)	0.36	(0.34, 0.37)
SALICON [13]	1.41	(1.39, 1.44)	0.53	(0.51, 0.54)	1.76	(1.72, 1.80)	0.39	(0.37, 0.41)
DR(eye)VE [21]	1.95	(1.87, 2.04)	0.50	(0.48, 0.52)	2.63	(2.51, 2.77)	0.35	(0.33, 0.37)
Ours (default)	1.24	(1.21, 1.28)	0.58	(0.56, 0.59)	1.71	(1.65, 1.79)	0.41	(0.40, 0.43)
Ours (HWS)	**1.24**	**(1.21, 1.27)**	**0.59**	**(0.57, 0.60)**	**1.67**	**(1.61, 1.73)**	**0.44**	**(0.42, 0.45)**

testing set to compare the different models. In order to test how well the models perform at important moments where drivers need to watch out, we further calculated the mean prediction errors on the subset of testing frames where the attention maps deviate significantly from the average attention maps of the corresponding videos (defined as KL divergence greater than 2.0). We will refer to these frames as non-trivial frames. Our models output predicted attention maps in the size of 64×36 pixels, but the DR(eye)VE model and the SALICON outputs in bigger sizes. For a fair comparison, we scaled the DR(eye)VE model and the SALICON model's predicted attention maps into 64×36 pixels before calculating the prediction errors.

Another important evaluation criterion of driver attention models is how successfully they can attend to the objects that demand human driver's attention, e.g. the cars in front, the pedestrians that may enter the roadway, etc. Therefore, we applied the same attended object analysis described in the Berkeley Deep-Drive Attention Dataset section. We used YOLO [22] to detect the objects in the videos of our dataset. We selected object categories that are important for driving and that have enough instances in both our dataset and the DR(eye)VE dataset for comparison (car, pedestrian and cyclist). We calculated the proportions of all the detected instances of those categories that were actually attended to by humans versus the models. The technical criterion of determining attended objects was the same as described in the Berkeley DeepDrive Attention Dataset section.

5.2   Evaluating Attention Predictor

Quantitative Analysis of Attention Prediction. The mean prediction errors of different models are summarized in Table 3 (measured in D_{KL} and CC) and Table S1 (measured in NSS and AUC) in supplementary materials. Both of our models significantly outperformed the DR(eye)VE model, the SALICON model and the baseline model in all metrics on both the entire testing set and the subset of non-trivial frames. Our model trained with HWS was essentially trained on a dataset whose distribution was altered from the distribution of the testing set. However, our HWS model showed better results than our default model even when being tested on the whole testing set. When being tested on

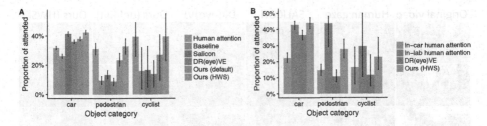

Fig. 5. Analysis of attended objects for human attention and different models tested on our dataset (A) and the DR(eye)VE dataset (B). Error bars show 95% bootstrapped confidence intervals

the subset of non-trivial frames, our HWS model outperformed our default model even more significantly. These results suggest that HWS has the power to overcoming the dataset bias and better leveraging the knowledge hidden in crucial driving moments.

The results of the attended object analysis are summarized in Fig. 5A. Cars turned out to be easy to identify for all models. This is consistent with the fact that a central bias of human attention is easy to learn and cars are very likely to appear in the center of the road. However, for pedestrians and cyclists, the DR(eye)VE model, SALICON model and baseline model all missed a large proportion of them compared with human attention ground-truth. Both of our models performed significantly better than all the other competing models in the categories of pedestrians and cyclists, and our HWS model matched the human attention performances the best.

Importantly, our HWS model did not simply select objects according to their categories like an object detection algorithm. Considering the category that has the highest safety priority, pedestrian, our models selectively attended to the pedestrians that were also attended to by humans. Let us refer to the pedestrians that were actually attended to by humans as the important pedestrians and the rest of them as non-important pedestrians. Among all the pedestrians detected by the object detection algorithm, the proportion of important pedestrians was 33%. If our HWS model were simply detecting pedestrians at a certain level and could not distinguish between important pedestrians and non-important pedestrians, the proportion of important pedestrians among the pedestrians attended to by our model should also be 33%. However, the actual proportion of important pedestrians that our HWS model attended to was 48% with a bootstrapped 95% confidence interval of [42%, 55%]. Thus, our HWS model predicts which of the pedestrians are the ones most relevant to human drivers.

Qualitative Analysis of Attention Prediction. Some concrete examples are shown in Fig. 6 (see supplementary information for videos). These examples demonstrates some important driving scenarios: pedestrian crossing, cyclist getting very close to the vehicle and turning at a busy crossing. It can be seen from these examples that the SALICON model and the DR(eye)VE model mostly

Original video Human gaze   SALICON   DR(eye)VE   Ours (default) Ours (HWS)

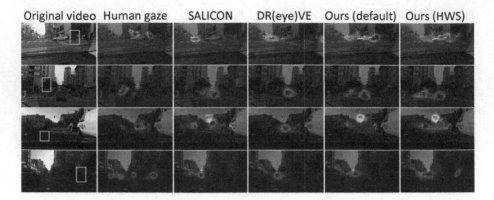

Fig. 6. Examples of the videos in our dataset, ground-truth human attention maps and the prediction of different models. The red rectangles in the original video column highlight the pedestrians that pose a potential hazard. Row 1: the driver had the green light, but a pedestrian was about to cross the road while speaking on a phone without looking at the driver. Another pedestrian was present in the scene, but not relevant to the driving decision. Row 2: the driver had a yellow light and some pedestrians were about to enter the roadway. Another pedestrian was walking in the same direction as the car and therefore not relevant to the driving decision. Row 3: a cyclist was very close to the car. Row 4: the driver was making a right turn and needed to yield to the crossing pedestrian. Other pedestrians were also present in the scene but not relevant to the driving decision (Color figure online)

only predicted to look at the center of the road and ignored the crucial pedestrians or cyclists. In the examples of row 1, 2 and 3, both our default model and HWS model successfully attended to the important pedestrian/cyclist, and did not give false alarm for other pedestrians who were not important for the driving decision. In the challenging example shown in row 4, the driver was making a right turn and needed to yield to the crossing pedestrian. Only our HWS model successfully overcame the central bias and attended to the pedestrian appearing in a quite peripheral area in the video frame.

Human Evaluation. To further test how natural and reasonable our HWS model's predicted attention maps look to humans, we conducted an online Turing Test. In each trial, a participant watched one driving video clip three times: the first time with no edit, and then two times in random order with the ground-truth human driver attention map and our HWS model's predicted attention map overlaid on top, respectively. The participant was then asked to choose whether the first or the second attention map video was more similar to where a good driver would look.

Note that the experiment settings and instructions were the same as the online study described in the dataset section, except that one compares model prediction against the in-lab driver attention maps, and the other compares the in-car driver attention maps against the in-lab driver attention maps. Therefore, the result of this Turing Test can be compared with the result of the previous online study. In total, we collected 462 trials from 20 participants. If our HWS model's predicted attention maps were perfect and indistinguishable from the ground-truth human driver attention maps, the participants would had to make random choices, and therefore we would expect them to choose our model prediction in about 50% of the trials. If our HWS model's prediction was always wrong and unreasonable, we would expect a nearly zero chosen rate for our model prediction. Our results showed that in 41% of all trials the participants chose our HWS model's predicted attention maps as even better than the in-lab human attention maps (see Table 2). In the previous online study, the in-car attention maps of DR(eye)VE only achieved a chosen rate of 29%. This result suggests that our HWS model's predicted attention maps were even more similar to where a good driver should look than the human driver attention maps collected in-car (permutation test p $= 4 \times 10^{-5}$).

5.3 Predicting In-car Driver Attention Data

To further demonstrate that our model has good generalizability and that our driver attention data collected in-lab is realistic, we conducted a challenging test: we trained our model using only our in-lab driver attention data, but tested it on the DR(eye)VE dataset, an in-car driver attention dataset. Note that the DR(eye)VE dataset covers freeway driving, which is not included in our dataset due to the small density of road user interactions on freeway. The high driving speed on freeway introduces strong motion blur which is not present in our dataset videos. Furthermore, drivers need to look further ahead in high speed situations, so the main focus of driver gaze pattern shifts up as the driving speed increases. In order to adapt our model to these changes, we selected 200 ten-second-long video clips from the training set of the DR(eye)VE dataset and collected in-lab driver attention maps for those video clips (already described in the Berkeley DeepDrive Attention Dataset section). We fine-tuned our HWS model with these video clips (30 min in total only) and the corresponding in-lab driver attention maps, and then tested the model on the testing set of the DR(eye)VE dataset (with in-car attention maps). The mean testing errors were calculated in D_{KL} and CC because the calculation of NSS and AUC requires the original fixation pixels instead of smoothed gaze maps and the original fixation pixels of the DR(EYE)VE dataset were not released. Our fine-tuned model showed a better mean value in KL Divergence and a worse mean value in CC than the DR(eye)VE model (see Table 4). But the 95% bootstrapped confidence intervals for the two models in both metrics overlapped with each other. So overall we concluded that our fine-tuned model matched the performance of the DR(eye)VE model. Note that the DR(eye)VE model was trained using the DR(eye)VE dataset and represents the state-of-the-art performance on this dataset.

We also calculated proportions of attended objects of important categories for our fine-tuned model and the DR(eye)VE model (Fig. 5B). Our fine-tuned model showed significantly higher proportions of attended objects in the car, pedestrian and cyclist categories and was more similar to the in-lab driver attention than

Table 4. Test results obtained on the DR(eye)VE dataset by the state-of-the-art model (DR(eye)VE) and our finetuned model. Mean and 95% bootstrapped confidence interval are reported

	KL divergence		Correlation coefficient	
	Mean	95% CI	Mean	95% CI
DR(eye)VE	1.76	(1.65, 1.87)	0.54	(0.51, 0.56)
Ours (finetuned)	1.72	(1.66, 1.81)	0.51	(0.48, 0.53)

the DR(eye)VE model. Note that we have shown in the Berkeley DeepDrive Attention Dataset section that humans rated the in-lab attention maps as more similar to where a good driver should look from a third-person perspective than the in-car attention maps.

6   Conclusions

In this paper, we introduce a new in-lab driver attention data collection protocol that overcomes drawbacks of in-car collection protocol. We contribute a human driver attention dataset which is to-date the richest and will be made public. We propose Human Weighted Sampling which can overcome common driving dataset bias and improve model performance in both the entire dataset and the subset of crucial moments. With our dataset and sampling method we contribute a novel human driver attention prediction model that can predict both in-lab and in-car driver attention data. The model demonstrates sophisticated behaviors and show prediction results that are nearly indistinguishable from ground-truth to humans.

References

1. Alletto, S., Palazzi, A., Solera, F., Calderara, S., Cucchiara, R.: DR(eye)VE: a dataset for attention-based tasks with applications to autonomous and assisted driving. In: Proceedings of the IEEE Conference on Computer Vision and Pattern Recognition Workshops, pp. 54–60 (2016)
2. Bazzani, L., Larochelle, H., Torresani, L.: Recurrent mixture density network for spatiotemporal visual attention. arXiv preprint arXiv:1603.08199 (2016)
3. Bruce, N., Tsotsos, J.: Saliency based on information maximization. In: Advances in Neural Information Processing Systems, pp. 155–162 (2006)
4. Bruce, N.D., Tsotsos, J.K.: Saliency, attention, and visual search: an information theoretic approach. J. Vis. **9**(3), 5–5 (2009)
5. Bylinskii, Z., Judd, T., Oliva, A., Torralba, A., Durand, F.: What do different evaluation metrics tell us about saliency models? IEEE Trans. Pattern Anal. Mach. Intell. **41**, 740–757 (2018)
6. Cavanagh, P., Alvarez, G.A.: Tracking multiple targets with multifocal attention. Trends Cogn. Sci. **9**(7), 349–354 (2005)

7. Cornelissen, F.W., Peters, E.M., Palmer, J.: The eyelink toolbox: eye tracking with matlab and the psychophysics toolbox. Behav. Res. Methods Instrum. Comput. **34**(4), 613–617 (2002)

8. Cornia, M., Baraldi, L., Serra, G., Cucchiara, R.: Predicting human eye fixations via an LSTM-based saliency attentive model. arXiv preprint arXiv:1611.09571 (2016)

9. Erdem, E., Erdem, A.: Visual saliency estimation by nonlinearly integrating features using region covariances. J. Vis. **13**(4), 11–11 (2013)

10. Fridman, L., Langhans, P., Lee, J., Reimer, B.: Driver gaze region estimation without use of eye movement. IEEE Intell. Syst. **31**(3), 49–56 (2016)

11. Groner, R., Walder, F., Groner, M.: Looking at faces: local and global aspects of scanpaths. In: Advances in Psychology, vol. 22, pp. 523–533. Elsevier (1984)

12. Harel, J., Koch, C., Perona, P.: Graph-based visual saliency. In: Advances in Neural Information Processing Systems, pp. 545–552 (2007)

13. Huang, X., Shen, C., Boix, X., Zhao, Q.: SALICON: reducing the semantic gap in saliency prediction by adapting deep neural networks. In: Proceedings of the IEEE International Conference on Computer Vision, pp. 262–270 (2015)

14. Krizhevsky, A., Sutskever, I., Hinton, G.E.: ImageNet classification with deep convolutional neural networks. In: Advances in Neural Information Processing Systems, pp. 1097–1105 (2012)

15. Kümmerer, M., Theis, L., Bethge, M.: Deep Gaze I: boosting saliency prediction with feature maps trained on ImageNet. In: International Conference on Learning Representations (ICLR 2015) (2015)

16. Kümmerer, M., Wallis, T.S., Bethge, M.: DeepGaze II: reading fixations from deep features trained on object recognition. arXiv preprint arXiv:1610.01563 (2016)

17. Liu, N., Han, J., Zhang, D., Wen, S., Liu, T.: Predicting eye fixations using convolutional neural networks. In: Proceedings of the IEEE Conference on Computer Vision and Pattern Recognition, pp. 362–370 (2015)

18. Liu, Y., Zhang, S., Xu, M., He, X.: Predicting salient face in multiple-face videos. In: Proceedings of the IEEE Conference on Computer Vision and Pattern Recognition, pp. 4420–4428 (2017)

19. Mannan, S., Ruddock, K., Wooding, D.: Fixation sequences made during visual examination of briefly presented 2D images. Spat. Vis. **11**(2), 157–178 (1997)

20. Murray, N., Vanrell, M., Otazu, X., Parraga, C.A.: Saliency estimation using a non-parametric low-level vision model. In: 2011 IEEE Conference on Computer Vision and Pattern Recognition (CVPR), pp. 433–440. IEEE (2011)

21. Palazzi, A., Solera, F., Calderara, S., Alletto, S., Cucchiara, R.: Learning where to attend like a human driver. In: 2017 IEEE Intelligent Vehicles Symposium (IV), pp. 920–925. IEEE (2017)

22. Redmon, J., Farhadi, A.: YOLO9000: better, faster, stronger. In: 2017 IEEE Conference on Computer Vision and Pattern Recognition (CVPR), pp. 6517–6525. IEEE (2017)

23. Rizzolatti, G., Riggio, L., Dascola, I., Umiltá, C.: Reorienting attention across the horizontal and vertical meridians: evidence in favor of a premotor theory of attention. Neuropsychologia **25**(1), 31–40 (1987)

24. Simon, L., Tarel, J.P., Brémond, R.: Alerting the drivers about road signs with poor visual saliency. In: 2009 IEEE Intelligent Vehicles Symposium, pp. 48–53. IEEE (2009)

25. Tawari, A., Kang, B.: A computational framework for driver's visual attention using a fully convolutional architecture. In: 2017 IEEE Intelligent Vehicles Symposium (IV), pp. 887–894. IEEE (2017)

26. Thomas, C.L.: OpenSalicon: an open source implementation of the salicon saliency model. Technical report. TR-2016-02, University of Pittsburgh (2016)
27. Underwood, G., Humphrey, K., Van Loon, E.: Decisions about objects in real-world scenes are influenced by visual saliency before and during their inspection. Vis. Res. **51**(18), 2031–2038 (2011)
28. Valenti, R., Sebe, N., Gevers, T.: Image saliency by isocentric curvedness and color. In: 2009 IEEE 12th International Conference on Computer Vision, pp. 2185–2192. IEEE (2009)
29. Wei, Y., Wen, F., Zhu, W., Sun, J.: Geodesic saliency using background priors. In: Fitzgibbon, A., Lazebnik, S., Perona, P., Sato, Y., Schmid, C. (eds.) ECCV 2012. LNCS, vol. 7574, pp. 29–42. Springer, Heidelberg (2012). https://doi.org/10.1007/978-3-642-33712-3_3
30. Xu, H., Gao, Y., Yu, F., Darrell, T.: End-to-end learning of driving models from large-scale video datasets. In: Proceedings of the IEEE Conference on Computer Vision and Pattern Recognition (2017)
31. Yu, F., et al.: BDD100K: a diverse driving video database with scalable annotation tooling. arXiv preprint arXiv:1805.04687 (2018)
32. Zhang, J., Sclaroff, S.: Saliency detection: a boolean map approach. In: 2013 IEEE International Conference on Computer Vision (ICCV), pp. 153–160. IEEE (2013)

Aligning and Updating Cadaster Maps with Aerial Images by Multi-task, Multi-resolution Deep Learning

Nicolas Girard[1(✉)], Guillaume Charpiat[2], and Yuliya Tarabalka[1]

[1] TITANE Team, Inria, Université Côte d'Azur, Sophia-Antipolis, France
{nicolas.girard,yuliya.tarabalka}@inria.fr
[2] TAU Team, Inria, LRI, Université Paris-Sud, Saclay, France
guillaume.charpiat@inria.fr

Abstract. A large part of the world is already covered by maps of buildings, through projects such as OpenStreetMap. However when a new image of an already covered area is captured, it does not align perfectly with the buildings of the already existing map, due to a change of capture angle, atmospheric perturbations, human error when annotating buildings or lack of precision of the map data. Some of those deformations can be partially corrected, but not perfectly, which leads to misalignments. Additionally, new buildings can appear in the image. Leveraging multi-task learning, our deep learning model aligns the existing building polygons to the new image through a displacement output, and also detects new buildings that do not appear in the cadaster through a segmentation output. It uses multiple neural networks at successive resolutions to output a displacement field and a pixel-wise segmentation of the new buildings from coarser to finer scales. We also apply our method to buildings height estimation, by aligning cadaster data to the rooftops of stereo images. The code is available at https://github.com/Lydorn/mapalignment.

Keywords: Alignment · Registration · Multi-task · Multi-resolution

1 Introduction

Having a precise map of buildings is crucial for numerous applications such as urban planning, telecommunications and disaster management [9]. In the field of remote sensing, satellite or aerial images are used to retrieve meaningful geolocalized information. This may be the location of man-made objects, animals or plants, or delimitation perimeters of semantic areas such as forests, urban areas and buildings. The general goal is to automatically produce a map of the world.

Electronic supplementary material The online version of this chapter (https://doi.org/10.1007/978-3-030-20873-8_43) contains supplementary material, which is available to authorized users.

Fig. 1. Crop of one of the test images. Green buildings: ground truth; red: misaligned [input]; blue: aligned [our output]. (Color figure online)

One of the challenges in remote sensing is to deal with errors in the data. Each pixel in an image can be geolocalized by knowing the position and angle of the satellite, as well as the digital elevation model which gives the elevation of every point on earth. These data contain uncertainty errors, especially the digital elevation model which typically has a spatial resolution of 10 m and a vertical resolution of 1 m [14]. Also, atmospheric effects introduce errors, which might be reduced to an extent [15], but might still be there. Thus even if an object is accurately detected in an image, its geolocalization error may be high. Human-made maps may also suffer from geolocalization errors, due to human error [16] or to simply a lack of precision in the source material (scanned cadaster data from local authorities). Therefore, large misalignments frequently occur between a remote sensing image and an existing map. We observed displacements of up to 8 m in OpenStreetMap [10], which translates to 27 px in a 30 cm/px image, and such displacements are not constant across the image.

There is a considerable amount of ground truth data available in the form of existing maps, that could potentially be used to learn the task of automatically mapping the world from remote sensing images, but it is useless in its current form because of such misalignments. We thus aim at correcting them.

Solving this alignment problem, also known as non-rigid image registration, can be formulated as the search for a dense displacement field between two given images: here, a cadaster map and a satellite photography. Each pixel of the first image is thus associated with a 2D displacement vector describing where it is mapped to in the second image. Non-rigid registration also arises notably in medical imaging, where different scans need to be aligned (scans of different patients, or of the same patient at different times, or of different modalities). Classically, alignment problems are classified in two categories: mono-modal or multi-modal, depending on whether the two images to be registered are taken by the same type of sensor or not.

Classical methods for mono-modal image alignment use image similarity measures or key-point descriptors such as SIFT [7] or HOG [3] to match parts of the 2 images with each other [11]. More recent methods use CNNs to predict the optical flow between two images [4]. These methods rely intrinsically on appearance similarities and thus cannot be extended to the multi-modal setting, which is our case of interest. Note e.g. that trees can cover part of the objects of interest in the RGB image while trees are not indicated on the cadastral map, so direct point-to-point appearance matching would fail. However a recent method considered structural similarity [18] to define a new feature descriptor for key-point matching.

These methods are not specific to certain types of images or objects, which is why they are widely used. However machine learning and more recently deep learning methods have achieved state-of-the-art performance on many computer vision problems by learning the best features for the task at hand. Several deep learning methods for image registration have been proposed, for instance Quicksilver [17] learns an image similarity measure directly from image appearance, to predict a dense deformation model for applications in medical imaging. However it works best for rather small displacements and with 2 image-like modalities. Also from the field of medical imaging, the fully-convolutional neural network U-Net [12] has been widely-used for image segmentation. Its use of skip-connections at intermediate levels of the network performs very well for predicting a spatially precise output that corresponds pixel-to-pixel to the input image. A new deep learning method for remote sensing imaging using a U-Net-like model has been proposed by [19], in a multi-resolution approach to predict large displacements. Indeed, solving for increasing resolutions iteratively has proved successful in a number of applications [2,5].

Another success in machine learning has been the use of multi-task learning [13]. The idea is to learn multiple tasks at the same time with a single neural network instead of one network per task. This allows the network to train better as it learns common features from all tasks while still being able to learn task-specific features. It also has the advantage of producing a single neural network, smaller and faster than the compilation of individual task-specific networks.

We propose a deep learning method that uses the multi-resolution approach from [19] and aims to improve the results by training the network with a multi-task objective. The primary objective is to directly compute a dense displacement map (or flow) that aligns the building cadaster to the image (for example building cadaster from OpenStreetMap). See Fig. 1 for a visual result of our alignment method. The second objective is to output a segmentation of the buildings from the image (otherwise known as pixel-wise classification) to help train the network and detect new buildings as well which can be used to update a map with missing buildings or recently-built buildings. The contributions of this work are:

(i) The design of a fully-convolutional neural network able to correct and update existing cadastral maps. Multi-task learning is used to improve alignment performance and to provide new building detection at no additional cost;

(ii) The use of intermediate losses inside the network to help gradients flow and improve final performance on both objectives;

(iii) Random dropping of input polygons, to force the detection of new objects.

After presenting the methodology in Sect. 2, we present our experimental setup in Sect. 3; we apply our method to the building alignment task and evaluate the results in Sect. 4. We show another applicative potential of our method on building height estimation, from a pair of images and misaligned building cadaster data, in Sect. 5.

2   Methodology

2.1   Objective Functions

Mathematical Modeling. Given two images A_1 and A_2 of same size $H \times W$, but of different modalities, e.g. with A_1 an RGB image (picture from a satellite) and A_2 a binary image (cadaster, indicating for each pixel whether it belongs to a building or not), the alignment problem aims at finding a deformation, i.e. a 2D vector field $\mathbf{f}$ defined on the discrete image domain $[1, H] \times [1, W]$, such that the warped second image $A_2 \circ (\mathrm{Id} + \mathbf{f})$ is well registered with the first image A_1. To do this, in a machine learning setting, we will provide examples of image pairs (A_1, A_2) as inputs, and ask the estimated deformation $\hat{\mathbf{f}}$ to be close to the ground truth deformation $\mathbf{f}_{\mathrm{gt}}$.

For the segmentation problem, only the RGB image A_1 is given as input, and the desired output is an image of same size, expressing building presence probability for each pixel. The ground truth segmentation is thus the perfectly-registered cadaster $A_2 \circ (\mathrm{Id} + \mathbf{f}_{\mathrm{gt}})$.

Displacement Field Map Cost Function. The displacement field map loss function is the mean squared error between the predicted displacement field map ($\hat{\mathbf{f}}$) and ground truth displacement field map ($\mathbf{f}_{\mathrm{gt}}$). However, the displacement cannot be predicted equally well on every pixel in the image. For example, building corners can be precisely matched, while building boundary pixels have ambiguous displacement along one dimension (the boundary), which is classically known as the aperture problem, and whereas pixels $\mathbf{x}$ inside homogeneous cadaster zones (i.e. far inside or outside buildings) suffer from ambiguity in both spatial dimensions and thus cannot hope for a precise displacement vector $\mathbf{f}(\mathbf{x})$. To take this into account, we distinguish 4 different classes of pixels on the input cadaster image A_2 (which can be seen as a misaligned polygon raster image): background, polygon interior, edge, and vertex, in decreasing difficulty order. We denote by $c(\mathbf{x}) \in \{1, 2, 3, 4\}$ the class of a pixel $\mathbf{x} \in [1, H] \times [1, W]$. We apply a different loss coefficient w_c on each pixel class c, making the loss a weighted average of square errors. The loss coefficients are of increasing values from background pixels to vertex pixels ($w_1 \leq w_2 \leq w_3 \leq w_4$). As pixel classes are unbalanced, the loss of a pixel $\mathbf{x}$ is normalized by the pixel count of its corresponding class, denoted by $n_{c(\mathbf{x})}$. The displacement field cost is thus defined as:

$$L^{\mathrm{disp}}(\hat{\mathbf{f}}) \;=\; \sum_{\mathbf{x}\in[1,H]\times[1,W]} \frac{w_{c(\mathbf{x})}}{n_{c(\mathbf{x})}} \left\| \hat{\mathbf{f}}(\mathbf{x}) - \mathbf{f}_{\mathrm{gt}}(\mathbf{x}) \right\|_2^2 \tag{1}$$

Segmentation Cost Function. As the task of aligning buildings requires to be able to detect where buildings are, we consider an additional segmentation task, to help the training. For each pixel $\mathbf{x}$, and for each class $c \in \{$background, polygon interior, edge, vertex$\}$ independently, we predict the probability $\hat{p}^c(\mathbf{x})$ that a pixel $\mathbf{x}$ belongs to class c. The associated loss function is the sum of class-specific cross-entropies $KL\left(\mathcal{D}(p_{\mathrm{gt}}^c) \,\|\, \mathcal{D}(\hat{p}^c)\right)$, where $p_{\mathrm{gt}}^c(\mathbf{x})$ is the binary ground truth (whether pixel $\mathbf{x}$ is of class c), and where $\mathcal{D}(p)$ stands for the distribution $(p, 1-p)$ over the two possibilities (of class c or not). We also apply different coefficients w_c' for each class, to put more emphasis on vertices than edges, and than interior and background ($w_1' \leq w_2' \leq w_3' \leq w_4'$). The segmentation cost function is thus:

$$L^{\mathrm{seg}}(\hat{\mathbf{p}}) \;=\; \frac{1}{HW} \sum_{\mathbf{x}\in[1,H]\times[1,W]} \sum_{c=1}^{4} w_c' \, KL\left(\mathcal{D}(p_{\mathrm{gt}}^c) \,\|\, \mathcal{D}(\hat{p}^c)\right) \tag{2}$$

2.2 Neural Network with Double Inputs and Outputs

To address both tasks (alignment and segmentation), the main building block of the method is designed as a neural network with 2 image inputs and 2 image outputs (see Fig. 2). It uses skip-connections at multiple levels in the network like U-Net [12]. Model inputs and outputs examples are shown in Fig. 3. The input image A_1 has 3 channels, with real values in $[-1, 1]$, standing for RGB. The input misaligned polygon raster A_2 has also 3 channels, with Boolean values in $\{0, 1\}$, corresponding to polygon interior, edge and vertices. The output displacement field map has 2 channels with real values in $[-1, 1]$, standing for the x and y components of the displacement vector. The output segmentation (or pixel-wise classification) has 4 channels: one for the background class, and three as for the input polygon raster.

The network is fully convolutional and uses only 3×3 convolutional kernels without padding, which reduces the image size slightly after every layer but avoids border artifacts. A 220×220 px input image thus leads to a 100×100 px output. The first layer of the A_1 input image branch has 32 convolutional filters. Then the number of filters doubles after each pooling operation. For the misaligned polygon raster input branch (A_2), the first layer requires 16 filters only, as polygon rasters are less complex than standard images. In total, the network has about 9 million trainable parameters. To train this network block, the ground truth displacement map has values in $[-4\,\mathrm{px}, 4\,\mathrm{px}]$ which are normalized to $[-1, 1]$ to match the output value range.

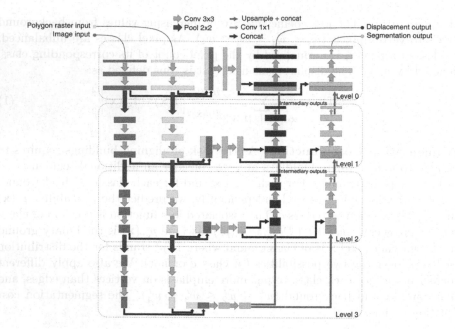

Fig. 2. Model architecture for one resolution. There are 4 different levels inside the network: one after each pooling operation in addition to the first level.

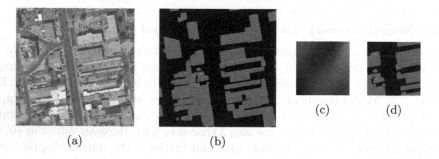

Fig. 3. (a) input image, (b) input misaligned polygon raster, (c) output displacement field map, (d) output segmentation.

2.3 Multi-resolution

From Coarse to Fine. The multi-resolution approach iteratively applies a neural network at increasing resolutions (see Fig. 4 for a diagram of the multi-resolution pipeline). By solving the alignment problem from coarse to fine resolutions, the difficulty at each resolution step becomes drastically lower than for the whole problem. At the first step, the network is applied to the inputs downscaled by a factor of 8. Assuming the initial displacements to predict are in the range $[-32\,\mathrm{px}, 32\,\mathrm{px}]$, the new low-resolution ones are within $[-4\,\mathrm{px}, 4\,\mathrm{px}]$ only, reducing significantly the search space. Then each next resolution step

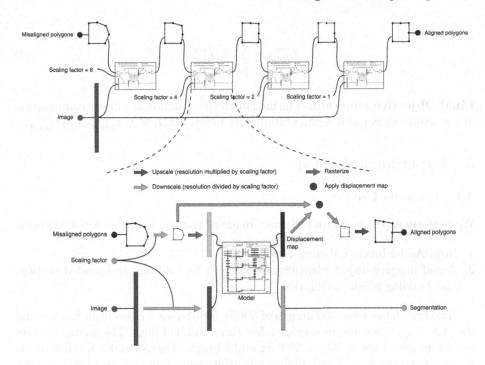

Fig. 4. Multi-resolution pipeline.

multiplies the image resolution by a factor 2, and supposes that the remaining, finer deformation to be found is within $[-4\,\text{px}, 4\,\text{px}]$ at that scale (the larger displacements having been found at the coarser scales). Note that we could multiply the resolution by a factor 4 at each step, but that, to allow for a scale overlap and increase stability, we keep a factor 2.

Intermediate Cost Functions. When training, the network quickly learns to output a null displacement map, as it is the average of the ground truth displacement maps, and is the best possible constant output. To help the gradients flow and avoid the network being stuck in a local minimum, we added intermediate outputs in the displacement map and segmentation branches at levels $l = 0, 1, 2$ of each resolution-specific block (see Fig. 2). The size of these intermediate outputs increases from inside the network block towards the final block outputs. The corresponding loss functions are applied to these intermediary outputs with different coefficients α_l, and denoted by L_l^{disp} and L_l^{seg}. As the training advances, the intermediary losses' coefficients α_l are pushed to zero so that only the final output is optimized. This helps the optimization process well:

$$L_{\text{total}}^{\text{disp}} = \sum_{l=0}^{2} \alpha_l L_l^{\text{disp}} \tag{3}$$

$$L_{\text{total}}^{\text{seg}} = \sum_{l=0}^{2} \alpha_l L_l^{\text{seg}} \tag{4}$$

Final Objective Function. The final objective function is a linear combination of the displacement and segmentation cost functions: $L = \lambda_1 L_{\text{total}}^{\text{disp}} + \lambda_2 L_{\text{total}}^{\text{seg}}$.

3   Experimental Setup

3.1   Datasets Used

We perform experiments on a dataset made of the two available following ones:

1. Inria Aerial Image Labeling Dataset [8],
2. Aerial imagery object identification dataset for building and road detection, and building height estimation [1].

The first dataset has 360 images of 5000×5000 px for 9 cities from Europe and the U.S. Each image has in average a few thousand buildings. The second dataset has 24 images of about 5000 × 5000 px and 1 image of about 10000 × 10000 px for 9 cities from the U.S. The building footprints were pulled from OSM for both datasets. We removed images whose OSM data is too misaligned, keeping images where it is relatively good. We split the second dataset into 3 sets: 8 images for training, 3 for validation and 3 for testing. To develop our method to generalize to new cities and capture conditions, each set does not contain images from the same cities under the same capture conditions as any of the other 2 sets. From the first dataset, 332 images were picked for training and 26 for validation. These datasets may seem small compared to other deep learning datasets which can contain millions of images, but because each image is very big, they provide enough data. For example, our testing dataset contains 13614 buildings. More information on the splitting of these datasets into train, validation and test sets can be found in Sect. 3 of the supplementary materials.

3.2   Data Preprocessing

Displacement Map Generation. The model needs varied ground truth displacement maps in order to learn, while the dataset is made of perfectly aligned image pairs only ($\mathbf{f} = 0$). We generate these randomly in the same way as described in [19], by generating normalized 2D Gaussian random fields added together for each coordinate (see Fig. 3(c) for an example). The displacements are then scaled so that the maximum absolute displacement is 32 px. The ground truth polygons are then inversely displaced by the generated displacements to compute the misaligned polygons which are then rasterized ($A_2 \circ (\text{Id} + \mathbf{f})$).

Scaling and Splitting into Patches. All the images of the datasets do not have the same ground sample distance (pixel width measured on the ground in meters), which is a problem for a multi-resolution approach which learns a specific model per resolution. As more than 90% of the images of our dataset have a ground sample distance of 0.3 m, we rescale the other images to that ground sample distance so that they all match. Then every data sample (image, misaligned polygon raster, and displacement map), which usually is of size 5000×5000 px, is rescaled to 4 different resolutions defined by the downscaling factors. For example a downscaling factor of 2 rescales the data sample to a size of 2500×2500 px, resulting in a ground sample distance of 0.6 m. Successive rescaling steps are performed as one, to limit interpolation errors of the scaling operation. Finally, data samples are split into patches of size $220 * \sqrt{2} = 312$ px with a stride of $100/2 = 50$ px, to account for rotations in the data augmentation step.

Classical Data Augmentations. To augment the dataset, classical augmentation techniques were used: perturb image brightness, contrast, saturation randomly, rotate by a random real angle $\theta \in [0, 2\pi]$, random horizontal flip and crop to the final input size of 220×220 px.

Random Dropping of Input Polygons. With displacements of only up to 4 px, it could be easy for the network to keep a small error by outputting, as a segmentation, just a copy of the input polygon raster A_2. This behavior does not allow the network to learn buildings from the input image A_1, and it cannot learn to detect new buildings either. To avoid this, we randomly drop (remove) polygons from the polygon raster input before feeding it to the network. This introduces a new hyper-parameter $keep\_poly\_prob \in [0, 1]$ which is the probability each input polygon is kept and actually fed to the network while training. This operation is also data augmentation in that it generates multiple possible inputs from one data sample.

3.3 Training

As shown in Fig. 4, 4 different models are used with downscaling factors 8, 4, 2 and 1. We trained 4 models independently for each downscaling factor. We used the Adam optimizer with batch size 32 on a GTX 1080 Ti. We used a learning rate of $1e^{-4}$ until iteration 25000 and then $0.5e^{-4}$ until the end (100000 iterations). We also used weight L_2 regularization with a factor of $1e^{-4}$. Table 1 summarizes the loss coefficients for the intermediate losses (Eqs. 3, 4) as well as for the different pixel classes (Eqs. 1, 2). We set $keep\_poly\_prob = 0.1$ to only keep 10% of input polygons, in order to learn new buildings on 90% of the buildings.

4 Cadastral Map Alignment

4.1 Results

To evaluate the method and its variations for the alignment task, we applied the full pipeline on the 3 images of the city of San Francisco from the second

Table 1. Intermediate loss coefficients α_l and class loss coefficients w_c, w_c'.

Up to iter.	2500	5000	7500	100000
α_0	0.50	0.75	0.9	1.0
α_1	0.35	0.20	0.1	0
α_2	0.15	0.05	0	0

	w_c	w_c'
Background ($c = 1$)	0	0.05
Interior ($c = 2$)	0.1	0.1
Edge ($c = 3$)	1	1
Vertex ($c = 4$)	10	10

Fig. 5. Several crops of test images. Green buildings: ground truth; red: misaligned [input]; blue: aligned [our output]. The right crop is an example of the segmentation output. (Color figure online)

dataset. For each image, we generated 10 different displacement maps for a more precise evaluation. For visual results of the alignment, see Fig. 5.

To measure the accuracy of the alignment, for any threshold τ we compute the fraction of vertices whose ground truth point distance is less than τ. In other words, we compute the Euclidean distance in pixels between ground truth vertices and aligned vertices, and plot the cumulative distribution of those distances in Fig. 6a (higher is better). The no alignment curves are for comparison and show the accuracy obtained if the output displacement map is zero everywhere.

We compared our method to Zampieri et al. [19], which we trained on the same dataset; its test accuracy is summarized in Fig. 6c. We also compare to Quicksilver [17]; however it could not handle the 32 px displacements we tested on (it gave worse results than no alignment), so we trained Quicksilver with images downscaled by a factor of 4 and displacements of 4 px maximum at the downscaled resolution. We compare this version of Quicksilver with the model of our method trained with the same downscaling factor for a fair comparison. Figure 6b shows the result of this comparison.

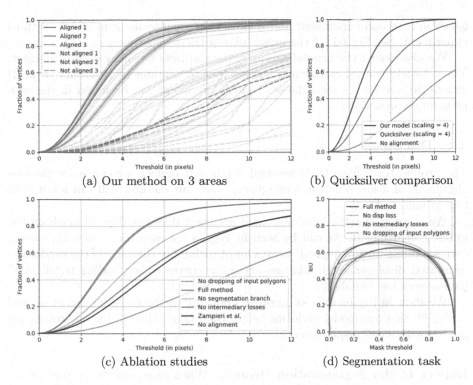

(a) Our method on 3 areas   (b) Quicksilver comparison

(c) Ablation studies   (d) Segmentation task

Fig. 6. Accuracy cumulative distributions and mean IoU values. Faded curves each correspond to one of the 10 polygon maps to align per image. Solid curves are the average. (Color figure online)

To test the segmentation of new buildings, we apply the model trained at the highest resolution (with a downscaling factor of 1) with just the image as input. The polygon raster input is left blank as would be the case with an empty map. In this extreme case, all buildings in the image are new (with respect to the empty polygon raster input). See the right image of Fig. 5 for an example of segmentation. We measure the IoU (Intersection over Union) between the ground truth polygons and the output polygon raster (which combines the polygon interior, edge and vertex channels of the model's output). The polygon raster has values between 0 and 1, we threshold it at various values to obtain a polygon mask. The IoU (Intersection of Union) is then computed for the 3 test images (see Fig. 6d for the mean IoUs).

We proceeded to ablation studies to measure the performance gains of the 3 main contributions of this work. For the alignment objective, we removed the segmentation branch in a first experiment, removed all intermediary losses in a second experiment and set the probability of dropping input polygons to 1 in a third experiment. See Fig. 6c for the mean accuracy cumulative distributions of these experiments. For the segmentation objective, we set the probability of dropping input polygons to 1 in a first experiment, removed all intermediary losses in a second experiment and removed the displacement branch in a third experiment. See Fig. 6d for the mean IoUs of these experiments.

We also tested the generalization across datasets by using a third dataset. The networks trained on this new dataset plus the dataset by Bradbury et al. [1] generalize well to the Inria dataset. This experiment can be found in the supplementary materials.

4.2 Discussion

The ground truth from OSM we used is still not perfect, we can see some misalignment of a few pixels in some places. But our method still can learn with this ground truth.

We observe that the final alignment accuracy does not depend much on the initial misalignment. As can be seen in Fig. 6a for each area, accuracy curves corresponding to "not aligned" have a lot of variability (because of the randomly-generated displacements), whereas accuracy curves corresponding to "aligned" have a very low variability.

We show in Fig. 6c that we improve upon the method of Zampieri et al. and in Fig. 6b that our model performs better than Quicksilver in the one-resolution setting with small displacements.

Impact of the Segmentation Branch. When removing the segmentation branch altogether, we globally lose accuracy on the alignment task. Figure 6c shows a drop of 22% for a threshold value of 4 px. The segmentation branch was initially added to stabilize the beginning of the training, it turns out it also improves the final performance of the network as well as providing a way to detect new buildings that do not appear in the input misaligned building map. We chose to classify polygon edges and vertices in addition to the very common polygon interior classification, in order to control how much the network has to focus on learning edges and vertices to optimize its cost function. It also gives more information compared to a classical building classification map. Classifying building edges allows for the separation of individual buildings that touch each other as can be seen in the right image of Fig. 5. The final goal of using the segmentation output is to vectorize the bitmap to obtain building polygons that can be added to an existing map. Detecting vertices, edges and interior of buildings should help this vectorization step which we hope to explore in a future work.

Impact of the Displacement Branch. When removing the displacement branch, we also lose accuracy on the segmentation task. Figure 6d shows a relative gain of the full method in terms of area under the curve of 4.6% compared to not using multi-task learning.

Impact of Intermediary Cost Functions. We lose more alignment accuracy when not using intermediary cost functions by setting $\alpha_0 = 1, \alpha_1 = 0$ and $\alpha_2 = 0$. Figure 6c shows a drop of 32% for a threshold value of 4 px. It also affects the segmentation task. Figure 6d shows a relative gain of the full method in terms of area under the curve of 8.3% compared to not using intermediary cost functions. This technique proves that using intermediary losses could improve semantic segmentation methods.

Impact of Randomly Dropping Input Polygons. If we set the probability of dropping input polygons to 0 (equivalent to not using this technique), the network almost does not output anything for the segmentation output, and consequently the IoU gets very low (see Fig. 6d). The reason is that it learns to output a building only when there is a building in the input. We checked that this technique does not decrease the performance of the alignment task: Fig. 6c shows that the 2 curves corresponding to using this technique (full method) and not using it (no dropping of input polygons) are equivalent.

5   2.5D Reconstruction of Buildings

5.1   Method

The alignment of building polygons can be used to solve the building height estimation problem to reconstruct 2.5D buildings from a stereo pair of images. The inputs to the method are 2 orthorectified satellite images captured from different views and a cadaster map of buildings which does not need to be precise. The first step consists in using our alignment method to align the building cadaster to the first image and to the second image. We then measure for each building the distance between the corresponding aligned buildings in both images. From this distance it is possible to compute the height of the building with trigonometry (assuming the ground is flat). For this we need to know the elevation (e_i) and azimuth (a_i) angles of the satellite when it captured each image i. We first used Eq. 19 from [6] which uses only elevation angles because they assume both images are captured from the same side of nadir and also that the satellite ground path goes through the captured area (meaning the azimuth angles are the same). We generalize their formula by including azimuth angles, thus linking the building height H to the distance D between the 2 aligned building polygons as:

$$H = D \frac{\tan(e_1)\tan(e_2)}{\sqrt{\tan^2(e_1) + \tan^2(e_2) - 2\tan(e_1)\tan(e_2)\cos(a_1 - a_2)}} \tag{5}$$

5.2   Results and Discussions

We applied this method to a pair of Pléiades satellite images of the city of Leibnitz. So that the accuracy can be quantified, ground truth buildings with

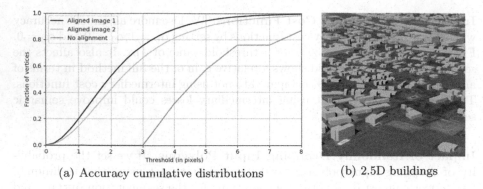

(a) Accuracy cumulative distributions   (b) 2.5D buildings

Fig. 7. Height estimation by alignment of polygons of one view to the image of the other view and vice versa.

a height attribute were given to us by the company Luxcarta along with the satellite images. Image 1 was captured with an elevation and azimuth angles of 76.7° and 212.9° respectively. For Image 2 those angles are 69.6° and 3.6°. We aligned the building polygons to the 2 images with our method; the accuracy of the alignment is displayed in Fig. 7a. The models of our method were trained on aerial images only and were applied as-is to these 2 satellite images. We use the same elevation and azimuth angles for every building of an image, as our data comprises the mean angles of the images only. In reality, the angles are not constant across the image and Eq. 5 can be used with different angles per building. See Fig. 7b for the 2.5D buildings obtained by this method. For each building we measure the difference between the ground truth height and the predicted height. We obtain a mean error of 2.2 m. We identified 2 sources of error:

1. Our model did not train on images far from nadir (lack of ground truth data at those angles). This is why Image 2 has lower alignment accuracy than Image 1: being farther from nadir, the network has more trouble with it.
2. Alignment errors get multiplied by a greater factor when the elevation angle is near nadir (closer to 90°) than when it is farther from it (closer to 0°).

These 2 sources of errors should be solved by the same solution: training the networks on images farther from nadir with good ground-truth.

6   Conclusions

The multi-task, multi-resolution method presented in this paper can be used to effectively solve the common problem of aligning existing maps over a new satellite image while also detecting new buildings in the form of a segmentation map. The use of multi-task learning by adding the extra segmentation task not only helps the network to train better, but also detects new buildings when coupled with a data augmentation technique of randomly dropping input polygons when training. Adding intermediate losses at different resolution levels inside the network also helps the training by providing a better gradient flow. It improves the performance on both alignment and segmentation tasks and could be used in other deep learning methods that have an image-like output which can be interpreted at different scales. Interestingly, multi-task learning also helps the segmentation task, as adding the displacement loss when training increases IoU.

We also tried our method on the task of building height estimation, generating simple but clean 3D models of buildings. We hope that our method will be a step towards automatically updating maps and also estimating 3D models of buildings. In the future we plan to work on the segmentation branch by using a better-suited loss for each output channel and a coherence loss between channels, to further improve map updating. We also plan to improve displacement learning by adding a regularization loss enforcing piece-wise smooth outputs, such as the BV (Bounded Variation) norm or the Mumford-Shah functional.

Acknowledgments. This work benefited from the support of the project EPITOME ANR-17-CE23-0009 of the French National Research Agency (ANR). We also thank Luxcarta for providing satellite images with corresponding ground truth data and Alain Giros for fruitful discussions.

References

1. Bradbury, K., et al.: Aerial imagery object identification dataset for building and road detection, and building height estimation, July 2016
2. Charpiat, G., Faugeras, O., Keriven, R.: Image statistics based on diffeomorphic matching. In: ICCV, October 2005
3. Dalal, N., Triggs, B.: Histograms of oriented gradients for human detection. In: CVPR, June 2005
4. Fischer, P., et al.: FlowNet: learning optical flow with convolutional networks. CoRR (2015)
5. Hermosillo, G., Chefd'Hotel, C., Faugeras, O.: Variational methods for multimodal image matching. Int. J. Comput. Vis. **50**, 329–343 (2002)
6. Licciardi, G.A., Villa, A., Mura, M.D., Bruzzone, L., Chanussot, J., Benediktsson, J.A.: Retrieval of the height of buildings from worldview-2 multi-angular imagery using attribute filters and geometric invariant moments. IEEE J. Sel. Top. Appl. Earth Obs. Remote. Sens. **5**, 71–79 (2012)
7. Lowe, D.G.: Distinctive image features from scale-invariant keypoints. Int. J. Comput. Vis. **60**, 91–110 (2004)
8. Maggiori, E., Tarabalka, Y., Charpiat, G., Alliez, P.: Can semantic labeling methods generalize to any city? The Inria aerial image labeling benchmark. In: IGARSS (2017)
9. Manfré, L.A., et al.: An analysis of geospatial technologies for risk and natural disaster management. ISPRS Int. J. Geo-Inf. **1**, 166–185 (2012)
10. OpenStreetMap contributors: Planet dump (2017). Accessed https://planet.osm.org
11. Ptucha, R., Azary, S., Savakis, A.: Keypoint matching and image registration using sparse representations. In: IEEE International Conference on Image Processing, September 2013

12. Ronneberger, O., Fischer, P., Brox, T.: U-Net: convolutional networks for biomedical image segmentation. In: Navab, N., Hornegger, J., Wells, W.M., Frangi, A.F. (eds.) MICCAI 2015. LNCS, vol. 9351, pp. 234–241. Springer, Cham (2015). https://doi.org/10.1007/978-3-319-24574-4_28
13. Ruder, S.: An overview of multi-task learning in deep neural networks. CoRR (2017)
14. Thompson, J.A., Bell, J.C., Butler, C.A.: Digital elevation model resolution: effects on terrain attribute calculation and quantitative soil-landscape modeling. Geoderma **100**, 67–89 (2001)
15. Wang, A.: Correction of atmospheric effects on earth imaging (extended inverse method). Math. Model. **9**, 533–537 (1987)
16. Wright, J.K.: Map makers are human: comments on the subjective in maps. Geogr. Rev. **32**, 527–544 (1942)
17. Yang, X., Kwitt, R., Niethammer, M.: Quicksilver: fast predictive image registration - a deep learning approach. CoRR (2017)
18. Ye, Y., Shan, J., Bruzzone, L., Shen, L.: Robust registration of multimodal remote sensing images based on structural similarity. IEEE Trans. Geosci. Remote Sens. **55**, 2941–2958 (2017)
19. Zampieri, A., Charpiat, G., Tarabalka, Y.: Coarse to fine non-rigid registration: a chain of scale-specific neural networks for multimodal image alignment with application to remote sensing. CoRR (2018)

SPNet: Deep 3D Object Classification and Retrieval Using Stereographic Projection

Mohsen Yavartanoo(iD), Eu Young Kim(iD), and Kyoung Mu Lee(✉)(iD)

Department of ECE, ASRI, Seoul National University, Seoul, Korea
{myavartanoo,shreka116,kyoungmu}@snu.ac.kr
https://cv.snu.ac.kr/

Abstract. We propose an efficient Stereographic Projection Neural Network (SPNet) for learning representations of 3D objects. We first transform a 3D input volume into a 2D planar image using stereographic projection. We then present a shallow 2D convolutional neural network (CNN) to estimate the object category followed by view ensemble, which combines the responses from multiple views of the object to further enhance the predictions. Specifically, the proposed approach consists of four stages: (1) Stereographic projection of a 3D object, (2) view-specific feature learning, (3) view selection and (4) view ensemble. The proposed approach performs comparably to the state-of-the-art methods while having substantially lower GPU memory as well as network parameters. Despite its lightness, the experiments on 3D object classification and shape retrievals demonstrate the high performance of the proposed method.

Keywords: 3D object classification · 3D object retrieval ·
Stereographic projection · Convolutional Neural Network ·
View ensemble · View selection

1 Introduction

In recent years, success of deep learning methods, in particular, convolutional neural network (CNN), has urged rapid development in various computer vision applications such as image classification, object detection, and super-resolution. Along with the drastic advances in 2D computer vision, understanding 3D shapes and environment have also attracted great attention.

Many traditional CNNs on 3D data simply extend the 2D convolutional operations to 3D, for example, the work of Wu et al. [36] which extends 2D deep belief network to 3D deep belief network, or the works of Maturana et al. [18] and Sedaghat et al. [25] where they extend 2D convolutional kernels to 3D convolutional kernels. Furthermore, Brock et al. [5] and Wu [35] proposed to build deeper 3D CNNs following the structures from inception-module, residual connections, and Generative Adversarial Network (GAN) to improve the generalization capability. However, these methods are based on 3D convolutions, thereby having high computational complexity and GPU memory consumption.

© Springer Nature Switzerland AG 2019
C. V. Jawahar et al. (Eds.): ACCV 2018, LNCS 11365, pp. 691–706, 2019.
https://doi.org/10.1007/978-3-030-20873-8_44

An alternate approach is based on projected 2D views of the 3D object to exploit established 2D CNN architectures. MVCNN [31] renders multiple 2D views of a 3D object and use them as an input to 2D CNNs. Some other works [1,26,28] propose to use the 2D panoramic views of a 3D shape. However, these methods can only observe partial parts of the 3D object, failing to cover full 3D surfaces.

To address all these limitations, we introduce a novel 3D shape representation technique using stereographic mapping to project the full surfaces of a 3D object onto a 2D planar image. This 2D stereographic image becomes an input to our proposed shallow 2D CNN, thereby reducing substantial amount of network parameters and GPU memory consumption compared to the state-of-the-art 3D convolution-based methods, while achieving high accuracy.

By taking advantage of multiple projected views generated from a single 3D shape, we propose *view ensemble* to combine predictions of most discriminative views, which are sampled by our view selection network. On the contrary, Conventional methods [1,20,28,31,33,34] simply aggregate the responses of all multiple views via max or average pooling.

2   Related Work

In this section, we review recent deep learning methods for 3D feature learning. These methods are categorized in term of different feature representations; (1) point cloud-based representations, (2) 3D model-based representations, and (3) 2D and 2.5D image-based representations.

Point Cloud-Based Methods: While previous works often combine hand-crafted features or descriptors with a machine learning classifier [4,9,11,32], the point cloud-based methods operate directly on point clouds in an end-to-end manner. In [6,16,21], the authors designed novel neural network architectures suitable for handling unordered point sets in 3D. Features based on point clouds often require spatial neighborhood queries, which can be hard to deal for inputs with large numbers of points.

3D Model-Based Methods: Voxel-based methods learn 3D features from voxels which represent 3D shape by the distribution of corresponding binary variables.

In 3D shapeNet [36], the authors proposed a method which learns global features from voxelized 3D shapes based on the 3D convolutional restricted Boltzmann machine. Similarly, Maturana and Scherer [18] proposed VoxNet which integrates a volumetric occupancy grid representation with a supervised 3D CNN. In a follow-up, Sedaghat et al. [25] extended VoxNet by introducing auxiliary task. They proposed to add orientation loss in addition to the general classification loss, in which the architecture predicts both the pose and class of the object. Furuya et al. [10] proposed Deep Local feature Aggregation Network (DLAN) which combines rotation-invariant 3D local features and their aggregation in a single architecture.

Sharma et al. [27] proposed a fully convolutional denoising auto-encoder to perform unsupervised global feature learning. In addition, 3D variational auto-encoders and generative adversarial networks have been adopted by Brock et al. [5] and Wu et al. [35], respectively. Furthermore, recent works [22,34] exploit the sparsity of 3D input using the octree data structure to reduce the computational complexity and speed up the learning of global features.

2D/2.5D Image-Based Methods: Image-based methods have been considered as one of the fundamental approaches in 3D object classification. Light Field descriptor (LFD) [8] by Chen et al. used multiple views around a 3D shape, and evaluates the dissimilarity between two shapes by comparing the corresponding two view sets in a greedy way instead of learning global features by combining multi-view information. Bai et al. [3] used a similar approach but using the Hausdorff distance between the corresponding view sets to measure the similarity between two 3D shapes.

Su et al. [31] proposed a CNN architecture that aggregates information from multiple views rendered from a 3D object which achieves higher recognition performance compared to single view based architectures. By decomposing each view sequence into a set of view pairs, Johns et al. [14] classified each pair independently and learned an object classifier by weighting the contribution of each pair, which allows 3D shape recognition over arbitrary camera viewpoint. To perform pooling more efficiently, Wang et al. [33] proposed a dominant set clustering technique where pooling is performed in each cluster individually. Kanezaki et al. [15] proposed RotationNet which takes multi-view images of an object and jointly estimates its object category and poses. RotationNet learns viewpoint labels in an unsupervised manner. Moreover, it learns view-specific feature representations shared across classes to boost the performance.

As an alternative approach, Gomez-Donoso et al. [12] proposed LonchaNet which uses three orthogonal slices from 3D point cloud as an input to three independent GoogLeNet networks, each network learning specific features for each slice. Cohen et al. [7] in Spherical CNNs proposed a definition for the spherical cross-correlation that is both expressive and rotation-equivariant. The spherical correlation satisfies a generalized Fourier theorem, which allows to compute it efficiently using a generalized Fast Fourier Transform (FFT) algorithm. Papadakis et al. [19] proposed PANORAMA that uses a set of panoramic views of a 3D object which describe the position and orientation of the object's surface in 3D space. 2D Discrete Fourier Transform and the 2D Discrete Wavelet Transform are computed for each view. Shi et al. in DeepPano [28], projected each 3D shape into a panoramic view around its principal axis and used a CNN for learning the representations from these views. To make the learned representations invariant to the rotation around the principal axis a row-wise max-pooling layer is applied between the convolution and fully-connected layers. to achieve better feature descriptor for a 3D object in the training phase, Sfikas et al. [1] use three panoramic views corresponding to the major axes and taking average pooling over feature descriptor of each view for the training of an ensemble of CNNs.

3   Proposed Stereographic Projection Network

In this section, we provide details of our proposed approach. We first describe
how to transform a 3D object into a 2D planar image using stereographic projection. Then, we give the detailed description of the proposed shallow 2D CNN
architecture, SPNet, followed by the procedures for view selection and view
ensemble.

3.1   Streographic Representation

Stereographic projection is a mapping that projects a 2D manifold onto a 2D
plane. Such a technique is well developed in the field of Topology and Geography
to project surface of the earth to a 2D planar map [30]. Since then, various
projection functions have been proposed to improve the quality of mapping.
In this work, we explore different types of projection functions showing that
stereographic projection preserves the more detailed surface structure of a 3D
object.

To construct the stereographic representation of a 3D object, we first normalize the 3D object such that a unit sphere can fully cover it. We then translate
the origin of the sphere to the center of the object assuming that the orientation
of the object is aligned. For each point p on the surface of the object, we denote
e as a unit vector from the origin o to the point p as shown in Fig. 1(a). By
assuming that the poles are aligned with the z-axis, image coordinates in 2D
mapped image can be determined by different types of projection functions as
follow:

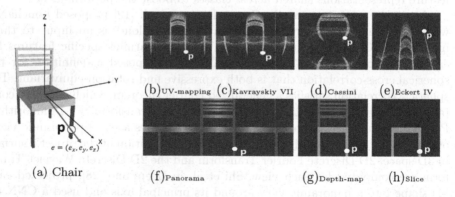

(a) Chair   (b) UV-mapping (c) Kavrayskiy VII (d) Cassini (e) Eckert IV

$e = (e_x, e_y, e_z)$

(f) Panorama   (g) Depth-map   (h) Slice

Fig. 1. 2D representation of surface of 3D object. (a) 3D mesh model with a point p
at the surface and its corresponding unit vector e from the origin 0. (b) (e) different
types of stereographic projection functions. (f) Panoramic view [1,26,28]. (g) Depth-
map [3,14]. (h) Slice-based projection [12].

UV Projection [30]:

$$u = 0.5 + \frac{\lambda}{2\pi}, \tag{1}$$

$$v = 0.5 - \frac{\phi}{\pi}, \tag{2}$$

Kavrayskiy VII Projection [30]:

$$u = \frac{3\lambda}{2}\sqrt{\frac{1}{3} - (\frac{\phi}{\pi})^2}, \tag{3}$$

$$v = \phi, \tag{4}$$

Eckert IV Projection [30]:

$$u = 2\lambda\sqrt{\frac{4 - 3\sin|\phi|}{6\pi}}, \tag{5}$$

$$v = \sqrt{\frac{2\pi}{3}}(2 - \sqrt{4 - 3\sin|\phi|}), \tag{6}$$

Cassini Projection [30]:

$$u = 2\arcsin(\cos\phi\sin\lambda), \tag{7}$$

$$v = \arctan 2(\frac{\tan\phi}{\cos\lambda}), \tag{8}$$

where, $\lambda = \arctan 2(e_x, e_y)$ and $\phi = \arcsin e_z$ refer to the longitude and the latitude, respectively.

After determining the UV coordinates of the 3D object in the 2D mapped image, we set a value of each pixel with the distance of the corresponding point p from the origin in the 3D object as shown in Fig. 1(a). We discretize the 2D image to have a size of 128×128. As shown in Fig. 1(b)-(h). We note that the stereographic representations of 3D object preserve more details about the shape of the 3D object compared to other approaches such as panorama [1, 26, 28], slice [12], and multi-view [15, 31] representations.

3.2   Network Architecture

We propose SPNet, a very shallow 2D CNN which consists of 4 convolutional layers and two fully connected layers. For each convolutional layer, we use a convolutional kernel of size 3×3 followed by tanh non-linearity and 2×2 max-pooling layers except for the last convolutional layer where we use global average pooling in place of max-pooling. Each side of inputs to all convolutional layers is zero-padded by 1 pixel to keep the feature map size unchanged. We also propose to add dropout after every layer except for the last fully connected layer to prevent over-fitting and for better generalization capability. The number of feature maps of our convolutional layers is 24, 32, 48, and 64, respectively. Details of the model are shown in Fig. 2.

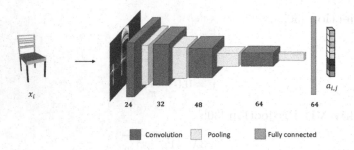

Fig. 2. Illustration of proposed SPNet, a shallow 2D convolutional neural network architecture. $a_{i,j}$ denotes the output from the last fully connected layer.

3.3 View Selection

To construct multiple view stereographic representations from a 3D object, we augment the data with azimuth and elevation rotations. We first rotate the object along the gravity axis, each rotated 45° intervals. We further generate more views through elevation rotations with 45° intervals. Both angles are sampled uniformly from $[0, 360°]$ to generate $N = 64$ views in total. Let us denote generated views of the object x_i as $\{v_{i,j}\}_{j=1}^{N}$ where i refers to the instance of the 3D object and j refers to the rotated instance of the corresponding 3D object.

All views $v_{i,j}$ are fed into the trained SPNet in Fig. 2 to extract the view-specific feature response maps $a_{i,j}$. All N view-specific features are then passed through a one-by-one convolutional layer to perform weighted-average over all view-specific features. The output is then used as a final prediction score map. The overall process of view selection is visualized in Fig. 3. The one-by-one convolutional layer in our view selection learns the importance of each view-specific features, thereby indicating the degree of contributions of each view to the final prediction. Once our view selection converges, we select M most discriminative views $\{v_{i,j}^{*}\}_{j=1}^{M}$ where $M \leq N$ by observing the highest weight values in the one-by-one convolutional kernel.

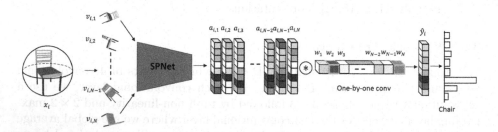

Fig. 3. Illustration of view selection and view ensemble. Both view selection and view ensemble adopt the same architecture but with different numbers of views to train each model. $a_{i,j}$ is the output of SPNet for the corresponding view $v_{i,j}$. Darker colors on the view-specific features $a_{i,j}$ and on the weights of the one-by-one convolutional layer denote higher values. Red boxes on the weights of the one-by-one convolutional kernel indicate the selected views. (Color figure online)

3.4 View Ensemble

Many recent works [13,17,23] have shown that the use of ensemble technique provides a significant boost to the classification performance. Thus, we also exploit the weighted-average over predictions of M selected views $\{v_{i,j}^*\}_{j=1}^M$ (Fig. 4).

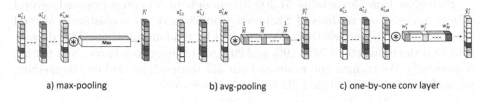

a) max-pooling b) avg-pooling c) one-by-one conv layer

Fig. 4. Comparison of different types of ensemble. Darker colors on each view-specific features and weights of the one-by-one convolutional kernel indicate higher values. (Color figure online)

We train our view ensemble model in Fig. 3 by using only the selected most important M views $\{v_{i,j}^*\}_{j=1}^M$. Moreover, we examine different types of aggregation for the predictions of M selected views:

Max-Pooling:

$$\hat{y}_i^* = \max_j\{a_{i,j}^*\}, \tag{9}$$

Avg-Pooling:

$$\hat{y}_i^* = \frac{1}{M}\sum_{j=1}^M a_{i,j}^*, \tag{10}$$

Weighted-Average:

$$\hat{y}_i^* = \sum_{j=1}^M w_j^* a_{i,j}^*, \tag{11}$$

where, $\hat{y}_i^*$ denotes the estimate of the object category label for each object x_i.

We have tested these three ensemble methods empirically and found that by learning the weights $\{w_j^*\}_{j=1}^M$ of the one-by-one convolutional layer properly, the weighted-average produces superior performance over the max-pooling and the average-pooling [1,20,28,31,33,34], as shown in Table 3.

4 Experimental Evaluation

4.1 Datasets

We have evaluated our method on the two subsets of the Princeton ModelNet large-scale 3D CAD model dataset [36] and the ShapeNet Core55, a subset of the ShapeNet dataset [24].

ModelNet-10 includes ten categories of 3991 and 908 models into training, and testing partitions, respectively. The dataset provides objects of same orientations.

ModelNet-40 contains 12,311 CAD models split into 40 categories that provides objects of same orientations. The training and testing subsets consist of 9843 and 2468 models, respectively.

ShapeNet Core55 contains 51,300 3D models in 55 categories and several subcategories. Two versions of ShapeNet Core55 exist (a) consistently aligned 3D models and (b) models that are perturbed by random rotations. This dataset split into three subsets of 70%, 10% and 20% for training, validation, and testing respectively. We trained and evaluated our 3D retrieval method on the training set and test set of the aligned 3D models, respectively.

4.2   Training

The baseline architecture of our CNN is shown in Fig. 2 which is smaller than the VGG-M network architecture that MVCNN [31] used. Table 1 shows the comparison of classification accuracy on the ModelNet-10 [36] of our baseline architecture and some famous Convolutional Neural Network architectures. To train SPNet, we used SGD optimizer with a learning rate of 0.01.

Table 1. Classification accuracy on ModelNet-10 with various network architectures for a single view.

Architectures	SPNet (ours)	VGG-16	ResNet-18	ResNet-32	ResNet-50	ResNet-101
Accuracy	**93.39%**	83.92%	91.74%	91.19%	92.18%	91.41%

4.3   Choice of Stereographic Projection

We have evaluated several stereographic projection models for the 3D classification task including UV, Kavrayskiy VII, Eckert IV, and Cassini [30]. Table 2 shows the test results on ModelNet-10 [36], where we can clearly observe that the UV-mapping outperforms the others. Since the UV-mapping is proven to be the best, we will use this mapping function in all subsequent experiments.

Table 2. Classification accuracy on ModelNet-10 with various mapping functions.

Mapping function	Accuracy
UV [30]	**93.39%**
Kavrayskiy VII [30]	93.17%
Eckert IV [30]	89.76%
Cassini [30]	92.51%
Depth-map (YZ-plane)	85.02%
Panorama (around Z-axis)	92.07%

4.4 Test on View Selection Schemes

We consider three view selection setups for the ensemble of the multi-view 2D stereographic representation to demonstrate the preference and power of our view selection approach.

Case (i): Major Axes. In this case, we set the viewpoints along three axes, x-axis, y-axis, and z-axis. The objects have same orientation namely that the viewpoint is along the x-axis. To obtain the two other viewpoints, each time we rotate the objects by $\theta = 90°$ and $\phi = 90°$ around z-axis and y-axis, respectively.

Case (ii): 12 MVCNN. In this case, we fix z-axis as the rotation axis. We place the viewpoints at $\phi = 30°$ from the ground plane and each time rotate the objects by $\theta = 30°$ around the z-axis to obtain 12 views for the object.

Case (iii): View Selection. Our view selection method which learns the view's influence by a one-by-one convolutional layer. We used the method on 64 different rotations by rotating the objects around z-axis and y-axis and then selected the views with the highest influence.

We compared the classification accuracy for these three view setup on the ModelNet-10 [36] with our view ensemble neural network architecture named SPNet_VE. Table 3 shows the comparison of classification accuracy on the ModelNct-10 [36] of plain and ensemble with the Max-pooling, Avg-pooling, and one-by-one convolutional layer as a weighted-average over the score features of the multi-view 2D representations. From these results, we observe that our learned weighted averaging of 5 views gives the best performance over other schemes, so that we use this ensemble model for our experiments.

4.5 3D Object Classification

We have first evaluated our baseline method SPNet in classification on both ModelNet-10 [36] and ModelNet-40 [36]. The performance of our model is measured by the average binary categorical accuracy.

We have compared our method with recent sate-of-the-art methods including 3D ShapeNet [36], GIFT [3], DeepPano [28], Multi-view Convolutional Neural Networks (MVCNN) [31], Geometry Image descriptor [29]. In addition to above methods the results are extended to include the following voxel based methods: ORION [25], 3D-GAN [35], VoxNet [18], O-CNN [34] and OctNet [22]. Table 4 summarizes the comparative results of classification on ModelNet-10 and ModelNet-40 in terms of GPU memory usage and the number of parameters during the training phase, and classification accuracy.

We note that in our approach, the view-ensemble model (SPNet_VE) boosts significant performance improvement over the baseline model (SPNet) by 3.9% and 4.0% on ModelNet-10 and ModelNet-40, respectively. Moreover, SPNet_VE achieved comparable results to those of the state-of-the-arts RotationNet [15], while requiring much less memory (2%) and network parameters (0.2%), respectively. Note also that there is a large gap between the average (94.82%) and

Table 3. Classification accuracy on ModelNet-10 with various view selection schemes.

View setup	#views	Max-pool	Avg-pool	One-by-one conv
Plain	1	93.39%	93.39%	93.39%
Major axes	3	95.15%	95.59%	96.26%
MVCNN	12	91.63%	92.51%	92.40%
View selection	1	93.39%	93.39%	93.39%
	2	95.82%	96.15%	96.15%
	3	95.59%	95.59%	96.26%
	4	95.15%	95.48%	96.58%
	5	94.05%	95.93%	**97.25%**
	6	94.16%	95.15%	97.03%
	64	90.64%	91.74%	91.52%

maximum (98.46%) accuracy of the RotationNet [15] which shows this method is not stable while our method showed consistent performances (97.25%) for each trial of training process.

4.6   Shape Retrieval

We have evaluated the view ensemble version, SPNet_VE with the learned five views for the 3D object retrieval task under three datasets, ModeNet-10 [36], ModelNet-40 [36] and ShapeNet Core 55 [24]. Table 5 shows the results of our retrieval experiment on the test sets of ModelNet-10 and ModelNet-40 with mean Average Precision (mAP) in comparison with other state-of-the-art methods.

We used the learned global features of our ensemble network before the last tanh activation function. Then, we applied the softmax function to create the best feature descriptors for all 3D objects. We sorted the most relevant 3D objects for each query from the test set by using both L_1 and L_2 distance metrics. Our SPNet_VE with L_1 achieved the best performance on ModelNet-10 and the second best on ModelNet-40. Note that the complexity of our model is much lighter than PANORAMA-ENN [1]; only 36% and 1% of the memory and parameters of PANORAMA-ENN are used, respectively.

Table 6 shows our results of the retrieval experiment on the large-scale normalized ShapeNet Core55 dataset. We tested our ensemble model by F-score, mean Average Precision (mAP) and Normalized Discounted Gain (NDCG) metrics in comparison to [3,10]. The Macro-averaged is an unweighted average over the entire dataset while the Micro-averaged gives an average over category. The proposed method outperformed the other methods by NDCG metric on both the Macro and Micro averaged.

Table 4. Classification results and comparison to state-of-the-art methods on ModelNet-10 and ModelNet-40. Also the number of parameters and GPU memory usage. VE indicates view ensemble.

InputModality	Method	GPU memory	Parameters	ModelNet class 10	class 40
Point clouds	PointNet [6]	-	3.5M	-	89.2%
	PointNet++ [21]	-	-	-	91.9%
3D Volume	ShapeNet [36]	60.5 MB	15M	83.50%	77.00%
	LightNet [2]	2 MB	0.3M	93.39%	86.90%
	ORION [25]	4.5 MB	0.91M	93.80%	-
	VRN [5]	129 MB	18M	93.60%	91.33%
	VRN Ensemble [5]	678 MB	93.5M	97.14%	95.54%
	VoxNet [18]	4.5 MB	0.9M	92.00%	83.00%
	FusionNet [2]	548 MB	118M	93.10%	90.80%
	3D-GAN [35]	56 MB	11M	91.00%	83.30%
	OctNet [22]	-	-	90.42%	-
	O-CNN [34]	-	-	-	90.6%
Others	Spherical CNNs [7]	-	1.4M	-	-
	LonchaNet [12]	-	15M	94.37%	-
2D Represen.	MVCNN [31]	331 MB	42M	-	90.10%
	MVCNN-MultiRes [20]	-	180M	-	91.40%
	RotationNet [15]	731 MB	42M	**98.46%**	**97.37%**
2.5D Represen.	DeepPano [28]	9.8 MB	3.27M	85.45%	77.63%
	PANORAMA-NN [26]	6.77 MB	2.86M	91.10%	90.70%
	PANORAMA-ENN [1]	42 MB	8.6M	96.85%	95.56%
	GIFT [3]	-	-	92.35%	83.10%
	Pairwise [14]	-	42M	92.80%	90.70%
	SPNet (ours)	3 MB	86K	93.39%	88.61%
	SPNet_VE (ours)	15 MB	86K	97.25%	92.63%

Figure 5 shows some of the retrieval cases on the test set of the ModelNet-10. The first column in the figure illustrates the queries and the remaining columns illustrate the corresponding retrieved objects in rank order. The red models indicate that the retrieved objects are in a wrong class with the queries. In other cases, the queries and the retrieved objects have the same classes. For instance, in the class of the dresser, the retrieved objects are so similar to the query while they are from different classes. The reason for these failure cases is that some objects from two different classes are hard to distinguish. Note that

Table 5. Comparison of retrieval results measured in mean Average Precision (mAP) on the ModelNet-10 and ModelNet-40 datasets.

Method	GPU memory	Parameters	ModelNet(mAP)	
			class 10	class 40
MVCNN [31]	331 MB	42M	-	79.5%
Geometry Image [29]	-	-	74.9%	51.3%
GIFT [3]	-	-	91.12%	81.94%
DeepPano [28]	9.8 MB	3.27M	84.18%	76.81%
3D ShapeNets [36]	-	-	68.3%	49.2%
PANORAMA-ENN [1]	42 MB	8.6M	93.28%	**86.34%**
SPNet_VE (L2)	15 MB	86K	92.94%	84.68%
SPNet_VE (L1)	15 MB	86K	**94.20%**	85.21%

Table 6. Retrieval results measured in F-score, mean Average Precision (mAP) and Normalized Discounted Gain (NDCG) on the normalized ShapeNet Core55. VE indicates View Ensemble.

Method	Micro-averaged			Macro-averaged		
	F-score	mAP	NDCG	F-score	mAP	NDCG
Kanezaki	**79.8%**	**77.2%**	86.5%	**59.0%**	**58.3%**	65.6%
Zhou	76.7%	72.2%	82.7%	58.1%	57.5%	65.7%
Tatsuma	77.2%	74.9%	82.8%	51.9%	49.6%	55.9%
FUruya	71.2%	66.3%	76.2%	50.5%	47.7%	56.3%
Thermos	69.2%	62.2%	73.2%	48.4%	41.8%	50.2%
Deng	47.9%	54.0%	65.4%	16.6%	33.9%	40.4%
Li	28.2%	19.9%	33.0%	19.7%	25.5%	37.7%
Mk	25.3%	19.2%	27.7%	25.8%	23.2%	33.7%
SHREC16-Su	76.4%	73.5%	81.5%	57.5%	56.6%	64.0%
SHREC16-Bai	68.9%	64.0%	76.5%	45.4%	44.7%	54.8%
SPNet_VE	78.9%	69.2%	**89.0%**	53.5%	39.2%	**69.5%**

our approach does not have any failure cases in the class of Chair and Toilet of the ModelNet-10. Figure 6 shows the confusion matrix for all 3D objects on the test set of ModelNet-10. The similarity is measured by L1 distance. Therefore, so lower values indicate higher similarities between pairs of objects.

| Query | Ranked Retrievals |

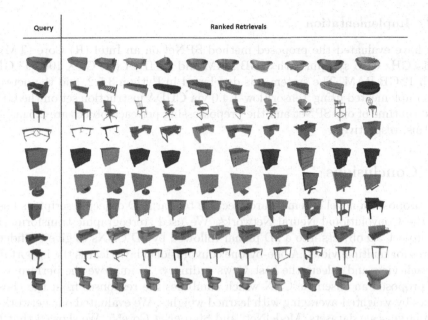

Fig. 5. Retrieval examples by the proposed SPNet_VE on the test set of the ModelNet-10 dataset. The first column illustrates the queries and the remaining columns show the corresponding retrieved models in rank order. Retrieved objects with blue and red colors are queries and failure cases, respectively. (Color figure online)

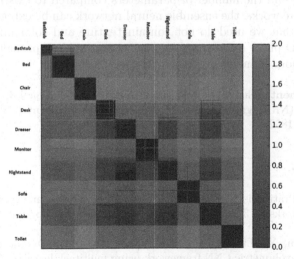

Fig. 6. Confusion matrix for 3D objects on the test set of the ModelNet-10. Values of the matrix show the similarity between pairs of 3D objects. Higher values indicate the two 3D objects have fewer similarities; see the color bar. (Color figure online)

4.7 Implementation

We have evaluated the proposed method SPNet on an Intel (R) Core (TM) i5 @ 3.4 GHz CPU system, with 32GB RAM and NVIDIA (R) GTX 1080 Ti GPU with 12 GB RAM. The system was developed in Python 3.5.2, and the network was implemented using TensorFlow-1.4.0 via CUDA instruction set on the GPU. The runtime of our SPNet and the prepossessing per each object are 2.5 ms and 120 ms, respectively.

5 Conclusions

We proposed a novel ensemble architecture to learn 3D object descriptors based on the Convolutional Neural Networks. We used stereographic transformation to project 3D objects into a 2D planar followed by 2D CNNs to give confidence scores for multiple views. A one-by-one convolutional layer learns the importance of each view and selects the best views ordinary. To improve the performance, we proposed an ensemble CNN which combines the responses from the chosen views by weighted-averaging with learned weights. We evaluated our network on two large-scale datasets, ModelNet, and ShapeNet Core55. We showed that the performance of the proposed method for the classification task is par to those of the state-of-the-art approaches, while outperforms most existing works in the retrieval task. Moreover, our proposed model is most efficient regarding GPU memory usage and the number of parameters compared to existing networks.

In the future works, the ensemble neural network can be extended. Moreover, The datasets that we used do not contain texture and color information. The one channel 2D plane represented by our stereographic representation could be extended to more channels if this information existed.

Acknowledgment. This work was supported by the National Research Foundation of Korea (NRF) grant funded by the Korea Government (MSIT) (No. NRF-2017R1A2B2011862).

References

1. Sfikas, K., Pratikakis, I., Theoharis, T.: Ensemble of panorama-based convolutional neural networks for 3D model classification and retrieval. Comput. Graph. **71**, 208–218 (2018)
2. Zhi, S., Liu, Y., Li, X., Guo, Y.: Toward real-time 3D object recognition: a lightweight volumetric CNN framework using multitask learning. Comput. Graph. **71**, 199–207 (2018)
3. Bai, S., Bai, X., Zhou, Z., Zhang, Z., Latecki, L.J.: Gift: a real-time and scalable 3D shape search engine. In: 2016 IEEE Conference on Computer Vision and Pattern Recognition (CVPR), pp. 5023–5032 (2016)
4. Behley, J., Steinhage, V., Cremers, A.B.: Performance of histogram descriptors for the classification of 3D laser range data in urban environments. In: 2012 IEEE International Conference on Robotics and Automation, pp. 4391–4398 (2012)

5. Brock, A., Lim, T., Ritchie, J.M., Weston, N.: Generative and discriminative voxel modeling with convolutional neural networks. CoRR abs/1608.04236 (2016)
6. Charles, R.Q., Su, H., Kaichun, M., Guibas, L.J.: PointNet: deep learning on point sets for 3D classification and segmentation. In: 2017 IEEE Conference on Computer Vision and Pattern Recognition (CVPR), pp. 77–85 (2017)
7. Cohen, T.S., Geiger, M., Köhler, J., Welling, M.: Spherical CNNs. In: ICLR (2018)
8. Ding-Yun, C., Xiao-Pei, T., Yu-Te, S., Ming, O.: On visual similarity based 3D model retrieval. Comput. Graph. Forum **22**(3), 223–232 (2003)
9. Frome, A., Huber, D., Kolluri, R., Bülow, T., Malik, J.: Recognizing objects in range data using regional point descriptors. In: Pajdla, T., Matas, J. (eds.) ECCV 2004. LNCS, vol. 3023, pp. 224–237. Springer, Heidelberg (2004). https://doi.org/10.1007/978-3-540-24672-5_18
10. Furuya, T., Ohbuchi, R.: Deep aggregation of local 3D geometric features for 3D model retrieval. In: BMVC (2016)
11. Golovinskiy, A., Kim, V.G., Funkhouser, T.: Shape-based recognition of 3D point clouds in urban environments, September 2009
12. Gomez-Donoso, F., Garcia-Garcia, A., Garcia-Rodriguez, J., Orts-Escolano, S., Cazorla, M.: LonchaNet: a sliced-based CNN architecture for real-time 3D object recognition. In: IJCNN, pp. 412–418 (2017)
13. Huang, H., et al.: Dynamical waveforms and the dynamical source for electricity meter dynamical experiment. In: 2016 Conference on Precision Electromagnetic Measurements (CPEM 2016), pp. 1–2 (2016)
14. Johns, E., Leutenegger, S., Davison, A.J.: Pairwise decomposition of image sequences for active multi-view recognition. In: Savva:2016:LSR:3056462.3056479, pp. 3813–3822 (2016)
15. Kanezaki, A., Matsushita, Y., Nishida, Y.: RotationNet: joint object categorization and pose estimation using multiviews from unsupervised viewpoints. In: CVPR (2018)
16. Klokov, R., Lempitsky, V.: Escape from cells: deep Kd-networks for the recognition of 3D point cloud models. In: ICCV, pp. 863–872 (2017)
17. Kumar, A., Kim, J., Lyndon, D., Fulham, M., Feng, D.: An ensemble of fine-tuned convolutional neural networks for medical image classification. IEEE J. Biomed. Health Inform. **21**(1), 31–40 (2017)
18. Maturana, D., Scherer, S.: VoxNet: a 3D convolutional neural network for real-time object recognition. In: IROS, pp. 922–928 (2015)
19. Papadakis, P., Pratikakis, I., Theoharis, T., Perantonis, S.: Panorama: a 3D shape descriptor based on panoramic views for unsupervised 3D object retrieval. IJCV **89**(2), 177–192 (2010)
20. Qi, C.R., Su, H., Nießner, M., Dai, A., Yan, M., Guibas, L.J.: Volumetric and multi-view CNNs for object classification on 3D data. In: CVPR, pp. 5648–5656 (2016)
21. Qi, C.R., Yi, L., Su, H., Guibas, L.J.: PointNet++: deep hierarchical feature learning on point sets in a metric space. arXiv preprint arXiv:1706.02413 (2017)
22. Riegler, G., Ulusoy, A.O., Geiger, A.: OctNet: learning deep 3D representations at high resolutions. In: CVPR, pp. 6620–6629 (2017)
23. Russakovsky, O., et al.: ImageNet large scale visual recognition challenge. IJCV **115**(3), 211–252 (2015)
24. Savva, M., et al.: Large-scale 3D shape retrieval from ShapeNet core55. In: Proceedings of the Eurographics 2016 Workshop on 3D Object Retrieval, 3DOR 2016, pp. 89–98 (2016)

25. Sedaghat, N., Zolfaghari, M., Brox, T.: Orientation-boosted voxel nets for 3D object recognition. CoRR abs/1604.03351 (2016)
26. Sfikas, K., Theoharis, T., Pratikakis, I.: Exploiting the panorama representation for convolutional neural network classification and retrieval. In: 3DOR (2017)
27. Sharma, A., Grau, O., Fritz, M.: VConv-DAE: deep volumetric shape learning without object labels. In: Hua, G., Jégou, H. (eds.) ECCV 2016. LNCS, vol. 9915, pp. 236–250. Springer, Cham (2016). https://doi.org/10.1007/978-3-319-49409-8_20
28. Shi, B., Bai, S., Zhou, Z., Bai, X.: DeepPano: deep panoramic representation for 3-D shape recognition. IEEE Signal Process. Lett. **22**(12), 2339–2343 (2015)
29. Sinha, A., Bai, J., Ramani, K.: Deep learning 3D shape surfaces using geometry images. In: Leibe, B., Matas, J., Sebe, N., Welling, M. (eds.) ECCV 2016. LNCS, vol. 9910, pp. 223–240. Springer, Cham (2016). https://doi.org/10.1007/978-3-319-46466-4_14
30. Snyder, J.P.: Flattening the Earth: Two Thousand Years of Map Projections. University of Chicago Press, Chicago (1993)
31. Su, H., Maji, S., Kalogerakis, E., Learned-Miller, E.: Multi-view convolutional neural networks for 3D shape recognition. In: ICCV, pp. 945–953 (2015)
32. Teichman, A., Levinson, J., Thrun, S.: Towards 3D object recognition via classification of arbitrary object tracks. In: 2011 IEEE International Conference on Robotics and Automation, pp. 4034–4041 (2011)
33. Wang, C.: Dominant set clustering and pooling for multiview 3D object recognition. In: BMVC (2017)
34. Wang, P.S., Liu, Y., Guo, Y.X., Sun, C.Y., Tong, X.: O-CNN: octree-based convolutional neural networks for 3D shape analysis. ACM Trans. Graph. **36**, 72:1–72:11 (2017)
35. Wu, J., Zhang, C., Xue, T., Freeman, W.T., Tenenbaum, J.B.: Learning a probabilistic latent space of object shapes via 3D generative-adversarial modeling. In: NIPS, pp. 82–90 (2016)
36. Wu, Z., et al.: 3D ShapeNets: a deep representation for volumetric shapes. In: CVPR, pp. 1912–1920 (2015)

SRC-Disp: Synthetic-Realistic Collaborative Disparity Learning for Stereo Matching

Guorun Yang, Zhidong Deng$^{(\boxtimes)}$, Hongchao Lu, and Zeping Li

Department of Computer Science,
State Key Laboratory of Intelligent Technology and Systems,
Beijing National Research Center for Information Science and Technology,
Tsinghua University, Beijing 100084, China
{ygr13,luhc15,li-zp16}@mails.tsinghua.edu.cn,
michael@mail.tsinghua.edu.cn

Abstract. Stereo matching task has been greatly improved by convolutional neural networks, especially the fully-convolutional network. However, existing deep learning methods always overfit to specific domains. In this paper, focus on domain adaptation problem of disparity estimation, we present a novel training strategy to conduct synthetic-realistic collaborative learning. At first, we design a compact model that consists of shallow feature extractor, correlation feature aggregator and disparity encoder-decoder. Our model enables end-to-end disparity regression with fast speed and high accuracy. To perform collaborative learning, we then propose two distinct training schemes, including guided label distillation and semi-supervised regularization, both of which are used to alleviate the lack of disparity labels in realistic datasets. Finally, we evaluate the trained models on different datasets that belong to various domains. Comparative results demonstrate the capability of our designed model and the effectiveness of collaborative training strategy.

Keywords: Stereo matching · Collaborative learning · Disparity · Guided label distillation · Semi-supervised regularization

1 Introduction

Disparity estimation aims to find corresponding pixels between rectified stereo images [18]. It is a fundamental low-level task in computer vision, which has a wide range of applications such as depth prediction [32], scene understanding [12] and robotics navigation [37]. In recent years, deep learning methods [6,24,26, 29,31,41,43] continuously improve the performance on specific scenes, while the domain adaptation for stereo matching gains more attention.

A popular pipeline for disparity estimation gets involved in matching cost computation, cost aggregation, disparity calculation, and disparity refinement [36]. Previous methods often manually design reliable features to describe

© Springer Nature Switzerland AG 2019
C. V. Jawahar et al. (Eds.): ACCV 2018, LNCS 11365, pp. 707–723, 2019.
https://doi.org/10.1007/978-3-030-20873-8_45

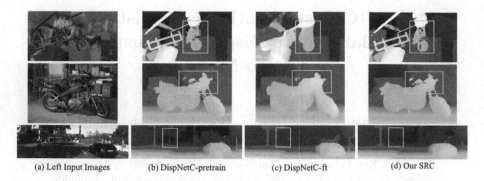

(a) Left Input Images   (b) DispNetC-pretrain   (c) DispNetC-ft   (d) Our SRC

Fig. 1. Examples of predicted results of DispNetC [29] and our SRC model. From top to down, we test the models on Scene Flow dataset [29], Middleburry Stereo dataset [35] and KITTI Stereo 2015 dataset [30]. From left to right, we give left input images and predicted disparity maps by DispNetC-pretrained, DispNetC-finetuned, and our SRC model. All of the disparity maps are colorized by the devkit [30]. With the SRC training, our model can adapt to various domains

image patches to localize matching correspondings [5,15,34]. These methods are easily affected by textureless areas, shadow regions, and repetitive patterns. Since the convolutional neural network (CNN) exhibits great representative capacity on image classification [25], several approaches replace above-mentioned hand-craft features with CNN features [28,43], which significantly increases the accuracy of disparity estimation. Inspired by the progress in semantic image segmentation task [7,27], modern stereo methods adopt fully-convolutional network (FCN) to learn disparity map [24,29]. These methods utilize siamese structure to process binocular inputs and design a correlation part to automatically encode matching costs. This structure enables an end-to-end disparity regression and further improves estimated accuracy and processing speed. In order to predict reasonable disparities on target scenes, these models are always pretrained on synthetic datasets and finely-tuned on realistic datasets. However, the resulted models are easily overfitted on specific domains. For example, in Fig. 1, the Disp-NetC model [29] pretrained on scene flow dataset is able to predict considerable results on synthetic scenes, but leading to mediocre outputs on realistic scenes. Meanwhile, the model finely-tuned on KITTI dataset [30] behaves well on road scenes, while suffering on indoor and virtual environments. From the above observation, existing deep methods cannot well address domain adaptation problem.

In this paper, our goal is to train better adaptable model for stereo matching. Instead of successively training on the synthetic and realistic dataset, we propose a novel synthetic-realistic collaborative (SRC) learning strategy, where virtual and real images are fused to train our network synchronously. We hope that the model maintains its properties on various domains through SRC training. Specifically, for virtual images in the synthetic dataset, high-quality disparity labels can be directly fetched to train the model in a supervised learning mode. For real images, since there are not enough disparity labels, we present two different schemes: 1) Guided label distillation. Here, an existing method is employed to generate disparity maps that are used as guided labels for the realistic dataset, and then the supervised training can be seamlessly migrated to the realistic dataset. 2) Semi-supervised regularization. Unlike the supervised loss computed between predicted disparities and labels, a photometric distance is measured between the source image and the reconstructed image at the referenced view. In our experiments, the reconstructed image is warped from source image at the other view based on the current predicted disparity map. Along with photometric distance, we also add smoothness constraints to penalize disparity incoherence. Thus the semi-supervised regularization means that either the supervised loss or the unsupervised photometric loss is selected depending on whether labels are provided or not. The experimental results in Sect. 4 illustrate that both of guided label distillation and semi-supervised regularization make sense.

To take full advantage of the capacity of SRC learning, we design an end-to-end disparity regression model. The encoder-decoder architecture is also adopted in our model, embedded with a shallow feature extractor and a correlation feature aggregator. We use the extractor to obtain image features and the aggregator to combine matching cost between stereo features. The following encoder is a ResNet-like model to learn disparity information. The decoder is composed of several deconvolutional blocks to regress the full-size disparity map. We evaluate the SRC models on different datasets across various domains, including indoor [35], outdoor [30] and virtual [29] scenes. Compared to the baseline models which are only trained on an individual dataset, the SRC model shows significant superiorities, especially on unseen domains. Besides, we set different ratios between synthetic dataset and realistic dataset to exploit data properties for SRC learning. Our main contributions are summarized below:

- We develop a compact model that integrates shallow feature extractor, correlation aggregator and encoder-decoder to regress disparity map in an end-to-end manner.
- We propose a novel synthetic-realistic collaborative learning strategy. Two schemes as guided label distillation and semi-supervised regularization, are presented to conduct SRC model training.
- Comparative results are evaluated on different stereo datasets across various domains, which demonstrates the effectiveness of our SRC strategy for domain adaption problem.

2   Related Work

Disparity estimation from stereo images has been studied for several decades. Scharstein et al. [36] provide a taxonomy of stereo algorithms and analyze the typical four-step pipeline. In this section, we would not track back to early stereo methods but focus on recent deep learning approaches.

Zbontar and LeCun [43] first introduce CNN to describe image patches and compute matching cost. Luo et al. [28] design a siamese structure embedded with a product layer to calculate marginal distributions over all possible disparities.

A multi-scale deep model presented by Chen *et al.* [8] leverages appearance data to learn disparity from a rich embedding space. Shaked and Wolf *et al.* [38] propose a highway network along with a hybrid loss to measure the similarity between image patches on multi-levels. Compared to traditional approaches, the above methods adopt CNN features to conduct matching cost computation and improve the accuracy of disparity prediction with a considerable margin. However, these methods are still time-consuming due to the post-processing steps or complex optimization framework.

Inspired by FCN used in semantic segmentation task [7,27], Mayer *et al.* [29] raise an encoder-decoder architecture called DispNet to enable end-to-end disparity regression. DispNet adopts a correlation operation as FlowNet [11] where the matching cost can be directly integrated to encoder volumes. Pang *et al.* [31] provide a cascade structure to optimize residues between predicted results and ground-truth values. Liang *et al.* [26] propose two-stage pipeline where the second sub-network is used to refine initial estimated disparity by measuring feature constancy. A few methods adopt three-dimensional convolutions to learn disparity. For example, Kendall *et al.* [24] integrate contextual information by 3D convolutions over a cost volume. A two-stream network proposed by Yu *et al.* [42] realizes cost aggregation and proposal selection respectively. Chang *et al.* [6] combine spatial pyramid network with 3D convolutional layers to incorporate global context information. Although these methods achieve state-of-the-art results on several stereo benchmarks by successively training on synthetic dataset [29] and realistic dataset [14,30], there remains the domain adaptation problem because their models always overfit to specific domains belonging to current training datasets. Unlike the common training schedule, we propose SRC training strategy, which makes our model more reliable to domain shifts.

Another class of approaches attempts to exploit other information to improve stereo matching. Guney and Geiger [17] introduce object-aware knowledge into MRF formulation to resolve possible stereo ambiguities. Yang *et al.* [41] combine the high-level semantic information to optimize disparity prediction. Song *et al.* [39] utilize the cues of edge detection to recover disparity details. In addition, several approaches [1,4,9,33] tackle semantic-level or instance-level information to improve the accuracy of optical flow which is a similar scene-matching task as disparity estimation. We argue that the introduction of other information may not be effective because domain adaptation is a wide-spread problem in vision tasks. Moreover, increased information also brings extra computations.

Recently, some unsupervised learning methods are proposed for depth prediction and scene matching. Garg *et al.* [13] estimate single-view depth by minimizing projection errors in stereo environment. Godard *et al.* [16] conduct left-right consistency check in a fully-differentiable structure. Yu *et al.* [22] fuse photometric loss and smoothness constancy to predict optical flow. Tonioti *et al.* [40] leverage on the confidence measures to finetune a standard stereo model. A guided flow method presented by Zhu *et al.* [45] employs FlowFields [2] to generate flow labels for flow learning. Our idea of SRC learning is inspired from these unsupervised methods. Concretely for the semi-supervised regularization,

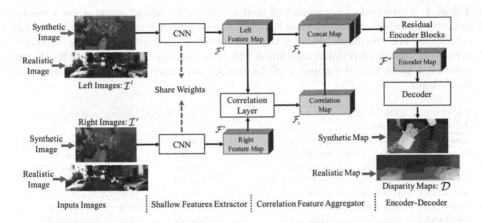

Fig. 2. Model architecture. The model can be divided into three parts: shallow feature extractor, feature aggregator and encoder-decoder. For SRC learning, the input data are fused with synthetic and realistic images

we combine the supervised loss and unsupervised loss together to train our model on the fusion set of synthetic and realistic data.

Our method follows the encoder-decoder architecture to regress disparity map. We utilize ResNet model [19] as the backbone and integrate the correlation part [11,29] to compute cost volumes between stereo pairs. Focus on the domain adaptation problem, SRC learning strategy is proposed to train the model. Specifically, for the lack of disparity labels in the realistic dataset, we provide two schemes as guided label distillation and semi-supervised regularization. Finally, our experimental results evaluated across different datasets demonstrate the effectiveness of the SRC-learning.

3   Method

In this section, we first describe the model architecture for disparity regression in Sect. 3.1 and then explain the SRC learning strategy, including the guided label distillation and semi-supervised regularization in Sect. 3.2.

3.1   Model Architecture

Our model is shown in Fig. 2 and layer structural definition is detailed in Table 1. Given a pair of images $\mathcal{I}^l$ and $\mathcal{I}^r$, the goal is to estimate the dense disparity map $\mathcal{D}$. We use the ResNet-50 [19] as the backbone of our model. According to data flow, the model can be divided into three parts: shallow feature extractor, correlation feature aggregator and encoder-decoder. For the inputs of network at training time, we fuse synthetic and realistic images to conduct SRC learning. Our model enables accurate prediction of disparity map.

Table 1. Layer-by-layer structure of model. The "conv_block" denotes the convolutional block, where a convolutional layer is followed by batch normalization and ReLU activation. The "res_block" denotes the residual block designed by [19]. The "corr_1d" denotes the single-directional correlation [29]. The "deconv_block" denotes the deconvolutional block that is composed of deconvolutional layer, batch normalization and ReLU layer.

Layer	Attributes	Channels I/O	Scaling	Inputs
1. Shallow feature extractor				
conv_block1_1	kernel size = 3, stride = 2	3/64	1/2	input stereo images
conv_block1_2	kernel size = 3, stride = 1	64/64	1/2	conv_block1_1
conv_block1_3	kernel size = 3, stride = 1	64/128	1/2	conv_block1_2
max_pooling	kernel size = 3, stride = 2	128/128	1/4	conv_block1_3
res_block2_1	kernel size = 3, stride = 1	128/256	1/4	max_pool_block1
res_block2_2	kernel size = 3, stride = 1	256/256	1/4	res_block2_1
res_block2_3	kernel size = 3, stride = 1	256/256	1/4	res_block2_2
res_block3_1	kernel size = 3, stride = 1	512/512	1/8	res_block2_3
2. Feature aggregator				
conv_block_pre	kernel size = 3, stride = 1	512/256	1/8	res_block3_1
corr_1d	max displacement = 32, single direction [29]	256/33	1/8	conv_block_pre
conv_trans	kernel size = 3, stride = 1	256/256	1/8	conv_block_pre
concat	aggregate corr_1d and conv_trans	(256 + 33)/289	1/8	corr_1d, conv_trans
3-1. Disparity encoder-decoder				
res_block3_2	kernel size = 3, stride = 1	409/512	1/8	concat
res_block3_3	kernel size = 3, stride = 1	512/512	1/8	res_block3_2
res_block3_4	kernel size = 3, stride = 1	512/512	1/8	res_block3_3
res_block4_1	kernel size = 3, stride = 1, dilated pattern	512/1024	1/8	res_block3_3
res_block4_2	kernel size = 3, stride = 1, dilated pattern	1024/1024	1/8	res_block4_1
res_block4_3	kernel size = 3, stride = 1, dilated pattern	1024/1024	1/8	res_block4_2
res_block4_4	kernel size = 3, stride = 1, dilated pattern	1024/1024	1/8	res_block4_3
res_block4_5	kernel size = 3, stride = 1, dilated pattern	1024/1024	1/8	res_block4_4
res_block4_6	kernel size = 3, stride = 1, dilated pattern	1024/1024	1/8	res_block4_5
res_block5_1	kernel size = 3, stride = 1, dilated pattern	1024/2048	1/8	res_block4_6
res_block5_2	kernel size = 3, stride = 1, dilated pattern	2048/2048	1/8	res_block5_1
res_block5_3	kernel size = 3, stride = 1, dilated pattern	2048/2048	1/8	res_block5_2
conv_block5_4	kernel size = 3, stride = 1	2048/512	1/8	res_block5_3
deconv_block1	kernel size = 3, stride = 2	512/256	1/4	conv_block5_4
deconv_block2	kernel size = 3, stride = 2	256/128	1/2	deconv_block1
deconv_block3	kernel size = 3, stride = 2	128/64	1	deconv_block2
disp_conv	kernel size = 3, stride = 1	64/1	1	deconv_block3

Shallow Feature Extractor. We use the shallow part of ResNet-50 model to extract image features $\mathcal{F}^l$ and $\mathcal{F}^r$. This part contains three convolutional blocks, a max-pooling layer and four residual blocks. It subsamples the input images in two stages: "conv_block_1_1" and "max_pool1", which results in 1/8 scaling to raw images. Compared with original images, the features obtained from shallow extractor are more robust to local context.

Correlation Feature Aggregator. A correlation layer [29] is adopted to compute cost volumes $\mathcal{F}^c$ between $\mathcal{F}^l$ and $\mathcal{F}^r$. We only perform single-direction search due to epipolar property. Both max displacement and padding size are set to 32 so that channels of $\mathcal{F}^c$ are 33. Besides, left features $\mathcal{F}^l$ are preserved

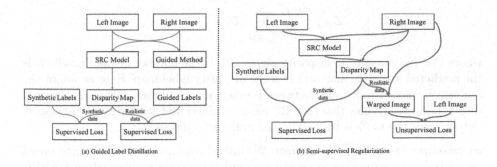

(a) Guided Label Distillation

(b) Semi-supervised Regularization

Fig. 3. Diagram of guided label distillation and semi-supervised regularization

for the detailed information on reference view. The cost volumes $\mathcal{F}^c$ and left features $\mathcal{F}^l$ are aggregated to form hybrid map $\mathcal{F}^h$. The feature aggregator integrates image features and matching information together for posterior disparity learning.

Encoder-Decoder. After feature aggregation, we feed hybrid map $\mathcal{F}^h$ into encoder-decoder to regress full-size disparity map $\mathcal{D}$. As depicted in Table 1, the encoder consists of 12 residual blocks. Several convolutional operations in residual blocks use dilation pattern [7] for larger receptive fields. In the decoder, we place three deconvolutional blocks to gradually upsample the spatial size of feature maps. An extra one-channel convolutional layer is appended at the end to regress full-size disparity map. Our model is also fully-convolutional so that it enables end-to-end disparity learning.

3.2 SRC Learning

As introduced in Sect. 1, the idea of SRC learning is to find an available training solution on fused datasets, especially on the realistic datasets. To enable training on real images, we explain two schemes below:

Guided Label Distillation. A direct way for collaborative learning on realistic dataset is that we adopt an existing method to generate disparity maps. Although the labels predicted by guided method are not exactly accurate as synthetic labels, we find they can help our model converge to a certain level. This scheme has two advantages: (1) The guided method can produce large amounts of disparity labels so that we do not need manual annotations or extra equipments, such as Lidar and depth camera. (2) It enables seamless supervised training on realistic datasets, which makes our model better adaptable to target domains.

In our experiments, we employ SGM algorithm [20] as the guided method. Since the generated disparity maps are not dense, we only measure loss on valid pixels. The loss function is expressed as:

$$\mathcal{L}_{sup} = \frac{1}{N_{\mathcal{V}}} \sum_{i,j \in \mathcal{V}} \|\mathcal{D}_{i,j} - \hat{\mathcal{D}}_{i,j}\|_1, \tag{1}$$

where $\mathcal{V}$ is the set of valid disparity pixels, $N_{\mathcal{V}}$ is the number of valid pixels, $\mathcal{D}$ is the predicted disparity map and $\hat{\mathcal{D}}$ is the disparity label map. Here we adopt the l_1 norm to measure distance between predictions and labels. The experimental results in Sect. 4.3 show that the SRC model trained with guided label distillation outperforms the models trained on the individual datasets.

Semi-supervised Regularization. We introduce unsupervised training based on spatial transformation to constitute semi-supervised regularization for SRC learning. As shown in Fig. 3(b), stereo images are fed to SRC model and we obtain predicted disparity map. Based on the disparity map, we warp the right image to left view and get the reconstructed image. Our image reconstruction adopts bilinear sampling where the output pixel is the weighted sum of nearest two input pixels [21]. Such sampling operation is differentiable and enables loss propagation. Compared with guided label distillation, semi-supervised regularization further gets rid of the dependence on guided method. Here, we measure the photometric loss [22] between source left image and reconstructed image on all pixels:

$$\mathcal{L}_p = \frac{1}{N} \sum_{i,j} \|\tilde{\mathcal{I}}_{i,j}^l - \mathcal{I}_{i,j}^l\|_1, \tag{2}$$

where $\mathcal{I}^l$ denotes source left image and $\tilde{\mathcal{I}}^l$ denotes reconstructed left image. In addition, we define smoothness loss to penalize discontinuity on disparity maps:

$$\mathcal{L}_s = \frac{1}{N} \sum_{i,j} [\rho_s(\mathcal{D}_{i,j} - \mathcal{D}_{i+1,j}) + \rho_s(\mathcal{D}_{i,j} - \mathcal{D}_{i,j+1})], \tag{3}$$

where $\rho_s(\cdot)$ is the spatial smoothness penalty implemented as generalized Charbonnier function [3]. The photometric loss and the smoothness loss are made as the unsupervised loss for realistic datasets. The overall semi-supervised loss is regularized as:

$$\mathcal{L}_{semi} = \delta \mathcal{L}_{sup} + (1 - \delta)(\lambda_p \mathcal{L}_p + \lambda_s \mathcal{L}_s), \tag{4}$$

where $\delta \in \{0, 1\}$, λ_p denotes the weight of photometric loss and λ_s denotes the weight of smoothness loss. When training SRC model with semi-supervised regularization, δ is set to 1 for synthetic data and 0 for realistic data.

4   Experimental Results

In this section, we fuse Scene Flow dataset [29] and Cityscapes dataset [10] to train the model, where the former is the synthetic dataset and the latter is the realistic dataset. The well-trained models are evaluated on Scene Flow test set [29], KITTI stereo 2015 [30] and Middlebury stereo 2014 [35] which represent virtual, outdoor and indoor domains, respectively. Related datasets and evaluation metrics are introduced in Sect. 4.1. Implementation details are described in 4.2. Ablation studies on guided label distillation and semi-supervised regularization are provided in Sects. 4.3 and 4.4, respectively. Finally, we compare our method with other methods in Sect. 4.5.

4.1   Datasets and Evaluation Metrics

The Scene Flow dataset [29] is a synthetic dataset for scene matching including disparity estimation and optical flow prediction. This dataset is rendered by computer graphics techniques with background scenes and 3D foreground models. It contains 22,390 images for training and 4,370 images for testing. Image size is $H = 540$ and $W = 960$.

The Cityscapes dataset [10] is a realistic dataset that is released for urban scene understanding. It provides stereo images and corresponding disparity maps which are pre-computed by SGM algorithm [20] so that we directly use these disparity maps as guided labels. Gathering the stereo pairs from different subsets, we can fetch over 20,000 images with the size of $H = 1024$ and $W = 2048$. These subsets contain "train", "validate", "test" and "extra train" sets.

The KITTI Stereo 2015 dataset is also released for real-world autopilot scenes. It contains 200 training and 200 testing image pairs. Since the disparity labels for testing set are not released, we evaluate our model on the training set. The average image size is $H = 376$ and $W = 1240$.

The Middleburry Stereo 2015 dataset [35] provides 30 pairs for indoor scenes, where 15 each for training and testing. This dataset offers different resolutions and we select quarter resolution for model evaluation.

We use the Scene Flow training split [29] and Cityscapes dataset [10] to train our model. To keep balance, we respectively choose $22,000$ images from Scene flow dataset and Cityscapes dataset so that a maximum number of $44,000$ images can be used for SRC training. The Scene Flow testing set [29], KITTI Stereo datasets [14,30] and Middleburry Stereo 2014 [35] are selected for model evaluation. We apply the end-point-error (EPE) and the bad pixel error (D1) as evaluation metrics, where the threshold in D1 is set to 3. For KITTI datasets, the errors in both non-occluded regions (Noc) and all pixels (All) are calculated. In addition, we depict colorized disparity maps and error maps for better visualization. In the error maps such as Fig. 4, blue areas represent correct predictions and red regions indicate mistaken estimates.

4.2   Implementation Details

Our model shown in Table 1 is implemented on a customized Caffe [23]. We use the "poly" learning rate policy where current learning rate equals to the base one multiplying $(1 - \frac{iter}{max\_iter})^{power}$ [5,44]. At training time, we set base learning rate to 0.01, power to 0.9, momentum to 0.9 and weight decay to 0.0001 respectively. The maximum iterations and batch size are set to $200K$ and 16 for ablation studies in Sects. 4.3 and 4.4. We select the GPU of NVIDIA Titan Xp for model training and testing.

For data augmentation, we adopt random resize, color shift and contrast brightness adjustment. The random factor is between 0.5 to 2.0. The maximum color shift along RGB axes is set to 10 and maximum brightness shift is set to 5. The contrast multiplier is between 0.8 and 1.2. The "cropsize" is set to 513×513 and batch size is set to 16.

For parameters in semi-supervised regularization Eq. 4, the loss weights λ_p and λ_s for photometric term and smoothness term are set to 1.0 and 0.1. The Charbonnier terms α, β and ϵ in smoothness loss term are 0.21, 5.0 and 0.001 as described in [22].

4.3   Ablation Study for Guided Label Distillation

We conduct four groups of experiments on guided label distillation. As described in Sect. 4.1, Scene Flow dataset [29] and Cityscapes dataset [10] are selected as synthetic and realistic dataset. Here, the guided labels for realistic data are pre-computed by SGM method [20]. The first column in Table 2 indicates the current dataset settings for training, where the values of "Synth." and "Real." denote the used ratios of synthetic and realistic images. For example, the values in first line of Group 4 are 1/8 and 1, which means 2, 750 synthetic images and 22, 000 realistic images are used for training.

Table 2. Results of guided label distillation.

Settings		Scene Flow [29]		KITTI Stereo 2015 [30]				Middleburry [35]	
Synth.	Real.	EPE	D1	Noc EPE	All EPE	Noc D1	All D1	EPE	D1
Group 1: Compare SRC-trained model with individual-trained models									
1	0	**2.89**	10.69	3.63	3.65	16.90	17.22	2.42	15.08
0	1	6.50	19.05	1.26	1.29	6.21	6.42	3.36	20.93
1	1	2.92	**10.33**	**1.21**	**1.23**	**5.91**	**6.15**	**1.82**	**12.10**
Group 2: SRC models trained with different amounts of data									
1/8	1/8	3.00	10.94	1.23	1.25	6.12	6.34	1.87	12.37
1/4	1/4	2.96	10.60	**1.20**	**1.22**	**5.83**	**6.09**	1.88	12.39
1/2	1/2	2.94	10.50	1.21	1.24	5.95	6.19	1.94	13.13
1	1	**2.92**	**10.33**	1.21	1.23	5.91	6.15	**1.82**	**12.10**
Group 3: SRC models trained with different amounts of realistic data									
1	1/8	2.99	12.00	1.24	1.26	6.32	6.59	1.88	12.16
1	1/4	**2.88**	**10.14**	1.24	1.26	6.18	6.44	1.84	**12.09**
1	1/2	2.96	11.02	**1.20**	**1.23**	5.97	6.21	1.88	13.01
1	1	2.92	10.33	1.21	**1.23**	**5.91**	**6.15**	**1.82**	12.10
Group 4: SRC models trained with different amounts of synthetic data									
1/8	1	3.18	12.25	1.23	1.25	5.99	6.18	2.11	14.16
1/4	1	3.05	11.48	**1.20**	**1.22**	5.91	6.13	2.08	13.33
1/2	1	3.00	10.75	1.22	1.24	**5.86**	**6.08**	1.88	12.90
1	1	**2.92**	**10.33**	1.21	1.23	5.91	6.15	**1.82**	**12.10**

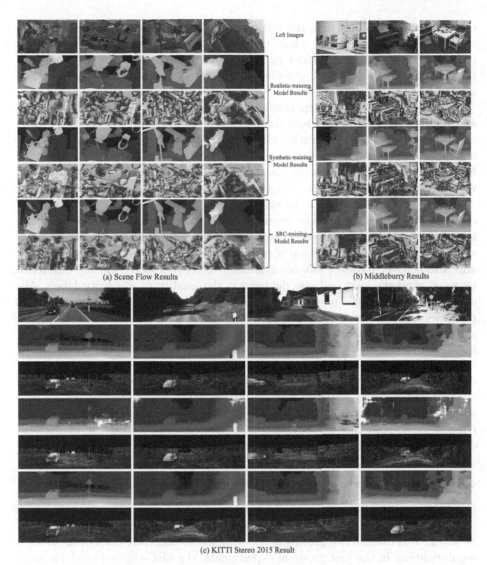

(a) Scene Flow Results   (b) Middleburry Results

(c) KITTI Stereo 2015 Result

Fig. 4. Qualitative results of SRC-trained models with guided label distillation. These results are tested on Scene Flow validation set [29], Middleburry Stereo 2014 dataset [35] and KITTI Stereo 2015 dataset [30] respectively (Color figure online)

The first group of experiments are performed to compare the SRC-trained model with synthetic-trained model and realistic-trained model. On scene flow validation set [29], the error rate of SRC-trained model is flat to synthetic-trained model and much lower than realistic-trained model. On KITTI Stereo 2015 dataset [30], the SRC-trained model performs much better than synthetic-trained model and also achieves higher accuracy than realistic-trained model.

On Middleburry dataset [35], the SRC-trained model outperforms the other two models with a large margin, where the EPE is reduced from 2.42 to 1.82 compared to synthetic-trained model, and the D1 error is improved by 8% compared to realistic-trained model. This group of experiments proves the effectiveness of guided label distillation.

In the second group of experiments, we hold the balance between synthetic and realistic datasets and reduce training data. We observe that the SRC models trained by 1/4 and 1/2 ratios yield similar accuracy to the full-data training model. When the ratio decreases to 1/8, the error rates increase on Scene Flow [15] and KITTI Stereo [30] datasets. Based on this group of experiments, we suggest 5k or more images to train SRC models for guaranteed quality.

In the third group, we fix the synthetic data ratio and increase the ratio of realistic data, and no significant improvement is gained from incremental realistic images. In contrast, we keep the quantity of realistic dataset and raise the ratio of synthetic images in fourth group of experiments. The results on Scene Flow [29] and Middleburry datasets [35] are gradually improved. Here, the key difference between synthetic and realistic datasets is the quality of disparity labels. We analyze that, when the model converges to a certain level during training, the potential errors in guided labels may hinder the further boosts. Nevertheless, a certain amount of guided labels for realistic dataset is still a prerequisite of SRC learning.

In Fig. 4, we show several qualitative examples of SRC-trained models on different scenes. From the colorized disparity maps and error maps, we find that the synthetic-trained model is keen to object edges, while the realistic-trained model behaves better consistency on big objects, such as road and car. The SRC-trained model combines the advantages to provide more reasonable predictions on various domains.

4.4   Ablation Study for Semi-supervised Regularization

For SRC learning by semi-supervised regularization, we calculate supervised loss for synthetic data and unsupervised loss for realistic data as described in Sect. 3.2. We conduct two groups of experiments to illustrate the effects of such regularization. In the first group of experiments, the SRC-trained model is compared to synthetic-trained and realistic-trained models. With synthetic labels, the SRC-trained model performs much better than realistic-trained model on all benchmarks. When fed with realistic data and constraints of photometric consistency, the SRC-trained model achieves higher accuracy on KITTI Stereo [30] and Middleburry [35] datasets than synthetic-trained model. These three experiments validate the semi-supervised regularization.

In the second group of experiments, we explore the impacts of different amounts of data. Similar to guided label distillation, we adopt four ratios of training data. With the increase of ratio, no remarkable improvement can be found on Scene Flow dataset [29] and Middleburry dataset [35], and a little progress emerges on KITTI dataset [30]. We argue that the quantity of training data is not the core factor for semi-supervised regularization. Besides, the overall

Table 3. Results of semi-supervised regularization.

Settings		Scene Flow [29]		KITTI Stereo 2015 [30]				Middleburry [35]	
Synth.	Real.	EPE	D1	Noc EPE	All EPE	Noc D1	All D1	EPE	D1
Group 1: Compare SRC-trained model with individual-trained models									
1	0	**2.89**	10.69	3.63	3.65	16.90	17.22	2.42	15.08
0	1	8.81	24.22	1.88	2.11	8.85	9.55	5.69	29.28
1	1	**2.89**	10.56	**1.39**	**1.50**	**7.14**	**7.74**	**2.33**	**15.01**
Group 2: SRC models trained with different amounts of data									
1/8	1/8	2.96	10.62	1.46	1.57	7.31	7.89	**2.19**	**13.86**
1/4	1/4	2.95	10.90	1.52	1.63	7.21	7.82	2.46	15.15
1/2	1/2	2.90	**10.49**	1.48	1.63	7.22	7.93	2.55	15.88
1	1	**2.89**	10.56	**1.39**	**1.50**	**7.14**	**7.74**	2.33	15.01

results of semi-supervised regularization are worse than guided label distillation. We analyze that the photometric loss measured between potential corresponding image patches only provides weak guidance. Compare with supervised loss computed on SGM labels [20], the unsupervised loss is easily influenced by ambiguities and illuminations. Even so, the semi-supervised regularization enables SRC learning without ground-truth labels or guided labels on realistic datasets (Table 3).

In Fig. 5, we show several predictive examples. In contrast to the realistic-trained model that is the purely unsupervised model, the SRC-trained model predicts more accurate disparities on edges, sharp positions, and small objects. Compared to synthetic-trained model, the SRC-trained model further reduces the errors on local ambiguity areas.

4.5 Compare with Other Methods

To exploit the potential of SRC-learning, we adopt guided label distillation, and we increase the training iterations from $200K$ to $500K$, and the batch size from 16 to 32. More training epoches further improve the performance of our model. We compare our SRC method to other classical or deep learning-based methods, including SGM [20], DispNetC [29], CRL [31], EdgeStereo [39] and iResNet [26]. The deep learning-based models [26,29,31,39] are pretrained on Scene Flow dataset without finely tuning on specific datasets.

We list the results of different methods in Table 4. We find all of the deep learning methods outperform classical SGM algorithm on three benchmarks. Although our SRC model ranks at penultimate on Scene Flow dataset [29], our method ranks second on both KITTI Stereo 2015 benchmark [30] and Middleburry dataset [35]. It is remarkable that KITTI Stereo 2015 dataset and Middleburry dataset are unseen in the training period so that it illustrates that our SRC-learning can help model better adapt to various domains. We believe that the SRC learning can be used as a general strategy for other deep learning-based stereo matching models.

Table 4. Comparative results to other methods.

Methods	Scene Flow [29]		KITTI Stereo 2015 [30]		Middleburry [35]		Running time (s)
	EPE	D1	All EPE	All D1	EPE	D1	
SGM [20]	7.29	16.18	5.02	14.79	8.29	25.35	1.47
DispNetC [29]	2.33	10.04	1.61	10.84	3.09	18.85	**0.05**
CRL [31]	1.67	6.70	1.40	8.18	1.77	13.47	0.16
iResNet [26]	**1.27**	**4.90**	**0.70**	**2.38**	1.74	11.06	0.13
EdgeStereo [39]	1.33	5.26	1.48	8.64	**1.57**	11.38	0.21
SRC (Ours)	2.72	8.45	1.12	5.64	1.67	**10.96**	0.29

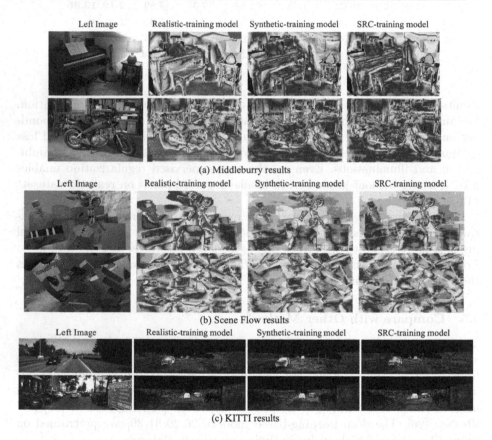

(a) Middleburry results

(b) Scene Flow results

(c) KITTI results

Fig. 5. Error maps of SRC-trained models with semi-supervised regularization. From top to down, we provide Scene Flow [29], Middleburry Stereo 2014 [35] and KITTI Stereo 2015 [30] examples, respectively. From left to right, we provide left input images and error maps by realistic-trained, synthetic-trained and SRC-trained models

5 Conclusion

As a core problem in low-level vision, disparity estimation is required to have the properties of fast speed, high accuracy, and adaptability to various domains.

In this paper, we develop a compact model that is composed of shallow feature extractor, matching feature aggregator and encoder-decoder. We also present SRC learning strategy for joint training on synthetic and realistic datasets. Two schemes, *i.e.* guided label distillation and semi-supervised regularization, are provided to mitigate for the lack of labels in realistic datasets. Our experimental results evaluated on different datasets demonstrate the effectiveness of our deep learning model and SRC strategy.

Acknowledgment. This work was supported in part by the National Key R&D Program of China under Grant No. 2017YFB1302200 and by Joint Fund of NORINCO Group of China for Advanced Research under Grant No. 6141B010318.

References

1. Bai, M., Luo, W., Kundu, K., Urtasun, R.: Exploiting semantic information and deep matching for optical flow. In: Leibe, B., Matas, J., Sebe, N., Welling, M. (eds.) ECCV 2016. LNCS, vol. 9910, pp. 154–170. Springer, Cham (2016). https://doi.org/10.1007/978-3-319-46466-4_10
2. Bailer, C., Taetz, B., Stricker, D.: Flow Fields: dense correspondence fields for highly accurate large displacement optical flow estimation. In: ICCV (2015)
3. Barron, J.T.: A more general robust loss function. arXiv preprint arXiv:1701.03077 (2017)
4. Behl, A., Jafari, O.H., Mustikovela, S.K., Alhaija, H.A., Rother, C., Geiger, A.: Bounding boxes, segmentations and object coordinates: how important is recognition for 3D scene flow estimation in autonomous driving scenarios? In: ICCV (2017)
5. Brown, M., Hua, G., Winder, S.: Discriminative learning of local image descriptors. TPAMI **33**, 43–57 (2011)
6. Chang, J.R., Chen, Y.S.: Pyramid stereo matching network. In: CVPR (2018)
7. Chen, L.C., Papandreou, G., Kokkinos, I., Murphy, K., Yuille, A.L.: DeepLab: semantic image segmentation with deep convolutional nets, atrous convolution, and fully connected CRFs. TPAMI **40**, 834–848 (2016)
8. Chen, Z., Sun, X., Wang, L., Yu, Y., Huang, C.: A deep visual correspondence embedding model for stereo matching costs. In: ICCV (2015)
9. Cheng, J., Tsai, Y.H., Wang, S., Yang, M.H.: SegFlow: joint learning for video object segmentation and optical flow. In: ICCV (2017)
10. Cordts, M., et al.: The cityscapes dataset for semantic urban scene understanding. In: CVPR (2016)
11. Dosovitskiy, A., et al.: FlowNet: learning optical flow with convolutional networks. In: ICCV (2015)
12. Franke, U., Joos, A.: Real-time stereo vision for urban traffic scene understanding. In: IV (2000)
13. Garg, R., B.G., V.K., Carneiro, G., Reid, I.: Unsupervised CNN for single view depth estimation: geometry to the rescue. In: Leibe, B., Matas, J., Sebe, N., Welling, M. (eds.) ECCV 2016. LNCS, vol. 9912, pp. 740–756. Springer, Cham (2016). https://doi.org/10.1007/978-3-319-46484-8_45
14. Geiger, A., Lenz, P., Urtasun, R.: Are we ready for autonomous driving? The KITTI vision benchmark suite. In: CVPR (2012)

15. Geiger, A., Roser, M., Urtasun, R.: Efficient large-scale stereo matching. In: Kimmel, R., Klette, R., Sugimoto, A. (eds.) ACCV 2010. LNCS, vol. 6492, pp. 25–38. Springer, Heidelberg (2011). https://doi.org/10.1007/978-3-642-19315-6_3
16. Godard, C., Mac Aodha, O., Brostow, G.J.: Unsupervised monocular depth estimation with left-right consistency. In: CVPR (2017)
17. Guney, F., Geiger, A.: Displets: resolving stereo ambiguities using object knowledge. In: CVPR (2015)
18. Hartley, R., Zisserman, A.: Multiple View Geometry in Computer Vision. Cambridge University Press, Cambridge (2003)
19. He, K., Zhang, X., Ren, S., Sun, J.: Deep residual learning for image recognition. In: CVPR (2016)
20. Hirschmuller, H.: Stereo processing by semiglobal matching and mutual information. TPAMI **30**, 328–341 (2008)
21. Jaderberg, M., Simonyan, K., Zisserman, A., et al.: Spatial transformer networks. In: NIPS (2015)
22. Yu, J.J., Harley, A.W., Derpanis, K.G.: Back to basics: unsupervised learning of optical flow via brightness constancy and motion smoothness. In: Hua, G., Jégou, H. (eds.) ECCV 2016. LNCS, vol. 9915, pp. 3–10. Springer, Cham (2016). https://doi.org/10.1007/978-3-319-49409-8_1
23. Jia, Y., et al.: Caffe: convolutional architecture for fast feature embedding. In: ACM MM (2014)
24. Kendall, A., et al.: End-to-end learning of geometry and context for deep stereo regression. In: ICCV (2017)
25. Krizhevsky, A., Sutskever, I., Hinton, G.E.: ImageNet classification with deep convolutional neural networks. In: NIPS (2012)
26. Liang, Z., et al.: Learning for disparity estimation through feature constancy. In: CVPR (2018)
27. Long, J., Shelhamer, E., Darrell, T.: Fully convolutional networks for semantic segmentation. In: CVPR (2015)
28. Luo, W., Schwing, A.G., Urtasun, R.: Efficient deep learning for stereo matching. In: CVPR (2016)
29. Mayer, N., et al.: A large dataset to train convolutional networks for disparity, optical flow, and scene flow estimation. In: CVPR (2016)
30. Menze, M., Geiger, A.: Object scene flow for autonomous vehicles. In: CVPR (2015)
31. Pang, J., Sun, W., Ren, J., Yang, C., Yan, Q.: Cascade residual learning: a two-stage convolutional neural network for stereo matching. In: ICCV Workshop (2017)
32. Rajagopalan, A., Chaudhuri, S., Mudenagudi, U.: Depth estimation and image restoration using defocused stereo pairs. TPAMI (2004)
33. Ren, Z., Sun, D., Kautz, J., Sudderth, E.B.: Cascaded scene flow prediction using semantic segmentation. In: 3DV (2017)
34. Revaud, J., Weinzaepfel, P., Harchaoui, Z., Schmid, C.: DeepMatching: hierarchical deformable dense matching. IJCV **120**, 300–323 (2016)
35. Scharstein, D., et al.: High-resolution stereo datasets with subpixel-accurate ground truth. In: Jiang, X., Hornegger, J., Koch, R. (eds.) GCPR 2014. LNCS, vol. 8753, pp. 31–42. Springer, Cham (2014). https://doi.org/10.1007/978-3-319-11752-2_3
36. Scharstein, D., Szeliski, R.: A taxonomy and evaluation of dense two-frame stereo correspondence algorithms. IJCV **47**, 7–42 (2002)
37. Schmid, K., Tomic, T., Ruess, F., Hirschmuller, H.: Stereo vision based indoor/outdoor navigation for flying robots. In: IROS (2013)
38. Shaked, A., Wolf, L.: Improved stereo matching with constant highway networks and reflective confidence learning. In: CVPR (2017)

39. Song, X., Zhao, X., Hu, H., Fang, L.: EdgeStereo: a context integrated residual pyramid network for stereo matching. arXiv preprint arXiv:1803.05196 (2018)

40. Tonioni, A., Poggi, M., Mattoccia, S., Di Stefano, L.: Unsupervised adaptation for deep stereo. In: ICCV (2017)

41. Yang, G., Zhao, H., Shi, J., Deng, Z., Jia, J.: SegStereo: exploiting semantic information for disparity estimation. In: Ferrari, V., Hebert, M., Sminchisescu, C., Weiss, Y. (eds.) ECCV 2018. LNCS, vol. 11211, pp. 660–676. Springer, Cham (2018). https://doi.org/10.1007/978-3-030-01234-2_39

42. Yu, L., Wang, Y., Wu, Y., Jia, Y.: Deep stereo matching with explicit cost aggregation sub-architecture. In: AAAI (2018)

43. Zbontar, J., LeCun, Y.: Stereo matching by training a convolutional neural network to compare image patches. JMLR **17**, 2 (2016)

44. Zhao, H., Shi, J., Qi, X., Wang, X., Jia, J.: Pyramid scene parsing network. In: CVPR (2017)

45. Zhu, Y., Lan, Z., Newsam, S., Hauptmann, A.G.: Guided optical flow learning. In: CVPR Workshop (2017)

Author Index

Printed in the United States
By Bookmasters